PRACTICALLY EVERYONE IS RAVING ABOUT THE PRACTICAL GUIDE TO PRACTICALLY EVERYTHING!

One *"of the most appealing gift books"* of the year. *"A most astonishing mix of the trivial and essential."*
—Christopher Lehmann-Haupt, *The New York Times*

"Open to any page and you're likely to find something you can use...this bulging paperback with all the right stuff is my pick for a stocking stuffer."
—Gene Shalit, *Today*

"This is the stuff inquiring minds want to know about—and brag about. News that people can use. Information that will save them money, time or grief."
— *The Times-Picayune*

"Like the classic early-American almanacs, [The Practical Guide] *is designed to tickle and intrigue readers as well as help them puzzle out the problems of daily life.* The Practical Guide *is alive with characters."*
—Kevin McManus, *The Washington Post*

"If you're as much of a reference book junkie as I am, The Practical Guide to Practically Everything *will occupy an honored place next to conventional almanacs."*
—Dave Kinchen, *The Register Herald*

"In this chubby, comprehensive volume, Consumer Reports *meets* The World Almanac. *The diligent reporting and amusing titles make a fine mix, whether you are just browsing or bent on self-education."*
—*Mademoiselle*

"Practical, nuts and bolts data on important aspects of daily life...as pleasurable to read as it is informative." —*Library Journal*

"Fun to read, good for the bookshelf. Practically everyone should own a copy of The Practical Guide to Practically Everything.*"*
—Judyth Rigler, *The San Antonio Express-News*

"If ever a book functioned as an instruction manual for almost every aspect of life, it's this ultimate consumer annual."
—Doug Hatt, *People*

WITH HUNDREDS OF EXPERTS TO SAVE YOU TIME AND MONEY IN 1998!

"A long life may not be good enough, but a good life is long enough."

Ben Franklin
Poor Richard's Almanac

THE PRACTICAL GUIDE TO PRACTICALLY EVERYTHING

1998 EDITION

PETER BERNSTEIN & CHRISTOPHER MA
EDITORS

RANDOM HOUSE NEW YORK

To our siblings and their families

Tom and Andi, Sam, Lee, and Will
Bill and Martha, Allison, Laura, and Michael
Louise, Kathryn and Sanford,
Emily, Hannah, and Eliza
Philip and Jennifer

In the preparation of this book, every effort has been made to offer current, correct, and clearly expressed information. Nonetheless, inadvertent errors can occur and information can change. The information in the text is intended to afford general guidelines on matters of interest. Accordingly, the information in this book is not intended to serve as legal, accounting, tax, or medical advice. Readers are encouraged to consult with professional advisers concerning specific matters before making any decision, and the editors and publisher disclaim any responsibility for positions taken by readers in individual cases or for any misunderstanding on the part of readers.

Earlier editions of this work were published in 1995 and 1996 by Random House, Inc.

Library of Congress Cataloging-in-Publication Data is available.

ISBN 0-375-75029-0

Random House website address: http://www.randomhouse.com/

Printed in the United States of America

98765432

Third Edition

CONTENTS

Chapter 1:
MONEY

Chapter 2:
HEALTH

Chapter 3:
EDUCATION

THE PRACTICAL GUIDE

Chapter 6:

TRAVEL

Chapter 7:

ENTERTAINMENT

Chapter 8:

COMPUTERS

Chapter 9:

AUTOS

Chapter 10:

SPORTS & GAMES

THE PRACTICAL GUIDE

Chapter 11:

FACTS FOR LIFE

INTRODUCTION

From the editors

DEAR READER,

When we published the first edition of *The Practical Guide to Practically Everything* in the fall of 1995, our goal was to provide up-to-date information and the very best advice from experts on all the subjects that can really make a difference in your daily life, from health and nutrition to money management and career planning, travel, and consumer technology. Our inspiration was the traditional almanacs made famous by Benjamin Franklin and other early-American publishers. This year, for the third edition, we have redoubled our commitment to making this book practical, valuable, and time saving, and have added many new experts and new features. For example, the Facts for Life chapter includes a Citizen's Guide to fill you in on everything from the ins and outs of jury duty to how to read a poll. There is also a Survival Guide to consult in case of fire, flood, hurricanes, and other disasters. This year's edition includes a new feature throughout the book, Cyber Sources, which point you to valuable resources available on the Internet.

We've been enormously gratified by the feedback we've gotten from the hundreds of people we've met or who have been kind enough to write or fill in the questionnaire that you will find at the back of the book (see page 787). Hardly a day passes in which there isn't something in the mail. This year we've heard from readers from all over the globe. A reader in Hong Kong, which reverted to Chinese rule on July 1, 1997, wanted to know more about stress management! Meanwhile, a reader at the Altona Correctional Facility in New York wanted to know about stretch marks and how to get rid of them. As always, we have tried to incorporate as many of your suggestions into this year's book as possible.

We are also thankful that some of you have written to call a mistake or two to our attention. A baseball fan noted that while we were correct in saying that Henry Aaron was the all-time leader in home runs, the total is 755—not the 714 we cited. Babe Ruth's total was 714, ranking him second. We stand corrected.

A major occupational hazard of writing a book called *The Practical Guide to Practically Everything* is that it is sometimes assumed that we know practically everything, which of course is anything but the case. *The Practical Guide to Practically Everything* needs the help of practically everyone to stay current and compelling. So whether you're a new reader or an old friend, please pass the word that *The Practical Guide* is back and hopes to hear from you.

Peter Bernstein and Christopher Ma

CONTRIBUTORS

Editors: Peter W. Bernstein and Christopher Ma

Managing Editor: Anna G. Isgro
Senior Editor: Mary Yee
Editorial Design: Janice Olson
Senior Writer: Michele Turk (HEALTH)
Maps and Illustrations: Steve McCracken
Charts and Graphics: David Merrill

Reporters: Jessica Beels (ENTERTAINMENT), Andrea Chipman (CAREERS, MONEY), Lucas Graves (COMPUTERS), Shannon Henry (MONEY, TRAVEL), Leila Kahn (COMPUTERS, EDUCATION, MONEY, SPORTS & GAMES), Jamie Krents (ENTERTAINMENT, AUTOS, SPORTS & GAMES), Christina Lowery (EDUCATION), Anna Mulrine (ENTERTAINMENT, FACTS FOR LIFE), Melissa Perenson (COMPUTERS), Sarah Roberts (COMPUTERS), Debbie Sanders (TRAVEL), Jeff Sheler (FACTS FOR LIFE), Ann Sherman (EDUCATION), Jay Strell (CAREERS, AUTOS), Molly Tschida (CAREERS, MONEY), Molly Ulam (TRAVEL), Leonard Wiener (MONEY), Drake Witham (EDUCATION)

Copy Editors: Eva Young, Evan Stone, Regina Allegra
Indexer: S.W. Cohen & Associates
Design Consultant: Rob Covey

CHAPTER ONE

MONEY

"The best places to invest, in the long term, are non-durable consumer goods and services."
—Elaine Garzarelli, Wall Street analyst
Page 2

"Maps and books aren't like sports cars or paintings. The market doesn't fluctuate."
—Paul Cohen, gallery director, Richard Arkway Inc.
Page 70

"You can retire in semiluxury on what would be a semi-starvation budget here."
—John Howells, author of *Choose Costa Rica*
Page 98

■ **WHAT'S AHEAD: INVEST** in companies that produce nondurable goods... **BUY** stocks and hold them for the long term... **FIND** a comfortable level of investment risk... **ALLO-CATE** a chunk of your portfolio to overseas stock... **SEARCH FOR** a second home with retirement in mind ... **COUNT** on quality to be your best investment in antiques and collectibles... **DONATE** five percent of your income to charity... **CONSIDER** doing your banking on the Internet... **START** saving for a comfortable retirement now...

INVESTING

STOCKS: Why you should continue to bet on stocks, PAGE 4   **RISK:** How to gauge the amount of risk you can handle, PAGE 7   **OVERSEAS:** Hot markets in Asia and Eastern Europe, PAGE 10   **DIVIDENDS:** The 10 companies with the biggest yields, PAGE 12   **BONDS:** Is an inflation-indexed bond for you? PAGE 14   **MUTUAL FUNDS:** The top 130 funds, PAGE 17   **INVESTMENT CLUBS:** How a club from Wyoming tripled its money, PAGE 30

EQUITIES
▼

PICK STOCKS LIKE A WALL ST. PRO

Look at the health of industrial sectors first, says a respected analyst

Buy low, sell high—it's the dream of all investors hoping to strike gold in the stock market. The strategy sounds simple, but as most investors know, timing the market is elusive at best. Rather than trying to divine the market, Elaine Garzarelli, a respected Wall Street analyst, uses a sector analysis approach to investing. Garzarelli evaluates 75 industrial sectors, selecting those that are poised to outperform the stock market as a whole.

Hard-charging and flamboyant, Garzarelli, now head of Garzarelli Capital, was a vice president at a major investment firm when she was 22. For 10 years she was Shearson's chief quantitative strategist, and for 11 consecutive years she has been named an all-star analyst by *Institutional Investor* magazine. Along the way, Garzarelli served as the model for Sigourney Weaver's role in the movie *Working Girl*.

Garzarelli is best remembered for her prescience in predicting the stock market crash of 1987. She slipped a bit in 1996, when she suddenly turned bearish, but *SmartMoney* came to her defense, pointing out that for the past four years her stock picks for the magazine outperformed the Standard & Poor (S&P) 500 by at least 12 percentage points.

We asked Garzarelli to provide some stock-picking advice for the average investor.

■ **What is your stock-picking philosophy?**

I first look at the health of the overall stock market and pick industries that can be expected to do well within the economic environment. Then I pick stocks in those industries, looking for strong performers, which are selling at a price that's relatively cheap compared to their highs.

In making an assessment, I look at the economic climate, monetary policy, and valuation (whether the market is too high or low based on earnings and interest rates). I also look at investor sentiment—the more bearish advisers are out there, the better the sentiment; the more bullish, the worse it is.

■ **What's your long view for the economy?**

We're looking for a slowing of growth, so the best places to invest in the long term are in stable growth sectors—such as nondurable consumer goods and services—that are driven by regular, automatic purchases. Even in a slow economy, consumers won't stop using their banks, or eating, smoking, reading, or taking their medicine. They won't cut off their phone service or insurance coverage.

ELAINE'S FAVORITE FIVE FOR THE LONG RUN

Garzarelli's top choices for investing are in sectors that can withstand a potential slowdown in the economy.

Company/ ☎	SYMBOL/ Business	Comment
McDonald's ☎ 800–659–6237	MCD Fast Food	A great opportunity in the restaurant sector. More than 50 percent of its sales are overseas.
Dell Computer ☎ 800–472–3355	DELL Technology	The computer hardware industry has the potential to outpace the S&P 500 earnings. Dell's fundamentals are strong.
Phillips Petroleum ☎ 918–661–6600	P Oil	The oil industry looks favorable. Phillips looks especially good because it is well priced.
Tenet Healthcare ☎ 805–563–7188	THC/Hospital Management	The health care sector has positive demographics and the potential to beat the S&P. Tenet is my number-one choice in this industry.
Philip Morris ☎ 800–343–0975	MO Tobacco	About 50 percent of sales are non-tobacco-related subsidiaries like Kraft Foods and Miller Brewing. I expect it to outperform the stock market by double-digits.

■ **Which sectors should be avoided?**

Stay away from the capital goods sectors, such as chemicals, steel, machine tools, electrical equipment, aluminum, other machinery, and manufacturing companies. These companies are less likely to begin major expansion programs during a slowing economic phase.

I'd also avoid light cyclical sectors like housing, autos, and appliances—anything that people can postpone purchasing.

■ **Which stocks do well in a downturn?**

Look at industries that led the way out of past recessions and find good stocks within those sectors. In the past, the industry groups that have shown big gains in the first 12 months after the market bottomed out are: leisure, retail drugstores, pollution control, newspaper publishing, homebuilding, airlines, electronics, trucking, semiconductor, broadcast media, and textiles and apparel. All these industries have shown average gains above 50 percent after the market bottomed out.

■ **How can an investor ride out a bear market?**

Average investors with a long-term horizon, should just hold on to their investments. Those with a shorter time frame should invest in more defensive industries, such as electric utilities and oil. The best advice is to buy stocks for the long term, not for short-term gains. We like to hold our selections at least for one year.

■ **Any advice for the investor reluctant to jump into the market?**

I suggest dollar-cost averaging into the stock market. (A strategy that involves putting a fixed amount of savings each month into the stock market.) A balanced mutual fund that invests in stocks, cash, and bonds is also a good start.

■ **What about investing in a sector mutual fund?**

Keep in mind that while sector funds may sound targeted, many contain surprises on closer inspection. Some mix metals mining with oil and gas drilling, for example, and call it Natural Resources. The trouble is, the oil and gas industry is far different from those of gold and silver, so you get a portfolio that's chronically underperforming. You need to look at a fund closely and identify if it is truly investing in those sectors that are attractive for the long term.

WHY YOU SHOULD NEVER SELL

On Wall Street, patience is almost always rewarded

The percentage of Americans who own stock has doubled in the past seven years, from 21 percent in 1990 to 43 percent in 1996. Not since the go-go stock market of the late '60s have households had so much of their money tied up in financial assets. With so much at stake, should the wise investor take some chips off the table?

A widely held belief says, no. Over the long term, argues Jeremy J. Siegel, a finance professor at the University of Pennsylvania's Wharton School, stocks beat every other investment. Says Siegel, "Most people should buy a diversified list of stocks and use that as nearly 100 percent of their long-term hold-

ings—and they should do that whether or not the valuations tend to be on the high side or on the low side when they buy." Siegel, whose strategy is detailed in his book, *Stocks for the Long Run* (Irwin, 1994), says it might be possible for some investors to time the market and buy and sell accordingly. But, he cautions, it's foolish to try. For truly long-term investing, says Siegel, there is never a bad time to buy stocks—or a good time to sell.

History is on his side. Measure stocks against bonds, cash, diamonds, you name it, and in the long run, stocks win. Stashing your cash in houses, gold, oil, or collectibles is considered smart during times of high inflation, which can hurt stocks and most bonds. But not over the long haul, according to R. S. Salomon, Jr. of STI Management, a Stamford, Conn., investment firm. After tracking the returns of different assets from the late 1970s to 1995, Salomon found that returns on tangible assets fluctuate wildly from year to year. In the long term, though, financial assets beat out collectibles and hard assets hands down.

Pit stocks against cash and again stocks are tops. (By cash, we mean money invested

---

■ THE BULLS ARE BEATING THE BEARS

This century's bull markets have lasted longer and moved farther than the bear markets. On average, they've lasted about two years with a near 85 percent increase in the Dow Jones Industrial Average. The current bull started running on October 11, 1990, and was still going strong as of February 12, 1997. The average bear market during this century lasted 410 days, during which the Dow dropped some 30 percent.

■ BEAR MARKETS

Beginning date	Ending date	Number of days	Loss in Dow	Mos. to recover
2/9/66	10/7/66	240	−25.2%	6
12/3/68	5/26/70	539	−35.9%	22
4/28/71	11/23/71	209	−16.1%	64
1/11/73	12/6/74	694	−45.1%	4
9/21/76	2/28/78	525	−26.9%	6
9/8/78	4/21/80	591	−16.4%	10
4/27/81	8/12/82	472	−24.1%	4
11/29/83	7/24/84	238	−15.6%	3
8/25/87	10/19/87	55	−36.1%	23
7/16/90	10/11/90	87	−21.2%	5

SOURCE: Ned Davis Research Inc.

■ BULL MARKETS

Beginning date	Ending date	Number of days	Gain in Dow
10/7/66	12/3/68	788	32.4%
5/26/70	4/28/71	337	50.6%
11/23/71	1/11/73	415	31.8%
12/6/74	9/21/76	655	75.7%
2/28/78	9/8/78	192	22.3%
4/21/80	4/27/81	371	34.9%
8/12/82	11/29/83	474	65.7%
7/24/82	8/25/87	1,127	150.6%
10/19/87	7/16/90	1,001	72.5%
10/11/90	——	2,316*	194.3%*

*As of February 12, 1997.

in three-month Treasuries or a first-rate money market fund, not the reserve you stash away for a rainy day.) Looking back 50 years, cash has beaten out stocks only 10 times, according to Ibbotson Associates, a Chicago research firm. One of the rare periods was between August 1990 and the end of 1994, when the returns of 30-day Treasury bills outperformed the Standard & Poor's 500 stock index by 3 percentage points and 20-year Treasury bonds by 15 percentage points. Usually, though, periods when cash is king have not lasted longer than 24 months. After accounting for inflation, cash has returned an average 0.5 percent per year since 1926, compared with 6.9 percent for the S&P 500, according to Ibbotson.

What's an investor to do when market indicators, such as the Dow Jones Industrial Average and the S&P 500 hit rocky patches? Hold on tight, say buy-and-hold advocates, the road will eventually smooth out. What's more, market averages can sometimes be deceiving. Take, for example, the 16 years between the market peak in 1966 to the low in the summer of 1982—perhaps the most abysmal period for stock market investors since the Great Depression of the 1930s. The Dow lost money at an average annual rate of 1.5 percent. The S&P gained a measly 0.9 percent annually. Treasury bills looked downright alluring with returns of 7 percent a year. But the picture wasn't as bleak as the market averages suggest. If you include stock dividend income, an important part of the market's total return, the S&P return jumps to 5.1 percent a year, according to Ibbotson. Also, not all stocks were losers. Returns for

...AND WHEN YOU SHOULD SELL

Even buy-and-hold advocates would agree that there is a difference between trying to time the market and trying to reassess your holdings. Is it time to unload a few stocks? Ask yourself these questions before you dump them. Responses were culled from the best advice of financial planners:

■ **Have a particular stock's underlying fundamentals changed?**

Study the company's financials and management history. Are there signs of serious trouble? A few quarters of poor results doesn't necessarily signal a dog, but some pros say when a company reports earnings decreases of 5 percent or more over a 12-month period, it's probably time to unload. Others say a considerable slowdown in a company's sales growth can also be a sell signal.

■ **How does the stock's performance compare with my goals for buying it?**

If the stock price is dipping well below your goals for those shares, it may be time to cut your losses. Some investors say if a stock price falls 30 percent, it's time to unload it. On the other hand, a stock that rises 30 percent may also be a candidate for a sell.

■ **How exposed to stocks is my portfolio?**

A diversified portfolio that combines stocks, bonds, and cash—like money markets and Treasury bills—is well buttressed against dips in the stock market. Even if stocks plunge 20 percent, say, you won't pulverize your holdings.

■ **What are the costs of dumping?**

You'll face hefty brokerage commissions when you sell. And you may have to fork over plenty in taxes if you sell and show a profit on the investment.

■ **Where would I invest the money?**

Determine what your investment alternatives are. Nearly all other investment options—bonds, money-market funds, Treasury bills, hard assets—won't beat stocks over the long haul. For inflation-beating returns, there's just no match for the stock market.

20 UNDERACHIEVERS WORTH A BET

Each year, the Council of Institutional Investors, a Washington, D.C.–based group of huge pension funds, puts out a list of 20 companies that are underachievers—or that are poised for a turn around. To make the list, a company must have total shareholder returns below its industry average for the year and for the five previous years. Once a company beats the S&P 500 on its five-year returns, it is removed from the list.

The Council has found that investing in the 20 companies has paid off nicely. In the year after a company makes the list, its share price has risen an average 14 percent above the S&P. Earnings also improved as the companies refocused their operations and restructured their assets.

Here's the 1997 list:

A&P	201-573-9700
ADVANCED MICRO DEVICES	408-732-2400
AUTODESK	415-507-5000
COMMUNITY PSYCHIATRIC CENTERS	415-831-1166
DILLARD DEPT. STORES	501-376-5200
FLEMING CO.	405-840-7200
GIDDINGS & LEWIS	414-921-9400
H&R BLOCK	816-753-6900
KMART	810-643-1000
MOORE CORP.	416-364-2600
NAVISTAR INTERNATIONAL	312-836-2600
NIAGARA MOHAWK POWER	315-474-1511
NORDSTROM	206-628-2111
NOVELL	801-226-8202
ORYX ENERGY	214-890-6000
OUTBOARD MARINE	847-689-6200
SHONEY'S	615-391-5201
STRIDE RITE	617-824-6000
UNICOM	312-394-7399
UNISYS	215-986-4011

SOURCE: Council of Institutional Investors, Washington, D.C.

small-company stocks actually rose 12.7 percent a year, including reinvested dividends.

Furthermore, market averages become less significant for investors who regularly pump money into stocks, regardless of share prices. A strategy called dollar-cost averaging helps manage the risk of stock market ups and downs. By investing a set dollar amount regularly, say, $100 a month, you get more shares when stock prices are low and fewer when prices are high. Over time, the practice reduces your average cost per share, improving your chances of becoming a slow but steady winner. Ibbotson figures that if you had put $100 every month into S&P 500 stocks between 1966 and 1982, you would have invested a total of $19,800. The total worth of your portfolio at the market low in August 1982, would have been $32,600, or 64 percent more than your cost.

The moral of the story: Don't panic during a bear market. There hasn't been one in seven years (see table on page 4), although chances are there's one around the corner. Since 1956, there have been nine downturns—an average of one every four or five years. The typical bear has lasted one year and taken 33 months to bounce back. But from 1932 to 1995, there has never been a 10-year period in which stocks have lost money.

That doesn't mean the wise investor should sit back and neglect his portfolio. Professionals say more important than which stocks you pick is how you allocate your assets. In times of a liquidity-swollen bull market, you should diversify more broadly into bonds and overseas investments, for example. (See page 10 on investing abroad.)

In the end, the best preparation for weathering a bear market may be to set realistic expectations for returns. From 1995 to mid-1997, stocks returned an annual average of a dizzying 30 percent, compared to 15.3 percent for the decade. But over the course of stock-market history, the average is a far lower 10.7 percent. Even if you set your sights at a 9 percent annual return, your stock portfolio is likely to quadruple in 16 years. No other single investment comes even close to that kind of consistent return.

EXPERT Q & A

THE RULES OF RISK TAKING

Find a level of investment risk that won't send you into a panic

When it comes to investing, dips and losses are bound to occur from time to time. The key is to set a course that will help you manage risk and the potential for losses. Perhaps no one has studied the subject of risk taking with more profundity than Peter L. Bernstein, a consultant to institutional investors and author of *Against the Gods: The Remarkable Story of Risk* (John Wiley & Sons, 1996). We asked Bernstein (no relation to this book's coeditor) for advice in helping the average investor understand the rules of risk taking. Here are his insights on learning to live with risk—and to soften the blow of those losses:

■ **How can the average investor manage risk?**

One way is to diversify. But diversification must be carefully carried out so that the various components of your portfolio have as little correlation as possible. Having lots of holdings is not the same as diversification; a few holdings with low correlation can do the job. For example, you get diversification by holding a small stock fund plus a bond fund; a large cap fund, plus a money-market fund; or a Japan fund plus a U.S. index fund.

The second, and perhaps more important way, is to refrain from taking risks you don't understand, or that would lead you to act in panic if your decision turns out to be wrong, as it frequently might. Fancy forms of risk management, like derivatives, are for full-time professionals. The average investor should stay away.

■ **So, diversification is still the key strategy?**

By its nature, diversification must be the key strategy for risk management. If we knew the future, we would put all our eggs in the basket that promised the greatest gain. But we don't know the future—that is what risk means. Diversification is acknowledging our inescapable ignorance of the future.

■ **Is it safe to rely on the market's past performance to determine future activity?**

Past performance helps us understand the conditions under which stocks produce high or low returns. In that sense, history is valuable, and I spend much of my time studying history for that very reason. But history can tell us perilously little about what will happen tomorrow, next month, or even the next 10 years.

FACT FILE:

DOGS OF THE DOW

■ *These 10 bargain stocks, often called the "Dogs of the Dow," are the 1997 highest-yielding stocks of the Dow Jones 30. At the beginning of each year, buy the bargain 10 for that year, hold them for one year and then repeat the process. You'll almost always beat the market.*

COMPANY	YIELD (%)*
PHILIP MORRIS	4.2
J.P. MORGAN	3.6
TEXACO	3.5
CHEVRON	3.3
EXXON	3.2
AT&T	3.0
GENERAL MOTORS	2.9
INTERNATIONAL PAPER	2.5
DUPONT	2.4
3M COMPANY	2.4

*As of Dec. 31, 1996. Yields are calculated by dividing the annual dividend by the stock price.
SOURCE: John Downes, editor of *Beating the Dow*, ☎800–477–3400.

■ Can a case be made for investing in cash?

Cash is important on two scores. First, the correlation between stocks and returns on cash equivalents like Treasury bills, or, even better, Treasuries with a two-year maturity, is lower than between stocks and bonds. So cash is a better diversifier than bonds, and cash would make possible a higher percentage of equities in the portfolio than would be possible with long-term bonds. Second, cash reduces anxiety and results in more rational decisions when unpleasant surprises occur.

■ Given the volatility of emerging markets, should the average investor avoid foreign investments?

International investing is essential and offers expected returns as high or higher than the

United States. If an asset has low correlation with other holdings, it may well reduce the volatility of the total portfolio, even if the asset itself is volatile. That is what well-planned diversification can accomplish.

But average investors should invest abroad only through mutual funds, because there is too little information available about foreign individuals to make wise choices.

■ What factors should an investor consider when determining his or her own asset mix?

The most important fact about investing is that we do not know what the outcome of our decisions will be. Our choices and forecasts will often be wrong. How we handle ourselves under those circumstances will, more than anything else, determine our success as investors. My experience tells me that nothing else matters as much. Acting in panic almost always is a big mistake, and almost always an irreversible one.

■ How much risk should an investor take?

All investors should take as much risk as they can stand, because the purpose of investing is to make one's wealth grow. But the primary and overwhelming consideration is not age or occupation or other assets or family responsibilities: it is the ability to keep cool under fire. This factor defies generalization—we each have to make our own choices. Do not take so much risk that you are unable to handle the situation when things go wrong, because they will go wrong from time to time.

■ What's the biggest risk an investor can take?

Acting in ignorance is the biggest risk. You should not buy stocks of companies whose products or business you do not understand. That's what mutual funds are for. I own directly no technology stocks and only a couple of major blue-chip healthcare stocks, because I am basically ignorant of what makes those companies tick. Stocks with funny names are anathema to me. When their prices fall, I will have absolutely no

FACT FILE:
BETTING ON BOWIE

■ *Would you risk your money on a rock star? David Bowie is the first entertainer to package himself as an investment. In early 1997, Fahnestock & Co., a New York investment firm, floated Bowie Bonds (7.9 percent, 10-year average-life bonds). The bonds, backed by Bowie's future music royalties, were rated single-A by Moody. Investors snapped up some $55 million worth.*

■ *Look for more celebrity securities. Dorsey & Whitney, a Minneapolis law firm, polled 1,000 Americans to determine the most bankable celebrities. Here are the top five they'd bet on:*

Oprah Winfrey	27%
Steven Spielberg	19%
Tiger Woods	15%
Michael Jordan	14%
Tom Cruise	8%

PETER LYNCH'S TEN COMMANDMENTS

Legendary stock-picker Peter Lynch, vice-chairman of Fidelity Investments and former head of its hugely successful Magellan Fund, preaches about the basics of good investing whenever he can find a pulpit. Much has been written about his stockpicking strategies. Here we've synthesized his approach into 10 basics—a list investors may want to consult before buying or selling:

1. DON'T TIME THE MARKET. It is futile to predict what will happen with the economy, interest rates, and the stock market. You can't time the market, so don't bother. If market-timing is so great, why aren't all market-timers fabulously rich?

2. TAKE THE LONG VIEW. Investors who were out of the market in 40 key months during the past 40 years showed returns that underperformed meager earnings from savings accounts.

3. DON'T WORRY—even though there's always something to worry about. In this century, we've had a correction of 10 percent or more about every two years. About every six years, we have a correc-

tion of 25 percent or more. It's only natural.

4. DON'T PULL OUT EARLY. Those who sell to avoid a bear market are sure to miss the rally that follows. If the risk is intolerable, maybe you shouldn't be investing in the first place.

5. DON'T FEAR BEAR MARKETS. They offer opportunities. A correction gives investors a good chance to pick up favorite stocks at bargain prices.

6. KNOW WHAT YOU OWN. Stock prices rise because corporate profits rise, and the same with dividends. There's a company behind every stock. Get to know that company, its management, its finances, its business.

7. AVOID LONG SHOTS. Stick to companies with good, stable management and healthy balance sheets.

8. RIDE OUT A RECESSION. Even if an economic slump drives down corporate profits by half, and stock prices follow suit, you'll still do better than investing in bonds, for example.

9. STICK WITH STOCKS. They outperformed bonds in eight of the nine decades in this century—and are likely to do so in this decade, too.

10. DON'T LISTEN TO ANYONE who makes comments like: "It's only $3. What can you lose?" "When it rebounds to $10, sell," or, "You missed that one, but can catch the next one."

idea whether to sell or buy more. And many other more knowledgeable investors will take advantage of me on the other side of any trade I make.

■ **What's your advice on weathering a bear market?**

Bear markets are opportunities, but only the cool headed will be in a position to take advantage of those opportunities. If you

were greedy and took too much risk in the bull market, such as refusing to cut back or buying even more as your stocks appreciated, you will be unable to weather the bear market. Prudence pays off big. It may cut returns on the way up, but it puts you in a position to do your buying when the great bargains are really there and the downside risks are getting smaller each day the market declines.

THE WORLD IS YOUR OYSTER

How to find the pearls in the universe of foreign markets

A n increasing number of financial analysts are suggesting that investors put some of their portfolio dollars into foreign stocks. Here's their rather convincing argument: the world economy is expanding, corporate profits are revving up, interest rates are heading down, inflation is leveling off, and many stocks in foreign firms are trading at bargain prices. What's more, since some foreign markets move in different cycles than U.S. markets over periods of five years or so, investing internationally can provide a hedge against a downturn in the American market. (See box, facing page.)

As enticing as those arguments may be, pumping money into foreign stocks is not for the faint hearted. The foreign markets can be volatile, to say the least. After spectacular gains in 1993—the average emerging market stock fund gained 72 percent—global markets crashed. The average fund lost 10 percent in 1994 and 7 percent in 1995. By 1996, however, investors were toasting an average 20 percent rise in European markets alone.

How much of a model portfolio should go overseas? Pension funds, huge investors of retirement monies, have been moving aggressively into foreign assets of late. Maria Fiorini Ramirez, international economist and president of MFR Inc., suggests that individual investors gradually shift to overseas securities, increasing the allocation by 5 percent per quarter until 30 percent of your portfolio is invested overseas. Ideally, she says one-third of these assets should go into fixed income securities, via international bond funds such as Templeton's Emerging Market Income Fund,

Lexington Ramirez Global Income Fund, or MFR Global Funds, and the rest in equities. For diversification, she suggests putting one third of the total foreign assets in emerging markets, the remainder in developed countries.

Which countries look good for the long term? We asked a number of investment advisers; here are some of their top choices:

ASIA

■ **INDONESIA.** An enticing country whose companies are expected to show an earnings growth rate of 18 percent, on average, for several years to come.

■ **MALAYSIA.** This country has had steady economic growth of more than 8 percent annually since 1988. Its inflation rate was a low 3.3 percent in 1996 and its currency has been appreciating against the dollar.

■ **PHILIPPINES.** The economy has evolved from agriculture to manufacturing. More plants are producing high-tech goods. The government's embrace of deregulation is attracting foreign investment, which is driving economic growth. The inflation rate is 4.4 percent and GDP growth is at about 5 percent.

■ **SOUTH KOREA.** This nation's economy is expected to expand 5 to 7 percent annually for a decade. South Korea is finally cracking open the door to outside investment in its stock market. Many argue that the Korean stock market is cheap.

LATIN AMERICA

■ **ARGENTINA.** Back on track after a few years of turmoil, Argentina's GDP should grow by 5 percent in 1997. Inflation is close to zero. Unemployment is high, but strong growth should add new jobs.

■ **BRAZIL.** This country has turned itself around, bringing inflation down from 2,000 percent a year to about 25 percent a year. Brazil's stock market is cheaply priced, at about 11 times earnings. Corporate profits are expected to rise nearly 30 percent in 1998.

COUNTRIES TO VISIT—AND THOSE TO AVOID

Which foreign markets should you invest in? Pick a country whose economy does not rise and fall in tandem with the American economy, suggests editors of the World Money Analyst, *an investment newsletter (☎ 800–898–4685). After studying emerging markets, they've identified countries whose economies are most and least linked with the U.S. economy, riding high during good times and in the dumps during bad. Here are the findings:*

TOO CLOSE FOR COMFORT

The following countries closely mimic the ups and downs of the U.S. economy.

Country	Correlation	Return*
Canada	0.59	1.6%
Netherlands	0.49	1.5
Sweden	0.46	−.09
Australia	0.43	−2.7
Belgium	0.42	0.4
United Kingdom	0.41	−3.9
France	0.41	1.5

* One-year returns as of March 31, 1997

A MIND OF THEIR OWN

These countries have the least correlation, making them safer investments.

Country	Correlation	Return*
India	−0.11	21.0
Colombia	0.03	19.6
Peru	0.08	13.5
Venezuela	0.09	−7.9
Taiwan	0.09	18.5
South Korea	0.12	-8.4
Chile	0.14	14.6
Brazil	0.16	29.5

■ **CHILE.** Many believe this is the tiger of Latin America. It's tops in terms of savings and investment. Average annual per capita growth since 1985 has been 4.8 percent. Analysts expect a 16 percent annual rise in corporate profits over the next five years.

EASTERN EUROPE

■ **ROMANIA.** Eastern Europe was an investor's dream in 1996. Hungary, Poland, and the Czech Republic showered shareholders with returns of 104 percent, 57 percent, and 29 percent respectively in 1996. Many think the region's next hot spot will be Romania, where the government is turning toward economic reforms and taking a more pro-investor stance. For the moment, the market is not directly available to U.S. investors, although it may be soon.

■ **RUSSIA.** The Russian stock market was up 139 percent in 1996, and many analysts believe it will rise further. The big draw: stocks are selling at rock-bottom prices. Of course, that's due largely to Russia's political instability, which brings volatility and lowers prices. But if you think the Bear can resolve its problems, then the time is ripe for you to invest in Russia.

AFRICA

■ **SOUTH AFRICA.** This market has been in the doldrums for years, turning in an abysmal performance in 1996. But some are turning bullish on South Africa, citing its average earnings growth of 20 percent or more and a price-to-earnings ratio of 10 or lower in early 1997. With inflation at its lowest in 24 years, and a surging trade surplus, the country deserves a new look.

NORTH AMERICA

■ **CANADA.** Tame inflation and a trading partner—the U.S.—that buys 80 percent of its exports augur well for corporate profits. Stock prices aren't cheap, however, and Canada's economy often mimics that of the U.S.

EUROPE

■ **PORTUGAL.** The numbers look good for this country. The 1996 inflation rate was a mere 3.3 percent, and unemployment held steady at 7.3 percent. More important, the deficit in relation to GDP is only slightly above 3 percent.

A LITTLE EXTRA DIVIDEND

Why companies whose payout climbs regularly are a good bet

I f the stock market has you jittery but you don't want to bail out altogether, look for stocks that have a habit of raising dividends year after year, no matter what. That's the strategy pushed by, among others, Peter Lynch, vice chairman of Fidelity Investments and manager of its Magellan fund for 13 years. (See box on page 9 for more of Lynch's stock-picking approach.) As Lynch explained in a 1996 issue of *Worth* magazine, investing in so-called dividend achievers is a way of getting the best of both worlds: Money to live on that normally comes from bonds, and growth that comes from stocks.

One reason that Lynch and others love dividend achievers is that these companies provide steadiness in rough times. Take, for example, American Home Products Corp., maker of Robitussin, Gulden's mustard, etc., which has had 44 years of dividend growth. If its stock were to skid 5 percent over the next year, an investor would still come out ahead, thanks to its 6 percent or so dividend. When directors raise dividends, they think future earnings will be good enough to allow the higher payouts, and they're usually right.

Lynch goes so far as to propose that investors sink 100 percent of their investment capital into a portfolio of companies that pay decent dividends. An easy way to invest in dividend achievers is to buy into an S&P 500 index fund, recently yielding about 3 percent. Or you can be more selective and choose a few dividend achievers from the list in *Moody's Handbook of Dividend Achievers*. (Cost: $24.95. Call: ☎ 800–342–5647, ext. 0546.)

Of the 13,200 publicly traded stocks tracked by Moody's, about 17 percent increased their dividends in 1996. Of those, 345 companies have raised dividends for at least 10 years in a row. Winn-Dixie Stores holds the title for the longest stretch of annual dividend hikes: 53 years. Close behind is Ohio Casualty Corp. at 51 years. Both companies ranked in the top third of Moody's list for total returns, that is, dividend income plus price appreciation.

The total returns of many of the dividend achievers compare favorably with other investments. And, when the bull market soars, the combination of price appreciation and reinvested dividends yielded some dazzling returns. Apogee Enterprises, for example, which topped Moody's 1996 list of total return achievers, had a total return of 136.7 percent.

■ TOP DIVIDEND ACHIEVERS

The top 10, ranked by the average annual dividend growth rate, 1986 to 1996.

Company	Industry	Growth rate
Fed. National Mortgage Assoc. (Fannie Mae)	Financial	46.2%
United Asset Mngmt.	Investment	45.5%
Travelers Group Inc.	Insurance	40.5%
Watts Industries Inc.	Manufacturing	39.5%
Student Loan Marketing Assoc. (Sallie Mae)	Financial	31.3%
Alex. Brown Inc.	Investment	30.5%
Raymond James Financial	Financial	26.9%
Brady (W.H.) Co.	Manufacturing	26.2%
Cintas Corp.	Business service	25.9%
Corus Bankshares Inc.	Financial	25.9%

■ TOP IN TOTAL RETURNS

The companies with the greatest stock-price appreciation plus dividends in 1996.

Company	Industry	Return rate
Apogee Enterprises Inc.	Glass/aluminum	136.7%
Frisch's Restaurants Inc.	Restaurant	89.0%
Flowers Industries Inc.	Food	83.6%
American Precision Ind.	Equipment	83.5%
United Carolina Bancshares	Banking	80.4%
Helmerich & Payne	Oil and gas	77.4%
Alex. Brown Inc.	Investment	74.5%
Diebold Inc.	Manufacturing	72.6%
Synovus Financial	Financial	72.2%
Eaton Vance Corp.	Investment	71.9%

SOURCE: *Moody's 1997 Handbook of Dividend Achievers.*

BONDS
▼
WHERE TO GET GOOD PAPER

Brokers, funds, and Uncle Sam all offer an on-ramp to bond investing

Once you've selected from the variety of available bonds—government bonds, U.S. Savings bonds, Treasury bills, Treasury notes, municipal bonds, and corporate bonds—how do you go about buying them? Depending on the type, you have several options.

Municipals and corporate bonds are bought through brokers. You can buy Treasuries through a bank, a broker, a mutual fund, or through a government program called Treasury Direct, ☎ 202-874-4000. The advantage of buying through the government is that there is no commission.

You also can open an account and learn about scheduled bond auctions. Two- and three-year bonds are available for a minimum $5,000 investment. Five- and 10-year notes require a minimum $1,000 investment.

For greater diversification, you can turn to bond funds (see table below). You can invest in small amounts and a professional manager runs the show. A drawback: Bond funds constantly trade bonds and don't hold them to maturity, so you lose the guarantee that you'll get a bond's face value at a certain date.

When investing in bond funds, scrutinize fees and other expenses. After all, the return is usually so low, why dish out 4 or 5 percent on fees? To determine a bond's true return, find out the yield and subtract the fund's annual expense ratio.

To learn more about fixed-income investments, try the Web site Bonds Online (http://www.bonds.com). You'll find links to bond tidbits around the Web and the Bond Professor, who offers investment basics, as well as a chance to submit your own questions.

■ CHOOSING A BOND STRATEGY
The determining factor is when you expect to cash in

TIME FRAME	TYPE OF BOND	COMMENTS
Less than 1 year	Any	■ You may want to consider a money market fund for stability of principal.
1–2 years	Short-term bond	■ If interest rates are stable or fall, you could get higher than money market fund yields as well as potential capital appreciation. If interest rates rise, this fund could still be a good choice. Unless rates rise substantially, you may still come out ahead of a money market.
2–4 years	Federal or state tax-free bond, mortgage bond, government bond, investment grade bond	■ If you're counting on the fund to supply you with a stream of income, keep in mind that higher yields can help compensate for some of the drop in the value of your account. If you invested to diversify a stock portfolio, keep in mind that the long-term price volatility of bonds is typically lower than that of stocks.
More than 4 years	Aggressive bond	■ Although interest rates can affect these funds, they tend to benefit from a healthy economy. Over the long term, income provides the bulk of total return in bond funds. If you are comfortable with the quality of risk, aggressive funds provide the highest income.

SOURCE: Fidelity Investments.

BONDS THAT BEAT INFLATION

Uncle Sam's indexed bonds could boost your long-term savings

Economists have long clamored for bonds that would eliminate the effects of inflation, which can be insidious. Inflation cuts the worth of a bond's coupon payments and its eventual redemption value. For example, if you bought a 30-year government bond in 1966 yielding 5 percent, the bond would now be worth only 85 percent of its original value, thanks to years of higher-than-expected inflation.

To remove some of that risk, the Treasury has begun issuing a new bond offering returns that rise and fall in line with inflation. The bonds are intended to help the average investor save for retirement, the kids' college tuition, and other long-term goals. The 10-year bonds are issued at a minimum denomination of $1,000 and pay interest twice a year.

Here's how they work. Say you invest $1,000, and the bonds are priced to yield 3 percent. If inflation rises at a 1 percent rate that year, you would get two interest payments totalling $30.30. If inflation rises to 2 percent, the value of the indexed note would be adjusted upward to $1,030 and interest would be paid on that amount. Your payments would come to $34.96. Adjustments are made every six months. After 10 years, assuming similar inflation, the investor would have received $351.57 in semiannual interest payments and would be paid $1,343.92 in principal at maturity.

There are a few trade offs. One is a lower coupon: recent bonds carried an initial interest rate of 3.45 percent, compared with 6.6 percent for a similar non-inflation-adjusted Treasury note. The other is that although the bonds are exempt from state and local taxes, you still have to pay federal taxes. And, both the interest income and the semiannual adjustments to principal are taxable, even though the adjustments are not paid out until maturity. For that reason alone, the bonds may be best suited for tax-deferred accounts like IRAs and 401(k)s.

Aside from buying the inflation-indexed bonds at a Treasury auction, you can also invest in them through mutual funds, sold by families such as Twentieth Century/Benham.

STAYING AHEAD OF THE CURVE

Want to know where bonds are headed? Consult the yield curve. The yield curve, which can be found in *The Wall Street Journal* or *Investor's Business Daily*, shows how interest rates and bonds of different maturities relate to each other.

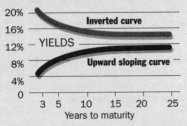

A normal curve moves upward, showing that interest rates rise as maturities increase. The curve turns downward, or inverts, when short-term rates are higher than long-term rates. When short- and long-term rates are about the same, the curve is flat—the market sees little difference between the short-term and long-term risks, so buying longer-term bonds gives you only a slight premium. When short-term yields exceed long-term yields, the curve inverts, a sign of a recession to come. In a recession, you want to be in long-term bonds; eventually the curve will normalize and the value of the bonds will rise.

HOW TO ANALYZE A MUTUAL FUND

There's no lack of information out there. Here's what to focus on

Mutual fund investors can't make perfect choices every time—too many variables are stacked against them. They need to compile the ideal portfolio, buy into a fund at precisely the right time, and bail out just before the precisely wrong time. But investors can stay a step ahead and avoid serious blunders by knowing the basics of analyzing a mutual fund's performance. Here are a few simple lessons in evaluating a fund:

■ **RETURN.** Many investors obsess over a fund's yield, which tells you the current income distributed annually. But the true test of any fund, even one bought for income, is total return. Total return measures the increases and decreases of your investment over time, assuming the reinvestment of dividends and subtracting the fund's costs. If you'd rather skip the mathematics involved in calculating a fund's total return, just call the fund company's toll-free number and ask for it.

When comparing the total returns of several funds, be sure you're comparing only figures calculated over the same time period, say January 1 to December 31. Determine if sales charges have been deducted from total returns before you compare fund results. Some funds and most financial publications report total returns before sales fees and other costs have been deducted. Then run year-by-year and cumulative comparisons, say, over five years or since the fund's inception. If most of the cumulative gains have been earned over the past year or two, you're looking at a fund that could burn out.

■ **RISK.** It isn't easy to calculate or compare how much risk a mutual fund assumes but getting an idea of risk is important. A few statistical measures that give an idea of a fund's risk include a fund's beta, alpha, and standard deviation. Beta measures the volatility of a fund's return against an index, such as the Standard & Poor's 500. Aggressive investors prefer funds with a beta above 1.0, which means the fund's returns have moved up and down more than the S&P as a whole. A more conservative choice would be a fund with a .75 beta, for example, meaning it was 75 percent less volatile than the market.

Alpha reports how much the fund's performance deviated from its expected return. A fund with a positive alpha did better than expected. A negative alpha means the fund underperformed.

Academics especially like a risk measure called standard deviation. It gauges how widely a fund's return swings from one time period to another. A fund with volatile returns is supposedly more likely to show a big loss in the future.

■ **INVESTMENT STYLE AND MIX.** Two funds can fall under the same general investment category but have very different styles that affect their performance. The reason: interpretations of terms such as "aggressive growth" may vary from fund to fund. The prospectus will give you a precise explanation of a fund's strategy and investment objective. (Funds often change their investment style or management team, making past performance a nearly useless measure.) Check out a fund's mix of investments, too. Exposure to a vulnerable industry or to volatile foreign stocks can go a long way toward explaining a fund's performance.

■ **LEVERAGE.** Many funds hedge against possible changes in interest rates or currency values with strategies that may be risky. Be sure you're comfortable with a fund's hedging strategy. Can the fund invest in risky derivatives, fill up on Latin American stocks, sell short? Often, the techniques help returns, but just as often they can cause deep losses. Scrutinize the prospectus.

■ **TAXES.** Don't ignore the tax implications of

GETTING TO KNOW A FUND'S STYLE

Funds are generally grouped according to investment objectives, so investors can compare apples with apples. Here are the categories Morningstar Inc. used to compile its rankings of the top 130 mutual funds, which begin on the facing page.

■ **AGGRESSIVE FUNDS:** Seek the rapid growth of capital, often through investment in smaller companies and with techniques involving greater than average risk, such as frequent trading, short selling, and leveraging.

■ **GROWTH FUNDS:** Invest primarily in equity securities. Current income, if it is considered at all, is a secondary objective.

■ **TOTAL RETURN FUNDS:** Include equity income funds that invest at least 65 percent of assets in equity securities with above-average yields, and growth and income funds that seek growth of capital and current income as near-equal objectives.

■ **INTERNATIONAL FUNDS:** Include stock funds, which generally invest at least 40 percent of their equity holdings in foreign stocks.

■ **SPECIALTY FUNDS:** Seek capital appreciation by investing in equity securities in a single industry, like health, technology, or natural resources.

■ **HYBRID FUNDS:** Have substantial holdings in both stocks and bonds, or hold securities that have characteristics of both stocks and bonds.

■ **CONVERTIBLE BOND FUNDS:** Invest primarily in bonds and preferred stocks that can be converted into common stocks.

■ **CORPORATE BOND HIGH-YIELD FUNDS:** Usually invest 65 percent or more of their assets in bonds rated below investment grade.

■ **CORPORATE BOND FUNDS:** Invest in fixed-income securities, primarily corporate bonds of various quality ratings. This category includes High-Qual-ity Corporate Bonds that have at least 65 percent of their holdings in securities rated A or higher.

■ **GOVERNMENT BOND GENERAL FUNDS:** Invest in a blend of mortgage-backed securities, Treasuries, and agency securities.

■ **INTERNATIONAL BOND FUNDS:** Seek current income with capital appreciation as a secondary objective by investing primarily in bonds denominated in currencies other than the U.S. dollar. Also includes Short-Term World income funds that seek higher yields than a money market fund and less fluctuation of their net asset value than a world bond fund.

■ **MUNICIPAL BOND FUNDS:** These funds seek income that is exempt from federal income tax through state or municipal bonds.

buying a particular fund, but don't get carried away by potential tax bills either. There's no doubt that taxes can take the fun out of a mutual fund gain. If you're shopping for a tax-free fund, avoid those that post most of their income in gains. If you're buying stock funds, find out when the fund posts its annual gains, usually at year-end, and wait until after that move to buy in.

But don't pick a fund just for its tax advantages. A study by the *No-Load Fund Analyst*, a newsletter based in Orinda, Calif., found that there's not much change in equity-fund rankings on an after-tax basis. So, the report suggests, investors should focus first on performance, not taxes. Use the tax analysis only when you're deciding between two similar funds with comparable gross returns.

THE 130 TOP MUTUAL FUNDS

Here Morningstar Inc., the Chicago-based investment information publisher, ranks the top 10 mutual funds in 13 different categories. The funds are ranked based on their three-year annualized return as of March 31, 1997. The rating column refers to Morningstar's exclusive five-star rating system. Notes explaining the rating system and various terms used throughout the tables can be found on pages 18 and 19.

FUND NAME	STYLE	TOTAL RETURN			M★ RATING	EXPENSE RATIO	MAX. SALES CHARGE	NET ASSETS $MM	PHONE
		1 YR.	3 YR.	5 YR.					
AGGRESSIVE GROWTH									
1. Alger Capital Appreciation B	MG	1.11	27.66	NA	★★★★	2.45	5.00	165.3	800–992–3863
2. Rydex Nova	LB	19.99	25.97	NA	★★★★★	1.31	0.00	385.6	800–820–0888
3. Alliance Quasar A	SG	9.80	22.89	15.83	★★★	1.79	4.25	280.4	800–227–4618
4. Alliance Quasar B	SG	8.90	21.98	14.81	★★★	1.03	4.00	217.0	800–227–4618
5. Alliance Quasar C	SG	9.03	21.97	NA	★★★★	2.61	1.00	62.1	800–227–4618
6. Oppenheimer Capital Ap A	MG	17.14	20.42	14.81	★★★	1.03	5.75	978.2	800–525–7048
7. Oppenheimer Capital Ap C	MG	18.14	19.34	NA	★★★★	1.90	1.00	17.0	800–525–7048
8. Kaufmann	SG	0.92	18.21	16.90	★★★★	2.17	0.00	540.0	800–237–0132
9. New USA Growth	MG	5.34	17.56	NA	★★	2.69	5.00	208.4	800–222–2872
10. USAA Aggressive Growth	SG	–5.70	17.52	11.02	★	0.74	0.00	690.4	800–382–8722
GROWTH									
1. White Oak Growth Stock	LG	23.16	27.85	NA	★★★★★	0.97	0.00	93.9	800–932–7781
2. Legg Mason Value Prim	LV	33.49	27.69	20.35	★★★★★	1.82	0.00	2318.1	800–577–8589
3. Mairs & Power Growth	MB	21.36	27.39	20.09	★★★★★	0.99	0.00	182.9	800–304–7404
4. Rydex OTC	LG	31.84	26.91	NA	★★★★★	1.33	0.00	137.7	800–820–0888
5. Pepp America-Abroad	LG	24.30	28.49	17.37	★★★★★	1.22	0.00	41.8	800–421–4004
6. Franklin CA Growth I	MG	15.09	26.40	20.55	★★★★★	0.71	4.50	244.5	800–342–5236
7. Torray	MV	19.12	26.22	18.89	★★★★★	1.25	0.00	182.5	800–443–3036
8. Dreyfus Appreciation	LG	22.92	25.18	15.19	★★★★	0.91	0.00	1132.0	800–645–6561
9. Dreyfus Large Company Value	LV	21.80	24.56	NA	★★★★★	1.25	0.00	79.8	800–645–6561
10. Fidelity Dividend Growth	MB	18.35	24.20	NA	★★★★★	0.99	0.00	79.8	800–544–8888
TOTAL RETURN									
1. Legg Mason Value Prim	LV	33.49	27.69	20.35	★★★★★	1.82	0.00	2318.1	800–577–8589
2. Torray	MV	19.12	26.22	18.89	★★★★★	1.25	0.00	182.5	800–443–3036
3. Rydex Nova	LB	19.99	25.97	NA	★★★★★	1.31	0.00	385.6	800–443–3038
4. Dreyfus Large Company Value	LV	21.80	24.56	NA	★★★★★	1.25	0.00	79.8	800–845–6561
5. Kemper-Dreman High Return A	LV	25.01	24.48	18.95	★★★★★	1.25	5.75	557.5	800–621–1048
6. Smith Breeden Equity Plus	LB	21.41	23.47	NA	★★★★★	0.90	0.00	12.5	800–221–3138
7. Victory Diversified Stock A	LB	19.18	22.89	17.06	★★★★	1.05	4.75	637.0	800–539–3863
8. Washington Mutual Investors	LV	19.10	22.79	17.04	★★★★	0.66	5.75	27704.4	800–421–4120
9. Selected American	LV	26.36	22.75	15.74	★★★★	1.09	0.00	1562.7	800–243–1575
10. Westwood Equity Ret	LB	19.09	22.63	17.81	★★★★★	1.50	0.00	58.3	800–937–8966

■ EXPERT LIST

FUND NAME	STYLE	TOTAL RETURN			M★ RATING	EXPENSE RATIO	MAX. SALES CHARGE	NET ASSETS $MM	PHONE
		1 YR.	3 YR.	5 YR.					
INTERNATIONAL EQUITY									
1. Wright EquiFund-Netherlands	ES	20.95	21.38	15.25	★★★★★	2.00	0.00	9.6	800–888–9471
2. Dean Witter European Growth	ES	22.90	19.92	19.66	★★★★★	2.23	5.00	1461.5	800–869–3863
3. Premier Growth A	LB	20.97	19.78	NA	★★★★	1.25	4.50	58.6	800–554–4611
4. Janus Worldwide	WS	20.24	19.39	18.76	★★★★★	1.01	0.00	6570.8	800–525–8983
5. Pioneer Europe A	ES	25.17	19.28	15.57	★★★★	1.93	5.75	122.1	800–225–6292
6. Premier Growth B	LB	20.02	18.91	NA	★★★★	2.00	4.00	115.6	800–554–4611
7. Pioneer Europe A	ES	24.08	18.88	NA	★★★★★	2.74	4.00	29.8	800–225–6292
8. American Cent-20thC Intl Dis	FS	29.25	18.67	NA	★★★★★	2.00	0.00	511.6	800–345–2021
9. Putnam Europe Growth A	ES	21.39	18.30	16.61	★★★★★	1.47	5.75	218.3	800–225–1581
10. Wright EquiFund-Nordic	ES	24.03	18.27	NA	★★★★★	2.00	0.00	5.8	800–888–9471
SPECIALTIES									
1. Fidelity Sel Electronics	T	33.09	34.96	33.36	★★★★★	1.22	3.00	1786.3	800–544–8888
2. Fidelity Sel Energy Service	N	31.15	31.80	23.29	★★★	1.58	3.00	443.7	800–544–8888
3. Fidelity Sel Health Care	H	13.35	30.65	15.10	★★★★	1.30	3.00	1374.1	800–544–8888
4. Fidelity Sel Home Finance	F	30.76	29.96	30.96	★★★★★	1.32	3.00	1174.7	800–544–8888
5. Vanguard Spec Health Care	H	14.19	27.88	18.59	★★★★★	0.45	0.00	3024.5	800–662–7447
6. Davis Financial A	F	30.72	27.79	23.97	★★★★★	1.18	4.75	125.5	800–279–0279
7. Fidelity Sel Regional Banks	F	29.69	27.30	24.92	★★★★★	1.40	3.00	838.3	800–544–8888
8. Putnam Health Sciences A	H	8.45	27.00	14.34	★★★★	1.10	5.75	1438.5	800–255–1581
9. State St. Research Glob Res A	N	42.12	26.75	24.23	★★★★★	1.75	4.50	87.3	800–882–0052
10. Seligman Communicate & Info A	T	15.21	26.54	26.56	★★★★	1.61	4.75	2483.8	800–221–2783
HYBRID									
1. Zweig Managed Assets C	IH	11.5	7.97	NA	★★★★	2.29	1.25	418.6	800–444–2706
2. Zweig Managed Assets A	IH	11.94	8.72	NA	★★★	1.59	5.50	113.9	800–444–2706
3. ZSA Asset Allocation	DH	11.20	9.19	NA	★★★	1.91	0.00	8.2	800–525–3863
4. Westwood Balanced Svc	DH	13.87	16.68	NA	★★★★	1.57	4.00	12.4	800–937–8966
5. Westwood Balanced Ret	DH	13.89	17.00	14.57	★★★★★	1.32	0.00	40.6	800–937–8966
6. Warburg Pincus Balanced	DH	8.34	15.12	12.86	★★★★	1.53	0.00	35.5	800–927–2874
7. Waddell & Reed Asset Stret B	DH	–0.85	NA	NA	NA	2.54	3.00	13.8	913–236–2000
8. Vista Balanced B	DH	11.00	12.79	NA	★★★	2.00	5.00	10.9	800–648–4782
9. Vista Balanced A	DH	11.79	13.82	NA	★★★	1.25	4.50	65.1	800–648–4782
10. Victory Balanced B	DH	12.46	14.34	NA	★★★	1.27	4.75	293.6	800–539–3863

EXPLANATION OF TERMS

STYLE
Growth-oriented funds **(G)** generally include companies with the potential to increase earnings faster than the rest of the market. Value-oriented funds **(V)** focus on stocks that are undervalued by the market. A blend of the two **(B)** may con-tain growth and value stocks, or stocks that exhibit both character-istics. Funds with medi-an-market capitaliza-tions of less than $1 billion are labeled small-company funds **(S)**. Funds with median market capitalizations between $1 billion and $5 billion are labeled medium **(M)** offerings, and funds with median market capitalizations exceeding $5 billion qualify for the large **(L)** label. Fixed-income funds are split into three maturity groups—short **(S)**, intermediate **(I)**, and long **(L)**—and three credit quality groups—high **(H)**, medium **(M)**, and low **(L)**. Funds with an average effective maturity of less than four years qualify as short-term bond funds; those with maturity longer than 10 years are long term. Other abbreviations used are: **ES** (Europ-ean Stock); **WS** (World Stock); **FS** (Foreign Stock); **T** (Technology); **N** (Natural Resources); **H** (Health); **F** (Finan-cial.); **IH** (Internat. Hybrid); **DH** (Domestic Hybrid). See page 16 for definitions. NOTE: There is no designation for a fund if its style is the same as its cate-gory (i.e., convertible, multisector bond, etc.)

TOTAL RETURN
Total return is calculat-

■ **EXPERT LIST**

FUND NAME	STYLE	TOTAL RETURN			M★ RATING	EXPENSE RATIO	MAX. SALES CHARGE	NET ASSETS $MM	PHONE
		1 YR.	3 YR.	5 YR.					
MULTISECTOR BOND									
1. EV Marathon Strategic Income		17.51	**11.87**	7.23	★★★★	2.18	3.00	131.8	800–225–6265
2. North American Strat Inc A		12.37	**10.75**	NA	★★★★★	1.50	4.75	15.5	800–872–8037
3. MFS Strategic Income A		11.36	**10.05**	8.23	★★★★	1.13	4.75	55.2	800–637–2929
4. North American Strat Inc C		11.77	**9.89**	NA	★★★★★	2.15	1.00	26.9	800–872–8037
5. North American Strat Inc B		11.77	**8.89**	NA	★★★★★	2.15	5.00	32.8	800–872–8037
6. Hancock Strategic Income A		10.40	**9.69**	8.52	★★★	1.03	4.50	407.7	800–225–5291
7. Phoenix Multi-Sector F/I A		13.07	**9.55**	10.11	★★★★	1.10	4.75	185.2	800–243–4361
8. MFS Strategic Income B		10.69	**9.33**	NA	★★★★★	1.80	4.00	34.8	800–637–2929
9. Van Kampen Am Cap Strat IncA		13.78	**9.23**	NA	★★★	4.11	4.75	42.0	800–421–5666
10. T. Rowe Price Spectrum Inc		7.83	**9.01**	8.80	★★★★★	0.00	0.00	1441.0	800–638–5660
CONVERTIBLE BOND									
1. Davis Convertible Secs A		24.93	**17.12**	NA	★★★	1.14	4.75	47.5	800–279–0279
2. Calamos Growth & Income A		12.93	**15.04**	13.64	★★★	2.00	4.75	8.4	800–823–7386
3. Pacific Horizon Captl Inc A		18.03	**14.49**	16.29	★★★★	1.23	4.50	307.4	800–332–3863
4. Calamos Convertible A		13.17	**14.08**	12.52	★★★	1.50	4.75	36.8	800–823–7386
5. Putnam Convert Income-Grth A		12.96	**13.93**	13.95	★★★	1.06	5.75	996.1	800–225–1581
6. Franklin Convertible Secs I		12.57	**13.38**	14.39	★★★★	1.02	4.50	155.3	800–342–5236
7. Putnam Convert Income-Grth B		12.13	**12.89**	NA	★★★	1.81	5.00	181.6	800–225–1581
8. Key SBSF Convertible Secs		13.76	**12.79**	12.94	★★★★	1.31	0.00	65.8	800–539–3863
9. Value Line Convertible		10.58	**12.42**	12.31	★★★	1.07	0.00	68.9	800–223–0818
10. Harris Ins Convertible		15.01	**12.10**	11.30	★★★	0.80	4.50	1.2	800–982–8782
CORPORATE BOND—HIGH YIELD									
1. Northeast Investors		17.57	**12.84**	14.73	★★★★★	1.02	0.00	1561.1	800–225–6704
2. Value Line Aggressive Income		14.78	**11.91**	11.98	★★★★★	1.22	0.00	93.2	800–223–0818
3. Fidelity Spartan High-Income		10.77	**11.82**	13.43	★★★★★	0.79	0.00	1931.4	800–544–8888
4. Seligman High-Yield Bond A		9.56	**11.73**	12.70	★★★★★	1.09	4.75	473.0	800–221–2783
5. MainStay Hi-Yield Corp Bd B		11.87	**11.43**	13.63	★★★★★	1.60	5.00	2604.3	800–522–4202
6. Franklin AGE High Income I		12.16	**11.41**	11.24	★★★★	0.70	4.25	2586.9	800–342–5236
7. Pilgrim America High-Yield A		14.15	**11.34**	11.70	★★★★★	1.00	4.75	34.5	800–334–3444
8. First Invest Fund for Inc A		11.24	**11.16**	11.79	★★★★	1.18	6.25	432.5	800–423–4026
9. Legg Mason High-Yield Prim		12.87	**10.89**	NA	★★★★★	1.50	0.00	269.0	800–577–8589
10. Federated High-Income Bond A		11.88	**10.88**	11.15	★★★★★	1.22	4.50	823.5	800–341–7400

ed by taking the change in investment value, assuming the reinvestment of all income and capital-gains distributions during the period, and dividing by the initial investment value. Total returns for periods over a year are expressed in terms of compounded average annual returns.

RATING
Morningstar rates a fund's return performance relative to its class based on total returns adjusted for maximum front-end and applicable deferred loads and redemption fees. It then calculates the fund risk, mindful that most investors' biggest fear is losing money. The fund's comparative Risk score is then subtracted from its Return score. The result is plotted along a bell curve to determine the fund's rating. The top 10 percent of the class receives five stars (highest); the next 22.5 percent receives four stars (above average); the middle 35 percent earns three stars (average); those lower still in the next 22.5 percent receive two stars (below average); and the bottom 10 percent get one star.

EXPENSE RATIO
The annual expense ratio expresses the percentage of assets deducted each fiscal year for fund operating expenses.

SALES CHARGE
Maximum level of various fees and sales charges imposed by a fund. A deferred sales charge (D) is paid when you sell a fund.

NET ASSETS
The mutual fund's year-end net assets, recorded in millions of dollars.

■ **EXPERT LIST**

FUND NAME	STYLE	TOTAL RETURN			M★ RATING	EXPENSE RATIO	MAX. SALES CHARGE	NET ASSETS $MM	PHONE
		1 YR.	3 YR.	5 YR.					
CORPORATE BOND									
1. CGM Fixed-Income	L	6.68	**11.57**	11.50	★★★★★	0.85	0.00	39.6	800–345–4048
2. Strong Corporate Bond	I	8.01	**10.29**	10.57	★★★★	1.00	0.00	306.6	800–368–1030
3. Alliance Bond Corp Bond A	L	10.47	**9.79**	12.56	★★★★	1.20	4.25	347.4	800–227–4618
4. Vanguard Preferred Stock	L	10.72	**9.71**	9.24	★★★★	0.39	0.00	301.5	800–662–7447
5. Managers Bond	L	7.31	**9.15**	8.91	★★★★	1.34	0.00	31.8	800–835–3879
6. Alliance Bond Corp Bond C	L	9.71	**9.04**	NA	★★	1.90	1.00	150.0	800–227–4618
7. Alliance Bond Corp B	L	9.63	**9.01**	NA	★★	1.90	3.00	446.1	800–227–4618
8. Invesco Select Income	L	6.44	**8.28**	8.53	★★★★	1.01	0.00	268.9	800–525–8085
9. Smith Barney Invsmt Gr Bd A	L	4.35	**8.17**	NA	★	1.11	4.50	199.6	800–451–2010
10. IDS Bond A	I	7.02	**8.17**	9.31	★★★★	0.78	5.00	2627.7	800–328–8300
GOVERNMENT BOND—GENERAL									
1. American Cent-Ben TarMat2015	L	1.21	**8.24**	9.39	★	0.85	0.00	111.0	800–331–8331
2. American Cent-Ben TarMat2020	L	0.63	**8.14**	10.01	★	0.61	0.00	862.7	800–331–8331
3. American Cent-Ben TarMat2010	L	1.23	**7.82**	10.18	★	0.67	0.00	104.1	800–331–8331
4. Franklin Strategic Mortgage	I	6.31	**7.63**	NA	★★★★	0.00	4.25	7.1	800–342–5236
5. Vanguard F/I GNMA	I	5.87	**7.62**	6.96	★★★★	0.29	0.00	7429.3	800–662–7447
6. Frankllin Tax-Adv U.S. Govt	I	6.22	**7.29**	6.87	★★★	0.67	4.25	315.0	800–342–5236
7. Smith Breeden Interm Dur Gov	I	5.92	**7.22**	8.08	★★★★	0.90	0.00	37.9	800–221–3138
8. Franklin U.S. Govt Secs I	I	5.99	**7.16**	6.60	★★★★	0.61	4.25	9797.1	800–342–5236
9. Fidelity Spartan Ginnie Mae	I	5.21	**7.15**	6.41	★★★★	0.62	0.00	447.7	800–544–8888
10. Vanguard Adm Lng Trm US Tr	L	2.95	**7.14**	NA	★★	0.15	0.00	192.5	800–662–7447
INTERNATIONAL BOND									
1. GT Global High-Income A		32.74	19.15	NA	★★★★★	1.69	4.75	196.7	800–824–1580
2. Bear Stearns Emg Markts Debt A		33.06	19.12	NA	★★★★★	2.00	3.75	35.3	800–766–4111
3. Scudder Emerging Mrkts Income		31.09	19.05	NA	★★★★★	1.44	0.00	388.7	800–225–2470
4. GT Global High-Income B		31.93	18.35	NA	★★★★★	2.34	5.00	270.6	800–824–1580
5. Alliance Global Dollar Gov A		32.24	18.35	NA	★★★	1.65	4.25	29.0	800–227–4618
6. Fidelity New Markets Income		40.31	17.85	NA	★★★	1.09	0.00	377.3	800–544–8888
7. Fidelity Adv Emerg Mkts T		39.43	17.74	NA	★★★	1.50	3.50	98.7	800–522–7297
8. Alliance Global Dollar Gov C		31.46	17.45	NA	★★★	2.35	1.00	20.3	800–227–4618
9. Alliance Global Dollar Gov B		31.43	17.42	NA	★★★	2.37	3.00	88.5	800–227–4618
10. Merrill Lynch Americas Inc D		22.85	16.90	NA	★★★	1.60	4.00	19.8	800–637–3863
MUNICIPAL BOND (National Long)									
1. Excelsior King-Term Tax-Ex		5.25	8.50	8.77	★★★★★	0.77	0.00	112.6	800–446–1012
2. Executive Investors Ins T/E		5.51	8.27	8.84	★★★★	0.50	4.75	15.4	800–423–4026
3. United Municipal High-Inc A		8.03	8.23	8.43	★★★★★	0.81	4.25	418.4	800–366–5485
4. Blanchard Flexible T/F Bond		5.44	7.92	NA	★★★★	1.05	0.00	21.9	800–829–3863
5. Voyageur Natl High-Yld Muni		7.76	7.71	7.98	★★★★★	0.85	3.75	55.8	800–553–2143
6. United Municipal Bond A		6.36	7.62	7.92	★★★	0.68	4.25	960.0	800–366–5465
7. Stein Roe High-Yield Munis		5.99	7.58	6.52	★★★★★	0.85	0.00	302.0	800–338–2550
8. Franklin High Yld T/F Inc I		7.10	7.58	8.30	★★★★★	0.61	4.25	4502.4	800–342–5236
9. Alliance Muni Income Natl A		6.83	7.49	7.23	★★★★	0.69	4.25	322.3	800–227–4618
10. T. Rowe Price Summit MuniInc		6.87	7.42	NA	★★★★★	0.50	0.00	17.6	800–638–5660

HOW THE TOP MUTUAL FUND FAMILIES STACK UP

Dreyfus, Fidelity, Vanguard—they are household names. But how do they differ from each other and from other big fund families? The table below compares the biggest families[1], including both no-load funds, which charge no fees or commissions when you buy or sell fund shares, and load funds, which do levy them. Front-end loads are sales charges paid before an investor's money goes into the mutual fund. With back-end loads, sales charges are paid when an investor redeems or sells shares. The average expense ratio is the annual expenses shareholders can expect shown as a percentage of the funds' assets. For example, Vanguard's 0.40 percent average expense ratio means that the group's average stock fund costs 40 cents per $100 in assets to run. The industry average is 1.34 percent.

Fund Family ☎ Business hours[2]	Assets in $billions / Type[3]	Number of funds	Best fund Worst fund[4]	Exp. ratio front (F) back (B)	Initial minimum investment	Min. check- writing
AMERICAN FUNDS ☎ 800–421–9900 8 am–8 pm, M–F	$198 **Load**	14 stk 11 bnd 3 mm[5]	**Washington Mutual Inv** *Tax–Ex Money Fnd. of America*	0.78% F	$250– $2,500	$250
DEAN WITTER INTERCAPITAL ☎ 800–869–3863 8 am–8 pm, M–F	$80 **Load**	19 stk 27 bnd 9 mm	**Dean Witter Euro Grow** *Dean Witter NY Muni MM*	1.75% B	$1,000– $10,000	$500
DREYFUS CORP. ☎ 800–782–6620 24 hours, 7 days	$84 **No Load**	19 stk 27 bnd 9 mm	**Dreyfus Disc Stock; Rtl** *Dreyfus Prem Agg Gro; A*	0.92%	$2,500– $25,000	$500
FIDELITY MGT. & RESEARCH ☎ 800–544–8888 24 hours, 7 days	$469 **No Load**	83 stk 43 bnd 23 mm	**Fidelity Select Electronic** *Fidelity Yen Perform*	0.91%	$2,500– $10,000	$500
FRANKLIN TEMPLETON ☎ 800–632–2180 9 am–11 pm, M-F; 11 am–8pm, Sa	$146 **Load**	29 stk 55 bnd 6 mm	**Franklin Stra:CA Grow;1** *Franklin NY TF*	0.65% F	$2,500 $10,000	$500
IDS MUTUAL FUND GRP. ☎ 800–328–8300 8 am– 8 pm, M–F	$76 **Load**	17 stk 16 bnd 3 mm	**IDS Precious Metals A** *IDS Tax–Free Money; A*	0.90% F 1.64% B	$2,000–	$500
MERRILL LYNCH ASSET MGT. ☎ 800–637–3883 9 am–5 pm, M–F	$175 **Load**	22 stk 27 bnd 28 mm	**Merrill Lynch Growth Fund; A** *Merrill Sh–Tm Global; B*	1.07% F 2.09% B	$250– $5,000	$500
PUTNAM INVESTMENT MGT. CO. ☎ 800–225–8806 8:30 am–8pm, M–F	$137 **Load**	28 stk 21 bnd 5 mm	**Putnam New Oppty; A** *Putnam CA Txex*	1.16% F	$500	$500
SMITH BARNEY INC. ☎ 800–221–8806 8 am–8 pm, M–F	$81 **Load**	28 stk 21 bnd 12 mm	**CG Cap Mkts:Sm Cap Gro** *Smith Barney Muni: CA MM; A*	0.86% F	$1,000– $10,000	**None**
VANGUARD GROUP ☎ 800–635–1511 8 am–9 pm, M–F; 9–4, Sa	$264 **No Load**	33 stk 24 bnd 9 mm	**Vanguard Primecap** *Vanguard NJ TX–Fr: MM*	0.40%	$500– $50,000	$250

NOTES: **1.** Federated Investors is omitted from this list because it sells largely through bank trust departments. **2.** Eastern Standard Time. **3.** Assets as of January 31, 1997. **4.** Based on growth rates from March 31, 1992 to March 31, 1997. **5.** mm means "money market."

SOURCES: Lipper Analytical Services Inc.; Investment Company Institute; company reports.

WHERE LESS EQUALS MORE

No-load funds not only have fewer up-front charges but better returns

These days, investors bristle at paying commissions and sales charges when similar versions of a product are available without a fee. Hence, the attraction of no-loads, or mutual funds that don't charge a fee or commission to buy or sell its shares. No-loads are grabbing more than 45 percent of sales. Small wonder that the big brokerage firms, long leaders of mutual funds with loads, or costly sales charges, are plunging into no-load waters.

Full-service broker Smith Barney offers a deluxe service that includes no-fee transactions on mutual funds, stocks, and bonds. Investors get access to mutual fund and other investment research, and personal investment advice. The program isn't completely fee-free. Loads are waived, but there is a small yearly charge for the research and advice services based on the value of an investor's funds. Prudential Securities also has a no-load plan and other giant load firms are sure to jump in with no-load offerings.

The newcomers are pining after the business being snatched away by wildly successful programs like OneSource, offered by discount broker Charles Schwab. The plan offers one-stop shopping, making hundreds of no-load funds accessible with one phone call. All reporting is conveniently consolidated in one statement. For the services, investors pay only a small transaction fee, if any.

The lines between no-load and load funds were starting to blur even before the big boys got into the act. Sales charges on many traditional load funds have been shrinking. Up-front loads—which are paid at the time a mutual fund is purchased—have dropped from 8.5 percent in the early 1980s to about 4.5 percent and are expected to fall further.

As the question of fees begins to recede, other differences between no-loads and loads loom larger. Which are riskier, for example, and which are better performers? Conventional wisdom holds that no-loads take more risks because they want to make a bigger splash and attract aggressive investors. Not so, says a study by Morningstar Inc., the mutual fund research company. Based on standard measures, no-loads actually proved less risky on average than loads. Even on performance, Morningstar found that no-loads came out slightly ahead over the long haul. Over a five-year period, returns for no-load diversified equity funds came to 10.78 percent, compared to 9.83 percent for funds with loads.

Investors should focus less on the distinctions between load and no-loads, Morningstar concluded, and more on the services provided by load funds—and whether that advice is worth the added expense.

■ **WHAT TO AIM FOR**

Your odds of getting better returns rise when you invest in lower-cost funds. Here are the average annual expenses you can expect for various stock and bond funds. A .77 percent expense ratio for municipal bond funds, for example, means the average such fund costs 77 cents per $100 in assets to run.

DIVERSIFIED U.S. STOCK FUNDS	1.29%
Aggressive growth	1.72%
Equity income	1.25%
Growth	1.28%
Growth and income	1.18%
Small company	1.37%
INTERNATIONAL STOCK FUNDS	**1.77%**
Diversified foreign	1.62%
Europe	1.90%
Pacific	1.84%
BOND FUNDS	
Corporate bonds	0.84%
Government bonds	0.91%
Municipal bonds	0.77%

SOURCE: Morningstar Inc.

WHY YOU CAN'T BEAT THE MARKET

A stock market guru makes the case for index funds

Why search for just the right stock fund or manager when you can do better by investing in an unmanaged index fund? That's the question posed by proponents of index funds, which buy the stocks in the Standard & Poor's 500 to get the same performance as the index. Critics of index funds ask, why settle for mediocrity when you could hit on a fund that soars? As the debate rages on, investors have poured nearly $40 billion into index funds.

To get an expert's perspective, we consulted Princeton University economist Burton Malkiel, author of the classic investment book, *A Random Walk Down Wall Street* (W. W. Norton, 6th ed., 1996). Malkiel has long argued that investing in the stock market is like taking a random walk. Or, as he has often stated, "A blindfolded chimpanzee throwing darts at the stock pages could select a portfolio that would do as well as the experts." Here are Malkiel's views on index funds.

■ Are index funds all they're cracked up to be?

I have argued for over 20 years that an indexing strategy—simply buying and holding the hundreds of stocks making up the broad stock market averages—is probably the most sensible one for individuals and institutional investors. With index funds, investors can buy different types of stocks and get the benefits of stock and bond investing with no effort, minimal expense, and big tax savings.

■ How have index funds performed?

Over the past 25 years, the Standard & Poor 500 Stock Index has outperformed about 70 per-

cent of active investment managers. In 1995, more than 80 percent of the pros were trounced by the index. Statistics show similar results for professional investors like pension fund managers. And they've done well compared with other indexes, too, like the Wilshire 5000 Stock Index.

■ What's the biggest advantage of index funds?

The biggest benefit is the tax advantage of deferring capital gains taxes, or avoiding them altogether if the shares are left to an heir. Switching from stock to stock involves realizing capital gains that are subject to taxes, which cut net returns substantially. Index funds don't trade from security to security and therefore avoid capital gains taxes.

■ How do index-fund fees compare with those of traditional funds?

Very favorably. Fund expenses for actively managed funds average more than 1 percent a year, compared to less than .2 of a point for the largest public index funds.

■ What about the criticism that index funds simply guarantee mediocrity?

Well, you can't boast about the fantastic gains you've made by picking stock market winners. But index fund investors are likely to get better results than those of the typical fund manager, whose huge fees and large portfolio turnover reduce returns. To many, the guarantee of playing at par with the stock market nearly every time is very attractive.

■ Which index funds do you like?

The popularity of Standard & Poor's 500 funds may have inflated their value. But indexing isn't simply buying the S&P 500. I also like funds that match other indexes such as the broader Wilshire 5000. Some good values may exist in small-cap stocks, in real estate investment trusts, and in foreign equities. There are funds that match those indexes, such as Morgan Stanley Capital International Index of European and Asian Stocks, as well as emerging-markets indexes. These index funds have also generally outperformed actively managed funds that invest in similar securities.

READY-MADE PORTFOLIOS

These funds decide for you how to balance your investments

Jittery about jumping into the stock market? Would you rather have someone else do the investment work for you? Many reluctant investors are calming their nerves these days by tossing out piles of prospectuses and investing in asset allocation funds. These funds serve as sort of mini portfolios that aim to give you the kind of balance you want.

Asset allocation funds invest broadly in stocks, bonds, and money market instruments. Their promise is to move your money among the various choices in order to seize maximum advantage of changing markets. Members of the extended family of asset allocation funds include balanced funds and the latest addition to the clan, lifestyle or life-cycle funds.

There are only a few hundred asset allocation funds around, a trickle in the large pool of 6,000 mutual funds. And they are fairly new—of the 200 funds tracked by Morningstar Inc., half are less than three years old. Even so, asset allocation funds managed to attract some $4.28 billion in assets in 1996, up from a mere $1.7 billion in 1995.

Not everyone is enamored of the funds. Some financial experts say investors may be paying plenty just to calm their jitters. Others wonder about the funds' usefulness. The question in their minds: Are they really the first brick in an investment portfolio—or are they just a mediocre investment choice for lazy investors? Here are some pros and cons of asset allocation funds.

■ Who would gain from investing in asset allocation funds?

New or tentative investors stand to gain because the funds' managers tackle the big decisions: how much to invest and where. They are good choices for investors who want to diversify beyond stock funds but who may not have a large enough portfolio to do so on their own. Each fund serves as a stand-alone portfolio, buying stocks, bonds and cash in varying proportions. They are also appealing for those who have the money to diversify but don't have an interest in devising their own asset allocation plan.

■ Who doesn't need them?

Anyone who is investing for the long haul and has the stomach for stocks probably doesn't need asset allocation funds. If your portfolio already includes several different kinds of funds, you may be in good shape on your own. Fund managers will jiggle those assets around more than you will, but you'll be paying for all the fine-tuning.

■ Are the fees higher?

Asset allocation funds trade a lot, making their brokerage costs somewhat higher than other mutual funds. While the costs aren't always reflected in a fund's expense ratio, they cut into returns. In general, you should aim for an expense ratio that is no higher than 1 percent. You may be willing to go higher if you know the fund has a superior portfolio manager. You can find out the manager's experience by calling the fund company directly.

■ What's the right mix?

Some asset allocation funds are geared for a certain stage of life, age, risk tolerance, investment goal, or some combination of these factors. The right mix depends mainly on how much time you have before you'll need the money. You can choose a portfolio geared to short-, intermediate-, or longer-term needs. It's rare for an investor to have to cash in an entire portfolio, so some money should almost always be left in equities, which have the best performance record over the long haul.

A first fund might be one that buys blue-chip companies or that mimics a market index. When choosing a first stock fund, you're better off passing by the hotshots, advises A. Michael Lipper, president of Lipper Analytical Services, a research and consulting firm in Summit, N.J. "Funds that are hot are the most likely to disappoint."

■ What's their record?

Not all assets take their lumps at the same time, which can work to the advantage of asset allocation funds. When the stock market plunged in 1987, for example, many asset allocation fund managers switched to bonds. The bond market rallied, limiting the funds' losses to about 11 percent, compared to about 30 percent for stocks as a whole.

As a group, asset allocation funds have turned in a fair, if not stellar performance. During the five-year period ending December 31, 1996, they returned 12.29 percent, compared with 17.25 percent for diversified equity funds and 7.39 percent for taxable fixed-income funds, according to Morningstar. But looked at individually, returns for asset allocation funds can swing wildly.

For example, take the Quest for Value Opportunity A fund, which invests heavily in stocks. Its total three-year return rate of 17.20 percent handily beat the S&P 500's 14.69 percent return. At the other extreme, the Mathers Fund, which pumps its assets largely into bonds, showed a three-year total return rate of a measly 0.88 percent. (See table below for a comparison of some other popular funds.)

■ How do the funds invest?

Diversifying and trying to time the stock market are two entirely different things and asset allocation funds shouldn't be in the forecasting business, say experts. "Most asset allocation funds move money around based on their forecast of how one asset class is going to do and that's awfully hard to predict," says John Markese, president of the American Association of Individual Investors.

If an asset allocation fund is making dramatic swings among various asset groups, it may be trying to time the market. Aggressive market timers—those that have more than 150 percent turnover rate—are best avoided. How can you find out that information? One way is to check with one of the independent mutual fund rating services such as Chicago-based Morningstar Inc.

■ How do you know what you're buying?

It's often hard to know what you're buying with mutual funds—and this can be especially true of asset allocation funds. Some fund managers have great flexibility in shifting into more appealing assets at any given time. Others operate under a ceiling of how much can go into a given asset group. You can get information on how much leeway a manager has by calling the fund. Ask what, if any, investing parameters are placed on a fund's manager.

If it's safety you're after, be leery of some asset allocation funds that invest in more volatile areas like emerging markets, gold, or commodity-based stock. The peso's devaluation in 1994, for example, really whacked some of the funds.

■ ASSETS AND LIABILITIES

Returns and expense ratios among asset allocation funds vary widely. Here's a snapshot of some of the more popular funds.

FUND	OBJECTIVE	TOTAL RETURN*	EXPENSE RATIO
DREYFUS ASSET ALLOCATION	High total return	14.15%	1.25%
FIDELITY ASSET MANAGER	Long-term reduced risk	7.53%	0.95%
GABELLI ABC	High total return	5.10%	2.09%
VALUELINE ASSET ALLOCATION	High total return	17.66%	1.38%

*One year total return as of March 31, 1997.

HOW MANY FUNDS SHOULD YOU OWN?

There's a danger in owning too many. Simplify your portfolio

You've heard the message by now: investing in mutual funds gives you the immediate benefit of diversification, which lowers risk without hurting returns. But investors fond of fund collecting could be heading for mediocre results or, even worse, diminishing returns.

The problem with piling on funds is that you may be duplicating what's already in your portfolio. "With two to four funds you can own 1,000 stocks of many kinds from all over the world. How many stocks do you need?" asks Eric Kobren, president of Insight Management Inc., a Wellesley, Mass., investment firm that publishes *Fidelity Insight*, an independent newsletter.

Indeed, a study by Professors Walt Taylor of the University of Southern Mississippi and Jim Yoder of West Georgia College found that a handful of stock funds are all you need to reduce risk. The study, which tracked 168 domestic stock funds from 1978 through 1989, found that most risk reduction, about 75 percent, occurred with just four funds. Beyond 15 funds, there was almost no lessening of risk.

Before you can consolidate wisely, says Kobren, look at the kinds of securities each fund owns. A good mix would include large-and small-company stocks and foreign stocks and bonds. Kobren believes just three well-chosen funds will do the job.

We asked Kobren to devise a diversified three-fund portfolio for a moderately aggressive investor and one for an investor with moderately conservative tastes. His choices for the more aggressive investor are Oakmark and Gabelli Growth funds that invest in large company stocks, and Mutual Discovery, which emphasizes small-company and international stocks. Kobren says this diversity gives the portfolio less volatility than the Standard & Poor's 500.

For the moderately conservative investor, Kobren suggests a mix of less risky large-company stock funds through Fidelity Growth and Income and Tweedy Browne Global Value funds, augmented with exposure to bonds through Vanguard's Intermediate U.S. Treasury fund. This mix, says Kobren, is about 75 percent less volatile than the S&P.

Here are Kobren's model portfolios, along with what percent of your assets to allocate to each fund and the funds' three-year return rates.

■ MODEL PORTFOLIOS: WHEN THREE FUNDS ARE ENOUGH

Eric Kobren argues that for most investors, three funds will more than do.

FUND	TYPE	% ALLOCATION	3-YEAR RETURN*	☎ PHONE
■ MODERATELY AGGRESSIVE				
OAKMARK	Large value	40%	20.5%	800–625–6276
GABELLI GROWTH	Large growth	30%	18.2%	800–422–3554
MUTUAL DISCOVERY	Small value	30%	19.5%	800–342–5236
■ MODERATELY CONSERVATIVE				
FIDELITY GROWTH & INCOME	Growth & income	40%	20.0%	800–544–8888
TWEEDY BROWNE GLOBAL VALUE	Global equity	30%	11.8%	800–432–4789
VANGUARD INTERMD US TREAS	Bond	20%	6.4%	800–662–7447

*As of April 1997.

FUNDS THAT SERVE WITH A SMILE

Some treat your money with the respect it deserves

Service is the name of the game in the crowded field of mutual funds. Many fund companies are looking to grab market share by bending over backward to cater to investors. Which companies provide the best service? DALBAR Inc., a Boston-based mutual fund research firm, tested about 75 mutual fund groups in 1996 before selecting a handful that provide kid-glove service to investors.

For the 1996 awards, DALBAR looked at more than 10,000 transactions designed to test 55 different aspects of service. The areas of service rated ranged from routine matters, such as opening an account and checking fund share prices, to whether dividends, annual reports, and tax statements were received on time, to the funds' representatives' confidence when giving responses. DALBAR invested about $180,000 of its own money in the funds and conducted more than 146,000 evaluations throughout the year before selecting the funds that would be awarded its excellence-in-service seal.

What should you do to get the best service from your funds? After many years of conducting its surveys, DALBAR has gleaned the following advice for investors:

■ **Ask how you can access your money efficiently.** Get a checkbook and check-writing privileges, so you can write yourself a check when you want cash from your account.

■ **Know how your money flows.** Find out beforehand how to transfer money between funds or switch from reinvesting dividends to taking them in cash, or vice versa.

■ **Ask who to call for advice or help.** Funds should be able to tell you how to use your investment as collateral for a loan. Some funds will issue a certificate acceptable to the lender; a stockbroker should be able to put your account on margin.

■ AND THE WINNERS ARE:

DALBAR doesn't reveal the losers, but here's the list of winners of the 1996 DALBAR Quality Tested Service Seal.

FUND	ASSETS	☎ PHONE
EVERGREEN KEYSTONE	$29.6 billion	800–343–2898
GALAXY FUNDS	$10.7 billion	800–628–0414
IDEX MUTUAL FUNDS	$1.7 billion	800–851–9777
INVESCO FUNDS GROUP	$15.6 billion	800–525–8085
KEMPER FUNDS	$38.5 billion	800–621–1048
MFS MUTUAL FUNDS	$42.3 billion	800–637–2929
THE MONTGOMERY FUNDS	$8 billion	800–572–3863
NEW ENGLAND FUNDS	$18.6 billion	800–225–7670
T. ROWE PRICE	$71.9 billion	800–225–5132
USAA MUTUAL FUNDS	$19.4 billion	800–531–8448
VAN KAMPEN AMERICAN CAPITAL	$37 billion	800–421–5666

THE BEST INVESTMENT NEWSLETTERS

Financial newsletters number in the hundreds—500 is a common estimate. So which tip sheets offer the most lucrative advice? For the rankings below, the Hulbert Financial Digest, the bible of comparative newsletter performance, examined scores of newsletters over 5-year and 10-year periods ending December 31, 1996. Hulbert used two measures to rate the performance of the portfolios recommended by the newsletters: total-return and risk-adjusted. In cases where a newsletter recommended more than one portfolio, its ranking was based on an average of all its portfolios. As benchmarks, Hulbert used the total returns of the Wilshire 5000 and returns on a Treasury bill portfolio. Risk-adjusted ratings are based on average monthly gains per unit of risk. The Wilshire 5000 is equal to 100, so the higher a newsletter's risk-adjusted rating, the better its performance. The best mutual fund newsletters are ranked similarly.

TOTAL RETURN RATINGS

The total returns of the Wilshire 5000 and returns on a Treasury bill portfolio were used for comparison.

■ TEN YEARS

	Total ret. (%)	Annualized ret. (%)
1. MPT Review	690.0	23.0
2. California Technology Stock Ltr.	523.7	20.1
3. New Issues	454.8	18.7
4. BI Research	423.7	18.0
5. Stockmarket Cycles	332.0	15.8
Wilshire 5000 total return	**293.2**	**14.7**
Treasury bill portfolio	**71.7**	**5.6**

■ FIVE YEARS

1. The Prudent Speculator	386.2	37.2
2. The Turnaround Letter	229.7	27.0
3. New Issues	202.7	24.8
4. The Insiders	198.0	24.4
5. California Technology Stock Ltr.	143.7	19.5
Wilshire 5000 total return	**100.4**	**14.9**
Treasury bill portfolio	**23.5**	**4.3**

■ MUTUAL FUNDS NEWSLETTERS, FIVE YEARS

1. Stockmarket Cycles	118.3	16.9
2. Equity Fund Outlook	100.9	15.0
3. Fundline	100.0	14.9
4. Timer Digest	99.4	14.8
5. Fund Profit Alert	91.2	13.8
Wilshire 5000 total return	**100.4**	**14.9**
Treasury bill portfolio	**23.5**	**4.3**

RISK-ADJUSTED RATINGS

Risk-adjusted ratings are assigned using the Wilshire 5000's rating of 100 as a benchmark.

■ TEN YEARS

	Risk adjusted rating
1. Investors Intelligence	136.8
2. Systems and Forecasts	126.8
3. Stockmarket Cycles	119.5
4. Fund Exchange	111.1
5. Zweig Performance Ratings Report	108.9
Wilshire 5000	**100.0**

■ FIVE YEARS

1. The Prudent Speculator	116.0
2. The Insiders	109.6
3. The No-Load Fund Investor	107.3
4. Fidelity Monitor	104.7
5. Richard E. Band's Profitable Investing	103.8
Wilshire 5000	**100.0**

■ MUTUAL FUNDS NEWSLETTERS, FIVE YEARS

1. The No-Load Fund Investor	107.3
2. Fidelity Monitor	104.7
3. Fidelity Insight	102.0
4. No-Load Fund Analyst	100.0
5. Personal Finance*	95.9
Wilshire 5000	**100.0**

*Average of fund portfolios.   SOURCE: *Hulbert Financial Digest*, 316 Commerce St., Alexandria, Va. 22314, ☎ 703-683-5905.

WHERE TO GET THE TOP NEWSLETTERS

Subscribing to a top newsletter might provide some good returns.

CALIFORNIA TECHNOLOGY STOCK LETTER
Mike Murphy, ed., $295
PO Box 308
Half Moon Bay, CA 94019
☎ 415–726–8495

THE CHARTIST
Dan Sullivan, ed., $150
PO Box 758
Seal Beach, CA 90740
☎ 310–596–2385

EQUITY FUND OUTLOOK
Thurman Smith, ed., $125
PO Box 76
Boston, MA 02117
☎ 617–397–6844

FIDELITY INSIGHT
Eric Kobren, ed., $99
PO Box 9135
Wellesley Hills, MA 02181
☎ 617–369–2100

FIDELITY MONITOR
Jack Bowers, ed., $96
PO Box 1270
Rocklin, CA 95677
☎ 800–397–3094

FUNDLINE
David Menashe, ed., $127
PO Box 663
Woodland Hills, CA 91365
☎ 818–346–5637

INVESTECH MUTUAL FUND ADVISOR
James B. Stack, ed., $175
2472 Birch Glen
Whitefish, MT 59937
☎ 800–955–8500

MPT REVIEW
Louis Navellier, ed., $275
1 East Liberty St., 3rd Fl.
Reno, NV 89501
☎ 800–454–1395

NEW ISSUES
Norman Fosback and Glen King Parker, eds., $95
3471 N. Federal Hwy.
Ft. Lauderdale, FL 33306
☎ 800–327–6720

NOLOAD FUND INVESTOR
Sheldon Jacobs, ed., $129
PO Box 318
Irvington, NY 10533
☎ 914–693–7420

OBERWEIS REPORT
James D. Oberweis, ed., $249
841 N. Lake
Aurora, IL 60506
☎ 630–801–4766

OTC INSIGHT
James Collins, ed., $195
PO Box 127
Moraga, CA 94556
☎ 800–955–9566

PERSONAL FINANCE
Stephen Leeb, ed., $39
1750 Old Meadow Rd.
McLean, VA 22102
☎ 703–905–8000

THE PRUDENT SPECULATOR
Al Frank, ed., $175
PO Box 1438
Laguna Beach, CA 92652
☎ 310–587–2410

RICHARD BAND'S PROFITABLE INVESTING
Richard Band, ed., $99
7811 Montrose Rd.
Potomac, MD 20854
☎ 301–340–1520

STOCKMARKET CYCLES
Peter Eliades, ed., $198
PO Box 6873
Santa Rosa, CA 95406
☎ 707–579–8444

SYSTEMS & FORECASTS
Gerald Appel, ed., $225
150 Great Neck Rd.
Great Neck, NY 11021
☎ 516–829–6444

TIMER DIGEST
Jim Schmidt, ed., $225
PO Box 1688
Greenwich, CT 06836
☎ 800–356–2527

TURNAROUND LETTER
George Putnam III, ed., $195
225 Friend St., Suite 801
Boston, MA 02114
☎ 617–573–9550

VALUE LINE INVESTMENT SURVEY
Value Line, Inc., $570
220 East 42nd St., NY, NY 10017–5891
☎ 800–634–3583

ZWEIG PERFORMANCE RATINGS
Martin Zweig, publ., $225
PO Box 360
Bellmore, NY 11710–0751
☎ 516–223–3800

WHY KLONDIKE IS KING

Here's how the Buffalo, Wyoming, investors' club became number one

The Beardstown Ladies may be the reigning queens of investment clubs, but the Klondike Investment Club, a group of down-to-earth investors in a tiny Wyoming town, wears the crown of number one investment club in America. The honor was bestowed on Klondike by Value Line, the New York research firm, and the National Association of Investors Corp. (NAIC), which oversees the nation's 27,500 investment clubs.

Nine-year old Klondike Club's record is stellar: a stock portfolio that grew at a compounded rate of 19.3 percent in 1996, compared with 15.7 percent for the Standard & Poor's 500 index. Klondike's 17 members range in age from 30 to 70 and include two teachers, a cattle rancher, a doctor, a lawyer, and two gas station operators—Dick Reimann, president of the club, and his son, Steve. We asked the elder Reimann to share some secrets of Klondike's success:

■ What is your stock-picking approach?
We look for undervalued stocks of companies that have long-term growth potential. Each member choses a stock recommended by a broker, friend, or a publication such as *Value Line*, a Standard & Poor's Report, *The Wall Street Journal*, or *Better Investing*, an NAIC publication. The member then gathers the company's balance sheet and profit and loss data from the past five years and runs the data through a program you can get through the NAIC. (☎ 800–583–6242). The program makes projections about the likelihood that a particular stock will go up or down.

We only pick stocks whose prices have a 3:1 likelihood of rising. We pay close attention to the price/earnings ratio to make sure that the stock is undervalued and also follow the *Value Line* reports of where the company is headed.

■ How do you attain diversification?
To minimize the risk of investing only in common stocks, we spread investments over several different industries. We sink our funds mostly into large company stocks, because they tend to have the best gains.

■ How do you know when to sell?
Club members monitor each company's stock price and performance on a monthly basis. If a particular stock starts to perform badly, we do a new study. We are more likely to sell if we see that the company's growth is flattening and that the company's industry has a dim outlook for the next several years.

■ How much of a stock do you buy?
We use the 100-shares rule because the commission rate is lower. Also, because the stocks we buy are usually undervalued and therefore cheaper, a profit on no fewer than 100 shares will justify all our research.

■ Any advice to others who want to form an investment club?
First, contact the NAIC, and when you're part of a club, find good, solid companies, and invest for the long term.

■ INVESTMENT CLUB HITS

The 10 most popular stocks held by the nation's clubs, ranked by dollar value of holdings as of the end of 1996:

	Value of holdings (millions)
AFLAC Inc.	$391.5
Merck & Co.	$208.2
McDonald's Corp.	$203.1
Intel Corp.	$197.1
PepsiCo	$163.9
Coca Cola Co.	$148.6
Johnson & Johnson	$128.9
General Electric	$122.6
Motorola	$114.4
Microsoft Corp.	$112.6

Source: National Association of Investors Corp.

EXPERT Q & A

FINDING THE BEST BROKER

The nation's top stock cop on what to expect from your stockpicker

Few people can talk about the brokerage business with more authority than Arthur Levitt, Jr., the chairman of the Securities and Exchange Commission (SEC) and the nation's top market cop. A former broker, Levitt headed the American Stock Exchange for more than a decade. As SEC chief since 1993, he has made investor protection and education a top priority. We asked Levitt for tips on how to find a good broker and what to do about an unethical one.

■ How do you pick the best broker?

The best brokers ask you questions before you invest to understand fully your financial goals and your tolerance for risk. This is the only way that they can recommend a portfolio that matches your needs. Most serious problems arise when a broker recommends a stock or other financial product simply to earn a commission, rather than considering whether the product fits your needs.

The important thing in picking a broker is to look him or her in the eye and ask some tough questions. What is the broker's philosophy on how best to meet your goals? Has the broker ever been disciplined for wrongdoing? Does the broker seem more interested in selling you a stock than getting to know your financial situation and your future financial needs? Ask questions that will help you determine if the chemistry is right and whether the broker will always put your interests first.

■ What else should an investor ask a potential broker?

First, find out how your broker gets paid. Typically, brokers are paid by commissions

that reward them for the quantity of business they do, not for the quality. Ask your broker a few questions, such as: Do you make more if I buy this mutual fund, for example, than if I buy this stock? Some brokerage firms allow you to pay a flat fee based on the amount of your assets under management. Ask the broker if you would be better off paying a flat fee or a commission.

■ How do I know if my broker is getting me the best price when I buy or sell stocks?

When your broker quotes you the price at which he'll sell you a stock or bond, ask how much he'd pay to buy it from you. The difference is the spread. You should ask your broker whether you could get a better price for a stock if you place a "limit" order, which specifies a price that falls in the middle of the spread. Also ask your broker if you could get a better price if he routed your order to a particular exchange or another market.

■ How do I know my municipal bond investments are in good hands?

Since early 1996, your broker has been able to obtain key data about the financial health of municipal bond issuers from national or state information centers. For example, your broker can find out if the bond issuer is delinquent on principal or interest payments, if its ratings have been downgraded, or if it has lost its tax-exempt status. Be sure to ask for this information.

■ In what other ways can investors better protect themselves?

Before you hire a broker, check out his record by calling the National Association of Securities Dealers' hot line (☎ 800–289–9999) or your state securities regulator. We also post records of SEC enforcement actions on the Internet *(http://www.fedworld.gov)*. Also, scrutinize your account statements for transactions that you didn't authorize, excessive commissions, and delays in executing orders. Complain if you suspect wrongdoing.

■ What should an investor do if he runs into a bad broker?

Most stockbrokers are honest professionals.

■ FEES: THE TALE OF THE TAPE

Brokerage firms are not created equal. In fact, the differences among them in commissions, fees, performance, and conduct are enormous, according to a 1996 report by the National Council of Individual Investors. The NCII studied the top 10 firms in the categories below. They found that the difference in commissions is up to 638 percent. From their survey, we picked the firms in each category with the highest and lowest brokerage commissions and annual IRA fees.

FULL SERVICE

Commissions*	AVERAGE	$160	
	HIGHEST	$177	Paine Webber
	LOWEST	$130	Everen Securities
Annual IRA fees	AVERAGE	$34	
	HIGHEST	$40	Smith Barney
	LOWEST	$30	A.G. Edwards, Dean Witter Reynolds, Edward Jones & Co.

BANK-AFFILIATED

Commissions*	AVERAGE	$101	
	HIGHEST	$150	Nations Securities
	LOWEST	$59	First Interstate Securities
Annual IRA fees	AVERAGE	$28	
	HIGHEST	$40	First Interstate Securities
	LOWEST	None	Citicorp Investment Services

DISCOUNTERS

Commissions*	AVERAGE	$60	
	HIGHEST	$89	Charles Schwab
	LOWEST	$25	Pacific Brokerage**
Annual IRA fees	AVERAGE	$18	
	HIGHEST	$40	Pacific Brokerage
	LOWEST	None	Olde Discount, Waterhouse Securities, Kennedy Cabot & Co.

DEEP DISCOUNTERS

Commissions*	AVERAGE	$32	
	HIGHEST	$39	Investors National, Marsh Block & Co.
	LOWEST	$24	Wall Street Equities
Annual IRA fees	AVERAGE	$27	
	HIGHEST	$60	Brown & Co.
	LOWEST	None	Kennedy Cabot & Co., Lombard Institutional

*Commissions based on 500 listed shares at $10. **Also a deep discounter.
SOURCE: National Council of Individual Investors.

But if you think you've encountered an unethical one, call our Office of Investor Assistance at ☎ 202–942–7040. We use "tips" from you to keep our securities markets free from fraud and bad brokers and bad financial planners. Report any problems promptly to the branch officer or the firm's compliance officer as well as to the NASD.

■ How do I settle a dispute with a broker?

Most investors agree to arbitrate disputes when they sign a customer agreement with a brokerage firm, so arbitration is the main route for settling disputes. You can file for arbitration with the NASD, or the New York Stock Exchange (☎ 212–656–3000), among other exchanges, or the American Arbitration Association (☎ 202–296–8510).

The SEC is working to improve the arbitration process in order to ensure that disputes are handled fairly. We're looking to expand the pool of arbitrators, give investors a greater say on who sits on their arbitration panel, and improve the training of arbitrators so that they better understand securities laws.

DISCOUNT BROKERS

TRADING ON THE CHEAP

Everything you need to know about discount brokers

Discount brokers account for about one-third of individual stock trades. Small wonder. While full-service brokerages provide customers with investment advice and other services, discount brokers stick to no-frills trading, passing the savings on to you. Cost-conscious investors can take a huge chunk out of commissions paid on trades by using discounters. But you have to know what you want and be comfortable making your own investment decisions.

When it comes to price breaks, discounters are great and getting better. While commissions at full-service brokerage firms have hovered around $246 per transaction for several years, deep discounters have slashed rates by 50 percent, according to Mercer Inc., a New York–based research firm. The average commission among the 10 cheapest dis-count brokers to trade 100 shares at $50 per share was $26.15 in 1996, according to Mercer. The same trade would cost an average $52.70 at the Big Three regular discounters— Charles Schwab, Fidelity, and Quick & Reilly—and $103 at a full-service brokerage.

Which discount brokerage offers the best deal? That's tough to say because they set their prices differently. Rates are often based on the total dollar value of a transaction, the number of shares purchased, or simply a flat fee for each type of transaction. Sometimes, small commissions and fees for non-routine trades are tacked on. Large dollar volume trades or those placed online often get further discounts at some firms.

As a result, some firms are cheaper for some trades and not for others. Before you pick a broker, advises the American Association of Individual Investors (☎ 312–280–0170), first compare the commissions the firm charges for the kinds of trades you're apt to make. Call the discounters directly, or use one of the surveys put out annually by Mercer (☎ 800–582–9854) or the AAII. After you've chosen a few candidates, ask for a commission schedule and description of services, fees, and bonus discounts. Keep in mind that some firms may charge a flat fee to open a new account, for example, and then high fees to wire funds or to get copies of reports.

■ TEN TOP DEEP DISCOUNTERS

Among these brokers with the cheapest commissions, Wall Street Equities charges the least to trade stocks. For bonds, Ceres is best at a low $18 commission.

Broker	☎	NUMBER OF Offices / Accounts	COMMISSION ON Min.	1 share @ $50	T bill*	Load funds	No-fee no-load funds
Brown & Co.	800–822–2021	10/10,000	$29	$29	$38	No	No
Ceres Securities	800–669–3900	1/NA	$18	$18	$18	Yes	Yes
Consolidated Financial	800–292–6637	1/3,000	$35	Neg.	$35	Yes	No
J. B. Oxford	800–500–5007	5/NA	$23	$23	$23	Yes	No
K. Aufhauser & Co.	800–368–3668	1/720,000	$25	$25	$39	Yes	No
Kennedy Cabot & Co.	800–252–0090	15/121,500	$20–$30	$20	$30	Yes	No
Lombard Institutional	800–566–2273	2/25,000	$34	$34	$34	Yes	No
National Discount Broker	800–888–3999	5/NA	$30	$30	$40	Yes	Yes
Pacific Brokerage Services	800–421–8395	4/120,000	$25	$25	$25	No	No
Wall Street Equities	800–447–8625	1/5,000	$15	$15	N/A	No	No

*$10,000 Treasury bill at auction.   SOURCES: Mercer Inc.; brokerage houses.

The Big Three discounters, and a few others, try to compete with full-service firms by offering research information, stock and bond picks, 24-hour phone service, asset management accounts with check-writing privileges and ATM cards, and margin accounts for trading instruments such as options, bonds, and certificates of deposit. Another plus is their extensive branch networks. The add-ons just keep coming. If you have an account with Schwab, for example, you now can also have dividends reinvested free, get a free retirement-planning software program, and a credit card that gives you points redeemable for free investment research.

Most discount brokerage customers use discounters for little more than trading stocks and bonds. But what if you wanted to get into zero coupon bonds, say, or futures? Which firm has the widest range of products? Discounters Jack White and Quick & Reilly were cited by *SmartMoney* magazine in July 1996 as tops in product offerings. Both carry futures trades, unit-investment trusts, and other esoteric investments. For investors who want to pick from a highly selective list of free no-load mutual fund offerings, Jack White wins again. White offers the most no-load, no-transaction-fee funds (805). Accutrade's 549 no-load, no-fees put it in second place.

But don't expect a lot of handholding. You'll get little account maintenance and even less personal attention. If more attention and greater control over the price you pay is what you're after, you're better off with a full-service broker. Often, says Andre Scheluchin, managing editor of *Mercer's 1997 Discount Brokerage Survey*, it's not impossible to negotiate a cut in commission with a full-service broker. In fact, you may end up paying only slightly more than with a discounter.

It's a smart idea to check out a brokerage firm thoroughly before doing business. Background information is available from the National Association of Securities Dealers (☎ 800–289–9999), or from the Central Registration Depository of your state securities agency, listed in the blue pages of the phone book.

EXPERT PICKS

BUYING STOCK AT WHOLESALE PRICES

Want to cut your broker out altogether? More and more companies are letting investors buy stock directly—even if it's their initial purchase in the company. What's the appeal? First, says Charles Carlson, editor of *DRIP Investor* newsletter (☎ 219–852–3220) and author of *Buying Stocks Without a Broker* (McGraw-Hill, 1996), you can save a bundle by bypassing expensive brokers. Second, you're not sacrificing service. Many no-load stock programs, as they're known, are administered by large banks and offer services such as automatic withdrawals from your bank account to make electronic payments and redemption services that sell stock by phone. You can't lose, says Carlson. "You get a nice breadth of services and pay little, if any, fees." Here are Carlson's 10 favorite no-load stocks for 1997.

COMPANY	☎	MINIMUM INITIAL INVESTMENT
BellSouth	888–887–2965	$500
Exxon	800–252–1800	$250
Lucent Technologies	888–582–3686	$1,000
McDonald's	800–774–4117	$1,000
Merck	800–774–4117	$350
Procter & Gamble	800–764–7483	$250
Regions Financial	800–922–3468	$500
Reuters Holdings	800–774–4117	$250
Southern Company	800–774–4117	$250
Tribune Company	800–924–1490	$500

NOTE: The Direct Stock Purchase Plan Clearinghouse can provide information for these plans as well as others (☎ 800–774–4117).

ONLINE **INVESTING**

REPLACING YOUR BROKER

Online trading is getting cheaper but there are risks

An investing revolution is underway on the Internet, as more brokers provide cheap stock-trading and easy-to-reach investor help. Not since the 1970s, when discount brokers first emerged, has there been so dramatic a shift in the way people invest their money. The big winners are online investors who can now buy and sell stock for as little as $9.99 per trade. Today, there are 1.5 million online brokerage accounts. Within five years they will swell to 10 million, according to Forrester Research, a consulting firm in Cambridge, Mass.

Upstarts like E*Trade and Datek Securities (see page 36 for online addresses) are at the forefront, offering cheap transaction fees and sites that give you investing data at the click of a mouse. You can invest as little as $1,000 with E*Trade and $2,000 with Datek. With Datek, if your order isn't executed in just one minute, you don't pay the $9.95 commission fee. The larger online brokers, such as Charles Schwab, PC Financial, Donaldson, Lufkin & Jenrette's cybertrading service, and American Express's InvestDirect, generally charge heftier fees. Charles Schwab for example, charges $29.95 per trade and has a $5,000 minimum. Yet, the same trade through a Schwab broker would run about $55 per 100 shares. Also, unlike some of the upstarts, the larger brokers typically let you trade bonds and mutual funds as well as stocks.

Beware of unexpected fees that some cyberbrokers collect, however. American Express's InvestDirect, for instance, charges $75 if you make fewer than five trades a year. PC Financial tacks on a $50 fee to close an IRA account. And cheap broker E*Trade bills 27¢ for every minute you spend on its computer site.

Another caveat: Investors who need individual advice are better off with traditional brokers. In fact, customer service in cyberspace is practically nonexistent.

Before you place your online order, be sure you've done your research. For an excellent primer on online investing, visit the American Association of Individual Investor's Web site, where you'll also find selected articles to sharpen your financial skills. For the computer-challenged, the AAII offers a paper guide—a good, thorough and unbiased source on online investing—called *The Individual Investor's Guide to Computerized Investing* ($24.95, ☎ 800–428–2244).

When researching potential investments, check out two fairly new and essential sources: Zacks Investment Research and Morningstar. *SmartMoney* magazine calls the Zacks site a "hands-down winner." It's chock full of statistics and commentary on overall investing trends. You'll find data on individual companies, including earnings estimates, what the analysts think, stock-price charts, and more. At the Morningstar site, you'll find loads of mutual fund information from daily updates to 10-year total returns on a huge database of funds. On top of that there are articles such as why a particular stock is cooling off, for example, or whether to take Social Security payments at age 62 or 65.

If you'd rather scrutinize the raw data, check out the Securities and Exchange Commission's Edgar database, which houses thousands of corporate and mutual fund filings, including prospectuses and corporate 10-Ks.

As always, when entering the world of message boards, arm yourself with skepticism. Message boards are often the venue for dubious investment pitches. From time to time, it pays to check several sites that monitor online scams: The National Fraud Information Center (http://www.fraud.org), which provides reports on financial fraud on the Internet and online services, and the SEC (http://www.sec.gov) and National Association of Securities Dealers (http://www.nasdr.com) sites, which warn investors about the latest online scams.

ONLINE TRADING POSTS

There's a ton of investment data and services on the Internet—from pages to research your targets, to sites for placing your order. Here's the lowdown on some of the more popular investment sites:

BROKERS

Dozens of discount brokers provide online trading. A sampling:

AMERICAN EXPRESS INVESTDIRECT
http://www.americanexpress.com/direct
☎ 800–658–4672
■ Hard to beat this offer: no minimum investment, and stock trades cost a low $27 per trade.

DATEK SECURITIES
http://www.datek.com
☎ 888–463–2835
■ Rock bottom fees of $9.99 per trade up to 5,000 shares. $2,000 minimum.

E. SCHWAB
http://www.eschwab.com
☎ 800–372–4922
■ Trade mutual funds and bonds, as well as stock. Sets a $5,000 minimum on investments. Gives an online commission discount of 20 percent. A flat $29.95 for Internet trades.

E*TRADE GROUP
http://www.etrade.com
☎ 800–786–2573
■ More than a trading hole, this site lets you get breaking news on individual companies. To set up an account, mail in your vital financial data and a $1,000 check to cover the minimum investment.

PC FINANCIAL NETWORK
http://www.pcfn.com
☎ 800–825–5723
■ The online arm of Donaldson Lufkin & Jenrette, this site charges a slightly higher $40 or so per trade, but sets no minimum.

RESEARCH

Visit these sites when doing nitty-gritty research.

AMERICAN ASSOC. OF INDIVIDUAL INVESTORS
http://www.aaii.org
■ A good primer on online investing; also has articles to sharpen the financial skills of more advanced investors.

EDGAR
http://www.sec.gov
■ This Security and Exchange Commission site holds reams of corporate filings, including 10-Ks, 10-Qs, prospectuses, etc..

MORNINGSTAR
http://www.morningstar.net
■ All you need to know about mutual funds—total returns, fees, risk levels, objectives, ratings, management facts, and more.

ZACKS INVESTMENT RESEARCH
http://www.zacks.com
■ The latest data on companies and their stock, including earnings histories, stock price charts, and analysts' opinions.

COMPANY SITES

Of the hundreds of company sites on the Web, these are both useful and jazzy.

IBM
http://www.ibm.com/Annual Report/1996
■ This sophisticated site lets you build your own charts of Big Blue's historical performance.

INTEL
http://www.intel.com/intel/finance
■ Aside from a snazzy annual report, you also get audio and slide shows from the company's annual meeting.

MICROSOFT
http://www.microsoft.com/msft
■ The report's financial tables can be converted into other languages and currencies, including for England, Canada, France, Germany, and Japan.

EXPERT SOURCES

TEN BOOKS WORTH THE INVESTMENT

Bookstores are bulging with tomes on how to invest your money. But separating treasures from trash can be an expensive and time-consuming process. With this in mind, we asked Yale Hirsch, editor of the 1997 Stock Trader's Almanac (☎ 800–477–3400) and a publisher of investment newsletters for 36 years, for his favorite titles of recent years. Here are his picks and comments.

CYBERINVESTING
David L. Brown, Kassandra Bentley, John Wiley & Sons, 1995, $24.95
■ Brown, creator of one of the best online financial information services, shows novice and seasoned investors how to unleash the potential of their PCs to spot investment opportunities.

WHAT WORKS ON WALL STREET
James P. O'Shaughnessy, McGraw-Hill, 1996, $29.95
■ This will be the stock market book of the '90s. O'Shaughnessy has taken all the notable market strategies and tested them on 34 years of data to discover what really works on Wall Street.

THE 100 BEST STOCKS TO OWN IN AMERICA
Gene Walden, Dearborn Financial, 4th ed., $22.95
■ Ranks the best 100 stocks, using a variety of formulas and criteria. Earning performance is the most important factor—if a company is able to raise earnings year after year, the stock price will follow.

GOD WANTS YOU TO BE RICH
Paul Zane Pilzer, Simon & Schuster, 1995, $23
■ An individual's success is good for all of society, argues Pilzer, because wealth begets wealth for everyone. A society's wealth is determined not by the supply of physical resources but by human ingenuity.

TRADERS' TALES
Ron Insana, John Wiley & Sons, 1996, $24.95
■ A collection of stories capturing the true flavor of Wall Street, from some of the best-known names in the business.

SOROS ON SOROS
George Soros with Byron Wien and Krisztina Koenen, John Wiley & Sons, 1995, $39.95
■ The world's most powerful and profitable investor today. Soros offers his views of investing and global finance, politics and the emerging world order.

BOOM: VISIONS AND INSIGHTS FOR CREATING WEALTH IN THE 21ST CENTURY
Frank Vogl and James

Sinclair, Irwin, 1996, $24.95
■ A comprehensive outline for the emerging market order, describing the dramatic evolution of global opportunities.

INVEST WITHOUT STRESS
Anne Farrelly, Camden Press, 1996, $25
■ A step-by-step encyclopedia that gives easy-to-digest answers to questions about any and all investments you may encounter.

SCHWAGER ON FUTURES: FUNDAMENTAL ANAYLSIS
Jack D. Schwager, John Wiley & Sons, 1995, $55
■ Shows traders how to apply analytical techniques to actual price forecasting and trading in virtually all futures contracts currently traded.

SCHWAGER ON FUTURES: TECHNICAL ANALYSIS
Jack D. Schwager, John Wiley & Sons, 1996, $60
■ Explores the structure and design of a variety of technical trading systems and demonstrates their applications in real market example.

REAL ESTATE

HOMEBUYER'S GUIDE: The top 130 housing markets in the country, PAGE 40 **MORTGAGES:** Which kind is right for you? PAGE 44 **LENDERS:** What to expect when you apply for a loan, PAGE 48 **REFINANCING:** When to trade in a mortgage, PAGE 51 **INSURANCE:** Tips for buying homeowner's policies, PAGE 52 **VACATION HOMES:** Best places to buy a second home, PAGE 54 **FORECLOSURES:** Where you can get land on the cheap, PAGE 55

PRICES
▼

WHAT WILL YOUR HOME BE WORTH?

Our expert says the value of your humble abode will rise

The good old days of solid housing profits are long gone. In fact, the heady '80s may have been an aberration. For some time now, home prices have done little more than march to the tune of the inflation rate. Over the past five years, inflation has averaged 3.1 percent a year, while the median increase in home sale prices during that time was 3.2 percent annually, according to Regional Financial Associates, a West Chester, Pa., economic consulting firm.

The picture for the rest of the century calls for more of the same, says John Tuccillo, chief economist for the National Association of Realtors. The economy will continue to be sturdy, and Tuccillo predicts low inflation and modest interest rates will keep the housing market strong throughout 1998. The favorable market is likely to encourage Generation Xers to purchase their first homes and baby boomers to upgrade their existing homes, says Tuccillo.

While real estate windfalls are unlikely in the late '90s, Tuccillo says conservative buyers could still see payoffs down the road—if they invest wisely. "If you're going to move into a house and stay 10 or 15 years, the things you've got to look for are good location and good quality. Ten or 15 years from now, those are the things that will really pay off." Here's what Tuccillo sees in his crystal ball for the future of housing.

■ **What's the outlook for home sales and prices?**

We will continue to see a strong housing market through 1998, but one declining in terms of numbers. We'll see the sales of existing and new homes come down 5 percent to 7 percent in 1998, but still remain within a good range. On average, housing prices have been rising in concert with inflation and will continue to do so, meaning home appreciation for most of the country will continue to average about 3 percent.

■ **Do you see any downturn looming in real estate?**

I don't see a downturn coming in 1998. The economy is moving along at a sustainable pace, employment is good, and we're looking at a housing market that has sufficent numbers of people who are looking to buy and sell.

■ **How far will mortgage rates go and which types of mortgages will be most popular?**

I would say that mortgage rates won't go

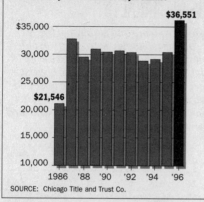

■ HOW MUCH DOWN? HOW MUCH A MONTH?

Homebuying costs in major markets

Initial outlay for a house in major market

$36,551

$35,000

30,000

25,000

$21,546

20,000

15,000

10,000

1986 '88 '90 '92 '94 '96

SOURCE: Chicago Title and Trust Co.

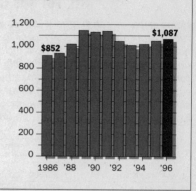

**The average monthly payment
(including taxes and insurance)**

1,200

$1,087

1,000 $852

800

600

400

200

0

1986 '88 '90 '92 '94 '96

higher than 8 percent. Fixed-rate mortgages will be in the 7 3/4 percent to 8 percent range. But rising interest rates in fixed-rate mortgages will increase the popularity of adjustable rates. For the last few years, the market has been a fixed-rate market; now we'll see some balance with more people using adjustable-rate mortgages.

■ When is a good time to refinance?

As a general rule of thumb, if the mortgage rate is 2 percentage points below your mortgage rate, it's a good time to refinance. The refinancing market has changed a bit, and now people refinance more quickly because it's easier to do. If you have a good purpose for refinancing, such as to fund an education or make investments, then it's likely that any time is a good time to refinance.

■ Will the future be kind to first-time buyers?

Interest rates are moderate, housing prices are pretty steady, and income and employment are growing. All of that adds up to a good opportunity for first-time home buyers.

■ How are babyboomers affecting the real estate market?

The major actions among that generation are coming from those who are now

beginning to trade up their homes to get in the right school districts and accommodate their growing families. Five years from now, the older boomers will be retiring or looking to retire, and will be buying retirement or additional homes.

FACT FILE:

MARRIED, WITH HOUSE

Characteristics and preferences of today's buyers:

■ *In a major shift, married home buyers returned to the housing market in a big way in 1996. The percentage of married couples buying homes rose to 70.2 percent in 1996, up from 66.4 percent the year before.*

■ *Low interest rates made fixed-rate mortgages the choice of 70 percent of buyers in 1996, up from 55.5 percent the previous year.*

■ *How many houses do buyers peruse before finding their dream home? Answer: 14.7.*

SOURCE: Chicago Title and Trust Co.

THE TOP 130 HOUSING MARKETS

Home prices rose throughout 1996 as a strong economy and stable mortgage rates encouraged many Americans to buy their first homes or trade up on older homes. The Midwest experienced the biggest increase in the median price of homes—up 4.4 percent from 1995, while the South, the region with the biggest concentration of affordable homes, had a 3.7 percent increase. On the west and east coasts, the median price of homes increased 2.7 percent. The following list shows the national median home prices for single-family detached and attached existing homes in various metropolitan areas across the country.

Metropolitan Area	1996 price	% change from '95
1. New Orleans, La.	$89,300	15.5
2. Sioux Falls, S.D.	$90,300	13.7
3. Detroit, Mich.	$112,600	12.9
4. Richland/Kennewick/Pasco, Wash.	$111,000	12.6
5. Waterloo/Cedar Falls, Iowa	$61,300	12.5
6. Portland, Ore.	$145,600	11.0
7. Mobile, Ala.	$83,500	10.3
8. Charleston, W.V.	$89,200	10.0
9. Green Bay, Wis.	$100,500	9.5
10. Houston, Texas	$85,700	9.0
11. Tallahassee, Fla.	$112,700	8.7
12. Trenton, N.J.	$135,800	8.6
13. Bergen–Passaic, N.J.	$200,200	8.6
14. Greenville–Spartenburg, S.C.	$105,300	8.4
15. Daytona Beach, Fla.	$75,200	8.4
16. Toledo, Ohio	$82,300	8.1
17. Lincoln, Neb.	$89,500	8.0
18. Charlotte–Gastonia–Rock Hill, N.C.	$117,400	7.9
19. Eugene–Springfield, Ore.	$116,200	7.9
20. Cedar Rapids, Iowa	$93,800	7.8
21. Ft. Lauderdale–Hollywood–Pompano Beach, Fla.	$115,800	7.7
22. Phoenix, Ariz.	$106,700	7.7
23. Kalamazoo, Mich.	$90,300	7.4
24. Louisville, Ky.	$94,800	7.1
25. Biloxi–Gulfport, Miss.	$78,800	6.9
26. Kansas City, Mo.	$100,200	6.8
27. Lake County, Ill.	$146,400	6.7
28. Amarillo, Texas	$75,000	6.7
29. Dallas, Texas	$103,100	6.6
30. Memphis, Tenn.	$95,000	6.0
31. San Francisco, Calif.	$265.900	6.0
32. Atlanta, Ga.	$103,100	6.0
33. Chattanooga, Tenn.	$92,500	6.0

Metropolitan Area	1996 price	% change from '95
34. Columbus, Ohio	$106,000	5.8
35. Grand Rapids, Mich.	$87,300	5.6
36. Greensboro/Winston-Salem/High Point, N.C.	$113,900	5.6
37. Baton Rouge, La.	$89,300	5.6
38. Youngstown–Warren, Ohio	$67,400	5.5
39. Miami, Fla.	$114,300	5.3
40. Peoria, Ill.	$74,300	5.2
41. Dayton–Springfield, Ohio	$92,700	5.1
42. Topeka, Kan.	$73,400	4.9
43. Monmouth–Ocean, N.J.	$143,000	4.8
44. San Antonio, Texas	$85,300	4.8
45. Minneapolis–St. Paul, Minn.	$113,500	4.7
46. Denver, Colo.	$134,400	4.6
47. El Paso, Texas	$75,700	4.6
48. Melbourne–Titusville–Palm Bay, Fla.	$83,000	4.5
49. Omaha, Neb.	$89,100	4.5
50. Lansing–E. Lansing, Mich.	$85,600	4.4
51. Pensacola, Fla.	$82,900	4.1
52. Little Rock–N. Little Rock, Ark.	$83,900	4.1
53. La Vegas, Nev.	$118,600	3.9
54. Shreveport, La.	$78,100	3.9
55. Hartford, Conn.	$134,300	3.6
56. Cleveland, Ohio	$112,400	3.6
57. Colorado Springs, Colo.	$119,000	3.6
58. Reno, Nev.	$142,500	3.6
59. Albuquerque, N.M.	$121,100	3.5
60. Knoxville, Ind.	$97,800	3.5
61. Lexington–Fayette, Ky.	$95,400	3.5
62. Jacksonville, Fla.	$87,400	3.4
63. Cincinnati, Ohio	$105,500	3.4
64. Akron, Ohio	$97,200	3.4
65. Saginaw–Bay City–Midland, Mich.	$67,800	3.4
66. Saint Louis, Mo.	$90,800	3.3

■ **HOMEBUYER'S GUIDE**

Metropolitan Area	1996 price	% change from '95
67. Tacoma, Wash.	$125,700	3.3
68. Davenport/Moline/ Rock Island, Iowa	$70,800	3.2
69. Gainesville, Fla.	$96,700	3.2
70. Anaheim–Santa Ana, Calif.	$213,800	3.1
71. Ocala, Fla.	$64,800	3.0
72. Tampa–St. Petersburg– Clearwater, Fla.	$82,800	3.0
73. Boise, Idaho	$102,400	2.9
74. Birmingham, Ala.	$115,600	2.8
75. Worcester, Mass.	$133,900	2.8
76. New York City–North N.J.– Long Island, N.Y.	$172,900	2.7
77. Springfield, Ill.	$79,300	2.7
78. Canton, Ohio	$88,900	2.7
79. Atlantic City, N.J.	$107,300	2.6
80. Seattle, Wash.	$164,000	2.6
81. Beaumont, Texas	$64,300	2.6
82. Washington, D.C.–Md.–Va.	$159,000	2.4
83. San Diego, Calif.	$174,300	2.4
84. Nassau–Suffolk, N.Y.	$158,700	2.4
85. Indianapolis, Ind.	$98,000	2.4
86. Ft, Worth–Arlington, Texas	$86,400	2.4
87. Aurora–Elgin, Ill.	$135,500	2.3

Metropolitan Area	1996 price	% change from '95
88. Salt Lake City–Ogden, Utah	$121,800	2.2
89. Oklahoma City, Okla.	$74,100	2.1
90. Charleston, S.C.	$94,700	2.0
91. Providence, R.I.	$116,800	2.0
92. Milwaukee, Wis.	$116,300	1.7
93. Orlando, Fla.	$90,500	1.3
94. Wichita, Kan.	$81,400	1.2
95. Spokane, Wash.	$100,300	1.2
96. Columbia, S.C.	$92,900	1.2
97. Richmond–Petersburg, Va.	$108,400	1.1
98. Norfolk–Va. Beach– Newport News, Va.	$106,100	1.0
99. Austin/San Marcos, Texas	$106,100	1.0
100. Chicago, Ill.	$148,300	0.9
101. Buffalo–Niagara Falls, N.Y.	$81,100	0.9
102. South Bend–Mishawaka, Ind.	$73,500	0.8
103. Pittsburgh, Pa.	$81,500	0.6
104. Rochester, N.Y.	$85,200	0.6
105. Des Moines, Iowa	$89,500	0.6
106. Albany–Schnectady– Troy, N.Y.	$106,100	0.2
107. Syracuse, N.Y.	$79,100	0
108. Montgomery, Ala.	$89,000	0
109. Boston, Mass.	$177,100	–0.2
110. Baltimore, Md.	$110,500	–0.2
111. Appleton, Wis.	$84,500	–0.4
112. Nashville, Tenn.	$111,200	–0.4
113. Rockford, Ill.	$89,400	–0.6
114. Ft. Myers–Cape Coral, Fla.	$77,900	–0.6
115. Tucson, Ariz.	$102,400	–0.9
116. Springfield, Mo.	$79,000	–0.9
117. Champaign, Ill.	$76,800	–1.0
118. Madison, Wis.	$126,100	–1.3
119. Tulsa, Okla.	$80,600	–1.6
120. Gary–Hammond, Ind.	$92,800	–1.6
121. Bradenton, Fla.	$90,200	–2.2
122. West Palm Beach–Boca Raton–Delray Beach, Fla.	$123,400	–2.7
123. Springfield, Mass.	$101,400	–2.7
124. Fargo, N.D.	$78,900	–3.0
125. Sarasota, Fla.	$105,300	–3.2
126. Sacramento, Calif.	$113,100	–4.6
127. New Haven–Meriden, Conn.	$127,400	–4.7
128. Los Angeles–Long Beach, Calif.	$167,100	–5.0
129. Honolulu, Hawaii	$333,500	–5.3
130. Corpus Christi, Texas	$81,700	–5.7

■ **A DECADE-LONG LOOK AT HOUSING PRICES**

The average price gain in 1996 was 3.7 percent—up from a flimsy 1.6 percent in 1995—as upper income buyers traded up. Here's a look at average home prices in major markets:

Average new home price $187,800

SOURCE: Chicago Title and Trust Co.

SOURCE: National Association of Realtors®.

MORTGAGES
▼

SHOULD YOU RENT OR BUY A HOME?

A formula for the biggest investment decision you're likely to make

It's often difficult to remember that buying a home is an investment fraught with some of the risks of Wall Street. And much as you might wish to own a place of your own, you might feel somewhat better about parting with your hard-earned down payment if you were convinced that you were making a savvy investment. A quick rule of thumb: You can assume you're probably better off renting if you do not itemize deductions on your tax returns or if you plan to move in a few years.

Gaylon Greer, professor of real estate at the University of Memphis, has devised a more sophisticated formula by adapting for potential homeowners a calculation used to decide whether to rent or buy. Keep in mind that Greer's calculation only considers the financial aspects of the decision. Here's how it works:

Consider the hypothetical predicament of Tracy and Jeff Summers, who are renting an apartment in Chicago for $1,200 a month. They are considering buying a similar-sized home for $200,000 and plan to live in the house for seven years.

■ **STEP 1:** Figure out the yearly financial cost for each scenario. For renting, that would be the Summers's annual rent of $14,400. For buying, it would be the after-tax costs of mortgage payments, property taxes, and maintenance.

Greer suggests estimating the annual maintenance costs at about 1 percent of the

---

■ **WHERE BUYING BEATS RENTING**

A deep dip in mortgage rates, along with higher rents, has made owning a house cheaper than renting in many areas nationwide.

In 51 of the 75 most populous metro areas, it is less expensive to own a four-bedroom house than to rent a two-bedroom luxury apartment, according to a study by the E&Y Kenneth Leventhal Real Estate Group in 1996. When the firm measured housing affordability in early 1994, renting was cheaper in most of the markets. Another finding: The most affordable housing can be found in Tornado Alley, or the area running from north of Texas to Missouri. In most of the West Coast, however, housing costs remain sky-high.

This table shows the percentage of median household income that goes toward paying housing costs—mortgage and rent—in the most affordable and least affordable areas across the country.

Metropolitan area	Single-family home costs*	Rental costs*
THE TEN MOST AFFORDABLE HOUSING MARKETS		
1. Oklahoma City, Okla.	15.3%	23.7%
2. Kansas City, Kan.	17.7	24.1
3. Houston, Texas	19.4	23.3
4. Tulsa, Okla.	17.5	25.2
5. St. Louis, Mo.	18.5	25.4
6. Central N.J.	22.2	21.8
7. Grand Rapids, Mich.	22.2	22.2
8. Salt Lake City, Utah	19.9	24.9
9. Dallas–Ft. Worth, Texas	20.2	24.9
10. Louisville, Ky.	21.9	23.5
THE TEN LEAST AFFORDABLE HOUSING MARKETS		
1. San Francisco, Calif.	57.3	42.7
2. Los Angeles, Calif.	46.0	34.4
3. Honolulu, Hawaii	40.8	39.2
4. Oakland–East Bay, Calif.	38.2	34.3
5. Miami, Fla.	35.4	35.5
6. San Diego, Calif.	34.2	36.6
7. Boston, Mass.	38.1	31.8
8. Pittsburgh, Pa.	33.8	34.9
9. El Paso, Texas	35.5	33.2
10. New York, N.Y.	35.4	32.4

*As a percentage of disposable median household income.
SOURCE: E&Y Kenneth Leventhal Real Estate Group.

house's value for a new home. For an older house, he suggests up to 3 or 4 percent. The local tax assessor can give you property tax rates.

The Summerses estimated spending about $2,000 a year on maintenance and paying $8,000 in property taxes. Their yearly mortgage payments come to approximately $16,000, assuming a $180,000 mortgage at 8.1 percent. However, the total yearly cost of buying is brought down substantially once you factor in the fact that property tax and mortgage payments are mostly tax deductible. Since the Chicago couple falls into the 39.6 percent income tax bracket, they can roughly estimate that the government pays that percentage of their costs. Therefore their total yearly costs for buying would be $16,000.

■ **STEP 2:** Figure how much you stand to recoup when you sell your house. You should expect anywhere from 8 to 10 percent of the final value to be consumed by transaction costs, such as brokerage and legal fees. After subtracting their transaction costs, the Summers estimate getting $290,000 for their house after living there for seven years. And they will still owe about $165,000 on their mortgage, so after taxes their net gain will be approximately $90,000.

■ **STEP 3:** Estimate how much you might make if you had invested your money in something other than a home—such as corporate or municipal bonds, or shares of corporate stock. You can use the table on this page to give you the value today of a dollar available at various points in the future. The table is based on an 8 percent rate of return on high-grade corporate bonds. This number can change—if it does you can use a present value table found in any finance book.

Each number corresponds to a year, so for year one, the factor will be .9259. Multiply that number by the annual cost of $16,000 to get a "present value equivalent" for the first year cost of ownership. Continue with similar calculations for each year you plan to live in the house. At the end you will add what you can expect to recoup from selling the house

and the down payment. You should end up with something like this. Parentheses indicate negative numbers, or costs.

Year	(Cost) or benefit	Factor	Present value equivalent
1	($16,000)	.9259	($14,814.40)
2	($16,000)	.8573	($13,716.80)
3	($16,000)	.7983	($12,772.80)
4	($16,000)	.7350	($11,760.00)
5	($16,000)	.6806	($10,889.60)
6	($16,000)	.6502	($10,403.20)
7	($16,000)	.5835	($9,336.00)
7*	$90,000	.5835	$52,515.00

Present value equivalent	
(Total)	**($31,177.80)**
Include:	
Down payment to buy	**($20,000.00)**
Net present value equivalent	**($51,177.80)**

* Sold in seventh year.

■ **STEP 4:** Go through the same calculation for renting—minus the down payment and net gain from selling. The lower cost is the best financial option.

Year	(Cost) or benefit	Factor	Present value equivalent
1	($16,000)	.9259	($14,814.40)
1	($14,400)	.9259	($13,332.96)
2	($14,400)	.8573	($12,345.12)
3	($14,400)	.7983	($11,495.52)
4	($14,400)	.7350	($10,584.00)
5	($14,400)	.6806	($9,800.64)
6	($14,400)	.6502	($9,362.88)
7	($14,400)	.5835	($8,402.40)

Present value equivalent	
(Total)	**($75,323.52)**

The bottom line for the Summerses: They should buy the house. Figuring the present value of their money, they will come out ahead by over $20,000 if they go ahead and purchase the home.

Of course, even if the result favors renting, you might still decide to buy the house you saw because it has such a lovely view from the kitchen window. That's simply a different definition of present value.

WHICH MORTGAGE IS FOR YOU?

It's hard to keep track of all the different kinds of mortgages currently being offered, much less choose the one that's the best deal for you. Here's an explanation of some of the most popular varieties, adapted from The Mortgage Money Guide, *published by the Federal Trade Commission, along with the pros and cons of each and some expert tips.*

FIXED-RATE MORTGAGE
Fixed interest rate, usually long term; equal monthly payments of principal and interest until debt is paid.

■ **PROS:** Offers some stability and long-term tax advantages.
■ **CONS:** Interest rates may be higher than other types of financing. New fixed rates are rarely assumable.

■ **EXPERT TIP:** Can be a good financing method, if you are in a high tax bracket and need the interest deductions.

FIFTEEN-YEAR MORTGAGE
Fixed interest rate. Requires down payment or monthly payments higher than 30-year loan. Loan is fully repaid over 15-year term.

■ **PROS:** Frequently offered at slightly reduced interest rate. Offers faster accumulation of equity than traditional fixed-rate mortgage.
■ **CONS:** Has higher monthly payments. Involves paying less interest but this may result in fewer tax deductions.

■ **EXPERT TIP:** If you can afford the higher payments, this plan will save you interest and help you

build equity and own your home faster.

ADJUSTABLE RATE MORTGAGE
Interest rate changes over the life of the loan, resulting in possible changes in your monthly payments, loan term, and/or principal. Some plans have rate or payment caps.

■ **PROS:** Starting interest rate is slightly below market. Payment caps prevent wide fluctuations in payments. Rate caps limit amount total debt can expand.
■ **CONS:** Payments can increase sharply and frequently if index increases. Payment caps can result in negative amortization.

■ **EXPERT TIP:** If your payment-capped loan results in monthly payments that are lower than your interest rate would require, you still owe the difference.

RENEGOTIABLE RATE MORTGAGE
Interest rate and monthly payments are constant for several years; changes possible thereafter. Long-term mortgage.

■ **PROS:** Less frequent changes in interest rates offer some stability.
■ **CONS:** May have to re-negotiate when rates are higher.

BALLOON MORTGAGE
Monthly payments based on fixed interest rate; usually short term; payments may cover interest only with principal due in full at end of term.

■ **PROS:** Offers low monthly payments.
■ **CONS:** Possibly no equity until loan is fully paid. When due, loan must be paid off or refinanced. Refinancing poses high risk if rates climb.

■ **EXPERT TIP:** Some lenders guarantee refinancing when the balloon payment is due, although they do not guarantee a certain interest rate.

GRADUATED PAYMENT MORTGAGE
Lower monthly payments rise gradually (usually over 5 or 10 years), then level off for duration of term. With adjustable interest rate, additional payment changes possible if index changes.

■ **PROS:** Easier to qualify for.

■ **CONS:** Buyer's income must keep pace with scheduled payment increases. With an adjustable rate, payment increases beyond the graduated payments can result in additional negative amortization.

SHARED APPRECIATION MORTGAGE

Below-market interest rate and lower monthly payments, in exchange for a share of profits when property is sold or on a specified date. Many variations.

■ **PROS:** Low interest rate and low payments.

■ **CONS:** If home appreciates greatly, total cost of loan jumps. If home fails to appreciate, projected increase in value may still be due, requiring refinancing at possibly higher rates.

■ **EXPERT TIP:** You may be liable for the dollar amount of the property's appreciation even if you do not wish to sell at the agreed-upon date.

ASSUMABLE MORTGAGE

Buyer takes over seller's original, below-market rate mortgage.

■ **PROS:** Lower monthly payments.

■ **CONS:** May be prohibited if "due on sale" clause is in original mortgage.

■ **EXPERT TIP:** Many mortgages are no longer legally assumable.

SELLER TAKE-BACK

Seller provides all or part of financing with a first or second mortgage.

■ **PROS:** May offer a below-market interest rate.

■ **CONS:** May have a balloon payment requiring full payment in a few years or refinancing at market rates, which could sharply increase debt.

■ **EXPERT TIP:** If an institutional lender arranges the loan, uses standardized forms, and meets certain other requirements, the owner take-back can be sold immediately to Fannie Mae. This enables seller to obtain equity promptly.

WRAPAROUND

Seller keeps original low-rate mortgage. Buyer makes payments to seller, who forwards a portion to the lender holding original mortgage.

■ **PROS:** Offers lower effec-

■ **HOW MUCH INCOME YOU NEED TO GET A MORTGAGE**

Figures are based on a 30-year loan and assume a down payment of 20 percent of purchase price.

Interest rate	$50,000 loan	$75,000 loan	$100,000 loan	$150,000 loan	$200,000 loan	$250,000 loan
6%	$16,754	$25,131	$33,508	$50,261	$67,015	$83,769
6.5%	$17,451	$26,176	$34,901	$52,352	$69,802	$87,253
7%	$18,163	$27,244	$36,325	$54,488	$72,651	$90,814
7.5%	$18,889	$28,334	$37,779	$56,668	$75,558	$94,447
8%	$19,630	$29,445	$39,260	$58,889	$78,519	$98,149
8.5%	$20,383	$30,574	$40,766	$61,149	$81,532	$101,915
9%	$21,148	$31,722	$42,296	$63,444	$84,593	$105,741
9.5%	$21,925	$32,887	$43,849	$65,774	$87,698	$109,623
10%	$22,711	$34,067	$45,423	$68,134	$90,845	$113,557
10.5%	$23,508	$35,262	$47,016	$70,523	$94,031	$117,539
11%	$24,313	$36,470	$48,626	$72,940	$97,253	$121,566
11.5%	$25,127	$37,690	$50,254	$75,380	$100,507	$125,634

NOTE: Calculations assume property taxes equal 1.5 percent of purchase price and hazard insurance costs 0.25 percent of purchase price.   SOURCE: Fannie Mae.

tive interest rate on total transaction.

■ **CONS:** Lender may call in old mortgage and require higher rate. If buyer defaults, seller must take legal action to collect debt.

■ **EXPERT TIP:** Wraparounds may cause problems if the original lender or the holder of the original mortgage is not aware of the new mortgage. Some lenders or holders may have the right to insist that the old mortgage be paid off immediately.

GROWING EQUITY MORTGAGE

Rapid payoff mortgage. Fixed interest rate but monthly payments may vary according to agreed-upon schedule or index.

■ **PROS:** Permits rapid pay-off of debt because payment increases reduce principal.

■ **CONS:** Buyer's income must keep up with payment increases. Does not offer long-term tax deductions.

LAND CONTRACT

Seller retains original mort-gage. No transfer of title until loan is fully paid. Equal monthly payments based on below-market interest rate with unpaid principal due at loan end.

■ **PROS:** Payments figured on below-market interest rate.

■ **CONS:** May offer no equity until loan is fully paid. Buyer has little protection if conflict arises during loan.

■ **EXPERT TIP:** Land contracts are being used to avoid the "due on sale" clause. The buyer and seller may assert to the lender who provided the original mortgage that the clause does not apply because the property will not be sold to the end of the contract. Therefore, the low interest rate continues.

BUY-DOWN

Developer (or other party) provides an interest subsidy that lowers monthly pay-ments during the first few years of the loan. Can have fixed or adjustable interest rate.

■ **PROS:** Offers a break from higher payments during early years. Enables buyer with lower income to qualify.

■ **CONS:** With adjustable rate mortgage, payments may jump substantially at end of subsidy. Developer may increase selling price.

■ **EXPERT TIP:** Consider what your payments will be after the first few years.

■ PAYMENTS MONTH-BY-MONTH

The following chart shows the maximum monthly amount you could spend for home payments and total monthly credit obligations at a variety of income levels and meet the guidelines required by most lenders. As a rule of thumb, no more than 28 percent of your gross monthly income should be used for your mortgage payment (principal, interest, taxes, insurance, condo fees, owners association fee, mortgage insurance premium) and no more than 36 percent of your gross monthly income should be going toward your mortgage payment plus all other monthly credit obligations (car loans, credit cards, utility payments).

Your gross annual income	Monthly mortgage payments	Maximum monthly credit obligations
$20,000	$467	$600
$30,000	$700	$900
$40,000	$933	$1,200
$50,000	$1,167	$1,500
$60,000	$1,400	$1,800
$70,000	$1,633	$2,100
$80,000	$1,867	$2,400
$90,000	$2,100	$2,700
$100,000	$2,333	$3,000
$130,000	$3,033	$3,900
$150,000	$3,500	$4,500
$200,000	$4,667	$6,000

SOURCE: *Unraveling the Mortgage Loan Mystery*, Federal National Mortgage Association.

They could jump considerably. Also check to see whether the subsidy is part of your contract with the lender or with the builder. If it's provided separately with the builder, the lender can still hold you liable for the full interest rate.

RENT WITH OPTION
Renter pays "option fee" for right to purchase property at specified time and agreed-upon price. Rent may or may not be applied to sales price.

■ **PROS:** Enables renter to buy time to obtain down payment and decide whether to purchase. Locks in price during inflationary times.
■ **CONS:** Payment of option fee. Failure to take option means loss of option fee and rental payments.

REVERSE ANNUITY MORTGAGE
Equity conversion. Borrower owns mortgage-free property and needs income. Lender makes monthly payments to borrower, using property as collateral.

■ **PROS:** Can provide homeowners with needed cash.
■ **CONS:** At end of term, borrower must have money available to avoid selling property or refinancing.

■ **EXPERT TIP:** You can't obtain a RAM until you have paid off your original mortgage.

SOURCE: *The Mortgage Money Guide,* Federal Trade Commission.

CYBER SOURCES

FINDING A MORTGAGE ON THE WEB

Want to spare yourself the hassle of shopping around from bank to bank for a good mortgage? Or, just curious about how large a mortgage you can afford? Then check out some of the more than 100 mortgage-related sites on the Web. Here are a few worth clicking into:

MR. CASH
http://www.mrcash.com
■ A folksy approach to relaying mortgage information from Consolidated Mortgage & Financial Services Corp.

COUNTRYWIDE
http://www.countrywide.com
■ Provides information on mortgages, equity lines, loans and services, and home and life insurance.

FANNIE MAE
http://www.fanniemae.com
■ The Federal National Mortgage Association's site provides all you need to know about mortgages and related subjects, as well as tools such as mortgage calculators.

HOMEBUYER'S FAIR
http://www.homefair.com
■ A directory of cost-of-living and housing data on 450 cities, as well as mortgage data and information for first-time buyers.

MORTGAGE MART
http://www.mortgage.com
■ Focuses primarily on mortgage financials. Includes updated rate information and a standard loan application form.

R-NET
http://www.clark.ne/pub/rothman/re.htm#calculators
■ Real Estate on the Net offers an overview of home buying and selling, as well as links to numerous related sites.

WHAT LENDERS WANT TO KNOW

You can speed up the loan application process by having the right information with you when you meet with your mortgage lender. Here— from the Federal National Mortgage Association, the government-chartered company otherwise known as Fannie Mae that buys mortgages from 3,000 lenders nationwide—are some of the things lenders look for:

■ **PURCHASE AGREEMENT/SALES CONTRACT:** Outlines the terms and conditions of the sale.

■ **YOUR ADDRESSES:** All from last seven years.

■ **EMPLOYMENT INFORMATION:** Name, address, and phone number of all employers for the past seven years.

■ **SOURCES OF INCOME:** Two recent pay stubs and your W-2 forms for the previous two years. Verification of income from social security, pension, interest or dividends, rental income, child support, and alimony may also be needed.

■ **CURRENT ASSETS:** The balance, account number, name and address of financial institutions for your savings, checking, and investment accounts. Recent statements should suffice. Real estate and personal property can also be listed on your application as assets.

Bring an estimate of market value.

■ **CURRENT DEBTS:** Names and addresses of all creditors plus account numbers, current balances, and monthly payments. Recent bank statements may be required.

■ **SOURCE OF DOWN PAYMENT.** May be savings, stocks, investments, sale of other property, or life insurance policies. May also be from relatives if money doesn't have to be repaid.

■ **DOES YOUR MORTGAGE LENDER MAKE THE GRADE?**
The best lenders help you refinance when rates fall. The following mortgage originators came out on top in a recent consumer survey by DALBAR Inc., a Boston research firm. Customers chose them as providers of the best service after the mortgage was granted. What makes the lenders stand out? Their willingness to provide refinancing when interest rates fall and help in special situations such as a sudden job loss or the death of a spouse, say satisfied customers.

Customers rated lenders on a scale of 4, very satisfied, 3, satisfied, 2, dissatisfied and 1, very dissatisfied.

RANK	COMPANY	RATING
1.	Source One Mortgage	3.64
2.	Chase Manhattan	3.63
3.	Weyerhauser Mortgage	3.50
4.	Glendale Federal Bank	3.43
5.	BancBoston	3.40
	Marine Midland Bank	3.40
6.	Director's Mortgage	3.38
	Keycorp	3.38
	BancOne	3.38
7.	American Savings Bank	3.33
	Barclays American	3.33
	Great Western Bank	3.33
8.	Countrywide Mortgage	3.31
9.	Home Savings	3.29
	Security Pacific Housing	3.29
10.	G.E. Capital	3.25

MAKING SENSE OF YOUR MORTGAGE PAYMENTS

These tables show what your monthly payments (principal and interest) will be assuming different interest rates and loan terms. For example, monthly payments for a $90,000, 30-year fixed mortgage at 8 percent would be $660.39. For amounts over $100,000, add the numbers for the amount equal to the amount of mortgage.

AMOUNT FINANCED	MONTHLY PAYMENTS (principal and interest)					
	5 years	10 years	15 years	20 years	25 years	30 years
6% ANNUAL PERCENTAGE RATE						
$25,000	$483.33	$277.56	$210.97	$179.11	$161.08	$149.89
$30,000	$579.99	$333.07	$253.16	$214.93	$193.30	$179.87
$35,000	$676.65	$388.58	$295.35	$250.76	$225.51	$209.85
$40,000	$773.32	$444.09	$337.55	$286.58	$257.73	$239.83
$45,000	$869.98	$499.60	$379.74	$322.40	$289.94	$269.80
$50,000	$966.65	$555.11	$421.93	$358.22	$322.16	$299.78
$60,000	$1,159.97	$666.13	$506.32	$429.86	$386.59	$359.74
$70,000	$1,353.30	$777.15	$590.70	$501.51	$451.02	$419.69
$80,000	$1,546.63	$888.17	$675.09	$573.15	$515.45	$479.65
$90,000	$1,739.96	$999.19	$759.48	$644.79	$579.88	$539.60
$100,000	$1,933.29	$1,110.21	$843.86	$716.44	$644.31	$599.56
7% ANNUAL PERCENTAGE RATE						
$25,000	$493.03	$290.28	$224.71	$193.83	$176.70	$166.33
$30,000	$594.04	$348.33	$269.65	$232.59	$212.04	$199.60
$35,000	$693.05	$406.38	$314.59	$271.36	$247.38	$232.86
$40,000	$792.05	$464.44	$359.54	$310.12	$282.72	$266.13
$45,000	$891.06	$522.49	$404.48	$348.89	$318.06	$299.39
$50,000	$990.06	$580.55	$449.42	$387.65	$353.39	$332.66
$60,000	$1,188.08	$696.66	$539.30	$465.18	$424.07	$399.19
$70,000	$1,386.09	$812.76	$629.18	$542.71	$494.75	$465.72
$80,000	$1,584.10	$928.87	$719.07	$620.24	$565.43	$532.25
$90,000	$1,782.11	$1,044.98	$808.95	$697.77	$636.11	$598.78
$100,000	$1,980.12	$1,161.09	$898.83	$775.30	$706.78	$665.31
8% ANNUAL PERCENTAGE RATE						
$25,000	$506.91	$303.32	$238.91	$209.11	$192.95	$183.44
$30,000	$608.29	$363.98	$286.70	$250.93	$231.54	$220.13
$35,000	$709.67	$424.65	$334.48	$292.75	$270.14	$256.82
$40,000	$811.06	$485.31	$382.26	$334.58	$308.73	$293.51
$45,000	$912.44	$545.97	$430.04	$376.40	$347.32	$330.19
$50,000	$1,013.82	$606.64	$477.83	$418.22	$385.91	$366.88
$60,000	$1,216.58	$727.97	$573.39	$501.86	$463.09	$440.26
$70,000	$1,419.35	$849.29	$668.96	$585.51	$540.27	$513.64

50 MONEY

■ HOMEBUYER'S GUIDE

AMOUNT FINANCED	MONTHLY PAYMENTS (principal and interest)					
	5 years	10 years	15 years	20 years	25 years	30 years
$80,000	$1,622.11	$970.62	$764.52	$669.15	$617.45	$587.01
$90,000	$1,824.88	$1,091.95	$860.09	$752.80	$694.63	$660.39
$100,000	$2,027.64	$1,213.28	$955.65	$836.44	$771.82	$733.76

9% ANNUAL PERCENTAGE RATE

AMOUNT FINANCED	5 years	10 years	15 years	20 years	25 years	30 years
$25,000	$518.96	$316.69	$253.57	$224.93	$209.80	$201.16
$30,000	$622.75	$380.03	$304.28	$269.92	$251.76	$241.39
$35,000	$726.54	$443.36	$354.99	$314.90	$293.72	$281.62
$40,000	$830.33	$506.70	$405.71	$359.89	$335.68	$321.85
$45,000	$934.13	$570.04	$456.42	$404.88	$377.64	$362.08
$50,000	$1,037.92	$633.38	$507.13	$449.86	$419.60	$402.31
$60,000	$1,245.50	$760.05	$608.56	$539.84	$503.52	$482.77
$70,000	$1,453.08	$886.73	$709.99	$629.81	$587.44	$563.24
$80,000	$1,660.67	$1,013.41	$811.41	$719.78	$671.36	$643.70
$90,000	$1,868.25	$1,140.08	$912.84	$803.75	$755.28	$724.16
$100,000	$2,075.84	$1,266.76	$1,014.27	$899.73	$839.20	$804.62

10% ANNUAL PERCENTAGE RATE

AMOUNT FINANCED	5 years	10 years	15 years	20 years	25 years	30 years
$25,000	$531.18	$330.38	$268.65	$241.26	$227.18	$219.39
$30,000	$637.41	$396.45	$322.38	$289.51	$272.61	$263.27
$35,000	$743.65	$462.53	$376.11	$337.76	$318.05	$307.15
$40,000	$849.88	$528.60	$429.84	$386.01	$363.48	$351.03
$45,000	$956.12	$594.68	$483.57	$434.26	$408.92	$394.91
$50,000	$1,062.35	$660.75	$537.30	$482.51	$454.35	$438.79
$60,000	$1,274.82	$792.90	$644.76	$579.01	$545.22	$526.54
$70,000	$1,487.29	$925.06	$752.22	$675.52	$636.09	$614.30
$80,000	$1,699.76	$1,057.20	$859.68	$772.02	$726.96	$702.06
$90,000	$1,912.23	$1,189.36	$967.14	$868.52	$817.83	$789.81
$100,000	$2,124.70	$1,321.51	$1,074.61	$965.02	$908.70	$877.57

11% ANNUAL PERCENTAGE RATE

AMOUNT FINANCED	5 years	10 years	15 years	20 years	25 years	30 years
$25,000	$543.56	$344.38	$284.15	$258.05	$245.03	$238.08
$30,000	$652.27	$413.25	$340.98	$309.66	$294.03	$285.70
$35,000	$760.98	$482.13	$397.81	$361.27	$343.04	$333.31
$40,000	$869.70	$551.00	$454.64	$412.88	$392.05	$380.93
$45,000	$978.41	$619.88	$511.47	$464.48	$441.05	$428.55
$50,000	$1,087.12	$688.75	$568.30	$516.09	$490.06	$476.16
$60,000	$1,304.54	$826.50	$681.96	$619.31	$588.07	$571.39
$70,000	$1,521.97	$964.25	$795.62	$722.53	$686.08	$666.63
$80,000	$1,739.39	$1,102.00	$909.28	$825.75	$784.09	$761.86
$90,000	$1,956.81	$1,239.75	$1,022.94	$928.97	$882.10	$857.09
$100,000	$2,174.24	$1,377.50	$1,136.60	$1,032.19	$980.11	$952.32

SOURCE: *The Mortgage Money Guide*, Federal Trade Commission.

REFINANCING
▼

WHEN TO TRADE IN A MORTGAGE

The right answer may be a lot sooner than you think. Here's why

The conventional wisdom is that interest rates have to drop 2 percent to make refinancing attractive. The conventional wisdom may be wrong. In fact, if you're planning to live in your house for many years, refinancing to a lower rate by as little as 1 percent can be profitable.

For a typical mortgage that involves refinancing costs of 1 percent of the total loan, the accounting firm of Ernst & Young figures that, if you can lower your interest rate by a single percentage point, the new loan will put you ahead after just 18 months.

Refinancing can give you other opportunities—like switching from a 30-year fixed mortgage to 15 years. The switch usually bumps up your monthly payments, but it will also reduce the overall cost of your loan, and the interest rate you pay will generally be about a half percentage point lower than a 30-year mortgage. Another benefit: You build up more equity in your home that you can tap into later. Recent data show that a third of the holders of 30-year mortgages choose 15-year loans when they refinance.

That may not be a good decision, though. For example: If you get a $150,000, 30-year mortgage at 7.3 percent, you will pay $229,208 in interest over the life of the loan. A 15-year mortgage at 6.8 percent would cost less than half that—$89,612. The difference in monthly payments is $304—$1,028 for the 30-year mortgage versus $1,332 for the 15-year mortgage.

But suppose you opt for the 30-year loan and invest the $304 difference in the stock market, where it earns 7 percent after tax. (The historic return on stocks is about 10 percent before taxes.) And suppose you also invest the extra tax savings generated by the longer-term loan. Since the loan amortizes more slowly than a 15-year mortgage, more of your monthly payment is tax-deductible interest. After 10 years, the 30-year loan looks like a much better deal. By the end of 15 years, the holder of the 30-year loan would have earned enough on his investment to pay off the remaining debt on the house and still have some $10,000 left.

After choosing a mortgage, you'll have to decide about refinancing costs: covering them at the outset by paying points or spreading them over the life of the loan by accepting a slightly higher interest rate. In most cases, you should opt for not paying points. By investing the money you would have paid in points, you can build up a tidy nest egg over the life of your mortgage, which should amount to more than you'd save if you paid the points and invested the amount you saved in lower interest costs. The bottom line: the best mortgage for you will be the one whose term most closely matches the time you expect to keep your house.

FACT FILE:

MONEY IN THE BANK?

■ *Payments and savings on a $100,000 mortgage refinanced to 7 percent.*

Current rate	Current monthly payment	Monthly savings at 7%	Annual savings at 7%
8.0%	$734	$69	$828
8.5%	$769	$104	$1,248
9.0%	$805	$140	$1,680
9.5%	$841	$176	$2,112
10.0%	$878	$213	$2,556
10.5%	$915	$250	$3,000
11.0%	$952	$287	$3,444
11.5%	$990	$325	$3,900
12.0%	$1,029	$364	$4,368
12.5%	$1,067	$402	$4,824
13.0%	$1,106	$441	$5,292

SOURCE: Mortgage Bankers Association of America.

INSURANCE
▼

THE PERILS OF OWNING A HOME

*Standard policies often don't cover
the possessions you prize the most*

If you're a proud homeowner, of course you
need home insurance (see "Policies to Keep
You Covered," page 83). And you may be
able to cut your premiums significantly by
taking advantage of the discounts insurers
offer (see the table below).

But that doesn't mean that you're suffi-
ciently covered. For example, your policy may
cover jewelry up to a specified amount against
certain named "perils," but if your necklace
is stolen and "theft" is not one of the named
perils, you're out of luck—unless you have a
rider, an extra piece of insurance that covers
special property in special circumstances. If
you own any of the following items, you might
consider adding a rider to your policy:

■ **JEWELRY.** Many basic home insurance policies exclude theft from named perils when
it comes to jewelry and limit coverage to a
maximum payout of $1,500. A jewelry
rider—also known as a "personal articles
policy"—should itemize each piece of jewelry insured, including its appraised value.

■ **SILVERWARE.** Silverware is generally covered for everything but theft and is usually
limited to $2,500 worth of coverage.

■ **ORIENTAL RUGS.** Standard homeowner policies limit the reimbursement for damage to
Oriental rugs to $5,000 on any one rug and
$10,000 total.

■ **ART OR ANTIQUES.** Basic policies usually
limit contents coverage to 50 percent to 75
percent of the face value of your homeowner's policy.

■ **COMPUTER GEAR.** Your homeowner's policy
may not cover the full cost of all your high-
tech gadgets, particularly if you have a
home office. It should cost $50 to $100 to
increase coverage to $10,000 from the stan-
dard $2,500 for office equipment.

■ DISCOUNTS FOR HOME INSURANCE

Some 20 million homeowners can cut their home insurance bills by up to 50 percent or
more, say experts, yet many are unaware they may qualify for discounts. Most insurers, for
example, will shave your premium if you let them know you've installed or upgraded a home
security system. To find out what you qualify for, call your insurance carrier and ask.

TYPE OF DISCOUNT[1]	STATE FARM	ALLSTATE	AMEX	AMICA	AETNA	USAA[3]
New Home	20%	25%	15%	20%	20%	20%
Less than 7 years old	3%	6%	2%	10%	12%	8%–18%
Less than 10 years old	NONE	NONE	NONE	4%	9%	2%–6%
Less than 12 years old	NONE	NONE	NONE	NONE	3%	NONE
Central alarm	15%	10%	15%	5%	20%	15%
Fire/smoke alarm	4%	3%	15%	2%	7%	2%
Sprinklers	10%	10%	NONE	13%	7%	8%
Home/auto combination	NONE	5%	15%	NONE	5%	NONE
Renovations	NONE	25%	15%	NONE	NONE	NONE
Retirees	NONE	10%	NONE	NONE	NONE	NONE
Customer for 3+ years	5%	NONE	NONE	NONE	NONE	NONE
Customer for 6+ years	10%	NONE	NONE	NONE	NONE	NONE
$1,000 deductible[2]	24%–33%	21%	25%	19%	22%	30%–32%

NOTES: **1.** Type and amount of discount may vary from state to state. **2.** Standard deductible ranges from $100 to $250.
3. Eligibility restricted to present and former U.S. military officers and their families.   SOURCE: Company reports.

A COTTAGE IN THE COUNTRY

Forget bigger digs, boomers are nudging prices up on second homes

Baby boomers have pretty much settled into their primary homes, but they won't sit still for long. A study by the American Resort Development Association in 1995 found that 35 percent of those polled believed there was a good chance they would buy vacation property within the next decade. Only 16 percent had a similar response in 1990.

The group most likely to buy a second home—35- to 54-year-olds with no kids at home—could double by the year 2000, according to *American Demographics* magazine.

With boomers set to charge into the vacation home market, prices of second homes could nudge upwards, says Karl Case, a principal in the Cambridge, Mass., real estate research firm, Case Shiller Weiss. That bodes well for early birds who get into the market now. We asked Case to give us the lowdown on the second-home market:

■ What should a buyer consider when looking for a home?

First and foremost, look at whether you are going to use it and enjoy it. Often buyers focus on the investment factor and forget that the most important part is the actual benefits you get from living in or using the home.

Other important considerations when looking for a vacation home are regional economic factors. How are the retail businesses in the area doing? Are the hotels running at capacity? Is there construction going on in the area? The financial sector is more cautious about making investments, so if investors are constructing hotels and building properties, somebody is financing all that growth, which is a good sign.

■ Is a second home a good investment?

Remember that the return on your investment includes your use of the home or renting it out. If you use it a lot, it's probably a good investment. If it's sitting vacant 9 or 10 months of the year, that's wasteful. Or if it's in a place that can't be occupied in the winter or summer, it doesn't make sense.

Of course, a buyer wants to buy a home in an improving market. But picking markets is like picking stocks: The ones we know are good are already expensive and the ones that aren't so strong are less expensive. Occasionally, you can find an underpriced market because of regional economic conditions. Often, property a little off the beaten track is usually significantly less expensive. If it's in a growing area, off the beaten track can become the beaten track.

You have to remember there's no free lunch, and you're taking a risk because you're buying a big asset, but there is less risk if it's something you're going to use and get pleasure from. And if there's enough of a market that you can get some rental income out of it, there are some tax advantages as well.

■ What areas of the country are appealing in terms of affordable vacation homes?

Vacationers in the Northeast tend to favor spots like Cape Cod, Maine, or Vermont. Right now, Cape Cod is very affordable, except for Martha's Vineyard. California is doing poorly, but the Midwest and Mountain States are doing well. There are probably good opportunities in spots where southern Californians normally vacation.

Florida is very affordable, and there are a lot of pockets in the South where there are vacation properties available, including some of the banks of North Carolina and parts of Georgia. Out West, southwestern Colorado near Telluride and a town called Ouray are good places. The areas around Jackson Hole and Aspen are always going to be popular.

■ What's the future for vacation home prices?

Vacation home prices will move upward as

THE HOT VACATION HOME MARKETS

The following vacation spots won out in a survey of second-home markets around the country, conducted by the CENTURY 21® real estate system. The survey studied factors such as home price appreciation between 1995 and 1996, the availability of recreational opportunities, and proximity to urban areas. More vacation home shoppers are buying with an eye toward using the retreat as a retirement home. Indeed, in some areas such as Brigantine Island, N.J. and Lake Gaston, Va., 50 percent of buyers had retirement in mind.

Location	Average price[1]	1995–1996 increase	Plan to retire	Nearest big city	Distance from nearest city (miles)
NORTHEAST					
Barnstable Village, Mass.	189,000	3%	40%	Boston, Mass.	62
Strasburg, Pa.	85,000	0%	10%	Philadelphia, Pa.	70
Waterbury, Vt.	112,500	2%	10%	Montpelier, Vt.	15
Brigantine Island, N.J.	135,000	5%	50%	Atlantic City, N.J.	.5
Penn Yan, N.Y.	55,000	0%	10%	Rochester, N.Y.	55
SOUTHEAST					
Ocean City, Md.	100,000	2%	25%	Salisbury, Md.	30
Lake Gaston, Va.	150,000	6.5%	50%	Richmond, Va.	70
Lake Marion, S.C.	80,000	3%	85%	Charleston, S.C.	70
Clayton, Ga.	95,000	7%	40%	Atlanta, Ga.	90
MIDWEST					
Brainerd, Minn.	224,500	10%	20%	St. Cloud, Minn.	65
Traverse City, Mich.	184,763	9.26	N/A[2]	Grand Rapids, Mich.	130
Boyne City, Mich.	250,000	7.5%	20%	Petoskey, Mich.	12
North Woods, Wis.	245,000	10%	N/A	Rhinelander, Wis.	30
Lake of the Ozarks, Mo.	103,000	8%	25%	Jefferson City, Mo.	55
WEST					
Scottsdale, Ariz.	$180,000	5 to 8%	N/A	Scottsdale, Ariz.	0
Sante Fe, N.M.	240,000	–2 to –5%	N/A	Sante Fe, N.M.	0
South Lake Tahoe, Calif.	145,000	4%	10%	Reno, Nev.	60
Bend, Ore.	200,000	0%	N/A	Bend, Ore.	0

NOTES: **1** Average price for a 1,500 sq. foot home. **2** N/A (not available). SOURCE: Century 21 Real Estate Corp.

baby boomers enter their prime earning years. Right now the people who buy vacation homes are the baby boomers—two-income earners in their late 30s or early 40s. Boomers are facing low interest rates, and they are also about to receive a substantial transfer of wealth from their parents. Many of the boomers have equity built up in their first homes. Diversifying into real estate is likely to be an attractive alternative for them.

■ What's the most valuable tip you would give someone looking for a second home?

People forget that owning a vacation house is like owning a small business. It's expensive to maintain. Unless you use it regularly, you'll have to find somebody you trust to maintain it because as in any vacant home, the pipes freeze, the basement floods, etc. It's not like buying a time share at a resort hotel, it can be very, very time consuming.

HOUSES ON THE CHEAP

Well, somebody has to buy these thousands of troubled properties

To many people, buyers of foreclosed properties are like vultures descending on luckless prey. But somebody has to buy the thousands of troubled properties on the market each year, and the plucky, patient buyers who survive the process are often rewarded.

The best time to close in on a troubled property is after the foreclosure process has been completed and the house is in the hands of the lender, says Ted Dallow, author of *How to Buy Foreclosed Real Estate for a Fraction of Its Value* (Adams Publishing, 1991). Such properties are called OREs, or owned real estate. By taking this route, rather than buying directly from the owner of a property in the foreclosure process, you'll eliminate surprises—such as tax liens on a house whose owner hasn't paid property taxes. Lenders are also usually anxious to unload the properties—on which they have to pay taxes and other expenses—and will chip away at prices.

Government agencies, such as the Veterans Administration and the Federal Housing Administration, and mortgage providers like Fannie Mae and Freddie Mac, have loads of foreclosed properties on their hands. The FHA alone forecloses on nearly 30,000 properties a year. The agencies advertise in the real estate section of local newspapers, running long lists of available properties. Fannie Mae (☎ 800–732–6643) will send you a list of its foreclosed properties. You can also locate foreclosed properties from real estate agencies, which often represent FHA and VA properties. Or, advises Dallow, go to local banks and talk with the officer in charge of foreclosure.

Once you spot a good prospect, try to find out how long the lender has held it, which will give you an idea of how eager he is to unload it. Then bargain hard to bring down the price, interest rate financing, and closing costs.

A PIECE OF THE DESERT AND A BURRO TO BOOT

Those newspaper ads touting sales of cheap public land are come-ons. Homesteading laws were repealed in 1976. Occasionally, though, the Department of the Interior's Bureau of Land Management (☎202–452–5125) sells off parcels of land considered to be "excess" public acreage.

■ Most of the land is in 11 western states, although there are some scattered parcels in the East. You can buy a few acres or a couple hundred.

■ Don't expect dirt cheap prices; the government can't accept offers below fair market value.

■ Dreaming of digs in the desert? You can buy up to 320 acres of arid or semi-arid land—but you'll have to install an irrigation system, which could run $250,000 or more.

■ Sales are usually held at a site near the property, but you can also send a sealed bid. After the bid is accepted, it will probably take a year or two before you get title to your property.

■ Want your own wild horse or burro? Some 6,000 wild horses and burros are put up for adoption each year by the BLM. You can adopt one for $125. After one year, if you show you can care for it satisfactorily, the BLM will give you title to the horse or burro. For more information about this program, call ☎ 800–417–9647.

COLLECTING

COLLECTIONS
▼

FINDING OBJECTS OF YOUR DESIRE

Trade secrets and rules of collecting from America's top auctioneer

Nearly everyone collects something, whether it's buttons, posters, or the art of fabulous old masters. "It's an innate trait," says John Marion, the nation's most famous auctioneer of fine art and antiques. "Throughout history, going back to the cave dwellers, people have collected objects." Few people can speak with more authority about collecting than Marion, who as chairman of Sotheby's North America for 20 years, brought down the gavel on some of the world's greatest treasures, including van Gogh's *Irises,* which sold for $53.9 million, and Renoir's *Au Moulin de la Galette,* which went for $78.1 million.

Marion began his first collection as a young boy, when he collected tiny cakes of soap that his father, who was also a famous auctioneer, brought back from his stays in luxury hotels. We asked Marion, author of *The Best of Everything* (Simon & Schuster, 1989), for advice on starting and maintaining a collection, and what to buy now for potential profit.

■ **Is collecting limited to the rich?**

Definitely not. That's a misconception that arises from the fact that whenever high-priced art is sold, the multimillion-dollar sales are widely publicized. That leads people to assume that all fine art is beyond the reach of the average person. The fact is that of the 200,000-plus lots sold at Sotheby's each year, more than half sell for under $5,000, and one quarter sell for $1,000 or less.

Once, nearly all of Sotheby's customers were professionals—dealers, museums, and the like—now it's more like less than half. The majority are individual collectors.

■ **What should one look for in starting a collection?**

First of all, look for what really fascinates you. Go to exhibitions of all types—American paintings, contemporary art, porcelain, you name it. Go to swap meets and flea markets, which are fun and affordable. Go to dealers, read about collectibles, join collectors' clubs.

Look for what adds to the quality of your life. For some people it's antique furniture, for others contemporary art, or arts and crafts. Collecting involves all kinds of objects at all price levels.

■ **Can collecting be profitable?**

If you pick objects the right way, yes. But in my experience the people who do best financially are not collecting for profit. They buy things because they like them. That's their impetus and, if they are lucky enough to

HOT TOYS OF YESTERYEAR

In a nod to nostalgia, baby boomers are rushing to collect memorabilia that harken to their salad days.

Many objects that were prized when boomers were babes are today's hot items. Original 1960s trolls, those cheap, neon-haired plastic figures, for example, are trading for $400 or so. And Pez candy dispensers, first produced in 1952, can fetch up to $2,000. Even staid auction houses like Sotheby's and Christie's are pushing boomer collectibles aggressively. We asked John Koenig, editor of *Toy Trader* (☎ 800–334–7165) which toys of yesteryear are hot today.

■ **STAR WARS.** Thanks to a boost from movie sequels, Star Wars action figures and other licensed products from Kenner are highly sought after. New Star Wars action figures sell out as quickly as they are released

and distributed. Some are being produced and shipped in shorter supply than others, causing an immediate upsurge in value.

■ **HOT WHEELS.** These die cast vehicles sold for a mere 75 cents in the 1970s and now fetch up to $2,000 each. The prices of original Hot Wheels in mint condition are rising faster than older toys, like Lionel trains. No scrapes or wear on the wheels, though, or they don't get top dollar.

■ **TV SHOWS OF THE 1970s.** Toys, lunchboxes, show figures— anything emblazoned with 1970s TV characters are in demand. Incredibly hot characters: Bionic Man, Dukes of Hazzard, and Charlie's Angels. Condition is paramount here, too.

collect things of high quality, they will make a profit because the objects get more and more rare as they are no longer produced and are constantly going out of circulation.

Often when the stock market is hurting the average investor, Americans do what Europeans have done for centuries, look for an investment that's portable, beautiful, a reminder of their cultural heritage, and a hedge against inflation. As long as people want to preserve the value of their capital, they will look for rare objects and the market for scarce objects can only go up relative to the value of money. The best of the best will bring top prices whenever it is offered—regardless of prevailing economic conditions.

■ **What are your current collections?**

I collect Federal style furniture and have a small collection of American paintings from the 19th and 20th centuries. Many years ago, I started buying small antiquities and stat-

ues—some Eygptian, Mayan, and Roman objects. It eventually became an obsession, as collecting often does, and over the years the collection has grown to include a 2,300-year-old Egyptian bust, a Han dynasty horse, and a few Pre-Columbian pieces. In the last few years, I have become interested in Native American art.

■ **What are some items worth collecting today for eventual profit?**

It's best to buy something that's in ample supply and of the best quality that you can afford. Autographs may be a good area. Today we have word processors, which put a limit on the hand-written word. But autographs and hand-written documents of the past are wonderful to have.

Looking toward Europe, the Eastern bloc countries have had wonderful artists and artisans whose works will at some point be traded openly and there will be great opportunities there. Another area is Latin America, where every country is highly attuned to the arts. An appealing factor about collecting Latin American art is that a lot of the currencies of these countries have suffered in the past decade, putting some of their better artworks at a disadvantaged price.

American collectibles are unaffected by currency fluctuations, making Americana attractive. When it comes to furniture, unlike European antiques, which could have been made in any one of a thousand cities and towns, almost all late–18th century American furniture was produced in seven seaport cities, limiting the supply and enhancing the value.

■ What's a good investment strategy for collecting art?

I advise a contrarian approach. Paintings of the West are more popular out west than in the east, for example, so easterners are at an advantage. When the oil industry took a hit a few years back, Western art was flying. As oil prices fell, fortunes tumbled and the market for Western art suffered. Although it's now recovered somewhat there are still opportunities there.

Keep in mind, however, that the thing that survives best is the object of top quality. And sometimes, the best bargain is the thing that seems so very expensive on the day it was bought. But the fact is, it will become more and more rare, and therefore appreciate in value.

■ Are prints a good investment?

Prints have some investing appeal, but you have to be careful what you buy and who you buy them from. There are many bogus prints done with a photomechanical process. Beware of anything that's advertised as part of a limited edition—the sellers are only limited by the number of orders they can take. The same for some collectibles—like plates, dolls, figurines—that are advertised in magazines. There is little residual value in them, in my opinion.

■ Does it pay to collect trendy objects, like dolls or toy trains?

In recent years so-called nostalgia collecting has become a powerful factor in the collecting world. Antique dolls range in price from $100 to more than $100,000 and the market is growing. Toy soldiers, games, Bakelite radios, Wurlitzer jukeboxes, circus art, movie posters, rock and roll memorabilia—any piece of yesterday that is treasured is today's collectible. Right now there are things at the toy store around the corner that, frightening as it may seem, could be tomorrow's collectibles.

■ How do you assess an object's value?

First, contact an expert in the field to determine if the object is genuine. Find out what similar items have sold for and, if possible, who is collecting those items. The condition of an object is very important. An item in top condition will fetch top dollar; one in poor condition will not.

■ How do you care for a collection?

If you take good care of an object, it will appreciate. If you have a pastel, for example, keep it out of the sun and moisture, which can harm it. Never hang any work of art over a working fireplace. Soot, smoke, and heat can ruin paintings. Antique furniture needs to be nourished or the wood will dry out, particularly in our centrally heated homes. Oriental carpets should be rotated occasionally to minimize damage caused by walking on them.

■ What are some rules of going to auction?

The auction business is seasonal. Virtually no sales are held in late July or in August. The most important auctions are usually held during November and May. You just register at the door, and you'll be given a numbered paddle.

There's nothing elitist about auction houses. They hold public exhibitions and the public is welcome to come and inspect the property. There's no need to feel ill at ease. Check out the catalogs that are available there. Sit in on an auction and get a feel for the prices and the marketplace. The auction house staff is eager to answer questions, whether you are a potential bidder, seller, or just curious.

:://

CYBER SOURCES

HOW MUCH IS THAT MASTERPIECE IN THE WINDOW?

By surfing the Web, collectors can find everything from price guides for paintings to who craves your old cookie jar. There are dozens of online art and antique trading networks and bulletin boards. These are among the best:

ANTIQUE & COLLECTIBLE EXCHANGE
http://www.worldint.com/ace

■ The original online marketplace for antiques and collectibles.

■ **Cost to sellers:** $195 per year for unlimited advertising, including color photos.

☎ 800–643–2204

ANTIQUE NETWORKING
http://www.smartpages.com/antique

■ Online database.

■ **Cost:** $4.95 per search; 50 searches for $25.

☎ 800–400–8674

ARTNET AUCTIONS PRICES ONLINE
http://www.artnet.com

■ Everything there is to know about the fine arts market.

■ **Cost:** Free software. Searches cost $1.75 per minute, reduced rates after the first hour.

☎ 800–4–ARTNET

CHRISTIE'S
http://www.christies.com

■ Online auction catalogs, schedules and highlights of sales.

■ **Cost:** Free.

☎ 212–546–1000

COLLECTOR'S ATLAS
http://www.worldint.com/atlas

■ Guide to art, antiques, and collectibles worldwide, or in your own hometown.

■ **Cost to sellers:** $45 to $300 to advertise.

☎ 800–643–2204

COLLECTOR ONLINE
http://www.collectoronline.com/collect

■ Want ads, an auction calendar, and an inventory of antiques for sale.

■ **Cost for buy/sell ads:** $10 per two weeks with photo.

☎ 800–546–2941

COLLECTOR'S SUPERMALL
http://www.csmonline.com

■ *Antique Trader* magazine's Web site got antiques and collectibles.

■ **Cost for ads:** $5 and up.

☎ 800–364–5593

INTELLASEARCH
http://www.intellasearch.com

■ Marketplace for antiques and collectibles.

■ **Cost:** $13 per month plus $25 to $45 for software.

☎ 800–947–5390

SOTHEBY'S
http://www.sothebys.com

■ Auction calendar, tips on collecting items the house sells, and information about artists.

■ **Cost:** Free.

☎ 212–606–7000

■ What are some good auction strategies?

Once you're ready to participate, the first thing to do is set a limit for yourself. Buying on impulse is the single biggest mistake a collector can make. Another strategy is to watch out for the peaks and valleys during an auction. Whenever there's a star object in a lot, everyone focuses on that object and fails to concentrate on the next object, leaving the field wide open to the few bidders who stayed cool and paid attention. I've seen items go for only a small fraction of their worth, because they followed the star item. Finally, remember that a successful bid is legally binding.

■ Is a return on a collecting investment guaranteed?

There is no foolproof way of predicting how a particular area will perform. But opportunities abound for the collector who is willing to do his homework. Whatever the dynamics of the market at the time you decide to jump in, you must ultimately be guided not by trends but by your heart and your head.

SIZING UP AN HEIRLOOM

Examine the finish, hardware, feet, and even the smell, says our expert

How can a casual buyer tell if that attractive antique chest is genuine, a reproduction, a mongrel, or a fake? Sam Pennington, editor of *Maine Antique Digest* (☎ 800–752–8521), says when you're trying to determine whether an antique is authentic, you should examine several things: finish, backboard, drawers, hardware, and feet. "Sometimes, even smell will help," says Pennington. "You shouldn't detect any oil or paint-type odor, which suggests the piece has been recently worked on. Good, early, untouched furniture gives off a wonderful nutty smell from inside the drawers. Once you smell it, you never forget it." Here are Pennington's tips on sizing up an antique chest, bed, mirror, and chair from the 18th to early 19th century.

CHEST OF DRAWERS

■ In American chests, backboards generally tell you a lot. Look at the back carefully. It's usually made of pine and should be well darkened with age and exposure to air and dirt.

■ The older or earlier the finish, the better. A piece should not be refinished or painted. It should have a uniform patina and age to it.

■ Pull out the drawers. Dovetails—a special type of tongue-in-groove joint—on drawers are important. They should be hand done. Often cabinet makers would number the drawers in pencil and the numbers are sometimes still visible. There should be no shellac or finish on the inside of the drawers. Glue or black gunk is a sign of repair. The color of the wood inside the drawers should vary. The bottom drawer should be darker in the front and lighter to the rear. The bottom of the bottom drawer should be darkest of all—it gets more exposure. The middle drawers, which get less exposure to light, shouldn't show as much darkness as the bottom drawer.

■ Look at the hardware. Is there an extra set of holes? Then the original hardware has probably been replaced.

■ Check out the feet. Do they look as old as the chest? If the feet have been replaced, the price of the piece goes way down.

ANTIQUE BED

■ Tastes in beds have changed over the years and many antique beds have been altered to changing tastes. As a result, beds don't bring a lot of money.

■ There were no king-size beds 100 years ago, of course, so if the bed's been used, the rails will probably have been lengthened. Another compromise you may have to accept is the addition of box spring holders.

■ Look at the legs. Most early beds were too high for modern tastes and people have cut off the legs.

■ Beds should be made of all hard woods, such as mahogany, maple, cherry, walnut, or birch. The main things to look for in the wood are signs of smeared stain or wood that doesn't match.

■ Antique beds should have hand-fashioned bedbolts holding them together.

■ If it's a tall poster bed, look for the original tester (pronounced "teester"), the framework that holds the cloth canopy over the bed.

■ If there is carving on the bed, be sure it's consistent with the bed's style and period.

ANTIQUE MIRROR

■ The nicest thing to find in a mirror is a label. Labeled furniture is rare but you find more labels on mirrors than on any other

HOW TO RECOGNIZE FAMOUS NAME ANTIQUES

English designers Thomas Chippendale, George Hepplewhite, and Thomas Sheraton helped make the 18th century the golden age of furniture.

CHIPPENDALE 1750–1785	HEPPLEWHITE 1785–1810	SHERATON 1790–1830

■ **CHAIR.** S-shaped curved legs and ball-and-claw feet. Back is fiddle-shaped with decorative carvings.

■ **CHAIR.** Distinctive shield-shaped chair backs. Legs usually tapered, with spade feet.

■ **CHAIR.** Thin, tapered legs. Brass castors under feet. Chair backs usually square or rectangular.

■ **CHEST.** Rococo carving often used. Big brass pulls on drawers. Legs curved, ball-and-claw feet common.

■ **CHEST.** Usually made of fancy woods, often with inlays. Feet curve outward. Oval brass drawer pulls.

■ **TABLE.** Typically drum-shaped. Curved and fluted legs. Top often covered with leather.

■ **MIRROR.** Frames made of thinly cut mahogany and often feature elaborate, pierced-scroll fretwork.

■ **MIRROR.** Frames are elaborate and heavily gilt. Typical design features a floral urn atop an oval inlay.

■ **TESTER CANOPY BED.** Foot and head posts usually lightly tapered. Edge of headboard arched or flat.

antique. It's nice to know who made the piece and it helps date it.

■ If the mirror was made before 1830, the back shouldn't have circular saw marks on it. It should have plane marks instead.

■ Look for major replacements. Curlicues, or ears, on a mirror often break and get replaced. A number of those round mirrors have eagles or gilded work on them—it's hard to tell if they were made in 1820 or 1920—but you want to look for obvious changes in the finish or breaks in the design. The early ones were made of gesso, plaster with gold leaf rubbed on to it.

■ If it's an early mirror, the glass will be wavy. You'll see some breaks in the reflectivity. More likely, though, the glass has been replaced. I'd rather have the original glass, if possible.

ANTIQUE CHAIR

■ A really early chair may have sat in a cellar or on a dirt floor and part of its feet may have rotted away. Look for replacement of the bottom three or four inches of the legs, which seriously lessens the value.

■ If the chair is upholstered, try to see the frame under the upholstery. See if it's the original frame and that no one has put in a bigger wing than was there, for example. Be very careful if it's the original upholstery; that makes the chair worth a lot more. You don't see much original upholstery anymore.

■ Beware of a chair that has screws in it. The chair will be unstable because screws don't hold well in wood under the stress of a chair.

■ A Windsor chair with its original paint is more valuable than if it's been stripped down. In a Windsor chair, the legs are generally made of maple or birch, the seat is usually pine, the spindles and back are hickory or ash, and the arms might be oak. So, to get a uniform color, Windsor chairs were painted. Collectors are really after a Windsor with the original paint.

STERLING TIPS FOR BUYING SILVER

Not only is used stuff better, you don't have to fork over a fortune

Opulence doesn't come cheap. Setting a dinner table for four with sparkling sterling silverware by top names like Tiffany, Georg Jensen, Gorham, or Christofle can set newlyweds or anyone else back about $3,000. One five-piece place setting of Jensen's popular Pyramid pattern, for example, goes for about $750.

There is a way to slice the price of silver: Buy it secondhand. Even aside from cheaper prices, says Connie McNally, managing editor of *Silver* magazine, "It's always best to buy silver on the secondary market because older silver is heavier and much better crafted than today's silver."

Auction houses are a good source for used silver. Big New York auction houses like Christie's and Sotheby's put silver on the block a few times each year, and many smaller houses across the country also hold silver auctions occasionally. All kinds of patterns go up for auction, says McNally. You can get a few pieces, or complete sets of silverware for 12, 18, or 24.

Buyers at auction pay a buyer's premium, usually an additional 15 percent above the purchase price. Even with the premium, though, the final cost is generally below retail. Tiffany's popular Take The Wave Edge pattern, for example, sells at retail for about $545 a place setting or $109 a piece. At a recent Christie's auction a service of 110 pieces sold for $5,520—or $51 a piece—including the premium. Sotheby's silver auctions often include Georg Jensen's Acorn pattern, a current favorite, for about $50 a piece. One piece of Acorn sells for $200 or so at retail.

Many novices shy away from auctions but they shouldn't. Nearly half the participants at silver auctions are amateurs. Dealers tend to keep their distance because the going auction prices may be a steal for consumers but they don't give dealers much room to turn around and sell the silver at a profit.

Another source for discount silver: dealers who specialize in secondhand and antique silver. You can find them at antique malls, flea markets, and in shops devoted solely to buying and selling silver at off-prices. Silver dealers are particularly good if you want to locate an odd piece or two to fill out your set, although chances of finding an entire set of the pattern you want are somewhat slim. If you're buying a complete set of silverware from a dealer, he may hesitate to reveal if it was assembled from a variety of sources. Be sure to inspect the pieces carefully to see if they are true matches and in comparable condition.

Specialized publications are another way to shop for silver for less. Magazines like *Silver* (☎ 619–756–1054), *Maine Antique Digest* (☎ 800–752–8521), and *Antiques and the Arts Weekly* (☎ 203–426–3141) run ads regularly from silver dealers, listing available patterns and prices. Or you can contact the dealers and request a search for pieces in your pattern.

A cautionary note from McNally: Buy from a reputable source and check silver carefully. Sometimes monograms, or initials of former owners, are removed from old silver, a process that can alter part of the pattern and remove some silver as well. One tell-tale sign is a dip or hollow area where the monogram used to be.

SILVER MARKS: LOOK FOR A LION OR A KING

Silver can be easily altered or imprinted with a phoney hallmark, so it pays to know your silver. Sterling silverware is made by mixing pure silver with copper or some other alloy to make it harder and more durable. Three grades of silver are commonly used: Sterling, which is 925 parts per 1,000 pure silver; English, at 975; and European Continental, at 800. To identify silver flatware, turn the piece over. You may need a magnifying glass to decipher the markings on the back.

Before 1860, American silversmiths marked their wares on the back with their initials or full name. Silver made in America after 1860 is marked with the word "sterling." Sometimes there may also be initials or a silver maker's identification. For example, the markings for American Gorham are a lion, an anchor, a "G" and the word "sterling."

British silver has a complete set of hallmarks, including when and where it was made. Look for a king's or queen's head, a lion, or a leopard, among assorted other markings. A lion signifies that the piece is sterling silver. A leopard's head means it was made in London. A king's or queen's head indicates that the piece was made during the reign of the monarch depicted. There are often other marks as well, which can be identified by referring to one of the many tomes on silver markings, such as *The Book of Old Silver* (Crown Publishers, 1937; available in libraries) by Seymour B. Wyler, the definitive source for silver marks.

The marking on European Continental silver is "800," the designation for Continental-grade silver. Russian pieces are engraved with an "840." Pieces with no markings are either silver plate or some other alloy. Silver plating, which began on a large scale in the 19th century, consists of a metal base with a thin silver coating, usually applied by electroplating. Silver plated ware sells for about one-third the price of sterling.

CONFESSIONS OF A FLEABITTEN JUNKIE

Make a list, pack a lunch, avoid hot collectibles, and always haggle

Flea markets carry something for everyone: affordable antiques, kitschy velvet paintings, new and old clothes, gems and costume jewelry, often plants and produce, and just plain junk. Every size pocketbook is represented—from 25¢ postcards to $2,000 restored Coke machines. The markets attract collectors and treasure hunters of all kinds, including the likes of Barbra Streisand and Michael Jackson, who have been spotted in flea markets from London to Pasadena.

The rules of flea-marketdom are easy. "What's your best price?" is a choice phrase that sellers expect to hear. Regulars don't expect miracle finds every time. They say that most dealers know the value of their goods and how much profit they are willing to forsake. Expert foragers say the best times to pick up bargains are on rainy mornings and late in the day, when dealers may be feeling desperate. Then again, latecomers miss the first pickings.

Mary Randolph Carter is an advertising executive for a tony New York designer during the week. But when the weekend comes she engages in her favorite sport, "junking," scouring flea markets, garage sales, auctions, and junk shops in search of hidden treasures. We asked Carter, author of *American Junk* (Viking Studio Books, 1994), for some tips on how to be a successful flea market forager.

✔ Junking really starts on Friday, when the local newspapers list tag sales, flea markets, and auctions coming up that weekend. I mark the ones that look interesting, cut them out and tape them in my notebooks.

✔ It helps to bring a small magnifying glass to look for chips, cracks, dates, marks, names of artists, and manufacturing trademarks. You should probably bring along a measuring tape, although I don't use one. I use my eye.

✔ For a long day of junking, you don't want to waste time stopping for food. Take along a cooler in the car filled with bottled water, juices, carrot sticks, fruit, and yogurt. You don't have to add junk food to junk hunting.

✔ Making a list of the things you're looking for helps keep you focused, especially if you're going to a huge market or auction.

✔ I prefer junking alone. Going with a friend can be fun, except when you fixate on the same things. Then we have a "who grabs it first gets it" code.

✔ There's a lot of stuff out there for a dollar or two. Take along 20 singles and a few fives or tens. Sometimes you can make a deal by saying, "Gee, I only have five dollars."

✔ Always haggle, unless the item is really cheap. Before I bargain, I accumulate a pile of things I'd like. A dealer is more apt to make a deal on a bunch of things rather than one item.

✔ Paintings are great—they're inexpensive and come in all sizes. It's nice to collect different themes, like dogs or landscapes.

✔ Junk shops are great places. It's more difficult to find great treasures at tag sales, garage sales, and yard sales. They sell mostly utilitarian junk. If you've had a bad day finding what you want at those kinds of sales, hit a good junk shop and get a good fix.

COLLECTIBLES THAT WON'T BREAK THE BANK

The law of supply and demand is what drives prices. An exquisite, rare piece is worthless if no one wants it. We asked Donald R. McLaughlin, an antique dealer and president of the World Antique Dealers Association, to pick items worth collecting that cost $500 or less. Before you buy, advises McLaughlin, pick an area and bone up on it by reading and visiting antique shops, auctions, and museums.

1. GLASS PIECES from the American brilliant period (1880–1905) retain their popularity. Typically the pieces are made of thick, heavy, clear glass and are elaborately worked.

2. AMERICAN POTTERY from the Arts and Crafts period (early 1900s) has skyrocketed in value but you can still buy much for under $500. Some of the pottery was made in Ohio by the Rookwood, Weller, and Roseville companies.

3. HEISEY GLASS, made in clear crystal and in a variety of colors, has retained its value. The pieces are signed with a diamond "H" and were made in Newark, Ohio, in the early 1900s to the late 1950s.

4. VICTORIAN JEWELRY has been popular for some time. Art Deco pieces, including jewelry that uses Bakelite, a heavy and durable plastic, are currently sought after.

5. SHELLEY BONE CHINA from England is a current craze. There are several hundred patterns of the fine bone china. Shelley dates from 1929 and is still made today.

6. ANTIQUE DOLLS—even those from the 40s, 50s, and 60s—have appreciated in value. Black dolls of all periods are also in demand, part of the larger market for black memorabilia.

7. QUALITY FURNITURE from the 1940s through 1960s. Pieces made especially for Williamsburg, for example, and any good Baker or other high-quality furniture made in Michigan and South Carolina. These will become the Americana of the future.

8. POLITICAL MEMORABILIA will always be popular. There's a big market for Civil War flags and Vietnam military items. Royalty memorabilia and coronation items from England, Germany, and Sweden are also sought after.

9. MARBLES from the turn of the century through the 1920s and 1940s were made of quality glass. They are hard to find but worth it. Some of the marbles, called sulfides, came with animal figures inside.

10. TOYS from the early 1900s. The better condition they're in, the more they'll increase in value. Newer toys should be bought in the original boxes. Banks disguised as ships, cars, horses, and other animals are especially in demand. Mechanical banks usually cost more than $500.

11. PREMIUMS that were given away by companies and radio stations are hot, especially gas station collectibles, such as little Sohio gas company tin banks, and advertising calendars and glasses. Radio premiums offered during old programs like *Orphan Annie* and *Dick Tracy* include badges, belt buckles, and secret decoders. You can sell a good radio premium ring for more than a gold or precious-stone ring.

12. SMALL SILVER ITEMS, like early silver boxes, and silver made in the South are good choices, as well as ornate silver made by Tiffany, Gorham, and some Chicago silversmiths. Also anything made by the Danish silversmith Georg Jensen, but especially the Acorn pattern, is sought after.

GEMSTONES
▼

BEYOND THE GLITTER

Everything you need to know about choosing the perfect ring

To the Greeks, diamonds were tears of the gods. To the Romans, they were splinters from falling stars. Today, the sparkling chunks of crystallized carbon are not only a girl's best friend but also a $2.6 billion business. More than three-quarters of all first-time brides get diamond engagement rings, according to industry figures. Unfortunately for grooms, tastes in engagement rings change with the wind. The wise groom would do well to keep up if he wants to get off on the right foot.

In the 1980s, the object of many a new bride's desire was a sapphire and diamond ring. The model: a large oval sapphire surrounded by 14 diamonds and set in 18-carat gold that Prince Charles presented to Lady Di when he popped the question. But, like their marriage, that style has hit on hard times. "She's no longer the model brides seek when they go into the state of matrimony,"says Eileen Farrell, communications director of the Jewelers of America.

Prospective brides now want rings that bring to mind homier models: their grandmothers. Industry officials say the current rage is antique rings, "retro" styles, and new diamond rings set in platinum—in short, the kind of ring that Grandma wore. Platinum, a highly durable metal that looks like silver but is pricier than both silver and gold, went out of fashion during World War II, but retailers now say it's the setting of choice for engagement rings and wedding bands.

Shopping for an engagement ring poses a dilemma: Does the groom scour the shops alone and surprise his intended with his choice? Or does he shop with the bride so that she gets what her heart desires? There are no hard answers, but retailers report that more couples comb the stores together, with the groom returning alone to make the purchase.

The average engagement ring costs about $1,600. Getting a good value requires knowing the four C's: cut, clarity, color, and carat weight. The size of the diamond shouldn't be the prime consideration. Size increases the cost, but it is almost meaningless if the stone is poorly cut, is flawed, or has poor color. Cut is actually most important because it sets apart the dull diamond from a dazzler.

Diamonds come in a variety of cuts, with the round or brilliant cut being the most popular—65 percent of diamonds sold in 1994 were round. Marquise, or a sort of diamond shape, followed at 24 percent and the rest were pear-shaped and assorted other cuts. More than half of engagement rings bought in 1994 were diamond solitaires, that is, unembellished with other gems.

Tiffany's and Cartier's may have a certain cachet, but they don't have a monopoly on fine diamonds. Just shop at a trustworthy jeweler who will be around if there's a problem or if you later decide to restyle the ring. But if it's an investment-quality ring you're after, the ones from the big name stores hold their value best. "Winston, Van Cleef & Arpels and Tiffany signify a certain quality of stones and a certain quality of classic design. People are willing to pay a premium for that," says John Block, jewelry director of Sotheby's New York. Small wonder that flashy real estate magnate Donald Trump presented his betrothed, Marla, with a 7.45-carat flawless, emerald-cut diamond from New York's Harry Winston, Inc. Unfortunately, that didn't guarantee a long marriage. The couple announced a separation in mid-1997.

■ **SOME POPULAR CUTS**

Brilliant   Marquise   Pear

Emerald   Oval   Square

PUTTING A LITTLE SPARKLE IN YOUR LIFE

The value of most gemstones is pretty steady compared to commodities like coffee and gold, changing no more than 10 or 15 percent in a year. But like any commodity, their value is tied to the vagaries of the global market-place—a mine strike can send prices up just as a glut can send prices down. With that in mind, these numbers were compiled by Richard Drucker, who publishes a guide to per-carat wholesale gem values, to give a feel for how gems are priced across a wide spectrum of quality. They are accurate as of January 1, 1997, and have been modified to reflect retail prices.

GEMSTONE	WEIGHT	GRADE			
		Commercial	Good	Fine	Extra Fine
RUBY	¹/₂ carat	$55	$550	$1,500	$3,000–$5,000
	1 carat	$150	$2,200	$4,900	$7,800–$14,400
SAPPHIRE	¹/₂ carat	$30	$125	$250	$600–$1,400
	1 carat	$100	$600	$1,600	$3,600–$6,500
EMERALD	¹/₂ carat	$30	$325	$1,200	$2,400–$4,500
	1 carat	$70	$1,350	$3,150	$5,800–$14,000
AMETHYST	1 carat	$2	$6	$14	$32–$44
	3 carats	$6	$24	$54	$108–$210
PINK TOURMALINE	1 carat	$30	$40	$100	$200–$300
	3 carats	$120	$210	$420	$810–$1,080
GREEN TOURMALINE	1 carat	$20	$40	$80	$150–$200
	3 carats	$90	$150	$360	$600–$900
PERIDOT	1 carat	$8	$24	$50	$80–$120
	3 carats	$24	$72	$150	$240–$360
AQUAMARINE	1 carat	$20	$50	$150	$380–$600
	3 carats	$90	$300	$900	$1,650–$2,550
RHODOLITE GARNET	1 carat	$4	$20	$40	$60–$120
	3 carats	$24	$120	$180	$270–$540
TANZANITE	1 carat	$70	$100	$240	$420–$600
	3 carats	$390	$750	$1,260	$2,010–$2,550

■ **DIAMONDS.** *The Gemological Institute of America has developed a grading system for diamonds measuring "the four C's": carat weight, color, clarity, and cut. The best diamond would be an "ideally cut DIF"*

COLOR is graded from D (the best) to Z. (D to M is the general range, though.)
CLARITY ranges from best to worst as follows: "internally flawless" (IF), "Very, very slightly included" (VVS1), VVS2, "Very slightly included" (VS1), VS2, "Slightly included" (SI1), SI2, "Imperfect" (I), I2, and I3.
CUT can range from ideal cut to poorly cut. (Well-cut is a good standard.)

GIA Standard	WEIGHT	COLOR / CLARITY			
		G / VS1	H / VS2	I / SI1	J / SI2
DIAMOND	¹/₂ carat	$3,300	$2,600	$2,100	$1,600
(well-cut)	1 carat	$10,800	$9,800	$8,200	$6,600

SOURCE: (For gemstone table) Richard Drucker, Publisher, *The Guide.*

?

MINTING A COIN COLLECTION

If you think collecting money will make you money, think again

One attraction of coin collecting is the beauty and historic value of what are essentially high-grade government documents. But no doubt the possibility of striking gold by discovering a rare and expensive coin buried in an old penny jar, say, is also a lure for America's two million numismatists. The chances of that happening are practically nil, according to veteran collectors. Coin collecting probably won't turn you into Midas, but if you're willing to bone up on the hobby, buy wisely, and wait patiently, you might even show a modest return for your efforts.

Meager monetary rewards haven't stopped coin collectors over the years. The hobby probably dates back to the Renaissance when royal families collected large copper coins struck during the days of the Roman Empire. As a result, coin collecting has become known as "the hobby of kings, the king of hobbies." We asked George Cuhaj, managing editor of the *Standard Catalogue of World Coins* (Krause Publications, $49.95) about the current trends in coin collecting:

■ Which coins make good collectibles right now?

U.S. coins in demand right now are large cents from 1793 to 1814, which were thicker and larger than today's quarter. Silver coins with the bust-image of Liberty (1796–1838) and those struck with the image of Liberty seated (1839–91) are also in demand.

You'll pay a premium for them, though. A Seated Liberty half dollar from 1856 to 1866, for example, goes for

$400 to $2,500. A Bust Design silver dollar dated in the 1820s retails for $700 to $1,200. The higher end of those price ranges is for coins in so-called brilliant, uncirculated condition—a top grade. You can find these coins in lesser condition for as little as $50 or so, but those aren't usually in demand and won't appreciate. Buy coins of the best quality you can afford. That way you stand the best chance of realizing a profit after a reasonable time.

■ Which foreign coins are appealing?

The better grade coins of Germany have always had good collector appeal. For example, a silver five-mark coin from the state of Hesse-Darmstadt, dating back to the 1890s sells for $1,700 to $2,500. Commemoratives issued by the Federal Republic of Germany in the 1950s have also appreciated. The Nuremberg Museum's five-mark commemorative goes for $1,200 to $1,600. Ancient coins in superior quality are also in demand.

■ Are ancient coins readily available?

Yes, you can get them at coin shows and through dealers of ancient coins. Coins are made of durable metals and age doesn't always play a part in a coin's price. You can collect coins from ancient Greece and Rome and pay just a few dollars.

■ How do you know they're not fakes?

Every ancient coin has its own personality. Coins today are very uniform. Old coins were struck by hand and are irregular in shape. They usually don't have complete dates or designs; those that do command higher prices.

The potential of buying a fake is there. Familiarize yourself with the coins , and go to a reputable dealer.

■ Can a collector make money from coins in circulation?

Finding rare or expensive coins in circulation has always been hard. Coins in circulation are usually too worn to be valuable. A novice collector simply trying to assemble a set of recent circulating coins will even have a hard time. For example, there are few so-called

PROFITING FROM BOTCHED-UP STAMPS

A printer's mishap can bring big rewards

Printing stamps is so simple a process these days that botched-up stamps are a rarity. On those rare occasions, collectors stand to win big. "The aristocrat of all errors is the invert stamp," says Wayne Youngblood, the publisher of *Stamp Collector and Stamp Wholesaler* (☎ 888–457–2873), referring to upside-down stamps.

But inverts have occurred only a handful of times over the years. In 1918, a biplane was printed upside down, for example, and in 1986 collectors discovered some upside-down candlestick stamps. The discovery of 160 inverted Richard Nixon stamps in 1995 caused quite a stir when one of the stamps sold for $14,500. But, in the end, the stamps' owner admitted that he had obtained the stamps not from the post office but from the printer, making them illegal.

The value of inverts depends on the stamp's age and how many misprints are around. Inverts can fetch from 15¢ for a 1962 botched-up stamp that was reproduced aplenty, to $225,000 for a very rare 100-year-old stamp commemorating Christopher Columbus.

More common printing errors include missing colors or omitted perforations. A recent example: In March 1996, a 50¢ stamp honoring aviation pioneer, Jacqueline Cochran, was sold with Cochran's name and title missing. The first of the stamps sold for several hundred dollars, but as others emerged in post offices across the country, values dropped to less than $100 per stamp—still a tidy return on a 50¢ investment.

For more stamp news, consult:

AMERICAN PHILATELIC SOCIETY
■ The oldest and largest with services that include insurance and certification. Annual memberships dues: $25
☎ 814–237–3803

LINN'S STAMP NEWS
■ All the stamp news fit to print. Cost: $2 per issue; $39 per year
☎ 800–448–7293

THE SCOTT CATALOG
■ Definitive numbers and prices. Cost: $34 per volume
☎ 800–572–6885

wheat ear pennies, those made before 1959, and few silver coins made before 1964 in circulation. If you find one somewhere, it's likely to be worn and have little resale value. You can buy one of these coins in uncirculated condition from a dealer, of course. You'll pay from about $50 to more than $200, depending on its quality, date and mark. But you'll do well when you resell it later, providing you've taken care of it.

I'm not sure if any modern coins will appreciate in value. Modern coins are utilitarian—they're meant to be spent.

■ Is this a good time to start a collection?
Right now there are lots of new issues being minted for circulation in the recently independent nations of the former Soviet Union. It's popular for collectors to fill out whole sets of coins from new countries.

An aspiring collector should visit coin shops, shows, and auctions, read trade publications, auction catalogs, and dealer fixed-price lists to get a feel for what's being offered. You can get a free sample of the major coin weeklies, *Numismatic News* (☎800–258–0929) and *Coin World* (☎800–253–4555).

Always buy the best quality that you can afford. But first enjoy the history of the coin, learn about its designers and heraldry, and about the times it was minted. Then, if it happens to increase in value, all the better.

EXPERT Q & A

THE NEW ALLURE OF OLD MAPS

Two experts shatter some myths about map collecting

If you're a civil war buff with a collection of old maps and other such memoribilia, you may be sitting on more than just a pile of dust-collectors. Antique maps are a growing interest among collectors and investors. Drawn by the artistry and history that old maps reveal, collectors are willing to pay hundreds of thousands of dollars to get their hands on good old ones.

Take Barry Ruderman, a 34-year-old bankruptcy lawyer in San Diego. He took a dip into the map market seven years ago with a $60 purchase of a map of his hometown. Since then, Ruderman has invested some $40,000 in maps and related materials, a collection now valued at up to $400,000. His goal is to retire from law in 10 years or so and become a full-time map dealer.

For insights on map collecting as a hobby and an investment, we tapped Ruderman and Paul Cohen, author of *Manhattan in Maps* (Rizzoli Publishing) and gallery director for Richard Arkway Inc. (☎800–453–0045), a prestigious source for antique maps. Here are their comments:

■ Are maps and related materials a good financial investment?

Nobody who has ever approached map collecting as an investment has gotten rich. Sure, you'll make money, but if that's your goal, you're better off putting your money in stocks and bonds. Map collectors collect because they love their subjects— be it maps from during the French-Indian War or Colonial America. A serious map collector's main goal is to assemble a good collection, not to make a good return on investment. (PC)

■ How does the map market compare to the stock market?

In some ways they're identical—there'll always be people selling wisely, and people buying foolishly—but the downside is that the maps aren't as liquid as stocks. You can't just call your broker and tell him to dump the map one day. You can make money if you hold on until the right buyer comes along, but if you're desperate to sell, you'll only get 40 to 70 percent of what it is really worth. (BR)

■ What kind of return is possible?

In 1989, an 1830 Stephen F. Austin map (published by H.S. Tanner) depicting Texas as a Republic, sold for about about $30,000—which was considered a high price at the time. The map later sold at auctiion for $100,000. (See table on facing page.) (BR)

But there are thousands of maps depicting Texas as a Republic, most not worth nearly as much. Knowing your history, and working with a good dealer can help you understand why certain maps are more valuable than others. (PC)

■ Do maps ever decrease in value?

Only if you buy badly. But if you buy well and work with a reputable dealer who accurately assesses the market value of a map, then you won't lose money. If you're willing to hold on to it, the value will accelerate a great deal. Maps and books aren't like sports cars or paintings. The market doesn't fluctuate. The prices may level off, but they will never go down. (PC)

■ What types of maps are best buys?

The most expensive maps usually retain value and increase in value the most. You can buy a really good map in the $5,000 to $10,000 dollar range. Maps that sell for $100 are fine for decorative purposes, but their value may be minimal. (PC)

■ **CHARTING AN UPWARD COURSE**

The rare maps market has been steaming in the past decade. Here's a sampling:

Map / Description	Date	1987 price	1997 price
De La Louisiane	1718		
Earliest map to name Texas and New Orleans		$2,800	$7,500
Das Ender Alter Der Werlt	1493		
Earliest obtainable map to show America		$4,000	$12,500
Map of the Most Inhabited Part of Virginia	1775		
Done by Thomas Jefferson's father		$4,500	$16,000
Occidentalis Americae Partis	1594		
Map of Caribbean from voyages by DeBry		$4,500	$11,000
Map of Texas	1830		
Depicts Texas as a Republic and parts of adjoining states		$30,000	$100,000

SOURCE: Richard Arkway Inc.

■ **Where is the big money in maps?**

Collectors will definitely see the value of their collections grow over time, but this type of investment won't bring the quick profits you see from active buying and selling. For instance, last year, I bought an atlas for $5,200 on a Monday, and then turned it around for $10,000 on Thursday. A few years ago, I bought an early English language map of the eastern seaboard for $1,000, and sold it a week later for $12,000. Not every transaction is as lucrative, but if you follow the market—know what things are worth, and keep tabs on buyers' preferences—you can manage some pretty high returns. (BR)

■ **Where can you find good maps?**

Auction houses or antique dealers like Sotheby's and Christie's are one source. But there are lots of maps and related materials that haven't found their ways to dealers yet. You might find a good bargain at a garage sale, library sale, or maybe at a local antiques store. But you have to really know what makes a map valuable and what makes it worthless. It takes a lot of work to search out the treasures from the trash, and at some point you have to decide whether it's worth it. (BR)

■ **What about reprints?**

There's a myth that reprints are worthless. Sure, it's true of modern day maps— those from the 19th and 20th centuries. But in the early days of colonial America, competitors of the original map-makers would simply copy the maps and reissue them. Some of these early reprints are as valuable as the originals. But steer clear of 19th century reprints of 17th century maps. These have little resale value. (PC)

■ **What's the most important thing to do when you're starting out?**

Find a dealer whom you trust and who will help you buy some good quality maps at a fair price. (PC)

Concentrate. Pick an area like your home town, or an event like the American Revolution, and learn all you can about maps during that period. This may expand later— you may start with San Francisco, for example, which naturally expands to Northern California, etc. But don't try to take on too big an area or time frame at once; you'll be overwhelmed and undereducated. (BR)

■ **Where can interested collectors learn more about map collecting?**

There's a wonderful old book by Seymour Schwartz, a long-time collector, and Ralph Ehrenberg who is in the maps division of the Library of Congress, called *The Mapping of America* (Abrams Press). It's beautifully illustrated, very readable, and really describes the early history of mapping. Historical books about mapping are far superior to books about collecting maps. You really have to appreciate the history before you can understand the value. (PC)

DOLLARS & SENSE

BILLS

EASING THE PAIN OF BILL PAYING

Online banks are proliferating. Here's what they have to offer

Banks are the ultimate inconvenience: The hours are limited, the lines are long, and you have to leave the comfort of your own home, of course. Why bother when you can do your banking—well, except for picking up a roll of quarters—electronically?

Online banking has been around for about a decade, although it's had a hard time gaining widespread acceptance. But as more people are hooked up to the Internet, online banking is taking off. By 2000, about 30 million households will be using some sort of home banking services, according to First Annapolis Consulting Inc.

More than 50 banks now offer electronic banking. To get onboard, first call your bank or check into its World Wide Web page (see list on facing page for some online addresses). Find out the range of services offered and the type of software you'll need. Most online banking is available around the clock, seven days a week. The comforts of home-banking come with a fee, however, which varies depending on the service. Prodigy Bill Payer, for example, is available to Prodigy users, who pay an additional $24 a year for the service, plus monthly fees that vary according to the bank. Two other popular software choices are Intuit's Quicken and Microsoft Money. Both are readily available at retail stores. Quicken goes for about $25 and Microsoft Money for about $30. (See box comparing services on facing page.)

Typically, online banking will get you access to your account balance, allow you to transfer funds from one account to another, and to pay your bills electronically. Some services will make your monthly mortgage and car payments automatically. Just be sure your balance will cover the payments; electronic checks can also bounce and you'll be liable for hefty overdraft fees. Some sophisticated programs let consumers initiate loans and even buy stocks or foreign currency.

When shopping for a bank, find out how it protects your data from computer hackers. Most likely, the data is encrypted, meaning it is scrambled as it travels through the Internet. Encrypted data are available only to those with the appropriate password or personal identification number. If a hacker manages to access the data, the bank generally takes responsibility for any losses to your account. Wells Fargo, for example, fully guarantees your losses if funds vanish from your account. Find out how much of the potential losses the bank is willing to assume before you sign on.

Many banks offer electronic banking merely to be competitive. But some banks are entering the business with real gusto. A recent survey by Dean Witter ranked the top 25 banks with the technology in place to service customers best. The winner: NationsBank, based in Charlotte, N.C. Nations has some 250,000 customers using its online banking program. In addition to an electronic bill paying service, customers can also track investments, create budgets, and even plan for retirement.

More and more banks are bypassing the software route and setting up shop directly on the Net. Among them are Bank of America and Wells Fargo. The first all-Internet bank was Security First Network Bank, which was born in cyberspace in 1995 and maintains a small physical office in Atlanta. When you visit the SFNB site, you enter a virtual bank lobby. To get started, click on one of the many options, such as rates, customer service, accounts, or security. Then conduct your business: open a checking account, make deposits, and transfer funds. Your money is insured by the FDIC and the bank is regulated by the Office of Thrift Supervision, which also oversees traditional savings banks.

Perhaps the biggest downside to online banking is learning to use the service. In a test done by *The Washington Post* recently, reporters found that that it took nearly one month between their initial call to the bank of their choice and the day they performed

CYBER SOURCES

Online addresses for finding your favorite bank teller:

- **Citibank** *http://www.citibank.com*
- **Crestar Bank** *http://www.crestar.com*
- **First Interstate Bank** *http://www.fibank.com/fi*
- **First Union** *http://www.firstunion.com*
- **MasterCard** *http://www.mastercard.com*
- **NationsBank** *http://www.nationsbank.com*
- **Security First National Bank** *http://www.sfnb.com*
- **Wells Fargo** *http://www.wellsfargo.com*
- **Visa** *http://www.visa.com*

their first regular online transaction. The time was spent mainly learning the new software program and fussing with download transactions and account registers. Eventually, however, the researchers found the trouble was well worth the convenience. They also found another benefit: The exercise gave them greater control over and understanding of their finances.

■ **BILL-PAYING OPTIONS**

Here's how four of the most popular programs compare in a range of features:

FUNCTIONS	CITIBANK DIRECT ACCESS	INTUIT QUICKEN	MICROSOFT MONEY 97	PRODIGY BILL PAYER USA
Printout of ATM record	✔	✔	✔	✔
Transfer $ bet. accounts	✔	✔	✔	✔
Pay bills electronically	✔	✔	✔	✔
Loan information/ application option	✔	Varies by bank	No	Only available at 2 banks
Stock information	Research, prices, purch. online	Research, prices available	Research, prices available	Payment by all, price quotes by 2 banks only
Buy travelers checks	✔	No	No	No
View credit card account and pay credit card bills	✔	✔	✔	✔
Order foreign currency	✔	No	No	Only at 2 banks

CAN I HAVE MY ALLOWANCE?

Free advice from Dr. Tightwad on teaching your kids about money

I f your spendthrift preteen regularly asks you for more pocket change and your college student treats her credit card like cash, you're not alone. There are ways, however, to teach your children how to manage their funds. We asked Janet Bodnar, a senior editor at *Kiplinger's Personal Finance* magazine who also writes a *New York Times* syndicated column under the alias "Dr. Tightwad," for her best advice on all the most vexing money questions you and your kids will confront from 6 to 60—give or take a few years!

■ **When should you start giving allowances, and how much**

FACT FILE:

A KID AND HIS MONEY

■ *An online site, Kids' Money, polled its young visitors on allowance practices in their homes. Here are the percentages of "yes" responses:*

DO YOU GET AN ALLOWANCE?	77%
DO YOU HAVE TO DO CHORES FOR IT?	71%
DO YOU HAVE TO PUT SOME OF IT IN SAVINGS?	37%
CAN YOU PRETTY MUCH SPEND IT AS YOU WISH?	69%
ARE YOU SATISFIED WITH YOUR ALLOWANCE?	64%

SOURCE: Kids' Money
(http://pages.prodigy.com/ kidsmoney)

should you give kids at different ages?

Start the allowance around the age of six or so, when the child is in the first grade and starting to learn about money in school. You should start with at least $1 a week, which pays for about two video games at the movies.

The average allowance for six- to eight-year-olds is $2 a week, but it also depends on whether a child is an older child or younger sibling. You can get away with less for an oldest child because he or she has nothing to look up to. If the child is a younger sibling, and older siblings are getting $3, you might find yourself giving him or her allowances at an earlier age and giving more than you would otherwise. For 9- to 11-year-olds, $4 a week is the average; for 12- to 13-year-olds, $6; for 14- and 15-year-olds, $10; and it tops out there.

■ **At what point during the week should you give your kids their allowance?**

On your payday you have money on your mind and cash in your pocket, so it's a good time to pay the kids. Sunday, at the beginning of the week, is also good. Parents tend to give allowances at the end of the week, and the kids spend it over the weekend.

■ **What should kids be required to pay for with their allowance?**

It will vary with the parents. It doesn't matter how much you require kids to pay for out of their allowance—as long as they pay for something. Young children should start by paying for the one thing that they most like to spend your money on—something within the dollar-a-week budget. As they get older, expand that. If they are getting $5 a week, it is reasonable to expect them to pay for movie admission, snacks, or rent video games.

■ **Should you give your kids a clothing allowance, and, if so, when?**

Clothing allowances are probably a good thing. This topic comes up around the age of 15. You really want kids to be able to spend money wisely. Ask them to go through their clothes and take an inventory of what they need. I recommend starting with catalogs. Say, for example, "I would typically spend $200 for you per season.

DO WORKING AND LEARNING MIX?

If you think that your teenager's after-school job is harming his or her future prospects, you may be mistaken. A study by Christopher Ruhm, an economics professor at the University of North Carolina at Greensboro, suggests that, on the contrary, such work can have a positive effect on long-term employment, fringe benefits, and occupational status. The study found the correlation is particularly strong for high school seniors. But, working can exact a short-term cost. A study by professors of psychology Laurence Steinberg of Temple University and Sanford Dornbush of Stanford University in the early '90s found that teens who worked 20 hours or more a week after school got grades half a letter lower than youngsters who worked fewer than 10 hours a week. Kids who spent more than 20 hours at work compensated for shorter hours spent on school work by cheating, copying assignments, and cutting classes more frequently. More alarming are the results of another Steinberg study: Teens who worked more than 20 hours a week used drugs and alcohol 33 percent more often than those who didn't work at all. Kids who work between 1 and 10 hours a week, however, tend to have slightly higher grade point averages and spend more time doing their homework than kids who are not employed.

■ THE REWARDS OF WORKING IN HIGH SCHOOL

Professor Ruhm's study examined the number of hours worked per week as a junior or senior in high school and annual earnings 6 to 9 years after high school graduation.

High school employment hours	Number of respondents	Annual earnings
JUNIOR WORK HOURS		
0	370	$13,856
1–20	553	$17,592
>20	139	$19,241
SENIOR WORK HOURS		
0	282	$12,765
1–20	494	$16,703
>20	289	$19,789

From "Is High School Employment Consumption or Investment?" Christopher J. Ruhm, University of North Carolina Greensboro and National Bureau of Economic Research. Revised: December 1994.

Here is the J. Crew or L.L. Bean catalog; if you had $200, how would you spend it? Some of those things you might be able to order from catalogs but other things you could get less expensively. " They learn if they want a $40 shirt, they'll have to get regular jeans, not designer jeans, etc. Take them shopping with you. Teach them what is flattering and what isn't; what is well made and what isn't. Give them a grasp of how much things really cost.

■ Should you pay kids for chores?

You should separate chores and allowances, or you end up paying kids for things they should be doing for free—cleaning up their rooms and taking out the trash, for example. I think kids should do additional chores and be paid on a chore-by-chore basis—this teaches them about working for pay, which is a fine value. Baby-sitting for younger kids, washing the car, cleaning the garage—if you can agree on a price, inspect the job, and pay for it, it saves time.

■ What about baby-sitting for siblings or family members?

It depends on the circumstance. If you have to run to the grocery store after school, no, but if it is something you would pay for—say, it's Saturday night and your child could go out and get another baby-sitting job—you should pay your kids just as you would anyone else. It is okay to pay less than the going rate as long as you don't take advantage of them.

■ How should parents advise children who make money from part-time jobs?

You don't want to give kids the wrong idea that

MAKING KIDS MONEY-SMART

Several studies show that today's kids know less about financial matters than did children 30 years ago. What's the best way for parents to teach their kids money skills? By being good role models and discussing family finances on a regular basis, say experts. Some teaching aids:

PUBLICATIONS

NATIONAL CENTER FOR FINANCIAL EDUCATION
☎ 619–232–8811
■ Kids' books about money. A catalog costs $2; it is also available online at *http://www.ncfe.org.*

CONSUMER FEDERATION OF AMERICA
1424 16th St. N.W., Suite 604, Washington, DC 20036
☎ 202–387–6121
■ Send self-addressed, stamped envelope for brochures about saving and spending.

FEDERAL RESERVE BANK OF NEW YORK
Publications Department
☎ 212–720–6130
■ Comic books about inflation, trade, etc.

A PENNY SAVED
Neale Godfrey and Tad Richards, Simon & Schuster, $18.95

■ A guide for teaching preschool-to-teenage kids the value of money. Covers spending, saving, lending, borrowing, taxes, and interest.

MONEY SMART KIDS (AND PARENTS, TOO!)
Janet Bodnar Kiplinger, Kiplinger Washington Editors, Inc., $12.95.
■ An all-in-one guide covering topics ranging from allowances and baseball card collections to gift-giving and college funds.

ONLINE

INVESTING FOR KIDS
http://tqd.advanced.org:80 /3096/index.htm
■ Bills itself as "designed by kids for kids." Three financially savvy high school students teach kids the principles of saving and investing by examining stocks, bonds, and mutual funds. A stock game teaches kids how the process works.

KIDS' MONEY
http://pages.prodigy.com/ kidsmoney/
■ Packed with information for parents and kids: money activities, parent surveys, recommended reading lists (with titles such as *Clothing Allowance: Real Life Training*), and links to other sites.

OTHER

STEINROE'S YOUNG INVESTOR FUND
☎ 800–338–2550
Min. investment: $1,000
■ For parents who want to teach their young kids about equities, this fund invests largely in stocks with kid-appeal, including Coca-Cola, Hershey's, and McDonald's. Includes newsletters, parents' guide, and computer game for older kids.

all money is discretionary. If they make $80 a week, they think that's great, but in the real world, $80 a week is not enough to live on. Nowadays kids can't graduate from high school and get a job that pays a living wage, so it is appropriate to make kids put some money away for college. You should say, if you want a part-time job, this is how much time you should work because your studies come first.

Kids seem to be able to handle 10 to 15 hours of work a week without too much suffering. But once it gets beyond that, there seem to be problems—especially after 20 hours a week. Family members don't see each other as often, and the parents don't seem to have as much control. But for some kids work is good, because if they are really unsuccessful in school, they can get job skills.

CREDIT CARDS
▼

A PRO'S PLASTIC PICKING POINTERS

Avoid the hype, be wary of rebates, and closely eye interest rate charges

I f your mailbox regularly fills up with preapproved credit card offers, you're not alone. But accepting every invitation is generally not a good idea—two cards are more than enough for most consumer needs. The most important thing for credit card shoppers to keep in mind when selecting a card is their own spending habits. We asked Ruth Susswein, executive director of Bankcard Holders of America (BHA), a consumer advocacy group, for tips on how to select and use credit cards wisely.

■ What is the most important thing to keep in mind when choosing a credit card?

Most people should base their decision on rate, because most people—about 70 percent—carry a balance and pay interest. The average balance is $1,800 and the average interest rate is 18 percent, so you want to do better than that.

If you are someone who doesn't pay interest and puts a lot of money on your card, then you are an ideal candidate for a rebate/frequent flyer card. Consumers who don't pay interest but spend less can still benefit from these cards, but it will take more time to earn a free trip or a rebate of real value. For example, if a person spends less than $3,000 a year on a rebate card, he or she is taking in $13 at the end of the year. The same person will spend over $300 in interest if he or she carries a balance. If you are going to use a rebate or airline mileage card, you should be using that card for all your expenses.

■ Should I take advantage of temporary low-rate, preapproved offers? Are there

disadvantages to changing cards regularly?

We haven't seen anyone hurt by rate-hopping. A lot of the plans are for six months, but we recommend that you go for a teaser rate that lasts a year. You may or may not be able to get an extension, because the bank is not looking to maintain that low rate. If things are competitive, the policy that month might be to extend the rate for six months.

■ Is it worth bargaining with my current issuer if I am offered a better rate?

Certainly. We recommend negotiating the rate. Before you even start looking for another card, it's worth a phone call.

■ My card no longer requires a minimum payment. Should I pay it anyway?

Many issuers have dropped their minimum payment entirely or lowered it. But even if you are paying $2 a month on every $100 of your balance, $1.50 of that will be interest. We recommend you always pay more than the minimum. You can also pay the balance off in full, and that is the best way to deal with a credit card, because then you're getting a free loan every month.

■ Any other pointers?

Make every effort to pay your bills on time, because many card issuers are penalizing consumers for paying their bills late, skipping payments, or going over their credit limit. We've seen issuers as much as double their rates for these consumers.

EXPERT SOURCES

If you've been denied credit within the past 60 days, you can check on your report at no cost. One of the four big credit-rating agencies can tell you how:

CSC Credit Serv.	☏ 800–392–7816
Equifax	☏ 800–685–1111
Trans Union	☏ 800–851–2674
TRW	☏ 800–392–1122

CONSUMER'S GUIDE

THE BEST AND MOST POPULAR CREDIT CARDS

We've listed the largest credit card issuers as well as the top low-interest, rebate, airline mileage, and secured credit cards in the following guide. The interest rates shown are as of January 1997, and can, of course, vary. Do check before signing up. We've listed the rates for standard cards in all cases; fees and perks for gold cards tend to be higher. Diner's Club and American Express cards are excluded here since they are charge cards and must be paid in full each month.

■ THE TEN BIGGEST CREDIT CARD ISSUERS

The 10 biggest credit card companies are ranked by numbers of card holders. While both Visa and MasterCard are widely accepted in the United States, cardholders who travel abroad should be aware that Visa is more frequently recognized overseas.

Issuer ☎	No. of accounts	Interest (standard card APR)[1]	Annual fee	Grace period (days)	Annual cost on $2,000 balance[2]	Card choices
1. DISCOVER ☎800-347-2686	39,200,000	19.40% VARIABLE	Classic: None Gold: $40	25	$388.40-$428.40	Discover
2. CITICORP ☎800-456-4277	25,100,000	17.90% VARIABLE	None	20-25	$358.00	Visa, MasterCard
3. CHASE MANHATTAN ☎800-242-7324	17,100,000	16.90% VARIABLE	None	30	$338.00	Visa, MasterCard
4. MBNA AMERICA ☎800-421-2110	21,200,000	17.24% VARIABLE	None	25	$344.80	Visa, MasterCard
5. AT&T UNIVERSAL ☎800-862-7759	18,400,000	18.40% VARIABLE	None	25	$368.00	Visa, MasterCard
6. FIRST CHICAGO ☎800-368-4535	16,300,000	18.40% VARIABLE	None	25	$368.00	Visa, MasterCard
7. HOUSEHOLD ☎800-477-6000	15,295,000	19.40% VARIABLE	Classic: None Gold: $39	25	$368.00-$427.00	Visa, MasterCard
8. FIRST USA ☎800-537-6954	12,500,000	13.99% Fixed	None	25	$279.80	Visa, MasterCard
9. CAPITAL ONE ☎800-933-5182	9,066,000	15.90% VARIABLE	None	25	$318.00	Visa, MasterCard
10. BANC ONE ☎800-436-7920	8,796,468	16.45% VARIABLE	Classic: $20 Gold: $40	25	$349.00-$369.00	Visa, MasterCard

■ THE FIVE BEST LOW-RATE CARDS*

Banks usually offer a range of interest rates that depend on the cardholder's perceived credit risk. Arkansas rates are also among the most attractive because of the state's strict usury laws. All these cards use the average daily balance method of calculating the balance; the difference is that some include new purchases, while others don't.

Issuer ☎	Interest (standard card APR)	Annual fee	Grace period (days)	Annual cost on $1,800 balance	Card choices	New purchases included or excluded
1. CITIZEN'S BANK (RI) ☎800-438-9222	5.9% FIXED	None	25	$106.20	Visa	Excluded
2. BANK OF BOSTON (MA) ☎800-252-2273	6.4% VARIABLE	$18	25	$137.70	Visa, MasterCard	Included
3. AMERICAN EXPRESS/CENTURION (True Grace) (UT) ☎800-467-8462	7.9% FIXED	None	25	$142.20	Optima	Excluded
4. AFBA INDUSTRIAL BANK (CO) ☎800-776-2265	8.5% FIXED	None	25	$153	Visa, MasterCard	Included

■ CONSUMER'S GUIDE

Issuer ☎	Interest (standard card APR)	Annual fee	Grace period (days)	Annual cost on $1,800 balance	Card choices	New purchases included or excluded
5. RUKEYSER'S WALL ST. CLUB/ UNION PLANTERS BANK (TN) ☎800–971–4653	8.15% VARIABLE	None	25	$151.20	MasterCard	Included

* National Issuers.

■ FIVE POPULAR REBATE CARDS

Consumers can now charge their way to rebates on just about everything. To get the greatest benefit, cardholders should make use of the rebates and charge all purchases to their cards.

Issuer ☎	Interest (standard card APR)	Annual fee	Grace period (days)	REBATE
1. AMERITECH/HOUSEHOLD BANK ☎800–695–2273	19.15% VARIABLE	None	25 (purch.) None (cash)	Cash rebate of 1% on purchases above $2,000; .5% for under $2,000. A 10% rebate on Ameritech calling calls.
2. CASHBUILDER/CHASE MANHATTAN ☎800–577–0635	15.65%– 17.65% VARIABLE	None	30 (purch.) None (cash)	Earn 1% rebate when monthly bill is $200 or more. Each month a balance is carried, 10% of interest charge is rebated. A check is issued when rebate reaches $500, or 3 years.
3. GE REWARDS/GE CAPITAL ☎800–677–1050	17.21% VARIABLE	None	25 (purch.) None (cash)	Tiered rebate structure; up to 2% cash back on annual purchases up to $10,000 ($140 annually). Discount coupons worth more than $2,500 annually.
4. GM/HOUSEHOLD BANK ☎800–947–1000	18.65% VARIABLE	Classic: 0 Gold: $39	25 (purch.) None (cash)	5% rebated on every $1 (up to $500 a year; $3,500 over 7 years). Redeemable toward purchase/lease of new GM car or truck (except Saturn). 5% rebate on balance transfers.
5. SMARTRATE/DISCOVER ☎800–347–2683	17.15%– 19.8% VARIABLE	None	25	Tiered cash rebate of .25% to 1% paid yearly with no maximum.

■ THE FIVE LARGEST AIRLINE MILEAGE CARDS

All major U.S. airlines offer a credit card, and the plans listed here have generous tie-in programs. American Express and Diner's Club also offer airline mileage plans.

Issuer ☎	Interest (standard card APR)	Annual fee	Annual cost on $1,800 balance	REBATE
1. AMERICAN AIRLINES AADVANTAGE/CITIBANK ☎800–843–0777	$17.65 VARIABLE	$50	$349.70	1 mile for each dollar charged; 2,500 bonus miles for new cardholders, 20,000 miles required for free ticket.
2. UNITED AIRLINES MILEAGE PLUS/FIRST CARD ☎800–537–7783	18.15% VARIABLE	Classic:$60 Gold:$100	$368.70– $408.70	1 mile for each dollar charged, 25,000 miles required for free trip in continental U.S., 50,000 mile limit per year.
3. CONTINENTAL ONE PASS/ MARINE MIDLAND BANK 800–850–3144	19.95% (GC) 18.95% (G) VARIABLE	Classic: $55 Gold: $75	$404.10– $406.10	1 mile for each dollar charged, 20,000 miles to obtain free ticket.
4. USAIR/NATIONS BANK ☎800–294–0849	18.15% VARIABLE	Classic: $35 Gold: $55	$343.70– $363.70	1 mile for each dollar charged, 2,500 mile bonus for new cardholders, 25,000 miles to obtain free ticket.
5. NORTHWEST WORLDPERKS/ FIRST BANK SYSTEM ☎800–285–8585	18% VARIABLE	Classic: $55 Gold: $85	$361– $391	1 mile for each dollar charged, 20,000 miles needed for free ticket.

■ CONSUMER'S GUIDE

■ FIVE GOOD SECURED CREDIT CARDS

For many, including students and those with bad or nonexistent credit histories, getting a credit card is a hurdle. "Secured" cards require cardholders to make a deposit to be held as collateral on which interest is paid. Interest tends to be high and credit limits low, but there are deals.

Issuer ☎	Interest (standard card APR)	Annual fee	Grace period (days)	Card choices	Minimum deposit/ interest
1. FEDERAL SAVINGS BANK (AR) ☎800–290–9060	10.2% VARIABLE	$39	25	Visa, MasterCard	$250/2.5%
2. CALIFORNIA COMMERCE BANK (CA) ☎800–222–1234	12% FIXED	$50	25	Visa, MasterCard	$300/2.25%
3. PEOPLE'S BANK (CT) ☎800–262–4442	16.9% FIXED	$25	25	MasterCard	$500/2.25%
4. BANCO POPULAR (NY) ☎800–232–6255	18% FIXED	$25	25	MasterCard	$500/3%
5. AMERICAN PACIFIC BANK (OR) ☎800–610–1201	17.4% FIXED	$25	30	Visa,	$400/4.5%

NOTES: **1.** Fixed rates can be changed within 15 days' notice. **2.** Annual cost on $2,000 balance includes annual fee, where applicable.   SOURCES: Top Ten Card Issuers, RAM Research (http://www.ramresearch.com). All other tables: Bankcard Holders of America (BHA).

Complete updated listings of these and other cards are available from Bankcard Holders of America, ☎ 540–389–5445. Top Ten Issuers Scoreboard available from RAM Research, ☎ 800–344–7714.

TIPS ON TIPPING

The following table reflects the standard gratuity rates in the United States. Overseas, traditions can differ from country to country; consult a guidebook for the country you will be visiting to learn the local customs.

■ AIRPORT

Car-rental shuttle driver	$1 per use
Hotel courtesy van	$1
if driver helps with luggage	$2
Taxi dispatcher	None
Taxi driver	10–15%
Car service	Gratuity included, or 15% of bill
Curbside baggage handler	$1–$1.50 per bag

■ HOTEL

Doorman for special service	$1–$2
baggage depending on number of bags	$1–$2
Bellhop for taking luggage to room	$1–$2 /bag
for delivering messages or packages	$1–$2 /del.
Message service	None
Housekeeper	$1–$2 per day
for special service	$1–$2 per day
Room service waiter	15–20%
(if service is included in the bill)	5% or $1 min.
Concierge for tickets, etc.	$5–$10

■ RESTAURANT

Coffee shop waiter	13–17% of bill
Maitre d' to get a good table	$5 for two
	$10 for four or more
(double amounts for five-star restaurants)	
Waiter	15–20% of bill
(if gratuities are included, an additional	
tip is warranted for special service)	
Wine steward	10% of wine bill
Bartender	15% of liquor bill
Hat/coat check	$1 per coat (or per person)
Door attendant	$1–$2 for cabs

■ OTHER

Parking valet	$1–$2 per use
Rail porter	$1 per bag
Barber	10–15%
Hairdresser	10–15%
Apartment doorman (at Christmas)	$10–$50

LONG DISTANCE

SAY HELLO TO CHEAP RATES

"Second tier" carriers can help slash your phone bill

There's no place to hide from the marketing blitz of long-distance carriers trying to lure customers. Not surprisingly, consumers have become skeptical of claims by AT&T, MCI, and Sprint that promise to slash their long-distance bills. So, where are the real bargains? The answer: The Big Three offer some, but increasingly, little-known second-tier providers like LCI International, Matrix, WorldCom, and Frontier, are where the action is.

These upstarts are snatching market share away from the Big Three, and for good reason. In many cases, they offer discount rates and quality service. How much money you save depends on your usage and calling habits. Do you use the phone sparingly? Are most of your calls placed during the day or at night? Do you call one geographic area frequently? All these factors should be considered before you choose your phone plan. We've researched plans offered by a variety of carriers and, with the help of the Telecommunications Research & Action Center (TRAC), a Washington, D.C. consumer group, have come up with the following guidelines:

■ **If you use your phone sparingly**, you'll benefit most from second-tier companies. They offer highly competitive rates at low volumes without the minimum monthly charges required by the Big Three. For example, AT&T has a flat rate, all-day-long calling plan for 15¢ a minute, and offers a less publicized 10¢ a minute rate with a $4.95 monthly charge. MCI discounts its own 15¢ flat rate to 12¢ a minute after the caller's bill reaches $25. But with second-tier Matrix, you get a flat rate of 14¢ a minute and no monthly minimums.

■ **An average daily phone user,** defined as one who makes 25 percent of calls during the day, 45 percent in the evening, and 30 percent at night or on weekends, has several options. Let's say you make 18 calls a month and talk for a total of 159 minutes. One option is a highly popular plan that offers one rate for calling anywhere in the country at any time of the day. For that option, the best deal is offered by Matrix, which would charge $26.58. With the Big Three, the tab would come: $27.65 with AT&T, $28.80 with Sprint, and $29.43 with MCI. The same caller opting for a flat-rate plan with multiple time periods would do well with WorldCom Home Advantage: the bill would come to $24.70, compared with $29.20 for AT&T.

■ **Heavy day users.** Those who use the phone heavily during the day and want to go with a one-period, flat rate would do best with Matrix ($22.44) and LCI ($23.51). By comparison Sprint would run $24.30, MCI $24.93, and AT&T $25.75.

EXPERT TIPS

Bugged by telemarketers? Here are some solutions.

■ **Don't hang up when you get a call**—at least not until you've told the salesperson that you want to be placed on the company's no-call list. All firms are required by law to keep lists of consumers who don't want to be disturbed.

■ **Get your name on a national list of folks who don't want to do business over the phone.** The Direct Marketing Association, which provides marketing information to 3,900 member companies, offers the free service. Write to:

DMA Telephone Preference Service, P.O. Box 9014 Farmingdale, NY 11735–9014

HOW TO BE A TELEPHONE TIGHTWAD

Getting the best deals requires determination and vigilance

■ **BE A FIGHTER.** Some of the best plans by long-distance providers are unadvertised and available only if you insist on them. Call your provider every few months to see if you can get a better deal.

■ **DON'T FALL FOR FLAT RATE PLANS.** The new flat rate plans that offer you the same rate 24 hours a day are generally best for daytime callers. If you typically call during nights and weekends—as most residential callers do—find a plan that discounts night and weekend calls.

■ **WATCH OUT FOR FEES AND MINIMUMS.** Monthly fees and minimum calling requirements are back into vogue. AT&T's new One Rate Plus now carries a $4.95 monthly fee. MCI charges a higher rate when you spend less than $25 a month. It also carries a $5 monthly minimum; if you make only $2 worth of calls, you'll be charged $5.

■ **AVOID LONG-DISTANCE IN-FORMATION CALLS.** These calls cost from 64¢ to 95¢ per call. Instead, try one of the free directory services on the Internet, or your local library, which may carry phone books from different states.

■ **NEVER PAY STANDARD RATES.** That's like paying the sticker price for a new car. Standard rate plans are mileage-banded and broken up into time periods that can cause your bill to climb if you are not careful. You can save by switching from the most expensive standard rate to the least expensive calling plan; sometimes you can stay with the same carrier.

SOURCE: Telecommunications Research and Action Center.

Heavy day users who prefer a flat rate but multiple-period plan, do best with Matrix's Small Office Home Office plan ($24.02) and LCI's All America Plan ($24.96). The Big Three would charge between $27.10 and $29.95.

■ **Night owls and weekend callers** are more likely to see savings from a multiple time period calling plan that discounts off-peak hours. For these callers, assuming an 18-calls-a-month profile, Matrix Smart World is the best deal at $23.94, compared with $25.80 for Sprint Sense and $25.95 for AT&T.

■ **Even high volume callers** can find bargains among the upstarts. Say you make 180 calls a month, mostly during the day, and pick a flat rate, multiple-period plan. Your best bet is Frontier Homesaver; your bill would run $220.95, versus more than $259 with AT&T and Sprint. Yet, when it comes to high-volume callers who choose a single-time period, flat-

rate plan, the Big Three offer the best deal: $188.20 with AT&T One Rate Plus and MCI One, versus $249.56 with LCI Flat Rate and $242.23 with Matrix Flat Rate I.

Another factor to consider before picking a plan is the billing increments used by the different providers. Frontier, LCI, Matrix, and MCI offer six-second billing increments on some or all their plans. AT&T, Sprint, and WorldCom bill only by the minute.

When it comes to perks and services, the second-tier companies are getting more competitive. All four offer calling cards, with surcharges that are the same as, or less than, those of the Big Three. All the upstarts provide residential 800 numbers. Matrix and WorldCom offer Internet service, and all but Matrix offer cellular long distance. Paging services are available from all except LCI. One big drawback: Matrix and Frontier can't place collect calls.

POLICIES TO KEEP YOU COVERED

If you read nothing else before you buy insurance, read this

Buying insurance is right up there with going to the dentist on most folks' list of things they hate to do. And worse, unlike going to the dentist, buying insurance requires some know-how. Studies by the nonprofit National Insurance Consumer Organization show that more than 9 out of 10 Americans buy and carry the wrong types and amounts of insurance coverage.

The insurance industry doesn't make it any easier. Sorting through all the policies offered requires the patience of a crossword puzzle addict and the mathematical skills of an astrophysicist.

Some simple guidelines can help, though. Find a strong, healthy company that tailors policies to the coverage you need, and then focus on getting the best value for your dollar. Here's how to figure out what kind and just how much coverage you really need for the most common varieties of insurance.

LIFE INSURANCE:

Your life insurance needs will vary over the course of your life, peaking as you cope with hefty mortgage payments and big tuition bills for your kids, and falling after you've retired.

■ **How much you need:** Whatever policy you buy, the most important thing is that you end up with enough coverage.

The amount of life insurance you need roughly correlates with your family's annual living expenses for the number of years you'll need the insurance. Add together all of your family's expenses for the years you'll need insurance. You should include future college costs, mortgage payments, costs to settle your estate and an emergency fund (typically, three months' salary). Then subtract all family income other than your salary. Be sure to include Social Security and pension payments as well as any income you may receive from your investments. Adjust both your future expenses and income to take account of inflation. The result of this calculation is how much life insurance you need. Some experts suggest an even simpler formula: multiply your annual take-home pay by five.

■ **What your options are:** Term insurance will pay your survivors a death benefit if you die while the contract is in force. It is often called "pure" insurance because it offers a death benefit without a savings component. A term life insurance policy can be locked in for 1 to 20 years. It is often the best—and cheapest—bet for families who want to provide for the future in the event of the loss of a breadwinner and who want to target the years when their insurance needs will be greatest.

A term insurance policy can often be rolled into a whole life policy later. "Whole life" (also called guaranteed-permanent) insurance provides a death benefit until you reach the age of 90 or 100, as long as you pay fixed premiums—premiums that cannot have unscheduled increases. Whole life insurance premiums are substantially higher at first than the same amount of term insurance, but term insurance premiums skyrocket as you get older. With whole life, you are betting that you will be around awhile, paying the higher premium at first and then averaging the cost out over a lifetime.

If you are older, the kids have graduated from college, and the mortgage is paid off, the fixed premiums of a whole life policy might be more attractive. These policies also offer an investment opportunity. Here, part of your premium payment is invested into a plan where earnings are tax deferred, so that the policy builds "cash value" over the years. At some point, the cash value of the policy should be enough to pay your premiums. "Cash-value" policies can help build wealth for you, and possibly your heirs—life insurance proceeds are not subject to income tax, or, for the most part, estate tax. However, they still need to be carefully evaluated. You should weigh each policy's returns against those you're getting from your other investments.

■ **What to watch out for:** Remember, the agent's computer models showing the projected returns are estimates, and are by no means guaranteed.

Not all policies that appear to provide fixed premiums and cash values are guaranteed-permanent insurance. Universal life, for example, is a form of cash-value insurance that combines term insurance with a "side fund" that is credited with earnings. Instead of making fixed premium payments, you have the flexibility to decide the size and frequency of your payments to the side fund, which accumulates interest on a tax-deferred basis. You get death-benefit protection as long as the amount in the side fund can cover the cost of the insurance.

If you make low payments to the side fund early on, you will have

to make sharply higher payments later to maintain death-benefit protection. This flexibility means that universal life can function more like term or guaranteed-permanent insurance, depending on how you fund it.

Variable life insurance products can be even riskier. You choose among the investment options offered by the insurance company—stocks, bonds, fixed-rate funds, etc. Depending upon how the investments perform, you either build up cash value in the policy or not.

DISABILITY:

Disability insurance may be the most important kind of insurance to have. Indeed, during the peak-earning years of your career, the possibility of suffering a long-term disability is considerably greater than the possibility of death. The Society of Actuaries says that a 35-year-old is three times likelier to become disabled for three months before reaching 65 than he is to die younger than 65.

■ **How much you need:** You can figure out how much disability insurance you need in the same way that you calculated your life insurance needs. Take your annual expenses and subtract your family's annual income without your salary. Buy as much disability insurance up to that level as you can. Generally, insurers will sell you only enough insurance to replace 60 percent of your income, so that, they say, you will have an incentive to return to work.

■ **What your options are:** The cost of disability income insurance depends on factors like your age, your profession, the amount of time you've worked or owned your business, whether you smoke and whether you're a man or a woman. Since women file for disability benefits more often than men, many insurance companies have begun to raise women's rates, while at the same time lowering the rates for men.

■ **What to watch out for:** Look for a policy that can't be canceled and has no

FACT FILE:

THE SPAN OF LIFE

■ *The average American born in 1990 can expect to live more than 26 years longer than his ancestor born in 1900.*

LIFE EXPECTANCY IN YEARS

Year born	Male	Female
1900	46.6	48.7
1910	48.6	52
1920	54.4	55.6
1930	59.7	63.5
1940	62.1	66.6
1950	66.5	72.2
1960	67.4	74.1
1970	68	75.6
1980	70.7	78.1
1990	72.7	76.1

SOURCE: 1995 *Life Insurance Fact Book Update*, American Council of Life Insurance.

increase in premium until you are 65. Get a cost-of-living adjustment provision, so that your benefits increase once a year for as long as you are disabled. You should also insist on a provision allowing you to boost your coverage as your income increases.

Pay particular attention to the definition of disability. Some insurers say you qualify for benefits if you are unable to do your job, others only if you are unable to do any job. Residual or partial disability benefits can be tacked on to provide a percentage of lost income if you take a lower-paying job because of your disability. Set as long a waiting period as you can afford before the benefits kick in—delaying payments for three months to a year can substantially reduce premiums. A final tip: You can usually earn substantial premium discounts from insurers simply by doing things such as supplying a copy of your tax return at application time or prepaying a few years' premium up front.

HEALTH:

You're probably covered by group health insurance by your employer, but if you're not, you can buy individual coverage that will meet your needs—at a higher cost.

■ **How much you need:** At a minimum, you should buy a catastrophic policy that protects you from serious and financially disastrous losses that can result from an illness or injury. You need to factor in how much you must absorb in deductibles and copayments.

■ **What your options are:** Even if you buy a comprehensive policy that covers most medical, hospital, surgical, and pharmaceutical bills, it won't cover everything. You may need additional single-purpose coverage. You may want a Medicare supplement policy to fill in the gaps in your Medicare coverage if you are over 65. Private insurers offer "MedSup" specifically to cover Medicare copayments and deductibles. Some also cover outpatient prescription drugs. Hospital indemnity insurance pays you cash benefits for each day you are

hospitalized, up to a designated number of days. The money can be used to meet out-of-pocket medical copayments or any other need. Specified disease policies—usually for cancer—are not available in every state. Even so, benefits are limited.

Depending on your age and circumstances, a long-term-care policy might be a good idea. This type of policy covers the cost of custodial care either in a nursing home or in your own home. The Health Insurance Association of America estimates that nursing home care costs $30,000 to $50,000 per year or more, depending on where you live. Having someone in your home three days a week to care for you can cost almost $7,500 a year. If those kinds of expenses make you shudder, a long-term-care policy can offer some relief. But remember this: If you are 65, there's slightly more than a 60 percent chance you'll never collect anything from a long-term-care policy.

■ **What to watch out for:** You can reduce your premiums by opting for a large deductible—you will

FACT FILE:

THE WAYS OF DEATH

■ *More than half the deaths in the United States stem from heart disease or cancer.*

CAUSES OF DEATH IN THE U.S.

Heart disease	32.4%
Cancer	23.6%
Cerebrovascular disease	6.7%
Influenza and pneumonia	3.6%
Diabetes	2.4%
Diseases of arteries, arteriole	1.9%
Chronic liver disease/cirrhosis	1.1%
Other diseases	21.9%
TOTAL NATURAL CAUSES	**93.7%**
Motor vehicle accidents	1.8%
Suicide	1.3%
Homicide	1.0%
Other accidents	2.1%
TOTAL EXTERNAL CAUSES	**6.3%**

SOURCE: *1995 Life Insurance Fact Book Update,* American Council of Life Insurance.

pay the entire amount due up to a certain limit. You may be able to save more by enrolling in a managed care plan, such as a health maintenance organization (HMO). If you have a problem getting insurance because of a preexisting condition, find out if your state is one of the growing number that have risk pools, which provide insurance for people who can't get it elsewhere.

HOMEOWNER'S:

It doesn't matter what you paid for your house. What you need to insure is the cost to rebuild it. The two figures can be wildly different.

■ **How much you need:** The conventional formula for gauging how much insurance you need on your home is to figure out how much it would actually cost to rebuild it, then tack on the extras, such as the cost of central air conditioning or a new furnace. If you can't afford insurance for 100 percent of the house's value, make sure you're covered for at least 80 percent. That way, if you suffer a partial loss—say, a fire destroys your bedroom—an insurer will likely cover the entire cost. If you're less than 80 percent insured, your insurer will only pay that percentage of partial damages.

■ **What your options are:** There are three types of homeowner's policies: cash-value, replacement cost and guaranteed replacement cost. Cash-value insurance is the least expensive. It will pay you whatever your valuables would sell for today, which is unlikely to buy you a similar new item. Replacement cost insurance will replace the item that was lost or damaged with something new, but not necessarily the same as the one you lost, because this type of insurance usually comes with a price cap. You'll be able to replace, say, your furnace, but not necessarily with the best model. Guaranteed replacement cost insurance has no cap and offers the best coverage. The only thing it generally will not cover is the cost of upgrading your house to meet building codes that may have changed since the policy was issued.

Homeowner's insurance also includes liability coverage. Most policies come with up to $300,000 worth of coverage. Unless your total assets are less than that, you should probably pay a little more and get more coverage. For example, experts counsel that if you have $200,000 to $500,000 in assets, you need about $1 million in liability coverage. The best way to do this is to buy an "umbrella policy" that covers both your home and car. Liability coverage comes fairly cheap. It's unlikely that a claim against you will exceed $300,000, so underwriters can afford to give you a price break. A $300,000 to $1 million umbrella liability policy will cost anywhere from $80 to $300 annually, the average being about $150. For another $1 million in coverage, double the price.

■ **What to watch out for:** Cash-value coverage may be a little risky, since an investment you made years ago that is still holding up—such as a good furnace—may now be worth just a fraction of its cost. Replacement-cost coverage, which usually costs 10 percent to 20 percent more, is preferable—and worth it. You should be sure to find out if there are any caps on what will be reimbursed for individual items, such as jewelry. For example, the amount you can recover if all of your jewelry is stolen may be, say, $1,000, if that is the amount of the cap for jewelry. If you have valuables that are worth more, you may want to buy more insurance by adding riders to your policy. This generally costs about $1.50 per $100 of insurance.

AUTO:

In most states, drivers are required to have liability insurance for each driver, for accidents, and for the other person's car in case of an accident.

■ **How much you need:** Generally, insurance experts counsel that you buy as much liability coverage as you're worth. You should also consider an "umbrella policy," described above, that covers both your home and car.

■ **What your options are:** Collision and com-

THE DOGS OF THE INSURANCE WORLD

The CFA Insurance Group is a nonprofit organization that promotes the interests of insurance buyers. Here is its list of coverage not worth buying.

■ **Air travel insurance:** It costs too much and pays back only about 10 cents for each dollar of premiums. It is not comprehensive. You're more likely to die from a heart attack.

■ **Rain insurance:** It pays if it rains a lot on your vacations.

■ **Life insurance if you're single:** If you have no dependents, there is no economic reason to buy life insurance since there is no economic catastrophe associated with your death.

■ **Life insurance if you're married with children and your spouse has a good job:** If one of you dies, can the other get along on one income? If so, perhaps no

life insurance is necessary beyond that which you have at work.

■ **Mail order life insurance:** Stay away unless you compare its price to annual renewable term insurance and find it cheaper.

■ **Insurance that pays only if you're hurt or killed in a mugging:** A classic example of "junk" insurance. This risk is covered by good life and health policies.

■ **Contact lens insurance:** The cost of a premium is about equal to the cost of a lens at a discount eyeglass store.

■ **Cancer insurance:** What good is a cancer in-

surance policy if you have a heart attack? To buy specific illness coverage is like buying toothpaste one squeeze at a time.

■ **Rental car insurance:** Your own auto insurance policy probably covers you if you do damage to a rental car. Also, many credit cards cover this.

■ **Life or health insurance sold to cover a car or other loan.**

■ **Health insurance that pays $100 a day while you are in the hospital in lieu of comprehensive coverage.**

■ **Health insurance on your pet.**

SOURCE: The CFA Insurance Group, Washington, D.C.

prehensive coverage accounts for 30 percent to 45 percent of your premium. If the cost of your collision and comprehensive insurance is more than 10 percent of your car's Blue Book value, it probably makes sense to drop it. Remember, though, that if you get into an accident, you'll have to decide if it's worth getting your car fixed.

Uninsured or underinsured motorist coverage also is sometimes desirable, but it is probably cheaper to purchase it in your home or life policy. You may be able to slash the price of your car insurance by adding safety or antitheft features to your car, maintaining

a safe driving record, or simply by driving a low number of miles each year.

■ **What to watch out for:** For an old jalopy, the insurance cost may not be worth the amount you'd receive in the event of an accident. The most you'll get if your car is damaged is the Blue Book value of the vehicle—not that much if your car is more than five years old.

A last tip: Medical payment, income replacement, and rental car insurance can add substantially to your premiums and may be covered elsewhere. Some credit card companies, for example, offer rental car insurance.

EXPERT SOURCES

HELP IS JUST A PHONE CALL AWAY

Some sources for insurance advice, discounts, and information

BASIC INFORMATION

General information and advice by phone:

NATIONAL INSURANCE CONSUMER HELPLINE
■ Sponsored by the insurance industry. Offers general information and advice about choosing the right policy, though it will not offer advice on specific products. It can help with life, health, home, and auto insurance.
☎ 800–942–4242

THE INSURANCE INFORMATION INSTITUTE
■ A nonprofit trade group for property and casualty insurers, answers questions on homeowners and car insurance.
☎ 212–669–9200
For information about fee-only insurance alliances in your area:
☎ 800–874–5662

THE HEALTH INSURANCE ASSOCIATION OF AMERICA
■ Provides information on health insurance.
☎ 202–824–1600

THE AMERICAN COUNCIL OF LIFE INSURANCE
■ The industry's trade organization.
☎ 202–624–2000

YOUR STATE INSURANCE DEPARTMENT
■ Can tell you what products and companies are available in your area. Usually able to assist consumers with complaints. Check directory assistance for toll-free number.

INDEPENDENT APPRAISERS

Unlike insurance agents, who get a commission, independent appraisers do not have a vested interest in the kind of insurance you buy.

THE CFA INSURANCE GROUP
■ A nonprofit public interest group. Provides general tips on buying any kind of insurance. An actuary will evaluate computer illustrations of cash-value policies you're thinking of buying or currently own for a flat $40 fee for the first one, $30 for each additional assessment, and $75 for second-to-die policies.
☎ 202–387–0087

THE LIFE INSURANCE ADVISERS ASSOCIATION
■ Charges an hourly fee to analyze a policy and help you identify exactly what you need.
☎ 800–521–4578

PRICE QUOTES

To shop insurance rates by phone without dealing with an agent:

INSURANCE QUOTE
■ Provides quotes free of charge over the phone for term insurance and whole life insurance.
☎ 800–972–1104

SELECTQUOTE
■ Identifies companies that give you the best rates for term insurance and sells policies by mail.
☎ 800–343–1985

QUOTESMITH
■ Will search pool of policies sold by independent agents and provide quotes free of charge.
☎ 800–556–9393

INSURANCE INFORMATION
■ Will find cheapest policies for $50 fee. Full refund if it doesn't save you $50 over your current policy.
☎ 800–472–5800

WHOLESALE INSURANCE NETWORK
■ Will give you prices for low-load policies.
☎ 800–808–5810

CONSUMER'S GUIDE

HAVING YOUR DAY IN SMALL CLAIMS COURT

Mad as hell at your neighbor who mistakenly cut down one of the trees on your property? Furious at the dry cleaner who ruined your new suit? Peeved at the mechanic who did everything but fix your car? Disputes like these, where the anger quotient is high and the dollar value relatively small, usually end up in small claims court. The filing fee is nominal, often $25 or less, and most cases are settled within two months. Although you can hire a lawyer to present your case, in most states, representation isn't necessary. Many states now send cases to mediators, who help the parties reach a compromise, and arbitrators, whose decisions are binding. The following are state-by-state guidelines from the National Center for State Courts in Williamsburg, Va.

State	Maximum dollar amount	Jury trials	Lawyers permitted
Alabama	$1,500	No	Optional
Alaska	$5,000	No	Yes
Arizona	$1,500	No	No
Arkansas	$3,000 [1]	No	No
California	$5,000	No	No
Colorado	$3,500	No	No
Connecticut	$2,000	No	Yes
Delaware	$15,000	No	Yes
District of Columbia	$5,000	Yes	Yes
Florida	$2,500	Yes	Yes
Georgia	$25,000 [2]	Yes [3]	Yes
Hawaii	$2,500 [4]	No	Yes
Idaho	$3,000	No	No
Illinois	$2,500	Yes	Yes
Indiana	$3,000	No	Yes
Iowa	$4,000	No	Yes
Kansas	$1,800	No	No
Kentucky	$1,500	No	Yes
Louisiana	$2,000	No	Yes
Maine	$3,000	No	Yes
Maryland	$2,500	No	Yes
Massachusetts	$1,500 [5]	Yes	Yes
Michigan	$1,750	No	Yes
Minnesota	$5,000	No	Yes
Mississippi	N/A	N/A	N/A
Missouri	$3,000	No	Yes
Montana	$3,000	No	No
Nebraska	$1,800	No	No
Nevada	$3,500 [6]	No	Yes
New Hampshire	$2,500	No	Yes
New Jersey	$2,000	No	Yes
New Mexico	N/A	N/A	N/A
New York	$3,000	N/A	Yes
North Carolina	$3,000	No	Yes
North Dakota	$3,000	No	Varies
Ohio	$2,000	No	Yes
Oklahoma	$3,000	Yes	Yes
Oregon	$2,500	No	No
Pennsylvania	$5,000	No	Yes
Rhode Island	$1,500	No	Yes
South Carolina	$2,500	Yes	Yes
South Dakota	$4,000	No	Yes
Tennessee	$10,000 – $15,000	No	Yes
Texas	$5,000	Yes	Yes
Utah	$5,000	No	Yes
Vermont	$3,500	Yes	Yes
Virginia	N/A	N/A	N/A
Washington	$2,500	No	No
West Virginia	N/A	N/A	N/A
Wisconsin	$4,000	Yes	Yes
Wyoming	$2,000	No	Yes

NOTES:

N/A=Information not available

Maximum dollar amount=maximum amount of suit

1. (Municipal Court); $300 (Justice of the Peace)
2. (Civil Court); $5,000 (Magistrate Court); $7,500 (Municipal Court)
3. Except Magistrate Court
4. Except in residential security deposit cases
5. $2,000 for District Court Department
6. (Justice Court); $2,500 (Municipal Court)

SOURCE: National Center for State Courts ©1996.

AN ACCOUNTANT YOU CAN TRUST

Half of Americans get help. Here's some help about finding help

Here's how the instructions on an IRS tax form no bigger than a postcard might read if we had a really simple flat tax: Write down your total income for 1997. Now, send it in.

Of course, that's not the type of flat tax most citizens have in mind. And it's unlikely that in our lifetime any tax form put out by the IRS will be that short and simple. But, there's no doubt that an awful lot of Americans find the current tax system too complicated—so complicated, in fact, that they shy away from doing their own taxes. Currently, about half of taxpayers pay for help to complete their returns.

If your affairs are plain vanilla—your income coming from wages and simple investments, for example, and your deductions are the typical ones of, say, mortgage interest, donations, and local tax—you shouldn't fear doing your own return. But some people prefer not to devote the time, no matter how straightforward their return. And professional help may be in order if you're grappling with complex areas—running a business or rental property, say, or you've been through a financial whirl because of a divorce or complex investment.

Picking the right help, however, requires a bit of effort. Anyone can hang out a shingle as a tax preparer, whether qualified or not. And someone skilled in dashing off simple returns could miss tax-saving breaks or run afoul of the rules when wading into a more complicated return. Remember, you are ultimately responsible for any extra tax, interest or penalties that are assessed because of goofs—not your accountant.

Recommendations from friends or rela-

tives are a good way to narrow the field when choosing a tax preparer. When a return involves special circumstances ask a preparer if he or she is familiar with what has to be done. Don't neglect local taxes—if you've moved from one state to another and owe tax in both, that can be daunting to some preparers. A preparer should match your tax style. If you're willing to take aggressive positions in gray areas, you won't be happy with a preparer who is very conservative, or vice versa.

Discuss fees up front. In many cases it's a flat amount. When charges are by the hour, ask for an estimate of the time needed. The cost can run from $50 or so on common returns to several hundred dollars for modestly involved ones—and up to several thousand dollars for elaborate ones. A lot depends on the type of preparer—listed below in order of generally rising expertise and cost.

■ **SEASONAL PREPARERS:** Operate only during the tax season; vary widely in knowledge; may be OK for common returns, but can fall behind on changes in the law and rules; check credentials and recommendations carefully.

■ **CHAINS:** Trained preparers, but many may be part-timers with limited knowledge beyond routine matters; a personalized, extra-cost service may be offered for complex or high-income returns; may be too conservative in trying to whittle tax for some tastes

■ **ENROLLED AGENTS:** Accredited by the IRS; must have worked as an IRS examiner or passed a stringent test; must take part in continuing education; good for all-year guidance. National Association of Enrolled Agents (☎800–424–4339) provides names of members.

■ **PUBLIC ACCOUNTANTS:** Full-time professionals, generally meet some state regulatory rules but with fewer educational requirements than certified public accountants (CPAs); often specialize in small businesses.

■ **CERTIFIED PUBLIC ACCOUNTANTS (CPAS):** Highly trained and regulated; range from small operations to national firms with many partners;

PREPARING IT RIGHT THE FIRST TIME

Some common tax errors to avoid before you sign the check

■ Make sure you have claimed all of your dependents, such as elderly parents who may not live with you.

■ Recheck your cost basis in the shares you sold this year, particularly shares of a mutual fund. Income and capital gains dividends that were automatically reinvested in the fund over the years increase your basis in the mutual fund and thus reduce a gain or increase a loss that you must report.

■ Fill out Form 8606, Nondeductible IRA Contributions, for your deposits to an IRA account if you don't claim any deductions for the contributions.

■ Are your W-2s and 1099s correct? If they're not, have them corrected so IRS records agree with the amount shown on your return.

■ If you are single and live with a dependent, see if you qualify for the lower tax rates available to a head of household or surviving spouse with a dependent child.

■ If you worked for more than one employer, be sure to claim the credit for any overpaid Social Security taxes withheld.

■ Check last year's return to see if there are any items that carry over to this year, such as capital losses or charitable contributions that

exceeded the amount you were previously able to deduct.

■ Don't report a state tax refund as income if you didn't claim an itemized deduction for the tax when it was originally paid.

■ If you adopted a child, check your eligibility for a tax credit of up to $6,000 for adoption expenses.

■ Complete Form 2119 after selling a home even if you defer tax by buying a replacement.

■ People 65 and older who don't itemize deductions should claim a special, higher-than-normal standard deduction.

big firms are often not geared to handle individual returns except for the wealthy; may be overkill; good for strategic planning.

■ **TAX ATTORNEYS:** Not for completing returns; useful for guidance on major estate or other tax planning; needed for tax litigation; may work with your accountant.

It's in your interest to help a preparer by supplying organized, complete, and pertinent records. You should have documentation to support your income and deductions, including tabulations of the amounts. Bring along your W-2 forms for wages. You may also need 1099 forms for interest and dividends, statements for the purchase and sale

price of securities you've traded, and receipts for business expenses. Ask what you should bring, and the degree of detail. You might save on the fee by tallying some totals yourself.

You can't expect a course in taxation, but when a return is complete it's reasonable to look it over and ask for explanations of items or calculations you don't understand.

A tax deduction for the cost of doing your return? Probably not. The fees are generally considered a miscellaneous deduction and nothing is deductible until the total of miscellaneous items tops 2 percent of your adjusted gross income. But fees related to a business tax schedule on your return may be deductible separately.

TWENTY-FIVE EASILY OVERLOOKED DEDUCTIONS

Expenses for everything from contact lenses to dry cleaning could help you lower your tax bill. IRS regulations allow many personal and business expenses to be deducted from your gross income before you figure your tax liability. The more you can subtract, the more you reduce the amount of your taxable income. Here's a list from Ernst & Young, one of the nation's largest accounting firms, of 25 deductions that are easily overlooked:

1. APPRAISAL FEES: When paid to determine value of a charitable gift or extent of a casualty loss.

2. BUSINESS GIFTS: No more than $25 to any one person per year.

3. CELLULAR TELEPHONE: When used in your business, or required by your employer, the cost of the phone may be deductible, plus phone calls made.

4. CHARITABLE EXPENSES FOR VOLUNTEER WORK: Twelve cents a mile for use of your car, plus out-of-pocket spending for such items as uniforms and supplies.

5. COMMISSIONS ON SALE OF ASSETS: Brokerage or other fees to complete a sale are taken into account when you figure your profit or loss (generally added to your cost for the asset).

6. CONTACT LENSES: Also include the cost of eyeglasses or cleaning solution.

7. CONTRACEPTIVES: Legitimate medical items include birth control pills. Also legal abortions.

8. DRUG AND ALCOHOL ABUSE TREATMENT: Includes meals and lodging when staying at a treatment center, but not programs to quit smoking.

9. EDUCATIONAL EXPENSES: To improve or keep up your skills at your current job.

10. EMPLOYMENT AGENCY FEES: Whether you get a new job or not; but not if you're looking for your first job or switching occupations. Résumé and travel costs also are deductible.

11. FOREIGN TAX: If you pay tax to another country on income from foreign investments, you can get a deduction or credit for those payments when figuring your U.S. tax.

12. GAMBLING LOSSES: Only up to the amount of reported winnings.

13. LAUNDRY SERVICE ON A BUSINESS TRIP: You needn't pack for an entire trip.

14. MOVING EXPENSES: When changing jobs or starting work for the first time, and only if new job must mean a 50-mile or longer extra commute if you don't move.

15. PREMIUM ON TAXABLE BONDS: Investors who buy taxable bonds for more than face value can gradually deduct the excess each year they own the bond.

16. MEDICAL TRANSPORTATION: If driving, you can claim 10¢ per mile plus tolls and parking.

17. ORTHOPEDIC SHOES: The extra amount over the cost of normal shoes.

18. PENALTY FOR EARLY WITHDRAWAL OF SAVINGS: When a certificate of deposit is cashed in before maturity, a penalty is deductible as an adjustment to income.

19. POINTS ON A HOME MORTGAGE: Deductible as a lump sum when paid on a loan to buy or remodel a main residence; deductible gradually over the life of the loan when paid to refinance a mortgage.

20. SELF-EMPLOYMENT TAX: Adjustment allows the self-employed to reduce taxable income by half their self-employment Social

Security and Medicare tax.

21. SPECIAL SCHOOLING: For the mentally or physically impaired when the school is primarily to help them deal with their disability.

22. SUPPORT FOR A VISITING STUDENT: Up to $50 per month in housing, food, and support for live-in exchange student is deductible—only

if you're not reimbursed.

23. TAX PREPARATION: Accountant's fees, legal expenses, tax guides, and computer programs.

24. WORK CLOTHES: When required for work, but not suitable for ordinary wear.

25. WORTHLESS STOCK: Claimed as a capital loss in

the year it first has no value. (Less than one cent per share generally is considered worthless.)

NOTE: Some deductions are limited. For example, only the portion of total medical expenses exceeding 7.5 percent of your adjusted gross income is deductible. "Miscellaneous" deductions, including most employment-related and investment expenses, are deductible only to the extent they exceed 2 percent of adjusted gross income.

SOURCE: Adapted from *The Ernst & Young Tax Guide 1997*, Peter W. Bernstein, ed., John Wiley & Sons, 1997.

TEN SOURCES OF TAX-FREE INCOME

The biggest stream of tax-free income for many people comes from Social Security benefits. It's wholly untaxed unless your income exceeds a certain level—roughly $25,000 for single people and $32,000 for couples. Here are other types of income that can elude income tax.

■ **CHILD SUPPORT:** Parents who collect child support from an ex-spouse do not report it as income.

■ **DISABILITY INCOME:** Worker's compensation benefits because of a job injury are generally not taxed.

■ **GIFTS:** Bequests and gifts are tax free; any gift or estate tax that may be due is paid by the giver.

■ **LIFE INSURANCE:** Beneficiaries don't pay tax on insurance proceeds, but an owner of a policy who cashes it in faces tax on proceeds that exceed the premiums paid.

■ **RENTAL OF A HOME:** Income from renting a vacation or other home for 14 or fewer days a year isn't taxable.

■ **SALE OF A RESIDENCE:** People 55 or older when they sell their principal residence can—once in a lifetime—permanently escape tax on up to $125,000 of any profit.

President Clinton has proposed letting people of any age escape tax on $250,000 (or $500,000 for a couple) every two years.

■ **U.S. SAVINGS BONDS:** Interest on bonds bought since 1990 can be wholly or partly tax free for parents who redeem the bonds to pay college tuition—but income and other limits apply.

■ **SCHOLARSHIPS:** Untaxed when the recipient is a candidate for a degree and the money is for tuition, fees, and supplies and isn't payment for work.

■ **MUNICIPAL BONDS:** Federal income tax doesn't apply to interest from state and local government obligations—but the interest could lift the amount of Social Security benefits subject to tax.

■ **WELFARE PAYMENTS:** Aid to families with dependent children, emergency disaster relief, compensation to crime victims— all can qualify as tax-free assistance.

IF THE IRS COMES KNOCKING

Chances are, you'll end up paying after an audit by the IRS

The IRS leaves a lot of returns unaudited, but its examiners can be obnoxiously nosey about the ones they do examine. At one time, IRS personnel may have left it at checking the validity of your tax deductions, these days they're on orders to do more snooping for income you may have neglected to report.

The IRS's lethal weapon of choice is what's popularly called a lifestyle audit. Examiners take a global view of your financial and family affairs to see if your reported income is sufficient to support the lifestyle you're enjoying. Besides asking you for receipts for charitable donations, proof of business expenses, and details of investment transactions, auditors today may ask how you can afford that car and a second home on your income. Questions about the amount of your mortgage payment, whether your children work, what appliances you've recently bought, where you went to college, and whether you've been divorced are also fair game.

The IRS's top audit targets are generally upper-income professionals, self-employed people, investors claiming big losses, and people with considerable income from tips—but no group is immune. About 80 percent of audits end up pulling in extra tax, so emerging unscathed is a long shot.

Audits come in three flavors. Least intimidating is a correspondence audit—usually a letter asking for documentation to back up a single item. More fearsome are office audits in which you go to an IRS office for a face-to-face probe that may cover more topics in greater detail. At the top tier are field audits, which most often involve business-related returns and are conducted by top-trained agents at a taxpayer's home or office. Office audits are most common, partly because budget restraints limit the number of face-to-face encounters the IRS can afford. But exams by mail are also often based on the least solid suspicion of wrongdoing, so they are often the easiest to successfully fight.

When the IRS contacts you, it has usually found at least something suspicious. Generally, it will be up to you to show why any proposed changes are wrong. Mail audits can often be handled on your own, but you may want guidance from an accountant on deeper probes.

You would be wise not to insist on total victory. Give the auditor a few small wins so the IRS can close your case and move on. But also be wary. The examiner may be friendly and even sympathetic, yet his or her job is to extract more tax from you. And like an elephant, the IRS never forgets: If you have been audited before, the IRS will remember. Don't repeat past mistakes.

■ WHO GETS CHECKED THE MOST BY THE IRS

A look at individual tax returns audited in 1996 shows that estates are the most likely to attract Uncle Sam's attention:

TYPE OF RETURN	PERCENTAGE AUDITED
PERSONAL	
Income under $100,000	1.48%
Income over $100,000	2.85%
SELF-EMPLOYED	
Gross revenue under $100,000	3.45%
Gross revenue over $100,000	4.09%
FARMERS	
Gross revenue under $100,000	1.59%
Gross revenue over $100,000	3.61%
ESTATES	
Assets under $1 million	7.85%
Assets $1 million to $5 million	21.42%
Assets over $5 million	49.33%

NOTE: Personal income is the total before subtracting investment or tax shelter losses.
SOURCE: Internal Revenue Service.

EXPERT Q & A

CHARITY BEGINS WITH YOU

Good causes abound. Here's what you should know before you give

A mericans gave nearly $144 billion to charity in 1995, and as federal budget cutbacks begin to be felt, demand for donations and competition among charities is expected to increase. Donors who want to make sure their hard-earned cash is put to the best use will have to choose between competing causes. We spoke with Stacy Palmer, managing editor of *The Chronicle of Philanthropy*, to get expert advice.

■ **What are the important things for people to keep in mind when choosing a charity?**

They really have to think hard about what causes they care about—not just the ones that solicit through the mail. It's only certain kinds of charity that raise money through the mail. It's the smaller, local social service charities that are going to be most affected by the federal cuts and are going to be really dependent on private donations. Arts groups are also going to be particularly hard hit.

■ **How much of your income should you give to charities?**

Charities recommend giving 5 percent of your income or your time, or some combination of the two. But most people don't give that much. For some charities, volunteer help is just as important as cash.

■ **What should potential donors beware of?**

Giving by telephone. That is where the most abuses occur. People should be extremely

---

■ **WHO GIVES AND WHO GETS**

Charitable giving rose by 10.8 percent in 1995, to an estimated $144 billion, but in many cases the numbers were just barely above inflation. Where are those dollars going?

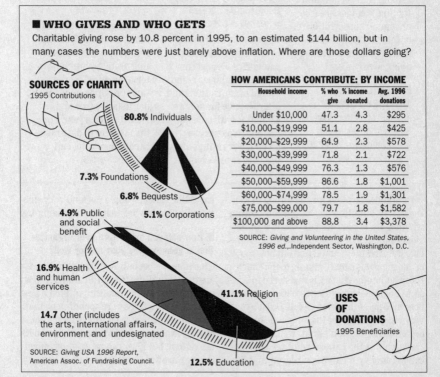

SOURCES OF CHARITY
1995 Contributions

80.8% Individuals
7.3% Foundations
6.8% Bequests
4.9% Public and social benefit
5.1% Corporations

16.9% Health and human services
14.7 Other (includes the arts, international affairs, environment and undesignated
41.1% Religion
12.5% Education

USES OF DONATIONS
1995 Beneficiaries

SOURCE: *Giving USA 1996 Report,*
American Assoc. of Fundraising Council.

HOW AMERICANS CONTRIBUTE: BY INCOME

Household income	% who give	% income donated	Avg. 1996 donations
Under $10,000	47.3	4.3	$295
$10,000–$19,999	51.1	2.8	$425
$20,000–$29,999	64.9	2.3	$578
$30,000–$39,999	71.8	2.1	$722
$40,000–$49,999	76.3	1.3	$576
$50,000–$59,999	86.6	1.8	$1,001
$60,000–$74,999	78.5	1.9	$1,301
$75,000–$99,000	79.7	1.8	$1,582
$100,000 and above	88.8	3.4	$3,378

SOURCE: *Giving and Volunteering in the United States, 1996 ed.,*.Independent Sector, Washington, D.C.

EXPERT SOURCES

WHO'S WATCHING OUT FOR YOUR MONEY?

Americans have been bombarded in recent years with media reports of unsavory fraud rings posing as charities and philanthropic organizations. How can you make sure your money is going to truly worthy causes? The following watchdog groups monitor charities around the country and issue regular reports that are available to the public:

NATIONAL CHARITIES INFORMATION BUREAU

19 Union Square West
New York, NY 10003
☎212–929–6300

■ Provides brief reports of nearly 400 charities in its *Wise Giving Guide,* published quarterly. Charities evaluated as to their management of finances, truth in fund-raising, and accountability. Single copies are free; an annual subscription costs $35. You can also find information online at *http://www.gize.org*

PHILANTHROPIC ADVISORY SERVICE

(Council of Better Business Bureaus) 4200 Wilson Blvd., Arlington, VA 22203
☎703–276–0100

■ Information about 250 of the most visible national charities, including programs, finances, fund-raising practices, and governance. PAS has a number of publications and a Web site: *http://www.bbb.org*

AMERICAN INSTITUTE OF PHILANTHROPY

4905 Del Ray Ave., #300
Bethesda, MD 20814
☎301–973–5200

■ Rates the finances of over 300 charities in 37 categories. Reports on executive salaries at individual organizations and offers advice for donors. Charities with substantial endowments are given lower ratings since they are seen as requir-

ing less in the way of donations. The quarterly *Charity Rating Guide and Watchdog Report* is available for $3 a copy; a one-year subscription costs $35.

EVANGELICAL COUNCIL FOR FINANCIAL ACCOUNTABILITY

PO Box 17456,
Washington, D.C. 20041
☎703–713–1414

■ This group publishes a list of over 850 accredited religious organizations that abide by a set of criteria specified by the Council. Updated member lists are free and issued twice a year. For the most up-to-date member information, call ☎ 800–323–9473.

careful and always ask for something in writing. They should ask the person calling whether he is paid to call—is he a professional solicitor, or is he volunteering for the charity? And they should find out how much of the money is actually going to the charity. Ask whether the charity is registered in your state. Some states require charities to be registered to make that kind of call. But it's very, very risky to give over the telephone to some organization you don't know well.

Watch out for callers who say they are raising money for dying children and dis-

eases like cancer. People respond very emotionally. That's where a lot of the scams are.

■ **How can you make sure your organization is going to use your money well?**

Charities —especially legitimate charities— are usually willing to send an annual report or their provisional tax return. That's how you can see what they are spending on their program expenses, their fund raising, etc. A charity is not required by law to send you its tax return, but if you show up at its offices, it is required to show the return to you.

PHILANTHROPIST'S GUIDE

CHARITIES THAT MAKE A DIFFERENCE

Each year, The Chronicle of Philanthropy *ranks charities according to their private income and the percentage of donations that are used for program support. Here are the largest foundations by category:*

CHARITY	LOCATION	PRIVATE INCOME ($millions)	SHARE FOR PROGRAMS (%)	TELEPHONE
■ **HUMAN SERVICES**				
Salvation Army	Alexandria, Va.	$644	85.53	703–684–5500
American Red Cross	Washington, D.C.	$466	96.53	202–639–3286
Catholic Charities	Alexandria, Va.	$419	83.32	703–549–1390
Second Harvest	Chicago, Ill.	$369	99.69	302–263–2303
YWCA of the USA	New York, N.Y..	$284	83.85	212–614–2700
■ **INTERNATIONAL**				
World Vision	Monrovia, Calif.	$240	80.48	818–303–8811
AmeriCares Foundation	New Canaan, Conn.	$145	97.23	203–972–5500
Larry Jones Int. Ministries	Oklahoma City, Okla.	$117	86.22	405–942–0228
MAP International	Brunswick, Ga.	$105	92.88	912–265–6010
■ **CONSERVATION**				
Nature Conservancy	Arlington, Va.	$209	81.34	703–841–5300
World Wildlife Fund	Washington, D.C.	$43	81.15	202–778–9753
North Shore Animal League	Port Washington, N.Y.	$26	83.84	516–883–7575
Ducks Unlimited	Memphis, Tenn..	$26	76.58	901–758–3825
Humane Society of the United States	Washington, D.C.	$25	56.73	202–452–1100
■ **HEALTH**				
American Cancer Society	Atlanta, Ga.	$382	64.66	404–841–0700
American Heart Association	Dallas, Texas	$256	74.31	214–373–6300
March of Dimes Birth Defects Found.	White Plains, N.Y.	$126	74.99	914–428–7100
Planned Parenthood Fed. of America	New York, N.Y.	$123	76.49	212–261–4300
American Lung Association	New York, N.Y.	$106	77.39	212–315–8700
■ **RELIGION**				
Campus Crusade for Christ Int.	Orlando, Fla.	$185	84.08	407–826–2200
Focus on the Family	Colorado Springs, Colo.	$88	80.68	719–531–3400
Billy Graham Evangelistic Assoc.	Minneapolis, Minn.	$84	73.14	612–338–0500
Christian Broadcasting Network	Virginia Beach, Va.	$83	94.60	804–579–7000

SOURCE: *The Chronicle of Philanthropy*, October 31, 1996.

The thing to keep in mind with small charities is that they tend to spend a lot on fundraising and administration, because they're getting started and trying to make their appeal. So it doesn't necessarily mean they're a fraud just because they're spending 30 to 40 percent on fund raising. Small charities are sometimes shunned because of that and they shouldn't be.

■ **What can you do if you think you have been taken advantage of by a fraudulent organization?**

You should report that right away. Go to your state attorney general. Most states have a person or an office that specifically works on consumer protection. The other thing to do is to call an organization like the Better Business Bureau.

RETIREMENT

HOT SPOTS
▼

HEADING SOUTH OF THE BORDER

Mexico and Costa Rica are luring more and more retired Americans

Many retirees dream of spending their golden years watching copper sunsets melt over silver oceans. But when they start making their plans, they find their retirement resources won't stretch to their dream paradises. Well, that depends on your chosen paradise. Thousands of Americans on shoestring budgets are retiring south of the border—in Mexico, Costa Rica, and other countries where the cost of living is about half that of many American cities. As John Howells, a noted travel writer puts it, "You can retire in semiluxury on what would amount to a semistarvation budget in the United States."

Between 150,000 and 200,000 Americans have chosen to spend their retirement in Mexico. About 25,000 retirees have moved to Costa Rica, with its high quality, yet inexpensive health care, balmy temperatures, and breathtaking beaches and rain forests. Howells, author of more than a dozen travel and retirement books, including *Choose Mexico* (Gate-way Books, 1997) and *Choose Costa Rica* (Gateway Books, 1996), has made Costa Rica his second home, living in a house he built in an enclave of about 300 other foreign retirees and expatriates.

Despite the exotic atmosphere, Howells warns that the lifestyle is not for everyone. "If you expect everything to be as it is back home, you are at a great disadvantage," he says. For one thing, the pace is so slow that going to the bank can take all morning; and plumbers and other service people do not feel obliged to honor appointments. Furthermore, Mexico and Costa Rica have experienced their share of political unrest: Laws, fees, currency value, and property rights change—and then change back just as quickly. Before you pack your bags and head south, Howells suggests considering some of the following factors:

■ **COST OF LIVING.** A retired couple can support a very comfortable lifestyle in Mexico with an income of $1,000 a month, says Howells. That amount would cover basics, such as a furnished rental apartment, food, utilities, entertainment, health care, and housekeeping. In areas off the beaten track, you can cover your basics for about $600 a month. In Costa Rica basics run between $800 and $1,000 dollars per month; for a more luxurious lifestyle count on spending about $1,200.

■ **HOUSING.** Your expenditures are contingent on your choice of neighborhoods. In Lake Chapala, a community outside Guadalajara,

Mexico, which has a strong American presence, a large two-bedroom furnished apartment rents for $400 to $600 dollars. A similar two-bedroom condo in a more exclusive neighborhood with a pool runs between $600 and $800. In Mexico City, that same apartment costs $1,000 to $3,000. Most Americans find that living quarters in the $400 to $600 range are spacious, comfortable, secure, and perfectly adequate. However, those who prefer to be closer to the culture and amenities of a lively commercial area—or choose an elaborate beach villa, can expect to shell out about $5,000 a month.

Even if you are are fairly sure you want to retire abroad, consider renting before buying or building a home. Doing so gives you time to decide if the lifestyle suits you and to choose the best location and housing. An important factor to consider about buying real estate in Mexico or Costa Rica is that it is difficult and expensive to get financing from a foreign bank. Interest rates fluctuate widely, and may range from 20 to 90 percent. Most Americans opt instead to sell their state-side home and use the proceeds to purchase foreign property outright. Because real estate laws in both countries are tricky, any venture should be overseen by a competent, English-speaking attorney.

■ **LEISURE ACTIVITIES.** According to Howells, foreigners living overseas form stronger social bonds than they would at home. In his community outside San Jose in Costa Rica, he says, "not two days go by without neighbors dropping in or sending an invitation to a cocktail party or trying to recruit you for their latest charity project."

In Mexico, one of the largest social organizations, the American Society of Mexico (☎011–52–5–202–4600) hosts events and serves as a referral service to other groups in Mexico. Resort towns like Acapulco and Puerto Vallarta offer weekend getaways, as well as every imaginable water sport.

■ **MAKING YOURSELF UNDERSTOOD.** If you settle in or near an American stronghold, you won't need to master Spanish to get by. But retirement advisers suggest you learn at least the

SENIOR SIGNPOSTS

It's never too soon to start planning retirement, nor is it ever too late. Here are the financial and legal mileposts you'll encounter as you look down the road and at what age you should expect them:

■ **AGE 55:** Minimum age for many senior communities. If you retire or lose your job, you can withdraw from your Keogh, 401(k), and profit sharing without tax penalty or having to annuitize. You can sell your house tax-free on a capital gain of up to $125,000.

■ **AGE 59 AND A HALF:** You can withdraw a lump sum from certain pension plans—IRA, Keogh, 401(k), without a tax penalty.

■ **AGE 60:** You qualify for senior discounts at stores, hotels, movies, etc.

■ **AGE 62:** You qualify for Social Security, but you'll get more if you wait until age 65.

■ **AGE 65:** If you're getting Social Security benefits, you are automatically enrolled in Medicare. If you're not on Social Security, you must apply for Medicare coverage.

■ **AGE 70:** Social Security benefits rise, if you're just starting; personal income—regardless of how much—doesn't reduce Social Security benefits.

■ **AGE 70 AND A HALF:** Start withdrawing from private plans, like Keogh and IRA, by April 1 or face tax penalties.

basics. "Even though Spanish isn't necessary, it's desirable," Howells says. "Your experience will be much more rewarding and the language will open doors for you socially and from a business standpoint." You can brush up on your Spanish at any number of inexpensive language schools prevalent in both Mexico and Costa Rica. For instance, the Mesoamerica Language Institute in San Jose, Costa Rica, offers a four-week program, combining instruction, conversation, field trips, and cultural events for less than $400 (☎011–506– 234–7682)

■ **HEALTH CARE.** Both Mexico and Costa Rica offer good health care, at costs below those in the United States. Generally, Medicare and private insurance don't cover medical care abroad, although there is some discussion about changing this policy. In the meantime, some retirees purchase out-of-country riders to their additional policies or special travelers' insurance. Many opt to buy local policies. Insurance from the American Society of Mexico, or the Mexican social security system, costs less than $250 a year, and generally covers medical, dental, eye care, prescription drugs, and hospitalization. Health insurance through the Costa Rican government costs about $150 per month, and covers doctors'

visits, medicine, and hospitalization.

In Mexico, public hospitals and health centers are inexpensive, although the quality of care can be erratic. Most foreigners prefer private clinics, where you can expect to find English-speaking doctors and up-to-date treatment and equipment. The top draw for many retirees who choose Costa Rica is the health care system, which is top-notch and inexpensive. A visit to a private doctor costs between $25 and $50. Howells claims that no hospital room in Costa Rica costs more than $80 dollars. "And that is for the top-of-the line," he says. "You get a private bath, beds for relatives to sleep over, and all the luxuries of a fine hotel."

■ **THE CITIZENSHIP QUESTION.** In Mexico, most retirees enter the country on a tourist visa that's valid for six months and renewable by leaving the country. Many other types of resident permits are available that afford additional privileges, including allowing you to bring in appliances, get a job, even start a business. In Costa Rica, most retirees also enter as tourists with a visa valid for 90 days. Some retirees ignore the expiration date, choosing instead to pay a modest penalty and tax when they leave the country. Like Mexico, Costa Rica offers many options for residency.

EXPERT SOURCES

FINDING YOUR OWN PLACE IN THE SUN

The following organizations can help you investigate overseas retirement.

THE AMERICAN SOCIETY OF MEXICO
Mexico City, Mexico
■ Cultural, social organization; referral service for other Mexican groups.
☎ 011–525–202–4600

MESOAMERICA LANGUAGE INSTITUTE
San Jose, Costa Rica
■ Language programs,

cultural events, field trips.
☎ 011–506–234–7682

INTERCONTINENTAL MEDICAL
■ For a list of reputable doctors and hospitals abroad.
☎ 800–426–8828

COSTA RICA TOURISM DEPT.
■ Residency and tourist information.

☎ 800–343–6332

MEXICAN NATIONAL TOURIST OFFICE
■ Ask for retirement and residency information.
☎ 212–755–7261

EMBASSY OF MEXICO
■ Ask for retirement and residency information.
☎ 202–728–1600

EXPERT Q & A

WHERE THE LIVING IS EASY

Baby boomers are forsaking Florida and finding new territory

Each year about 2 million folks take their gold watches and head for the easy life. Not all join the exodus to the Sun Belt, though. In fact, the vast majority of retirees remain in their own hometowns. A tiny number—1 of every 70—make less-than-dramatic moves within their own state. Only about 5 percent actually pack up and move out of state, say retirement experts.

While that percentage sounds low, the ranks of retirement migrants add up to nearly half a million, a figure that's expected to rise significantly as baby boomers start hitting retirement age. By the year 2000, the number of Americans over 65 is expected to exceed 29 million.

Retirement experts say we'll see plenty of changes in retirement patterns in years to come. Some trends are already emerging. For one, more new retirees continue to work to some degree: 25 percent now hold seasonal or part-time jobs. For another, many relocating retirees are looking beyond Florida to more unusual locales. Increasing numbers are picking college towns, for example.

What factors should a new retiree consider before choosing a place to live out the golden years? We posed that question and others to David Savageau, author of *Retirement Places Rated* (Macmillan, 1995).

■ **Which states are retirees choosing?**

The Sun Belt states—Florida, Arizona, Texas, New Mexico, Nevada—have always attracted retirees and continue to do so. But the new trend is to look outside the Sun Belt. Many are turning to Washington state, Oregon, Colorado, Montana, and, in New England, Ver-

mont and Maine. Though still minor players compared to Florida, the appeal of these states will rise as more baby boomers retire.

■ **Why are some states more appealing than others?**

States with no taxes on personal income—Florida, Nevada, Texas, and Washington state—have historically lured retirees. South Dakota, Wyoming, and Alaska also have no taxes on personal income, although most people don't think of them as good places to retire.

Many states allow you to avoid taxes on retirement income. Mississippi, for example, has no tax on social security or pension benefits. Georgia has generous exemptions on retirement income, as does Colorado.

■ **Will baby boomers differ in their retirement patterns?**

Yes, they won't be choosing idle retirement, that is, you won't find them lying on beaches and playing bridge. They are more adventurous and will look at nontraditional places like the Northwest, Colorado, the Carolinas, and New England states. They'll be willing to discover new places to live—college towns, mountain resorts, small towns.

In compiling my book, I've starting seeing boomers who are retiring. Many of them are former federal, state, or municipal employees taking early retirement. They're setting up bed-and-breakfast inns and seeking out places like Durango and Grand Junction, Colo., and Sandpoint, Idaho.

■ **What should you look for in a retirement place?**

Most important is the cost of living. Your retirement location should cut your cost of living by at least 20 to 33 percent, money that you'll need later in life. Primary targets for cuts should be taxes and housing costs.

Look at the local quality of life: access to health care, the climate, and personal safety. I would advise looking for nontraditional places that have four seasons—not spots that are uniformly paradise. Ideally, the place should be situated in the midst of protected land, such as a national park, that will let you get outdoors and also provides a draw for

THE VERY BEST PLACES TO RETIRE

In his book Retirement Places Rated, *David Savageau graded 183 potential retirement spots across the country. He took into account seven factors: housing, climate, personal safety, availability of services and leisure activities, and the availability of part-time work. No spot rated a perfect 100. Here are Savageau's picks for the top 20 retirement places, the area's score, and its most attractive features.*

PLACE	SCORE	SELLING POINTS
1. Las Vegas, Nev.	84.47	Potential for part-time work
2. St. Petersburg–Clearwater, Fla.	83.88	Leisure activities and affordable housing
3. Bellingham, Wash.	83.25	Leisure activities
4. Fort Collins–Loveland, Colo.	83.09	Leisure activities and personal safety
5. Medford-Ashland, Ore.	82.37	Low cost of living
6. Tucson, Ariz.	82.26	Availability of services
7. Coeur d'Alene, Idaho	82.12	Leisure activities and low cost of living
8. Traverse City, Mo.	81.77	Affordable housing and personal safety
9. Phoenix–Mesa–Scottsdale, Ariz.	81.66	Potential for part-time work
10. Melbourne, Fla.	81.38	Affordable housing and leisure activities
11. Savannah, Ga.	80.95	Affordable housing and availability of services
12. Daytona Beach, Fla.	80.73	Low cost of living
13. Fort Myers–Cape Coral, Fla.	80.54	Potential for part-time work and leisure activities
14. Fayetteville, Ark.	80.18	Affordable housing and low cost of living
15. Gainesville, Fla.	80.08	Services and affordable housing
16. San Diego, Calif.	79.96	Potential for part-time work and services
17. San Antonio, Texas	79.78	Affordable housing and services
18. Camden, Me.	79.33	Personal safety, services and leisure activities
19. Austin, Texas	79.26	Services and affordable housing
20. Port Angeles–Sequim, Wash.	79.09	Personal safety and services

tourism. Twenty years later when it comes time to dispose of the home, the place will be well-positioned for a sale.

Another bit of advice: Stay within a major media market. That's important not only for entertainment and information, but also because the trend is away from center cities to outlying areas.

■ Why the trend toward retiring in college towns?

They have rich, year-round calendars—academic, athletic, arts, and culture. For their scale, college towns provide a higher level of human services, such as public transportation, health care, education, and voluntary organizations than other towns.

College towns are good rental markets, with professors and students coming and going. If you're retiring and you don't know if you should buy, I advise renting until you're sure. You can become a landlord and rent out to graduate students, for example, or become a tenant. By renting you avoid most of the cost of living differences involved in buying or living in an overpriced house.

Some good college towns are Bloomington, Ind., Princeton, N.J., Boulder, Colo., and Charlottesville, Va. Some aren't great. College Park, Md., for example, is within the commuting range of big city problems, making it a less desirable place to retire.

ELDER COMMUNITIES
▼

SURE BEATS A NURSING HOME

These days, you have a plethora of choices. Here's how to sort them out

The graying of America is in full swing: the over-85 group grew 275 percent between 1960 and 1994, according to the Census Bureau's latest data. Combined with longer life spans, Americans can expect to spend a fourth of their lives retired.

Not long ago, nursing homes were about the only option. Today, elders can pick from a variety of retirement communities. There are nearly 700 such communities in the country, a figure that's expected to double in the next decade. Finding the right place requires a lot of legwork. And most have waiting lists ranging from 6 months to 10 years.

Before starting the search, advises Robert Greenwood of the American Association of Homes and Services for the Aging, ask yourself just what services you'll need. Do you need help with personal care? Do you need special meals? Will you need transportation? Do you intend this to be your last move?

We've tapped the experts and scoured the resources on retirement communities. Here's the lowdown, along with some pros and cons of each option.

■ **CONGREGATE HOUSING OR INDEPENDENT LIVING.**
These communities are the ticket for active seniors who want to live independently but don't want to do chores like mowing the lawn and shoveling drives. Residents live in apartments, condos or single-family homes. The community provides the groundskeepers, social activities, and recreational facilities, which often include a golf course, swimming pools, and health clubs. The communities also offer security. Housing generally sells at market rates for comparable properties in the area. The commu-

nities charge monthly fees, which vary widely and which can be hefty.

For those still able to care for themselves, these communities are a good choice. But residents must provide their own health care, so a move to an independent-living setting probably won't be the last move the elder makes.

■ **ASSISTED LIVING.** This type of housing is for seniors who need help with personal care, such as dressing and grooming, but don't require 24-hour attention. Services vary widely from place to place. Some won't accept seniors who need wheelchairs, for example, or who have continence problems. Some offer housekeeping, others don't.

To determine if a community is right for you, inspect the place. Residents don't own their own rooms or units. Ask which room you would be given. Would you get the same room after a hospital stay? Can you come and go at will? Is transportation available? When are health care providers on duty?

Assisted-living communities cost a bundle. Monthly fees can run from $1,000 to more

---

FACT FILE:

EVE'S GARDENS

■ *One-time nursing home director, William Thomas, found that residents exposed to children, animals, and plants required fewer medications and were generally less depressed. Now many nursing homes are following Thomas's pioneering philosophy. One such concept, the Eden Alternative, is used in more than 100 nursing facilities nationwide. Some sites share space with day care centers and summer camps. At some homes, dogs, cats, chickens—even llamas—are in residence. The result: drug costs are decreasing.*

SOURCE: For more information on homes using these methods, call the National Citizens' Coalition for Nursing Home Reform, ☎202–332–2275.

than $3,000. There may also be entry deposits and other charges. Medicare and Medicaid usually won't help foot the bills.

When a resident's health declines, many places allow nurses to come in and help with the care. Fees for the services are tacked onto monthly charges.

■ **NURSING HOMES.** Nursing homes, which provide 24-hour care, have been tarnished with a bad reputation. Many deserve it, according to *Consumer Reports*, which conducted a year-long investigation and concluded that "many facilities range from inadequate to scandalous and the good ones are hard to find."

To find a good one, visit as many facilities as possible. By law, nursing homes must make government inspection reports available to the public. Look for any deficiencies and violations of health and safety laws.

The best places to get the lowdown on specific nursing homes, according to *Consumer Reports*, are the offices of the state ombudsmen, who serve as advocates for nursing home residents. (Call your state office on aging for the number of your ombudsman.)

Nursing homes cost about $40,000 to $70,000 a year. Who pays? Residents, long-term health care insurance, and Medicaid. To qualify for Medicaid, however, a senior must impoverish himself to about $3,000 and enough to cover his burial. Before signing a nursing home contract, ask if the place will guarantee a Medicaid bed as soon as the patient is eligible and if they'll guarantee a return bed after a hospital stay. Find out if costs for things like laundry and TV are covered by the daily rate and if they are covered by Medicaid.

■ **LIFE-CARE COMMUNITIES.** Also called continuing-care retirement communities, these are good places for seniors who don't want to move more than once. They offer a lifetime guarantee of room, board, and access to health care. Such communities include independent-living and assisted-living facilities, and nursing homes—on the same site or nearby.

You usually sign a contract that guarantees residence for life and pay a lump-sum entrance fee that can range from $40,000 to $400,000. There are also hefty monthly fees to cover utilities, property taxes, maintenance services, and such. Some communities are resident-owned: Members buy stock in proportion to the square footage of their apartments and put up money to buy the community's services and amenities. If the resident leaves, a portion or all of the fee is refunded.

HOW TO BAIL OUT EARLY

You don't have to wait until you're 65 to enjoy the good life.

Jim Rogers was a high-charged Wall St. investor when at 37, he dropped out to pursue his fantasy: retire early and motorbike around the world. Starting in 1990, Rogers lived out his adventure, logging 65,065 miles in 22 months. He recounts the tale in his book, *Investment Biker* (Random House, 1994). Not everyone who checks out early is as financially well-cushioned as Rogers was. But, even for him, early retirement held a few surprises, as he explains:

■ **FOCUS.** *"People who retire early, especially if they're young, need to have a focus. I knew I wanted adventure but because I didn't have a clear idea, I was exploding in all directions, wasting a lot of time."*

■ **YOU'LL NEED PLENTY OF MONEY.** *"Don't forget, Social Security won't kick in at 42 and it costs more to retire at 40 or 50 than after 65, when you may have less energy."*

■ **NO REGRETS.** *"I exult in what I've done. By retiring early, you get to do things you've only dreamed of and still be young enough to enjoy them."*

■ **JUST DO IT.** *"Someday it will be too late. Why would anyone want to say: 'I'm glad I kept working and got to be a senior vp, but I never got to visit the Nile.' Everybody has dreams. Never living those dreams is a terrible tragedy."*

NEST EGGS

HOW MUCH DO YOU NEED TO RETIRE?

More than you think. And, the onus is on you to find the funds

A good rule of thumb is that you'll need at least 70 percent of your annual preretirement income to maintain your standard of living during retirement. That may sound high, but isn't in reality. True, those who retire at 65 can expect to spend less on housing, food, and transportation. But beyond that age, health care costs go way up. As a result, reports a study by Georgia State University's Center for Risk Management and Insurance Research, retirees will need 70 to 85 percent of what they earned before retiring.

Where does the average retiree's income come from? For those pulling in more than $20,000 a year in retirement income, the largest chunk, 39 percent, comes from personal savings and investments. Employer pensions contribute 15 percent and continued employment by one or both spouses provides 26 percent. Only 20 percent comes from Social Security benefits, according to the Treasury Department. But both Social Security and traditional pension plans are undergoing changes. Increasingly, the onus is on workers to fund their own retirement.

Two-thirds of Americans have never tried to figure out how much money they'll need when they retire. To get an idea of whether you'll have enough money for a comfortable retirement, first calculate the amount equal to at least 70 percent of your income. Then figure out if your retirement nest egg—including savings, 401(k)s, other pension plans, and Social Security benefits—will generate enough income. The table on the next page, developed by Westbrook Financial Advisers,

---

CYBER SOURCES

THE PLANNING STARTS HERE

Seniors are taking to the Internet in droves—some 20 percent of households headed by folks age 60 or older own a PC, according to Computer Intelligence in La Jolla, Calif. Cyberspace is chockablock with sites to plan retirement, calculate finances, and enjoy the company of other retirees. Some must-stops:

AARP WEBPLACE
http://www.aarp.org

■ Make this your first stop for orientation on retirement-planning options. Run by the American Association of Retired Persons, this site offers information on financing your retirement and links to other home pages, such as the Alzheimer's Association, that can provide additional help.

SENIORNET
http://www.seniornet.org

■ Visit this home page, or find the SeniorNet sites on America Online and the Microsoft Network, to meet older adults for e-mail exchanges and chat sessions on topics like health, leisure, travel, etc.

SENIORS-SITE
http://www.seniors-site.com

■ Get information on grandparenting, death

and dying, education, financing, housing, medicine, nutrition, travel, the Internet, and lots more.

TORRID TECHNOLOGIE'S RETIREMENT PLANNER
http://www.awa.com/softlock/tturner/401k

■ A good financial source. A retirement-planning worksheet is provided. Just plug in your finances and it will calculate how much you need to retire.

Inc., a New Jersey retirement planning firm, will help you determine if you're putting enough aside. Since people are living longer these days; plan as if you and your spouse will live to 92, so you don't outlive your savings.

If you find you're not saving enough, how you face up to that shortfall depends on your age and how you are allocating your assets. No one type of investment always comes out on top, so diversifying makes sense. The level of risk you're willing to take is also important.

T. Rowe Price, the mutual fund family, has devised three possible retirement-investment strategies. The risk-averse, or those near retirement, should consider putting 40 percent of their assets into growth-oriented investments such as stocks or stock funds, 40 percent in bonds, and 20 percent in ultra-safe vehicles like Treasury bills, money market funds, and CDs.

If you are some years before retirement and can tolerate a moderate degree of risk, or if you are near retirement and want to assume risk because you have other assets or sources of income, you should emphasize growth stocks, in a mix that includes 60 percent stocks, 30 percent bonds, and 10 percent Treasury bills or money market funds.

If you have a long way to go before you retire and can stomach greater risk for potentially greater returns, consider a portfolio of 80 percent stocks and 20 percent bonds. Over the period 1950–1994, this strategy would have shown the greatest rewards, according to T. Rowe Price. An investor would have seen inflation-adjusted returns of 6.9 percent, compared to 4.4 percent from the risk-averse mix and 5.7 percent for the moderate-risk mix. But, of course, it was also the most volatile— swinging from gains of 42.6 percent in the best year to a 20 percent loss in its worst year.

Inflation can flatten your savings. To keep your money growing at an inflation-beating rate, be sure you are getting at least 2 to 4 percent returns after inflation. Historically, stocks that return an average 10 percent are the best way to outpace inflation.

Sixty-six percent of Americans nearing retirement age regret not saving sooner. Saving for retirement isn't easy, especially if you're already 40-something. According to Merrill Lynch, the investment firm, the average baby boomer household saves at only one-third the rate needed to ensure a cozy retirement. The moral of this story: It's never too soon to start planning your retirement.

■ ARE YOU SAVING ENOUGH?

This table, developed by Westbrook Financial Advisers, will tell you if you have enough put aside to live well during your golden years. Find your approximate savings goal, then look at the number below the age when you want to call it quits. That's the amount you would receive in current dollars for the rest of your life, including Social Security benefits, assuming a 3 percent annual inflation rate, a life expectancy of 92, and that the money is invested at 6.5 percent.

SAVINGS	AGE 50	AGE 55	AGE 62	AGE 65
$50,000	$8,875	$10,701	$14,428	$17,332
$100,000	$11,195	$13,168	$17,192	$20,276
$200,000	$15,836	$18,100	$22,721	$26,165
$300,000	$20,476	$23,033	$28,250	$32,054
$400,000	$25,116	$27,965	$33,779	$37,943
$500,000	$29,757	$32,898	$39,308	$43,832
$600,000	$34,397	$37,830	$44,837	$49,721
$700,000	$39,037	$42,763	$50,366	$55,610
$800,000	$43,678	$47,696	$55,895	$61,499
$900,000	$48,318	$52,628	$61,424	$67,388
$1,000,000	$52,958	$57,561	$66,953	$73,277

SOURCE: Westbrook Financial Advisers, Ridgewood, N.J., and New Canaan, Conn.

SOCIAL SECURITY
▼

WHAT TO EXPECT FROM UNCLE SAM

It's not a golden handshake, but, at least, it's something

A retiree would have a tough time surviving on Social Security benefits alone. The average Social Security benefit paid to a 65-year-old retiree in 1996 was a meager $13,060. You can start taking Social Security benefits at age 62 but you'll suffer a permanent 20 percent cut in benefits. If you wait until 65 or beyond, you could get up to several thousand dollars more a year.

Keep in mind that legal changes have extended the age at which people will start getting Social Security payments in the future. The full retirement age will be increased in gradual steps. For example, benefits start at age 65 and 2 months for those born in 1938, at 65 and 4 months for those born in 1939, 65 and a half for those born in 1940, 65 and 8 months for those born in 1941, and 65 and 10 months for those born in 1942. Those born between 1943 and 1954 will have to wait until they reach 66. The steps increase until those born in 1960 reach full retirement age at age 67.

Working beyond your full retirement age can help you get higher Social Security payments because higher lifetime earnings mean higher benefits. But working while you're getting Social Security could lower your benefits. If you are 62 to 64 and earn more than $8,040, you could reduce your payments by $1 for every $2 you earn over the limit. If you are 65 to 69 and earn more than $11,160, your Social Security benefits are cut by $1 for every $3 you earn over your limit. Once you've hit 70, your benefits can't be cut, though, no matter how much you earn.

The table on this page estimates your annual benefits if you retire at 65. But benefits depend on your earnings history and that of your spouse, so you may want to contact the Social Security Administration, ☎800–772–1213, for a more accurate estimate.

With Congress tampering with Social Security, the future of benefits is unclear. Under current law, if you receive income in addition to Social Security benefits, and your adjusted income is more than $34,000 ($44,000 for couples), up to 85 percent of your benefits could be included in your taxable income. Congress has been tinkering with the amount subject to tax and inevitably will do so again.

At greatest risk are future Social Security benefits for those with higher incomes. Congress will most likely pass legislation restricting or eliminating their benefits. Within the next decade, predicts Ted Benna, author of *Escaping the Coming Retirement Crisis* (Pinon Press, 1995), it's possible that a person whose annual retirement income falls in the $40,000 to $50,000 range will see shrinking benefits. And those in the higher income ranges—say, $80,000 or above—probably won't get any benefits.

On another front, Social Security taxes have been climbing for two decades—from 5.85 percent of wages in 1977 to 7.65 percent in 1990. During that time, the maximum tax payable jumped from $965 to $4,682. The so-called FICA taxes are expected to shoot up further, predicts Benna, carving out 20 percent of your wages within the next 15 years.

■ WHAT SOCIAL SECURITY OWES YOU

The estimated benefits shown below assume that you work steadily over the years and retire when you turn 65. They do not reflect automatic cost-of-living adjustments.

ANNUAL WORKING INCOME	ANNUAL BENEFITS	
	Worker only	Worker and spouse
$20,000	$9,420	$14,124
$30,000	$13,564	$18,840
$40,000	$13,812	$19,992
$50,000	$14,532	$21,792
$61,200 or more	$14,976	$22,464

SOURCE: Social Security Administration, 1997.

HOW TO NURTURE YOUR 401(K)

*The man with a plan tells you how
to maximize your savings*

More and more workers are pumping money into their retirement piggy banks through 401(k) plans. The plans get their awkward name from a 1978 tax code provision that created them and are available through employers. A 401(k) lets participants invest pretax earnings in a personal account where money grows tax-free until retirement. There's an extra bonanza: Some employers will match employees' contributions.

The amount a participant can contribute in any one year is limited by the IRS and the employer. The 1997 maximum set by the IRS is $9,500, subject to certain complex restrictions. Most employers are expanding the number of investment choices they offer, which typically include a combination of company stock, money market funds, and stock and bond mutual funds. Despite their appeal, experts say 25 percent of those eli-

gible for 401(k)s don't participate, and an overwhelming number contribute less than they are allowed by law.

For help on how to nurture your 401(k), we turned to benefits consultant Ted Benna, the father of 401(k)s. In 1980, Benna created the first 401(k) plan for his own consulting firm. Today, he runs the 401(k) Association, a Langhorne, Pa., advocacy firm. Benna predicts that assets in all 401(k)s will bulge to more than $1 trillion by the end of 1998.

■ What's the big appeal of 401(k)s?

Normally, experts cite benefits like tax savings, or a company's matching contribution, or the ability to borrow or withdraw money when you need it. But I say the most important benefit is that they help participants become successful savers. They force you to save every pay period. They reverse the normal spend-save cycle, that is, I spend and intend to save but never have anything to save. A 401(k) makes saving the first priority.

■ Are they superior to traditional pension plans?

One is not clearly superior. Traditional pension plans are wonderful if you manage to spend virtually all your career in one place and stay until retirement. But they are pretty rotten for employees who move from job to job, or who willingly or unwillingly retire in their mid-to-late 50s. That's because most of a pension plan's value builds from

---

■ SIZING UP THE BIG BOYS' PLANS

Not all 401(k) plans are created equal, even among the nation's largest companies. The maximum percentage of salary that an employee can contribute and the amount that an employer will match vary from company to company. So do the number and type of investments. Here's a scorecard comparing the plans of some of the largest companies.

Company	Max. employee pretax contribution	Employer match	INVESTMENT OPTIONS		
			Money market	Stocks	Bonds
AT&T (management)	16%	67%	1 fund	5 funds	2 funds
EXXON	14%	100%	0	2 funds	1 fund
GENERAL ELECTRIC	17%	50%	1 fund	1 fund	3 funds
GENERAL MOTORS (salaried employees)	15%	25%	1 fund	35 funds	4 funds
IBM	12%	50%	1 fund	4 funds	2 funds

SOURCE: Company reports.

55 to 65. The high cost of pension buildup is one reason that downsizing companies target older employees.

For employees who are mobile, 401(k)s are definitely more beneficial. The ideal would be to work for a company that gives you both and most big companies still do.

■ What would a smart 401(k) plan look like in terms of asset mix?

That depends on how old you are and your investment goals. An aggressive strategy for a working 40-year-old would be to put 100 percent into stocks for an annual return of about 10.3 percent. For a person near retirement age, an aggressive plan would call for a mix of 60 percent stocks and 40 percent bonds. A conservative mix for a 40-year-old would be: 20 percent in stocks, 60 percent in bonds, and 20 percent in other fixed-income instruments.

For higher, most-aggressive rates of return, active workers need to put money in more volatile investments, like growth stocks. Retirees can probably get good rates by sticking to a mixture of more stable blue chip stocks, high-quality bonds, and other fixed-income vehicles.

■ Is a buy-and-hold strategy a good one for 401(k)s?

Yes, I normally recommend that people planning their retirement establish a strategy in terms of their investment objectives and stick to it and not get blown in the wind by what the stock market does every day.

■ There have been reports of possible misuse of 401(k) plan contributions. Should participants in 401(k)s be worried about fraud?

Yes and no. There have been cases where small companies started a 401(k) and a few months later went out of business and there was no money in the plan. But there are 250,000 plans out there and the number of cases where this happens is very small.

Where there's more need for concern is in a company of fewer than 25 employees that may be in serious financial difficulty. But larger employers have never been cited for improperly funding their plans.

One-half of the workforce has no form of private retirement coverage. For small companies, 401(k)s can cost about $3,000 and be complex to administer. We've come up with a 401(k) starter plan for very small employers that only costs between $500 to $700 to administer. Interested employers can call ☎800–320–401K.

■ What happens when a 401(k) participant switches companies?

You can transfer your fund directly into another company-sponsored plan or into an individual retirement account (IRA). You can also get a cash payment to roll the money over into an IRA. But getting the cash requires tax-withholding, so it's more advantageous to do a direct rollover.

One option that people are not commonly familiar with is that if their benefit payment is more than $3,500, they are allowed to leave it in their company plan.

■ Is taking a loan from your 401(k) wise?

No, it should be a last resort. For most people it's tough to repay the loan and continue to contribute to the plan. If you have an employer who's matching your contribution, you're missing out because you may not be able to put in the maximum amount allowed and repay the loan at the same time.

■ Will a good 401(k) alone provide adequate retirement income?

It certainly will. But you have to start early—at least at age 30. Also, between your contributions and your employer's matching, you have to save at least 10 percent of your income. And you have to invest it aggressively. You can't afford to have it sit in money-market investments, for example.

■ What happens when participants retire? Do they just enjoy their 401(k) windfall?

People are living 20 to 25 years in retirement these days and they have to continue to be active in managing their retirement money. The old idea of converting it to fixed income was okay when people lived 10 years during retirement. Today you must reinvest more aggressively during your retirement.

NEST EGGS
▼

DON'T GIVE UP ON YOUR IRA

It may not be deductible but earnings compound tax-free

The thrill is long gone from Individual Retirement Accounts. They lost a lot of their appeal a decade ago when the law allowing tax-deductible contributions for most employed individuals was changed. But IRAs may still be a worthwhile tax saver for some workers, and in recent years Washington has been abuzz with proposals to resuscitate them as a wealth-building tool. Recent proposals have included allowing more people with higher incomes to deduct deposits, giving savers a choice of tax-free withdrawals instead of a deduction, and easing restrictions on withdrawals before age 59¹/₂. (More generous rules, though, might include curbs on how much people who fund an IRA could put into a 401(k) retirement plan at work.)

A break that took effect for 1997 can help single-income families. Until now, a couple

EXPERT TIP

Though withdrawals from an IRA are generally not allowed without a tax penalty until you reach age 59½, you can begin pulling money out sooner if the withdrawals are in a series of substantially equal annual payments linked to your life expectancy. There are several approaches and formulas are tricky, so you may want some professional guidance.

could deposit $2,250 a year (total) to IRAs if one spouse had a job. The cap is now $4,000, the same as for a couple in which both spouses work. As this book was going to press, other major IRA rules were unchanged. These rules bar employees who are eligible for a retirement plan at work from fully deducting deposits to an IRA unless their adjusted gross income is below $40,000 on a joint return or $25,000 on a single return. (A partial deduction is allowed when incomes are less than $10,000 above those amounts.) IRAs remain a potent tool for employees not covered by a plan at work. These workers can make fully deductible deposits regardless of their income. But there's a trap: If one spouse is in a retirement plan at work, a deduction could be barred for either spouse.

Even without a deduction, an IRA can yield a tax benefit: Investment earnings in the account can compound without a yearly tax bite. That translates into bigger returns from stocks, certificates of deposit, or other assets into which an IRA's balance is put. But the benefits of tax-deferred compounding become significant only after many years of reinvestment.

Taking money out of an IRA can be tricky. Withdrawals are fully taxed if you got deductions for your deposits and partly taxed if you didn't. Currently, moreover, withdrawals before age 59¹/₂ are generally subject to a penalty of 10 percent off the top, plus regular tax. And 'after age 70¹/₂, you must begin taking out money at a pace designed to deplete the account over your life expectancy.

These rules do not apply when you remove money to switch investments—from an IRA at one mutual fund to another fund, for example. You can make an unlimited number of direct transfers when the firm holding your IRA sends the withdrawal directly to a new account. But if you make a rollover yourself, you can do that only once every 12 months for each IRA you have (you can have as many as you wish). The funds being rolled over can remain in your hands for no more than 60 days or they'll be taxed and subject to the 10 percent withdrawal penalty.

SELF-EMPLOYED
▼

WHERE TO STASH YOUR CASH

*If you want to retire in style,
consider one of these savings plans*

The self-employed are different from the run-of-the mill working stiff: They can salt away a sizable portion of their income each year and shelter it from taxation. A tax deduction for deposits to a retirement plan provides an immediate reward, while investment earnings in the account compound without a tax bite. The money isn't taxed until withdrawn.

In the easiest maneuver, under the current law, you can divert up to 13.0435 percent of your self-employment income to an IRA-like simplied employee pension (SEP) plan, up to a maximum annual contribution of $24,000. The paperwork is minimal and mutual funds and others offer ready-made plans.

More complex are Keogh retirement plans. They can shelter more income than a SEP and withdrawals may qualify for more favorable tax treatment. But, as with SEPs, withdrawals before age 59 1/2 are generally subject to a 10 percent early withdrawal penalty.

The most popular type of Keogh is a so-called profit-sharing plan. It's flexible since you can vary the share of income that you save each year. As with a SEP, a maximum of 13.0435 percent of self-employment income— up to $24,000 a year—can be set aside. (Self-employment income in these cases is what is left after subtracting business expenses and the deduction you get for half of your self-employment Social Security tax.)

An antidote for people who feel constrained by the $24,000 limit is to fund a money purchase Keogh plan. You'll be locked into saving a fixed percentage of income, but that can be up to 20 percent—to a maximum annual contribution of $30,000. Want greater flexibility on making deposits? Many advisers suggest that you can open both a profit sharing and a money purchase plan. You get a combined contribution limit of 20 percent and a top deposit of $30,000, yet can set the fixed money purchase deposit low enough to be manageable.

Don't be misled by rules that say you can put 15 percent of your income in a SEP or profit-sharing Keogh, or up to 25 percent into a money purchase Keogh or a paired profit-sharing and money purchase plan. Those percentages apply to self-employment income after you have subtracted the deposit itself. That's tricky math. It's easier to use the equivalent limits of 13.0435 and 20 percent of income before subtracting the deposit.

The most aggressive savings tactic is to open what's known as a defined benefit Keogh plan. Someone who is, say, 10 or 15 years from retirement can shelter a very large portion of income since these plans generally allow whatever is needed to be set aside to fund a predetermined retirement benefit. These plans, however, are the most complex of all and you'll need professional help setting one up.

People who hire employees may face an extra burden. They may have to provide retirement benefits for workers if they fund a SEP or Keogh for themselves. But look on the bright side; you'll not only be funding your own retirement but helping others look forward to life on Easy Street, as well.

EXPERT TIP

The deadline to open a new Keogh plan for 1997 is generally December 31, but deposits for 1997 can be made until the filing deadline in 1998 for your '97 return, including any extension you get. For a SEP, you have until the filing deadline for your 1997 tax return, including any extension, to both set one up and make a contribution.

THE RICH DIE RICHER

And so can you. A noted trust and estates lawyer tells you how

The very rich are different from you and me, as F. Scott Fitzgerald once noted. One big difference is that even after they leave their worldly fortune, the rich manage to shield it from the tax man. What lessons can a person of average means learn from how the wealthy plan their estates? William D. Zabel, a senior partner with Schulte Roth & Zabel, a New York and Palm Beach law firm, has given legal advice to very rich clients for more than 30 years. "With some sophistication and planning," says Zabel, author of *The Rich*

FACT FILE:

PITY THE HARRIMAN HEIRS

■ *Before Ambassador to France, Pamela Harriman, died suddenly in 1997, she had already forked over some $10 million to the heirs of third husband W. Averell Harriman. They had accused her and her advisers of squandering $40 million of the more than $100 million she had inherited upon Averell's death. Nor did the Democratic doyen die smartly. According to* The Washington Post, *Harriman did not set up a trust to shelter the estate from taxes, so her heirs can expect a hefty bill from the IRS.*

Die Richer and You Can Too (William Morrow and Co., Inc. 1995), "everyone can make estate and gift taxes essentially voluntary rather than mandatory." Here are some pointers:

■ How do the rich die richer?

Most Americans pay little, if any, attention to estate planning. The rich, however, are accustomed to trying to preserve and protect their money and they focus heavily on estate plans.

■ How hefty are estate taxes and what are some tax-saving techniques?

Every American citizen has a one-time $600,000 exemption from federal, estate, and gift taxes ($1.2 million for a couple). A transfer of these amounts can be made during your lifetime as a gift or at death through a will or a trust. Beyond that exemption, estate taxes kick in, with rates between 37 and 55 percent, and an extra 5 percent surcharge for estates of $10 million to $21 million.

Some tax-saving techniques include setting up a charitable trust to defer or eliminate taxes, setting up a family foundation that will get the money that would have gone to taxes, and freezing the value of a closely held business. Another strategy is to make low-interest loans to children to avoid gift taxes.

■ How much of an estate that's left to a spouse can be given free of estate and gift taxes?

Under federal tax laws, no matter how rich you are, you can leave 100 percent of your estate to your spouse free of estate and gift taxes. Still, you can restrict what happens to your estate after your spouse dies—an important factor to consider if there are children from a former marriage. The most common device used is a so-called QTIP trust (qualified terminable interest property). Simply put, you would say: "I give all the income for life to my wife but at the death of my wife the property will pass to my children."

■ How can gifts to children and grandchildren escape gift taxes?

Each year, you can give $10,000 ($20,000 per couple) to as many recipients as you wish free of gift taxes. The best time to make these gifts is early in January of each year so death during the year won't preclude the gifts.

During your lifetime you can also pay college or medical costs tax-free for children, grandchildren, or others. But payment must be made directly to the school or the provider of the medical services.

■ What's a good way to restrict the use of money left to kids?

Setting up a trust is the traditional way. You can include conditions that require children not to smoke or drink, for example. You can indicate that if they don't complete their education, they won't get the money. One way to provide incentive for children to earn money is to set up a trust that will match income produced. You can't include conditions that are against public policy, such as requiring that a son divorce his wife.

■ What about giving to charity?

The most common tax technique is the charitable remainder trust, of which there are several varieties. Such a trust allows you to sell an asset without incurring a capital gains tax; increase your life income and your spouse's income; and get an immediate charitable income-tax deduction. At the death of both spouses, the income goes to the charity of their choice. This sort of trust lets you have your charitable cake and still eat a good part of it.

■ How useful are life insurance trusts as tax shelters?

A so-called irrevocable life insurance trust is the safest and most effective means of leaving substantial funds to children free of all death taxes. You can leave an unlimited amount of insurance proceeds to your spouse tax-free, but that doesn't avoid death taxes, it only defers them. The primary purpose of a life insurance trust is to avoid an estate tax in both spouses' estates and leave the insurance proceeds to younger generations tax-free. There's an added benefit: You can pass millions of dollars to grandchildren and escape estate taxes and the fairly new tax called the generation-skipping tax. In very high brackets, this

■ THE ESTATE TAX BITE

Your heirs only pay the top rate on the top end of your estate.*

If estate is above this base	Your tax is this...	Plus this % over base
$600,000	$0	37%
$750,000	$55,500	39%
$1,000,000	$153,000	41%
$1,250,000	$255,500	43%
$1,500,000	$363,000	45%
$2,000,000	$588,000	49%
$2,500,000	$833,000	53%
$3,000,000	$1,098,000	55%
$10,000,000	$4,948,000	60%
$21,040,000	$11,572,000	55%

* Table does not account for taxable gifts.
SOURCE: Internal Revenue Service.

tax can almost double the death taxes for assets left to grandchildren.

■ What's the difference between an executor, a trustee, and a guardian? How should they be chosen?

An executor carries out the terms of the will. He or she collects the assets, has them appraised, invests or sells them, pays the death taxes, if any, and distributes the assets according to the will. A trustee oversees property that's held in trust and administers it for the benefit of the trust's beneficiaries.

Choose them *very* carefully: If they turn out to be the wrong person for the job, they can destroy the value of a will or estate plan. Family members, friends, lawyers, accountants, or bank and trust company officials can be chosen as trustees and executors. Integrity and good judgment are the most important factors to look for.

Guardians are surrogate parents for children whose parents die unexpectedly. It's vital for parents, regardless of their assets, to appoint guardians for their children. Otherwise, a court will do it for them. Blood relatives are usually chosen, but the best guardians are those who share the same traditions and values as the parents, and, of course, who have a willingness to love and care for the minor children.

DO YOU NEED A WILL?

The answer is probably yes. Here's why and what it should include

More than half of American adults do not have wills, according to the American Association of Retired Persons. True, if your estate is under $600,000—and that's the case for most Americans—your heirs may be exempt from paying estate taxes, but that doesn't mean that you don't need a will. What are the potential consequences of not planning for the disposition of your estate? For some expert answers, we spoke with Boston attorney Alexander Bove, the author of *The Complete Book of Wills & Estates* (Henry Holt, 1989).

■ What happens if I don't have a will?

If you have no will, your estate will end up in probate court and many important decisions will be out of your hands. Normally, you name an executor, a trusted friend or family member who is responsible for determining taxes, assets, bills, and debts to be paid on your estate. Without a will, the court becomes the executor and your estate is divided under state laws.

■ What are the most important components of a will?

As a rule, wills are broken up into two parts. Bequests include specified property, such as amounts of money, real estate, and stocks that are left to a designated beneficiary. The residue is everything else, or everything not specifically defined, and will normally go to the primary beneficiary of the estate, usually a spouse, children, or both. Only property in your name at the time of your death can be passed on to your heirs.

■ What are living wills, health care proxies, and durable powers of attorney, and why are they important?

A living will is a declaration that indicates whether you would want to be kept alive by artificial means in the event that you are diagnosed with a terminal illness.

A health care proxy allows you to appoint someone to make medical decisions for you.

A durable power of attorney names someone to make financial transactions for you. If you don't have a durable power of attorney, and if your assets or property need to be transferred, your beneficiaries would have to go to probate court in order to appoint a conservator or guardian.

■ How often should I update my will?

Whenever there is a major change in the tax laws, or if there is a change in your family or your family's finances.

■ How can I provide for minor children?

If you have minor children, you should be sure to name a trusted relative or friend as the guardian who will be responsible for the "person and property" of the minors.

■ What is the difference between a will and a living trust?

A living trust is a legal document that you create while you are alive; you can transfer assets to the trust while you are alive, and the trust governs the assets. You may be your own trustee. Whatever is in the trust does not have to pass through probate. Whatever you do not put into the trust goes into a will.

A living trust—including a will, a durable power of attorney, and health care proxy—and a living will are the typical documents in a modern estate plan.

■ How much should I pay to have a will drawn?

That depends on the complexity of the estate. The process of drawing up a will can range between $50 and $5,000, depending on how complicated it is. Often the amount of property is not as important a factor as the family circumstances.

CHAPTER TWO

HEALTH

"Most people eat their way into having high cholesterol."
—Dr. James Cleeman, National Institutes of Health
Page 139

"When you're in love with a man's potential, you're not looking at him as a person—you see him as a project."
—Barbara De Angelis, psychologist
Page 164

"Basically, menopause is perfectly natural."
—Dr. Susan Love, author of *Dr. Susan Love's Hormone Book*
Page 169

■ **WHAT'S AHEAD: WEIGH** the costs and benefits of diet centers... **EXPECT** the hype over DHEA to continue despite incomplete research... **CREATE** your own beauty style with the right makeup... **LEARN** the potential risks of hormone replacement therapy before you make a decision... **CONDUCT** a home test for HIV... **PREVENT** birth problems before you conceive... **SCRUTINIZE** HMOs through the new report cards...

GETTING FIT

WEIGHT LOSS

▼

THE HIDDEN COSTS OF DIETING

Ways to trim your waistline without trimming your wallet

For many Americans dieting is a way of life. Despite their efforts, though, one-third of adults are overweight compared with one-fourth two decades ago. Most people are well aware of the health risks of being overweight; they also know that the only sure-fire formula for losing weight is a combination of exercise and a healthy diet. Still, at one time or another, most dieters turn to commercial weight loss centers, nutritionists, liquid diets, pills, and newfangled fitness contraptions.

A major problem with these attempted solutions, is that dieters often lose more than a few pounds—they also spend a small fortune for fleeting benefits. Americans shell out more than $33 billion a year on products and services to help them lose weight, according to the American Dietetic Association. Throwing money at the problem doesn't guarantee results. In fact, there's no clear connection between the cost of any given weight loss method and its effectiveness at achieving permanent weight loss. If that's the case, why not look for economical ways to trim your figure? We asked weight-loss specialists, doctors, nutritionists, and fitness experts for tips on losing weight without being financially squeezed. Here's their advice.

■ **FORGET QUICK FIXES.** Gimmicks don't work. Losing weight and keeping it off requires changing your lifestyle and your mindset—not an easy undertaking. Before throwing away money on programs that don't match your lifestyle, do some research, advises Dr. Larry Richardson, a Houston physician and president of the American Society of Bariatric Physicians. "Sometimes people spend a lot of money on something they heard about from friends or on a TV infomercial," he says. "They follow second- or third-hand advice wholeheartedly without investigating it first."

There are many inexpensive ways to gather information: sign up for free educational classes, nutritional counseling or introductory weight-loss programs given by a local hospital or HMO; buy a good nutrition or exercise book or borrow one from the library; and take advantage of the health and dieting home pages on the Internet. A good place to start is CyberDiet (*http://www. cyberdiet.com*), which offers information on how to figure your daily caloric requirements, recipes, etc.

■ **CUSTOMIZE YOUR DIET PLAN.** Many dieters pay top dollar for commercial weight loss plans and either don't complete the program or soon regain the weight they lost. The key to permanent weight loss is finding a program that fits your food preferences and lifestyle, says Anne Fletcher, a registered dietitian and diet book author "Even though something worked for a celebrity or your mother or brother, it may not work for you," she says.

The 250 dieters chronicled in Fletcher's book, *Eating Thin for Life: Food Secrets and Recipes From People Who Have Lost Weight & Kept It Off* (Chapters, 1996), lost an average of 63 pounds and kept it off for at least three years. While many failed at weight loss programs, they learned to piece together bits and pieces of programs that worked for them. "Instead of saying I blew it with Weight Watchers or Jenny Craig, go back and look at what worked in those programs," suggests Fletcher. If eating four grapefruits or bowls of cabbage soup a day didn't work, but packing your lunch every day did, then incorporate that lesson into your weight-reduction plan.

■ **GET TO WORK IN THE KITCHEN.** Many weight-loss programs involve using prepackaged foods, prepared by a diet center or purchased at the supermarket. Prepared foods can help in teaching how to control portions, but they cost two to three times as much as the raw ingredients required to make the meal from scratch. "Some of the foods labeled diet are automatically marked up, but if you buy regular products and eat less of them, you save money," advises Dr. Denise Bruner, a weight-loss specialist in Arlington, Va. "If you spend a few extra minutes in the kitchen putting a piece of chicken in the microwave and steaming vegetables, for example, you'd have a less expensive and more nutritious meal," she says.

■ **FIND COST-EFFECTIVE WORKOUTS.** Exercise is the other major component of weight loss. But high-priced spa memberships or fancy training equipment aren't needed to reap the benefits of exercise. "Nobody has to join anything or buy anything," says Millicent Betts, a certified fitness instructor and personal trainer in Chantilly, Va. "Instead, invest in a good pair of walking shoes. For results, it's the best and cheapest thing you can do." Other inexpensive and effective exercise tools include elastic bands, a mini-trampoline, and aerobic videotapes. More sophisticated home exercise equipment can be worth the cost—if it's not lying idle.

If you need the motivation of belonging to a health club, shop for one that gives you punch for your dollar. Staff credentials are important. Before joining a club, have a staff

---

■ **DOES YOUR WEIGHT FIT YOUR HEIGHT?**

The latest guidelines, which apply to both men and women regardless of age, prescribe acceptable ranges rather than specific weights because people of the same height may have different amounts of muscle and bone. The farther you are above the healthy weight range for your height, the higher are your risks of developing weight-related health problems.

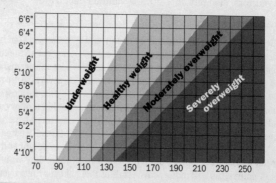

6'6"
6'4"
6'2"
6'
5'10"
5'8"
5'6"
5'4"
5'2"
5'
4'10"

70 90 110 130 150 170 190 210 230 250

Underweight   Healthy weight   Moderately overweight   Severely overweight

DIETER'S GUIDE

A DIET CENTER FOR EVERY TASTE

Americans spend more than $33 billion a year on diet foods, gadgets, and weight-loss services, according to the American Dietetic Association. If you need to lose lots of weight, consult a physician first. If you're looking to shed just a few pounds, a gentle nudging and a weekly weigh-in may be all you need. Before you spend a dime, though, be sure to conduct a thorough investigation and sign up for no more than you need.

DIET CENTERS
JENNY CRAIG INC
■ Comprehensive program with preplanned menus and prepackaged foods.
$ $99 for basic program, plus about $70 a week for prepackaged meals.
☎ 800–43–JENNY

NUTRI/SYSTEM
■ All-inclusive program emphasizes use of prescription weight-loss drugs; pre-packaged foods available.
$ $499 for one year, plus food and medications.
☎ 800–321–THIN

SUPPORT GROUPS
TOPS CLUB
■ Members stick to diets recommended by their doctors, then rely on weekly meetings for support. TOPS stands for Take Off Pounds Sensibly.
$ $20 annual fee, plus nominal weekly fees.
☎ 800–932–8677

WEIGHT WATCHERS
■ Calorie-controlled diet, weigh-ins, peer support. Optional foods available in supermarkets.
$ $20 to $30 to enroll, plus $12 a week for meetings. No fee for lifetime members.
☎ 800–651–6000

OVEREATERS ANONYMOUS
■ Adheres to 12-step model. Members follow their own diets and discuss trials and tribulations. Some 7,000 local chapters.
$ Voluntary contributions at each meeting.
☎ 505–891–2664

MEDICALLY-SUPERVISED PROGRAMS
MEDIFAST
■ Diet designed for rapid weight loss in those at least 30 percent over ideal body weight. Must use provided foods.
$ $65 to $85 per week, including meals; cost of physician visits varies.
☎ 800–638–7867

OPTIFAST
■ Designed for those who need to lose 50 pounds or more. A customized food program and counseling.
$ Varies greatly with individual program. Insurance reimbursement may be available.
☎ 800–662–2540

member perform a fitness evaluation and draw up an exercise plan for you. Consistent use of the club will help justify the cost, of course. Engaging a personal trainer can be expensive but can also make workouts more effective. To defray the cost, Betts advises meeting with the trainer less frequently or training with a partner.

■ **GET MOTIVATED.** Losing weight on your own is, of course, the best money-saver. Half of the dieters in Fletcher's book lost weight by using no-cost strategies such as accepting weight loss as a permanent lifestyle change and devising ways to nip small weight gains in the bud.

But the most important lesson they learned is that money can't buy motivation and commitment—the real secret to weight loss. Explains Fletcher, "Successful dieters want to lose weight and stay at the new weight more than they want to engage in behavior that keeps them overweight."

EXPERT LIST

LET THE GAMES BEGIN

Find a hill and climb it, pick a path and jog it. It doesn't take a big budget to get in shape, as the following analysis from Dr. David R. Stutz, *author of* 40+ Guide to Fitness *(Consumer Reports Books, 1994), illustrates.*

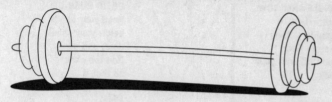

ACTIVITY	IMPROVES HEART AND LUNG FITNESS[1,2]	BURNS CALORIES[1,2]	TONES AND BUILDS MUSCLES[2]	LOWERS STRESS[1]
AEROBIC DANCE	Very good	Very good	Poor	Very good
ALPINE SKIING	Fair	Fair	Good	Good
BASEBALL	Fair	Fair	Fair	Good
BASKETBALL	Very good	Very good	Fair	Good
BICYCLING	**Excellent**	**Excellent**	Good	**Excellent**
BOWLING	Poor	Poor	Fair	Good
CROSS-COUNTRY SKIING	**Excellent**	**Excellent**	Fair	**Excellent**
FISHING (SITTING)	Poor	Poor	Fair	**Excellent**
FOOTBALL	Good	Good	Fair	Good
GARDENING	Poor	Fair	Fair	**Excellent**
GOLF	Poor	Poor	Poor	Good
HIKING AND CLIMBING	Very good	Very good	Fair	**Excellent**
HOCKEY	Very good	Very good	Fair	Good
HORSEBACK RIDING	Fair	Fair	Fair	**Excellent**
JOGGING AND RUNNING	**Excellent**	**Excellent**	Fair	**Excellent**
JUMPING ROPE	**Excellent**	**Excellent**	Fair	Very good
MARTIAL ARTS	Very good	Very good	Very good	Good
RACQUETBALL AND SQUASH	Very good	Very good	Fair	Good
ROWING AND CANOEING	**Excellent**	**Excellent**	Very good	**Excellent**
SAILING	Poor	Poor	Fair	**Excellent**
SKATING OR ROLLERBLADING	Good	Very good	Fair	Good
SOCCER	Very good	Very good	Fair	Good
STAIR CLIMBING	Good	Good	Very good	Very good
SWIMMING LAPS	**Excellent**	**Excellent**	Good	**Excellent**
TENNIS	Good	Good	Fair	Good
VOLLEYBALL	Good	Good	Fair	Good
WALKING (NORMAL)	Fair	Good	Poor	**Excellent**
WALKING (SPEED)	Very good	Very good	Fair	**Excellent**
WEIGHT TRAINING	Fair	Good	**Excellent**	Good
WOODWORKING	Poor	Poor	Fair	Very good

NOTES: **1.** Largely dependent upon duration of activity. **2.** Largely dependent upon intensity of effort.
SOURCE: Dr. David R. Stutz.

BUILDING STRENGTH AND ENDURANCE

The American College of Sports Medicine recommends these exercises to build strength. Be sure to exhale on exertion and to inhale when returning to start.

■ ARMS, SHOULDERS, AND CHEST

SINGLE-ARM ROW: Pull weight to shoulders, then ease to floor. Don't lift with your back.

CHAIR PUSH-UP: Keep your hands below your shoulders, and position the chair so that it doesn't slide.

■ ABDOMINALS

SHOULDER CURL-UP: Lift your back off the floor. But don't sit all the way up; it may strain your back. Use a pad if possible.

■ LOWER BODY

SEATED STRAIGHT-LEG LIFT: Raise your entire leg off the chair by keeping the knee locked. Good for the quadriceps, the muscle that extends the leg.

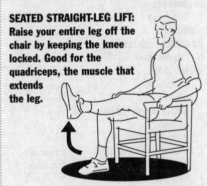

PRONE NECK LIFT: Keep hands up and lift neck. But avoid arching it backward.

SOURCE: *American College of Sports Medicine Fitness Book,* Human Kinetics, 1992.

■ LESS-EFFECTIVE TRADITIONAL EXERCISES

BICYCLES   **DONKEY KICKS**   **KNEE BENDS**   **JUMPING JACKS**

STAY FLEXIBLE IN WHAT YOU DO

Stretching is important before and after workouts. Limber up with this routine from the American College of Sports Medicine.

■ NECK

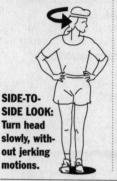

SIDE-TO-SIDE LOOK: Turn head slowly, without jerking motions.

■ SHOULDER, CHEST, AND BACK

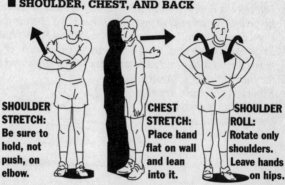

SHOULDER STRETCH: Be sure to hold, not push, on elbow.

CHEST STRETCH: Place hand flat on wall and lean into it.

SHOULDER ROLL: Rotate only shoulders. Leave hands on hips.

■ ABDOMINALS AND LOWER BACK

STANDING CAT STRETCH: Don't arch your back.

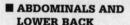

KNEE TO CHEST: One knee at a time, then both. Keep hands under thighs.

SEATED TOE TOUCH: Keep legs straight, toes pointed. Don't bounce.

■ LOWER BODY

WALL LEAN: Keep your back heel on the ground and feet turned inward.

QUADRICEPS STRETCH: Bring foot gently toward buttocks. Don't bounce.

■ LESS-EFFECTIVE TRADITIONAL EXERCISES

HURDLER STRETCH   **BACK BENDS**   **THE PLOW**   **STANDING TOE TOUCH**

A RACE FOR THE WHITE HOUSE

During the Kennedy administration, the man in the Oval Office exhorted his fellow Americans to test their fitness in a 50-mile walk. Now, the President's Council on Physical Fitness and Sports has issued a new challenge to children ages 6 to 17. Children who score at or above the following levels for their age and sex on all five of the suggested events qualify for the President's Physical Fitness Award and are eligible for both a presidential commendation and a badge.

AGE	Curl-ups (per minute)	Shuttle run (seconds)	V-sit reach (inches)	Sit and reach (centimeters)	1-mile run (minutes)	Pull-ups
BOYS						
6	33	12.1	3.5	31	10:15	2
7	36	11.5	3.5	30	9:22	4
8	40	11.1	3.0	31	8:48	5
9	41	10.9	3.0	31	8:31	5
10	45	10.3	4.0	30	7:57	6
11	47	10.0	4.0	31	7:32	6
12	50	9.8	4.0	31	7:11	7
13	53	9.5	3.5	33	6:50	7
14	56	9.1	4.5	36	6:26	10
15	57	9.0	5.0	37	6:20	11
16	56	8.7	6.0	38	6:08	11
17	55	8.7	7.0	41	6:00	13
GIRLS						
6	32	12.4	5.5	32	11:20	2
7	34	12.1	5.0	32	10:36	2
8	38	11.8	4.5	33	10:02	2
9	39	11.1	5.5	33	9:30	2
10	40	10.8	6.0	33	9:19	3
11	42	10.5	6.5	34	9:02	3
12	45	10.4	7.0	36	8:23	2
13	46	10.2	7.0	38	8:13	2
14	47	10.1	8.0	40	7:59	2
15	48	10.0	8.0	43	8:08	2
16	45	10.1	9.0	42	8:23	1
17	44	10.0	8.0	42	8:15	1

SOURCE: President's Council on Physical Fitness and Sports.

BODY SHAPE

WHY AN APPLE IS NOT A PEAR

Weight around the belly is riskier than around the hips

How your weight is distributed may be even more important than how much weight you have in the first place, at least when it comes to determining risks to your health. If you are carrying around too much weight around your waist, your health is at far greater risk than if you are carrying extra weight around your hips, buttocks, and thighs.

All of that excessive fat around the belly, has been found by researchers to be associated with an increased risk of breast and uterine cancer, heart disease, and diabetes, as well as a host of other ailments.

To assess whether your weight distribution puts you at higher risk, ask yourself whether your body more closely resembles the shape of an apple or the shape of a pear. "Apples" are often bigger at the waist than in the hips—traits found more often in men than in women. "Pears," on the other hand, carry their weight low. Their waists are smaller than their hips and they are usually women.

A more precise assessment can be obtained by measuring your hips and waist, and then dividing your waist measurement by your hip measurement. If the result is greater than 0.80 for women or 1.0 for men, it puts you squarely in the apple category. Another way to assess fat distribution is to measure your waistline: Men with a 40-inch or greater waistline and women with a 35-inch or greater waistline might benefit from directing some energy toward taking off some pounds in the right places.

Researchers at the University of Glasgow suggest an even easier way to gauge your health risks from carrying too much weight in the wrong places. Their recent study found significantly higher health risks among women whose waists measure more than 34.5 inches and for men whose waists exceed 40 inches. Their advice: To ward off health problems, keep your waist size to 31.5 inches if you are a woman, and to 37 inches if your chromosomes make you a "he."

EXERCISING TO YOUR HEART'S CONTENT

Checking your pulse rate is one of the best ways to gauge whether you're exercising hard enough to improve your heart and lungs. The American Heart Association advises that you push your heart beat during exercise to between 50 percent and 70 percent of your maximum heart rate (calculated by subtracting your age from 220). Anything lower than 50 percent does little for your heart's conditioning; anything higher than 75 percent can cause problems unless you're in superb shape. When you're just starting an exercise program, cardiologists recommend aiming for the lower part of the target heart zone and gradually stepping up your pace.

AGE	Target heart rate beats per minute	Maximum heart rate
20	100–150	200
25	98–146	195
30	95–142	190
35	93–138	185
40	90–135	180
45	88–131	175
50	85–127	170
55	83–123	165
60	80–120	160
65	78–116	155
70	75–113	150

IMPORTANT NOTE: A few high blood pressure medicines lower the maximum heart rate and thus the target zone rate. If you are taking high blood pressure medications, call your physician to find out if your exercise program needs to be adjusted.

WHAT IT TAKES TO BE A TROPHY BODY

Follow Miss Galaxy's advice to give your muscles tone and definition

Ever wonder how some amateur athletes can run a marathon even though they appear to be out of shape? How could they possibly be fit enough to run 26 miles, yet appear so flabby? Aerobic exercises improve cardiovascular fitness and endurance and can help you lose weight, but they don't necessarily tone or sculpt your muscles. Even if you're an avid jogger, swimmer, or cyclist, and can run, paddle, or pedal forever, your muscles still may not be as toned as you'd like them to be.

The only way to achieve muscle definition is to lift weights or do strength training, or anaerobic, exercises that use the body's weight as resistance, says Ursula Sarcev, winner of the 1994 Miss Galaxy fitness competition. Miss Galaxy's advice is borne out by the American College of Sports Medicine, which recommends that both aerobic and anaerobic exercise be included in any balanced physical fitness program. Women, in particular, may reap benefits from a program of weight training. According to a recent report in the *American Journal of Health Promotion*, strength training not only improves the muscle strength of women in their 40s but also boosts their body image and self-esteem far more than walking for exercise.

Designing a training regimen should take into account the physique with which you begin. A general rule of thumb: How much weight you lift depends on whether you want to build muscle mass or merely tone and shape your muscles. If you carry more weight and body fat than you are happy with in a certain area, you'll want to go with lighter weights and higher repetitions, say, 25 to 30, to help burn fat. "Don't use too much weight in areas you want to slim down because you'll

---

■ DUMBBELL FLIES:
Tones the pectoral chest muscles without making you look like a bodybuilder.

Lie on your back on a bench with a small dumbbell in each hand. Hold your arms out to the side with your arms bent and your wrists turned toward each other. Lift up toward the ceiling, then bring both arms back down to the side. If you raise the bench so it's on an incline, you'll work muscles higher in your chest. If you lower the bench so your head is below your torso, you'll work the lower chest muscles.

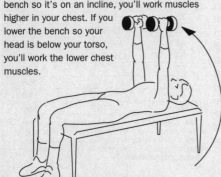

■ BICEP CURLS:
Tones and shapes the biceps; builds muscles if more weight is used.

Hold a dumbbell in each hand and stand with your arms at your side and your palms facing forward. Curl the dumbbell up toward your chest and turn your wrist out when you are at the end of the curl. Lower the weight slowly because you're resisting weight and strengthening your muscles as you go down, too. Do 15 to 20 repetitions, alternating arms or lifting both at the same time.

end up building up that area," advises Sarcev. If you're trying to put on weight in specific areas, go with heavier weights and do fewer reps, about 8 to 10.

A professional body builder, Sarcev says that the key to achieving maximum results is proper form. For starters, always contract your muscles from the moment you start an exercise until you're finished. "You're not doing anything if you just lift up and down," she explains. "It's not about how much weight you lift, but about how hard you squeeze." Also, you want to make sure that you extend your muscle entirely with each repetition. "The biggest mistake I see is when people don't have full range of motion, which is like working half the muscle," says Sarcev. "You'll make much more progress if you use less weight, but use the full range of motion."

Even if you don't have access to a gym, you can invest in inexpensive equipment, such as small free weights, that will help you slim down or build up specific muscle groups. Miss Galaxy recommends these exercises to tone you up and shape common trouble spots.

■ LEG RAISES:
The best way to tone the lower abdomen.

To begin, hang from a bar and lift your legs straight in front of you as high as possible, at least at a 90-degree angle. Eventually try to work up to 15 to 20 leg raises, but try not to swing. It's a difficult maneuver, so beginners should start by lifting their knees up while someone helps balance them.

■ LUNGES:
Trims and tones the quadriceps in the legs and gluteal muscles in the buttocks. Using dumbbells adds resistance and helps build muscle rather than slim you down.

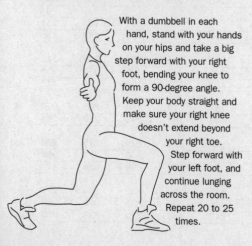

With a dumbbell in each hand, stand with your hands on your hips and take a big step forward with your right foot, bending your knee to form a 90-degree angle. Keep your body straight and make sure your right knee doesn't extend beyond your right toe. Step forward with your left foot, and continue lunging across the room. Repeat 20 to 25 times.

■ STEP-UPS:
A simple exercise, yet far more effective at trimming and toning the buttocks than the step machine.

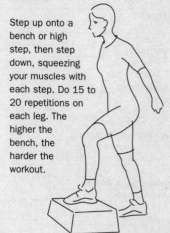

Step up onto a bench or high step, then step down, squeezing your muscles with each step. Do 15 to 20 repetitions on each leg. The higher the bench, the harder the workout.

WORKOUT BENEFITS AT A GLANCE

From puttering around to Olympic skiing, the estimated calories burned during 30 minutes of activity depends on body weight and intensity of effort.

ACTIVITY	WEIGHT						
	105	120	135	150	165	180	195
DAILY ACTIVITIES							
Work, sedentary office	36	41	46	51	56	61	66
Cooking	60	68	77	85	94	102	111
Cleaning (heavy)	107	123	138	153	169	184	199
AEROBICS							
Low-impact dance	119	136	153	170	188	205	222
High-impact dance	167	191	215	239	263	286	310
Water	95	109	122	136	150	163	177
ALPINE SKIING							
Moderate (recreational)	119	136	153	170	188	205	222
Vigorous (steep slope)	167	191	215	239	263	286	310
BASEBALL	119	136	153	170	188	205	222
BASKETBALL							
Half-court	143	164	184	205	225	245	266
Full-court (slow)	191	218	245	273	300	327	355
Full-court (fast break)	315	360	405	450	495	540	585
BICYCLING							
10–12 mph	143	164	184	205	225	245	266
12–14 mph	191	218	245	273	300	327	355
14–16 mph	239	273	307	341	375	409	443
BOWLING	72	82	92	102	113	123	133
CALISTHENICS							
Light	107	123	138	153	169	184	199
Heavy	191	218	245	273	300	327	355
CROSS-COUNTRY SKIING							
2.5 mph	167	191	215	239	263	286	310
4–5 mph	191	218	245	273	300	327	355
FISHING							
Sitting	60	68	77	85	94	102	111
Standing	84	95	107	119	131	143	155
FOOTBALL							
Playing catch	60	68	77	85	94	102	111
Touch or flag	191	218	245	273	300	327	355
GARDENING	95	109	123	136	150	164	177
GOLF							
Pulling cart	119	136	153	170	188	205	222
Carrying clubs	131	150	169	187	206	225	244
HIKING AND CLIMBING							
Cross-country hiking	143	164	184	205	225	245	266
Rock climb (mountain trek)	191	218	245	273	300	327	355
Rock climb (vigorous)	253	289	325	361	398	434	470
HORSEBACK RIDING							
Leisure riding	95	109	123	136	150	164	177
Posting to trot	143	164	184	205	225	245	266
Galloping	188	215	242	269	296	323	350

■ EXERCISER'S GUIDE

ACTIVITY				WEIGHT			
	105	120	135	150	165	180	195
ICE OR ROLLER SKATING/BLADING							
Sustained moderate	167	191	215	239	263	286	310
Vigorous (9+ mph)	215	245	276	307	338	368	399
JOGGING AND RUNNING							
12 min./mile pace	191	218	245	273	300	327	355
10 min./mile pace	239	273	307	341	375	409	443
8 min./mile pace	298	341	384	426	469	511	554
6 min./mile pace	382	436	491	545	600	655	709
JUMPING ROPE							
Slow	191	218	245	273	300	327	355
Moderate	239	273	307	341	375	409	443
Fast	286	327	368	409	450	491	532
MARTIAL ARTS							
Tae kwon do, karate, judo	239	273	307	341	375	409	443
Tai chi	95	109	123	136	150	164	177
RACQUET AND COURT GAMES							
Racquetball (social)	167	191	215	239	263	286	310
Racquetball (competitive)	239	273	307	341	375	409	443
Handball and squash	286	327	368	409	450	491	532
ROWING AND CANOEING							
Leisurely	84	95	107	119	131	143	155
Vigorous sustained	167	191	215	239	263	286	310
Very vigorous	286	327	368	409	450	491	532
SAILING							
Leisurely	72	82	92	102	113	123	133
Racing	109	136	153	170	188	205	222
SOCCER							
Casual	167	191	215	239	263	286	310
Competitive	239	273	307	341	375	409	443
SWIMMING							
Laps freestyle (moderate)	191	218	245	273	300	327	355
Laps freestyle (fast)	239	273	307	341	375	409	443
TENNIS							
Social doubles	119	136	153	170	188	205	222
Social singles	157	180	202	225	248	270	293
Competitive doubles	172	196	221	245	270	295	319
Competitive singles	227	259	291	324	356	389	421
VOLLEYBALL							
Leisurely	74	85	96	106	117	128	138
Competitve	167	191	215	239	263	286	310
WALKING							
24 min./mile pace	72	82	92	102	113	123	133
20 min./mile pace	84	95	107	119	131	143	155
17min./mile pace	95	109	123	136	150	164	177
15 min./mile pace	107	123	138	153	169	184	194
12 min./mile pace	119	136	153	170	188	205	222
WEIGHT TRAINING							
Free weights or machines	143	164	184	205	225	245	266
Circuit weight training	191	218	245	273	300	327	355

SOURCE: Dr. David R. Stutz.

HOW TO STAY OFF THE BENCH

The N. Y. Knicks' doc on avoiding injuries and healing quickly

Professional athletes "play hurt," it is often said, and no wonder, for getting hurt is as much a part of most pro athletes' careers as collecting paychecks. Football great Joe Montana suffered serious injuries to his throwing arm, basketball legend Larry Bird was plagued by back pain and tennis star Martina Navratilova is known for her weak knees.

But sports injuries aren't limited to the pros. Weekend athletes are also prone to injury because they tend to overdo exertion even though they're out of shape. Usually it's minor damage, resulting in annoying aches and pains, but as you get older, you get more susceptible to serious injuries because your muscles aren't as strong as they once were. Scientists have found that many people, even those who get regular aerobic exercise, suffer rapid erosion of muscle mass after age 45 or so.

Weight training can help ward off injury by counteracting the subtle muscle atrophy that accompanies aging, and it can also play a role in recuperation. In general, it's safe to resume activity and do strengthening exercises a couple of days after the swelling and pain subside, says Dr. Norman Scott, chief of orthopedics at Beth Israel Medical Center North in New York City. Scott, also the team physician for the New York Knicks basketball team and the 1992 Olympic basketball team (known as "The Dream Team"), says there's little difference between the injuries sustained by recreational and professional athletes, except the pros are more likely to suffer serious injuries because they play with more force. Below, Scott helps explain what causes

some common athletic injuries, how to avoid them, and what to do if you get laid up:

NECK: *Serious neck injuries are rare among athletes other than those who participate in contact sports like football and rugby. However, weightlifting, wrestling, even racquet sports like tennis can cause chronic aches and pains, especially flare-ups along the nerve route.*

■ **CAUSES:** Neck injuries in older amateur athletes are usually a sign of arthritic changes (joint inflammation), which are often totally asymptomatic. Strenuous neck movements often result in an inflammation that is associated with pain running down the arm into the fingers.

■ **PREVENTION:** Better overall conditioning is the best way to prevent neck injuries.

■ **TREATMENT:** If discomfort is acute, avoid exercise and don't stretch the muscle. Apply ice immediately and don't apply heat until 48 to 72 hours after the injury occurs. If necessary, take nonsteroidal anti-inflammatory medications like Motrin, Advil, or Aleve (the same is true of all minor injuries).

BACK: *Almost any sport that requires trunk rotations, as in golf or racquet sports like tennis and racquetball.*

■ **CAUSES:** Most back injuries are muscular in origin, but, depending on your age, back pain can also be due to arthritic changes like osteoarthritis or degenerative arthritis.

■ **PREVENTION:** The best way to prevent back pain is through good overall conditioning and following a good stretching program to increase flexibility.

■ **TREATMENT:** Apply ice early on, then apply heat after 72 hours. Water therapy like swimming helps decrease spasms. Try gentle stretching exercises, including an abdominal strengthening workout.

SHOULDER: *Pitching, racket sports, golf, lifting weights, and other activities where you put your arm in an overhead position.*

■ **CAUSES:** The most common cause is bursitis, an inflammation of a normal structure called the bursa. Shoulder injuries are much more common as a person gets older due to muscle atrophy. Damage to the rotator cuff, a group of tendons that allows you to raise your arm up and down, is usually caused by repetitive motions like pitching a baseball.

■ **PREVENTION:** A program for stretching and strengthening muscles can reduce your chances of getting a shoulder injury.

■ **TREATMENT:** Continue to move the shoulder; if you don't, it can freeze up very quickly. Rotate your arms and shoulder, moving your hand in front of your body, then backwards, and up and down; also try to stretch from side to side, bringing your right hand over to touch your left shoulder.

KNEE: *Any sport that requires a pivoting motion, like tennis and basketball; runners are also prone to knee injuries.*

■ **CAUSES:** The knee is a joint that's especially susceptible to injuries, usually caused by sudden rotational movements.

■ **PREVENTION:** Develop very strong leg muscles by biking, lifting weights, and using step machines.

■ **TREATMENT:** Follow the RICE principle: Rest (but don't completely immobilize it), Ice, Compression (wrap the knee to reduce swelling), and Elevation. Apply ice for 48 hours, then progress to strengthening exercises. Sprained ligaments will need 3 to 12 weeks of rehabilitative exercise, but a torn ligament or cartilage may need surgery.

ANKLE: *Ankle injuries are common in any sport that requires a lot of running, such as jogging, racquet sports, baseball, and football.*

■ **CAUSES:** Sprains and strains are common injuries that occur when the joint or ligaments connecting bones are overstretched or twisted.

■ **PREVENTION:** Make sure you warm up—and your sneakers aren't untied.

■ **TREATMENT:** Again, follow the RICE principle, applying ice immediately. If the swelling is slight, you can exercise the following day, but keep your ankle wrapped or wear high-top sneakers. Try strengthening exercises a couple of days after swelling and pain subside.

ELBOW: *Besides tennis, you can develop tennis elbow from any sport that requires you rotate your hand up and down repeatedly, as when you swing a golf club incorrectly.*

■ **CAUSES:** Tennis elbow (pain in the forearm and wrist) is a very common injury caused by too much tension on the tendons around the bony prominence of the elbow.

■ **PREVENTION:** Strengthening exercises, like squeezing a rubber ball, build muscles in your forearm.

■ **TREATMENT:** Apply ice. If necessary, take anti-inflammatory medications.

■ WHERE BRUISES COME FROM

Below are the estimates of the number of product-related injuries that occurred while playing various sports in 1995, derived from data collected in hospital emergency rooms. The sports that result in the greatest number of injuries aren't inherently more dangerous than other sports, however, since far more people play a sport like basketball than golf.

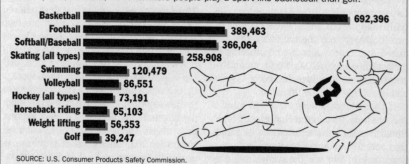

Sport	Injuries
Basketball	692,396
Football	389,463
Softball/Baseball	366,064
Skating (all types)	258,908
Swimming	120,479
Volleyball	86,551
Hockey (all types)	73,191
Horseback riding	65,103
Weight lifting	56,353
Golf	39,247

SOURCE: U.S. Consumer Products Safety Commission.

HEALTHY EATING

DHEA: Can a dietary supplement really keep you young? PAGE 135 **ZINC:** It's still no cure for the common cold, PAGE 136 **MINERALS:** An essential guide, PAGE 137 **CHOLESTEROL:** What you need to know to control it, PAGE 139 **FISH:** Health benefits depend on what kind you eat, PAGE 141 **FRUIT:** A buyer's guide to ripeness, PAGE 144 **COFFEE:** A quick tour of beans around the world, PAGE 146 **SAFETY:** Tips to avoid food poisoning, PAGE 148

EXPERT Q & A

A LEAFY WAY TO LOOK AT LIFE

For those whose appetite is being ruined by all those diet studies

Eat this. Avoid that. Take dietary supplements. Forget it, on second thought. Every week, it seems, there's another medical study that either touts the benefits of a diet rich in one or another vitamin, or dashes the hopes that some previously favored nutrient can help ward off disease and keep you in the pink of health.

For those who want a bottom line, however, the newest dietary guidelines from the U.S. Department of Health and Human Services (HHS) and the U.S. Department of Agriculture (USDA) provide one: Eating a varied, balanced diet that meets the recommended dietary allowances (RDAs) for various nutrients will help you reduce the risk of disease and live a long, healthy life.

If that sounds obvious, keep in mind a recent study that found that most people think they eat a more nutritious diet than they actually do. Asked to record in diaries what they in fact ate, the study's subjects discovered that they consumed far more fat-filled junk food than they thought they did, and that their intake of fruits, vegetables, and whole grains didn't begin to satisfy the guidelines urged by the USDA's food pyramid.

Here, Dr. Walter Willett, chairman of the nutrition department at the Harvard School of Public Health, puts the latest nutrition research in perspective:

■ What is the relationship between diet and disease?

We thought for a long time that diet influenced heart disease and cancer, but now it also seems important for preventing diseases like cataracts. We've also learned that while some aspects of diet are probably undesirable and to be avoided, eating foods that are protective, such as fruits and vegetables, seems to be more important.

■ What benefits are there from eating lots of fruits and vegetables?

There are dozens of studies that show reduced risk of various cancers—lung, colon, prostate, stomach, and breast—among people who eat a lot of fruits and vegetables. There's additional evidence that high intake of vitamin C can help in cataract prevention. It also appears that vitamins and minerals, like folic acid, in the diet seem to be critical in preventing birth defects, and may also help protect against heart disease and some cancers. Macular degeneration, a common cause of blindness, is also related to low intake of fruit and vegeta-

THE ASIAN PYRAMID

People in Asian countries tend to live longer than Americans. Scientists think this may be attributed in part to a diet that features very little meat.

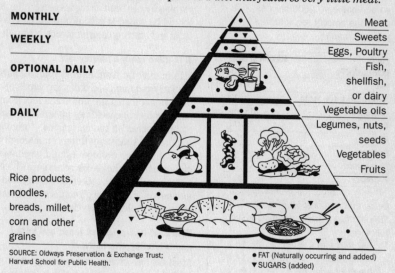

MONTHLY — Meat

WEEKLY — Sweets / Eggs, Poultry

OPTIONAL DAILY — Fish, shellfish, or dairy

DAILY — Vegetable oils / Legumes, nuts, seeds / Vegetables / Fruits

Rice products, noodles, breads, millet, corn and other grains

SOURCE: Oldways Preservation & Exchange Trust; Harvard School for Public Health.

● FAT (Naturally occurring and added)
▼ SUGARS (added)

bles, particularly dark green leafy vegetables.

Diets rich in vegetables and fruits probably contain other nutrients that are not well-recognized. For example, phytochemicals, chemicals found in plant foods that prevent cancer in people, are probably important. And there's evidence that people who eat a lot of foods containing fiber have a considerably lower risk of heart disease.

■ What are antioxidants and what role do they play in protecting against disease?

We are constantly being bombarded with oxidative stresses—molecules that can damage DNA and other cell structures. Some of these stresses come from cigarette smoke and sunlight, but many are produced by the normal working of the cells' machinery. Antioxidants are compounds that prevent damage due to oxidative stress. Some antioxidant vitamins derived from the diet, such as vitamin C and E, and carotenoid compounds such as lycopene also protect us from these stresses. We can get most antioxidants adequately from

our diet, except possibly for vitamin E, if we eat enough fruits and vegetables.

■ What are the benefits of vitamin E?

Many studies show that people who take vitamin E supplements of 200 IU a day or more have a lower risk of heart attack. You can't get this much from your diet, however. The final answer is not in, and until further studies are concluded, many physicians and nutritionists think it is reasonable for middle-aged people to take vitamin E supplements.

■ Who should take folic acid supplements?

All women of reproductive age should take a folic acid supplement, which is found in multi-vitamins, for prevention of birth defects. There is also substantial evidence that folic acid can reduce the risk of heart attack and colon cancer, although this is not yet proven.

■ What's the optimum amount of fat intake?

Fat has been labeled the worst aspect of the

■ VITAL INGREDIENTS

How much is too much? How little is too little? The FDA recommends the following for a healthy diet, assuming a daily intake of 2,000 calories— about the amount required by a young woman.

FOOD COMPONENT	MAXIMUM DAILY VALUE
Fat	65 g
Saturated fatty acids	20 g
Cholesterol	300 mg
Total carbohydrate	300 g
Fiber	25 g
Sodium	2,400 mg
Potassium	3,500 mg
Protein*	50 g

*The DV for protein does not apply to certain populations; for these groups, FDA nutrition experts recommend the following:

Children 1 to 4 years:	16 g
Infants less than 1 year:	14 g
Pregnant women:	60 g
Nursing mothers:	65 g

NUTRIENT	MINIMUM DAILY VALUE
Vitamin A	5,000 International Units (IU)
Vitamin C	60 mg
Thiamin	1.5 mg
Riboflavin	1.7 mg
Niacin	20 mg
Calcium	1.0 g
Iron	18 mg
Vitamin D	400 IU
Vitamin E	30 IU
Vitamin B 6	2 mg
Folic acid	0.4 mg
Vitamin B 12	6 micrograms (mcg)
Phosphorus	1 g
Iodine	150 mcg
Magnesium	400 mg
Zinc	15 mg
Copper	2 mg
Biotin	0.3 mg
Pantothenic acid	10 mg

SOURCE: U.S. Food and Drug Administration.

diet. We've known for a long time, however, that it's the type of fat that's important. There's little evidence that body fat is related to the amount of fat in the diet. We've seen a steady decline of total fat in recent years, yet obesity has been on the increase. Efforts should be aimed at getting a healthier type of fat and limiting calories modestly overall.

■ Is there really a healthy fat?

Minimizing fat from animal sources, particularly red meat and dairy fat, which are high in saturated fat, and trans fats from partially hydrogenated vegetable oil like vegetable shortening and margarine, is what's important. Almost anything commercially fried should be avoided. Liquid vegetable oils are a better choice. We're not sure which are the healthiest, but there are many studies showing that olive oil confers beneficial effects on cholesterol levels.

■ Are fat-free prepared foods and baked goods healthy alternatives?

Most fat-free sweets and baked goods are loaded with sugar instead of fat; they may actually be worse than some products with fat. There's evidence that eating refined carbohydrates like white bread or white rice has a worse effect on blood cholesterol than a diet with a lot of monounsaturated fat: Low-fat, high-carbohydrate diets tend to lower HDL cholesterol (the good cholesterol) as well as LDL cholesterol (bad cholesterol). Eating lots of sugar also displaces other nutrient-rich sources of calcium from the diet. In many cases, it's better to substitute a good fat for a bad fat than to replace it with a sugar or refined carbohydrate, which still has lots of calories.

■ Is it necessary to limit salt in the diet?

Extra salt in the diet will tend to increase blood pressure slightly, but still importantly. The best thing to do is cut down slowly and then it won't be missed. Most salt in our diet comes from commercially prepared foods, so beware. Although one study found that low-salt intake might be associated with heart disease, there's not much evidence that low salt intake is a problem in this country.

THE HOME VITAMIN SHELF

Your body needs vitamins to form blood cells, build strong bones, and regulate the nervous system, but it can't generate most of them on its own. Here are the FDA's daily values for essential vitamins and the foods that contain them.

VITAMIN A

DAILY VALUE:	5,000 international units
1 scrambled egg:	420 IU
1 cup nonfat milk:	500 IU
1 nectarine:	1,000 IU
1 piece watermelon:	1,760 IU

■ **WHAT IT DOES:** Aids in good vision; helps build and maintain skin, teeth, bones, and mucous membranes. Deficiency can increase susceptibility to infectious disease.

■ **WHAT IT MAY DO:** May inhibit the development of breast cancer; may increase resistance to infection in children.

■ **FOOD SOURCES:** Milk, eggs, liver, cheese, fish oil. Plus fruits and vegetables that contain beta carotene. You need not consume preformed vitamin A if you eat foods rich in beta carotene.

■ **SUPPLEMENTATION:** Not recommended, since toxic in high doses.

VITAMIN B1 (THIAMIN)

DAILY VALUE:	1.5 milligrams
1 slice enriched white bread:	0.12 mg
3 oz. fried liver:	0.18 mg
1 cup black beans:	0.43 mg
1 oz. dry-hull sunflower seeds:	0.65 mg

■ **WHAT IT DOES:** Helps convert carbohydrates into energy. Necessary for healthy brain, nerve cells, and heart function.

■ **FOOD SOURCES:** Whole grains, enriched grain products, beans, meats, liver, wheat germ, nuts, fish, brewer's yeast.

■ **SUPPLEMENTATION:** Not necessary, not recommended.

VITAMIN B2 (RIBOFLAVIN)

DAILY VALUE:	1.7 milligrams
1 oz. chicken:	0.2 mg
1 bagel:	0.2 mg
1 cup milk:	0.4 mg
1 cup cooked spinach:	0.42 mg

■ **WHAT IT DOES:** Helps cells convert carbohydrates into energy. Essential for growth, production of red blood cells, and health of skin and eyes.

■ **FOOD SOURCES:** Dairy products, liver, meat, chicken, fish, enriched grain products, leafy greens, beans, nuts, eggs, almonds.

■ **SUPPLEMENTATION:** Not necessary and not recommended.

VITAMIN B3 (NIACIN)

DAILY VALUE:	20 milligrams
1 slice enriched bread:	1.0 mg
3 oz. baked flounder or sole:	1.7 mg
1 oz. roasted peanuts:	4.2 mg
1/2 chicken breast:	14.7 mg

■ **WHAT IT DOES:** Aids in release of energy from foods. Helps maintain healthy skin, nerves, and digestive system.

■ **WHAT IT MAY DO:** Megadoses lower high blood cholesterol.

■ **FOOD SOURCES:** Nuts, meat, fish, chicken, liver, enriched grain products, dairy products, peanut butter, brewer's yeast.

■ **SUPPLEMENTATION:** Large doses may be prescribed by doctor to lower blood cholesterol. May cause flushing, liver damage, and irregular heart beat.

VITAMIN B5 (PANTOTHENIC ACID)

DAILY VALUE:	7 milligrams
8 oz. nonfat milk:	0.81 mg
1 large egg:	0.86 mg
8 oz. low-fat fruit-flavored yogurt:	1.0 mg
3 1/2 oz. liver:	4.57 mg

■ **WHAT IT DOES:** Necessary for healthy metabolism and production of essential body chemicals.

■ **FOOD SOURCES:** Whole grains, beans, milk, eggs, liver.

■ **SUPPLEMENTATION:** Not necessary, not recommended. May cause diarrhea.

VITAMIN B6 (PYROXIDINE)

DAILY VALUE:	2.0 milligrams
1 bran muffin:	0.11 mg
1 cup lima beans:	0.3 mg
3 oz. cooked bluefin tuna:	0.45 mg
1 banana:	0.7 mg

■ **WHAT IT DOES:** Vital in chemical reactions of proteins and amino acids. Helps maintain brain function and form red blood cells.

■ **WHAT IT MAY DO:** May help to boost immunity in the elderly.

■ **FOOD SOURCES:** Whole grains, bananas, meat, beans, nuts, wheat germ, brewer's yeast, chicken, fish, liver.

■ **SUPPLEMENTATION:** Large doses can cause numbness and other neurological disorders.

VITAMIN B12

DAILY VALUE:	6.0 micrograms
1/2 chicken breast:	0.29 mcg
1 large egg:	0.77 mcg
1 cup nonfat milk:	0.93 mcg
3 1/2 oz. lean beef flank:	3.05 mcg

■ **WHAT IT DOES:** Necessary for development of red blood cells. Maintains normal functioning of nervous system.

■ **FOOD SOURCES:** Liver, beef, pork, poultry, eggs, milk, cheese, yogurt, shellfish, fortified cereals, and fortified soy products.

■ **SUPPLEMENTATION:** Not usually necessary, but people who are on strict vegetarian diets may need supplementation.

VITAMIN C (ASCORBIC ACID)

DAILY VALUE:	60 micrograms
1 orange:	70 mcg
1 green pepper:	95 mcg
1 cup cooked broccoli:	97 mcg
1 cup fresh orange juice:	124 mcg

■ **WHAT IT DOES:** Helps promote healthy gums and teeth; aids in iron absorption; maintains normal connective tissue; helps in the healing of wounds. As an antioxidant, it combats the adverse effects of free radicals.

■ **WHAT IT MAY DO:** May reduce the risk of lung, esophagus, stomach, and bladder cancers, as well as coronary artery disease; may prevent or delay cataracts and slow the aging process.

■ **FOOD SOURCES:** Citrus fruits and juices, strawberries, tomatoes, peppers, broccoli, potatoes, kale, cauliflower, cantaloupe, brussels sprouts.

■ **SUPPLEMENTATION:** 250–500 mgs a day for smokers and anyone not consuming several fruits or vegetables rich in C daily. Larger doses may cause diarrhea.

VITAMIN D

DAILY VALUE:	400 international units
1 oz. cheddar cheese:	3 IU
1 large egg:	27 IU
1 cup nonfat milk:	100 IU

■ **WHAT IT DOES:** Strengthens bones and teeth by aiding the absorption of calcium. Helps maintain phosphorus in the blood.

■ **WHAT IT MAY DO:** May reduce risk of osteoporosis, forestall breast and colon cancers.

■ **FOOD SOURCES:** Milk, fish oil, fortified margarine; also produced by the body in response to sunlight.

■ **SUPPLEMENTATION:** 400 IU for vegetarians, the elderly, those who don't drink milk or get sun exposure. Toxic in high doses.

VITAMIN E

DAILY VALUE:	30 international units
1/2 cup boiled brussels sprouts:	1.02 IU
1/2 cup boiled spinach:	2.7 IU
1 oz. almonds:	8.5 IU

■ **WHAT IT DOES:** Helps form red blood cells. Combats adverse effects of free radicals.

■ **WHAT IT MAY DO:** May reduce the risk of esophageal or stomach cancers and coronary artery disease; may prevent or delay cataracts; may boost immunity in the elderly.

■ **FOOD SOURCES:** Vegetable oil, nuts, margarine, wheat germ, leafy greens, seeds, almonds, olives, asparagus.

■ **SUPPLEMENTATION:** 200–800 IU advised for everybody; you can't get that much from food, especially on a low-fat diet.

BIOTIN (VITAMIN B)

DAILY VALUE:	300 micrograms
1 cup cooked enriched noodles:	4 mcg

CAN DHEA KEEP YOU FOREVER YOUNG?

The latest potion in the search for perpetual youth

Explorer Ponce de Leon's search for the fountain of youth continues unabated among Americans. Recently held out as the magic elixir for stopping aging was melatonin, a hormone taken as a dietary supplement. While it's still popular, closer scrutiny revealed that melatonin's much-touted benefits require further investigation. Now comes the latest drug purporting to stop the ravages of time—a dietary supplement called DHEA.

DHEA is a hormone secreted by the adrenal gland beginning at around age seven. The levels of DHEA peak between ages 25 and 30, then progressively drop off to about 10 percent by age 70. It is believed that dwindling levels of DHEA may be responsible for degenerative changes associated with aging. Researchers suspect that replacing levels of the lost hormone can ward off some of old age's most debilitating diseases by tricking the body into thinking it is still young.

Can popping DHEA tablets, which can be bought at health food stores and supermarkets, really make you feel and look younger? The converted swear by it, citing effects such as improved memory, restored muscle tone, weight loss, a boost in energy and libido, and fewer diseases. Research on lab animals does show that huge doses of DHEA can prolong lifespan, enhance the immune system, and prevent diabetes, obesity, some cancers, and atherosclerosis. There's little proof, however, that DHEA can confer the same benefits on humans.

New research conducted at the University of California's San Diego School of Medicine, shows that both men and women can indeed benefit from taking DHEA. In one study, volunteers over age 50 were given either a 50 milligram dose of DHEA or a placebo for 12 months. Roughly 67 percent of male volunteers and 84 percent of female volunteers reported feeling better, and having a better ability to cope with stress.

Researchers caution, however, that taking DHEA tablets is not advisable until further studies are done to determine its effectiveness as well as its potential effects on the young. What's more, taking DHEA can cause some unseemly side-effects, including acne, oily skin, irritability, and excessive facial hair in women—hardly the miracle cure Ponce de Leon had in mind.

---

1 large egg:	11 mcg
1 oz. almonds:	23 mcg

■ **WHAT IT DOES:** Important in metabolism of protein, carbohydrates, and fats.

■ **FOOD SOURCES:** Eggs, milk, liver, mushrooms, bananas, tomatoes, whole grains.

■ **SUPPLEMENTATION:** Not recommended.

FOLATE (VITAMIN B)

(Also called Folacin or folic acid)

DAILY VALUE:	400 micrograms
1 orange:	47 mcg
1 cup raw spinach:	108 mcg
1 cup baked beans:	122 mcg
1 cup asparagus:	176 mcg

■ **WHAT IT DOES:** Important in synthesis of DNA, in normal growth, protein metabolism. Reduces risk of certain birth defects, notably spina bifida and encephaly.

■ **WHAT IT MAY DO:** May reduce the risk of cervical cancer.

■ **FOOD SOURCES:** Leafy greens, wheat germ, liver, beans, whole grains, broccoli, asparagus, citrus fruit, and juices.

■ **SUPPLEMENTATION:** 400 mcg, from food or pills, for all women who may become pregnant, to help prevent birth defects.

SOURCE: U.S. Food and Drug Administration; *Food Values of Portions Commonly Used*, Jean A. P. Pennington, Harper & Row, 1980.

THE HOPE AND HYPE OF ZINC

Are zinc-laced lozenges the cure for the common cold?

What irony. Scientists have made huge strides in discovering penicillin and vaccines for virulent diseases like polio and tuberculosis, but they have yet to find a cure for an annoying human ailment—the common cold. For a time, it seemed as if a cure was in sight. Researchers at the Cleveland Clinic Foundation reported in 1996 that zinc lozenges, available in health food stores and pharmacies, can reduce the symptoms and duration of a cold. By the time the winter flu season hit, stores couldn't keep zinc on the shelves, despite its fairly hefty cost of up to $10 for 50 lozenges. As it turns out, though, it's unclear whether the Cleveland study holds out more promise than it can deliver.

It wasn't the first time the curative powers of zinc—found naturally in beans, red meat, seafood, eggs, and whole grain cereals and breads—have been investigated. In fact, seven previous studies have looked at zinc lozenges as potential cold cures. The results were mixed: Three found beneficial effects, and four concluded that taking zinc did not alleviate cold symptoms. All the hoopla regarding the Cleveland study derives partly from the fact that the results were published in a well-regarded medical journal, *The Annals of Internal Medicine*.

All the media attention surprised even the study's senior researcher, Dr. Michael Macknin, chairman of the Cleveland Clinic's department of general pediatrics. "The scientific evidence justifies further investigation," says Macknin, "but it doesn't justify a national craze." Macknin and his researchers studied 99 volunteers within 24 hours after the onset of their cold symptoms. Half were given a lozenge containing 13.3 milligrams of zinc; the other half took a placebo. Both groups were asked to chart their cold symptoms. The results showed that taking zinc tablets regularly cut the cold's duration by nearly half: from 7.6 days, to 4.4 days, on average.

In addition, those who took zinc reported a reduction in coughing, headaches, hoarseness, nasal congestion, nasal drainage, and sore throats. They saw no significant reduction, however, in fever, muscle aches, scratchy throats, or sneezing. Promising—but no miracle cure, says Macknin. "The symptoms went away faster and the cold went away faster, but zinc is not something you pop in your mouth and suddenly you're cured," explains Macknin, who considers his work a preliminary investigation that requires confirmation by further research.

What's more, 90 percent of the volunteers reported side effects, albeit minor ones, from ingesting zinc. About 80 percent cited a chalky, unpleasant aftertaste—similar to the taste of chewing an antacid tablet. For 10 percent, the taste was so foul that they dropped out of the study. Another reported side effect was nausea, experienced by 20 percent.

Those intent on giving zinc a try should follow some precautions, says Macknin. For one thing, zinc should not be taken simultaneously with vitamin C tablets—the combination can deactivate the zinc. (Mixing zinc with other over-the-counter cold remedies does not appear to be harmful, however.) Further, there is no evidence that zinc can ward off a cold before it strikes. In fact, warns Macknin, taking megadoses of zinc over long periods can be harmful, possibly causing a decreased white blood cell count and lower copper levels, which can impair the body's ability to fight infection.

Macknin is now researching the effects of zinc on children. Until those results are in, he advises parents not to give zinc to children. "I think it's safe, but I'm not sure it works," says Macknin. So far, children don't seem to be favorably inclined to take the stuff: Six volunteers—students in grades 1 through 12—have dropped out of the study. They didn't like the taste of zinc.

THE MINERAL MINDER

Minerals help your body form bones, regulate the heart, and synthesize enzymes, but experts say too many, or too few, can lead to heart disease, diabetes, or even cancer. Here are the FDA's daily values and where to get them.

CALCIUM

DAILY VALUE:	1 gram
1 cup hard ice cream:	0.18 g
1 cup nonfat milk:	0.3 g
2 oz. cheddar cheese:	0.41 g
8 oz. nonfat yogurt:	0.45 g

■ **WHAT IT DOES:** Helps form strong bones and teeth. Helps regulate heartbeat, muscle contractions, nerve function, and blood clotting.

■ **WHAT IT MAY DO:** May reduce the risk of high blood pressure, high cholesterol, colon cancer, and kidney stones (see page 138).

■ **FOOD SOURCES:** Milk, cheese, butter and margarine, green vegetables, legumes, nuts, soybean products, hard water.

■ **SUPPLEMENTATION:** Most Americans don't consume enough calcium, but megadoses are not recommended. High intakes may cause constipation and increase some men's risk of urinary stones.

IRON

DAILY VALUE:	18 milligrams
1 slice whole wheat bread:	1 mg
3 scrambled eggs:	2.1 mg
3 oz. lean sirloin steak, broiled:	2.6 mg
3 oz. fried liver:	5.3 mg
1 packet instant oatmeal:	6.7 mg

■ **WHAT IT DOES:** Vital in forming hemoglobin (which carries oxygen in blood) and myoglobin (in muscle).

■ **FOOD SOURCES:** Red meat, poultry, liver, eggs, fish, whole-grain cereals, and breads.

■ **SUPPLEMENTATION:** Often (but not always)

advised for dieters, strict vegetarians, menstruating women, pregnant women, infants, and children. Large doses may damage the heart, liver, and pancreas.

PHOSPHORUS

DAILY VALUE:	1 gram
6 scallops:	0.2 g
1 cup nonfat milk:	0.25 g
3 oz. broiled trout:	0.26 g
1 cup tuna salad:	0.28 g
1 cup low-fat cottage cheese:	0.34 g

■ **WHAT IT DOES:** Helps form bones, teeth, cell membranes, and genetic material. Essential for energy production.

■ **FOOD SOURCES:** Nearly all foods, including red meat, poultry, liver, milk, cheese, butter and margarine, eggs, fish, whole-grain cereals and breads, green and root vegetables, legumes, nuts, and fruit.

■ **SUPPLEMENTATION:** Not recommended. Deficiencies in Americans are virtually unknown. Excessive intake may lower blood calcium level.

POTASSIUM

DAILY VALUE:	3,500 milligrams
1 cup nonfat milk:	406 mg
1 banana:	451 mg
1 baked potato, with skin:	844 mg
1 cup cooked spinach:	839 mg

■ **WHAT IT DOES:** Needed for muscle contraction, nerve impulses, and function of heart and kidneys. Aids in regulation of water balance in cells and blood.

■ **WHAT IT MAY DO:** May fight osteoporosis and help lower blood pressure.

■ **FOOD SOURCES:** Unprocessed foods such as fruits, vegetables, and fresh meats.

■ **SUPPLEMENTATION:** Not usually recommended. Take only under a doctor's advice and supervision.

■ **EXPERT LIST**

IODINE

DAILY VALUE:	150 micrograms
1 oz. cheddar cheese:	12 mcg
1 tsp. iodized salt:	400 mcg

■ **WHAT IT DOES:** Necessary for proper thyroid gland function and thus normal cell metabolism. Prevents goiter (enlargement of thyroid).

■ **FOOD SOURCES:** Milk, cheese, butter and margarine, fish, whole-grain cereals and breads, iodized table salt.

■ **SUPPLEMENTATION:** Not recommended. Widely dispersed in the food supply, so even if you eat little iodized salt, you probably get enough iodine.

FACT FILE:

GRINDING DOWN KIDNEY STONES

■ *A long-held suspicion was that a high-calcium diet might cause kidney stones, which form when calcium combines with a body chemical called oxalate. However, a recent study found that women on a high-calcium diet are less likely to develop kidney stones.*

■ *Out of 91,000 women studied over a 12-year period, those who consumed more than 1,100 milligrams of calcium daily were 35 percent less likely to develop kidney stones than women who took in fewer than 500 milligrams.*

■ *Benefits came from consuming calcium-rich foods, not supplements. Women who took supplements were 20 percent more likely to develop kidney stones than those who didn't.*

SOURCE: *Annals of Internal Medicine*, 1997.

MAGNESIUM

DAILY VALUE:	400 milligrams
1 tbsp. peanut butter:	28 mg
1 baked potato:	55 mg
1/2 cup cooked spinach:	79 mg

■ **WHAT IT DOES:** Aids in bone growth, basic metabolic functions and the functioning of nerves and muscles, including the regulation of normal heart rhythm.

■ **FOOD SOURCES:** Milk, fish, whole-grain cereals and breads, green vegetables, legumes, nuts, and hard water.

■ **SUPPLEMENTATION:** Not usually recommended. Deficiency is rare.

ZINC

DAILY VALUE:	15 miligrams
8 oz. low-fat fruit yogurt:	1.52 mg
1 cup boiled lentils:	2.5 mg
3.5 oz. roast turkey, dark:	4.4 mg

■ **WHAT IT DOES:** Stimulates enzymes needed for cell division, growth, and repair (wound healing). Helps immune system function properly. Also plays a role in acuity of taste and smell.

■ **FOOD SOURCES:** Red meat, fish, seafood, eggs, milk, whole-grain cereals and breads, legumes.

■ **SUPPLEMENTATION:** Not recommended, except by a doctor for the few Americans who have low zinc levels.

COPPER

DAILY VALUE:	2 milligrams
2/3 cup seedless raisins:	0.31 mg
1 oz. dry roasted pistachios:	0.34 mg
1/2 cup boiled mushrooms:	0.39 mg

■ **WHAT IT DOES:** Helps in formation of red blood cells. Helps keep bones, blood vessels, nerves, and immune system healthy.

■ **FOOD SOURCES:** Red meat, poultry, liver, fish, seafood, whole-grain cereals and breads, green vegetables, legumes, nuts, raisins, mushrooms.

■ **SUPPLEMENTATION:** Not recommended. A balanced diet includes enough copper.

SOURCE: U.S. Food and Drug Administration; *Food Values of Portions Commonly Used*, Jean A. P. Pennington, Harper & Row, 1980.

CHOLESTEROL IN A NUTSHELL

Cut saturated fat intake and exercise to lower your "bad" cholesterol

Cholesterol is "bad" except when it's "good." Having high cholesterol is unhealthy except when it's the type that's desirable. If you're confused about the role of cholesterol in the body, here is Dr. James Cleeman, coordinator of the National Cholesterol Education Program (NCEP) at the National Heart, Lung, and Blood Institute of the National Institutes of Health, to explain:

■ What is cholesterol?

Cholesterol is a waxy substance that's an important component of cell membranes and is important in making hormones. When too much cholesterol circulates in the blood, however, it leaves deposits on the walls of the arteries, including the coronary arteries that supply the heart. Over time, the buildup of cholesterol and fatty substances, called plaque, gets larger and thicker and starts to impede the flow of blood. In some cases, a clot may also form. When that happens, the flow of blood to that vessel may completely stop, robbing the heart muscles of oxygen and causing a heart attack. Plaque can also cause angina—pain caused by too little blood flow to a portion of the heart muscle.

■ How much cholesterol is unhealthy?

In people age 20 and over, a total cholesterol count of less than 200 mg/dL is considered desirable. A cholesterol count between 200 and 239 mg/dL is considered borderline high, and 240 or greater is too high. In children 2 to 19, acceptable total levels are less than 170 mg/dL, 170 to 199 mg/dL is borderline, and 200 mg/dl and above is high.

■ What's the difference between "good" cholesterol and "bad" cholesterol?

Cholesterol is carried along in the blood combined with protein, forming a package called a lipoprotein, which is essentially a transport mechanism. Low-density lipoprotein (LDL) is the vehicle by which cholesterol is transported to the cell; high-density lipoprotein (HDL) is thought to be the vehicle by which cholesterol is transported away from the cells to the liver for excretion. LDL is known as "bad" cholesterol because it's the major culprit in atherosclerosis, which develops when plaque is deposited in the arteries. HDL, on the other hand, is "good" cholesterol because it prevents cholesterol from building up in artery walls. The lower the HDL, the higher the risk for heart disease.

■ What gives a person high cholesterol?

Two important factors are what you eat and heredity. Most people eat their way into having high cholesterol through high intakes of saturated fat (the chief culprit). There aren't many whose genetic makeup is so bad that they're going to have high cholesterol no matter what they do.

■ How often should cholesterol tests be taken?

People 20 and older should have both a total cholesterol and HDL-cholesterol test, which can be done without fasting, at least once every five years. If those are fine, you don't have to have further tests. But if there's a problem, then you should have a complete lipoprotein profile to determine your LDL cholesterol level. In children 2 to 19, cholesterol levels should be measured if a parent has high blood cholesterol or if a parent or grandparent developed heart disease before age 55.

■ What are the best ways to lower cholesterol?

First, watch the composition of your diet. For the roughly 40 million people who need cholesterol lowering but don't have coronary heart disease already, a Step One diet is the place to begin. A Step One diet takes 8 to 10 percent of its calories from saturated fat, about 30 percent from total fat, and allows less than 300 milligrams a day of dietary cholesterol. Try that for a period of time, rechecking your cholesterol at four to six weeks, and then again at three months.

If that's not lowering your cholesterol enough, you need to move to the Step Two diet, which reduces the saturated fats to less than 7 percent of calories and the cholesterol to less than 200 milligrams a day. For a patient who has coronary disease and has already had a heart attack or angina, the Step Two diet would be the first step.

■ Which foods should be eaten or avoided?

To reduce saturated fat and cholesterol, substitute lower-fat items for higher fat ones: Drink skim or 1% milk instead of whole or 2% milk, limit yourself to no more than six ounces a day of skinless chicken, fish and lean cuts of meat, and concentrate on fruits, vegetables, and grains. Organ meats and eggs yolks are also very high in dietary cholesterol and should be restricted.

If you are overweight, you will lower your LDL cholesterol and raise your HDL cholesterol if you lose weight. By reducing your weight, you also lower your risk of coronary disease. Physical activity can also help lower LDL cholesterol and raise HDL cholesterol, even if you don't need to lose weight.

■ Who should take drugs to reduce cholesterol?

For people without heart disease, drugs would be considered if dietary therapy doesn't work after about six months, but they would be added to the dietary therapy, not substituted for it. For the patient with coronary disease whose LDL cholesterol level is far above the goal of 100, cholesterol lowering drugs should be considered from the start of treatment, together with diet and physical activity. It is estimated that 85 percent of coronary patients could benefit from cholesterol lowering, but only about 29 percent of them are actually doing diet therapy and only 25 percent are taking cholesterol-lowering medications. These 12 to 13 million patients account for about half of the approximately 1.5 million heart attacks that occur each year.

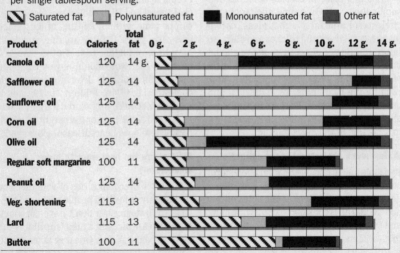

■ FAT ATTACK

Saturated fat slows down the elimination of cholesterol in your bloodstream, and that can lead to heart disease. Here are some household oils listed by saturated fat content per single tablespoon serving.

▨ Saturated fat   ▨ Polyunsaturated fat   ■ Monounsaturated fat   ■ Other fat

Product	Calories	Total fat	0 g.	2 g.	4 g.	6 g.	8 g.	10 g.	12 g.	14 g.
Canola oil	120	14 g.								
Safflower oil	125	14								
Sunflower oil	125	14								
Corn oil	125	14								
Olive oil	125	14								
Regular soft margarine	100	11								
Peanut oil	125	14								
Veg. shortening	115	13								
Lard	115	13								
Butter	100	11								

SOURCE: U.S. Department of Agriculture.

A FISHY WAY TO LIVE LONGER

The benefits of eating fish may depend on what kind you choose

Here's a fishy debate: Does eating fish help ward off heart disease? There's plenty of evidence—including the two most recent studies—that suggests that eating fish may lower a person's risk of death from heart disease. However, a larger, earlier study found no such effect.

In the latest study, researchers at Northwestern University Medical School in Chicago conducted a follow-up of the famous Western Electric study, which was started in 1957 on 1,800 company employees. The researchers found that the men surveyed about their diet and health habits who eat at least seven ounces of fish—the equivalent of one large can of tuna fish—a week are less likely to die of heart attacks than men who don't eat fish. In a report in *The New England Journal of Medicine,* the researchers concluded that eating fish led to an overall reduction of 42 percent in deaths over 30 years among fish-eaters, but the study did not specify what type of fish they ate. The researchers took into consideration the age, cholesterol level and blood pressure, weight, education level, and alcohol consumption of the men and whether they smoked cigarettes.

Another study, conducted in 1996 by researchers at the University of Washington in Seattle, where moderate seafood consumption is a way of life, compared the diets of a group of Seattle-area residents who suffered cardiac arrest with a second group of randomly chosen people in the same 24- to 74-year-old age group. Researchers looked not only at how much fish was eaten by the subjects, but also at the level of fatty acids in the participants' blood cell membranes.

■ **HEART HEALTHY WITH FISH OIL**

While the effectiveness of omega-3 fish oil has not been conclusively shown to prevent heart disease, here's a lineup of the fish and shellfish with the highest concentrations of the oil. Fish caught in the wild generally contain more omega-3 than farm-raised fish.

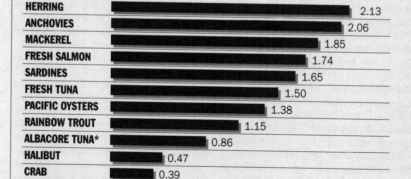

Grams of omega-3 fatty acids per 3.5 ounces of fish

HERRING	2.13
ANCHOVIES	2.06
MACKEREL	1.85
FRESH SALMON	1.74
SARDINES	1.65
FRESH TUNA	1.50
PACIFIC OYSTERS	1.38
RAINBOW TROUT	1.15
ALBACORE TUNA*	0.86
HALIBUT	0.47
CRAB	0.39
FLOUNDER	0.26

* Canned in water. Tuna packed in water has more omega-3 than tuna packed in oil.

SOURCE: University of Washington Cardiovascular Health Research Unit, *Washington Post* staff reports.

■ **HOW TO CLEAN A FISH**

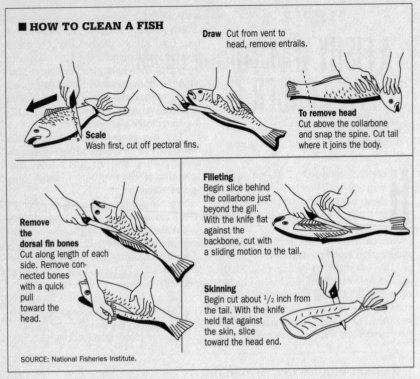

Draw Cut from vent to head, remove entrails.

Scale
Wash first, cut off pectoral fins.

To remove head
Cut above the collarbone and snap the spine. Cut tail where it joins the body.

Remove the dorsal fin bones
Cut along length of each side. Remove connected bones with a quick pull toward the head.

Filleting
Begin slice behind the collarbone just beyond the gill. With the knife flat against the backbone, cut with a sliding motion to the tail.

Skinning
Begin cut about 1/2 inch from the tail. With the knife held flat against the skin, slice toward the head end.

SOURCE: National Fisheries Institute.

Cardiac arrest, which occurs when the heart suddenly stops beating, appears in about two people per 10,000, and is responsible for about one-quarter of deaths from heart disease, says lead researcher David Siscovick, co-director of the Cardiovascular Health Research Unit at the University of Seattle.

The Seattle study suggests that even modest consumption of fish rich in omega-3 fatty acids (a type of oil unique to fish) reduced the risk of cardiac arrest. Researchers found that eating the equivalent of one to two servings of fish a week, depending on the type of fish, cuts in half the risk of cardiac arrest. When at least 5 percent of the fatty acids in a person's cell membranes were composed of omega-3 fatty acids, that person lowered his risk of cardiac arrest by 70 percent. Although studies in animals have found similar results, it's not clear why omega-3 fatty acids reduce the risk of heart attack.

What is evident, says Siscovick, is that "when it comes to these types of fatty acids,

you are to a large extent what you eat." Increasing your dietary intake of these fatty acids by eating fish like salmon, albacore tuna, herring, and mackerel once or twice a week "results in changes that may influence short- and long-term health in a matter of days or weeks," says Siscovick. The research suggests that frying fish reduces some of the benefits, so it's best to grill, broil, or poach.

However, a much larger study by researchers at Harvard found that eating fish doesn't appear to prevent heart disease. The Harvard investigators questioned more than 44,000 apparently healthy men about their eating habits, then monitored their health for six years. The study, which focused on overall risk of heart disease, not just cardiac arrest, found that men who ate fish frequently—up to seven times a week—were just as likely to be stricken with and die from heart disease as those who ate it once a month. Even taking fish oil supplements conferred no additional benefits.

GOURMET'S GUIDE

THE CATCH OF THE DAY

These days Americans can get fish caught in waters the world over in supermarkets and restaurants. But according to the National Fisheries Institute's study of data collected by the National Marine Fisheries Service, most Americans' idea of fish is still the old standby: canned tuna. If you're one of these folks and you want to expand your taste horizons, the guide below will help you decide between bluefish and mahi mahi the next time you're in the grocery store or scanning the restaurant menu.

FISH ⇨ SOURCE ● **TYPE OF MEAT** ○ *FLAVOR*

SEA BASS ⇨ Northeast Atlantic coast ● **Dark** ○ *Light to moderate*

STRIPED BASS ⇨ Atlantic and Pacific coastal waters; also farm-raised ● **Light** ○ *Light to moderate*

BLUEFISH ⇨ Atlantic coastal waters ● **Dark** ○ *Light to moderate*

CARP ⇨ Freshwater lakes, ponds worldwide ● **Light** ○ *Wild carp may taste muddy*

FARMED CARP ⇨ Farms worldwide ● **Light** ○ *Farmed carp is light to moderate*

CATFISH ⇨ Lakes, ponds, and rivers; also farmed ● **White** ○ *Wild catfish may taste muddy*

FARMED CATFISH ⇨ Farms worldwide ● **White** ○ *Farmed catfish light to moderate*

COBIA ⇨ Mid-Atlantic from U.S. to Argentina ● **White** ○ *Light to moderate*

COD ⇨ North to mid-Atlantic or North to mid-Pacific, depending on species ● **White** ○ *Very light, delicate*

FLOUNDER ⇨ Atlantic, Pacific coasts, Asian Pacific coast, and Bering Sea ● **White** ○ *Very light, delicate*

GROUPER ⇨ Tropical and subtropical coastal waters and Atlantic coast ● **Light** ○ *Very light, delicate*

HALIBUT ⇨ North Atlantic or Pacific coast, depending on species ● **White** ○ *Very light, delicate*

LAKE HERRING ⇨ Lakes and rivers in Canada and northern U.S. ● **Light** ○ *Light to moderate*

MACKEREL ⇨ Atlantic or Gulf coast, Pacific, European Atlantic coast, Indian Ocean ● **Light** ○ *Pronounced flavor*

MAHI MAHI ⇨ Off Hawaii and Florida, Gulf Stream, Pacific Calif. to S. America ● **White** ○ *Light to moderate*

MONKFISH ⇨ North to mid-Atlantic ● **Light** ○ *Light to moderate*

ORANGE ROUGHY ⇨ Deep ocean waters off New Zealand and Australia ● **White** ○ *Very light, delicate*

PIKE ⇨ Rivers and streams worldwide ● **Light** ○ *Light to moderate*

POLLOCK ⇨ North Pacific or both sides of North Atlantic and the North Sea ● **Light** ○ *Light to moderate*

RED SNAPPER ⇨ Gulf coast and Atlantic coast from North Carolina to Florida ● **Light** ○ *Light to moderate*

SALMON ⇨ Northern Atlantic or Pacific, rivers when spawning; also farmed ● **Light** ○ *Light to moderate*

SAND SHARK ⇨ Western Atlantic ● **Light** ○ *Light to moderate*

SMELT ⇨ Lakes, rivers, and northern Atlantic and Pacific coasts ● **Light** ○ *Very light, delicate*

SWORDFISH ⇨ Off Calif., New England, Hawaii, Spain, Japan, Greece, S. America ● **Light** ○ *Light to moderate*

RAINBOW TROUT ⇨ North American rivers and streams; also farmed ● **Light** ○ *Very light, delicate*

TUNA ⇨ Tropical to temperate waters worldwide ● **Dark** ○ *Light to moderate*

WALLEYE ⇨ Northern North American lakes and rivers ● **Light** ○ *Very light, delicate*

WHITEFISH ⇨ Northern United States and Canadian lakes ● **White** ○ *Light to moderate*

SOURCE: National Fisheries Institute.

THE PICK OF THE LOT

A grocery shopper's guide to choosing fresh fruits

For many consumers, buying fresh produce is like a game of roulette. There's no telling whether their fruits and vegetables will be fresh and ripe at home because they don't know how to choose produce at the grocery store.

Even some shoppers who consider themselves knowledgeable produce pickers are misinformed. Contrary to popular belief, watermelon thumping, cantaloupe shaking, and pineapple plucking are not valid tests for determining ripeness, according to the Produce Marketing Association.

Experts there offer these tips for choosing the ripest of the most popular fresh fruits:

■ APPLES
Fruit should be firm, well-colored, and mature. Should have no soft spots or broken or shriveled skin.

■ APRICOTS
Plump fruit with golden-orange color. When

FACT FILE:

FRUITS THAT DO NOT RIPEN AFTER HARVEST:

■ Apples	■ Cherries
■ Grapefruit	■ Grapes
■ Lemons	■ Limes
■ Oranges	■ Pineapples
■ Strawberries	■ Tangerines
■ Tangelos	■ Watermelons

---

ripe, flesh will yield to gentle pressure when touched. Avoid hard and overly firm fruit.

■ AVOCADOS
When ripe, fruit yields to gentle pressure when touched. Firm avocados will ripen at room temperature. Should have no bruises or hard and soft spots.

■ BANANAS
Look for firm, bright-colored fruit without bruises. Fully ripe when skin turns yellow with brown and black flecks. Can be purchased green and stored at room temperature to ripen.

Only refrigerate ripe bananas. Refrigeration will turn skins black, but will not affect fruit quality.

■ CANTALOUPES
Will have a cantaloupe smell, yield to pressure on the blossom end, and have a yellowish cast under the netting when ready.

Leave cantaloupes at room temperature to soften and become juicier.

■ CHERRIES
Should be plump with firm, smooth, and brightly colored skins and intact stems. Avoid cherries with blemished, rotted, or mushy skins or those that appear either hard and light-colored or soft, shriveled, and dull.

■ GRAPEFRUIT
Should be firm, springy to the touch, heavy for size, well shaped, and thin-skinned.

Grapefruit may show russeting (browning of the peel) or regreening, which do not affect fruit quality.

■ GRAPES
Bunches should be well colored with plump fruits firmly attached to green, pliable stems. Grapes should not leak moisture.

■ HONEYDEWS
Will have a creamy yellow skin and a slightly soft blossom end. An unripe honeydew has white skin with a green tint and a hard blossom end, and will ripen at room temperature.

Choose melons that are heavy for their size and are well shaped. Unlike cantaloupe, honeydew does not have a distinctive aroma.

■ KIWIFRUIT

Choose firm, plump, light brown kiwi that gives slightly to the touch. Harder fruit can be purchased and ripened at room temperature at home.

■ LEMONS

Should have a pleasant citrus fragrance. Should be firm, heavy for size, and have thin smooth skins.

■ LIMES

Should be plump and heavy for their size, with glossy skin.

■ NECTARINES

Look for a creamy yellow background color without any green at the stem end. Firm fruits can be ripened at home. When they yield slightly to pressure, they're ready to eat.

■ ORANGES

May regreen after harvest, but this is natural and does not indicate unripeness. To get the juiciest fruit, choose oranges that feel heavy for their size.

■ PEACHES

Fruits should smell peachy and have no tinge of green in the background color of the skin. The amount of red blush does not indicate ripeness. Buy peaches that are fairly firm and a little soft. They should give a bit when squeezed in the palm of the hand. Stored in a paper bag, they will soften and get juicier, but not sweeter.

■ PEARS

Will yield to gentle pressure near the stem end and side when they are ready to eat. Ripen at home at room temperature.

■ PINEAPPLES

Will have a strong pineapple aroma. Should be heavy for their size, well shaped and fresh-looking with dark green crown leaves and a dry, crisp shell. Ripeness is not indicated by

EXPERT TIP

To speed the ripening of soft fruits such as avocados, bananas, kiwis, nectarines, peaches, pears, plums, and tomatoes, store them in a paper bag with an apple. The apple will boost the partly ripe fruit's exposure to ethylene, a gas required for ripening.

—The Produce Marketing Association

shell color or pulling crown leaves.

■ PLUMS

Choose plump fruit with good color for the variety. Skin should be smooth, without breaks or discolorations. Flesh should be fairly firm to slightly but not excessively soft. To ripen at home, store in a paper bag.

■ STRAWBERRIES

Should be plump, firm, well rounded, and have an even bright red color with natural shine. Caps should be fresh-looking, green, and in place. When possible, avoid fruit that is white near the caps. This is called white shoulders, and it can mean two things: either the fruit was picked too soon, or the berries are fully ripe but missing some color due to a lack of sunshine.

■ TANGERINES

Look for fruit with deep, rich color and "puffy" appearance. Good-quality fruit should be heavy for its size. Avoid fruit with soft or water-soaked spots or mold.

■ WATERMELONS

Should have a dull (as opposed to shiny) rind, a dried stem, and a yellowish underside where the watermelon has touched the ground. Immature watermelons have a shiny rind and a white, pale green, or light yellow underside. Thumping does not indicate ripeness.

COFFEE
▼

A WORLDWIDE BEAN TOUR

From the mountains of Colombia to Java, beans to suit every palate

Coffee beans are like wine grapes. Where they are grown and how they are raised shapes their taste profoundly. Even the most casual of coffee drinkers will taste the difference, for instance, between the light-bodied coffee produced from beans cultivated in the high Sierras in southern Mexico and the "buttery" full body and spicy aroma of Indonesian-grown coffees. For a taster's tour of coffees around the world, sip on:

■ **CENTRAL AND SOUTH AMERICA.** Coffees from south of the U.S. border are usually light-to-medium bodied with clean lively flavors. Colombian coffees have a brisk snappy quality—called "acidity" by coffee connoisseurs although it has nothing to do with pH factor. Their aroma is heady and distinctive. Costa Rican beans, particularly those from the mountainous Pacific region known as Tres Rios, are medium-bodied when brewed, with a tangy aroma. Guatemalan beans, particularly those from the Antigua region, produce a richer and more complex flavored coffee than any other Central American variety. Kona coffee is smooth and even. Although it is raised in Hawaii, not Latin America, it is a close cousin to that region's products in taste and aroma.

■ **EAST AFRICA.** Medium to full-bodied generally, the coffees of East Africa combine the brisk, refreshing quality found in Central American coffees with flavors that seem floral or resemble fine red wine at times. Kenyan coffee is especially known for its combination of heartiness and winelike flavor. The Arabica beans native to Ethiopia produce a brew that is medium-bodied with a deep, near-floral aroma and taste. Arabian Mocha is smooth, delicate, winy, and aromatic all at once. It comes from Yemen, where coffee was first grown. It is sometimes blended with Java beans from Indonesia to produce Arabian Mocha Java.

■ **INDONESIA.** Full-bodied and smooth, Indonesian coffees are quite different in taste and aroma from those of Latin America. Indonesian coffees often have exotic floral or spice-like aspects to their aroma and flavor. The best-known coffee from the region is Estate Java, which is rich and full-bodied with a deep spicy aroma.

SOURCE: Adapted from "The World of Coffee," Starbucks Coffee Company, 1995.

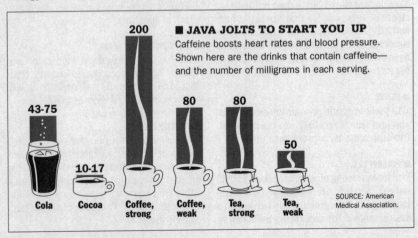

■ **JAVA JOLTS TO START YOU UP**
Caffeine boosts heart rates and blood pressure. Shown here are the drinks that contain caffeine—and the number of milligrams in each serving.

Cola	Cocoa	Coffee, strong	Coffee, weak	Tea, strong	Tea, weak
43-75	10-17	200	80	80	50

SOURCE: American Medical Association.

TEA

BREWS FIT FOR AN EMPEROR

The world's greatest tea masters on the perfect cup of tea

For more than two millennia tea has been extensively cultivated in the East, especially in China. Yet most consumers are unfamiliar with the growing and production processes required to develop fine teas. That is not the case for Donald R. Wallis and Roy Fong, founders of the American Tea Masters Association based in San Francisco. An organization for tea cognoscenti, the Tea Masters Association imports connoisseur-grade tea from Chinese tea farmers who raise their crops according to the Association's demanding standards. The group then sells these stocks to its members, at $150 to $2,500 a pound. Some 421 varieties of the finest teas are available, and nonmembers can order through a catalog as well.

Not everyone can match Wallis and Fong's tea connoisseurship. (Wallis drinks 20 to 30 cups a day.) But even an introduction by them to the world of tea will delight you. Their report:

The tea plant, *Camellia sinensis*, is a member of the large family of flowering camellias that often decorate parks and gardens. The world's most popular beverage today, tea is produced everywhere from China to South America. The best known is black tea, although technically it is actually reddish in color. The mislabeling is thought to date to the 1600s, when a dark oolong tea from the Wu Yi mountains in China may have been exported via Dutch traders to Europe, and thanks to its dark color, incorrectly named black tea. Today, other types of tea, such as green, oolong, yellow, white, and puerh, are also popular.

In Western countries, tea is usually sold in teabags that infuse within a matter of seconds and produce a drink, referred to in its liquid form as liquor, which is somewhat more astringent than loose whole-leaf teas.

Every tea has an optimum technique for preparation, but the consumer can rely on a few basic tips. To avoid a bitter liquor, many commercial teabags may often be improved by steeping for 30 seconds or less in an open cup with very hot but not boiling water—temperatures generally not exceeding 185 degrees F. The resulting liquor will exhibit a lighter, sweeter flavor, and the bag may be infused a second or third time. Properly prepared tea should not taste bitter.

Loose whole-leaf tea is usually best prepared fresh by the cup. Loose green teas also enjoy lower temperature water and may be improved by steeping them for only a minute or two. The liquor is then drained from the leaves using a small utility strainer or the lid of a Chinese covered teacup (gaiwan) to retain the leaves in the cup. The leaves may be used again for additional infusions with slightly increased water temperature and steeping time, as desired. All subsequent infusions should be completed within an hour or so of the first immersion.

White and yellow teas are prepared in a similar manner. Loose red (black), oolong, and puerh teas may be prepared at higher water temperatures, but for the gourmet palate never at the boiling point. To the gourmet, tea is not a strong, coarse beverage that overwhelms the senses with bitter vengeance, but a smooth, sweet, and subtle taste sensation.

EXPERT SOURCE

For more information on tea connoisseurship or a catalog of special teas for mail order, contact:

The American Tea Masters Association
41 Sutter Street #1191
San Francisco, CA 94104
☎ 415–775–4227

F O O D

BLAST BACTERIA AT THE SOURCE

A new inspection system is in place, but it pays to take precautions

Food scares have become commonplace in recent years. In March 1997, 163 Michigan schoolchildren contracted the liver infection, hepatitis A, by eating strawberries imported from Mexico and processed in California. Some 25,000 cases of hepatitis A are reported to the Centers for Disease Control and Prevention annually. Millions of Americans get some form of food poisoning each year, resulting in up to 9,000 fatalities.

Some common sources are poorly processed foods, unpasteurized dairy products, and tainted meat, poultry, and seafood. The U.S. Department of Agriculture recently instituted a new inspection system to help identify tainted products, but the agency warns that some will probably continue to slip through. Here are precautions you can take:

■ **CLEAN KITCHEN EQUIPMENT.** Clean cutting boards with hot water and soap, or run them through a dishwasher. Always wash counter tops, utensils, dish cloths, and hands after exposure to raw meats and fish. Clean sponges in a dishwasher. Washing surfaces with an antibacterial cleanser is recommended.

■ **MELT WITH CARE.** Thaw frozen seafood and meat in the refrigerator, not at room temperature. Place them on a plate to catch juices.

■ **AVOID RAW FISH.** If you love raw shellfish or sushi, eat it only at reputable restaurants.

■ **FINISH THE JOB.** Undercooked ground meat and chicken, and raw eggs pose a major risk of food poisoning. Cooking at high temperatures can destroy most organisms. (See chart at right.)

■ **GERM WARFARE**
Use temperature to kill bacteria before they make you sick.

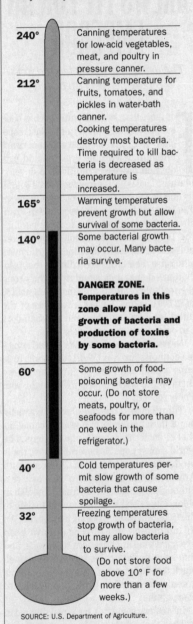

240°	Canning temperatures for low-acid vegetables, meat, and poultry in pressure canner.
212°	Canning temperature for fruits, tomatoes, and pickles in water-bath canner. Cooking temperatures destroy most bacteria. Time required to kill bacteria is decreased as temperature is increased.
165°	Warming temperatures prevent growth but allow survival of some bacteria.
140°	Some bacterial growth may occur. Many bacteria survive.
	DANGER ZONE. Temperatures in this zone allow rapid growth of bacteria and production of toxins by some bacteria.
60°	Some growth of food-poisoning bacteria may occur. (Do not store meats, poultry, or seafoods for more than one week in the refrigerator.)
40°	Cold temperatures permit slow growth of some bacteria that cause spoilage.
32°	Freezing temperatures stop growth of bacteria, but may allow bacteria to survive. (Do not store food above 10° F for more than a few weeks.)

SOURCE: U.S. Department of Agriculture.

EXPERT PICKS

THE JAMES BEARD COOKBOOK HALL OF FAME

The Cookbook Hall of Fame recognizes books that have significantly influenced the way we think about food and honored authors who possess an exceptional ability to communicate their gastronomic vision via the printed page. The first cookbook was inducted into the Hall of Fame in 1977.

1996 FRENCH PROVINCIAL COOKING, *Elizabeth David, Michael Joseph, 1960, out of print*

1995 LE TECHNIQUE *and* **LA METHODE,** *Jacques Pépin, Times Books;* Le Technique, *1976;* La Methode, *1979, out of print*

1994 GREENE ON GREENS, *Bert Greene, Workman Press, 1989*

1993 ALICE LET'S EAT, AMERICAN FRIED AND THIRD HELPINGS (THE TUMMY TRILOGY), *Calvin Trillin, FS&G, 1994*

1992 SIMPLE FRENCH FOOD, *Richard Olney, Macmillan, 1992*

1991 THE SILVER PALATE COOKBOOK, *Julee Rosso and Sheila Lukins with Michael McLaughlin, Workman Press, 1982*

1990 THE FOOD OF FRANCE and **THE FOOD OF ITALY,** *Waverley Root, Random House, 1992*

1989 THE ART OF EATING, *M. F .K. Fisher, Macmillan, 1990*

1988 No award given

1987 FOODS OF THE WORLD *(18 volumes, 1969–1972), Time-Life Books*

1986 MASTERING THE ART OF FRENCH COOKING, VOLUMES ONE AND TWO, *Volume One by Julia Child with Simone Beck and Louisette Bertholle; Volume Two by Julia Child with Simone Beck, Knopf, 1970*

1985 THE AMERICAN WOMAN'S COOKBOOK, *edited by Ruth Berolzheimer, Culinary Arts Institute, 1948, out of print*

1984 GEORGE AUGUSTE ESCOFFIER COOKBOOK COLLECTION, *George Auguste Escoffier, Van Nostrand Reinhold, 1979*

1983 THE JAMES BEARD COOKBOOK, *James Beard, Dutton, 1970, out of print*

1982 THE BETTY CROCKER COOKBOOK, *edited by Marjorie Child Hustad, Bentham, 1987, out of print*

1981 THE NEW YORK TIMES COOKBOOK, *Craig Claiborne, HarperCollins, 1990*

1980 THE CORDON BLEU COOKBOOK, *Dione Lucas, Little , Brown, 1947*

1979 THE FANNIE FARMER COOKBOOK, *Fannie Merritt Farmer, Knopf, 1983*

1978 THE JOY OF COOKING, *Irma Rombauer, Dutton, 1991*

1977 THE SETTLEMENT COOKBOOK, *Mrs. Simon (Lillian) Kander, Simon & Schuster, 1976*

■ SELECTED JAMES BEARD FOUNDATION 1997 COOKBOOK AWARD WINNERS

COOKBOOK OF THE YEAR

THE BOOK OF JEWISH FOOD: AN ODYSSEY FROM SAMARKAND TO NEW YORK, *Claudia Roden, Alfred A Knopf, 1996*

SINGLE SUBJECT

THE PASTA BIBLE, *Christian Teubner, Silvio Rizzi, and Tan Lee Leng,Penguin , 1996*

HEALTHY-FOCUS

MOOSEWOOD RESTAURANT LOW-FAT FAVORITES, *The Moosewood Collective, Clarkson Potter, 1996*

VEGETARIAN

1000 VEGETARIAN RECIPES, *Carol Gelles, Macmillan USA, 1996*

LOOKING GREAT

CONTACTS: Lenses that can protect your eyes from sun damage, PAGE 152 **MAKEUP:** An expert's tips on creating your own look, PAGE 153 **BALDNESS:** New treatment options offer hope for patients with thinning hair, PAGE 155 **COSMETIC SURGERY:** A guide to common procedures, PAGE 156 **SKIN:** Laser technology can help erase wrinkles, PAGE 159 **COSTS:** What cosmetic surgeons charge to fix your nose or tuck your tummy, PAGE 161

SKIN CARE
▼

LESSONS FROM THE AGING WARS

You can't erase genetic makeup; you can avoid damage from the sun

At first, it's merely a few laugh lines around your eyes, then tiny wrinkles appear around the mouth. Gradually, eyelids begin to droop and a double chin shows up uninvited. As inevitable as the aging process may be, however, there is great variability in how youthful different people appear at the same age. Everyone wants to look like Grace Kelly at age 50, Audrey Hepburn at age 60, or Claudette Colbert at 70, but few people take the preventive measures necessary to maintain youthful-looking skin.

Two factors are critical in determining how your skin ages: genetics and sun exposure. To some extent your skin's appearance is predetermined by genetic traits inherited from your parents. In addition, fair-skinned people are more likely than the more dark-complexioned to age prematurely or to develop skin cancer from sun exposure. That's because the fairer-skinned have less pigment to protect them from the sun's rays and are more susceptible to the process known as photoaging, which comes from the cumulative exposure a person receives to the sun.

Photoaging actually plays a bigger role in your skin's appearance than your chronological age. Skin can age as a result of getting too much sun over a short period of time, as well as from the gradual damage of long-term exposure. But most damage occurs by the time you reach age 18. "If you were dealt a bad hand genetically, and you want to make sure you don't get advanced signs of aging, the best thing you can do is avoid the sun," explains Dr. Cherie Ditre, a prominent Philadelphia dermatologist and researcher. Below is a guide to what you can expect of your skin from your 20s through your 50s, and what you can do to combat the toll of time:

■ **THE TWENTIES.** "No one is as gorgeous as a woman in her early 20s. This is the best you're ever going to look," says Dr. Wilma Bergfeld, head of clinical research for the department of dermatology at the Cleveland Clinic Foundation and past president of the American Academy of Dermatology. By the time you reach the late 20s, fine lines will probably develop around the mouth and eyes and be noticeable when you wear makeup. If you become pregnant, you may develop brown spots on your face, either now or later; sun exposure exacerbates the problem.

But how fast your skin ages depends on whether you stay out of the sun and use sunscreen religiously (see box). Other skin-

THE SHIELD YOU NEED AGAINST THE SUN

Sun smarts begin with a cream or lotion with a rating of at least SPF 15

It's hard to pinpoint when Americans went around the bend in worshiping the bronzed god, but Hollywood no doubt bears a large measure of blame. Even before George Hamilton or Annette Funicello's antics proved that the suntanned had more fun, moviegoers had already been subjected to years of glamorous palm-tree and fun-in-the-sun imagery.

That cinematic fantasy, happily perpetrated by suntan lotion advertising, remains alive today. According to a recent survey for the American Academy of Dermatology, 59 percent of Americans view a tan as a sign of health and find that it enhances appearance.

The key to being "sun smart" is to use a sunscreen on exposed skin whenever you're outside. To help you choose the appropriate level of protection, the U.S. Food and Drug Administration now requires all sunscreen makers to rate the protective power of each product. A sunscreen with a sun protection factor (SPF) of 2, for example, allows you to stay in the sun without getting burned for twice as long as would otherwise be possible without a screen; an SPF of 8 gives you eight times the protection, and so on. Words of wisdom to keep in mind:

■ **Choose a sunscreen with at least SPF 15.** Dermatologists say this is necessary to ensure the filtering out of most UV-B rays, the part of the ultraviolet light spectrum most responsible for sunburn and skin cancer.

■ **Make sure the sunscreen also guards against UV-A rays.** SPF only addresses a sunscreen's ability to guard against UV-B radiation. Researchers have recently discovered that another kind of ultraviolet radiation, known as UV-A, harms the skin's connective tissue, resulting in visible aging and contributing to skin cancer in some cases.

■ **Reapply sunscreen after exercise or swimming.** Water magnifies the power of ultraviolet rays, ensuring that you will burn even more quickly in the water than on the beach unless the sunscreen you use is water-resistant. Even if it is, it's a good idea to reapply it after leaving the water to ensure full protection.

saving strategies include not smoking, controlling your weight, and maintaining good health. "It's like anything else—if you wait until the damage is done, it's pretty hard to turn it around," says Bergfeld.

■ **THE THIRTIES.** The first real signs of aging usually become apparent after age 30. That's when you'll start to notice more fine wrinkles, see the skin on your eyelids begin to droop, and find the circles under your eyes becoming darker and maybe even puffy. Smokers will develop even more lines around their eyes and mouth.

For many women, the discovery of those first few wrinkles are enough to send them directly to the cosmetics counter. Happily, some products show promise in counteracting the damaging effects of the sun. There's no doubt, says Bergfeld, that simply moisturizing can reduce fine wrinkling up to about 16 percent.

If you're looking for something more potent, moisturizers containing alpha hydroxy acids (AHAs) derived from fruit, sugar cane, or lactic acid exfoliate, or shed the upper layer of skin, exposing newer skin. Recent research by Dr. Ditre, a clinical assistant professor of dermatology at Hahnemann University Hospital and Abington

Memorial Hospital near Philadelphia, suggests that using AHAs can even reverse some of the signs of photoaging. In a study of 17 adults with severely sun-damaged skin, a lotion with a 25 percent concentration of AHA thickened the outer layers of the skin, increased its elasticity, and lightened age spots. (Over-the-counter formulations contain anywhere from a 2 percent to 10 percent concentration of AHA and prescription formulas have about 15 percent.) There is no evidence, however, that you can prevent wrinkles or turn back the aging clock with AHAs, even in the higher concentrations found in prescription-only formulas. AHAs, says, Ditre, are "not a facelift in a jar."

■ **THE FORTIES.** Between ages 40 and 50, your skin loses its collagen and elastin (tissues that keep skin firm and plump), which means wrinkles get bigger and deeper and your skin begins to sag. In addition, your skin gets drier and appears more sallow, pores get larger, eyelids droop more, frown lines show themselves, and flat brown spots called liver or age spots appear.

FACT FILE:
CONTACTS CAN PROTECT AGAINST THE SUN

■ *Most people know that their skin needs sun protection. But too much sun can also increase the risk of developing premature cataracts or degeneration of the retina. Now there are contact lenses that can absorb the sun's harmful rays. A study by Dr. Nadia-Marie Quesnel of the University of Montreal College of Optometry found that contact lenses with a built-in UV filter provide better protection against UV rays than regular contacts. However, warns Quesnel, UV-blocking lenses don't eliminate the need for sunglasses.*

At this stage, says Bergfeld, you should routinely inspect your face and body for potentially cancerous lesions and investigate any suspicious moles or growths, because you're more susceptible to developing skin cancer. (By the year 2000, skin cancer is expected to be the most widely diagnosed cancer in the United States.)

If you already have extensive wrinkling, you may be a candidate for Retin A at this age. Recently reformulated and renamed Renova, the acne cream derived from Vitamin A has long been prescribed to fight wrinkles, even though it was only recently approved by the Food and Drug Administration (FDA) to treat sun-damaged skin. As the first wrinkle cream to be approved by the FDA, Renova diminishes fine wrinkles and lightens and smoothes skin that has turned brown or rough. Renova cannot increase elasticity, eliminate deep wrinkles, or rejuvenate dull or sallow skin, however. "It can't turn a woman who's never taken care of her skin into a youthful 20-year-old," says Bergfeld, "but it can bring about an impressive skin change that people notice."

Drawbacks shouldn't be ignored, however. Most people who use it experience temporary redness, dryness, itching, peeling, and a slight burning sensation. For pregnant women and nursing mothers, the medication is entirely off-limits. Moreover, the cream has no lasting benefits if you stop using it.

■ **THE FIFTIES.** The changes that began two decades ago evolve still more—deeper wrinkles, especially around the eyes and mouth; sagging, dry skin; and age spots. By now, your wrinkles are clearly noticeable if you've spent a lot of time tanning yourself over the years, or if you smoke. You're also more likely to see wrinkles if your weight has fluctuated significantly. "It's like stretching a balloon," says Bergfeld. "If it collapses after a while, the skin is real wrinkled and the wrinkles are exaggerated." Aesthetically at least, it's better to keep on a few extra pounds because it acts as a filler, says Bergfeld. "Aging women may have to put up with a fatter body for a better-looking face."

FACE TO FACE WITH CHRISTIE BRINKLEY

Tips from a top makeup artist to the world's most beautiful women

Are you unhappy with your looks? Plagued by freckles or a prominent nose? Do you think your lips are too small or too big? Well, take heart in the fact that even supermodels like Christie Brinkley, Kate Moss, and Christy Turlington struggle with beauty crises and skin care woes, according to Bobbi Brown, who is makeup artist to these beauties and others such as Meg Ryan, Tina Turner, and Brooke Shields. Brown believes the problem lies not with women but with conventional notions of beauty.

The key to being perceived as pretty, says Brown, author of *Bobbi Brown Beauty: The Ultimate Beauty Resource* (HarperCollins, 1997), is to exude self-confidence, by being satisfied with your looks and developing an individual beauty style. "My crusade is to make women comfortable in their own skin," says Brown, founder of Bobbi Brown Essentials, a line of cosmetic and skin care products. We asked Brown how cosmetics can help you achieve a face you can love. Here, Brown offers her expertise.

■ **DON'T FIX IT, ENHANCE IT.** First of all, things like a small mouth and big nose are traits, not flaws. Sadly, women who have these features have been taught not to like them. The challenge is to reverse this way of thinking. For me, the question is not how do you fix it? It's taking the features that make you who you are, and making the most of them. Accept the features you have, learn to feel good about them, and start playing them up.

■ **USE THE RIGHT FOUNDATION.** Flaws like uneven skin colorations and dark circles under the eyes should be concealed. But it has to be done naturally. A bad concealer looks worse than dark circles. It's important to use a yellow-toned concealer. Using the right foundation for your skin is key. I only apply oil-free foundation on oily skin because most women need some moisture. The trick to finding the right foundation is to apply it on the side of your face. If it disappears, then it's the right one.

■ **DON'T COVER UP WRINKLES.** The closest thing I've found to a miracle in skin care is alpha hydroxy acid, which gives the skin a smoother look. Don't try to cover up wrinkles. Instead, apply a brighter blush on the cheeks or line the eyes to make them more prominent.

■ **DIET AND EXERCISE TO RESCUE LACKLUSTER SKIN.** I've found that the more you exercise and feel healthy, the younger and fresher you look. If I eat well, I look good. Drinking a lot of water also works for me, both by staving off my appetite and giving my skin a clearer plumped-up appearance.

■ **CHANGE YOUR MAKEUP SEASONALLY.** In the summer, wear less makeup, softer more pastel colors, and a bronzer instead of foundation. In the fall, wear moisturizer and foundation and richer lipstick colors like plums and burgundies. Changing the color of your lipstick is not an absolute necessity every season. I wear nude lipstick year-round, and a lot of women who wear red lipstick do the same thing. But the easiest and quickest way to change your look is by changing lipstick color.

■ **DON'T TAKE TRENDS TOO FAR.** Makeup that appears on the runway isn't necessarily meant to be worn on the streets. Don't take trends too literally. For example, if a model is wearing black lipstick on the runway, you might want to go for a darker tone than you normally wear. If the look is lots of shine, use shimmer on select spots, not everywhere. It's what works on you that matters.

■ **MAKE MAKEUP LAST.** The trick to having makeup last for hours is to layer creamy and dry textures. A concealer, for example, is

A LITTLE MAKEUP GOES A LONG WAY

Cosmetic counters are bursting with beauty products. Which ones really work wonders? Here are some of the favorite beauty aids of top makeup artist Liz Michael, along with her comments:

FOUNDATION

VIRTUAL SKIN FOUNDATION
by Prescriptives
■ A natural matte finish that's completely oil free and really lasts all day. For normal to oily skin.

LIQUID MAKEUP
by Stila
■ Ultra-sheer finish, oil-free, and a great selection of colors.

SATIN FOUNDATION
by M.A.C
■ An emollient formula that makes skin look dewy and young. Incredible on older skin.

POWDER & BLUSH

POWDER
by Le Clerc
■ An ultra-fine powder with a slight yellow undertone, it's a natural for fair to medium skin. Banane is the most popular color.

POMMETTE
by Lancôme
■ Cream blush with an ultra-soft, satin finish that gives skin a soft glow.

EYESHADOW, PENCILS & MASCARA

COMPACT DISC EYESHADOW IN BROWN #7
by Estée Lauder
■ A basic brown that looks good on anyone.

SATIN TAUPE
by M.A.C
■ A grayish brown frost with a hint of silver. A little glamorous, yet natural.

ALL ABOUT EVE
by Nars
■ An eyeshadow duo with champagne and beige that has a sheer, transparent finish with a satin shimmer. Ultra bare look, but it opens eyes.

SHADOWLINER
by Clinique
■ A soft eyelining pencil that's powder-like, velvety, and blends easily.

FRINGE BENEFITS MASCARA
by Origins
■ Silky and glossy, with an exceptional brush.

LIPCOLOR

SHEER INDOLENCE
by Poppy
■ The best natural lipcolor. A soft, pink-brown, it suits almost everyone.

SHEER LIPSTICK, PLUM STAIN
by Prescriptives
■ Sheer, with a little more color than your lips. Looks good on most women.

RAISIN
by Face Stockholm
■ A deep, red brown—a great red color.

SKIN CARE PRODUCT

CALMING COMPOSITION
by Aveda
■ A light oil for sensitive, dry, or irritated skin, which removes makeup and soothes the skin. Use it as a treatment or as a moisturizer.

---

moist and will stay on only if you layer it with a dry powder. I can't emphasize enough how important powder is for locking in makeup. Also, lipstick will stay on longer if you apply color with a lip pencil over it. And using moistened eyeshadow to line your eyes instead of a pencil will result in longer-wearing eye liner.

■ **EXPECT BAD BEAUTY DAYS.** Most women tend to put more makeup on when they're having a bad day, but that only makes matters worse. If you're not looking your best, skip the foundation that day. Use a tinted moisturizer and blush instead. And drink lots of water. On a bad day, I wear a baseball cap and sunglasses.

HAIR LOSS

DON'T WANT TO BE LIKE MIKE?

From minoxidil to hair transplants, what you can do to treat balding

When it comes to hair loss, men are often as vain about their looks as many women. Eager to restore hair to its youthful fullness, balding men spend thousands of dollars on "miracle cures" and other desperate measures to salvage their locks and their looks. "It's so traumatic, they'll go to any lengths to get their hair back," says Dr. Deirdre Marshall, associate clinical professor of plastic surgery at the University of Miami Medical School and chief of plastic surgery at the Miami Veterans Hospital. Fortunately, balding men today have many treatment options.

The least invasive option is using Rogaine (minoxidil), the only proven medical method to thwart hair loss and grow new hair. Rogaine is available over-the-counter (about $30 for a month's supply) and works best in men with typical male pattern baldness—in which the hair line is receding at the corners of the forehead and crown—and in women with thinning hair. However, spraying Rogaine on thinning hair daily doesn't have a dramatic effect on its growth, and the new hair is baby fine. Also, Rogaine is not suitable for people with some medical conditions such as high blood pressure.

The only tried-and-true hair replacement method is a hair transplant, a surgical technique that involves moving tiny pieces of the scalp from the back of the head, where hair is plentiful, to the area on top or in front of the head, where balding is occurring.

Today's transplant technology makes it possible to perform more refined grafts, such as "minigrafts," in which two to six follicles are transplanted in tiny clusters or circles, and "micrografts," in which groups of just one to four hairs transplanted in a staggered pattern. The effect is a more natural hairline than with earlier approaches using 25 to 50 hairs. However, the new procedures are more difficult and time consuming.

The best candidates for transplants are men with typical male pattern baldness and most women, who tend to lose hair all over. Men and women should consider undergoing transplant surgery as soon as they start to lose hair, says Dr. Barry Resnik, a clinical instructor of dermatology at the University of Miami Medical School: "When you have enough hair, it looks imperceptible."

There are other less common procedures, such as the scalp flap, in which a chunk of scalp (with hair) is removed from the back of the head and moved to the front. Another option is a scalp reduction. In this procedure, the bald spot is cut out of the top of the head, then the skin with hair is pulled higher on the head and the edges are sewn together.

The average cost of a transplant is $2,100, but more than one surgery is often necessary. And, says Dr. Marshall, "If patients keep going bald, and they want to have a normal-looking hair pattern, they'll have to come back and have more transplants."

While there's no board certification required of doctors who treat hair loss, most are dermatologists or plastic surgeons. Be sure to select a well-trained doctor who's performed the surgery often.

EXPERT TIPS

Anthony Santangelo of the American Hair Loss Council advises on how not to pick a hairpiece:

■ **Don't choose one with too much hair.**

■ **Don't pick an unrealistic hairline. A 40-year-old, for example, shouldn't have bangs.**

■ **Don't try to cover up gray hair with a hairpiece. If you have some gray, match the piece with it.**

THE NEXT BEST THING TO BEING REAL

Facial implants and chemical peels have joined tummy tucks and nose jobs in the panoply of cosmetic procedures that appearance-conscious Americans are resorting to in increasing numbers. The American Society of Plastic and Reconstructive Surgeons provides this guide to today's most-elected interventions with nature.

BREAST ENLARGEMENT

Augmentation Mammoplasty. Enhances the size and shape of breasts using artificial implants.

■ **PROCEDURE:** Lasts 1 to 2 hours. Local anesthesia with sedation, or general. Usually outpatient.

■ **SIDE EFFECTS:** Temporary swelling, change in nipple sensation, bruising, breasts sensitive to stimulation for a few weeks.

■ **RECOVERY:** Back to work in 2 to 4 weeks. More strenuous activity after 4 to 6 weeks or more. Fading and flattening of scars: 3 months to 2 years.

■ **RISKS:** Blood clots. Infection. Bleeding under the skin flap. Poor healing resulting in conspicuous scarring or skin loss. Need for a second operation.

■ **DURATION:** Permanent.

BREAST LIFT

Mastopexy. Raises and reshapes sagging breasts by removing excess skin and repositioning remaining tissue and nipples.

■ **PROCEDURE:** Lasts 1 1/2 to 3 1/2 hours. Local anesthesia with sedation, or general. Usually outpatient. Some-

times inpatient 1 to 2 days.

■ **SIDE EFFECTS:** Temporary bruising, swelling, discomfort, numbness, dry breast skin. Permanent scars.

■ **RECOVERY:** Back to work in a week.

■ **RISKS:** Thick, wide scars; skin loss; infection. Unevenly positioned nipples. Permanent loss of feeling in nipples or breast.

■ **DURATION:** Variable; gravity, pregnancy, aging, and weight changes may cause new sagging. May last longer when combined with implants.

CHEMICAL PEEL

Phenol, trichloracetic acid (TCA). Restores wrinkled, blemished, unevenly pigmented or sun-damaged facial skin, using a chemical solution to peel away skin's top layers. Works best on fair, thin skin with superficial wrinkles.

■ **PROCEDURE:** Takes 1 to 2 hours for full face. No anesthesia—sedation and EKG monitoring may be used. Usually outpatient. Full-face phenol peel may require admission for 1 to 2 days.

■ **SIDE EFFECTS:** Both: Temporary throbbing, tingling, swelling redness; acute sensitivity to sun. Phenol: Permanent lightening of treated skin; permanent loss of ability to tan.

■ **RECOVERY:** Phenol: Formation of new skin in 7 to 21 days. Normal activities in 2 to 4 weeks. Full healing and fading of redness in 3 to 6

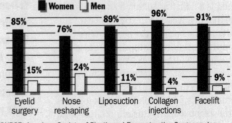

■ **SEX DISTRIBUTION**

Eyelid surgery is most popular among women, but men prefer to have their noses altered.

Sex distribution of aesthetic procedures, 1996.

■ Women □ Men

	Women	Men
Eyelid surgery	85%	15%
Nose reshaping	76%	24%
Liposuction	89%	11%
Collagen injections	96%	4%
Facelift	91%	9%

months. TCA: New skin within 5 to 10 days.

■ **RISKS:** Both: Tiny whiteheads (temporary); infection; scarring; flare-up of skin allergies, fever blisters, cold sores. Phenol: Abnormal color changes (permanent); heart irregularities (rare).

■ **DURATION:** Phenol is permanent, although new wrinkles may form as skin ages. TCA is variable (temporary).

COLLAGEN/FAT INJECTIONS

Plumps up creased, furrowed, or sunken facial skin; adds fullness to lips and backs of hands. Works best on thin, dry, light-colored skin.

■ **PROCEDURE:** Lasts 15 minutes to 1 hour per session. Collagen: usually no anesthesia; local may be included with the injection. Fat requires local anesthesia. Outpatient.

■ **SIDE EFFECTS:** Temporary

stinging, throbbing, or burning sensation. Faint redness, swelling, excess fullness.

■ **RISKS:** Collagen: allergic reactions including rash, hives, swelling, or flulike symptoms; possible triggering of connective-tissue or autoimmune diseases. Both: contour irregularities; infection.

■ **DURATION:** Variable, from a few months to as long as a year.

DERMABRASION

Mechanical scraping of the top layers of skin using a high-speed rotary wheel. Softens sharp edges of surface irregularities, including acne and other scars and fine wrinkles, especially around mouth.

■ **PROCEDURE:** Lasts a few minutes to 1½ hours. May require more sessions. Anesthesia: Local, numbing spray, or general. Usually outpatient.

■ **SIDE EFFECTS:** Temporary

tingling, burning, itching, swelling, redness. Lightening of treated skin, acute sensitivity to sun; loss of ability to tan.

■ **RECOVERY:** Back to work in 2 weeks. More strenuous activities in 4 to 6 weeks. Fading of redness in about 3 months. Return of pigmentation/sun exposure in 6 to 12 months.

■ **RISKS:** Abnormal color changes (permanent). Tiny whiteheads (temporary). Infection. Scarring. Flare-up of skin allergies, fever blisters, cold sores.

■ **DURATION:** Permanent, but new wrinkles may form as skin ages.

EYELID SURGERY

Blepharoplasty. Corrects drooping upper eyelids and puffy bags below the eyes by removing excess fat, skin, and muscle. (May be covered by insurance if used to improve vision.)

■ **PROCEDURE:** Lasts 1 to 3 hours. Usually, local anesthesia with sedation, occasionally general. Usually outpatient.

■ **SIDE EFFECTS:** Temporary discomfort, tightness of lids, swelling, bruising. Temporary dryness, burning, itching of eyes. Excessive tearing, sensitivity to light for first few weeks.

■ **RISKS:** Temporary blurred or double vision; blindness (extremely rare). Infection. Swelling at corners of eyelids; tiny whiteheads. Slight asymmetry in healing or

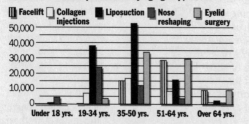

■ **AGE DISTRIBUTION**

People want nose work first, but face lifts become increasingly popular as the years go by.

Number of aesthetic procedures by age group, 1996.

Legend: Facelift | Collagen injections | Liposuction | Nose reshaping | Eyelid surgery

Y-axis: 0, 10,000, 20,000, 30,000, 40,000, 50,000
X-axis: Under 18 yrs. | 19-34 yrs. | 35-50 yrs. | 51-64 yrs. | Over 64 yrs.

SOURCE: American Society of Plastic and Reconstructive Surgeons, Inc.

scarring. Difficulty in closing eyes completely (rarely permanent). Pulling down of the lower lids (may require further surgery).

■ **RECOVERY:** Reading in 2 or 3 days. Back to work in 7 to 10 days. Contact lenses in 2 weeks or more. Strenuous activities, alcohol in about 3 weeks. Bruising and swelling gone in several weeks.

■ **DURATION:** Several years to permanent.

FACE-LIFT

Rhytidectomy. Improves sagging facial skin, jowls, and loose neck skin by removing excess, tightening muscles, redraping skin. Most often done on men and women over 40.

■ **PROCEDURE:** Lasts several hours. Anesthesia: Local with sedation, or general. Usually outpatient. Some patients may require short inpatient stay.

■ **SIDE EFFECTS:** Temporary bruising, swelling, numbness, and tenderness of skin; tight feeling, dry skin. For men, permanent need to shave behind ears, where beard-growing skin is repositioned.

■ **RECOVERY:** Back to work in 10 to 14 days. More strenuous activity in 2 weeks or more. Bruising gone in 2 to 3 weeks. Limit exposure to sun for several months.

■ **RISKS:** Injury to the nerves that control facial muscles, loss of feeling (usually temporary but may be permanent). Infection. Poor healing, excessive scarring. Change in hairline.

■ **DURATION:** Usually about 5 to 10 years.

FACIAL IMPLANTS

Change the basic shape and balance of the face using care-

fully styled implants to build up a receding chin, add prominence to cheekbones, or reshape the jawline. Implants may be natural or artificial.

■ **PROCEDURE:** Lasts 30 minutes to 2 hours. Anesthesia: Local with sedation, or general. Usually outpatient. Occasionally requires overnight stay.

■ **SIDE EFFECTS:** Temporary discomfort, swelling, bruising, numbness and/or stiffness. In jaw surgery, inability to open mouth fully for several weeks.

■ **RECOVERY:** Back to work in about a week. Normal appearance in 2 to 4 weeks. Activity that could jar face after 6 weeks or more.

■ **RISKS:** Shifting or imprecise positioning of implant, or infection around it, requiring a second operation or removal. Excess tightening and hardening of scar tissue around an artificial implant ("capsular contracture"), causing an unnatural shape.

■ **DURATION:** Permanent.

FOREHEAD-LIFT

Brow-lift. Minimize forehead creases, drooping eyebrows, hooding over eyes, furrowed forehead, and frown lines by removing excess tissue and redraping skin. Most often done on people over 40.

■ **PROCEDURE:** Length: 1 to 2 hours. Anesthesia: Local with sedation, or

---

FACT FILE:

GRACE KELLY, WHERE ARE YOU?

■ *"Celebrities set the tone for what we think of as beauty," says Dr. Alan Matarasso, associate clinical professor of plastic surgery at Albert Einstein College of Medicine in New York City. Some people—especially women—request the facial features of a star. Some of the more common requests: Claudia Schiffer's lips, Sharon Stone's nose, and 15 years after her death, Grace Kelly's facial shape. Most surgeons warn patients, however, that changing a feature won't make them look exactly like the celebrity.*

general. Usually outpatient.
■ **SIDE EFFECTS:** Temporary
swelling, numbness, head-
aches, bruising. Possible
itching and hair loss for
several months. Change in
hairline.
■ **RECOVERY:** Back to work in
7 to 10 days. More strenuous
activity after several weeks.
Bruising gone after 2 to 3
weeks. Limited exposure to
sun for several months.
■ **RISKS:** Injury to facial
nerve, causing loss of
motion, muscle weakness,
or asymmetrical look.
Infection. Broad or excessive scarring.
■ **DURATION:** Usually about 5
to 10 years.

HAIR REPLACEMENT SURGERY
*Fill in balding areas with
the patient's own hair using
a variety of techniques including scalp reduction, tissue expansion, strip grafts,
scalp flaps, or clusters of
punch grafts.*

■ **PROCEDURE:** Lasts 1 to 3
hours. Some techniques
may require multiple pro-
cedures over 18 months
or more. Anesthesia: Usu-
ally local with sedation.
Flaps and tissue expansion
may may be done under
general anesthesia. Usually
outpatient.
■ **SIDE EFFECTS:** Temporary
aching, tight scalp. An
unnatural look in early
stages.
■ **RECOVERY:** Back to work:
usually in 2 to 5 days. More
strenuous activities after 10

A LIGHT TOUCH-UP FOR YOUR FACE
*High-tech lasers do a great job with facial
creases, but it's a pricey new technique*

A new technique known as laser resurfacing that literally zaps wrinkles off your face is the latest high-
tech innovation to stave off the signs of aging.

The CO_2 laser, the type used for aesthetic treatments
such as removing visible blood vessels, port wine stains,
birthmarks, and tattoos, produces intense, short bursts
of light that vaporize skin tissue. The laser removes thin
layers of damaged skin, smoothes the skin's surface, and
allows new collagen to form, giving skin a tighter
appearance. Laser resurfacing (also known as laser-
brasion or laser peeling) can remove age spots, soften
fine wrinkles, lift droopy eyelids, and heal acne scars.

Sound too good to be true? Well, consider the cost:
about $3,000 to $5,000 to "resurface" the entire face and
roughly $2,000 for specific areas like crow's feet—fees
that are rarely covered by health insurance.

Despite its high price tag, laser resurfacing is quickly
becoming one of the most popular cosmetic procedures
because it's safer and more precise than another popular nonsurgical method of smoothing aging skin—
chemical peels that use various types of acid to exfoliate
and remove the superficial layers of skin. Unlike moderate or deep-depth chemical peels that can scar the skin
or cause an infection, laser resurfacing doesn't cause
significant scarring and is bloodless and relatively
painless. While skin will appear red for a couple of
weeks, and a flushed look may persist for more than a
month, "The laser is probably a safer way to do skin
resurfacing because you can see how deep into the skin
you're going," says New York City plastic surgeon Dr.
Paul Weiss. With chemical peels, he explains, you only
know how deep you go by the type of chemical used.

A caveat: Laser resurfacing has only been performed
for a few years and there are no studies yet proving its
long-term safety and effectiveness. "Because the procedure doesn't have a long track record, we have to be cautious in whom we recommend it to," says Dr. Weiss. A
further caution: Patients considering laser resurfacing
should make sure the dermatologist or plastic surgeon
has ample experience in this procedure because in the
wrong hands, the laser could burn facial skin.

days to 3 weeks. Final look: may be 18 months or more, depending on procedure.
■ **RISKS:** Unnatural look. Infection. Excessive scarring. Failure to "take." Loss of scalp tissue and/or transplanted hair.
■ **DURATION:** Permanent.

LIPOSUCTION

Suction-assisted lipectomy. Improve body shape using tube and vacuum device to remove unwanted fat deposits that don't respond to dieting and exercise. Locations include chin, cheeks, neck, upper arms, above breasts, abdomen, buttocks, hips, thighs, knees, calves, ankles.

■ **PROCEDURE:** Lasts 1 to 2 hours or more, depending on extent of surgery. Anesthesia: Local, epidural, or general. Usually outpatient. Extensive procedures may require short inpatient stay.
■ **SIDE EFFECTS:** Temporary bruising, swelling, numbness, burning sensation.
■ **RECOVERY:** Back to work in 1 to 2 weeks. More strenuous activity after 2 to 4 weeks. Swelling and bruising may last 1 to 6 months or more.
■ **RISKS:** Infection. Excessive fluid loss leading to shock. Fluid accumulation. Injury to the skin. Bagginess of skin. Pigmentation changes (may become permanent if exposed to sun).
■ **DURATION:** Permanent, with sensible diet and exercise.

MALE BREAST REDUCTION

Gynecomastia. Reduce enlarged breasts in men using liposuction and/or cutting out excess glandular tissue. (Sometimes covered by medical insurance.)

■ **PROCEDURE:** Lasts 1¹/₂ hours or more. Anesthesia: general or local. Usually outpatient.
■ **SIDE EFFECTS:** Temporary bruising, swelling, numbness, soreness, burning sensation.
■ **RECOVERY:** Back to work in 3 to 7 days. More strenuous activity after 2 to 3 weeks. Swelling and bruising subsides in 3 to 6 months.
■ **RISKS:** Infection. Excessive fluid loss leading to shock. Fluid accumulation. Injury to the skin. Bagginess of skin. Pigmentation changes (may become permanent if exposed to sun). Excessive scarring if tissue was cut away. Need for second procedure to remove additional tissue.
■ **DURATION:** Permanent.

NOSE SURGERY

Rhinoplasty. Reshape nose by altering size, removing hump, changing shape of tip or bridge, narrowing span of nostrils, or changing angle between nose and upper lip. May relieve some breathing problems .

■ **PROCEDURE:** Length: 1 to 2 hours or more. Local anesthesia with sedation, or general. Usually outpatient.
■ **SIDE EFFECTS:** Temporary swelling, bruising around eyes and nose, and headaches. Some bleeding and stuffiness.
■ **RECOVERY:** Back to work or school in 1 to 2 weeks. More strenuous activities after 2 to 3 weeks. Avoid hitting nose or sunburn for 8 weeks. Final appearance after a year or more.
■ **RISKS:** Infection. Small burst blood vessels resulting in tiny, permanent red spots. Incomplete improvement, requiring additional surgery.
■ **DURATION:** Permanent.

TUMMY TUCK

Abdominoplasty. Flatten abdomen by removing excess fat and skin and tightening muscles of abdominal wall.

■ **PROCEDURE:** Lasts 2 to 5 hours. Anesthesia: General, or local with sedation. In- or outpatient.
■ **SIDE EFFECTS:** Temporary pain. Swelling, soreness, numbness of abdominal skin, bruising, tiredness for weeks or months.
■ **RECOVERY:** Back to work in 2 to 4 weeks. More strenuous activity after 4 to 6 weeks or more. Fading and flattening of scars in 3 months to 2 years.
■ **RISKS:** Blood clots. Infection. Bleeding under the skin flap. Poor healing resulting in conspicuous scarring or skin loss. Need for a second operation.
■ **DURATION:** Permanent.

SOURCE: American Society of Plastic and Reconstructive Surgeons, Inc.

PAY AND PLAY AS YOU GO

From Manhattan to Hollywood, what plastic surgery costs

Procedure	CALIFORNIA	NEW YORK	FLORIDA	TEXAS
BREAST AUGMENTATION	$3,077	$4,105	$2,700	$3,004
BREAST LIFT	$3,541	$5,163	$3,375	$3,219
BREAST RECONSTRUCTION				
Implant alone	$2,588	$3,832	$2,839	$2,382
Tissue expander	$3,392	$4,222	$3,049	$2,787
Latissimus dorsi	$5,408	$6,468	$4,989	$5,073
TRAM (pedicle) flap	$6,152	$8,159	$6,892	$6,227
Microsurgical free flap	$6,484	$6,812	$7,773	$7,334
BREAST REDUCTION	$4,885	$6,426	$5,229	$4,732
BREAST REDUCTION IN MEN	$2,414	$3,652	$2,597	$2,292
BUTTOCK LIFT	$3,618	$5,821	$2,993	$3,215
CHEEK IMPLANTS	$2,106	$2,892	$1,783	$1,788
CHEMICAL PEEL				
Full face	$1,638	$1,969	$1,638	$1,622
Regional	$684	$1,027	$625	$626
CHIN AUGMENTATION				
Implant	$1,420	$2,050	$1,347	$1,207
Osteotomy	$2,164	$2,850	$2,067	$2,239
COLLAGEN INJECTIONS PER 1 CC	$281	$340	$284	$270
DERMABRASION	$1,634	$2,075	$1,716	$1,479
EYELID SURGERY				
Both uppers	$1,702	$2,180	$1,597	$1,451
Both lowers	$1,765	$2,277	$1,588	$1,468
Combination of both	$3,049	$3,977	$2,611	$2,591
FACE-LIFT	$4,547	$6,625	$4,464	$4,304
FAT INJECTION				
Head/neck	$822	$873	$833	$718
Trunk	$728	$1,413	$917	$584
Extremities	$787	$1,568	$873	$530
FOREHEAD-LIFT	$2,474	$3,431	$2,175	$2,266
LIPOSUCTION—any single site	$1,960	$2,450	$1,782	$1,481
MALE-PATTERN BALDNESS				
Plug grafts–per plug	$799	$653	$23	$1,348
Strip grafts–per strip	$555	$1,000	$600	$750
Scalp reduction–all stages	$2,536	$2,625	$2,800	$1,000
Pedicle flap–all stages	$2,613	$3,500	$3,600	N/A
Tissue expansion–all stages	$3,109	$3,000	$2,275	$5,000
NOSE RESHAPING (primary)				
Open rhinoplasty	$3,268	$4,386	$3,129	$3,084
Closed rhinoplasty	$3,110	$4,659	$3,045	$2,715
NOSE RESHAPING (secondary)				
Open rhinoplasty	$3,085	$4,359	$3,343	$2,919
Closed rhinoplasty	$3,028	$4,742	$3,330	$2,872
RETIN-A TREATMENT per visit	$308	$133	$73	$85
THIGH LIFT	$3,898	$5,568	$3,288	$3,222
TUMMY TUCK	$4,120	$5,151	$4,002	$3,814

SOURCE: American Society of Plastic and Reconstructive Surgeons, Inc., 1997.

SEXUALITY

CONTRACEPTIVES: The options for lovers, PAGE 165   **RU-486:** The latest on the controversial abortion pill, PAGE 166   **MASSAGE:** Always start from the ground up, PAGE 167   **MENOPAUSE:** Should women opt for hormone replacement? PAGE 169   **AIDS:** Protease inhibitors offer help, but no cure, PAGE 172   **TESTS:** Confidential at-home screening for HIV, PAGE 173   **STDS:** Common diseases and treatments, PAGE 174

COURTSHIP
▼

THE REAL RULES OF MATCHMAKING

Every solid relationship should pass through four stages

By now, nearly every adult, single or married, is familiar with the bestseller, *The Rules: Time-Tested Secrets for Capturing the Heart of Mr. Right* (Warner Books, 1995). The book aims to teach single women how to lure a man into accompanying her to the altar. Not everyone agrees with the calculated tactics. One of them is psychologist and relationship expert, Barbara De Angelis, who has penned a rebuttal called *The Real Rules: How to Find the Right Man for the Real You* (Dell Publishing, 1997). De Angelis, who has written seven books on personal relationships, argues that women don't need to rely on "bad, recycled, antiquated advice" to find a partner. Instead of relying on tricks to trap a man into marriage, she proposes that women follow her 25 "real rules" for forming a solid relationship. Here De Angelis offers her views on the mating game.

■ How do your "real" rules differ from the old rules?

The real rules aren't about trying to be what a man wants you to be so he'll marry you. Instead, the real rules are about becoming who you really are and finding a man who loves you because of it. The real rules won't teach you how to get a man, they teach you how to get the right man.

■ What's wrong with the traditional approaches?

The old rule was that the goal of a woman's life is to find a man and get married. This rule is based on the negative principle of fear—fear of being alone, fear of being unattractive, and fear of making one wrong move and blowing a whole relationship. This approach means you're never acting from your most powerful self. In addition, when you follow the old rule, you focus your energy on the getting part of the process as opposed to focusing it on whom you're getting. And one day you wake up and realize you're in a relationship that's not at all what you want with someone not at all whom you want.

■ Why shouldn't women play a few games in relationships?

Playing games is the wrong way to get the right man. The basis for most games is deception, secrecy, and competition. None of those belong in your love life. Men who respond to

THE ROAD THAT LEADS TO MR. RIGHT

First came The Rules: Time-Tested Secrets for Capturing the Heart of Mr. Right *by Ellen Fein and Sherrie Schneider. Then, relationship expert Barbara De Angelis brought forth* The Real Rules: How to Find the Right Man for the Real You. *Both proffer advice on how a woman can win the heart of a special man—yet their approaches are about as different as the sexes. Here are the dueling rules at a glance.*

THE RULES		THE *REAL* RULES
Make Mr. Right obsessed with having you by his side by making yourself seem unattainable	❤	Become the confident unique woman you really are and find a man who loves the real you
Don't stare at a man; don't talk too much, or open up too fast when you first meet	❤	Be yourself. If you like someone, let him know
Don't call him and only rarely return his calls	❤	Don't play games
Stop dating him if he doesn't buy a romantic gift for your birthday or Valentine's Day	❤	Judge a man by the size of his heart, not his wallet
Hold off. Don't rush into bed too soon	❤	Become emotionally close before becoming sexually intimate
Don't date a married man	❤	Don't date any man who isn't completely available
Don't stop following the rules until a ring is on your finger	❤	Make a loving, healthy relationship your goal

these games—those who see themselves as the hunter and you as the prey—are men you should stay away from.

■ How should a woman behave on entering a relationship?

Treat men the way you want them to treat you. For instance, if you want him to be honest with you, be honest with him. The same goes for being respectful, considerate, and not being manipulative. Even if you forget all else, if you adhere to this real rule, you'll probably make the right decisions about how to act or what to say. And be yourself. If a man doesn't like the real you, then he's not for you.

■ What warning signs should a woman look for in an initial meeting with a man?

When you meet someone you really like or find yourself falling in love, you're busy paying attention to other things such as how good it is to have someone special in your life, and fantasizing about your future together.

Women don't pay enough attention to warning signs because we often don't want to see them. Most of us are looking for reasons to fall in love or get married, not reasons to disqualify someone.

I've learned that so much of the hurt, heartache, and disappointment we experience in love can be avoided if we just pay more attention at the beginning of a relationship. Stay focused on what you're looking for in a partner and what you're trying to avoid. Pay attention to the warning signs of potential problems. For example, it could signal a problem if he dislikes talking about his feelings, avoids discussing his past, or always needs to be in charge.

■ Do you advise following a "don't ask," "don't tell" approach in the beginning, so a man won't think a woman is being pushy?

No. The first few dates are exactly when you should be asking a man questions to help you decide whether to become more involved.

What's the point of waiting until you're already in love and perhaps sexually intimate to find out the truth? The time to check someone out is long before you have sex and before you let him into your heart. One reason we don't ask our new boyfriends more questions is that we don't want to know the answers, but what you don't know can hurt you.

■ If you find a man who has "potential," should you try to change him?

Don't fall in love with a man's potential. When you're in love with a man's potential, you're not looking at him as a person—you see him as a project. Having a healthy relationship with a person means loving him for who he is now, not loving him in spite of his situation, or in the hopes of whom he will change into tomorrow.

■ When is the right time to become sexually involved?

Having sex too soon is one of the most common and most hurtful mistakes women make. You should not base this important decision on how much time has passed, but instead on how much true emotional closeness and compatibility has been established. Wait until you are emotionally intimate before becoming sexually intimate. That means you should feel a strong bond between your hearts and share a closeness you don't experience with anyone else. You should have verbally shared deep feelings for one another, preferably feelings of love.

Don't mistake lust, or intense sexual chemistry, for compatibility. You should also be intellectually intimate before you become sexually intimate. That means you should spend at least twice as much time talking and learning about one another as you do fooling around. Of course, you should also discuss birth control and sexually transmitted diseases before you become sexually intimate.

■ Is it wrong to apply a little pressure to get a man's commitment?

Never pressure a man into making a commitment. Commitment is something you can't capture from someone—it has to be given freely and that's why it's so precious.

When you're in the right relationship with the right man, you will both know at the right time that you are meant to spend the rest of your life together.

■ How do you get to the commitment stage?

A lot of commitment problems can be avoided if we understand that making a commitment isn't about deciding one day to marry someone. Instead, relationships should go through four stages of commitment; each stage requires the couple to make a decision. In the first three months, there should be a commitment to be sexually and emotionally monogamous. In three to six months there should be a commitment to work toward partnership. This is a crucial stage of a relationship during which you become more emotionally involved. Therefore, you want to be sure you're making the right decisions before making yourself even more vulnerable. Don't stay in a developing relationship for more than four to six months without getting a commitment.

The third phase of commitment, which can be made as early as six months but could take much longer, is to spend your immediate future together and work towards a long-term relationship. The final commitment is to spend the rest of your lives together. Instead of feeling pressured to make a premature commitment to marriage, you and your partner can decide one step at a time and feel confident that when you decide to marry, you'll both be ready.

■ Can you ever be certain that your current boyfriend is the right one for you?

Nothing in life is absolutely certain, but if you learn as much as you can about love, intimacy, and compatibility, you can be very sure that you have chosen the right partner. The key is to look for a person with good character, not simply a good personality. Personality is the way someone presents himself to the world, the way he expresses himself on the outside. Character is someone's essence on the inside. Character determines how a person will treat himself, you, and one day, your children. It is the foundation of a healthy partnership.

BETTER SAFE THAN DISMAYED

Birth control techniques don't work unless they're used regularly. The following efficacy rates, estimates based on the percentage of women who would avoid pregnancy in the first year of use, are provided by the Alan Guttmacher Institute. Methods that are dependent on conscientious use are subject to a greater chance of human error and reduced effectiveness. Without contraception, some 85 percent of sexually active women would likely become pregnant within a year.

MALE CONDOM
84 to 98 percent effective

■ **USE:** Applied immediately before intercourse; used only once and discarded. Effectiveness largely depends on proper, consistent use. Nonprescription.

■ **RISKS:** Rare irritation and allergic reactions.

■ **STD PROTECTION:** Latex condoms help protect against all sexually transmitted diseases, including herpes and HIV.

SPERMICIDES USED ALONE
70 to 97 percent effective

■ **USE:** Applied no more than an hour before intercourse. Nonprescription.

■ **RISKS:** Rare irritation and allergic reactions.

■ **STD PROTECTION:** Unknown.

DIAPHRAGM WITH SPERMICIDE
82 to 94 percent effective

■ **USE:** Can be inserted 6 hours before intercourse and left in place up to 24 hours, but additional spermicide must be inserted if intercourse is repeated. Effectiveness depends largely on proper use. Prescription.

■ **RISKS:** Rare irritation and allergic reactions; urinary tract infections.

■ **STD PROTECTION:** May protect against pelvic infections and certain STDs.

CERVICAL CAP WITH SPERMICIDE
84 to 94 percent effective

■ **USE:** Can be inserted up to 8 hours prior to intercourse and should remain in place at least 6 hours afterwards but no more than 24 hours. May be difficult to insert. Prescription.

■ **RISKS:** Abnormal Pap test; vaginal or cervical infections.

■ **STD PROTECTION:** None.

PILLS
97 to 99 percent effective

■ **USE:** Pill must be taken on daily schedule, regardless of the frequency of intercourse. Prescription.

■ **RISKS:** Water retention, weight gain, bleeding, breast tenderness, hypertension, mood change, and nausea. In rare cases, blood clots, heart attacks, strokes. Not usually recommended for women who smoke, especially over age 35.

■ **STD PROTECTION:** Confers some protection against pelvic inflammatory disease.

IMPLANT (NORPLANT)
99 percent effective

■ **USE:** Effective 24 hours after implantation for approximately seven years; can be removed by physician at any time. Requires prescription, minor outpatient surgical procedure.

■ **RISKS:** Menstrual cycle irregularity; headaches, breast tenderness, and weight gain; may subside after first year.

■ **STD PROTECTION:** None.

INJECTION (Depo-Provera)
99 percent effective

■ **USE:** One injection every three months. Prescription.

■ **RISKS:** Amenorrhea, cramps, weight gain, other side effects similar to Norplant.

■ **STD PROTECTION:** None.

IUD
99 percent effective

■ **USE:** After insertion, stays in until physician removes it. Can remain in place for 1 to 10 years, depending on the type. The IUD should

OPTIONS FOR THE MORNING AFTER

The controversial RU-486 may be here soon

Efforts to introduce RU-486, the French "abortion pill," to American women have met with vehement opposition from abortion foes for nearly a decade. The drug, known here as mifepristone, has been widely used in other countries and appears ready for final approval by the U.S. Food and Drug Administration.

A woman undergoing this so-called medical abortion would follow a two-step regimen. First she would take mifepristone tablets, which interfere with progesterone production, interrupting the pregnancy. Then, 36 to 48 hours later, she would take another drug, misoprostol, which induces contractions. For most women, the pills induce abortion within four hours, but if that should fail, a surgical abortion would be required.

While using RU-486 takes longer than a surgical abortion and is slightly less effective, it can be performed much earlier in the pregnancy than surgical abortions, which usually aren't done until the sixth week of pregnancy. In fact, researchers find that the drug is most effective within the first seven weeks of pregnancy.

Already available to women is a less publicized drug combination, which can also safely and effectively terminate pregnancy within the first nine weeks. According to one study, administering two drugs, methotrexate and misoprostol, in succession, effectively terminated pregnancies in 96 percent of the 178 cases studied.

To induce an abortion using these drugs, a woman is first injected with methotrexate, which interrupts the growth of the embryo. Then, three to seven days later, the woman receives a suppository of misoprostol, which causes uterine contractions, cramping, and bleeding. Typically, it takes a few days for the abortion to occur, although it can take up to a few weeks. In addition, about one-quarter to one-half of women who take the drugs need a second suppository to induce the abortion.

Anesthesia is not required for abortions using either mifepristone or the methotrexate and misoprostol combination. However, both modes of medical abortion typically cause heavy bleeding, abdominal cramps, and pain. Mifepristone can cause nausea, headache, and fatigue; methotrexate typically causes nausea, vomiting, and diarrhea.

only be used by women in monogamous relationships because multiple partners may increase the risk of developing or aggravating pelvic inflammatory disease. Prescription.

■ **RISKS:** Cramps, bleeding, pelvic inflammatory disease.

■ **STD PROTECTION:** None.

PERIODIC ABSTINENCE
53 to 86 percent effective

■ **USE:** Requires the woman to frequently monitor her body's functions and periods of abstinence; effectiveness depends on accurately predicting when ovulation will occur. Can be used in conjunction with barrier methods to increase effectiveness.

■ **RISKS:** None.

■ **STD PROTECTION:** None.

SURGICAL STERILIZATION
99 percent effective

■ **USE:** Vasectomy (for men) is a onetime procedure usually performed in a doctor's office under local anesthesia; tubal ligation (for women) is a onetime procedure performed in an operating room and requires the use of general anesthesia. Both procedures are considered permanent but can sometimes be reversed.

■ **RISKS:** Pain, infection, and, for tubal ligation, possible surgical complications and bleeding.

■ **STD PROTECTION:** None.

WELL-KNEADED RESPITES

The pleasures of foot massage have been treasured for centuries

In the opening of the film *Pulp Fiction*, Vincent and Jules, hitmen with a knack for scintillating dialog, can be found debating the meaning of a foot massage after their boss orders that his wife's chaperon be thrown from a window. His transgression? He gave the boss's spouse a foot massage.

The lure of the foot massage isn't difficult to understand. It's indulgent, seductive, sensual—and clearly off limits unless it's done by an intimate partner. What else confers so much pleasure?

Exactly.

In fact, the feet were considered a private part long before Hollywood declared them decadent. In ancient China, society girls willingly subjected themselves to having their feet bound to become more desirable to men. The crippling procedure involved folding the toes underneath the foot and compressing the arch by wrapping tight bandaging around the heelbone and forefoot. Women with Golden Lotuses—perfectly shaped tiny feet—set the standard for beauty and were highly alluring to male suitors. But Golden Lotuses weren't just a status symbol; they

■ ON WINGED FEET

The quickest way to a person's soul may be through his soles.

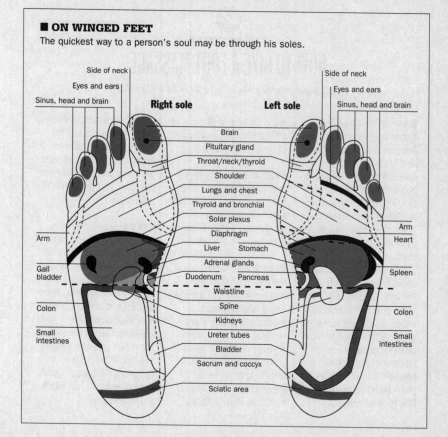

were also considered an erotic body part—regarded as a woman's most desirable physical asset.

Today, instead of subjecting themselves to the pain of foot-binding, women are more likely to pamper their feet with pedicures and foot massages that make their feet look and feel more attractive. Properly done, a foot massage can be refreshing, making tension disappear from the entire body. What's more, there's evidence that a therapeutic foot massage technique known as reflexology not only relieves stress and tension, but improves circulation, alleviates minor aches and pains brought on by stress, and promotes healing.

How does it work? There are thousands of nerve endings in the feet connected to nerves throughout the human body and when muscles tighten, it restricts blood flow to the area of the body under stress. Every body part and organ is connected to a reflex point on a person's foot and by massaging the foot in specific points on this map, it soothes the corresponding body parts.

By applying pressure to an area just below the ball of the foot, for example, you can help relieve a stomachache. Pushing about an inch higher will comfort and refresh the lungs (you can only work the heart by applying pressure to the left foot). "All of this is based on the belief that the body has the power to heal itself," explains Lucy Ostergren, a reflexologist at the New Age Health Spa in Nerversink, N.Y. "When the nerves relax, then the muscles relax, when the muscles relax, then the blood flows more freely."

EXPERT TIPS

HOW TO GIVE A FOOT MASSAGE

A little technique goes a long way in reflexology

Imagine that a Lilliputian-size person is contained inside your foot, and his body parts correspond with various reflex points on the soles of your feet. For instance, the big toe is connected with the head, the spine runs vertically along the inside of the feet, and the intestines, colon, liver, and pancreas are in the arch of the foot. Of course, it takes practice to find the reflex points and some are more difficult to find than others, but there's no harm in trying. Here, Susan Ciminelli, owner of the Susan Ciminelli Day Spa in New York City, explains how to give a reflexology foot massage in three easy steps:

STEP 1: Warm the foot and knead it a little to get the circulation going. Rub a little lotion or aromatic oil on your hands to make it easier to massage.

STEP 2: Start at the top of the foot with the big toe and work down to the heel, using your thumb or knuckle to gently push each point. If you push gently and hold a reflex point, it will send a message to sedate the corresponding body part, but if you "pulse" the point by pushing in and out, it will stimulate the connecting part. Never pump or pulse the adrenal points or the intestine (see graphic), just push in and hold them.

STEP 3: Gently rub the sensitive areas and hard spots to help break up calcium deposits. If you hit a point that hurts, you've found a trouble spot. For example, if someone has a stomachache, when you massage the corresponding reflex point, it's going to hurt. When that happens, push gently and hold the points, but don't pump them.

▼

A WARY SECOND LOOK AT ESTROGEN

Weigh the risks of hormones, says women's health advocate Dr. Love

For millions of women heading toward midlife, no health question looms larger than whether to take hormones during menopause. Doctors routinely prescribe drugs like Premarin, an estrogen derived from pregnant mare's urine, to ease menopause symptoms such as hot flashes, insomnia, and night sweats. Many doctors are also prescribing the drugs to ward off heart disease and osteoporosis. Despite the popularity of hormones, there are drawbacks, including a possible increase in a woman's chance of getting breast cancer.

The problem is it's too soon to tell. "We know very little about the risks and benefits of hormone replacement therapy," says women's health advocate Dr. Susan Love, "so we're really making decisions based on inadequate information." The decision to take hormones should be left to the woman, argues Love, an adjunct professor of surgery at the University of California at Los Angeles and author of *Dr. Susan Love's Breast Book* (Addison-Wesley, 1995) and *Dr. Susan Love's Hormone Book* (Random House, 1997).

A vocal critic of hormone therapy, Love argues that menopause is not a disease that needs curing with drugs, but a natural life stage. Here, she explains how the 40 million or so American women who will enter menopause in the coming decade should determine if and when to take supplemental hormones:

■ **What are the most important factors to consider in deciding whether to take hormone therapy?**

Basically, you have to divide the decision into two parts. First, you have to decide whether to take hormones for the relief of menopause symptoms. Some women have severe symptoms; some are able to cope with their symptoms, some are not. The symptoms are transient, though, lasting two to three years. You may want to take hormone therapy for two to five years and then gradually taper off. As far as we know, there's not a lot of downside to this approach.

The second reason to take hormones is to prevent diseases that may or may not happen. There's some suggestion that hormones might reduce the risk of heart disease. There is also evidence that there's a reduction in bone fractures that come with osteoporosis. But there may be better ways to accomplish this than by taking drugs for 30 years. We also know there's some risk of breast cancer, but we don't know how much. Some women may not get heart disease, but they may get breast cancer. What's needed is a higher standard for the degree of risk you're willing to accept or not accept—and that's not being done.

■ **What can women do until more is known about the benefits and risks of hormone replacement therapy?**

We know very little now. The Women's Health

FACT FILE:

IT'S IN THE TIMING

■ *Reaping the benefits of hormone replacement therapy may depend on how and when you use it, according to a recent report in the New England Journal of Medicine.*

■ *A study of 60,000 women found that short-term therapy (10 years) can increase longevity by 37 percent. However, the health benefits then taper off.*

■ *Although the women still faced a 20 percent lower mortality rate than women not taking hormones, they were also more susceptible to breast cancer.*

Initiative, the largest clinical trial of women ever conducted, won't be completed until 2008. Until we get some answers, women need to look at their own health and their genetics, and make what they believe are good decisions, realizing that the decision may change with time. Your life may change or the data may change. More data will come in and we may find hormone therapy doesn't really prevent heart disease. Or, you may decide to take hormones and your sister may get breast cancer and so you decide to stop.

■ What are the health benefits and risks of estrogen therapy?

We know that estrogen prevents bone loss, but it doesn't build bone. Out of 100 women taking estrogen from age 50 on, maybe two hip fractures can be prevented. We don't know much about the effect on heart disease or Alzheimer's, but we're looking at studies. When you compare women taking hormones to women who aren't, indeed those taking the drugs have less heart disease. However, those women also have a higher socioeconomic status, are more likely to go to a physician, and to treat their high blood pressure and high cholesterol. So we don't know whether hormones make you healthy or whether it's just that healthy women take hormones.

It's also likely that we are overemphasizing the benefits and underemphasizing the risk of breast cancer. When you look at the women who were in the breast cancer study, between 60 percent and 80 percent had had a hysterectomy. That's an important factor because most women who have a hysterectomy and their ovaries removed at a young age also have a decreased risk of breast cancer. As a result, we might be underestimating the breast cancer risk. In addition, even though physicians are less likely to put women at risk of breast cancer on hormones, you still see a 30 percent to 50 percent higher risk of breast cancer among those on hormones—even though they're a select group.

■ Why shouldn't all post-menopausal women be on hormone therapy?

Basically, menopause is perfectly natural. We're not supposed to have high levels of hormones our whole lives, and it may even be dangerous to have them. We need high levels during our reproductive years, but then the body shifts down. And estrogen deficiency isn't the cause of osteoporosis and heart disease. These are diseases of aging, not of menopause. Even calling the therapy estrogen replacement implies that you're replacing something that's missing rather than adding something that isn't supposed to be there—namely progesterone and estradial. They're not normal, they're drugs.

We shouldn't kid ourselves about what we're doing. What we're saying really is that premenopausal women are normal and that postmenopausal are diseased and need to be made to be like premenopausal women.

■ What are some alternative remedies for treating short-term menopause symptoms and for preventing osteoporosis and heart disease?

Lifestyle changes plus alternative treatments like using herbal remedies and acupuncture often work better and have fewer side effects than hormone therapy. For example, 90 percent of heart disease can be prevented by not smoking, eating a healthy diet, and exercising. Exercise alone can also help prevent breast cancer and osteoporosis. For most women, lifestyle changes are all they need, but these options aren't often suggested.

■ If a woman decides to take hormones as a preventative, are there any guidelines on when to start and stop taking them?

Women may want to hold off on hormone therapy in their 50s, waiting instead until their 70s. In order to gain benefits in terms of heart disease and osteoporosis, you must be on the drugs at the time you get the disease—it's not a cumulative thing. Likewise, if you stop taking hormones, then the breast cancer risk decreases. Since the average heart attack in women occurs at age 76, and the average age of hip fracture is 80, you might be better off starting hormone therapy later.

There is no clear message. This is where we are at the moment, but stay tuned. This is nowhere close to being figured out.

IMPOTENCE

A NEW MUSE FOR AN OLD PROBLEM

Preventive maintenance can spare many men difficulties in bed

Doctors say the scenario is common: During a routine check-up, a man discusses a variety of minor ailments. But the patient doesn't mention the real reason he's there until he's walking out the door and says, "By the way…" So-called doorknob diagnoses are frequent with men who suffer from impotence, a condition that afflicts 10 to 20 million American men. Yet, most are reluctant to seek treatment because they feel uncomfortable discussing their sex lives, even with their doctors.

The embarrassment need not be chronic. While impotence was long regarded as a psychological problem for which few medical treatments were available, doctors have come to realize that its causes are usually physiologic in nature. They have now begun to treat impotence, technically called erectile dysfunction, as they would any other illness.

Sufferers must confront the fact that most treatments for impotence are still not user-friendly, however. "Treatment of erectile dysfunction is more complex than just writing a prescription," says James Barada, assistant professor of surgery at Albany Medical College and head of the Center for Male Sexual Health in Albany. "The best of all possible worlds is the most minimally invasive approach that gives the most patient satisfaction." For instance, Barada now uses a drug delivery system called MUSE (medicated urethral system for erection) as a first line of treatment, although it's still considered experimental. By inserting an applicator into the urethral opening in the penis, MUSE releases a pellet of alprostadil, a drug usually injected by needle, causing a temporary erection.

In a recent study reported in the *New England Journal of Medicine*, 1,500 men with chronic impotence due to medical causes were asked to use either MUSE or a placebo at home for three months. The researchers found that 65 percent of those who used Muse were able to achieve erections sufficient for intercourse at least once, compared to 18 percent of the men who received a placebo. One-third of those who used the device reported mild pain, although only a fraction dropped out of the study because if it.

More established treatment falls into three main categories: vacuum constriction devices, contraptions that pump air out of a cylinder to create a vacuum, causing an erection; penile prostheses, a plastic implant that can be pumped into the erect position; and penile injection therapy, which involves injecting a drug into the penis that increases blood flow. The Food and Drug Administration recently approved Caverject, the only injectable drug approved specifically for the treatment of impotence. Although a generic version of the drug, alprostadil, has been used for over a decade, the new formula has become the treatment of choice.

All three are tried and true remedies that can help a man achieve an erection sufficient for sexual intercourse, yet

FACT FILE:

HOW COMMON IS IMPOTENCE?

■ *Studies show that 40 percent of men at age 40 suffer from impotence; 50 percent at age 50, 60 percent at age 60, and it doesn't get better.*

■ *Two of the most common medical conditions associated with impotence are diabetes and heart disease. High blood pressure can also impair circulation, injuring the lining of blood vessels, leading to blocked arteries and impotence.*

each has advantages and drawbacks. For example, penile injections of alprostadil are expensive ($15 to $30 per shot), can cause discomfort, and may result in a prolonged erection. Penile implants offer the highest satisfaction, but require surgery and can cost up to $15,000, says Barada. Vacuum devices are the least expensive although they are awkward to use. Fortunately, many health insurance plans cover the cost of treatment for impotence.

Recent guidelines by the American Urological Association recommend all three types of treatment as safe and effective. The report warns against experimental therapies like blood vessel surgery and use of a natural plant substance called yohimbine, neither of which appears to be effective.

Because many men are reluctant to embrace existing forms of impotence treatment, researchers are at work developing an anti-impotence drug in pill form. In three clinical trials, Viagra (generic name: sildenafil) significantly improved men's ability to attain erections. In one trial of 351 men, between 65 percent and 88 percent reported improved erections (the success varied depending on the dose), compared to just 39 percent of those who took a placebo. Viagra is still undergoing clinical trials, however, and will likely take a few more years to get FDA approval.

Perhaps the best news is that despite its prevalence, impotence is not an inevitable part of aging. Medical problems that arise as men age, such as prostate cancer, diabetes, hypertension, high cholesterol, and obesity increase the risk of impotence. But age itself is not a risk factor, says Barada. In fact, to some extent impotence can be prevented by implementing lifestyle changes. "There are things you can do to maintain an active, vigorous, and long-standing sexual life," explains Barada. Most important, don't smoke. Smoking is the biggest risk factor for impotence, explains Barada, who says 50 percent of his patients are or were smokers. In addition, keeping weight down and controlling blood pressure and cholesterol can also ward off impotence. These are small prices to pay, considering that once a man becomes impotent, the problem can be treated, but not cured.

THE DRAMA OF AIDS INHIBITORS

Drugs offer AIDS sufferers hope, but it's too soon to declare victory

Fifteen years after the AIDS epidemic began, new drugs have begun to transform the disease, offering hope that a diagnosis of AIDS may no longer be a death sentence. Instead, many of the roughly 1 million Americans now infected may be able to live with AIDS just as if they had any other chronic, treatable illness.

These wonder drugs, a new class of anti-AIDS drugs known as protease inhibitors, thwart the virus's capacity to replicate itself when they are used in combination with older drugs like AZT. Attempts to contain HIV have been most successful when three of the nine available AIDS drugs, including a protease inhibitor, are used together in what's known as a triple drug therapy.

Studies show that these combination cocktails can suppress the AIDS virus in the blood to below detectable levels, a feat no other anti-AIDS drug has accomplished. In two separate, small-scale studies conducted last year by New York researchers, only one of the 16 AIDS patients who had followed the triple-drug therapy showed detectable levels of HIV in the blood after nearly one year of treatment.

Researchers continue to follow the drugs' effects on those infected with HIV, as pharmaceutical companies work to further refine protease inhibitors. For example, preliminary research suggests that the latest version, a drug called Viracept, is safer and more convenient than its predecessors, which require patients to adhere to a complicated regimen of dozens of pills a day. In the first study on humans, Viracept reduced HIV levels in the blood to undetectable levels in 81 percent of the 700 patients who were given it along with two other drugs. Viracept has yet to receive FDA approval, however.

Public health experts say that the new medications have already prolonged the lives of some people infected with HIV. The Centers for Disease Control and Prevention (CDC) reported a 13 percent drop in AIDS mortality during the first half of 1996, compared with the same period the previous year. New York, which has the largest concentration of infected people in the country, recently reported a 30 percent decline in the number of AIDS-related deaths from 1995 to 1996.

Anecdotal evidence suggests that the drugs are having a dramatic effect on the lives of some patients. People literally preparing to die have been rejuvenated and resumed normal lifestyles. Hospitals across the country report that admissions are down, and that the average length of hospital stays for AIDS-related problems has also dropped. Even though the drugs are expensive—more than $10,000 for a year's supply—two studies released in early 1997 suggest that the new drug regimens have already reduced the total cost of AIDS treatment, primarily because they have reduced the length of hospital stays.

Despite all the positive developments, researchers and public health experts are reluctant to refer to the new therapies as a cure. The FDA has pushed through the approval of many of the latest drugs quickly, which means that their long-term effects are still uncertain. In addition, some people can't tolerate the drugs, and the drugs don't completely prevent replication of the virus, even if a patient's health seems to have dramatically improved.

HIV TESTS: THE NEXT GENERATION

A home test kit that is reliable and easy to administer

Few diseases have ever garnered as much public attention in such a short time as AIDS. Yet health officials estimate that two-thirds of Americans at risk for contracting HIV still have not been tested—meaning they don't know if they have the virus and if they might be infecting others.

In the hopes of encouraging more people to learn if they are HIV-positive and to seek treatment if needed, the U.S. Food and Drug Administration (FDA) recently authorized a do-it-yourself test kit, called Home Access. Home testing is not only convenient, it's also very reliable. Research in 1997 studied some 1,200 participants as they administered the Home Access test to themselves. The results, the study found, were just as effective as professionally conducted HIV tests at medical facilities.

The test involves pricking your finger with a lancet to draw a small blood sample, then smearing the blood on a speci-

men card. The card is mailed in an enclosed prepaid envelope to a medical laboratory for analysis. Results of Home Access tests can be obtained within a week by calling a toll-free number and punching in your identification number. The testing service also provides professional pre- and post-test counseling and offers medical and social service referrals via its toll-free numbers.

Home Access guarantees confidentiality, which is not always the case with HIV testing at most medical facilities. Anonymous testing ensures that a person's HIV status won't be released to insurance companies or employers, who may deny health insurance or behave in a discriminatory way if they discover that an individual tests positive.

Home Access costs $29.95; Home Access Express runs $44.95 but provides results within three business days. Both are available in pharmacies or by calling ☎ 800–THE–TEST.

EXPERT LIST

IT HAPPENS SOME NIGHTS

The chances of contracting a bacterial sexually transmitted disease such as syphilis or gonorrhea, or a viral STD like herpes, are about 1 in 29 for men and women who have multiple sex partners, according to a recent study. Following are descriptions of the most common STDs from the Centers for Disease Control and Prevention, along with some possible symptoms and treatments.

DISEASE	HOW SPREAD	SYMPTOMS	TREATMENT
BACTERIAL VAGINOSIS	Sexual intercourse. Possibly through towels and wet clothing	Grayish vaginal discharge	Metronidazole
CHLAMYDIA	Vaginal or anal intercourse; mother to child during birth; hand-to-eye contact if hands have infected discharge	Vaginal discharge, painful urination, vaginal bleeding in women. Burning during urination, urethal discharge in men	Tetracycline, doxycycline, erythromycin (for, pregnant women), chlortetracycline (for eyes)
CRABS	Contact with infected person or using his/her towels, clothes or bedding	Intolerable itching in genital or other areas	Kwell lotion; clean clothes, towels, bed linens
GENITAL WARTS	Sexual intercourse, oral sex	Women: small, painless warts in labia, vulva, cervix or anus. Men: warts on penis or scrotum	Laser beam; podophyllin, trichloracetic acid.
GONORRHEA	Sexual intercourse, oral sex; mother to child during birth; hand-to-eye contact	Thick milky discharge, burning, painful urination, pain in lower abdomen, vomiting, rash, chills, fever, pain in wrists, and extremities. (Almost all men show symptoms; women may be asymptomatic)	Ceftriaxone, erythromycin (for (pregnant women)
HERPES	Sexual intercourse, oral sex	Tingling, itching in genital area, legs, buttocks; sores, blisters	Keep sores clean and dry; xylocaine cream or ethyl chlo ride may ease pain
HIV INFECTION / AIDS	Sexual intercourse, anal sex, blood transfusions, infected needles	Fatigue, weight loss, swollen glands, fever, night sweats, bronchial infections, sores, loss of appetite, trouble swallowing, recurrent yeast infections (women)	Protease inhibitors in combination with AZT and other drugs
NONGONOCOCCAL URETHRITIS	Sexual intercourse	Often none; sometimes penal discharge and inflamed urethra	Tetracycline; doxycycline, erythromycin
SCABIES	Sexual contact, towels, clothes, furniture	Intense itching, red bumps on torso or hands	Kwell; eurax for pregnant women
SYPHILIS	Sexual or skin contact, mother to child at birth	Painless genital sore, rash, sore throat, swollen joints, aching bones, hair loss	Penicillin; doxicline, tetracycline

HAVING CHILDREN

PRENATAL CARE
▼

WHEN A MOTHER HAS TO WORRY

The right time to take care of your baby is before you conceive

Once a woman learns she's pregnant, she's likely to revamp her lifestyle by eating balanced meals, and avoiding cigarettes and alcohol. What many women may not realize is that fetal development begins 17 days after conception—just three days after the first missed menstrual period—and continues until day 56 of the pregnancy. Because most women aren't aware of the fact that they're pregnant until after this critical period, they miss a vital window for improving their chances of delivering a healthy baby.

"We have to change the outdated paradigm that the time to take care of yourself is when you look pregnant," says Merry-K. Moos, research associate professor in the obstetrics and gynecology department at the University of North Carolina. A leading proponent of what's known in the medical community as preconceptional care, Moos says the first step is to educate women early about behaviors that can harm a fetus, and about healthy habits that can improve the outcome of their pregnancy. Because more than half of all pregnancies are unplanned, any woman with the potential of becoming pregnant should consider preconceptional counseling, says Moos. In reality, most women consult a doctor about six to eight weeks after conceiving.

A preconceptional visit involves a series of tests, including screening for existing medical conditions and for any family history of genetic defects. The visit can prevent a lot of potential problems for mother and child, says Dr. Richard Johnston, medical director of the March of Dimes Birth Defects Foundation and professor of pediatrics at Yale University School of Medicine. "It's a critically important health visit, even though it is not built into the system now." Indeed, a recent Gallup survey found that only 26 percent of 2,000 women aged 18 to 45 who had been pregnant, had talked with their doctor before becoming pregnant.

EXPERT SOURCE

Want to learn more about pre-pregnancy care? The March of Dimes is sponsoring a nationwide campaign to inform women about steps that will improve the chances of having a healthy baby. For more information:

☎ **888-MODIMES**

Studies suggest that adopting a healthy lifestyle before conceiving can increase the chances of having a healthy baby. While nothing can guarantee a perfect birth every time, the following advice can raise the odds.

■ **TAKE FOLIC ACID:** Studies show that a daily dose of folic acid in the very early stages of pregnancy reduces by 50 to 70 percent the likelihood of having a baby with a neural tube defect, such as spina bifida and anencephaly (the absence of a brain). The FDA recommends that all women of childbearing age consume at least .4 milligrams of folic acid each day. Folic acid is found in some foods, such as leafy greens, but, advises Johnston, "The only sure way for a woman to get enough folic acid is to take a vitamin every day." By 1998, folic acid will be added to all enriched foods like flour and rice.

■ **PUT ON JUST ENOUGH WEIGHT:** Many women gain 40 to 50 pounds while pregnant, putting them at an increased risk for complications, including diabetes, high blood pressure, and an increased likelihood of birth by cesarean section. On the other hand, being underweight can lead to low birth-weight babies. The ideal weight gain for a woman of normal weight, according to the American College of Obstetrics and Gynocologists (ACOG), is 25 to 35 pounds. Women should not try to lose weight during pregnancy.

■ **EXERCISE:** There's evidence that moderate to high-intensity exercise can be good for both mother and her fetus. Exercise can boost energy and ease discomforts associated with pregnancy, such as backache, constipation, and varicose veins. A 1996 study suggests that regular exercise during the first 20 weeks of pregnancy reduces a woman's chances of developing pregnancy-induced high blood pressure. While some doctors still advise pregnant patients to avoid exercise, ACOG insists that it's safe for most healthy women. Of course, some sports, like downhill skiing, which can harm the fetus, are off limits.

■ **DON'T SMOKE OR DRINK:** After drug abuse, smoking cigarettes has the most harmful effect on a developing fetus; alcohol constumption can also be damaging.

"Smoking is the number-one cause of preventable infant mortality," says Moos. Studies show that smoking doubles a woman's risk of having an ectopic pregnancy (a pregnancy outside the uterus). It also increases the chances of miscarriage and of delivering a low-birth-weight baby, as well as a baby with a higher risk of having an attention deficit hyperactivity disorder.

While there is no question that excessive alcohol consumption during pregnancy is a leading cause of preventable mental retardation, learning disabilities, and fetal alcohol syndrome, it is unclear how much alcohol causes harm. The only way to be safe is to refrain from drinking while pregnant, says Johnston. He adds, however, an occasional drink shouldn't be harmful. "No amount of alcohol has been proven safe. Depending on how much risk you want to take," says Johnston, "you'll drink a little or not at all."

■ **GROWTH OF THE FETUS FROM 8 TO 40 WEEKS**

Fetal development has already begun 17 days after conception. While the average pregnancy lasts 280 days from the last menstrual period, it is normal to give birth anywhere from 37 to 42 weeks after the last period.

Week	8	12	16	20	24	28	32	36	40
Length	1 in.	3 in.	6.5 in.	10 in.	13 in.	14.5 in.	16 in.	18 in.	20 in.
Weight	0.07 oz.	0.6 oz.	5 oz.	12 oz.	1.3 lb.	2 lb.	3.5 lb.	5.5 lb.	7.5 lb.

SOURCE: *American Medical Association Encyclopedia of Medicine*, Random House, 1989.

DRUG SIDE EFFECTS THAT HARM BABIES

You can't be too careful when you are pregnant. Beware of what these agents could do to the fetus

AGENT	REASONS USED	EFFECTS
ALCOHOL	Part of regular diet, social reasons, dependency.	Growth and mental retardation.
ANDROGENS	To treat endometriosis.	Genital abnormalities.
ANTICOAGULANTS Warfarin (Coumadin, Panwarfin) and dicumatrol	To prevent blood clotting; used to prevent or treat thromboembolisms (clots blocking blood vessels).	Abnormalities in bones, cartilage, and eyes; central nervous system defects.
ANTITHYROID DRUGS Propylthiouracil, iodide, and methimazole (Tapazole)	To treat an overactive thyroid gland.	Underactive or enlarged thyroid.
ANTICONVULSANTS Phentoin (Dilantin), trimethadione (Tridione), paramethadione (Paradione), valproic acid (Depakene)	To treat epilepsy and irregular heartbeat.	Growth and mental retardation, developmental abnormalities, neural tube defects.
CHEMOTHERAPEUTIC DRUGS Methotrexate (Mexate) and aminopterin	To treat cancer and psoriasis.	Increased rate of miscarriage, various abnormalities.
DIETHYLSIBESTROL (DES)	To treat problems with menstruation, symptoms of menopause and breast cancer, and to stop milk production; previously used to prevent preterm labor and miscarriage.	Abnormalities of cervix and uterus in females, possible infertility in males and females.
LEAD	Industries involving lead smelting, paint manufacture and use, printing, ceramics, glass manufacturing, and pottery glazing.	Increased rate of miscarriage and stillbirths.
LITHIUM	To treat the manic part of manic-depressive disorders.	Congenital heart disease.
ORGANIC MERCURY	Exposure through eating contaminated food.	Brain disorders.
ISOTRETINOIN (Accutane)	Treatment for cystic acne.	Increased rate of miscarriage, developmental abnormalities.
STREPTOMYCIN	An antibiotic used to treat tuberculosis.	Hearing loss.
TETRACYCLINE	An antibiotic used to treat a wide variety of infections.	Underdevelopment of tooth enamel, incorporation of tetracycline into bone.
THALIDOMIDE	Previously used as a sedative and a sleep aid.	Growth deficiencies, other abnormalities.
X-RAY THERAPY	Medical treatment of disorders such as cancer.	Growth and mental retardation.

SOURCE: *Planning for Pregnancy, Birth, and Beyond*, American College of Obstetricians and Gynecologists, 1993.

MEDICAL CHECKS IN THE WOMB

Today's tests for genetic defects make far more information available

Ten tiny toes, 10 tiny fingers: The emotional climax of any pregnancy comes when the doctor places the newborn baby on the mother's belly and assures the parents that he or she is healthy. But many mothers no longer have to wait until the child is born to learn whether their baby is likely to be healthy. As more women postpone having children until their mid- to late 30s, genetic tests that offer women a chance to learn the likelihood that the baby will have a serious birth defect are being administered far more frequently.

Below, Lee Fallon, a certified genetic counselor and supervisor of genetic counseling at the Genetics and IVF Institute in Fairfax, Va., answers some of the most common questions asked about genetic testing by prospective parents:

■ Which birth defects are most common?

Two of the most common birth defects are congenital heart defects and cleft lip and palate. One in 500 to 1,000 babies is born with either cleft lip or cleft palate, or both, and one in 100 to 200 is born with heart defects. Two other common birth defects are neural tube defects such as spina bifida (a damaged spinal cord) and anencephaly (the absence of a part of the brain) and chromosomal abnormalities such as Down's syndrome, the most common type of serious chromosomal disorder.

■ At what age are women at risk of having a baby with chromosomal abnormalities?

A woman in her 20s has about a 1 in 500 chance of having a baby with a chromosomal abnormality. It's about 1 in 380 by age 30, 1 in 180 at age 35, 1 in 100 by age 38, and 1 in 50 by age 41; then it doubles almost every year after that. However, 80 percent of children with Down's syndrome are born to women in their 20s, many of whom, because they face less risk, are not advised or choose not to undergo more advanced diagnostic tests.

■ What is the AFP test?

The AFP test is a blood test that measures a chemical called alpha-fetoprotein (AFP), which is produced inside the liver of the fetus. If the spinal fluid were leaking into amniotic fluid, there would be a higher concentration of AFP in the amniotic fluid, and therefore a higher level would usually get into the blood of the mother.

The test, which is normally offered to all pregnant women, is most accurate at detecting spina bifida and anencephaly, which are suspected when there's an elevated AFP level, but it can also help detect Down's syndrome.

■ What is ultrasound screening and who should have it done?

An ultrasound test is usually offered only when there's another risk factor for a genetic disorder or birth defect like a family history or an abnormal AFP test. Ultrasound uses sound waves that emit from a transducer (a reverse microphone) and bounce off structures. It allows us to look at the physical development of the baby and get a general picture of the legs, arms and body. The denser the structure, such as bone, the brighter the image. For example, a birth defect like anencephaly is very accurately picked up on ultrasound because you can see the part of the skull that's not formed.

■ How likely are these basic screening tests to detect problems?

The AFP Plus test detects 80 to 85 percent of cases of spina bifida and about 65 percent of Down's syndrome, which means that almost one in three cases would not show up. When ultrasound is done after 18 weeks, it will detect most serious heart defects and more than 50 percent of neural tube defects, and it's even more likely to detect major physical problems.

■ WHEN FAMILY HISTORY BECOMES DESTINY

Some defects are more likely to recur if parents already have one child with the defect.

DISORDER	RISK OF HAVING A FETUS WITH THE DISORDER		
	Overall		With one affected child
DOMINANT GENE			
Polydactyly	1 in 300 to 1 in 100		50%
Achondroplasia	1 in 23,000		50%
Huntington's disease	1 in 15,000 to 1 in 5,000		50%
RECESSIVE GENE			
Cystic fibrosis	1 in 2,500	White persons	25%
Sickle-cell anemia	1 in 625	Black persons	25%
Tay-Sachs disease	1 in 3,600	Ashkenazi Jews	25%
Beta-thalassemia	1 in 2,500- 1 in 800	Persons of Mediterranean descent	25%
X-LINKED			
Hemophilia	1 in 2,500	Men	50% for boy, 0% for girl
CHROMOSOMAL			
Down's syndrome	1 in 800	Average risk increases with mother's age	1%–2%
Klinefelter syndrome	1 in 800	Men	No significant increase
Turner syndrome	1 in 3,000	Women	No significant increase
MULTIFACTORAL			
Congenital heart disease	1 in 125		2%–4%
Neural tube defects	1 in 1,000 to 1 in 500		2%–5%
Cleft lip/cleft palate	1 in 1,000 to 1 in 500		2%–4%

SOURCE: *Planning for Pregnancy, Birth, and Beyond*, American College of Obstetricians and Gynecologists, 1993.

■ Are further tests necessary if the results of AFP and ultrasound are normal?

It's important to understand the difference between screening tests like AFP and ultrasound and diagnostic tests like amniocentesis or chorionic villus sampling (CVS). A screening test doesn't give you a yes or no answer; it just tells you if your risk is average or above or below average, whereas diagnostic tests almost always give you a yes or no answer. If you have an abnormal result from a screening test, you most likely have a healthy pregnancy, but you may want to have a diagnostic test. A normal result on a screening test doesn't mean you have a healthy pregnancy, but your chances of developing certain problems are lower than most.

■ What's the difference between amniocentesis and the diagnostic test CVS?

Amniocentesis involves withdrawing about a tablespoon of amniotic fluid by inserting a thin needle through the mother's abdomen. Cells in the fluid shed from the baby can be used to determine if the baby has a chromosomal or genetic abnormality. CVS involves removing a small amount of cells called the chorionic villi that form the placenta by inserting either a catheter into the cervix or a needle into the mother's abdomen, then genetic tests are performed on the cells.

■ Who should undergo diagnostic tests?

These tests are usually offered only to women who will be age 35 or older at the time their baby is due, unless there's another indication, such as if a woman has already had a baby with a chromosomal abnormality or there's another hereditary risk. Amniocentesis may also be offered to women at least 14 weeks pregnant because of an AFP or ultrasound finding, but the window of opportunity has closed by that time to perform CVS, which is done between 10 and 13 weeks of pregnancy. Most facilities will provide these tests to younger women if requested, but most insurers consider it optional and would not cover the cost. (Amniocentesis costs about $1,500; CVS costs $1,500 to $1,800).

■ How does a woman decide which diagnostic tests to undergo?

Whether to undergo any of these tests is the decision of the woman or the couple. Amniocentesis is the more commonly available test. CVS is usually performed if a woman desires results early in her pregnancy, if a woman has had a previous pregnancy with chromosomal abnormalities, or if the couple is at risk of having a child with a genetic disease. However, CVS isn't available everywhere.

■ How effective are amniocentesis and CVS at detecting abnormalities?

Both amniocentesis and CVS have greater than 99 percent accuracy in detecting chromosomal abnormalities.

■ What are the risks associated with the various screening and diagnostic tests?

The AFP and ultrasound screening tests pose no risk to the baby; both amniocentesis and CVS carry a risk of causing miscarriage. On average in the U.S., the risk of miscarriage associated with CVS is one in 100 to 200, and it's one in 200 to 400 for amniocentesis.

■ What factors should a couple consider in deciding whether a woman should be tested?

Couples should think about whether the information the test provides has a real benefit such as peace of mind or being able to make a decision about the pregnancy. Some decide to have the test because they feel that any risk of an abnormality would justify finding out. Others decide to have the test not based on the statistics, but on fear of the unknown.

■ Do some women over age 35 choose not to undergo any screening tests?

People who decide not to have testing done feel they would not do anything different in the pregnancy and taking a risk—however small—of losing that pregnancy is too great of a tradeoff. If there is a problem, the choices available are limited. Because we can't cure these conditions, the options are continuing the pregnancy knowing the diagnosis or terminating the pregnancy.

INFERTILITY
▼

NEW WAYS TO START A FAMILY

Options for couples having trouble conceiving are greatly expanded

L ate marriages and biological clocks are frequent factors. Environmental toxins, previous surgery, and declining sperm counts may also play a role. And sometimes there's no explanation why about 1 out of every 12 couples in the United States has been reported unable to conceive in a year of trying. This is despite the fact that more than half of women trying to conceive already had at least one child. The experience can be emotionally and financially draining, not to mention disappointing, since many couples don't get to bring home a baby even after trying for years.

In some cases the causes of infertility seem clear cut. The age of the mother is one of the biggest factors that influence the ability to conceive because as women age, they are less likely to ovulate. Certain women who don't release enough eggs can be treated with a fertility drug such as Clomid. (There's evidence that women who take some of these fertility drugs face a greater risk of ovarian cancer, although that's still unclear.) Other factors that can prevent successful conception include tubal scarring and blockage, poor sperm quality, or a low sperm count.

The procedures used to correct these problems vary. Sometimes couples just need to adjust their schedules (see box), undergo minor surgery to correct problems in their reproductive organs, or take prescription medications to conceive. But others must subject themselves to demanding and costly tests and treatments like hormone injections, egg retrieval, and embryo transfers.

So-called assisted reproductive technologies have become incredibly advanced since the birth of Louise Brown through in vitro fertilization (IVF) in 1978. Newer technologies such as gamete intrafallopian transfer (GIFT) and zygote intrafallopian transfer (ZIFT) have also become more widespread. With GIFT, the sperm and egg are inserted into the fallopian tubes, where fertilization occurs naturally. For IVF and ZIFT, fertilization of the eggs by the sperm takes place in the laboratory and the fertilized egg is placed directly into the woman's uterus for IVF, or her fallopian tubes for ZIFT.

One area that has progressed tremendously is in treating male infertility, which accounts for as much as 40 percent of all cases. For example, intracytoplasmic sperm injection (ICSI), which involves injecting a single sperm into an egg, then returning the egg to the uterus, is a technique designed to overcome infertility caused by weak or abnormal sperm. The aggressive procedure has made it possible for men with extremely low sperm counts or defective sperm to become fathers. However, the five-year-old technique may lead to what is known as inherited infertility, a condition in which newborns develop the same genetic problem that caused their fathers' infertility.

But these high-tech treatments have their limits. There's little evidence that recreating the same procedure more than four to six times increases the likelihood of pregnancy. Yet one of the most difficult decisions is when to quit. When a couple thinks they've done everything they can, the decision is sometimes complicated by a doctor's optimism that he or she can find a treatment that will work.

Some fertility clinics publish exaggerated success rates, which can also inflate couples' confidence that eventually they will conceive. In fact, the Federal Trade Commission has won cease and desist agreements against five clinics that ran misleading ads. The success rate for assisted reproductive technologies averages about 20 percent, ranging from 21 percent for IVF to almost 30 percent for GIFT and ZIFT. Although only one in seven couples conceive on the first try using more established assisted reproductive technologies like IVF, the success rate increases after several tries.

Only 10 states require insurance companies to cover such procedures, which can cost anywhere from $6,000 to $10,000 a try. One study estimated that the cost of IVF can range from $66,000 for a couple that conceives after the first try to up to $800,000 for couples that try repeatedly to conceive.

THE BEST DAY TO TRY YOUR LUCK

Time your lovemaking to the day of ovulation if you're hoping to conceive

Recent research may make it easier for couples to conceive simply by clarifying exactly when a couple is most likely to conceive. The study, conducted by researchers at the National Institute of Environmental Health Sciences and published in the *New England Journal of Medicine*, concluded that a woman's chances of becoming pregnant are greatest if she has sexual intercourse on the day of ovulation (when the egg is released from the ovary), or in the five days before she ovulates.

The finding challenges the conventional wisdom that a woman is fertile from about three days prior to ovulation to about three days afterward. Most surprising was the finding that a woman's chances of conceiving after ovulation are virtually nil. Not one of the study's 221 women who were trying to become pregnant conceived as a result of having intercourse after they ovulated, while 10 percent of those who had intercourse five days before ovulating and 33 percent of those who had intercourse on the day of ovulation became pregnant. To take advantage of this timing information, women must first predict when they will ovulate, which they can do by either using over-the-counter ovulation tests or by charting basal body temperature.

SUCCESSFUL ADOPTIONS

To avoid pitfalls, examine your motivation before you begin

Parental rights battles like the "Baby Jessica" and "Baby Richard" cases have made Americans more aware of the anguish associated with adoption. While most adoptive parents don't experience that degree of trauma, they routinely have to contend with endless waits, exorbitant costs, and bureaucratic runarounds. Deb Harder, program director of Adoptive Families of America, a nationwide nonprofit agency that provides information and assistance to adoptive parents, has the following advice on how to avoid being victimized or caught up in "the system."

■ **Examine what's motivating you to adopt.** The first step for anyone considering adoption is to make sure you're firmly committed to rearing and nurturing a child. Look very carefully at your skills and strengths as a person and how they translate to being an effective parent. If you're dealing with infertility, it's important to have gone through a grieving process and acknowledge that you're unlikely to bear children. You should look at adoption not as a second best option, but as an alternative to bearing a child.

■ **Decide what kind of child you will be an effective parent for.** Many families only consider adopting a healthy, same-race infant, and don't think of a child born in another country or one with special needs. Some folks are prepared to parent a child with special needs, but others might not be equipped to. Likewise with kids from other cultural backgrounds. You have to consider how you are going to incorporate that heritage into day-to-day life.

■ **Learn state laws.** Among the first things a family should do is contact their state department of social services and talk to an adoption supervisor to find out what they are legally required to do to complete an adoption in their state.

■ **Choose the type of adoption you're interested in.** One of the first decisions is whether you'd like to adopt through a public agency, which primarily works with kids in foster care and group home settings—and rarely handles healthy, same-race infants, or a private agency, which specializes in healthy, same-race infants and children with special needs, and in some cases arranges international adoptions. You can also opt for an independent, or private adoption, in which adoptive parents work with a lawyer or other non-agency adoption provider to find a birth parent or child. There are certain risks with private adoptions and more of a safety net with an agency.

■ **Assess the costs.** The cost of adopting a child ranges from $8,000 to $20,000, depending on the type of adoption. International adoptions tend to be more expensive, because there are hidden costs such as long-distance calls and travel expenses. Private adoption has the reputation of being more expensive, because the costs usually aren't set up front, while some agencies may charge on a sliding scale basis.

Different agencies have different fee structures, services, and missions. Try to get details about the services they provide and insist that they assign a service to each fee.

■ **Expect to be scrutinized during the selection process.** Many private agencies allow birth mothers a say in choosing which couple they want to adopt their child. Agencies can and do compile a book of dossiers with biographical information about prospective families for birth mothers to review. Your age may also be a factor. One reason many adoptive parents look at international programs is that some agencies have a 35- to 40-year-old age cap for adoptive parents, but many international programs have wider age ranges.

■ **Be honest during the "home study."** All prospective adoptive parents must undergo a home study, a means by which agency personnel can assess the qualities needed to be an effective parent with what your qualities are. It's not unlike applying for a mortgage. For example, they assess what's motivating you to adopt, how you were parented, and how you plan to discipline the child. They'll also ask for references and look at your finances and psychological stability. If you have a criminal history or a history of psychiatric illnesses, you don't want to lie about the situation—it will cause greater problems than if you're up front and explain what's what.

■ **Decide whether you want an open or confidential adoption.** In years past, you could be fairly sure an adoption would be confidential and records would be sealed. But open adoption, in which the birth and adoptive families establish communication, is becoming more common. If the agency allows open adoption, consider what degree of openness you're interested in. It's a highly emotional time for adoptive and birth parents, so it's hard to assess what you're going to be comfortable with long-term.

■ **Find out how quickly adopted children go home with adoptive families.** The number of families seeking to adopt is greater than the number of healthy, same-race infants available, which means the wait can take anywhere from 9 to 24 months. It varies more than it used to because of the degree of openness in the process these days, which also means you have greater opportunity to be selected ahead of time. The agency should be able to give you a time line as to what to expect, but bear in mind that nothing is written in granite. Be flexible, but assertive. Remember, the agency will control if and when your child comes home to you.

■ **Make sure the people you're working with are reputable.** The people you're working with must be competent, qualified, and ethical or the whole thing is jeopardized. If you opt for a private adoption, don't go to a family lawyer unless he or she has experience in adop-

tion. And bear in mind that just because a lawyer knows how to complete an adoption according to the letter of the law doesn't mean he or she has a background in the sociological and psychological aspects of adoption. If you are trying to arrange an international adoption, be aware that what is culturally acceptable in other countries may be way outside of our experience or what we deem acceptable. For example, many international programs will request "gifts" that may look like bribes in the U.S.

■ **Weigh the risks and benefits of "legal risk."** In an agency adoption, the baby usually stays with a foster family during a waiting period mandated by the state (from 48 hours to three months), until the adoption becomes final. But if you arrange what's called legal risk, you take custody of the adopted child immediately after birth, but the birth parents can come forward and reclaim the child during that period. You can arrange this through both agency and private adoptions, but most agencies don't tell you it's an option unless you ask. Chances are you'll immediately bond with the child, so it's an extremely painful experience for adoptive families to go through to have the birth mother renege, and if they do, there's not a lot of recourse.

EXPERT SOURCES

For more information and publications about adoption, contact one of the following organizations:

Adoptive Families of America
☎ 800–372–3300

National Council for Adoption
☎ 202–328–1200

The National Adoption Center
☎ 800–TO–ADOPT

GROWTH

WATCHING THEM GROW AND GROW

You can't control a child's height, but weight is another matter

Few processes can be as engrossing to parents as watching their child grow and trying to divine how tall or thin their precious offspring might eventually be. Often, though, the process can also be worrisome. Is the child eating enough or too much? Does a child's slow growth mean he or she has a deficiency of growth hormones? While no one has yet figured out how to predict a child's full adult weight and height, there are plenty of tools, such as the growth charts below, to help you determine if your child's growth is in the normal range.

Infants grow at an incredible pace—doubling their weight in the first four to five months and tripling it by the time they are one. By the end of their first year, their height increases by 50 percent. By age three, a child's head is almost 90 percent of its adult size.

Heredity greatly determines a child's ultimate height. Generally, tall parents produce tall children, and short parents have short children. In some cases, parents may suspect that their "too short" child has a deficiency of growth hormones, which are produced by the pituitary gland. Only a doctor can determine if a child has extreme growth problems that warrant growth hormone therapy. Because of

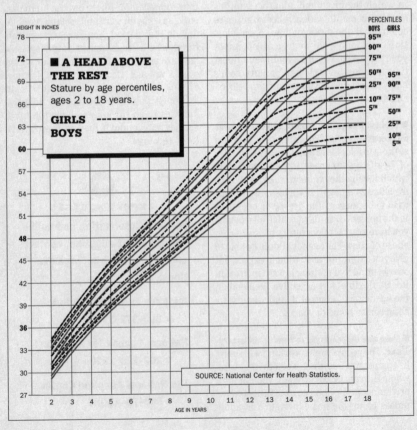

HEIGHT IN INCHES

■ A HEAD ABOVE THE REST
Stature by age percentiles, ages 2 to 18 years.

GIRLS - - - - - - - - - -
BOYS ——————

PERCENTILES
BOYS GIRLS

SOURCE: National Center for Health Statistics.

AGE IN YEARS

potential side effects, hormone drugs are prescribed only for severe growth retardation.

A child's weight is greatly affected by the parents' eating habits. The high-fat, high-calorie average American diet, together with a lack of exercise, are causing a sharp rise in the rate of childhood obesity. By some estimates, 25 percent of children are obese. Studies show that a family history of obesity is a strong indication that a child will be obese.

As a rule of thumb, children are considered obese if their weight is 20 percent or more above the expected weight for their height. To help an overweight child shed excess pounds, pediatricians suggest making good nutrition and exercise a family affair, instead of isolating the child who has the problem.

In between regular pediatric visits, parents can keep tabs on their child's growth rate by using the charts below, which are similar to the ones used in a pediatrician's office. To plot the child's height, find the vertical line for his or her age at the bottom of the height chart. Locate the horizontal line for the child's height on the left side of the chart, and mark the point at which the two lines cross. Do the same for the weight chart, using the child's weight.

The numbers on the curved lines represent percentiles. For example, if your daughter weighs 125 pounds at age 12, she is in the 90th percentile. This means that about 90 percent of normal girls weigh less than she does and about 10 percent weigh more. Parents should keep in mind, though, that these are simply statistical measures; only a pediatrician can determine whether a certain percentile is normal or abnormal for a particular child.

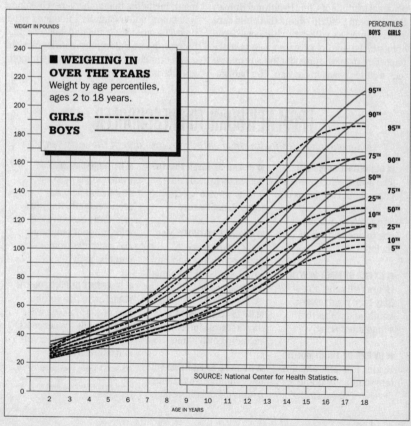

WEIGHING IN OVER THE YEARS
Weight by age percentiles, ages 2 to 18 years.

GIRLS ----------------
BOYS ———————————

SOURCE: National Center for Health Statistics.

WHO'S BRINGING UP BABY?

It's not who provides the care, but the quality that counts

One of the toughest decisions facing new mothers who return to work is where to look for good child care. Some solid new research about the quality of the nation's day care may help allay the fears of parents reluctant to place their babies in the arms of strangers.

A nationwide study conducted by the National Institute of Child Health and Human Development (NICHD) found that child care does not interfere with early childhood development; the quality of care given is more important than who provides the care or how long a child spends in day care. If a babysitter interacts frequently with a child, his or her intellectual development will exceed that of a child who doesn't get proper attention.

These findings support earlier research suggesting that for children to thrive in a day-care center, the facility must have a high ratio of staff to children, and the staff must be attentive to each child. "The amount of language that is directed to the child is an important component," says Sarah Friedman, coordinator of the NICHD study. "Language input can predict a child's acquisition of cognitive and language skills, which are the bedrock of school readiness."

The NICHD study confirmed the conclusions of an earlier study by the same researchers. A key finding in both studies: day care in itself does not harm the mother-child bond. The most important factor influencing a child's development is the home environment, including the mother's psychological well-being, and the family's financial situation. The latest study did find, however, that the more hours children spent in day care, the greater the chances that they and their mothers interacted poorly.

FROM NEWBORN TO PRESCHOOLER

A developmental timeline of a child's progression in the early years

■ **DURING FIRST MONTH:** The average daily weight gain: about two-thirds of an ounce; the average daily height increase: one to one-and-a-half inches

■ **BY END OF FIRST MONTH:** Hears well generally. May turn head toward family and voices that sound interesting

■ **BY END OF THIRD MONTH:** Begins to babble and imitate some sounds and to develop a social smile

■ **BY END OF SEVEN MONTHS:** Responds to own name and uses voice to express joy and displeasure

■ **BY FIRST BIRTHDAY:** May walk two or three unassisted steps and can say "Dada" and "Momma" and respond to "no"

■ **BY 15 TO 18 MONTHS:** Says several simple words, including own name

■ **BY 18 TO 24 MONTHS:** Follows simple instructions; begins make-believe play

■ **BY THIRD BIRTHDAY:** Understands most sentences and uses pronouns and some plurals. Can also express a wide range of emotions and separates from parents easily

■ **SOMETIME DURING FOURTH YEAR:** Has active vocabulary of 300 to 1000 words. Understands the concepts of "same" and "different" and tells stories

SOURCE: Adapted from *Caring for Your Baby and Young Child*, American Academy of Pediatrics, Bantam Books, 1993.

THE CHILD WHO CAN'T SIT STILL

Ritalin's use in treating the hyperactive child has more than doubled

To skeptics, ADHD is a much overstated rationale for behavior that is only to be expected in children. But to families with children who seem constantly hyperactive, impulsive, and inattentive, learning to recognize and get help for Attention Deficit Hyperactivity Disorder is crucial. The controversial malady has become so prevalent, according to the National Institute of Mental Health, that there is a child who suffers from it in every classroom in the country. Increasingly, adults are claiming to have the disorder as well.

To treat the disorder, doctors typically prescribe Ritalin, a stimulant drug that calms hyperactive children and perks up inattentive ones. A recent study found that Ritalin use increased two-and-a-half times between 1990 to 1995. The trend has raised a number of concerns. Some fear that too many are being treated unnecessarily for ADHD and Attention Deficit Disorder (ADD), a similar malady in which children are inattentive, but not impulsive or hyperactive. Critics maintain that misdiagnosis of ADHD, which is typically identified by age seven, is rampant. They say pediatricians and psychiatrists are too quick to diagnose it, without doing a complete medical and psychological evaluation to rule out other illnesses. Critics also claim doctors are too rash in prescribing medication, perhaps in an effort to appease frustrated parents.

Parents of children on Ritalin, meanwhile, also voice concerns. Some worry that Ritalin will stunt their child's growth, although research shows little cause and effect in most children. It can, however, decrease appetite

and cause insomnia and nausea, side effects that often subside after a month or so. In addition, there's little evidence that the drug poses any long-term health consequences, says veteran ADHD researcher James Swanson, director of the Child Development Center and professor of pediatrics, psychiatry and social sciences at the University of California-Irvine. Here, Swanson offers guidance in understanding the treatment of ADHD:

■ When and where should parents seek help if they suspect that their child may have ADHD?

All children are inattentive, hyperactive, and impulsive to some extent, but the severity has to be great enough to cause impairment. Treatment should be sought when there is notable impairment, usually a significant disruption at home or school. Schools are often the first to recognize it. After that parents typically go to their pediatrician or a child psychiatrist or maybe a pediatric neurologist. If there's no interest in treating ADHD with medication, a child psychiatrist might be able to deal with the problem through behavior modifications.

■ What is the preferred approach to treating ADHD?

Medication has a beneficial effect in 70 percent to 80 percent of children. It's the most well-established treatment. But medication alone probably isn't enough by itself to have long-term impact. School-based intervention and behavioral treatment are the other components to supplement any effect the medication might have and to make short-term effects persist. Parents are taught to use reinforcement, such as punishment and stimulus control; treatments based on the same principles of behavioral modification are then also used at school.

■ Which children are candidates for drug therapy?

It depends on the preference of the parents. Most kids would be tried on drug therapy because it's so well accepted. It's sort of the cultural norm here, whereas in other countries, it's not. ADHD is fifty times more likely to be recognized and treated in the United States than in England, for example.

■ Why are so many more kids taking drugs like Ritalin nowadays?

There's been a dramatic increase because of an increased perception of the problem since 1990, when the education law changed. Before then, schools were reluctant to identify and refer children, but now they are free to do so. As a result, we see twice as many referrals because we have two sources—parents and schools. Groups like Children and Adults with Attention Deficit Disorder (CHADD) have also been very effective in educating people about the fact that this is a real disorder. Those factors have given rise to an increase in the number of parents thinking maybe their child has the problem.

■ Is ADHD overdiagnosed and overtreated?

It's reaching the point where the prevalence is probably being matched by recognition and treatment. Approximately 6 percent of boys and 1.5 percent of girls are diagnosed with ADHD. That has increased from about 2 percent to 3 percent 10 years ago and less than 5 percent 5 years ago. The real question is whether it's the right children. Some of the

children who have the disease aren't recognized as having it and some who are recognized may not have it. The total may be right, but the mix may not be.

■ What are realistic expectations about what Ritalin can do to control ADHD?

What to expect is clear: Ritalin decreases symptoms and reduces aggression. However, it doesn't have any effect on positive interaction or cognitive ability, although a lot of the studies haven't looked at the long-term effect of the medication. There have been limited effects on academic achievement, and maybe there's a way to prescribe the drug so that it would elicit better academic achievement. Also, not every patient responds to it.

■ Why is Ritalin so much more popular than similar drugs?

Ritalin is used in 80 percent of cases because it has slightly fewer side effects and is very effective in so many people. The medications haven't changed since about 1960. We need some improvement in medications. For example, it's inconvenient to give the drug two or three times a day so we're working with pharmaceutical companies on a longer acting form as well as new designs for medications.

■ RECOMMENDED CHILDHOOD IMMUNIZATION SCHEDULE

The Centers for Disease Control, the American Academy of Pediatrics, and the American Academy of Family Physicians are America's leading authorities on childhood immunization. Below is their unified immunization schedule, released in January 1997.

Vaccine	First dose	Second dose	Third dose	Fourth dose	Fifth dose	Sixth dose
Hepatitis B[1]	Before 2 mos.	1–4 mos.[2]	6–18 mos.			
Diphtheria, Tetanus, Pertussis (DTP or DTaP)[3]	2 mos.	4 mos.	6 mos.	15–18 mos.	4–6 yrs.	11–16 yrs.[4]
H. influenza (type B)	2 mos.	4 mos.	6 mos.[5]	12–15 mos.		
Polio[6]	2 mos. (IPV)	4 mos. (IPV)	12–18 mos. (OPV)	4–6 yrs. (OPV)		
MMR	12–15 mos.	4–6 yrs. or 11–12 yrs.[2]				
Chicken Pox[1]	12–18 mos.[7]					

NOTES: 1. Unvaccinated children should be vaccinated between ages 11 and 12. 2. Allow at least one month after previous dose before administering next. 3. DTaP is the preferred vaccine. 4. Td is recommended if at least five years have elapsed since last dose. 5. Children who get an H. influenza vaccine known as PRP–OM do not require a dose at 6 months, but still require the booster. 6. Two polio vaccines are now licensed in the U.S.: the IPV and OPV, and this is one of three schedules parents can choose from. 7. Susceptible children may receive a vaccine at any time after their first birthday.

SOURCE: Centers for Disease Control, the American Academy of Pediatrics, and the American Academy of Family Physicians, 1997.

DOCTORS & MEDICINE

HOSPITALS: America's best treatment centers, PAGE 193 **EXPERT Q & A:** How to choose the right doctor, PAGE 200 **GENERIC DRUGS:** When paying less is hip, PAGE 205 **PAIN:** A guide to over-the-counter drugs, PAGE 207 **MEDICATIONS:** Drugs that treat depression, PAGE 208 **CAREGIVING:** A former First Lady's advice, PAGE 210 **PROSTATE CANCER:** When men should seek treatment, PAGE 214 **ALTERNATIVE MEDICINE:** Biofeedback may be of help, PAGE 216

HMOs

EXAMINING YOUR HEALTH PLAN

Before you pick a medical plan, scrutinize industry report cards

Comparison shopping is the norm when it comes to making a major purchase like a car, yet when it comes to selecting a managed health care plan, the decision is usually given little thought. Most Americans base their choice simply on word-of-mouth advice or the plan's cost. One reason is that, until recently, little information was available to compare the quality of care offered by the nation's 593 HMOs (health maintenance organizations). But a new nationwide movement is changing all that. So-called medical report cards are arming employers, and consumers, with a wealth of data that compare the quality of managed care plans, and provide tools to help them make the right choices.

Some of the report cards are the work of business coalitions that include large employers and nonprofit groups. Some are published by the health care plans themselves. The report cards use various criteria to measure how HMOs compare in terms of cost, quality, and ease of access. For example, they assess how well a plan delivers preventive services such as childhood immunizations, cholesterol screenings, mammograms, and pap smears. They also consider the percentage of members who undergo serious operations such as coronary bypass, angioplasty, hysterectomy, and cesarean sections.

A major advance came in 1996, when the National Commission for Quality Assurance (NCQA), the main accrediting body for HMOs and the leader in developing measures for health plan performance, launched the first national database of information. The report, called Quality Compass, assesses 250 health plans. It is based on per-

EXPERT SOURCE

The National Commission for Quality Assurance (NCQA) began a voluntary accreditation process for HMOs in 1991, which has become another useful tool for evaluating the quality of managed care plans. Consumers can find out the accreditation status of up to three managed care plans they may be considering by calling ☎ 202–955–5697.

formance measures called HEDIS (the Health Plan Employer Data and Information Set), which apply uniform criteria in analyzing a health plan. "To compare plans used to be difficult because you were comparing apples with oranges," explains Linda Ruth, benefits consultant at Hewitt Associates, a consulting firm which also helps companies devise their own report cards. "From 1997 forward, we're looking much more at apples with apples," says Ruth.

HEDIS measurements are quickly becoming the most widely accepted method of analyzing managed care plans. "HEDIS is the gold standard of report cards in that it's accepted by health plans and employers alike," says Ruth. Most of the report cards are designed to help companies make more informed decisions about which plans to offer employees, but many employers are passing on the information to employees. However, many consumers are having difficulty using the report cards to their advantage because of their complexity.

What should a consumer look for? First, narrow down your choices to two or three affordable plans that offer the benefits you're after. (See "Making HMOs Suit You," on facing page, for factors to consider when picking an HMO.) Once you've done that, says Ruth, look at all the statistics on the report cards that refer to the quality of care given by the plans. That should be a prime consideration.

Try also to ascertain the satisfaction rate of the plan's members, says Carol Cronin, senior vice president of Health Pages, a consumer health information company. Obtaining such data is not easy. Cronin cautions that often what appears on the report cards in this area does not tell you much because member satisfaction is lumped together instead of categorized, making it seem that all members are relatively satisfied. A more telling statistic is the number of complaints that have been filed against a plan, figures that appear on some but not all report cards. Another helpful measurement, according to Cronin, is physician turnover, which can be determined by looking at the names of doctors who remain in the plan from report card to report card. If you're in the market for a new primary care doctor, you'll also want to know how many of the listed doctors have "closed" practices, meaning they don't take new patients from that managed care plan.

To gauge the validity of a report card, you may want to ask whether the data have been audited by an outside company. An external audit ensures that the information was collected in a uniform manner.

While report cards are becoming more sophisticated and reliable, there are limitations. One of the weakest areas is the emphasis on process, or whether a plan offers certain services, rather than on how effective that care is. Another drawback: report cards typically evaluate the health plan and not the performance of a specific doctor or hospital. "The next generation of report cards will also evaluate a plan's doctors and the hospitals they use," predicts Cronin. "After all, the degree to which a managed care plan is good is highly dependent upon the doctors and hospitals in the plan."

Despite their shortcomings, early evidence suggests that report cards are effecting change in health care. A California study showed that over a period of six years, doctors at one hospital were able to cut the rate of cesareans from 31 percent to 15 percent of all deliveries, by using report cards that compared their doctors' cesarean-section rates with those of doctors in other hospitals. Likewise, the use of similar report cards in a hospital in New Orleans helped reduce the rate of cesareans by 30 percent during a six-month period. "If you believe the old adage that what gets measured, gets done, there's no question that report cards have helped managed care plans improve their processes," says Ruth. "Now they have a way of finding out how they're doing against a benchmark, and they can say, 'I know where I am and where I want to be,' and they can figure out how to fill that gap." And, HMO report cards will go a long way toward arming consumers with information to help them make more informed health plan decisions.

EXPERT TIPS

MAKING HMOs SUIT YOU

It takes skill and assertiveness to get the most out of the new plans

Members of managed care health plans take heart: Recent research has shown that the quality of care in managed care health plans is generally as good as in fee-for-service situations. A 1996 study by KPMG Peat Marwick, a financial services and consulting firm, of 11 million patients treated in cities with a high level of managed care found that the 3,700 hospitals surveyed reported significantly lower costs, shorter lengths of stay, and lower mortality rates than the national average. Another study of 8,000 heart attack survivors found that those enrolled in health maintenance organizations (HMOs) were less likely to undergo angioplasty (surgery to enlarge blood vessels) than those patients insured by other health care plans, yet short-term survival rates were about the same. To ensure top treatment, you have to be your own health care watchdog, however. Geraldine Dallek, director of health policy for Families USA, a national, nonprofit health consumer group, offers this advice on how to be a savvy medical consumer in the changing world of health care:

■ **Analyze each health care plan according to your special needs.** Look at a plan in terms of what medical conditions you or your family members will need to be treated for. If you have a special problem or concern, make sure the plan will provide you access to the drugs, specialists, or hospitals you need. And don't make a decision solely on cost, unless you

---

■ **THE NEW HEALTH CARE LANDSCAPE**

Fewer than a quarter of all Americans insured through employer-sponsored health plans still see doctors on a fee-for-service basis.

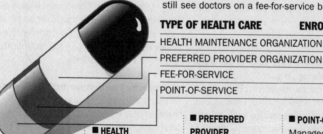

TYPE OF HEALTH CARE	ENROLLMENT
HEALTH MAINTENANCE ORGANIZATION	33%
PREFERRED PROVIDER ORGANIZATION	31%
FEE-FOR-SERVICE	18%
POINT-OF-SERVICE	17%

■ **FEE-FOR-SERVICE**
Private care where the patient chooses any doctor he or she wants to see. The patient pays according to the service rendered.

■ **HEALTH MAINTENANCE ORGANIZATION (HMO)**
Managed care where the patient is limited to seeing doctors employed by the HMO, and there is a set fee for the visit, no matter what service is performed.

■ **PREFERRED PROVIDER ORGANIZATION (PPO)**
Managed care where the patient chooses from a list of specific doctors in his or her area and pays a set fee for the consultation, no matter what service is performed.

■ **POINT-OF-SERVICE**
Managed care where the patient chooses from a list of doctors a primary care physician who coordinates all of his or her care. Patients who want to see a specialist must obtain the primary care physician's approval first.

SOURCE: KPMG Peat Marwick LLP, survey of employer-sponsored health benefits, 1996.

can't afford anything but the cheapest plan.

■ **Find out what's covered, and what's not, before you sign up with a health plan.** If you're concerned about special medical needs or problems, ask which services are covered in the benefits package offered and which have to be paid for out-of-pocket. Be sure to ask your doctor if the plan imposes any limits on his ability to talk to you about your medical needs.

■ **Ask your primary care doctor which, if any, plans he or she participates in.** You may not want to join an HMO if you've already established a relationship with a physician not on the list. However, you can opt for a point-of-service plan that allows you to go outside the HMO's network of providers for an additional fee.

■ **Learn when referrals are allowed, and when they're not.** Most HMOs require that patients first see a primary care doctor, who determines whether you need to see a specialist. Sometimes decisions are not in the primary care doctor's hands. Ask him under what circumstances he would give a referral, and whether somebody else approves referrals, which is likely the case if you're in an HMO. If you have a particular illness like Multiple Sclerosis (MS), make sure your plan allows you access to a specialist in MS.

■ **Compare the out-of-pocket costs of the health plans you're considering.** In many fee-for-service plans you pay an annual deductible and a percentage of each medical bill. Look at how much your monthly premium and deductibles will be as well as your maximum out-of-pocket costs—it could be $2,500 or $12,000. If you're in an HMO, you may have to pay a fixed amount, and in a PPO, a percentage of the cost of each visit. Managed care plans are generally cheaper than fee-for-service plans, but be sure to compare co-payment requirements for prescription drugs and office visits for HMOs.

■ **Know which hospitals and network of providers you'll be limited to if you sign up.** Many people are reluctant to enroll in managed care plans because they're concerned that if they get sick the plan won't allow them to get the best possible treatment at so-called centers of excellence. If you're not satisfied with the choice of hospitals, try a preferred provider organization (PPO), which usually offers a range of hospitals in the plan, or an HMO with a point-of-service option.

Make sure you look at the whole range of providers. With some HMOs you don't actually receive medical care from the HMO's total network, or main group of doctors, but from a contracting medical group or independent practice association (IPA), a network of providers that contracts with the HMO. So the HMO may have a wonderful list of doctors, but that isn't going to help you at all. For example, your care could be very limited if your IPA only has two heart specialists they've contracted with.

■ **Use the coordinated care and preventive services provided by managed care.** There are benefits to joining a managed care plan aside from reduced cost. In the best plans, somebody really is coordinating your care and making sure you get the referrals you need, and that's a huge plus. HMOs do a very good job of providing preventive care because it's very cost-effective. They make it easy to get preventive care, and it's paid for, so patients are much more willing to get preventive services like a physical, pap smear, mammography or immunizations.

■ **Raise a fuss if you think your needs aren't being met.** When you're in a managed care plan, you need to take responsibility for making sure that what needs to get done gets done. If you're denied a service you think is critical, you should first talk to your primary care doctor. You can also file a grievance with the HMO challenging a health care provider's judgment and requesting that a decision not to provide or pay for care be reconsidered. All HMOs have grievance procedures, although they do vary. If need be, investigate whether there's an outside group available to help you. Some communities have nonprofit advocacy groups and at least half of all states have hot lines that you can call to complain and ask for an investigation if you have a grievance.

EXPERT LIST

THE BEST HOSPITALS IN AMERICA

Each year, the magazine U.S. News & World Report *publishes a special report ranking America's best hospitals in 16 categories. The magazine's rating system was designed by the National Opinion Research Center, a social-science research group at the University of Chicago. The model combines three years' worth of reputational surveys conducted by the magazine, death-rate statistics, and a collection of measures, specific to each specialty, which physicians and social-science researchers believe reflect quality of care. To be considered for this study, a hospital must meet one of three criteria: be affiliated with a medical school, or have 9 of more of 18 specific items of technology, or be a member of the Council of Teaching Hospitals.*

■ **AIDS:** Hospitals and doctors specializing in treating patients infected with HIV, the virus that causes AIDS, have several newer medications to work with in addition to AZT. Combinations of these drugs can supress HIV for longer periods and improve survival. As a result, much HIV treatment is now provided on an outpatient basis at the top hospitals.

HOSPITAL	OVERALL SCORE	Reputational score	Mortality rate	Technology score (of 9)	Discharge planning (of 3)	R.N.s to beds
1. San Francisco General Hospital Medical Center	100.0	59.3%	0.94	7.5	2	2.21
2. Johns Hopkins Hospital, Baltimore*	71.8	35.3%	0.91	9.0	3	1.36
3. Massachusetts General Hospital, Boston*	59.4	24.4%	0.76	9.0	1	1.40
4. University of California, San Francisco Medical Center*	53.6	19.0%	0.70	9.0	3	1.41
5. UCLA Medical Center, Los Angeles*	51.0	18.8%	0.68	9.0	1	1.03
6. University of Miami, Jackson Memorial Hospital*	43.5	15.8%	0.95	6.5	3	1.49
7. Memorial Sloan-Kettering Cancer Center, New York*	42.1	11.7%	0.80	8.0	2	1.56
8. New York University Medical Center*	38.6	10.9%	0.88	8.5	3	0.91
9. Northwestern Memorial Hospital, Chicago*	37.6	8.9%	0.59	7.5	3	0.99
10. New York Hospital—Cornell Medical Center*	36.9	11.7%	0.99	8.0	2	0.93
11. Montefiore Medical Center, Bronx, N.Y.*	36.0	9.1%	0.98	8.0	3	1.52
12. Duke University Medical Center, Durham, N.C.*	35.0	4.4%	0.78	9.0	3	1.73
13. Rush-Presbyterian—St. Luke's Medical Center, Chicago*	33.7	5.4%	0.65	9.0	1	1.07
14. UCSD Medical Center, San Diego*	33.5	3.7%	0.67	8.0	3	1.73
15. University of Washington Medical Center, Seattle*	33.5	3.8%	0.68	8.0	2	1.88
16. New England Deaconess Hospital, Boston*	32.9	6.7%	0.80	7.0	2	1.00
17. Beth Israel Hospital, Boston*	32.7	4.7%	0.72	7.0	2	1.53
18. Stanford University Hospital, Stanford, Calif.*	32.3	4.8%	0.78	7.5	3	1.18
19. Mayo Clinic, Rochester, Minn.*	31.9	4.9%	0.67	7.5	3	0.83
20. Mount Sinai Medical Center, New York*	31.2	5.3%	0.97	8.5	3	1.39

TERMS:

REPUTATIONAL SCORE: Percentage of board-certified doctors surveyed in 1994, 1995, and 1996 who named the hospital.

MORTALITY RATE: Comparison of actual to expected deaths. Rate is specialty-specific except for AIDS and gynecology.

TECHNOLOGY SCORE: Relates to high-tech services. Points vary by specialty.

DISCHARGE PLANNING: Availability of staffed social work department and patient-representative services.

R.N.S TO BEDS: Number of full-time registered nurses relative to number of beds.

* Indicates member of Council of Teaching Hosptials.

SOURCE: Reprinted from *U.S. News & World Report,* August 12, 1996.©1996.

AIDS HOSPITALS (CNT'D)	OVERALL SCORE	Reputational score	Mortality rate	Technology score (of 9)	Discharge planning (of 3)	R.N.s to beds
21. Hospital of the University of Pennsylvania, Philadelphia*	30.5	3.5%	0.81	7.0	3	1.52
22. Columbia-Presbyterian Medical Center, New York*	30.1	6.7%	1.16	9.0	2	1.17
23. New England Medical Center, Boston*	29.7	0.9%	0.81	8.0	3	2.16
24. Brigham and Women's Hospital, Boston*	28.6	3.6%	0.78	6.5	3	0.76
25. Cook County Hospital, Chicago*	28.5	1.2%	0.55	7.0	3	1.49

■ **CANCER:** Cancer is a group of diseases in which cells grow uncontrollably and spread throughout the body. Although cancer diagnoses and deaths continue to climb, the quality of life for many cancer patients has improved thanks to less disfiguring surgery, drugs to control chemotherapy's side effects, and better pain control.

HOSPITAL	OVERALL SCORE	Reputational score	Mortality rate	Technology score (of 7)	R.N.s to beds	Proced. to beds
1. Memorial Sloan-Kettering Cancer Center, New York*	100.0	72.4%	0.89	6.0	1.56	8.74
2. University of Texas M.D. Anderson Cancer Ctr., Houston*	99.7	68.8%	0.18	6.5	1.49	8.51
3. Dana-Farber Cancer Institute, Boston	68.8	47.1%	0.06	3.0	6.16	11.33
4. Johns Hopkins Hospital, Baltimore*	55.7	32.6%	0.44	7.0	1.36	1.62
5. Mayo Clinic, Rochester, Minn.*	47.6	28.9%	0.47	5.5	0.83	3.55
6. Stanford University Hospital, Stanford, Calif.*	35.2	17.2%	0.64	5.5	1.18	2.17
7. University of Washington Medical Center, Seattle*	30.7	11.6%	0.56	6.0	1.88	1.81
8. Duke University Medical Center, Durham, N.C.*	30.2	10.9%	0.63	7.0	1.73	3.14
9. University of Chicago Hospitals*	28.2	8.4%	0.44	7.0	1.63	2.71
10. University of California, San Francisco Medical Center*	25.6	7.7%	0.47	7.0	1.41	0.96
11. Massachusetts General Hospital, Boston*	25.3	8.0%	0.70	7.0	1.40	2.79
12. Roswell Park Cancer Institute, Buffalo	23.4	7.5%	0.49	5.5	2.92	14.56
13. Indiana University Medical Center, Indianapolis*	22.2	4.1%	0.57	7.0	1.76	1.59
14. Fox Chase Cancer Center, Philadelphia	20.7	6.1%	0.21	4.0	1.90	9.68
15. University of Michigan Medical Center, Ann Arbor*	19.8	2.1%	0.45	7.0	1.45	1.64
16. UCLA Medical Center, Los Angeles*	19.7	3.0%	0.47	7.0	1.03	1.89
17. Barnes-Jewish Hospital, St. Louis*	18.9	3.3%	0.58	6.5	1.00	1.69
18. Hospital of the University of Pennsylvania, Philadelphia*	18.4	2.5%	0.71	6.0	1.52	2.33
19. Mary Hitchcock Memorial Hospital, Lebanon, N.H.*	18.4	0.5%	0.50	7.0	1.49	1.92
20. University of Iowa Hospitals and Clinics, Iowa City*	18.3	1.4%	0.57	7.0	1.31	1.62
21. Rush-Presbyterian—St. Luke's Medical Center, Chicago*	18.2	1.9%	0.48	7.0	1.07	1.65
22. Georgetown University Hospital, Washington, D.C.*	18.1	1.2%	0.49	5.0	1.63	2.11
23. University of Virginia Health Sciences Ctr., Charlottesville*	17.9	0.0%	0.54	7.0	1.77	1.94
24. Mount Sinai Medical Center, New York*	17.9	4.2%	1.03	6.5	1.39	2.38
25. Vanderbilt University Hospital and Clinic, Nashville*	17.7	1.4%	0.64	7.0	1.34	1.94

TERMS:

REPUTATIONAL SCORE:
Percentage of board-certified doctors surveyed in 1994, 1995, and 1996 who named the hospital.

MORTALITY RATE:
Comparison of actual to expected deaths. Rate is specialty-specific except for AIDS and gynecology.

R.N.S TO BEDS:
Number of full-time registered nurses relative to number of beds.

PROCEDURES TO BEDS:
Number of surgical and nonsurgical procedures relative to the number of beds. Specialty-specific.

TECHNOLOGY SCORE:
Relates to high-tech services. Points vary by specialty.

* Indicates member of Council of Teaching Hospitals.

SOURCE: Reprinted from U.S. News & World Report, August 12, 1996.©1996.

■ EXPERT LIST

■ **CARDIOLOGY:** Many hospitalizations are due to congestive heart failure, in which the heart cannot adequately pump blood. An increasing number of people are living with this condition, thanks to improved survival of patients with coronary artery disease—which can set the stage for heart failure—and to better treatment of heart failure itself. Top cardiology hospitals perform transplants in heart-failure patients who do not respond to drug and diet therapy.

HOSPITAL	OVERALL SCORE	Reputational score	Mortality rate	Technology score (of 9)	R.N.s to beds	Proced. to beds
1. Cleveland Clinic*	100.0	54.6%	0.65	8.5	1.10	9.10
2. Mayo Clinic, Rochester, Minn.*	96.0	52.9%	0.75	8.0	0.83	10.43
3. Massachusetts General Hospital, Boston*	67.6	30.6%	0.64	9.0	1.40	8.68
4. Duke University Medical Center, Durham, N.C.*	58.2	23.7%	0.74	9.0	1.73	7.09
5. Texas Heart Institute—St. Luke's Episcopal, Houston*	53.6	28.0%	1.22	8.0	1.31	11.20
6. Emory University Hospital, Atlanta*	49.3	21.7%	0.88	9.0	0.87	9.39
7. Brigham and Women's Hospital, Boston*	48.3	23.7%	0.94	7.0	0.76	5.92
8. Stanford University Hospital, Stanford, Calif.*	44.9	18.3%	0.87	8.0	1.18	7.20
9. Johns Hopkins Hospital, Baltimore*	35.2	13.8%	1.16	9.0	1.36	5.01
10. University of California, San Francisco Medical Center*	33.2	6.5%	0.76	9.0	1.41	2.77
11. Barnes-Jewish Hospital, St. Louis*	30.0	8.4%	0.92	9.0	1.00	5.35
12. Cedars-Sinai Medical Center, Los Angeles*	29.6	7.9%	0.87	8.0	1.04	7.90
13. Columbia-Presbyterian Medical Center, New York*	29.1	9.7%	1.12	9.0	1.17	4.72
14. Methodist Hospital, Houston*	28.9	10.9%	1.13	8.0	1.03	7.15
15. Beth Israel Hospital, Boston*	28.9	4.0%	0.77	8.0	1.53	11.60
16. Mount Sinai Medical Center, New York*	27.5	3.3%	0.78	8.5	1.39	3.74
17. UCLA Medical Center, Los Angeles*	26.8	3.2%	0.68	9.0	1.03	4.55
18. University of Alabama Hospital at Birmingham*	26.7	9.4%	1.19	7.0	1.42	7.76
19. Hospital of the University of Pennsylvania, Philadelphia*	26.6	1.7%	0.76	9.0	1.52	4.95
20. University of Chicago Hospitals*	26.3	1.6%	0.77	9.0	1.63	4.46
21. William Beaumont Hospital, Royal Oak, Mich.*	25.6	2.5%	0.85	9.0	1.51	10.65
22. New York Hospital—Cornell Medical Center*	25.2	4.6%	0.88	9.0	0.93	3.85
23. University of Washington Medical Center, Seattle*	25.0	0.4%	0.70	9.0	1.88	4.29
24. University Hospitals of Cleveland*	24.3	0.5%	0.79	9.0	1.84	4.99
25. Baylor University Medical Center, Dallas*	23.9	4.2%	0.91	8.0	1.19	6.89

■ **ENDOCRINOLOGY:** Endocrinology involves diagnosing and treating disorders of the endocrine glands, such as diabetes, infertility, osteoporosis, thyroid disorders, high cholesterol and hormone-producing tumors. At large medical centers, endocrinologists are often "hidden specialists" who consult with other specialists.

HOSPITAL	OVERALL SCORE	Reputational score	Mortality rate	Technology score (of 7)	R.N.s to beds
1. Massachusetts General Hospital, Boston*	100.0	63.8%	0.59	7.0	1.40
2. Mayo Clinic, Rochester, Minn.*	95.1	63.4%	0.68	5.5	0.83
3. University of California, San Francisco Medical Center*	48.3	23.6%	0.45	7.0	1.41
4. Johns Hopkins Hospital, Baltimore*	42.8	22.3%	0.88	7.0	1.36
5. Barnes-Jewish Hospital, St. Louis*	37.9	20.4%	0.93	6.0	1.00
6. New England Deaconess Hospital, Boston*	32.6	14.0%	0.57	6.0	1.00
7. Brigham and Women's Hospital, Boston*	29.7	12.9%	0.55	5.0	0.76
8. UCLA Medical Center, Los Angeles*	29.1	12.1%	0.66	6.0	1.03
9. Parkland Memorial Hospital, Dallas*	28.9	11.4%	0.81	6.0	1.61

■ **EXPERT LIST**

ENDOCRINOLOGY HOSPITAL (CNT'D)	OVERALL SCORE	Reputational score	Mortality rate	Technology score (of 7)	R.N.s to bed
10. University of Chicago Hospitals*	28.9	9.7%	0.62	7.0	1.63
11. University of Michigan Medical Center, Ann Arbor*	27.5	9.4%	0.71	7.0	1.45
12. University of Washington Medical Center, Seattle*	26.0	8.6%	0.79	7.0	1.45
13. Vanderbilt University Hospital and Clinic, Nashville*	25.8	6.8%	0.43	7.0	1.34
14. Duke University Medical Center, Durham, N.C.*	24.7	7.6%	0.78	7.0	1.73
15. University of Virginia Health Sciences Ctr., Charlottesville*	23.7	6.6%	0.75	7.0	1.77
16. Stanford University Hospital, Stanford, Calif.*	23.2	5.8%	0.09	6.0	1.18
17. Columbia-Presbyterian Medical Center, New York*	20.5	6.8%	1.14	7.0	1.17
18. Hospital of the University of Pennsylvania, Philadelphia*	20.5	2.5%	0.55	7.0	1.52
19. University Hospital, Denver*	20.3	2.6%	0.35	6.0	1.62
20. Beth Israel Hospital, Boston*	19.7	4.2%	0.78	6.0	1.53
21. University of Texas M.D. Anderson Cancer Ctr., Houston*	18.9	1.0%	0.23	7.0	1.49
22. University of Iowa Hospitals and Clinics, Iowa City*	18.8	3.8%	0.82	7.0	1.31
23. Cleveland Clinic*	18.7	4.2%	0.73	6.5	1.10
24. Mount Sinai Medical Center, New York*	18.1	4.6%	1.18	6.5	1.39
25. Medical University of South Carolina, Charleston*	18.0	0.6%	0.32	6.5	1.76

■ **GYNECOLOGY;** The top hospitals in gynecology, almost always linked with obstetrics, manage problems ranging from cancers of the female reproductive tract to uterine fibroids to premature labor. These institutions can help women conceive and ensure that they carry their pregnancies to term.

HOSPITAL	OVERALL SCORE	Reputational score	Mortality rate	Interns and res. to beds	Technology score (of 8)	R.N.s to beds	Proced. to beds
1. Johns Hopkins Hospital, Baltimore	100.0	30.8%	0.91	0.68	8.0	1.36	0.43
2. Mayo Clinic, Rochester, Minn.	93.9	29.6%	0.67	0.61	6.0	0.83	1.12
3. University of Texas M.D. Anderson Cancer Ctr., Houston	70.5	19.3%	0.19	0.77	7.0	1.49	0.82
4. Brigham and Women's Hospital, Boston	69.2	18.9%	0.78	1.80	6.0	0.76	0.65
5. Massachusetts General Hospital, Boston	63.9	15.9%	0.76	1.20	8.0	1.40	0.67
6. Duke University Medical Center, Durham, N.C.	44.5	9.2%	0.78	0.94	8.0	1.73	0.55
7. Los Angeles County—USC Medical Center	44.2	10.0%	0.67	1.40	5.5	1.19	0.04
8. Parkland Memorial Hospital, Dallas	42.7	9.9%	1.07	1.07	7.0	1.61	0.12
9. Memorial Sloan-Kettering Cancer Center, New York	41.6	8.7%	0.80	0.90	7.0	1.56	0.52
10. Cleveland Clinic	40.7	8.7%	0.68	0.89	7.5	1.10	0.55
11. UCLA Medical Center, Los Angeles	38.6	6.8%	0.68	1.55	8.0	1.03	0.50
12. University of Chicago Hospitals	37.2	5.0%	0.64	1.80	8.0	1.63	0.36
13. University of California, San Francisco Medical Center	36.3	6.2%	0.70	1.04	8.0	1.41	0.25
14. Hospital of the University of Pennsylvania, Philadelphia	35.4	4.3%	0.81	1.94	8.0	1.52	0.37
15. Stanford University Hospital, Stanford, Calif.	33.0	6.7%	0.78	0.69	6.5	1.18	0.55
16. Columbia-Presbyterian Medical Center, New York	32.5	6.5%	1.16	1.10	8.0	1.17	0.27
17. Northwestern Memorial Hospital, Chicago	31.8	6.7%	0.59	0.45	7.0	0.99	0.43
18. Yale–New Haven Hospital, New Haven, Conn.	29.8	5.1%	0.90	1.19	7.5	0.95	0.60
19. Vanderbilt University Hospital and Clinic, Nashville	28.5	3.5%	0.95	1.47	8.0	1.34	0.39
20. New York Hospital—Cornell Medical Center	27.4	5.1%	0.99	0.80	8.0	0.93	0.24
21. University of Washington Medical Center, Seattle	27.4	2.6%	0.68	1.05	8.0	1.88	0.60
22. University of Michigan Medical Center, Ann Arbor	27.1	2.3%	0.90	1.67	8.0	1.45	0.42

◼ **EXPERT LIST**

GYNECOLOGY HOSPITALS (CNT'D)	OVERALL SCORE	Reputational score	Mortality rate	Interns and res. to beds	Technology score (of 8)	R.N.s to beds	Proced. to beds
23. Cedars-Sinai Medical Center, Los Angeles	26.9	5.3%	0.98	0.65	7.0	1.04	0.54
24. University of North Carolina Hospitals, Chapel Hill	26.6	3.4%	1.11	1.42	7.5	1.43	0.45
25. New York University Medical Center	26.4	3.8%	0.88	1.30	7.5	0.91	0.29

◼ **NEUROLOGY:** Stroke is one of the major disorders treated by neurologists. Leading neurology hospitals are equipped with the imaging tools needed to diagnose stroke and other ailments of the brain and nervous system, such as multiple sclerosis and dementia.

HOSPITAL	OVERALL SCORE	Reputational score	Mortality rate	Technology score (of 7)	R.N.s to beds
1. Mayo Clinic, Rochester, Minn.*	100.0	56.9%	0.78	5.5	0.83
2. Masschusetts General Hospital, Boston*	90.5	46.0%	0.79	7.0	1.40
3. Johns Hopkins Hospital, Baltimore*	82.3	41.7%	0.88	7.0	1.36
4. Columbia-Presbyterian Medical Center, New York*	58.6	28.1%	1.02	7.0	1.17
5. University of California, San Francisco Medical Center*	53.7	22.3%	0.79	7.0	1.41
6. Cleveland Clinic*	40.5	13.5%	0.59	6.5	1.10
7. UCLA Medical Center, Los Angeles*	37.1	11.8%	0.68	6.0	1.03
8. Duke University Medical Center, Durham, N.C.*	35.5	10.1%	0.77	7.0	1.73
9. Hospital of the University of Pennsylvania, Philadelphia*	33.4	8.6%	0.76	7.0	1.52
10. Barnes-Jewish Hospital, St. Louis*	33.0	10.3%	0.76	6.0	1.00
11. New York Hospital—Cornell Medical Center*	29.9	9.3%	0.89	7.0	0.93
12. University of Miami, Jackson Memorial Hospital*	29.2	8.6%	0.91	4.5	1.49
13. University of Iowa Hospitals and Clinics, Iowa City*	25.7	3.8%	0.72	7.0	1.31
14. University of Washington Medical Center, Seattle*	25.0	2.1%	0.61	7.0	1.88
15. Shands Hospital at the University of Florida, Gainsville*	24.7	3.1%	0.38	7.0	1.09
16. University of Michigan Medical Center, Ann Arbor*	24.3	6.0%	1.15	7.0	1.45
17. University of Ilinois Hospital and Clinics, Chicago*	24.2	2.5%	0.34	5.0	1.81
18. University of Chicago Hospitals*	24.1	1.5%	0.57	7.0	1.63
19. University of Texas M.D. Anderson Cancer Ctr., Houston*	24.1	1.5%	0.15	7.0	1.49
20. New York University Medical Center*	23.4	3.1%	0.66	6.5	0.91
21. Rush-Presbyterian—St. Luke's Medical Center, Chicago*	23.2	2.2%	0.44	7.0	1.07
22. Stanford University Hospital, Stanford, Calif.*	22.7	3.1%	0.75	6.0	1.18
23. Beth Israel Hospital, Boston*	22.5	1.0%	0.64	6.0	1.53
24. Mount Sinai Medical Center, New York*	22.4	3.0%	0.84	6.5	1.39
25. Georgetown University Hospital, Washington, D.C.*	22.0	1.4%	0.70	5.0	1.63

TERMS:

REPUTATIONAL SCORE: Percentage of board-certified doctors surveyed in 1994, 1995, and 1996 who named the hospital.

MORTALITY RATE: Comparison of actual to expected deaths. Rate is specialty-specific except for AIDS and gynecology.

INTERNS AND RESIDENTS TO BEDS: The number of doctors in training relative to number of beds.

R.N.S TO BEDS: Number of full-time registered nurses relative to number of beds.

PROCEDURES TO BEDS: Number of surgical and nonsurgical procedures relative to the number of beds. Specialty-specific.

TECHNOLOGY SCORE: Relates to high-tech services. Points vary by specialty.

DISCHARGE PLANNING: Availability of staffed social work department and patient-representative services.

* Indicates member of Council of Teaching Hosptials.

SOURCE: Reprinted from *U.S. News & World Report*, August 12, 1996.©1996.

■ **EXPERT LIST**

■ **ORTHOPEDICS:** This branch of surgery deals with bones, joints, and muscles. One of the most common procedures is hip replacement in patients with arthritis or other debilitating diseases.

HOSPITAL	OVERALL SCORE	Reputational score	Mortality rate	Technology score (of 5)	R.N.s to beds	Proced. to beds
1. Mayo Clinic, Rochester, Minn.*	100.0	48.5%	0.50	4.0	0.83	6.08
2. Massachusetts General Hospital, Boston*	90.0	40.2%	0.57	5.0	1.40	2.81
3. Hospital for Special Surgery, New York*	89.0	39.7%	0.04	4.5	1.12	21.28
4. Johns Hopkins Hospital, Baltimore*	49.1	18.9%	0.65	5.0	1.36	1.23
5. Duke University Medical Center, Durham, N.C.*	39.8	13.0%	0.58	5.0	1.73	1.78
6. Cleveland Clinic*	34.1	10.4%	0.48	4.5	1.10	2.39
7. UCLA Medical Center, Los Angeles*	33.1	10.9%	0.70	5.0	1.03	1.88
8. University of Iowa Hospitals and Clinics, Iowa City*	28.9	8.2%	0.69	5.0	1.31	1.25
9. University of Washington Medical Center, Seattle*	27.7	6.0%	0.50	5.0	1.88	1.76
10. Hospital for Joint Diseases—Orthopedic Inst., New York*	27.4	6.4%	0.06	4.0	1.10	9.06
11. University of Michigan Medical Center, Ann Arbor*	23.1	5.2%	0.85	5.0	1.45	1.25
12. Stanford University Hospital, Stanford, Calif.*	22.5	4.1%	0.54	4.0	1.18	3.04
13. Hospital of the University of Pennsylvania, Philadelphia*	22.2	4.3%	0.80	5.0	1.52	1.80
14. Harborview Medical Center, Seattle*	21.4	5.3%	1.15	3.5	2.25	1.25
15. Los Angeles County—USC Medical Center*	20.6	3.8%	0.40	3.5	1.19	0.21
16. Thomas Jefferson University Hospital, Philadelphia*	20.1	2.7%	0.41	4.0	1.38	0.99
17. University of Texas M.D. Anderson Cancer Ctr., Houston*	20.1	2.2%	0.08	5.0	1.49	0.74
18. University of Chicago Hospitals*	19.3	1.5%	0.27	5.0	1.63	1.56
19. Vanderbilt University Hospital and Clinic, Nashville*	19.2	2.3%	0.60	5.0	1.34	1.79
20. Rush-Presbyterian Medical Center, Chicago*	18.8	2.2%	0.54	5.0	1.07	1.98
21. Beth Israel Hospital, Boston*	18.1	0.8%	0.48	4.0	1.53	2.99
22. Columbia-Presbyterian Medical Center, New York*	17.7	3.6%	1.37	5.0	1.17	1.58
23. UCSD Medical Center, San Diego*	17.6	1.1%	0.30	4.0	1.73	1.18
24. Green Hospital of Scripps Clinic, La Jolla, Calif.*	17.2	0.0%	0.25	4.0	1.48	6.18
25. Northwestern Memorial Hospital, Chicago*	17.2	2.0%	0.55	4.0	0.99	2.06

■ **UROLOGY:** One of the major controversies in the field of urology today is how aggressive doctors should be in detecting and treating prostate cancer. Prostate surgery and radiation treatments can sometimes have detrimental results, including incontinence and impotence.

HOSPITAL	OVERALL SCORE	Reputational score	Mortality rate	Technology score (of 8)	R.N.s to beds	Proced. to beds
1. Johns Hopkins Hospital, Baltimore*	100.0	55.3%	0.89	7.5	1.36	1.32
2. Mayo Clinic, Rochester, Minn.*	83.8	44.3%	0.57	6.5	0.83	3.76
3. Cleveland Clinic*	54.7	25.1%	0.60	7.0	1.10	1.60
4. UCLA Medical Center, Los Angeles*	52.3	23.4%	0.57	7.0	1.03	2.29
5. Massachusetts General Hospital, Boston*	50.1	22.3%	0.81	8.0	1.40	2.21
6. Barnes-Jewish Hospital, St. Louis*	40.5	17.3%	0.77	7.0	1.00	1.52
7. Duke University Medical Center, Durham, N.C.*	38.8	14.0%	0.67	8.0	1.73	1.86
8. University of Texas M.D. Anderson Cancer Ctr., Houston*	33.9	10.4%	0.27	7.0	1.49	1.93
9. Memorial Sloan-Kettering Cancer Center, New York*	32.7	10.3%	0.68	7.0	1.56	2.82
10. Stanford University Hospital, Stanford, Calif.*	31.0	11.2%	0.79	6.0	1.18	2.15
11. Baylor University Medical Center, Dallas*	30.5	9.4%	0.62	7.0	1.19	1.57
12. New York Hospital—Cornell Medical Center*	30.1	10.5%	0.76	8.0	0.93	1.43

■ EXPERT LIST

UROLOGY HOSPITALS (CNT'D)	OVERALL SCORE	Reputational score	Mortality rate	Technology score (of 8)	R.N.s to beds	Proced. to beds
13. University of California, San Francisco Medical Center*	28.3	6.7%	0.50	8.0	1.41	1.79
14. University of Michigan Medical Center, Ann Arbor*	23.0	3.8%	0.66	8.0	1.45	1.40
15. University of Washington Medical Center, Seattle*	22.5	2.7%	0.54	8.0	1.88	1.58
16. Brigham and Women's Hospital, Boston*	21.8	5.6%	0.66	6.0	0.76	1.19
17. Hospital of the University of Pennsylvania, Philadelphia*	21.7	2.8%	0.66	8.0	1.52	2.76
18. Indiana University Medical Center, Indianapolis*	21.5	4.8%	1.13	8.0	1.52	2.76
19. Columbia-Presbyterian Medical Center, New York*	21.1	5.1%	0.93	7.0	1.17	1.67
20. Northwestern Memorial Hospital, Chicago*	20.8	4.3%	0.71	7.0	0.99	1.54
21. University of Iowa Hospitals and Clinics, Iowa City*	20.4	2.8%	0.69	8.0	1.31	1.28
22. Emory University Hospital, Atlanta*	20.2	4.6%	0.79	7.0	0.87	2.47
23. Thomas Jefferson University Hospital, Philadelphia*	20.0	2.0%	0.60	7.0	1.38	1.01
24. Los Angeles County—USC Medical Center*	18.6	2.7%	0.63	5.0	1.19	0.18
25. UCSD Medical Center, San Diego*	18.6	0.7%	0.34	6.5	1.73	1.67

■ **PEDIATRICS:** The field of pediatrics covers adolescents as well as children and infants; doctors at top centers often subspecialize in a specific age group. In the *U.S. News & World Report* rankings, this medical specialty is ranked solely on reputational scores from physician surveys conducted in 1994, 1995, and 1996. To make the list, hospitals had to be recommended by at least 3 percent of the board-certified specialists polled in the appropriate field.

HOSPITAL	Reputational score
1. Childrens Hospital, Boston	41.8%
2. Children's Hospital of Philadelphia	28.3%
3. Johns Hopkins Hospital, Baltimore	27.8%
4. Childrens Hospital Los Angeles	12.1%
5. Children's Nat. Medical Ctr., Washington, D.C.	9.0%
6. Children's Memorial Hospital, Chicago	8.9%
7. Children's Hospital of Pittsburgh	8.8%
8. Children's Hospital, Denver	8.8%
9. Mayo Clinic, Rochester, Minn.	8.0%
10. Children's Hospital Medical Ctr., Cincinnati	7.9%
11. Columbia-Presbyterian Medical Ctr., New York	7.1%
12. Univ. Hosps. of Cleveland (Rainbow Babies and Children's Hosp.)	6.7%

HOSPITAL	Reputational score
13. UCLA Medical Center, Los Angeles	5.6%
14. St. Louis Children's Hospital	4.9%
15. Duke University Medical Ctr., Durham, N.C.	4.6%
16. Massachusetts General Hospital, Boston	4.6%
17. Texas Children's Hospital, Houston	4.3%
18. Univ. of Washington Medical Ctr., Seattle	4.3%
19. Stanford University Hospital, Stanford, Calif.	4.1%
20. Univ. of California, San Francisco Medical Ctr.,	3.8%
21. Children's Hospital and Medical Ctr., Seattle	3.5%
22. St. Jude Children's Research Hosp., Memphis	3.2%
23. Univ. of Michigan Medical Ctr., Ann Arbor	3.1%
24. Univ. of Miami, Jackson Memorial Hosp.	3.0%

TERMS:

REPUTATIONAL SCORE: Percentage of board-certified doctors surveyed in 1994, 1995, and 1996 who named the hospital.

MORTALITY RATE: Comparison of actual to expected deaths. Rate is specialty-specific except for AIDS and gynecology.

INTERNS AND RESIDENTS TO BEDS: The number of doctors in training relative to number of beds.

R.N.S TO BEDS: Number of full-time registered nurses relative to number of beds.

PROCEDURES TO BEDS: Number of surgical and nonsurgical procedures relative to the number of beds. Specialty-specific.

TECHNOLOGY SCORE: Relates to high-tech services. Points vary by specialty.

DISCHARGE PLANNING: Availability of staffed social work department and patient-representative services.

* Indicates member of Council of Teaching Hospitals.

SOURCE: Reprinted from *U.S. News & World Report*, August 12, 1996.©1996.

WHAT TO LOOK FOR IN A DOCTOR

Dr. C. Everett Koop on finding the right doctor in today's environment

L ike it or not, managed care is rapidly replacing fee-for-service medical treatment in the lives of most Americans. Understandably, the change has provoked great confusion and concern about the quality of medical care today. One common complaint is that doctor-patient trust has been destroyed by the dollars-and-cents mentality that now pervades the profession.

Former United States Surgeon General C. Everett Koop is a longtime consumer health advocate and author of a self-help guide, *Dr. Koop's Self-Care Advisor: The Essential Home Health Guide* (Time Life Medical, 1996), to help educate health care consumers and encourage them to take a more active role in the health care decisions affecting them. Here, Dr. Koop discusses how consumers can get the most out of a visit to the doctor:

■ How should patients choose a doctor?

With 66 percent of the country now in managed care, most people don't have much choice. The patients with the greatest leeway are those on Medicare. But if you do have a choice of doctors, one of the things I think people find most helpful is referrals from patients who are satisfied with their doctor. If a doctor doesn't listen to you or doesn't communicate, that's not a doctor to seek out unless there's something very special about him and his knowledge.

■ How can patients determine whether their doctor is qualified to treat their condition, or whether they need to see a specialist?

That's a real tough one. If you have an honest primary care physician and you ask, "Do you know as much about what you want me to do as a specialist would," a good answer would be, "No, I don't, but I know enough so that I'm doing the right thing for you." Depending on your confidence in your doctor, you would accept that. You don't have to know everything to be able to do the right thing. It's the tricky situations where a difference of opinion can make a real difference in the patient's quality of life, or even life itself. Sometimes people understand by attitude, innuendo, and body language what their doctor's comfort level is with what he's telling them.

■ What if you do need a specialist?

Many people know a doctor, he may even be a friend they don't use professionally, who can recommend a specialist. Patients can also ask what a doctor's background is. If your primary care physician thinks you should see a specialist, ask whether this person has board certification—which means he has passed an exam recognizing his expertise in a particular field of medicine. If you visit the doctor you've been referred to, and he says, "You ought to have X, Y, and Z done," you say, "Are there other options?" When he answers, ask, "How often have you done X, Y, and Z, and what are the results?" The more that patients ask, the more honesty they're going to get from physicians.

■ Is there any statistically reliable way to gauge a physician's skill?

In many places now, the batting average of doctors and hospitals in the management of certain problems is being made available. In Pennsylvania, for instance, every doctor who does open heart surgery is not only listed with his mortality rate overall, but also his mortality rate in different hospitals where he works. You have pretty good objective evidence, all based on the same kind of statistics. Say your cardiologist says that there are three surgeons to consider in your town, and you can see that one has a 95 percent success rate, one a 92 percent rate, and one an 89 percent. That gives you a place to go. You then can talk to the doctor with the lowest rating and he may say, "I'm different than the other two because I take every patient that comes my way, and sometimes I take very high-risk patients, and of course they tend to have more problems than the others, while my competitor only takes patients that he knows he's going to succeed with." There are ways you can ferret out the answers you want, but it takes digging.

■ How can patients get their doctor to listen to their questions and help ensure successful treatment?

Most people know in general what their problem is before they go see a doctor; at least their symptoms point to something they fear. Patients should write down their symptoms and complaints so that they don't forget any of them. More important, they should write down the questions they want to ask their doctors. Experience shows that when their own health is concerned, a lot of things fly out of patients' heads in their doctor's office.

■ What if seeing a doctor is intimidating?

One of the things patients must realize is, there's no foolish question and there's no question that they can ask that the doctor hasn't heard before. If you don't understand what a doctor is telling you, ask to have it put in plain language. Your doctor may get annoyed with you, but you're paying for his service and you're entitled to be satisfied when you leave his office.

■ When do you recommend getting a second opinion?

Second opinions are very important for surgical procedures, especially those that even the laity knows are not always successful, like operations for lower back pain. Then there are the situations where one doctor says you need your gallbladder out and "I can do that through three little incisions with a laparoscope and you'll be out the next day," and another doctor says, "You need an old-fashioned surgical procedure"— then a second opinion is necessary. Insurance companies are willing to pay for second opinions because if the second opinion is not to have surgery and the patient believes it, they save money.

■ Is it harder to get a second opinion when you're in a managed care situation?

With any HMO you have a built-in constraint on referrals because they're trying to save money. So you probably don't have as many referrals outside the HMO. You might be able to choose from more than one specialist within the plan, but patients may be suspicious that all the specialists work for the same boss and are giving them the party line. Second opinions also benefit managed care companies, and managed care companies are as liberal with second opinions as they are with any referrals outside of their own group.

■ What questions should patients ask before undergoing surgery?

Ask about your particular situation and why it's absolutely necessary to have surgery. Then ask about the risk versus the benefit and whether you have something that is premalignant or just a nuisance that is bothering you. If you ask questions like this, you can weigh whether the surgery's risk is relatively small and is worth the benefit. I don't think patients should think about the economics of it if it's at all possible to do so.

■ Should patients in an HMO question a decision not to treat their condition?

They have every right to. One of the sad things about managed care is that in some systems the physician gets docked for doing too much—if he has too many referrals, if his prescriptions are too expensive, if he is seeing too many patients for 20 minutes instead of 15. That all comes out in the computer and he could get less income at the end of the month. No matter how bad fee-for-service is, with ethical physicians you always knew the doctor had the ability to be the patient's advocate, whereas in an HMO system the doctor is primarily an advocate for the company and himself. It's the same thing for a test. If a doctor says, "You ought to have a stress test," some people won't think the system should be charged for that. They should say, "Doctor, talk to me about why you think it's important that I should have the test." But that demands a frankness with doctors that patients are frequently loath to show.

FEES FOR SERVICE WHEN THE TAB'S ON YOU

Each year, the publication Medical Economics *compiles data on medical charges by physicians in private, office-based practices across the country. The figures below represent median fees for a variety of medical procedures in 1996. The survey sample was designed to be representative by type of practice, age, geographic region, and gender. Overall, the survey found that fees for medical services and procedures increased about 3 percent over the previous year.*

PEDIATRICIANS

History, examination of normal newborn	$125
Immunization, DPT	$27
MMR virus vaccine	$45
Circumcision, clamp procedure, newborn	$124

Dilation and curettage (for abortion)	$696
Dilation and curettage (diagnostic)	$600
Laparoscopy with fulguration of oviducts	$1,184

OBG SPECIALISTS

Circumcision, clamp procedure, newborn	$148
Total hysterectomy, abdominal	$2,465
Complete OB care, routine delivery	$2,158
Routine delivery by family physicians	$1,654
Complete OB care, cesarean section	$2,500

GENERAL SURGEONS

Total hysterectomy, abdominal	$2,017
Appendectomy	$1,122
Laparoscopy, surgical; appendectomy	$1,366
Cholesystectomy	$1,755
Laparoscopy, surgical; cholecystectomy	$2,200

■ OFFICE VISIT FEES FOR A NEW PATIENT

Consider the AMA's evaluation of a new patient in which the physician must: 1. compile a comprehensive history; 2. undertake a comprehensive exam; 3. perform medical decision making of moderate complexity. In a case whose description is adapted here from the journal *Medical Economics*, the problems are of moderate to high severity, typically requiring 45 minutes of physician time. Examples might include a patient in his mid-60s experiencing chest pains possibly related to cardiologic difficulty, or a woman in her mid-30s with an infertility problem.

	East	South	Midwest	West	Urban	Suburban	Rural
Cardiologists	$147	$125	$125	$150	$150	$150	$110
Family physicians	$90	$100	$100	$125	$100	$100	$100
Gastroenterologists	$135	$127	$120	$150	$147	$125	N/A
General practitioners	$95	$80	N/A	$100	$100	$75	$80
General surgeons	$105	$110	$100	N/A	$114	$105	$107
Internists	$104	$105	$110	$131	$125	$105	$100
OBG specialists	$125	$100	$95	$131	$117	$110	$100
Orthopedic surgeons	$118	$125	$119	$149	$125	$125	N/A
Pediatricians	$75	$85	$80	$99	$90	$90	$75
All surgical specialists	$116	$110	$102	$127	$119	$110	$102
All non-surgeons*	$100	$100	$100	$124	$114	$102	$99
All doctors	$104	$100	$100	$125	$117	$106	$100

*Includes family physicians and general practitioners.   SOURCE: *Medical Economics*, Continuing Survey, 1996.

■ **EXPERT LIST**

Inguinal hernia repair, age five and over	$1,065
Gastrectomy with gastroduodenostomy (partial stomach removal for ulcers)	$2,511
Modified radical mastectomy	$2,108
Excision of cyst fibroadenoma from breast tissue, one or more lesions	$617

ORTHOPEDIC SURGEONS

Colles' fracture, closed manipulation	$621
Open treatment of hip fracture	$2,597
Knee arthroscopy with meniscectomy	$2,150
Total hip arthroplasty	$4,536
Diagnostic knee arthroscopy	$1,006
Total knee arthroplasty	$4,500

CARDIOVASCULAR SURGEONS

Replacement of aortic valve with cardiopulmonary bypass	$5,000
Insertion of permanent pacemaker with transvenous electrodes, ventricular	$1,500

Coronary artery bypass, with three coronary venous grafts	$5,500
Replacement, mitral valve, with cardiopulmonary bypass	$5,000
Ascending aorta graft, with cardio-pullmonary bypass, with coronary reconstruction	$6,500

NEUROSURGEONS

Cranioplasty for skull defect, larger than 5-cm. diameter	$3,500
Craniotomy for evacuation of hematoma	$4,499
Neuroplasty, median nerve at carpal tunnel	$1,135
Neuroplasty, major peripheral nerve, arm or leg	$1,500
Diskectomy, anterior and osteophytec-tomy, cervical, single interspace	$3,737
Laminectomy, more than two vertebral segments; lumbar	$4,178

SOURCE: *Medical Economics*, Continuing Survey. 1996. Copyright ©1996 by Medical Economics Company. Reprinted by permission from MEDICAL ECONOMICS magazine.

■ **OFFICE VISIT FEES FOR AN ESTABLISHED PATIENT**

Doctors' fees tend to be higher in the East and West than in the Midwest and South. In one situation whose AMA description is adapted from the publication *Medical Economics*, the doctor seeing an established patient for an office or other outpatient visit must deal with at least two of three components: 1. an expanded problem-focused history; 2. an expanded problem-focused examination; 3. medical decision making of low complexity. Usually, the problems presented are of low to moderate severity (e.g., an office visit for a patient in his mid-50s, for managing hypertension).

	East	South	Midwest	West	Urban	Suburban	Rural
Cardiologists	$60	$53	$53	$55	$58	$57	N/A
Family physicians	$44	$44	$45	$55	$47	$48	$40
Gastroenterologists	$60	$54	$45	$55	$60	$50	N/A
General practicioners	$50	$42	$45	$49	$50	$45	$40
General surgeons	$55	$49	$49	N/A	$50	$50	$46
Internists	$55	$50	$48	$55	$50	$50	$42
OBG specialists	$71	$50	$50	$60	$60	$55	$50
Orthopedic surgeons	$59	$55	$53	$56	$53	$60	N/A
Pediatricians	$50	$45	$45	$53	$45	$48	$44
All surgical specialists	$60	$50	$50	$56	$53	$55	$50
All non-surgeons*	$50	$45	$45	$55	$50	$50	$42
All doctors	$53	$48	$48	$55	$50	$50	$45

*Includes family physicians and general practitioners.   SOURCE: *Medical Economics*, Continuing Survey, 1996.

THE PATIENT'S BILL OF RIGHTS

Patients should be considered partners in their hospital care. The American Hospital Association has proposed a patient's bill of rights to help make your care as effective as possible.

WHILE YOU ARE A PATIENT IN THE HOSPITAL, YOU HAVE THE RIGHT:

■ To CONSIDERATE and respectful care.

■ To BE WELL INFORMED about your illness, possible treatments, and likely outcome and to discuss this information with your doctor. You have the right to know the names and roles of people treating you.

■ To CONSENT TO OR REFUSE a treatment, as permitted by law, throughout your hospital stay. If you refuse a recommended treatment, you will receive other needed and available care.

■ To HAVE an advance directive, such as a living will or health-care proxy. These documents express your choices about your future care or name someone to decide if you cannot speak for yourself. If you have a written advance directive, you should provide a copy to the hospital, your family, and your doctor.

■ To PRIVACY. The hospital, your doctor, and others caring for you will protect your privacy as much as possible.

■ To EXPECT that treatment records are confidential unless you have given permission to release information or reporting is required or permitted by law. When the hospital releases records to others, such as insurers, it emphasizes that the records are confidential.

■ To REVIEW your medical records and to have the information explained, except when restricted by law.

■ To EXPECT that the hospital will give you necessary health services to the best of its ability. Treatment, referral, or transfer may be recommended. If a transfer is recommended or requested, you will be informed of risks, benefits, and alternatives. You will not be transferred until the other institution agrees to accept you.

■ To KNOW if this hospital has relationships with outside parties that may influence your treatment and care. These relationships may be with educational institutions, other health-care providers, or insurers.

■ To CONSENT OR DECLINE to take part in research affecting your care. If you choose not to take part, you will receive the most effective care the hospital otherwise provides.

■ To BE TOLD of realistic care alternatives when hospital care is no longer appropriate.

■ To KNOW about hospital rules that affect you and your treatment and about charges and payment methods. You have the right to know about hospital resources, such as patient representatives or ethics committees that can help you resolve problems and questions about your hospital stay and care.

YOU HAVE RESPONSIBILITIES AS A PATIENT. You are responsible for providing information about your health, including past illness, hospital stays, use of medicine. You are responsible for asking questions when you do not understand information or instructions. If you believe you can't follow through with your treatment, you are responsible for telling your doctor.

The hospital works to provide care efficiently and fairly to all patients and the community. You and your visitors are responsible for being considerate of the needs of other patients, staff and the hospital. You are responsible for providing information for insurance and for working with the hospital to arrange payment, when needed.

Your health depends not just on your hospital care but, in the long term, on the decisions you make in your daily life. You are responsible for recognizing the effect of lifestyle on your personal health.

A hospital serves many purposes. Hospitals work to improve people's health; treat people with injury and disease; educate doctors, health professionals, patients, and community members; and improve understanding of health and disease. In carrying out these activities, their institution works to respect your value and dignity.

THE SAVINGS FROM NO-BRANDS

The do's and don'ts of using generic drugs to cut your bills

Cost-conscious consumers have long known that they can save 30 percent to 50 percent of their prescription drug bills by using generic rather than brand-name drugs. As the average price of prescription drugs climbs year after year, more and more people are growing wise to the ways of generic drugs, whose prices have remained steady. In 1985, 14 percent of prescriptions were filled with generic drugs compared with approximately 43 percent in 1996.

In fact, one way managed care plans keep costs down is by urging their members to use generic rather than brand-name prescription drugs. But many consumers aren't sure whether it's safe to substitute their prescriptions with generic drugs, or if they're as effective or reliable as brand-name drugs. Dr. Brian Strom, a professor of biostatistics and epidemiology and director of the Center for Clinical Epidemiology and Biostatistics at the University of Pennsylvania, helps explain the similarities and differences between brand-name and generic drugs:

■ What are generic drugs and how do they differ from brand-name drugs?

All drugs have generic or scientific names that identify their active ingredients. The active ingredient in generic drugs—what makes a drug work—is the same as in brand-name drugs, and it's in the same amount. In some cases, it's exactly the same drug, but it has a different name. The only question is whether the manufacturing process may have changed things. The process of man-

ufacturing the drugs may vary and the fillers—the inactive ingredient in drugs—may be different.

■ Are generic drugs as reliable as brand-name drugs?

In the 1980s, there was a scandal involving brand-name drugs marketed in generic form that had not undergone the proper testing. But consumers no longer have to worry whether generic drugs are safe. People can have allergic reactions to a generic drug's inactive ingredients, but the same problem can occur with the inactive ingredients in a brand-name drug. Brand-name companies give the impression that generic drugs aren't as reliable, but if you looked at the drug recalls by the Food and Drug Administration (FDA), that's not at all clear. With drugs that have been FDA-approved as generically equivalent, there are extremely few, if any examples that have been shown to be unsafe or unequal.

■ How does the FDA evaluate drugs?

The FDA process is rigorous. Before a brand-name drug can be marketed, its manufacturer has to go through extensive testing in people to make sure that it's safe and effective. If a drug manufacturer changes the manufacturing process, or if it markets a generic drug, it has to measure the rate of drug absorption and demonstrate that roughly the same amount of the drug appears in the blood in roughly the same time as the brand-name drug.

There's no test of the generic drug's effectiveness, however—only whether it absorbs in the body at roughly the same rate as its brand-name counterpart.

■ Why are generic drugs less expensive than brand-name drugs?

Generic drug manufacturers charge just what it costs to manufacture the drug, whereas brand-name drug manufacturers base their prices on the market rate, and are hugely profitable ventures. In addition, brand-name manufacturers make a huge investment in testing many, many drugs that don't work and are never marketed.

Generic drug manufacturers don't incur the initial, expensive costs of developing and testing drugs. And generic drugs—which are sometimes made by the same companies that manufacture brand-name drugs—aren't advertised.

■ Are generic drugs always less expensive?

A generic drug will almost always be cheaper than the brand-name drug. But it's important to check the prices from one pharmacy to the next, because prices can vary for the same drugs.

■ Why are some drugs not available in generic form?

When a new drug is marketed and sold in the United States, patent laws prevent any drug manufacturer from producing the same drug until the patent expires. Until recently, patents on new drugs barred a drug from being sold in generic form for 17 years. The world trade agreement extended patent protection three years so the United States complies with the rest of the world's patent rules, which allow 20-year patent protection on new drugs. That means that some drugs, like the world's largest-selling drug, Zantac, won't be available in generic form until a few years later than expected. (A generic version of Zantac, used to treat ulcers, is expected to be available shortly.)

■ Can generic and brand-name drugs be used interchangeably?

In general, it's fine to take a generic drug instead of a brand-name drug, but switching back and forth may be ill-advised. If you're taking a certain class of drugs, the so-called critical dose drugs, you shouldn't change back and forth because the rate of absorption could be slightly different. Since most drugs are given in larger doses than necessary, if you take a little more of these drugs, you could have a problem. For example, people who take blood thinners, anti-seizure medications, and some diabetes drugs should check with their pharmacist or doctor to find out whether the drug is a critical dose drug.

■ A DRUG BY ANY OTHER NAME...

Here's a sample of cost differences between brand-name drugs and their generic equivalents. By using generics, your savings can sometimes be substantial.

DRUG BRAND NAME / Generic name	Dosage/Quantity Uses	Average price Brand / Generic
ATIVAN Lorazepam	**1 mg. tablet/60** To treat anxiety disorders.	$46.10 $5.49
CARDIZEM Diltiazem HCl	**60 mg. tablet/90** To treat high blood pressure and reduce chest pain.	$62.94 $37.17
DIABINESE Chlorpropamide	**250 mg. tablet/60** To treat diabetes.	$47.24 $5.76
ELAVIL Amitriptyline	**25 mg. tablet/90** To treat diabetes. To treat diabetes.	$36.48 $5.49
HYTONE Hydrocortisone	**2.5%. cream/30 g.** To reduce itching and redness of skin caused by irritants like poison ivy.	$21.14 $8.65
KEFLEX Cephalexin	**500 mg. capsule/20** To prevent and treat bacterial infection.	$57.20 $8.49
LOPRESSOR Metroprolol	**50 mg. tablet/60** To treat cardiovascular problems like high blood pressure.	$83.74 $30.10
PERCOCET Oxycododone/APAP	**5 mg./325 tablet/90** To relieve pain.	$60.86 $12.91
VENTOLIN/PROVENTIL Albuterol Sulfate	**4 mg. tablet/90** To treat asthma and other lung problems.	$47.63 $12.44

SOURCE: Health Care Financing Administration, 1994.

OFF-THE-SHELF PAIN RELIEF

Do you always reach for the same over-the-counter pain reliever whether you have a throbbing headache, a swollen ankle or premenstrual cramps? Certain painkillers work wonders with some conditions, but should be avoided in other situations. Here's a guide to help you choose the appropriate over-the-counter pain reliever:

ASPIRIN

■ **USES:** The granddaddy of painkillers, this anti-inflammatory drug reduces fever, relieves muscle stiffness and joint pain caused by some forms of arthritis, and may help migraine headache sufferers. Aspirin is the only pain reliever also shown to reduce the risk of heart attack or stroke.

■ **WARNINGS:** Like all anti-inflammatory drugs (including ibuprofen, naproxen sodium, and ketoprofen), aspirin can upset the stomach, and should be avoided by those who experience stomach problems like ulcers or heartburn. It can also raise blood pressure and cause bleeding. If you take a blood thinner, don't use aspirin or other anti-inflammatory drugs.

ACETAMINOPHEN

Tylenol

■ **USES:** Acetaminophen provides immediate relief for pain and fever without causing stomach irritation, bleeding, or nausea that can occur with anti-inflammatory drugs. It's

also a more effective fever-fighter for children, and is the best choice for post-operative pain and for people taking blood thinners, because anti-inflammatory drugs can cause bleeding. However, because it's not anti-inflammatory, acetaminophen won't reduce swelling or stiffness.

■ **WARNINGS:** Acetominophen should not be mixed with alcohol. Heavy drinkers and people with liver, renal, or kidney disease should avoid using the drug.

IBUPROFEN

Advil, Motrin, Nuprin

■ **USES:** Ibuprofen provides immediate relief for headaches, fever, and inflammation and is especially effective for menstrual cramps. Like all anti-inflammatory pain relievers, ibuprofen can also relieve minor aches and pains.

■ **WARNINGS:** Like aspirin, ketoprofen, and naproxen sodium, ibuprofen can upset the stomach and may cause other gastrointestinal problems. It should be avoided by peo-

ple with asthma, high blood pressure, kidney disease, and cirrhosis, and those taking lithium or diuretics.

KETOPROFEN

Orudis KT, Actron

■ **USES:** Orudis KT and Actron were approved as over-the-counter drugs in 1995 to reduce fever and relieve the discomforts of arthritis, menstrual cramps, and other pains. Ketoprofen provides fast relief yet seems to cause fewer stomach problems than other anti-inflammatory drugs.

■ **WARNINGS:** Precautions are the same as for aspirin and ibuprofen.

NAPROXEN SODIUM

Aleve

■ **USES:** Naproxen sodium is effective at reducing pain and fever for 8 to 12 hours, a longer period of time than acetaminophen, ibuprofen, or ketoprofen. It's an anti-inflammatory, but it's gentler on the stomach than aspirin.

■ **WARNINGS:** Precautions are the same as for aspirin and ibuprofen.

▼

MINDING YOUR MENTAL HEALTH

Substantial relief for sufferers of depression and anxiety

Depression and anxiety are closely related mental illnesses that are among the most common psychiatric problems suffered by Americans. In recent years there have been a number of advances in treating mental disorders with psychoactive drugs, but each medication has its drawbacks. Following is a guide to help understand depression and anxiety and the medications available to treat the disorders:

DEPRESSION

Ten million American adults will suffer a bout of depression this year alone, according to the National Institute of Mental Health (NIMH). Women are twice as likely to be afflicted as men. The telltale symptoms include persistent feelings of sadness or irritability, changes in weight or appetite, impaired sleep or concentration, fatigue, restlessness, thoughts of death or suicide, and loss of interest in sex.

Even though the disorder is very common, nearly two-thirds of depressed people don't get treatment because they don't seek it or their symptoms aren't recognized, according to NIMH. Primary care physicians are the health care providers most likely to see depressed patients, but they're also most apt to underdiagnose and undertreat it, says Dr. John Whipple, staff psychiatrist at New Beginnings Health Care in Topeka, Kansas.

Untreated, prolonged depression is associated with higher rates of heart attack and stroke, especially in older people. Further, it's estimated that at least half of all people who commit suicide are severely depressed.

Yet depression is a very treatable illness.

According to NIMH, 80 to 90 percent of those with serious depression can improve significantly, restoring normal function. The most common treatments for depression are psychotherapy and antidepressant medications, which are often used in combination.

When should a person seek treatment for depression? According to Whipple, a major factor to consider is the duration of the depression. "If someone has struggled with it for many months wihtout resolution and it's clearly getting worse," says Whipple, "or if it was triggered by stress, but the stress is gone and the depression is still there, then these are reasons to start medications."

ANXIETY

Experiencing anxiety at some point in life is normal, but for people who suffer anxiety disorders, it becomes overwhelming and completely disrupts one's life. Anxiety disorders encompass several distinct disorders:

■ **PANIC DISORDERS** occur when a person experiences recurrent panic attacks, which are overwhelming, immobilizing fears with no apparent cause.

■ **GENERALIZED ANXIETY DISORDERS** are characterized by unrealistic, persistent fears or concerns that something bad is going to happen.

■ **PHOBIAS** occur when people dread a situation or object and go to great lengths to avoid it. Examples include fear of heights (acrophobia) and agoraphobia (fear of being trapped).

■ **OBSESSIVE-COMPULSIVE DISORDERS** result in persistent irrational thoughts such as contamination that are relieved by repeating routine acts like washing your hands.

■ **POST-TRAUMATIC STRESS DISORDER** afflicts survivors of extraordinary trauma, such as war or violent crime.

Although anxiety disorders are more common than depression, people who suffer depression are more likely to seek treatment than those with anxiety disorders. According to the Anxiety Disorders Association of

PROZAC ISN'T ALWAYS THE ANSWER

Below is an outline of the major classes of psychoactive medications used to treat anxiety disorders and depression. All are antidepressants except the benzodiazepines, which are used to depress or slow the central nervous system.

SELECTIVE SEROTONIN REUPTAKE INHIBITORS (SSRIS)

Prozac (fluoxetine), Paxil (paroxetine), Zoloft (sertraline)

■ **USES:** To treat panic disorder, social phobias, and obsessive-compulsive disorder.Often the first course of treatment for depression.

■ **PRECAUTIONS:** SSRIs may cause insomnia, drowsiness, anxiety, agitation, diarrhea, headache, and nausea, and can disrupt sexual function.

TRICYCLICS (TCAS)

Elavil (amitriptyline), Norpramin (desipramine), Tofranil (imipramine), Anafranil (clomipramine), Pamelor (nortriptyline), Sineqan (doxepin)

■ **USES:** To treat generalized anxiety disorder and

obsessive-compulsive disorder.

■ **PRECAUTIONS:** Side effects include weight gain, dry mouth, blurred vision, drowsiness, heart rhythm disturbances, insomnia, constipation, decreased sexual ability, dizziness, headache, nausea, difficulty urinating and sleeping.

MONOAMINE OXIDASE INHIBITORS (MAOIS)

Marplan (isocarboxazid), Nardil (phenelzine), Parnate (tranylcypromine)

■ **USES:** To treat depressed patients who have failed to respond to other treatments, can't tolerate side effects of other drugs, or have an atypical form of depression. Also used to treat social phobias.

■ **PRECAUTIONS:** Can produce toxic food-drug

interactions known as the "cheese reaction," which can cause severe hypertension, headaches, and heart palpitations. Patients taking MAOIs must avoid a substance called tyramine, found in most types of cheese, beer, yeast, wine, chicken liver, lox, soy sauce, and licorice.

BENZODIAZEPINES

Valium (diazepam), Ativan (lorazepam), Xanax (alprazolam)

■ **USES:** To treat generalized anxiety disorderr.

■ **PRECAUTIONS:** Physical dependency to benzodiazepines, causing withdrawal symptoms such as anxiety, insomnia, and agitation when treatment is stopped. May cause drowsiness; cannot be taken with alcohol.

America, only 23 percent of those who suffer an anxiety disorder will undergo treatment. Untreated, anxiety disorders can lead to depression, suicide, substance abuse, and an increased risk of heart attack.

Both antianxiety medications and cognitive behavioral therapy, which teaches patients how to allay their fears and modify anxiety-producing behaviors, can relieve the symptoms of all types of anxiety disorders. Receiving both treatments simultaneously appears more effective than either one alone,

says Dr. Jack Gorman, professor of clinical psychiatry at the Columbia University College of Physicians and Surgeons.

It's also common to be afflicted with two distinct anxiety disorders or to experience symptoms of both depression and anxiety at the same time. Gorman estimates that 50 percent of people with anxiety disorders will ultimately develop depression: "All of the anxiety disorders are frequently complicated by depression, and when they are, it's a good idea to use medications."

A HELPING HAND FOR CAREGIVERS

A former First Lady's sage advice for those who care for the infirm

Rosalynn Carter, wife of former president Jimmy Carter, learned about caring for the dying long before the word caregiving entered the lexicon. As a young girl in Georgia, she helped nurse her terminally ill grandfather and father. Her experiences resulted in a book, *Helping Yourself Help Others* (Times Books, 1994), which Carter says she wrote to help the 22 million American families who serve as caretakers. Carter, who is currently caring for her ailing mother, is the honorary chairperson of the Last Acts Coalition, a new umbrella group composed of organizations that deal with end-of-life issues. Here are some words of wisdom from the former First Lady:

■ What effect does caring for a seriously ill relative have on a family?

It's usually a shock to families. People are so often thrust into the role of caregiver and most are not prepared for it. It can be devastating, especially when you are dealing with a disability that demands full-time care. But even if the care is given only a few hours a day, most caregivers feel guilty that they aren't spending more time with the ill person. Or, if they take a few minutes for themselves, they also feel guilty.

Life is very lonely and frustrating for those who take care of someone. That's why caregivers are three times as likely to be depressed and more likely to abuse drugs and alcohol.

■ What can caregivers do to relieve their burden?

We did a survey of caregivers in our local area and found that what they needed most was information about their loved one's particular illness and about whether they were doing their best for the sick person. But caregivers also need to learn that if they don't care for themselves, the quality of the help they can give is diminished.

It is very important for caregivers to have some outlet—a hobby such as gardening around the house, for example. Take a break without feeling guilty about it. Pay attention to yourself and appreciate your own efforts. It's also important to find support groups with whom you can share information about an illness and find out where to go for help.

■ When should families start thinking about and planning for dying?

It's often difficult to make decisions in a crisis situation, so it's important to prepare ahead of time. Think about who will care for you and make arrangements for it now. We also have to change our attitudes towards death and dying. Dying is a natural phenomenon; it shouldn't be thought of as a failure on anyone's part. At the Last Acts Coalition, we're trying to change our culture's attitudes. We need to recognize death as a natural act of life and be prepared for it when it comes.

■ What can be done to avoid unnecessary pain and suffering?

Families need to talk about what they want to happen if they are confronted with death. Talk about it before the time comes so that every member of the family is aware of your wishes. In my book, I advocate living wills for people, but we've found that even living wills are not sufficient. Many times the wills don't follow patients from hospitals to nursing homes, for example.

One of the goals of the Last Acts campaign is to change the curriculum for doctors. We've learned that doctors have not had training in death and dying; they're taught to heal people and they feel like failures if they don't succeed. That needs to change. Also, families don't like to give up loved ones by letting them die, so they allow all kinds of measures to be taken, such as allowing loved ones to be hooked up to tubes.

A PRIMER ON BREAST CANCER

Knowing the risk factors will cut your risk of being a victim

Breast cancer is the most common form of cancer among American women. According to the American Cancer Society, 184,000 American women develop breast cancer and 44,000 die of the disease annually. Although more women now die of lung cancer and heart disease, breast cancer is the leading cause of death in women aged 40 to 55. Dr. A. Marilyn Leitch, chair of the American Cancer Society's Breast Cancer Subcommittee and an associate professor in surgical oncology at the University of Texas/Southwestern Medical Center, explains the risks, the precautions that should be followed, and the treatment options that are available:

■ Do one in eight women really develop breast cancer?

The numbers sound so much more horrifying if you don't look at the risk in relation to a woman's age. One in 8 women will get breast cancer assuming a lifespan of 85 to 90 years. If you live to age 60, your risk decreases to about 1 in 29, if your lifespan is 50, it's about 1 in 40, and at age 40, 1 in 65.

■ What are the symptoms of the disease?

The most common symptom is a painless mass found during a breast self-exam. Less common signs are nipple discharge, a change in the appearance of the skin on the breast such as redness or nipple dimpling, or a lump or swelling under the arm.

■ Who is most at risk of breast cancer?

All women—and men to a minor degree—are at risk of breast cancer. Advancing age is the most important risk factor—the older a woman gets, the more likely she is to get breast cancer. Roughly 77 percent of women diagnosed with breast cancer in a given year are over age 50.

■ Are there other factors that predispose a woman to developing breast cancer?

Yes, but these aren't as important as a woman's age. They include a prior diagnosis of breast cancer or a family history of breast cancer (the closer the relative is, the greater the risk). Having a breast biopsy in the past which shows abnormal changes in the breast's fibrocystic tissue, menstruating at an early age or having a late menopause, never having a baby, or getting pregnant for the first time after age 30 are also risk factors.

■ What can women do to protect themselves from the disease?

Self-exam is the most common way to detect breast cancer. All women—with or without risk factors—should be doing breast self-exams every month by the time they are age 20. It's ideal to do the exam about five to

---

■ FEAR OF DYING

Breast cancer is one of the most haunting problems facing women, yet there's evidence that *fear* of cancer is disproportionate to its actual incidence. A 1992 Gallup poll of more than 1,000 women found that breast cancer is by far the disease women are most concerned about, even though they are more likely to die of other causes:

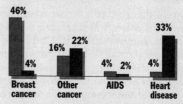

What women saw as most serious threats:
What women actually die of:

Breast cancer	Other cancer	AIDS	Heart disease
46% / 4%	16% / 22%	4% / 2%	4% / 33%

SOURCE: National Center for Health Statistics.

seven days after a woman's period starts, when breasts are the least tender or full. Post-menopausal women should perform self-exams at the same time each month. Statistically, most women aren't going to detect any abnormalities, but if something seems out of the ordinary, you'll be able to detect it because you'll be familiar with how the breast tissue feels. Examination by a health care professional can also help detect breast cancer. Between the ages of 20 and 40, women should be examined by their doctor every two to three years, and every year after age 40.

■ What is a mammogram and is the procedure safe?

A mammogram is an X ray of the breast that can detect smaller tumors before they can be felt in physical exams. Mammograms are the second most common method of detecting breast cancer. The theoretic risk of radiation is extremely low compared to the risk of getting breast cancer. Today, the technical aspects of doing mammographies have become very rigorous, and women are only exposed to very low doses of radiation. In addition, the Mammography Quality Standards Act, which requires mammography facilities to be certified by the Food and Drug Administration, ensures that high-quality equipment and technicians are used.

■ Who should get mammograms?

The American Cancer Society has recently revised its guidelines. It now recommends that a woman should have her first mammogram by age 40, then a mammogram every year thereafter.

■ Are mammograms effective in younger women?

One of the arguments for not doing mammograms in women aged 40 to 49 is that their breasts are more dense, so it's hard for the X ray to see through them. But that's become less of an issue in the past decade as mammography technique has improved. There's no question that there's a benefit to a woman who has her cancer diagnosed early—she has more treatment options and she's going to live longer. A review published last year that analyzed various studies showed that mammography screening can reduce mortality in women under age 50 by 24 percent.

■ How much do mammograms cost?

A diagnostic mammogram costs more than a screening mammogram because it requires more work on the part of the technician and the radiologist. A screening mammogram costs between $65 and $100, and a diagnostic mammogram usually costs anywhere from $100 to $150, although the price varies depending on where you are in the country. Most insurance carriers cover routine mammographies, although some have stopped paying for mammograms for women under age 50 because of the revised guidelines.

■ What does it mean if a woman finds a lump during a self-exam?

Sometimes a lump is just a thickening in the breast tissue that does not need further treatment, but all women who find a lump should have it checked by their primary care doctor to determine whether it's what's called a dominant mass. If it is, women over 30 should have a mammogram to evaluate the lump and a biopsy in which a needle is inserted into the lump to determine whether it's a solid tumor or a fluid-filled cyst. If it's solid, the cells will be examined under a microscope to determine if the lump is benign or malignant.

■ What are the treatment options once you're diagnosed with breast cancer?

Most women with breast cancer are candidates for a breast-saving surgery called lumpectomy, which involves removing the cancerous tumor in the breast and lymph nodes under the arm, then getting radiation treatment to the entire breast. Women can also choose a mastectomy, which involves removing the breast, then they can have the breast reconstructed afterward if they want.

■ What are the chances of beating the disease through various treatments?

It depends on the stage of disease when patients are treated. The majority of women diagnosed with breast cancer can certainly expect to be alive in five years, but the earlier you detect it, the better your odds of surviving the disease. In five years, roughly 95 percent of white women whose tumor is confined to the breast and 75 percent of women whose tumors have spread to the lymph nodes will be alive. However, the survival rates are consistently lower for black women; we don't know whether it's because they don't have access to care or because of biologic differences. In 1995, the National Cancer Institute (NCI) announced the first decrease in the incidence of breast cancer mortality in decades, but it was primarily for white women. The mortality rate actually increased for black women.

■ Can a low-fat diet or exercise reduce your risk of breast cancer?

It seems there is some relationship between obesity, a high-fat diet, and the development of breast cancer. Breast cancer is more common in countries where there's a high fat content in the diet, like the U.S., and is quite low in countries that have a lower fat content, like Japan. The decreased risk may be related to reducing the level of estrogen in the body. Younger women who are very athletic and

women who have multiple pregnancies have fewer menstrual periods, which may have a protective effect because fewer hormones are produced, and women who are overweight tend to produce more estrogen. A 1994 study suggests that women who exercise when they're first menstruating through their reproductive years can greatly reduce their risk of premenopausal cancer, possibly because it can reduce the number of menstrual cycles. A couple of studies have suggested that reduction of weight and fat in the diet improves outcome even after a woman develops breast cancer.

■ Now that a gene thought to be associated with breast cancer has been identified, should women undergo genetic testing for breast cancer?

At the present time, there is not a single test readily available to the average woman to determine her risk of developing breast cancer. However, women with a family history of breast cancer should contact a university medical center involved in studying genetic risks of breast cancer in high-risk populations to learn about genetic testing and to donate their blood, which might help researchers learn more about the disease.

■ PERFORMING A BREAST SELF-EXAMINATION

1. Once a month, after your period, examine your breasts. Get to know their shape and texture, and be alert to changes. Raise each arm above your head and turn from side to side, looking for changes in appearance.

2. Squeeze the nipple to check for discharge. Check surface for peculiarities. Orange-peel texture could indicate a lump.

3. Lie on your back with your arm by your side. Using the flat of your hand, work around the outer parts of the breast in a clockwise direction.

4. Raise arm over head. Check inner parts of the breast, along collarbone and into armpit. Stretching the skin makes detection easier.

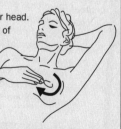

PROSTATE CANCER
▼

THE PROBLEM WITH MANHOOD

Diagnosis is easier than ever, but there's a debate about treatment

Bob Dole is among the afflicted. So is retired general Norman Schwarzkopf and junk bond developer Michael Milken. Nearly a quarter-million American men develop prostate cancer each year, making it the most common cancer in men, and after lung cancer, the second leading cancer killer among men.

Detecting prostate cancer is easier than ever, thanks to a blood test called the PSA (see box, facing page), which enables doctors to detect small tumors confined to the prostate. Most doctors agree that not all prostate cancers need to be treated, but it remains unclear which patients with localized prostate cancer will benefit from treatment, and no method exists to measure how effective those treatments are. "If we knew that finding can-

cer early would improve the chances of survival, we would have no problem treating everyone with prostate cancer," says Dr. Mark Austenfeld, a urologist at the University of Kansas Medical Center and a member of a special American Urological Association (AUA) study panel on the subject.

Prostate cancer is typically diagnosed late in life and grows slowly. In fact, only 1 in 10 cancers ever becomes aggressive, or life-threatening, and many men with prostate cancer will die with the disease, not of it. Studies of autopsy results suggest that almost half of all men aged 70 to 80 have prostate cancer at the time of death, and the majority of men over age 90 have the disease—often without knowing it—yet they die of other illnesses. Unfortunately, it's difficult to determine accurately which cancers will advance quickly and spread, and which might remain harmless for as long as a decade without progressing.

Some doctors adopt a "surveillance" approach, examining the patient periodically to determine if the disease is spreading rather than rushing to treatment. Other doctors err on the side of caution, treating most cases by either removing the prostate with an increasingly common surgical procedure called radical prostatectomy, or administering radiation therapy that kills the cancer cells.

To help clarify the treatment options, the American Urological Association recently released guidelines for both doctors and patients that spell out factors to consider when choosing a treatment:

■ **Consider the stage and grade of a tumor.** A patient's prognosis depends on the grade and stage of his tumor. That means estimating the size of the tumor and the extent to which it has spread to other parts of the body. A grade is assigned to a tumor based on the results of an ultrasound test and biopsy, procedures that help determine how aggressive the tumor is, or how quickly it's expected to grow. Patients with small, low-grade tumors fare better than patients with high-grade tumors, regardless of the type of treatment. Some patients with low-

FACT FILE:

A TOMATO A DAY

■ *A study by Harvard University researchers suggests that tomatoes in the diet can help ward off prostate cancer. Men who ate at least 10 servings a week of tomato-based products had a 45 percent less chance of getting prostate cancer; men who ate at least 4 servings lowered their risk by 20 percent. The reduced risk may be derived from the antioxidant lycopene, abundant in tomatoes.*

THE GUIDELINES FOR GETTING TESTED

As all men of a certain age know, a digital rectal exam in the doctor's office was for years the only screening test available to detect prostate cancer. But a more accurate test has now been developed that measures the amount of a protein in the blood called "prostate-specific" antigen. The higher a man's PSA count, the greater the possibility that he has some prostatic disease.

The PSA test does have limitations: It will yield positive results in two-thirds of the men who take it, but only 30 to 40 percent of those with high PSA levels will actually have prostate cancer. PSA levels are also elevated in men with an enlarged prostate, a noncancerous condition known as benign prostatic hyperplasia, or BPH. An even more precise test may soon become available. Known as the "free PSA" test, it isolates free-floating PSA, which is common in men with prostate cancer, rather than measuring total PSA levels like the current test. The new test is expected to lower the high false-positive rate, greatly reducing the number of unnecessary biopsies. But more research is necessary before the free PSA test is widely used, according to the American College of Physicians.

Here's what men should keep in mind:
■ All men, especially African American men and men with a family history of prostate cancer, are at risk.
■ There are no symptoms in the disease's early stages, but there will be urinary difficulties and some pain as it progresses.
■ The American Cancer Society and the American Urological Association recommend that all men age 40 and older have an annual digital rectal exam (DRE). African American men and those with a family history should also have an annual PSA test beginning at age 40. All men 50 and older are advised to undergo a DRE and a PSA test annually. However, a task force convened by the U.S. Public Health Service advises against routine prostate cancer screening because there's not enough evidence that early detection saves lives.

The American College of Physicians advises men to discuss the PSA test with their doctor before undergoing the test.

---

grade tumors diagnosed at an early stage may choose surveillance as a treatment option.

■ **Take into account a patient's age, health, and life expectancy.** Because it's difficult to accurately determine the grade and stage of the cancer, doctors also rely on a patient's age, health, and life expectancy at the time of diagnosis to determine whether he's a good candidate for treatment. According to the guidelines, a man's life expectancy should be at least 10 years to be considered a candidate for treatment because that's how long it usually takes prostate cancer to spread and become fatal. The younger a man is the more likely he will benefit from treatment because the disease will probably progress during his lifetime if left untreated. Regardless of the size and grade of the tumor, prostate cancer needs to be treated in someone age 50 or younger, says Austenfeld.

■ **Understand the side effects of treatment.** Some patients are reluctant to undergo prostate surgery because it may result in impotence and pain. But removal of the entire prostate greatly reduces the likelihood that the cancer will recur. With radiation therapy, the risk of impotence and incontinence is somewhat less, but the cancer may recur because the prostate remains in place.

Because the best treatment for prostate cancer remains unclear, patients need to be involved in making decisions, particularly if their case is borderline. Says Austenfeld: "We can't definitely say which treatments are preferable so we have to rely to some extent on patient preferences."

THERAPIES YOU CAN USE

Biofeedback, visual imagery, and yoga may have uses

Homeopathy? Acupuncture? Massage therapy? Ten or 20 years ago these practices were dismissed as black magic by medical doctors and regarded with suspicion by most Americans. But alternative therapies are entering mainstream medicine. In 1993 the National Institutes of Health opened an Office of Alternative Medicine to oversee scientific research on alternative therapies. The federally funded agency recently awarded grants to eight specialty centers charged with evaluating various alternative therapies. A landmark study on alternative medicine published in the *New England Journal of Medicine* found that in a single year alternative approaches were used by more than one-third of Americans to treat a serious illness—with an out-of-pocket cost of $10 billion. Dr. James Gordon, the founder and director of the Washington, D.C.–based Center for Mind-Body Medicine and author of *Manifesto for a New Medicine: Your Guide to Healing Partnerships and the Wise Use of Alternative Therapies* (Addison-Wesley, 1996), discusses the changing status of alternative therapies:

■ **What is alternative medicine and how does it differ from holistic or mind-body medicine?**

Alternative medicine is basically everything your physician didn't learn in medical school. It uses the techniques of other healing systems, cultures, and approaches as an integral part of medical care. Holistic medicine, which comes from the Greek word *holos*, meaning whole, was developed in the 1970s to describe medicine that understood the whole person in his or her total environment and appreciated that a human being was different from and greater than the sum of his or her parts. Mind-body medicine refers to the effects of the mind on the body and the reciprocal effects of the body on the mind. It emphasizes the largely untapped power we all have to affect our health simply by using our minds through biofeedback, visual imagery, meditation, and relaxation. Some physical exercises, like yoga and tai chi, can also profoundly affect mental and emotional function.

■ **How does alternative medicine differ from conventional medicine in its approach to treating illness?**

The understanding that dominates our health care is that if somebody has a disease, we have to go in and find out what the biological basis is and develop something to solve the biological problem. When you focus on a specific biological reaction and develop a drug for that, like antibiotics, you destroy the bacteria you want to destroy. But in the process you may wipe out all the other bacteria and affect the immune system negatively. A more holistic approach might be to ask, "What can people do for themselves to strengthen their immune system so they don't get infections?" Instead of attacking the disease process as if it were the offender, you strengthen the whole human being so the disease process no longer has a place.

Most of the people I've seen come because conventional medicine has not done what they hoped it would do. Some of the studies coming out are having an effect, too. When a good study comes out that shows that garlic can lower cholesterol, people have to say, "Well, maybe there's something to it." Where we have made significant gains—for example, in cardiovascular disease—those gains have mostly come about because of patterns in diet and exercise rather than anything we've developed as far as drugs or surgery go.

■ **Which alternative treatments are the best-established?**

The best evidence shows that we can use our

CHIROPRACTIC'S RIGHTFUL USE

Established medicine may not like it, but chiropractors do help some

Should you trust a chiropractor? The very notion makes many medical doctors, disturbed by what they see as a growing trend by chiropractors to tout themselves as primary care providers capable of treating the entire family, cringe.

But spinal manipulation—the mainstay of the nation's 50,000 licensed chiropractors—is increasingly being accepted by medical authorities as a means of controlling low back pain. Spinal manipulation involves adjusting by hand the 24 vertebrae stacked on top of each other, to restore normal movement in the joints

A panel assembled by the Agency for Health Care Policy and Research (AHCPR), a branch of the U.S. Department of Health and Human Services, found that spinal manipulation is safe during the first month a patient experiences low back symptoms, as long as there has been no nerve damage. Medical doctors maintain that people with chronic low back pain require a multidisciplinary effort because the short-term benefits conferred by spinal manipulation will disappear quickly.

"Manipulation is a very reasonable option for people who don't want to take medication," says Dr. Paul Shekelle, an internist at the West Los Angeles Veterans Administration Medical Center. Shekelle led a 1990 study by the RAND Corporation that also found that spinal manipulation can provide short-term relief from acute low back pain. There's only a one in a million occurrence, says Shekelle, that a serious complication will result from spinal manipulation of the lower spine.

In a 1992 article published in the *Journal of Family Practice*, Peter Curtis, a family physician at the University of North Carolina, and Geoffrey Bove, a doctor of chiropractic conducting research at Massachusetts General Hospital, suggest choosing a chiropractor who:

■ primarily treats musculoskeletal disorders with manual therapy like spinal manipulation

■ doesn't charge a lump sum before treatment begins

■ graduated from a school accredited by the Council on Chiropractic Education, 4401 Westown Parkway, Suite 120, W. Des Moines, IA 50265, ☎ 515–226–9001.

Bove says that the notion that once you start seeing a chiropractor, you must keep going, is a myth. If you don't see any results after three or four weeks of treatment, warns Bove, you should question whether your chiropractor's approach is likely to work—just as you would with a medical doctor.

---

minds to change in a positive direction many physiological functions that were believed to be beyond our voluntary control 30 years ago. For example, you can lower blood pressure, relieve pain, and improve functioning in asthma patients. There's a good deal of evidence that relaxation therapies like biofeedback, hypnosis, and visual imagery are effective for treating insomnia and pain. There are also very good studies on acupuncture and herbal therapies; they're just not known in this country because most of them have been done in Asia and Europe.

Other research focuses on the use of chiropractic to treat lower back pain and on the effectiveness of homeopathic remedies for a variety of conditions including hay fever in children and arthritis. Studies of therapeutic touch show that when people trained as healers bring their hands close to other people, it relaxes them and improves their physiological functioning.

■ **How do nutrition and exercise fit in?**

They are also considered alternative therapies, because they're not ordinarily a part of physicians' practices. There's no real understanding of the use of nutritional supplementation or of diets like the Mediterranean diet, which can help prevent cardiovascular disease. The same with exercise. Most doctors know a bit about aerobic exercise, but they don't know anything about yoga or tai chi, which are enormously helpful in treating many chronic conditions. For example, there are many studies done in India where people have used yoga as part of the treatment for asthma, arthritis, hypertension, anxiety, and depression—with good results.

■ What should patients look for in a physician who practices alternative medicine?

At a minimum, every physician using alternative approaches should know about relaxation therapies, self-awareness, meditation, nutrition, and exercise. Beyond that, it's hard to know which system will be most effective. Sometimes you'll have a sense of which techniques are most important to you. For example, if you have a bad back or musculoskeletal problems, it's best to go to someone who knows manipulation in addition to conventional medicine. If you have food allergies, clearly you want somebody who knows about nutrition. If you have chronic pain, acupuncture is a good bet. It's important to work with someone who knows at least one approach well but won't beat you over the head with it whether it works or not.

■ How does the relationship between alternative practitioners and their patients differ from the typical doctor-patient relationship?

It involves a teaching relationship—which is not primarily the kind of relationship conventional doctors have with patients. What you want are people who are going to help you learn how to take care of yourself, not people who are going to make you dependent on them. Alternative medicine practitioners often use groups as a way of maximizing therapeutic work, because we've found that people can help each other make real changes not only in psychology, but in basic biological processes, simply by sharing their experiences.

The most striking study was done at Stanford University, where one group of women with breast cancer received the conventional medical treatment—surgery, chemotherapy, and sometimes radiation—and another group, in addition, met together with a psychiatrist once a week for an hour and a half for a year. Women in the support group lived on average 18 months longer than women not in the support group.

■ Does insurance cover alternative therapies?

A lot of things are considered part of general medical treatment—so if I'm a doctor and I do homeopathy or nutritional counseling, that's covered. Most plans also cover chiropractic, and in some states acupuncture. But that's not the case for many of the services by practitioners who are not medical doctors.

■ What should a patient do if his doctor is reluctant to discuss alternative therapies?

Roughly 70 percent of patients receiving alternative therapies don't discuss it with their doctor because they fear their doctors will not only not be sympathetic, but will be angry with them. That has to change. Part of being a scientist is keeping an open mind and waiting until all the evidence is in. If patients find doctors irritated with them, or condescending, for being interested in alternative therapies, it's time to say, "That's unacceptable; take a look at the evidence. I need you to help me and not make uninformed judgments."

■ Are there any dangers to using alternative medicine?

Any health care practitioner should be optimistic and inspire hope, but I would be wary of anyone who promises miracles. One of the shortcomings of alternative medicine is that some practitioners think their method is going to cure everything. And some alternative practitioners have an antagonism toward traditional medicine. You need someone who can see the strengths and weaknesses of all the approaches. Alternative therapies can be used just as stupidly as conventional therapies.

CHAPTER THREE

EDUCATION

EXPERT QUOTES

"There is no need for a child to have organized activity like sports or music before the age of five or six."
—David Elkind, professor of child study, Tufts University
Page 226

"In talking animal books, boys are definitely the default setting."
—Kathleen Odean, author of *Great Books for Girls*
Page 232

"Too many students put all their eggs in the early decision basket."
—Steven Antonoff, author of *The College Finder*
Page 234

■ **WHAT'S AHEAD: STAY TUNED** to state efforts to develop content standards for their school systems... **CHECK** online for resources that can help your child do his homework... **FIND OUT** about colleges around the world via the Internet... **CONSIDER** the pros and cons of applying for "early admission" to college... **KNOW** the financial aid options available for graduate school... **LEARN** new skills or earn a diploma without leaving your home... **JOIN** a book club or start your own...

K THROUGH 12

SCHOOL REFORM
▼

PUTTING SCHOOLS TO THE TEST

Will the drive for education standards hit your school?

When asked recently how challenging America's public high schools are, one-half of 1,300 teenagers polled replied: Not challenging enough. The poll, conducted by the nonprofit group Public Agenda, reaffirms what everyone from Bill Clinton to education experts to teachers and parents has been harping on for years: American schools need tougher standards and a greater emphasis on math and basic reading. As Education Secretary Richard Riley put it, "We're teaching dead-end math classes with nominal work, and administering watered-down testing. Students are socially promoted and then graduated." A frequently cited international study, conducted by the Department of Education several years ago, showed that American eighth graders ranked 28th in the world in math and 19th in science, although the scores have improved slightly since then.

Federally sponsored efforts to identify what every student should know by grades 4, 8, and 12 have been a cornerstone of the Clinton administration's educational program, Goals 2000, approved by Congress in 1994. But efforts at national standards and tests came under attack by those who fear too much federal meddling in the classroom. A poll conducted by *The Wall Street Journal* found that 47 percent of all adults believe the federal government should not be involved in establishing a national test for reading and math. For the short term, at least, the drive for national standards appears to be an uphill fight.

At the state level, however, standards-setting is taking firm root. Today, 48 states either have or are developing mandatory tests. Only Iowa and Wyoming have not yet adopted any testing. But having state standards is no assurance that the problem is resolved. Research by the National Assessment of Educational Progress (NAEP), a Washington-D.C. group, found, for example, that although Wisconsin and Louisiana reported that 88 percent of their students performed well in reading tests, by NAEP standards only 35 percent in Wisconsin and 15 percent in Louisiana were adequate readers. Where does the discrepancy lie? Many state standards are not set high enough, according to Marc Tucker, director of the National Center for Education and the Economy (NCEE) in Washington, D.C. Says Tucker, "States need to be more ambitious in their goals. We have lower expectations of our kids than most industrialized countries. Enormous evidence suggests that if you ask more of kids they will deliver."

EXPERT SOURCES

GETTING A FIX ON THE NEW STANDARDS

Booklets containing the curricular standards being developed by educators for the nation's schools come in a variety of core subjects. They attempt to describe all a student should know by a certain grade level— both the content and how a student should be able to demonstrate such knowledge. Prices for the booklets range from $7 to $25. To obtain copies of the standards for different disciplines, contact:

ART EDUCATION

Music Educators National Council
1806 Robert Fulton Dr.
Reston, VA 20191
☎ 800–828–0229

CIVICS AND GOVERNMENT

Center for Civic Education
5146 Douglas Fir Rd.
Calabasas, CA 91302
☎ 800–350–4223

ENGLISH AND LANGUAGE ARTS

National Council of Teachers of English
1111 W. Kenyon Rd.

Urbana, IL 61801
☎ 800–369–6283

FOREIGN LANGUAGES

American Council on the Teaching of Foreign Languages
6 Executive Blvd.
Yonkers, NY 10701–6801
☎ 914–963–8830

GEOGRAPHY

Council for Geographic Education
Room 16A Leonard Hall
Indiana University of Pennsylvania
Indiana, PA 15705
☎ 412–357–6290

UNITED STATES HISTORY

National Council for the Social Studies
3701 Newark St., N.W.
Washington, D.C. 20016
☎ 202–966–7840

MATHEMATICS

National Council of Mathematics
1906 Association Dr.
Reston, VA 20191
☎ 703–620–9840

SCIENCE

National Research Council
2101 Constitution Ave., N.W.
Washington, D.C. 20418
☎ 202–334–1399

The push by the federal government to raise state standards is gaining momentum. Of the states that already have standards, at least seven have changed theirs to match federal benchmarks, which now exist for the arts, business, civics, English, foreign languages, geography, mathematics, and science. Other states are using the federal guidelines together with a variety of other sources to revamp their stated standards. Some states differ on the length of time a student should spend on a given subject, others on the content of the curriculum, still others on what every child must prove he or she knows.

Another prominent effort to develop a comprehensive set of standards for all major academic disciplines is being spearheaded by the NCEE in conjunction with the Learning Research and Development Center of the University of Pittsburgh. Called New Standards, the effort is notable because it attempts to measure students against international benchmarks and specifies what students need to know in each subject by a given age. The program also spells out how students should demonstrate their knowledge and skills, and provides teachers and schools with the tests to measure students' performances. One aspect of its system could allay the fears of those who balk at national standardized tests: An individualized portfolio system, which shows a variety of a student's work, including writing samples and math and science assignments, over a period of time. At several points during the year, the teacher reviews the material and assesses a student's progress.

READ THIS FOR YOUR CHILD'S SAKE

Lighten up, parents. Pushing reading too early is a big mistake

To be a good reader in school is to be considered smart. To be a bad reader, far too often, is to be labeled stupid. Research over the past few decades shows that difficulty in reading is due not to inferior intelligence but to specific learning disabilities that are neurological disorders, which can be helped and sometimes corrected through proper training. Still, parents go to extraordinary lengths to ensure that their child master the art of reading—from reading to the child while still *in utero* to buying a Speak & Spell when the child is a mere two years old. Harvard School of Education professor Jean Chall, author of *Learning to Read, the Great Reading Debate* (McGraw Hill, 1970) and other seminal books in the education field, shares her perspective on teaching reading:

■ At what age should a child learn to read?

That is difficult to answer as every child varies greatly. Traditionally, American schools teach children at age six, but many schools begin teaching informally in kindergarten and pre-kindergarten. I am wary of telling parents to start too early, because if a child does not immediately succeed, the parent has a hard time relaxing and letting the child go at his or her own pace.

■ Which teaching method works best?

Over the years, research has proved that the use of both—the "whole language" method and the "phonic"—is the best way for a child to master reading. While the "whole language" approach, which includes reading to children and getting them interested in both the activity of reading and the story they are reading, is helpful, phonics must be taught. Children must be taught that one of the squiggles they see on a page is a "p" and another a "b" and that those two letters sound different and are written differently. Getting the print off the page requires a different ability than being able to understand the meaning of what is written. It is very important for normal progress, and especially for children at risk, that both methods be taught.

■ How do you lay the groundwork for reading in a young child?

You can start developing the skills needed in reading at a very young age. Again, I caution parents to not push their children too fast. Besides reading to children, parents can start "ear training" their child by playing rhyme games. This develops the child's ability to discern different sounds and to realize that certain words begin, look, and sound same. In reading to children, parents also can point to words as they go, teaching the child that the funny lines on the page are the words you are saying. All of this "early teaching" should not be a serious thing. It should be a fun activity. There is plenty of time for serious learning later.

■ When should you "get serious"?

Once a child is in school, the learning of reading is inevitably more serious. If children do not already know how to identify and write letters, and to recognize words, they start to learn it in a systematic way. I am reluctant to tell parents when to teach reading to their children, as they often embark on too serious a task too early for the child.

■ How many children suffer from learning disabilities?

Most schools cite a 10 to 15 percent learning disability rate among their student body; some as high as 20 percent. Many children have some kind of reading difficulty.

■ What if your child is having difficulty with reading?

You must get a professional diagnosis. While

ACQUIRING A SECOND TONGUE

English has always been the "American language," but because of the global economy, foreign language ability is increasingly important for Americans. Starting when a child is young is critical, argues Nancy Rhodes, who is associate director for English language and multi-cultural education at the Center for Applied Linguistics in Washington, D.C. Rhodes offers this advice on training children to speak foreign tongues:

■ **Start foreign language training early.** After 12 or 13, it is very difficult to learn a language and be able to speak it like a native speaker. Young kids like playing with language and are not embarrassed by making strange sounds, so it's ideal for them to learn a foreign language. If you wait until kids are in adolescence, they are very inhibited and worried about how they appear to their peers.

■ **Don't worry that studying a foreign language will harm a child's native language ability.** All of the research shows that studying another language actually enhances your native language abilities. By the time children in foreign language immersion programs get to fifth or sixth grade, they score as well or better in English than their peers who have been studying only in English.

■ **If you have a choice, select a program that integrates foreign language instruction into the rest of the curriculum.** About a fifth of the elementary schools in the U.S. teach some type of foreign language. It could be just an introduction, or it could be an immersion experience in which the foreign language is the medium of instruction, so that the students are learning language as well as their content areas through the foreign language. The successful programs are integrated into the school day so that everybody sees foreign language as part of the curriculum.

■ **When a family is multilingual, be as consistent as possible about who speaks what.** Children can learn five or six different languages. The important thing is to separate the languages. If the mother speaks English, for example, and the father speaks Spanish, they should try to keep those roles the same. Do not be surprised or alarmed, however, if a young child mixes the languages he or she hears. This is normal and a phase. Do not react with impatience. Remember that by teaching a foreign language early, you are imparting a great gift.

the teacher might say the child is merely disinterested but will get over it, disinterest or poor performance in reading can stem from a number of things, some being very specific learning disabilities that can be identified and worked on. Correcting these early can circumvent a lot of potential problems for the child later in school. Learning disabilities have now been shown to be neurological problems that can be corrected with the proper training.

■ **What kind of specialist is it best to see?**

Every school should have a reading specialist that can assess your child and explain to you why the child might be experiencing difficulty. If the school has no specialist, ask about private tutors, talk to other parents, consult a local university, but find an outside specialist. It is very tricky for parents to deal with their own child's learning disabilities and I most certainly do not recommend it.

DOES MUSIC MAKE YOU SMARTER?

Intriguing research suggests music helps develop spatial reasoning

When champions of the liberal arts argue that there's more to education than just reading, writing, and arithmetic, music and arts are often cited for their value in stimulating students' creativity and expanding their cultural horizons. Now there is evidence that students who receive formal musical training may enjoy higher standardized test scores and demonstrate greater powers of spatial reasoning than students who do not get this experience.

According to data released by the College Entrance Examination Board, for instance, students who reported coursework or experience in music performance scored 23 points higher on the verbal portion of their Scholastic Assessment Test (SAT) in 1995, and 19 points higher on the math component of the

exam than the entire pool of test-takers. Students who reported taking music appreciation classes at school scored 33 points higher on their verbal SAT and 26 points higher on the math portion of the test than the test-taking universe as a whole.

While it is impossible to establish any cause-and-effect relationship between musical training and academic performance based on the SAT data, two recent studies by researchers at the Center for the Neurobiology of Learning and Memory at the University of California at Irvine suggest that there may indeed be a causal link between music and spatial intelligence. Spatial intelligence is the ability to perceive the visual world accurately, to form mental pictures of physical objects, and to recognize when objects differ physically. Having well-developed powers of spatial reasoning is considered crucial for excelling at complex mathematics and playing chess, among other things.

In one of the two studies, the UC Irvine team led by psychologist Frances Rauscher and neuroscientist Gordon Shaw compared the spatial reasoning abilities of 19 preschool children who took music lessons for eight months with the performance of a demographically comparable group of 15 preschool children who received no music training. The researchers found the first group's spatial reasoning dramatically better. The team also reported that the ability of the music students to do a puzzle designed to measure their spatial reasoning powers rose significantly during the experiment.

A second study, which replicated and expanded on results of an earlier study in the journal *Nature* in 1993, found that when college students listened to 10 minutes of Mozart's piano sonata K.448, their spatial IQ scores rose more than when these students spent the same amount of time sitting in silence or performing relaxation exercises. Curiously, the researchers observed no improvement in the students' spatial skills after 10 minutes of listening to the avantgarde composer Philip Glass or to a highly rhythmic dance piece, suggesting that hypnotic musical structures do nothing to improve spatial skills.

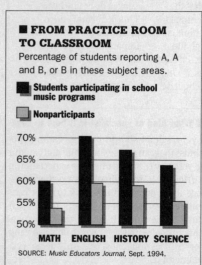

■ FROM PRACTICE ROOM TO CLASSROOM

Percentage of students reporting A, A and B, or B in these subject areas.

■ Students participating in school music programs

▨ Nonparticipants

70%
65%
60%
55%
50%

MATH ENGLISH HISTORY SCIENCE

SOURCE: *Music Educators Journal*, Sept. 1994.

■ STARTING YOUNG

The median age musicians start lessons is 9.4 years. Age when all current or former players first learned to play:

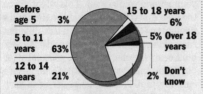

Before age 5 — 3%
5 to 11 years — 63%
12 to 14 years — 21%
15 to 18 years — 6%
Over 18 years — 5%
Don't know — 2%

■ FIRST TEACHERS

Where current or former players learn to play. Total exceeds 100 percent due to multiple response.

Took private lessons	40%
Took lessons at school	26%
Taught self	17%
Took band or orchestra at school	16%
Parent or family member taught	5%
Friend taught	4%

■ TUNE-IN TIME

What makes players start an instrument:

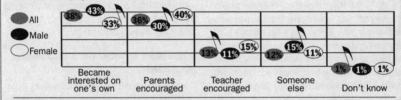

- All
- Male
- Female

	Became interested on one's own	Parents encouraged	Teacher encouraged	Someone else	Don't know
All	38%	36%	13%	12%	1%
Male	43%	40%	11%	15%	1%
Female	33%	30%	15%	11%	1%

■ CHOOSE YOUR INSTRUMENT

The 10 most popular musical instruments, and what beginners will pay for them:

INSTRUMENT	ALL PLAYERS	MALE	FEMALE	BEGINNER PRICE RANGE
PIANO	34%	17%	50%	$1,200–$3,200
GUITAR	22%	36%	8%	$160–$200 (acoustic) $180–$300 (electric)
DRUMS	6%	11%	1%	$600–$800; individual drum $150
FLUTE	5%	2%	8%	$235–$400
ORGAN	4%	1%	7%	$250–$550
SAXOPHONE (ALTO)	4%	5%	3%	$475–$800
KEYBOARD	4%	4%	4%	$250–$550
CLARINET	4%	1%	6%	$250–$400
TRUMPET	3%	6%	1%	$345–$500
VIOLIN	3%	2%	4%	$285

■ THE TEEN BEAT

What teenagers say about the benefits of music:

It is an activity a child can enjoy all his or her life	91%	Performing in front of others helps develop poise and confidence	51%
It helps instill appreciation of arts and culture in general	90%	It helps develop child's creativity	49%
It helps children make friends	72%	It provides a child with another means of self-expression	48%
It teaches children self-discipline	62%	Teens who play an instrument are less likely to get in trouble with the law	47%
It provides a sense of accomplishment	57%		

SOURCE: Reprinted with permission from the National Association of Music Merchants.

THE CHILD WHO DOES TOO MUCH

The more activities kids take on, the less enriched their educations are

Every parent knows the exasperation that comes from having a child who "acts up"—whether it be the 5-year-old who is terrorizing other children at nursery school, the 7-year-old who throws a fit every morning before leaving the house, or the 10-year-old who refuses to do her homework. What can a parent do in such cases? Dr. David Elkind, a leading child development expert, shares his views about how to evaluate and cope with your child's behavior. Elkind is professor of child study at Tufts University and author of *The Hurried Child* (Addison-Wesley, 1988) and *Ties That Stress* (Harvard University Press, 1994):

■ How can you tell the difference between a child who is acting up because of stress, and one who is precocious and simply wants more stimulation?

Parents experience very different demands from children depending on what that child is experiencing. For example, a gifted child might demand constant stimulation to try to satisfy his or her voracious appetite for information—a chorus of whys ringing in your ears all day. That's very different from a child who battles for attention and presents parents with strain and power struggles.

You need to look at how many demands there are on a child. Is he having to adapt to too many places and people each day (e.g., school, daycare, baby-sitters)? The more changes a child experiences in a day, the more stress he feels. Also, if you are troubled or there is distress in the family, your child's behavior will often mirror it.

■ What can be done to relieve stress at school?

Increasingly, with so many early education programs, educators are assuming that children know their numbers and letters at a younger and younger age. This might not be the case, and it is no reflection on the child's intelligence—different children have different rates of development. If your child has a September or October birthday, especially for boys, you may want to wait a year before enrolling him. This is much preferred to starting your child and then having him repeat a year. There is such a stigma for kids who are held back that if you are considering holding your child back a year, I recommend allowing him to continue to the next grade, and providing additional tutoring.

■ How many activities can a child manage adequately?

There is no need for a child to have any organized activity like sports or music before the age of five or six. For school-age children, a sport, a musical instrument, and maybe a "peer activity" like scouts is plenty. These should not take more than a few hours a week. It is very important for a child not to have all his time programmed. Children must learn to manage their own time. I see a lot of new college students who simply do not know how to manage their time because they had such "planned" lives.

■ How do you allow a child to manage his or her own time, yet limit television or video watching?

You can lay down some ground rules. For instance, you allow your child a certain number of hours of Nintendo per week, and the rest must be spent doing other things. You are not saying that he or she can't do something, but you are setting limits on it.

■ What's the best way to help a child deal with a stress that won't go away, like a death, divorce, or a move?

The most important thing is to talk to your child and help him or her deal with

HOW TO RAISE A MORAL CHILD

Empathy is the key to developing morality, says Dr. Stanley Greenspan

"Children are going to learn morality not from what you tell them, but from how you treat them," says child psychiatrist Stanley Greenspan, whose latest book, *The Growth of the Mind and Its Endangered Future* (Addison-Wesley, 1996), discusses how children develop their sense of morality. The way a child is treated is crucial, says Greenspan, whose research has shown that morality depends on a person's ability to feel empathy for someone else, and to have empathy a child must first develop what Greenspan calls "a sense of shared humanity." That sense of shared humanity, or "buying into the human race," comes from a child experiencing intimacy and warmth in a relationship with another person, whether that figure is the child's parents, relative, or other close contact. It's impossible to develop a concern for others, Greenspan argues, unless someone in your life has shown concern for you.

That sense of shared humanity is only the starting point, however, for encouraging morality in children. "You can't empathize with someone else unless you can picture what the other person wants and desires and are able to put yourself in the other's shoes," says Greenspan. "If you can't put yourself in another's shoes, you can't really contemplate how your actions are going to affect them."

Empathy is essential, Greenspan says, because it helps guide children's judgments in cases where there may not be a clear-cut rule to follow, and a child may have to decide how to handle a moral dilemma on his own. If you simply tell a child, "You don't do this, you don't do that," says Greenspan, some children will obey out of a fear of being "a bad person," without really understanding what that means. Such children have what Greenspan calls "a concrete sense of morality, and can just as soon be immoral as moral" if a new authority figure with less savory rules appears. To make moral judgments, stresses Greenspan, "the kind we want in our Supreme Court justices, comes from a sense of empathy."

his or her feelings. If someone has died, it's very important for the child to talk about that person and to articulate how he or she feels. Similarly, if a child sees something frightening on TV, the child needs to talk about it and be allowed to work through his or her emotions.

■ When is professional help advisable?

While there are cases where a child needs therapy, a parent must be very careful. Being sent to see someone can label the child as abnormal and become yet another form of stress. When there is a problem for which a parent wants to seek professional counseling, this should be done as a family. A child does not become emotionally distressed overnight, but over a period of years as a result of

family behavior patterns. Even when a child is experiencing a physiological problem, such as Attention Deficit Disorder, the parents need counseling as well.

■ What is the biggest mistake parents make in helping children deal with life's stresses?

One of the biggest mistakes is to think that bad experiences prepare children for other bad experiences. I believe that the more good experiences parents can give their children—doing things with their children, giving them loving and successful experiences—the better they feel about themselves, the better the relationships they have with their parents, the better they are able to cope when something difficult does happen.

A HELPING HAND AT DAY'S END

Some sound advice on how a parent can aid in after-school work

For parents eager to help their children's learning, getting involved with homework is one of the best methods. Yet all too often, homework becomes a battleground for wars of words between parent and child.

"The relationship [of parent helping the child] is supposed to go on for years," says Joyce Epstein, who has studied homework issues extensively as director of the Johns Hopkins Center on Families, Communities, Schools and Children's Learning. "You have to be careful that one night of confrontation doesn't ruin you for 12 years of school."

To develop good family communications, says Epstein, it's important how a parent talks to a child about school. "Many parents are told or advised to ask their child, 'How was school today?' as a way of interacting," says Epstein. "Better to ask: 'Show me something you learned in math today,' because that makes the youngster demonstrate and re-create, rather than comment on nothing." From there, she says, parents can build the kind of interaction that will not only help the child's work but will improve the way the parent and child communicate. Other pitfalls that parents must avoid include:

■ A confrontational attitude in which the parent challenges the child, rather than allowing the child to demonstrate what he or she has learned.

■ Giving up the guidance role too early, particularly with adolescents. Studies have found, says Epstein, that parents tend to talk less to their children as they reach high school, even though these students continue to need positive interaction on their work.

■ Taking on the teacher role, which sets up resistance in the child.

Epstein's research has shown a strong connection between parents' involvement in learning activities at home and gains in skills in reading and other subject areas. Concerned about lost learning opportunities at home, Epstein and a team of Hopkins educators designed TIPS (Teachers Involve Parents in Schoolwork)—homework assignments in which students discuss something interesting about their schoolwork with someone at home. Instead of dittoed exercises to be done in one night, homework becomes a source of games, interviews, and experiments conducted by the child with the help of a parent over a period of two to three days.

Epstein's research reveals that middle-school teachers who systematically involve families are more likely to see parents as allies, and to foster good communication between parent and child about school and homework. In the TIPS model, parents take on a variety of roles. For a lesson on the use of proper nouns, students play a game with the parent naming proper nouns from a list of common nouns such as *cereal* and *tennis shoe*. For a lesson called "Test Your Nerves," the parent is the test subject in an experiment in which a child observes and charts nervous reactions, such as blinking. All of the activities conclude with discussion on whatever phenomenon is studied.

"Schools are calling for more homework," says Epstein. "But what is really needed is better homework. Instead of assigning another page of math problems, teachers need to step back and see how to engage children in extra minutes of thought."

■ **FOR MORE INFORMATION:** TIPS manuals and activities booklets are available for elementary and middle grades. Write: Dissemination Office, Center on Families, Communities, Schools and Children's Learning, The Johns Hopkins University, 3505 N. Charles Street, Baltimore, MD 21218, or call ☎ 410–516–8808.

CYBER SOURCES

THE TUTOR IN YOUR COMPUTER

Students of all ages, equipped with a computer and access to the Internet, can tackle tough homework assignments without lifting a reference book. The World Wide Web and online services, such as America Online, offer access to thousands of resources—from dictionaries to experts in quantum physics. However, users should be wary: Because of the often undocumented nature of cyber-information, it's difficult to know how reliable any piece of information may be. For that reason, students are advised to tap into solid, reputable resources, such as those described below. These sites are generally suitable for students aged 10 to 18.

GENERAL REFERENCE

AMERICA ONLINE

■ The best online service for homework help. Besides an extensive array of reference resources, AOL retains teachers to answer students' questions by e-mail. There's a chat room with tutors to respond to immediate homework-related questions on just about any subject. The downside: It may be tough to post your query; the chat room gets lots of traffic.

RESEARCH IT!
http://www.itools.com/research-it/research-it.html

■ A one-stop-shop for Webster's dictionary; Roget's thesaurus; French, Spanish, Italian, German, Czech, and Japanese translators; a French verb conjugation tool; *Bartlett's Quotations;* maps, plus more.

ASK AN EXPERT
http://www.askanexpert.com/ask anexpert/

■ This site includes hundreds of links to experts who answer e-mail inquiries on a range of subjects.

MATHEMATICS AND SCIENCE

THE MATH FORUM
http://forum.swarthmore.edu/

■ Sponsored by Swarthmore College, this is perhaps the Web's best math resource. Most helpful is Dr. Math, which features a stable of college students who answer questions in all areas of mathematics.

THE NINE PLANETS
http://www.seds.org/billa/tnp/

■ A detailed guide to planets, as well as other phenomena in the solar system.

MAD SCIENTIST NETWORK
http://medicine.wustl.edu/~ysp/ MSN/MAD.SCI.html

■ Scientists from around the globe offer expertise on all manner of scientific subjects. Archives of previously answered questions can be searched by subject.

THE WHY FILES
http://whyfiles.news.wisc.edu/

■ This National Science Foundation site features reports on phenomena in a variety of fields. It also has links to related sites on the Internet and a search engine.

PERIODIC TABLE OF ELEMENTS
http://mwanal.lanl.gov/CST/ imagemap/periodic/periodic.html

■ Los Alamos National Laboratory has assembled the table, which has links to

---

■ **WEB GUIDES**
Each of the sites below is a compendium of Web sources for students. The references included in the compendiums are chosen for their usefulness.

KID'S WEB	http://www.npac.syr.edu/textbook/kidsweb/
THE INTERNET PUBLIC LIBRARY	http://www.ipl.org/
THE VIRTUAL LIBRARY	http://www.w3.org/vl/
THREE RIVERS FREE-NET HOMEWORK HELP.	
	http://trfn.clpgh.org/Education/K12/homework.html

■ CYBER SOURCES

detailed material about the attributes and history of each element.

SOCIAL SCIENCES
THOMAS
http://thomas.loc.gov

■ This Library of Congress site presents in-depth information about current Congressional bills; texts of historical documents; and links to related Web sites.

THE AMERICAN PRESIDENT
http://www.grolier.com/presidents/preshome.html

■ Presented by Grolier, the

encyclopedia company, this site offers everything you ever wanted to know about the executive branch, individual presidents, and their administrations.

U.S. CENSUS BUREAU
http://www.census.gov/stat_abstract/

■ This is the definitive site for demographic and economic reports and statistics such as family income, poverty levels, etc.

LITERATURE
THE COMPLETE WORKS OF

WILLIAM SHAKESPEARE
http://the-tech.mit.edu/Shakespeare/works.html

■ As the title suggests, you get full texts of all the Shakespearian works; a search engine helps you locate textual references.

PROJECT BARTLEBY
http://www.cc.columbia.edu/acis/bartleby/

■ Columbia University's expanding online library of literature and reference works, including editions of Strunk's and Fowler's respective writing manuals.

FONTS OF KNOWLEDGE AND POWER

Compact discs tolled the death knell for multivolume print encyclopedias several years ago: Discs are compact and far less expensive. Here we compare the four top home CD-ROM encyclopedias, including special features and comments for each. Prices are as of March 1997.

	BRITANNICA CD97 *Encyclopaedia Britannica Inc.*	COMPTON'S INTERACTIVE *The Learning Company*	GROLIER MULTIMEDIA *Grolier Interactive, Inc.*	MICROSOFT ENCARTA 97 *Microsoft Corp.*
☎	800–747–8503	800–227–5609	203–797–3530	800–426–9400
PRICE	$299 for CD; $50 online updates	$49.95, free monthly updates	$49.95, free monthly updates	$79.95 (deluxe) $54.95 (standard)
ONLINE VERSION	http://www.eb.com	Available through AOL and Prodigy	http://www.grolier.com	No online version
ONLINE COST	$14.95 per month or $150 per year		$49.95 plus $5 registration fee	
FEATURES	66,000 articles, the Merriam-Webster Collegiate Dictionary, pictures and maps, interface with Netscape Navigator.	37,000 articles, Webster's New World Dictionary/Thesaurus, free updates, and a planetarium that lets users see night sky from any location.	50,000 articles, free monthly updates, and sound, video, and animation.	31,000 articles, American Heritage Dictionary,and 18 free monthly updates, then a one-time $20 fee.
COMMENT	Well-written, in-depth coverage of topics. No video and audio but twice as much detail as the others. However, online updates cost an extra $50 a year.	Its best feature is Showmaker, which lets the user prepare customized multimedia.	An interactive atlas has a zoom feature and more than 1,200 maps.	Outstanding multi-capabilities, featuring 60 degree panoramic views (Windows 95 or NT only), combined audio, video, and text presentations.

KEEPING GIRLS ON THE FAST TRACK

Single-sex education is only one way to help young women's self-esteem

Sixty percent of elementary school girls say they are "always happy the way I am." Fewer than half that many high school girls feel the same. Teenage girls are much more likely than boys to say they are "not smart enough" or "not good enough" to achieve their dreams. Moreover, when specifying what they disliked about themselves, girls tended to name a physical trait, whereas boys targeted a talent or ability. These disturbing findings were published in a study of 3,000 girls and boys by the American Association of University Women in 1991. The blow to girls' confidence documented in the report may manifest itself in a host of self-destructive behaviors. According to the National Institute of Mental Health, about 20 percent of high school and college-age girls suffer from an eating disorder.

Some educators argue that the way to stem the precipitous drop in girls' self-esteem is to encourage single-sex education for young women. Here, Susan McGee Bailey, executive director of the Center for Research on Women at Wellesley College and principal author of the report "How Schools Short-change Girls," discusses the research and argues that it is important to change how and what we teach boys and girls, rather than simply divide the sexes:

■ **Are girls really at a disadvantage in mixed-sex classrooms?**

Studies show that boys receive more of a teacher's attention than do girls. They tend to be more assertive than girls and to have that quality encouraged by their teachers, whereas girls are not. Because of this, girls and shyer boys begin to feel inhibited and self-conscious about speaking out.

The message being sent to both sexes is: "It's okay for boys to behave this way and if they do, they will get attention. However, it's not okay for girls to behave this way." This message that good girls are those who listen well and remain quieter is all wrong. We need boys to be good listeners just as much as we need girls to be good speakers.

■ **Do girls benefit from the experience of single-sex education?**

We have to be extremely careful in talking about the benefits and drawbacks of single-sex education because the research is very limited. Although many girls and women who have been to all-girls schools seem to have benefited from the experience, all of these schools are private. We must look at what is possible in the public school system and assess what is causing an unequal educational experience for boys and girls.

■ **What is it about an all-girls school that seems to benefit students?**

Girls' schools often use more women as examples in teaching—more women's experiences and women as role models. Many girls say they feel less inhibited and a more integral part of the class in such schools. They say it is easier to pursue and excel at typical "boy things," such as math and science, with no stigma attached.

In addition, many who have attended all-girls schools claim that because of the absence of boys in the school day, there is less emphasis on physical appearance than in a coeducational school. But all-girls schools can reinforce stereotypical gender roles just as easily as mixed-sex schools. I believe mixed-sex schools can provide positive rather than negative experiences to girls as well as boys if we change the way we teach.

■ **What can teachers in a mixed-sex school do to combat sexism in the classroom?**

Students need to talk about what their perceptions of the issue are. Some boys might argue that the girls in the class are favored while girls will contend that boys blurt out

ONCE UPON A TIME, THERE WAS A STRONG GIRL

Finding nontraditional girl characters in children's literature

As a librarian for 15 years, Kathleen Odean has devoted considerable time sifting through children's literature to find books that show girls stepping out of traditional roles for their sex. The result is her book, *Great Books for Girls* (Ballantine, 1997), in which Odean promotes titles that offset sexism. Here Odean, a former member of the prestigious Caldecott and Newbery Award Committees, offers her thoughts on picking good books for girls:

■ I look for books that defy stereotypes—girls who like sports, insects, snakes, and motorcycles. I look for girl characters who initiate adventures, who don't wait to be rescued, but instead, do the rescuing. There are so many stories about girls who sacrifice for the good of the family. But why should we always read about girls playing a self-sacrificing role?

■ Some examples of strong girl characters include Beverly Cleary's series about Ramona Quimby, which show girls being looked up to by boys. *Anna Banana and Me* by Lenore Blegvad is about a girl who keeps doing daring things, and a boy who follows her and does things he wouldn't have tried.

Climb or Die by Edward Myers is about a girl and her younger brother who crash in the mountains. She helps him by using skills she learned at wilderness camp.

■ In talking animal books, boys are definitely the default setting. *Winnie the Pooh*, *Wind in the Willows*, *Frog and Toad*—all are wonderful books, but the main characters are males. In the last few years, however, we've seen more females in great books like *Poppy* by Avi and *The School Mouse* by Dick King-Smith.

■ Classics like *Anne of Green Gables* and *Little Women* are books I recommend, but if you read them closely, many 19th-century books have subtle lessons that aren't part of my goal. Parents gravitate toward stories they loved as children, but it's regrettable if they miss books written in the last 10 or 20 years. For example: *Dealing with Dragons* by Patricia C. Wrede, a fantasy about a princess who hates being a princess, and *Tuck Everlasting* by Nathalie Babbott, about a 10-year-old girl who helps out a wandering family. They are beautifully written and almost always have happy endings.

the answers all the time and don't give them a chance. Once the issue is on the table and is recognized, then the entire class—teachers and students—can deal with how to change.

■ **How can parents help a daughter who may be suffering in school because of gender?**

Parents need to be supportive and reinforce that support when their daughters do speak out and take a chance. Girls need to feel that their parents are proud of them when they do step outside the "traditional girl model."

Parents should also encourage their daughters to be involved in a single-sex activity, such as Girl Scouts or an all-girls team. Girls learn to appreciate other girls and therefore to think more highly of themselves.

■ **When do girls most need to spend time with other girls?**

The middle-school years are particularly important. That's when girls are beginning to question themselves and are trying to figure out how they can be popular with boys, etc. This is the time that girls are shown to have a tremendous drop in their self-esteem. It's at this time that they need confidence and need to feel good about being strong and outspoken, smart, and to feel good about their bodies.

COLLEGE & GRAD SCHOOL

ONLINE: Click here for the college of your choice, PAGE 235 **TESTS:** Ways to get ready for the SAT, PAGE 236 **SOFTWARE:** Packages that help you prepare for the SAT, PAGE 237 **RANKINGS:** The best colleges in America, PAGE 238 **BEST VALUES:** Good colleges for the money, PAGE 244 **PROFESSIONAL SCHOOLS:** The best institutions for law, business, and medicine, PAGE 250 **FINANCIAL AID:** Options for helping meet the high cost of tuition, PAGE 256

ADMISSIONS

CLAIMING A SEAT EARLY

Many students should worry more about fitting in than getting in

Deciding on the right college has traditionally been a springtime ritual for high school seniors. But the stakes have changed in the college admissions game, as more schools and students push to make the decision earlier. Last year an estimated 100,000 students applied under early admission plans; some of the elite schools filled more than half of their incoming freshman class with early admissions applicants.

Rules vary from school to school, but generally early admissions applicants must apply to their first-choice schools by November 1 of their senior year. At that time, they make an ironclad commitment to attend that school if accepted. The college generally notifies applicants by mid-December. Students who are not accepted early may still be admitted in the regular admissions process, but they must wait until April to learn whether they have been accepted.

Early decision making isn't for everyone, says Steven Antonoff, an educational consultant and author of *The College Finder: 475 Ways to Choose the Right School for You* (Ballantine, 1993). Of the more than 2,000 students Antonoff has advised during his 15-year career, only 10 percent, he says, were good candidates for filing early applications. Here Antonoff shares his expertise:

■ **Why isn't the early admissions strategy for everyone?**

Most seniors in the first few weeks of school haven't devoted enough time to considering which college best suits their interests and lifestyles. Many students feel pressure from peers, parents, or school counselors to apply early, and end up picking a college that's a poor fit. A student considering early admissions should start the college planning process early in the junior year by undergoing testing, visiting schools, reading catalogs, and broadening their community involvement or other extracurricular activities.

■ **What is the difference between "early decision" and "early action"?**

In an early decision plan, the college application itself is a contract signed by the student, parents, and school counselors agreeing that if the student is accepted, he or she will attend that school. The student cannot apply to any other schools and must withdraw any applications already submitted elsewhere.

Early action plans are less common but more flexible. The student also applies in the fall of senior year and is notified by mid-December. But the acceptance decision is deferred until the spring, usually around May 1. The student has the chance to apply to other schools and to compare offers before locking into a decision.

■ What does it mean when an applicant's early decision application is "deferred" by a college?

It means the application will be reevaluated during the general admissions process. But what it should mean to parents and students is that it's way past time to get on the ball and look at other schools. Too many students and parents put all their eggs in the early decision basket. If it doesn't work out they are left high and dry.

■ Are students who wait until spring at a disadvantage?

No. Most schools are generally consistent in terms of the criteria they use to evaluate the quality of students they accept during both admissions rounds. In the early decision round, the applicants are generally highly qualified students with good SAT scores, high grade point averages, and exceptional community involvement. It makes sense that a higher percentage of these students would be admitted than during the regular admissions period where the qualifications of applicants can vary widely.

■ Should an outstanding, well-rounded student of exceptional abilities even worry about second or third college choices?

There are 150,000 high schools in the country, which means that many valedictorians and salutatorians, and at least 1,000 times that many star athletes, concert violinists, and champion debaters. I see many parents and students whose goal is to get into the biggest name school they can. Students feel if they don't apply for early admissions, their chances of getting in are jeopardized. That's untrue. My view is parents and students should spend less time worrying about getting in and more time thinking about fitting in.

■ Does financial aid dry up by the time spring applicants apply?

No. I've never heard of a school running short of aid before the needs of all the students they've accepted have been taken care of, regardless of when they were accepted. It would be foolhardy for a school to be in a position of not having financial aid available for its spring choices, especially since those students presumably have the option of comparing aid packages offered by their other choices. I've found that if a school admits a student, it will do everything in its power to ensure that the student can afford it—through grants, loans, or work-study programs.

■ What are the greatest benefits of making an early decision?

The student can relax and enjoy senior year. The family can begin financial planning earlier, and spare themselves hundreds of dollars in application fees to other schools.

■ What are some disadvantages?

One disadvantage is that a student doesn't get the chance to compare financial aid packages. Students with three or four acceptance offers can see vast differences in the scholarship or loan amounts among the schools and use the information in picking a school. With the early decision process, you take the offer or leave it. The only way for a student to renege on an early decision contract, in fact, is to leave it. If a family feels the financial aid offered by the school is insufficient to cover costs, the student can back out of the contract without a penalty.

■ Where should a student or a parent go for guidance on the early decision process?

College handbooks offer the most up-to-date information on a particular school's early admissions policies. But the first stop should be the school counselor. If a family wants more hands-on, personal assistance, they can call the Independent Educational Consultants Association (☎ 800–808–4322) for a free directory of educational advisers in their area.

CYBER SOURCES

THE COLLEGE SHOPPING MALL

Finding the right college has never been easier, thanks to the Internet. Nearly every college worth the name has a site. An applicant can find information about schools around the world, apply online, even take virtual campus tours. Search engines let you compile a list of colleges based on your preferences in categories such as location, tuition expenses, and extracurricular activities. Here are some good starting points for your online college search:

COLLEGE BOARD ONLINE
http://www.college-board.org
■ The best place to begin. Brought to you by the SAT folks, this site is packed with information on pre-college testing and online test registration, as well as advice on picking a school and finding financial help. The site is working to make available a generic application, accepted by some 550 colleges, and proprietary applications used by 200 colleges.

THE PRINCETON REVIEW
http://www.review.com
■ Opinions and data on more than 300 top colleges. You'll find pre-college test samples here that you can download and use to practice away.

YAHOO'S HIGHER EDUCATION INDEX
http://www.yahoo.com/edu cation/higher education
■ An all-encompassing set of links to colleges, test-preparation companies, sites handling financial aid, you name it. Lists two-year and four-year schools alphabetically or by state.

CHRISTINA DEMELLO'S COLLEGE AND UNIVERSITY HOME PAGES
http://www.mit.edu:8001/ people/cdmello/univ.html
■ Lists Web sites for thousands of colleges throughout the world and offers links to other indexes.

THE COMMON APPLICATION
http://www.nassp.org/ser-vices/commapp.htm
■ Offers a four-page generic application form, accepted by more than 160 colleges.

COLLEGELINK
http://www.ultranet.com/ biz/collegelink
■ E-mail your application data to College-Link. This service enters the data into an electronic version of the

application of each of your college choices and then sends you a print-out. The first application is free; additional colleges cost $5.00 each.

U.S.NEWS ONLINE COLLEGES AND CAREER CENTER
http://www. usnews. com/ usnews/EDU/college
■ From *U.S. News & World Report,* featuring among other services the magazine's annual college rankings and a forum that answers questions related to filing applications.

FIN-AID: THE FINANCIAL AID INFORMATION PAGE
http://www.finaid.org
■ Everything you ever wanted to know about financial aid, from where to find it to how to get it.

FASTWEB
http://www.finaid.org /finaid/fastweb.html
■ A search engine with descriptions of 180,000 scholarships, fellowship, grants, and loans.

PREPPING FOR THE SATs

Bone up and you could raise your score by about 100 points

A rmed with sharpened number two pencils, nearly 2 million students each year take the Scholastic Assessment Test (SAT), a three-hour test of verbal and math abilities. About 5 percent of them will have bolstered their test-taking skills with short-term cram courses. And at least half of the students will have spent hours poring over study manuals or mousing their way through software programs designed to prepare them for taking the tests.

Should every student facing the SAT do some prepping? If so, is a classroom course a better route to honing SAT skills than a guidebook or a software program? Bob Schaeffer, public education director for the National Center for Fair and Open Testing, in Cambridge, Mass., says some students require little or no preparation, whereas others need extensive help. A student's first step

toward gauging how much help he may need should be to get a copy of an SAT practice test, available from the school guidance office or from the College Board (☎ 212–713–8000). If your score is within the range of the school you would like to attend, Schaeffer advises passing up the prep tools. But if your scores aren't up to par, then it's time to explore resources that will give you the extra boost.

The range of SAT help tools includes software programs, guidebooks, and classroom courses. Students who are comfortable on the computer would do well to invest in a software program designed for SAT preparation. (See box on facing page.) Those who are self-motivated can probably benefit from using one of the hundreds of SAT guides available in bookstores. Students requiring a more disciplined approach may want to try classroom courses.

When it comes to guides, some of the best-known publishers are Kaplan, Arco, and the Princeton Review. They each publish six or seven different guides and change the titles each year, so it's hard to pin down which are the best-sellers. In recent years, the crop has grown to include lesser-known titles such as *The SAT for Dummies* (IDG Books Worldwide) and *Panic Plan for the SAT* (Peterson's). All the guides are a hefty weight and sell for about $20.

The best way to find one that's right for you is to browse through a few. As you do, keep in mind the following questions: Does the book include practice tests that mimic the actual SAT format and length? Does it offer explanations or simply provide answers to questions? And does it explain the test structure and offer test-taking strategies?

For students searching for a good classroom review course, the undisputed leaders in the field are also Kaplan (☎ 800–KAP–TEST) and The Princeton Review (☎ 800–2–REVIEW), commercial companies that offer SAT prep courses. The courses run about six weeks and cost between $500 and $700. Class size is limited to ensure that each student gets personalized attention. Both companies offer financial aid to needy students.

Many good and less expensive local programs can be found, but because the quality

---

■ **DATES TO REMEMBER**

If you are taking the SATs during the 1997–98 school year, here's when to do it. Online registration is available at *http://www.collegeboard.org*

1997–1998 test dates	Registration deadlines	Late regis. deadlines
Oct. 4, 1997	Sep. 9, 1997	Sep. 13, 1997
Nov. 1, 1997	Sep. 26, 1997	Oct. 8, 1997
Dec. 6, 1997	Oct. 30, 1997	Nov. 14, 1997
Jan. 24, 1998	Dec. 9, 1997	Dec. 30, 1997
Mar. 28, 1998*	Feb. 20, 1998	Mar. 4, 1998
May 2, 1998	Mar. 26, 1998	Apr. 10, 1998
June 6, 1998	Apr. 30, 1998	May 15, 1998

* SAT I only.
SOURCE: College Entrance Examination Board.

SIZING UP TEST SOFTWARE

Preparing for SATs may not be everyone's idea of fun, but much of the software designed to help actually makes honing critical math and verbal skills entertaining. Many programs provide immediate feedback, comparing the student's score with students at hundreds of schools. Most generate personalized study plans, and all are readily available at local computer- and bookstores. Here are some of the more popular titles.

CLIFFS STUDYWARE FOR SAT I
Cliff's Studyware, $49.95

■ Provides numerous practice drills and skill-building exercises, including four full-length practice tests. The program lets you skip back and forth between questions, just as you might do during the actual exam. The skills drills are especially useful, although explanations of answers are often too brief. The software comes with a 450-page guide.

THE ULTIMATE TRAINER FOR THE SAT
Davidson & Associates, $59.95

■ This program by a well-known maker of children's educational software is a best-seller. A pretest identifies your strengths and weaknesses. The program then designs a personal training schedule with up to 12 hours of practice in areas such as vocabulary or algebra, for example. As you proceed, you are given detailed strategies for handling certain types of questions.

ROADTRIP FOR THE SAT/ACT
Kaplan, $29.95

■ This creative program is full of entertaining videos, animation, sound, and graphics. Roadtrip puts students behind the wheel, steering you through virtual exits that lead to test-taking strategies and skill builders. The program re-creates actual test conditions—a loud cough or a droning helicopter can be heard at times during the seven practice tests. You can also download additional questions from AOL.

INSIDE THE SAT
The Princeton Review, $29.95

■ Gets good reviews for its irreverence and sense of humor. Designs are friendly: You start in a school with a dozen doors leading to classes in different academic areas. Comical scenes and animation make the exercises entertaining. In addition, the program teaches test-taking smarts, such as when to use a calculator or when to make an educated guess.

SCOREBUILDER FOR THE SAT
The Learning Co.. $49.95

■ Provides a straightforward, well-organized review of the exam, the types of questions it contains, and strategies for answering them. The program offers one of the easiest-to-follow study plans and does a thorough job of providing a solid review, rather than suggesting tricks for beating the test writers.

of instruction can vary, experts advise researching them carefully. Some high schools also offer classroom reviews, but again, the caliber of teaching and content can vary enormously between schools.

Does prepping pay off in the end? Absolutely, says Schaeffer, who adds that with preparation SAT scores can rise an average 100 points. Of course, how well the preparation works depends on a student's effort.

Whether you prepare or not is your choice, but at the very least, advises Schaeffer, read the SAT registration booklet carefully—it contains specific and vital instructions for taking the test. "Anyone who waits to read the directions during the test is wasting time."

THE BEST COLLEGES IN AMERICA

Every year U.S. News & World Report *publishes a widely followed special report that ranks America's best colleges and universities by several objective measures such as test scores and student/faculty ratios, as well as by academic reputation. Highlights from the 1996–97 survey appear below.*

■ BEST NATIONAL UNIVERSITIES

The 229 national universities from which these top-ranked institutions were selected have comprehensive program offerings, place great emphasis on faculty research, and award many Ph.D.'s. In 1996 Yale outranked Harvard, which had finished first five years in a row.

Rank / School	Overall score	Academic reputation	SAT / ACT 25th–75th percentile	Freshmen in top 10% of HS class	Acceptance rate	Student / faculty ratio	Education expenditures per student
1. Yale University (Conn.)	100.0	3	1350—1550	95%	20%	9/1	$45,507
2. Princeton University (N.J.)	99.8	1	1340—1550	92%	14%	8/1	$32,417
3. Harvard University (Mass.)	99.6	3	1370—1560	92%	12%	12/1	$42,902
4. Duke University (N.C.)	98.7	11	1290—1470	87%	29%	14/1	$31,652
5. Massachusetts Inst. of Technology	98.3	1	1380—1540	97%	27%	10/1	$37,376
6. Stanford University (Calif.)	96.8	3	1330—1530	87%	19%	13/1	$36,643
7. Dartmouth College (N.H.)	96.5	11	1330—1520	88%	23%	10/1	$31,491
8. Brown University (R.I.)	96.2	11	1290—1470	86%	21%	13/1	$23,889
9. California Institute of Technology	95.5	7	1400—1580	97%	27%	6/1	$73,967
9. Northwestern University (Ill.)	95.5	11	1260—1440	81%	40%	12/1	$29,760
11. Columbia University (N.Y.)	95.4	11	1341—1438	84%	24%	18/1	$32,738
12. University of Chicago	95.3	3	1270—1470	74%	71%	7/1	$40,686
13. University of Pennsylvania	95.2	11	1270—1440	83%	33%	6/1	$32,022
14. Cornell University (N.Y.)	94.8	7	1250—1440	81%	34%	13/1	$22,285
15. Johns Hopkins University (Md.)	94.6	7	1280—1460	76%	43%	14/1	$61,704
16. Rice University (Texas)	94.1	18	1260—1530	85%	26%	8/1	$25,878
17. University of Notre Dame (Ind.)	93.0	30	1230—1410	82%	39%	13/1	$15,874
17. Washington University (Mo.)	93.0	24	1180—1380	67%	56%	10/1	$54,020
19. Emory University (Ga.)	92.9	30	1230—1390	81%	51%	14/1	$30,163
20. Vanderbilt University (Tenn.)	90.6	24	1220—1370	64%	58%	13/1	$25,490
21. University of Virginia	89.2	18	1210—1390	79%	42%	15/1	$14,142
22. Tufts University (Mass.)	89.1	41	1200—1380	62%	43%	13/1	$20,226
23. Georgetown University (D.C.)	88.5	28	1240—1420	74%	22%	11/1	$20,924
24. University of Michigan—Ann Arbor	87.7	11	25—30	64%	69%	16/1	$16,293
25. U. of North Carolina—Chapel Hill	87.2	21	1120—1330	73%	35%	14/1	$18,398
25. Wake Forest University (N.C.)	87.2	65	1180—1380	71%	43%	14/1	$49,051
SCHOOLS RANKED 27TH TO 50TH							
27. University of California—Berkeley	86.9	7	1180—1430	95%	39%		$16,374
28. Carnegie Mellon University (Pa.)	85.9	21	1240—1430	62%	54%		$25,791
29. Brandeis University (Mass.)	85.1	41	1300	57%	66%		$17,690
30. University of Rochester (N.Y.)	83.5	55	1140—1350	56%	61%		$29,834
31. Univ. of California—Los Angeles	83.2	21	1100—1340	97%	42%		$21,500
32. Lehigh University (Pa.)	82.6	65	1130—1320	49%	60%		$15,503

■ **EXPERT LIST**

Rank / School	Overall score	Academic reputation	SAT / ACT 25th–75th percentile	Freshmen in top 10% of HS class	Acceptance rate	Student / faculty ratio	Education expenditures per student
33. College of William and Mary (Va.)	81.5	30	1200—1390	73%	49%		$10,757
34. Univ. of California—San Diego	80.5	41	1110—1330	95%	54%		$20,875
35. New York University	80.4	41	1160—1360	60%	47%		$24,135
36. Tulane University (La.)	79.6	55	1170—1370	56%	73%		$18,548
37. University of California—Irvine	78.7	49	980—1230	90%	73%		$16,779
38. Boston College	78.4	55	1200—1370	69%	38%		$12,301
38. Case Western Reserve Univ. (Ohio)	78.4	49	1210—1450	69%	77%		$19,940
40. University of California—Davis	78.0	41	1039—1281	95%	71%		$17,073
41. Univ. of Wisconsin—Madison	75.9	18	24—29	43%	71%		$11,999
42. University of Washington	75.8	28	1020—1260	40%[1]	65%		$16,677
43. Univ. of Southern California	75.7	37	1070—1310	44%	70%		$18,580
44. Syracuse University (N.Y.)	73.8	55	1070—1290	33%	66%		$15,418
45. Yeshiva University (N.Y.)	73.0	103	1090—1310	N/A	84%		$23,039
46. George Washington University (D.C.)	71.7	65	1140—1330	42%	55%		$16,855
46. Univ. of California—Santa Barbara	71.7	65	1010—1220	93%	81%		$10,568
48. Georgia Institute of Technology	71.6	30	1240—1410	73%[2]	62%		$13,416
48. Texas A&M Univ.—College Station	71.6	49	1020—1280	49%	69%		$10,284
50. U. of Illinois—Urbana—Champaign	71.2	24	24—29	50%	72%		$11,154

NOTES: Schools with the same numbered rank are tied. Reputational surveys conducted by Market Facts Inc. **1.** Data reported to *U.S. News* in previous years and not submitted in form requested. **2.** Data reported to *U.S. News* in previous years.

■ **BEST NATIONAL LIBERAL ARTS COLLEGES**
The 160 liberal arts colleges from which these outstanding schools were picked are highly selective in their admissions and award more than 40 percent of their degrees in the liberal arts each year.

Rank / School	Overall score	Academic reputation	SAT / ACT 25th–75th percentile	Freshmen in top 10% of HS class	Acceptance rate	Student / faculty ratio	Education expenditures per student
1. Swarthmore College (Pa.)	100.0	3	1320—1500	87%	34%	9/1	$26,504
2. Amherst College (Mass.)	99.2	1	1280—1480	78%[4]	19%	8/1	$22,674
3. Williams College (Mass.)	98.7	1	1320—1520	83%	26%	9/1	$23,602
4. Wellesley College (Mass.)	96.6	3	1270—1450	83%	39%	10/1	$25,797
5. Pomona College (Calif.)	94.2	6	1320—1490	77%	34%	9/1	$22,333
6. Haverford College (Pa.)	93.9	6	1290—1450	80%[4]	37%	11/1	$19,121
7. Middlebury College (Vt.)	92.3	9	1230—1400	65%	36%	10/1	$23,472
8. Bowdoin College (Me.)	92.2	6	1270—1420[3]	74%	30%	11/1	$20,480
9. Carleton College (Minn.)	92.0	5	1270—1450	73%	51%	11/1	$18,870
10. Bryn Mawr College (Pa.)	91.5	9	1210—1420	71%	58%	9/1	$22,416
11. Davidson College (N.C.)	90.2	15	1230—1390	77%	36%	12/1	$19,738
12. Smith College (Mass.)	89.7	9	1203—1360	57%	49%	10/1	$22,059
13. Washington and Lee University (Va.)	89.5	25	1270—1420	74%	31%	10/1	$17,739
14. Wesleyan University (Conn.)	89.2	9	1260—1430	65%	36%	11/1	$18,460
15. Claremont McKenna College (Calif.)	89.1	15	1270—1440	73%	41%	10/1	$19,836
16. Grinnell College (Iowa)	88.6	9	1210—1400	60%	74%	9/1	$21,164

■ EXPERT LIST

Rank / School	Overall score	Academic reputation	SAT / ACT 25th–75th percentile	Freshmen in top 10% of HS class	Acceptance rate	Student / faculty ratio	Education expenditures per student
17. Vassar College (N.Y.)	88.4	15	1230—1380	58%	48%	10/1	$17,829
18. Colby College (Me.)	88.0	18	1200—1350	65%	38%	12/1	$18,430
19. Mount Holyoke College (Mass.)	86.8	22	1124—1329	58%	65%	9/1	$21,390
20. Colgate University (N.Y.)	85.9	18	1220—1380	56%	41%	12/1	$17,044
21. Trinity College (Conn.)	85.8	29	1170—1330	43%[4]	57%	10/1	$19,021
22. Bates College (Me.)	85.7	18	1230—1360[3]	51%	37%	10/1	$18,805
23. Barnard College (N.Y.)	85.3	18	1210—1370	61%[4]	45%	10/1	$14,323
24. Oberlin College (Ohio)	84.7	9	1200—1400	50%	65%	11/1	$18,006
25. Hamilton College (N.Y.)	84.4	29	1150—1320	43%	48%	10/1	$18,732
SCHOOLS RANKED 26TH TO 40TH							
26. Connecticut College	83.4	29	1170—1340	44%	50%		$16,609
27. College of the Holy Cross (Mass.)	83.2	33	1190—1360	57%	50%		$13,608
28. Colorado College	83.1	25	1190—1340	46%	60%		$16,434
29. Sarah Lawrence College (N.Y.)	83.0	43	1120—1290	37%[3]	59%		$15,682
29. University of the South (Tenn.)	83.0	38	1180—1340	53%	64%		$21,738
31. Bucknell University (Pa.)	82.7	25	1190—1320	50%	55%		$15,421
32. Macalester College (Minn.)	82.6	22	1230—1410	54%	54%		$16,687
33. Kenyon College (Ohio)	81.3	25	1160—1350	40%	72%		$14,632
34. Franklin and Marshall College (Pa.)	80.6	33	1170—1350	53%	69%		$17,082
34. Union College (N.Y.)	80.6	43	25—29	47%	52%		$15,938
36. Scripps College (Calif.)	79.8	33	1120—1300	50%	80%		$19,847
37. Reed College[5] (Ore.)	79.3	22	1250—1450[6]	N/A	71%[6]		$16,351[7]
38. Occidental College (Calif.)	79.0	33	1080—1310	57%	67%		$19,462
39. Lafayette College (Pa.)	78.9	38	1090—1280[4]	37%	60%		$17,881
40. Bard College (N.Y.)	78.6	48	1170—1400[4]	49%	53%		$15,979

NOTES: Schools with the same numbered rank are tied. Reputational surveys conducted by Market Facts Inc. **3.** Data based on fewer than 51 percent of enrolled freshmen. **4.** SAT I and/or ACT not required. **5.** School refused to fill out *U.S. News* survey. **6.** Data reported to Wintergreen/Orchard House Inc. **7.** Data reported to U.S. Department of Education.

■ **BEST REGIONAL UNIVERSITIES**

These institutions award a full range of bachelor's degrees and at least 20 master's degrees each year. Schools in this category have been subdivided into four regions. The top 15 from each of the four regions:

Rank / School	Overall score	Academic reputation	Student selectivity	Faculty resources	Financial resources	Retention rank	Alumni satisfaction
NORTH							
1. Villanova University (Pa.)	100.0	1	6	75	16	2	60
2. Providence College (R.I.)	98.8	3	8	62	34	1	14
3. Fairfield University (Conn.)	96.0	3	13	54	13	3	54
4. Loyola College (Md.)	95.0	3	5	107	29	8	25
5. University of Scranton (Pa.)	94.4	9	14	41	28	4	21
6. Rochester Inst. of Tech. (N.Y.)	93.3	2	10	36	4	44	62
7. College of New Jersey	92.9	6	1	67	55	14	110
8. Ithaca College (N.Y.)	92.7	6	15	9	21	17	44

■ **EXPERT LIST**

Rank / School	Overall score	Academic reputation	Student selectivity	Faculty resources	Financial resources	Retention rank	Alumni satisfaction
9. Simmons College (Mass.)	92.2	13	24	7	3	23	20
10. SUNY Col. Arts & Sci.—Geneseo	91.6	6	2	136	128	11	52
11. St. Joseph's College (Pa.)	91.3	9	3	112	51	13	48
12. St. Michael's College (Vt.)	90.2	9	48	106	18	6	15
13. Quinnipiac College (Conn.)	90.0	38	12	21	46	7	10
14. Hood College (Md.)	89.8	9	41	13	14	32	12
15. Alfred University (N.Y.)	88.1	13	36	34	7	34	18
SOUTH							
1. University of Richmond (Va.)	100.0	1	1	1	1	1	6
2. Rollins College (Fla.)	88.9	7	12	5	4	3	21
3. James Madison University (Va.)	86.1	2	5	61	92	2	26
4. Stetson University (Fla.)	85.8	3	26	2	6	8	23
5. Mary Washington College (Va.)	81.5	9	2	58	85	4	10
6. Centenary College of Louisiana	79.5	21	7	3	9	24	25
7. Samford University (Ala.)	78.3	4	10	21	18	23	99
8. Loyola University New Orleans	77.9	7	27	4	12	32	62
9. The Citadel (S.C.)	77.6	4	80	51	41	6	20
10. Converse College (S.C.)	77.3	32	36	7	14	15	8
11. Harding University (Ark.)	77.1	32	4	64	55	10	2
12. Queens College (N.C.)	75.6	32	30	8	10	31	14
12. Spring Hill College (Ala.)	75.6	21	21	54	19	17	11
14. Appalachian State University (N.C.)	75.1	9	23	42	77	7	56
15. Mercer University (Ga.)	74.7	9	28	6	13	60	45
MIDWEST							
1. Creighton University (Neb.)	100.0	1	12	3	1	9	13
2. Valparaiso University (Ind.)	95.2	3	3	52	4	5	4
3. Drake University (Iowa)	92.7	1	5	9	8	14	36
4. University of Dayton (Ohio)	92.6	4	17	16	5	4	46
5. John Carroll University (Ohio)	91.5	4	31	30	24	3	25
6. Butler University (Ind.)	91.2	7	8	13	6	12	19
7. Bradley University (Ill.)	90.2	4	23	11	21	8	27
8. Xavier University (Ohio)	89.6	7	24	24	10	11	11
9. Calvin College (Mich.)	87.5	7	13	59	30	16	3
10. Drury College (Mo.)	87.2	19	7	27	9	28	1
11. University of Evansville (Ind.)	85.8	13	6	29	25	21	31
12. College of Mount St. Joseph (Ohio)	85.7	60	41	17	38	1	5
13. Baldwin-Wallace College (Ohio)	85.6	13	20	46	26	7	55
14. North Central College (Ill.)	85.4	23	10	37	15	29	2
14. University of St. Thomas (Minn.)	85.4	11	40	77	20	6	70
WEST							
1. Trinity University (Texas)	100.0	1	2	2	1	2	22
2. Santa Clara University (Calif.)	89.6	2	12	94	6	1	10
3. Loyola Marymount University (Calif.)	88.3	5	21	4	4	3	19
4. University of Redlands (Calif.)	86.9	11	19	1	2	15	13
5. Linfield College (Ore.)	85.0	11	5	10	23	6	3

■ **EXPERT LIST**

Rank / School	Overall score	Academic reputation	Student selectivity	Faculty resources	Financial resources	Retention rank	Alumni satisfaction
6. **Gonzaga University** (Wash.)	83.7	3	6	18	20	11	24
7. **St. Mary's College of California**	82.4	14	9	8	26	5	18
8. **University of Portland** (Ore.)	81.0	8	18	20	24	14	15
9. **Pacific Lutheran University** (Wash.)	80.9	8	34	42	16	7	20
10. **Whitworth College** (Wash.)	80.5	5	10	67	29	12	12
11. **Seattle University**	80.1	5	38	3	8	27	32
12. **Mount St. Mary's College** (Calif.)	79.7	20	8	50	10	10	26
13. **Cal Poly—San Luis Obispo**	78.0	3	3	51	53	24	30
14. **St. Mary's Univ. of San Antonio**	76.9	14	28	12	33	13	65
15. **Univ. of the Incarnate Word** (Texas)	76.3	37	40	37	59	9	2

■ **BEST REGIONAL LIBERAL ARTS COLLEGES**

The schools from which these colleges have been identified are generally less selective than the national liberal arts colleges. Over half of the bachelor's degrees they award are in occupational, technical, and professional fields. The top 10 schools from each region:

Rank / School	Overall score	Academic reputation	Student selectivity	Faculty resources	Financial resources	Retention rank	Alumni satisfaction
NORTH							
1. **Susquehanna University** (Pa.)	100.0	1	4	41	8	6	9
2. **Stonehill College** (Mass.)	97.2	3	2	56	37	1	18
3. **St. Anselm College** (N.H.)	94.7	2	25	52	41	3	19
4. **Elizabethtown College** (Pa.)	94.2	5	3	11	14	17	25
4. **Le Moyne College** (N.Y.)	94.2	5	16	8	52	5	27
6. **Grove City College** (Pa.)	93.8	5	1	87	87	2	53
7. **Rosemont College** (Pa.)	93.5	32	20	3	3	10	12
8. **Regis College** (Mass.)	92.5	11	53	14	5	9	3
9. **King's College** (Pa.)	90.9	5	42	12	36	7	16
10. **St. Vincent College** (Pa.)	90.5	16	9	47	25	11	14
SOUTH							
1. **Lyon College** (Ark.)	100.0	5	1	3	2	43	21
2. **Emory & Henry College** (Va.)	97.0	3	46	18	24	3	2
3. **Mary Baldwin College** (Va.)	96.4	2	43	54	6	1	24
4. **Berry College** (Ga.)	95.1	1	12	52	11	10	29
5. **Roanoke College** (Va.)	93.4	3	42	17	14	6	20
6. **John Brown University** (Ark.)	91.7	15	3	37	23	11	9
7. **Eastern Mennonite University** (Va.)	91.4	15	40	68	9	2	7
8. **Asbury College** (Ky.)	90.6	9	18	36	36	20	5
8. **Columbia College** (S.C.)	90.6	9	32	32	16	13	13
10. **Coker College** (S.C.)	89.3	48	53	2	32	7	8
MIDWEST							
1. **St. Mary's College** (Ind.)	100.0	2	15	1	5	1	23
2. **Hillsdale College** (Mich.)	97.1	2	1	5	3	11	32
3. **St. Norbert College** (Wis.)	93.8	2	13	6	37	5	15

■ **EXPERT LIST**

Rank / School	Overall score	Academic reputation	Student selectivity	Faculty resources	Financial resources	Retention rank	Alumni satisfaction
4. Principia College (Ill.)	93.5	24	50	2	2	3	50
5. Otterbein College (Ohio)	92.6	5	27	35	27	2	22
5. Taylor University (Ind.)	92.6	9	3	36	36	4	28
7. Ohio Northern University	92.1	5	7	22	9	10	21
8. Marietta College (Ohio)	91.2	17	45	3	7	8	18
9. Millikin University (Ill.)	90.1	1	23	32	16	14	42
10. Mount Union College (Ohio)	89.3	9	10	11	52	13	13
WEST							
1. Texas A&M Univ.—Galveston	100.0	3	5	1	9	5	34
2. Albertson College (Ida.)	98.5	13	4	2	3	6	18
3. George Fox University (Ore.)	93.5	2	7	33	25	10	7
4. LeTourneau University (Texas)	93.2	3	12	11	39	7	10
4. Texas Lutheran College	93.2	3	9	15	31	12	6
6. Pacific Union College (Calif.)	92.4	13	8	41	15	3	12
7. Oklahoma Baptist University	91.0	6	3	14	44	14	9
8. Evergreen State College (Wash.)	90.7	1	19	62	30	2	19
9. Northwest Nazarene College (Ida.)	89.5	19	10	26	12	9	8
10. College of Santa Fe (N.M.)	89.3	8	31	4	11	11	45

SOURCE: *U.S.News & World Report, America's Best Colleges 1996 College Guide,* ©U.S.News & World Report.

■ **A WORD ON METHODOLOGY**

The *U.S. News* methodology for ranking America's colleges and universities has two components: a reputational survey taken among college administrators, together with a collection of more objective statistical measures of an institution's educational quality.

REPUTATION: According to *U.S. News*, over 4,200 college presidents, deans, and admissions directors participated in the 1996 survey of academic reputations. Participants were asked to score only institutions in the category to which their own schools belonged. The respondents were expected to assign each school to one of four quartiles based upon their assessment of a school's academic quality, and an average score was computed for each school.

STUDENT SELECTIVITY: In measuring selectivity, the survey took into account the acceptance rate and actual enrollment of students offered places in the admissions process, the enrollees' high school class rankings, and the average or midpoint combined scores on the SATs or ACTs.

FACULTY RESOURCES: Faculty resources were judged by the ratio of full-time students to full-time faculty, excluding professional schools (such as law, dental, and medical), as well as the percentage of full-time faculty with Ph.D.'s or other top terminal degrees, the percentage of part-time faculty, the average salary and benefits for tenured full professors, and the size of the undergraduate classes.

FINANCIAL RESOURCES: This was calculated by dividing the institution's total expenditures for its education program during the previous year, including such things as instruction, student services, libraries and computers, and administration, by its total full-time enrollment.

ALUMNI SATISFACTION: This measure was derived from the average percentage of alumni giving during the two previous years. While figures for alumni giving do not appear in all the tables for space reasons, they were factors in compiling the overall rankings.

THE BEST VALUES ON CAMPUS

With the cost of a college education increasing faster than most family incomes, value has become a key factor for many students when it comes to choosing a school. To enable families to relate the cost of attending to the quality of education involved, U.S. News & World Report developed a "best value" rating system that identifies colleges that score high on overall quality as well as reasonableness of cost. The "best values" are based on an institution's "sticker price," the published price for tuition, room, board, and fees. For many students, the actual price of attending that college will be less because of merit awards and need-based grants.

■ NATIONAL UNIVERSITIES

Rank/ BEST VALUES	Total Cost
1. U. of North Carolina—Chapel Hill	$15,193
2. Texas A&M Univ.—College Station	$12,713
3. University of Washington	$14,383
4. Rice University (Texas)	$18,025
5. University of Florida	$11,600
6. University of Iowa	$13,020
7. Univ. of Wisconsin—Madison	$14,860
8. Florida State University	$11,460
9. SUNY—Binghamton	$13,446
10. University of Virginia	$18,312
11. University of Kansas	$11,666
12. Univ. of Tennessee—Knoxville	$10,374
13. Univ. of Minnesota—Twin Cities	$14,350
14. University of Georgia	$11,920
15. Georgia Institute of Technology	$15,108
16. University of Texas—Austin	$12,891
17. Rutgers—New Brunswick (N.J.)	$14,411
18. Ohio University	$13,047
19. U. of Illinois—Urbana—Champaign	$15,369
20. Univ. of California—Los Angeles	$18,469
21. University of California—Berkeley	$19,458
22. University of California—Irvine	$17,713
23. Baylor University (Texas)	$13,010
24. University of California—Davis	$17,934
25. Iowa State University	$11,988
26. University of Kentucky	$11,934
27. Auburn University (Ala.)	$11,792
28. Pennsylvania State University	$16,424
29. College of William and Mary (Va.)	$19,386
30. Ohio State University—Columbus	$15,242
31. Univ. of California—San Diego	$19,429
32. University of Hawaii—Manoa	$12,590
33. SUNY—Buffalo	$14,469
34. California Institute of Technology	$23,663
35. Univ. of Missouri—Columbia	$14,782
36. Northwestern University (Ill.)	$24,162
37. University of Delaware	$16,280
37. University of Notre Dame (Ind.)	$23,807
39. Michigan State University	$16,979
40. University of Arizona	$12,875
41. Univ. of California—Santa Barbara	$18,634
42. Michigan Technological University	$13,515
43. Allegheny University (Pa.)	$13,098
44. Miami University—Oxford (Ohio)	$15,354
45. Indiana University—Bloomington	$15,615
46. Virginia Tech	$14,867
47. Wake Forest University (N.C.)	$23,700
48. SUNY—Stony Brook	$14,084
49. North Carolina State U.—Raleigh	$14,291
50. Purdue Univ.—West Lafayette (Ind.)	$15,160

■ NATIONAL LIBERAL ARTS COLLEGES

1. St. Mary's College of Maryland	$14,775
2. Washington and Lee University (Va.)	$20,535
3. Wheaton College (Ill.)	$17,650
4. Centre College (Ky.)	$18,420
5. Grinnell College (Iowa)	$22,060
6. Wabash College (Ind.)	$19,252
7. St. Olaf College (Minn.)	$19,550
8. University of the South (Tenn.)	$21,425
9. Birmingham-Southern College (Ala.)	$18,270
10. Southwestern University (S.C.)	$18,424
11. Furman University (S.C.)	$19,818
12. Thomas Aquinas College (Calif.)	$19,200
13. Gustavus Adolphus College (Minn.)	$19,350
14. Carleton College (Minn.)	$25,410
15. Macalester College (Minn.)	$22,983
16. Wellesley College (Mass.)	$26,970
17. Amherst College (Mass.)	$27,815
18. DePauw University (Ind.)	$21,224
18. Hampden-Sydney College (Va.)	$19,960
20. Claremont McKenna College (Calif.)	$25,050
21. Davidson College (N.C.)	$25,457
22. Swarthmore College (Pa.)	$28,230

■ **PARENT'S GUIDE**

23. Rhodes College (Tenn.)	$21,660
23. Williams College (Mass.)	$28,050
25. Illinois Wesleyan University	$20,834
26. Agnes Scott College (Ga.)	$20,480
27. Colorado College	$23,850
28. Earlham College (Ind.)	$22,310
29. Pomona College (Calif.)	$27,570
30. Haverford College (Pa.)	$27,700
31. Lawrence University (Wis.)	$23,197
32. Beloit College (Wis.)	$22,210
33. Bowdoin College (Me.)	$27,760
34. Bryn Mawr College (Pa.)	$27,980
34. Knox College (Ill.)	$22,440
36. Smith College (Mass.)	$27,458
37. Sweet Briar College (Va.)	$21,625
38. Bucknell University (Pa.)	$25,420
39. Middlebury College (Vt.)	$28,410
40. Whitman College (Wash.)	$24,233

■ **REGIONAL UNIVERSITIES**

NORTH

1. College of New Jersey	$12,752
2. Gallaudet University (D.C.)	$12,160
3. SUNY Col. Arts & Sci.—Geneseo	$13,259
4. Towson State University (Md.)	$12,508
5. Millersville U. of Pennsylvania	$13,766
6. Rutgers—Camden (N.J.)	$14,411
7. St. Bonaventure University (N.Y.)	$17,513
8. Chestnut Hill College (Pa.)	$18,770
9. Trinity College (D.C.)	$19,070
10. Gwynedd Mercy College (Pa.)	$17,900

SOUTH

1. The Citadel (S.C.)	$9,792
2. Murray State University (Ky.)	$8,880
3. Univ. of Tennessee—Chattanooga	$9,474
4. Harding University (Ark.)	$11,082
5. Mississippi College	$10,242
6. Winthrop University (S.C.)	$10,522
7. Meredith College (N.C.)	$10,990
8. Appalachian State University (N.C.)	$11,417
9. James Madison University (Va.)	$13,246
10. University of North Florida	$10,990

MIDWEST

1. Truman State University (Mo.)	$9,342
2. South Dakota State University	$8,808
3. University of Northern Iowa	$10,136
4. Univ. of Wisconsin—Oshkosh	$10,590
5. Univ. of Wisconsin—Whitewater	$10,900
6. Univ. of Wisconsin—Eau Claire	$12,012

7. Drury College (Mo.)	$13,666
8. Central Michigan University	$12,367
9. Creighton University (Neb.)	$16,936
10. Valparaiso University (Ind.)	$16,310

WEST

1. Abilene Christian University (Texas)	$11,920
2. Cal Poly—San Luis Obispo	$13,532
3. Western Washington University	$13,274
4. California State Univ.—Fresno	$13,104
5. University of St. Thomas (Texas)	$14,008
6. Univ. of the Incarnate Word (Texas)	$14,500
7. St. Mary's Univ. of San Antonio	$14,712
8. Trinity University (Texas)	$19,189
9. Oral Roberts University (Okla.)	$14,256
10. Westminster Col. of Salt Lake City	$14,628

■ **REGIONAL LIBERAL ARTS COLLEGES**

NORTH

1. Grove City College (Pa.)	$10,130
2. York College of Pennsylvania	$9,890
3. St. Vincent College (Pa.)	$16,910
4. Seton Hill College (Pa.)	$16,780
5. Le Moyne College (N.Y.)	$18,140

SOUTH

1. Mississippi Univ. for Women	$7,343
2. Mississippi Valley State Univ.	$7,770
3. Flagler College (Fla.)	$8,990
4. Louisiana College	$9,389
5. Union University (Tenn.)	$9,784

MIDWEST

1. Dordt College (Iowa)	$13,800
2. Alverno College (Wis.)	$13,268
3. Cedarville College (Ohio)	$13,302
4. Muskingum College (Ohio)	$14,530
5. Concordia College (Neb.)	$13,690

WEST

1. Oklahoma Baptist University	$10,310
2. McMurry University (Texas)	$10,117
3. Texas A&M Univ.—Galveston	$12,666
4. Bartlesville Wesleyan College (Okla.)	$11,200
5. Okla. Christian U. of Science and Arts	$11,350

METHODOLOGY NOTE: These ratings were based on the quality rankings for *U.S. News & World Report's* 1996 edition of *America's Best Colleges*, divided by the total of tuition, required fees, and room and board for the 1996–97 academic year. The higher the ratio of quality (a school's overall score) to price, the better the value. Because the best values are by definition at the better schools, only a proportion of all schools were considered.

FINANCIAL AID

▼

LOOKING TUITION BILLS IN THE EYE

Know your options for meeting the staggering cost of college today

The average cost for a year at a private four-year college was $20,361 in the 1996–97 school year. Without some financial assistance from the government, educational institutions, or other private sources, more than half of college students would come up short at tuition time. Jack Joyce, manager for information and training services at the College Board, sponsors of the SATs and an organization dedicated to broadening access to higher education, has this advice for students and families on applying for financial aid.

■ Who is eligible for financial aid?

Well over half the students that are in college, and in some institutions, probably three-quarters of the students enrolled. But there is no one income number or other characteristic that determines a student's eligibility for aid.

■ How is a student's eligibility for financial aid determined?

At least two application forms and two formulas are used to determine a student's eligibility for financial aid. The most commonly used process starts with an application form that's called the Free Application for Federal Student Aid, or FAFSA. It collects a fairly limited amount of information on a family's income and assets. That information is used in the "federal methodology," which is a formula approved by Congress to determine a student's eligibility for federal financial aid programs.

Many colleges that have their own non-federal financial aid collect some additional information on what is called the CSS/Financial Aid PROFILE™. That form requests more details about a family's assets situation, including such things as home equity, and a little more information on other expenses the family has, such as medical and dental expenses. It is used to support a more traditional and sensitive need analysis. This formula, known informally as the Institutional Methodology, was developed with the intent of providing a reasonable guideline as to a family's ability to contribute toward college costs.

■ Does it matter if the student is applying to a private or a state school?

In general, students applying to a state institution or public university where federal financial aid is all that is available would probably have to complete only the FAFSA. If they are applying to private colleges or universities, they would also be asked to complete the PROFILE. Students should understand that forms and procedures do change from year to year. It's important for a student to ascertain what application forms are required for financial aid and what kind of deadlines the colleges, universities, and scholarship programs have.

■ Do both the federal and institutional methodologies look at stocks and other investments to see if a student qualifies?

There is no consideration of assets in the federal formula for a family whose taxable income is less than $50,000 and who files one of the simplified versions of the federal tax return, the 1040A or 1040EZ. For others, both methodologies collect and consider information on assets, including the value of stocks and bonds and anything else that would generate interest or dividend income.

■ How does family size affect a family's eligibility for financial aid?

The number of siblings and the size of the household is an important consideration. The other important factor is the number of family members enrolled in college at the same time. A family might not be eligible for much financial aid this year, but next year, when the family's twins are enrolled, the family would suddenly be eligible for considerably more aid.

■ What are the major loan options and what are their differences?

The Stafford loan is the most widely available option. Right now it comes in two flavors. The first is available to families as part of the Federal Family Education Loan Programs (FFELP). The eligibility is determined by the school, which helps the family apply for the loan through a private lender, but the government pays the interest on the loan while the student is enrolled in school. For the past couple of years there's been a parallel program called the Federal Direct Student Loan Program. That program eliminates the private lender as the middle man and has the school not only determine eligibility for the loan but actually deliver the loan proceeds to the student. But from the student's perspective the differences are transparent. In both cases the terms are the same, the repayment obligation is the same, and the amount they can borrow is the same.

There is also the Perkins Loan Program, which is available to the neediest of students. The amount of money a college has for this program varies from school to school and depends on how many students an institution has applying for financial aid. Because it is intended for students with the highest need, it is a little more competitive than the Stafford program.

■ Are there any other loans?

Thanks to a major change in the FFELP and Direct Loan programs, a student who is not eligible for a loan based on need would still be eligible for an unsubsidized Stafford loan, in which the student would be responsible for the interest that accrues while she or he was in school. The student can either arrange to pay the interest while enrolled or opt to have the interest capitalized while he or she attends school and then repay both principal and interest later. Compared to a commercial loan, it would still be an attractive option.

In addition, there is the Federal PLUS loan, which is available to parents as opposed to the students themselves. Right now a parent would be able to borrow as much as the full cost of education for a son or daughter, minus any financial aid, including subsidized or unsubsidized Stafford loans, regardless of income level. Repayment would generally begin within 60 days of the receipt of the loan. The interest rate is similar to the Stafford loan, but it's determined a little differently each year. Some families advocate home equity loans or home equity lines of credit as a more attractive option. There are others that have investments they may draw upon. But PLUS is a source for a number of parents.

■ WHAT A YEAR OF COLLEGE COSTS

Going to college these days can pose a financial burden on students and their families. Here's a look at average academic expenses in 1996–97.

SECTOR		TUITION AND FEES	BOOKS AND SUPPLIES	ROOM AND BOARD	TRANS- PORTATION	OTHER EXPENSES	ESTIMATED TOTAL EXP.
TWO-YEAR PUBLIC	Resident	$1,394	$591	N/A*	N/A	N/A	N/A
	Commuter	$1,394	$591	$1,801	$935	$1,189	$5,910
PRIVATE	Resident	$6,673	$589	$4,231	$583	$998	$13,074
	Commuter	$6,673	$589	$1,875	$951	$1,254	$11,342
FOUR-YEAR PUBLIC	Resident	$2,966	$615	$4,152	$572	$1,344	$9,649
	Commuter	$2,966	$615	$1,806	$948	$1,412	$7,747
PRIVATE	Resident	$12,823	$615	$5,361	$535	$1,027	$20,361
	Commuter	$12,823	$615	$1,879	$851	$1,183	$17,351

*Sample too small to provide meaningful information.
SOURCE: College Entrance Examination Board, 1996.

THE ABC'S OF GREEK LIFE

There's more to it than goldfish swallowing and panty raids

Secret handshakes and childish pranks are still a mainstay of fraternity and sorority life, but the wildest of the antics typified in the '70s movie hit *Animal House* have generally been relegated to the past. After some bad publicity regarding drinking and dangerous hazing practices, universities have clamped down on the worst offenses, even yanking a group's charter if violations are found. Many societies have themselves taken steps to polish up their image in order to survive in a climate less tolerant of disruptive behavior.

Hundreds of organizations fall under the category of Greek Letter Societies, including honor societies, professional organizations, social groups, and others devoted to community service. Here is a primer on fraternities and sororities, focusing on the more familiar social organizations—including the 63 members of the National Interfraternity Council and the 26 sororities that compose the National Panhellenic Conference. The pros, cons, and costs of going Greek follow.

TIES THAT BIND

Going away to college can be exciting, as well as lonely and intimidating. For many students, a sorority or fraternity serves as a family unit away from home, and a ready-made social life. Further, the groups offer a venue for taking part in leadership roles and community service, and perhaps making vital contacts for a future career.

Becoming a member can make extreme demands on a student's time, however. The rites associated with pledging, or making a commitment to join a sorority or fraternity, can take up 15 to 20 hours a week. Once you join, you must attend meetings and a whirlwind of social events. Some students find it hard to keep up with schoolwork, other interests, and friends who are not part of the Greek system.

THE RITES OF HAZING

The process of hazing, or undergoing often demeaning exercises to prove your worthiness to join a society, has been denounced by universities and the national organizations. Most states have made hazing a felony, although many of the activities are secretive, making the law hard to enforce. At least one large fraternity has cut back its pledging period from five months to two weeks in the hope of shortening the period during which hazing is typically at its worst.

Many schools and chapters are working to resolve the abuse of alcohol in faternities and sororities. A Harvard University study found that 86 percent of students who live in a frat house are binge drinkers, compared with 45 percent of those not affiliated with a fraternity. A number of national chapters have instituted rules that prohibit the purchase of alcohol with membership funds. Several of the largest fraternities also recently announced that by the year 2000, their

---

FACT FILE:

FAMOUS GREEKS

■ *Post-collegiate fame is not assured, but going Greek didn't hurt the following:*

Brad Pitt	*Sigma Chi*
Elizabeth Dole	*Delta Delta Delta*
Farrah Fawcett	*Delta Delta Delta*
Georgia O'Keeffe	*Kappa Delta*
Jane Pauley	*Kappa Gamma*
Robert Redford	*Kappa Sigma*

A WALK DOWN FRATERNITY ROW

*Here's a snapshot of five of the largest fraternities and sororities,
along with some vital statistics*

FRATERNITY	Symbol	Initiates	Chapters	Colors	Flower	Philanthropy
Lambda Chi Alpha (Lambda Chi)	ΛXA	225,000	220	Purple, green, and gold	White rose	North American Food Drive
Sigma Chi (Sig Chi)	ΣX	240,000	228	Blue and old gold	White rose	Children's Miracle Network
Sigma Phi Epsilon (Sig Ep)	ΣΦE	212,000	265	Purple and red	Violet and dark red rose	Project America
Tau Kappa Epsilon (Teke)	TKE	207,000	290	Cherry red and gray	Red carnation	Special Olympics
Sigma Nu (Sig Nu)	ΣN	190,854	210	Black, white, and gold	White rose	Varies with local chapters
SORORITY						
Chi Omega* (Chi O's)	XΩ	235,000	173	Cardinal and straw	White carnation	Varies with local chapters
Delta Zeta (D. Z.)	ΔZ	170,000	168	Old rose and vieux green	Killarney rose	Aid to the deaf and hearing impaired
Alpha Chi Omega (Alpha Chi)	AXΩ	155,000	135	Scarlet and olive green	Scarlet carnation	Victims of domestic violence; Easter Seals
Zeta Tau Alpha (Zeta's)	ZTA	146,000	139	Steel gray and turquoise	White violet	Susan G. Komen Breast Cancer Foundation
Alpha Delta Pi* (A. D. Pi)	AΔΠ	133,998	134	Azure blue and white	Woodland violet	Ronald McDonald House

*Data based on information reported in 1991. (Other data as of March 1997.) SOURCES: National chapter headquarters.

chapters will be virtually alcohol-free. In addition, many Greek houses have started mandatory education programs addressing issues such as alcoholism, drug abuse, and date rape.

PLEDGING TO STUDY

One benefit of fraternity or sorority membership is mandatory participation in a structured study program. Most new initiates are required to spend 10 to 14 hours a week in a study hall. Whether the sessions are focused on academic work, however, or on socializing with new pledge brothers or sisters, depends largely on who is monitoring the group.

Research shows that during the orientation period, the grade point averages of new pledges fall well below university averages. Many professors and candid Greek members agree that grades suffer as a result of time pressures placed on new pledges.

THE COST OF BELONGING

Dues and fees associated with joining a fraternity or sorority vary greatly from campus to campus. What seems to be constant is that housing costs are about the same in a chapter house or a dorm. Fraternity or sorority members can expect to pay between $500 and $1,500 a semester in chapter dues. Some chapters charge the entire amount up front, others bill by event. On top of that, figure in incidentals, such as rush outfits, Greek-letter T-shirts, party costumes, and favors that members often swap—to mention just a few.

LEARNING MORE

Your school's Student Affairs Office can put you in touch with the Greek Advisory Office or Panhellenic Council. These organizations offer timely information on when and how to apply for membership, the status of each chapter on campus, and costs involved.

AMERICA'S BEST PROFESSIONAL SCHOOLS

There will always be a market for lawyers, MBA's, and doctors, but these professions, like others, have had to change with the times. Increasingly, new graduates are expected to be as well trained in the practical demands of the daily work environment as in classroom theory. U.S. News & World Report *found that America's best law, business, and medical schools recognize this trend and have begun to revamp their curricula to reflect the needs of their new students. Here from the magazine's 1997 survey are the top 25 institutions from each of the categories:*

■ THE TOP LAW SCHOOLS

There are 179 accredited law schools in the United States. In *U.S. News & World Report*'s 1997 survey, Yale University led the pack. Almost half of Yale law graduates start their legal careers with a judicial clerkship.

Rank / Schools	Overall score	Reputational rank by Academics	Judges/ lawyers	Student selec.	Faculty resources	Placement success	Median LSAT score	Accept. rate(%)	Bar pass. rate in juris. (%)	Juris. bar pass. rate (%)	Employ. 9 mos.after grad. (%)
1. Yale University (Conn.)	100.0	1	1	1	1	1	171	6.6	96.5	79/N.Y.	99
2. Harvard Univ. (Mass.)	99.5	1	1	2	4	2	169	13.0	96.4	79/N.Y.	97
3. Stanford Univ. (Calif.)	98.5	6	1	3	3	3	167	12.2	91.1	73/Calif.	97
4. Univ. of Chicago	98.1	1	1	5	8	7	169	23.2	97.0	86/Ill.	96
5. Columbia Univ. (N.Y.)	97.9	1	1	7	5	8	168	19.7	93.0	79/N.Y.	97
6. New York University	97.3	6	9	6	2	4	168	22.7	94.2	79/N.Y.	97
7. Univ. of Mich.–Ann Arbor	96.1	1	1	10	9	16	167	30.9	89.0	70/Mich.	93
8. Univ. of Virginia	95.3	6	7	8	22	5	166	25.9	87.7	76/Va.	99
9. Univ. of Calif.–Berkeley	95.0	6	7	4	27	9	166	18.3	90.4	73/Calif.	95
10. Duke Univ. (N.C.)	94.5	14	9	9	13	6	168	31.6	94.0	79/N.Y.	98
11. Univ. of Pennsylvania	94.1	10	9	11	12	12	165	29.3	91.0	79/N.Y.	95
12. Cornell Law School (N.Y.)	93.6	10	12	13	10	13	165	24.8	96.0	79/N.Y.	96
13. Georgetown Univ. (D.C.)	92.7	14	12	12	14	14	166	28.0	90.5	79/N.Y.	97
14. Northwestern Univ. (Ill.)	92.5	10	12	13	6	25	164	20.5	94.7	86/Ill.	90
15. Univ. of Southern Calif.	91.3	18	25	16	7	11	165	23.2	84.0	60/Calif.	94
16. Vanderbilt Univ. (Tenn.)	88.4	17	17	18	47	10	163	30.0	90.0	79/Tenn.	97
17. UCLA School of Law	88.3	16	16	19	23	30	162	22.8	88.8	73/Calif.	93
18. Univ. of Texas–Austin	85.5	10	12	20	49	43	162	28.3	91.9	82/Texas	90
19. U.of Ill.–Urbana	85.4	23	25	34	24	19	161	33.1	89.6	87/Ill.	94
20. U.of Minn.–Twin Cities	84.9	18	25	21	53	24	163	37.3	97.0	88/Minn.	96
21. U. of Notre Dame (Ind.)	84.4	35	20	22	34	23	163	26.3	97.1	86/Ill.	95
22. Boston College	83.8	24	20	26	48	27	162	26.4	91.9	84/Mass.	88
23. G. Washington Univ. (D.C.)	83.6	24	20	27	56	21	161	20.0	89.0	75/Md.	92
24. Univ. of Iowa	82.5	18	29	36	18	48	160	35.1	78.0	75/Iowa	91
25. Wash. and Lee Univ. (Va.)	82.3	35	35	15	11	56	165	27.8	80.5	76/Va.	89

NOTE: Jurisdiction refers to the state where the largest number of graduates took the test for the first time—not always the same as the state where the school is located.

SOURCES: *U.S. News & World Report* and the schools. Reputational surveys conducted by Market Facts Inc. Response rates to reputational surveys: academics, 70 percent; lawyers and judges, 33 percent. *U.S. News & World Report* (March 10, 1997).

■ THE TOP BUSINESS SCHOOLS

There are 300 accredited M.B.A. programs in the United States. After a slowdown in the market for MBA's in the early 1990s, companies are hiring again thanks to a robust economy. Here are the schools that corporate recruiters and others surveyed regard among the best.

Rank / Schools	Overall score	Reputational rank by Academics	Recruiters	Rank Student selec.	Placement success	Avg. '96 GMAT score	'96 avg. undergrad. GPA	'96 accept. rate (%)	'96 med. starting salary	Employ. 3 mos.after grad. (%)
1. Stanford University (Calif.)	100.0	1	3	1	1	711	3.60	7.4	$82,000	98.9
2. Harvard University (Mass.)	99.5	1	2	2	4	670*	3.50	12.8	$80,000	96.4
3. Univ. of Pennsylvania (Wharton)	99.1	1	4	7	2	662	3.41	14.7	$79,000	100.0
4. Mass. Institute of Tech. (Sloan)	98.7	1	4	9	3	650	3.50	15.1	$78,000	98.8
5. University of Chicago	98.1	1	8	3	10	680	3.40	25.0	$65.000	98.4
6. Northwestern U. (Kellogg) (Ill.)	97.8	1	1	8	11	660	3.40	16.0	$70,000	93.6
7. Columbia University (N.Y.)	97.5	9	10	6	5	660	3.45	14.8	$83.000	96.2
8. Dartmouth College (Tuck) (N.H.)	97.2	12	11	4	6	670	3.40	12.6	$70,000	98.3
9. Duke Univ. (Fuqua) (N.C.)	96.5	9	7	13	8	646	3.33	20.5	$67,500	98.5
10. Univ. of Calif.–Berkeley (Haas)	96.0	7	12	11	12	652	3.42	13.3	$70,000	93.7
11. Univ. of Virginia (Darden)	95.6	12	9	15	9	660	3.10	18.9	$66.000	98.1
12. U. of Michigan–Ann Arbor	95.5	7	6	16	14	645	3.30	28.0	$65,000	99.1
13. New York University (Stern)	94.9	16	19	14	7	646	3.30	20.9	$70,583	97.0
14. Carnegie Mellon Univ. (Pa.)	93.6	12	18	22	13	640	3.20	30.8	$67,200	96.6
15. Yale University (Conn.)	93.5	18	17	5	22	675	3.39	23.5	$65,000	91.5
16. U. of N.C. Chapel Hill (Kenan-Flagler)	93.2	16	16	19	16	630	3.30	19.8	$60,000	96.8
17. Univ. of Calif.–LA (Anderson)	91.8	9	13	10	38	651	3.50	17.5	$65,000	82.2
18. Univ. of Texas–Austin	91.7	18	13	21	24	630	3.29	27.3	$60,000	97.3
19. Indiana Univ.–Bloomington	91.0	18	20	33	17	630	3.20	44.7	$61,500	95.2
20. Cornell Univ. (Johnson) (N.Y.)	90.7	12	15	18	36	637	3.30	25.4	$64,000	85.1
20. U. of Rochester (Simon) (N.Y.)	90.7	18	29	26	20	630	3.25	36.0	$58,500	97.4
22. Ohio State U. (Fisher)	89.8	24	29	31	18	611	3.30	23.2	$61,000	97.8
23. Emory Univ. (Goizueta) (Ga.)	89.2	35	28	25	19	626	3.30	33.0	$60,000	96.7
24. Purdue Univ. (Krannert) (Ind.)	89.1	22	21	40	21	603	3.20	20.7	$63,700	93.6
25. U. of Maryland–Coll. Park	87.8	35	53	12	27	640	3.41	18.9	$53,000	95.0

*Signifies a *U.S. News* estimate.
SOURCES: *U.S. News & World Report* and the schools. Reputational surveys conducted by Market Facts Inc. Response rates to reputational surveys: academics, 56 percent; corporate recruiters, 34 percent. *U.S. New & World Report* (March 10, 1997).

■ THE TOP MEDICAL SCHOOLS

Among the 125 accredited medical schools in the United States, Harvard ranked first in the *U.S. News* survey. It also ranked first in the magazine's survey of specialty programs—for drug and alcohol abuse, internal medicine, pediatrics, and women's health.

Rank / Schools	Overall score	Reputational rank by Academics	Intern/ res. dir.	Rank Student selec.	Faculty resources	Placement success	Avg. '96 MCAT score	'96 Accept. rate(%)	NIH research '96 total	Faculty student ratio
1. Harvard Univ. (Mass.)	100.0	1	2	4	2	1	11.3	5.4	$452,263,730	6.4
2. Johns Hopkins Univ. (Md.)	99.7	1	1	3	3	3	11.3	5.4	$196,000,000	3.6
3. Duke Univ. (N.C.)	95.2	3	3	9	5	11	11.0	2.9	$126,332,612	3.1
4. Univ.of Calif.–San Francisco	94.8	5	11	1	20	6	12.0	3.8	$167,914,455	2.0
5. Washington Univ. (Mo.)	94.7	5	9	2	17	8	11.7	4.6	$155,976,863	2.1

252 EDUCATION

■ EXPERT LIST

Rank / Schools	Overall score	Reputational rank by		Rank			Avg. '96 MCAT score	'96 Accept. rate(%)	NIH research '96 total	Faculty student ratio
		Academics	Intern/ res. dir.	Student selec.	Faculty resources	Placement success				
6. Yale Univ. (Conn.)	94.4	7	7	6	9	9	11.1	4.4	$153,735,334	2.4
7. Univ. of Pennsylvania	94.2	7	5	11	20	4	11.0	5.2	$187,500,000	2.0
8. Columbia U. Coll. of Physicians and Surgeons (N.Y.)	93.6	11	6	12	6	7	11.1	7.2	$156,038,073	2.9
9. Univ. of Mich.–Ann Arbor	92.1	7	4	8	17	15	11.3	4.7	$111,571,472	2.1
10. Stanford Univ. (Calif.)	90.2	3	8	7	47	12	11.1	3.5	$119,809,033	1.2
11. U. of Calif.–Los Angeles	89.5	13	17	13	26	5	10.9	3.9	$186,420,000	1.7
12. Cornell Univ. (N.Y.)	88.1	15	10	22	17	10	10.6	2.8	$132,388,000	2.1*
13. Univ. of Washington	87.0	7	13	43	20	2	10.1	18.0	$201,987,811	2.0
14. Vanderbilt Univ. (Tenn.)	86.6	16	15	5	9	25	11.2	4.8	$76,684,769	2.4
15. Baylor Coll. of Med. (Texas)	85.1	16	16	15	15	21	10.8	7.9	$84,514,237	2.2
16. Univ. of Chicago	83.2	11	14	29	26	19	10.3	2.7	$86,569,754	1.7
17. Univ. of Pittsburgh (Pa.)	82.8	22	26	18	9	18	10.7	6.8	$93,430,365	2.4
18. Case Western Univ. (Ohio)	82.0	16	18	42	9	14	10.0	3.7	$115,923,000	2.4
19. Emory Univ. (Ga.)	79.9	22	19	24	8	29	10.3	3.1	$67,200,940	2.8
20. Univ. of Calif.–San Diego	79.3	16	38	14	47	16	10.9	5.3	$102,715,440	1.2
21. U. of Texas SW Med. Cr–Dallas	78.8	13	20	19	63	23	10.6	11.0	$81,474,363	1.0
22. Yeshiva U./ Albert Einstein Coll. of Med. (N.Y.)	78.0	30	38	21	6	20	10.6	4.9	$85,241,863	2.9
23. New York University	77.7	30	25	17	23	27	10.7	8.4	$70,801,750	1.9
24. Mayo Medical School (Minn.)	76.4	30	21	16	1	42	10.7	2.4	$49,513,322	8.7
25. Northwestern Univ. (Ill.)	75.4	22	12	26	37	38	10.4	5.7	$57,768,357	1.5

*Signifies a *U.S. News* estimate.
SOURCES: *U.S. News & World Report* and the schools. Reputational surveys conducted by Market Facts Inc. Response rates to reputational surveys: academics, 50 percent; intern residency directors/medical schools, 45 percent; intern residency directors/primary care, 34 percent. *U.S. News & World Report* (March 10, 1997).

■ A WORD ON METHODOLOGY:

The *U.S. News* methodology for ranking America's top law, business, and medical schools has three components: a reputational survey taken among faculty members and professionals in the field, a collection of more objective statistical measures of an institution's educational quality, and a measure of the degree of success in placing graduating students in positions within three months of graduation.

REPUTATION: *U.S. News* conducted two surveys in 1996 for each professional school. The first asked deans and faculty members to rate the reputation of the accredited schools. The second asked practicing professionals to select the top 25 schools in their professions. In the case of law schools, 1,310 practicing lawyers and judges were asked to rate each law school based on the appraisals of the work of recent graduates of that school.

STUDENT SELECTIVITY: In measuring selectivity, the surveys took into account median undergraduate grade point averages, the proportion of applicants enrolled in the school, and the students' scores in the Law School Admission Test, Graduate Management Admission Test, or Medical College Admission Test, whichever was applicable.

FACULTY RESOURCES: Faculty resources were judged on total expenditures per student for instruction, student-to-teacher ratio, and supporting services, such as titles in the law library, in the case of the law schools list.

PLACEMENT SUCCESS: This was measured only for the law and business schools. It was calculated by looking at the percentage of the graduating class employed full and part-time at graduation or shortly thereafter.

RESEARCH ACTIVITY: This measure applied only to the medical schools list. It was based on the total dollar amount of research grants awarded to the school and its affiliated hospitals by the National Institutes of Health.

THE BEST GRADUATE SCHOOLS IN AMERICA

If attending graduate school figures into your plans, a recent study by the National Research Council (NRC), a highly respected research organization, is must-reading. In 1995, the NRC released comprehensive ratings of the best graduate schools in the United States. The evaluation of 3,634 doctoral programs in 274 universities nationwide took more than four years to complete and involved over 8,000 faculty members. Ratings were based on a combination of factors, including scholarly quality, educational effectiveness, and change in program quality over the last five years. (Duplicate rankings are ties.)

Rank	Quality	Effec-tiveness
ART HISTORY		
1. Columbia University	4.79	4.29
1. New York University	4.79	4.32
3. University of California Berkeley	4.67	4.18
4. Harvard University	4.49	4.11
5. Yale University	4.44	4.36
6. Princeton University	4.04	3.78
7. Johns Hopkins University	3.93	3.46
8. Northwestern University	3.83	3.57
9. University of Pennsylvania	3.80	3.51
10. University of Chicago	3.74	3.49
COMPARATIVE LITERATURE		
1. Yale University	4.70	4.30
2. Duke University	4.51	3.80
3. Columbia University	4.44	3.82
4. Harvard University	4.37	3.81
5. Princeton University	4.32	3.96
6. Cornell University	4.31	3.78
7. Johns Hopkins University	4.18	4.12
8. University of California Irvine	4.06	3.63
9. Stanford University	4.05	3.75
10. University of California Berkeley	4.00	3.83
ENGLISH LANGUAGE & LITERATURE		
1. Yale University	4.77	4.43
1. University of California Berkeley	4.77	4.53
1. Harvard University	4.77	4.14
4. University of Virginia	4.58	4.27
5. Duke University	4.55	3.98
5. Stanford University	4.55	4.30
7. Cornell University	4.49	4.43
8. University of Pennsylvania	4.47	4.24
8. Columbia University	4.47	3.91
10. University of Chicago	4.41	4.20
LINGUISTICS		
1. Massachusetts Institute of Technology	4.79	4.39
2. Stanford University	4.59	4.01

Rank	Quality	Effec-tiveness
3. University of California Los Angeles	4.56	4.17
4. University of Massachusetts Amherst	4.44	4.44
5. University of Pennsylvania	4.16	3.68
6. University of Chicago	3.97	3.64
6. University of California Berkeley	3.97	3.40
8. Ohio State University	3.80	3.46
9. Cornell University	3.78	3.89
10. University of California Santa Cruz	3.66	3.80
MUSIC		
1. Harvard University	4.59	4.26
2. University of Chicago	4.53	4.32
3. University of California Berkeley	4.51	4.11
4. City University of New York Graduate School and University Center	4.41	3.79
5. Yale University	4.40	4.11
6. Princeton University	4.39	4.18
7. University of Pennsylvania	4.35	3.79
8. University of Rochester	4.24	4.03
9. University of Michigan	4.16	4.03
10. U. of Illinois Urbana-Champaign	4.11	3.60
PHILOSOPHY		
1. Princeton University	4.93	4.56
2. University of Pittsburgh	4.73	4.43
3. Harvard University	4.69	3.77
4. University of California Berkeley	4.66	3.66
5. University of Pittsburgh Program in History and Philosophy of Science	4.47	4.26
6. University of California Los Angeles	4.42	4.01
7. Stanford University	4.20	4.02
8. University of Michigan	4.15	3.88
9. Cornell University	4.11	4.14
10. Massachusetts Institute of Technology	4.01	3.91
RELIGION		
1. University of Chicago	4.76	4.01
2. Harvard University	4.73	4.10
3. Princeton University	4.33	3.89

■ EXPERT LIST

Rank	Quality	Effec-tiveness
4. Duke University	4.25	3.90
5. Emory University	4.05	3.59
6. University of Virginia	3.96	3.46
7. Vanderbilt University	3.85	3.50
8. Princeton Theological Seminary	3.84	3.61
9. University of California Santa Barbara	3.82	3.33
10. Jewish Theological Seminary	3.74	3.26
10. University of Pennsylvania	3.74	3.22

BIOCHEMISTRY & MOLECULAR BIOLOGY

Rank	Quality	Effec-tiveness
1. University of California San Francisco	4.84	4.73
2. Massachusetts Institute of Technology	4.83	4.68
2. Stanford University	4.83	4.59
4. University of California Berkeley	4.81	4.66
5. Harvard University	4.80	4.44
6. Yale University	4.59	4.32
7. California Institute of Technology	4.57	4.41
8. University of Wisconsin Madison	4.55	4.30
9. University of California San Diego	4.53	4.37
10. Johns Hopkins University	4.38	4.26
10. Columbia University	4.38	4.25

CELL & DEVELOPMENTAL BIOLOGY

Rank	Quality	Effec-tiveness
1. Massachusetts Institute of Technology	4.86	4.66
2. Rockefeller University	4.77	4.54
3. University of California San Francisco	4.76	4.57
4. California Institute of Technology	4.73	4.68
5. Harvard University	4.70	4.33
6. Stanford University Sch. of Medicine	4.55	4.39
7. University of California San Diego	4.50	4.15
8. University of Washington	4.48	4.23
9. Washington University	4.39	4.24
10. Yale University	4.37	4.22

ECOLOGY, EVOLUTION, & BEHAVIOR

Rank	Quality	Effec-tiveness
1. Stanford University	4.51	4.23
1. University of Chicago	4.51	4.31
3. Duke University	4.49	4.33
4. Cornell University	4.44	4.24
5. University of California Davis	4.42	4.12
6. Princeton University	4.34	3.96
7. University of Washington	4.30	4.20
8. University of California Berkeley	4.29	4.15
9. University of Wisconsin Madison	4.18	4.13
10. State U. of New York Stony Brook	4.12	3.86
10. University of Texas Austin	4.12	3.77

MOLECULAR & GENERAL GENETICS

Rank	Quality	Effec-tiveness
1. Massachusetts Institute of Technology	4.88	4.75
2. University of California San Francisco	4.87	4.80

Rank	Quality	Effec-tiveness
3. Harvard University	4.77	4.55
4. California Institute of Technology	4.51	4.47
5. Stanford University	4.48	4.44
6. University of California San Diego	4.44	4.17
7. University of Wisconsin Madison	4.33	4.40
8. Yale University	4.32	4.29
9. Johns Hopkins University	4.26	4.01
10. University of California Berkeley	4.21	4.18

NEUROSCIENCES

Rank	Quality	Effec-tiveness
1. University of California San Diego	4.82	4.48
2. Yale University	4.76	4.44
3. Harvard University	4.73	4.33
4. University of California San Francisco	4.66	4.45
5. Stanford University	4.64	4.56
6. Columbia University	4.58	4.29
7. Johns Hopkins University	4.47	4.33
8. Washington University	4.43	4.42
9. University of California Berkeley	4.32	4.12
10. California Institute of Technology	4.30	4.22
10. University of Pennsylvania	4.30	4.17

PHARMACOLOGY

Rank	Quality	Effec-tiveness
1. Yale University	4.45	4.32
2. U. of Texas Southwestern Medical Center	4.39	4.04
3. University of California San Diego	4.36	3.87
4. Johns Hopkins University	4.21	4.22
5. Duke University	4.18	4.03
6. Vanderbilt University	4.17	4.15
7. Harvard University	4.14	4.00
8. University of North Carolina Chapel Hill School of Arts and Sciences	4.03	3.99
9. University of Washington	4.02	4.01
9. University of Pennsylvania	4.02	4.02

PHYSIOLOGY

Rank	Quality	Effec-tiveness
1. Yale University	4.48	4.38
2. University of California San Diego	4.47	4.25
3. University of Pennsylvania	4.27	3.95
4. University of California Los Angeles	4.23	4.02
5. University of California San Francisco	4.21	4.00
5. Baylor College of Medicine	4.21	3.84
7. University of Washington	4.20	4.10
7. Stanford University	4.20	4.17
9. University of Virginia	4.19	3.83
9. Columbia University	4.19	3.83

AEROSPACE ENGINEERING

Rank	Quality	Effec-tiveness
1. California Institute of Technology	4.61	4.43
2. Massachusetts Institute of Technology	4.54	4.31
3. Stanford University	4.50	4.26

■ EXPERT LIST

Rank	Quality	Effec-tiveness
4. Princeton University	4.30	4.03
5. University of Michigan	4.05	3.80
6. Cornell University	3.93	3.75
7. Purdue University	3.71	3.46
8. University of Texas Austin	3.67	3.64
9. Georgia Institute of Technology	3.66	3.49
10. University of California San Diego	3.62	3.27
10. University of California Los Angeles	3.62	3.44

BIOMEDICAL ENGINEERING

Rank	Quality	Effec-tiveness
1. Massachusetts Institute of Technology	4.62	4.17
2. University of California San Diego	4.45	4.43
3. University of Washington	4.35	3.85
4. Duke University	4.33	3.63
5. University of Pennsylvania	4.28	3.82
6. Johns Hopkins University	4.25	4.09
7. University of California San Francisco	4.19	3.89
8. University of California Berkeley	4.08	3.84
9. University of Utah	3.97	3.69
10. Rice University	3.94	3.95

CHEMICAL ENGINEERING

Rank	Quality	Effec-tiveness
1. University of Minnesota	4.86	4.57
2. Massachusetts Institute of Technology	4.73	4.43
3. University of California Berkeley	4.63	4.43
4. University of Wisconsin Madison	4.62	4.37
5. University of Illinois Urbana-Champaign	4.42	4.28
6. California Institute of Technology	4.41	4.24
7. Stanford University	4.35	4.31
8. University of Delaware	4.34	4.21
9. Princeton University	4.14	4.02
10. University of Texas Austin	4.08	3.73

CIVIL ENGINEERING

Rank	Quality	Effec-tiveness
1. Massachusetts Institute of Technology	4.61	4.47
2. University of California Berkeley	4.56	4.22
3. Stanford University	4.44	4.29
4. University of Texas Austin	4.42	4.27
5. University of Illinois Urbana-Champaign	4.41	4.23
6. Cornell University	4.30	4.08
7. California Institute of Technology	4.27	4.42
8. Princeton University	3.99	3.89
9. Northwestern University	3.96	3.73
10. University of Michigan	3.90	3.82

ELECTRICAL ENGINEERING

Rank	Quality	Effec-tiveness
1. Stanford University	4.83	4.68
2. Massachusetts Institute of Technology	4.79	4.61
3. University of Illinois Urbana-Champaign	4.70	4.57
4. University of California Berkeley	4.69	4.46
5. California Institute of Technology	4.46	4.34

Rank	Quality	Effec-tiveness
6. University of Michigan	4.38	4.17
7. Cornell University	4.35	4.08
8. Purdue University	4.02	3.94
9. Princeton University	4.01	4.00
10. University of Southern California	4.00	3.71
10. University of California Los Angeles	4.00	3.79

MATERIALS SCIENCE

Rank	Quality	Effec-tiveness
1. Massachusetts Institute of Technology	4.61	4.22
2. Northwestern University	4.47	4.08
3. Cornell University	4.35	4.10
4. University of California Berkeley	4.33	4.08
5. University of Illinois Urbana-Champaign	4.29	3.93
6. Stanford University	4.24	4.00
7. University of Massachusetts Amherst	4.20	4.21
8. University of California Santa Barbara	4.18	3.65
9. Pennsylvania State University	3.97	3.83
10. University of Pennsylvania	3.79	3.62

MECHANICAL ENGINEERING

Rank	Quality	Effec-tiveness
1. Stanford University	4.77	4.50
2. Massachusetts Institute of Technology	4.65	4.45
3. University of California Berkeley	4.54	4.50
4. California Institute of Technology	4.35	4.30
5. University of Michigan	4.22	4.00
6. Princeton University	4.19	4.09
7. Cornell University	4.15	3.99
8. University of Minnesota	4.09	3.85
9. University of Illinois Urbana-Champaign	4.07	4.02
10. University of California San Diego	4.04	3.59
10. Purdue University	4.04	4.01

ASTROPHYSICS & ASTRONOMY

Rank	Quality	Effec-tiveness
1. California Institute of Technology	4.91	4.75
2. Princeton University	4.79	4.38
3. University of California Berkeley	4.65	4.53
4. Harvard University	4.49	3.92
5. University of Chicago	4.36	3.85
6. University of California Santa Cruz	4.31	4.14
7. University of Arizona	4.10	3.69
8. Massachusetts Institute of Technology	4.00	3.68
9. Cornell University	3.98	3.97
10. University of Texas Austin	3.65	3.39

CHEMISTRY

Rank	Quality	Effec-tiveness
1. University of California Berkeley	4.96	4.72
2. California Institute of Technology	4.94	4.75
3. Harvard University	4.87	4.57
3. Stanford University	4.87	4.57
5. Massachusetts Institute of Technology	4.86	4.70
6. Cornell University	4.55	4.40

■ EXPERT LIST

Rank	Quality	Effec-tiveness
7. Columbia University	4.54	4.37
8. University of Illinois Urbana-Champaign	4.48	4.38
9. University of Wisconsin Madison	4.46	4.26
9. University of Chicago	4.46	4.20
9. University of California Los Angeles	4.46	4.00

COMPUTER SCIENCES

Rank	Quality	Effec-tiveness
1. Stanford University	4.97	4.60
2. Massachusetts Institute of Technology	4.91	4.62
3. University of California Berkeley	4.88	4.58
4. Carnegie Mellon University	4.76	4.38
5. Cornell University	4.64	4.47
6. Princeton University	4.31	3.84
7. University of Texas Austin	4.18	3.81
8. University of Illinois Urbana-Champaign	4.09	3.93
9. University of Washington	4.04	4.05
10. University of Wisconsin Madison	4.00	3.87

GEOSCIENCES

Rank	Quality	Effec-tiveness
1. California Institute of Technology	4.87	4.63
2. Massachusetts Institute of Technology	4.67	4.52
3. University of California Berkeley	4.45	4.09
4. Columbia University	4.38	4.14
5. Stanford University Program in Geophysics	4.33	3.96
6. University of California San Diego	4.23	4.06

Rank	Quality	Effec-tiveness
7. University of Chicago	4.22	4.03
8. Harvard University	4.20	3.80
9. Stanford University	4.15	4.06
9. Cornell University	4.15	3.71

MATHEMATICS

Rank	Quality	Effec-tiveness
1. University of California Berkeley	4.94	4.37
1. Princeton University	4.94	4.69
3. Massachusetts Institute of Technology	4.92	4.57
4. Harvard University	4.90	4.58
5. University of Chicago	4.69	4.64
6. Stanford University	4.68	4.41
7. Yale University	4.55	4.11
8. New York University	4.49	4.26
9. University of Michigan	4.23	3.84
9. Columbia University	4.23	3.94

OCEANOGRAPHY

Rank	Quality	Effec-tiveness
1. University of California San Diego	4.69	4.21
2. Massachusetts Institute of Technology	4.62	4.31
3. University of Washington	4.31	4.07
4. Columbia University	4.30	4.00
5. Oregon State University	3.88	3.46
6. University of Rhode Island	3.68	3.53
7. University of Hawaii Manoa	3.50	3.11
8. State U. of New York Stony Brook	3.49	3.28

PAYING FOR YOUR GRAD SCHOOL MEAL TICKET

Plan on working at least part-time and borrowing a bunch to pay the tab

Federal financial aid for graduate students is similar to aid for undergraduates, according to Bart Astor, editor of *College Planning Quarterly*, with a few key differences: Graduate students are not eligible for such major federal scholarship programs as the Pell Grant, but the federal Stafford and Direct Loan programs have higher maximum amounts students can borrow; and all grad students are considered independent of their parents (i.e., only the student's income—and spouse's, if appropriate—is used to determine the expected contribution for federal aid).

Another big difference is in how grad students pay for their education. Most graduate school aid comes from sources other than the federal government, and is not based on need. Also, a majority of grad students attend school part-time and maintain full-time jobs elsewhere; many receive tuition assistance from their employers. Of full-time students, many are awarded teaching and research assistantships or work for professors and are funded by research grants. Students attending the professional schools (medicine, law, etc.) usually do not work and have to borrow large amounts to pay for their schooling. There are private loan programs available to these students; the schools themselves can lead students in the right direction.

■ **EXPERT LIST**

Rank	Quality	Effec-tiveness
9. Florida State University	3.48	3.28
10. University of Maryland College Park	3.42	3.17

PHYSICS

Rank	Quality	Effec-tiveness
1. Harvard University	4.91	4.71
2. Princeton University	4.89	4.69
3. Massachusetts Institute of Technology	4.87	4.64
3. University of California Berkeley	4.87	4.49
5. California Institute of Technology	4.81	4.61
6. Cornell University	4.75	4.54
7. University of Chicago	4.69	4.55
8. U. of Illinois Urbana-Champaign	4.66	4.39
9. Stanford University	4.53	4.35
10. University of California Santa Barbara	4.43	3.91

STATISTICS & BIOSTATISTICS

Rank	Quality	Effec-tiveness
1. Stanford University	4.76	4.44
1. University of California Berkeley Program in Statistics	4.76	4.33
3. University of California Berkeley Program in Biostatistics	4.43	4.01
4. Cornell University	4.37	4.06
5. University of Chicago	4.34	4.09
6. University of Washington Program in Biostatistics	4.21	4.08
7. Harvard University	4.17	3.80
8. University of Wisconsin Madison	4.06	4.07
9. U. of Washington Program in Statistics	4.01	3.85
10. Purdue University	4.00	3.61

ANTHROPOLOGY

Rank	Quality	Effec-tiveness
1. University of Michigan	4.77	4.40
1. University of Chicago	4.77	4.19
3. University of California Berkeley	4.51	3.93
4. Harvard University	4.43	3.67
5. University of Arizona	4.11	3.60
6. University of Pennsylvania	3.94	3.68
7. Stanford University	3.71	3.63
8. Yale University	3.67	3.43
8. University of California Los Angeles	3.67	3.50
8. University of California San Diego	3.67	3.44

ECONOMICS

Rank	Quality	Effec-tiveness
1. University of Chicago	4.95	4.63
1. Harvard University	4.95	4.33
3. Massachusetts Institute of Technology	4.93	4.71
4. Stanford University	4.92	4.58
5. Princeton University	4.84	4.69
6. Yale University	4.70	4.01
7. University of California Berkeley	4.55	4.05
8. University of Pennsylvania	4.43	3.91

Rank	Quality	Effec-tiveness
9. Northwestern University	4.39	4.04
10. University of Minnesota	4.22	4.08

HISTORY

Rank	Quality	Effec-tiveness
1. Yale University	4.89	4.55
2. University of California Berkeley	4.79	4.50
3. Princeton University	4.75	4.48
4. Harvard University	4.71	4.02
5. Columbia University	4.63	4.29
6. University of California Los Angeles	4.59	4.07
7. Stanford University	4.56	4.44
8. University of Chicago	4.49	4.20
9. Johns Hopkins University	4.42	4.37
10. University of Wisconsin Madison	4.37	4.33

POLITICAL SCIENCE

Rank	Quality	Effec-tiveness
1. Harvard University	4.88	4.17
2. University of California Berkeley	4.66	4.13
3. Yale University	4.60	4.24
3. University of Michigan	4.60	4.31
5. Stanford University	4.50	4.02
6. University of Chicago	4.41	3.83
7. Princeton University	4.39	3.91
8. University of California Los Angeles	4.25	3.62
9. University of California San Diego	4.13	3.70
10. University of Wisconsin Madison	4.09	3.86

PSYCHOLOGY

Rank	Quality	Effec-tiveness
1. Stanford University	4.82	4.64
2. University of Michigan	4.63	4.40
3. Yale University	4.62	4.31
4. University of California Los Angeles	4.61	4.05
5. University of Illinois Urbana-Champaign	4.58	4.36
6. Harvard University	4.48	4.09
7. University of Minnesota	4.46	4.33
8. University of Pennsylvania	4.35	4.18
9. University of California Berkeley	4.33	4.03
10. University of California San Diego	4.32	4.12

SOCIOLOGY

Rank	Quality	Effec-tiveness
1. University of Chicago	4.77	4.26
2. University of Wisconsin Madison	4.74	4.61
3. University of California Berkeley	4.56	3.60
4. University of Michigan	4.39	4.08
5. University of California Los Angeles	4.36	3.79
6. University of North Carolina Chapel Hill	4.31	4.00
7. Harvard University	4.18	3.58
8. Stanford University	4.08	3.77
9. Northwestern University	4.07	3.61
10. University of Washington	4.03	3.73

SOURCE: National Research Council.

LIFELONG LEARNING

COURSES: Technology offers new ways to learn outside the classroom, PAGE 260 **RETIREMENT:** Spending the golden years in a college town, PAGE 261 **LIBRARIES:** Carnegie Foundation president Vartan Gregorian shares his choices for the world's top libraries, PAGE 262 **BOOKS:** The New York Public Libary's list of books that have most influenced life in the 20th century, PAGE 263 **CLUBS:** How to join or start a book group, PAGE 266

SKILLS
▼

THE NEW JOB RULE: RETOOL

Nearly all workers need retraining to avoid obsolescence

A re you worried about being nudged down a rung on the career ladder? Or has downsizing pushed you right off? Either way, you're a candidate for retraining. In fact, even if your feet are securely planted on your current career rung, professionals say the way to stay grounded in today's job market is to further your education and gain new skills. "Don't wait until your job is in peril to start thinking of job training possibilities," says William Hamrick, vice president of training and development for Snelling Personnel Services, a Dallas-based firm. Instead, employees of all stripes should be flexible and stay on top of—even anticipate—industry changes, says Hamrick.

The past two decades have transformed the character of companies and the workforce as firms struggle to gain a competitive edge by cutting costs and outsourcing work. To stay employed in the new economy, workers need new credentials and skills. Here are some essentials for preventing obsolescence.

■ **MAINTAIN COMPUTER PROFICIENCY.** The most important skill in which workers are deficient, says Saul Rosen, associate executive director of New York City's Consortium for Worker Education, is computer proficiency. "Almost everyone who walks through our doors needs to learn basic computer skills or upgrade existing skills," he says. No matter who you are or what you do, there is no excuse for computer illiteracy or for not keeping up with changing technology and software in your field.

■ **LOCATE A RETRAINING PROGRAM.** Many companies provide retraining courses in-house. Perhaps the most ambitious of such programs is offered by Motorola Inc., maker of cellular phones. Fifteen years ago, the company began what is now known as Motorola University. Employees put in at least 40 hours of training each year, choosing from more than 600 courses, ranging from English as a second language to post-doctoral physics. It's unlikely that your company offers such an extensive program, but you can find similar courses available at local community colleges, community centers, and libraries. You can also learn about other programs through your state's labor department.

■ **FIND FUNDING.** More than 90 percent of major companies offer continuing education benefits today. You may also be able to get some funding through the federal Job Training Partnership Act program, which gives

■ **STAY PROFESSIONALLY CURRENT: IT'S THE LAW**

Many states are trying to increase the quality of services offered by the nation's professionals by mandating continuing education. Below are the number of states that required continuing education, by profession, in 1996:

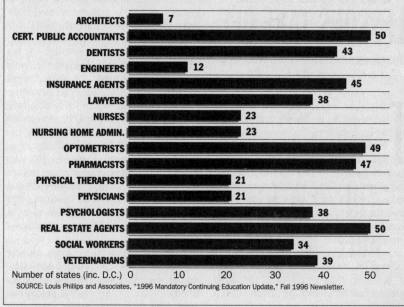

Profession	Number of states
ARCHITECTS	7
CERT. PUBLIC ACCOUNTANTS	50
DENTISTS	43
ENGINEERS	12
INSURANCE AGENTS	45
LAWYERS	38
NURSES	23
NURSING HOME ADMIN.	23
OPTOMETRISTS	49
PHARMACISTS	47
PHYSICAL THERAPISTS	21
PHYSICIANS	21
PSYCHOLOGISTS	38
REAL ESTATE AGENTS	50
SOCIAL WORKERS	34
VETERINARIANS	39

Number of states (inc. D.C.)   0   10   20   30   40   50

SOURCE: Louis Phillips and Associates, "1996 Mandatory Continuing Education Update," Fall 1996 Newsletter.

states federal monies to operate training programs for disadvantaged and dislocated workers. The U.S. Department of Labor handed states some $1.3 billion in 1997 for such training programs. Navigating your way through the maze of state programs is tough, but not impossible. The federal government is planning one-stop career centers nationwide to help workers find retraining assistance. But, for now, you can learn about them through your state's labor department or a local city or county elected official.

■ **LEARN TO WEAR MANY HATS.** A major trend in the workplace is the integration of a wide variety of skills and responsibilities into a single job. You may be required, for example, to be a salesperson as well as a manager, technical expert, and computer whiz. Many colleges are working to prepare workers to be multifaceted. The New School for Social Research in New York City, for example, offers degree programs designed for man-

agers in human resources, health services, and in the nonprofit sector. The courses recognize that to be successful in these fields, more than basic management skills are required. A program offered by Johns Hopkins in Baltimore is designed for managers within the criminal justice system, recognizing that it will take training that goes well beyond criminology and basic management to be a police chief of a large city like New York.

■ **DON'T BREAK STATE LAWS.** Many states mandate continuing education for a variety of professionals, from real estate agents to home health aides to lawyers. (See chart above.) Mandatory training means workers must complete a certain number of hours of study provided by an approved institution or attend a certain number of hours of conferences and workshops. Contact your state's labor department to find out about specific requirements in your field.

▼

LONG-DISTANCE LESSONS TAKE OFF

Computers and videos are becoming the classrooms of the future

The stigma once attached to learning via correspondence courses is wearing off as long-distance learning meets the high-tech world. Courses are delivered via satellite broadcasts, interactive video, online computer services, the Internet, and plain old snail mail. The options are endless: work toward an MBA, earn a certificate in hotel management, debate the fine points of Shakespearean tragedies—or even attend a seminary.

"Individuals all over the globe, in all walks of life, have access to almost any kind of program they can dream up," says Michael Lambert, executive director of the Distance Education Training Council (DETC), an accrediting agency based in Washington, D.C. The ranks of folks who are beefing up their résumés and furthering their education by remote learning are growing. Precise numbers are hard to come by, but the online service provider Compu-Serve estimates that more than 4 million individuals are learning via computer. Another 3 million are enrolled in study programs conducted by mail, video, satellite TV, and telephone, according to the DETC.

A good starting point for locating more traditional correspondence courses is the DETC, which currently screens and accredits 70 long-distance study institutions. Course offerings are far-flung: advanced gun repair offered by the Modern Gun School, freelance journalism by International Correspondence Schools, and nutrition sciences by the National Institute of Nutritional Education, to mention just a few examples. Although many of the newer course offerings require using a computer, many others use audio and visual tapes, pre-prepared workbooks and lessons, and nothing more technical than the telephone or the post office to communicate with instructors.

When it comes to online courses, colleges and universities are crowding the information superhighway. More than 75 institutions offer online degree programs, according to CompuServe's Education Forum. Many universities are not so much designing courses to fit the new technology as applying the technology to existing, solid courses. In June 1997, Duke University grad-

---

CYBER SOURCES

RESOURCES THAT HELP YOU GO THE DISTANCE

Want to learn more about the potential of long-distance learning? These resources can guide you through the maze of programs, from online to video to correspondence courses:

DISTANCE EDUCATION AND TRAINING COUNCIL
1601 18th St., N.W.
Washington, D.C. 20009-2529
☎ 202–234–5100
http://www.detc.org
■ List of 70 accredited programs and hundreds

of courses.

PETERSON'S EDUCATION AND CAREER CENTER
http://www.petersons.com
■ Details on 58 long-distance university programs, as well as

helpful study tips.

YAHOO
http://www.yahoo.com
■ Check out the education pages for upcoming conferences and links to universities.

uated its first class of students with virtual master's degrees from its business school. Even venerable Harvard University is bowing to the trend: MBA candidates can take refresher courses in basics like accounting or computer skills, via the World Wide Web.

Contact with teachers, professors, and other students varies greatly from course to course. An MBA program offered by Colorado University, for example, allows students to "attend" class by VCR and file homework electronically at their convenience. A mystery writing class at a DETC-accredited school requires students to log onto their computers at a given time each week for a "class discussion."

Needless to say, the quality of the programs can range from excellent to subpar. Currently, no certification system exists for online programs, although the American Council on Education, a Washington-D.C. group, is working to establish guidelines for the industry.

When choosing a program, go with a school that has a good reputation and whose on-campus courses are accredited. If it's a diploma you're after, be certain that the school offers a full load of courses that leads to a degree. Another factor to consider is whether the school treats credits earned online in the same way as those earned on campus. Furthermore, all credits should be interchangeable, so that a student can start out on campus and switch to online learning, or vice versa, without any disruption in coursework.

Which schools are at the forefront of online learning? Stephen Wright, a Penn State professor, has studied the remote-learning universe. In a recent long-distance learning workshop conducted by the University of Notre Dame, Wright identified the following as universities with solid programs and ambitious plans to adapt them to new technology: University of California-Extension, University of Nebraska-Lincoln, Pennsylvania State University, University of Iowa, University of Missouri, Columbia University, University of Minnesota, and University of Wisconsin Extension School.

LEARN TO STAY YOUNG

Retiring alumni and faculty are increasingly choosing their old college towns as places to spend their later years. In the past 10 years, more than 50 retirement communities have opened in college towns from Minneapolis, Minn., to Charlottesville, Va., and experts expect that number to increase fourfold in the next decade. Some are open only to that school's alumni and former faculty, others to anyone interested in living in a college town.

What's the appeal? Mostly, the chance for retirees to be near others who have similar backgrounds, have led interesting lives, and maintain an interest in intellectual and social pursuits. Events in college retirement communities can include everything from basketball games to French farces to lectures by leading intellectuals. In addition, residents generally have use of college facilities and can take or audit classes.

The cost of such stimulating living varies. You may be asked to pay a membership fee that can range from $50,000 to more than $250,000. Monthly fees for services such as food, transportation, and cleaning can range from $1,000 to more than $3,000. Sometimes the monthly fees are a fixed rate for all services, but charging residents for only what they use is increasingly common.

For more about college retirement communities, consult *University Linked Retirement Communities* (Haworth Press, 1994), coedited by Leon Pastalan, a professor at the University of Michigan. Pastalan has rated the nation's best campus retirement communities. Among his top choices: Meadowwood at the University of Indiana (☎ 812–336–7060), The Colonnades at the University of Virginia (☎ 804–448–8983), and University of Minnesota Retirees Association (☎ 612–625–4700).

GETTING LOST IN THE STACKS

The favorite libraries of noted bibliophile Vartan Gregorian

Asking Vartan Gregorian to name his 10 favorite libraries is like asking him to list his favorite 10 colors. "The world is full of a myriad of beautiful hues, and there are hundreds of wonderful libraries," says Gregorian, president of the Carnegie Foundation and former president of Brown University. The following "is not an objective list of great institutions," says Gregorian, who once headed the New York Public Library. "It is more a personal reflection" on some of his favorite libraries. His selections and commentary:

First, of course, must be the New York Public Library (*http://www.nypl.org*), where I spent eight rich years. The NYPL is in a class by itself in the sheer size and diversity of its holdings, and because of its writers' room where so many major works of both fiction and nonfiction were done, from Robert Caro's multivolume biography of Lyndon Johnson to Rachel Carson's *Silent Spring*.

Next I think of the Library of Congress (*http://lcweb.loc.gov*), our nation's premier library. No country in the world boasts a greater national library, and what a glory it is for a nation barely 200 years old that did not have the patronage of an aristocracy to shape its beginnings.

Another favorite is the British Library (*http://portico.bl.uk*), which was, is, and I hope will remain one of the great libraries of the world. On a similar scale is the Bibliothèque Nationale (*http://www.bnt.fr*) in Paris, of which I have personal memories from having spent many happy days there. Unlike our Library of Congress, the Bibliothèque Nationale began as a royal collection as early as the 15th century, and one can hardly imagine the depth

and variety of its holdings.

Also in Europe is the Vatican Library, with its universal holdings on every possible topic and its current accessibility, which ranks it as one of the great libraries in the world. At Oxford is the Bodleian Library, and in Cambridge, the King's College Library.

The greatest university library in the United States is Harvard's Widener Library (*http://www.harvard.edu*), which along with its sister libraries at Harvard, is a universe apart. Some of the public university libraries are also spectacular, such as the one at the University of Illinois in Urbana (*http://www.grainger.uiuc.edu*), which is, with about 8 million books, the fourth largest library in the U.S. after the Library of Congress, the NYPL, and Harvard.

There are also the specialized, independent research libraries, which tend to be somewhat unknown but are much beloved and have absolutely irreplaceable materials. The most famous of these perhaps is the Pierpont Morgan Library, which is only a few blocks from the NYPL and contains all that money could buy, beginning early in this century when Morgan began his collecting.

Others of this type of library, founded by wealthy and enlightened individual collectors, are the Huntington Library, near Los Angeles, and the Folger Library in Washington, D.C. The Folger began as a library for the study of Shakespeare and has since branched out productively to a library for the study of Renaissance England.

Only after I went to Brown University did I realize that on that campus is the very prototype and model of all such libraries in the United States, the John Carter Brown Library (*http://www.brown.edu/Facilities/University Libr*). It is the greatest in the world for the study of the history of the expansion of Europe to America between 1492 and 1825.

Finally, there are our town and small city libraries. Surely it was one of the greatest philanthropic acts of all time that Andrew Carnegie built some 1,600 public libraries in the U.S. The tradition of making reading material available easily and freely continues. One can hardly overestimate their value in the success of this country.

EXPERT LIST

BOOKS THAT SHAPED THE 20ᵀᴴ CENTURY

To celebrate its centennial in 1995, the New York Public Library mounted an exhibit of books that its staff considered among the most influential of the 20th century. For more discussion of what makes these books great, see The New York Public Library's Books of the Century *(Oxford University Press, 1996).*

LANDMARKS OF MODERN LITERATURE

Anton Chekhov. **Tri sestry [The Three Sisters]**, *1901*

Marcel Proust. **A la recherche du temps perdu [Remembrance of Things Past]**, *1913–27*

Gertrude Stein. **Tender Buttons**, *1914*

Franz Kafka. **Die Verwandlung [The Metamorphosis]**, *1915*

Edna St. Vincent Millay. **Renascence and Other Poems**, *1917*

William Butler Yeats. **The Wild Swans at Coole**, *1917*

Luigi Pirandello. **Sei personaggi in cerca d'autore [Six Characters in Search of an Author]**, *1921*

T. S. Eliot. **The Waste Land**, *1922*

James Joyce. **Ulysses**, *1924*

Thomas Mann. **Der Zauberberg [The Magic Mountain]**, *1924*

F. Scott Fitzgerald. **The Great Gatsby**, *1925*

Virginia Woolf. **To the Lighthouse**, *1927*

Federico García Lorca. **Primer Romancero gitano [Gypsy Ballads]**, *1928*

Richard Wright. **Native Son**, *1940*

W. H. Auden. **The Age of Anxiety: A Baroque Eclogue**, *1947*

Ralph Ellison. **Invisible Man**, *1952*

Vladimir Nabokov. **Lolita**, *1955*

Jorge Luis Borges. **Ficciones [Fictions]**, *1944: 2nd augmented edition, 1956*

Gabriel García Márquez. **Cien años de soledad [One Hundred Years of Solitude]**, *1967*

Toni Morrison. **Song of Solomon**, *1977*

NATURE'S REALM

Maurice Maeterlinck. **La vie des abeilles [The Life of the Bee]**, *1901*

Marie Sklodowska Curie. **Traité de radioactivité [Treatise on Radioactivity]**, *1910*

Albert Einstein. **The Meaning of Relativity**, *1922*

Roger Tory Peterson. **A Field Guide to the Birds**, *1934*

Aldo Leopold. **A Sand County Almanac**, *1949*

Konrad Z. Lorenz. **Er redete mit dem Vieh, den Vögeln und den Fischen: King Solomon's Ring [King Solomon's Ring: New Light on Animal Ways]**, *1949*

Rachel Carson. **Silent Spring**, *1962*

Smoking and Health, *Known as* **The Surgeon General's Report**, *1964*

James Watson. **The Double Helix: A Personal Account of the Discovery of the Structure of DNA**, *1968*

Edward O. Wilson. **The Diversity of Life**, *1992*

PROTEST & PROGRESS

Jacob Riis. **The Battle with the Slum**, *1902*

W. E. B. DuBois. **The Souls of Black Folk**, *1903*

Upton Sinclair. **The Jungle**, *1906*

Jane Addams. **Twenty Years at Hull-House**, *1910*

Lillian Wald. **The House on Henry Street**, *1915*

Lincoln Steffens. **The Autobiography of Lincoln Steffens**, *1931*

John Dos Passos. **U.S.A.**, *1937*

John Steinbeck. **The Grapes of Wrath**, *1939*

James Agee and Walker Evans. **Let Us Now Praise Famous Men**, *1941*

Lillian Smith. **Strange Fruit**, *1944*

Paul Goodman. **Growing Up Absurd**, *1960*

James Baldwin. **The Fire Next Time**, *1963*

Malcolm X. **The Autobiography of Malcolm X**, *1965*

Randy Shilts. **And the Band Played On**, *1987*

Alex Kotlowitz. **There Are No Children Here**, *1991*

COLONIALISM & ITS AFTERMATH

Joseph Conrad. **Lord Jim**, *1900*

Rudyard Kipling. **Kim**, *1901*

■ **EXPERT LIST**

Mohandas K. Gandhi. **Satyagraha [Non-Violent Resistance],** *1921–40*

E. M. Forster. **A Passage to India,** *1924*

Albert Camus. **L'étranger [The Stranger],** *1942*

United Nations Charter, *1945*

Edward Steichen. **The Family of Man: The Photographic Exhibition Created by Edward Steichen for the Museum of Modern Art,** *1955*

Chinua Achebe. **Things Fall Apart,** *1958*

Frantz Fanon. **Les damnés de la terre [The Wretched of the Earth],** *1961*

Jean Rhys. **Wide Sargasso Sea,** *1966*

Tayeb el-Salih. **Mawsim al-Hijra ila al-Shamal [Season of Migration to the North],** *1969*

V. S. Naipaul. **Guerrillas,** *1975*

Buchi Emecheta. **The Bride Price,** *1976*

Ryszard Kapuściński. **Cesarz [The Emperor],** *1978*

Rigoberta Menchú. **Me llamo Rigoberta Menchú y ási me nacio conciencia [I, Rigoberta Menchú],** *1983*

Marguerite Duras. **L'amant [The Lover],** *1984*

MIND & SPIRIT

Emile Durkheim. **Le suicide: étude de sociologie [Suicide: A Study in Sociology],** *1897*

Sigmund Freud. **Die Traumdeutung [The Interpretation of Dreams],** *1900*

Havelock Ellis. **Studies in the Psychology of Sex,** *1901–28*

William James. **The Varieties of Religious Experience: A Study in Human Nature,** *1902*

Kahlil Gibran. **The Prophet,** *1923*

Bertrand Russell. **Why I Am Not a Christian,** *1927*

Margaret Mead. **Coming of Age in Samoa,** *1928*

Jean-Paul Sartre. **L'étre et le néant [Being and Nothingness],** *1943*

Dr. Benjamin Spock. **The Common Sense Book of Baby and Child Care,** *1946*

The Holy Bible. Revised Standard Version, *1952*

Paul Tillich. **The Courage to Be,** *1952*

Ken Kesey. **One Flew Over the Cuckoo's Nest,** *1962*

Timothy Leary. **The Politics of Ecstasy,** *1968*

Elisabeth Kübler-Ross. **On Death and Dying,** *1969*

Bruno Bettelheim. **The Uses of Enchantment,** *1976*

POPULAR CULTURE & MASS ENTERTAINMENT

Bram Stoker. **Dracula,** *1897*

Henry James. **The Turn of the Screw,** *1898*

Arthur Conan Doyle. **The Hound of the Baskervilles,** *1902*

Edgar Rice Burroughs. **Tarzan of the Apes,** *1912*

Zane Grey. **Riders of the Purple Sage,** *1912*

Agatha Christie. **The Mysterious Affair at Styles,** *1920*

Dale Carnegie. **How to Win Friends and Influence People,** *1936*

Margaret Mitchell. **Gone with the Wind,** *1936*

Raymond Chandler. **The Big Sleep,** *1939*

Nathanael West. **The Day of the Locust,** *1939*

Grace Metalious. **Peyton Place,** *1956*

Dr. Seuss. **The Cat in the Hat,** *1957*

Robert A. Heinlein. **Stranger in a Strange Land,** *1961*

Joseph Heller. **Catch-22,** *1961*

Truman Capote. **In Cold Blood: A True Account of a Multiple Murder and Its Consequences,** *1965*

Jim Bouton. **Ball Four: My Life and Hard Times Throwing the Knuckleball in the Big Leagues,** *1970*

Stephen King. **Carrie,** *1974*

Tom Wolfe. **The Bonfire of the Vanities,** *1987*

WOMEN RISE

Edith Wharton. **The Age of Innocence,** *1920*

Carrie Chapman Catt. **Woman Suffrage and Politics: The Inner Story of the Suffrage Movement,** *1923*

Margaret Sanger. **My Fight for Birth Control,** *1931*

Zora Neale Hurston. **Dust Tracks on a Road,** *1942*

Simone de Beauvoir. **Le deuxième sexe [The Second Sex],** *1949*

Doris Lessing. **The Golden Notebook,** *1962*

Betty Friedan. **The Feminine Mystique,** *1963*

Maya Angelou. **I Know Why the Caged Bird Sings,** *1969*

Robin Morgan, editor **Sisterhood Is Powerful: An Anthology of Writings from the Women's Liberation Movement,** *1970*

Susan Brownmiller. **Against Our Will: Men, Women, and Rape,** *1975*

Alice Walker. **The Color Purple,** *1982*

ECONOMICS & TECHNOLOGY

Thorstein Veblen. **The Theory of the Leisure Class: An Economic Study of Institutions,** *1899*

Max Weber. **Die protestantische Ethik und der Geist des Kapitalismus [The Protestant Ethic and the Spirit of Capitalism],** *1904*

Henry Adams. **The Education of Henry Adams,** *1907*

John Maynard Keynes. **The General Theory of Employment, Interest and Money,** *1936*

Milton Friedman. **A Theory of the Consumption Function,** *1957*

John Kenneth Galbraith. **The Affluent Society,** *1958*

Jane Jacobs. **The Death and Life of Great American Cities,** *1961*

Helen Leavitt. **Superhighway—Super Hoax,** *1970*

E. F. Schumacher. **Small Is Beautiful: A Study of Economics as if People Mattered,** *1973*

Ed Krel. **The Whole Internet: User's Guide & Catalog,** *1992*

UTOPIA & DYSTOPIAS

H.G. Wells. **The Time Machine,** *1895*

Theodor Herzl. **Der Judenstaat [The Jewish State],** *1896*

L. Frank Baum. **The Wonderful Wizard of Oz,** *1900*

J. M. Barrie. **Peter Pan in Kensington Gardens,** *1906*

Charlotte Perkins Gilman. **Herland,** *1915*

Aldous Huxley. **Brave New World,** *1932*

James Hilton. **Lost Horizon,** *1933*

B. F. Skinner. **Walden Two,** *1948*

George Orwell. **Nineteen Eighty-four,** *1949*

Ray Bradbury. **Fahrenheit 451,** *1953*

Anthony Burgess. **A Clockwork Orange,** *1962*

Margaret Atwood. **The Handmaid's Tale,** *1985*

WAR, HOLOCAUST, TOTALITARIANISM

Arnold Toynbee. **Armenian Atrocities: The Murder of a Nation,** *1915*

John Reed. **Ten Days That Shook the World,** *1919*

Siegfried Sassoon. **The War Poems,** *1919*

Jaroslav Hašek. **Osudy dobrého vojáka Svejkā za svêtové války [The Good Soldier Schweik],** *1920–23*

Adolf Hitler. **Mein Kampf,** *1925*

Erich Maria Remarque. **Im Westen nichts Neues [All Quiet on the Western Front],** *1928*

Anna Akhmatova. **Rekviem [Requiem],** *1935–40*

Ernest Hemingway. **For Whom the Bell Tolls,** *1940*

Arthur Koestler. **Darkness at Noon,** *1941*

John Hersey. **Hiroshima,** *1946*

Anne Frank. **Het Achterhuis [The Diary of a Young Girl],** *1947*

Winston Churchill. **The Gathering Storm,** *1948*

Mao Zedong. **Quotations from Chairman Mao,** *1966*

Dee Alexander Brown. **Bury My Heart at Wounded Knee: An Indian History of the** American West, *1970*

Aleksandr I. Solzhenitsyn. **The Gulag Archipelago, 1918–1956: An Experiment in Literary Investigation,** *1973*

Michael Herr. **Dispatches,** *1977*

Art Spiegelman. **Maus: A Survivor's Tale, 2 vols.,** *1986–91*

OPTIMISM, JOY, GENTILITY

Sarah Orne Jewett. **The Country of the Pointed Firs,** *1896*

Helen Keller. **The Story of My Life,** *1903*

G. K. Chesterton. **The Innocence of Father Brown,** *1911*

Juan Ramón Jiménez. **Platero y Yo [Platero and I: An Andalusian Elegy],** *1914*

George Bernard Shaw. **Pygmalion,** *1914*

Emily Post. **Etiquette in Society, in Business, in Politics, and at Home,** *1922*

P. G. Wodehouse. **The Inimitable Jeeves,** *1923*

A. A. Milne. **Winnie-the-Pooh,** *1926*

Willa Cather. **Shadows on the Rock,** *1931*

Irma S. Rombauer. **The Joy of Cooking: A Compilation of Reliable Recipes with a Casual Culinary Chat,** *1931*

J. R. R. Tolkien. **The Hobbit,** *1937*

Margaret Wise Brown. **Goodnight Moon,** *1947*

Harper Lee. **To Kill a Mockingbird,** *1960*

Langston Hughes. **The Best of Simple,** *1961*

Elizabeth Bishop. **The Complete Poems, 1927-1979,** *1983*

READING
▼

BOOK CLUB BONANZA

Where folks can meet, greet, and expand their minds

Book clubs were popular in this country long before Oprah Winfrey gave them a boost by launching her television book discussions in late 1996. During the last century, groups of women frequently gathered for conversations on literature and culture. Today there are more than 250,000 book clubs nationwide, according to Rachel Jacobsohn, author of *The Reading Group Handbook* and founder of the Association of Book Group Readers and Leaders, based in Highland Park, Ill.

Want to get in on the "group activity rage of the '90s," as *Publisher's Weekly* calls the phenomenon? You have several options besides tuning into Oprah: join an existing book club or start your own. The benefits of book clubs,

EXPERT PICKS

By devoting one show a month to a book of her choice, the queen of talk-shows, Oprah Winfrey, has created a book club for the masses. Here are five of her picks:

- ■ *The Deep End of the Ocean* by Jacquelyn Mitchard
- ■ *Song of Solomon* by Toni Morrison
- ■ *The Book of Ruth* by Jane Hamilton
- ■ *She's Come Undone* by Wally Lamb
- ■ *Stones from the River* by Ursula Hegi

says Jacobsohn, include personal enrichment, social interaction, and a chance to further your education. Here Jacobsohn offers some pointers for joining or starting a club.

■ Consider how often a club meets, the length of meetings, number of members, book selections, and members' qualifications. Be sure your interests are compatible with other members. Do you want a group that meets primarily to socialize, or do you prefer to devote time to delving seriously into a book?

■ An ideal member is not necessarily one who shares your taste in literature. One of the great things about a book club is that you will read books you might never have picked yourself. If you're forming your own club, put the word out to more than your immediate circle of friends.

■ Groups can vary in size from 5 members to more than 25. The optimum size is 12 to 16, which means between 8 and 10 members will most likely attend each meeting.

Book clubs generally meet once a month for two hours. More frequent meetings are for avid readers, or for discussing shorter pieces, such as short stories or chapters of books.

■ How a group selects titles varies. In some clubs, members take turns picking a book and leading the discussion. Others have a committee that selects the titles, while others brainstorm as a group and vote on a list.

■ Discussion leaders should create a list of questions and select passages to read and discuss. Also gather supplemental information that will aid in understanding the book, such as the author's biography, the story's setting, etc. (Many publishers offer guides to facilitate book group discussions. Check with your local bookstore.)

■ If you buy your books in bulk, a member should contact a bookstore and inquire about a discount. Bookstores are increasingly offering special services to clubs. They are also good places to find out about local book clubs that you might want to join.

CHAPTER FOUR

CAREERS

EXPERT QUOTES

"Without a mastery of networking, you are probably in for a long and difficult search."
—Clyde Lowstuter, coauthor of *Network Your Way to Your Next Job, Fast*
Page 268

"Companies are looking for other ways to reward employees rather than adding to base pay."
—Mary Lowe, marketing coordinator, William M. Mercer, Inc.
Page 279

"Don't rely just on the advice of well-meaning friends, who often don't know as much as they tell you they do."
—Richard Bolles, author of *What Color Is Your Parachute?*
Page 291

■ **WHAT'S AHEAD: THINK** twice before painting your office green or yellow... **EXPECT** more companies to use temporary workers... **SEARCH** for new jobs on the Internet... **WRITE** a résumé that will get you noticed... **AVOID** these gaffes on your next interview... **FIND OUT** your company's perks for relocating... **LEARN** management skills by reading these books... **BE SURE** you have what it takes to start your own business... **THINK TWICE** before painting your office green or yellow... **BEAT** burnout on the job with simple relaxation techniques...

GETTING STARTED

STRATEGIES
▼

MASTERING THE NETWORK GAME

A step-by-step plan for finding your next job

The word conjures up images of the let's-do-lunch Hollywood crowd, but when you are in the market for a new job—no matter what field you're in—networking is essential. Nearly 80 percent of all jobs are found through a previous contact, say career experts. Simply put, networking is the process of using your resources and connections to gain an advantage. "You can have the best résumé in the world and interview superbly, but without a mastery of networking, you are probably in for a long and difficult search," says Clyde Lowstuter, cofounder of Robertson Lowstuter Inc., an executive career consulting firm, and co-author of *Network Your Way to Your Next Job, Fast* (McGraw-Hill, 1995). Here, Lowstuter lays out the rules for playing the networking game successfully.

■ **LIST YOUR CONTACTS.** Start networking for a new job only after you have made all attempts to strengthen your current posi-

tion. If that fails, start networking by putting together a résumé that clearly, crisply, and concisely identifies your professional accomplishments, roles, and responsibilities. Next, make a list of all of your colleagues, past and present employers, school associates, friends, relatives, neighbors—anyone who might be able to help you. Your list should contain 50 to 150 names.

■ **ORGANIZE YOUR LIST.** Divide your list into primary and secondary contacts. Your primary network is made up of individuals you know personally, people who will field your calls and help you. The secondary contacts are names of individuals you glean from primary contacts. Don't prejudge or eliminate any contacts who may not be in your industry or socioeconomic group. They may know others who can help.

■ **BE DIRECT.** When you place a networking call to a contact, quickly get to the reason for your call. Let him know if you are employed but looking for a job, willing to relocate, or unemployed. Don't beat around the bush—come out and ask for contacts in your desired company, industry, or location. You can legitimize a follow-up call by asking, "Is it okay if I send you a copy of my résumé or call you next week?" It's surprising how many people don't think of forwarding their résumés to their networking contacts.

■ **GATHER INFORMATION.** Do not use your net-

WHERE ALL THE JOBS ARE—AND AREN'T

Are you in a growing or declining job market? Here's a snapshot of where job growth is hottest across the country. Bars on the map show the percentage increase in jobs in 1996.

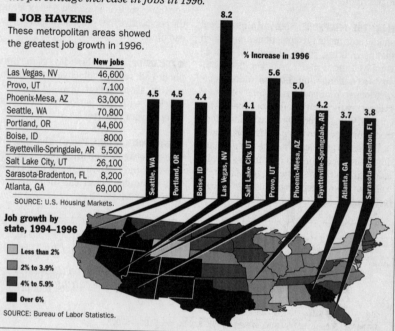

■ **JOB HAVENS**
These metropolitan areas showed the greatest job growth in 1996.

	New jobs
Las Vegas, NV	46,600
Provo, UT	7,100
Phoenix-Mesa, AZ	63,000
Seattle, WA	70,800
Portland, OR	44,600
Boise, ID	8000
Fayetteville-Springdale, AR	5,500
Salt Lake City, UT	26,100
Sarasota-Bradenton, FL	8,200
Atlanta, GA	69,000

SOURCE: U.S. Housing Markets.

Job growth by state, 1994–1996

☐ Less than 2%
▨ 2% to 3.9%
▨ 4% to 5.9%
■ Over 6%

SOURCE: Bureau of Labor Statistics.

% Increase in 1996

working calls as a job interview attempt. Reassure your contacts that you are calling to find out about their industry, competition, and related fields, and to generate some visibility for yourself. Networking calls should be unthreatening, no-obligation discussions based on trust, respect, and rapport.

■ **DON'T TALK TOO MUCH.** You should be speaking about 40 percent or less of the time. The more you get the other person to talk and answer your questions, the greater the chance of getting additional leads. Always behave warmly and positively toward your contacts, regardless of how little information they give or effort they expend.

■ **POSE MEANINGFUL QUESTIONS.** Try to get specific information from your contact by asking things like: What has your career path been?

What are the job's positive and negative aspects? What skills, abilities, and contacts should one have to succeed in this role? Who do you know who is already successful in this role? What other experts in this field do you recommend I contact for other perspectives?

■ **DEVELOP A VERBAL RESUME.** This will help you to present yourself professionally, powerfully, and clearly over the telephone. The verbal résumé should be about two minutes long. Think of it as an advertising commercial filled with "sound bites." In single sentences, state concisely your primary career goals and briefly outline where you were born and raised. In about five seconds, state your degrees, major subjects, and schools you attended. When networking on the telephone, stand up and gesture as you talk. Practice with a tape recorder beforehand.

Be confident, enthusiastic, and bold. Always express an interest in the other person. For example, ask, "What are you working on? How can I help you?" Find a reprint of a relevant newspaper article or book title to pass along.

■ **HIT THE TELEPHONE.** Your minimum goal should be to make 10 connections a day, which means making 20 to 30 calls. If you're employed and sitting in an office, that's obviously a challenge and your networking may take longer. Your goal with primary contacts is to secure three to five additional names per contact. With secondary contacts, shoot for a minimum of one to three additional names.

When you get a lead, ask the contact some qualifying questions to be sure it's a solid lead. Find out when they last spoke, how well they know each other, and if your contact minds if you use his name.

■ **BE PERSISTENT.** If your contact is having difficulty coming up with names, try to keep him on the line awhile. Share some of your positive career search results. Ask if he knows any of the firms, organizations, or individuals you are targeting. If you get the cold shoulder from someone—no big deal, maintain the perspective that you just caught him at a bad time.

■ **FOLLOW UP.** Within three days of the initial phone call, send a contact your résumé and a letter. Always ask if it would be okay to check in with him periodically to update them on your progress.

■ **KNOW WHEN TO QUIT.** There's a balance to be struck between informing people of your progress and hounding them. Respect people's schedules. Never call a contact more than three times.

TEN CUTTING-EDGE JOBS FOR WOMEN

Each year, Working Woman *magazine compiles a report on the hottest careers for women. Here's the 1996 list of jobs on the cutting edge.*

JOB   **$ Salary**   ✔ *Women's Appeal*

ANIMATOR $ Entry, **$27K–$60K**; midlevel, **$40K–$100K**; top, **$100K–$300K**.
✔ *Still male-dominated at top levels, but overall little pay disparity.*

BIO-TECH PATENT LAYWER $ Entry **$32K–$60K**; midlevel, **$125K–$160K**; top, **$160K–$210K**.
✔ *Women make up 40 percent of all patent lawyers.*

BUSINESS-SOFTWARE DESIGNER $ Junior engineer, **$42K**; senior, **$57K**; manager, **$86K**; director, **$100K**.
✔ *High growth but still male-dominated.*

CHEMICAL ENGINEER $ Entry, **$23K–$37K**; midlevel, **$47K–$62K**; top, **$80K+**.
✔ *One-third of all chemical engineers are women. Because companies are actively recruiting women, many start off with higher salaries than men.*

CONSTRUCTION MANAGER $ Civil engineer, **$29K–$70K**; supervisor (engineer), median **$60K**.
✔ *One of the fastest-growing areas for women entrepreneurs.*

DENTIST $ Ranges **$50K–$230K**; oral surgeons, up to **$230K**.
✔ *Flexible hours; more than 70 percent of dentists have their own practice.*

EMPLOYEE-ASSISTANCE PROGRAM MANAGER $ Entry, **$22K+**; midlevel, **$50K**; top, **$90K**.
✔ *The number of companies using EAPs has risen 40 percent.*

ENVIRONMENTAL ECONOMIST $ Entry, **$30K**; midlevel, **$50K**; top, **100K+**.
✔ *Consulting offers flexible hours and plenty of autonomy.*

EXECUTIVE-SEARCH CONSULTANT $ Entry, **$50K–$60K**; midlevel, **$150K–$200K**; top, **$300K–$500K**.
✔ *Excellent pay and good place for jumping to other fields.*

FINANCIAL PRODUCTS SALESPERSON $ Entry, **$50K–$60K**; midlevel, **$70K–$135K**; top **$300K–$500K+**.
✔ *More women are investing money and often want women as advisors.*

SOURCE: *Working Woman* magazine (July–August, 1996).

THE 30 FASTEST-GROWING PROFESSIONS

The best job opportunities often are not where the most jobs are, but instead where the most growth is. Explosive growth in a relatively small pool indicates an industry in need of a rapid infusion of labor. Overall, the projected rate of growth will be slower than it has been in years past. From 1983 to 1994, total employment grew 24 percent, but projected growth by the year 2005 is only 13.9 percent.

The service-producing industries will be unaffected by this sluggish growth. The aging U.S. population and medical advances will create a boom for health-care services, which will account for almost one-fifth of all future job growth. Also, there will be growth in the computer science and systems analysis fields. The following numbers from the U.S. Bureau of Labor Statistics show the 30 professions expected to experience the fastest growth.

■ **PROJECTED EMPLOYMENT GROWTH BY 2005**

Occupation	Jobs in 1994	Anticipated % change	Anticipated no. of new jobs
Homemaker–home health aides	598,000	107	640,000
Computer scientists and systems analysts	828,000	91	755,000
Physical therapy assistants and aides	78,000	83	64,000
Occupational therapy assistants and aides	16,000	82	13,000
Physical therapists	102,000	80	81,000
Human services workers	168,000	75	125,000
Services sales representatives	612,000	72	441,000
Occupational therapists	54,000	72	39,000
Medical assistants	206,000	59	121,000
Paralegals	111,000	58	64,000
Medical record technicians	81,000	56	45,000
Special education teachers	388,000	53	206,000
Correctional officers	310,000	51	158,000
Operations research analysts	44,000	50	22,000
Guards	867,000	48	415,000
Speech-language pathologists and audiologists	85,000	46	39,000
Private detectives and investigators	55,000	44	24,000
Surgical technologists	46,000	43	19,000
Dental assistants	190,000	42	79,000
Dental hygienists	127,000	42	53,000
General office clerks	2,946,000	NA	26,000
Teacher aides	932,000	39	364,000
Securities and financial services sales representatives	246,000	37	90,000
Emergency medical technicians	138,000	36	49,000
Management analysts and consultants	231,000	35	82,000
Radiologic technologists	167,000	35	59,000
Employment interviewers	77,000	35	27,000
Social workers	557,000	34	187,000
Preschool teachers and child-care workers	1 million+	33	358,000
Restaurant and food service managers	526,500	33	192,000

SOURCE: U.S. Bureau of Labor Statistics.

WHAT SHOULD I BE WHEN I GROW UP?

The clueless might get some clues from a psychological profile

The title of a recently published book captures the thought: *I Can Do Anything, If I Only Knew What It Was* (by Barbara Sher and Barbara Smith, Delacorte, 1994). But what is it? One way to find out is to take a personality test. The tests are becoming increasingly popular among individuals to help determine what career may best suit them. You can take them on the cheap by buying modified versions in a book. But the full-dress tests, administered by career counselors, psychologists, or psychiatrists, can cost hundreds of dollars—and produce uncertain results.

The Rorschach test, invented in the 1920s, was the first and is still widely used by psychiatrists. It is supposed to reveal an individual's underlying personality through his or her reaction to a series of inkblot designs. More popular these days are the Myers-Briggs Type Indicator and the Strong Interest Inventory. Unlike the Rorschach, both involve completing a lengthy questionnaire and attempt to gauge an individual's interests and temperament through the answers.

Until recently, personality tests were thought to be best only for individuals looking to change careers in midstream, but, increasingly, the tests are being administered to people of all ages and at various stages of their lives. Some colleges are administering the tests to freshmen to help students plan their short-term and long-term goals. College career centers give the tests to graduating seniors before heading into the "real" world. In the business world, many corporations are using the tests to determine hirings (and promotions), saving the company the expense of hiring an individual whose personality does not complement the job or work environment. "These tests help people to understand what motivates them," says Irene Mendelson, a professional career counselor and president of BEMW Inc., in Bethesda, Md. "It also gets

OTHER PLACES TO FIND THE REAL YOU

The perfect job probably doesn't exist but these tomes can help you find one that works for you:

100 BEST COMPANIES TO WORK FOR IN AMERICA
by Robert Levering and Milton Moskowitz (Plume, 1996).
■ A thorough guide to the best employers, including information on salary, benefits, and responsiveness to workers and clients. Also describes company values, missions, and culture. Use this guide

to help you determine which company best suits your personality.

ZEN AND THE ART OF MAKING A LIVING: A PRACTICAL GUIDE TO CREATIVE CAREER DESIGN
by Lawrence G. Boldt (Penguin Books, 1993).
■ Practical career advice for job seekers at all stages of the game. A dash of Zen spirituality

spices up this guide for discovering the true you.

WHAT COLOR IS YOUR PARACHUTE? (1997 ED.)
by Richard Bolles (Ten Speed Press).
■ This book has been a best-seller since it was first published 25 years ago. It is considered essential for job hunters and career changers alike.

at the underlying issues in their lives and allows them to work and understand themselves better."

Most professionals agree that taking the test under the supervision of an accredited career counselor or psychiatrist is the best option—and the most expensive. Most of the tests cost between $200 and $300, which includes follow-up counseling sessions.

Here's a brief assessment of the two most popular tests:

■ **MYERS-BRIGGS TYPE INDICATOR (MBTI).** The most popular of the personality tests, the MBTI categorizes people based on four scales of personal preferences: extroversion-introversion, sensing-intuition, thinking-feeling, and judging-perceiving. The answers place individuals in one of 16 personality groups. Once MBTI identifies your type, a counselor will provide you a list of job fields best suited for you. The drawback of MBTI is that it's a personality, not a skills, test.

If you decide to take the test yourself, take a look at *Do What You Are,* by Paul Tieger and Barbara Barron-Tieger (Little, Brown and Co., 1995). The book includes a list of careers that appeal to the different MBTI personality types.

■ **STRONG INTEREST INVENTORY.** Many counselors recommend taking this test in conjunction with Myers-Briggs. The interest inventory collects information about an individual's interests and recommends potential occupations based on work activities involved, the traits of the working environment, and personality characteristics that can affect work. Individuals are categorized by one of the six occupational types (realistic, investigative, artistic, social, enterprising, and conventional) that correspond with a list of career options. This test works best for college students or individuals with a college degree.

Before taking either test, you should contact a professional career counselor (or call the National Board for Certified Counselors ☎ 910–547–0607). Or check with the career office at a local university. Many allow students or alumni to take these tests free.

GETTING HIRED
▼

JOB HUNTING IN CYBERSPACE

Forget the classifieds. You'll find them plus lots more online

No job hunt is complete these days without a trip to the online job supermarket. Most online services, such as America Online and CompuServe, offer their own sites and résumé-posting services. But the real action is on the World Wide Web, where job bank sites and those offering employment advice are constantly springing up. There are dozens of résumé database services, hundreds of job-related bulletin boards, and a slew of employment-related sites sponsored by individual companies.

The major career sites now list more than 500,000 openings. Not too long ago, job listings were targeted mainly to computer and high-tech types; now nearly half the job postings are in nontech fields like sales, nursing, and banking. One place to get your bearings is the employment site offered by the Yahoo browser (*http://www.yahoo.com/Business_and Economy/Employment/Jobs*), which serves up a list of more than 170 linked sites. The Companies link, for instance, sends Net cruisers to a list of nearly 200 companies seeking workers, with descriptions of the firms; similarly, the government site lists openings within federal departments and agencies.

Many services help you tailor your job search, as well as provide a spot to post your résumé. E-Span (see page 274 for good online sources) allows you to store a "user profile" of desired job specifications, by various categories, so that you can run a customized search of its job bank whenever you log on. As openings arise that match your profile, E-Span will notify you by e-mail. Most of the larger sites cover all the career bases, including chat areas where you can get feedback on your résumé from other job hunters, tips on

CYBER SOURCES

WANTED: HELP FOR THE JOBLESS

New job-related Web sites appear on the Internet almost every day, but finding the most valuable sites can be time-consuming. First-time surfers might want to browse a bit, but there are some good general sites that will point you toward specialized jobs and give you a broader idea of what is out there. We listed some of our favorite picks. Aim your browser at one of these:

AMERICA'S JOB BANK
http://www.ajb.dni.us

■ A service of the U.S. Department of Labor and state employment agencies, this site is free for employers and job hunters. Contains a huge database for low- to mid-level salaried jobs. Search by category, employer, and location. Links to stats about future job growth.

CAREERPATH
http://www.careerpath.com

■ Fast, easy to use, and lists a wide variety of openings. Connects users to the classified pages of newspapers like the *Boston Globe, Chicago Tribune, Los Angeles Times, New York Times, Washington Post,* and *San Jose Mercury News.*

CAREERMOSAIC
http://www.careermosaic.com

■ This site is heavily used by recruiters across the country. More than 36,000 job hunters have posted their résumés here for free. The jobs database is extensive. Also provides links to more than 250 other career resources, as well as job hunting tips.

E-SPAN EMPLOYMENT DATABASE SEARCH
http://www.espan.com

■ Gives users access to the interactive Employment Network with links to job banks across the country. The Network stores information on your background, experience, and job preferences for a customized search. You can also post your résumé on E-Span and get job hunting and interviewing tips.

MONSTER BOARD
http://www.monster.com

■ Ads here come from companies, not newspapers. A wealth of offerings, including an online job fair, where you can learn about firms that will be recruiting in your area.

writing cover letters, referrals to career advisory services, and updated listings of headhunters and job fairs around the country.

Figures on the success rate of online job hunts are hard to come by, but some experts say companies are impressed by the initiative of job seekers who are Internet-savvy. For their part, many employers say they like the medium because it's inexpensive and effective. As more players get on board, experts say online job searches will become easier and more productive. Already, more and more headhunters are using Web sites to gather executive résumés. In early 1996, only a dozen or so headhunters had Web sites; one year later, more than 100 outfits were reachable online, according to *Executive Recruiter News*, a New Hampshire newsletter.

Another plus is that posting your résumé online gets you visibility you can't get by mailing paper résumés. Keep your online résumé short, so that it's easy to skim and faster for an employer to download. Always include your e-mail address, if you have one.

There are many good resources to help you navigate the sometimes muddled waters of online employment sites. Among them: *Be Your Own Headhunter Online* by Pam Dixon and Sylvia Tierston (Times Books, 1995), and a quarterly bulletin called *NetWords*, published by Exec-U-Net, a career-counseling service (☎ 800–637–3126).

TEMPORARY JOBS

▼

THE TEMPTATIONS OF TEMPING

Companies are test-driving workers before hiring

Temporary jobs have long been little more than a way to pay the rent while hunting for full-time work. But times have changed in the temping business. So much so that temping is now becoming an attractive avenue for landing a good, permanent job. The ranks of temporary workers have exploded in recent years—from 1.3 million in 1991 to 2.3 million strong in 1996. More important, companies are increasingly tapping temps to fill full-time jobs: About 40 percent of temp workers sent on an assignment get offers of full-time employment, according to the National Association of Temporary and Staffing Services.

Nor is temping limited to those in search of secretarial and receptionist jobs, as was once the case. More companies are turning to professional temps for special projects and long-term assignments. In the legal field, for example, there were 40,000 temp lawyers in 1995, up from 10,000 in 1992. By 2005, the number is expected to rise by 56 percent, according to the Bureau of Labor Statistics.

Employers are snapping up temps for several reasons. "Companies are changing the way they hire," says Gretchen Kresky, a manager with Manpower Inc., one of the biggest temp agencies. "First, they are hiring temporary people to be sure there is a job to be filled. At the same time, they can measure the quality of the temp's work."

From the job seeker's perspective, temping holds great appeal. For one thing, it's a good way to gain experience and hone skills, making it a smart career move for new grads and mid-career transplants. What better way to test different career options while collecting a salary? Many temp agencies are also providing free training that can give candidates a leg up on the competition. For those with limited computer skills, even a few days of training can boost their wages up to 25 percent, say temping experts. For more advanced employees, some agencies provide free training in areas such as marketing, executive management, and high-tech fields. Such courses can cost thousands of dollars elsewhere.

Large temp agencies have even eliminated what once was one of temping's biggest drawbacks: finding affordable health insurance. Many of the largest agencies now provide employees with comprehensive health insurance—and vacation—plans. Ironically, all these pluses may be working against temps. As more job seekers turn to temping, the field will become more competitive, meaning it may be harder to land plum assignments. Then again, insecurity is also a hallmark of full-time work.

■ TEMPING IN THE BIG LEAGUES

More than 200 agencies nationwide specialize in placing technical and professional workers. Here are the nation's top five, along with their employment specialties, in descending order of emphasis.

AGENCY	EMPLOYMENT SPECIALTY	NUMBER OF OFFICES	☎ TELEPHONE
Olsten Corp.	Industrial, medical, office-clerical	1,200	516–844–7800
Manpower, Inc.	Industrial, technical, professional, office-clerical	1,000	414–961–1000
Kelly Services, Inc.	Industrial, office-clerical, technical, professional	850	810–244–4874
INTERIM Services, Inc.	Industrial, medical, office-clerical, technical, professional	700	954–938–7600
Adia Services, Inc.	Industrial, medical, office-clerical, technical, professional	579	415–610–1000

SOURCES: National Association of Temporary and Staffing Services; Manpower, Inc.

A RESUME THAT WORKS OVERTIME

Writing a killer résumé means paying close attention to detail

When it comes to job hunting, your résumé does the legwork for you. Yet, the odds facing your résumé are astounding: Human resource managers say they spend only about 30 seconds to 4 minutes reading most curriculum vitae. For every 1,470 résumés submitted for a job opening, only one job offer is tendered and accepted, according to career consultant Richard Bolles. To narrow the odds against it, your résumé must be a finely tuned document that garners attention and gets results. We've consulted résumé experts for advice on what to do and what to avoid in writing an effective résumé.

■ Picking the proper font or typeface is a crucial decision, says Lloyd Raines, a career counselor at American University. He suggests a simple, clean font such as New Times Roman, Arial, or Palatino. The role of the font is to invite the reader into the content. "It should be aesthetically pleasing and not too busy," says Raines.

■ Page margins—left, right, top, and bottom—should be a minimum of .6 of an inch and a maximum of one inch. The font size for the content of the résumé should be a minimum of 10 points and a maximum of 12 points; your name should be a 14 or 15 point size.

■ Use a visual marker—a medium-sized round bullet works best—to tick off achievements at a job. Bullets let you set off information without having to use another font or underlining, italicizing, or using boldface, all of which should be limited or avoided.

WHAT YOU SHOULDN'T DO AT THE INTERVIEW

You left the interview believing you'd aced it. But the interviewer never called again. Sure, there are mercurial managers, but maybe you're unknowingly committing some interviewing gaffes. Maryanne Rainone, vice president of Heyman Associates Inc., an executive search firm, offers these don'ts:

■ **DON'T** let your eyes wander to the floor, ceiling, or walls of the interviewer's office. Basic a tip as it may be, maintaining eye contact with the interviewer is essential.

■ **DON'T** forget to do your homework. Know the company's hot issues before going into an interview. Read the daily papers and check the Internet for the most up-to-date information about company performance and any breaking news.

Learn a bit about the company's corporate culture by reading business magazines.

■ **DON'T** interrupt or answer too quickly. Listen carefully to questions and answer each one before elaborating on other points. Be specific and give examples.

■ **DON'T** fudge. Specifically, don't misrepresent salary or benefits. A potential employer may ask you to produce a pay stub or a tax form that shows your former salary. If it shows that you have exaggerated, you will be eliminated immediately.

■ **DON'T** forget to maintain your professionalism, including on your home answering machine. More than one prospective employer has been turned off by a wacky answering machine message.

■ The length of the perfect résumé is a controversial topic. Some experts adhere to the one-page-only rule. Others say that rule is too limiting, causing many people to omit valuable material. Raines advises breaking the one-page rule if your experience warrants it. But be sure to make it no less than one page and a third and no more than two pages.

■ A résumé that looks good is only half the challenge, of course. Presenting your work experience in a unique and thoughtful manner sets you apart from other job applicants. General descriptions of work duties make a résumé ineffective. Instead, relay specific contributions you made and how you applied particular skills.

■ Many companies use computers to scan résumés for key words; résumés that don't include those words are automatically discarded. Toss in words like "generated new business," "increased sales," and "introduced new systems," which the computer is apt to pick up.

■ If you have an e-mail address, include it on your résumé. Employers are using e-mail to contact applicants. Don't include your work phone number, unless you have a direct line or a voice mailbox, or don't care if your employer discovers you are job hunting.

■ After finding even one spelling error, most employers will discard your résumé. Don't trust computerized programs to check the spelling on your résumé. They won't catch homonyms, for example. Don't trust yourself, either. Have someone else review the résumé for spelling and grammatical errors.

■ Should you list hobbies and interests? Recent college grads would do well to list them so that an employer gets a well-rounded picture. Some extracurricular activities can give any résumé a boost. Volunteer work, for example, indicates community involvement, and playing team sports shows an ability to work well in a group. At very least, say experts, the information gives employers a hook for an interview conversation.

EXPERT SOURCES

PICK A PARAGON OF PERFECTION

Writing a résumé is fairly formulaic. Career counselor Lloyd Raines and other experts urge résumé writers to leaf through books that provide good sample résumés and find one to emulate. The following are among the best:

TRASHPROOF RÉSUMÉS: YOUR GUIDE TO CRACKING THE JOB MARKET
by Timothy D. Haft (Random House/Princeton Review, 1995)
■ Sample résumés galore, along with tips to keep yours out of a hiring manager's recycling bin.

THE RÉSUMÉ GUIDE FOR WOMEN OF THE 90'S
by Kim Marino (Ten Speed Press, 1996)

■ The author offers actual résumés from the files of her company, Just Resumes, based in Santa Barbara, Calif. A companion book, *The College Student's Résumé Guide*, is a good resource for recent grads.

RÉSUMÉ POWER: SELLING YOURSELF ON PAPER
by Tom Washington (Mt. Vernon Press, 1996)
■ Not limited to paper

résumés, this book includes tips for compiling an effective résumé for use on the Internet, along with samples of electronic résumés.

ENCYCLOPEDIA OF JOB-WINNING RÉSUMÉS
by Myra Fournier (Round-Lake, 1996)
■ Sample résumés for just about any professional field, from engineering to the publishing world.

PAY & PERKS

SALARIES
▼

ARE YOU READY FOR A RAISE?

Companies are still tightfisted but you can fatten your paycheck

Today's economy seems tailor-made for rewarding workers with generous raises: The labor market is tight, consumer confidence is rising, and anxieties over downsizing and job security are receding. So, why are healthy merit raises becoming as obso-

FACT FILE:

GET TO WORK

■ *Chief executives got a 54 percent pay raise in 1996 compared to 3 percent for the average factory worker.*

■ *How long would a hot dog vendor at Disneyland have to work to earn what Disney CEO Michael Eisner made in 1996? The answer: 17,852 years.*

SOURCE: AFL–CIO (http://www.paywatch.org)

lete as manual typewriters? The answer points to a radical change in the ways companies are compensating workers.

First, a look at the raises picture. Average increases came to 4.1 percent in 1996, according to consulting firm William M. Mercer Inc. Some sectors, such as retailing and services, were more generous to their workers; others, like the mining, transportation, and utilities industries, were downright miserly. But even the highest increases—4.5 percent in retailing—were a far cry from the 5.5 percent hikes common in 1990. The scenario for the future appears equally grim: A survey of more than 2,500 companies conducted by Mercer found that pay increases will remain at 4.1 percent for 1997, making it the fifth year in which average salary increases have fallen below 5 percent. Newer members of the workforce may have trouble recalling the last time there were double-digit salary hikes: They occurred in 1981, when raises averaged more than 10 percent.

Why are companies still stingy after all these years? The corporate explanations for stagnating wages are depressingly familiar: domestic and foreign competition, and a shifting of more of the burden for rising health-care costs to employees. These factors temper the wage pressures that would normally build as unemployment falls. Actually, though, the low-raise trend reflects more than economics. It points to major changes in compensation patterns that are sweeping corporate

EXPERT TIPS

BEST WAYS TO GET THAT RAISE

In this era of downsizing, the last thing most people want to do is risk their job by asking for a raise. While it is never possible to predict exactly how your boss will react, there are a few mistakes you want to make sure to avoid. Alisa Mosley, director of Career Connections at the University of South Carolina, offers some tips for employees looking to increase their take-home pay.

■ **TIMING IS EVERYTHING**
Don't ask for more money when your firm has just lost a major contract. Similarly, if your company has gone through difficult times, downsizing, or just released earnings that are down, you'd do better holding off. If you have recently done something that wasn't particularly positive, you wouldn't want to call attention to yourself, either.

If you work for a large organization that has a formal human resources policy, probably the best time to ask for a raise is at your performance review. If you're working for a small company without a structured policy, the best time to approach your boss is when you've done something that's really had a positive impact on

the organization (e.g., you've made a big sale, brought in a new client, implemented a new computer system, etc.).

■ **DO YOUR HOMEWORK**
If you really feel that you're being underpaid compared with others doing the same work, get some general salary information for that position that you could quote—professional associations publish salary surveys and state employment services also publish statistics. But keep in mind that salaries for the same position can vary from place to place. So the more localized the information, the better. Don't try to find out how much your coworkers are being paid if your company prohibits this practice.

■ **DON'T TAKE A NEGATIVE APPROACH**
When enumerating the reasons why you deserve a raise, note accomplishments, not sacrifices made. Don't assume that you deserve a raise just because you've been there a long time or because someone else got a raise. You need to be able to demonstrate your contribution and worth to an organization.

■ **AVOID BLACKMAIL**
Be assertive, but not aggressive. Clearly state what you want and why you deserve it. If you use an ultimatum as part of your raise negotiation, you need to be prepared to follow through. Don't threaten to quit unless you are willing to walk out the door.

America. "Companies are looking for other ways to reward employees rather than adding to base pay," says Mary Lowe, marketing coordinator at Mercer. "They are getting creative with lump-sum bonuses."

Some employers are trying to compensate for stagnant salaries by improving working conditions. For example, many are offering more flexible time schedules. Nearly 50 percent of companies are considering flex

time, up from the 45 percent that do so currently. One of every five employers is considering offering workers the opportunity to telecommute, up from 15 percent in an earlier survey.

But the biggest change in the workplace is the rise of so-called alternative compensation schemes. These plans run the gamut from onetime bonuses to a range of merit-based and incentive-based programs. About

WHY YOU BOTH NEED TO WORK

Salaries have barely budged, but living costs have exploded.

In 84 percent of American households, both husband and wife work outside the home. In most cases, that second paycheck is not just a luxury—it's needed to keep up with life's rising major expenses, which have shot up even faster than the paychecks of top male executives. The median income of families rose only 8.4 percent in real terms between 1975 and 1995, according to Census Bureau data, even though women more than doubled their time in the workforce. By comparison, the cost of living has gone through the roof.

On top of the huge income and cost disparities, two-career families also face a penalty in their paychecks, reports *Fortune* magazine. Two management professors, Joy Schneer at Ryder University in New Jersey and Frieda Reitman at Pace University, studied 236 male managers in 1993. All were married with children. The researchers found that, on average, the men married to women who worked full-time or part-time earned 32 percent less than men married to non-working women.

Here's how some everyday expenses have risen within the last 20 years.

■ UP AND UP

Percentage increase in the inflation-adjusted costs of major living expenses between 1975 and 1995.

TAXES	30.2
NEW HOUSE	30.9
NEW CAR	65.8
PUBLIC COLLEGE TUITION	36.4
PRIVATE COLLEGE TUITION	66.5
DAYCARE	202.2
MEDIAN FAMILY INCOME	8.4

61 percent of large and medium-sized companies now offer some kind of variable pay, such as profit-sharing and bonus awards, up from 47 percent in 1990, according to consultants Hewitt Associates. The upshot: Smart employees hankering for fatter paychecks will have to perform big. Bonuses will be tied directly to their contributions to the company's return on equity or productivity gains, for example. Nor can workers rest on their laurels. Employees will be expected to re-earn rewards by meeting performance targets that rise each year. The strategies keep base pay low, but they also allow recognition of achievements that improve the bottom line. And the new incentives can be a way to wangle a bigger paycheck, even if the amount isn't guaranteed from year to year.

When it comes to getting ahead in today's business world, workers are faced with several options. One is to look for companies with beefy incentive programs in industries with high labor demands and above-average growth. Not surprisingly, prospects for a raise are higher in fields that are booming, such as telecommunications, computers, nursing, systems analysis, law, financial management, medicine, and marketing. Jobs in these fields are expected to pay above-average raises, with some high-tech professions hitting hikes of 6 to 7 percent, according to economists at *Business Week*. Steer clear of jobs in government and education, however, where raises are expected to grow a puny 3.5 percent.

Another option is to pursue opportunities in areas of the country where labor is in demand, such as the Midwest. A new study by consulting firm Challenger, Gray & Christmas, identifies the states that have the lowest rates of unemployment nationwide. The top 10 states are: Nebraska, Utah, South Dakota, North Dakota, New Hampshire, Iowa, Minnesota, Missouri, Wisconsin, and Kansas.

WHAT 100 OCCUPATIONS PAY

Updated every two years by the Bureau of Labor Statistics, the Occupational Outlook Handbook *is a treasure trove of useful information. The book covers the training and education needed, earnings, working conditions, and employment prospects for jobs from accountant to zoologist. Below are the salaries of 100 occupations from that book. In real life, of course, salaries can vary considerably by region, level of experience, and other factors, but the list does give a good comparison of average incomes.*

TITLE	NO. OF JOBS	STARTING SALARY	MEDIAN SALARY[1]	TOP SALARY
■ **EXECUTIVE, ADMINISTRATIVE, AND MANAGERIAL OCCUPATIONS**				
ACCOUNTANT	962,000	$27,900 yr.	$25,400–$77,200 yr.	$84,500 yr.
FUNERAL DIRECTORS	26,000	N/A	$44,062–$62,506 yr.	N/A
HOTEL MANAGERS	105,000	N/A	$57,000 yr.	$81,000 yr.
INSPECTORS	157,000	$18,700–$41,000 yr.	$26,630–$62,970 yr.	N/A
ADVERTISING AND MARKETING MANAGERS	461,000	$22,000 yr.	$44,000 yr.	$98,000+ yr.
PERSONNEL MANAGERS	513,000[3]	$25,800–$38,700 yr.	$25,000–$52,800	N/A
RESTAURANT MANAGERS[2]	526,500	N/A	$28,600 yr.	$45,000+ yr.
EXECUTIVE CHEFS	526,500	N/A	$37,000 yr.	$43,000+ yr.
■ **PROFESSIONAL SPECIALTY OCCUPATIONS**				
ENGINEERS	1,327,000	$34,100–$55,300 yr.	$46,600 yr.	$105,700 yr.
ARCHITECTS	91,000	$24,700 yr.	$38,900–$50,000 yr.	$110,000+ yr.
ACTUARY	17,000	$36,000 yr.	$46,600–$72,700 yr.	$96,000 yr.
SYSTEMS ANALYSTS[3]	828,000	$35,000–$54,000 yr.	$44,000 yr.	$69,400+ yr.
MATHEMATICIANS	14,000	$30,300–$35,600 yr.	$35,000–$52,500 yr.	N/A
STATISTICIANS	14,000	N/A	$56,890–$60,510 yr.	N/A
BIOLOGICAL SCIENTISTS	118,000	$22,900–$48,000 yr.	$37,500 yr.	$73,900+ yr.
CHEMISTS	97,000	$29,300–$52,900 yr.	$45,400–$66,000 yr.	N/A
METEOROLOGISTS	6,600	$22,000–$37,000 yr.	$50,540 yr.	N/A
ASTRONOMERS AND PHYSICISTS	20,000	N/A	$64,000	$77,000
LAWYERS	656,000	$37,000–$80,000+ yr.	$115,000 yr.	$1 million+ yr.
ECONOMISTS	48,000	$27,600 yr.	$70,000 yr.	$95,000 yr
PSYCHOLOGISTS	144,000	N/A[4]	$26,000–$58,000 yr.	N/A
URBAN PLANNERS	29,000	$28,300 yr.	$30,000–$42,000	$63,000 yr.
HUMAN SERVICES WORKERS	168,000	$13,000–$20,000 yr.	$18,000–$27,000 yr.	N/A
SOCIAL WORKERS	557,000	N/A	$17,500–$30,000 yr.	$44,000 yr.
PROTESTANT MINISTERS	300,000	N/A	$40,000 yr.	N/A
RABBIS	4,225	N/A	$38,000–$62,000 yr.	N/A
ROMAN CATHOLIC PRIESTS	51,000	N/A	$29,000	N/A
ARCHIVISTS	19,000	$18,700–$41,100 yr.	$50,000	$100,000
LIBRARIANS	148,000	$28,300 yr.	$35,000–$58,200 yr.	N/A
ELEMENTARY SCHOOL TEACHERS	1.6 million	$20,000–$25,000 yr.	$36,400	N/A

■ EXPERT LIST

TITLE	NO. OF JOBS	STARTING SALARY	MEDIAN SALARY[1]	TOP SALARY
DENTISTS	164,000	N/A	$97,450–$132,500 yr.	N/A
PHYSICIANS	539,000	N/A	$156,000	N/A
VETERINARIANS	56,000	$30,694	$59,188 yr.	N/A
DIETITIANS	53,000	N/A	$29,600–$41,600 yr.	N/A
OCCUPATIONAL THERAPISTS	54,000	N/A	$39,634 yr.	$49,392 yr.
PHYSICAL THERAPISTS	102,000	N/A	$37,596 yr.	$61,776+ yr.
PHYSICIAN ASSISTANTS	56,000	$44,176	$53,284 yr.	N/A
REGISTERED NURSES	1,906,000	N/A	$682 wk.	$1,005 wk.
SPEECH-LANGUAGE PATHOLOGISTS	85,000	N/A	$693 wk.	N/A
WRITERS and EDITORS	272,000	$18,000	$30,000–$60,000 yr.	N/A
PHOTOGRAPHERS	139,000	N/A	$25,100 yr.	$46,300+ yr
DANCERS	24,000	$475 wk.	$610 wk.	N/A

■ TECHNICIAN AND RELATED SUPPORT OCCUPATIONS

TITLE	NO. OF JOBS	STARTING SALARY	MEDIAN SALARY	TOP SALARY
EKG TECHNICIANS	15,000	N/A	$18,396 yr.	$22,985 yr.
EMERGENCY MEDICAL TECHNICIANS	138,000	$19,919–$23,861 yr.	$23,330–$33,962	N/A
NUCLEAR MEDICINE TECHNICIANS	13,000	N/A	$35,027	$41,598
AIRCRAFT PILOTS	90,000	$13,000–$27,900 yr.	$37,500–$81,000 yr.	$200,000
AIR TRAFFIC CONTROLLERS	23,000	$22,700	$59,800	N/A
COMPUTER PROGRAMMERS	537,000	$25,000–$54,000	$38,400 yr.	$60,600+ yr.
ENGINEERING TECHNICIANS	685,000	$16,590 yr.	$34,530–$51,060 yr.	N/A
PARALEGALS	110,000	$14,000–$32,000 yr.	$31,700	N/A

■ MARKETING AND SALES OCCUPATIONS

TITLE	NO. OF JOBS	STARTING SALARY	MEDIAN SALARY	TOP SALARY
CASHIERS	3,005,000	$4.25 hr.	$228 wk.	$421+ wk.
COUNTER AND RENTAL CLERKS	341,000	$4.25 hr.	$266 wk.	$586+ wk.
INSURANCE AGENTS and BROKERS	418,000	N/A	$31,620 yr.	$69,900+ yr.
REAL ESTATE AGENTS	374,000	N/A	$593 wk.	$1,447+ wk.
SERVICE SALES REPRESENTATIVES[4]	612,000	$24,600–$31,600 yr.	$28,800–$32,900 yr.	N/A
TRAVEL AGENTS	122,000	N/A	$21,300 yr.	$38,400+ yr.

■ ADMINISTRATIVE SUPPORT OCCUPATIONS

TITLE	NO. OF JOBS	STARTING SALARY	MEDIAN SALARY	TOP SALARY
BANK TELLERS	559,000	N/A	$15,300 yr.	$24,200 yr.
COMPUTER OPERATORS	259,000	$20,000–$31,500 yr.	$21,300 yr.	$39,500+ yr.
GENERAL OFFICE CLERKS	2,946,000	$13,000 yr.	$19,300 yr.	$32,200+ yr.
MAIL CLERKS	127,000	N/A	$322 wk.	$437 wk.
MAIL CARRIERS	320,000	$25,240 yr.	$34,566 yr.	N/A
SECRETARIES	3.3 million+	N/A	$26,700 yr.	$38,400 yr.
STENOGRAPHERS, COURT REPORTERS, MEDICAL TRANSCRIPTIONISTS[5]	105,000	N/A	$399 wk.	$790+ wk.
TEACHER AIDES	932,000	N/A	$8.29–$8.77 hr.	N/A
TELEPHONE OPERATORS	310,000	N/A	$398 wk.	$604+ wk.
DATA ENTRY KEYERS	1.1 million	N/A	$17,600 yr.	N/A

■ EXPERT LIST

TITLE	NO. OF JOBS	STARTING SALARY	MEDIAN SALARY[1]	TOP SALARY
■ SERVICE OCCUPATIONS				
CORRECTIONAL OFFICERS	310,000	$19,100 yr.	$22,900 yr.	$57,100 yr.
FIREFIGHTERS	284,000	N/A	$630 wk.	$975+ wk.
POLICE OFFICERS	682,000	N/A	$34,000–$42,800 yr.	$62,100 yr.
SHORT–ORDER COOKS	760,000	N/A	$6.50 hr.	N/A
WAITERS	1.8 million+	N/A	$256 wk.	$430+ wk.
BARTENDERS	373,000	N/A	$299 wk.	$514+ wk.
DENTAL ASSISTANTS	190,000	N/A	$329 wk.	N/A
MEDICAL ASSISTANTS	206,000	N/A	$7.51–$13.12 hr.	N/A
OCCUPATIONAL THERAPY ASSISTANTS	16,000	N/A	$25,300	N/A
PHYSICAL THERAPY ASSISTANTS and AIDES	78,000	$22,500 yr.	$24,000	N/A
COSMETOLOGISTS	709,000	N/A	$14,800	N/A
PRESCHOOL TEACHERS	1 million+	N/A	$260 wk.	$430+ wk.
FLIGHT ATTENDANTS	105,000	$12,700 yr.	N/A	$40,000 yr.
HOMEMAKER–HOME HEALTH AIDES	598,000	$4.90–$6.86 hr.	$5.69–$8.11	N/A
JANITORS	3,168,000	N/A	$293 wk.	$407+ wk.
■ MECHANICS, INSTALLERS, AND REPAIRERS				
ELEVATOR INSTALLERS	24,000	$410–$574 wk	$820 wk.	$923 wk.
AUTOMOTIVE BODY REPAIRERS	209,000	N/A	$456 wk.	$790+ wk.
AIRCRAFT MECHANICS	119,000	$8.70–$13.56 hr.	$36,858 yr.	$53,872 + yr.
VENDING MACHINE REPAIRERS	19,000	N/A	$8.30 hr.	$22 hr.
■ CONSTRUCTION TRADES OCCUPATIONS				
CARPENTERS[6]	992,000	N/A	$424 wk.	$785 + wk
CARPET INSTALLERS	66,000	N/A	$412 wk.	$751+ wk.
ELECTRICIANS	528,000	N/A	$574 wk.	$971+ wk.
PAINTERS[6]	439,000	N/A	$381 wk.	$721+ wk.
PLUMBERS[6]	375,000	N/A	$530 wk.	$970+ wk.
■ PRODUCTION OCCUPATIONS				
BUTCHERS	351,043	N/A	$329 wk.	$702+ wk.
JEWELERS	30,000	N/A	$400 wk.	N/A
MACHINISTS	376,000	N/A	$520 wk.	$880+ wk.
TOOL AND DIE MAKERS	142,000	N/A	$660 wk.	$1,130+ wk.
POWER PLANT OPERATORS	43,000	N/A	$857 wk.	N/A
TREATMENT PLANT OPERATORS	95,000	N/A	$27,100 yr.	$42,100 yr.
PRINTING PRESS OPERATORS	244,000	N/A	$432 wk.	$787+ wk.
BUS DRIVERS	568,000	N/A	$401 wk.	$758+ wk.
TRUCK DRIVERS	2,900,000	N/A	$8.06–$14.87 hr.	N/A

NOTES: **1.** In general, employees of the federal government earn less than those in the private sector. **2.** Includes assistant managers; represents all restaurant and food service managers. **3.** Includes computer scientists. **4.** Earnings depend on performance. Some sales reps are paid a straight salary, while others work solely on commission. Incentive pay can add up to 75 percent of base salary. **5.** Court reporters generally earn higher salaries. **6.** Excluding the self-employed, who sometimes earn more.

SOURCE: *Occupational Outlook Handbook,* Bureau of Labor Statistics, Spring 1996.

MORE CHOICES, LESS COVERAGE

Here's the deal: You get lots of options but lots more of the cost

The news about employee benefits will hardly seem like news to the average American worker: benefits have been getting skimpier over the past few years. A 1995 survey of 929 firms by the U.S. Chamber of Commerce found that employee benefits decreased by 0.8 percent in 1994 measured by dollars spent per employee per year. That is in contrast to an 8.6 percent increase posted in 1994.

The most striking trend concerns medical benefits: Most employers decreased their share of medical costs per employee in 1994 after a significant increase in 1993. This was largely due to employers passing more of the cost on to workers, and more employees entering managed care programs. To slash medical costs, smaller firms, in particular, are increasingly joining co-ops for health insurance. Overall, all medically related benefits, including health insurance, disability, dental insurance, and wellness programs, decreased $241 per employee in 1994, after increasing $491 the previous year. Meanwhile, corporate payments to pension accounts have grown.

The extent to which employees have been losing benefits, of course, depends on where they work. Generally, large firms provide more benefits than small firms. Also, benefits vary from industry to industry. In 1994, manufacturing firms paid, on average, $16,253 per employee in benefits; nonmanufacturing firms just $14,333.

The best advice for benefit-hungry employees: Go west. Employers in the western states are more generous than those in the Rust Belt. Companies in the western United States had 43.4 percent of payroll going to benefits in 1994. Companies in the East North-Central United States (Illinois, Indiana, Michigan, Ohio, and Wisconsin) spend just 38.5 percent of payroll costs on benefits. What accounted for the difference? Many workers in the West are younger and more mobile, the Chamber of Commerce survey found, and better benefits attract better workers.

Chances are your company—whether it's large or small—now offers you as many benefit choices as there are items at the salad bar in the company cafeteria. Here are some of the current benefit choices.

■ **PENSION AND INVESTMENT PLANS.** The trend is toward defined contribution plans, in which employer contributions are matched by the employee, and away from traditional defined benefit plans, which put a greater emphasis on the employer's guarantee of a retirement income. Defined contribution plans—of which 401(k)s are the most common—can be taken with you if you change jobs or start your own business. New federal legislation is designed to make retirement benefits more portable. Also, many companies, concerned about their future liability for retired employees who are financially unstable, are offering investment education seminars and a greater choice of investment plans.

■ **HEALTH CARE.** More companies are moving away from traditional fee-for-service plans and toward managed care. Nearly two-thirds of companies were following this trend in 1995, according to *Money* magazine. But many firms are also offering a wider selection of managed care options and helping their workers to choose the plans that are best for them. As more fee-for-service doctors join managed care plans, employees in traditional health programs might find they can save money by changing to an HMO—without necessarily losing the physicians they are familiar with.

■ **LIFE INSURANCE.** The main differences are between plans that are fully employer-paid, and those that depend on employee contributions. Some companies offer a combination of both. Most core plans provide a cash payout equal to one times the employee's most recent annual salary, sometimes with a cash maximum.

■ **DISABILITY INSURANCE.** Employers differ in their formulas for calculating short-term disability payments. Some companies use the "salary continuation method" in which employees receive their entire salary (or a percentage of their salary depending on the years they have worked) for a defined period of time before long-term disability benefits kick in. Other employers use the "accrual" method. Your benefits are based on the amount of time you've worked for the company. Unlike other benefits, however, this one is crucial for all jobholders. Workers should consider buying supplemental coverage if their disability benefit will not replace at least 60 percent of their current compensation to age 65.

■ **FLEXIBLE BENEFITS.** Increasingly, you can order your benefits à la carte. Each employee receives a certain number of credits to use as he or she sees fit. For instance, you may be able to "buy" additional vacation days with part of your salary, "sell" credits for cash, or use them to purchase extra life insurance or health insurance. Employees covered under their spouse's health plan might want to cash in their own health benefits and invest the money in a company stock purchase plan or some other savings options. An increasing number of companies also let you put a percentage of your pretax salary in "spending accounts" for health or "dependent care." Flexible schedules are also on the rise, as is the number of companies offering emergency and "sick-child" centers, *Money* found. And a number of firms are now offering cash or benefit credits for employees who quit smoking or lose weight.

RELOCATION PERKS WORTH THE MOVE
Some factors to consider if your company wants you to transfer

Long gone is the organization man who dutifully accepted a company transfer and whose family followed faithfully behind. Companies are increasingly aware that relocation is a burden on workers: spouses are yanked from careers, children from schools, and the family from its community. A study by the Conference Board, a New York research firm, shows that most workers won't take it anymore. More than 50 percent of employers said employees have turned down relocation offers, citing concerns about children and spouses.

If relocation is in the cards for you, be sure your employer's offer is worth the move. Compare your company's perks with this list of what other employers are offering, based on a 1996 survey of 196 firms by Atlas Van Lines, the moving company:

■ More than 50 percent of companies allow employees to take two expense-paid trips to find housing in the new location; 42 percent let the spouse take two house-hunting trips; 47 percent pay for five to nine days of house-hunting trips.

■ Nearly 70 percent pay all fees associated with the purchase or sale of a house; 34 percent purchase the employee's former residence; 70 percent pay a lease-termination penalty; 41 percent pay a lump sum for temporary living and house-hunting expenses.

■ More than 70 percent pay to move an unlimited weight of the employee's belongings; 92 percent pay a moving company to do all the packing; 43 percent cover storage of some possessions.

■ Nearly 30 percent of companies help spouses find jobs at the new location. Employers either find work for them with other companies or pay job-hunting fees.

IS YOUR COMPANY FAMILY-FRIENDLY?

Some progressive employers can help you juggle kids and work

Many employers tout themselves as being family-friendly, but what does that really mean? Here Barbara Reisman, executive director of the New York–based Child Care Action Committee, which has been fighting for family rights within the workplace for more than a decade, answers questions about finding and securing family-friendly benefits.

■ What are the most important benefits you should look for in an employer?

The following benefits are becoming common in the more family-friendly companies, and are not unreasonable requests.

- ■ Flexible work time or work space (allowing parents to work at home).
- ■ Part-time work options with benefits.
- ■ Paid parental leave.
- ■ Child-care support, whether it be on- or near-site child care, financial support for employees' child-care needs, emergency or backup child care, before- and after-school care, or contributions to local child-care facilities.
- ■ Information and resources to help employees find dependent care.
- ■ Paid sick-child days (not vacation or employees' own sick days).
- ■ Phase-back work option for new moms (allowing employees to return to work part-time or work from home).

■ Legally, what does a company have to provide?

Under the Family and Medical Leave Act (FMLA), companies that employ 50 or more have to provide unpaid leave, with a job guarantee and continued benefits for 12 weeks in the case of a birth, adoption, or extended illness of child, or if your spouse or other dependent is chronically ill.

■ What if I work for a small company?

While not required by law, many small companies offer family-friendly benefits with little difficulty. One of the most important and cost-effective things a small company can do is look for ways to improve child-care programs already in operation. Small companies can make contributions to local child-care providers, and then arrange for their employees to receive special rates, etc.

Pretax set-asides for dependent care is another easy thing for small companies to do because it doesn't cost them any money. Each month, employees can set aside a certain amount of their pretax paycheck to be used for dependent care. They are then reimbursed at a later date.

■ What can you do to make your company more family-friendly if quitting and looking for another employer isn't an option?

Talk to other employees and find out if they're facing the same issues. Find out what your employer's competition offers. As a group, make a list of concerns and suggestions. Present your requests directly to your employer or human resources person.

It's always best to present your concerns in a nonconfrontational manner. Illustrate how these benefits will help the employer and employees alike. Get the company to recognize that it's in both of your interests to address these needs.

■ How do I do that?

A number of recent studies have established that employees who worry about family obligations or child care are not productive workers. Employees who must take sick days or leave work early because they don't have reliable child care cost employers time and money.

At Du Pont, for example, employees can participate in corporate-sponsored work-life programs that ease some of their family and child-care burdens. Du Pont's programs

THE 10 BEST COMPANIES FOR WORKING MOMS

Employers who welcome each new kid in the family as if their own

Working Mother magazine annually compiles a list of the 100 best companies for working mothers. The magazine selects companies based on a number of criteria, including pay, opportunities for women to advance, child care, and other family-friendly benefits such as job sharing and flexible hours.

Benefits that were once considered revolutionary, such as job sharing and sick-child days, have become commonplace in many work settings—as the stiff competition for the *Working Mother* list illustrates. A trend at the very best companies is providing financial aid for employees to adopt children. The top 10 employers in the magazine's 11th annual survey (presented in alphabetical order here) welcome each new kid into the family as if it were their own:

Barnett Banks, *Jacksonville, Fla.*
Eli Lilly & Co., *Indianapolis, Ind.*
Hewlett-Packard, *Palo Alto, Calif.*
IBM, *Armonk, N.Y.*
Johnson & Johnson, *New Brunswick, N.J.*
MBNA America Bank, N.A., *Newark, Del.*
Merck & Co., Inc., *Whitehouse Sta., N.J.*
Nationsbank Corporation, *Charlotte, N.C.*
Patagonia, Inc., *Ventura, Calif.*
Xerox Corporation, *Stamford, Conn.*

All the companies on the *Working Mother* top 10 list, with the exception of Eli Lilly, have appeared in the magazine's previous top 10 lists. In fact, IBM has been something of a pioneer in family friendliness among corporations—this is its 9th straight year on the list.

SOURCE: *Working Mother* (October 1996).

---

include a program that links employees to emergency child care and reimbursement of dependent care expenses if an employee has an overnight business trip. A recent study shows that more than 60 percent of employees surveyed said the work-life programs strengthened their relationship with their employer, 75 percent said the service helps their companies retain valuable employees, and employees who use the work-life programs are the most committed employees in the company.

■ If a fellow employee is allowed flexible hours, does the company have an obligation to make me a similar offer?

No, but companies tend to be concerned about equity issues. Consult with the employee who has flexible hours and find out more about his or her situation. Then explain to your employer that since flexible time has made the other employee more productive, it's bound to have the same effect on you. Do your research and have your case well thought out before you present anything to your boss.

■ Do fathers have to be extended the same benefits as mothers?

The Family and Medical Leave Act applies to both fathers and mothers, and has to be adhered to in a nondiscriminatory manner. Beyond that, companies have no obligation to provide fathers with flex-time or phase-back time after a new baby. Fathers can get those benefits, but they must speak up first.

■ How do I find out more about child care and other family-friendly initiatives?

Call Child Care Aware at ☎ 800-424-2246 to find out about resources and referral agencies in your area. Child Care Aware can also tell you which organizations provide useful publications on a variety of child-care topics.

▼

HOW TO GET YOUR JOB BACK

What to do if you need to take time off to care for a loved one

All politicians say they are pro-family and now they have a law to prove it. The 1993 Family and Medical Leave Act (FMLA) stipulates that all government agencies and all private employers with more than 50 employees must provide up to 12 weeks of unpaid, job-protected leave for an employee for any of the following reasons: the birth or adoption of a child; the care of an immediate relative with a serious health condition; or medical leave for the employee if he or she is unable to work because of a serious health condition. Here, from the Labor Department's *Compliance Guide to the Family and Medical Leave Act*, are answers to some of the most commonly asked questions about the new law.

■ Does the law guarantee paid time off?

FMLA leave is generally unpaid. However, in certain circumstances the use of accrued paid leave—such as vacation or sick leave—may be substituted for the unpaid leave required by the law. FMLA is intended to encourage generous family and medical leave policies. For this reason, the law does not diminish more generous existing leave policies or laws.

■ Does FMLA leave have to be taken in whole days or weeks, or in one continuous block?

The FMLA permits leave for birth or placement for adoption or foster care to be taken intermittently, in blocks of time or by reducing the normal weekly or daily work schedule—subject to employer approval. Leave for a serious health condition may be taken intermittently when "medically necessary."

■ Are there employees not covered by the law?

Yes. About 60 percent of U.S. workers (and about 95 percent of U.S. employers) are not covered. To be eligible for FMLA benefits, an employee must: (1) work for a covered employer; (2) have worked for the employer for at least a year; (3) have worked at least 1,250 hours over the prior 12 months; and (4) work at a location where at least 50 employees are employed by the employer within 75 miles.

■ What do I have to do to request FMLA leave from my employer?

You may be required to provide your employer with 30 days' advance notice when the need for leave is "foreseeable." When the need for the leave cannot be foreseen, you must give your employer notice as soon as "practicable." You may need to submit documentation from the health-care provider treating you or your immediate family member.

■ Will I be allowed to return to the same job?

Ordinarily you will be restored to the same position you held prior to the leave, with the same pay and benefits, if the position remains available. You may be restored to an "equivalent" position rather than to the position you held before taking the leave, if the previous position is not available. An equivalent position must have pay, benefits, and terms and conditions of employment equivalent to the original job.

■ Do I lose all benefits when I take unpaid FMLA leave?

Your employer is required to maintain health insurance coverage on the same terms it was provided before the leave began. In addition, the use of FMLA leave cannot result in the loss of any employment benefit that accrued prior to the start of your leave.

■ What if I believe my employer is violating the law?

You can file, or have someone file on your behalf, a complaint with the Employment Standards Administration, Wage and Hour Division, or you can file a private lawsuit.

SMART MOVES

CLOTHING: How to dress on dress-down days, PAGE 290   **EXPERT TIPS:** A top headhunter on how to get noticed, PAGE 292   **LEADERSHIP:** Success may be in the books, PAGE 293   **BOSSES:** Dealing with office bullies, PAGE 295   **STRESS:** Ways to beat burnout, PAGE 297   **ENTREPRENEURS:** What it takes to be your own boss, PAGE 299   **START-UPS:** Online help for setting up shop, PAGE 301   **HOME BUSINESSES:** The hottest home-based businesses, PAGE 302

GETTING AHEAD
▼

WHAT COLOR IS YOUR NEW CAREER?

A guidance guru's secrets for making a successful switch

The typical American worker can expect to have two or three different careers during his professional life. In light of the recent savage restructuring of corporate America, that estimate appears to be far too conservative, say employment experts. So, what's the best way to make a smooth transition to a new career? We asked Richard Bolles, author of the wildly popular *What Color Is Your Parachute?* (Ten Speed Press, 1997), a sort of bible for first-time job seekers and seasoned career switchers.

■ **How do I know when I'm ready for a career change, and not just bored in my current job?**

You can determine that by asking yourself the following questions:
1. Do I like my present boss or bosses, and do I enjoy working for them?
2. Do I like my coworkers, and enjoy working with them?
3. Do I like what I do—the tools I work

with, the product I produce, the information I disseminate, or the people I am trying to help?
4. Am I using the skills I most love to use?
5. Do I really like the field I am in?

If your answer to either of the first two is "No," you should consider changing your job, though not necessarily your career. But if your answer to any of the last three questions is "No," you probably need to think about changing careers.

■ **Let's say I know I want to make a career change but don't know what I want to do.**

There are two ways to solve this common puzzle. First, think about all the people you know or see in a given week. Ask yourself if any of them has a job you would really like to have. If so, what is that job? Second, identify your favorite skills and fields of interest. Your skills are verbs ending in "ing," such as "designing," "writing," "researching," "sewing," and the like. They are transferable from one field to another. Fields of interest are nouns, like "stamps," "computers," "gardens," "design," and "insurance." Your favorite transferable skills, plus your favorite fields of interest will define a new career.

■ **Once I've decided what I'd like to do, how do I find a job that matches my skills and interests?**

If you know the skills you'd like to use, and the field you'd like to be in, but are not clear

CLOTHES THAT WORK ON FRIDAYS

Ambitious employees are well aware of the dress code for climbing the corporate ladder—navy or gray suits for men, navy jackets and beige or gray skirts for women. But what is appropriate attire for casual dress days?

Image consultants say you shouldn't wear your regular office wardrobe on casual Fridays, otherwise, you jeopardize your everyday effectiveness. Besides, here's where you really get a chance to express your individuality. So, what do you don on dress-down day? Some expert tips:

■ Unless you work in an ultra-relaxed office, to be taken seriously, you should dress a notch more conservatively than your peers. Tip: Your sartorial model should be your boss or someone at least one level above you.

■ Your wardrobe should consist only of clothes made from natural fibers, such as cotton, wool, and linen. For shirts, chambray or oxford-cloth button-downs work for men and women. Tan or navy slacks in lightweight wools are good choices for both also.

■ Men should buy casual business wear in the same conservative men's stores they frequent for their regular business clothes. Women should follow their lead, buying from the ladies' departments of those same traditional stores.

■ Both men and women should keep a navy blazer on hand for an unexpected meeting or if a client drops by. Cashmere and gabardine are good fabrics for a blazer.

as to which career it all points to, there's an easy way to find out. Talk to people in the field. Make use of the Yellow Pages to contact them, if necessary. Ask what kinds of careers in that field require the skills you have identified as your favorites. Keep going, until you find some answers you like.

■ If I want to break into an entirely new field, where and how do I start a job search?

Once you have identified the career, talk to at least five people who are doing that work. Again, the Yellow Pages can help identify people in that line of work. Also, your local librarian can help you locate the associations of companies in that field and you can contact them. If you are skilled on the Internet, see what turns up in the way of news groups and other information about that career.

When talking to people in your targeted career, ask these four questions: How did you get your job? What do you like most about it? What do you like least? Who else would you recommend I talk to about this career? Since you're talking to workers and not employers, and you're asking them how they found their job, you'll get plenty of ideas about ways to find work in the field. If your source lives nearby and the career still interests you—and it might not—ask him if you can observe him at work for a day to see what the job involves in detail.

■ How much attention should I pay to career lists that point to the fastest-growing jobs, for example?

Let's look at such a list. [Editor's note: See our list, page 271.] According to the 1997 edition of my book, the fastest-growing occupations between now and 2005 are predicted to be:

Personal and home care aides, systems analysts, computer engineers, physical and corrective therapy assistants, electronic pagination systems workers, physical therapists, residential counselors, and human services workers. Anything there grab you? If so, great. But if not, let's note this simple fact: No two such lists agree because no one really knows which careers are going to grow the fastest. It's all guesswork.

What is the most challenging aspect of changing careers?

Most challenging is taking the time to identify your favorite skills and fields of interest. The process, if done right, takes a full weekend. Next comes taking the time to interview workers in your new career before going job hunting. Most people want to leap over these two essential preliminary steps. Consequently, their career change is often a sort of "out of the frying pan, into the fire" experience.

If I'm changing careers at midlife, how do I compete with younger candidates?

Know your skills better, know the field better, and be a harder worker. Come in earlier, stay later, miss fewer days. Finally, you have to be able to tell an employer why you can do the work better than the other candidates, whether they're younger or older. In short, spend more time preparing for a career change by doing an inventory of yourself and by doing informational interviews, before attempting to launch a new career.

Should I work with a career counselor? If so, what should I expect?

The rule is: don't rely just on the advice of well-meaning friends. Instead, master the process of changing careers through your own self-study course. Less than $20 for a helpful book may be all you need to spend. But if that doesn't work, look for other low-cost resources—seminars, testing, counseling—available through a community college, library, or chamber of commerce.

Only when you have exhausted these sources should you turn to a paid career counselor. When you do, find one who charges by the hour. (Fees are generally the same as those of a competent therapist.) You should not have to sign anything before you begin counseling and you should be able to end the hourly meetings at any time. The counselor's stated goal should be to teach you how to change careers yourself, rather than trying to do it all for you. Visit at least three counselors before choosing the one you feel is most competent.

What about using a headhunter?

Headhunters generally work for employers, who have hired them. They typically look for candidates who already work for organizations or companies and are tops in their field. A career-changer's chances of being of interest to a headhunter are slim. Still, it can't hurt to send your résumé to a headhunter, as long as it doesn't take too much of your time.

What if I identify a dream career but can't find a job in that field?

Your backup is to pick up your list of favorite skills and fields of interest, each ranked in order of preference. Show this list to everyone you know and ask them which careers or jobs the list might suggest to them. Then interview workers in the careers that interest you. Your dream may have more than one form, but you should never give up on that dream.

FACT FILE:

WHY YOU CAN'T WORK ON MONDAYS

■ *For many people, Monday is the least productive day of the week. Experts say it's only natural: workers are feeling the stress of having to return to work after a pleasurable weekend. What day is most productive? Tuesday, studies show. After that, the pre-weekend slump sets in and builds throughout the rest of the week.*

■ *The big surprise is that any work gets done at all. Every day, the average employee gets 3.18 phone calls, 13.6 e-mail messages, 8.8 fax documents, and 5.1 message slips, according to a Gallup poll.*

EXPERT Q & A

HOW TO GET YOUR HEAD HUNTED

A top headhunter on what it takes to get on a "most wanted" list

Headhunters prowl the corporate jungle, trying to lure the best and brightest managers and executives from one company to another. So why hasn't your phone rung with a juicy job offer? One of the nation's leading headhunters, Gerard Roche, has spent over 30 years at the New York City executive search firm of Heidrick & Struggles, Inc. His clients have included IBM, Kodak, and Westinghouse.

■ How do you get a headhunter's notice?

Do an extraordinary job at the job you're in, and get a track record where you get recognition. The thing that will get our attention is your reputation at what you're doing in front of you. Nothing else is even nearly as important. If you succeed to a high extent, we'll sniff you out.

One way to get noticed is to be active in your industry—attend association meetings, give a speech, write an article, or get a top newsmagazine to quote you. Do whatever you can to be unique and let people know you're a leader. A strong reputation and résumé are mostly gained through individual effort, not public relations departments.

■ Say you're ready to move on. Is it wise to approach a headhunter yourself?

This is a networking game. I get thousands of résumés a week, so just sending a résumé isn't the best move. If you want to approach a top headhunter, get somebody who you think knows him to recommend that he pay special attention to you. If you want to use a book to look up names, Jim Kennedy's *Getting Behind the Résumé—Interviewing Today's Candidates* (Prentice Hall, 1987) is as good as any.

■ If a headhunter calls, how forthcoming should you be?

It's strictly a matter of whether you're the one pursuing a job, or the one being pursued. If you're secure in a position with an established reputation and not looking for a job—which is the type of people we normally go after—listen, see what the person has to offer, then respond as you see fit and feel comfortable doing.

If you're looking for a job, never take a headhunter's call raw. Ask if you can call back; this gives you a chance to find out exactly who it is who's calling, then call back when it's convenient for you.

How forthcoming you are depends on how badly you're interested in a new job. Even if you're looking, you should still have a certain amount of detached interest.

■ Sure, headhunters are hired to search for CEOs. What if you're a smaller fish in the corporate pond?

It's simple—just do your job. If you excel, we'll pick you up on our screen. If you spend most of your time trying to get our attention, you're probably not going to get it.

EXPERT SOURCE

Down and out and looking for a new job? You may be red meat for headhunters. To find them, check out the *Directory of Executive Recruiters* (Kennedy Publications, $44.95), which provides information on search firms. *Executive Recruiter News* publishes a directory of 120 search firms that place executives temporarily ($24.95). For a copy of either publication, call ☎ 800–531–0007.

LEADERSHIP
▼

MANAGEMENT BY THE BOOK

Literary classics for a good read as well as a few leadership pointers

I f you thought reading Shakespeare was only for English literature students, you're in for a surprise. John K. Clemens, a professor of management at Hartwick College in Oneonta, N.Y., has been using literature, including Shakespeare, to teach managerial skills to business students. The literary case studies are now being used by about 70 business school professors across the country. Clemens, who is executive director of the Hartwick Humanities in Management Institute, recommends the following literary classics for managers in search of a good read as well as a few leadership pointers.

■ **HERMAN MELVILLE'S** *BILLY BUDD, SAILOR.* In this Melville novel, a leader must choose between adhering to a rigid organizational policy and doing what he believes is morally right. The case presents an opportunity to explore the problems that arise when company decisions are based on rules rather than circumstance, and understanding the difference between doing the right thing and doing things right. Also, nearly everyone can relate to the book's primary conflict: the effects of one coworker's dislike for another.

■ **JOHN MASEFIELD'S** *THE BIRD OF DAWNING.* Observe the birth of a leader, as protagonist Cyril Trewsbury is unexpectedly thrust into a position of power and must learn through trial and error which leadership techniques work best. The most important lessons here concern recognizing the ways in which one might transform one's vision into reality, and the critical but often unappreciated importance of challenging employees or coworkers to do more than even they thought possible.

■ **MARTIN LUTHER KING'S** *LETTER FROM A BIRMINGHAM JAIL.* This is a classic lesson in how language is a leader's most effective tool. King's masterful oratorical skills come across just as strongly on paper. He also reveals in great clarity his four steps for organizational change. This "recipe" can be used in any social setting including modern corporations.

■ **CHIEF JOSEPH.** In his writings, Native American leader Chief Joseph offers an in-depth look at three styles of leadership, the types of organizations they are associated with (bureaucratic, entrepreneurial, and integrative), and the problems and benefits unique to each of them. This reading offers one of the big lessons for survival in a changing business environment: A corporation ought to look more like a collection of tribes than a monolithic organization. With "tribalism" comes agility, common beliefs, "local" knowledge, and perhaps most important, respect for the individual.

■ **SHAKESPEARE'S** *HENRY IV AND HENRY V.* Shakespeare's exploration into the lives of these two kings (and their differing leadership styles) offers lessons on the emergence of a leader, important personal and political traits of leaders, and what works and what doesn't. To lead you must first be a follower. Prince Hal was a great follower, and, subsequently, as king he was a great leader.

■ **HOMER'S** *ILIAD.* This epic poem tells the story of the anger of the great warrior Achilles and the terrible consequences that his community (the Greek army) endured because of it. Clearly, the major figures in Homer's epic are driven by compelling needs and forces not immediately apparent. Once discovered, however, they help to reveal the inner workings of leadership in any setting.

■ **DAVID MAMET'S** *GLENGARRY GLEN ROSS.* This dark play presents a leader whom most readers will not admire. Yet he is in a difficult position, forced to pursue goals that may be unattainable, using an organization that is often untrustworthy and ineffectual. Analyzing him and the other characters in the play

MOVIES FOR MANAGERS

All it may take to learn how to be a leader is to plunk yourself down, pop in a video, and take in the show. Or so says John Clemens, who is studying 50 films for their potential to teach inspirational—or cautionary—tales about leadership under a grant from the W. K. Kellogg Foundation in Battle Creek, Michigan. Here, he gives a quick overview of the top five films with management lessons:

12 O'CLOCK HIGH
directed by Henry King, starring Gregory Peck and Hugh Marlowe. 1950.

■ This film dramatizes the impact of appropriate leadership style. Watch as two leaders use distinctly different approaches to try to rebuild a bomber group suffering from low morale and heavy losses. Note how one leader succeeds and the other fails.

LORD OF THE FLIES
directed by Peter Brook, starring James Aubrey and Tom Chapin. 1963.

■ Here, a fledgling leader grasps for group cohesion. His failure to coalesce his team resonates for anyone who has witnessed mediocre management. The compelling portrayal of this young leader's challenger shows how quickly a breakaway group can "kill" the organization.

12 ANGRY MEN
directed by Sidney Lumet, starring Jack Klugman, Henry Fonda, and Ed Begley, Sr. 1957.

■ One of the most important aspects of leadership ability is the capacity to sense others' actions. In this film, which shows a jury agonizing over the fate of an alleged murderer, students are asked to predict the order in which the 12 jurors change their votes from guilty to innocent. To do so, they must be astute observers of human behavior.

THE CAINE MUTINY
directed by Edward Dmytryk, starring Humphrey Bogart. 1954.

■ This film about the crew of a minesweeper, the USS *Caine*, provides key lessons in team building and group structure. See how difficult it is for leaders to gain compliance with their desires, let alone their orders. Watch the infamous Captain Queeg as he factionalizes his crew and turns their dislike to hate. This is the ultimate cautionary tale of leadership.

DEAD POETS SOCIETY
directed by Peter Weir, starring Robin Williams and Ethan Hawke. 1989.

■ No managerial task is more difficult than creating change. Here, a young English teacher at a straitlaced boys boarding school makes an ill-starred effort to move it from dictatorship to democracy, providing an unforgettable example of the challenge of change.

surprisingly reveals human qualities that students can identify with. Readers can evaluate the management strategies used in this organization and decide what, if anything, they have to do with the organization's fate.

■ **WILLIAM GOLDING'S** *LORD OF THE FLIES.* This story portrays leadership development and conflict among a group of boys marooned on a desert island. It also explores the alternative ways a subordinate leader can wrest control of the group from an elected leader. The story clearly demonstrates the importance of collaboration and compromise, rather than competition, in achieving organizational objectives.

BULLY BOSSES FROM HELL

*They tyrannize the workplace.
Here's how to escape their clutches*

The American workplace can be a brutal place. On any given day, according to Columbia University psychologist Harvey Hornstein, one in five people gets abused by a boss. Using questionnaires filled out by nearly 1,000 men and women over an eight-year period, Hornstein estimates that over 90 percent of U.S. workers experience some form of abusive behavior during their working life.

In his study of managerial abuse, *Brutal Bosses and Their Prey* (Riverhead Books, 1996), Hornstein discusses what separates "bully bosses" from those who are merely "tough, but fair" managers. Here he describes brutal bosses and how to deal with them.

■ **Are there any places where bully bosses tend to exist more than others?**

No, and that's the scary part. By the end of our research, almost all industries were equally represented. Gender was equally represented. Blue-collar workers and white-collar executives were all represented. In some cases, the abuse may have taken different forms—usually verbal or physical—but I don't know that the pain was any less in each case. Abuse occurs in the boardroom as well as on the shop floor. There really are no differences. Some abuse literally occurred in manholes where utility workers were working, as well as on the 68th floor.

■ **Which kind of bully bosses are people likely to encounter?**

Our evidence suggests conquerors, performers, and manipulators (see box, next page, for descriptions) are the most common. Power organizations focus you on power. That's the name of the game, that's what the trade is about. Turf and power are the issues. It's what's traded. And the subordinates are the ones made to suffer.

However, I have found dehumanizers, blamers, and rationalizers most frequently arise in organizations facing issues such as downsizing or other measures that are taken in the face of difficult times. Whenever companies are making a transition, these three seem to pop up.

■ **What is the most effective way to deal with a bully boss?**

From an individual perspective, what works well is to try and find protection within the organization. This can usually be found through an ombudsperson, a grievance committee, or even by pursuing legal options. Options do exist, but not always.

One of the reasons I wrote the book was to enable workers to "learn the patterns of the predator." What triggers them? What kinds of issues are their major concerns? And how do workers try to avoid them? In many cases it was quite literally physically avoiding bosses at times when they are at their most volatile. That's how a lot of folks survive working for these kinds of people.

■ **What if you can't avoid them?**

When you are attacked, it's important to make a good faith response. Focus on the content of what's being said, not on the curses. Focus on the meaning of the message, not the malevolence. Otherwise you just inflame them.

■ **What about confronting bully bosses when they are being abusive?**

That may be the noble thing to do, but it is often the costly thing to do—very costly. Most of the time you pay the price. If you don't lose your job, you certainly get labeled as someone who is a troublemaker. You get pushed into positions that are undesirable. That's the potential downside of taking legal action or invoking other forms of protection. And that's why people are afraid to do it.

A SPOTTER'S GUIDE TO BRUTAL BOSSES

In his book, Harvey Hornstein identifies six different types of "brutal bosses." Here's his description of each.

■ **CONQUERORS.** Concerned with power and making sure it's not undermined in any way, they use words to bludgeon you. They want to make you feel small. They are the classic schoolyard bullies.

■ **PERFORMERS.** These types are threatened by anyone who challenges their competence, or whom they perceive as outperforming themselves. Rather than take a subordinate's performance as a plus for their camp, they see it as a minus for themselves. Their favorite weapon is to belittle. They are known to put comments in your personnel file without telling you, and criticize your work without giving you a chance to explain or respond. They are also the types to ask for positive comments to affirm their own self-worth You end up not giving honest feedback, but rather absolute approval.

■ **MANIPULATORS.** Concerned with how they are being valued, whether people like them and care about them is what's important. They will attack you personally. Their weapon is to smear your reputation. They take credit for your successes, but will attribute their failures to you or anyone else who is around. You can't win with these folks.

■ **DEHUMANIZERS.** They turn people into numbers. They look at you as simply cogs. They have a machinelike view of human beings and the social world. That permits them to abuse. It's much easier to abuse someone when the target of your abuse is seen as a "thing" rather than a person.

■ **BLAMERS.** They write off their harm by saying that you and the others "deserved it." This is the blame-the-victim attitude. They will say, "I didn't do a bad thing. They deserved what happened to them."

■ **RATIONALIZERS.** These brutal bosses don't blame the victim of abuse, but use abuse to justify a greater cause. Rationalizing brutal bosses say things such as, "Just helping out the organization," or "Well, someone had to do it." They use these self-justifying terms to cover up their own feelings about the abuse they have inflicted.

I just heard of a case the other day, where a woman took legal action and it's taken two years to go to court. Two years! And her attorney told her that this was a cut-and-dried case. And there is still no remedy. Of course now no one in the company wants this woman working for them, although up until the time this event occurred, she was a choice employee. It's not easy.

The shortcoming of these solutions is that they really don't solve the problem from an organizational perspective. The brutal characters are still there. And even if you get out of their way, and mitigate the harm that's coming your way, they are still free to roam the corridors and beat up on someone else. So the organization hasn't solved the problem.

■ **Does senior management need to step in and address the bully boss problem?**

Yes, exactly. Ways to do that include introducing progressive management tools such as 360-degree feedback, which gives employees a greater voice and makes them more equal. It gives them access to senior level management and puts bosses at all levels on notice that their misbehavior will be part of the record and will not go unnoticed.

STRESS
▼

HOW TO BEAT BURNOUT

Smart ways to deal with that "take this career and shove it" feeling

B asketball star Michael Jordan did it. So did Harvard University president Neil Rudenstine and "Far Side" cartoonist Gary Larsen. All three—to name just a few—recently took breathers in their careers to combat battle fatigue. Millions of Americans report that they are burned out, job-weary, bored, frustrated, overworked, or just plain stressed out. A 1992 study of job and personal life stress on 28,000 workers, for example, found that more than half of them reported some degree of career burnout.

Relax, help is just ahead. Cynthia Scott is a clinical psychologist and the author of 10 books on achieving optimal happiness and performance in the workplace. Founding principal of the San Francisco–based firm Changeworks Solutions, she has served as a consultant to executive and management teams from such companies as National Semiconductor and the IRS. Her advice:

■ **KNOW THE BURNOUT SIGNS.** The best indication of burnout is your day-to-day relationship with your immediate supervisor. Supervisors who communicate, share information, collaborate, and allow some control over how work is done produce less burnout in their coworkers. Research suggests burnout is less related to how much pressure people feel than to how meaningful they find their work. People who work hard but love what they do don't get burned out—unless they're working around abusive people or doing a job without a clear goal related to it.

■ **DO AT HOME WHAT YOU CAN'T DO AT WORK.** If you don't have a lot of control in the workplace, you may need to take on more control at home. Vacuum the rug, clean the house, plant a garden, take up a sport—anything that moves your body, lets the tension out, and gives you control. If your work involves long assignments, go home and do things with a quick finishing point. If you're working on real choppy, quick stuff, do something at home that has some longevity, like building a ship in a bottle. If you're isolated all day, go home and talk all night. If you talk to people all day, spend a quiet night reading. Whatever you do, don't get into numbing yourself; that can lead to alcohol and drug abuse, and isn't a real release.

■ **KNOW WHEN TO TAKE A STEP BACK.** If things at work are really getting to you, take a day off and get some distance. Ask yourself: Is the problem short-term stress that you know will be over soon? If I'm overloaded with a short-term stressor, I might just go off for an hour and do something nice for myself. If it's a long-term pressure that doesn't stop—like a long commute you have every day—taking an hour off won't do anything. For a chronic pressure like this, you need to ask yourself, "Is it going to get better?" Then see what options might work.

■ **GET INPUT FROM FAMILY AND FRIENDS.** I call it bringing together your "board of directors"—the people who know you from different stages of your life. Have a pizza party, bring everyone together, and get their opinions just like you would in a business meeting. It's important to get the perspective of other people, because they each have a different view of you and a different time frame. They can often help you deal with some things you didn't think you could do anything about.

■ **SEEK THE TRUTH ABOUT YOUR JOB STABILITY.** It's better to actually get laid off than to worry about it. People have their worst anxieties when they don't have information. If you know that you're losing your job in three months or three weeks, you can learn coping strategies. If you hear a bunch of "wells" and "maybes," you stay in a perpetual state of anxiety. You need clarity and the truth. Approach your boss and ask what's going on; this releases you to take other action. If your boss won't be specific, ask him, "Can you at least take this to the next level of understanding?" The more you know, the better.

■ **LEARN WHAT WOMEN KNOW ABOUT STRESS.** Women inherently have had more opportunities to develop and practice dealing with multiple onslaughts of stress—and establish coping capabilities. Women have had to juggle roles of home and work much more, and the same skills work in each venue. The more traditional male role has been full of onslaughts, but in a narrower vector. In the past, because women didn't have traditional power and authority, they had to get it by sharing their experiences with others in a "friendship network." That's why in many ways women have more success with these new workplaces that are team-based. They

also often have a higher emotional literacy, so they can express their concerns—and don't mind doing so to another person. Only now are men getting some permission to have feelings.

■ **BRING WORK CONCERNS OUT IN THE OPEN.** I'm always a fan of not "choking on it"—of trying to communicate how you feel. Try saying to your boss, "That last comment you made really made me feel devalued, and I'm not sure what role I have in this project now. Could we try and work it out?" If a problem is really stressful, and you don't want to deal with it, do something to get yourself centered again. Try deep breathing or taking a walk—just get out of the stressful situation.

■ **USE MENTAL IMAGERY AND CALMING TECHNIQUES.** If you're doing some awful task, you need a place where you can go mentally via imagery to get through it and get a sense of ease. People choose lots of different things, like lying on the couch, going to the seashore, or sitting in their bathtubs.

I encourage people to always have one image ready. If you practice this kind of self-care strategy, you can meditate and go to your safe place mentally whenever you want—even as you're being screamed at by your boss. You can have your eyes open and be attempting to listen, but the rest of you is thinking your way into your place of ease. Sometimes time to unwind is needed to alleviate stress. If you've just left an awful meeting with your boss, take the stairs instead of the elevator. Ease the butterflies in your stomach by breathing in as you take each step to let out tension and get oxygen to your brain.

■ **LEARN HOW TO JUDGE THE STRESS LEVEL OF YOUR JOB.** Jobs that are high demand but have low control are the most stressful. It's more about position than occupation. For instance, a nurse working in a clinic has high demand and low control, with no way of knowing how many patients will be coming in each shift. Firemen have high demand, but it comes in spurts—fires are often followed by long periods of downtime—so it's actually not as stressful.

■ **WHERE THE STRESS IS— AND ISN'T**

How stressful is your job? The *National Business Employment Weekly Jobs Rated Almanac* (John Wiley, 1995) evaluated 250 occupations considering factors such as deadlines, confinement, public meetings, hazards, environmental conditions, and degree of stamina required. Scores were adjusted to reflect the average number of hours per week a job was likely to entail. These jobs surfaced as most and least stressful.

MOST STRESSFUL	LEAST STRESSFUL
1. U.S. president	Med. records technician
2. Firefighter	Janitor
3. Sr. corp. executive	Forklift operator
4. Race car driver (Indy class)	Musical instrument repair
5. Taxi driver	Florist
6. Surgeon	Actuary
7. Astronaut	Appliance repair
8. Police officer	Medical secretary
9. NFL football player	Librarian
10. Air-traffic controller	Bookkeeper

WANT TO BE YOUR OWN BOSS?

Learn to minimize the risks before taking the plunge

Entrepreneurs are bursting out all over as workers look for more flexible schedules and high-tech tools such as e-mail, desktop publishing, and the Internet ease the way There are now some 20 million small businesses, with nearly 171,000 start-ups cropping up in 1996 alone. The ranks of full- and part-time workers who toil in home offices have swelled to some 35 million.

The other side of the picture: The eight-year survival rate for small businesses is a low 30 percent. The fact is, being your own boss isn't easy. So before taking the plunge, keep in mind that self-employment can be financially and emotionally draining, says Jane Applegate, a nationally syndicated columnist and author of *Jane Applegate's Strategies for Small Business Success* (Plume, 1995). Applegate says that the self-employed need all the agility of a plate spinner at the circus to keep those plates perched on spindly poles from crashing down. Applegate offers the following advice on launching your own business:

■ How do I decide which business to go into?

Base the decision on skills you already have. It doesn't make sense to change careers completely, unless you plan to go to school or take special training classes. Figure out if the work you are doing for your current employer is salable and if you can promote those services or goods to former clients and customers after you leave your job. The best way to test the market is to conduct your own short survey asking people if they would buy the goods or services you have to offer.

■ What research should I do before starting a business?

Before you quit your job and sink your savings into a business, sign up for classes, attend seminars, and consider volunteering in a business similar to the one you have in mind. Meet with other small-business owners—they'll probably tell you more than you ever wanted to know. You can also get free counseling through your local Small Business Development Center. Another program, sponsored by the Small Business Administration, is called SCORE, for the Service Corps of Retired Executives. This team of volunteers will provide answers to many small-business questions.

■ How much of my own money should I invest?

That depends on the business you're setting up. If you plan to open a retail store, you will need money to buy merchandise, and pay rent and the staff—all before you make your first sale. A service business usually needs less capital to get started. No matter what sort of business you start, as a general rule, set aside twice as much as you think you'll need. And sock away at least six months' worth of living expenses—it always takes longer to get off the ground than you expect.

■ How do I attract business investors?

You need more than a dream to share with investors—you need a well-written business plan that will serve as a personal and professional road map. Most major accounting firms offer free business-planning guides, and there are many good planning resources on the market and the Internet.

■ What are the best sources of financing?

Friends, family, shirttail relatives, and colleagues are best. Many entrepreneurs think venture capitalists fund most new businesses, but in reality, they reject about 99 percent of the deals they consider. On the other hand, so-called angel investors—typically professionals looking to invest in a nearby business—put up about $6 out of every $10 invested in very small firms. The International Venture Capital Institute publishes a list of venture capital clubs, where angels meet several times a year. (To get a copy of the list, send a check or money order for $49.95 to IVCI, Box 1333, Stamford, CT, 06904.)

■ What about bank loans?

Many banks shun high-risk start-ups, but if you have a substantial net worth or other investments you can probably get a bank loan for your new business. If you don't qualify, try to get a loan guarantee from the Small Business Administration, which guarantees up to 90 percent of the loan value. Small Business Investment Companies, a group of private companies, offer government-backed loans and equity investments. (You can get a list of SBICs by sending a $20 check or money order to the National Association of Small Business Investment Companies, P.O. Box 2039, Merrifield, VA, 22116.)

FACT FILE:

BEST AND WORST STATES FOR ENTREPRENEURS

■ *Looking for the right area to start a new business? Cognetics, Inc., a consulting firm, evaluated the entrepreneurial climate across the country, using factors like proximity to universities and airports, and a skilled labor force. The results:*

TOP 10	WORST 10
1. Utah	Alaska
2. Arizona	Montana
3. Nevada	Iowa
4. Alabama	Wyoming
5. Virginia	North Dakota
6. Georgia	Connecticut
7. Colorado	New York
8. Tennessee	West Virginia
9. Florida	Pennsylvania
10. New Mexico	Oklahoma

SOURCE: Cognetics, Inc., Cambridge, Mass., 1996.

■ When can I expect a profit?

If you are selling a product, you can potentially make money from day one. Other businesses, such as manufacturing or exporting, can take years to pay off. Service businesses may also take longer to build a clientele.

■ How can I compete with a giant in my industry?

Entrepreneurs competing with a Goliath say the only way to succeed is to figure out a unique way of selling your products. You can't outspend a big corporation, so outsmart it: provide better and faster service, more personal attention, more intelligent sales people, or a unique approach.

■ How much should I pay myself?

There is no magic formula—just be sure that you are able to take something home. Calculate your total living expenses for a few months and put that in the bank before you open the business. You don't want to sacrifice your family and your home for the business venture.

■ What are promising areas for start-ups?

The best areas for the self-employed are business-to-business services and anything that helps busy, two-career families, such as kiddie transportation services, home catering, tutoring, and daycare for the elderly.

■ What sacrifices will I need to make?

Be prepared to give up a steady paycheck, a worry-free life, and time for fun and family. You could be sacrificing your company's pension or 401(k) plan, so try to set up an IRA or a small business pension plan to protect yourself when you retire.

■ What are some benefits?

You'll enjoy a roller-coaster ride full of adrenaline and the potential to make more money than you ever dreamed of. You can also expect enormous flexibility, a sense of accomplishment, and a realization that though you work hard, all the money will come straight back to you and your family.

CYBER SOURCES

ONLINE HELP FOR START-UPS

Setting up shop, getting financial backing, and finding the right marketing tools are essential for starting your own business. These sites can help take some of the drudgery out of those research chores.

ABOUT WORK

http://www.aboutwork.com

■ This site offers wisdom on what works to attract customers. There's also a chat room where you can discuss and share ideas on business financing and marketing plans with fellow entrepreneurs.

DATABASE AMERICA

http://databaseamerica.com

■ You'll find useful material for helping sell a variety of products and services, as well as tools to help you build your own mailing list.

ENTREPRENEURIAL EDGE MAGAZINE

http://edgeonline.com

■ Index your business card here for free. Tap the expertise of others, and get schedules of upcoming conferences and quick updates on business news.

INC. MAGAZINE

http://www.inc.com also AOL (keyword: Inc)

■ You can set up a home page for free and establish an online presence for your business at the Inc. site. You also get access to scores of busi-

ness articles, including interviews with other entrepreneurs.

SMALL BUSINESS ADMINISTRATION

http://www.sbaonline.sba.gov

■ Offers financing information and pointers to the SBA's field offices, as well as shareware programs that can be downloaded. At the SCORE site *(http://www.sbaonline.sba. gov/SCORE)*, a team of volunteer retired executives is available to provide useful answers to your business questions.

THE FASTEST-GROWING FRANCHISES

Which franchises are hot these days? In Entrepreneur *magazine's annual Franchise 500, franchises are rated on many factors, including the length of time they have been in business, the number of franchises and company-owned units, start-up costs, growth rates, and percentage of terminations.*

ENTREPRENEUR'S TOP 10 FASTEST-GROWING FRANCHISES

NAME	SERVICE	GROWTH (1995–96)	☎ TELEPHONE
McDonald's	Hamburgers, chicken, salads	+2,665	708–575–5645
Yogen Fruz Worldwide	Frozen yogurt and ice cream	+1,699	905–479–5235
Subway	Submarine sandwiches and salads	+1,343	203–876–6688
Jani-King	Commercial cleaning services	+985	972–991–5723
7-Eleven	Convenience store	+833	214–841–6776
Snap-On Tools	Professional tools and equipment	+718	414–656–5088
Novus Windshield Repair	Windshield repair	+692	612–944–2542
Coverall Cleaning Concepts	Commercial office cleaning	+452	619–584–4923
Coldwell Banker	Residential real estate brokerage	+412	201–560–1380
Blimpie International, Inc.	Submarine sandwiches and salads	+386	770–980–9175

THE HOTTEST HOME-BASED JOBS

Make a handsome living without leaving your front door. Here's how

Y ou can't beat this commute: Roll out of bed, go down the hall, switch on your computer, and you're at the office. More than 13 million Americans, according to *Money* magazine, are now running businesses from home. Another 6 million or so work for corporations from home an average of a day and a half a week. Roughly half of the home-based businesses are service firms, says an AT&T survey, ranging from consulting to graphic design. The rest are primarily in sales, technical and administrative support, and repair services.

Judging by the money they make, home entrepreneurs aren't just home visiting the fridge: One study by IDC/Link, a New York City market research firm, found that full-time home-business owners earn an average of $58,000 annually. A 1996 *Money* poll discovered that 20 percent reported that their businesses grossed between $100,000 and $500,000 last year, while 14 percent paid themselves annual salaries of $50,000 to $250,000.

Sound appealing? Paul and Sarah Edwards are the authors of *The Best Home Businesses for the 90s* (Tarcher/Putnam, 1994) and cohosts of weekly cable television and radio shows on the subject. They can be reached via CompuServe's Working From Home Forum and on their Web page *(http://www.homeworks.com)*. Here are their picks of some of today's hottest home-based careers:

SPECIALTY CONSULTING

Large companies are eliminating departments or staff positions, but they still want the service the department or person provided. At the same time, small businesses are growing, but they can't afford to hire people to do train-

ing, public relations, or graphic design. So they contract out for those services.

Some of the best specialty consulting fields are technical—software engineers and people who can provide technical and scientific expertise. People in human resources, health administration, education, law, and business can also find lots of work.

An up-and-coming niche position is the "business coach," who works with individuals, often the president of a small business. Coaches ask—and answer—questions that the client would get from a staff and VPs if he or she were the CEO of a large company. You don't need an MBA, just good skills at recognizing problems.

■ **TYPICAL ANNUAL GROSS REVENUE:** $30,000–$120,000 per year (billing 15–30 hours a week, 40 weeks a year, at $50–$100 an hour).

■ **POTENTIAL DOWNSIDE:** Selling yourself as simply a "marketing consultant" can get you nowhere fast; pick a specialty and stick to it.

BUSINESS PLAN WRITER

The market here is smaller businesses that are growing. When they're seeking venture capital or money from a lender, most companies need a business plan that goes beyond what they might get in a software program.

Independent plan writers should consider teaching a course at a local college. Frequently people who take how-to courses in computer programming or writing business plans will realize the professor knows more than they ever will—and make a job offer.

■ **TYPICAL ANNUAL GROSS REVENUE:** $20,000–$100,000. (Median of $55,000 based upon writing 10 plans per year at $5,000 each and editing 10 plans at $500 each.)

■ **POTENTIAL DOWNSIDE:** Vulnerable to economic cycles. Because you're dealing with companies in a state of flux, legal or collection problems may arise.

DESKTOP VIDEO PUBLISHER

As the number of cable channels expands, more advertising is needed to support them. Someone working from home is in a great position if he or she can do a decent, quick job producing commercials for local businesses. Related work includes making business pro-

THE FENG SHUI OF YOUR OFFICE

For thousands of years the Chinese have practiced the art of feng shui, which translated literally means "wind and water." The goal of feng shui is to create a balance between individuals and their surroundings, whether in the home or workplace. When it comes to your office, feng shui proponents believe placement of your furniture can affect your performance, attitude— even whether you get a promotion or a pink slip. Experts offer these tips on arranging your office furniture for good feng shui.

■ Place your desk so that you have the security of a solid wall behind you. Be sure that you have space in front of you and most importantly that you have a clear view of the doorway. Never have your back facing the door, a highly vulnerable position. If you must, place a mirror in front of you to reflect any arriving visitors.

■ An office should not have a pointed or sloping ceiling, which creates an overly stimulating and distracting aura, more suitable for a children's playroom. Such a room is not conducive to sustained thinking. If your office has such a ceiling, place a mobile or chime to deflect the energy created by the acute ceiling angles.

■ Choose colors carefully. White is considered a color of mourning for the Chinese, therefore, pure white walls are to be avoided. Green signifies growth and tranquillity and yellow represents longevity. Soft green would work well for a bedroom and yellow for a kitchen, but when it comes to an office, cream colors, warm off-white tints, and beige tones are recommended.

■ Plants and flowers are thought to bring customers and money to a business. Fishbowls and aquariums also encourage money-making activities and when placed in an office are thought to absorb bad luck.

posals and how-to videos, as well as designing Web pages and producing CD-ROMs.
■ **TYPICAL ANNUAL GROSS REVENUE:** $35,000–$150,000.
■ **POTENTIAL DOWNSIDE:** Huge start-up costs of $10,000–$30,000 for equipment, which must be kept updated. Huge learning curve for those with no prior video or hardware experience.

INFORMATION BROKERING

This position is an investigative reporter, marketing researcher, and librarian rolled into one. The highest incomes go to those who do competitive intelligence—the gathering of information (what a company's competitors are doing, what's happening to the industry, etc.) before marketing decisions are made.

■ **TYPICAL ANNUAL GROSS REVENUE:** $17,500–$75,000.
■ **POTENTIAL DOWNSIDE:** You have to be good at drumming up business, or you can starve.

TEMPORARY HELP SERVICES

Specialize. Develop your database and contacts, then target a very identifiable number of businesses (attorneys, chiropractors, etc.).
■ **TYPICAL ANNUAL GROSS REVENUE:** $70,000 (minus payroll; assumes you have 10 employees working 15 hours a week, $21 an hour).
■ **POTENTIAL DOWNSIDE:** Start-up costs are high ($9,000–$31,000), because your workers get paid before you do. Working capital alone of $5,000–$20,000 is needed to keep folks paid between monthly billing cycles.

WHAT'S NAUGHTY, WHAT'S NICE

Stick to fruit baskets, golf balls, and other gifts of nominal value

With workplaces increasingly sensitive to ethical questions, gift giving at the office can be a virtual minefield. W. Michael Hoffman, executive director of the Center for Business Ethics at Bentley College in Waltham, Mass., discusses the rules of office giving.

■ How should employees treat gifts from clients or contractors?

Some corporations set a dollar amount, but it's better to say that gifts can have only a "nominal value." It's very hard to police a dollar amount. If someone gives you a ballpoint pen, you have a good idea of the cost. The pen is a way of saying "don't forget us," but it's not going to convince you to do business with a company. If, on the other hand, someone gives you a Mont Blanc pen, that kind of crosses the line.

The real purpose of corporate ethics policies is to try to get employees to think about what they are accepting and, if needed, to check the company's ethics policy. If it is a gift that could be perceived by someone to influence, or in fact actually change, your decision about whether you would do business with that supplier over other suppliers, it should be returned.

■ Should an employee give a gift to his or her supervisor?

Gifts from a subordinate to a supervisor are particularly sensitive; if the gift is too expensive, coworkers could say that the gift giver is trying to gain an edge. That could create resentment and be seen as being improper if not unethical. It puts both the giver and the recipient in an awkward position, perhaps even influencing improperly a judgment. For instance, if the supervisor wants to promote an employee and then gets a set of golf clubs from that employee, the supervisor could feel uneasy about giving the promotion.

■ Should a supervisor give a gift to a subordinate?

Recognition for employees is fine, but this does not necessarily mean a gift. The supervisor is better off recognizing an employee through salary. As a rule, though, nominal gifts hold true for the boss-employee relationship as well as the other way around. This is a matter more of common sense than ethics. In internal office giving, the main rule of thumb is to try to avoid giving gifts that could be seen as trying to win favor or influence.

FIT FOR A CHAIRMAN

Chances are you haven't given a lot of thought to what you sit on at the office. But Richard Holbrook, an ergonomics expert who runs an industrial design firm in Pasadena, Calif., has. His thoughts:

■ **FIT COMES FIRST.** Find a chair that fits your body.
■ **BEWARE CUSHY SEATS.** You don't

want too much weight concentrated on your seat bones.

■ **AVOID LONG CUSHIONS.** If you can't get against the backrest, you can't get a comfortable, healthy posture.
■ **KEEP MOVING.** The best way to stay pain-free is to avoid spending hours on end at your desk. Take a break every hour to walk around.
■ **BACKRESTS AND ARMRESTS.** A chair with good back support gets the spine back into the natural "S curve" equilibrium.

CHAPTER FIVE

HOUSE & GARDEN

■ **WHAT'S AHEAD: TRY** doing some home renovation yourself... **KNOW** what it will cost to remodel different rooms in your house... **CHOOSE** the right color paint to enhance every living space in the house... **LOOK FOR** the plants that will solve problem spots in your garden... **PLAN** your garden to attract butterflies and hummingbirds... **ASK** your veterinarian about the latest innovations in treating your pet... **GIVE** pit bulls another chance... **RETHINK** what you may be feeding the family dog...

AROUND THE HOUSE

EXPERT Q & A

MAKING YOUR HOUSE A HOME

A pro's advice on tackling remodeling jobs

You bought a house that looks like a time capsule for the 1970s—avocado-green kitchen, pink-mosaic-tiled bathrooms, and bright orange carpeting throughout. You decide to renovate, but what changes should you tackle on your own and what jobs are better left to the experts?

We consulted Steve Thomas, host of the acclaimed television series *This Old House*, and self-proclaimed victim of "renovator's disease." Thomas, who is the author of *This Old House Kitchens* (Little, Brown, 1992) and *This Old House Baths* (Little, Brown, 1993), undertook his first home renovation project in 1974. Since then, he has renovated an 1836 Colonial Revival and an 1846 Greek Revival home, among numerous others. Here's Thomas's advice on tackling remodeling jobs in any home, no matter how humble.

■ **Which remodeling jobs can a homeowner take on without too much difficulty?**

It really depends on your skill level. If you're

willing to put in the time to do a quality job, just about anyone can improve the cosmetic appearance of their home with some fresh paint and new wallpaper, for example. Another type of remodeling job that can be accomplished with few skills but a substantial amount of sweat equity is landscaping. Though most homeowners often overlook its importance, landscaping is one of the few renovations that can dramatically increase the value of your home. You should treat landscaping as another renovation project that needs to be well planned and budgeted.

■ **Which jobs are better left to the experts?**

Any job that is potentially dangerous or involves meeting building codes should be done by a licensed expert. That would include electrical, plumbing, heating, and roofing work. In addition, any job that has to do with critical structural elements, such as load-bearing walls, should be done by a pro.

■ **What's a good starting point for a novice to gain more expertise?**

One of the best ways to enhance your level of experience is to specialize in an area of renovation, such as painting or carpentry. Focusing on one aspect will allow you to build upon your experience and over time to acquire more skills and better tools. You should start with a simple project. Building a deck, for example, requires relatively average carpentry skills, but you can learn a tremendous

HOW LONG IS A LIFETIME?

Nothing really lasts forever, of course, but some materials do have greater durability. If you're undecided about whether to put down vinyl or ceramic tiles in your new kitchen, for example, this life-expectancy list can help.

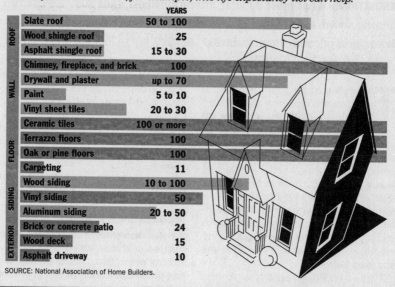

		YEARS
ROOF	Slate roof	50 to 100
	Wood shingle roof	25
	Asphalt shingle roof	15 to 30
WALL	Chimney, fireplace, and brick	100
	Drywall and plaster	up to 70
	Paint	5 to 10
	Vinyl sheet tiles	20 to 30
	Ceramic tiles	100 or more
FLOOR	Terrazzo floors	100
	Oak or pine floors	100
	Carpeting	11
SIDING	Wood siding	10 to 100
	Vinyl siding	50
	Aluminum siding	20 to 50
EXTERIOR	Brick or concrete patio	24
	Wood deck	15
	Asphalt driveway	10

SOURCE: National Association of Home Builders.

amount about renovation by going through the process. It's a good starting point—from getting the proper permit to creating a good set of plans and buying the right tools.

■ **What are some of the common pitfalls that do-it-yourself remodelers encounter?**

For one thing, they generally underestimate the time it's going to take to complete the project. When budgeting, they fail to allow for a contingency of at least 25 percent to cope with unforeseen problems. In many renovations, especially older homes, unexpected difficulties can arise and you need to allow time and money to resolve them.

Often, they underestimate the importance of the design process. It's crucial to work with a design professional who can not only help you create the home you want, but also has the foresight to articulate the details of the process from the structural to the ornamental.

Another pitfall is a tendency to take the lowest bid from a contractor, which may end up costing a homeowner more in the end. It's wise to solicit bids from a number of contractors and compare them carefully. For a successful bid competition, you'll need to provide complete and detailed specifications to ensure that everybody is bidding on exactly the same project. The more decisions you can make about materials, finishes, and detailing before asking for bids, the easier it will be to select a contractor and the fewer problems you will have once he begins the job.

■ **How can pitfalls be avoided?**

Having a a great set of detailed plans will ensure that the work is done in the correct sequence and that the job goes smoothly for all involved. This will require you to become more involved in the process and to make major decisions early. But in the long run, homeowners who invest a substantial amount of time in the planning phase can potentially save between 20 and 30 percent in the overall cost of their renovation.

DOES IT PAY TO REMODEL?

What most popular alterations cost from coast to coast

The place is finally yours, but it needs work, and you're not sure where to start. Every house is different, of course, but some remodeling projects offer a better payback than others. Each year *Remodeling* magazine puts some of the most popular home improvement projects to the test, asking real estate agents in 60 cities how much the project would add in the first year to a mid-priced house in an established neighborhood. The results are instructive: Buyers will pay for state-of-the-art kitchens, luxurious master bed and bath suites, family rooms, and extra bedrooms.

Here's a region-by-region breakdown of the projects. The estimates for average construction costs come from Craftsman Book Company of Carlsbad, Calif., HomeTech

Information Systems of Bethesda, Md., and R. S. Means Company of Kingston, Mass. Actual prices can vary widely depending on materials, labor costs, and design.

MINOR KITCHEN ADDITION

■ **Project description:** In a functional but outdated 200-square-foot kitchen with 30 lineal feet of cabinetry and countertops, refinish cabinets, install new energy-efficient wall oven and cooktop, new laminate countertop, mid-priced sink and faucet, wall covering and resilient flooring, and fresh paint. Includes new raised-panel wood doors on cabinets.

REGION	JOB COST	RESALE VALUE	COST RECOUPED
East	$9,706	$8,794	91%
South	$7,480	$7,974	107%
Midwest	$8,170	$7,095	87%
West	$8,672	$8,259	95%
National	$8,313	$7,891	95%

MAJOR KITCHEN REMODEL

■ **Project description:** Update outmoded, 200-square-foot kitchen with design and installation of new cabinets, laminate countertops, mid-priced sink and faucet, energy-efficient wall oven, cooktop and ventilation system, built-in microwave, dishwasher, garbage disposal, custom lighting, new resilient flooring, and painted woodwork and ceiling. Features 30 lineal feet of semi-custom-grade wood cabinets and counter space, including 3-by-5-foot center island.

REGION	JOB COST	RESALE VALUE	COST RECOUPED
East	$22,871	$21,946	96%
South	$18,659	$19,365	96%
Midwest	$21,186	$16,628	78%
West	$22,333	$18,821	84%
National	$21,262	$19,190	90%

BATHROOM ADDITION

■ **Project description:** Add a second full bath to a house with one-and-a-half baths. The 6-by-8-foot bath should be within the existing floor plan in an inconspicuous spot convenient to bedrooms. Include cultured marble vanity top, molded sink, standard bathtub with shower, low-profile toilet, lighting, mirrored medicine cabinet, linen storage, vinyl wallpaper, and ceramic tile floor and walls in tub area.

REGION	JOB COST	RESALE VALUE	COST RECOUPED
East	$12,702	$11,094	87%
South	$9,959	$10,576	106%
Midwest	$11,468	$8,840	77%
West	$12,445	$11,709	94%
National	$12,452	$11,863	95%

BATHROOM REMODEL

■ **Project description:** Update an existing 5-by-9-foot bathroom that is at least 25 years old with new standard-size tub, toilet, and solid surface vanity counter with integral double sink. Install new lighting, faucets, mirrored medicine cabinet, and ceramic tile floor and wall in tub/shower area. Vinyl wallpaper elsewhere.

REGION	JOB COST	RESALE VALUE	COST RECOUPED
East	$9,194	$7,304	79%
South	$7,186	$6,550	91%
Midwest	$8,252	$5,423	66%
West	$9,061	$6,642	83%
National	$8,423	$6,480	73%

FAMILY ROOM ADDITION

■ **Project description:** In a style and location appropriate to the existing house, add a 16-by-25-foot, light-filled room on a new crawl space foundation with wood joist floor framing, matching wood siding on exterior walls, and matching existing fiberglass roof. Include drywall interior with batt insulation, hardwood tongue-and-groove floor, and 180 square feet of glass, including atrium-style exterior (doors, windows, and two operable skylights). Tie into existing heating and cooling.

REGION	JOB COST	RESALE VALUE	COST RECOUPED
East	$34,901	$30,037	86%
South	$27,523	$25,289	92%
Midwest	$31,773	$21,968	69%
West	$33,186	$28,636	86%
National	$31,846	$26,483	83%

MASTER SUITE

■ **Project description:** On a house with two or three bedrooms, add over a crawl space a 24-by-16-foot master bedroom with walk-in closets. Master bath includes dressing area, whirlpool tub, separate ceramic tile shower, and a double-bowl vanity. Bedroom is carpeted; floor in bath is ceramic tile.

REGION	JOB COST	RESALE VALUE	COST RECOUPED
East	$39,758	$32,681	82%
South	$31,032	$30,348	98%
Midwest	$35,995	$25,972	72%
West	$39,103	$33,119	85%
National	$36,472	$30,530	84%

HOME OFFICE ADDITION

■ **Project description:** Convert an existing 12-by-12-foot room into a home office. Install custom cabinets configured for desk, computer workstation, and overhead storage, and 20 feet of plastic laminate desktop. Rewire room for computer, fax machine, and other electronic equipment as well as cable and telephone lines. Include drywall interior and commercial-grade, level-loop carpeting.

REGION	JOB COST	RESALE VALUE	COST RECOUPED
East	$8,706	$6,146	71%
South	$7,145	$4,903	69%
Midwest	$7,957	$4,373	55%
West	$8,605	$6,271	73%
National	$8,103	$5,423	67%

ATTIC BEDROOM

■ **Project description:** In a house with two or three bedrooms, convert unfinished attic with rafters to 15-by-15-foot bedroom and 5-by-7-foot shower/bath. Add four new windows and a 15-foot shed dormer. Insulate and finish ceiling and walls. Carpet unfinished floor. Extend existing heating and central air conditioning to new space. Retain existing stairs.

REGION	JOB COST	RESALE VALUE	COST RECOUPED
East	$24,864	$19,604	79%
South	$19,658	$16,752	85%
Midwest	$22,440	$16,389	73%
West	$24,396	$23,589	97%
National	$22,840	$19,084	84%

REPLACE SIDING

■ **Project description:** Replace 1,250 square feet

of existing siding with new vinyl or aluminum siding, including trim.

REGION	JOB COST	RESALE VALUE	COST RECOUPED
East	$5,792	$4,412	76%
South	$4,824	$4,033	84%
Midwest	$5,185	$3,574	69%
West	$6,031	$3,912	65%
National	$5,458	$3,983	73%

REPLACE WINDOWS

■ **Project description:** Replace 10 existing 3-by-5-foot windows with aluminum-clad windows, including new trim. Replace sashes, frames, and casings.

REGION	JOB COST	RESALE VALUE	COST RECOUPED
East	$6,462	$5,370	83%
South	$5,334	$4,276	80%
Midwest	$5,937	$3,843	65%
West	$5,805	$4,653	69%
National	$6,112	$4,536	74%

DECK ADDITION

■ **Project description:** Add a 16-by-20-foot deck of pressure-treated pine supported by 4 x 4 posts set in concrete footings. Include built-in bench, railings, and planter, also of pressure-treated pine.

REGION	JOB COST	RESALE VALUE	COST RECOUPED
East	$6,172	$4,459	72%
South	$5,433	$4,676	86%

Midwest	$6,084	$3,581	59%
West	$6,531	$4,400	67%
National	$6,172	$4,459	72%

TWO-STORY ADDITION

■ **Project description:** Over a crawl space, add a 24-by-16-foot two-story wing with a first floor family room and a second floor bedroom with full bath. Features a prefab fireplace in family room, 11 windows and atrium-style exterior door, carpeted floors, and painted drywall. Five-by-8-foot bath has fiberglass bath/shower, standard-grade toilet, wood vanity with ceramic sink top, ceramic tile flooring, mirrored medicine cabinet with light strip above, and wallpapered walls. Add new heating and cooling system to handle addition.

REGION	JOB COST	RESALE VALUE	COST RECOUPED
East	$60,279	$49,675	82%
South	$47,687	$44,372	94%
Midwest	$55,087	$40,622	74%
West	$59,693	$50,274	84%
National	$55,687	$46,236	83%

For a complete 1996–97 *Cost vs. Value Report*, send a check for $8.95 to Hanley-Wood, Inc., One Thomas Circle, NW, #600, Washington, D.C., 20005, Attn. Cost vs. Value Reprints.

SOURCE: *Remodeling* magazine, October 1996.
©Hanley-Wood, Inc.

■ **HOW REMODELING PROJECTS DEPRECIATE**

A new garage is your best bet for increasing the long-term value of your house.

PROJECT	PERCENTAGE OF ORIGINAL RENOVATION COSTS ADDED TO THE VALUE OF HOUSE AFTER		
	1 YEAR	3 YEARS	5 YEARS
Kitchen renovation	77%	62%	47%
Bathroom renovation	77%	62%	44%
Roof replacement	69%	52%	39%
Fireplace addition	76%	68%	61%
Swimming pool addition	53%	42%	31%
One-car garage	84%	78%	71%
Wood deck addition	79%	66%	55%
Solar room addition	72%	61%	53%
Living/dining/family room update	79%	59%	37%

SOURCE: Marshall & Swift National Cost-Reporting Service.

A CONTRACTOR YOU CAN TRUST

Your sanity and bank balance are at stake. How to avoid mistakes

Sometimes even the most intrepid do-it-yourselfer is cowed by a home repair or renovation project. That's when it's time to call in a professional. But being certain that you're hiring a dependable contractor is tricky. Most contractors are reliable and hardworking, insists Thomas Kraeutler, a veteran home inspector and president of HomeChek of New Jersey, Inc. But to guard against the few who aren't, here he suggests ways to avoid a home improvement disaster.

BID APPLES TO APPLES

Know exactly what you want before you pick up the phone and call any contractor. Pick out specific products (by brand name, model, and style) to include in the renovation. Tell the contractors which brand and style you've chosen. Don't leave the choice of materials to the contractor—you're likely to get the cheapest stuff available.

CONTRACT WITH YOUR CONTRACTOR

For jobs costing more than a couple of hundred dollars, have a written agreement. Make sure the contract states what is to be done, in as much detail as possible, and when it is to be completed. A common complaint is that the job takes longer to complete than a contractor estimated. To avoid this, include a "time of essence" clause, which charges the contractor penalties if the work takes too long. The contractor should also set forth a payment schedule. As a general rule, put up a small down payment and space out the remainder. Reserve at least 25 percent of the total amount for a final payment

and release it only when you're completely satisfied with the work.

If a contractor doesn't give you a contract, you can draw up one of your own. Or you can write the contractor a letter that outlines everything discussed. For a minor repair, the letter could simply read: "This confirms that you have agreed to fix my leaky toilet for $50. Per our agreement, I'll look forward to seeing you next Tuesday at 3 p.m. Thank you for your assistance."

CHECK INSURANCE

A contractor must have full insurance—this includes worker's compensation as well as general comprehensive liability insurance. Some contractors skimp on insurance, leaving you exposed in the case of an accident. When checking insurance, make sure the contractor provides a "certificate of insurance," which names you as an "additional insured." This guarantees that the contractor's insurance company will attempt to notify you if the policy is canceled for any reason. Also, be sure to check the policy limit of the general comprehensive coverage. A basic policy offers a limit of $50,000. This isn't very much coverage in today's litigious world. For peace of mind, insist on at least $300,000 coverage.

KEEP A WRITTEN RECORD

Good documentation of the job is crucial if something goes wrong later or if disputes arise. Keep written notes of starting and stopping times, how many people are working, and what's getting (or not getting) done. This is especially important if you are paying for the job by the hour. Also, for bigger jobs, keep notes of conversations you've had with contractors about problems, changes, etc.

GET AN OUTSIDE REVIEW

If any question arises about the quality of the job, have the work inspected by an independent professional, such as a home inspector. With all contracts, be sure to have them reviewed by your attorney before signing. The expense of such a review can be well worth it in the event of future problems.

THE SECRET LIFE OF PAINT

A color specialist on how to make your home beautiful with pigment

Each season, paint manufacturers debut scores of new paint colors with such imaginative names as Treasure, Lucia Blue, and WinterMoss. While these names may be pleasing to the ear, they are of little help when it actually comes to choosing a color for the walls of your living room or kitchen. Here, architectural color consultant Donald Kaufman has some genuinely practical tips for choosing paint for the home. Kaufman, coauthor with Taffy Dahl of *Color: Natural Palettes for Painted Rooms* (Clarkson Potter, 1992), has worked with renowned architects I.M. Pei and Philip Johnson, and has his own line of paint colors, The Donald Kaufman Color Collection (☎ 201–568–2226).

■ **Start by noticing which colors are already in and around your home.** An old rug, a painting, a stone terrace outside the house, or even a favorite pair of pants may provide the perfect inspiration. Computers can help turn these colors into paint, but they have limited formulas. Getting a painter to mix the paint often results in more complex colors.

■ **Understand the psychological effects of color.** People have different reactions to cool and warm colors. Cool colors—especially blues and violets—tend to create a sense of darkness and depression. They are the most difficult to use successfully because of these unsettling effects. Warm colors—reds, oranges, and yellows—are generally more pleasing and fulfill the basic human need for light. For this reason, they account for nearly 90 percent of the paints on store shelves. Warm colors are a safe choice for the dining room and kitchen because they improve the look of food. They also flatter the skin color of guests surrounding the table. If a cool color is a must, use green or a blue that has some yellow in it.

■ **Take the time to test samples.** A major complaint about final paint jobs is that they are too bright. Colors on a paint swatch appear twice as bright and twice as light when applied to a wall. Therefore, an adequate mock-up is essential. Paint a five-foot-wide sample swath from floor to ceiling. Block out existing colors with your hand and see how the new colors interact with the room and especially with the color of the floor. Look at the test area at different times of the day to see how it reacts to fluctuations in natural light and to artificial light at night. People who want to paint a brightly colored room a neutral color should prime the entire room before trying samples. Reflected light from strong colors will alter the perceived color of the mock-up.

■ **Brighten rooms.** The common solution to a dark room is throwing white paint on the walls to reflect more light. But the lack of light generally makes the white room look washed-out and gray. A better solution is to use a warmer and deeper color, which often can provide the luminosity that is missing from the room. Yellows are particularly effective, because the color value can be kept light enough while still adding warmth.

■ **Enlarge living spaces.** If you have light-colored floors, choose a deeper wall color and a light ceiling color to reflect the floor. Walls will appear to recede above the floor. If you have dark floors, keep walls and ceiling light and the same color. Eyes are attracted to contrast, and high contrast between walls and ceiling closes spaces. Some people think they can lift a ceiling by painting it white.

That is often the case, because a white ceiling reflects more light. But if there's already plenty of light, similarly colored walls and ceiling can make a room appear more open and atmospheric.

■ **Use the same trim color throughout a number of rooms.** The wall color in each room will make the trim appear different. Keep the trim lighter than the walls. Using darker trim colors can be beautiful, but it is much more difficult to pull off.

■ **Think about how the colors of adjoining rooms interact.** Colors in abutting rooms tend to reinforce each other—which can have dramatic or unpleasant results. A subtle beige room can appear much stronger if viewed from a subtle blue room, and vice versa. Also, thinking about rooms as a series of colors can make cramped quarters seem roomier. For a three-room apartment, if the kitchen and living room have light, warm colors, a bedroom with stronger and deeper colors can provide a perfect escape.

■ **Address the architecture.** Architectural details can be divided into two categories—structural and decorative. Neutral colors work better with structural details such as columns or door frames. Something that looks like it provides support is not the place for a pale peach color. Decorative colors would be more appropriate with friezes and other ornate moldings.

■ **Use top-of-the-line paint from any of the major manufacturers.** It lasts the longest and provides the best coverage. Don't overlook regional paint companies. Their top paints are just as good and sometimes better. But preparation is all-important. Clean, smooth surfaces lead to the best results.

■ **And remember, there are no bad colors.** Colors change and create different perceptions depending on where and how they are used. A very bright, garish green might seem a bad color for a dining room, but it could be absolutely beautiful as a thin stripe underneath crown molding in a beige living room.

NOT ALL PAINTS ARE CREATED EQUAL

Before you paint yourself into a corner, know your oil from your latex

When it comes to paint, there are two basic options: oil or latex. Convention has it that oil paint is more durable, has more sheen, hides brush strokes better, and is easier to clean when dry.

Today's latex paint equals the performance of oil on many of these scores. And because it's easy to use, latex now is the most popular type of paint on store shelves. With latex paint, there's less odor, drying times are shorter, brushes clean up with water, and errant paint splatters can be wiped away with a damp sponge. It also costs less and is better for the environment—latex paint contains fewer volatile organic compounds.

Oil paint is less forgiving. Odors are stronger, drying time can take a day, and cleanup requires turpentine or paint thinner. But in damp areas such as the kitchen and bathroom, it is better at repelling water.

For this reason, many professionals insist that oil makes a superior exterior paint. Latex paint, though, has a porous quality, which allows it to breathe. In homes where a lot of interior water vapor exits through exterior walls, use of latex paint can limit peeling. Keep in mind that both types of exterior paint cost more because of additional resins, pigments, and mildewcides.

Sheen is also an important factor to consider. Glossier finishes are harder and more durable. Use them in high wear or high humidity areas, such as on woodwork or in kitchens and bathrooms. Low luster finishes generally have greater hiding power. Use them on walls and ceilings.

PUT A LITTLE SPRING IN YOUR SOFA

If you're in the market for a new sofa, you're probably wondering what makes a $2,000 sofa any different from one that costs a mere $600. The difference lies in the frame, padding, cushions, springs, fabric, and finish:

■ **PADDING:** Sofas often wear at the arms because the maker has scrimped on padding. The better sofas have a layer of cotton or polyfiber over a layer of foam. Cheaper sofas have fabric right on top of the foam.

■ **FABRIC:** The grade of a fabric determines the price, but is not a measure of the fabric's durability. Grades are based largely on fiber content and on how much waste results from matching the pattern. For durability, consider spending the extra $50 or so for treating the sofa with fabric protection.

■ **SPRINGS:** Eight-way hand-tied springs used to be a sign of a top-notch sofa. No more. Many less expensive sofas also have them, although they are of inferior quality. A better question: How many rows of springs are used in the seat? The best use four rows.

■ **FRAME:** Maple and other hardwoods that grip nails well make the best frames. The wood should be kiln-dried to prevent shrinkage and warping. The best frames are $1^1/_2$ inches thick. (Experts refer to it as a $^6/_4$ frame.) To keep a sofa from sagging, joints and legs must be firmly attached to the frame. The best joints are double- or triple-doweled at the top corners and firmly attached with reinforcing blocks where the arms meet the seat.

■ **CUSHIONS:** Top-quality foam cushions are made from virgin foam with a density of 2.2 pounds per cubic foot. Accept no less than 1.8. Lower-density foam deteriorates more quickly. If you're looking for a soft down cushion, be sure the cushion has at least 30 percent down feathers in it. Otherwise, you'll be paying for down and getting far less.

■ **FINISH:** Attention to detail makes a difference. In a high-quality sofa, seams are straight, pleats lie flat, corners fill out, and cushions have metal zippers.

BEDS YOU WON'T LOSE SLEEP ON

Almost a third of life is spent sleeping, so take your mattress seriously

Your mattress sags, creaks, wobbles, and sways. It's probably time to toss this relic and invest in a new one. Is there any purchase that's more personal? Dr. Howard Levy of the Emory Spine Center in Atlanta, Ga., believes that a mattress should be firm and support the natural curves of the spine. Many of his colleagues agree. In a recent survey by Levy of orthopedic surgeons, he found that of the 134 respondents, 67.7 percent recommended a firm mattress, 8.9 percent hard, 1.6 percent a waterbed, and just under 1 percent a soft mattress. The next time you go mattress shopping, keep these tips in mind from the Better Sleep Council:

■ **SUPPORT:** Wear comfortable clothes to your local mattress retailer, so you can lie down on a number of mattresses. The best ones support your body at all points. Pay attention to your shoulders, hips, and lower back. Too little support can result in back pain; too much can lead to uncomfortable pressure.

■ **SPACE:** Sleepers toss and turn 40 to 60 times a night. If you are constantly fighting your partner for space, it may be time to upgrade to a queen- or king-size bed. Both are several inches longer and wider than the standard double bed.

■ **COIL COUNT:** The common innerspring mattress gets its support from tempered steel coils. A full-size version should have more than 300 coils, a queen-size more than 375, and a king-size more than 450.

■ **WIRE GAUGE:** The lower the number, the thicker, stronger, and more durable the wire. Stronger coils generally provide better support. Many manufacturers are introducing wire-engineered innersprings that employ lighter wire. They claim these systems make less noise and offer more support. Lie down and shift positions—it's the best way to test these claims and to see which mattress lends your body's curves the most support.

■ **COVER:** Look for superior stitching, quality seams, and an extra-soft surface. Don't buy a bed based solely on a pretty treatment.

■ **PADDING:** Layers of upholstery insulate and cushion the body from the innersprings. Once you've purchased a mattress that meets your comfort needs, remember to flip it regularly from head to toe. This extends mattress life and helps prevent creating an uncomfortable impression in the padding.

■ **FOUNDATION:** Don't blame a bad night's sleep on the mattress alone. The foundation, or box spring, may also be showing some signs of wear and tear. A mattress and its companion foundation are designed to work as a system. Putting a new mattress on an old foundation can reduce the life and comfort of a mattress.

■ **WARRANTIES:** Top brands generally come with 15 years' protection against product defects, but don't let the salesperson sell you a mattress based solely on the warranty. Let comfort and support guide your decision.

■ **FOAM MATTRESSES:** Made of a solid core or different types of foam laminated together, these mattresses should come with a minimum density of 2.0 pounds per cubic foot. High-resilience polyurethane and the more traditional latex, or synthetic rubber, mattresses provide the best performance.

■ **WATERBEDS:** Whether full motion or waveless, make sure the mattress vinyl is a minimum of 20 mil. in thickness, and pay close attention to seam durability. Even if you live outside of California, look to see if the system meets California Waterbed Standards.

LIGHTING
▼

FIXING THE LIGHT FANTASTIC

The right lighting will flatter, accent, and fill a home with warmth

For years lighting design has been nearly an afterthought for many residential architects and general contractors. The attitude was, what more could there be than a ceiling-mounted fixture in the center of the room or a homeowner's table lamps? But such light fixtures often tend to call attention to themselves and cast shadows in unflattering ways. Here, lighting designer Randall Whitehead, the owner of Light Source, a lighting store in San Francisco, and author of *Residential Lighting: Creating Dramatic Living Spaces* (Rockport Publishers, 1993) and *Lighten Up* (Light Source Publishing, 1996), tours the home and offers some advice on lighting.

■ **THE ENTRY.** The entrance sets the mood and tone for the rest of the house. In the entryway, lighting can be used to open up the space and provide a welcoming environment for guests. Make sure lights create a warm glow. Avoid harsh shadows by using uplighting instead of recessed downlights.

■ **THE LIVING ROOM.** The goal here is to create a soft island of illumination that invites people in to relax and converse. Layering the light creates an environment that is humanizing and dramatic. Wall sconces and torchères can generally provide ambient illumination, which softens shadows on people's faces and fills the room with a soft glow. Recessed adjustable fixtures or track lighting can be utilized to provide the necessary accent light for artwork, plants, or table-

BULBS THAT LIGHT UP YOUR LIFE

The right light takes the right bulb, as the following guide shows

■ **FLUORESCENT.** California, the bellwether of eco-friendly laws, now mandates that ambient lighting in new or remodeled kitchens and baths be fluorescent. Once derided for its cold, unfriendly illumination, advancements in fluorescent technology have increased its usefulness: There are over 200 color variations, and dimming possibilities are much greater than before. Now people can use energy-efficient fixtures without totally sacrificing the warm glow of more traditional light sources.

■ **INCANDESCENT.** This was the first light source created, and it still has a strong hold over the general public with its warm, amber illumination. But its color tonality shifts colors within a given space—reds turn orange, whites go yellow, and blues shift to green. Be aware of this when you choose paints and fabrics.

■ **QUARTZ AND TUNGSTEN HALOGEN.** These light sources are a recent improvement in incandescent lighting. They provide a whiter source of illumination, so colors are truer. Quartz lamps also produce twice as much illumination as standard lamps so you have a more energy-efficient source by using less wattage for the same amount of light.

■ **H.I.D.** (High Intensity Discharge). These lamps are used mostly in commercial and landscape lighting. Most streetlights use these lamps, but the mercury vapor and metal halide varieties are seeing more use in residential landscape designs.

tops. But be sure not to let accent lighting overpower you or your company.

■ **THE DINING ROOM.** This is where dramatic lighting can come into play. Wall sconces are a good source of ambient lighting in this room. A chandelier should only give the illusion of providing the lighting in the room, as otherwise it will be too bright or distracting. Using recessed, adjustable fixtures on either side of the chandelier will produce the necessary focal point lighting for the table, without eclipsing the decorative fixture.

■ **THE KITCHEN.** With today's open floor plan designs, the kitchen should be as inviting as the rest of the house. Mount fluorescent lights above cabinets, so light is bounced off the walls and ceilings, providing ambient lighting. Lights under cabinets provide good, unobstructed task light for the counters. Pendant-hung fixtures can be used for task light where cabinets are not present. Skylights can provide a cheery feeling during the day, and, through the use of fluorescent fixtures mounted in them, will avoid becoming "black holes" at night. A pot rack over a center island may appear to be a perfect idea, but how do you light work surfaces without creating shadows by trying to light through pots and pans? If you have sloped ceilings, special care must be taken to select fixtures that don't glare into people's eyes. Also, remember that an all-white kitchen is going to require dramatically less light than a kitchen with dark wood cabinets.

■ **BATHROOMS.** Lighting at the mirror is most important. Vertically mounted strip fixtures generally provide the best task light. Wall sconces or fluorescent strip fixtures mounted above cabinets, ledges, or beams provide the necessary ambient illumination.

■ **BEDROOMS.** It is important that there is good color-corrected light, especially in closets, to aid in the selection of properly color-matched clothes. Aside from the usual ambient light concerns, easily adjustable reading lamps at the bed are a must. A "panic switch" for outside lighting is often a desirable feature.

EXPERT TIPS

FRAME THE WORLD AROUND YOU

A picture's display can be the difference between wow! and ho-hum

For millennia, people have understood the importance of using a frame to separate a work of art from its surroundings. Ancient Pompeians framed wall paintings with lines of painted color, while artists in the Middle Ages used wood carved in an ornate Gothic style. Here, Greg O'Halloran (GOH), conservation framer at A.P.F., Inc., in New York, Lou Stovall (LS), archival framer and master printer at Workshop, Inc., in Washington, D.C., and Andrew LaBonte (AL), manager of Boston framers Haley & Steele, discuss how to frame art and display it in the home.

THE FRAME

✔ "A good framer will allow the art to make the choice. If you look at the art, it really can talk to you in terms of what is supposed to surround it. If it is done correctly, you can make a second-rate work of art look like a museum piece. For example, you can't take a scoop molding and put it on an 1850s Bierstadt. A period piece should have a style of frame from the same period. It really has to be a marriage of frame and art." (GOH)

✔ "Aside from aesthetics, the frame has to be sturdy enough to hold the artwork in the glass. A large work requires large moldings. Using a thin frame for a more streamlined look requires extra supports on the back. When it comes to frame styles, the options include gold leaf, burnished frames, ones with antiquing, ornamented styles, and plainer models. Generally, people match the frame to the style or period of the art. However, a lot of modern art really works extremely well with antique frames, even very heavily ornamented, gold-leaf frames. It even works well with modern decor." (AL)

✔ "You frame for the art. In rare cases, it's okay to frame the art to complement the living environment where the art will be located. Generally speaking, you want the molding to have some sensitivity to the furniture in the room. If you have traditional furniture, you would probably want a traditional frame, such as carved wood. If you have modern or contemporary furniture, you would go for a simple wood, or, most likely, a metal frame. If you have a dining room with brass wall sconces, you might want a brass frame. If you are hanging over wonderful, natural wood paneling, you would probably want a nice maple or cherry frame." (LS)

THE MAT

✔ "You always want acid-free, 100 percent cotton mats. You can have single, double, or triple mats. Mats set the work back from the glass for protection and give a nice surrounding. I tend to frame with white mats. I don't think much of colored mats, because the art should speak for itself. If the artist required more color around the border, he would have indicated it. But if you are hanging in a dark room painted deep red or forest green, you might consider a colored mat. It softens the blow between the darkness of the room and the art. Mat widths range from 2 1/2 to 5 or 6 inches. If something is larger than 36 by 40 inches, chances are you would want a 5 1/2- or 6-inch band around it. Anything under 20 inches square, you would want something 2 1/2 or 3 inches." (LS)

✔ "The bottom border is usually a small increment larger than the top and sides, for visual balance. If you make the margins all the same, the bottom will

actually end up looking narrower—it's an ancient principle of proportion. For this reason, columns in Greek architecture are wider at the bottom, and, usually on a chest of drawers, the bottom drawers are wider than the top drawers. A common border size is 3 inches on the top and sides and 3 1/4 on the bottom. Instead of using color mats, I paint lines or panels on the mat in the traditional English and French style. Usually, you see this style of mats used on decorative pieces, botanicals, landscapes, things like that. I also wrap mats in pure silks or pure linens. For instance, on Beacon Hill, if someone has watered silk wallpaper, I will do silk mats for their pictures. Silk mats also go well on master drawings." (AL)

HANGING THE PICTURE

✔ "With anything large, you want to use Plexiglas because it is light and won't break if the work falls from the wall. With something of value, you want to use UV reflective glass or Plexiglas to diminish the damaging effects of light. Also, you want to place the art on walls washed by light rather than on those with direct light. If you are going to install art lights, you want to place them on the ceiling 30 inches from the wall and at an angle so that light shows brightest on either edge of the frame. You don't want to have the lights on all the time, though. All light takes a toll." (LS)

✔ "One of the largest causes of damage to art and frames is that they fall off the wall. The wire breaks or mounting screws pull out—so make sure the hardware is top quality. To hang the art on masonry walls, use a masonry screw or drill a hole and insert a lead slug and a lag screw. If you have Sheetrock, traditional hangers will support up to 100 pounds. Anything heavier than that, or if the walls are plaster, I use molly bolts. You should also avoid putting adhesives like glue or tape on the artwork. There are a lot of mechanical mounts that hold the art and work very well." (AL)

PROTECT YOUR CASTLE FROM TIME

From stuck windows to trickling toilets, here's how to fix it yourself

The roof leaks, the basement is damp, and the toilet won't stop running. For many homeowners, such a scenario represents their worst nightmare. But who can afford to call a plumber at the first sign of a leak? Here, Thomas Kraeutler and George Pettie, president and vice president, respectively, of the home inspection firm HomeChek of New Jersey, provide a repair and maintenance guide that will help you protect your number one investment.

LEAKY ROOF

Watch out for unscrupulous contractors who try to sell you a new roof that you don't need. Most roof leaks can be remedied with minor flashing repair. Look for loose or deteriorated flashing around chimneys and vent pipes. Fill any gaps with a good asphalt roof cement. A neatly applied bead of sealant from a caulking gun is better than a thick, troweled-on application.

Loose flashing should be tightened up with masonry nails before resealing. Expect to seal flashing every two years. If sealing doesn't fix the problem, the roof shingles may be in fact worn out. To check your roof for signs of wear and tear, look for cracked, curled, or broken shingles. If the worn area is small, it can be repaired by replacing the old shingles or patching with asphalt roof cement. If all of the roof looks this way, entire replacement is best. Shingles that are allowed to deteriorate can cause major leaks leading to expensive repairs.

WET BASEMENT

Kraeutler and Pettie recount how one homeowner recently attempted to fix a leaky basement by calling a waterproofing contractor. Quotes ranged from $7,500 to $20,000. Yet the homeowner was eventually able to correct his outside drainage and easily fix the problem for under $500.

In fact, good gutters and properly sloping soil on a home's exterior can fix 99 percent of wet basement problems. Start by cleaning out gutters, downspouts, and underground drain pipes. A water hose is very useful for flushing out debris. When the accumulated mess in downspouts and drain pipes proves stubborn, rent a power auger to clear a passageway. If the gutter system doesn't empty into underground pipes, be sure to install downspout extensions that carry water 4 to 6 feet from the foundation. Also, inspect gutters for leaks and sags. Aluminum gutters can be sealed with polyurethane or butyl caulk. Ideally, copper and steel gutters should be resoldered, but they

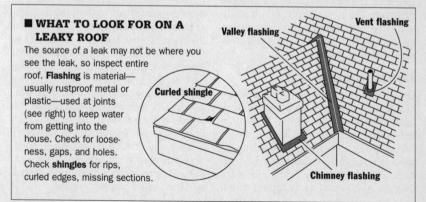

■ **WHAT TO LOOK FOR ON A LEAKY ROOF**

The source of a leak may not be where you see the leak, so inspect entire roof. **Flashing** is material—usually rustproof metal or plastic—used at joints (see right) to keep water from getting into the house. Check for looseness, gaps, and holes. Check **shingles** for rips, curled edges, missing sections.

Valley flashing

Vent flashing

Curled shingle

Chimney flashing

■ WHEN TO FIX IT, WHEN TO JUNK IT

To help you decide whether to repair or replace an appliance, consult the chart devised by Thomas Kraeutler below. In one typical scenario, you're stuck with an air conditioner that dies because the compressor is seven years old. An entirely new system would cost $2,500, but the compressor repair alone would be $850. According to the chart, a seven-year-old central air conditioner has a low risk of repetitive failure, so it's okay to spend up to 50 percent of the replacement cost on repair. Since the $850 repair cost is 50 percent of the replacement value, go ahead and call for service.

APPLIANCE:	ESTIMATED REPLACEMENT COST[1]	AGE RANGE RISK OF FAILURE[2]: % REPAIR COST LIMIT		
		Low Risk	Medium Risk	High Risk
FURNACE	$1,500–$2,500	up to 12 years: 30%	12–24 years: 20%	25 years & up: 10%
WATER HEATER	$350–$700	up to 7 years : 30%	7–14 years: 20%	15 years & up: 10%
CENTRAL A/C	$1,500–$3,000	up to 8 years: 50%	8–15 years: 30%	16 years & up: 10%
REFRIGERATOR	$700–$1,500	up to 8 years: 40%	8–15 years: 30%	16 years & up: 20%
KITCHEN RANGE	$700–$1,400	up to 15 years: 30%	15–25 years: 20%	26 years & up: 10%
DISHWASHER	$350–$750	up to 10 years: 40%	10–15 years: 30%	16 years & up: 20%
WASHER	$350–$700	up to 10 years: 40%	10–15 years: 30%	16 years & up: 20%
DRYER	$350–$700	up to 10 years: 50%	10–20 years: 40%	21 years & up: 10%
BUILT-IN MICROWAVE	$400–$800	up to 4 years: 20%	4–10 years: 15%	11 years & up: 10%
GARBAGE DISPOSAL	$150–$350	up to 1 year[3]	1 year & up: Always replace	—

NOTES:
1. Assumes replacement with like kind and quality as original appliance.
2. Risk of failure or breakdown increases with age. Percentage indicates minimum cost of repair limit. If cost of repair is greater than percentage of replacement cost shown, then replacement is recommended. If cost of repair is less than percentage of replacement cost show, then repair is likely to be cost-effective.
3. Repair disposals only if under manufacturer's warranty. Otherwise, always replace.

can be resealed with a similar caulk. Repair sags by removing the spikes that hold the gutter in place, raising the gutter so that it slopes evenly to downspouts, and nailing the gutter back in place.

To keep rainfall from collecting near foundation walls, soil should slope downward 6 inches over the first 4 feet from the foundation wall. Thereafter, it can be graded more gradually. Use clean fill dirt (not topsoil). Tamp the fill dirt down to the correct slope and finish with a layer of topsoil and grass seed, mulch, or stone.

EXTERIOR JOINTS AND GAPS

Open joints and gaps in the outside envelope of a house waste energy and provide easy entry for insects and vermin. Gaps often exist where siding meets trim, where electric cables or pipes enter the building, or where the sill of the house meets the foundation. For cracks up to 1/4 to 5/16 inches, a smooth, even bead of caulk applied with a caulking gun is best. For wider openings, use an aerosol spray foam insulation. Let the foam expand to fill cracks and slice away the excess after a day's drying time.

STUCK WINDOWS

Stuck windows are an inconvenience as well as a potential hazard, because they can impede escaping from fire. Most stuck windows are painted shut on the inside, outside, or both. With double-hung windows, place the heels of your hands on either end of the sash's top rail and rap sharply upward. Start with light impacts and don't get violent. If the sash doesn't move, cut the painted joint between the sash and the window stop or weatherstripping. Repeat the process on the outside. If cutting sash joints fails, work a putty knife deep into the joint between stop and sash. If it still won't budge, it may be necessary to remove the stop. Removing the stop will chip paint and requires careful carpentry skills.

BATHROOM CAULKING AND GROUTING

Neglecting to replace old grout and tired caulking in the bathroom is one of the most common home maintenance failures. It may not seem to be a big problem, but over time, the ceramic tiles loosen, allowing moisture to damage underlying wall materials. To prevent headaches later on, old grout, especially at horizontal tile joints where water penetration is greatest, should be scraped out. Before replacing grout, thoroughly wash tiles and joints with a tub and tile cleaner and then rinse.

Faucet, control, and spout joints in the shower or tub also should be well sealed. If they are not, remove the faucet escutcheon plates. Many of these plates have small set screws that must be loosened first. Some plates can be unscrewed after you've removed the faucet handles. Using a putty knife or blade scraper, remove all old caulking, dirt, mildew, and soap residue. Finish cleaning with a tub and tile cleaner and then rinse thoroughly. Next, seal all faucet penetrations with a good adhesive caulk. Before reinstalling the escutcheon plates, run a bead of caulk around the plates' mating edges. Tighten the plates against the wall and run another bead of caulk around the outside, where the plates meet the wall.

Don't neglect replacing the worn-out caulk between the tub and the wall tile. Dig out the old caulk to full depth with an old screwdriver or sharp utility knife. Squirt tub and tile cleaner in the joint. Remove all residual caulk, grout, dirt, and mildew by working a rag or paper towel with a putty knife into the gap. Keep working until the towel comes out clean and dry. To seal the gap, run a bead of caulk into the joint. Placing a strip of masking tape along the tile just above the tub results in a neat, crisp edge. The caulk should fill the joint $1/4$- to $3/8$-inch deep. Smooth in the caulk with your finger, wipe away excess from the tub and tile, and then let dry for several hours.

TRICKLING TOILETS

Toilets are one of the most used, yet least understood home appliances. They have two basic moving parts: the flush valve, which lets water out of the tank and down the drain; and the fill valve, which lets the toilet fill up after the flush cycle is complete. Small leaks in either of these valves can waste thousands of gallons of water in the course of a year. Here's how to tell if your valves are leaking:

To test the flush valve, open the top of the tank and pour a small amount of food coloring into the water. After an hour, if there is any colored water in the bowl, the flush valve is leaking and should be replaced.

To test the fill valve, open the top of the tank and find the hollow plastic pipe that sticks up from the bottom of the tank. The water level should be about an inch below the top of the pipe. If the water level is even with the top, the fill valve may be leaking or improperly adjusted and should be repaired or replaced. Next, flush the toilet and watch the top of the valve. If any water squirts up, you may have a leaky seal, which also means you need a new fill valve.

Both of these parts are easy to replace and cost less than $10. Fluidmaster makes good replacement valves with clear instructions that teach you how to do the job. You can find them at any home center.

■ HELP FOR A LEAKING TOILET

Most leakages in a toilet can be traced to problems in one of two places. Here's where they are inside the tank:

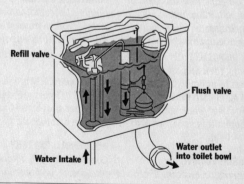

Refill valve

Flush valve

Water Intake ↑

Water outlet into toilet bowl

FIRST YOU USE 'EM, THEN YOU LOSE 'EM

Many household products contain hazardous chemicals that, if not discarded properly, can do lasting harm to the environment. Here's how to dispose of them and some homemade alternatives that you can use the next time around.

HOUSEHOLD CHEMICALS

ABRASIVE CLEANING POWDER

Corrosive, irritant, contains trisodiumphosphate, ammonia, and ethanol.

■ **DISPOSAL:** Rinse container thoroughly, then it may be sent to landfill; also check with water treatment plants—certain bacteria may detoxify the material.

■ **ALTERNATIVES:** Use baking soda or borax, or rub area with half a lemon dipped in borax (toxic to children and pets).

AMMONIA-BASED CLEANER

Corrosive, irritant, contains ammonia and ethanol.

■ **DISPOSAL:** Same as abrasive cleaner.

■ **ALTERNATIVES:** Use undiluted white vinegar.

BLEACH CLEANER

Corrosive, contains sodium or potassium hydroxide, hydrogen peroxide, sodium or calcium hypochlorite.

■ **DISPOSAL:** Fully use products, then dispose of waste, can be at landfill.

■ **ALTERNATIVES:** For laundry, use ¹/₂ cup white vinegar, baking soda, or borax per load.

DISINFECTANT

Corrosive, contains diethyl-ene or methylene glycol, sodium hypochlorite, and phenols.

■ **DISPOSAL:** If products are fully used and rinsed, and no waste remains in container, it may go to landfill, if necessary.

■ **ALTERNATIVES:** Mix ¹/₂ cup borax with 1 gal. boiling water. Not a disinfectant, however.

DRAIN CLEANER

Corrosive, contains sodium or potassium hydroxide, sodium hypochlorite, hydrochloric acid, and petroleum distillates.

■ **DISPOSAL:** Store safely until community organizes hazardous waste program.

■ **ALTERNATIVES:** Pour in ¹/₂ cup baking soda followed by ¹/₂ cup vinegar; let set for 15 minutes, follow with boiling water; snake or plunger.

FURNITURE POLISH

Flammable, contains diethylene, glycol, petroleum distillates, and nitrobenzene.

■ **DISPOSAL:** Same as drain cleaners.

■ **ALTERNATIVES:** Mix 3 parts olive oil to 1 part vinegar. For water stains, use toothpaste on damp cloth.

HOUSEHOLD BATTERY

Contains mercury, zinc, silver, lithium, and cadmium.

■ **DISPOSAL:** Recycle your waste, bring to a gas station or reclamation center.

■ **ALTERNATIVES:** Solar power, wind-up watches, rechargeables (may contain toxic heavy metals).

MOTHBALLS

Contain naphthalenes and paradichlorobenzene.

■ **DISPOSAL:** Same as abrasive cleaner.

■ **ALTERNATIVES:** Cedar chips or blocks; clean clothes well, put in airtight storage bag.

OVEN CLEANER

Corrosive, contains potassium or sodium hydroxide and ammonia.

■ **DISPOSAL:** If products are fully used and rinsed, and no waste remains in container, it may go to landfill.

■ **ALTERNATIVES:** Let mixture of 2 tbs. castile soap, 2 tsp. borax, and 2 cups water set in oven for 20 minutes; scrub with baking soda and salt.

PHOTOGRAPHIC CHEMICALS

Corrosive, irritant, contain silver, acetic acid, hydroquinone, sodium sulfite.

■ **DISPOSAL:** Store safely until community organizes a hazardous waste program.

■ **ALTERNATIVES:** Unknown.

POOL CHEMICALS
Corrosive, contain muriatic acid, sodium hypochlorite, and algicide.

■ **DISPOSAL:** Rinse container thoroughly and it may be sent to landfill; check with water treatment plants, as certain bacteria may detoxify the material.

■ **ALTERNATIVES:** Disinfectants: ozone or UV-light system. pH: consult baking soda box for amount to add for proper pH.

RUG AND UPHOLSTERY CLEANER
Corrosive, contains naphthalene, perchloroethylene, oxalic acid, diethylene, and glycol.

■ **DISPOSAL:** Store safely until community organizes a hazardous waste program.

■ **ALTERNATIVES:** Clean with soda water or baking soda paste, then vacuum.

TOILET BOWL CLEANER
Corrosive, irritant, contains muriatic (hydrochloric) or oxalic acid, paradichlorobenzene, and calcium hypochlorite.

■ **DISPOSAL:** Same as oven cleaner.

■ **ALTERNATIVES:** Coat bowl with paste of lemon juice and borax (toxic to children), let set, then scrub.

PAINTS
ENAMEL OR OIL-BASED PAINT
Flammable, toxic. Contains aliphatic and aromatic hydrocarbons, some pigments.

■ **ALTERNATIVES:** Latex or water-based paint.

■ **DISPOSAL:** Recycle wastes by bringing to service station or reclamation center.

LATEX OR WATER-BASED PAINT
May be toxic. Contains ethylene glycol, glycol ethers, phenyl mercuric acetate, some pigments, resins.

■ **DISPOSAL:** Check with water treatment plants; waste can be disposed of at some treatment plants where certain bacteria can detoxify the chemical; also may be recycled.

■ **ALTERNATIVES:** Latex without the above ingredients or limestone-based (whitewash) paint.

RUST-PROOFING COATING
Flammable, toxic. Contains methylene chloride, petroleum distillates, toluene, xylene, some pigments.

■ **DISPOSAL:** Should be safely stored until community organizes a hazardous waste program.

■ **ALTERNATIVES:** Unknown.

PAINT THINNERS, TURPENTINE
Toxic, flammable. Contain alcohol, acetone, esters, ketones, turpentine, petroleum distillates.

■ **DISPOSAL:** Check for disposal at local water treatment plants.

■ **ALTERNATIVES:** Use water in water-based paints.

PAINT AND VARNISH REMOVER
Flammable, toxic. Contains acetone, ketones, alcohol, xylene, toluene, methylene chloride.

■ **DISPOSAL:** Wastes should be safely stored until community organizes hazardous waste program.

■ **ALTERNATIVES:** For lead-free paint, use sandpaper or scraper and heat gun.

WOOD PRESERVATIVE
Flammable, toxic. Contains copper or zinc naphthenate, creosote, magnesium fluorosilicate, petroleum distillates, chlorinated phenols (PCP).

■ **DISPOSAL:** Wastes should be safely stored until community organizes hazardous waste program.

■ **ALTERNATIVES:** Use water-based wood preservatives. (Note that these products may still contain some of the ingredients mentioned above.)

STAIN AND VARNISH
Flammable, toxic. Contains mineral spirits, glycol ethers, ketones, toluene, xylene.

■ **DISPOSAL:** Wastes should be safely stored until community organizes a hazardous waste program.

■ **ALTERNATIVES:** Use latex or water-based finishes.

SOURCE: Environmental Hazards Management Institute, Durham, N.H.

GARDENING

HERBS: Tips on growing and using herbs, PAGE 327   **SOIL:** An expert's advice on preparing the foundation for a great garden, PAGE 330 **WILDLIFE:** How to attract butterflies and hummingbirds, PAGE 335 **ROSES:** No-fuss varieties for no-mess gardeners, PAGE 336   **BULBS:** A guide to planting favorite choices, PAGE 337   **TREES:** When and how to prune, PAGE 339   **LAWNS:** The best grasses for your region, PAGE 340

PROBLEM SOLVING

▼

PERFECT PLANTS FOR TOUGH PLACES

What garden doesn't have problem spots? Here's a guru to help

Nearly every garden has a tough spot, where the sun doesn't shine, or shines too much, or the drainage is poor, or the kids have made it a place to play ball. Instead of altering the nature of those problem spots, it's often easier to find plants that are suitable for the particular condition, advises Elvin McDonald, senior garden editor of *Traditional Home* magazine. A noted gardening authority and author of numerous books, including *The 400 Best Garden Plants* (Random House, 1995), McDonald offers his solutions to some frequently encountered gardening problems.

■ **Which plants do you recommend for shady areas?**

A number of plants thrive in the shade. Hostas, impatiens, hardy ferns, violets, and astilbe, which is a plant with plumy spikes of countless tiny flowers, are all good shade plants. Astilbe and impatiens are especially nice because they bring color to hosta and fern gardens. All are perennials except for impatiens, which are annuals in most parts of the country. Along the Gulf Coast, impatiens live sometimes two or three years until there is a freeze.

Other good possibilities are blue phlox, violets, hardy begonias, hardy primrose, and dicentra, also known as bleeding hearts.

■ **Which plants do well in very sunny spots?**

For very sunny places, you may want to try the purple coneflower, rudbeckia, daylily, and peony. All of them do well just about anywhere in the country, except for peonies, which don't do well in the deep South because there is not enough chilling. Showy sedum, a succulent that blooms in the late summer and fall, also likes sun. Bedding geraniums, garden mums, lavender, zinnias, and cosmos like sun, too.

■ **How should sloped areas around a house be treated?**

If an incline is too steep for mowing a lawn safely, plant a low-upkeep groundcover, like pachysandra, myrtle, or ajuga, along with shrubs and understory trees. If the slope is extremely steep, install retaining walls in a series of terraces and then plant whatever you wish.

■ **What do you recommend for clay soil?**

This is a common problem in much of the country. Sometimes, the answer is to install raised planting beds and fill them with well-

■ WHERE THE GROWING ZONES FALL

Most plant catalogs specify the regions in which perennial plants thrive. The standard USDA zones are defined by the minimum temperatures each region reaches in an average year; the 11 zones are shown.

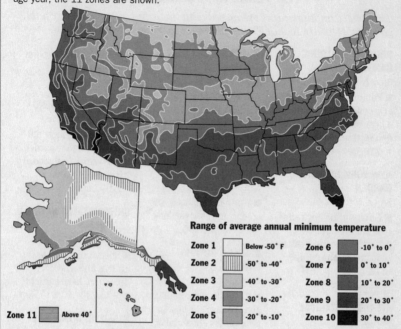

Range of average annual minimum temperature

Zone 1	Below -50° F	Zone 6	-10° to 0°
Zone 2	-50° to -40°	Zone 7	0° to 10°
Zone 3	-40° to -30°	Zone 8	10° to 20°
Zone 4	-30° to -20°	Zone 9	20° to 30°
Zone 5	-20° to -10°	Zone 10	30° to 40°

Zone 11 — Above 40°

prepared planting soil. If you are planting directly in clay soil, you should incorporate lots of well-rotted compost. Dig the clay soil 8 inches deep and add at least 4 inches of compost. You can fork or rototill the compost in. You can also treat soil that is too sandy the same way—add lots of well-rotted compost.

■ Should gardeners in arid parts of the country stick to indigenous plants?

Not necessarily. They might try selecting plants that are drought-tolerant, such as yucca, gaillardia, gaura, and callirhoe. Or they could choose plants from places that have common temperatures, amount of rainfall, or other similar factors.

■ Are there plants that can flourish in very wet spots in a garden?

Very wet areas must be drained. One system often used is the French draining system, which involves installing drain tiles into the earth to carry off excess water. Or a smart solution is to plant a bog garden using plants that like wet conditions. Some such plants are marsh marigold, cattail, Louisiana iris, spider lilies, and yellow flag, a tall yellow iris that's almost a weed. Bog gardens are meant to be wild places and you want a plant that will colonize and take off.

■ What about areas that might be frequently trampled upon by kids and dogs?

Groundcovers aren't a good solution for high-traffic areas. They are quickly damaged by frequent foot traffic. Fine-textured lawns aren't the answer either. Instead, select a lawngrass seed mixture that's recommended for playing fields and high traffic. Your local garden center can suggest the right grass for your region. Or use gravel or bark mulch. Shingletoe is especially good under swings.

TEN TERRIFIC PUBLIC GARDENS

The American landscape is scattered with thousands of spectacular public gardens. Here are 10 that Elvin McDonald considers among the best.

BROOKLYN BOTANIC GARDEN
Brooklyn, NY
- Famous for its systematic collection of plants in a beautiful designed garden setting.
☎ 718–622–4433

NEW YORK BOTANICAL GARDEN
Bronx, NY
- Outstanding herb and rose gardens. A newly refurbished conservatory reopened to the public in 1997.
☎ 718–817–8700

ATLANTA BOTANICAL GARDEN
Atlanta, GA
- Beautiful display of rare and endangered plants; also a gorgeous conservatory.
☎ 404–876–5859

MOODY GARDENS
Galveston, TX
- Famous pyramid-shaped rain-forest greenhouse built to withstand hurricane force winds.
☎ 409–744–1745

HUNTINGTON BOTANICAL GARDENS
San Marino, CA
- World-class bonsai, succulent, and rose gardens.
☎ 818–405–2100

CHICAGO BOTANIC GARDEN
Glencoe, IL
- Its walled perennial garden is one of the best in the country. Outstanding educational programs.
☎ 847–835–5440

HOLDEN ARBORETUM
Kirtland, OH
- Famous for its woody (trees and shrubs) plant collection.
☎ 216–946–4400

LONGWOOD GARDENS
Kennett Square, PA
- Perhaps the most outstanding display garden in the world. Included are 20 theme gardens.
☎ 610–388–1000

UNITED STATES NATIONAL ARBORETUM
Washington, DC
- Spectacular display of azaleas and a nearly three-acre herb garden.
☎ 202–245–2726

MISSOURI BOTANICAL GARDEN
St. Louis, MO
- A geodesic dome houses a full-fledged tropical rain forest.
☎ 314–577–5100

It's cushiony and breaks falls, reducing skinned knees and elbows.

Remember that you grow a lawn for children to play on, but if there's a path worn on it, then maybe a path belongs there—not grass.

■ Which factors should be taken into account when locating flower gardens?

I am strongly in favor of moving so-called foundation plantings, shrubs that developers usually plant near homes, to the perimeter of the property. That way the large area immediately surrounding the house is a more private place that can be used to plant flowers, edibles, herbs, and fragrant and butterfly-attracting plants.

Typical foundation plantings grow up and smother the house, shade out the windows, and make the house dismally dark inside. They also are good places for thieves to hide.

I believe we should rethink the placement of shrubs and trees, and claim the front yard for ourselves. Often, the front yard is the sunniest and best place for a garden. I'm not talking about turning it into a natural habitat that is unkempt or could harbor pestilence, but rather a beautiful private place.

EXPERT TIPS

HERBS FOR ALL SPACES

*Fragrant, tasty, and beautiful—
plant them outdoors or in*

Patches of garden that seem to sprout nothing but weeds should not be written off. "If you can't grow anything else," says gardening and food writer Sally Freeman, "herbs are the answer." Herbs have a long, noble history. They've been used to flavor food, prepare medicinal brews, beautify gardens—even line the pockets of merchants, as they tried to fill the demand for herbs and spices during the Middle Ages.

Growing herbs isn't difficult, as Freeman, author of *Herbs for All Seasons* (Penguin, 1991) and *Every Woman's Guide to Natural Home Remedies* (Holt, 1997), explains here.

■ **ESSENTIALS FOR AN HERB GARDEN.** Ideally, there are three essentials for an herb garden: good drainage, plenty of sunlight, and light soil enriched with compost. Try to keep your garden away from trees; the roots rob soil of moisture and nutrients.

But many herbs will do well without all three. Rosemary doesn't mind some shade. Basil, fennel, dill, Italian parsley, and chives do well in soil suitable for growing vegetables. Peppermint doesn't mind wet conditions. Thyme tolerates acid soil, while lavender requires more alkalinity than most herbs.

■ **INDOOR HERB GARDENS.** If your windows face south, you should have adequate light for even sun-loving herbs, such as dill, coriander, oregano, thyme, and marjoram. If your windows face in other directions, you should be able to grow rosemary, sweet woodruff, or bay laurel in natural light. You may have to augment natural light with special lighting.

Be sure to place herb containers as far as possible from radiators and other heating appliances, in a room that is cool, moist, and well ventilated. On very cold winter days they should be placed away from windows.

■ **GROWING FROM SEED.** Most herbs will grow easily from seed, germinating in five to seven days. There are exceptions. Lavender can take up to a month to germinate. Rosemary is best propagated by cuttings, and French tarragon, which is more flavorful than the Russian variety and preferable for cooking, must be propagated by root division. Parsley can be very difficult to germinate. Italian parsley is easier to grow than regular parsley, and, to my mind, tastes better.

■ **FERTILIZER OF CHOICE.** Compost is best because it won't burn the tender roots. Enrich your compost pile by including some weeds, especially dandelion, whose long roots bring up minerals from deep in the soil. A layer of mulch conserves moisture and suppresses weeds in the summer.

■ **WATERING HERBS.** Water herbs as soon as the soil feels dry. Rosemary, especially, should never be allowed to dry out. You may need to water every day. Your herbs will also appreciate a daily misting.

■ **TASTE-TESTING HERBS**

Sally Freeman's favorite recipe is herbed chicken:

**3–3½ lb. whole broiler or fryer
1 medium onion
3–4 cloves garlic, chopped
½ teaspoon dill
½ teaspoon coriander
⅛–¼ teaspoon cayenne**

■ Wash the chicken and pat dry. Lightly salt the inside of the cavity.

■ Cut small slits in the skin and insert pieces of garlic. Sprinkle chicken with dill, coriander, and cayenne.

■ Roast for 1½ hours at 350 degrees in close-fitting ceramic vessel with tight-fitting lid or in cast-iron enamelware. No need to baste.

TOOLS

PRUNERS AND SPADES TO DIE FOR

Wooden handles cause few blisters, anvil pruners cut most sharply

The gardening rage in recent years has brought forth an abundance of top-quality tools, many of them fashioned after classic English tools. But at current prices, equipping yourself fully can be quite an investment, so you must choose wisely.

Materials are important. Metal tools should be made from tempered, heat-treated, or forged metal. Stainless steel tools are most expensive, but they are also the strongest and should last you a lifetime. Choose wooden-handled tools over metal ones whenever possible because they are less likely to cause blisters. Hickory and ash wood make the best handles. Handles made from Douglas fir will be weak and should be avoided. And make sure that there are no cracks or flaws of any kind in the wood before buying.

Look for pitchforks with springy stainless steel tines, and hoses made from rubber or Flexogen last longer than plastic ones.

Bamboo lawn rakes are the lightest and easiest to handle. They're usually the best for raking leaves. But for raking leaves within flower beds, use a rake that is rubber-tipped. It won't damage the plants.

Here is the advice of gardening expert Alastair Bolton, who did his spadework at the National Arboretum before becoming a private gardening consultant in Washington, D.C.:

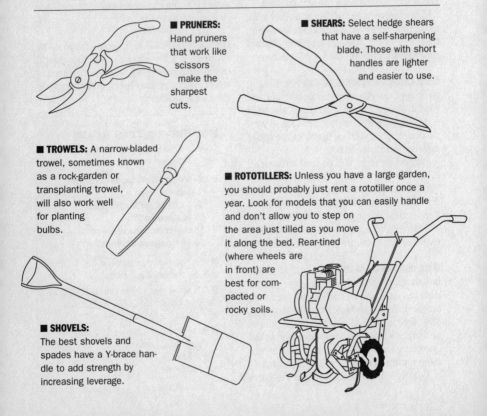

■ **PRUNERS:** Hand pruners that work like scissors make the sharpest cuts.

■ **SHEARS:** Select hedge shears that have a self-sharpening blade. Those with short handles are lighter and easier to use.

■ **TROWELS:** A narrow-bladed trowel, sometimes known as a rock-garden or transplanting trowel, will also work well for planting bulbs.

■ **ROTOTILLERS:** Unless you have a large garden, you should probably just rent a rototiller once a year. Look for models that you can easily handle and don't allow you to step on the area just tilled as you move it along the bed. Rear-tined (where wheels are in front) are best for compacted or rocky soils.

■ **SHOVELS:** The best shovels and spades have a Y-brace handle to add strength by increasing leverage.

TOOLS AND EQUIPMENT TO DO THE JOB

Where to get a great rake or the best English trowel, the best new seeds and plants. Plus, other resources for a beautiful garden

TOOLS

AMES
P.O. Box 1774
Parkersburg, WV 26102
■ Good selection of child-sized tools.
☎ 800–624–2654

E. C. GEIGER
P.O. Box 285
Harleysville, PA 19438
■ Tools, equipment, soil testers, fertilizers, etc.
☎ 800–443–4437

LANGENBACK
P.O. Box 1420
Lawndale, CA 90260
■ Top-of-the-line English and other imported tools.
☎ 800–362–1991

SMITH & HAWKEN
25 Corte Madera
Mill Valley, CA 94941
■ Tools, gifts, clothing.
☎ 800–776–3336

SEEDS AND PLANTS

W. ATLEE BURPEE & CO.
300 Park Ave.
Warminster, PA
18974–4818
■ Seeds, bulbs, shrubs, and gardening supplies.
☎ 800–487–1447

GEO. W. PARK SEED CO.
1 Parkton Ave.
Greenwood, SC
29647–0001
■ Seeds, plants, and gardening supplies.
☎ 864–223–7333

JACKSON & PERKINS
1 Rose Lane
Medford, OR 97501
■ Wide selection of roses and perennials, also garden accessories.
☎ 800–854–6200

SHEPHERD'S GARDEN SEEDS
30 Irene St.
Torrington, CT 06790
■ Specialty vegetable, herb, and flower seeds.
☎ 860–482–3638

THOMPSON & MORGAN
P.O. Box 1308
Jackson, NJ 08527
■ English catalog with over 2,500 varieties of flower and vegetable seeds.
☎ 800–274–7333

WAYSIDE GARDENS
1 Garden Lane
Hodges, SC 29695–0001
■ Large selection of perennials, trees, and shrubs.
☎ 800–845–1124

WHITE FLOWER FARM
Litchfield, CT 06759–0050
■ Perennials, bulbs, trees, and shrubs. Excellent catalog with detailed plant and growing instructions.
☎ 800–503–9624

BOOKS

AMERICAN HORTICULTURAL SOCIETY ENCYCLOPEDIA OF GARDEN PLANTS
Christopher Brickell, ed., Macmillan, 1989, $59.95
■ A comprehensive volume of information on most of the trees, shrubs, flowers, and foliage plants grown in American gardens.

READER'S DIGEST ILLUSTRATED GUIDE TO GARDENING
Carroll C. Calkins, ed., Reader's Digest Association, 1989, $30
■ If you had no other source, you could develop terrific skills with this book alone. Easy-to-understand and has excellent illustrations.

ONLINE

GARDENET
http://www.trine.com/GardenNet
■ Browse and buy from big-name seed and flower companies, order supplies, share the woes of pruning with fellow gardeners, and find out about flower shows and other horticultural events around the world.

DIG AND YOU SHALL REAP

Start with a soil test and a little nutrition for dirt that's lacking

Soil is the foundation for any garden. The effort given to its preparation will, to a large degree, determine the success of your garden. While soil quality varies widely depending on location, and your local agricultural extension service is likely to be the best information source about the soil in your region, some steps to soil preparation apply to any yard. Chris Curless, a horticulturist at White Flower Farm, the famous Litchfield, Conn., grower and supplier of ornamental plants to home gardens in the United States and Canada, explains how to get your garden ready for planting:

■ **Test your soil to find out how well it will support plant growth and what you might have to do to improve it.**

A soil test will show your soil pH and how to adjust it if needed, as well as the levels of specific nutrients to determine fertilizer needs. Extension services can perform these lab tests on your soil and give you a detailed profile of what you've got in your yard. Most plants prefer a slightly acidic-to-neutral soil. Your soil test will indicate how much lime or sulfur needs adding if adjustment is required. It will also recommend what other nutrients may be needed as supplements.

■ **Mark the area for your garden before you dig.**

If it's a simple shape like a rectangle or square, stakes and string are an easy way to do this. For a curved bed, a garden hose will allow you to make smooth bends. Mark the edge of the bed with white spray paint or powdered lime so you know exactly where you

want to dig. It's easy to think you know and still get lost in the middle of your digging.

■ **Remove existing grass to get to the soil.**

If you are going to put a border into a lawn, you want to get rid of the turf. If it's a large, relatively flat area, consider renting a sod cutter—a heavy, gas-powered machine. It's not great at corners and awful on a hillside because it weighs about 300 pounds, but for flat areas it is very fast. Smaller mechanical gadgets are also available to cut turf. But the tried-and-true method is to use a sharpened spade to undercut the turf. Since you're removing the top inch or so of soil and a lot of green material, put it in the compost pile so you can use it again in the future.

■ **Add a hefty layer of organic matter.**

Next, spread three to six inches of organic matter on top of the entire area with a rake. Organic matter benefits all kinds of soil, whether it's light and sandy or heavy. In a sandy soil, organic matter improves moisture retention; in a heavy, clayey soil it improves the drainage. Remember: if you're planting woody stock or perennials, you have only one chance to work the soil like this, so take advantage of the opportunity. Some good types of organic matter include aged manure, peat moss, or leaf mold. In some areas of the South, ground-up pine bark is recommended because it lasts longer in warm, moist soil. If you need to add soil amendments, spread them evenly on top of the organic matter.

■ **Thoroughly mix the organic matter and other additions into the soil.**

The next step is digging. I think turning the soil to a depth of a shovel is enough. Many books recommend double-digging—which means digging twice as deep—but for most people, that's just way too much work.

Start at one corner and work your way backward, so you don't compact the area you have turned. Break up big clods as you go. Digging and incorporating the organic matter and fertilizer creates air spaces in the soil, making it easier for the roots of your plants to get around. The goal of all this is to make it easier for plants to grow.

A VEGETABLE FOR EVERY POT

Most vegetables are easily grown from seed. For plants that require a long growing season, you can start the seeds growing indoors during winter months, then transplant the seedlings into your garden after the last frost. Your local agricultural extension service or plant nursery can tell you the best time to plant in your area. How deep should you sow the seed? As a general rule, plant at a depth four times the seed's diameter.

Vegetable *When to sow*	Days to germinate	Light	Space between plants (in.)	rows	Days to harvest
ARTICHOKE *Start indoors 8 to 10 weeks before last frost, then transplant outdoors*	7–14	Full sun	36	3 ft.	90–100 after transplanting
ARUGULA *Early spring, as soon as soil can be worked*	7–14	Full sun to partial shade	8–12	18–24 in.	35–45
ASPARAGUS *Best to start with year-old roots. Plant in spring; comes back every year.*		Full sun to partial shade	15	3 ft.	First harvest in second or third year
BEANS, bush *After last frost*	7–14	Full sun	4	2 ft.	45–60
BEANS, lima *After last frost*	7–12	Full sun	6–8	18 in.	55–75
BEANS, pole *After last frost*	7–14	Full sun	36	4 ft.	45–65
BEANS, pole lima *After last frost*	7–12	Full sun	6–8	18 in.	88–92
BEETS *After last frost*	7–14	Full sun	3	15 in.	49–60
BROCCOLI *Start indoors 5 to 7 weeks before last frost, then transplant outdoors*	5–10	Full sun	24	30 in.	50–65
BRUSSELS SPROUTS *Start indoors 5 to 7 weeks before last frost, then transplant outdoors*	5–10	Full sun	18	2 ft.	78–100
CABBAGE, Chinese *After last frost*	4–10	Full sun to partial shade	12	18 in.	43–55
CABBAGE, head *Start indoors 5 weeks before soil can be worked in spring, then transplant outdoors*	4–10	Full sun to partial shade	18	2 ft.	50–95 after transplanting
CARROTS *As soon as soil can be worked in spring*	12–17	Full sun	3	14 in.	60–75
CAULIFLOWER *Start indoors 5 to 7 weeks before soil can be worked in spring, then transplant outdoors*	5–10	Full sun	18	2 ft.	45–75 after transplanting
CELERY *Start indoors 10 to 12 weeks before last frost, then transplant outdoors*	21–28	Full sun	6	2 ft.	98–105 after transplanting
CORN, sweet *After last frost*	7–10	Full sun	10	3 ft.	66–92
CUCUMBER *After last frost and soil has warmed*	7–10	Full sun	48	6 ft.	55–62
EGGPLANT *Start indoors 8 to 10 weeks before last frost, then transplant when soil has warmed*	7–10	Full sun to partial shade	24	3 ft.	50–70 after transplanting
KALE *As soon as soil can be worked in spring; also in early fall for winter crop*	5–10	Full sun	12–15	2 ft.	55–65

■ PLANTER'S GUIDE

Vegetable When to sow	Days to germinate	Light	Space between		Days to harvest
			plants (in.)	rows	
LEEK	7–12	Full sun	2	1 ft.	110–145 from planting seed
Start indoors 6 to 10 weeks before last frost, then transplant outdoors; or sow outdoors 3 weeks before last frost					
LETTUCE, butterhead and Romaine (Cos)	7–10	Full sun to partial shade	6	14 in.	60–75
As soon as soil can be worked in spring; resow every 2 weeks into fall for continuous harvest					
LETTUCE, crisphead	7–10	Full sun to partial shade	10	14 in.	56–84
As soon as soil can be worked in spring; resow every 2 weeks into fall for continuous harvest					
LETTUCE, leaf	7–10	Full sun to partial shade	6	14 in.	45–50
As soon as soil can be worked in spring; resow every 2 weeks into fall for continuous harvest					
MELONS (cantaloupe/muskmelon, honeydew)	5–10	Full sun	36	6 ft.	68–88 from planting seed
After last frost and the soil has warmed; or, for earlier harvest, start indoors 4–6 weeks before last frost, then transplant outdoors after soil has warmed					
OKRA	7–14	Full sun	10	2–4 ft.	50–60
After last frost and soil has warmed					
ONIONS	10–14	Full sun	2	15 in.	85–120 after transplanting
Start seeds 12 weeks before last frost, then transplant outdoors; or grow from sets instead of seed and plant sets after last frost					
PARSNIPS	21–28	Full sun	3	18 in.	100–120
After last frost					
PEANUTS	7–10	Full sun	12	30 in.	120–135
After last frost					
PEAS	7–14	Full sun	8	2 ft.	62–72
As soon as the soil can be worked in spring					
PEPPERS	10–20	Full sun	24	2 ft.	65–75 after transplanting
Start indoors 8 to 10 weeks before last frost, transplant outdoors after soil has warmed					
POTATOES	From tubers	Full sun	12	3 ft.	60–80
As soon as soil can be worked in spring					
PUMPKIN	7–10	Full sun	60	12 ft.	80–120
After last frost					
RADISH	5–10	Full sun to partial shade	2	14 in.	22–28
As soon as soil can be worked in spring					
SPINACH	7–14	Full sun to partial shade	3	14 in.	39–45
As soon as soil can be worked in spring					
SQUASH, summer	7–14	Full sun	48	3 ft.	45–52
After last frost and soil has warmed					
SQUASH, winter	7–14	Full sun	60	6 ft.	75–110
After last frost and soil has warmed					
SWEET POTATOES	From plants	Full sun	12	3 ft.	90–120
After last frost and soil has warmed					
SWISS CHARD	7–10	Full sun to partial shade	9	18 in.	60–63
After last frost					
TOMATOES	7–14	Full sun	36	3 ft.	55–85 after transplanting
Start indoors 6 to 8 weeks before last frost; transplant outdoors after soil has warmed					
TURNIPS	7–14	Full sun	3	15 in.	35–60
After last frost					
WATERMELON	7–14	Full sun	96	8 ft.	65–100
After last frost and soil has warmed					

FERTILIZING
▼

FEED THE PLANT THAT FEEDS YOU

Here's when and how to side-dress your vegetable plants

How should you nurture your vegetables to ensure a bountiful harvest? The best way is to give them a fertilizer boost. Most commercial fertilizers contain three major plant nutrients: nitrogen, phosphorus, and potassium. Nitrogen is essential for leafy growth; phosphorus promotes root and fruit development; and potassium encourages general vigor. On the package labels you'll find a set of numbers that refers to the percentage of each of the three ingredients in the product. The ingredients are always listed in the same order. For example, a fertilizer labeled 10-15-10 contains 10 percent nitrogen, 15 percent phosphorus, and 10 percent potassium.

Here are some guidelines for choosing the right fertilizer for your garden.

■ Granular fertilizers are standard for long-term release of nutrients. Incorporate them into soil before planting. Use liquid fertilizers when you need to give plants a quick boost during the growing season.

■ Most vegetables benefit from another application of granular fertilizer after they have begun to flower and set fruit. This midseason boost is called side-dressing. Sprinkle the fertilizer along each row of plants and mix it into the soil. Water well.

■ For leafy crops, such as spinach and lettuce, use a fertilizer that has a higher ratio of nitrogen. For other vegetables, use a higher ratio of phosphorus.

■ Chemical fertilizers can't improve soil. To improve the soil, use organic materials, such as leaf mold, peat moss, and manure, which provide many nutrients to the soil but perhaps not all or enough for optimum plant growth. For that reason, you may want to supplement organics with chemical fertilizers.

EXPERT SOURCES

PLANTING THE SEEDS OF YESTERYEAR

For years, the only way to grow the vegetables popular in your great-grandmother's day was to get heirloom seeds through specialty catalogs devoted to saving a bit of horticultural history. But more and more gardeners are recognizing the appeal of antique varieties—so much so that Burpee, one of the country's most popular seed companies, recently launched an heirloom catalog for the mainstream gardener. What's the attraction? It's not so much nostalgia as taste. Decades of hybridizing have produced hardier modern vegetables, but at the expense of aroma and flavor. Gourmet gardeners claim the taste of old-fashioned varieties can't be beat. The following sources offer a wide selection:

W. ATLEE BURPEE & CO.
300 Park Ave.
Warminster, PA
18974—4818
☎ 800–888–1447

SEED SAVER'S EXCHANGE
3076 N. Winn Rd.
Decorah, IA 52101
☎ 319–382–5990

SEEDS BLUM
HC33 P.O. Box 2057
Boise, ID 83706
☎ 208–342–0858

HOMEMADE CURES FOR PESTS AND DISEASES

Organic gardening specialists recommend these do-it-yourself recipes for ridding your garden of unwanted visitors.

COOKING OIL SOLUTION

Effective against eggs and immature insects.

- 1 cup cooking oil
- 1 tbsp. liquid dish soap

■ Mix oil and soap. Use 2¹/₂ tsps. per 1 cup of water. Pour into a spray bottle and spray surface and undersides of leaves. Apply once every 2 to 3 weeks until pest is gone.

BAKING SODA SOLUTION

Usually effective in preventing foliage fungus, especially on roses.

- 1 tbsp. baking soda
- 1 gal. water
- ¹/₂ tsp. insecticidal soap

■ Dissolve baking soda in the water. Mix in the soap and pour into a spray bottle. Test this solution on just a few leaves before spraying an entire plant. Some plants may be sensi-

tive and the solution may need to be diluted to prevent foliage discoloration. Spray to cover the top and underside of foliage about twice a week from spring through early fall.

GARLIC-PEPPER SOLUTION

Effective against a wide range of chewing insects and animals.

- 2 cloves garlic
- 1 tsp. liquid detergent
- 2 tsps. cooking oil
- 1 tbsp. cayenne pepper
- 2 cups water

■ Put all the ingredients in a blender and mix until the garlic is thoroughly pureed. Spray solution on affected plants. Reapply as needed.

BORDEAUX MIXTURE

Effective against common

fungal disease. Often used on small fruits.

- 2 heaping tbsps. fresh hydrated spray lime
- 2 level tsps. copper sulfate crystals
- 3 gals. water

■ Dissolve lime in 2 gallons of water. In a separate container, dissolve the copper sulfate in 1 gallon of water. Add the copper sulfate solution to the lime solution. Strain the solution through a cheesecloth directly into a sprayer. Spray to cover foliage. When dry, it forms an insoluble copper precipitate that prevents fungal spores from entering and infecting plants. Begin applications in spring, repeat once every 7 to 14 days through early fall. Don't apply during cool and wet weather.

INSECTS THAT WILL SET YOU FREE

You can use natural predators to fight insect pests. Here are some friendly enforcers and what they can help control, as well as some places to get them:

■ **ASSASSIN BUG:** Aphids, caterpillars, leafhoppers, and a variety of beetles.

■ **LADYBUGS:** Aphids, chinch bugs, rootworms, scale, spider mites, weevils, whiteflies.

■ **PRAYING MANTIS:** Aphids, beetles, caterpillars, flies, leafhoppers.

■ **ROBBER, SYRPHID, AND TACHINID FLIES:** Aphids, Japanese beetles, leafhoppers, mealybugs, scale, caterpillars.

SOURCES

Planet Natural	☎ 800–289–6656
Gempler's	☎ 800–272–7672
Peaceful Valley	☎ 916–272–4769

▼

BUTTERFLY GARDENING

The winged beauties will visit if you create an alluring home

Everyone loves butterflies, so much so that public butterfly gardens and zoos are proliferating. There are 130 or more throughout the country, and the number is growing. Creating your own garden to attract butterflies is a fairly easy undertaking. Plant what butterflies like to eat, drink, and use for resting and laying eggs, and they will likely pay a visit. Here are some essentials for enticing butterflies to your garden:

■ **WHERE TO PLANT THE GARDEN.** Most butterflies are sun lovers. Pick a spot that gets at least five to six hours of full sun. Sheltering the garden from the wind with a hedge or vine-covered lattice increases chances that butterflies will settle long enough to lay eggs. You can also attract butterflies to your windowsill, balcony, or rooftop by planting some of the flowers recommended below in large containers or window boxes.

■ **WHAT TO PLANT.** Groupings of flowers that create large splashes of color are more effective than single plants. Butterflies like brightly colored blossoms with short flower tubes that let them reach the nectar with their probosces. Some butterfly preferences include: milkweed, dogbane, Joe-Pye weed, purple coneflower, thistle, aster, goldenrod, lilac, zinnia, cosmos, strawflower, marigold, verbena, and tickseed sunflower.

Some common plants that serve as hosts for caterpillars are: Queen Anne's lace, which provides food for the larva of the eastern black swallowtails; milkweed, which feeds monarchs; dill and parsley for various swallowtails; and thistle and hollyhock for painted ladies.

■ **OTHER LURES.** Butterflies take in salt and minerals by sipping from mud puddles. Create a shallow puddle in your garden to serve as a drinking hole. Place some flat stones in the garden, which butterflies can use as resting spots. Also, try scattering around pieces of rotting peaches or plums and putting out small, flat containers filled with sugar water.

■ **PEST CONTROL.** Never use pesticides in or near a butterfly garden. To control pests, try using predatory insects or insecticidal soaps. A healthy butterfly garden will usually attract beneficial insects, such as lady beetles, praying mantis, and lacewings, which help the garden care for itself.

TO LURE A HUMMINGBIRD

If hummingbirds live in your area you can attract them to your garden. The frenetic little bird—the smallest species is the size of a bumble bee—is fascinating to watch. It hovers like a helicopter, moving forward, sideways or backwards at speeds of up to 200 wingbeats per second.

Hummers are attracted to red, tubular flowers. The National Wildlife Federation suggests planting, among others: trumpet honeysuckle, trumpet creeper, cardinal flower, scarlet penstemon, scarlet morning glory, cypress vine, scarlet paintbrush, scarlet salvia, bee balm, fire pink, scarlet petunia, red buckeye, geiger tree, scarletbrush, and coral bells.

You can also attract hummers by hanging a red feeder outdoors in the shade, not too close to a window. Fill the feeder with a solution of four parts water to one part sugar. Clean the feeder every three days using a brush and mild soap. Rinse well.

EXPERT TIPS

WE PROMISE YOU A ROSE GARDEN

Raising roses may not need a ton of chemicals and constant worry

The rose's reputation as an aristocrat is well deserved—it is a regal flower that requires the attention usually reserved for royalty. But rose lovers need not quit their jobs and sell their silver to grow beautiful roses in their gardens. For 15 years, rose breeders Ping Lim and Martin Nemko have been combing the world for the most disease-resistant and beautiful rose varieties, and they have been cross-breeding them to create super-roses. Nemko, who serves as a consultant to the Minnesota-based firm Bailey's Nurseries, a leading breeder of easy-care roses, offers these tips for the busy gardener:

■ **Choose disease-resistant varieties.** Most varieties of roses become so diseased that they look like they were dunked in weed killer unless bombarded each week with enough chemicals to make Saddam Hussein proud. But a few widely available rose varieties, such as Cliffs of Dover, Sun Flare, and Flower Carpet have disease-resistant genes. By choosing healthy varieties, you can pretty much chuck the sprayer. If you look closely, you might notice an insect or two or a nibbled leaf or bloom, but you don't need to get compulsive about your rosebushes. In most areas of the country, the stalwart varieties listed below (see box) should look just fine without a weekly shower of Orthene and Daconil 2787.

■ **Use an automated watering system.** During the growing season, roses love to drink, but you can quench their thirst while saving water, too. Just use a timer that's hooked up to plastic irrigation spritzers. Many home or garden centers sell kits—the two-gallon per hour size works best. Set the timer to water every other day for 30 minutes.

■ **Feed your bushes just once a year.** When the ground starts to warm in the spring, place a time-release fertilizer such as Osmocote+Iron directly underneath the spritzers. The fertilizer you select should be a once-a-growing-season formulation.

NO-FUSS ROSES FOR NO-MESS GARDENERS

Rose breeder Martin Nemko recommends these roses, arranged by color, if you don't have time for hassles. Unless otherwise noted, Nemko's picks are 2 to 3 feet tall and wide and can be found at most well-stocked nurseries.

WHITE

■ **GOURMET POPCORN:** Dark green foliage covered in a cloud of white.

■ **CLIFFS OF DOVER:** 18 in. tall and perhaps the healthiest of all.

YELLOW

■ **SUN FLARE:** The glossiest forest-green foliage you'll ever see on a rose.

PINK

■ **FLOWER CARPET:** A great way to cover a 4- to 5-foot-wide space.

■ **CAREFREE DELIGHT:** Hundreds of old-fashioned roses on a newly bred plant.

■ **CAREFREE WONDER:** A well-mannered 3-foot-tall by 2-foot-wide plant.

■ **HAPPY TRAILS:** The perfect plant for a hanging basket or cascading in a rock garden.

■ **ALEXANDER MCKENZIE:** Winter-hardy and especially bred for the North.

RED

■ **CHAMPLAIN:** Another rose that flourishes in northern climes.

PLANTER'S GUIDE

A BULB LOVER'S FAVORITE CHOICES

*They can come back to brighten the same spot for decades,
or you can dig them up and move them to a new home.*

	Height (in.)	Planting depth (in.)	Planting time	Blooming time
SPRING-FLOWERING BULBS				
CROCUS *Crocus* species	3–5	3–4	EARLY FALL	EARLY SPRING
CROWN IMPERIAL *Fritillaria imperialis*	30–48	5	EARLY FALL	MIDSPRING
DAFFODIL *Narcissus* species	12	6	EARLY FALL	MIDSPRING
DUTCH IRIS *Iris xiphium*	24	4	EARLY FALL	LATE SPRING
FLOWERING ONION *Allium giganteum*	48	10	EARLY FALL	LATE SPRING
GRAPE HYACINTH *Muscari botryoides*	6–10	3	EARLY FALL	EARLY SPRING
HYACINTH *Hyacinthus orientalis*	12	6	EARLY FALL	EARLY SPRING
SNOWDROP *Galanthus nivalis*	4-6	4	EARLY FALL	EARLY SPRING
TULIP (early) *Tulipa* species	10–13	6	EARLY FALL	EARLY SPRING
TULIP (Darwin hybrid) *Tulipa* species	28	6	EARLY FALL	MIDSPRING
TULIP (late) *Tulipa* species	36	6	EARLY FALL	LATE SPRING
WINDFLOWER *Anemone blanda*	5	2	EARLY FALL	EARLY SPRING
SUMMER-FLOWERING BULBS				
ANEMONES *Anemone* species	18	2	**NORTH:** EARLY SPRING **SOUTH:** LATE FALL	LATE SUMMER
BUTTERCUP *Ranunculus*	12	2	**SOUTH:** LATE FALL	MIDSUMMER
CROCOSMIA *Crocosmia* species	24	4	APRIL-MAY	MID- TO LATE SUMMER
DAHLIA (dwarf varieties) *Dahlia* species	12	4	AFTER LAST FROST	LATE SUMMER
DAHLIA (large varieties) *Dahlia* species	48	4	AFTER LAST FROST	LATE SUMMER
GALTONIA *Galtonia candicans*	40	5	APRIL-MAY	MID- TO LATE SUMMER
GLADIOLUS (large flower) *Gladiolus* species	60	3–4	APRIL-JUNE	MIDSUMMER
GLADIOLUS (small flower) *Gladiolus* species	30	3–4	APRIL-JUNE	MIDSUMMER
LILY *Lilium* species	36–84	8	FALL OR EARLY SPRING	ALL SUMMER
TIGER FLOWER *Tigridia paronia*	16	3	EARLY SPRING	MID- TO LATE SUMMER

■ HEIGHT AND DEPTH

A bulb that is planted deep will not
necessarily grow tall.

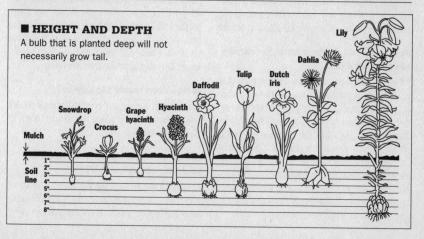

FROM ROOT TO BRANCH

Tree-planting is usually a fall pursuit. Here's how to do it

The selection of trees is one of the largest investments and most important decisions that a homeowner may face in landscaping a property. A well-chosen tree on the right site can transform even the plainest house into a home with visual appeal. Frank Santamour, research geneticist and tree expert at the National Arboretum in Washington, D.C., has been providing practical advice on growing trees for many years. Here he shares his experience and knowledge on tree selection and planting techniques.

■ What factors go into selecting a tree for a landscape?

First of all you look at ultimate size. You don't want to plant a tree that's going to get too big during the time you are paying off your house. Consider then what type of tree you want—evergreen or deciduous, flowering, or something that may have other attractions, like colored leaves in the autumn, or colored leaves all season. Finding trees that have practically no disease or insect problem is also important.

■ What should you look for at the nursery when buying a tree?

Most of the trees at nurseries are sold in containers nowadays. Look for a tree that has a large enough container so that a pretty decent portion of the root system will be intact. It's very difficult to make any judgments when you are viewing a plant at a nursery, because even a plant with a really tacky root system can look good if it's kept watered. You can't pop it out of the container to see the roots. So you've got to go on the general reputation of the nursery.

■ How about mail order trees?

I would stay away from them, quite frankly. There are some firms with a pretty decent reputation, but there are many horror stories—poor quality, small plants. Specialty items can be an exception, but go to your local nursery first and ask if they can get it for you. They should know where to get the best quality material.

■ When is the best time for planting?

That depends on where you live. I come from New England, and we plant in the spring because fall comes a little fast. Ideally, spring planting is done before growth begins, though with container-grown plants, you can plant a little later. In most of the United States, fall planting is also good. When you plant in the fall, wait until after the buds have set on the tree and growth has ceased, and do not fertilize afterward, which could promote new growth on the tree that sets it up for a killing frost.

■ How should a new tree be planted?

One of the myths people have is that they must fill a planting hole with manure and peat moss to make a nice home for the tree. If the tree is going to survive, the roots have to get out of that hole. In most areas, your home soil is worthless. My recommendation is to dig a hole twice the size of the container. When you take the tree out of the container, cut down the roots to promote their growth outward. Make enough room in the hole so the roots can escape that bound mess. Otherwise, they will continue to circle. When you backfill the hole, use what you have taken out of the hole—beat it up and put it back. If you have to amend the soil, use some loam or sandy loam. Do not plant the tree too low.

■ How deep should the hole be?

If the plant comes in a container, look where the soil level is and plant it just a tad high in the ground. It's going to settle in.

■ Should the burlap be removed if the roots are covered with it?

If there are any ties, burlap, plastic wrap, or anything, remove it. In the days when burlap was burlap, it might have rotted, but now, with the synthetic things being used, it's just a tragedy to leave them. The roots just can't get out. More trees die because of a lack of planting care than any other factor, although they don't die immediately. At least unwrap the burlap to let those roots get out.

■ What should you do once a tree has been planted?

Mulch. It keeps the soil relatively warm; if you are planting in the fall, it might allow more root growth before the cold weather sets in. It also keeps the lawn mower and weeding equipment away from the tree. I recommend about a 2-inch layer of mulch.

■ How about watering?

Absolutely the first thing you have to do is water, and make sure the plant is well-seated. Keep the tree watered in times of stress without overwatering.

■ Should new trees be staked?

The average homeowner is dealing with a tree that has a trunk with a 2- to $2\frac{1}{2}$-inch maximum caliper. If it's well planted, well watered in originally, and well sited, it's not going to blow over. Just tamp it down.

■ Should you fertilize your tree?

Most trees do not need fertilization, but if your tree is in your lawn, and you fertilize your lawn, don't worry about it. If you do fertilize, use a slow-release fertilizer. A common mistake is when people use lawn fertilizers with weedkillers. This material leaches into the ground and is taken up by the roots. Eventually it's going to get your tree.

■ Should a newly planted tree be pruned?

Tree growth promotes root growth. The only pruning that should be done on a newly planted tree is if there is a broken branch.

■ PRUNING TREES

Once a tree is established, it will need periodic pruning. The best time to prune deciduous trees is in winter, when trees are dormant—it's also easier to see the problem branches and the general shape of the tree without the leaves. If you're pruning an evergreen tree, wait until spring. Remember to prune with a light hand; overpruning can destroy your tree's look—and your investment.

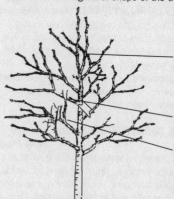

■ Crossing branches
When branches rub against each other, they may damage the bark and make the tree susceptible to disease and insects.

■ Dead, diseased, or broken branches
Cut back to a healthy branch.

■ Crowded branches
Thinning weak branches improves the tree's shape and allows better air circulation and light penetration.

■ HOW TO PRUNE

When pruning a tree, be sure that you cut just above a branch's slightly swollen base at the point where that branch meets another branch. This base consists of plant tissues that help the cut to heal. Leaving too much of a stub creates a conduit for diseases to attack the tree.

If you want to shorten a branch that's grown too long, make a cut on the branch just above a bud at a 45-degree angle. Pick a bud facing the direction that you want a new branch to grow.

THE GRASS IS ALWAYS GREENER

To pick the best grass seed for your lawn, take into account the growing region (defined by humidity level and mean temperature), microclimate (how much sun the lawn gets throughout the day), maintenance time, and expected foot traffic.

BAHIAGRASS *Paspalum* **Gulf Coast**
■ This wide, coarse-bladed grass is not particularly attractive, but its ruggedness and deep root system make it good for erosion control.

MICROCLIMATE	FOOT TRAFFIC	MAINTENANCE
Sunny to partly shady	High	Low

BENTGRASS *Agrostis* **Northern**
■ Often used on putting greens, this high-maintenance grass should be used only on low-traffic areas or where soft-soled shoes are worn.

MICROCLIMATE	FOOT TRAFFIC	MAINTENANCE
Sunny to partly shady	Low	High

BERMUDAGRASS *Cynodon* **Southern**
■ Fast-growing, this wide-bladed grass requires frequent edge-trimming, but will tolerate high traffic. Popular in the South for its vigor and density.

MICROCLIMATE	FOOT TRAFFIC	MAINTENANCE
Sunny	High	Medium to high

BUFFALOGRASS *Buchloe* **West Central**
■ Like wheatgrass, a native turf that is thick and rugged, requires low maintenance and will not grow over 4 or 5 inches if left unmowed. It is very tolerant of drought.

MICROCLIMATE	FOOT TRAFFIC	MAINTENANCE
Sunny	Medium	Low

CARPETGRASS *Axonopus* **Southern**
■ Coarse but sensitive to wear, this grass is used primarily on hard-to-mow places because of its low maintenance and slow growth rate.

MICROCLIMATE	FOOT TRAFFIC	MAINTENANCE
Sunny	Low	Low

CENTIPEDEGRASS *Eremochloa* **Southern**
■ A good "middle-of-the-road" grass—easy to care for, will tolerate some shade, and is vigorous and attractive. It requires two seasons to grow.

MICROCLIMATE	FOOT TRAFFIC	MAINTENANCE
Sunny to partly shady	Low	Low

KENTUCKY BLUEGRASS *Poa* **Northern**
■ The most popular of cool-season grasses for its beauty and ruggedness and flexibility. It will excel with minimum maintenance almost anywhere.

MICROCLIMATE	FOOT TRAFFIC	MAINTENANCE
Sunny to partly shady	Medium to heavy	Low to high

PERENNIAL RYEGRASS *Festuca* **Northern**
■ This quick-growing and reasonably hardy grass is used in seed mixes to provide cover and erosion control while the other seeds take root.

MICROCLIMATE	FOOT TRAFFIC	MAINTENANCE
Sunny to partly shady	Medium	Medium to high

ST. AUGUSTINE GRASS *Stenotaphrum*
South Atlantic
■ Dense and spongy, this low-growing, coarse-textured grass is prized for its high shade tolerance. Not available in seed form, but usually sold as fairly inexpensive sod.

MICROCLIMATE	FOOT TRAFFIC	MAINTENANCE
Sunny to shady	Medium	Medium to high

TALL FESCUES *Festuca* **Northern**
■ Though it is a cool-season grass, this tough, wide-bladed turf has good heat tolerance and grows well in areas with a steep range of weather. Often used on play-

■ **LAWNGROWER'S GUIDE**

grounds because of its ruggedness.

MICROCLIMATE	FOOT TRAFFIC	MAINTENANCE
Sunny to partly shady	Heavy	Medium

WHEATGRASS *Agropyron* **High plains**

■ Thick and tough, this grass is native to the high plains of the Northwest. It withstands weather extremes and heavy traffic and needs mowing about once a month.

MICROCLIMATE	FOOT TRAFFIC	MAINTENANCE
Sunny	High	Low

ZOYSIA *Zoysia* **Southern**

■ Takes root very quickly and crowds out other grasses and weeds. It turns a not entirely unattractive straw yellow in cold weather and requires little maintenance in general. Heat- and drought-tolerant.

MICROCLIMATE	FOOT TRAFFIC	MAINTENANCE
Sunny to partly shady	High	Low to medium

SOURCE: Dr. H. A. Turgeon, Pennsylvania State University.

EXPERT TIPS

LAWNS FIT FOR A PRESIDENT

You may not have to worry about helicopters leaving holes in your lawn, but White House horticulturist Dale Haney has some tips for starting and maintaining a lawn that will work anywhere. Haney has been keeping the grounds of the House since 1974.

■ Depending on your soil, you may have to fertilize before seeding. Use a nitrogen-rich fertilizer— say 8 to 12 percent. Rototill it into the soil. Then seed and fertilize— about 1 pound of fertilizer and 6 pounds of grass seed per 1,000 square feet.

■ It's very important to keep the seed wet until germination. This takes about two weeks. When the grass is about 3 inches tall, cut it to 2 inches. After that, start mowing it to about 3 inches. Don't spray for weeds until you've mowed it three or four times, otherwise you'll damage the grass before it has established itself.

■ After a lawn is established, mow and water it once or twice a week. Watering at night during the summer can invite fungal problems caused by standing water and high humidity. It's better to water during the day. It takes heat stress off the grass and keeps the roots from coming up to the top.

■ Keep putting down fertilizer at a half-rate throughout the growing season. This helps establish more root growth than top growth during the heat of summer— especially important because constant watering leaches nutrients from the soil.

■ Get rid of dead grass at the end of summer. In late August or early September the first year, and every four or five years after that, rent a thatching machine to remove the lower layer of thatch and put down some more fertilizer and seed. That should get you ready for winter and a healthy lawn for next spring.

HOUSEPLANTS FOR EVERY WINDOW

*How to match up a plant's light, temperature, and humidity needs
to the location in your home or office that will best provide them.*

■ **NORTH WINDOWS:** Receive no direct sun—but, if unobstructed, they do receive good light.
Plants grown in a shaded north window during the winter months would appreciate extra
light. When choosing plants for a dark window, remember that plants with variegated leaves
require more light than ones with strictly green leaves. Consult the key below.

PLANT	WATER	TEMPERATURE	HUMIDITY	FERTILIZER
CAST-IRON PLANT *Aspidistra eliator*	WD	I	MEDIUM	INTERMEDIATE
FERN, BIRD'S NEST *Asplenium nidus*	EM	I	HIGH	LOW
FIG *Ficus pumila*	EM	I	HIGH	LOW
PHILODENDRON, VELVET LEAF *Philodendron scandens var. micans*	W	I	HIGH	LOW
PRAYER PLANT *Maranta leuconeura*	EM	W	MEDIUM	INTERMEDIATE
SAGO PALM *Cycas revoluta*	W	I	MEDIUM	LOW
SPATHE FLOWER *Spathiphyllum*	EM	W	MEDIUM	INTERMEDIATE
WANDERING JEW *Zebrina pendula*	EM	I-W	MEDIUM	INTERMEDIATE

■ **EAST AND WEST WINDOWS:** Both are excellent for growing houseplants. East windows
tend to be cooler than west. If you can't grow the following plants in east or west windows,
they should do fine in a south window—but add some shading during the day in the summer, especially for ferns.

PLANT	WATER	TEMPERATURE	HUMIDITY	FERTILIZER
BROMELIAD	W	I	MEDIUM	LOW
CAPE PRIMROSE *Streptocarpus*	W	I	HIGH	HIGH
FERN, BOSTON *Nephrolepsis exaltata*	W	I	HIGH	LOW
IVY, GRAPE *Cissus rhombifolia*	EM	I	MEDIUM	INTERMEDIATE
LILY, AMAZON *Eucharis grandiflora*	EM	I-W	MEDIUM	HIGH
LILY, KAFFIR *Clivia miniata*	W	I	MEDIUM	INTERMEDIATE
LADY PALM *Rhapsis excelsa`*	W-EM	I	HIGH	INTERMEDIATE
NORFOLK ISLAND PINE *Araucaria heterophylla*	EM	C	MEDIUM	LOW
BEGONIA REX *Rex begonia*	EM	I	HIGH	HIGH
ROSARY VINE *Ceropegia woodii*	WD	I	LOW	INTERMEDIATE
RUBBER PLANT *Ficus elastica*	W	W	MEDIUM	LOW
SHAMROCK PLANT *Oxalis*	EM	I	MEDIUM	LOW
FIG, WEEPING *Ficus benjamina*	W	W	MEDIUM	LOW
VIOLET, AFRICAN *Saintpaulia*	W	I-W	MEDIUM	HIGH

KEY:

WATER:
WD: Water thoroughly, let dry fully before rewatering.
W: Water thoroughly but don't let it totally dry out
before rewatering.
EM: Keep soil evenly moist, but don't let
it stand in water. Top inch of soil
should always feel moist.

TEMPERATURE:
C: Cool: 45° nights, 55° to 60° days.
I: Intermediate: 50° to 55° nights, 65°
to 70° days.
W: Warm: 60° nights, 75° to 80° days.

HUMIDITY:
LOW: 20 to 40 percent.
MEDIUM: 40 to 50 percent.
HIGH: 50 to 80 percent.

FERTILIZER:
HEAVY: Use balanced fertilizer recommended
for frequent feeding, feed each watering.
INTERMEDIATE: Feed every other week with a
balanced fertilizer.
LOW: Feed about once per month with a
balanced fertilizer.

■ **INDOOR GARDENER'S GUIDE**

■ **SOUTH WINDOWS:** South windows receive the most light. During the summer months they even can be too bright for many kinds of houseplants—you may need to shade them a bit. All of these plants, while preferring south windows, can also be grown in east or west exposures.

PLANT	WATER	TEMPERATURE	HUMIDITY	FERTILIZER
ALOE	WD	I	LOW	LOW
BEGONIA, TRAILING Cissus discolor	EM	I	MEDIUM	INTERMEDIATE
CACTUS	WD	I-W	LOW	LOW
GERANIUM Pelargonium	W	I	MEDIUM	LOW
GERANIUM, STRAWBERRY Saxifraga stolonifera	W	I	MEDIUM	LOW
IVY Hedera helix	EM	I	MEDIUM	INTERMEDIATE
IVY, GERMAN OR PARLOR Senecio mikanioides	WD	I	LOW	INTERMEDIATE
JADE PLANT Crassula argentea	W	I	LOW	LOW
PASSION FLOWER Passiflora	EM	I	MEDIUM	INTERMEDIATE
POMEGRANATE, DWARF Punica granatum 'Nana'	EM	I	MEDIUM	INTERMEDIATE
SHEFFLERA, HAWAIIAN Erassaia arboricola	W	I	LOW	INTERMEDIATE

SOURCE: American Horticultural Society.

SHEDDING LIGHT ON HOUSEPLANTS

Fluorescent bulbs are best because they don't throw off a lot of heat

Unless you have a sunroom or greenhouse, the biggest dilemma of having plants indoors is providing them with enough light. Even if you have windows, they may be less than ideal if they're facing in a direction that gets little sun, or if they're shaded by a tree or porch overhang. Plants suffering from light deprivation are often lanky, with pale or yellowed leaves. Luckily, you can lend a helping hand with artificial lighting.

The best type of artificial light is fluorescent. Incandescent light doesn't provide the right kind of light for optimal growth, and it also produces lots of heat, which can burn your plants. Fluorescent light comes in several varieties: the standard ones, which you can find at any hardware store or home improvement center, are fine for growing small plants such as African violets, but for larger plants, go for higher-output fluorescents, which emit much more light and can be found at most well-equipped garden centers or through mail-order gardening supply catalogs. Bear in mind, too:

■ When growing plants under artificial light, choose those that prefer low to medium sunlight.

■ Keep your plants very close to the light source—no more than 6 to 12 inches away. The intensity of light diminishes drastically the farther away you move from it. To increase intensity, add more fluorescent tubes, grouped together.

■ Rearrange your plants regularly around their light source to ensure that they all receive equal exposure. The greatest amount of light is emitted from the center of a fluorescent tube.

■ Leave the lights on 14 to 16 hours each day. A couple of hours daily won't suffice. But don't leave the lights on all the time; plants need periods of darkness for rest.

PETS

DOG BREEDS: A dog's breed is no guarantee that it will make a good companion, PAGE 346 **DOGGIE BILLS:** How much you'll need to raise Fido, PAGE 347 **CANINE HEALTH:** Holistic medicine is for the dogs, PAGE 348 **CAT BREEDS:** A guide to picking a pet, PAGE 349 **SHOTS:** Vaccinations to keep your pet healthy, PAGE 351 **EXOTICS:** The cost and care of a hedgehog, python, or an African Gray parrot, PAGE 353

TRENDS

▼

A NEW AGE IN PET CARE

*Medical and high-tech advances
are helping vets help pets*

A pet is much more than a best friend, according to a recent survey by the American Animal Hospital Association: More than 78 percent of pet owners think of their pets as children. And nearly 50 percent of female pet owners rely more on their pet than a spouse or child for affection. As a result, says veterinarian Dr. Merry Crimi, "Pet owners are demanding the same kind of care for their pets as they can get for themselves and their families." The pet care business is responding with medical and technological advances that are helping pets live longer and healthier lives. Dr. Crimi, president of the American Animal Hospital Association and director of the Gladstone Veterinary Hospital in Milwaukie, Oregon, discusses the latest advances in caring for your pet.

■ **FAREWELL TO FLEAS.** The most radical changes in veterinary medicine within the past two years have occurred in flea control.

Until recently, pet owners had few choices: use flea powders and collars on their pets and spray the yard with chemicals.

Today, new options include pills and topical spot-on solutions. The pills prevent flea eggs from hatching, and the skin treatments kill fleas on contact for 30 days. Both are available at your vet's office. A 4- to 6-month supply of flea pills or spot applications costs between $30 and $40, depending on the size of your pet. Treatment for a cat, for example, would come to about $5 a month.

New advances in outdoor flea control are available that contain nematodes, live organisms that feed on flea larvae. These products reduce harm to the environment, as well as to humans, animals, and insects.

■ **COMPUTER ID.** A new way to identify your pet involves implanting a tiny microchip—about $1/4$ to $1/3$ inch long—under the skin of just about any animal. The result is a lifetime ID that can't be lost or removed. The information can be read by scanners now used by animal control centers and humane societies. So if your dog strays and ends up at one of these centers, the scanner reads the identification number that traces the pet back to you.

The chip is injected by a vet with a device that looks like a syringe and needle. The cost of the procedure runs from $35 to $60, depending on the kind and size of animal you own.

■ **PATCHING UP PAIN.** The new patch technology that's so popular for humans—estrogen patches for women, nicotine patches for smokers—is now being used on animals. If an animal is in pain after an accident, or is having a major dental procedure, we can apply a time-release patch that will steadily relieve the pain, rather than having to wait until the animal needs another dose of pain killer. Time-release patches are a little bit expensive—around $25 to $35 for a patch that lasts 3 to 5 days. But that's close to the cost of any good pain control medication. At the vet's office, an owner can choose between the patch technology and standard medication. Most owners pick patches because they don't have to get up in the middle of the night or come home from work to redose their pets.

■ **MODIFYING YOUR PET'S BEHAVIOR.** Shelters and humane groups destroy millions of dogs and cats each year because of the animals' behavior problems. That's more than the number killed each year by any disease. But behavior problems like aggression, digging, barking, biting, and house-soiling can now be resolved through behavior counseling programs. The earlier in a puppy or kitten's life that behavior problems are picked up, the greater the success in resolving them. Pets can get behavior counseling at special clinics or through veterinarians or specialists that your vet can recommend. Many counselors will even come to your home.

A pet's behavior can also be modified with drugs. Until a few years ago, information on treating animals with drugs was limited, but now we can treat disorders such as car sickness, aggression, and separation anxiety with a combination of behavior training and drug treatments.

■ **DIAGNOSIS AND SURGERY.** Ultrasound and endoscopy have been around for humans for many years, but they are now becoming affordable and more routinely used to diagnose and treat animal problems. They have revolutionized exploratory surgery. If an animal has a serious heart problem, or can-

WHAT'S IN A NAME?

Ever hear of a St. Francis Terrier? If not, you're probably not alone. The breed is neither new nor exotic. In fact, it's little more than an improved and rechristened pit bull. The new moniker is the brain child of the folks at the San Francisco SPCA, who think pit bulls suffer from an image problem. "To single out the breed as aggressive and dangerous is a bum rap for the pit bull," says Lynn Spivak of the San Francisco SPCA. "Any dog can bite. Pit bulls are also sweet, docile, and loving."

As a result of the breed's bad rep, the SPCA was having difficulty finding homes for stray pit bulls—until it hit on a novel public relations strategy. Why not put pit bulls through training, give them a "Good Doggie Behavior Diploma" upon graduation, and change their name to something more owner-friendly? Hence, St. Francis Terriers, named after the animal-loving patron saint of their city.

To get a diploma and become a St. Francis Terrier, a pit bull must undergo training and pass tests such as being sociable with other dogs, accepting a friendly stranger, and following instructions. Adoptions of the improved pit bulls are way up, says Spivak. "We've had greater demand than we can fill."

cer, for example, it can be diagnosed without having to make any incisions. The result is lower costs and less stress for owners.

Pet surgery has also come a long way. Dogs no longer need to go blind from cataracts. Cataracts can be removed surgically and artificial lenses can be implanted. And pets that suffer from chronic hip or knee deformities can have their joints replaced surgically, just like humans.

DOG ● BREEDS
▼

PICKING A CANINE COMPANION

A dog's breed is no guarantee that it will act according to the book

Every dog has its own personality. But some breeds are better suited to being jostled by children than others, while the circumstances of other pet lovers may require quite different choices. Here, veterinarian Sheldon L. Gerstenfeld suggests which dogs make good pets for families with children, owners with active lifestyles, and people who are older and looking for easy pet companionship. Gerstenfeld is the author of seven books about pet

---

■ **COMMON CONGENITAL DEFECTS IN DOGS**
Before selecting a best friend, check this list for potential problems.

■ **COCKER SPANIEL:** Cataracts, kidney disease, hemophilia, spinal deformities, behavior abnormalities

■ **COLLIE:** Deafness, epilepsy, hemophilia, hernia

■ **DACHSHUND:** Bladder stones, diabetes, cleft lips and palate, jaw too long or short, spinal deformities, limbs too short

■ **GERMAN SHEPHERD:** Cataracts, epilepsy, kidney disease, bladder stones, hemophilia, cleft lips and palate, behavior abnormalities

■ **LABRADOR RETRIEVER:** Cataracts, bladder stones, hemophilia

■ **TOY POODLE:** Epilepsy, nervous system defects, collapsed trachea, diabetes, spinal deformities, limbs too short, skin allergies, behavior abnormalities

---

care, including *The Dog Care Book* (Addison-Wesley, 1989). He also writes a pet column for *Parents* magazine.

DOGS FOR CHILDREN

■ **GOLDEN RETRIEVER:** Easygoing, active, and alert, golden retrievers have the best temperaments. They love to interact with kids and to play ball. The adult female weighs 50 to 60 pounds; the adult male 70 to 90 pounds. They need to be groomed and fed, and that teaches kids about being responsible. The golden retriever is the seventh most popular breed of the American Kennel Club (AKC).

■ **LABRADOR RETRIEVER:** Black, yellow, and chocolate Labs are known for being even-tempered and friendly. They are always ready to play, and kids can just lie on them. Adult dogs weigh 60 to 70 pounds. They need grooming, so they also teach kids to be responsible.

Avoid the Chesapeake Bay retriever, which has a curlier coat. It can be a little nasty and unpredictable and will bite more readily than the others. Labrador retrievers are the fifth most popular AKC breed.

■ **COLLIE:** These are sweet dogs. They're gentle and predictable and won't bite around your kids. They're easy to train and really want to please. Adult collies weigh about 50 pounds and their long hair requires grooming. The rough-coated collie, which is what Lassie is, is the 9th most popular AKC breed; the smooth-coated collie is the 13th most popular.

■ **STANDARD POODLE:** A gentle dog that is very intelligent. A standard poodle will let a kid lie on it. You need to groom them, but a fancy haircut is not necessary. Poodles, including miniature and standard, are the most popular breed in the United States. Because they are so popular, prospective owners have to watch out for puppy-mill degradation. The larger they are, the less active they are and the more exercise they need. Adult standard poodles weigh 50 to 55 pounds.

DOGS FOR THE ACTIVE PERSON

■ **GREYHOUND:** They are a little aloof, but also very gentle. Most are adopted from the racetrack. Greyhounds have a regal personality and don't slobber with affection like a retriever. They're also very athletic, so they're good for active people. Adult greyhounds weigh 70 to 80 pounds. High-strung and easily upset by sudden movements at times, greyhounds are the 105th most popular AKC breed.

■ **BOXER:** Animated, with outgoing personalities, boxers respond readily to playfulness. They are the 24th most popular AKC breed. Prospective owners looking for a dignified dog, however, should be wary of the boxer: They tend to drool and snore.

■ **TERRIER:** Terriers start out their morning as if they had eight cups of coffee, so they are good for an active person. I'd recommend the bull terrier, which was bred for pit fighting. They are always ready to frolic and so need firm training, but they are also known for their sweet personalities. The adult bull terrier weighs in at about 50 pounds. It is the 65th most popular AKC breed.

■ **ENGLISH COCKER SPANIEL:** These are sweet dogs, and they haven't been inbred. They're playful and alert at all times and great for children and active people. The English cocker spaniel is a medium-size dog with long hair. An adult usually weighs 23 to 25 pounds, 3 to 11 pounds more than its cousin, the American cocker spaniel. The English cocker is the 64th most popular AKC breed.

DOGS FOR OLDER PEOPLE

■ **CHIHUAHUA:** If they are from a good breeder, they will have a good personality. Chihuahuas have short hair, so they don't need a lot of grooming and so are a good choice for an older person living alone. The Chihuahua is the smallest of all the breeds. They can be yappy and clannish at times. An adult Chihuahua weighs about 3 pounds and is the 21st most popular AKC breed.

■ **MINIATURE POODLE:** These poodles are intelligent. And they're good for older people because they're small and don't

shed a lot. They love attention. Again, the poodle is the most popular AKC breed, so owners have to make sure the dog is not inbred. All poodles are fast learners; generally the smaller they are the faster they learn. The adult miniature poodle weighs in at about 15 pounds.

■ **TOY POODLE:** These dogs love to be cuddled and are intelligent. They have to be groomed, but they don't shed, so there's not much hair to clean up. The adult toy poodle weighs less than 10 pounds. It is the brightest of all the toys and will demand its owner's continuous attention. Because of the toy poodle's popularity, inbreeding can be a problem.

■ **YORKSHIRE TERRIER:** These dogs are small, easy to care for, and can be picked up. They weigh about 7 pounds and have silky long, draping hair. Their coats require grooming, however, which may not be good for an elderly person who doesn't have the energy, or who has arthritis. The Yorkshire terrier is the 14th most popular AKC breed.

FACT FILE:

BRINGING UP BABY

■ *Dogs make wonderful companions, but they don't come free, as these cost estimates from the Humane Society of the United States indicate.*

Adopting a dog from a shelter	$55
First-year vaccinations	$200
Each year thereafter	$65
Initial training	$50–$100
Each year thereafter	$50–$200
Other annual veterinary care [1]	$135
Annual feeding	$115–$400
Annual toys, grooming supplies	$160
Grooming, per visit [2]	$50
Annual flea and tick care	$80
Daily boarding	$21–$30

1. 1991 figures. 2. Varies with size and breed.

EXPERT Q & A

A WELLNESS GUIDE FOR ROVER

A holistic approach to health can help your pooch, too

What's good for the goose is good for the gander, goes the familiar saying. The same is often true of dog owners and their pets. But while health-conscious dog owners may be eating organically grown veggies and fruits, jogging regularly, and practicing yoga to deal with the stresses of daily living, the family dog is often stuck inside the house with a bowl of food that has the nutritional equivalent of a candy bar. Just as more people are advocating a holistic approach to human health care—the concept of caring for the whole rather than the individual parts—pets need the same care. So argues Wendy Volhard, author with veterinarian Kerry Brown of *The Holistic Guide for a Healthy Dog* (Macmillan/Howell Book House, 1995), who has this advice on taking care of your canine companion.

■ Why is a new form of animal care necessary?

What was traditionally used is no longer working. For one thing, standards in commercial dog food were changed in 1985. Most of the protein in commercial dog food now comes from cereal grains, which has the effect of turning a carnivore into a semi-vegetarian. Dog food is also subjected to great heat in processing, which destroys nutrients. Although dog food is fine as supplement, it lacks animal protein, vitamins, and amino acids, and therefore shouldn't be a dog's sole source of nutrition.

Vaccines are also a problem. They actually break down a dog's immune system. Some dogs get 47 vaccines before they are six months old, though some are combined into one shot so it doesn't seem like that many. In contrast, a puppy in the 1970s was more likely to get only two vaccines in the first six months of life. All vaccines, no matter what the sequence, should be given in minimum intervals of three weeks.

Owners are often totally unaware of these health issues until there is a sickness or behavioral problem with their dog. The majority of dogs are put to sleep because of behavior problems.

■ What should dog owners feed their pets?

Start with dog food, but realize it doesn't meet all your dog's nutritional needs. In addition to the regular serving of wet or dry dog food, you should give your dog fresh raw beef for protein every day. It needs to be raw because a dog's system is set up to digest raw, not cooked meat. For calcium, feed the dog cottage cheese, yogurt, or a five-minute cooked egg with the shell—a pure form of calcium. Then give him a serving of fresh raw vegetables. Any vegetable is fine. Then give the dog a vitamin/mineral mix that is designed for dogs. Extra vitamin C and B-complex should finish off the meal. But don't mix the dog food with the other food—give it to the dog separately.

■ How much exercise does a dog need?

Running in the backyard is not enough. Dogs really need one hour in the morning and one hour in the afternoon of exercise. For little dogs, some of that can be running around and playing in an apartment or house. But big dogs need to get outside. Get up earlier and go to the park. People are busy, but that's something they need to consider before they decide to take care of a dog. For people who are too busy, a new cottage industry has sprouted up—daycare for dogs.

■ What kind of dog training should be done?

Training should be positive, with a reward rather than punishment. All dogs need to be trained. It makes them easier to live with. It's worth an eight-week course—you'll be able to take them everywhere with you and they'll have a lot of freedom.

CAT BREEDS
▼

ALL THE CATS' MEOWS

From pharaohs' favorites to loving tabbies, choose your companion

Celebrated for their highly independent nature, cats have been everything from lap companion to religious idol in the pages of human history. Today, over 200 million cats reside in American homes, making them nearly as popular as dogs for household pets. Here's the book on the best, brightest, most elegant, and most cuddly cats from which to choose.

■ **ABYSSINIAN:** One of the oldest known breeds, their slender, elegant, muscular bodies were often featured in paintings and sculptures in ancient Egyptian art. Abyssinians have arched necks, large ears, almond-shaped eyes, and long, tapered tails. The Abyssinian's soft and silky medium-length coat is one of its most unusual features. Each hair has two or three distinct bands of black or dark brown, giving the breed a subtle overall coat color and lustrous sheen. Abyssinians also can have a rich copper-red coat. They are particularly loyal and make good companions.

■ **AMERICAN CURL:** The name comes from the breed's unique curled ears, which curl away from the head to make it look as if this cat is always alert. The American curl is moderately large, with walnut-shaped eyes. Its ears are straight at birth, and curl within 2 to 10 days. A relatively rare breed, the American curl usually weighs 5 to 10 pounds. Curls are short-haired, and their coats come in all colors possible. Even-tempered and intelligent with a playful disposition, American curls adore their owners and display affection in a quiet way. They adapt to almost any home, live well with other animals, and are very healthy.

■ **AMERICAN SHORTHAIR:** The descendants of house cats and farm cats, American shorthairs are easy to care for and resistant to disease. They have big bones and are docile and even-tempered. The breed is strongly built, with an agile, medium to large body. They have a short, thick coat that ranges in colors from black to white to red to tabby.

■ **AMERICAN WIREHAIR:** Uniquely American, the breed began as a spontaneous mutation in a litter on a farm in New York in 1966. Its dense coarse coat is hard to touch and sets these cats apart from any other breed. Some also have curly whiskers. The breed is active and agile and has a keen interest in its surroundings. Although it is quiet and reserved, owners find the breed easy to care for.

■ **BALINESE:** Related to the Siamese, it has a long silky coat, but unlike most long-haired cats, its coat doesn't mat. Endowed with a long, muscular body, the Balinese can come in several colors, including seal point, blue point, and chocolate point. Intelligent, curious, and alert, the Balinese is as affectionate and demonstrative as the Siamese, but it isn't as talkative and has a softer voice.

FACT FILE:

TALLYING A TABBY'S TAB

■ *From the Humane Society of the United States, estimates of what it costs to be a cat owner on average:*

Adopting a cat from a shelter	$25
First-year vaccinations	$200
Each year thereafter	$27
Other annual veterinary care[1]	$80
Annual feeding[1]	$145
Annual kitty litter	$78
Annual toys, grooming supplies	$160
Daily boarding	$10

1. 1991 figures.

■ **BRITISH SHORTHAIR:** Perhaps the oldest natural English breed, the British shorthair is enjoying new popularity. These cats tend to be reserved, devoted, and good companions. Because of their dense coats, they also are easy to groom.

■ **BURMESE:** Known as the clown of the cat kingdom, the Burmese thrives on attention and is very gregarious. It has a compact body and a glossy coat. Burmese live well with children and dogs. They are smart, loyal, and devoted. Despite their hefty appetites, they seldom are fat. They are very expensive, though, costing as much as $1,500.

■ **CORNISH REX:** The Cornish Rex has the body of a greyhound, huge ears set high on its head, and large eyes. These cats fastidiously groom themselves—and their human companions. If that's not to your liking, choose another cat, since the problem may be impossible to eliminate. The Cornish Rex are excellent choices for people who love cats but dislike cat hair, because they have an undercoat but no outer coat.

■ **DEVON REX:** Devons are considered a mutant breed. The mature female averages 6 pounds; the male averages 7.5 pounds. Devons have a full, wavy coat, large eyes, a short muzzle, prominent cheekbones, and huge low-set ears. They are very curious and refuse to be left out of anything. People with allergies to cat hair can happily live with a Devon Rex because they do not shed.

■ **EXOTIC SHORTHAIR:** Sometimes called the "Teddy Bear" cat, exotic shorthairs have a medium-to-long coat that does not mat. They will jump in your lap to take a nap, but generally prefer cooler places to sleep. They are very quiet but tireless—they will retrieve a toy until you get tired of throwing it.

■ **JAPANESE BOBTAIL:** The Japanese consider bobtails a symbol of good luck. They are medium-sized and muscular with a short tail that resembles a rabbit's. They have high cheekbones, a long nose, and large ears. Active, intelligent, and talkative, their soft voices have a whole scale of tones. They almost always speak when spoken to. Japanese bobtails are good travelers and good with dogs and children.

■ **MAINE COON CAT:** The Maine coon cat was chosen as best cat at the first cat show ever held in America. It is a native American long-hair. Originally a working cat, it is a very good mouser. The Maine coon cat is solid and rugged. It has a smooth, shaggy coat and is known for its loving nature and great intelligence. The breed is especially good with children and dogs.

■ **ORIENTAL SHORTHAIR:** The extremely long Oriental shorthair is medium-sized and are choosy eaters at times. They are easy to care for and make a practical pet. The Cat Fanciers' Association says, "Their innate sensibility verges on psychic. Once communication is established, you'll never need an alarm clock, or wonder where the cat is when you arrive home from work."

■ **PERSIAN:** The most popular breed, Persians have long, flowing coats that require an indoor, protected environment and regular combing and bathing. Persians have a massive head and a very round face. They have short, thick necks and legs and broad, short bodies. Persians have gentle personalities that fare best in serene households.

■ **RUSSIAN BLUE:** Fine-boned, with short hair and a regal appearance, Russian blues are clean, quiet cats that don't shed a lot. They are very intelligent and are well attuned to the moods of their owners. They generally do well in a house full of kids and dogs.

■ **SIAMESE:** Like dogs, Siamese cats will fetch and do tricks, talk a lot, and follow their owners around the house. They have blue eyes, and a dark, raccoonlike "mask" around them. They have long svelte bodies and short, finely textured coats. Siamese cats have distinctive voices and are intelligent, dependent, and affectionate. But because they have been highly inbred, they can be extremely timid, unpredictable, or aggressive.

PREVENTIVE CARE
▼
BOOSTING YOUR PET'S WELL-BEING

Vaccinations will keep your dog or cat free of many common diseases

Since the discovery in the 18th century that it was possible to build up immunities against certain diseases in both people and animals by injecting them with tiny amounts of living virus, hundreds of vaccines have been created. By immunizing pets in their early months and bolstering the protection with annual "booster" vaccinations, pet owners can shield their animals from diseases that often are highly contagious to other animals and, in cases such as rabies, pose a serious threat to humans as well. Here, from the American Veterinary Medical Association, is a rundown of the diseases against which your dog or cat should be immunized.

BOTH CATS AND DOGS

■ **RABIES:** A viral disease that can attack the central nervous system of all warm-blooded animals, including humans. It is fatal if not treated. Most states require dog and cat owners to vaccinate their pets against rabies. The disease is transmitted by saliva, which is usually transferred by a bite from an infected animal and is frequently found in wild animals, such as skunks, raccoons, and bats.

There are two types of rabies—"dumb" and "furious." Both cause a departure from normal behavior. Animals with furious rabies will have a period immediately prior to death in which they appear to be "mad," frothing at the mouth and biting anything that gets in their way. Dumb rabies differs in that there is no "mad" period. Instead, paralysis, usually of the lower jaw, is the first sign. The paralysis spreads to limbs and vital organs and death quickly follows. Wild animals that are unusually friendly and appear to have no fear of man or domestic animals should be avoided and reported immediately to the police or animal control authorities.

Rabies is almost totally preventable by vaccination. Dogs and cats should receive an initial rabies vaccination by the age of three

■ CALLING THE SHOTS ON YOUR PET'S HEALTH

The American Veterinary Medical Association recommends the following vaccination schedule:

Disease	First	Second	Third	Revaccination intervals (months)
■ **DOGS**				
Distemper	6–10	10–12	14–16	12
Infectious canine hepatitis (CAV-1 or CAV-2)	6–8	10–12	14–16	12
Parvovirus infection	6–8	10–12	14–16	12
Bordetellosis	6–8	10–12	14–16	12
Parainfluenza	6–8	10–12	14–16	12
Leptospirosis	10–12	14–16		12
Rabies	12	64		12 or 36*
Coronavirus	6–8	10–12	12–24	12
■ **CATS**				
Panleukopenia	8–10	12–16		12
Viral rhinotracheitis	8–10	12–16		12
Caliciviral disease	8–10	12–16		12
Rabies	12	64		12 or 36*
Feline leukemia	10	12 & 24 or 13–14*		12

Column header: AGE AT VACCINATION (IN WEEKS) spans First, Second, Third.

* Check with your veterinarian for type of vaccine.   SOURCE: American Veterinary Medical Association.

to four months. Protection lasts from one to three years. Regular boosters are required.

DOGS ONLY

■ **CANINE BORDETELLOSIS:** Caused by bacteria in the respiratory tracts of many animals, it is the primary cause of kennel cough. Besides the cough, some dogs suffer from a purulent nasal discharge. Transmission usually occurs through contact with other dogs' nasal secretions. Vaccination is generally administered by nasal spray.

■ **CANINE DISTEMPER:** A highly contagious viral disease, canine distemper is transmitted by direct or indirect contact with the discharges from an infected dog's eyes and nose. Early signs are similar to those of a severe cold and often go unrecognized by the pet owner. The respiratory problems may be accompanied by vomiting and diarrhea. A nervous system disorder may also develop. The death rate from canine distemper is greater than 50 percent in adult dogs and even higher in puppies. Even if the dog survives, distemper can cause permanent damage to a dog's nervous system, sense of smell, hearing, and sight. Partial or total paralysis is not uncommon.

■ **CANINE LEPTOSPIROSIS:** A bacterial disease that harms the kidneys and can result in kidney failure. Vomiting, impaired vision, and convulsions are all tipoffs. Transmission results from contact with the urine of infected animals, or contact with something tainted by the urine of an infected animal.

■ **CANINE PARAINFLUENZA:** A viral infection of the respiratory tract, it is frequently accompanied by other respiratory viruses and is usually spread through contact with the nasal secretions of other dogs.

■ **CANINE PARVOVIRUS (CPV):** A serious problem because the virus withstands extreme temperature changes and even exposure to most disinfectants. The source of infection is usually dog feces, which can contaminate cages and shoes and can be carried on the feet and hair of infected animals.

CPV attacks the intestinal tract, white blood cells, and heart. Symptoms include vomiting, severe diarrhea, a loss of appetite, depression, and high fever. Most deaths occur within 48 to 72 hours after the onset of clinical signs. Infected pups may act depressed or collapse, gasping for breath. Death may follow immediately. Pups that survive are likely to have permanently damaged hearts.

■ **INFECTIOUS CANINE HEPATITIS:** Caused by a virus that can infect many tissues, the disease usually attacks the liver, causing hepatitis. In some instances a whiteness or cloudiness of the eye may accompany the disease. Another strain of the same virus can cause respiratory tract infections. These viruses are transmitted by contact with objects that have been contaminated with the urine from infected dogs. Infectious canine hepatitis is different from human hepatitis.

CATS ONLY

■ **FELINE PANLEUKOPENIA:** Also known as feline distemper, the disease comes from a virus so resistant that it may remain infectious for over a year at room temperature on inanimate objects. Spread through blood, urine, feces, nasal secretions, and fleas from infected cats, the virus causes high fever, dehydration, vomiting, and lethargy and destroys a cat's white blood cells. It is 50 to 70 percent fatal, but immunity can be developed through vaccination of kittens and annual boosters.

■ **FELINE LEUKEMIA VIRUS:** A disease of the immune system that is usually fatal, its symptoms include weight loss, lethargy, recurring or chronic sickness, diarrhea, unusual breathing, and yellow coloration around the mouth and the whites of the eyes. Confirmation of the virus requires a blood test. Fortunately, there is a new vaccine that provides protection.

■ **FELINE VIRAL RHINOTRACHEITIS, FELINE CALICIVIRUS, AND FELINE PNEUMONITIS:** All three are highly infectious viruses of the respiratory tract, for which vaccinations are available.

EXOTIC ANIMALS
▼

YOU HAVE A PET WHAT?

Creatures that get the neighbors talking are the "in" thing

Pop star Michael Jackson has an entire menagerie of exotic animals at his Los Angeles retreat, Neverland Ranch. But it's not necessary to be an international celebrity or a member of royalty to own an exotic pet today. Animals as unusual as miniature donkeys, mute swans, African bush babies, and reindeer can even be ordered from a popular catalog called the "Animal Finders Guide."

One indication of the current boom in exotic animals comes from the U.S. Fish and Wildlife Service, which reports that between 1980 and 1992 "legal animal shipments," which require official government notification, grew from 45,000 to 70,000. Many exotic animals are also brought into the country illegally each year, according to animal experts.

But taking animals out of their natural environments and selling them to people who are often uncertain how to care for them can endanger both the animals and their owners. "Any time you deal with an exotic animal, you are dealing with a tremendous amount of the unknown," says Richard Farinato, director of the captive wildlife protection program at the Humane Society of the United States.

Like hairstyles and skirt lengths, exotic animal fashions shift frequently. For example, the movie *Jurassic Park* caused a boom for pet reptiles. But when the animals are no longer wanted, says Farinato, they are often abandoned. In the Washington, D.C. area, for instance, so many pot-bellied pigs were cast off by fickle owners that an animal sanctuary had to be established as a refuge for these animals. That sanctuary now has a waiting list.

Many exotic pets aren't so lucky. Half of all birds and reptiles shipped to the U.S. die before they arrive. Some states have laws against owning exotic pets. California and Georgia, for example, ban most exotic animals. All of the exotic pets that Farinato describes below are perfectly legal in the United States. Even so, he advises, don't buy a pet just because it's unusual and cute; make sure you know exactly what's needed to take care of it. "There's no such thing as an easy-care pet," he warns.

■ **HEDGEHOGS.** A favorite character in children's books, hedgehogs are the most popular exotic pet today. They are usually an African species, which means they are accustomed to a tropical environment. Because they are small and cute, says Farinato, "they were tailor-made for a boom." Most people keep pet hedgehogs in an aquarium, which is a very unnatural place for animals that are burrowers. Hedgehogs eat live insects and are nocturnal. That means they are usually asleep when the owner is awake—not the ideal arrangement if you want a companion. **Cost: $50 to $300**

■ **IGUANAS.** A popular Christmas gift item, iguanas are being brought in by the thousands from South and Central America. Young iguanas are usually about six to eight inches long, but they can grow to six feet. If they get that large, they can be dangerous because of their large tails and long nails, especially to small children. Even worse, iguanas naturally harbor salmonella, a bacteria commonly associated with food poisoning, in their digestive tracts. This can be deadly to children or anyone with a weak immune system, such as people with AIDS.

The Centers for Disease Control and

Prevention has reported an increased incidence of salmonella illness in 12 states, all linked to exposure to iguanas and other reptiles. Natives of the tropics, iguanas need an enclosure where the temperature is kept at 78 to 95 degrees Fahrenheit. Without that heat, the lizard will refuse to eat and become lethargic. Iguanas eat plants and insects, although their diet in the wild consists mainly of flower petals.
Cost: $25 to $100

■ **SUGAR GLIDERS.** Native to Australia, and similar to a flying squirrel in appearance, these animals are now bred mostly in captivity. They are a nocturnal species with extremely sharp teeth, which can make balancing one on your shoulder a risky endeavor. Most owners keep them in small cages. At chow time, sugar gliders require a diet of fresh fruits. Unless you have the time to buy and cut up fruit for them every day, which few people do, this is not the pet for you. **Cost: $100**

FACT FILE:

HOUSEHOLD FAVORITES

■ *More than 40 percent of pet owners talk to their pets on the phone or through an answering machine.*

■ *Twenty-five percent of pet owners blow-dry their pet's hair after a bath.*

■ *More than 50 percent of dog and cat owners give their pets a human name, such as Molly, Sam, or Max.*

■ *Nearly 60 percent of owners bury their pets on family property when they die; 25 percent have them cremated.*

SOURCE: American Animal Hospital Association.

■ **BALL PYTHONS.** As pythons go, they're not the biggest around, but ball pythons do grow to about three to five feet. They are also extremely finicky eaters, preferring live rodents. Few will eat dead animals. In fact, some are so particular that they will only consume a certain color live rodent. These snakes can be dangerous; even a three-foot python is a constrictor. A small child with a snake around his neck could be in big trouble. As with most exotic pets, Farinato advises: "Don't keep these animals near small kids."
Cost: $40 to $100

■ **BENGAL CATS.** A hybrid of a wild and domestic cat, Bengals are finding their way into more people's homes. They range in size from a large housecat to a large bobcat when fully grown. While they are manageable as infants, they get wilder and more unpredictable, not to mention bigger, as they grow up. Bengals eat what other cats eat, including commercial cat food.
Cost: $300 to $500

■ **AFRICAN GRAY PARROTS.** One of the longest-living animals around, African Gray parrots can last 50 to 80 years. In fact, they can often outlive their owners. As pets they are very demanding. If it's not part of a flock, the bird needs to develop a close one-on-one relationship with the owner. Without that relationship, the parrot will become neurotic and start pulling out its feathers. To forge this bond, the owner must talk to the bird often and feed it by hand. In return for this close personal attention, a happy African Gray is one of the most talkative birds around.
Cost: $700 to $1,500

■ **OSTRICHES, EMUS, AND RHEAS.** Sold mainly for their meat until recently, these birds are beginning to find favor as pets. While acquiring an ostrich is something that most people will want to leave to Michael Jackson, emus and rheas are more affordable—and not as large.
Cost: Ostriches: $10,000 to $20,000; Emus: $1,000; Rheas: $100 to $1,000

CHAPTER SIX

TRAVEL

■ **WHAT'S AHEAD: TAKE** a vacation during the off-season to save big... **SEEK** out sharks on your next diving expedition... **DISCOVER** the favorite sights of park rangers at their national parks... **EXPERIENCE** a quiet retreat at a monastery or convent... **EXPLORE** the magnificent ruins of ancient Egypt along the banks of the Nile... **SPEND** a weekend at a romantic bed and breakfast inn... **CRUISE** on one of the latest mega-ships... **CHECK OUT** the Internet when planning your next trip...

HOT SPOTS

CONTRARIAN TRAVEL

THE PLEASURES OF OFF-SEASON

The rewards of touring during low season are more than monetary

Travel during peak season can often be more hassle than fun. In the summer months, for example, Greece is a magnet for tourists of all ages. And the prospects of glimpsing rare treasures in London's British Museum in July are downright discouraging. Why fight the crowds if you can travel off-season? The benefits of off-season travel are many, not least of which are reduced airfares and hotel rates. By vacationing when the crowds recede, you can save between 20 and 50 percent, particularly if you choose a tour package.

Some spots lure tourists year-round. You're not apt to find any off-season bargains in places like Aspen, Colo., for example, which is a hot ski resort in winter and an arts-festival haven in the summer. We've scoured the off-season possibilities, keeping in mind that a vacation shouldn't necessarily include extreme cold, sleet, hail, or avalanches. Here is a sampling of some choice values.

GREEK ISLANDS—SANTORINI

☞ *Best time to visit: in the spring and fall, when temperatures are mild.*

■ One of the lures of the Greek islands is the comparatively inexpensive fares and hotel rates, even during peak summer months. Consequently, summertime tourists swarm the Cyclades, a group of islands off the coast of Athens. These picturesque islands can best be appreciated in the relative calm after Labor Day, or in the early days of spring.

At the southern tip of the Cyclades is Santorini, perhaps the most dramatic island in the Mediterranean. It's also one of the most interesting archaeologically. Perched on the edge of a volcanic crater, it rises out of the ocean to a height of 300 feet. As you approach

by water, you see an extraordinary sight of multicolored volcanic cliffs, dotted with tiny white-washed, cubist-like towns. Hillsides are spotted with the terraced slopes of grape vineyards.

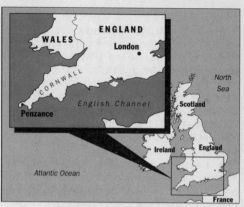

■ **MAJOR ATTRACTIONS:** Santorini's 4,000-year-old Minoan ruins in the ancient town of **Akrotini** are required viewing. Although a volcanic eruption destroyed the town in the 16th century B.C., you can still see remnants of the narrow streets and house foundations. Return to the present with a visit to the small artists' colony of Oia, with its whitewashed houses and cobalt and turquoise bay. Be sure to visit the **Archaeological Museum,** just north of the town of Fira, which contains relics of the Cycladic and Minoan periods, as well as of the later Dorian, Hellenic, and Roman periods. The Venetian castle of **Skaros** sits imperially at the tip of the island.

Santorini is also a good base from which to visit other Cycladian islands; most are accessible by ferry. If you're musically inclined, the two-week-long international Classical Music Festival takes place in September. For details, contact the Petros Nomikos Conference Center at Fira, Santorini. ☎ 0286–22 231

✈ **GETTING THERE:** Delta flies nonstop to Athens from New York. In peak season, early June to mid-September, round-trip fares go for about $1,100. During off-season (except for the Christmas holidays), rates fall to about $500. Spring travelers recently took advantage of an American Express 12-day tour of Greece and the Aegean, including airfare, first-class hotels, meals, and a short cruise for about $1,400.

WHERE TO STAY:

$$ La Perla, offered by Ivy International Ventures, comprises seven villa apartments in Oia overlooking the sea. Low-season rates are $163 double occupancy, including maid service and Continental breakfast, for a savings of about 20 percent from peak season. ☎ 800–719–5260

ENGLAND—LONDON AND PENZANCE

☞ *Best time to visit: in September, October, April, and May, when the weather is still pleasant. Winter months are damp and cold.*

■ London may well be the world's most diverse city—culturally, ethnically, and aesthetically. Just like most major cities, London is teeming with tourists in the summer months. But off-season travelers can enjoy London's rare sights more comfortably when visitors are fewer, fares are reasonable, and the cultural season is in full swing. Of course, you may have to brace yourself for the possibility of dampness and drizzle.

A fun detour from London if you have the time takes you to the harbor town of Penzance at the southwest tip of Cornwall. There's plenty to explore in and around town: ancient moors, jagged cliffs, unspoiled coastline, tiny fishing villages, and, believe it or not, palm trees. On the way back to London, be sure to stop at Stonehenge in Salisbury, the site of the famed Druidical monoliths.

■ **MAJOR ATTRACTIONS:** In London, after visiting Buckingham Palace, the Tower of London, and Westminster Abbey, take off for the city's lesser-visited delights. On Queen Victoria Street are the 20-foot Roman walls of the **Temple of Mithras** discovered 18 feet below street level, during excavations in 1954. The **Chapel Royal of Saints Peter and Vincula,** where Anne Boleyn and Catherine Howard prayed before they were beheaded, is beautiful and poignant. **St. Peter's Church** is a tiny gem of a Georgian-style building on Vere Street.

Besides the **British Museum,** where you'll find everything from an exquisite pre-Christian Portland vase to a 2,000-year-old corpse found in a Chesire bog, there's a treasure trove of lesser-known but equally impressive museums. On the city's periphery are the early 17th-century **Ham House,** the Palladian-style **Marble Hill House,** and **Hatfield House,** where Bloody Queen Mary imprisoned her younger half-sister, Elizabeth. Also worth a visit is the 300-year-old **Woburn Abbey,** which contains portraits of royalty. (A tip: Get a Great British Heritage Pass from a travel agent before your trip. It lets you into all of the National Trust properties, plus many others.)

For more mundane pleasures, visit some of London's famous shops. Go to **Bond Street** for upscale treasures and the **Portobello Road Market** for remarkable bargains. For half-price theater tickets, try the SWET booth in Leicester Square.

The sights in Penzance are a sharp contrast to London's urbanity. Walk along Chapel Hill, which is lined with old Georgian town houses and fishermen's cottages. Stop at the **Museum of Nautical History,** in a re-created 18th-century battle ship. Nearby is the castle of **St. Michael's Mount,** on an islet that rises 250 feet from the sea and is accessible by a causeway.

✈ **GETTING THERE:** Delta, British Air, and American Airlines are among the carriers that fly to London. During peak season you can expect to pay about $740 round trip from New York to London. During off-season, you can find fares as low as $314. From London's Paddington Station, it's a seven-hour train ride to Penzance.

WHERE TO STAY:

$$ The Rembrandt, a charming three-star hotel in Knightsbridge, opposite the Victoria and Albert Museum and a short walk from Harrods, is also easy on the pocketbook. From May through August, rates are $269 per night, double occupancy; in early winter, rates fall to $129. ☎ 800–424–2862

$$ In Penzance, the **Abbey Hotel** is located on a narrow street in the town's oldest section and overlooks the harbor. Peak season rates go for about $150 per night and drop to about $115 during off-season. ☎ 01736–36906

THE CARIBBEAN—ST. JOHN

☛ *Best time to visit: mid-April to late summer, when the winter crowds recede but before the hurricane season.*

■ The same pleasures you find in the packed winter season on the island of St. John (and most of the Caribbean) can be yours if you visit from spring to late summer. Avoid late August and September, when hurricane season is in full swing. Summers on the islands are a bit more sultry, but not much: Caribbean temperatures vary only about 5 percent throughout the year.

About two-thirds of St. John is a protected national park, providing opportunities for beachside relaxation, hiking, biking, bird-watching, enjoying nature, and hopping to nearby islands.

■ **MAJOR ATTRACTIONS:** The underwater trail at **Trunk Bay** is particularly good for beginning snorkelers. Another top snorkeling spot is at **Lameshur Bay.** Visit the spectacular cliffs at **Ram Head** and the **Annaberg Plan-**

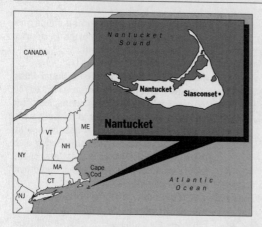

tation, a restored 18th-century Danish sugar mill. **Mongoose Junction** is one of the prettiest places to shop in the Caribbean.

✈ **GETTING THERE:** American Airlines flies to St. John via St. Thomas. Fares during the peak season go for about $600, versus off-season rates of about $500 or less.

WHERE TO STAY:

$$$ Caneel Bay is a posh resort on 170 acres of greenery, flowers, and beaches. It has tennis courts, a large swimming pool, and three restaurants. Peak season doubles, at $350–$750 per night, can be had for $225–$550 in low season. ☎ 800-928-8889

$ Maho Bay Camps consists of more than 100 cabin-like "eco-tents" on a hillside. Each tent, which sleeps up to six, goes for $95 during peak season and drops to $60 in off-season. ☎ 800–392–9004

MASSACHUSETTS—NANTUCKET

☛ *Best time to visit: in early September through late October. Late March to the end of May is also pleasant.*

■ Motorists clog New England roads during the fall to view the splendid foliage. Why fight the traffic when you can take an hour-and-45-minute ferry ride from Cape Cod to Nantucket? You'll see the changing leaves and a lot more.

After Labor Day, the crowds in tiny Nantucket subside and life returns to a slower pace. It may be too cool for much beach bum-

ming, but there's plenty else to enjoy. Nantucket, with its cedar-shingled cottages, white picket fences, and cobblestone streets, is a step back into an early 19th-century whaling village, which it once was. The island is a designated National Historic District. Because of its small scale and narrow streets, walking and biking are the best ways to sightsee.

■ **MAJOR ATTRACTIONS:** The **Nantucket Whaling Museum** and the **Museum of Nantucket History** (closes at the end of September), describe traditional island industries such as whaling, candle making, and sheep shearing. Take a bike ride through the sweet-smelling moors of heather and cranberry. Or go on a whale-watching excursion (through mid-September). From Memorial Day to Columbus Day, 14 historic houses are open to the public; an $8 ticket from the Nantucket Historical Association will get you into all of them. The village of **Siasconset,** formerly an actor's colony, is worth a visit. For $10 per person, you can get an overview tour of the island with the Robert Pitman Grimes Historic Nantucket Tours (☎ 508–228–9382).

✈ **GETTING THERE:** Take the $10 ferry ride from Hyannisport or Wood's Hole, Mass. Or fly to Nantucket from Boston on Nantucket Airlines. Round-trip fares are about $130. ☎ 800–635–8787 or 508–228–6252

WHERE TO STAY:

$$$ Nashagwisset, a replica of an old whaling village, consists of 90 two-story houses and tennis courts. In peak season expect to pay $1,700 per week for a double. In off-season a double can go for $170 per day. ☎ 508–228–0625

$$$ Wauwinet is a gray-shingled house on a private beach. There are tennis courts and two restaurants. Hop aboard the Topper, a 21-foot ship that takes you on free cruises around the island. Peak-season doubles start at $210 per night, falling to $190 in off-season. ☎ 800–426–8718

▼

ISLAND-HOPPING AROUND THE GLOBE

Some spots that castaways would die for

By nature, islands retain a unique style that can be determined quickly, perhaps in a matter of minutes. How do you like your islands? Robinson-Crusoe isolated, or culturally stimulating? We've put together a handful of islands that ooze style, while disproving Edna St. Vincent Millay's moan, "There are no islands anymore." These places are not only natural paradises but also offer attractions that will rivet your attention, and hold it for more than just one week.

MAHE
59 sq. mi.; pop.: 59,500 ☛ *The Seychelles*

■ Once thought to be the actual Garden of Eden, Mahe is the largest of the Seychelles, a group of 100 or so islands in the Indian Ocean off the coast of Africa. *USA Today* recently cited the Seychelles as the top vacation hot-spot of the '90s. Mahe's mountainous coastal road is lined with expansive white beaches and massive outcrops of granite dating back millions of years. You can smell the scents from the cinnamon, tea, nutmeg, and vanilla plantations. Beaches are magnificent, with pure water, coral reefs, and no pollution—environmental laws are strictly enforced. Wildlife include rare birds, such as the paradise flycatcher and sooty tern, and the giant tortoise.

Mahe's capital port, Victoria, retains elements of British colonialism; a statue of Queen Victoria and a Big Ben clock are prominent in the center square. The cultural and racial diversity of the Seychelles is reflected in tin-roofed Chinese and Indian shops and restaurants. Houses are a brightly colored French Colonial style.

■ **MAIN ATTRACTIONS:** The **Sans Souci Pass** leads deep into the rain forest. At the top of the pass is a kiosk that sells exotic spices. The southern coastline is wild and lovely, with unparalleled views of lagoons, bays, and neighboring islands. At **Mahe Beach** and **Beau Vallon** the water is calm and clear, great for swimming, snorkeling, and other water activities.

A trip to one of the tea plantations, as well as the **Morne Seychellois National Park,** are good side excursions. Resort-type attractions are plentiful, including facilities for golf, tennis, and disco and folk dancing. Well worth the two-hour ferry ride is a visit to the island of **Praslin,** a sort of natural Shangri-la. Here you'll find thousands of Coco de Mer palms, some nearly 900 years old. And, if you're lucky, you might catch a glimpse of the rare black parrots that inhabit the island.

WHERE TO STAY:

$$$ The **Equator Grande Anse Residence** is a rustic seaside hotel surrounded by tropical gardens. ☎ 218–78228

$ The **Auberge d'Anse Boileau** is a small thatched-roof inn. ☎ 248–7660.

☎ **Tourism:** 248–225–256 (U.S. Embassy in Mahe), or 212–687–9766 (Embassy of Republic of Seychelles in N.Y.)

MOOREA
37 sq. mi.; pop.: 9,000 ☛ *French Polynesia*

■ If you had to pick a spot on which to be shipwrecked, Moorea is the island to choose. This island is part of French Polynesia, an island chain between Tahiti and the Easter Islands. Its beauty has lured the adventuresome for centuries, from Captain Cook to Gauguin. The islands are characterized by verdant mountains, jungle valleys, and palm-crested pristine beaches. The best time to visit is during the dry season from May through October. Winter can be hot, humid, and rainy.

■ **MAIN ATTRACTIONS:** Moorea is undoubtedly one of the world's most beautiful islands—a painter's heaven of jagged peaks and spires, white sand beaches, and two placid bays in the north. The island's main road along the coast is bordered by papaya, coconut, and breadfruit trees, and sweet-smelling hibiscus and Tahitian gardenias. Inland, the lookout point of **Belvedere** commands one of the most impressive panoramic views in the Pacific. Be sure to visit the **Tiki Village,** which features native arts, crafts, and dancing. Also ask at your hotel about arrangements for taking a "Dolphin Quest" tour, which takes you into the waters to meet these friendly creatures.

WHERE TO STAY:
All-inclusive package deals are the best way to visit Moorea. One good deal, offered by **Islands in the Sun** (☎ 800–828–6877), starts in Los Angeles, stops overnight at the Royal Tahitier Hotel in Papeete, and then proceeds by air to Moorea. You stay at **Club Bali Hai** on Cook's Bay, one of the island's most scenic spots, for six days before returning to L.A. From April 1 to December 31, the package goes for about $890 a person (meals are not included). Club Med (☎ 800–258–1633; ask for Tahiti desk) offers an all-inclusive seven-night package for $1,800 to $1,900 a person.
☎ **Tourism:** 212–838–7800, ext. 253

BORNHOLM
436 sq. mi.; pop.: 44,936 ☛ *Denmark*

■ Off the coast of Denmark, Bornholm is referred to as the Pearl of the Baltic. Unlike its chilly mother country, Bornholm has a sunny, temperate climate. Its landscape is varied: A steep rocky northern coast with coves and salt marshes, and a huge rift valley. Teyn, the largest fishing village, lies in the north, as does the small village of Sandvig, noted for its charming harbor and old-fashioned half-timbered houses. In the center is

Akerhely, a town dating back to 1346 and renowned for its profusion of flowers. Fishing villages dot the east and west coasts. At the island's southern end is the Dueodde Strand, a mammoth sand dune of what natives claim is the world's finest sand.

■ **MAIN ATTRACTIONS:** Sand and sun need not be the main attractions on this ancient island. There are medieval stone buildings to check out, including four fine examples of Nordic medieval round churches, built between 1150 and 1200. A zoological park is located in an unused quarry near **Allinge.** In the tiny **Borholm Museaum,** you are treated to an unusual exhibit on the history of clockmaking, an old island industry. On the eastern coast is the hamlet of **Gudhjem-Melstad,** a three-harbor village of picturesque 17th- and 18th-century houses and cobblestone streets. A network of bike paths, moderately priced hotels, and fine beaches make this a good island to explore with teenagers and younger children. An old-fashioned amusement park called **Braendesgardshaven,** featuring a row boat pond, a toy factory, and a deer and nature park, also appeals to families.

WHERE TO STAY:
$$$ The **Strandholellet** is a distinctive old hotel near the harbor in Sandvig. ☎ 45-56/48-03-14
$$ The **Hotel Bornholm** in the Dueodde Woods has doubles, apartments, and bungalows. ☎ 45-56/48-07-09
$ Good options for the budget-conscious are the well-run youth hostels. One of these, the **Dueodde Youth Hostel,** is located in a wooded area near a sandy beach and offers facilities for golf and tennis. ☎ 45-56/48-81-19
☎ **Tourism:** 45–56–95–00

GRAHAM ISLAND
2,491 sq. mi.; pop.: 3,000 ☛ *Queen Charlotte Islands, British Columbia*

■ Off the coast of Canada, Graham Island is the largest of the Queen Charlotte Islands (known as Haida Gwaii to the native peoples), a group of some 150 islands and islets.

Sometimes called the Canadian Galapagos, these are moody islands in a misty, wind-swept region with unspoiled wilderness. A strange twist of nature left the islands untouched by the Ice Age, resulting in temperate rain forests, the evolution of unique plant and animal species, including some of the world's biggest trees. Graham's western coast is climatically wild and subject to pounding seas, but its eastern coast is protected by the Pacific Japanese current, accounting for its temperate climate and lush canopy of rain forest. May and August are the driest months.

■ **MAIN ATTRACTIONS:** The port village of Queen Charlotte City is just west of the ferry terminal at which you arrive from the mainland. Fishing, canoeing, and boating tours start here. From the top of nearby **Sleeping Beauty Mountain,** you get panoramic views of the village. Free primitive campgrounds are scattered throughout the island. Some 2,000 native Haida people live on the islands. The town of **Skidegate** is home to many of the Haida artists and craftsmen. Displays of native artifacts and totem poles can be found at the Ed Jones Haida museum in the village of Haida. Aficionados of rare birds, such as marbled godwits and dowitches, will love the **Delkatla Wildlife Sanctuary,** north of Masset. At Masset Inlet, peregrine falcons and killer whales can be spotted.

WHERE TO STAY:
   $ The **Premier Hotel** is a handsomely restored 1910 Heritage-style building. ☎ 250–559–8451
   $ **Weavers Inn Motel** situated in the ranching community of Tl'ell has a beautiful rural setting. ☎ 250–557–4491
☎ **Tourism:** 250–559–4742

BANDA NEIRA
59 sq mi.; pop.: 59,500 ☛ The Banda islands, Indonesia

■ The Bandas are the original Spice Islands, renowned through history for their natural beauty. Banda Neira is one of the seven tiny-islands, a subgroup of the world's largest archipelago, which constitutes Indonesia. More than 13,000 islands in this archipelago straddle the equator, from the Indian and Pacific oceans, linking Asia and Australia. **Bandeira,** the only town on Banda Neira, has Mediterranean-style houses and shops, a pretty Dutch Reform Church, and a neoclassic governor's house. The street behind the market is lined with once-grand old houses of the 19th century *perkeniers*, or Dutch planters. At the island's northeast corner is **Malole,** a coral-reef beach ideal for snorkeling and swimming.

■ **MAJOR ATTRACTIONS:** Explore the numerous remains of Dutch forts and visit the **Reunah Budaya Museaum,** located in an old Dutch villa. The hills afford fantastic views of the sea and nearby islands. The Banda Sea is deep, blue, and pure, making water sports a big activity here. Dazzling coral gardens lie between Banda Neira and two of the other Banda islands, Gunung Api and Banda Lontar, which combine to form a spectacular natural harbor. Within paddling distance of each other and Banda Neira, the islands are well worth a visit.

WHERE TO STAY:
$$$ The **Hotel Laguna,** located on the waterfront, is well equipped for water sports. ☎ 62–910–21018
   $ The **C Delfika** Guesthouse is located in an old Dutch mansion. ☎ 62–910–21027
☎ **Tourism:** 212–879–0600

TASMANIA
67,800 sq.mi.; pop.: 472,600 ☛ Australia

■ Off Australia's southern coast, Tasmania (see also story on page 408 in Adventure) is often considered the most beautiful of the continent's states—replete with colonial-style villages, huge untouched forests, thousands of lakes, beaches, moors, and pastures grazed by sheep. It has a temperate climate, with the warmest months and the least rainfall occurring in January and February. Wildlife here includes marsupials and many varieties of birds.

The distances on Tasmania are easy to manage by car, although the landscape is

EXPERT SOURCES

SWIMMING WITH THE SHARKS

For many, sharks still have a reputation as wanton predators, but scientists are finding that they are intelligent creatures that can be trained to distinguish between the hand that feeds them and the prey they eat (mostly fish). Apparently the word is getting out: Some 200,000 travelers now set out to swim with sharks every year. For safety, it's best to go on an organized trip with a diver versed in shark behavior. Here are some shark-diving operators:

THE BASKING SHARK EXPERIENCE
Legends Travel, Isle of Man (England)

■ The basking shark is the second largest fish in the world, some 35 feet long and weighing 5 tons. The guide is a research scientist with 13 years of experience with sharks. Lodging is in a family-run hotel in the charming Celtic village of Dalby.
☎ 44–1624–843551

CORAL DIVERS
Nassau, the Bahamas

■ Daily shark dives in the waters of the Caribbean. Dives are led by an experienced shark feeder.
☎ 242–362–1263

UNDERSEA EXPLORER PROGRAM
Osprey Reef in the Coral Sea (off the coast of Australia)

■ A shark research program studying many different species in a vast Coral Sea area. Experienced divers can hook up with research scientists.
✉ P.O. Box 615, Port Douglas, Queensland, Australia 4871
FAX ☎ 61–70–995914

MAD DOG EXPEDITIONS
Cape Town, South Africa

■ This group conducts shark research and conservation-oriented programs with the South African White Shark Research Institute. Headquarters are based in a luxurious eco-farm resort about 100 miles south of Cape Town.
☎ 800–4–MADDOG, or 212–744–6763

---

quite varied. In the west are impenetrable forests and windswept coastal cliffs. The north is mainly farmland. From the town of Launceston, the closest point to the mainland, it's a three-hour drive to Hobart, a city in the south with stone buildings around a waterfront that serves as a hub for cruise ships and yachts.

Tasmania was established in the early 1800s as a penal colony by the English, who wiped out the aboriginal tribes. Later, they attempted to re-create English towns, complete with farms, orchards, and villages. **Port Arthur,** in the south, is the site of the infamous penal colony, with buildings constructed by convicts.

■ **MAIN ATTRACTIONS:** In the Central Highlands is **Cradle Mountain–Lake St. Clair**

National Park. It is immense, largely untouched, and partly accessible for outdoor activities. In the southern village of **Richmond,** you can visit a museum dedicated to the island's penal past. Tasmanians are avid fishermen. Thanks to the abundance of slow-moving streams and generally shallow lakes, Tasmanian waters are ideal for fly fishing. For the best trout fishing, head for the Central Highlands, where creeks and rivers abound.

WHERE TO STAY:
- **$ Prospect House** in Richmond is an old colonial residence. ☎ (002) 62 2207
- **$** The **Old Bakery Inn,** in Launceston is a nicely restored, small hotel. ☎ (003) 31 7900
- ☎ **Tourism:** 03–62–33–8011 (Hobart); or 708–296–4900 (Aussie Helpline in Illinois)

THE CARIBBEAN'S HIDDEN TREASURES

Let's face it, the Caribbean islands have become America's tourist playground. As a result, many of the most popular ones, such as the American Virgins and Puerto Rico, can be incredibly crowded. More than 2,700 islands make up the Caribbean islands in a 2,500-mile-long arc stretching from just south of Florida to the coast of Venezuela. If you want to follow the sun far from the madding crowds, here are some great choices: seven tiny, off-the-beaten-path Caribbean islands. But don't worry about being too far from civilization—the larger islands are just a plane or boat ride away.

LITTLE CAYMAN

10 sq. mi.; pop.: 100 ☛ Cayman Islands, Greater Antilles

■ The southernmost and smallest of the three Caymans, this island is a thin limestone, coral, and salt marsh spit. A dive spot at **Bloody Bay Wall** plunges to 1,200 feet. Jacques Cousteau referred to it as one of the best dive sites in the world. The island flats offer great bonefishing. Bird-lovers can feast their eyes on rare native and migrating birds, including the West Indian whistling duck and the endangered Cayman parrot.

☛ **INSIDE SCOOP:** It may be far from the action on Grand Cayman, and largely undeveloped, but the electricity supply is reliable and telecommunications topnotch. More birds here than people.

✈ **GETTING THERE:** Island Air ☎ 809–949–5252; Cayman Airways ☎ 800–422–9626

WHERE TO STAY:
Pirates Point Resort is a secluded, 10-cottage hotel that's a top choice among divers. Its restaurant dishes up great food.
Rates: $125–$180 (per night, double occupancy).
☎ 345–948–1010
Little Cayman Beach Resort is a modern, all-inclusive resort. **Rates:** $475–$525 for 3 nights for divers, $409–$464 for nondivers. ☎ 809–948–1033

ANEGADA

15 sq. mi.; pop.: 250 ☛ British Virgin Islands

■ Twenty miles north of Virgin Gorda's North Sound, Anegada is a flat mass of coral. The most isolated of the British Virgin Islands, it is mostly under the jurisdiction of the BVI National Parks Trust, which includes a bird sanctuary for flamingos, herons, ospreys, and terns, as well as a population of 2,000 wild goats, donkeys, and cattle. Good bonefishing can be found, as well as beaches for snorkeling and diving.

☛ **INSIDE SCOOP:** This is no luxury resort island, although Princess Di and Ted Kennedy both found their way here. It is peaceful, natural, and laid-back. Boating near the surrounding coral reefs can be dangerous, as many sunken wrecks testify.

✈ **GETTING THERE:** Gorda Aero Services from Tortola. ☎ 800–433–7300

WHERE TO STAY: The **Anegada Reef Hotel** is a no-luxury affair, with few amenities. **Rates:** About $230 for a double. ☎ 809–495–8002

SABA

5 sq.mi.; pop.: 1,200 ☛ Netherlands Antilles, Leeward Islands

■ Relatively remote, this tiny Dutch island has not fallen prey to massive development. Ringed by steep cliffs, Saba lacks wide beaches and flatlands. Dormant Mt. Scenery rises 2,855 feet above sea level. Toylike villages, narrow paths, red-roofed houses with picket fences and gingerbread trim dot the mountainside. One road, aptly called the Main Road, serves the entire island, and there are few

■ **ISLAND-HOPPER'S GUIDE**

shops, inns, and resorts. But you can enjoy 18 botanical hiking trails, a tropical rain forest, undersea gardens, a marine park, 29 great dive sites, and deep-sea fishing.

☛ **INSIDE SCOOP:** Proficient hikers may want to tackle the 1,064 stone steps up **Mt. Scenery.** Others are advised to take the road.

✈ **GETTING THERE:** On WINAIR, it's a 15-minute flight from St. Maarten; or by a catamaran ferry, also from St. Maarten, which takes about one hour.

WHERE TO STAY:
Willard's of Saba is set high on a mountainside and has a heated pool, tennis courts, and sweeping views from its balconies and gardens. **Rates:** $150–$300. ☎ 011–599–4–62498
The **Gate House** has six

guest rooms, and is situated in a quiet village, inappropriately named Hell's Gate. **Rates:** $60–$80. ☎ 001–599–4–62416

LES SAINTES TERRE-DE-HAUT

3 sq. mi.; pop.: 1,500 ☛ *French West Indies (Leewards), Lesser Antilles*

■ Descendents of Norman and Breton sailors live on this island, whose main industry is fishing. Bourg is a miniature French-style village filled with brightly colored houses. There are few cars here, so the best way to explore is on foot. A fine hike leads to the island's highest point, Le Chameau. An old stone citadel awaits you there, with panoramic views of nearby islands. Other attractions include flowering cactus gardens and Fort Napoleon, from which no

shot has ever been fired. The island is, however, a perfect spot for deep-sea diving and snorkeling.

☛ **INSIDE SCOOP:** French cooking prevails here—from classical to nouvelle cuisine to spicy Creole. You'll find small, modestly priced restaurants but no nightlife—not even a movie theater.

✈ **GETTING THERE:** Air Guadeloupe from nearby Guadeloupe ☎ 011–590–82–47–00; ferry from Guadeloupe via ATE ☎ 011–590–83–12–45

WHERE TO STAY:
Auberge des Petits Saints is set on a hillside amid tropical gardens. Inside, rooms are furnished with antiques. **Rates:** $80–$140. ☎ 590–99–50–99
Hotel Bois Joli is situated on the beach, affording

■ **FINDING YOUR WAY IN THE ISLANDS**
The Caribbean islands and the Bahamas together form the West Indies. The islands between the Atlantic and the Caribbean Sea—true Caribbean—are called the Antilles. For more information on the above islands, call:

Caribbean Tourism Organization .. ☎ 212–682–0435

Saba Tourist Office .... ☎ 800–722–2394

Bequia Tourist Board .... ☎ 809–458–3286

St. Vincent Board of Tourism .... ☎ 809–457–1502

views of Pain-de-Sucre Bay.
Rates: $147–$276.
☎ 590–99–52–53

BEQUIA
7 sq. mi.; pop.: 5,000 ☛ *St. Vincent's and the Grenadines, Windward Isles*

■ Bequia is an old whaler's island seemingly little changed by time. Boat-building is a major activity. Be sure to visit **Paget Farm,** an old whaler's village. The yacht basin at Admiralty Bay hosts the annual Easter Regatta. Princess Margaret Beach is recommended for snorkeling. Devil's Table, a site with fish, coral, and the remains of a shipwreck, is a good dive spot.

☛ **INSIDE SCOOP:** Hope Beach on the Atlantic side is secluded but the surf is rough. The Bullet at north point has rays, barracuda, and nurse sharks.

✈ **GETTING THERE:** LIAT 809–458–4841; ferry, the MV *Admiral* from Kingston, Jamaica; or mail boat or schooner from St. Vincent's.

WHERE TO STAY:
Plantation House, an elegant hotel with a peach-and-white facade and wraparound porch, overlooks Admiralty Bay. It is surrounded by 10 acres of lush gardens. **Rates:** $320–$350. ☎ 809–458–3425
The Frangipani sits on the waterfront in Port Eliza-

beth, the island's only town.
Rates: $40–$120.
☎ 809–458–3255

MUSTIQUE
12 sq. mi.; privately owned ☛ *Windward Isles*

■ This island 18 miles south of St. Vincent is a retreat for the rich and famous. Its 52 houses are privately owned, though some are available for rent. (Princess Margaret and Mick Jagger rent out their villas.) The island's big attractions are its natural beauty: wooded hills, grassy valleys, and white sand beaches surrounded by coral reefs. Horseback riding is big here.

☛ **INSIDE SCOOP:** Basil's Bar is a popular gathering place.

✈ **GETTING THERE:** Mustique Airways from Barbados ☎ 800–526–4789; or private yacht.

WHERE TO STAY:
Cotton House is an 18th-century stone-and-coral plantation house with an antique decor. **Rates:** $325–$550. ☎ 809–456–4777
Firefly Guest House, the island's only guest house, is small and moderately priced. **Rates:** $80–150. ☎ 809–456–3414

MAYREAU
1.5 sq.mi.; pop.:250 ☛ *St Vincent's and the Grenadines, Windward Isles*

■ Situated halfway between St. Vincent and Grenada, this island is only accessible by boat—an advantage for those who enjoy real tranquillity and beautiful natural surroundings. No cars or phones, and only one road, create an 18th-century atmosphere. Saline Bay on the leeward coast is lined with sea grapes. Beaches are laden with shells, driftwood, and rock crystals. Station Hill, the island's highest point, is where most people live.

☛ **INSIDE SCOOP: Salt Whistle Bay** has one of the world's most magnificent beaches with powdery white sand shaded by palms and flowering bushes.

✈ **GETTING THERE:** From Barbados fly to Union Island, where the hotel's motor launch will meet you for the 20-minute trip; or take the mailboat MV *Snapper* from Union Island.

WHERE TO STAY:
Salt Whistle Bay Club is composed of stone cottages separated from the water by a palm grove. Amenities include diving and boat excursions, water sports, and hiking. **Rates:** $300–$490. ☎ 800–561–7258
Dennis' Hideaway is less expensive and offers good food, wonderful views, and clean, simple rooms. **Rates:** $50–$70. ☎ 809–458–8594

THE NEXT BEST THING TO A DESERT ISLAND

The beach might be the best place to beat the heat but most of the time it is not the best place to beat the crowds. Fortunately, there are still a few beaches as yet ungirded by tarmac, summer homes, or boardwalks. Often requiring a hike or a ferry ride, these wilderness beaches reward the extra effort with a guaranteed secluded spot at the shore. Stephen Leatherman (also known as Dr. Beach) is a leading coastal ecologist at the University of Maryland who has been exploring beaches all over the country for the last 20 years studying the effects of coastal erosion. His annual best beach survey (see below) always makes headlines. Here are his picks for the best wilderness beaches in the country.

JASPER BEACH
Near Machiasport, Maine

■ Named for the smooth pebbles of jasper, a reddish volcanic rock from the glacial cliffs found in this area. It's a 10- to 20-minute trek from the parking lot to see the eagles.

HIGHLAND LIGHT BEACH
Near Truro, Massachusetts

■ The heather-covered cliffs of Outer Cape Cod are reminiscent of the Scottish highlands. A short trek from Cape Cod Light, which is accessible by paved road.

HAMMOCKS BEACH
On Bear Island, just south of Borgue Banks and More-head City, North Carolina

■ Access to this four-mile-long island is only by pedestrian ferry. No buildings but for a park concession. No vehicles allowed.

PADRE ISLAND
About 20 miles south of Corpus Christi, Texas

■ The longest barrier island in the world—over 110 miles in length. There is some development at the

two ends. Travel is best by off-road vehicle.

LITTLE RIVER
Near Mendocino, California

■ Due to the deep water just offshore and the coastal upswelling of ice-cold water, not a good swimming beach, but great for hiking.

SHI SHI BEACH
Part of Olympic National Park, Washington

■ This area is only reached

by a 13-mile hike on which you will see a variety of wildlife. Shi Shi is next to a large Indian reservation, where permission is required to venture.

KALALAU BEACH STATE PARK
On the Napali coast on the island of Kauai, Hawaii

■ The number-one eco-tourism resort destination in Hawaii. There is an 11-mile hiking trail.

■ AND THE WINNERS ARE...
In his annual survey of best beaches in the country, Stephen Leatherman evaluates over 50 criteria, including beach cleanliness, number of sunny days, sand softness, and number of lifeguards. He takes first-place beaches out of the running in subsequent years.

1997 BEST BEACHES
1. Hulopoe Beach, Hawaii
2. Kailua, Hawaii
3. Caladesi Island, Fla.
4. Hamoa, Hawaii
5. Wailea, Hawaii
6. Cape Florida, Fla.
7. Hanalei Beach, Hawaii
8. Kaunaoa, Hawaii
9. Fort Desoto Park, Fla.
10. St. Joseph Peninsula, Fla.
11. Delnor-Wiggins Pass, Fla.
12. St. George Island, Fla.
13. Perdido Key, Fla.
14. Ocracoke Island, Fla.
15. East Hampton Beach, N.Y.
16. Westhampton Beach, N.Y.
17. Bald Head Island, N.C.
18. Coast Guard Beach, Mass.
19. Clam Pass, Fla.
20. Sand Key Park, Fla.

PREVIOUS WINNERS
1992 Bahia Honda, Fla.
1993 Hapuna, Hawaii
1994 Grayton Beach, Fla.
1995 St. Andrews, Fla.
1996 Lanikai, Hawaii

BEYOND HAWAII'S BIG ISLAND

These three are just as beautiful but less traveled

Hawaii is a long way from anywhere, so you'll want to choose your sites carefully. Of the eight Hawaiian islands, it's possible to visit only six: Kahoolawe is uninhabited and Niihau is privately owned. The popular islands, Oahu, Maui, and Hawaii, known as the Big Island, are still a visitor's paradise but one that must be shared with hordes of other tourists. What's more, these meccas suffer from ensuing ills like gridlock and scenery marred by relentless resort development. Fortunately, there are three other Hawaiian options—paradises that are less-trod and perhaps more inviting. Here's a guide.

KAUAI
533 sq. mi.; pop.: 51,000

■ Of all the islands, Kauai has the most beautiful natural scenery, thanks partly to its abundant rainfall. The top of Mt. Waialeale (5,238 ft.) is the rainiest place on earth. The interior is virtually inpenetrable.

■ **MAIN ATTRACTIONS:** For water sports, head for **Nukolii Beach Park** or **Mahaulepu Beach,** with its reef-protected shoreline and pocket beaches. It also has 100-ft. sand dunes. Horseback riding is big here, particularly in **Waimea Canyon.** Two great golf courses are the Princeville Makai and the Kiele.

The **Grove Farm Homestead** presents a picture of life on a 19th-century plantation. The climb to the top of Waialeale provides a unique (and wet) experience. **Kilauea National Wildlife Refuge** is home to many exotic birds and other animals.

There are many gems of beaches all around the island down little dirt roads. The village of **Hanalei,** the setting for the movie *South Pacific,* is worth a visit. **Pakala Beach** is perfect for all water sports, except swimming.

Inside scoop: Smith's Tropical Paradise is a tourist trap in the form of a theme park.

WHERE TO STAY:

$$$ Princeville Resort is the retreat-of-choice of the wealthy. The premier hotel is the **Princeville Hotel.** ☎ 800–325–3535. The **Outrigger Kauai Beach Hotel** is a horseshoe-shaped complex, surrounding a pool and waterfalls. ☎ 800–688–7444.

$ **Waimea Plantation,** set in a coconut grove, is one of the island's most secluded spots. ☎ 800–992–4632. The **Rosewood B&B** offers rooms in an 80-year-old plantation house. ☎ 808–822–5216. **Keapana Center** is a hilltop B&B with nearby hiking and beach opportunities. ☎ 800–822–7968.

MOLOKAI
263 sq. mi.; pop.: 6,900

■ Much of the island is hard to access. The coast in the north has the world's highest sea cliffs. Kamakou (4,970 ft.), the tallest mountain, is surrounded by jungles and pools. The west is dry and features the island's one resort complex. The south is flat, with offshore coral reefs. The interior is remote and largely privately owned. Many of the beaches are for admiring rather than swimming.

■ **MAIN ATTRACTIONS:** Kamakou Preserve is a 2,774-acre wildlife refuge. Contact the Nature Conservancy (☎ 808–553–5236) to visit. For a taste of Africa, visit the **Molokai Ranch Wildlife Park,** with animals mostly from Tanzania and Kenya.

Kawakiu Beach is a nature preserve and good swimming beach. One of the island's prettiest non-swimming beaches is **Pohakuloa Beach.** Hiking and biking are especially nice on an unpaved road beginning west of Kanuakakai along 9 miles of isolated beach.

Visit the **Kalokoeli Fish Pond,** an ancient type of fish pond unique to Hawaii. A strenuous, but rewarding, hike is into the **Halawa Valley,** where Moaula Waterfall cascades some 250 feet.

Inside scoop: There are very few restaurants here, so you might want to consider renting a condo with a kitchenette. Nightlife is practically nonexistent. There is, however, local music at the Pau Hana Inn. ☎ 800–432–MOLO or 808–553–5342).

WHERE TO STAY:

$$$ The best hotel is at the **Kaluakoi Hotel and Golf Club.** The course is excellent and it is located right on Kepuhi Beach. ☎ 800–552–2721. **Paniolo Hale** are condo units with ocean views. ☎ 800–552–2731.

$ **Honomuni House** is a cottage in a garden setting with a stream and waterfall. ☎ 800–558–8383. **Kamalo Plantation Bed & Breakfast** is surrounded by fruit trees. ☎ 808–558–8236.

LANAI

140 sq. mi.; pop.: 2,200

■ Formerly owned largely by the Dole Pineapple Co., Lanai is now being eyed by business interests intent on developing tourism. For the time being, however, this small island retains much of its old plantation ambience.

■ **MAIN ATTRACTIONS:** Garden of the Gods is a rock garden whose foundation consists of unusual lava and rock formations. The abandoned villages of Kaunolu and Keomuku are fun to explore. A nice hike is up the Munro Trail from Lanai City to the summit of Mt. Lanihale.

There are golf courses at each of the twin resorts. The best beach is **Hulopoe,** with its partly protected swimming area. Snorkeling and scuba diving are excellent.

The black Luahiwa rocks with their ancient petroglyphs are worth seeing. A remote beach great for walking is **Lopa,** near Keomuku Village.

Inside scoop: If you go hiking or biking, be sure to carry your own water; there is practically no surface water on the island.

WHERE TO STAY:

$$$ The **Lodge at Koele** is situated in the highlands among the cool Norfolk pine trees for which the island is famous. ☎ 800–321–4666. The **Manele Bay Hotel** is a luxury beach resort offering views of Hulopoe Bay. ☎ 800–321–4666.

$ **Hotel Lanai** is an old-fashioned inn with a front porch and wicker chairs. ☎ 800–321–4666.

EXPERT PICKS

NO HOOPS, BUT PLENTY OF HULA

Hula dances are stories in motion—spicy tales of love, war, and beauty. Ray Fonseca, who runs a hula school, suggests the following places to watch hula.

HULA KODAK SHOW
Waikiki

■ The performances are a bit touristy but still a lot of fun and a great introduction to the hula.

U.S.S. CONSTITUTION
Big Island

■ Once a week, there are great hula performances on this huge liner.

HAWAII NANI LOA
Hilo, Big Island

■ The hotel's nightly performances feature Fonseca's students.

MERRIE MONARCH FESTIVAL
Hilo, Big Island

■ Thousands of dancers compete in a three-day festival held around Easter.

HULA ONI E
Honolulu

■ Every October, 5- to 12-year-olds hula dance at the Hilton Hawaiian Village.

QUEEN LILIUOKALANI KEIKI COMPETITION
Oahu

■ A very traditional and prestigious competition held every August.

WHERE ROMEOS CAN TAKE JULIETS

Marriage may well be life's greatest adventure. Here are some places to start the journey, chosen by the editors of Honeymoon Magazine *(☎ 305–662–5589) as the most unusual honeymoon spots in the world.*

AMAZON RAIN FOREST
Ecuador

❤ Visit Vilcabamba, Ecuador, otherwise known as the "Valley of the Elders," with its astonishing number of centenarians. Take a cruise to the Galápagos Islands to view the interesting wildlife there. Best place to stay: Hacienda Cusin, in Otavalo.

BANFF SPRINGS
Canadian Rockies

❤ The Banff Springs Hotel in Alberta has been a vacation mecca since it opened in 1888. There are majestic mountains, glacial lakes, and other breathtaking scenery. The hotel includes a 35,000-square-foot spa and fitness center.

CHICHÉN ITZÁ
Yucatán Peninsula, Mexico

❤ Just a couple of hours drive from Cancún, all that remains of this former Mayan ceremonial city are centuries-old ruins, including a pool where virgins were once sacrificed. (For more about Mayan ruins, see page 422.) Visitors can climb to the top of one of the towering temples. Bordering the ruins, the Mayaland Hotel (☎ 800–235–4079) is a lush tropical hideaway with a local mariachi band.

GREAT BARRIER REEF
Australia

❤ This is the longest barrier reef on earth, teeming with tropical fish, colorful coral, giant clams, and other large marine animals. For day trips or deluxe live-aboard boats, call Taka Dive ☎ 800–241–7690.

VOLCANOES NATIONAL PARK
Hawaii

❤ By day, hike together through the mists surrounding the volcanoes. At night, watch fountains of lava shooting up from recesses of the earth. A helicopter tour gives great views. The most unusual hotel in Hawaii is Kona Village (☎ 800–325–5555), in Kailua-Kona, featuring thatch-roofed cottages. (For more about Hawaii, see pages 368–369.)

THE LION'S CITY
Singapore

❤ You can stay at the beautifully renovated Raffles Hotel and visit Sentosa, a theme-park island with a beach, an aquarium, and a model Asian village.

REVENTAZON RIVER
Costa Rica

❤ There's good rafting on the Reventazon River. You can hike around the Poas Volcano or visit a butterfly farm. The Casa Turire (☎ 503–531–1111), a Spanish-style hacienda located in the middle of a coffee and macadamia nut plantation, is a nice place to stay.

"STINGRAY CITY"
Grand Cayman Island

❤ This is a "must dive," according to *Skin Diver* magazine. A top diving site, the water at Stingray City is quite shallow, so the stingrays can be fed by adventuresome snorkelers.

YUCATÁN PENINSULA
Belize

❤ The world's second-largest barrier reef lies just off the Peninsula. It's worth taking in the famous blue hole, a 480-foot-deep limestone sinkhole, with giant stalactites in an ancient cavern. Call Lighthouse Reef ☎ 800–423–3114 for more information.

CRYSTAL CAVES
Bermuda

❤ Wonderful diving and snorkeling, beautiful pink-sand beaches and fantastic limestone caves. For romantic luxury, stay at Grotto Bay Beach Hotel & Tennis Club (☎ 800–582–3190).

GREAT FAMILY-FRIENDLY GETAWAYS

A vacation with kids can be challenging at best. When you want to bask in the sun, they're ready for hustle and bustle. And how do you keep the refrain of "I'm bored" from ringing in your ear? One solution is to take them to resorts that cater to families with kids. Pamela Lanier, author of Family Travel, The Complete Guide *(Lanier Publishing International, 1996), has traveled with her large family for over 20 years. As she puts it, she has traveled "with babies, from the rambunctious toddler years to the reckless phase of late teens and early twenties." Here are some of Lanier's choices of great family resorts.*

HAWK'S CAY RESORT AND MARINA, *Duck Key, Fla.*

■ A 60-acre private island, this resort offers a tropical setting, fantastic dining, and kids' programs that run year-round. There's also a dolphin educational program for adults and kids 10 and older in the on-site dolphin facility. Participants get to swim in the pool with these creatures and interact with them.
☎ 800–432–2242

FONTAINEBLEAU HILTON RESORT
Miami Beach, Fla.

■ Year-round recreational activities and fun for kids, teens, singles, adults, and families, as well as supervised field trips for kids to local attractions.
☎ 800–932–3322

HILTON HAWAIIAN VILLAGE
Honolulu, Oahu, Hawaii

■ Free year-round kids' programs feature children's Olympics, bird shows, cruises, treasure hunts, games, storytelling, and excursions to local hot spots. Lunch and snacks

are provided.
☎ 800–445–8667

MARRIOTT'S TAN-TAR-A RESORT
Osage Beach, Mo.

■ The motto here is "Kids need vacations, too!" Tan-Tar-A has a permanent children's facility with supervised fun: cooking, finger-painting, golf, ice skating, bowling, swimming, and more.
☎ 800–392–5304

MOHONK MOUNTAIN HOUSE
New Paltz, N.Y.

■ Nature and the great outdoors are the focus here for older kids; toddlers are kept occupied with indoor activities. Children's programs run nearly all day, from 9:30 a.m. to 12:30 p.m. and again from 2 to 5 p.m.
☎ 800–772–6646

MOUNTAIN LAKE HOTEL
Pembroke, Va.

■ Stay at the spot where the movie *Dirty Dancing* was filmed. Days are packed with family fun: chess with a life-size outdoor chessboard, horseshoes, tennis, paddleboats, fishing, and

hiking along the Appalachian Trail. At nighttime there are music campfires, magic shows, and, of course, dancing.
☎ 800–346–3334

RANCHO BERNARDO INN
San Diego, Calif.

■ Expertly-run camps will please kids ages 5 to 17. On the program: swimming, golf, crafts, make-a-movie day, family barbecues, and lots more. Camps run in August, and during Christmas and Easter holidays.
☎ 800–854–1065

SOUTH SEAS PLANTATION
Captiva Island, Fla.

■ The resort is on a beautiful setting on the tip of this tiny island. The Captiva Kids Club and Teenagers in Paradise programs keep kids hopping: volleyball tournaments, pool parties, moonlight movies, crab races, up-close inspections of abundant wildlife, and much more.
☎ 800–237–3102

SPLIT ROCK RESORT
Poconos, Pa.

■ An all-season family

resort that rocks with fun: bowling, bumper bowling, bumper boats, indoor and outdoor pools, miniature golf, pontoon rides, and a movie theater. Two bedroom suites are available with full kitchen, microwave, and dishwasher.
☎ 800–255–7625

SUNRIVER RESORT
Sunriver, Ore.

■ Cabins sleep 8 to 10 people. Among the available activities: swimming, biking on a 30-mile trail network, rafting on the Deschutes River, and exploring the Alpine wilderness.
☎ 800–547–3922

TAMARRON
Durango, Colo.

■ Half-day and full-day camps focus on activities for kids ages 4 through 12, including hiking, arts and crafts, singing by the campfire, and feeding horses and other farm animals.
☎ 800–678–1000

FOR ROMANCE, YOU CAN'T BEAT B & B'S

For charm and comfort, few accommodations can match B&B's. The following are among the best, according to an annual survey by Pamela Lanier, author of The Complete Guide to Bed & Breakfasts, Inns and Guesthouses.

THE LEGACY OF WILLIAMSBURG B&B
930 Jamestown Rd.
Williamsburg, VA 23185

■ A colonial inn surrounded by trees and beautiful gardens. Guests enjoy the use of a tavern, grand living room, library, and a billiard room.
☎ 800–962–4722

CAPTAIN FREEMAN INN
15 Breakwater Rd.
Brewster, Cape Cod, MA 02631

■ An old sea captain's mansion built in 1860. There's a 140-foot mahogany wraparound porch. Guest rooms are furnished with antiques and canopy beds.
☎ 800–843–4664

THE LAMPLIGHT INN
P.O. Box 70, 231 Lake Ave.
Lake Luzerne, NY 12846

■ Breakfasts are served on a wraparound porch

with views of the Adirondack Mountains. Innkeepers Gene and Linda Merlino are gracious and attentive to every detail.
☎ 518–696–5294 or 800–262–4668

KEDRON VALLEY INN
Route 106
South Woodstock, VT 05071

■ Innkeepers Max and Merrily Comins' collection of antique quilts is displayed throughout the house. The staff at the award-winning restaurant is Paris-trained.
☎ 802–457–1473, or 800–836–1193

THE VERANDA
P.O. Box 177, 252 Seavy St.
Senoia, GA 30276

■ Built in 1906, this inn was placed on the National Register of Historic Places in the 1970s. A breakfast specialty is an

original Veranda recipe of mushrooms served over eggs or spread on toast.
☎ 770–599–3905

THE WEDGEWOOD INN
111 W Bridge St.
New Hope, PA 18938

■ Inside, antiques and Wedgewood china are displayed throughout. The house was built in 1870 on an older foundation dating from 1720.
☎ 215–862–2570

JOSHUA GRINDLE INN
P.O. Box 206
44800 Little Lake Rd.
Mendocino, CA 95460

■ The Inn sits on a hill above Mendocino, with views of the ocean beyond. Rooms have private baths and are furnished with Early American antiques.
☎ 707–937–4143, or 800–474–6353

HOUSES IN THE COUNTRY

Visiting the grandest of Britain's grand old homes

As the backdrop for many a film, from *Brideshead Revisited*, shown on public television many years ago, to Emma Thompson's 1996 Oscar-winning adaptation of Jane Austen's *Sense and Sensibility*, the English country house has always had an air of class. And no wonder. These houses represent the finely tooled tradition of 400 years of pomp and circumstance and epitomize a level of decorative arts and architecture that is impossible to re-create today.

Neither castle nor palace, the rise of the English country house is directly linked to the early subjugation of the feudal aristocracy and ecclesiastical influence in England by Henry VIII (he didn't like the idea of his nobles living in castles, where they could defend themselves). Because English country houses essentially descended from squires' houses, their exteriors are markedly absent of the extreme architectural distinctions that characterized aristocratic palaces in other European countries.

Today, owing to the immense cost of upkeep, over 400 of these houses are open to the public for at least part of the year. Around 200 are operated by the National Trust, while others are run under a variety of arrangements. You're unlikely to visit them all. Here are some of the most significant, chosen by Fred Maroon, author of *The English Country House: A Tapestry of Ages* (Pavilion Books, 1988).

HADDON HALL
Bakewell, Derbyshire. 14th–early 17th centuries

■ Haddon Hall was originally a medieval manor house and a defensive wall dates from the 12th century. From medieval times onward, Haddon Hall was updated, but there were no major alterations after the early 17th century. As a result, the house contains some of the most authentically historic rooms in England, such as the cavernous kitchen, which still has medieval cupboards, and the 16th-century parlor.

LONGLEAT
Warminster. Late 16th century; altered late 19th century

■ Begun in 1547, Longleat House is considered the first Great House of English Renaissance style. Built on the ruins of an ancient priory, it marks a departure from the fortified look of the medieval house. The early Elizabethan architecture emphasizes a tall, compact building, with many windows, and the Renaissance ideals of balance and symmetry.

Longleat is situated in a park designed by

Capability Brown. The interior was redone around 1860 in the Italian style, but retains the traditional great hall. The library contains Henry VIII's Great Bible of 1541 and several original editions of Chaucer.

CHATSWORTH
Bakewell, Derbyshire. Late 17th, early 18th and 19th centuries

■ One of the most majestic houses in England, it was begun in the mid-1500s by Sir William Cavendish and his Lady, the famous Bess of Hardwick, who kept Mary, Queen of Scots a prisoner here. The exterior of the house is massive and austere. The painting collection includes works by Rembrandt, Veronese, Frans Hals, Poussin, Van Dyck, Reynolds, Sargent, and Lucien Freud. There are magnificent gardens and even a canal.

HARDWICK HALL
Chesterfield, Derbyshire. Late 16th century

■ Hardwick Hall, built by Bess of Hardwick between 1590 and 1597 near the family seat at Chatsworth, is situated on a hilltop with an expansive vista, surrounded by walled court-yards and gardens. It is perhaps the most impressive and least altered of the grand Elizabethan Renaissance houses. The 166-foot-long gallery contains huge glass windows, which were unusual for that time. The house is full of tapestry and fine embroidery, much of it done by Bess herself.

KNOLE
Sevenoaks, Kent. Mid- to late 15th century, enlarged 16th and 17th centuries

■ Knole was the childhood home of Vita Sackville-West, the lover of writer Virginia Woolf, who memorialized the house in her book *Orlando*. The house is an excellent example of the early Jacobean period (1600–1650) with its trademark shaped gables, grand hall, and the seven courtyards. The great staircase is a fine example of the new fashion of treating a staircase as a highly decorative entity.

HATFIELD HOUSE
Hatfield, Hertfordshire. Early 17th century

■ Hatfield House is more like a palace than a private house, fitting for its owners the Cecils, who have provided many of England's greatest statesmen. Built in 1608 by Robert Cecil, the first Earl of Salisbury, and Minister to Elizabeth I and James I, it is one of the finest examples of Jacobean architecture, with its classical symmetrical exterior, impressive wide staircase (the intricate Mannerist carving on it is world famous), and great state rooms.

CASTLE HOWARD
Malton, Yorkshire. Early to mid-18th century

■ The setting for the TV series *Brideshead Revisited*, Castle Howard was designed by Sir John Howard. Horace Walpole said of it: "I have seen gigantic palaces before, but never a sublime one." The finest example of the rare English classical Baroque style, which emphasized grandeur and flamboyance, construction of this building took the greater part of the 18th century. Rubens's famous painting *Salome* hangs here.

BLENHEIM PALACE
Woodstock, Oxfordshire. Early 18th century

■ Queen Anne and a grateful Parliament provided funds for Blenheim as a gift to John Churchill, the first Duke of Marlborough, for his famous victories over France. Winston Churchill was born in the cloakroom during a ball that his mother was attending at the time. The house is in the English Baroque style, but with a great deal of rustication. Capability Brown designed the park, replete with lakes and formal gardens.

SYON HOUSE
Brentford, Greater London. Rebuilt mid-16th century, altered late 18th century

■ Still owned by the family who built it, Syon House is set amid 80 acres of picturesque parkland along the Thames, not far from London. Although most of the rather banal exteriors date from the 15th and 16th centuries, the interior of the property was extensively remodeled by renowned neoclassicist Robert Adam in the 1700s. The grand entrance hall is is one of the most magnificent in Britain.

EUROPE'S MOST CHARMING INNS

Small European hotels with charm and character can be difficult to find through tourist agencies and guides. But Karen Brown has made that her specialty. She has been traveling through Europe for the past 20 years, evaluating small inns, hotels, and bed and breakfasts and publishing 12 discerning guidebooks of her discoveries—all part of Karen Brown's Country Inn *series (Travel Press, ☎ 415–345–9117). Here are some of her choices of the best ones in or near some of the continent's most popular destinations. The hotels are chosen for their charm and most of them offer excellent value. Prices are approximate and for 1997.*

FRANCE

HÔTEL DES QUARTRE DAUPHINS, *Aix-en-Provence*

■ This small, cheerful hotel is located in the old quarter of Aix. The rooms are simply but tastefully decorated with prints and dried flowers. The top rooms with exposed beams have the most character.
$ Double: 326–386 francs
☎ 42.38.16.39
FAX 42.38.60.19

HÔTEL LE HAMEAU, *St.-Paul-de-Vence*

■ A true country inn yet only a five-minute drive from Nice and the Riviera. It is a converted farm, nestled amid fruit trees and flower gardens in one of the classic hill-perched villages of the Riviera. It's one of the best values in southeast France.
$ Double: 390–620 francs; Suite: to 720 francs
☎ 93.32.80.24
FAX 93.32.55.75

HÔTEL LIDO, *Paris*

■ This family-run inn is safe, comfortable, and quiet. Situated right around the block from the elegant Place de la Madeleine, its location cannot be beat. The decor is lovely, with antiques, Oriental rugs, tapestries, and carved-wood paneling. Open all year.
$ Doubles 830–980 francs
☎ (1) 42.66.27.37
FAX (1) 42.66.61.23

SWITZERLAND

ROTE ROSE, *Reggensberg*

■ This country hotel is located in a medieval walled town 15 miles from Zurich. To stay in comparable quarters in Zurich would cost three times as much. The Rote Rose is beautifully restored and includes a fantastic rose garden.
$ Single: 280–330 Sw. francs
☎ (01) 85.31.013,
FAX (01) 85.31.559

HÔTEL LES ARMURES, *Geneva*

■ President Clinton paid a visit here when he was last in town. Originally a private residence that dates back to the 17th century, the hotel is located in the old quarter of the city. A quiet, elegant place with real old-world charm and a very good, reasonably priced restaurant.
$ Double: 368–540 Sw. francs
☎ (022) 310.91.72
FAX (022) 310.98.46

GERMANY

HOTEL MONDIAL, *Berlin*

■ This newly built hotel is a little antiseptic but everything is done tastefully. The Mondial has a darkened glass exterior and an outside shaded sitting area from which you can watch the action along the Kurfürstendamm, Berlin's main shopping street.
$ Double: DM 220–480; Suite: from DM 700
☎ (030) 884110
FAX (030) 88411150

DOM HOTEL, *Cologne*

■ In the pedestrian square near Cologne's magnificent cathedral, this old-world hotel is characterized by formal public rooms, marble stairways, luxurious bedrooms, and antique furniture. In the spring and summer an outside café offers informal dining right

in front of the cathedral.
$ Double: DM 430–730;
Suite: DM 740–1,150
☎ (0221) 20240
FAX (0221) 2024444

SPLENDID HOTEL, *Munich*
■ This hotel is located on the Maximilianstrasse, Munich's most chic street. There is a comfortable salon with antiques and Oriental carpets. The guest rooms have painted armoires and wooden beds.
$ Double: DM 265–325;
Suite: DM 450
☎ (089) 296606
FAX (089) 2913176

HOTEL ABTEI, *Hamburg*
■ One of the top 25 hotels in Germany, this converted private residence is personally run by an owner who insists on the finest of everything, including fresh flowers throughout, excellent service, and handsome furnishings. Although not inexpensive, it is one of the best values in Hamburg.
$ Double: DM 350–450;
Suite: DM 450–490
☎ (040) 442905
FAX (040) 449820

HOTEL BULOW RESIDENZ, *Dresden*
■ In a baroque building that dates from 1730, this small, elegant hotel is just a short walk from the major museums and historic sites of Dresden. It has a beautiful vine-covered courtyard for breakfast, elegant formal restaurant for dinner, and a

cozy piano bar for aperitifs.
$ Double: DM 440–490;
Suite: DM 490–600
☎ 0351–80030
FAX 0351–8003100

AUSTRIA
HOTEL ELEFANT, *Salzburg*
■ A charming, small family-owned inn that has been in the same family for generations. The building is over 700 years old and has served as an inn for 400 years. It is much less expensive than others in the area.
$ Double: AS 1,290–1,820
☎ 0662–84.3397
FAX 0662–84.01.09.28

ROMISCHER KAISER, *Vienna*
■ Located just off the Kärntnerstrasse, the major commercial street, and only blocks from the opera, this hotel has a rather formal atmosphere and impeccable service. It is expensive but has a great deal of charm.
$ Double: AS 2,150–2,950
☎ (1) 51.27.751
FAX (1) 51.27.75.113

ITALY
HOTEL D'INGHILTERRA, *Rome*
■ Costing less than most other deluxe hotels, this is one of the best small ones in Rome. It has a superb restaurant and a charming wood-paneled bar. Ask for one of the rooms with small breakfast terraces, which have wonderful views.
$ Double: Lire 445,000–520,000

☎ (06) 69.981
FAX (06) 69.92.22.43

VILLA BRUNELLA, *Capri*
■ The beach is just down the hillside and the center of town a 10-minute walk away. The views of the island and the ocean from the terraced guest rooms are outstanding.
$ Double: Lire 350,000–450,000
☎ (081) 83.70.122.
FAX (081) 83.70.430

HOTEL PIERRE MILAN, *Milan*
■ This small hotel is located in the historic Sant' Ambrogio district. It is expensive but offers an elegant atmosphere with excellent service. Each room has its own decor.
$ Double: Lire 400,000–540,000
☎ (02) 72.00.05.81
FAX (02) 80.52.157

HOTEL LOGGIATO DEI SERVITI, *Florence*
■ A fabulous value in a city where hotels are either outrageously priced or inexpensive and dreary. The hotel is situated on an arcaded square and occupies a building that dates to the 16th century. Although not deluxe, it provides excellent accommodations and service. The hotel is filled with antiques. Everything is white, bright, and cheerful.
$ Double: from Lire 270,000
☎ (055) 21.91.65
FAX (055) 28.95.95

■ **EXPERT PICKS**

SPAIN
HOTEL COLON, *Barcelona*
■ This hotel is fairly large and replete with an old-world atmosphere. It is located in the Barrio Gothico, the section of the city that dates from medieval times. The rooms have high ceilings; some are terraced and face the city's most famous cathedral.
$ Double: Ptas 23,500–35,500
☎ (3) 30.11.404
FAX (3) 31.72.915

TABERNA DEL ALABARDERO, *Seville*
■ This small seven-room hotel is one of the best buys in Spain. Only a short walk from Seville's cathedral, the hotel is operated by one of the most famous restaurants in town, which takes up most of this historic three-floor converted house. The hotel rooms are located on the top two floors around an iron-railed gallery beneath a skylight.
$ Double: Ptas 24,000
☎ (5) 45.60.637
FAX (5) 45.63.666

HOTELVILLA REAL, *Madrid*
■ This well-run antique-filled hotel is one of the best-value luxury hotels in Madrid. The hotel has an old-world ambience and an attentive staff. The rooms are plush, large, and most have balconies facing onto a small plaza in the middle of Madrid's famous triangle near the Prado Museum.
$ Double: from Ptas 34,600
☎ (1) 42.03.767
FAX (1) 42.02.547

IRELAND
THE CLARENCE, *Dublin*
■ A luxury boutique hotel in the heart of Temple Bar's trendy stores and vibrant nightlife. Built in 1852, the hotel has been completely refurbished, while retaining all the historic architectural features.
$ Double: £130–145; Suite: £300–1,500
☎ (01) 6707800
FAX (01) 6709000

THE QUAY HOUSE, *Clifton*
■ Paddy and Julia Foyle have refurbished this one-time harbormaster's house, blending old, modern, and unconventional in a charmingly idiosyncratic way with little jokes and quirks, such as the "vegetarian alley," a corridor of hunting trophies. Bedrooms vary from traditional to bohemian.
$ Double: £60–80
☎ (095) 21369
FAX (095) 21608

ENGLAND
KNIGHTSBRIDGE GREEN HOTEL, *London*
■ Close to Harrods and Hyde Park and just a few yards from the Knightsbridge tube station, this hotel stands out for its friendly staff, superb location, and reasonable prices. Every room is large and air-conditioned.
$ Double: £125; Suite: £145
☎ (0171) 5846274
FAX (0171) 2251635

OLD PARSONAGE HOTEL, *Oxford*
■ A wisteria-covered building that dates from 1660. The rooms are small and the floors uneven, but the place really feels like Merry Olde England, albeit with TVs and phones. The largest bedrooms are in the original house.
$ Double: £150–155; Suite: from £180
☎ (01865) 310210
FAX (01865) 311262

THE QUEENSBERRY HOTEL, *Bath*
■ This simple but very attractive hotel is a bargain. It is a converted mansion, and many of the rooms have high ceilings and ornate moldings. There is also an excellent restaurant on the premises.
$ Double: £115–180
☎ (01225) 447928
FAX (01335) 44065

SCOTLAND
MALMAISON, *Edinburgh*
■ For a city hotel, this is a surprisingly good value. The architecture is traditional, but the decor is stylishly modern. Bedrooms come with satellite TV, CD player, and telephone. Beds are large and bathrooms gleamingly modern.
$ Double: £85–120
☎ (0131) 5556868
FAX (0131) 5556999

EXCHANGES
▼

FINDING A HOME AWAY FROM HOME

You can save a king's ransom by swapping your castle

A beach house in Carmel, a condo in Captiva, an apartment on the Champs Elysées—imagine vacationing at each and paying little more than the airfare. This may sound too good to be true, but for the thousands of Americans who swap their homes with like-minded travelers, it's no daydream. Bill Barbour, author of *Home Exchange Vacationing: Your Guide to Free Accommodations* (Rutledge Hill Press, 1996), says home-swapping is rising at a 20 percent annual rate. He and his wife Mary have exchanged homes some 80 times.

The hot spots for home exchanges in the United States are California, Florida, and major East Coast states. Popular destinations abroad are Great Britain, France, and Italy. House-swapping is not a difficult undertaking. To get started, list your home with a home exchange agency such as Intervac or HomeLink (see pages 379–380). It generally costs less than $100 to list a home, but you must take care of setting up an exchange with the homeowner in your chosen destination.

The first step, says Barbour, is to pick a few preferred destinations, and decide how long you want to visit (the average exchange is two to three weeks). Start planning 9 to 12 months before you intend to travel. When listing with an agency, describe your home in great detail, including amenities, and access to tourist attractions, as well as any pets. For an additional fee, you can include a picture of your home. About 75 percent of home swappers also exchange the use of their cars, which can mean substantial savings.

Once your home has been listed, you will be contacted by interested parties, who will also provide information about themselves and their properties. You can also make contact with people whose properties interest you. "Those who are most successful at exchanges actively send out a lot of offers rather than wait for people to call them," says Karl Costabel, owner of HomeLink. Barbour says he receives roughly 90 letters between December and March requesting exchanges for his condo on Sanibel Island, Fla.

Many people swap homes to cut vacation expenses, but seasoned swappers insist there are other advantages. For one, house swapping makes you feel more like a house guest than a tourist. In addition, there is someone staying in your own house while you're away, which may be safer than leaving it vacant.

Still, the folks staying in your home are strangers and isn't that inviting trouble? "The kind of things people think of—returning to find your furniture gone or pizza crust all over the floor—those things don't happen," says Costabel, whose company has been in the business for nearly 40 years. "It's not the same as renting out your home. The other people don't forget that you're in their home too."

In a recent survey, Barbour asked 1,000 experienced home swappers whether they had ever had any problems. "Not one had ever heard of something being stolen," he says. His worst experience was returning to find a few broken plates, although he admits to having accidentally broken a few in some of the homes he's occupied.

Those still queasy about having strangers in their homes can engage full-service agencies, such as Agency Alpha International (☎310–472–7216), which screen potential guests and prospective homes for clients. Agency owner Janavee Citron says she checks out many properties herself. Citron says she recalls only one catastrophe, a last-minute swap she arranged for an apartment that turned out to be "an absolute dump."

After finding a match, you and the other party must work out all details, such as how to swap house and car keys, for example, and who pays for housecleaning services and feeds the pet. This phase of the process is crucial to ensure that your mutual expectations are met and that ground rules are laid down.

VILLA RENTER'S GUIDE

PALACES THAT COULD BE YOURS

The best way to save money on a vacation rental home is to bypass the middleman. You can save 20 to 30 percent by renting directly through the owner. Options include writing the local tourist board or looking through the classified sections of college alumni magazines. Rental agencies, on the other hand, offer the convenience of an experienced pro minding the details. Some resources:

RENTAL AGENCIES

If you use a rental agency, try to choose one with a local agent based near the town in which you intend to rent. That way, you'll have someone to contact in case anything goes wrong.

AT HOME ABROAD
New York, New York

■ Caters to an upscale market. Rates from $1,000 to $25,000 per week for villas, castles, and apartments in the Caribbean, Europe, and Mexico. Requires a $25 registration fee.
☎ 212–421–9165
FAX: 212–752–1591

BARCLAY INTERNATIONAL
New York, New York

■ Specializes in apartment and villa rentals in most of the major cities around the world. Properties include flats in some luxury hotels. Catalogs are available.
☎ 800–845–6636
(New York State residents: 212–832–3777)

BRITISH TRAVEL INTERNATIONAL
Elkton, Virginia

■ Properties in France, Britain, Spain, Portugal, and Italy, including over 4,000 b&b's in Britain. (The

agency can arrange bus and flexi-passes to Britain at ☎ 540–298–1395.) A color catalog is available for a fee.
☎ 800–327–6097

CREATIVE LEISURE INTERNATIONAL
Petaluma, California

■ Properties primarily in Hawaii, the Caribbean, and Mexico. Will arrange everything from airfare to baby-sitting.
☎ 800–426–6367

EUROPA LET
Ashland, Oregon

■ Listings in Europe, Mexico, Hawaii, the Caribbean, and the Pacific Islands. A good choice for sailors seeking seaside homes. There is a $50 booking fee.
☎ 800–462–4486

HOMES AWAY
Toronto, Canada

■ Rentals in the south of France and Umbria and Tuscany in Italy.
☎ 800–374–6637

INTERHOME
Fairfield, New Jersey

■ In its 32nd year and with over 18,000 listings in 11 European countries, Interhome is one of the oldest and largest home rental

agencies in the world. Florida rentals also available.
☎ 201–882–6864

RENT A HOME INTERNATIONAL
Seattle, Washington

■ Listings in Europe, Australia, the Caribbean, Mexico, the U.S., Canada, and Central America. Prices from $700 to $50,000 per week. Numerous catalogs are available for $15. You can also get information and see color photos online at http://www.rentavilla.com
☎ 206–789–9377

AGENCY ALPHA INTERNATIONAL
Los Angeles, California

■ Full-service home exchange and leasing in France and England. Optional car exchanges.
☎ 310–472–7216

RENTER'S LIST HOME EXCHANGE

An economical way to take a vacation. Usually there is a listing fee, but other arrangements are left to the homeowners.

HOMELINK INTERNATIONAL
Key West, Florida

■ Formerly Vacation Exchange Club. Listings in

■ **VILLA RENTER'S GUIDE**

U.S. (including Hawaii), Canada, Mexico, Europe, the Caribbean, Australia, and South Africa. Membership fee is $83.
☎ 800–638–3841

INTERVAC
■ International and domestic listings.
☎ 800–756–4663

RENTING BY COUNTRY
Renting through an institution abroad can be challenging. But it also can save you money.

ENGLAND
■ **LANDMARK TRUST:** A charitable trust that preserves everything from medieval halls to concrete bunkers by restoring them and renting them to vacationers. Prices during high season range from $320 per week for simple two-person accommodations to $2,200 for a manor hall for 15. A catalog of all 163 properties costs $19.50.
✉ RR1, Box 510, Brattleboro, VT 05301
☎ 802–254–6868

■ **NATIONAL TRUST HOLIDAY BOOKING OFFICE:** Determined travelers can find real bargains at this branch of the National Trust. From July through August, prices range from $300 to $1,200 per week, mostly for old cottages. The Royal Oak Foundation, a sister organization in New York, can send you a brochure of over 200 rental properties. Cost is $7.50.

✉ 285 West Broadway New York, NY 10013–2299
☎ 212–966–6565

FRANCE
■ **FEDERATION NATIONALE DES GITES RURAUX DE FRANCE:** An organization that preserves old country houses and promotes rural tourism. The network consists of over 50,000 houses and modest apartments, or gites.
✉ 35 Godot de Mauroy, 75009 Paris, France
☎ (011–33–1) 49–70–75–75

■ **THE FRENCH EXPERIENCE:** Rents more upscale French gites. In the high season, July and August, prices range from $400 to $750 per week. It also handles about 50 small hotels, as well as short-term rentals (in Paris). You can get information online at *http://www. frenchexperience.com*
✉ 370 Lexington Ave., New York, NY 10017
☎ 212–986–1115

GERMANY
■ **RING DEUTSCHER MAKLER:** A private association of German rental agencies. All of the reputable rental agencies are registered with it.
✉ Mönckebergstrasse 27, D-2 0095, Hamburg, Germany

☎ 011–49–40–331210

ITALY
■ **GRAND LUXE INTERNATIONAL:** Full-service rental agency that lists villas, castles, farmhouses, and apartments all over Italy. A catalog costs $8.50. The agency also arranges events such as weddings and family reunions in Italy.
✉ 165 Chestnut St., Allendale, NJ 07401
☎ 201–327–2333

SCANDINAVIA
■ **SCANAM WORLD TOURS:** Rents private homes throughout Scandinavia.
✉ 933 Highway 23, Pompton Plains, NJ 07444
☎ 800–545–2204

■ **SCANDINAVIAN DANCENTER:** Offers Danish rentals only. Material is written in German and Danish.
✉ Sotorvet 5, DK 1371 Copenhagen, Denmark
☎ 45–3333–0102

■ **SWEDISH TRAVEL & TOURISM COUNCIL:** A resource for rentals all over Sweden.
✉ P.O. Box 4649, Grand Central Station, New York, NY 10163
☎ 212–949–2333

SCOTLAND
■ **NATIONAL TRUST SCOTLAND:** This is the Scottish equivalent of the National Trust in England.
✉ 5 Charlotte Square, Edinburgh, Scotland EH2 4DU,
☎ 011–44–31–243–9331

EXPERT'S PICKS

THE BEST PLACES TO BED DOWN IN AMERICA

Here are the top-ranked hotels from four of the most respected travel authorities. The American Automobile Association (AAA) and the Mobil Travel Guide *both release a yearly list of the nation's best hotels. Also in the hotel rating game are two well-known travel publications: the* Hideaway Report, *a newsletter, and* Condé Nast Traveler *magazine. AAA and Mobil utilize roving teams of inspectors, whereas* Hideaway *and* Condé Nast *rely on reader polls. To appear on our list, a hotel had to get top marks from at least two of the four authorities we consulted. Eleven hotels—marked by hollow checks—made it onto all four lists.*

HOTEL	☎	HIDEAWAY	CONDE NAST	AAA	MOBIL
AUBERGE DU SOLEIL, Rutherford, CA	800–348–5406	✔	✔		
THE BOULDERS, Scottsdale, AZ	800–553–1717	✔	✔	✔	✔
THE BROADMOOR, Colorado Springs, CO	800–634–7711		✔	✔	✔
THE CARLYLE, New York, NY	800–227–5737	✔	✔		✔
THE CLOISTER, Sea Island, GA	800–732–4752	✔	✔		✔
C LAZY U RANCH, Granby, CO	303–887–3344			✔	✔
FOUR SEASONS, Boston, MA	800–332–3442	✔	✔	✔	
FOUR SEASONS, Chicago, IL	800–332–3442	✔	✔	✔	
FOUR SEASONS–RITZ-CARLTON, Chicago, IL	800–332–3442	✔	✔	✔	
FOUR SEASONS, Washington, DC	800–332–3442	✔	✔	✔	
FOUR SEASONS RESORT, Maui, HI	808–874–8000	✔	✔	✔	
FOUR SEASONS HOTEL, Newport Beach, CA	800–332–3442		✔	✔	
FOUR SEASONS, New York, NY	800–332–3442	✔	✔	✔	✔
FOUR SEASONS, Philadelphia, PA	800–332–3442		✔	✔	
FOUR SEASONS–OLYMPIC, Seattle, WA	800–332–3442		✔	✔	✔
GRAND HERITAGE–CLIFT, San Francisco, CA	415–775–4700	✔	✔		
GRAND WAILEA BEACH RESORT, Maui, HI	808–875–1234		✔	✔	
THE GREENBRIER, White Sulphur Springs, WV	800–624–6070	✔	✔	✔	✔
HALEKULANI, Oahu, HI	800–367–2343	✔	✔	✔	
HOTEL BEL-AIR, Los Angeles, CA	800–648–4097	✔	✔		✔
INN AT LITTLE WASHINGTON, Washington, VA	703–675–3800	✔	✔	✔	✔
THE LITTLE NELL, Aspen, CO	800–525–6200	✔	✔	✔	✔
LODGE AT KOELE, Lanai, HI	800–321–4666	✔	✔		
LODGE AT PEBBLE BEACH, Pebble Beach, CA	800–654–9300	✔	✔		
MANSION ON TURTLE CREEK, Dallas, TX	800–527–5432	✔	✔	✔	✔
MARRIOTT'S CAMELBACK INN, Scottsdale, AZ	800–242–2635		✔	✔	✔
MAUNA LANI BAY, Big Island, HI	800–367–2323	✔	✔	✔	
MEADOWOOD, St. Helena, CA	800–458–8080	✔	✔		
THE PENINSULA, Beverly Hills, CA	800–462–7899	✔	✔	✔	✔
THE PHOENICIAN, Scottsdale, AZ	800–888–8234	✔	✔		✔
RITZ–CARLTON BUCKHEAD, Atlanta, GA	800–241–3333	✔	✔	✔	
RITZ–CARLTON, Boston, MA	800–241–3333	✔	✔		
RITZ–CARLTON, Laguna Niguel, CA	800–241–3333	✔	✔	✔	✔
RITZ–CARLTON, Naples, FL	800–241–3333	✔	✔	✔	✔
RITZ–CARLTON, San Francisco, CA	800–241–3333	✔	✔	✔	✔
STOUFFER RENAISSANCE WAILEA BEACH RESORT, HI	800–992–4532		✔	✔	✔
ST. REGIS, New York, NY	800–759–7550	✔	✔	✔	✔
SCOTTSDALE PRINCESS, Scottsdale, AZ	800–344–4258		✔	✔	
VENTANA INN, Big Sur, CA	800–628–6500	✔	✔		
WILLIAMSBURG INN, Williamsburg, VA	800–447–8679		✔		✔
WINDSOR COURT, New Orleans, LA	800–262–2662	✔	✔	✔	

WHERE THE TOUGH GO SHOPPING

A traveler's guide to great bargains around the world

Inveterate shoppers have a knack for finding the best buys, no matter where they are. But true shopaholics might want to plan their next travel itinerary around the global retail calendar. Here are some of the best seasonal sales worldwide, compiled by Jennifer Farley, formerly contributing editor of *Delta Sky* magazine and shopping columnist for the *Houston Weekly*.

■ **BANGKOK:** If you love jewelry, go to the annual Bangkok Gems & Jewelry Fair (Queen Sirikit National Convention Center, 60 New Rajadapisek Rd., Klong Toey; call the Thai Trade Center in New York, ☎ 212–466-1777; held in March). Thailand is the world's second-largest manufacturer of jewelry; prices are low to moderate even for top-of-the-line goods. Loose stones are a special value.

■ **CHICAGO:** In early December, the School of the Art Institute of Chicago (112 S. Michigan Ave.; Student Union Office; ☎ 312–345–3589) offers for sale original paintings, sculpture, ceramics, photographs, and textiles—most items costing under $50. Admission is free.

■ **HONG KONG:** The semiannual sale at Joyce (202 The Landmark; ☎ 852/2525-3655; and the Galleria, 9 Queen's Road. Central; ☎ 852/2810-11220; in July and January) offers bargains on leading fashion designers, including Karl Lagerfeld, Dolce & Gabbana, and Calvin Klein. Prices are up to 30 percent off.

■ **LOIRE VALLEY:** Antique lovers will rejoice in the two-day auction held at the 17th-century Chateau de Cheverny (contact Flore de Brantes, Chateau du Fresne, Authon, France; ☎ 33-54/80-33-04, FAX 33-54/80-34-41; held in May). This auction of local families' superfluous heirlooms is organized by the daughter of a neighboring American marquise.

■ **LONDON:** Several hundred thousand patrons appear for the first day of Harrods' semiannual sale (Knightsbridge; ☎ 44-171-730-1234; held mid-July, and in January). Among the deals: half-price reductions on women's fashions, furnishings, and Oriental carpets and 30 percent discounts on accessories.

■ **NEW DELHI:** Asia's largest handicrafts bazaar, the Indian Handicrafts & Gifts Fair (Pragati Maidan; ☎ 91-11/600-871 or 91-11/687-5377, FAX 91-11/606-144; end of January) is primarily for wholesalers and retailers, but any shopper can revel in the 215,000-square-foot fair that includes woodcrafts, textiles, fashion jewelry, carved stone, papier-mâché, musical instruments, and more.

■ **NEW YORK CITY:** Bibliophiles will love the New York Book Fair (Seventh Regiment Armory, 643 Park Avenue; contact Sanford L. Smith & Associates, ☎ 212–777–5218; held in April), where they can find reasonable, first-edition, out-of-print, and rare books.

A fashion benefit for The Lighthouse, a group that helps the blind, is held in early April, also at the 7th Regiment Armory. (Contact The Lighthouse, 111 East 59th St., N.Y. ☎ 212–821–9200.) Tickets are $100 but you could recoup the cost by saving big on clothing from designers like Anne Klein and Chanel.

■ **PARIS:** Lines start forming early in the morning at the twice yearly sale at Hermès (24 Rue du Faubourg–St. Honoré; ☎ 33-1/40-17-48-10; held in June and January). Shoppers can bag the designer's famously expensive silk and leather accessories at up to 50 percent off.

■ **ROME:** Established in 1925 as a small leather and fur workshop, Fendi (36-40 Via Borgognona, ☎ 39-6/679-7641; and 76 Via Piave; Rome, ☎ 39-6/486-868; July and January) offers a broad array of the store's famous leather goods, furs, and men's and women's apparel discounted up to 50 percent.

FAMOUS FOOD CRITICS' FAVORITE PICKS

It's a big country with food that's getting better all the time, so coming up with the best restaurants in America could be a daunting task. We tackled it by asking the food critics in 10 cities to list their favorites. Prices listed are for dinner.

RESTAURANT ♦ Address ☎ **Phone** ✦ Cuisine § **Prices** ✍ Critic's comment

■ **ATLANTA:** *Christiane Lauterbach, the dining critic for* Atlanta *magazine, suggests some of the finer places to dine.*

BACCHANALIA ♦ 3125 Piedmont Rd. ☎ **404-365-0410** ✦ American § **Prix Fixe $40**
✍ *American cuisine in a romantic small house. Restaurant is chef-owned and has a great wine list.*

CANOE ♦ 4199 Paces Ferry Rd., NW ☎ **770-43CANOE** ✦ American § **Entrees $13 to $18**
✍ *Creative American cuisine in a glamorous location on the Chattahoochee River.*

THE DINING ROOM ♦ 3434 Peachtree Rd. NE ☎ **404-237-2700** ✦ Creative continental § **Prix Fixe, $56, $80 w/ wine.**
✍ *The best restaurant in Atlanta; renowned chef Gunter Seeger creates daring and fresh seasonal cuisine.*

PRIME ♦ 3393 Peachtree Rd., Lenox Square Mall ☎ **404-266-1440** ✦ American § **Entrees $18 to $20**
✍ *Steak and sushi in a prime location. A steakhouse for the '90s.*

RIVIERIA ♦ 519 E. Paces Ferry Rd. ☎ **404-262-7112** ✦ French § **Entrees $19.50 to $31.50**
✍ *Traditional French cuisine with a Mediterranean accent by star chef Jean Banchet.*

■ **BOSTON:** *Corby Kummer, senior editor at* The Atlantic Monthly *and the restaurant critic for* Boston *magazine, makes his picks.*

AUJOURD'HUI ♦ 200 Boylston St. ☎ **617-451-1392** ✦ French § **Entrees $32 to $44**
✍ *Impressive in every way, including cost, this gracious restaurant overlooking the Public Gardens always offers space, comfort, and superb food.*

BLUE ROOM ♦ One Kendall Sq. ☎ **617-494-9034** ✦ Asian § **Entrees $16 to $22**
✍ *Chef Steve Johnson, a leading light of the younger generation, cooks exciting, hearty brasserie food with Asian influence near the Boston area's best movie theater.*

HAMERSLEY'S BISTRO ♦ 553 Tremont St. ☎ **617-423-2700** ✦ French Provençal § **Entrees $19 to $28**
✍ *Boston's only true Provençal bistro, with an overlay of Parisian sophistication. Chef Gordon Hamersley sets the city's standards.*

METROPOLIS CAFE ♦ 584 Tremont St. ☎ **617-247-2931** ✦ Italian/American § **Entrees $13 to $19**
✍ *Seth Woods serves satisfying Italian-tinged American food and lots of it at this small, casual, popular spot in the gentrified South End.*

RIALTO ♦ One Bennett St. ☎ **617-661-5050** ✦ Mediterranean § **Entrees $19 to $29**
✍ *Chef Jody Adams and pastry chef Heather Adams please the well-heeled of Cambridge at this lively, polished, Mediterranean-style brasserie at the Charles Hotel in the heart of Harvard Square.*

■ **CHICAGO:** *Phil Vitell, restaurant critic for the* Chicago Tribune, *shares his picks.*

ARUNS ♦ 4156 N. Kedzie Ave. ☎ **312-539-1909** ✦ Thai § **Entrees $13.95 to $25.95**
✍ *Even though the room is full of authentic Thai art, the real treasures can be found on the plates.*

EVEREST ♦ 440 South La Salle St. ☎ **312-663-8920** ✦ American § **Entrees $28 to $34**
✍ *The 40th-floor view is as high as the culinary standards at this routinely wonderful dining room.*

GIBSON'S BAR AND STEAKHOUSE ♦ 1028 N. Rush St. ☎ **312-266-8999** ✦ American § **Entrees $12 to $32.75**
✍ *In a city renowned for top-quality steakhouses, this one gets my vote for number one.*

SPRUCE ♦ 238 E. Ontario St. ☎ **312-642-2757** ✦ American § **Entrees $17 to $24**
✍ *A fine-dining American newcomer that is quickly making a name for itself.*

TOPOLOBAMPO FRONTERA GRILL ♦ 445 N. Clark St. ☎ **312-661-1434** ✦ Mexican § **Entrees $14 to $25, Grill, $8 to $18**
✍ *Two restaurants in one space, Topolobampo is a smaller, more upscale dining room, while Frontera is more crowded and casual. Both offer unsurpassed regional Mexican food.*

■ **DINER'S GUIDE**

■ **DALLAS:** Dallas Morning News *lifestyles editor Dotty Griffith's favorites are less upscale than the renowned Mansion at Turtle Creek, and a little more off the beaten path.*

CITY CAFE ♦ 5757 W. Lovers Lane   ☎ 214-351-2233   ✦ Regional American   § **Entrees $13 to $19**
🖹 *Seasonally based, creative food with a menu that changes every two weeks.*

MATT'S RANCHO MARTINEZ ♦ Lakewood Plaza, 6312 La Vista Dr.   ☎ 214-823-5517   ✦ Tex-Mex   § **Entrees $7.25 to $15.75**
🖹 *Stupendous chiles rellenos.*

THE PALM RESTAURANT ♦ 701 Ross Ave. at Market   ☎ 214-698-0470   ✦ American   § **Entrees $14 to $25**
🖹 *Steaks, lobsters, and the beautiful people crowd.*

STAR CANYON ♦ 3102 Oaklawn Ave., Suite 144   ☎ 214-520-7827   ✦ New Texas   § **Entrees $14 to $23**
🖹 *Sophisticated food with Texas roots. Favorite dish: chilled shrimp and jicama soup with buttermilk and basil.*

MIPIACI ♦ 14854 Montfort Dr.   ☎ 214-934-8424   ✦ Northern Italian   § **Entrees $20 and up**
🖹 *Lots of fresh pasta and fresh herbs (they grow their own on the roof).*

■ **LOS ANGELES:** *Irene Virbila, the restaurant editor for the* Los Angeles Times, *made picks that reflected the fusion of styles found in southern California cuisine.*

ALTO PALATO ♦ 755 N. La Cienega, West Hollywood   ☎ 310-657-9271   ✦ Italian   § **Entrees $13.50 to $28.50**
🖹 *Authentic Italian cooking at moderate prices. Terrific thin-crusted Roman pizza, wonderful pasta and regional dishes, great gelato, and the best espresso and cappuccino in Los Angeles.*

CAMPANILE ♦ 624 S. La Brea Blvd.   ☎ 213-938-1447   ✦ California-Mediterranean   § **Entrees $20 to $30**
🖹 *Fabulous morning pastries, rustic breads, truly seasonal Californian-Mediterranean cooking—and killer desserts from one of America's premier pastry chefs.*

CHINOIS ON MAIN ♦ 2709 Main St., Santa Monica   ☎ 310-329-9025   ✦ East-West fusion   § **Entrees $23 to $50**
🖹 *Wolfgang Puck's—the creator of L.A. restaurant/institution, Spago—best restaurant yet.*

JOE'S ♦ 1023 Abbot Kinney Blvd., Venice   ☎ 310-399-5811   ✦ Californian   § Entrees $15 to $18
🖹 *Owner and chef Joe Miller's very personal cooking in a fun bohemian setting. He's great with fish. There's a four-course prix fixe menu at $30 and $38.*

VALENTINO ♦ 3115 Pico Boulevard, Santa Monica   ☎ 310-829-4313   ✦ Italian   § **Entrees $18 to $25**
🖹 *Possibly the best Northern Italian restaurant in North America. Instead of ordering from the menu, ask chef Piero Selvaggio to prepare a series of small courses.*

■ **MIAMI:** *Not just for retirees anymore, Miami these days is hot, filled with celebrities and great restaurants. Geoffrey Tomb, a restaurant critic at* The Miami Herald, *surveys the scene.*

CHEF ALLEN'S RESTAURANT ♦ 19088 N.E. 29th Ave., Miami Beach ☎ 305-935-2900 ✦ Fusion-American § **Entrees $22.95 to $29.95**
🖹 *Don't miss the 16-ounce veal chop with double mustard sauce, wild-mushroom risotto, and ginger-flavored calabaza.*

EAST COAST FISHERIES ♦ 300 West Flagler St., Miami   ☎ 305-577-3000   ✦ American   § **Entrees $9 to $45**
🖹 *Very fresh fish served in indigenous old riverside fish house off the beaten track.*

ASTOR PLACE BAR AND GRILL ♦ 956 Washington Ave., Miami Beach   ☎ 305-532-8934   ✦ Western   § **Entrees $15.95 to $27.95**
🖹 *Beautifully redone hotel with "cowboy" barbeque and trendy food. Desserts are special and palatial.*

OSTERIA DEL TEATRO ♦ 1443 Washington Ave., Miami Beach   ☎ 305-538-7850   ✦ Italian   § **$14 to $24**
🖹 *Excellent Italian food and maybe the best restaurant in town. Emphasis is on seafood.*

THE RALEIGH RESTAURANT ♦ 1775 Collins Ave., Miami Beach ☎ 305-534-1775   ✦ Creative American   § **Entrees $9 to $19**
🖹 *A 1940s gem; the ghost of Esther Williams lives here. Sit outside and order the warm goat cheese–potato cakes.*

■ **NEW YORK:** *In a city full of great restaurants, it was tough, but Florence Fabricant, a food and restaurant columnist for* The New York Times, *managed to select five for top honors.*

LE BERNARDIN ♦ 155 W. 51st St.   ☎ 212-489-1515   ✦ French   § **Entrees $68**
🖹 *The ultimate in seafood in the hands of chef Eric Ripert is as sublime as ever, witness truffled sea scallops and foie gras in cabbage.*

NOBU ♦ 105 Hudson St.   ☎ 212-219-0500   ✦ Fusion   § **Dinner $45 to $55**
🖹 *The most inventively delicious food in town: Deep-fried kelp adorns lobster nuggets or caviar on seared tuna.*

■ **DINER'S GUIDE**

PICHOLINE ▶ 35 W. 64th St.   ☎ 212-724-8585   ✦ American/Provençal   § **Entrees $24 to $34**
  ✍ Notable for stylish food that is well conceived and full of flavor, this lively place also has a splendid array of cheeses.

REMI ▶ 145 W. 53rd St.   ☎ 212-581-4242   ✦ Italian   § **Entrees $15 to $28**
  ✍ Francesco Antonucci unerringly commands pasta, risotto, foie gras, anchovies, duck, salmon, and zabaglione.

RESTAURANT DANIEL ▶ 20 E. 76th St.   ☎ 212-288-0033   ✦ French   § **Entrees $31 to $37**
  ✍ Sophisticated haute cuisine? Hearty peasant fare? Daniel Boulud is the master of both and serves his creations in a warmly comfortable dining room.

■ **SAN FRANCISCO:** *The challenge to good eating is the transient nature of restaurants in San Francisco, says Michael Bauer, the* San Francisco Chronicle's *restaurant critic. His picks:*

THE FRENCH LAUNDRY ▶ 6040 Washington St., Yountville   ☎ 707-944-2380   ✦ French   § **Prix Fixe $49**
  ✍ The $49 menu includes five courses, all reminiscent of a three-star country restaurant in France.

FRINGALE ▶ 570 Fourth St. at Bryant   ☎ 415-543-0573   ✦ French   § **Entrees $10 to $15**
  ✍ The best casual French restaurant in San Francisco; don't miss the mussels flecked with parsley and fried garlic.

MASAS ▶ 648 Bush St.   ☎ 415-989-7154   ✦ French   § **Prix Fixe $68 to $75**
  ✍ A great special-occasion restaurant with a four- to six-course classic French menu.

YANK SING ▶ 427 Battery St.   ☎ 415-781-1111   ✦ Chinese   § **Entrees $10 to $15**
  ✍ Unparalleled dim sum, minced squab in crunchy lettuce cups, and Peking duck with sweet, doughy buns.

ZUNI CAFE ▶ 1658 Market   ☎ 415-552-2522   ✦ American   § **Entrees $10 to $28**
  ✍ Great people-watching and casual food. Signature dishes: chicken with bread salad and hamburger on focaccia.

■ **SEATTLE:** *Tom Sietsema, former restaurant critic for the* Seattle Post-Intelligencer *and now national restaurant producer and food critic for* Sidewalk, *Microsoft's online entertainment and restaurant guide, still loves to dine in Seattle. Here are his favorite spots:*

CAFE CAMPAGNE ▶ 1600 Post Alley   ☎ 206-728-2233   ✦ French   § **Entrees $9.95 to $15.95**
  ✍ A charming, casual, golden-glowing room reminiscent of Paris' best neighborhood watering holes. Delicious, too.

LAMPREIA ▶ 2400 First Ave.   ☎ 206-443-3301   ✦ American   § **Entrees $17 to $24**
  ✍ No one nods to seasonal cuisine with such elegance and sophistication as chef Scott Carsberg, whose often brilliant cooking is framed in a chic, understated setting.

PALACE KITCHEN ▶ 2030 Fifth Ave.   ☎ 206-448-2001   ✦ Continental/American   § **Entrees $15 to $19**
  ✍ A loud and friendly place that reminds one of a stage set. Known for its wide-ranging menu, cool crowd, and white-hot bar (the only place to sit).

PIROSMANI ▶ 2220 Queen Ann Ave.   ☎ 206-285-3360   ✦ Georgian/Mediterranean   § **Entrees $13 to $22**
  ✍ Inspired food from the Republic of Georgia, which also embraces the sunny flavors of the Mediterranean.

SHIRO'S ▶ 2401 Second Ave.   ☎ 206-443-9844   ✦ Japanese   § **Entrees $15 to $19**
  ✍ Anticipate the finest sushi around from a master chef who combs the best markets twice a day looking for what is absolutely fresh and dear.

■ **WASHINGTON:** *Phyllis Richman, the food critic for* The Washington Post, *recommends:*

GALILEO ▶ 1110 21st St., NW   ☎ 202-293-7191   ✦ Italian   § **Entrees $19.95 to $29.95**
  ✍ Chef Roberto Donna's pappardelle and risotto with first-of-the-season alba truffles are famous.

GERARD'S PLACE ▶ 915 15th St., NW   ☎ 202-737-4445   ✦ French   § **Five-course special $55**
  ✍ Chef Gerard Pangaud cooks simple dishes of great sophistication. Try his lobster with a ginger-lime sauce.

INN AT LITTLE WASHINGTON ▶ Middle & Main St., Washington, Va.   ☎ 703-675-3800   ✦ New American   § **Full course $78 to $98**
  ✍ Self-taught American chef Patrick O'Connell coaxes wonders out of local ingredients such as Virginia ham, Chesapeake Bay crabs, berries, and herbs. A bit of a drive from the District.

KINKEAD'S ▶ 2000 Pennsylvannia Ave., NW   ☎ 202-296-7700   ✦ American   § **Entrees $14.50 to $24**
  ✍ Regional seafood shines here in an informal and energetic atmosphere.

OBELISK ▶ 2029 P St., NW   ☎ 202-872-1180   ✦ Italian   § **Prix Fixe $38**
  ✍ A tiny restaurant that personifies Italian simplicity—excellent wine and grappa.

GETTING THERE

AIR TRAVEL
▼

FLYING SMART, FLYING SAFE

A checklist for worrywarts who fear they might not beat the odds

Even the most sanguine of flyers were taken aback in 1996 when two major disasters occurred within months of each other: a ValuJet flight that crashed into the Florida Everglades killing 110, and a TWA flight that exploded into the Atlantic off Long Island killing 230. In the face of such catastrophes, there's almost no amount of reassurance that can allow a white-knuckled flyer to sit back, relax, and enjoy the flight. Not the fact that despite the disasters, only one in every 2 million passengers died in a commercial airline accident in 1996 (it's 1.4 times more likely that you'll be struck by lightning). Nor the fact that even if your plane did crash, these days one-third of the passengers survive, up from one-quarter not very long ago. With 50 percent of the world's air traffic, the United States has only 8 percent of the fatalities, according to the Federal Aviation Administration (FAA).

Does your fate depend on what airline you're flying? Yes, and on a host of other factors, according to Mary Schiavo, former inspector general for the Department of Transportation (DOT) and author of the controversial book *Flying Blind, Flying Safe* (Avon Books, 1997). In her book, Schiavo attacks the FAA and the airline industry for not doing enough to ensure the safety of flyers. Schiavo investigates the many factors that affect flying safety, such as aircraft age and size, the airport you're flying into and out of, pilot training, manufacturers' errors, security, and weather.

Schiavo concludes that airline travel is not only unsafe but isn't likely to improve in the future. In fact, with the number of air passengers slated to increase, the number of fatalities will also surely rise. Schiavo predicts a 77 percent rise in fatal accidents by the year 2003, if safety measures are not improved. The U.S. government says it is trying to do its part: The FAA and the DOT have announced a "zero accidents" goal and are spending billions on programs in different areas, including upgrading obsolete aircraft-control equipment.

Most of the burden, however, falls on airline manufacturers and the carriers themselves. So far, newer planes are proving to be safer than older models. And, to counter terrorist bombs that might be planted in airplane cargo, many airlines are looking at ways to outfit aircraft with explosion-proof

TAKING THE FEAR OUT OF FLYING

Air-travel phobia is surprisingly widespread: Some 64 percent of women and 36 percent of men have it. If you fear flying, the Institute for Psychology of Air Travel in Boston, Mass., suggests first consulting The Fearful Flyers Resource Guide *(Argonaut Entertainment, $13.95) by Barry Elkus and Murray Tieger, which lists seminars, self-help tapes, and books for phobics.Here are some of the Institute's tricks for keeping air fright from encroaching:*

■ **GET TO THE AIRPORT EARLY.** Rushing causes anxiety that won't vanish once you're on board. Plan to arrive at least 1 hour beforehand for domestic flights and 2 hours for international flights, giving you enough time to go through security, settle down, and walk onboard in a relaxed state.

■ **EAT SOMETHING NUTRITIOUS.** Cut back on caffeine and sugar the day before your flight. Protein and unrefined carbohydrates fortify you best.

Have a snack or meal at least every 3½ hours while you are flying.

■ **TRY TO RELAX.** You can help control your anxiety with relaxation techniques. Try deep-breathing exercises and listen to the relaxation tapes often available on the airline's audio channels. Or, pick a relaxing scene, such as lying on a beach watching the waves rush in and out. Focus solely on that scene.

■ **PICK THE RIGHT SEAT.** Many fearful flyers

become claustrophobic, that is, fear being closed in. Breathing deeply from the diaphragm can help. So can your choice of seats. Choose a forward aisle seat on a wide-body plane, allowing you to move around more freely.

■ **DON'T HIDE YOUR QUALMS.** Let the flight attendants know that you have a fear of flying. They will generally go out of their way to help you. Asking the crew for a tour of the cockpit can also help put you at ease.

---

cargo containers. Beyond leaving it up to the airlines, there are actions that passengers themselves can take. Here are some factors you may want to consider before you fly:

■ **CHECKING UP ON YOUR AIRLINE.** Statistics on airline safety can be elucidating—and sometimes misleading. Southwest Airlines often tops the safety lists, while Continental and Delta generally turn in a poorer showing. Yet, Southwest has an advantage in that its routes are in an area of the country that has generally good weather; many of the airlines with lower safety records fly routes that crisscross the Northwest, where frequent poor weather conditions makes flying more dangerous.

The picture is less cloudy when it comes to budget and commuter carriers, whose safety

records are generally poorer than those of the majors. The worst record belongs to Miami Air, a small regional carrier, which turned in a high score of 110 accidents and safety incidents for every 100,000 passengers, according to the FAA's data for 1991 to 1995. Says Todd Curtis, a Seattle-based air safety analyst, "If you have a choice between a small regional airline and a large jet, take the jet."

■ **THE VIEW FROM THE AIRPORT.** Not all airports are created equal. Schiavo reports that of the 19 U.S. airports that accommodate planes of all sizes, pilots fear six in particular. Three of them—Washington-National, New York's LaGuardia, and San Diego—are surrounded by city neighborhoods and have intersecting runways. Boston's Logan airport is plagued by poor snow removal and other runway hazards. Idaho's Sun Valley airport is so situated that a landing plane barely clears a mountain range. Similarly, Alaska's Juneau airport is surrounded by glaciers and mountain peaks.

Even so, of the world's largest 50 airports, New York's JFK has had the most crashes—22 since 1965. Chicago's O'Hare is second, and Los Angeles International and London's Heathrow tie for third, with 12 accidents each.

■ **HOW OLD IS YOUR PLANE?** The data on the state of U.S. aircraft are not encouraging. The life of a plane is typically 20 years, but in 1996, 1,000 of the 4,000 jets in U.S. airline fleets were older than 20; 500 dated back more than 25 years. Older planes suffer from corrosion, wear, and stress fractures. In addition, "avionics and electronic equipment are aged, as is the wiring," according to Schiavo.

The oldest aircraft operated by major domestic carriers are: ValuJet's DC-9s (average age: 26.6 years), Northwest's DC-9s (25.8), US Airways Shuttle's Boeing 727s (25.2), Midwest Express's DC-9s (25.2), and TWA's DC-9s (25), according to FAA data for 1996.

Because safety is directly related to the amount of material and space under your seat to absorb the energy of the impact, you have a better chance of surviving a crash if you're on one of the bigger planes, such as the Boeing 757s and 767s.

■ **A SENSE OF FALSE SECURITY.** For most of the 19 major U.S. airports, metal detectors are the primary means of detecting explosives. FAA tests of bomb and weapon detection rates by metal detectors at major airports have found that they are extremely effective. But when they tested more sophisticated bomb materiel, most detectors found the substances only about half the time. More reliable security systems are available, but as of the end of 1996 only three were in place: two in Atlanta and one in San Francisco.

■ **FINDING OUT THE FACTS.** Before you check in at the gate, check out the site of the National Transportation Safety Board (http://www.ntsb.gov), and the FAA's Internet page (http://www.faa.gov). All the latest incidents are posted, ranging from crashes to turbulence that results in injury, as well as the types of planes that each airline flies. If you're traveling abroad, call the FAA (☎ 800–FAA–SURE) to determine if your destination has been cited for failing to meet international safety standards. The International Airline Passengers Association (☎ 972–404–9980) provides safety information on most carriers worldwide.

■ HOW SAFE IS YOUR AIRLINE?

On any given day, more than 1.5 million passengers fly safely in one of America's major airlines. Here's how the nine biggest carriers compare, from the best to worst safety record:

CARRIER	NO. OF PASSENGERS	ACCIDENTS AND INCIDENTS (PER 100,000 PASSENGERS)	NEAR MISSES IN THE AIR
SOUTHWEST	2,606,206	1.5	0.9
AMERICA WEST	997,347	3.9	1.8
US AIRWAYS	4,418,100	4.6	0.6
UNITED	3,672,909	4.7	1.4
TWA	1,353,526	5.4	0.5
NORTHWEST	2,727,858	5.5	1.0
AMERICAN	4,425,578	5.9	1.1
DELTA	4,865,814	6.3	0.9
CONTINENTAL	2,452,472	6.8	0.8

SOURCE: Federal Aviation Administration, 1991–1995.

THE BEST AIRLINES IN THE SKY

Results of the surveys are in. Here are the facts to help you pick

May we have the envelope, please? Southwest Airlines won top carrier honors for the second consecutive year in the 1997 Airline Quality Rating Report of America's nine largest airlines. American Airlines remained in second place.

The AQR Report, conducted by the National Institute of Aviation Research at Wichita State University and the University of Nebraska at Omaha, is different from other surveys: it relies on objective data, not the opinions of passengers. The scores are based on 19 weighted factors including such things as mishandled baggage, average cost per seat-mile, and on-time performance. The numbers are crunched according to a complicated formula and an "airline quality rating" is produced. Southwest earned top marks in the AQR Report for average on-time percentage and for losing the least baggage among the major U.S. carriers (see table on page 390). On the other hand, Southwest placed second, behind American, among the airlines most likely to bump passengers involuntarily from their flights.

Other surveys, based on passenger opinions, produced quite different, and not entirely comparable, results. When *Frequent Flyer* magazine, for example, polled its readers about the nine largest U.S. carriers, Delta came out on top for overall service, placing first in 9 of 21 categories, such as baggage delivery speed, both short-haul and long-haul service, in-flight amenities, airport check-in, gate location, seating comfort, service with a smile, and on-time arrival. American Airlines came in a not-so-close second, earning first places in four categories:

food service, food quality, availability of seat preference, and keeping flyers informed of schedule delays. United placed third.

Condé Nast Traveler's annual airline survey includes large and small airlines—not just the Big Nine included in the AQR and *Frequent Flyer* reports. Midwest Express came in number one, with 66.9 percent of the respondents grading it as "excellent" or "very good." It also came in tops for food and comfort/service (it has extra-wide leather seats). United and Delta received high scores for their frequent flyer programs: United's Mile Plus was voted tops by 53.6 percent of the survey's respondents, Delta's Sky Miles by 45.4 percent.

Interestingly, the *Condé Nast* results mirror a 1995 Zagat survey, the most comprehensive of the consumer preference studies with over 9,000 respondents. Midwest Express was the only American carrier in Zagat's top 10 of international and domestic

FACT FILE:

THE SKINNY ON LOW-FAT MEALS

■ *Do airline meals billed as low-fat really fit the bill? A Physicians' Committee for Responsible Medicine's survey of seven major airlines showed that the meals can differ in fat by as much as 41 percent.*

■ **The lowest-fat meal:** *United Airlines' vegetarian steak and pasta with curry sauce with a mere 6.3 percent fat.* **A distant second:** *Continental Airlines' green pepper stuffed with vegetarian chili, nuts, and raisins (27.7 percent).* **The loser:** *Delta Airlines' vegetarian spinach ragout (47.9 percent). One shudders to think of the fat content in Delta's regular fare.*

airlines. The top three overall: Singapore Airlines, Swissair, and Cathay Pacific.

When *Condé Nast Traveler* asked its readers' opinions of international carriers, the clear favorite was again Singapore Airlines, which has been number one since 1989. In the magazine's 1996 survey, 72.1 percent of respondents rated Singapore Airlines as "excellent" or "very good." The airline's strengths included scheduling, cabin comfort/service, baggage handling, and food (best of all airlines). Swissair placed second in the international survey, with the upstart Virgin Atlantic coming in at third. Three U.S. airlines made the international top 20: Alaska Airlines (14th), United (16th), and Delta (19th).

With all the different surveys, it's sometimes hard to square the results. For instance, by the AQR Report's objective criteria Southwest was tops, but it placed sixth overall in the *Frequent Flyer* poll and and seventh in the *Condé Nast Traveler* survey. Indeed, Southwest rates poorly among *Condé Nast* readers when it comes to cabin comfort, ser-

vice, and food—criteria that the AQR Report doesn't consider as a matter of course, unless there have been consumer complaints. The report does, however, consider cost per seat-mile in its rankings, where a budget carrier like Southwest excels.

Of course, many of the airlines that did not rank overall at the top of the surveys have some strong suits going for them. For instance, TWA was touted in *Frequent Flyer*'s survey as having the most comfortable seats, and Northwest for the best frequent flyer program. For travelers with lots of carry-ons, America West won for overhead storage. For those who value promptness, Delta came in first for on-time arrival, although Southwest had the best ratings for overall on-time performance—it scored first for on-time departure and second for on-time arrival.

And, when it comes to most improved, Continental is a sure winner: It moved from last in overall quality in the 1996 AQR report to fifth in 1997.

EXPERT PICKS

STACKING UP AMERICA'S BIG AIRLINES

The National Institute for Aviation Research at Wichita State University (☎ 316–978–3845) and the Aviation Institute at the University of Nebraska at Omaha (☎ 402–554–3424) combined forces to produce the 1997 Airline Quality Rating Report, which analyzes 19 objective criteria and assigns each of America's big nine carriers an "air quality rating." Below are the results for 1997 report and some of the factors that went into the ratings.

Airline	Mean airline quality rating	Average on time (percentage)	Bags mishandled per 10,000 pass.	Denied boardings per 10,000 pass.	Average age of fleet (years)	Phone
1. SOUTHWEST	0.306	.818	39.6	2.39	7.5	800–435–9792
2. AMERICAN	0.033	.723	54.7	0.79	8.9	800–433–7300
3. UNITED	0.031	.739	67.3	0.54	10.7	800–241–6522
4. DELTA	−0.017	.712	51.9	1.30	10.6	800–221–1212
5. CONTINENTAL	−0.095	.766	40.5	0.19	9.4	800–235–9292
6. NORTHWEST	−0.100	.766	53.4	0.56	18.3	800–225–2525
7. US AIRWAYS	−0.267	.757	51.4	1.34	11.5	800–428–4322
8. AMERICA WEST	−0.275	.704	43.8	4.36	19.0	800–221–2000
9. TRANS WORLD	−0.302	.687	61.2	0.87	13.4	800–525–0280

SOURCE: National Institute for Aviation Research, Wichita, Kan., and Aviation Institute, Omaha, Neb.

TICKETS
▼

IF YOU'RE BUMPED FROM A FLIGHT

How to turn bad news to good news when your plane is overbooked

The departure lounge is overflowing. The gate attendant announces the flight is overbooked. Should you accept the airline's offer for another flight? David S. Stempler, president of Air Trav Advisors, offers some counsel.

■ What is overbooking?

For any given flight, a certain percentage of people will not show up for whatever reason. Airline companies track the average no-show rate for specific routes and over-book accordingly. If the no-show rate is usually about 10 percent, the airline then books the flight at 110 percent capacity.

■ How do I avoid being bumped from an overbooked flight?

You should get to the airport early, check in early, and get to the gate early. But watch out: sometimes just checking in at the gate doesn't necessarily count—your options change from airline to airline. Your best bet to avoid being bumped is to actually be on the plane as soon as possible. Possession is nine-tenths of the law.

■ If I volunteer to be bumped, what should I expect in the way of compensation?

Usually, the airlines start with the minimum that they can get away with, which is about $200. You're at the mercy of the lowest offer from other bidders though, so if the airline offers a free ticket, you should grab it. Be warned: the savvy traveler will ask when the next guaranteed trip to his

EXPERT PICKS

A REPORT CARD ON FREQUENT FLYER PROGRAMS

Earning miles may be easier, but on many airlines you need more miles to get a reward. Many airlines have increased the number of miles needed to get a free domestic ticket from 20,000 to 25,000, although America West and TWA remained at 20,000. The many ways to earn miles without flying are listed in The Miles Guide, *available at ☎ 800–333–5937. Here's how Randy Petersen, editor of* InsideFlyer *magazine (☎ 719–597–8889), rates the airlines' frequent flyer programs. Peterson has analyzed frequent flyer programs since their inception in 1981.*

PROGRAM	Grade	EASE OF EARNING		BLACKOUT		SEAT AVAILABILITY		Customer Service	Hotel Partners	Tie-Ins
		Dom.	Int.	Dom.	Int.	Dom.	Int.			
Northwest WorldPerks	B+	B+	A	B	A	A	C	**A+**	B	B
American AAdvantage	B+	**A+**	B–	A	C	A	C	C	A	A
United Mileage Plus	B+	A–	B	B	C	A	C	A	A	A–
US Airways Dividend Miles	B	B	B	A	C	A	C	B	A	B+
Amer. West FlightFund	B	B	B–	A	B	A	C	**A+**	B–	B–
Alaska Mileage Plan	B	B	B	B+	C	A–	C	B+	B	A–
Continental OnePass	B–	B+	B–	C–	D+	B	C	A–	B	B+
Delta SkyMiles	B–	B	B	C	D	A	C	A–	A	B
Southwest Rapid Rewards	B–	C	NA	**A+**	NA	**A+**	NA	A–	F	D
TWA Freq. Flight Bonus	C+	B–	C	C	D	B	C	B	C–	B–

EXPERT TIPS

ARE YOU IN THE SAFEST SEAT?

Since in most accidents, an aircraft travels with its nose down as well as bumping along the ground for a bit after impact, it stands to reason that sitting in one of the front rows won't increase your chances of survival. But are some seats on a plane really safer than others? Experts usually duck the question since there are so many possible crash scenarios, but here are some precautions you can take when reserving a seat:

■ **BOYCOTT BULKHEAD ROWS.** Seats that face the bulkheads and interior dividers provide more legroom, but they can also be more hazardous. Serious head injuries resulting when passengers hit their heads on the walls during air turbulence and landings top the list of non-crash injury concerns. The FAA, airlines, and safety researchers are looking into ways to lessen the danger, such as shoulder belts and airbags. Currently, only the Boeing 777, which has cushioned walls, passes the new federal standards. Until an appropriate solution is designed for other aircraft, airline crash injury specialists at the National Institute for Aviation Research advise passengers who are taller than average to sit elsewhere: the taller the person, the greater the chance of hitting the bulkhead.

■ **REQUEST A WINGSIDE SEAT:** Seats close to the aircraft wings are structurally more sound and have better support.

■ **LOOK FOR AN EXIT ROW:** Sitting by an emergency exit not only provides more legroom but also allows easier escape from fire and smoke dangers. But wherever you sit, be sure to count the number of rows you are from an exit; that way, if the lights go out, you can still find your way to safety.

■ **SETTLE FOR A GOOD BOOK:** Video screens or phone sets in the seat back, increasingly common in planes now, may make your trip more enjoyable, but they also add danger. Like the bulkhead, these stiff objects may cause head injuries. You're better off staring at a plain seat back.

destination is available or risk being stranded on standby. Also, ask yourself what out-of-pocket expenses you will incur in waiting for the next plane, and if the airline will cover them.

■ **What are my rights if I end up being bumped against my will?**

When you buy a ticket, you've made a contract with the airline. Before you do anything, you have to make sure you've held up your end. Did you check in on time, for instance? Also, if the airline can get you to your destination within an hour of your originally scheduled time, it is free of any liability. Between one and two hours, though, it has to pay the amount of a one-way ticket to your destination (maximum $200). After that, the compensation doubles.

In all cases you get to keep the original ticket to use on another flight or can turn it in for a refund. Also, the Supreme Court has said that you can sue for compensatory damages to recoup whatever loss the delay might have cost you. If, for instance, being bumped forced you to miss a cruise that was paid for in advance, you can sue for the amount of that cruise, though the airline will probably try to get you to the cruise late rather than have to pay for the whole thing.

AIRFARES
▼

DO'S AND DON'TS OF CHEAP FLYING

Coupons, regional airlines, and "split fares" can save you money

As the editor and publisher of *Best Fares* magazine, Tom Parsons has been studying the ins and outs of airline pricing and helping travelers fly cheaply since 1983. Here Parsons gives some money-saving tips.

DO

■ **Search for and use discount coupons.** Parsons says that airlines offer 350 to 400 unadvertised and unpublished travel deals every year. Most can be had by redeeming discount coupons that are distributed by retail outlets and with specific products. An example of one such program: people who bought

three rolls of Kodak film at a participating drug store could request a mail-in certificate redeemable for four $60-off coupons good on American Airlines. This sort of coupon can usually be used during fare wars to further reduce already low prices.

■ **Look into niche and regional airlines.** Several small airlines now offer service between select areas at very low prices. These airlines concentrate on specific pockets, usually limiting their flights to only a handful of cities, and deep-discount their ticket prices to make up for their lack of name recognition and to encourage passengers to fly the short haul rather than drive.

■ **Take advantage of "split fares."** Surprisingly, splitting fares may enable a traveler to combine two cheap tickets for much less than the cost of the original single ticket, especially with the aforementioned rise of niche markets. Rather than buying a single ticket from Dallas to Kansas City, for example, Parsons suggests that a consumer look into the option of flying from Dallas to Tulsa, Oklahoma, and then from Tulsa to Kansas City.

ALL'S FAIR IN THE FARE WARS

If this week's fare is half of what you paid last week, here's what to do:

You've already bought your ticket when you see the ad in the newspaper: a lower fare on the same route. Getting your ticket rewritten for the lower fare—and pocketing the savings—is not always possible. First you must meet all the qualifications listed in the ad in the small print: there must be the right number of days in advance of your trip; you must have been booked to travel when the fare applies; and there must still be seats available in the cheaper fare category. Even then, you might be charged $50 or so to have your ticket rewritten.

Don't give up if the first airline person who answers tells you your ticket is nonrefundable and nonchangeable, though.

Insist on speaking with a supervisor. Also, move fast. The number of seats available at the lower fare is probably limited. Even if you meet all the restrictions, you will not be able to claim one of the cheap seats unless they are still unsold when you call.

A travel agent can give you further assistance. Some agents now guarantee you the lowest fare through use of a computer that monitors reservations systems overnight. Your agent may call you when a lower fare pops up. (You certainly won't hear about it from the airline.) If the agent is still holding your tickets, he or she could rewrite your ticket at the new price even before you open your morning paper.

THE GUY SITTING NEXT TO YOU PAID LESS

Because airlines assign various fare levels to the seats in a plane, passengers in the same section are likely to have paid different prices. Below is a view of what people paid on an American Airlines flight from Miami to New York.

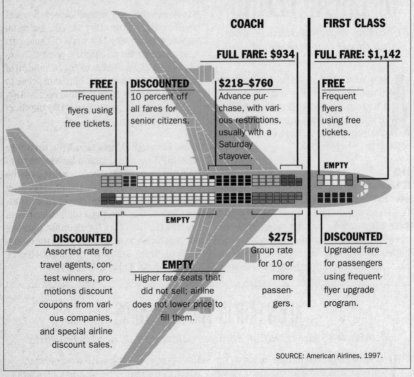

COACH

FIRST CLASS

FULL FARE: $934

FULL FARE: $1,142

FREE
Frequent flyers using free tickets.

DISCOUNTED
10 percent off all fares for senior citizens.

$218–$760
Advance purchase, with various restrictions, usually with a Saturday stayover.

FREE
Frequent flyers using free tickets.

EMPTY

EMPTY

DISCOUNTED
Assorted rate for travel agents, contest winners, promotions discount coupons from various companies, and special airline discount sales.

EMPTY
Higher fare seats that did not sell; airline does not lower price to fill them.

$275
Group rate for 10 or more passengers.

DISCOUNTED
Upgraded fare for passengers using frequent-flyer upgrade program.

SOURCE: American Airlines, 1997.

■ **Consider flying to and from alternative cities.** Some air routes are significantly cheaper than others. If you are willing to make the journey to and from an out-of-the-way airport before and after a long trip, you may be able to save big. A one- or two-hour drive, according to Parsons, can take as much as 70 percent off of a single ticket price. Washington, D.C., flyers, for example, should consider making the trek to the airport in nearby Baltimore, and Chicago flyers should look into flying by way of Milwaukee.

DON'T
■ **Buy tickets immediately.** Most discount fares need only be purchased 14 days in advance.

Buying sooner may simply mean a loss of future savings, because people who buy early can't get any money back when prices drop. Buy tickets immediately only if you wish to travel during busy holidays like Christmas or New Year's Day.

■ **Specify a flight time.** Tell travel and flight reservation agents that a cheap ticket is more important than, say, arriving at nine in the morning. The relationship between time and cost is not always obvious, so you should inquire about the least expensive times to fly a chosen route—some cost more than others, and some special fares only apply at specific times.

AIRFARES
▼

FOUR WAYS TO FLY FOR PEANUTS

Couriers, consolidators, charters, and rebaters are cheap—but tricky

In 1959, when *How to Travel without Being Rich* was a hot seller, a 10-day trip from New York to Paris including airfare, lodging, and sight-seeing cost $553. Today, that price would elude even the most serious of cost-cutters. But bargains still abound for travelers willing to do some research. (For ways to find bargains online, see page 405.)

AIR COURIERS

The absolute cheapest way to fly is as a courier. Although most large courier companies such as FedEx and UPS use their own couriers, smaller companies use "freelance couriers." A typical courier fare can be as low as one-fourth of the regular airline economy class fare. Last-minute tickets are especially cheap.

In exchange for a drastically reduced fare, couriers have minimal duties. After booking a flight with a company, the courier meets a representative of the company at the airport a few hours before departure. The agent hands over baggage checks for the cargo and other paperwork to the courier. The courier then boards the plane and, on arrival at his international destination, accompanies the cargo through customs. Once through customs, the courier hands over the paperwork to the company agent. After that he is free to go.

■ **DRAWBACKS:** Because air courier companies use a courier's allotted baggage space for cargo, couriers generally are limited to carry-on baggage only. More important, courier travel can be unreliable. On rare occasions, for instance, courier companies will cancel or postpone their shipments because of last-minute cargo changes. In this instance, if a courier does not have flexible travel plans and cannot wait for the next courier flight, he or she may have to buy a full-fare economy ticket from a regular airline.

■ **WHERE TO GO:** Most courier flights leave from New York, Los Angeles, San Francisco, or Miami. The best way to find them is to join the International Association of Air Travel Couriers, ☎561-582-8320. A one-year membership costs $45; you get a bimonthly bulletin and access to twice-daily updates of available courier flights online or via fax.

CONSOLIDATORS

Consolidators are the Price Club of airline travel—large brokerage houses that buy blocks of tickets from airlines at wholesale prices and then pass the savings on to individual flyers. Airlines sell to consolidators at reduced prices because they fear that the tickets would otherwise go unsold. Consolidators buy seats mostly on established carriers for flights that are headed to overseas destinations. Travelers booking flights with consolidators can save anywhere from 20 to 50 percent off the price of a regular ticket.

■ **DRAWBACKS:** Most consolidators are reliable, but to protect against illegitimate businesses, travelers should use a credit card whenever possible. Consolidator tickets are nonrefundable, so a traveler who cannot use his or her ticket will most likely end up eating the fare. Consolidator tickets typically are not honored by other airlines, so ticket holders who miss their flights or whose flights are canceled will have to wait for another flight on the issuing airline. Also, flights generally are not direct and sometimes have as many as three stops.

■ **WHERE TO GO:** Travel agents rarely volunteer information about consolidator tickets. Should a travel agent plead ignorance, it may help to suggest that he look up the fare in *Jax Fax*, ☎ 800-952-9329, a monthly newsletter that lists consolidator fares and is widely distributed to travel agents. Consolidator fares are also listed in small ads in the travel sections of major newspapers like *The New York Times* and *USA Today*. For flights from

Europe, the Air Travel Advisory Bureau in London, ☎ 44–1–636–5000, has a complete listing of consolidators (or, as they are called in Britain, "bucket shops").

CHARTER FLIGHTS

Charter flights offer savings that are competitive with consolidator tickets, but generally they are only for nonstop routes. Charter companies are able to profit by running less often than regularly scheduled airline flights and by booking to complete capacity. On transatlantic flights especially, travelers can save between $200 and $400.

Charters also are a good alternative for those who like to fly first class but don't want to pay for it. *Consumer Reports Travel Letter* editor Ed Perkins says, "One of the best values around is the premium class service on some of the transatlantic charters. First class on charter planes is a third of the price of regular airlines with many of the same amenities."

■ **DRAWBACKS:** Infrequency of flights and overcrowding of planes are common complaints. If a charter flight is canceled close to departure, there usually are no other planes available, nor will a charter ticket be honored on another airline. Travelers can often have a lengthy wait for another flight, or worse, will have to pay full fare on a regular airline. Also, despite the aforementioned first-class options, charter flights are not known for luxury service. The meals often come in a brown bag, and you're packed in like the proverbial sardine.

■ **WHERE TO GO:** Travel agencies are an excellent source for charter listings. Charter companies also advertise heavily in the travel sections of major newspapers.

REBATERS

Rebaters are "no-frills" travel agents who pay the ticket buyer all or part of the commission they are paid by airlines for selling the ticket. Rebaters profit by charging a flat fee for making a reservation and issuing a ticket to the buyer. For example, a traveler headed from New York to Stockholm might be quoted a round-trip fare of $800. By using a rebater, the fare would drop to $750. The reason: Rebaters refund their commission, in this case, $80 or 10 percent of the fare. They then tack on a $20 fee to issue the ticket and sometimes an extra $10 to make the reservation. Still, the total price of the ticket is $50 less than it would have been with a regular travel agent.

■ **DRAWBACKS:** For the money saved by using a rebater, a traveler gives up a lot in service. A rebater will make a reservation and issue a ticket, but all other travel details, such as seat assignments, hotel reservations, and ground transportation, will need to be made by the traveler. "The amenities a consumer loses using a rebater instead of a full-service travel agent are not worth the savings unless you are buying expensive tickets," Perkins says.

■ **WHERE TO GO:** One of the most prominent rebaters is Travel Avenue in Chicago, ☎ 800–333–3335. In addition, *Consumer Reports Travel Letter*, ☎ 800–234–1970, lists major rebaters throughout the country once a year.

FACT FILE:

LOOKING FOR THE LAVATORY?

■ *Some airlines are more generous than others when it comes to outfitting planes with bathrooms. Here are the ratios of passengers-to-lavatories for airlines that fly Boeing 737–200 jets:*

AIRLINE	ECON. CLASS	FIRST CLASS
AMERICA WEST	105	8
US AIRWAYS	102	8
UNITED	101	8
DELTA	95	12
CONTINENTAL	90	10

SOURCE: *Consumer Reports Travel Letter.*

RIDING THE RAILS TO ROMANCE

The world's best train trips—at practically stowaway prices

"There isn't a train I wouldn't take, no matter where it's going," wrote Edna St. Vincent Millay. No doubt, the poet would have jumped at the chance to purchase a railway pass that guarantees unlimited travel for a set price during a set period—had they been available in her day. Usually it takes only one or two trips for you to come out ahead, as compared with a regular round-trip ticket. With the help of Eleanor Hardy, vice president and tour director of the Society of International Railway Travelers (IRT), we've sorted through the vast array of train options. Below are some terrific train treks around the world. (For more information, contact IRT, which sponsors membership tours and publishes a newsletter for those who like to set off on their own but want pointers on the best buys and routes: ☎ 800–IRT–4881.)

AUSTRALIA

Air travel across this continent is more practical, but riding the rails affords better views. The scenery is varied and exotic—outback, rain forest, lakes full of black swans and masses of kangaroos and kookaburras. RailAustralia offers two kinds of passes, Austrailpass and Austrail Flexi-Pass. Because many of the major rail services are heavily patronized, advance reservations are often necessary.

■ **PRICE RANGE:** The Austrailpass no longer offers first class passes, only economy. Costs range from $407 for a 14-day pass to $634 for a 30-day pass. Travel is unlimited, including on metropolitan trains. With the Austrail Flexi-Pass economy class runs from $336 for an 8-day pass to $878 for a 29-day pass. The pass must be used within six months.

■ **TRAIN TIP:** Train lovers should not miss a ride on the luxurious Queenslander, which travels a 1,000-mile journey from Cairns to Brisbane through the rain forest and coral-fringed coast of Queensland. Inside the Queenslander, you'll find orchids in every room, a lively piano bar, and a gem of a dining car. Everyone here goes first class, so economy riders must temporarily upgrade their tickets, and all railpass holders must pay a supplement. The Queenslander runs from April to January.
☎ ATS Tours: 800–423–2880

CANADA

VIARail links Montreal's old-world milieu, Vancouver's mountain views, and the arctic tundra. The Canrail Pass allows unlimited coast-to-coast economy-class travel for 12 days within a 30-day period.

■ **PRICE RANGE:** The cost of the Canrail Pass depends on the time of year. For traveling during the peak season (June 1–October 15), it's $421; off-peak, it's $288.

■ **TRAIN TIP:** VIARail's restored stainless steel fleet has been updated with advanced suspension systems and showers in berths. On the run between Jasper and Vancouver, you can catch exhilarating views of the Canadian Rockies. You may want to upgrade your pass to upper-berth accommodations on this route; in addition to other amenities, you will receive access to the Park Car, whose dome roof lets you relax under the stars. Food and service are excellent. Travelers are advised to book early on this highly popular trip.
☎ VIARail: 800–561–3949

EUROPE

The Continent's railways, which serve more than 30,000 cities, have united to offer plenty of pass options: you can focus on just one country, a couple, or all. To help you compare prices and set your itinerary, Rail Pass Express offers a complete online database showing the prices for passes as well as for point-to-point tickets (http://www.eurail.com). *Also, American Youth Hostels offers free assistance to anyone in making European rail plans.*

■ **PRICE RANGE:** The well-known Europass encompasses Germany, France, Italy, Spain, and Switzerland. Consumers are given 11 options for adult fares, ranging from a three-country, 5-day pass ($316); to a five-country, 15-day pass ($736). All adult fares are first-class; all youth fares (for ages 12 to 25) are second-class. Thus, adults traveling with youths must either upgrade the youth pass to first-class, sit separately, or choose to sit in the second-class areas without getting a price break. To ease this dilemma, Europass has instituted a 50 percent discount for the second person in a party of two for all first-class fares; however, the pair must travel together at all times. Travelers can add countries—Austria, Belgium/Luxembourg/Netherlands, Greece, and Portugal—for nominal fees ranging from $29 to $90. A Eurail Pass makes sense only if you plan to do a lot of city hopping across the continent. It allows for unlimited travel in 17 countries during a specified time, ranging from 15 days for $522 to 3 months for $1,468. Additionally, there are flexi-passes that range from 10 days of travel in two months for $616 to 15 days in two months for $812.

■ **TRAIN TIP:** The Society of International Railway Travelers offers the following tips regarding Eurail passes. First, tailor your pass to a pre-determined itinerary and buy it from a travel agent or the agencies listed here before you leave the United States. Whenever you arrive at a train station, have the pass validated by a railway official in the station's ticket office. Passes are not presented to train conductors. Reservations are needed for many trains, including EurCity, InterCity, TGV, and ICE trains, and for all sleepers and couchettes.

Gena Holle, editor of *Inter-*

national Railway Traveler, highly recommends the line from Nice, France, to Livorno, Italy. This scenic route along the banks of the Mediterranean offers a chance to stop off at Cinqueterre, a unique spot made up of five beautiful seaside towns all connected by walkways.

☎ Rail Europe: 800–438–7245
   (*http://www.raileurope.com*)
☎ American Youth Hostels: 202–783–4943
☎ Rail Pass Express: 800–438–7245
   (*http://www.eurail.com*)

INDIA

Indian Railways boasts the world's largest railroad system, running more than 7,000 passenger trains daily. The rails offer a better alternative to driving, given the crowded cities and potentially rugged roads elsewhere. Although steam locomotives are still in use, extensive modernization is under way with super-fast trains in production.

■ **PRICE RANGE:** Indrail passes come in three classes: air-conditioned; first class (which varies from line to line, but often specifies an air-conditioned chair car); and second-class, usually crowded non–air-conditioned cars. For unlimited travel within a specified period, costs run from $10 for a half-day, second-class pass to $1,060 for a 90-day, air-conditioned-class pass. Regular tickets may be cheaper if you're planning only one or two trips, but the passes make it easier to get reservations. Tickets can be bought at travel agencies in the country or at the major railway offices and reservation counters.

■ **TRAIN TIP:** Delays and strandings at stations used to be common because of telex failures, but faxes now offer a more reliable backup system for rail reservations. *India by Rail* (Globe Pequot Press, 1994) describes some of the more scenic routes. Trains tend to be slow (52 mph), so you have time to soak in the views.

You can catch some terrific views aboard the Darjeeling

Himalayan Railway. With a railroad gauge measuring just two feet across, the Darjeeling is among the world's narrowest trains. En route to Darjeeling it passes through plantations before climbing 2,258 feet above sea level to one of the highest railway stations in Asia at Goom. Palace on Wheels, a luxury train with saloon cars custom-built for the Maharajas and Viceroys, makes an 8-day journey through former royal kingdoms.

☎ Hari World Travels, Inc.: 212–997–3300

JAPAN

The extensive Japan Railway (JR) system rivals that of continental Europe for speed and convenience, and it reaches nearly every tourist spot. Rail passes offer a great investment: an economy-priced 7-day pass with unlimited travel can cost less than one round-trip ticket between some cities—even less than a cab ride from Narita airport to downtown Tokyo.

■ **PRICE RANGE:** Passes come in two classes: superior, also called "green," and ordinary. Both include travel on most Shinkansen (bullet trains) and all ferries. Fares run from $280 for a 7-day ordinary pass to $768 for a 21-day superior.

■ **TRAIN TIP:** The Twighlight Express is Japan's finest overnight sleeper train. Named for the fantastic setting-sun views along the coast of the sea, the Twighlight travels four times a week between Osaka, Kyoto, and Sapporo. A superb dining car serves Japanese and French food; a lounge car offers panoramic views when the weather is clear. Accommodations range from standard berths to private rooms with bath, TV, and phones.

☎ TBI Tours: 800–223–0266

UNITED KINGDOM

Riding the rails through the United Kingdom is a great way to tour England, Scotland, Wales, and Northern Ireland. BritRail pass holders can travel throughout the area, training it from London to the rest of Britain.

■ **PRICE RANGE:** For unlimited consecutive days of travel, costs run from $249 for a second-class 8-day pass to $815 for a first-class 1-month pass. BritRail flexi-passes range from four days of second-class travel for $199 to 15 days of first-class travel for $615. All passes must be used within one month. The BritIreland pass allows for travel in Britain and Ireland, and includes a catamaran trip across the Irish Sea. Prices start at $335 for 5 days of travel within one month.

■ **TRAIN TIP:** Stephen Forsyth, the only U.S. distributor of the Thomas Cook Overseas Timetable (a must-have for rail travelers, ☎ 800–FORSYTH), recommends the short trip from Southhampton to Bournemouth; it travels through the New Forest, created in the 1200s, and past thatched-roofed cottages framed by flowers. At the forest's southeast corner is Buckler's Hard, a museum town where shipbuilding was a mainstay.

☎ Rail Pass Express: 800–551–1977

U.S.A.

America's passenger rail system, Amtrak, serves 530 stations in 45 states, over a 23,000-mile system. It operates some 230 trains each day, carrying 55 million passengers a year. Amtrak's Explore America pass is a convenient way to see a good part of the country for a low price. It's good for 45 days and includes three scheduled stops. In setting up its routes and fares, Amtrak has divided the country into three regions by drawing two lines from north to south: Chicago to New Orleans and Denver to Albuquerque. You can buy unlimited travel in one region, two, or three. The eastern region includes Montreal.

■ **PRICE RANGE:** Explore America passes run $228 for one region in peak; $198 for off-peak (after August), or $378 across the country in peak, $318 for off-peak.

■ **TRAIN TIP:** The Coast Starlight from Los Angeles to Seattle is Amtrak's most popular trip. The scenic ride along the Pacific shore to the snow-crested Cascades takes about 35 hours, but first-class passengers are kept busy with wine tastings, live entertainment, and fine dining.

☎ Amtrak 800–872–7245

WHERE EVERYTHING IS SHIPSHAPE

The way cruise ships are being outfitted these days, the passengers hardly realize that they're at sea. The newest boats contain practically everything anyone could possibly want—except, perhaps, sandy beaches. Here's a highly selective guide to cruise ships, new and old, plying the high seas.

THE MEGAS

The biggest ships just keep getting bigger. Carnival Cruise Line's 100,000-ton Destiny, which set sail in 1996, will be topped by the Princess Line's Grand Princess, with a tonnage of 105,000, which is scheduled to begin sailing in mid-1998. And Royal Caribbean is planning to launch two even bigger ships, each at 130,000 tons, in 1999 and 2000. These mega ships are fully equipped with multi-level dining rooms, larger cabins, and revolving-stage theaters, among many other amenities.

DESTINY

Carnival Cruise Line

■ **WHERE:** Year-round, 7-day cruises to eastern and western Caribbean. Home port: Miami.

■ **WHO:** Mass market.

■ **ON BOARD:** There's a 15,000-foot, two-level Nautica spa, which is 25 percent larger than those on other Carnival ships. Sixty percent of the cabins have ocean views, and 60 percent of those in turn have private balconies.

☎ 800–327–9501

GALAXY

Celebrity Cruises

■ **WHERE:** Western Caribbean from Ft. Lauderdale. Vancouver inside passage.

■ **WHO:** Adults ages 35 to 60, with a median income of $50,000 and over.

■ **ON BOARD:** One of the most technically advanced ships in terms of interactive systems and computer programs.

☎ 800–437–3111

GRANDEUR OF THE SEAS

Royal Caribbean Cruise Line

■ **WHERE:** The eastern Caribbean, year-round. Home port: Miami.

■ **WHO:** Mass market. 1,950 passengers, with average age of 43 and a median income of $50,000 or more.

■ **ON BOARD:** More square feet of glass than on any other ship afloat. With a cruising speed of 22 knots per hour, it is one of the speediest ships.

☎ 800–327–6700

GRAND PRINCESS (1998)

Princess Cruises

■ **WHERE:** The Caribbean only, on a year-round basis.

■ **WHO:** This will be a family-oriented ship accommodating 2,600.

■ **ON BOARD:** This huge ship will offer plenty of views; 750 of the cabins will have verandas.

☎ 800–421–1700

LUXURY ON A SMALL SCALE

These ships accommodate 250 passengers or less. The appeal is attentive service. The cuisine is apt to be first-class. Life on board is generally unstructured and low-key. Entertainment is often cabaret style. For those looking for more mental stimulation, many of the ships also provide lectures on a variety of subjects. Exercise focuses on water sports.

SEA GODDESS I & II

Cunard

■ **WHERE:** Sea Goddess I operates 7-day cruises to the Caribbean, spring and fall, Amazon in winter, Mediterranean in summer. Sea Goddess II goes to Asia in winter, east Mediterranean in summer.

■ **WHO:** 116 passengers—predominantly executives and professional types; predominantly couples, half from North America and half from Europe.

■ **ON BOARD:** A "country club" atmosphere, with lots of water sports, a spa, dancing, and just relaxing. All drinks are included.

☎ 800–221–4770

DECK BY DECK

Your cabin's location can have a profound effect on your enjoyment of a cruise. The higher you go, for example, the more likely you are to suffer the ill effects of the ship's pitching and rolling. On the other hand, if you are too close to the nightlife, you might not get much sleep. No two ships are alike, but here is what you generally can expect on various decks.

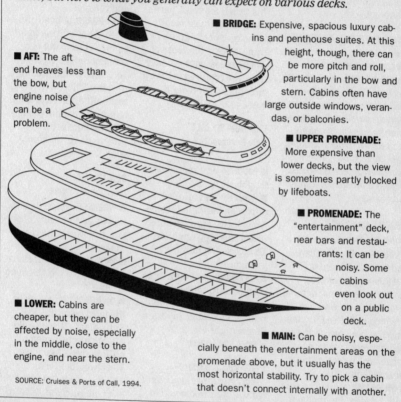

■ **AFT:** The aft end heaves less than the bow, but engine noise can be a problem.

■ **BRIDGE:** Expensive, spacious luxury cabins and penthouse suites. At this height, though, there can be more pitch and roll, particularly in the bow and stern. Cabins often have large outside windows, verandas, or balconies.

■ **UPPER PROMENADE:** More expensive than lower decks, but the view is sometimes partly blocked by lifeboats.

■ **PROMENADE:** The "entertainment" deck, near bars and restaurants: It can be noisy. Some cabins even look out on a public deck.

■ **LOWER:** Cabins are cheaper, but they can be affected by noise, especially in the middle, close to the engine, and near the stern.

■ **MAIN:** Can be noisy, especially beneath the entertainment areas on the promenade above, but it usually has the most horizontal stability. Try to pick a cabin that doesn't connect internally with another.

SOURCE: Cruises & Ports of Call, 1994.

SEABOURN'S PRIDE & SPIRIT
Seabourn Cruise Line

■ **WHERE:** Europe, Asia, Alaska, Mediterranean, and Caribbean.

■ **WHO:** 204 passengers. Median age is 45 to 50—apt to include financiers, professionals, members of the English upper class, and the "glitterati;" 70 percent are repeat passengers.

■ **ON BOARD:** These ships are larger than the Goddesses, with more facilities and entertainment, and larger cabins. The fares are higher too.
☎ 800–929–4747

SONG OF THE FLOWER
Radisson Seven Seas Cruises

■ **WHERE:** Summers in Europe, winters in Asia.

■ **WHO:** 214 passengers; likely to be well educated, include active executive types, 45+, as well as many retirees.

■ **ON BOARD:** Cheaper than Goddesses, but cabins not as beautifully decorated as Goddesses or Seabourns. This is a spotless ship, with

wonderful space, great service. The atmosphere is low-key and unpretentious. This ship can enter ports inaccessible to larger ones.
☎ 800–333–3333

BEST FOR YOUR BUCKS
Ever wonder if you are overpaying for a cruise vacation? Well, very often you are. Maybe you don't need all that pampering or supreme cuisine. But on the other hand, you probably don't care to travel "troop-ship" style, either. These ships were selected because they give you good value for your money.

REGENT RAINBOW
Regency Cruises
■ **WHERE:** 4-day Mexican and Caribbean cruises.
■ **WHO:** 960 passengers, mostly Americans in the 40 to 60 age range who like to live modestly. Recently, the ship has been attracting a number of foreigners because of its reputation for excellent value.
■ **ON BOARD:** A midsize ship with no glitz, but modern and comfortable. Wide range of entertainment from classical music to cabaret and western. There is also afternoon tea.
☎ 800–388–5500

ECSTASY
Carnival Cruise Line
■ **WHERE:** 3-day, year-round cruises to Bahamas from Florida and 4-day cruises to Key West and Cozumel.

■ **WHO:** Vacationers of all ages in search of good value and lively experience.
■ **ON BOARD:** If you like Las Vegas-style glitz and action, this ship is for you. There's also a large fitness facility and excellent children's programs to keep the younger set busy. (Passengers under 21 are are required to have a cabinmate 25 or older.)
☎ 800–327–9501

ENCHANTED ISLE
New Commodore Cruise Line
■ **WHERE:** 7-day, year-round Caribbean cruises.
■ **WHO:** Budget-minded upper- and middle-income Americans. Many groups travel this ship and there is an increasing number of younger people.
■ **ON BOARD:** A comfortable, relaxed ship, with spacious deck space, quite personalized service, and elaborate theme nights.
☎ 800–237–5361

THE TALL SHIPS
"Tall Ships" are replicas of old sailing schooners that sail under canvas—with ropes and salt spray, and moonlit nights at ocean level. The modern versions of these ships come in two styles: authentic replicas that depend on the sails to get places, and the so-called sail-cruise ships that are largely powered.

LILI MARLEEN
Peter Deilmann Reederei

■ **WHERE:** Caribbean and Baltic.
■ **WHO:** Experienced seamen and mature, older professionals and retirees.
■ **ON BOARD:** A beautiful 3-masted barkentine (one square-rigged and two schooner-rigged masts). You can assist in sailing the ship. There are candlelit dinners in a handsome dining room with menus featuring international cuisine.
☎ 800–348–8287

SEA CLOUD
Sea Cloud Cruises
■ **WHERE:** East Caribbean in winter and many different itineraries the rest of the year.
■ **WHO:** Available for charter with a passenger capacity of 69.
■ **ON BOARD:** This may be the most beautiful Tall Ship afloat—also the oldest. Formerly owned by millionairess Marjorie Merriweather Post. There's handcrafted carved oak paneling, antique furniture, and fine original oil paintings. (Note: Sea Cloud Cruises is based in Hamburg, Germany.)
☎ 011–49–40–369–0272

THE POLYNESIA
Windjammer Barefoot Cruises, Ltd.
■ **WHERE:** 6-day cruises around the Caribbean (the itinerary depends on the wind).

EXPERT TIPS

IF SHUFFLEBOARD ISN'T YOUR THING

And you like staring at salt water, a trip on a freighter may be just the ticket

Before turning to poking fun at Washington pooh-bahs (*Thank You for Smoking* and *The White House Mess*), Christopher Buckley penned *Steaming to Bamboola*, a first-person account of his trip from South Carolina to the North Sea on a tramp freighter. Freighter travel is still available to the general public today. *Ford's Freighter Travel Guide and Waterways of the World* (Ford's Travel Guides, 19448 Londelius St., Northridge, CA 91324) publishes semiannual listings of itineraries for more than a hundred different vessels. But freighter travel isn't for everybody. Buckley's counsel:

Those who like shuffleboard, mints on their pillow at night, and driving golf balls off the after deck, read no further. Freighter travel is not for you. It's also not for people with medical conditions, because there's no doctor on board. That's why only 12 people are allowed on board at once. But for those who enjoy reading or rereading the classics and long, long hours of boring, endless blue salt water, this is your trip. It's a reader's vacation—or a writer's vacation. Nelson Algren reread all of Hemmingway's works while on a freighter from San Francisco to Yokohama, then wrote about the experience in *Diary of a Sea Voyage—or Hemingway All the Way.*

A generation ago, you could go down to the dock, talk to a freighter captain, and get a job and berth on board. I arranged to work with the crew to pay my way on a freighter; you can't do that today. But a freighter is still less expensive than traveling on a cruise ship—and you're not going to have Kathie Lee Gifford twirling around telling you to eat more shrimp.

My first freighter trip came when I was 17 and about to start college; I saw a bit of the world at a young age, and developed a real relationship with the men on board. I only made $20 a week, but felt rich because I could buy cigarettes for $1 a carton and beer for $3 a case at the ship store.

It's like apples and oranges between the way I traveled and a freighter trip today. I doubt someone traveling now would be able to really get to know the crew, or to sample the local whorehouse with them. I guess going by freighter is still kind of a romantic idea, but if you're looking for romance, this ain't it.

■ **WHO:** Singles, retirees, families, and young marrieds. A high record of repeat passengers.
■ **ON BOARD:** A legendary old fishing schooner. Some cabins are made over into bachelor quarters. Singles and other theme cruises are featured. Life onboard is ultra casual—wear shorts and expect no frills.
☎ 800–327–2602

SIR FRANCIS DRAKE
Tall Ship Adventures
■ **WHERE:** Year-round, 3- to 7-day cruises, usually around the British Virgin Islands.
■ **WHO:** Young and middle-aged couples and singles. Median age is mid-40s.
■ **ON BOARD:** This is an authentic 3-masted ship that has been in service since 1917. Not as luxurious as the Sea Cloud, and not as simple as the Polynesia. All cabins have private baths (unlike Polynesia). Very casual.
☎ 800–662–0090

SURF THE WEB BEFORE YOU FLY

The Web may make travel agents as obsolete as steamer trunks

Do you want to get your hands on cheap airfares, low hotel rates, and great package deals to the earth's most idyllic spots? Travel agents aren't the sole proprietors of that information anymore. It's all out there in the World Wide Web. By the year 2000, the online travel business is expected to take in $3 billion of the estimated $360 billion Americans spend on business and pleasure travel each year.

Nearly every airline offers online booking services. The sites provide updates on the particular airline's flight schedules, fares, as well as any available last-minute discounts. Bargains abound: Many fares are 30 percent to 75 percent below typical coach fares. There are some restrictions, such as Saturday departures and early weekday returns. To get in on rock-bottom prices, register at a carrier's Web site and you will receive electronic messages, usually on a Wednesday, of fares that are good for the coming weekend. You then book the tickets online or by calling the toll-free number provided.

Ticketing is the most basic of the Web's travel services, however. You can plan every detail of your trip online, from reserving a hotel room to renting a car to booking theater tickets. Some sites serve as electronic guidebooks, spewing out everything from weather conditions to local customs. Others offer tips from overcoming the fear of flying, to best places to whale watch to the most challenging hikes in the mountains, and more.

There are a few downsides to online travel services. For one, when you sign onto a travel site, you're giving your e-mail address and, as a result, should brace yourself for electronic junk mail. Once you're targeted as a skier, for example, you'll get an avalanche of ads for ski trips and equipment. In addition, cyber bargains come and go swifly, which means you'll need to spend time aplenty mousing around the Web for the perfect deal.

A GUIDE TO THE TRAVEL GUIDES

Which guides are best? Here, Martin Rapp, a travel consultant and contributing editor at Travel & Leisure, *evaluates some of the more popular guides .*

■ **AAA.** If you're on the road and just want to find a place to stay, these guides are very useful. The maps and "Tripticks" (succinct notebook-style maps) are excellent.

■ **BIRNBAUM.** Their strength is special sections like "Unexpected Pleasures and Treasures." They don't give prices, but rather indicate "expensive" or "cheap," which doesn't really help. The driving itineraries are not extensive, but a good starting point.

■ **FODOR'S AND FROMMER'S.** Great for people who want to see the sights but are not adventurous. For a wider choice of hotels and restaurants in the medium- and lower-price range, I like Frommer's guides. Fodor's are dependable, middle-of-the-road books with which you really can't go wrong.

■ **LONELY PLANET.** These books are rooted in the budget end. The India book is probably the best guide ever for that country.

■ **MICHELIN "RED GUIDES."** The most detailed restaurant and hotel guides for Europe, with the most accurate prices. The city maps are superb and thorough, including one-way streets, parking areas, hotels, restaurants, and other attractions.

ONLINE SITES WORTH THE VISIT

*These travel sites can help save you a bundle on fares, as well as unearth
new deals and destinations—even if you're a seasoned traveler.*

AMERICA ONLINE'S TRAVEL CHANNEL
Keyword: TRAVEL

■ Offers a smorgasbord of services. For those shopping around for a good deal but not sure where they want to travel, AOL's site lists the best package deals it finds around the world for each month of the year. It also has thumbnail sketches of many worldwide destinations and personal reviews of top choices.

EPICURIOUS
http://www.epicurious.com

■ This *Condé Nast Traveler* site has extensive databases on travel destinations around the world. A feature called How Annoying is Your Airline? boils down the statistics on late arrivals, lost baggage, etc. Another called Deal of the Week offers up the best current deal. A recent bargain: seven nights in Jamaica for $548.

EXPEDIA
http://www.expedia.com

■ This Microsoft site books hotels, reserves rental cars, gets you tickets to shows in your vacation spot, and more. Its Fare Tracker page lets you type in up to three destinations and then will notify you by e-mail with the best flight deals to those places.

FODOR'S
http://www.fodors.com

■ Features seasonal hot spots in regular guides, such as the 30 best ski resorts. This site also offers reviews of travel books and a personal trip planner that lets you design a complete vacation. Fact lists include helpful tips such as government health and travel advisories, world weather forecasts, and toll-free numbers for airlines, trains, buses, car rental agencies, and hotels.

LET'S GO TRAVEL
http://www.letsgo.com

■ Takes a cue from the popular books of the same name that are written by college students and updated yearly. Like the books, the site offers low-budget, high-adventure travel information. Armchair travelers can pretend they are researchers for the *Let's Go Travel* guides, setting up a virtual tour that you choose from hotlinks to get to a new destinations.

Simulated trips include an espionage adventure in Russia and a trip to a cursed village in Ireland.

1TRAVEL.COM
http://www.1travel.com

■ Will locate the lowest airfares among the more reputable consolidators that offer discount tickets and then send you a quote by e-mail within 24 hours.

THE TRIP
http://www.thetrip.com

■ Touted as the "ultimate site for the business traveler." Corporate types can track flights, view U.S. city maps and airport plans, and check out events at their destination.

SABRE INTERACTIVE TRAVELOCITY
http://www.travelocity.com

■ A flashy site run by the parent company of American Airlines puts 700 maps, CD-ROMs, atlases, and guidebooks at your fingertips. A chat room lets you pick up travel tips, such as how to pack your bags and how to take great snapshots. Also available: weather alerts, guides to U.S. parks, and detailed travelogs.

ADVENTURE

EGYPT

SEE THE NILE CLEOPATRA-STYLE

Cruising by the land of pyramids and pharaohs

Caesar reputedly told Cleopatra that he would relinquish all his treasures if she would show him the Nile. Even today, it's hard to cruise up this river of ancient history and not be moved by the experience. The land is rich in icons of cultural history—pyramids, tombs of the pharaohs, ancient temples. Interspersed are glimpses of ordinary life: farming villages, children playing, and women washing clothes, just as they have for centuries.

Romantic as it may be, a trip to the Middle East requires precautions, however. There are some concerns about food safety—be finicky about what you eat and drink. Tourists are also advised to be aware of pickpockets and scam artists. Before planning a trip to the Middle East, it's also wise to check with the U.S. State Department (☎202–647–5225) for any official alert concerning travel to the area.

Perhaps the most care-free mode of traveling to the Nile is with a guided tour, of which there are a number of reputable ones

(see box, next page). Here's what not to miss on a Nile cruise.

■ **CAIRO.** Most tours start in this crowded, exciting city with colorful bazaars and world-famous museums. The Museum of Antiquities, containing the mummy room and the treasures of King Tutankhamen, is worth at least a morning's visit. A short drive takes you to Memphis, the ancient capital with its gargantuan statue of Ramses II. In nearby Giza, you'll find three pyramids and the colossal Sphinx.

■ **LUXOR.** On the east bank of the Nile, Luxor is an agricultural center full of ancient monuments, including the Temple of Luxor, which dates to 1380 B.C. The nearby village of Karnak is home to Karnak Temple, an extraordinary edifice where through the years pharaohs recorded their names and deeds. Many of the unearthed treasures found at Karnak are in the Luxor Museum of Ancient Egyptian Art.

■ **THEBES.** On the west bank, opposite Luxor and Karnak, is the necropolis of Thebes, ringed with rugged mountain peaks. From the heights, the Valley of the Kings, some distance away, presents an awesome panorama. Queen Nefertari's tomb has been recently reopened so that you can view the brilliantly restored interior frescoes. Also at Thebes is the mortuary temple of Hatshepsut, the first female pharaoh. At Deir el-Medina, you'll

PYRAMID SCHEMES WORTH CONSIDERING

These tour operators are experienced in Nile travel. Package tours are not cheap—they typically range from $3,200 to $4,000 per person.

ESPLANADE TOURS

■ Generally 12-day tours including airfare via British Airways. Consist of 5 nights in deluxe Cairo hotels, 7-night cruises on a 5-star deluxe vessel. Cost: about $3,900 per person. An add-on excursion to Abu Simbel costs an extra $250.
☎ 800–426–5492

OVERSEAS ADVENTURE TRAVEL

■ An eco-tourism group whose corporate board of directors includes luminaries such as Sir Edmund Hillary (the first European to scale Mt. Everest) and Rodrigo Carazo, former Costa Rican president. The group conducts a 16-day trip including airfare from New York or Boston via Egypt Air, for about $3,400. Nile-cruise tour leader is Ahmed Fakhry, a noted Egyptologist.
☎ 800–221–0814

ABERCROMBIE & KENT

■ An English firm that has conducted tours to Egypt for 17 years. Groups are limited to 24, and Egyptologists conduct tours. A good introductory tour is the 11-day Nile Explorer, with a 5-day cruise along the Nile from Cairo to Aswan and including Abu Simbel. From New York to London to Egypt the tour goes for about $3,500.
☎ 800–323–7308

THOMAS COOK HOLIDAYS

■ This British travel agency has a variety of plans, including a design-your-own-tour option. A 9-day tour leaving from London costs about $1,500.
☎ 01733 332255, or any Cook agency worldwide

SPECIAL EXPEDITIONS

■ A 10-day trip to the Nile leaves London via British Airways. A tour of Cairo is followed by a four-day cruise to Aswan and Abu Simbel. Cost: about $3,300 per person.
☎ 800–762–0003

---

find the tombs of workers as well as depictions of everyday life.

■ **EDFU.** This tiny town contains the best preserved temple in Egypt, the temple of the eagle-headed god Horus, which took 200 years to build. It is spectacular and intricate, with dark, mysterious chambers.

■ **KOM OMBO.** Kom Ombo lies 29 miles north of Aswan on the eastern bank of the Nile. Here is the Greco-Roman temple devoted to two gods: Sobek, the Crocodile God, and Haroeris, the Sun God.

■ **ASWAN.** This oasis-like town is the site of the famous Aswan Dam, one of the marvels of the world. Aswan is beautiful in its own right.

Its riverfront is jammed with shops, floating restaurants, and docks for feluccas, the traditional Egyptian vessels. A number of islets lie in the middle of the river: Elephantine Island, the largest, rich in antiquities; Kitchener's Island has botanical gardens of African and Asian plants. Set high on the cliffs behind Aswan is the handsome mausoleum of the late Aga Khan.

■ **ABU SIMBEL.** Many tours fly back to Cairo from Aswan, but a side trip to Abu Simbel, at the southernmost tip of the Nile, is well worth taking. A 30-minute plane ride takes you to this town, where you'll find two terrific temples of Ramses II, with colossal stone representations of Ramses and his beautiful wife, Nefertari.

JUST FOR THE TREK OF IT

*A world-wise veteran chooses
10 classics not to be missed*

The current vogue for trekking can be traced, in part, to the post-1960s crowd who traveled the world, exploring non-Western cultures and becoming inadvertent wanderers along the way. Today, trekking has gone mainstream. Tony trekking companies with glossy brochures offer deluxe trips to every imaginable corner of the globe. You can take your pick from a classic trek in Nepal to a pure wilderness experience in New Zealand. And you pay Ritz-Carlton prices to sleep in tents under the stars.

The immense popularity of trekking is sparking some environmental concerns. Once-pristine environments have become less so as trekkers have passed through. Cultures once isolated from outside influences now experience them with fair regularity.

We asked veteran trekker Robert Strauss, who has trekked on six continents and written numerous books on the subject including *Adventure Trekking: A Handbook for Independent Travelers* (Mountaineers, 1996), to pick what he considers to be the world's 10 classic treks. Strauss also provided the names of the outfitters listed.

KENYA

■ A five-day trek to Point Lenana (16,350 feet) in Mt. Kenya National Park (camping or staying in mountain huts en route) can be done with or without porters and guides. Rain forest on the lower slopes gives way to bamboo groves that thin into moorland—and, at higher altitude, the extraordinary giant species of groundsel and lobelia. Wildlife in the area includes elephants, buffalo, monkeys, and rock hyrax. Appropriate high-altitude experience and sufficient warm and waterproof gear are essential. Daily fees for park entry and camping are payable in advance.

■ **OUTFITTERS:**
Tusker Trail & Safari Co. ☎ 800–747–2728
Africatours ☎ 800–23–KENYA

PERU

■ The Inca Trail, a once-secret passage between Cuzco and Machu Picchu, the legendary lost city of the Incas, was rediscovered in 1911. The three-day trek features high passes, forests, and ancient ruins. It is strenuous in parts and often crowded, since it is easily the most well-known trekking destination in South America. For improved security, travel in a group and keep an eye on your tent and possessions.

■ **OUTFITTERS:**
Exploration Inc. ☎ 800–446–9660
International Expeditions ☎ 800–633–4734

VENEZUELA

■ In the southeast of the country is La Gran Sabana, a region renowned for its many tepui, or tablelike mountains of sandstone. The Roraima tepui rises 9,216 feet and is accessible via the village of San Francisco de Yuruaní. The trek to the top takes about five days. The trail starts in flat savanna, rises through rain forest, passing waterfalls and streams before the final steep ascent to the stepped plateau. It is strenuous in parts; take warm gear for the cold nights, rainproofs, and insect repellent. Hiring local guides is advisable. Overnighting en route consists of sleeping under rock overhangs or in caves.

■ **OUTFITTERS:**
Condor Adventures ☎ 800–729–1262
Southwind Adventures ☎ 800–377–WIND

TASMANIA

■ The delightful island state of Tasmania is a bushwalking magnet. (See also story on page 362 in Hot Spots.) Weather can change with amazing speed, so be prepared with cold-weather and wet-weather gear. In the center of the island, the popular, 50-mile-long Overland Track in the Cradle Mountain–Lake St. Clair National Park can be covered in a week or less. The trailheads at Cynthia Bay and Waldheim, at the southern and northern ends

GADGETS AND GIZMOS TO KEEP YOU OUT OF TROUBLE

An array of new gadgets—and improvements on old ones—ensures that civilization is never too far away. The gizmos are not infallible, of course—they can break and do not always work properly in deep valleys or under thick tree cover. Think of them as accessories, not substitutes for real wilderness skills. Most items can be found in specialty catalogs and outlets such as Sharper Image, Haverhill's, Herrington, and REI Outdoor Gear.

GLOBAL POSITIONING SYSTEM (GPS Unit)
Start around $200

■ Plug in data and the unit tells you where you are. It can also calculate your estimated time of arrival.

DATA SCOPE
About $450

■ How far and in which direction is that mountain? When will the sun set into the sea? This 5" x 30" monocular by KVH puts range, direction, or time data directly in the field of view.

NIGHT VISION SCOPES
Start $360–$400

■ Cold War Russian technology went into this light-intensifying scope by

Edmund Scientifics to help guide you around the campsite in the dark.

CELLPHONE RECEPTION AMPLIFIERS
About $25

■ This pocket-sized, wireless antenna picks up and amplifies phone signals indoors or outdoors.

LIGHTNING WARNING DEVICE
About $150

■ At the rumble of distant thunder, LED's Sky-Scan can warn you of impending lightning, whether it's 4 miles or 40 miles away.

NEAT LITTLE COMPASS
About $10

■ Only 2" by 3", the Silva compass has a direction

finder, moving bearing ring, magnifier, and three map-reading scales.

WATER PURIFIER
About $70

■ The compact PUR Voyage Purifier weighs only 11 oz., but in a pinch it will make water in the wilderness potable.

WINDMILL LIGHTER
About $50

■ This butane lighter produces 800°F heat and is good for 30,000 lights.

POCKET 35MM
About $200

■ The pocket-sized Olympus Rangefinder is fully automatic and recalls the great 35mm's of the prewar past.

---

of the park respectively, are served by a shuttle bus during the prime summer season. Permits are issued by park offices at both points.

■ **OUTFITTERS:**
Adventure Center ☎ 800–227–8747
Mountain Travel–Sobek ☎ 800–227–2384

NEW ZEALAND

■ Tramping (the New Zealand term for hiking/trekking) has become a passion for the locals. At the southern end of the South Island lies Mt. Aspiring National Park and Fiordland National Park, which are straddled by the Routeburn Track. This very popular

three-day tramp has great alpine scenery and passes through valleys covered by rain forest. A booking system for huts and campsites on the Routeburn has recently been introduced. (Less crowded tracks in the same area are The Greenstone and The Caples.) Information is available from the Department of Conservation (DOC) in Queenstown, which provides a transport base to access the northern end of the trail; Te Anau is convenient for the southern end.

■ **OUTFITTERS:**
Down Under Answers ☎ 800–788–6685
Swiss Hike, Olympia, WA ☎ 360–754–0978

CORSICA

■ GR20 (GR for Grande Route) passes through the national park (Parc Naturel Régional de la Corse) in the interior and extends 86 miles from Calenza in the north to Conca in the south—almost the full length of this Mediterranean island. There are beech and pine forests, aromatic scrub (maquis), high pasturelands, exposed mountaintops, and wild pigs with an aggressive craving for hikers' victuals! The walk can be split into two by starting in the middle at Col de Vizzavona. (The prime season for the northern section is early summer; autumn is best for the southern section.) You'll need at least two weeks to complete the full route, which requires fitness and experience in dealing with exposed terrain and major elevation changes. Unattended mountain huts (rifugios) provide shelter, but you need to carry your own food. Camping is prohibited within the park.

■ OUTFITTERS:

Himalayan Travel ☎ 800–225–2380

Adventure Center ☎ 800–227–8747

GREENLAND

■ A demanding terrain, lack of trails (for navigation at these latitudes you'll need to adjust your compass), and fickle weather make this destination at the Arctic Circle a challenge even for experienced trekkers. The five- to six-day trek between Qaqortoq, the major town in southern Greenland, and Igaliku offers the scenic variety of icebergs, bays, waterfalls, and boulder fields. There are also Norse church ruins dating back to medieval times.

■ OUTFITTERS:

Greenland Travel, Denmark ☎ +45 (33-13-10-11)

Black Feather, Canada ☎ 800–5RIVER5

ALASKA

■ Three-quarters of Alaska is protected wilderness. Backcountry trekking through Denali National Park is regulated through zoning and permit quotas. Free permits are issued a day in advance by the Visitor Access Center (VAC). Once you have your permit, a shuttle bus will drop you off at your assigned zone. The park has no marked trails; hikers find their way with topographical maps. Denali, which is dominated by Mount McKinley, America's highest mountain at 20,320 feet, is accessible from Anchorage by car, bus, and rail.

■ OUTFITTERS:

Sunlight North Expeditions, Anchorage, AK

☎ 907–346–2027

Hugh Glass Backpacking Co., Anchorage, AK

☎ 907–344-1340

NEPAL

■ The main gateway for the Annapurna region is the town of Pokhara. The Annapurna Conservation Area Project (ACAP), based in Pokhara, provides regional support for minimizing impact on the environment. The Annapurna Circuit is a trekking tour de force: it passes through alpine forests to arid semidesert characteristic of Tibet; crosses over the Thorong La pass with dazzling views at 17,650 feet; and drops into the Kali Gandaki gorge, the world's deepest. The full circuit takes around 18 days for seasoned trekkers putting in some 7 hours of hiking each day. Be prepared for the effects of high altitude and a possible wait to cross the pass if it's snowbound. The trail has plenty of teahouses and lodges en route.

■ OUTFITTERS:

Himalayan High Treks ☎ 800–455–8735

PAKISTAN

■ The northernmost region of Pakistan, where four mountain ranges (Himalaya, Hindu Kush, Pamirs, and Karakorum) meet, boasts the largest number of high peaks in the world. The Concordia trek, which passes through this area, is rated as one of the world's best. Because of the travel restrictions here, your best bet is to go on a trip organized through a tour operator. From the trailhead in Askole, the trek takes two weeks or longer, crossing awesome wilderness and glaciers into a natural amphitheater where colossal mountains (K2, Gasherbrum, Chogolisa, Broad Peak, and others) soar above you.

■ OUTFITTERS:

Snow Lion Expeditions ☎ 800–525–TREK

Wilderness Travel ☎ 800–368–2794

THE LAST GREAT PLACES ON EARTH

Progress exacts its price, but these 9 spots are still pristine and wild

The great wildernesses have long been a challenge to the more adventurous travelers. Whatever their reasons—self-renewal, getting back to nature, or just to see what's there—adventurers have risked life and limb to get to these, until recently, blank spots on the map. Yet these wildernesses are the last best places for adventure travel, not only because they have wild rivers, unclaimed mountains, and unpenetrated rain forest, but because just to travel through them is an adventure—a reminder of where we came from.

Now, with the advent of adventure tour operators as well as the inevitable roads and airstrips, you can visit these remote areas with relative ease. Although tourism does have an impact on wilderness, many conservationists view it as a major factor in the preservation of these places, providing governments and local peoples with an economic incentive to protect their natural resources.

Jim Fowler, co-host of Mutual of Omaha's *Wild Kingdom*, author of *Jim Fowler's Wildest Places* (Time-Life Books, 1993), conservationist, and worldwide explorer, has lived with Bushmen in the Okavango Delta, rafted down wild rivers in Sumatra, rappelled down cliffs in Patagonia, and wrestled crocodiles and boa constrictors in Africa and South America. He knows the wildernesses of the world in a way that very few do. Here is his list of the wildest places in the world that should tempt any modern-day adventurer.

TORRES DEL PAINE, *Chile*

■ Designated a world biosphere reserve by the United Nations, this park comprises 935 square miles of pristine Patagonian wilderness. One of the world's most wind-battered places, it has great extremes of climate and contains some of the least-explored regions. The mountain peaks that pierce through the perpetual storm clouds are so steep that they were not successfully climbed until the 1950s. Runoff from huge ice fields feeds dense forests replete with lakes, streams, and prowling 150-pound pumas and dwarf deer. In mountain meadows there are herds of guanacos (relative of the llama). Farther down in the pampas, Darwin's rhea (a 3-foot-high flightless bird) grazes.

■ **JUMPING-OFF POINT.** Punta Arenas, the southernmost city in the world. Hotel Explora, bordering the park, provides comfortable accommodations for those who are averse to roughing it (☎ 56–2–228–8081; FAX 56–2–228–4655. In the U.S., you can also fax 800–858–0855).

■ **ESSENTIAL EQUIPMENT.** The best wind and wet weather clothing that you can afford.

SKELETON COAST, *Namibia*

■ When people refer to Namibia's Skeleton Coast as a place of haunting beauty, they aren't just using a figure of speech. The bones of lost adventurers, shipwrecked sailors, and dead animals lie here in perpetuity, preserved by the salt and lack of rain. At the same time, garnet crystals shimmer in the sun, shifting sands settle in curved dunes called *barchans*, and underground streams nourish long corridors of trees and bushes such as acacia and mopane. Wildlife—including elephants, black rhinos, and ostriches—flourish along this protected 300-mile strip of the Atlantic coast.

■ **JUMPING-OFF POINT.** Walvis Bay, a large town where there are inland camping areas with huts being developed for tourists.

■ **ESSENTIAL EQUIPMENT.** Wind and sun protection, especially bandannas and scarves for the face. Boots that lace up to keep sand out.

■ **TRAVEL ADVISORY.** Don't sleep on the beach. There are giant carnivorous land crabs, a foot tall and several feet wide. Much of the water is polluted; filter and boil it before using.

GUNUNG LEUSER NATIONAL PARK, *Indonesia*

■ The 3,120-square-mile park preserves what

is left of one of the world's most unusual and fastest-disappearing wildernesses. (Indonesia is the world's leading exporter of tropical hardwood.) This forest is haven to one of the richest varieties of plant and animal species found anywhere. Fowler reports that this is where he saw the largest concentrations of butterflies he has ever seen, massed in migration, sipping moisture on small sand beaches. The best way to visit this wilderness is along the Alas River, which descends through 10,000-foot-high Mount Alas.

■ **JUMPING-OFF POINT.** Madian, a city located several hours' drive from the Alas river. Mountain Travel–Sobek (☎ 800–227–2384) is one of the few operators that run rafting trips here.

■ **ESSENTIAL EQUIPMENT.** Extra insect repellent for brown jumping leeches, which can jump through the eyelets of your boots. Also, because of the humidity, avoid using waterproof tents; instead, sleep on a hammock underneath a tarpaulin.

ROYAL CHITWAN, *Nepal*

■ When malaria was eradicated in the 1950s, poachers and settlers streamed into the region, and the endangered rhino was decimated within a decade. With little time to lose, the king of Nepal established a rhino sanctuary. Today, the sanctuary is the 360-square-mile Chitwan National Park, which contains the best-preserved section of a jungle that used to run the entire length of southern Nepal. Within this region live a recovering Asian rhino population of 400 (a quarter of the world's total), tiger, king cobra, crocodile, and the sloth bear, which attacks unprovoked.

Despite the dangerous animals, this is one of the easier wild places to explore. Knowledgeable native guides from the villages can be hired. For less intrepid and more affluent explorers, elephant safaris are conducted from the Tiger Top Lodge (see below).

■ **JUMPING-OFF POINT.** Tiger Top Lodge inside the park has an airstrip where planes from Katmandu land. Contact Durbar Marg, P.O. Box 242, Katmandu, Nepal (TELEX: 2216 Tiger Top NP). Reserve 6 to 12 months in advance.

■ **ESSENTIAL EQUIPMENT.** Elephantback is the recommended mode of travel for viewing tigers and rhinoceroses.

WOLONG NATURE RESERVE, *China*

■ The western half of Sichuan province is one of the world's most densely populated places; the rugged eastern half is one of the greatest remaining wildernesses. If you take the tortuous two-week bus trip from Chengdu east to Lhasa in Tibet—aside from Litang (the highest settlement in the world)—you would just see pure wilderness.

The Wolong reserve preserves ecosystems ranging from 11,000-foot mountains to tropical rain forest. Also found here are some of the world's most famous endangered animals, including snow leopards and the largest remaining population of giant panda.

■ **JUMPING-OFF POINT.** From Chengdu, capital of Sichuan province, it is an 11-hour bone-jarring bus drive to the dormitories for ecotourists in Wolong Reserve.

■ **ESSENTIAL EQUIPMENT.** Although dormitories have mattresses, you won't regret bringing your own sleeping bag. Also, exchanging of gifts is customary in this region, so bring plenty of trinkets (preferably baseball hats).

■ **TRAVEL ADVISORY.** Watch out for the alcohol that is served at the dormitory; it is similar to moonshine.

LAKE BAIKAL, *Russia*

■ Lake Baikal is the oldest, the largest, the deepest, and one of the cleanest lakes in the world. It contains 20 percent of the world's freshwater (more than all five Great Lakes combined). Surrounding the lake is the world's largest contiguous forest, which extends more than 3,000 miles from the Ural mountains in the west to the Sea of Japan. The lake lies in a deep rift valley surrounded by tall mountains, which accounts for its high endemism; of the more than 2,500 species of plants and animals that live here 1,500 are unique to the lake. Some of the species include the Baikal seal (the only freshwater seal in the world), the sable, and the giant fish-eating flatworm.

■ **JUMPING-OFF POINT.** From Irkutsk on the southern tip of Lake Baikal take a launch or helicopter to Barguzin camp on the northern wild part of the lake.

■ **ESSENTIAL EQUIPMENT.** A cot—to avoid the

HE'D GO ANYWHERE—AND HE HAS

Travel pointers from the world's most-traveled man

Ever spin the globe, wondering what some far-off place is like? Well, John Clouse doesn't—because he's probably been there. Listed in the *Guinness Book of World Records* as the world's most-traveled man, Clouse, a 72-year-old lawyer, has been known to spend four months a year globetrotting. Here he offers some travel tips.

■ **What do you take when you travel?**

I take things that I can wash. Sometimes, I save old socks and underwear and things that I can throw away. I always dress down, but I usually bring a suit and tie just for those places that won't let you in if you are not wearing them. For shoes, I like something flexible and low-cut, like sneakers.

■ **Do you have tips on visiting dangerous places?**

Don't tell the driver until you get in the car—otherwise he won't take you. Also, always go in the morning; the revolutionaries and terrorists usually stay up late!

■ **What are some spectacular places that are often overlooked by tourists?**

Lake Naivasha in Kenya is one of the most gorgeous places on earth—like the Garden of Eden. Namibia has spectacular horizons and a beautiful feeling of openness. On Irian Jaya, Djajapura, with its dense foliage, hills, and inlets, is one of the most beautiful harbors in the world.

■ **Where is the most romantic place?**

Paris is the most romantic place on earth, but everyone knows that. Tahiti has been overrun, but the islands near it, such as Moorea and Raiatea, have that romance that people associate with the South Pacific. The landscape has a softness and femininity to it with palm trees swaying and beautiful intoxicating sultry breezes.

■ **Any other tips for the traveler?**

Bring a beautiful person of your sexual orientation. Sex always enhances a trip; it's also nice to share a trip with someone else.

---

rodents that live around the park. Also, fishing gear: Lake Baikal is a great place to fish.

ANTARCTIC PENINSULA

■ The landscape almost belongs on another planet. There are floating icebergs 50 miles wide, millions of penguins, and mirrorlike reflections of mountain peaks. After crossing the stormy seas of the Drake Passage, you enter a tranquil land of black still water, rock, and ice. However, the coast, skies, and seas teem with wildlife, including the 700-pound leopard seal and the giant albatross, the world's largest bird.

Because of the intense cold and ferocious terrain, terrestrial adventure is only for the very hardiest of adventure seekers. For all other travelers, cruise ships equipped with zodiac landing craft suffice. Fowler recommends including the Falkland Island, South Georgia Island, and the Ross Ice Shelf on your itinerary.

■ **JUMPING-OFF POINT.** Falkland Islands

■ **ESSENTIAL EQUIPMENT.** Your ship should have Russian ice breakers and two engines, in case the krill, the ubiquitous crustaceans that surround Antarctica, clog one of the ship's engines.

RORAIMA (THE LOST WORLD),
Venezuela, Guyana, Brazil

■ This equatorial ecosystem is vast, diverse, hot, wet, and primeval. Throughout the tropical forest are unique flat-topped mountains called "tepuis." It was these tepuis that inspired Conan Doyle's *The Lost World*. The

LIONS AND TIGERS AND BEARS, OH MY

You never know when you might confront a bear in the woods or a lion in the bush. Some beast-by-beast advice from adventurer Jim Fowler

not alone in an area inhabited by lions.

■ **RHINO:** Rhinos have bad eyesight and only attack if panicked. If you encounter a rhino, make sure that you give it plenty of distance.

■ **BROWN BEAR OR SLOTH BEAR:** Be aggressive and make a lot of noise. If you act submissive, you risk being attacked.

■ **GRIZZLY BEAR:** Act submissively, but if the bear is about to attack you, challenge it.

■ **TIGER:** Tigers will usually not attack unless they are able to sneak up on you or you have your

back turned. In Nepal, for instance, natives wear a mask with eyes in the back to scare them off. If you do encounter a tiger, act aggressively. Hopefully, this is enough to make the largest predator in the world flee.

■ **LION:** Lions will usually not attack people unless they do not have anything else to eat. Nevertheless, make sure that you are

■ **GORILLA:** When a gorilla attacks you, kneel down and don't look it in the eye.

tallest of the tepuis, Mount Roraima, has become a famous site for professional mountain climbers. In addition, Angel Falls, the largest waterfall in the world (20 times the height of Niagara Falls), is located here. Diamond snakes, giant anaconda snakes up to 20 feet long, and vampire bats are common.

■ **JUMPING-OFF POINT.** From Caracas, Venezuela, fly into Canaima, a small town at the outskirts of Canaima National Park. For the remotest parts there are landing fields in Guyana that can be reached from Georgetown, its capital.

■ **ESSENTIAL EQUIPMENT.** Machetes, light hammocks (the local ones are superior to ones from the States), and tarpaulins (instead of A-tents). Make sure that you have mosquito nets to fit the hammock to avoid getting buzzed by vampire bats.

MOUNTAINS OF THE MOON,
Zaire, Rwanda, Uganda

■ Located in a region with live volcanoes, the Mountains of the Moon comprise some of the most varied wildernesses in Africa. High, wet, and cold, these equatorial mountains support strange vegetation such as forests of gigantic lobelias (a plant that grows only a few feet high in North America) and rare animals such as the mountain gorilla. Mount Margherita soars to 16,000 feet.

■ **JUMPING-OFF POINT.** Kahuzi Biega in Zaire

■ **ESSENTIAL EQUIPMENT.** A good ski jacket and lots of clothing for layering.

■ **TRAVEL ADVISORY.** Locate your campsite away from a game trail and your hammock high enough so that if a lion chasing its prey goes through your camp, it will go under you.

INTO THE HEART OF AFRICA

There are more destinations for today's adventurer into the bush

For years, if you were heading out on a safari, you headed for the game parks of Kenya and Tanzania in East Africa—most notably Serengeti National Park, the Ngorongoro Conservation Area, and Masai Mara Natural Reserve—where huge herds of animals still wander across the plains. Nowhere else in Africa can you see such a vast collection of wildlife in its natural habitat. And there are safari options for every type of traveler from the pampered who treasure their creature comforts to the rugged outdoors person who doesn't mind being without a hot shower.

These days, however, others parts of Africa also beckon. The civil war that ravaged Uganda is over and outsiders are once again starting to visit the region, where gorilla and other primates can be seen. More notably, southern Africa (Namibia, Zimbabwe, and Botswana) is becoming a favored spot now that the political strife and guerrilla skirmishes that terrorized the region have seemingly ended.

Instead of the endless wide open savannahs of eastern Africa, immense swamps and forests predominate in southern Africa. In general, safaris to the southern part of the continent offer more options for the active tourist—from walking safaris to expeditions on elephant and horseback. Also, night drives are much more common, an activity prohibited in national parks in eastern Africa. Such forays afford a different perspective on the wild kingdom, since some animals, like leopards, are nocturnal.

Below, with the help of Gaby Whitehouse, former director of planning for Harvard's Comparative Museum of Zoology, John Hemingway, former chairman of the African Wildlife Foundation, and Peter Alden, co-author of the *The National Audubon Society Field Guide to African Wildlife* (Random House, 1995), is an assessment of the best game-viewing spots, and camps and lodges not to be missed in Africa. Note: for a successful safari, timing is all. At certain times of the year the animals you wish to see may be away on migration or dispersed amid thick vegetation during the rainy season, so plan ahead.

EAST AFRICA

KENYA

■ Kenya has the highest concentrations of animals and tourists. Its biggest draw is the greatest game migration on the planet, which moves from the Serengeti in Tanzania up to the Masai Mara every year. Over a million wildebeests and hundreds of thousands of zebra can be found here from mid-July to mid-September. The best places to see game are in central Kenya at the national parks—Tsavo, Samburu, Amboseli, and Masai Mara (which boasts the largest lion population in Africa). Visitors to the national parks must be able to countenance the crowds as well as the constraints of watching the game from within an open safari vehicle.

Kenya is also one of the best places in the world to see birds; over 1,000 species of birds live here in a variety of different habitats. In addition, Kenya has some of the most varied and distinctive tribal cultures in Africa, including the Masai, who still maintain their traditional nomadic life.

EXPERT PICK ☛ Little Governors Camp. One of the smaller fixed-tented camps located near the epicenter of wildlife viewing, this camp is a welcome escape from the more mass-market tourist camps in the Masai Mara preserve.
✑ P.O. Box 48217, Nairobi; ☎ 254–2–33104

TANZANIA

■ Tanzania has Kenya's game without the crowds, albeit this is in good part due to its less-developed tourist facilities and much bumpier roads. The Serengeti and the

Ngorongoro Crater (the largest caldera in the world and the best place to see black rhino in Africa) abound with large herds of zebra and wildebeest. Like Kenya, tourists are restricted to safari vehicles in the national parks. For more adventurous walking or canoe safaris, head south to the Selous Game Reserve, the largest wildlife preserve in Africa, uninhabited except for a half dozen small tourist camps.

EXPERT PICK ☞ Tarangire Safari Lodge. Like the permanent tented camps of the old days—simple, secluded, and with a setting that cannot be beat. It is perched on a cliff overlooking a mini rift valley filled with zebras and wildebeests.
✎ Factory area, plot 2/3, Box 1182, Arusha
☎ 255–57–6886/6896

UGANDA

■ This landlocked country is mostly forested and mountainous, with a terrain reminiscent of Asia—very green, with terraced farming. Having recently emerged from a time of terror and political instability, Uganda is one of the most exciting places to visit in Africa right now. It is the best place in Africa to see primates and also the only safe place (safe from warring humans that is) where one can comfortably see gorillas. Visitors to the primate forests—the most notable of which is called the Bwini or Impenetrable Forest—must be ready for hard hikes and prepared for occasional deluges of rain.

EXPERT PICK ☞ Buhoma Gorilla Camp. One of the few outfitters with an established presence in Uganda, this is a very comfortable fixed-tented camp from which hikes are arranged into the primate-inhabited forests. Run by Abercrombie & Kent (see box on page 418 for how to contact).

SOUTHERN AFRICA

BOTSWANA

■ One of the most popular safari countries in southern Africa, Botswana has incredible wildlife, comfortable isolated safari lodges, and good transportation. The government has been successful so far in keeping out the large mass-market tent camps and lodges, which makes Botswana a more expensive place to visit than other African countries. While much of the country is arid and desertlike, the Okavango delta, in the northern part of the country, is like a primordial oasis. The only inland delta in the world, the Okavango is a lush swamp whose numerous rivulets and waterways empty directly into the Kalahari desert; the best way to explore it is by canoe. It's also one of the few bodies of fresh water in Africa where westerners can swim without worrying about parasites. In addition, this wilderness contains more plant species than all the rain forests of West and Central Africa combined. Adjoining the Okavango, the Moremi Reserve and Chobe National Park have one of the most varied and greatest concentrations of wildlife (including some of the largest elephant herds) in Africa. Botswana is also, together with Namibia, home to the majority of the 60,000 Bushmen in Africa.

EXPERT PICK ☞ Xaxaba Tented Camp. A small tented camp in the western and most remote part of the Okavango delta, Xaxaba is a particularly good location to see wildlife, since it is the camp that is located farthest away from the hunting preserves.
✎ P.O. Box 147, Maun, Botswana
☎ 267–660–351

ZIMBABWE

■ This is one of the all-around best countries to go on a safari. Zimbabwe has a good tourist infrastructure, excellent conservation programs, and offers perhaps the widest variety of safari options, including walking, kayaking, houseboat safaris, and some of the best white-water rafting in the world. In addition, the camps and lodges here are usually small scale, have good food, and offer personalized service. Seven percent of the country is protected, and the national parks—especially Mana Pools, located on the Zambezi river gorge—offer opportunities to see one of the greatest concentra-

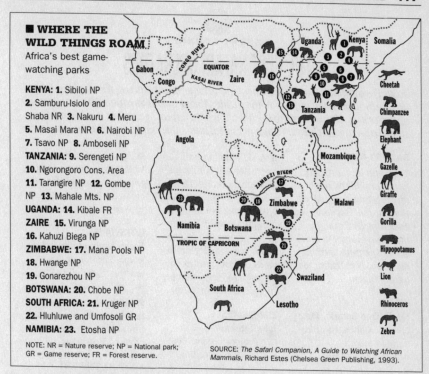

■ WHERE THE WILD THINGS ROAM

Africa's best game-watching parks

KENYA: 1. Sibiloi NP
2. Samburu-Isiolo and Shaba NR **3.** Nakuru **4.** Meru
5. Masai Mara NR **6.** Nairobi NP
7. Tsavo NP **8.** Amboseli NP
TANZANIA: 9. Serengeti NP
10. Ngorongoro Cons. Area
11. Tarangire NP **12.** Gombe NP **13.** Mahale Mts. NP
UGANDA: 14. Kibale FR
ZAIRE: 15. Virunga NP
16. Kahuzi Biega NP
ZIMBABWE: 17. Mana Pools NP
18. Hwange NP
19. Gonarezhou NP
BOTSWANA: 20. Chobe NP
SOUTH AFRICA: 21. Kruger NP
22. Hluhluwe and Umfosoli GR
NAMIBIA: 23. Etosha NP

NOTE: NR = Nature reserve; NP = National park; GR = Game reserve; FR = Forest reserve.

SOURCE: *The Safari Companion, A Guide to Watching African Mammals*, Richard Estes (Chelsea Green Publishing, 1993).

tions of wildlife during the dry season.

EXPERT PICK ☛ Victoria Falls Hotel. Located by the falls, the highest in Africa, this is one of the continent's grand old hotels. The terrace is perfect for high tea as well as for viewing the sunsets.
✏ P.O. Box 10, Victoria Falls, Zimbabwe
☎ 800–521–7242 (For reservations in U.S.)

ZAMBIA

■ More of a challenge to get to and travel through than other African countries, Zambia rewards the intrepid traveler. The Luangwa Valley is one of the most beautiful places in Africa. Crisscrossed by numerous rivers, the valley is home to many birds, African buffalo, hippos, crocodiles, zebras, and elephants. Walking and night safaris are readily available.

EXPERT PICK ☛ Chibembe Lodge. A 40-bed lodge and base for walking safaris. The lodge has a pool and landscaped grounds.

✏ Eagle Travel, Permanent House, Cairo Road, Box 35254, Lusaka;
☎ 260–1–229060/226857

MALAWI

■ There is not much tourism in Malawi, although there are numerous game-watching opportunities. Lake Malawi, which takes up a fifth of the country, contains over 300 varieties of fish, the greatest diversity of tropical freshwater fish of any lake in the world; it's also an excellent snorkeling spot. Zomba plateau, an enormous 8,000-foot plateau that topographically looks like Switzerland—except for the plethora of brilliantly colored orchids, and the leopards and antelope roaming about—can be explored on horseback.

EXPERT PICK ☛ Club Makokola. This hotel's comfortable rooms located right on the beach offer beautiful views of Lake Malawi.
✏ P.O. Box 59, Mangochi, Malawi
☎ 265–584–244 FAX 265–584–417

THE BEST SAFARI OPERATORS

John Hemingway, board member and former chairman of the African Wild-life Foundation, recommends the guides listed below as among the best safari operators in Africa. Generally, his choices are small-scale but highly professional operations that arrange personalized safaris and small group tours.

SAFARI GUIDES

Trips run by old Africa hands provide an opportunity to see a side of Africa that few tourists do. If you book directly through these operators, you may get a 15 percent discount that would otherwise go to a travel agent.

KENYA:
Flame Tree Safaris, Ltd.
Chrissie Aldrich, Box 82, Nanyuki, Kenya
☎ 254–176–22053
■ Chrissie Aldrich arranges mobile tented camp and walking tours on private preserves.

TANZANIA:
Richard Bonham Safaris
P.O. Box 24133, Nairobi, Kenya, ☎254–2–882521
TELEX 25547 BONHAM
■ Outfitted author and photographer Peter Matthiessen for the safari chronicled in *Sand Rivers* (out of print). Conducts walking tours and other expeditions in Tanzania and in Kenya.

UGANDA:
Abercrombie & Kent
1420 Kensington Road, Oak Brook, IL 60521
☎800–323–7308

■ A&K is not a small operation—it runs trips all over the world—but it is one of the few outfitters with a presence in Uganda. Trips there, however, are contingent upon ever-changing security conditions in that country, so be prepared for a change in a planned trip there.

ZIMBABWE:
John Stevens
C/o Fothergill Island, Post Bag 2081, Kariba, Zimbabwe; FAX 263–61–2253
■ Stevens is a guide who operates small walking safaris, canoe safaris, and mobile tented camp safaris from a seven-bed tented camp located near the Zambezi river.

ZAMBIA:
Robin Pope Safaris Ltd.
P.O. Box 320154, Lusaka, Zambia
■ From Tena Tena camp, a small base camp set on the Luangwa River, Robin Pope conducts walking safaris and movable tent safaris.

MALAWI:
Heart of Africa Safaris
P.O. Box 8, Lilongwe, Malawi, ☎ 265–740848

■ Run by David Foote, a well-known operator who arranges horseback safaris in the high country as well as walking safaris.

BOTSWANA:
Soren Linderstrom Safaris
Private Bag, Maun, Botswana; ☎ 267–660–994; FAX: 267–660–493
■ Linderstrom specializes in mobile photography safaris to remote parts of Botswana.

SAFARI TRAVEL AGENTS

Safari travel agents can book lodges, safaris, and tented camps throughout Africa as well as make travel arrangements.

■ **BUSHBUCK SAFARIS**
48 High St., Hungerford, Berkshire, Eng., RG17 One
☎011–44–1–488–684702
FAX 011–44–684868

■ **OVERSEAS ADVENTURE TRAVEL**
629 Mt. Auburn St. Cambridge, MA 02138
☎800–221–0814

■ **AFRICAN TRAVEL**
1000 East Broadway Glendale, CA 91205
☎800–421–8907

RAIN **FORESTS**
▼

GLORIES OF THE WET AND WILD

More life thrives in these tropical habitats than anywhere else

Tropical rain forests occupy only 7 percent of the earth's land surface, yet they contain over half its living organisms. What makes all that life possible is warm weather—averaging 80 degrees—and, of course, rain—lots of it. Tropical rain forests average 100 to 400 inches of rainfall a year, whereas New York City receives 43 inches a year and San Francisco only about 20 inches a year.

In contrast to other places on earth, most of the plant life in rain forests is in the treetops. Below this primary canopy is a secondary one where shrubs and smaller trees grow. Plant life on the forest floor is limited because of the lack of light.

Where should one go to witness the glories of the rain forests up close? Thomas Lovejoy, special adviser to the Smithsonian Institution, and Russell Mittermeier, president of Conservation International, suggested these South American spots; James Castner, a tropical scientist and author of *Rain Forests: A Guide to Research and Tourist Facilities* (now out of print), who has visited these forests, recommended the best lodges in which to stay.

COSTA RICA

Costa Rican rain forests do not have the staggering variety of species or sheer density of plant and animal life of the most significant rain forests in the world, such as those along the eastern Andes. However, they contain about 5 percent of the world's plants and animals.
RATE OF DEPLETION: *Costa Rica has the highest annual rate of deforestation in Central America.*

PARQUE NACIONAL CORCOVADO
On the Peninsula de Osa, about 115 miles southeast of San José.

■ The largest primary lowland rain forest in Costa Rica. Over 400 species of birds live here, including scarlet macaws. The park is also home to pumas, ocelots, tapirs, and jaguars, as well as numerous rare butterflies and the almost extinct Harpy eagle.

MONTEVERDE CLOUD FOREST RESERVE
A four-hour drive north of San José.

Situated on a mountain 4,600 feet above sea level, the reserve is a tropical cloud forest where constant low clouds hover in the treetops, creating a highly humid environment. The park contains over 2,000 species of wildlife, including mantled howler monkeys. Also, one of the last remaining nesting sites of the quetzal, reputedly the most beautiful bird in the world.

EXPERT PICK ☛ **Costa Rica Expeditions** operates small deluxe eco-sensitive lodges in both Corcovado, at the edge of the forest on the beach, and in Monteverde National Park—with Jacuzzis, fireplaces, and excellent food. ✆ Mikail Kaye, Costa Rica Expeditions, ☎ 506-257-0766   FAX 506–257–1665 E-MAIL: *Crexped@sol.Rasca.Co.Cr*

EASTERN SLOPES OF THE ANDES
This area extends from the southern part of the Colombian Amazon through Ecuador and Peru. Norman Myers, a leading expert on biodiversity, says these rain forests constitute the richest biotic zone on earth.
RATE OF DEPLETION: *According to Myers, 90 percent of the original forest will have been converted to agriculture or have been damaged by extractive industries by the year 2000, and 50 percent of the species will have disappeared or be near extinction.*

YASUNI NATIONAL PARK
The Oriente region of Ecuador.

■ The lakes in Yasuni National Park are home to piranhas and caimans (relatives of the crocodile). A number of Indian tribes also live here, including the Waorani, who until recently have avoided contact with outsiders.

EXPERT PICK ☛ La Selva Lodge, located on Garzacocha Lake, accommodates 35, is easily accessible, and has won eco-tourism awards.
☞ Eric Schwartz, La Selva Lodge, 6 de Diciembre 2816, P.O. Box 1712–635 Quito, Ecuador
☎ 593–2–550–995/554–686   FAX 567–297

TAMBOPATA-CAUDANO RESERVE AREA AND NATIONAL PARK

About 40 miles south of Puerto Maldonado in the Madre de Dios region of Peru.

■ This park is contiguous with the Madidi National Park in Peru, and together the two form the largest uninterrupted rain forest on earth. Tambopata-Caudano is also the best place to see butterflies—over 1,100 species live here. In addition, this park has the largest known macaw lick in South America.

EXPERT PICK ☛ The Explorers Inn is located only 100 meters from the Tambopata River. It has accommodations for 75 in seven bungalow-style buildings. There is a bar, library, and a bathroom in each room, but no electricity.
☞ Dr. Max Gunther, Peruvian Safaris S.A. Garcilazo de la Vegas 1334, P.O. Box 10088, Lima, Peru
☎ 51–1–431–304–7   FAX: 51–1–432–88–66

MANU NATIONAL PARK

About 75 miles northeast of Cuzco in Peru.

■ AND DON'T FORGET YOUR RAIN GEAR

The following groups organize eco-sensitve expeditions to many of the rain forests discussed here.

INTERNATIONAL EXPEDITIONS
Helena, Ala.   ☎ 800–633–4734

MOUNTAIN TRAVEL/SOBEK EXPEDITIONS
El Cerrito, Calif.   ☎ 800–227–2384

VICTOR EMANUEL NATURE TOURS
Austin, Texas   ☎ 800–328–8368

FIELD GUIDES
Austin, Texas   ☎ 512–327–4953

RAIN FOREST VENTURES
Gainesville, Fla.   ☎ 352–371–6439

■ This rain forest is the largest biosphere reserve zone in South America. It has the highest documented diversity of life in the world, containing an estimated 8,000 plant species, 200 animal species, and over 900 species of birds.

EXPERT PICK ☛ The Manu Lodge is a small, remote but comfortable rustic building built from mahogany logs taken from the Manu River. It accommodates 25 guests. A small electric generator powers appliances, and latrines are a short walk away. The food is simple, but good.
☞ Boris Gomez, Manu Nature Tours, Avenida Pardo 1046, Cuzco, Peru
☎ 51–84–252721   FAX 51–84–234793
E-MAIL: *MNT@Amauta.RCP.NET.PA*

ATLANTIC FOREST REGION RAINFOREST, BRAZIL

This belt of rain forest once extended along the coast of South America; today, only a small portion remains. Up to half of the plant species found here are not found anywhere else. The forest contains the largest variety of primates in South America— over 24 different species.
RATE OF DEPLETION: *Most of the remaining rain forest is partially protected, but it still faces threats from expanding agriculture, logging, and industrial development.*

ITATIAIA NATIONAL PARK

Located halfway between Rio de Janeiro and São Paulo near the town of Itatiaia, Brazil.

■ This park, with its numerous hiking trails, is very accessible. Over 100 plants found here are endemic to the Atlantic rain forest. Itatiaia National Park is also home to the pale-throated three-toed sloth and the red-breasted toucan.

EXPERT PICK ☛ Rustic accommodations are available in the park and should be booked 30 days in advance during the busy season. There are also several hotels in the park's perimeter.
☞ Administração do Parque Nacional de Itatiaia, Caixa Postal 83657, Itatiaia 27580–000 RJ, Brazil
☎ 0243–52–1652

GOING FOR THE GREEN

When it comes to defining "eco-tour," lexicographers must be scratching their heads. Like "natural," "eco-tour" is a label used to sell such a wide variety of offerings that it has almost lost its meaning. To help clear things up, we went to Lisa Tabb, editor and publisher of EcoTraveler magazine. Tabb defines a successful eco-tour as "a trip that provides a financial incentive for communities to preserve intact cultures and ecosystems." Here, she recommends trips that epitomize eco-tourism at its best.

SAIL IN THE GALAPAGOS

■ Small sailboats glide noiselessly among these starkly beautiful islands, enabling you to get up close to multitudes of rare reptiles and birds.
☞Mountain Travel–Sobek
☎800–227–2384

POLAR BEAR WATCHING IN MANITOBA

■ From October through November, this outfit operates trips out in Manitoba in southern Canada. Tundra buggies keep you propped up high enough to safely get within 10 feet of a polar bear.
☞Tundra Buggy Tours
☎204–675–2121

CAMEL TREK IN ISRAEL

■ Live like a Bedouin for seven days as you plod across Israel's Negev desert by camelback.
☞Society for Protection of Nature of Israel, 3 Hasfela St., Tel Aviv, Israel
☎011971–369–0644

THE MAYAS IN BELIZE

■ In southern Belize, outside of Punta Gorda, you can hike from Mayan village to Mayan village staying along the way in Mayan guest houses and eating with Mayan families.
☞Mayan Guesthouse Program, Nature's Way, 65 Front St., Punta Gorda, Belize
☎ 501–7–22119

TRACKING GAME IN SOUTH AFRICA

■ Conservation Corporation owns some of the highest-end lodges in South Africa. At Phinda lodge you stay in a glass-walled cabin, propped high enough above the bush to allow lions to meander underneath. There are expeditions for tracking rhinos, giraffes, and elephants with reformed poachers-turned-guides.
☞For U.S. bookings: Baobob Safari Tours
☎415–391–5788;
Park East Tours
☎800–223–6078; or
Abercrombie & Kent
☎800–323–7308

ABORIGINES IN AUSTRALIA

■ Spend eight days on a reserve where non-Aborigines are allowed only with special permission. There you will sleep under the stars and meet Pitjantjatjara elders who speak only their native tongue.
Adventure Center
☎510–654–1879 (ask about Desert Track Tours)

YURT-TO-YURT CROSS-COUNTRY SKIING IN IDAHO

■ Cross-country ski all day long in the Sawtooth Mountains and then return to a backcountry yurt where a gourmet meal, hot mulled wine, and a wood-burning sauna await.
☞Bob Jonas, Sun Valley Trekking ☎208–788–9585

CAMP ON A VIRGIN ISLAND

■ This is your basic beautiful Caribbean beach resort, but the lodging at Maho Bay camp on St. John in the U.S. Virgin Islands is made from recycled plastic, the bread is baked in a solar oven, and the food is organic.
☞Maho Bay Booking, 17A E. 73rd. St., NY, NY 10021
☎800–392–9004

TOURISME VERT IN FRANCE

■ For as little as $50 a night you can stay at a farmhouse inn and eat gourmet food with a working farmer.
☞Maison de Gites, 35 rue Godot-de-Mauroy, 75439 Paris Cedex 09

THE PYRAMIDS NEXT DOOR

Mayan ruins are as magnificent as those in Egypt—and a lot closer

Scattered throughout Central America are more ancient cities and ruins than are found in all of Egypt. They are from the Mayan civilization, the most advanced and longest lived in ancient America. Starting in 300 B.C., the Mayans built metropolises that rivaled those of Rome and Greece—complete with large pyramids, ornate palaces, and temples.

Mayan civilization was highly developed. The people built libraries and developed a calendar more accurate than that of the Spanish, who arrived in the 1520s and conquered them. Their understanding of astronomy enabled them to predict lunar and solar eclipses. But in A.D. 900, because of war and possibly diminishing natural resources, Mayan civilization began to decline.

La Ruta Maya, also known as Mundo Maya, is a 1,500-mile route that runs through the lands of the Maya—western Honduras, northern Belize, Guatemala, El Salvador, and the Mexican states of Yucatán, Quintana Roo, Tabasco, Campeche, and Chiapas. Mostly paved, the route is a modern creation, dedicated to the preservation of Mayan heritage and wildlife habitats. Although most travelers will not have time to travel the whole route, below is a list of some of the most significant Mayan cities, compiled with the help of Gordon Willey, professor of archaeology at Harvard, and Joyce Kelley, author of *An Archeological Guide to Mexico's Yucatán Peninsula* (University of Oklahoma Press, 1993).

CALAKMUL, Campeche, Mexico

Calakmul was one of the largest Mayan cities. It is estimated that over 60,000 people have lived here at one time. One of the oldest Mayan sites, it was established around 1500 B.C. So far, 6,500 structures have been mapped at Calakmul, including a 175-foot-high, 500-square-foot pyramid. From the top of it one can see the Danta Pyramid at El Mirador, another preclassic Mayan city over 20 miles away.

Only recently, Calakmul, located in a large jungle reserve, was reachable only by an overgrown jeep path. However, now a road has been built into the site, and travel time from the main road is only several hours.

■ **NEARBY:** The principal attractions are the Calakmul Reserve, a few under-visited but significant Mayan sites, and the lively ambience of small Mexican farm towns such as Escarcega. An excellent place from which to make day excursions, Escarcega offers a variety of budget accommodations.

CHICHÉN ITZÁ, Yucatán, Mexico

Over 3 million people visit Chichén Itzá each year; it is the most well known and most extensively excavated Mayan city. Built around A.D. 500, it was the most important city in the late classic period. Between the 11th and 13th centuries, this was where some of the last great Mayan buildings were constructed. Of all the Mayan cities, Chichén Itzá has the most varied architecture and sculpture, due in part to the influence of the Toltec Indian civilization of central Mexico.

■ **NEARBY:** Most of the tourist facilities near Chichén Itzá are overpriced. The resorts of Cancún (a two-hour drive away) and the coast immediately south of it have some of the world's flashiest and most famous resorts.

UXMAL, Yucatán, Mexico

Uxmal has some of the finest of the restored ruins and is considered by many to be the most beautiful of the Mayan cities. Many important satellite sites such as Kabah, Sayil, and Labnó are nearby.

Uxmal is where Mayan civilization reached its apogee in the years between A.D. 800 and 1000. The Governor's Palace is testimony to the Mayan's knowledge of astronomy. The central doorway of this 24-room building is aligned with the path of the planet Venus. At the bright planet's southern sol-

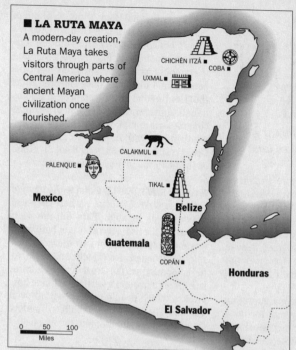

■ LA RUTA MAYA

A modern-day creation, La Ruta Maya takes visitors through parts of Central America where ancient Mayan civilization once flourished.

CHICHÉN ITZÁ ■
COBA ■
UXMAL ■
CALAKMUL ■
PALENQUE ■
TIKAL ■
Mexico
Belize
Guatemala
COPÁN ■
Honduras
El Salvador

0   50   100
Miles

winter solstice, the sun enters a doorway, hits the back wall, and appears to descend the stairway into a tomb.

■ **NEARBY:** Adjacent to the ruins is a campground where bohemian tourists eat the same psychedelic mushrooms that the Maya did. About 30 miles away are two famous waterfalls, Agua Azul and Misol-Ha.

TIKAL, Tikal National Park, Guatemala

Tikal was a great commercial and political power from 100 B.C. to A.D. 900. Plaza Mayor features well-restored buildings dating from 200 B.C. The 212-foot-tall temple is the second-tallest pyramid built by the Mayans.

■ **NEARBY:** The area known as the Petén is one of the most remote on the Ruta Maya. Eighteen miles from Tikal is Flores, the regional capital of the Petén, where accommodations are expensive and often crowded. A pleasant and inexpensive alternative place to stay is El Gringo Perdido campground on Lake Petén Itzá.

COPÁN, Honduras

The southernmost Mayan city, Copán lies in one of the most remote parts of Honduras. For more than 1,000 years, Copán was a center of culture and learning. The Hieroglyphic Stairway is composed of 2,500 blocks of stone and records the history of 17 rulers of a single royal dynasty. Fine pottery, jewelry, and jade carvings are on display at the Museo Regional de Arqueológica near the site.

■ **NEARBY:** Copán Ruinas, one of a number of interesting Spanish colonial villages in the area, is situated a few miles from the ruins. There are some small hotels here that offer simple but comfortable lodgings. About 10 miles from Copán is Agua Caliente, where one can swim in hot springs.

stice, the doorway is suffused with light illuminating the throne in the courtyard, as well as a temple on a hilltop 10 kilometers away.

■ **NEARBY:** Several hours' drive away is Mérida. Built by the Spanish in the 16th century, Mérida has fine examples of Spanish colonial architecture, excellent cuisine, a vibrant nightlife, and is a good departure point for many day trips to the Gulf Coast.

COBA, Quintana Roo, Mexico

Located in a jungle, the mainly unexcavated ruins of Coba, connected by Mayan limestime causeways, cover an area of 20 square miles. From the 140-foot-high Nohoch Mul pyramid, the views across the jungle and of the other ruins are magnificent.

■ **NEARBY:** About 25 miles away is Tulum, a Mayan site by the sea, south of which are pristine beaches bordered by verdant jungles.

PALENQUE, Chiapas, Mexico

In 1952, an excavation uncovered the intact tomb of Lord Pacal, one of the greatest Mayan kings, who ruled the city in the 7th century. At

VIETNAM
▼

BACK TO THE RICE PADDIES

An old Asia hand's tour of the beautiful, war-ravaged land

I t's probably the last place a Vietnam vet expected he would ever visit again. At the height of the Vietnam War there were over half a million American soldiers stationed in this faraway land. The last Americans left in 1975 as Saigon fell, evacuated from the roof of the American embassy by helicopter. It wasn't America's finest hour.

These days, former Vietcong guerrillas are laying out the welcome mat for once-reviled capitalists. Whether there are bitter memories of the war, of course, remains to be seen. Bombing targets are now tourist traps. But the countryside, dotted with rice paddies and pagodas, is still as beautiful as it always was, and the cities are teeming with energy. Saigon, once known as the Paris of the Orient, may one day soon reclaim the moniker. Stanley Karnow covered the Vietnam War as a journalist and later wrote *Vietnam: A History* (Viking/Penguin, 1984), which was also a PBS television series. Here are his sight-seeing recommendations:

■ **(HO CHI MINH CITY) SAIGON.** Saigon still has the look of a 19th-century French provincial capital. The architecture from that time predominates, with a legacy that includes a replica of the Paris Opera and a Cathedral of Notre Dame. The most interesting and beautiful building is the old French City Hall, called the Hôtel de Ville—now the headquarters of the Ho Chi Minh's People's Party. Visitors are not allowed inside, but the elegant facade is worth going to see, especially at night when it is covered with little lizards called geckos.

The Continental Hotel, which was built in 1880 and was the setting of Graham Greene's novel *The Quiet American*, has the most distinctive accommodations in town. Around the famous terrace bar (now an enclosed air-conditioned pizzeria), once referred to as the "Continental Shelf," secret agents, journalists, underworld figures, and prostitutes congregated during the Vietnam War. For traditional Vietnamese fare, the Lemon Grass restaurant at 63 Dong Khoi St. is one of the tastiest and most atmospheric.

■ **CAODAI GREAT TEMPLE.** Outside the town of Tay Ninh, west of Saigon, is where the see of Caodaism is located. This unique sect, founded in the 1920s, incorporates both western and eastern icons: among the venerated spirits are Victor Hugo, Gandhi, and Lenin. At the compound are the Great Temple, administrative offices, and a herbal medicine hospital to which people travel from all over Vietnam. The large temple is built on nine levels, which represent the steps to heaven.

■ **MEKONG DELTA.** Some of the most savage fighting during the Vietnam War took place in the picturesque countryside of the Mekong delta. Cantho, a small city in Tien Giang province, is an excellent place from which to take a boat trip through the mangrove forest swamps and tall grasses, where the Vietcong sought refuge from American bombs. Another interesting place to visit is Mytho, the capital of Tien Giang province, where the boat trips are much more expensive because they are controlled by the government.

■ **DALAT.** A six-hour drive from Saigon, this beautiful, largely French-built hill town is one of the most scenic cities in Vietnam. Long a resort area as well as an escape from the stultifying heat of the Mekong delta, wealthy Vietnamese and French expatriates built some outstanding villas here. Among the great houses is the old emperor's palace, now the Palace Hotel, owned and operated by an American. Because both sides used the area as a getaway from the war there was not the destruction here that occurred in the rest of the country.

ANGKOR WAT'S MAGNIFICENT TEMPLES

During the reign of terror in Cambodia that followed the end of the Vietnam War, the Khmer Rouge killed thousands of their countrymen. However, except for a few bullet holes, the brutal regime left largely intact the ruins of what was once the most magnificent city in Indochina, Angkor. Now, most of the land mines around the site have been removed and Angkor's numerous and elaborate temples are once again beguiling visitors.

The earliest of the ruins collectively known as Angkor date from the 9th century when King Jayavarman established a capital at Rouluous, southeast of the modern town of Siem Reap. At its height, the Khmer empire extended from the coasts of Vietnam to the borders of Burma. Angkor Wat, the most famous of the ruins, as well as one of the better preserved, was built in the 12th century. The walls of Angkor Thom, one of the successive capitals in the area, enclose a space larger than that of any medieval European city.

The Khmer cities were allegorical representations of the heavens, built around temples constructed atop natural or manmade hills. Most of the architecture combines Hindu and Buddhist symbolism. Angkor Wat boasts the longest bas-relief in existence, extending over 12,000 feet.

If you go: Allow at least two or three days to adequately take in the most significant sites near Angkor. There are daily flights from Phnom Penh to Siem Riep, and occasional direct flights from Ho Chi Minh City in Vietnam. A small town oriented toward tourism, Siem Riep has a variety of accommodations, from budget to luxury. Most travelers arrive as part of tour groups. However, Angkor is accessible to the independent traveler. For more information, contact Phnom Penh tourism (FAX) 855–23–26043.

■ **HANOI.** One of the oldest cities in Asia, Hanoi is more subdued than Saigon, but recently it has started to emulate Saigon's frenetic moneymaking pace. Architecturally, Hanoi is more interesting and unique. A style called Norman Pagoda, a hodgepodge of French and Asian architecture, predominates here. The 36 area streets (each named for a separate craft: weavers, dyers, goldsmiths, etc.) have a lively marketplace where you'll find some of the most talented artisans and craftspeople in Indochina. Ten miles outside Hanoi is the village of Bat Trang, whose 3,000 inhabitants pursue a tradition of ceramic making that goes back over six centuries.

■ **HA LONG BAY.** Occupying a central place in Vietnamese mythology, art, and history, the strangely shaped islands of Ha Long Bay are truly among the most magnificent sights in Vietnam. Situated about a 12-hour drive north of Hanoi, the over 1,600 limestone islands look magical with their grottoes, caves, dense foliage, and secret beaches. Here is where a strange Loch Ness–type monster supposedly prowls. Ho Chi Minh's old summer villa is located here. You can rent a boat for around $50 a day and go exploring throughout the islands and caves.

■ **SE PA.** This area is just beginning to be discovered by Western tourists. Se Pa is a French hill station that was built in the remote mountains of northwest Vietnam and abandoned during the colonial war in the 1950s. Today, it bears little trace of this or any other Western influence. About a 12-hour train trip from Hanoi, Se Pa is an excellent base from which to visit the Hmong, Zao, and Tay tribes who still practice their traditional cultures. From the town, arrangements can be made to climb Fan Si Pan, which, at 10,300 feet, is the highest mountain in Vietnam.

SLOW BOATS THROUGH EUROPE

With your craft moving at a snail's pace, you won't miss a thing

Before roads, canals and rivers were the major thoroughfares of Europe, crisscrossing the fields and wending their way through towns. Almost all the major cities of Europe were built on the banks of a river. Canals are hardly the avenues of commerce they once were, but they haven't fallen into total disuse. Pleasure boats and refitted barges laden with tourists now ply the waterways. At 8 to 12 mph, the scenery hardly goes whizzing by—and that's the beauty and charm of this antiquated mode of travel. The canals pass through some of the oldest and most picturesque parts of many European towns. It's possible for passengers to disembark for a leisurely walk or bicycle ride. The quarters on board have been modernized. Depending on the barge, the food can be of gourmet standard.

FACT FILE:

ALONG EUROPE'S WATERWAYS

■ *Approximate lengths of (mainly) interconnected navigable rivers and canals*

England and Wales	3,500 miles
Scotland	167 miles
Ireland	500 miles
France	5,000 miles
Germany	4,430 miles
Belgium	969 miles
Netherlands	4,600 miles

There are several barge options: Hotel barges are the most leisurely way to go; you don't have to maneuver boats into locks, and meals, cocktails, and excursions are included. However, the price can run to $300–$500 per person per day. Less pricey are self-driven barges, which accommodate 4 to 10 people. Many of these are converted commercial vessels and can be steered by a beginner, after a minimal amount of instruction. In France the average price of a four-person self-drive barge is about $1,000 a week.

We asked Hugh McKnight, one of the pioneers in the self-drive barge vacation who has taken barge trips throughout Europe for the past 30 years and is the author of many books on barges, including *Cruising French Waterways* and *Slow Boat Through Germany* (available through Shepperton Swan Ltd. in England ☎ 44–181–01932), to recommend the continent's best barge trips.

ENGLAND

■ **LEEDS AND LIVERPOOL CANAL.** This early 19th-century waterway in the north of England connects the east and west coasts via the rugged moorland scenery of Yorkshire and Lancashire. The canal features stone-built locks, many manually operated swing bridges, and appealing small mill towns.

■ **RIVER THAMES.** A historic and beautiful river with locks and weirs, crossing southern England from London to Gloucestershire and the Cotswolds. Famous towns and cities include Windsor (an 11th-century royal castle), Henley (Europe's premier rowing regatta), and the university center of Oxford.

SCOTLAND

■ **CALEDONIAN CANAL.** This early 19th-century engineering feat provides a coast-to-coast navigation through the Scottish Highlands from Fort William to Inverness. Spectacular "staircase" (multiple-chambered) locks and lengths of artificial canal link a series of natural lakes, including Loch Ness, renowned for its elusive monster.

IRELAND

■ **RIVER SHANNON.** The longest waterway in

WHERE TO RENT-A-BARGE

Author, barge veteran, and trip guide Hugh McKnight offers these suggestions. He can be reached in England at ☎ 44–181–01932.

HOTEL BARGES & SHIPS

U. K. W. H. LTD.
■ British waterways.
✇1, Port Hill, Hertford, SG14 1PJ ☎ FAX (441992) 587392

HIGHLAND MINI-CRUISES
■ Luxury barge cruises in Scotland's Caledonian Canal.
✇Muirtown Top Lock, Caledonian Canal, Inverness, Scotland, IV3 6NF ☎ (441463) 711913

RENT A CANAL CRUISER

CROWN BLUE LINE LTD.
■ Britain, France, Netherlands, also Erie Canal, USA.
✇8 Ber St., Norwich, Norfolk, NR1 3EJ. Great Britain ☎ (441603) 630513

HOSEASONS HOLIDAYS
■ Britain and France.
✇Sunway House, Lowestoft, Suffolk, NR32 3LT, Great Britain ☎ (441502) 501010

FRENCH COUNTRY CRUISES
■ Trips in France, Netherlands, and Mecklenburg/Germany.
✇Andrew Brock Travel Ltd, 54 High St East, Uppingham, Rutland, LE15 9PZ, Great Britain ☎ (441572) 821330

EMERALD STAR LINE
■ Irish waterways.
✇Star Line, 47 Dawson St., Dublin, Ireland ☎ 353–1–6798166

---

the British Isles, navigable from the south coast and via lakes large and small to the border of Northern Ireland. A 19th-century canal has been restored to provide a link with the huge and island-studded Lough Erne. This route is very thinly populated.

FRANCE

■ **CANAL DU MIDI ROUTE.** Together with the Canal lateral à la Garonne, the largely 17th-century Canal du Midi provides a navigable link through southern France from the Mediterranean to the Atlantic. Locks, buildings, and aqueducts are all over 300 years old.

■ **RIVER MEUSE.** From its upper reaches near the city of Nancy, this canalized river is one of the most beautiful in all Europe, especially as it passes through the Ardennes forests near the border with Belgium.

■ **WATERWAYS OF ALSACE.** The Canal de la Marne au Rhin and associated waterways in the northeastern part of the country have a Germanic character. Radar-operated locks are totally automatic as the route passes through pine forests in the valley of the Zorn River.

GERMANY

■ **RIVER RHINE.** The Rhine runs for 640 miles through Europe. The uppermost reaches (Strasbourg to Switzerland) are canalized with giant ship locks. Elsewhere, it flows unimpeded, especially through the castle-filled Rhine Gorge (Bingen to Koblenz). The river is most conveniently visited aboard one of the many large cruise ships, which take four to five days exploring the major part of the river.

■ **RIVER LAHN.** The Lahn is a Rhine tributary, branching off near Koblenz and terminating in the cathedral city of Limburg. Although the river is only 40 miles long, a return journey can easily fill a week, for every one of the towns and villages en route is well worth exploring.

■ **MECKLENBURG LAKES.** This is a complicated network of interconnected lakes north of Berlin in former East Germany. Because the area has been practically untouched by development since the 1930s, one of its attractions is the large number of traditional pre–World War II privately owned pleasure craft.

HIKING
▼

SIX WONDERFUL SWISS WALKS

The scenery is unsurpassed and backpacks are unnecessary

No one thought of climbing around in the Alps for fun until the great influx of British travelers arrived in Switzerland in the 19th century. Of course the Swiss had been hiking around the mountains for a millennium, but in their case it was work. Today, people hike for recreation from Katmandu to Kandersteg. Many Europeans, especially, spend their summer holidays in the mountains hoofing it and an increasing number of Americans are quite literally following in their footsteps.

True to their stereotype of hyper-efficiency, the Swiss have transformed the art of walking into a science. Not only are there a plethora of signposts at every fork in the footpath, but the distance to various points is indicated down to the minute. People of all ages and abilities are able to knock about the mountains with the reassurance that they can stop practically whenever they want to for refreshment or a rest. Throughout the mountains, tramways, trains, and cable cars run so that one can cross high passes or access otherwise hard-to-reach hillside villages. There's no need to carry a heavy backpack, either. Your bags can be shipped for a modest fee from one destination to the next, and local inns and hotels will gladly fetch your gear for you after you've checked in. There's no camping in the Alps, but you can stay at Swiss Alpine Club huts at the top of many mountain passes or hotels or pensions in most villages. Even the remotest spot isn't terribly far from a train that can speed you to Zurich or Geneva or anywhere else in Switzerland in a matter of hours. The hiking season, however, is short: from June to late August, when the first snows usually arrive.

We asked Eve Preminger, a judge in New York City's Surrogate Court who spends most of her summers walking in the Alps, for her favorites hikes. The hikes chosen are moderate to slightly challenging, meaning that anyone in reasonably good physical shape should be able to handle them comfortably. (Walking poles, available at most outdoor equipment stores, are advisable; they make descents, especially, less wearing on your knees.) Most of the chosen hikes can be accomplished in a day. But the most satisfying way to experience the Alps is to plan a walking trip of, at least, 3 to 4 days.

The walks are chosen from three of Switzerland's most scenic cantons: Valais, noted for its vineyards and for being one of the most inaccessible regions of Switzerland; Graubünden with its rural villages, and magnificent vistas of lakes, meadows, and mountains; and the Bernese Oberland, the southern part of the canton of Bern, with its famous Jungfrau.

VALAIS WALKS

Valais, in the southern part of the country along the Italian border, is the most mountainous region in Switzerland, containing the country's 10 highest mountains.

ZERMATT to HORNLIHUTTE
Round trip: 10 miles ➤ *Altitude: 6,300 ft.*
➤ *6–7 hours*

■ Start and, perhaps, stay in Zermatt, one of the great mountain villages of the world, dominated by the legendary Matterhorn. The town allows no cars, which contributes to its pristine air and quality of timelessness, and which is also enhanced by the horse-drawn carriages lining the single main thoroughfare, the Bahnhofstrasse. On either side are grand chalets, antique buildings, and fashionable boutiques and not-so-fashionable T-shirt shops. Of special note is the alpine museum, which has exhibits on mountain ascents.

Although the village can be very crowded in the summer, five minutes by foot takes you to an extensive network of pleasant walks. First take the cable car, skipping the trail that passes underneath the car, to the Hotel Schwarzee, which provides views of

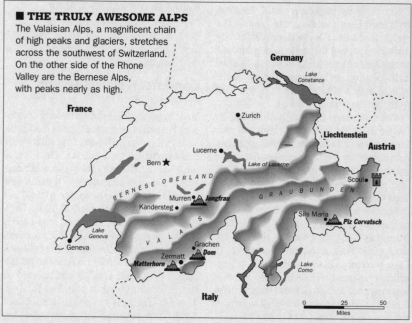

■ **THE TRULY AWESOME ALPS**
The Valaisian Alps, a magnificent chain of high peaks and glaciers, stretches across the southwest of Switzerland. On the other side of the Rhone Valley are the Bernese Alps, with peaks nearly as high.

France

Germany

Lake Constance

Zurich

Liechtenstein

Austria

Lucerne

Bern ★

Lake of Lucerne

BERNESE OBERLAND

Scuol

Murren Jungfrau

GRAUBÜNDEN

Kandersteg

VALAIS

Sils Maria

Piz Corvatsch

Lake Geneva

Geneva

Grächen Dom

Zermatt

Matterhorn

Lake Como

Italy

0   25   50
Miles

the Matterhorn and the Gorner Glacier. From the hotel it is about a three-hour hike to Hornlihutte, a little mountain inn that serves as the base camp for hardy souls preparing to climb the Matterhorn. This lonely, pyramid-shaped mountain can only be attempted by experienced climbers with technical climbing skills, but for hikers, there are some lovely walks. You can spend the night at the Hornlihutte, which is operated by the Swiss Alpine Club, then get up at 4 a.m. and breakfast with the mountaineers attempting to climb the summit, or you can walk back to Zermatt the same day and dine more elegantly.
☎ Zermatt tourist office: (4128) 66 11 81

GRACHEN to SAAS FEE
9 miles ➤ *Altitude: 6,200 ft.* ➤ *6–7 hours*

■ Saas Fee is separated from Zermatt by the Dom (14,941 ft.), the highest peak of the Mischabel range. Although lesser known than Zermatt, Saas Fee rivals it as one of the most spectacular mountain villages in the Valais. Like Zermatt, no cars are allowed. The environs allow for relatively easy walks as well as challenging hikes into the heights

overlooking the Saas valley. There are 170 miles of clearly marked trails.

For this hike take the bus to Grächen and hike back to Saas Fee above the Saas valley. It is a demanding hour's hike along ridge trails with a few steep sections and occasional drop-offs. About half an hour from Saas Fee, on the forested trail (inaccessible by car) is the Fletchorn Inn, perched on a cliff with a terrace that has a spectacular view. A famous chef, Irma Douce, presides. It is very informal, but the food is excellent.
☎ Saas Fee tourist office: (4128) 57 14 57

GRAUBÜNDEN WALKS
Located in the east of Switzerland, Graubünden is the largest Swiss canton—and the least populated. It is known for its rural villages, magnificent vistas, and some of the best-known resorts in Europe.

SCHUOL to FTAN
7 miles ➤ *Altitude: over 6,200 ft.* ➤ *1 1/2 hours*

■ Make your base in Guarda, a small village founded in 1197 and not that much different now from what it was then. The village lies in the midst of the Engadine, one of the country's most beautiful mountain ranges. The region is one the oldest and most culturally distinctive parts of Switzerland; people speak Romansch, which is linguistically not related to Indo-European languages. Access to the village is by a 20-minute walk by footpath from the train station.

The walk starts in Schuol, 20 minutes by foot from Guarda. Before you embark on your hike, cross over the Inn river to the Tarasp castle, a beautifully preserved medieval structure perched on its own demi-mountain. Then from Schuol, take the lift up the mountain and head for the ridge trail going west. There's a panoramic vista looking south to the snowcapped mountains that divide Switzerland from Italy. The trail descends through the woods into Ftan, a charming old town. In Ftan, perched on its own precipice with magnificent views, is the Hotel Paradiso, which is expensive but very good. From Ftan, you can take a 45-minute walk or bus back to Schuol.

☎ Guarda Tourist office: (4181) 862 23 42

SILS-MARIA to SGRISCHES LAKE and back
6 miles ➤ *Altitude: 6,200 ft.* ➤ *3–4 hours*

■ Sils-Maria is a small (pop. under 500) and quiet resort in the upper Engadine. The village lies at the beginning of the Engadine valley on a slope beneath the peak of Piz Corvatsch and between the lakes of Silvaplana and Sils. The German philosopher Friedrich Nietzsche, not known for his uplifting prose, lived here from 1881 to 1888—one can visit the room where he stayed. He called the little hamlet "the loveliest corner of the earth." There are still horse-drawn excursions up the Fex Valley—the most beautiful in the Bernina Massif.

A pleasant excursion is to take the Furtcillas lift from Sils-Maria and then hike up to Sgrishches Lake. Half an hour before you get there, there is a charming little alp (literally a hill or mountain) with a farmhouse where you can get fresh milk. At the lake you can take a chilly swim, then walk down the Fex Valley, making a circular hike. Stop at the Hotel Sonne for dinner, then proceed back to Sils-Maria.

☎ Sils-Maria tourist office: (4182) 4 52 37

BERNESE OBERLAND WALKS

The southern part of the canton of Bern, where the Jungfrau, one of Switzerland's most famous peaks, dominates the landscape.

KANDERSTEG to BLUMSLIALPHUTTE
6 miles ➤ *Altitude: 10,900 ft.* ➤ *4 hours*

■ At the north end of the 9-mile-long Lotschberg Tunnel (which links Bern and the Rhone Valley), Kandersteg lies in a lush valley with cattle-grazed alpine meadows. The town, a hiker's paradise, has a variety of trails, ranging from easy to difficult. Skip the trail and take the lift up to the Hotel Oeschinensee—the veranda of the hotel overlooking the Lake Oeschinensee is one of the most scenic spots in Switzerland to have lunch. Tall, imposing pine trees grow on the edge of the lake and there's a waterfall at one end. At the end of the lake, a path leads onward and upward to Blumslialphutte, a hut atop Hohturli—a demanding hike. Stay overnight at the Swiss Alpine Club–operated hut, which sits on the edge of a glacier, or return to Kandersteg.

☎ Kandersteg tourist office: 41-75-2233

GRIESALP to MURREN
10 miles ➤ *Altitude: 6,100 ft.* ➤ *7 hours*

■ Start from the tiny hamlet of Griesalp nestled high up in the mountains. You can stay at the Pension Golderli, a charming, simple inn with a superb valley view. The first hour and a half of the walk winds through mountain meadows. After another hour and a half you reach Ober Durrenberg, at 6,000 feet, the highest occupied farm in Europe. Here you can have refreshments and, if you wish, spend the night in a hayloft in the barn. A two-hour difficult hike from Ober Durrenberg takes you to the top of Sefinenfurkepasse, a pass where you begin a spectacular walk down into Mürren. Halfway down, stop at a little hut called Rotstockhutt for a rosti, a Swiss potato dish. As you descend, you'll see the Eiger, Monch, and Jungfrau, three of the most famous mountains in Switzerland. Mürren (pop. 350) is located on a rocky shelf overlooking the Lauterbrunnen Valley in the shadow of the Jungfrau massif.

☎ Griesalp tourist office: (4135) 55 16 16

▼

WHITE WATER RUNS THROUGH IT

Ten rafting journeys the whole family can enjoy

White-water rafting isn't for the faint of heart, but it isn't just for daredevils, either. Outfitters all across the country now offer trips for families. Children generally need to be 11 and up, as well as reasonably good swimmers. But those are the only requirements, plus perhaps an ample supply of adrenaline. We asked Jeff Bennett, a contributing editor at *Canoe and Kayak* magazine and author of *The Complete White-water Rafter* (McGraw Hill/Ragged Press, 1996), for his picks of the 10 best white-water rafting trips for families, along with the best guides.

SOUTH FORK OF THE AMERICAN RIVER
California ➤ 21 miles ➤ Class III

■ This stretch of river has long been California's most popular commercial trip. Dozens of Class II and III rapids, rich gold-era history, and easy access to big cities combine with sunshine and scenic rolling hills to create the perfect family trip. The big thrills happen at the river's two Class III rapids, Troublemaker and Satan's Cesspool.

■ **OUTFITTERS:**
Beyond Limits Adventures ☎ 800–234–7238
Tributary Whitewater Tours ☎ 916–346–6812
Whitewater Voyages ☎ 800–488–7238

DESCHUTES RIVER
Oregon ➤ 13 to 98 miles ➤ Class III

■ Running through the heart of Oregon's high-desert country, the Deschutes River provides a suprisingly sunny getaway for Pacific Northwesterners accustomed to damp, drizzly weather. Rafters can enjoy a bouncy one-day jaunt down the crowded Maupin section, or opt for a two- to five-day canoeing trip down the Deschutes's more remote corridors. Stair-stepped basalt cliffs, grassy meadows, and world-class fishing holes add to the experience.

■ **OUTFITTERS:**
Ewing's Whitewater ☎ 800–538–7238
Hunter Expeditions ☎ 503–389–8370
Rapid River Rafters ☎ 800–962–3327

SALMON RIVER, UPPER MAIN
Idaho ➤ up to 35 miles ➤ Classes II to III +

■ Just 90 minutes north of Sun Valley, the headwaters of the Salmon River cut a path through the Sawtooth National Recreation Area. At normal summer flows, the Salmon's emerald currents slip past smooth granite boulders and towering pines, occasionally erupting into series of big roller-coaster-style waves.

■ **OUTFITTERS:**
The River Company ☎ 800–398–0346
Triangle C Ranch Whitewater ☎ 208–774–2266
White Otter Outdoor Adventures ☎ 208–726–4331

SNAKE RIVER (GRAND TETON)
Wyoming ➤ 30 miles ➤ Classes I to II

■ One of the best ways to soak in the breathtaking beauty of Great Teton National Park is to float the Snake River downstream from Jackson Lake. You can comfortably gawk at the Teton's distant spires or search the banks for moose, bears, otters, and a variety of waterfowl.

■ **OUTFITTERS:**
Barker-Ewing Float Trips ☎ 800–365–1800
Fort Jackson Float Trips ☎ 800–735–8430
OARS ☎ 800–346–6277

COLORADO RIVER, GLENWOOD CANYON
Colorado ➤ 10 to 15 miles ➤ Classes II to III

■ Just three hours from downtown Denver, the Glenwood Canyon section of the Upper Colorado River carves a narrow, cliff-lined gorge alongside Interstate 70. Layers of sandstone, limestone, and granite rise from the riverbed, while cavalcades of big waves accent the toughest rapids.

■ **OUTFITTERS:**
Blazing Paddles Raft Adventures ☎ 970–925–5651
Blue Sky Adventures ☎ 970–945–6605
Timberline Tours ☎ 800–831–1414

■ A QUICK GUIDE TO WHITE-WATER RAPIDS

River conditions can vary widely and unpredictably. The following ratings were developed to give those unfamiliar with a river a feel for what they are getting into—before they get into it.

■ **CLASS I:** Flat water, some current.

■ **CLASS II:** Small waves.

■ **CLASS III:** Big waves, requires maneuvering through "hydraulic holes" in which the water breaks back on itself over a rock.

■ **CLASS IV:** Big waves, many rocks, and very fast, powerful water. Requires precise maneuverability. Not fun to swim in if you make a mistake.

■ **CLASS V:** Pushing the limits of navigability, should be done only by experts. Extremely steep gradient of river: 30- to 40-foot drops. Mistakes or capsizing will result in injury or possibly death.

■ **CLASS VI:** Pushing the absurd. Paddlers on the West Coast define it as not runnable. Those on the East recommend it only for experts, lunatics, or both. Injury or death is a distinct possibility.

Rio Grande, State Park and Racecourse sections

New Mexico ➤ *6.5–10.8 miles* ➤ *Classes II to III+*

■ The Rio Grande River rises along the eastern flanks of the southern Colorado Rockies, then flows 1,887 miles south to the Gulf of Mexico. Near Taos, N.M., it enters a spectacular and challenging gorge known as the Taos Box. To catch a taste of the Box but without the hazards of big rapids, families and the less adventuresome can paddle the Rio Grande's State Park and Racecourse sections near the quaint town of Pilar.

■ **OUTFITTERS:**
Far Flung Adventures ☎ 800–359–4138
New Wave Rafting Company ☎ 505–984–1444
Rio Grande Rapid Transit ☎ 800–222–7238

Kennebec River

Maine ➤ *6 to 12 miles* ➤ *Classes III to IV+*

■ Controlled releases from the Central Maine Power Company's Harris Station Dam guarantee reliable summertime flows, while memorable rapids like Magic Falls ensure tons of excitement. For a more sedentary experience through the Kennebec wilderness, run the Carry Brook section.

■ **OUTFITTERS:**
New England Outdoor Center ☎ 800–634–7238
North Country Rivers ☎ 800–348–8871

Youghiogheny River

Pennsylvania ➤ *7.5 miles* ➤ *Classes II to IV*

■ The lower Youghiogheny was the first river east of the Mississippi to be commercially rafted. Tracing a serpentine path through the Laurel Mountains near Ohiopyle State Park, the Lower Youghiogheny alternates between challenging rapids and calm pools. Although scheduled launch times help keep the river traffic in check, plan your trip ahead of time, as over 100,000 people run it every year!

■ **OUTFITTERS:**
Mountain Streams & Trails ☎ 800–245–4090
White Water Adventures ☎ 800–992–7238
Wilderness Voyageurs ☎ 800–272–4141

Ocoee River

Tennessee ➤ *4.5 miles* ➤ *Class III to IV*

■ Recently made famous by hosting the 1996

EXPERT PICKS

THE ULTIMATE RIVER RAFTING TRIP

Going down the Colorado through the Grand Canyon

"The type of experience that makes people go home and quit their jobs," is how Jeff Renakee, veteran river rat and author of *River Days: A Collection of Essays* (Fulcrum Press, 1988), refers to a rafting trip through the Grand Canyon. In Renakee's years as a guide on the river, he never saw anyone glad to go home. The trip, along 226 or 270 (depending where you get off) unspoiled miles of the Colorado River, is the longest and wildest river trip in the lower 48 states.

Nothing matches the magnitude of the Grand Canyon and the stupendous force that created it. Along the edge of the canyon is writ the geologic history of the last two billion years—from the relatively recent Jurassic period, 1.2 million years old, to the bottom layer of Vishnu rock, at approximately 2.0 billion years, some of the oldest rock in the world.

Three-quarters of the trips down the river are via motorized boats, which whisk though the canyon in about 6 days. Kim Crumbo, author of *A River Runner's Guide to the History of the Grand Canyon* (Johnson Press, 1981), and a former guide who has been down the canyon over a hundred times, recommends non-motorized boats, because they don't interfere with the majestic quiet of the canyon. It takes 12 to 18 days to make the trip in a nonmotorized boat; from Memorial Day to December they are the only craft allowed on the river.

The most common type of nonmotorized craft are oar boats, where one or two river guides control the oars while passengers sit back and take in the scenery. For more adventurous types who want an active participatory experience, a few companies run paddle boats where everyone paddles.

Rafting down the canyon may be the experience of a lifetime, but many people have to wait part of a lifetime to do it. The number of people allowed each year has been frozen at the 1972 limit of 20,000—roughly 800 trips down the river. For a commercial trip that averages about 25 passengers, you have to plan at least a year in advance. If you are an experienced rafter, you can apply for a permit, but these days, the average wait for private trips is 12 years. The best times to go are in the spring and the fall, when it's less crowded, and more temperate. Average summer highs are 106 degrees.

■ **FOR MORE INFORMATION:** Call Rivers and Oceans (☎ 800–473–4576) for rafting outfitters and availability.

Olympic white-water competitions, the Ocoee has long been a favorite among southeastern rafters. A healthy gradient and an endless assortment of boulders combine to form nearly continuous rapids on the section between the Ocoee Diversion Dam and its powerhouse downstream.

■ **OUTFITTERS:**
Nantahala Outdoor Center ☎ 800–232–7238
Ocoee Outdoors ☎ 800–533–7767
Southeastern Expeditions ☎ 800–868–7238

Nantahala River
North Carolina ➤ *8 miles* ➤ *Classes II to III*

■ The Nantahala, just east of Great Smoky Mountains National Park, runs along a valley thick with rhododendron, mountain laurel, and princess trees. Nantahala Falls (a sharp Class III+) highlights the trip.

■ **OUTFITTERS:**
Nantahala Outdoor Center ☎ 800–232–7238
USA Raft ☎ 800–872–7238
Wildwater Ltd. ☎ 800–451–9972

HEAVENLY PLACES TO REST YOUR WEARY SOUL

Christian monasteries have opened their doors to strangers in search of rest and reflection since the 6th century, when St. Benedict, founder of Western monasticism, made it a tenet that guests be received "as Christ himself." Robert Regalbuto, author of A Guide to Monastic Guest Houses *(Morehouse, 1997, ☎800–877–0012), has been visiting monasteries and convents across the nation and in Canada since he was in prep school. Here are some of his favorites:*

ABBAYE CISTERCIENNE D'OKA

Trappist monks (Roman Catholic)

♱ A large stone monastery with orchards, vegetable gardens, a dairy, and an apiary, surrounded by woodlands.
Oka, Quebec J0N 1E0, Canada
☎ 514–479–8361

BAY VIEW VILLA

Servants of the Immaculate Heart of Mary (Roman Catholic)

♱ Located on the beach at Saco Bay, this old-fashioned house has ocean and woodland views. There are 33 rooms.
Saco, ME 04072
☎ 207–283–3636

BETHLEHEM HOUSE

Order of the Sisters of St. Anne (Episcopal)

♱ An island of tranquillity in downtown Chicago. Room for only five guests. No meals included.
Chicago, IL 60610
☎ 312–944–9641

CONVENT OF ST. BIRGITTA

A Roman Catholic order of nuns

♱ The spacious guesthouse of this convent is close to woodlands and gardens.
Darien, CT 06820
☎ 203–655–1068

CONVENT OF ST. HELENA

Episcopal

♱ The convent is a large residence in the Capital Hill area of Seattle.
Seattle, WA 98112
☎ 206–325–2830

CRIEFF HILLS COMMUNITY

Presbyterian

♱ Picturesque stone and wood buildings surrounded by farmland.
Puslinch, Ontario N0B 2J0, Canada
☎ 519–824–7898

HOLY CROSS ABBEY

Benedictine monks (Roman Catholic)

♱ The Gothic revival buildings of this monastery are on the National Register of Historic Places.
Canon City, CO 81212–1510
☎ 719–275–8631

INCARNATION PRIORY

Order of the Holy Cross (Episcopal) and an order of Roman Catholic monks

♱ The only joint Anglican and Roman Catholic venture in the world. The monastery is mostly empty during the day.
Berkeley, CA 94709
☎ 510–548–3406 Episcopal
☎ 510–548–0965 Catholic

LEO HOUSE

Sisters of St. Agnes (Roman Catholic)

♱ Originally created to provide temporary safe haven for German immigrants, this convent on West 23rd St. has 60 rooms and can board up to 100 guests.
New York, NY 10011–2289
☎ 800–732–2438

MONASTERY OF ST. MARY AND ST. JOHN

Episcopal

♱ Overlooking the Charles River, this monastery is an architectural masterpiece near Harvard Square.
Cambridge, MA 02138
☎ 617–547–7330

OUR LADY OF GUADALUPE BENEDICTINE ABBEY

Benedictine monks and Oblate sisters (Roman Catholic)

♱ In the secluded Pecos River Valley, this abbey is a center for charismatic renewal.
Abiquiu, NM 87510
☎ 505–843–3049

■ **EXPERT PICKS**

THE RETREAT HOUSE
Camaldolese monks (Roman Catholic)

✟ Immaculate Heart Hermitage is located on 500 acres in the St. Lucia mountains with great views of the Pacific. Monks here practice the hermetical life.
Big Sur, CA 93920
☎ 408–667–2456

ST. AUGUSTINE'S HOUSE
✟ Located outside Detroit, with beautiful views, this is the only Lutheran monastery in the U.S.
Oxford, MI 48371
☎ 313–628–5155 (office)

ST. HILDA'S HOUSE
Community of the Holy Spirit (Episcopal)

✟ This convent is located in Manhattan. Some of the sisters are experienced craftswomen who merchandise their wares.
New York, NY 10025
☎ 212–932–8098

ST. JOHN'S CONVENT
Sisterhood of St. John the Divine (Anglican)

✟ The convent is close to the many cultural attractions of Toronto.
Willowdale, Ontario M2N 2J5, Canada
☎ 416–226–2201

ST. LEO ABBEY
Benedictine monks (Roman Catholic)

✟ Distinguished by a 2,100-pound marble crucifix at the center of the sanctuary, the monastery is situated on a lakefront in the Florida countryside.
Saint Leo, FL 33574
☎ 352–588–2881

ST. MARGARET'S HOUSE
Episcopal

✟ A beautiful stone convent house on the grounds of historic St. Luke's Episcopal Church.
Philadelphia, PA 19144
☎ 214–844–9410

ST. PAUL'S PRIORY
Order of Benedictines/Sisters of Jesus Crucified (Roman Catholic)

✟ Priory and guest house are surrounded by gardens with views of Newport Harbor. Prepare your own meals from a stocked refrigerator.
Newport, RI 02840
☎ 401–847–2423

SKETE OF THE RESURRECTION OF CHRIST
Synod of Bishops of the Russian Orthodox Church in Exile

✟ This monastery was once an ordinary suburban home. The highly traditional religious service featuring incense and elaborate vestments make this one of the most impressive Russian Orthodox liturgies outside of Russia.
Minneapolis, MN 55432
☎ 612–574–1001

WESTON PRIORY
Benedictine Monks (Roman Catholic)

✟ Located in a beautiful village, Weston Priory is well known for its crafts and liturgical music.
Weston, VT 05161
☎ 802–824–5409

EXPERT TIPS

Author Robert Regalbuto says accommodations are typically spare but surroundings can be splendid.

■ A guest must be prepared to abide by customs, however, which vary. Generally, monasteries and convents impose periods of quiet and often some of the services and parts of the compounds are off-limits to visitors.

■ Lodging usually includes meals, which are provided for a donation or modest fee. A day's room and board costs between $20 and $40 a person at most of these monasteries and convents.

■ Guest facilities are limited at most of these retreats, so make reservations well in advance.

NATURAL TREASURES

NATIONAL PARKS
▼

PARK RANGERS' SECRET SPOTS

An inside look at some hidden park treasures

Visitors storm America's national parks at the rate of 270 million a year. The parks collectively encompass some of the largest protected wilderness in the world. Yellowstone alone, for example, is about two-thirds the size of Connecticut. Yet few visitors venture beyond the major tourist attractions. Often it's on the trails less taken and roads less traveled that you can discover a park's true treasures. We canvassed park rangers from Maine to Wyoming to find out about little-known facets of the parks—after all, rangers know more about their parks than anyone. Here five rangers reveal some special spots and useful inside tips for the next time you visit these national treasures.

ACADIA NATIONAL PARK, *Maine*

❝One of my favorite places is Little Cranberry Island. In the summer you can take a ferry or mail boat out there—a 40-minute round-trip cruise. The ferry runs several times a day in the summer and no reservations are taken. On the ride out, you get a nice view of the mountains. You can imagine what explorer Samuel de Champlain saw when he was cruising the coast here. It's fun to stop along the way at the park's museum of maritime history and island life. It has some wonderful historical items dating back to the early 1800s. On Little Cranberry Island there's a country store and a fishing dock where you can watch the lobster fishermen come and go. And there are beautiful, rocky beaches to explore."

Wanda Moran

YELLOWSTONE NATIONAL PARK, *Wyoming*

❝A typical visitor stays a day and a half. Some major features like Yellowstone Lake, the canyon, Mammoth Hot Springs, can be seen from a car or by taking short walks.

But most visitors don't venture into the hundreds of square miles in back country. There are 200 lakes, hundred of creeks and rivers, 10,000 hot springs, mud pots, and steam vents that aren't on the main route. The park also has most of the earth's geysers. We also know of at least 130 waterfalls. The only way to find them is to hike many, many miles up the streams and discover them.

For example, there's one on Forest Creek that no one has ever heard of. It's 100 feet high and there's no access to it other than slugging up the stream. Twin Falls is a little-known falls discovered in the 1880s by an early superintendent, who named it and put it on the map, but then it was forgotten. He called it Twin Falls because it was two drops of water, one on top of the other. It's amazing that such a spectacular feature can remain unknown in 1997, but that's Yellowstone for you."

Lee Whittlesey

GREAT SMOKY MOUNTAINS NATIONAL PARK, *Tennessee*

❝ Cades Cove is a large valley in the mountains. You drive along and suddenly it just opens up before you—almost 3,000 acres big. It's quite impressive, and because it's so open it's the best place to see wildlife like deer, bears, red wolves, and river otters.

At Cades Cove you can take an exceptional walk along the Gregory Ridge trail, which is almost six miles. It starts at an elevation of about 2,000 feet and climbs to 5,500 feet. The walk takes you through four different forest habitats before you emerge into a big, grassy area called Gregory's Bald, which has spectacular views of the park. At the end of July, the flame azaleas bloom in red, yellow, and orange. From a distance it looks like the mountaintop is on fire."

Steve McCoy

GLACIER NATIONAL PARK, *Montana*

❝ One of the unique features of Glacier is that you can see dramatic vistas and wildlife from your car. A good place to do so is on the Going-to-the-Sun Road, a 52-mile road that was created in 1932. It rises up over Logan Pass (no relation to me) to an elevation of 5,200 feet. The road is carved right out of the cliffs, so if you're driving on the outside of the road, it's quite a thrill.

We're part of the grizzly bears' ecosystem and I can't think of any area in the park where you wouldn't come across signs of their presence. There are also elk, moose, deer, cougars, wolverine, bighorn sheep, mountain goats, and several resident bald eagles. The gray wolf has also moved down from Canada, denning here for the first time in 50 years."

Charlie Logan

BRYCE CANYON NATIONAL PARK, *Utah*

❝ The hoodoos—beautiful columns of rock carved out of a cliff edge with spi-

---

BILL AND HILLARY'S EXCELLENT ADVENTURE

George Bush fled to Kennebunkport, and Ronald Reagan escaped to his ranch in southern California, but the current White House occupant has no fixed retreat. For two consecutive summers, Bill Clinton and family chose to unwind in Wyoming's Grand Teton and Yellowstone National Parks. For those headed to the parks and wishing to follow the First Family's footsteps, here's the itinerary:

On their first trip, First Lady Hillary and daughter Chelsea hiked the trails and rode horseback in and around Grand Teton. The family toured nearby Yellowstone, stopping at Old Faithful, where Bill Clinton delivered a speech before the geyser dutifully erupted.

The following year, the Clintons drove to the top of Yellowstone's Mt. Washburn and had a picnic. Then they hiked $8^1/2$ miles on the Mt. Washburn Spur Trail, which allowed them a grand view of the park, but not its tranquillity—hordes of reporters trailed them on their jaunt.

---

rals and pinnacles—are what make Bryce Canyon so famous. But most people miss the canyon when it looks its best—at sunrise and in the early evening. The cliffs face eastward, so when the sun rises it lights up the hoodoos, making it a stunningly beautiful place.

There's an 18-mile rim drive in the park with four points that look out into the Bryce amphitheater. Any of those overlooks is a great place to be at sunrise. You can stand on the rim and see out for over 100 miles.

But my favorite thing to do is to view the night sky and the stars. With the clean air and the lack of city lights and pollution, on a good night you can see a couple thousand stars."

Dave Mecham

NATIONAL PARKS

WHERE THE CROWDS AREN'T

Places you've never heard of are just as beautiful as Yellowstone

Getting away from it all is getting more difficult all the time in America's national parks. Increasingly, people are running into the same urban ills that they are trying to escape: traffic jams, pollution, and even crime. While most people go for the blockbusters such as Yellowstone and Grand Canyon, there are parks just as magnificent and just as resource-rich with significantly fewer visitors. These lesser-known parks in many cases lie farther from population centers or just don't yet have local T-shirt and calendar industries.

There's a strong argument to be made that the undervisited reserves are the way national parks are meant to be. Without the car horns and camera-toting tourists, they better preserve that sense of yesteryear—and besides, you can grab a campsite at the last minute, instead of having to reserve a year in advance.

Noted National Park expert and Yale his-

EXPERT SOURCE

The U.S. Government Printing Office publishes an excellent guide to the less well known but in many cases no less spectacular parks called *National Parks: Lesser-Known Areas* ($1.75). To order a copy, contact the GPO at ☎202-512-1800, or the Consumer Information Center at ☎719-544-3142.

tory professor and department chair Robin Winks once sleuthed some important national secrets in a book called *Cloak and Gown*, about the CIA's involvement on college campuses. Here, Winks puts his formidable abilities to decidedly more pleasurable national secrets—the lesser-known national parks (see his choice list below). No armchair intellectual, Winks did his homework for a recent book, *The Rise of the National Park Ethic* (Yale University Press, 1996), a history of the National Park system, by visiting all 369 units then in the National Park System. He is researching and working on a second book, a hard-nosed guide that describes all 374 units now in the National Park system and rates them according to the quality of visitor experience.

CUMBERLAND ISLAND NATIONAL SEASHORE

40,743 visitors per year ☞ *33,900 acres*
Nearest big town: Accessible via the National Park Service ferry, from St. Mary's, Ga., 95 miles from Savannah

■ Cumberland Island, the largest of Georgia's Atlantic barrier islands, is also the most unspoiled. The southernmost of Georgia's Golden Isles, it has magnificent beaches, dunes, maritime forests, salt marshes, and a number of old estates, as well as raccoon, deer, and loggerhead turtles. The island can be reached only by ferry. Accommodations are available in five campsites on the island.
✉St. Mary's, GA 31558–0806
☎912–882–4336

VOYAGEURS NATIONAL PARK

224,181 visitors per year ☞ *218,034 acres*
Nearest big town: Duluth 280 miles

■ Much of the park is accessible only by boat (free canoes are available from the Park Service). There is, in fact, only one road. This wilderness is composed of 70,000 acres of dense forest, 30 lakes, and 900 islands teeming with wildlife, including a pack of timber wolves. The area has remained relatively unchanged from the days of trappers and explorers.
✉International Falls, MN 56649–8904,
☎218–283–9821

AMERICA'S NATIONAL TREASURES

NATIONAL HISTORIC SITE
1. Grant-Kohrs Ranch, Deer Lodge, Mont.

NATIONAL MONUMENTS AND PRESERVES
2. Aniakchak, King Salmon, Alaska

NATIONAL PARKS
3. Acadia, Bar Harbor, Maine
4. Channel Islands, Ventura, Calif.
5. Glacier, West Glacier, Montana
6. Grand Canyon, Ariz.
7. Grand Teton, Moose, Wyo.
8. Great Basin, Baker, Nev.
9. Great Smoky Mountain, Gatlinburg, Tenn.
10. Lassen Volcanic, Mineral, Calif.
11. North Cascades, Sedro Woolley, Wash.
12. Olympic, Port Angeles, Wash.
13. Rocky Mountain, Estes Park, Colo.
14. Voyageurs, Internat'l Falls, Minn.
15. Yellowstone, Wyo.
16. Yosemite, Calif.
17. Zion, Springdale, Utah

NATIONAL SEASHORES
18. Cumberland Island, St. Mary's, Ga.

WILDERNESS AREAS
19. Box Death Hollow, Escalante, Utah
20. Everglades, Homestead, Fla.
21. Frank Church River of No Return, Challis Nat'l Forest, Challis, Idaho
22. Pecos, Sante Fe Nat'l Forest, Pecos, N.M.
23. Pemigewasset, White Mt. Nat'l Forest, Plymouth, N.H.
24. Popoagie, Shoshone Nat'l Forest, Lander, Wyo.
25. Sylvania, Ottawa Nat'l Forest, Ironwood, Minn.
26. Weminuche, San Juan Nat'l Forest, Bayfield, Colo.
27. Wrangell-St. Elias, Copper Center, Alaska

Legend: National Forest / National Park / National Monument / National Wildlife Refuge and/or National Wilderness Areas

GRANT–KOHRS RANCH NATIONAL HISTORIC SITE

29,350 visitors per year ☛ *3,973 acres*
Nearest big town: Butte 45 miles

■ This was one of the largest and best-known ranches in the country at the end of the 19th century. Today, the ranch is almost unchanged: cowboys still gallop by, herds of cattle bellow, and the smells of a working ranch waft through the place. In addition, the site preserves the original log buildings, the main Victorian-style ranch house, and an impressive collection of saddles, wagons, buggies, and other artifacts.
✉ Deer Lodge, MT 59722-0790
☎ 406-846-2070

GREAT BASIN NATIONAL PARK

88,024 visitors per year ☛ *77,180 acres*
Nearest big town: Salt Lake City 230 miles

■ Situated in one of the most rugged and remote parts of the country, this park is reminiscent of the wide open Old West. It has vast stretches of desertlike open country, dramatic tall mountains, including the 13,063-foot Wheeler Peak, which descends to the Great Basin, one of the lowest points in the state. Among the park's attractions are ancient bristlecone pines, which, at 4,000 years old, are among the oldest living things in the world. Lehman Cave, one of the largest limestone caves in the country; and remnants of Pleistocene lakes.
✉ Baker, NV 89311-9700
☎ 702-234-7331

NORTH CASCADES NATIONAL PARK

19,323 visitors per year ☛ *504,781 acres*
Nearest big town: Seattle 115 miles

■ This is one of those hike-all-day-and-not-see-anyone-else parks, largely because Washington's other better-known park, Olympic, is more accessible. Northern Cascades is sometimes called the American Alps because of its numerous immense jagged glaciers — 318 in all. This enormous wilderness boasts 248 lakes, 1,700 species of plants, 207 species of birds, and 85 species of mammals, including grizzly bears and cougars.
✉ Sedro Woolley, WA 98284
☎ 360-856-5700

CHANNEL ISLANDS NATIONAL PARK

175,226 visitors per year ☛ *249,354 acres*
Nearest big town: Ventura on the coast is about 14 miles away by boat or plane

■ Because of the abundant wildlife here, which includes the world's largest creature, the blue whale, biologists often refer to these five tiny islands off the California coast as North America's Galapagos. Among the other animals that can be seen are sea lions, sea otters, pelicans, and cormorants. Remains of Spanish farms offer examples of how some of the earliest settlers in California lived.
✉ Ventura, CA 93001-4354
☎ 805-658-5700

LASSEN VOLCANIC NATIONAL PARK

385,489 visitors per year ☛ *106,372 acres*
Nearest big town: Chester 35 miles

■ Before Mount St. Helens erupted in 1980, Lassen Peak was considered the most active volcano in the lower 48 states. The park provides an excellent vantage point from which to observe volcanic action—fumeroles, bubbling mud pots, and hissing hot springs dot the landscape. There are also 150 miles of hiking trails through densely forested areas.
✉ Mineral, CA 96063
☎ 916-595-4444

ANIAKCHAK NATIONAL MONUMENT AND PRESERVE

1,193 visitors per year ☛ *137,176 acres in the Monument and 465,603 acres in the Preserve*
Nearest big town: Anchorage 400 miles

■ This wilderness is the most remote and difficult to visit in the National Park System. The quickest way to get to the focal point of Aniakchak, which is a giant crater, one of the largest in the world, is to fly into it. However, be forewarned if you're contemplating this feat: For every 10 attempts, only one is successful, because winds are constantly closing the only gap a plane can enter. Inside the crater, Surprise Lake's waters course through the wall of the crater to form the Aniakchak River.
✉ King Salmon, AK 99613-0007
☎ 907-246-3305

NATIONAL PARKS
▼

...AND WHERE THE CROWDS ARE

Folks flock to the 10 most popular parks for a reason

Italy has Venice. China, the Great Wall. The United States, its national parks, which altogether account for the largest protected wildernesses in the world. Collectively, the national parks draw some 270 million visitors a year. Unfortunately, the popularity of the parks is proving ruinous to their health. Unless visits drop off, which seems unlikely, or major changes are made in crowd management, many of our natural treasures could be in jeopardy. Pollution, traffic jams, and honky-tonk resorts are part of many people's experience in the national parks, especially the most popular ones. While there are 54 national parks, the 10 most popular parks account for over half the visitors.

The environmental threat posed by rapidly increasing tourism has been compounded by severe budget cutbacks that have curtailed park rangers' ability to provide services and keep parks clean. Many roads and sewer systems built in the 1930s and '40s have not been maintained. Recently, a failing sewer at Yosemite National Park, which wasn't repaired due to a lack of funds, almost polluted the water supply of San Francisco.

To stave off the ecological threat tourism has become, and to adapt to its shrinking budget, the National Park Service is getting back to nature. Roads are closing and in many cases just not being repaired; gift shops are being razed; and new construction is at a standstill. In addition, backcountry camping is now increasingly regulated by a new permit system.

With a little foresight, you can steer clear of the crowds and parking problems. If you're planning to visit one of the 10 most popular parks during the summer, try to make reservations far in advance. While some campsites are on a first-come, first-served basis, a large number can be reserved through the National Park Service's Destinet system, ☎ 800–365–2267.

Following are the 10 most popular national parks ranked by popularity (as of 1996) and a description of the most interesting tracks they have to offer—beaten or otherwise.

1. GREAT SMOKY MOUNTAINS NATIONAL PARK

8.62 million visitors per year ☛ *800 square miles* ☛ *Largest national park east of the Rockies*

■ A world unto itself, Great Smoky Mountains National Park has over 1,500 species of flowering plants, 10 percent of which are considered rare, and over 125 species of trees—more than in all of Europe. In addition, there are 200 species of birds, about 50

■ THE BIGGEST PARKS

The largest parks cover more ground than some of our smallest states

NATIONAL PARK OR STATE	ACRES
1. Wrangell–St. Elias, Alaska	8,331,604
2. Gates of the Arctic, Alaska	7,523,888
3. Denali, Alaska	5,000,000
4. Katmai, Alaska	3,716,000
5. Death Valley, Calif.	3,367,628
6. Glacier Bay, Alaska	3,225,284
CONNECTICUT	**3,118,080**
7. Lake Clark, Alaska	2,636,839
8. Yellowstone, Wyo.	2,219,790
9. Kobuk Valley, Alaska	1,750,421
10. Everglades, Fla.	1,506,499
11. Grand Canyon, Ariz.	1,217,158
12. Glacier, Mont.	1,013,572
13. Olympic, Wash.	922,163
14. Big Bend, Tex.	801,163
15. Joshua Tree, Calif.	793,954
RHODE ISLAND	**675,200**

SOURCE: *Backpacker* magazine, December 1994.

species of fish, and 60 species of mammals, including wild hogs and black bears.

A hike or drive from mountain base to peak is equivalent to the entire length of the Appalachian Trail from Georgia to Maine in terms of the number of species of trees and plants—every 250 feet of elevation is roughly equivalent to 1,000 miles of distance on the trail. A quarter of the park is virgin forest, the largest concentration east of the Mississippi.

In addition to its natural attributes, Great Smoky Mountains has farms, churches, cabins, and gristmills left by the mountain people who moved away when the park was created in 1934. The park has been designated a United Nations International Biosphere Reserve as well as a World Historical Site.
✐ Gatlinburg, TN 37738, ☎ 615–436–1200

■ **PEAK SEASON TIPS:** During the summer, in the lower elevations, expect haze, humidity, and afternoon temperatures in the 90s—and terrible traffic jams. Cades Cove is generally less crowded.

■ **CAMPING:** Sites at most campgrounds are on a first-come, first-served basis. Camping in the backcountry and the campgrounds at Cades Cove and Smokemont are open year-round. Look Rock and Elkmont are closed in the winter.

There is one camping facility, LeConte Lodge, located on the park's third-highest peak, Mt. LeConte (elevation 6,593 feet), a six-hour hike from the main road. Cabins do not have electricity or running water, but do include beds and hot meals. For information and reservations, call ☎ 423–429–5704.

■ **BEST ONE-DAY TRIP:** Entering the park from Gatlinburg, continue on U.S. 441, and stop at the Newfoundland Gap, where there are spectacular views of the mountains. From there, turn onto Clingmans Dome Road (closed in the winter), which ends at a parking lot where there is a strenuous half-mile hike to a lookout tower atop 6,643-foot Clingmans Dome—the highest peak in the park. Back on U.S. 441, continue to the Smokemont Campground, where the easy, two-mile Chasten Creek Falls Trail meanders along a stream through a hardwood forest ending at one of the park's many waterfalls.

■ **BEST EXPERIENCE:** The Great Smokies is one of the premier places in the East to enjoy magnificent fall foliage. The season lasts from September through October. Peak time: October 15 to October 31.

2. GRAND CANYON NATIONAL PARK

4.36 million visitors per year ☛ *1,904 square miles* ☛ *The 277-mile canyon is nearly a mile deep in places*

■ A Grand Canyon sunset is glorious, but even during the day, the canyon walls' many layers of stone refract hues of red, yellow, and green light. On a good day, you can see 200 miles across vast mesas, forests, and the Colorado River.

The park consists of three different areas: the North Rim, the South Rim, and the Inner Canyon, which is accessible only by foot, boat, or mule. The North Rim and the South Rim are only 9 miles apart as the eagle flies, but 214 miles by road.

The different rims are located in entirely different temperate climate zones. The North Rim on average is 1,000 feet higher and is heavily forested with blue spruce and alpine vegetation. It is open only from May to late October. The more popular South Rim is closer to population centers and has the juniper bushes and Gambel oak typical of the arid Southwest. The Inner Canyon is desertlike; temperatures there often exceed 110 degrees in the summer.
✐ Grand Canyon, AZ 86023
☎ 520–638–7888

■ **PEAK SEASON TIPS:** The South Rim is crowded all year. To escape the masses, take one of the many trails off East Rim Drive to a private spot overlooking the canyon, or try the North Rim.

■ **CAMPING:** For lodging reservations in the North and South Rims, including Phantom Ranch, ☎ 303–297–2757.

■ **BEST ONE-DAY TRIP:** The West Rim Drive offers wonderful views of the main canyon. In the summer, it is open only to buses, which can be taken from the visitor center. A paved trail runs along the South Rim. All hikes into the canyon are strenuous.

■ **BEST EXPERIENCE:** A raft ride down the Col-

SURE WAYS TO BEAT THE CROWDS

Travel in the off-season has its own rewards—and its own perils

Traffic on the main roads slows to a crawl, people are everywhere. Morning drive time in New York City? No, it's the summer rush to the nation's most popular national parks. Traffic has gotten so bad at some parks that tourists can spot wildlife simply by looking where other cars have pulled over to the side of the road to gawk.

The surest way to beat the crowds is to visit in the off-season. From June through October, Great Smoky National Park typically gets over a million visitors a month, but roughly half that number visit in the months between November and April, when temperatures in the lower elevations average about 50 degrees and occasionally reach into the 70s—perfect hiking weather, in other words.

There are other off-season rewards, too. At Rocky Mountain National Park, the bighorn sheep come down from higher elevations in May to feed on the mud deposits, and wildflowers there are spectacular in the spring. Yosemite National Park's waterfalls rush from the melting winter snows. In the fall, the foliage in many parks is absolutely superb. September is the sunniest month at Rocky Mountain National Park. And Grand Teton National Park is open all winter, allowing access to excellent cross-country skiing.

Of course, seasonal difficulties abound. There are, for instance, sudden snowstorms at Yellowstone National Park as early as September. And spring weather at Zion National Park is unpredictable; flash floods are not uncommon. Mammoth Cave can be especially dank in the dead of winter.

If such perils are too daunting for you, it is possible to avoid the masses in the summer simply by venturing into the backcountry. Most visitors don't wander very far from their cars.

---

orado River is a great way to enjoy the splendor of the canyon. Motorboat trips take 7 to 10 days, raft trips take 10 to 12 days, and trips on wooden dories usually last 18 days, though 3- to 8-day partial trips can be arranged. Call the park for a list of outfitters licensed by the National Park Service.

3. YOSEMITE NATIONAL PARK

3.96 million visitors per year ☛ 1,170 square miles ☛ Home of the giant sequoia

■ Yosemite's majestic granite peaks, groves of ancient giant sequoia trees, and waterfalls (including Yosemite Falls, which at a height of 2,425 feet is the nation's highest) inspired some of the earliest attempts at conservation in the United States. In 1864, Congress enacted laws protecting the valley. Journalist Horace Greeley noted that he knew of "no single wonder of Nature on earth which can claim a superiority over the Yosemite." And naturalist John Muir, whose efforts led to the park's formation, said of the valley, "No temple made with hands can compare with Yosemite."

The enormous park occupies an area comparable to Rhode Island, with elevations of up to 13,114 feet.

✉ Yosemite National Park, CA 95389
☎ 209–372–0200

■ **PEAK SEASON TIPS:** During the busy summer months, avoid the seven-mile Yosemite Valley, which attracts the hordes.

■ **CAMPING:** Of the 18 campgrounds in Yosemite, the 5 main ones in the valley offer "refugee-style camping"—over 800 campsites crammed into a half-mile of space. For more room and better views, try one of the eight Tioga Road campgrounds. There also are five tent camps on the High Sierra Loop Trail. Campers can obtain meals, showers, and cots there. Reservations are advised.

Reservations are required year-round in

Yosemite Valley's auto campground and for Hodgdon Meadow, Crane Flat, and Tuolumne Meadows campgrounds. Other campgrounds are operated on a first-come, first-served basis. Reservations may be made up to, but no earlier than, eight weeks. Reservable campsites fill up quickly from mid-May to mid-September. Your best bet for snagging a spot is to start calling the Destinet reservation number at 7 a.m. Pacific Standard Time eight weeks in advance of the date you want to camp.

■ **BEST ONE-DAY TRIP:** Avoid the congested route to Yosemite Valley, grab a tour bus and get off at either shuttle stop 7, for an easy half-mile, 20-minute hike to Lower Yosemite Falls, or shuttle bus stop 8, for a strenuous one- to three-hour round-trip hike to Upper Yosemite Falls. Other sites include the Native American Yosemite Village and El Capitan, a 3,000-foot face that is popular with rock climbers.

4. OLYMPIC NATIONAL PARK
3.38 million visitors per year ☛ 1,441 square miles ☛ The best example of virgin temperate rain forest in the country

■ On a relatively isolated peninsula with no roads traversing it, Olympic is one of the most pristine of the nation's parks. It has been referred to as the "last frontier." It divides into three distinct environments: rugged coastline, virgin temperate rain forest, and mountains, at the foot of which is the largest intact strand of coniferous forest in the lower

EXPERT TIP

The dramatic domes and soaring pinnacles in Yosemite make it one of the best places in the world for rock climbing. The Yosemite Mountaineering School and Guide Service offers beginning through advanced classes from April to mid-October; for information, call: ☎ 209–372–1244.

48 states. The park also has 60 active glaciers.
✉Port Angeles, WA 98362
☎360–452–4501

■ **PEAK SEASON TIPS:** Though three-quarters of the precipitation falls from October 1 to March 31, Olympic still receives more rain than any other area in the United States. Always bring rain gear.

■ **CAMPING:** The main coastal campgrounds of Kalaloch and Mora provide privacy and a sense of wilderness. For an even greater sense of solitude, try one of the two smaller campgrounds, Ozette Lake or Ericson's Bay. (The latter is accessible only by canoe.) All of the coastal campgrounds are available on a first-come, first-served basis.

The Hoh campground is the largest in the rain forest. The four smaller campgrounds, especially the 29-site July Creek campground on Quinault Lake, have more privacy and better wildlife-watching.

On the mountain, the Deer Park campground (elevation 5,400 feet) makes an excellent base from which to explore.

Most of the 17 developed mountain campgrounds are available on a first-come, first-served basis, but group reservations at Kalaloch and Mora can be made through the Kalaloch park ranger, ☎360–962–2283, or the Mora park ranger, ☎360–374–5460.

■ **BEST ONE-DAY TRIP:** On a drive up Route 101, you can take in the park's harbor seals, gigantic driftwood, and tide pools teeming with activity along the coast. On the right, you'll pass a sign for the world's largest cedar tree. Get off onto the spur road to the Hoh Rain Forest visitor center. There is a ³/₄-mile round-trip hike that winds through the dense rain forest at the end of the road. Back in your car, turn onto the road to the Mora campground, where there are several short scenic trails along the beach.

5. YELLOWSTONE NATIONAL PARK
3.04 million visitors per year ☛ 3,400 square miles ☛ The largest concentration of geysers and hot springs in the world

■ The center of what is now Yellowstone Park erupted 600,000 years ago. The explosion left behind a 28-by-47-mile crater that contained the world's greatest concentration of geothermal phenomena, including hot springs, fumaroles, steam vents, mud pots, and over 300 geysers. Among the geysers is Steam Boat, which shoots columns of water a record 350 feet high.

Yellowstone is the second-largest park in the lower 48 states, encompassing an area larger than the states of Delaware and Rhode Island combined. It is also the oldest park in the country, established in 1872. It has the largest mountain lake (Yellowstone Lake, with 110 miles of shoreline); the biggest elk population in America (90,000 strong); and is the last place in the country where there is a free-ranging herd of bison (3,500 of the woolly beasts).

✉ Yellowstone National Park, WY 82190

☎ 307–344–2002

■ **PEAK SEASON TIPS:** This is one of the coldest parks in the continental United States. Be prepared for winter weather at all times. The park receives half its nearly 4 million visitors in July and August. To avoid the crowds, head for the backcountry.

■ **CAMPING:** The 13 campgrounds at Yellowstone are available on a first-come, first-served basis except for Bridge Bay, where reservations can be made through Destinet. Winter camping is available only at Mammoth campground.

■ **BEST ONE-DAY TRIP:** From the west entrance, drive along Grand Loop Road to the mile-long Upper Geyser Basin, where boardwalks and trails run among the most outstanding geothermal phenomena in the world. Continue on to Yellowstone Lake.

6. ROCKY MOUNTAIN NATIONAL PARK

2.96 million visitors per year ☛ *414 square miles* ☛ *One of the highest regions in the country: 114 mountains above 10,000 feet*

■ On both sides of Rocky Mountain National Park's 44-mile Trail Ridge Road, the highest paved road in America, are craggy snow-capped mountain peaks shrouded in clouds, alpine fields ablaze with wildflowers, and crystal-clear mountain lakes. Elk, deer, moose, coyotes, marmots, ptarmigan, and bighorn sheep—the sym-

bol of the park—can often be seen.

✉ Estes Park, CO 80517, ☎ 303–586–1399

■ **PEAK SEASON TIPS:** The road to Bear Lake is jammed in the summer. Consider spending most of your time on the park's west side; it's less spectacular but also less crowded, and there are better chances to see wildlife.

■ **CAMPING:** There are five campgrounds in the park, each with a seven-day camping limit. For reservations to Moraine Park and Glacier Basin campgrounds, call Destinet. The other three are available on a first-come, first-served basis. In the summer, Timber Creek, on the west side of the park, is recommended—it doesn't fill up until about 1:30 p.m. Aspenglen and Longs Peak, where one begins the ascent to the summit, are often full by 8 a.m. Privately owned campgrounds also are available.

■ **BEST ONE-DAY TRIP:** For a sampling of the varied topography, take Fall River Road to the Alpine visitors center at Fall River Pass, 11,796 feet above sea level. Drive back along Trail Ridge Road. If time permits, turn off Trail Ridge Road onto Bear Lake Road, which winds past lakes and streams to Bear Lake, where there is an easy ²/₃-mile nature walk around the lake and a 1.1-mile hike to Dream Lake. A less crowded trail nearby is the Glacier Gorge Junction Trail to Alberta Falls. Those who are in peak physical condition may want to try Longs Peak Trail, a strenuous 8-mile hike at 14,000 feet.

EXPERT TIP

Yellowstone is one of the few national parks where snowmobiles are permitted (from December through February). In addition, snow coaches—buses on skis—are a unique way to travel in the winter. Call Amfac Parks and Resorts for reservations and rentals:

☎ **307–344–7311.**

■ **BEST EXPERIENCE:** Eighty percent of the park's trails can be ridden on horseback, and there are two historic ranches at the center of the park. Horses can be rented in Glacier Basin and Moraine Park.

7. ACADIA NATIONAL PARK

2.71 million visitors per year ☛ *54 square miles* ☛ *The highest coastal mountains on the East Coast*

■ The park is made of two islands and a peninsula: Mount Desert Island (accessible by a land bridge), Isle au Haut, and Schoodic Peninsula.

Artists and writers flocked to Mount Desert Island in the 1850s, attracted by its natural beauty. In the 1890s, wealthy vacationers, inspired by the paintings, came and built opulent "cottages," many of which were destroyed by fire in 1947.

The park's proximity to the ocean gives it a milder climate than that of the mainland, which helps it to sustain more than 500 varieties of wildflowers and makes it one of the best places on the eastern seaboard to take in fall foliage. The park also is known as the Warbler Capital of the United States. Over 275 species of birds, including 26 varieties of warblers and the endangered peregrine falcon, inhabit the park's birch and pine forests.

☞ Bar Harbor, ME 04609, ☎ 207–288–3338

■ **PEAK SEASON TIPS:** Expect bumper-to-bumper traffic on the Park Loop Road on the east side of Mount Desert Island in the summer. To avoid crowds, try the island's much less crowded western side or take a ferry trip either to Baker Island or to Isle au Haut. June is the best month to see forest birds; August is the best month for sea birds.

■ **CAMPING:** The landscaped Blackwoods campground on the east side of Mount Desert Island has 310 campsites. It is open all year. Reservations are advised.

On the less crowded west side is the 200-site Seawell campground, which is open only during the summer. You have to hike in from a parking lot to reach it, but it's worth the effort. Sites are available on a first-come, first-served basis only.

Particularly remote are Isle au Haut's five small lean-to shelters. Here you can escape the cars and crowds without sacrificing convenience. The ferry there lands at a nearby hamlet where you can get provisions.

■ **BEST ONE-DAY TRIP:** From the visitor center, take Park Loop Road to the 3.5-mile road that leads to Cadillac Mountain, where a short, paved trail winds around the 1,530-foot mountain, the highest coastal mountain in the United States. Back on Park Loop Road, turn around and continue down the East Coast. Stop at Sand Beach for a dip and the 1.4-mile Great Head Trail for a hike around a rocky, forested peninsula. Continue on Park Loop Road to Route 3 and turn onto Route 198. Look for Hadlock Pond Carriage Road Trail where there is a 4-mile loop across three granite bridges. This trail goes past the highest waterfall in the park and is one of the best places to enjoy the color of flowering plants in the spring.

■ **BEST EXPERIENCE:** From mid-June to mid-October, you can take the charming carriage ride through the park that is offered by the Wild Wood Stables, ☎ 207–276–3622.

If carriages are too tame for you, this also is one of the few national parks where snowmobiles are allowed. The network of carriage roads provides excellent terrain.

8. GRAND TETON NATIONAL PARK

2.54 million visitors per year ☛ *485 square miles* ☛ *Best part of the beautiful Teton range*

■ There are not many places in the world where you can literally stand next to a mountain. Imagine then Grand Teton, where the mountains rise out of the relatively flat Jackson Hole Valley like granite skyscrapers.

Another geological oddity formed during the ice age, Jackson Hole Valley looks as if some gargantuan infant sculpted it out of Play-Doh. When the valley formed, little driblets from the glaciers formed rocky deposits, called moraines, around the six sparkling mountain lakes that were incongruously punctured into the landscape.

Winding gently through this strange valley is the Snake River, along the banks of which grow willows, cottonwoods, and the

THESE SITES ARE HISTORY IN THE MAKING

Here are some of the newest sites and parks to receive a legislative blessing. Since most are still being developed, call for the status of visitor facilities.

CANE RIVER CREOLE NATIONAL HISTORICAL PARK

■ Established in 1714, Louisiana's Cane River is the oldest permanent settlement in the Louisiana Purchase territory. The site includes the Oakland and Magnolia Plantations and the historic district in the town of Natchitoches. Scheduled to open in 1998. ☎318–357–4237

NEW ORLEANS JAZZ NATIONAL HISTORICAL PARK

■ Over the next three to five years, this site will become an educational park dedicated to preserving and interpreting the history of jazz, a uniquely American musical form. Plans include live performances. ☎504–589–3882, ext. 106

NICODEMUS NATIONAL HISTORIC SITE

■ The town of Nicodemus in northern Kansas preserves a number of buildings and sites from the westward colonization movement of emancipated slaves in 1878–80. ☎316–285–6911

TALL GRASS PRAIRIE NATIONAL PRESERVE

■ Located in east central Kansas, this 11,000-acre site preserves a remnant of the tall grass prairie that once covered the Midwest. Also here are historic buildings from the late 1800s, including a country schoolhouse, and a hiking trail. ☎313–273–8494

WASHITA BATTLEFIELD NATIONAL HISTORICAL SITE

■ This site, located east of Cheyenne, commemorates the battle between General George Custer and Chief Black Kettle in 1868, in which the Chief and more than 100 Cheyennes, including women and children, were killed. While there are no federal facilities, the Oklahoma Historical Society operates the Black Kettle Museum in Cheyenne. ☎915–837–8247

NEW BEDFORD NATIONAL HISTORICAL SITE

■ Once the whaling capital of New England, this site will recreate whaling and shipbuilding activities, as well as preserve historical structures. ☎617–223–5001

BOSTON HARBOR ISLANDS NATIONAL RECREATION AREA

■ Current plans include development of the 30 islands off the coast of Boston. Emphasis will be on historical events and the business and cultural evolution of the islands. ☎617–223–5001

---

blue spruces in which bald eagles prefer to nest. Beavers have built dams up and down the river, forming wetlands that have an incredibly dense concentration of wildlife, including bears, elk, moose, trumpeter swans, sandhill cranes, and Canada geese. ✉Moose, WY 83012, ☎307–739–3300

■ **PEAK SEASON TIPS:** From June through August, the crowds are near Jenny Lake, which has sand beaches and sometimes is warm enough for a quick swim.

■ **CAMPING:** Campgrounds are generally open from late May to October. In summer, Jenny Lake tent campground fills the fastest and has a seven-day camping limit—the other five parks have two-week limits. Camping at all five campgrounds is available on a first-come, first-served basis.

■ **BEST ONE-DAY TRIP:** Beginning at the south entrance on Route 191, stop at Mentor's Ferry and the Chapel of the Transfiguration for a look at the dwellings of some of the area's first pioneers. Then drive north along Teton Park Road to Lupine Meadow and take the spur road to the trailhead, where, if you're in good physical shape, you can try a difficult hike to Amphitheater Lake near the timberline. Head back up Teton Road for a stop at South Jenny Lake, located at the bottom of the tallest Teton peak. An easy six-mile hike there circles the lake and affords spectacular views. Finally, stop at Colter Bay for a one-mile hike that loops around the wetlands.

■**BEST EXPERIENCE:** In winter, horse-drawn sleighs take visitors to see the herd of 11,000 elk that live in the valley.

9. ZION NATIONAL PARK

2.27 million visitors per year ☛ *229 square miles* ☛ *The 319-foot Kolub Arch is the world's largest sandstone formation*

■ Nineteenth-century Mormons named the main canyon in this park Zion after the Heavenly City and gave religious names to many of the brilliantly colored rock formations. The park's outstanding features include massive stone arches, hanging flower gardens, forested canyons, and isolated mesas.

The varied topography and plant life of the canyon have been caused by differences in the amount of water that reaches the various parts of the park. The microenvironments shelter a wide variety of animals, from black bears to lizards.

✉Springdale, UT 84767, ☎801–772–3256

■ **PEAK SEASON TIPS:** Expect traffic jams on summer weekends, when over 5,000 cars visit the park. The west side is less crowded.

■ **CAMPING:** The park's two camp grounds are open year-round on a first-come, first-served basis. There are picnic areas with fire pits and flush toilets, but there are no hookups for RVs. Campers should arrive before 11:00 a.m. for the best chance at getting a spot.

■ **BEST ONE-DAY TRIP:** A spectacular stretch of Utah Route 9 descends 2,000 feet in 11 miles into the park. As you enter the half-mile-wide canyon, the road turns into Zion Canyon Scenic Drive and runs north to the Temple of Sinawava. Riverside Walk, an easy 2-mile round-trip and the most popular trail in the park, begins here.

10. MAMMOTH CAVE

2.4 million visitors per year ☛ *82 square miles* ☛ *The largest cave in the world*

■ The Mammoth Cave consists of over 336 miles of the underground passages that have been explored and mapped. Native Americans first came 4,000 years ago and used it for over 2,000, leaving behind many artifacts.

Two-thirds of the park's land topography is called karst, characterized by sinkholes, cave entrances, and "disappearing" streams. There are nearly 100 sinking streams called "pnors" that disappear abruptly into holes in the ground. The cave also has some plant and animal species that have been isolated from the outside world for more than a million years. In fact, there are five species of animals unique to the cave.

✉Mammoth Cave, KY 42259

☎502–758–2328

■ **PEAK SEASON TIPS:** Most visitors come in June, July, and August. Be sure to make reservations for cave tours weeks in advance. Cave temperature is a cool 54 degrees year-round, so bring a light jacket or sweater.

■ **CAMPING:** There is a hotel, lodges, and cottages in the park, as well as four campgrounds—one large enough to accommodate large groups and horses. Camping in the backcountry is permitted year-round; camping elsewhere is closed in the winter. Call the Mammoth Cave Hotel at ☎ 502–758–2225 for more information.

■ **BEST ONE-DAY TRIP:** The park has over 70 miles of trails. Rangers offer guided nature walks. Hiking and camping are permitted in the park, and there are 30 miles of river available for fishing and canoeing, but the greatest attraction is, of course, the cave itself. After or before your cave tour, you may want to take the short $3/4$-mile hike on the Cedar Sink Trail to see good examples of the area's karst topography. You may also want to take the one-hour boat tour down the Green River.

■ **BEST EXPERIENCE:** Visiting the caves. Ranger-conducted tours cater to many levels of interest and can last from 45 minutes to nearly an entire day. Because of the popularity of the tours, be sure to make reservations well in advance by calling ☎ 800–967–2283.

ALL OF AMERICA'S CROWN JEWELS

America has designated over 80 million square miles as 54 National Parks for the enjoyment of its citizenry and the generations to come. The parks, how to get in touch with them, and their claims to fame

NATIONAL PARK ☎ Telephone number for information ✔ **Claim to fame** ☞ *Special activities*

ALASKA

DENALI ☎ 907-683-2294 ✔ **Mt. McKinley, N. America's highest mountain** ☞ *Dog sledding, cross-country skiing, hiking*

GATES OF THE ARCTIC ☎ 907-456-0281 ✔ **Greatest wilderness in N. America** ☞ *River running, fishing, mountaineering*

GLACIER BAY ☎ 907-697-2232 ✔ **Tidewater glaciers, wild terrain from ice to rain forest** ☞ *Sea kayaking, fishing*

KATMAI ☎ 907-246-3305 ✔ **Alaskan brown bears, the world's largest carnivores** ☞ *Sport fishing, kayaking*

KENAI FJORDS ☎ 907-224-3175 ✔ **300-sq.-mile Harding Ice Field, varied rain forest** ☞ *Sea kayaking, charter boats*

KOBUK VALLEY ☎ 907-442-3890 ✔ **Entirely north of the Arctic Circle** ☞ *Canoeing, exploring archaeological sites*

LAKE CLARK ☎ 907-271-3751 ✔ **Headquarters for red salmon spawning** ☞ *Charter river trips, fishing*

WRANGELL-ST. ELIAS ☎ 907-822-5234 ✔ **Chugach, Wrangell, & St. Elias mtns. meet here** ☞ *Rafting, x-country skiing*

AMERICAN SAMOA

PARK OF AMERICAN SAMOA ☎ 011-684-633-7082 ✔ **Paleotropical rain forests, coral reefs** ☞ *Bird-watching, sunbathing*

ARIZONA

GRAND CANYON ☎ 520-638-7888 ✔ **The mile-deep canyon itself** ☞ *River rafting, hiking, mule rides*

PETRIFIED FOREST ☎ 520-524-6228 ✔ **Petrified trees, Indian ruins** ☞ *Self-guided auto tours, photography*

SAGUARO ☎ 520-733-5100 ✔ **Greatest variety of desert life in N. America** ☞ *Photography, bird-watching, hiking*

ARKANSAS

HOT SPRINGS ☎ 501-624-3383 ✔ **Some 950,000 gals. of water a day flow through 47 thermal springs** ☞ *Hot baths*

CALIFORNIA

CHANNEL ISLANDS ☎ 805-658-5700 ✔ **Seabirds, sea lions, and unique plants** ☞ *Scuba diving, bird-watching*

DEATH VALLEY ☎ 619-786-2331 ✔ **Lowest point in Western Hemisphere** ☞ *Photography, jeep riding, horseback riding*

JOSHUA TREE ☎ 619-367-7511 ✔ **20- to 40-foot Joshua trees, stunning dunes** ☞ *Wildlife-watching, nature walks*

KINGS CANYON ☎ 209-565-3341 ✔ **The enormous canyons of the Kings River** ☞ *Hiking, photography*

LASSEN VOLCANIC ☎ 916-595-4444 ✔ **Huge lava-flow mountains, steaming sulfur vents** ☞ *X-country, downhill skiing*

REDWOOD ☎ 707-464-6101 ✔ **Redwood forests and 40 miles of scenic coastline** ☞ *Whale-watching, guided kayaking*

SEQUOIA ☎ 209-565-3341 ✔ **Giant sequoias include General Sherman, the largest living tree** ☞ *Hiking, fishing*

YOSEMITE ☎ 209-372-0200 ✔ **Granite peaks and domes, and the nation's highest waterfall** ☞ *Skiing, rock climbing*

COLORADO

MESA VERDE ☎ 970-529-4461 ✔ **Pre-Columbian cliff dwellings and other artifacts** ☞ *Guided lectures, exhibits*

ROCKY MOUNTAIN ☎ 970-586-1399 ✔ **Trail Ridge Rd., highest in the lower 48** ☞ *Mountain climbing, horseback riding*

FLORIDA

BISCAYNE ☎ 305-230-7275 ✔ **Pristine wilderness, living coral reefs** ☞ *Glass-bottom boat tours, snorkeling, scuba*

DRY TORTUGAS ☎ 305-242-7710 ✔ **Largest all-masonry fort in the west** ☞ *Fishing, snorkeling, scuba diving*

EVERGLADES ☎ 305-242-7710 ✔ **Largest remaining subtropical wilderness in U.S.** ☞ *Backcountry canoeing, fishing*

HAWAII

HALEAKALA ☎ 808-572-9306 ✔ **Inactive volcano, chain of pools linked by a waterfall** ☞ *Sunrise- and sunset-watching*

HAWAII VOLCANOES ☎ 808-985-6000 ✔ **Devastation from volcanic eruptions** ☞ *Backpacking, bird-watching*

450 TRAVEL

■ VISITOR'S GUIDE

KENTUCKY
MAMMOTH CAVE ☎ 502-758-2328 ✔ Longest recorded cave system in the world ☞ *Cave tours, cave boating*

MAINE
ACADIA ☎ 207-288-3338 ✔ Cadillac Mountain, highest on East Coast north of Brazil ☞ *Boat tours, skiing*

MICHIGAN
ISLE ROYALE ☎ 906-482-0986 ✔ The largest island in Lake Superior ☞ *Lake kayaking, hiking*

MINNESOTA
VOYAGEURS ☎ 218-283-9821 ✔ Thirty lakes and over 900 islands ☞ *Canoeing, x-country skiing, ice-skating*

MONTANA
GLACIER ☎ 406-888-7800 ✔ Nearly 50 glaciers, glacier-fed streams, lakes ☞ *Excursion-boat cruises, snowshoeing*

NEVADA
GREAT BASIN ☎ 702-234-7331 ✔ Ice field on 13,063-ft. Wheeler Peak, Lehman Caves ☞ *Fishing, climbing, spelunking*

NEW MEXICO
CARLSBAD CAVERNS ☎ 505-785-2232 ✔ U.S.'s deepest cave (1,593 ft.) and largest chambers ☞ *Guided cave tours*

NORTH DAKOTA
THEODORE ROOSEVELT ☎ 701-623-4466 ✔ The arid badlands, Roosevelt's Elkhorn Ranch ☞ *Fishing, photography*

OREGON
CRATER LAKE ☎ 541-594-2211 ✔ Deepest lake in the U.S. (1,932 feet) ☞ *Boat tours, snowmobiling, x-country skiing*

SOUTH DAKOTA
BADLANDS ☎ 605-433-5361 ✔ The scenic western badlands ☞ *Hiking, wildlife-watching*
WIND CAVE ☎ 605-745-4600 ✔ Beautiful limestone cave and the scenic Black Hills ☞ *Spelunking, cave tours, hiking*

TENNESSEE
GREAT SMOKY MOUNTAINS ☎ 423-436-1200 ✔ Loftiest range in the East, diverse plant life ☞ *Hiking, photography*

TEXAS
BIG BEND ☎ 915-477-2251 ✔ Rio Grande passes through canyon walls for 118 miles ☞ *Horseback riding, fishing*
GUADALUPE MOUNTAINS ☎ 915-828-3251 ✔ Portions of world's most extensive fossil reef ☞ *Hiking, historic sites*

UTAH
ARCHES ☎ 801-259-8161 ✔ Giant arches, pinnacles change color as the sun shifts ☞ *Interpretive walks, auto tours*
BRYCE CANYON ☎ 801-834-5322 ✔ Colorful, unusually shaped geologic forms ☞ *X-country skiing, snowshoeing*
CANYONLANDS ☎ 801-259-3911 ✔ Canyons of Green, Colorado rivers ☞ *Mountain biking, backcountry drives, rafting*
CAPITOL REEF ☎ 801-425-3791 ✔ Waterpocket Fold, a 100-mile-long wrinkle in earth's crust ☞ *Hiking, photography*
ZION ☎ 801-772-3256 ✔ Unusual geologic formations–Kolub Arch, world's largest at 310 feet ☞ *Hiking, photography*

VIRGINIA
SHENANDOAH ☎ 540-999-3400 ✔ The scenic Blue Ridge Mountains ☞ *Skyline Drive, horseback riding, nature walks*

VIRGIN ISLANDS
VIRGIN ISLANDS ☎ 809-775-6238 ✔ Secluded coves, white beaches fringed by lush hills ☞ *Snorkeling, swimming*

WASHINGTON
MOUNT RAINIER ☎ 360-569-2211 ✔ Greatest single-peak glacial system in U.S. ☞ *Skiing, snowshoeing, climbing*
NORTH CASCADES ☎ 360-856-5700 ✔ Half the glaciers in the U.S., 318 are active ☞ *Backpacking, hiking*
OLYMPIC ☎ 360-452-4501 ✔ One of the biggest temperate rain forests in the world ☞ *Mountain climbing, fishing*

WYOMING
GRAND TETON ☎ 307-739-3399 ✔ The flat Jackson Hole Valley and the Teton mountains ☞ *Hiking, climbing, skiing*
YELLOWSTONE ☎ 307-344-7381 ✔ World's largest concentration of geothermal phenomena ☞ *Skiing, snowmobiling*

SOURCE: National Park Service; individual parks.

THE BEST NATIONAL PARK GUIDES

The National Park Service publishes an excellent series of guides with color photos and maps; for more information call ☎ 304–535–6018. Michele Morris, senior editor of Backpacker *magazine, also recommends:*

IN PRINT

CAMPER'S GUIDE TO U.S. NATIONAL PARKS: Where to Go and How to Get There (Volumes 1 & 2)

Mickey Little and B. Morva, Gulf Publ., Houston, Texas, 1994, $18.95 per volume

■ More recreation and less backpacking, this book is especially good for families and beginning campers. It has maps of all the parks, plus tips about hiking.

THE COMPLETE GUIDE TO AMERICA'S NATIONAL PARKS

Jane Bangley McQueen, ed., National Park Foundation, $15.95

■ A handy reference guide to all the national parks. Practical information on permits, fees, and useful climate tables.

THE ESSENTIAL GUIDE TO WILDERNESS CAMPING AND BACKPACKING

Charles Cook, Michael Kesenel Publ. Ltd., 1994, $24.95

■ Provides comprehensive information on all the national parks with good tips on hiking and backpacking. Includes a good thumbnail guide to camping in national forests and a listing of notable trails.

NATIONAL GEOGRAPHIC GUIDE TO THE NATIONAL PARKS OF THE UNITED STATES

Elizabeth L. Newhouse, ed., National Geographic Society, 1992, $24

■ Perfect for the windshield tourist, this book is packed with itineraries, quick hikes, and beautiful pictures.

AMERICA'S WILDERNESS

Buck Tilton, Foghorn Press, 1996, $19.95

■ This book covers the nitty-gritty of every designated Wilderness Area in the country (more than 600 in all) managed by the National Park Service and other federal agencies. It also includes "10 best" recommendations by the author for everything from backpacking to hunting to kayaking.

ONLINE

NATIONAL PARK SERVICE HOME PAGE

http://www.nps.gov

■ Offers brief but useful information on the parks and links to the home pages of major parks.

NATIONAL PARKS ELECTRONIC BOOKSTORE

http://www.npeb.org/books.html

■ On this home page you can order specialized publications, such as park guides and books about regional flora, fauna, and history, which are sold at many of the national parks and public lands.

NATIONAL PARKS AND CONSERVATION ASSOCIATION

http://www.npca.org

■ A nonprofit citizen group that is dedicated to preserving the Appalachian Trail and the national parks. The site provides information on various activities and provides a link to the latest issue of *National Parks* magazine.

GORP (GREAT OUTDOORS RECREATION PAGES)

http://www.gorp.com

■ This commercial Web site has a vast array of offerings, including detailed reports on national parks, forests, wildlife refuges, etc. You'll also find information on hiking, biking, fishing, skiing, caving, etc., as well as tours of wilderness areas.

CATCH A GLIMPSE OF A BIGHORN

A wildlife expert on the best places to see some magnificent animals

It seems to be an inexorable law that as the human population expands, wild animal species decline. Viewing large numbers of wild animals in a relatively pristine habitat is increasingly a rare experience. But it's still possible—even in America. We asked Mark Damian Duda, a noted wildlife expert who has worked as a consultant to over 30 state fish and wildlife agencies, for the best places to see wildlife in their natural habitat in the United States. His choices are drawn from his book, *Watching Wildlife* (Falcon Press, 1995), which provides information on seasonal migrations, tips on how to watch wildlife, and helpful photography pointers. A series of state guides to wildlife are also available from Falcon Press ($5.95–$8.95).

BIGHORN SHEEP

Located along Interstate 70, about halfway between Denver and Vail, the Georgetown Viewing Site is probably the most accessible place for viewing Rocky Mountain bighorn sheep. Between 175 and 200 bighorns occupy the rocky cliffs along the north side of Clear Creek Canyon. Fall and winter are the best times to look for them. (There's a lookout tower shaped like a ram's horns.) An exhibit includes interpretative displays and mounted viewing scopes.
■ **WHERE:** Georgetown Viewing Site, Georgetown, Colorado, ☎303–297–1192.

MANATEES

The gentle, slow-moving, endangered Florida manatee is a large aquatic mammal, typically 10 feet long and weighing 1,000 pounds. Manatees live in shallow, slow rivers, river mouths, estuaries, saltwater bays, and shallow coastal areas. In recent years, more than 200 manatees have used the Kings Bay area as wintering grounds.
■ **WHERE:** Crystal River National Wildlife Refuge, Florida, ☎352–563–2088.

ROCKY MOUNTAIN ELK

During September and October, bull elk bugle as a physical release and to challenge other males during the fall rut. Bugling usually begins an hour before sunset and starts off as a low, hollow sound, rising to a high-pitched shriek, culminating in a series of grunts.
■ **WHERE:** Horseshoe Park, Rocky Mountain National Park, Colorado, ☎970–586–1399.

■ WINTERING ELK

When snow comes to high country in the Grand Tetons, elk migrate from their high-elevation summer range to winter range in the valley. Almost 7,500 elk inhabit the area. Elk arrive in early November and return to the high country in early May. In the winter, visitors can view elk from a horse-drawn sleigh. Sleighs run from late December to March, 10 a.m. to 4 p.m. daily. Tours operate from the National Museum of Wildlife Art, three miles north of Jackson on U.S. Highway 26/191.
■ **WHERE:** National Elk Refuge, Jackson Hole, Wyoming, ☎307–733–9212.

SANDHILL CRANES

For about five weeks in early spring (usually starting in March), more than three-quarters of the world's population of sandhill cranes gathers along the Platte River in central Nebraska. More than 500,000 of these stately birds rest and fatten up here on their way back to breeding grounds in the Arctic.

The local chamber of commerce sponsors a three-day program known as "Wings over the Platte," which includes bus tours, seminars, and wildlife art exhibits.
■ **WHERE:** Platte River, Nebraska. For more information contact: Field Supervisor, U.S.

Fish and Wildlife Service, ☎308–382–6468 or Grand Island/Hall County Convention and Visitors Bureau, Nebraska, ☎800–658–3178.

CALIFORNIA AND STELLER'S SEA LIONS

After descending more than 200 feet in an elevator to Sea Lion Caves on the coast of Oregon, you will find dim light, the hollow sound of waves crashing against cliffs, and the echoed barks of hundreds of Steller's sea lions (present year-round) and California sea lions (present from September to April). Sea lions swim and loaf below a cliff-top observation deck.
■ **WHERE:** Sea Lion Caves, Oregon ☎541–547–3111.

MEXICAN FREE-TAILED BATS

On warm summer evenings in the Chihuahuan Desert, thousands of Mexican free-tailed bats exit in a whirling, smokelike column from the natural mouth of Carlsbad Caverns. An estimated 300,000 bats inhabit the caverns. They emerge at dusk to feed on moths; other flights occur in late August and September, when young bats born in June join the evening ritual.

Flight Amphitheater, which is located at the mouth of the cavern, seats up to 1,000 people. Park rangers offer programs about the bats from Memorial Day to Labor Day prior to the evening flights. But don't expect to see bats if you visit during the winter—they will have migrated to Mexico.
■ **WHERE:** Carlsbad Caverns National Park, New Mexico, ☎505–785–2232.

BALD EAGLES

One of the largest concentrations of wintering bald eagles in the lower 48 states occurs at the Skagit River Bald Eagle Natural Area in northern Washington State. More than 300 bald eagles gather along the river's gravel bars between 7 a.m. and 11 a.m. to feed on spawned-out salmon. The eagles feast here between November and early March, with peak numbers occurring in mid-January.
■ **WHERE:** Skagit River, Mount Baker–Snoqualmie National Forest, Washington. For more information contact: The Nature Conservancy, Washington Field Office, ☎206–343–4344; Mount Baker Ranger District, Sedro Woolley, Washington, ☎360–856–5700; or Washington Department of Wildlife, ☎206–775–1311.

EXPERT LIST

WHERE TO WATCH THE WHALES

Thar she blows, according to the World Wildlife Fund. Here are the spots where whales are most likely to spout off.

WHERE *Country* ◗ Access ✔ Whales ◗ Peak season

S. OCEAN WHALE SANCTUARY *Antarctica.* ◗ Boat access only. ✔ **Humpback, southern right, minke whales.** ◗ Summer.
SAMANA BAY *Dominican Republic.* ◗ Boat and shoreline access. ✔ **Humpback, pilot, Bryde's whales** ◗ Jan.–March.
CAMPBELL RIVER *British Columbia.* ◗ Shoreline, sailboat access. ✔ **Minke and orcas (killer whales).** ◗ June–Sept.
CAPE COD *Massachusetts.* ◗ Boat access only. ✔ **Humpback, fin, northern right, minke, pilot whales.** ◗ April–October.
BAJA CALIFORNIA *Mexico.* ◗ Shoreline and boat access. ✔ **Gray, blue, and humpbacks.** ◗ Almost year-round.
LOFOTEN ISLANDS *Norway.* ◗ Boat access only. ✔ **Sperm, minkes, and orcas.** ◗ Summer.
KAIKKOURA *New Zealand.* ◗ Boat, shoreline access. ✔ **Sperm whale, orcas, also Hector's & dusky dolphins.** ◗ Year-round.
WHALE ROUTE *South Africa.* ◗ Shoreline access. ✔ **Southern right, humpback, Bryde's, orca.** ◗ August–Nov.
PATAGONIA *Argentina.* ◗ Boat and shoreline access. ✔ **Southern right whale and orcas.** ◗ June–Dec.
SHIKOKU *Japan.* ◗ Boat access only. ✔ **Bryde's whales** ◗ Year-round.

INTO THE WILDERNESS

Wilderness areas—some 96 million acres—are the most strictly protected lands in the country. "Carry out what you carry in" policies are enforced so that, in the words of the 1964 Wilderness Act, "the imprint of man's works" remains "substantially unnoticeable." Buck Tilton, a freelance columnist for outdoor magazines, has written America's Wilderness Areas *(Foghorn Press, 1996), a comprehensive guide. Here are his top picks.*

PEMIGEWASSET
■ One of the most extensive roadless areas in the East, this is New Hampshire's largest wilderness. Almost the entire forest was removed for timber between 1890 and 1940, but 55 years of regeneration have brought it back.
White Mountain National Forest, Pemigewasset Ranger District, Plymouth, NH
☎603–536–1310

EVERGLADES
■ Florida's "river of grass," 6 inches deep and 50 miles wide, forms the heart of this 1,296,500-acre wilderness area.
Homestead, FL
☎305–242–7700

SYLVANIA
■ This area contains 35 deep lakes (many edged with white sand), 84 established campsites, and a well-maintained trail system.
Ottawa National Forest, Ironwood, MI
☎906–932–1330

FRANK CHURCH RIVER OF NO RETURN
■ Besides Alaska, no area provides a wilderness experience to match its magnitude (it lies in six national forests). The canyon carved by the Main Salmon River lies deeper than the Grand Canyon.
Chellis National Forest, Middle Fork Ranger District, Chellis, ID
☎208–879–4101

POPO AGIE
■ This rugged area encompasses about 25 miles of the southern Wind River Mountain Range. A perennial snowfield lies along the Continental Divide.
Shoshone National Forest, Washakie Ranger District, Lander, WY
☎307–332–5460

WEMINUCHE
■ Colorado's largest and most popular wilderness has 63 ice-blue high country lakes and 500 miles of trails, including the Continental Divide Trail and the Colorado Trail.
San Juan-Rio Grande National Forest, Monte Vista, CO
☎719–852–5941

PECOS
■ Much of Pecos lies in the high country of New Mexico and features the 13,103-foot South Truchas Peak, the second highest in the state.
Sante Fe National Forest, Pecos Ranger District, Pecos, NM
☎505–757–6121

BOX–DEATH HOLLOW
■ Vertical gray and orange walls of Navajo sandstone stand above two canyon tributaries of Utah's Escalante River.
Dixie National Forest, Escalante Ranger District, Escalante, UT
☎801–826–5400

WRANGELL–ST. ELIAS
■ The largest unit of the National Park System, this Alaskan wilderness holds 9 of North America's 16 highest peaks, the 90-mile-long and 4,000-foot-thick Bagely Icefield, and the Malaspina Glacier, which is 50 percent larger than the state of Delaware.
National Park Service, Copper Center, AK
☎907–822–5234

COZY CABINS IN THE WOODS

Almost all the comforts of home in the middle of the wilderness

America's national parks contain some of the best-preserved rustic hotels in the United States. These capacious lodges were often built with stones and trees hewn directly from the stunning landscapes they occupy in an attempt to re-create the great outdoors indoors. But suppose you yearn for a less refined experience, yet decidedly more appealing than sleeping on a bed of pine needles. Rustic cabins offer a happy middle ground, and the national parks have a variety of offerings. Many of the cabins were built during the Great Depression by the Civilian Conservation Corps; the Park Service is not allowing any new construction. Rates range from $12 to $130 a night per person depending on the location, type of cabin, and whether meals are provided.

Whether you like your accommodations with amenities and gourmet meals or prefer something spartan and closer to nature, here are some of the best places to stay in the national parks.

RUSTIC LODGES
AHWAHNEE HOTEL
Yosmite National Park, California

■ Dating from 1925, this hotel's assymmetrical rock columns and varied levels convey the impression of a mountain range. The concrete exterior is dyed to match the redwood forest. The floor-to-ceiling stained glass windows offer splendid views of the soaring walls of Yosemite Valley. Open year-round.
☎ 209–252–4848

BRYCE CANYON LODGE
Bryce Canyon National Park, Utah

■ Atop a mesa overlooking the colorfully hued stone walls of Bryce Canyon, the lodge and adjacent cabins are classic examples of rustic architecture. A cedar-shingled roof, stone masonry, wrought-iron chandeliers, and liberal use of solid log beams give an Old West feel. Open April to November.
☎ 303–297–2757

EL TOVAR LODGE
Grand Canyon National Park, Arizona

■ Only 50 feet from the South Rim of the Grand Canyon, El Tovar was one of the first railroad destinations resorts—promotional literature described it as a combination of "Swiss chalet and Norway villa." With Indian murals and crafts throughout, it is among the most eclectic hotels in the national parks. It is also one of the most luxurious, with first-rate gourmet meals. Open year-round.
☎ 303–297–2757

LAKE MACDONALD LODGE
Glacier National Park, Montana

■ Lying atop a small rise, the western façade of the hotel faces out across Lake MacDonald, the largest lake in the park, with views of the magnificent snow-capped mountain beyond. Open May to October.
☎ 602–207–6000

NORTH RIM LODGE
Grand Canyon National Park, Arizona

■ Lying on the edge of the North Rim, the lodge offers an inexpensive alternative to El Tovar. Built into the side of the rim, its several levels actually step down from the canyon rim. The many terraces and observation decks offer breathtaking views of the canyon. Open mid-May to mid-October.
☎ 303–297–2757

OLD FAITHFUL INN
Yellowstone National Park, Wyoming

■ Built in 1904, this is the first national park building constructed in a style harmonious with its natural surroundings. The hotel boasts a seven-story-high log lobby. Many rooms have views of the world-famous Old Faithful geyser nearby. Open early May to mid-October.
☎ 307–344–7311

OREGON CAVES CHATEAU
Oregon Caves National Monument

■ Located in the Siskiyou Mountains, this hotel actually spans a small gorge. A stream runs through the first-floor dining room and disappears outside into a forest. Open May through October—part of the year at "bed and breakfast" rates; the rest of the year as a full-service hotel. Call for a schedule.

☎ 503–592–3400

PARADISE INN
Mount Rainier National Park, Washington

■ One of the earliest ski resorts in the country, the inn lies at an elevation of 5,400 feet. The silvery exterior is made from timbers that were aged 30 years before construction of the building in 1916. Open mid-May to October.

☎ 360–569–2275

WAWONA HOTEL
Yosemite National Park, California

■ The largest existing Victorian hotel complex within a national park, and one of the best preserved in the country, Wawona also contains the studio of Thomas Hill, one of the great painters of the Hudson River School. Open April to November continuously and intermittently throughout the year. You have a choice of rooms with or without baths.

☎ 209–252–4848

ROSS LAKE RESORT
Ross Lake National Recreation Area, Washington

■ The resort consists of 10 rustic cabins and 3 bunkhouses on floating log rafts along the steep shoreline of Ross Lake in the Ross Lake National Recreation Area. All cabins have stoves and fireplaces. The modern cabins have baths; the little cabins have outside facilities. You can hike 2 miles in or go by boat. Open mid-June to the end of October. Book at least a year in advance.

☎ 206–386–4437

COZY CABINS
APPALACHIAN MOUNTAIN CLUB CABINS
White Mountains National Forest, New Hampshire

■ These 8 "backcountry huts," each a day's hike apart, sleep 36 to 90, and include meals and bunks. The most spectacular is Lakes of the Clouds Hut on Mt. Washington, 5,050 feet above sea level. Open late spring until early October. One of two self-service huts is Carter Notch Hut. You get a bunk, pillow, and blanket, and use of a kitchen. There is running water and toilets but no shower or electricity.

☎ 603–466–2727

CAPE LOOKOUT CABINS
Harker's Island, North Carolina

■ The only undeveloped part of the Outer Banks, these islands can be reached by boat or ferry. Each island has 20 to 30 cabins that sleep 2 to 12 people. There is no electricity, and you must bring your own supplies. However, there are bathrooms and hot and cold water. The busy time is during the fall fishing season. Open year-round.

☎ 919–225–4261

CEDAR PASS LODGE
Badlands National Park, South Dakota

■ Bison and pronghorn and bighorn sheep can be seen from these cabins. There are also fossil beds formed 37 million years ago during the Oligocene epoch. The 24 pine cabins are heated and air-conditioned, have showers and baths, and sleep 4 to 6. Meals are served nightly. The cabins are available from April to October.

☎ 605–433–5460

GRANITE PARK CHALET
Glacier National Park, Montana

■ Dating from 1914, the 11-room Granite Park Chalet and Sperry Chalet, a sister lodge, lie deep in the wilderness. Hike in or rent a horse. No reservations are needed—just show up at the Apgar visitor center about 24 hours in advance. It is a steep 5-mile hike up to the hut. This is bear country—bring pepper spray in case of an encounter with a grizzly.

☎ 406–387–5654

HALEAKALA NATIONAL PARK CABINS
Haleakala National Park, Hawaii

■ Cabins are a 4- to 10-mile hike into a volcanic wilderness of striking lava scenery, unusual plants, and exotic birds. Three cabins sleep up to 12 people and have wood-burning stoves, bunks, pit toilets, and firewood. The cabins are very popular and only available through a monthly lottery. Write at least 2¹/₂ months in advance of a planned visit and address requests to Haleakala National Park, attn: Cabins, P.O. Box 369, Makawao, HI 96768.

HIGH SIERRA TENT CAMPS
Yosemite National Park, California

■ Reachable only on foot or on horseback, this is a series of tent camps spaced 8–10 miles apart. The most remote camp is Merced Lake, which sleeps up to 60. There is a separate bath building with showers and a dining room. Applications are on a lottery basis and are accepted from October through November for the following summer. Open mid-June to mid-September. Mule rentals available.
☎209–252–4848

KETTLE FALLS HOTEL
Voyageurs National Park, Minnesota

■ Voyageurs is a paddler's dream with more than 30 lakes. Accessible by ferry, about a half mile from the historic Kettle Falls Hotel, are 12 separate units in 4 cabins that sleep 4 to 6 people. All rooms have baths, and some, fully equipped kitchens. Bedding, towels, and cleaning service are included and meals can be had at the nearby Kettle Hotel. Closed mid-October to mid-May.
☎ 888–534–6835

LA CONTE LODGE
Great Smoky Mountain National Park, Tennessee

■ It takes a good part of a day to hike to these cabins located on the third-highest peak in the Smokies. There are 7 one-room and 3 group cabins; bathroom facilities are in a separate structure, no showers. Open March through November, but start booking in October for the following summer.
☎423–429–5704

MAHO BAY CAMP
Virgin Islands National Park

■ Half the island of St. John and much of its shoreline is national park. Its pristine coral reefs are a perfect place for snorkeling and there are miles of mountain trails for hiking. Maho Bay Camp, built on wooden platforms with walkways to preserve the vegetation beneath, consists of canvas- and screen-covered tent cottages that sleep 5 to 6 people. Beds, linens, cooking facilities, and fans are provided. Book at least a year in advance. There is a restaurant on the premises.
☎800–392–9004

NORTH CASCADES STEHEKIN LODGE
North Cascades National Park, Washington

■ Situated on the banks of Lake Chelan, North Cascades Stehekin Lodge is a complex of fully equipped cabins that sleep 2 to 8 people, but it's accessible only by boat or a day-long hike. There is a restaurant, cross-country ski trails, and fishing boats.
☎509–682–4494

PHANTOM RANCH
Grand Canyon National Park, Arizona

■ Accessible only by mule, foot, or raft, Phantom Ranch is a series of 14 cabins and other buildings about 10 miles from Grand Canyon Village on the South Rim. All but one of the cabins are for mule travelers (mules are rented); each can sleep up to 10 people. The remaining one is for hikers and sleeps 4. Cabins have baths, electricity, and heat. Meals are included. Open year-round. Book 6 to 11 months in advance. The reservation desk opens on November 30.
☎303–297–2757

POTOMAC APPALACHIAN TRAIL CLUB CABINS
Shenandoah National Park, Virginia

■ Some of the cabins for rent in the Shenandoah were original settlers' homes. The 26 operated by the Potomac Appalachian Trail Club sleep 8 to 12 people and are reached by hiking from ¹/₅ to 4 miles along backcountry trails. All have fireplaces or woodstoves, outhouses, and even dishes. Corbin, a 2-story cabin at the end of Corbin Cabin Cut-off Trail, is on the National Register of Historic Buildings. It sleeps up to 12 people.
☎703–242–0315

PATHS ACROSS THE NATION

Some are no wider than a fat guy, all are of scenic or historic value

While they may not have hiked it top to bottom, most Americans have heard of the Appalachian Trail. Many are unaware, though, that the Appalachian belongs to a much larger system of trails. In 1968, Congress passed the National Trails Assistance Act to establish a national trail system. The trails fall into two categories: national scenic trails, which are protected scenic corridors for outdoor recreation, and national historic trails, which recognize prominent past routes of exploration, migration, and military action and may consist of no more than a series of roadside markers. The entire system includes 19 trails and covers most of the country.

NATIONAL SCENIC TRAILS

Benton MacKaye, the man who created the Appalachian Trail, thought it should be no wider than the space required by the average fat man. The majority of the trails are open to hikers only, although some allow mountain bikes and horses. Many are works in progress and have large sections closed to the public. Call ahead to inquire about available sections, allowable modes of transportation, and camping permits.

APPALACHIAN NATIONAL SCENIC TRAIL

Length: 2,159 miles ☛ The first interstate recreational trail, the Appalachian was conceived in 1921 by Benton MacKaye as a national preserve parallel to the East Coast. Beginning in Georgia and ending in Maine, the trail hugs the crest of the Appalachian Mountains and is open only to hikers. There are shelters every 6 to 12 miles, making it possible to hike the entire span without leaving the trail. Approximately 175 people hike the entire length of the trail every year, while millions of other hikers find inspiration and adventure on shorter segments.
☞ Appalachian Trail Conference, Harpers Ferry, WV 25425, ☎ 304–535–6278

CONTINENTAL DIVIDE NATIONAL SCENIC TRAIL

Length: 3,100 miles ☛ The Continental Divide Trail provides spectacular backcountry travel through the Rocky Mountains from Mexico to Canada. It is the most rugged of the long-distance trails. About 75 percent of the entire 3,100 miles is finished in some form, and the Forest Service hopes to complete the rest by the year 2000. (It is possible for the more adventurous to hike from border to border now, though.) The longest continuous finished stretch reaches 795 miles from Canada through Montana and Idaho to Yellowstone National Park, and there is another solid 400-mile stretch through Colorado. The trail is open to hikers, pack and saddle animals, and, in some places, off-road motorized vehicles.
☞ Continental Divide Society, Baltimore, MD 21218, ☎ 410–235–9610

FLORIDA NATIONAL SCENIC TRAIL

Length: 1,300 miles ☛ The Florida Trail extends from Big Cypress National Preserve in south Florida to just west of Pensacola in the northern part of the Florida Panhandle. Formed in 1964, the trail will eventually extend through Florida's three national forests to Gulf Islands National Seashore in the western panhandle. The trail passes through America's only subtropical landscape, making it especially popular with winter hikers and campers. Side-loop trails connect to nearby historic sites and other points of interest. At present, Forest Service officials estimate that about 600 miles of the trails are in place and open to public use.
☞ Florida Trail Association, Gainesville, FL 32064, ☎ 352–378–8823

ICE AGE NATIONAL SCENIC TRAIL

Length: 1,000 miles ☛ At the end of the Ice Age, some 10,000 years ago, glaciers

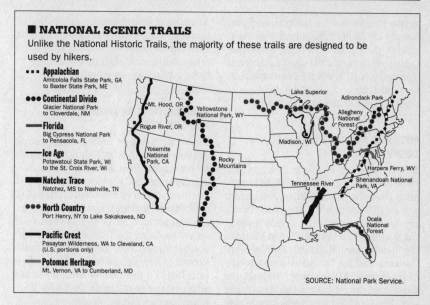

■ NATIONAL SCENIC TRAILS

Unlike the National Historic Trails, the majority of these trails are designed to be used by hikers.

- **▪ ▪ ▪ Appalachian**
  Amicolola Falls State Park, GA
  to Baxter State Park, ME

- **● ● ● Continental Divide**
  Glacier National Park
  to Cloverdale, NM

- **▬ Florida**
  Big Cypress National Park
  to Pensacola, FL

- **▬ Ice Age**
  Potawatoui State Park, WI
  to the St. Croix River, WI

- **▬ Natchez Trace**
  Natchez, MS to Nashville, TN

- **● ● ● North Country**
  Port Henry, NY to Lake Sakakawea, ND

- **▬ Pacific Crest**
  Pasaytan Wilderness, WA to Cleveland, CA
  (U.S. portions only)

- **▬ Potomac Heritage**
  Mt. Vernon, VA to Cumberland, MD

Map labels: Lake Superior; Adirondack Park; Mt. Hood, OR; Yellowstone National Park, WY; Allegheny National Forest; Rogue River, OR; Madison, WI; Yosemite National Park, CA; Rocky Mountains; Harpers Ferry, WV; Shenandoah National Park, VA; Tennessee River; Ocala National Forest

SOURCE: National Park Service.

---

retreated from North America and left at their southern edge a chain of moraine hills made of rocks and gravel that the glaciers had accumulated along their journey. In Wisconsin, this band of hills zigzags across the state for 1,000 miles from Lake Michigan to the St. Croix River. Almost half the trail is open to the public, and certain sections are sometimes even used for marathons, ski races, and super-long-distance running.

✎ National Park Service, Madison, WI 53711
☎ 608–264–5610

NATCHEZ TRACE NATIONAL SCENIC TRAIL

Length: 110 miles ☛ The trail lies within the boundaries of the as yet uncompleted Natchez Trace Parkway, which extends 450 miles from Natchez, Miss., to Nashville, Tenn. The parkway will commemorate the historic Natchez Trace, an ancient path that began as a series of animal tracks and trails used by Native Americans. It was later used by early explorers, "Kaintuck" boatmen, post riders, and military men, including Andrew Jackson after his victory at the Battle of New Orleans. Segments near Nashville (26 miles), Jackson (20 miles), and Rocky Springs (15 miles), which is near

Natchez, are close to completion. There also are about 20 shorter "leg-stretcher" trails throughout. The Park Service hopes to connect the entire 445 miles within the next 10 to 20 years.

✎ Natchez Trace Parkway, Tupelo, MS 38801
☎ 800–305–7417 or 601–680–4004

NORTH COUNTRY NATIONAL SCENIC TRAIL

Length: 3,200 miles ☛ Conceived in the mid-1960s, the North Country National Scenic Trail links the Adirondack Mountains with the Missouri River in North Dakota. The trail journeys through the grandeur of the Adirondacks, Pennsylvania's hardwood forests, the canals and rolling farmland of Ohio, the Great Lakes shorelines of Michigan, the glacier-carved lakes and streams of northern Wisconsin and Minnesota, and the vast plains of North Dakota—not to mention nine national forests and two national parks. About half of the trail is now completed for hiking.

✎ National Park Service, Madison, WI 53711
☎ 608–264–5610

PACIFIC CREST NATIONAL SCENIC TRAIL

Length: 2,638 miles ☛ Running along the spectacular shoulders of the Cascade and Sierra Nevada mountain ranges from Canada to Mexico, the Pacific Crest Trail is the West Coast counterpart to the Appalachian Trail. It passes through 25 national forests and seven national parks.

☛ U.S.D.A. Forest Service, Portland, OR 97204, ☎ 503–326–3644

POTOMAC HERITAGE NATIONAL SCENIC TRAIL

Length: 700 miles ☛ The trail commemorates the unique mix of history and recreation along the Potomac River. Although it was established only in 1983, park officials say that much of the trail is already in place: the 18-mile Mount Vernon Trail in Virginia, the 70-mile Laurel Highlands Trail in Pennsylvania, and the 184-mile towpath of the Chesapeake and Ohio Canal. The last 20 or so miles of the trail along the Chesapeake and Ohio provide a wonderful bicycle ride that ends in the heart of Washington, D.C.

☛ National Park Service National Capital FDO, Washington, D.C. 20242, ☎ 202–208–4797

NATIONAL HISTORIC TRAILS

National historic trails are somewhat more conceptual than national scenic trails. Their objective is to preserve any historic remnants of the trail rather than provide a continuous footpath across its entire length. The "trails" often are no more than a series of roadside signs that direct travelers to historic sites or markers, though foot trails do appear from time to time at the roadside stops. The main exception to this description is the Iditarod in Alaska.

IDITAROD NATIONAL HISTORIC TRAIL

Length: 2,450 miles ☛ The trail was made famous by prospectors and their dog teams during the Alaska gold rush at the turn of the century. Most of the trail is usable only during Alaska's six-month winter, when rivers and tundra are frozen. Each year, the 1,150-mile Iditarod sled dog race is run along the trail from Anchorage to Nome. Other events include the 210-mile Ididasport race for skiers, mountain bikers, and snowshoers, and the Alaska Gold Rush Classic Snowmachine Race.

A network of shelters is being installed by the Bureau of Land Management and the Iditarod Trail Committee.

☛ Bureau of Land Management–Anchorage District, Anchorage, AK 99687

☎ 907–267–1207

JUAN BAUTISTA DE ANZA NATIONAL HISTORIC TRAIL

Length: 1,200 miles ☛ In 1775, a party of 200 Spanish colonists led by Col. Juan Bautista de Anza set out from Mexico to establish an overland route to California. The band of 30 families, a dozen soldiers, and 1,000 head of cattle, horse, and mule spent three months traversing the deserts of the Southwest before reaching the California coast and another three months traveling up the coast to what is now San Francisco. There they established a presidio, or military headquarters, that is still in use today.

☛ National Park Service, Western Region Division of Planning, San Francisco, CA 94107, ☎ 415–427–1446

LEWIS AND CLARK NATIONAL HISTORIC TRAIL

Length: 3,700 miles ☛ President Thomas Jefferson in 1803 doubled the area of the United States by purchasing from France 885,000 square miles of land west of the Mississippi River. The following year he commissioned Meriwether Lewis and William Clark to explore and map his $125 million "Louisiana Purchase." They took the Missouri River upstream from what is today Wood River, Ill., and eventually

EXPERT SOURCE

The first comprehensive guide to America's trails, *Trails Across America* by Arthur and Marjorie Miller (Fulcrum, 1996, $19.95), describes all the National and Historic Trails and includes maps of each one.

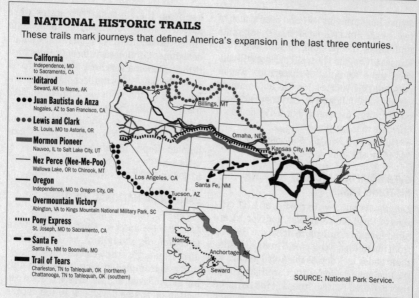

■ **NATIONAL HISTORIC TRAILS**

These trails mark journeys that defined America's expansion in the last three centuries.

— **California**
Independence, MO to Sacramento, CA

······ **Iditarod**
Seward, AK to Nome, AK

●●● **Juan Bautista de Anza**
Nogales, AZ to San Francisco, CA

●●● **Lewis and Clark**
St. Louis, MO to Astoria, OR

▬ **Mormon Pioneer**
Nauvoo, IL to Salt Lake City, UT

— **Nez Perce (Nee-Me-Poo)**
Wallowa Lake, OR to Chinook, MT

— **Oregon**
Independence, MO to Oregon City, OR

▬ **Overmountain Victory**
Abington, VA to Kings Mountain National Military Park, SC

'''''' **Pony Express**
St. Joseph, MO to Sacramento, CA

– – **Santa Fe**
Santa Fe, NM to Boonville, MO

▬ **Trail of Tears**
Charleston, TN to Tahlequah, OK (northern)
Chattanooga, TN to Tahlequah, OK (southern)

SOURCE: National Park Service.

reached the Pacific Ocean at the mouth of the Columbia River in 1805. State, local, and private interests have established motor routes, roadside markers, and museum exhibits telling the Lewis and Clark story along the route.

National Park Service, Madison, WI 53711
☎ 608–264–5610

MORMON PIONEER NATIONAL HISTORIC TRAIL

Length: 1,300 miles ☛ Mormon emigration was one of the principal forces of settlement of the West. Seeking refuge from religious persecution, thousands of Mormons in 1846 left their settlement in Nauvoo, Ill., where church founder Joseph Smith had lived. Smith and his followers spent the next winter in the Council Bluffs, Iowa, and Omaha, Neb., areas. Early in 1847, Brigham Young led an advance party west along the Platte River to Fort Bridger, Wyo., where they turned southwest and eventually came to the Great Salt Lake. The 1,624-mile route through five states generally is marked with a logo and closely follows the trail's historic route.

National Park Service, Salt Lake City, UT 84145, ☎ 801–539–4093

NEZ PERCE (NEE-ME-POO) NATIONAL HISTORIC TRAIL

Length: 1,170 miles ☛ The Nez Perce in 1877 were forced to leave their ancestral homelands in the Wallowa Valley of the Oregon Territory and move to the Lapwai Reservation in Idaho. Hostilities broke out between white settlers and some of the Nez Perce during the journey. Three of the settlers were killed. The U.S. Army was called in, and five bands of the Nez Perce, one of them led by Chief Joseph, headed north across the Rocky Mountains hoping to find refuge in Canada. They eluded capture for months, but just short of reaching the Canadian border in Montana, they were captured by the army and forced to settle in Oklahoma. Within two years, they were returned to Idaho and Washington. Joseph became an eloquent spokesman for peace until his death in 1904.

U.S. Forest Service, Nez Perce National Historic Trail Coordinator, Missoula, MT 59807, ☎ 406–329–3511

OREGON NATIONAL HISTORIC TRAIL

Length: 2,170 miles ☛ The Oregon Trail was the pathway to the Pacific for fur traders, gold seekers, missionaries, and emigrants of every stripe. Beginning in 1841 and over a span of two decades, an estimated 300,000 emigrants undertook the five-month journey from Kansas to Oregon. The trail corridor still contains some 300 miles of discernible wagon ruts and 125 historic sites. The approximate route can be followed by car; there are also opportunities to travel by foot, horse, or mountain bike in many places.

✐ National Park Service, Salt Lake City, UT 84145, ☎ 801–539–4094

OVERMOUNTAIN VICTORY NATIONAL HISTORIC TRAIL

Length: 300 miles ☛ In the fall of 1780, citizens of Virginia, Tennessee, and North Carolina formed a militia to drive the British from the southern colonies. This trail marks their 14-day trek across the Appalachians to the Piedmont region of the Carolinas. There they defeated British troops at the Battle of Kings Mountain, setting in motion events that led to the British surrender at Yorktown and the end of the Revolutionary War. Much of the trail is now roadway; only a 20-mile portion remains as a foot trail across the mountains.

✐ National Park Service, Atlanta, GA 30303 ☎ 404–562–3123

SANTA FE NATIONAL HISTORIC TRAIL

Length: 1,203 miles ☛ After Mexican independence in 1821, U.S. and Mexican traders developed this trail using American Indian travel and trade routes. It quickly became a commercial and cultural link between the two countries. It also became a road of conquest during the Mexican and Civil wars. With the building of the railroad to Santa Fe in 1880, the trail was largely abandoned. Of the 1,203 miles of the trail route between Old Franklin, Mo., and Santa Fe, N.M., more than 200 miles of wagon ruts remain visible; 30 miles of them are protected on federal lands.

✐ National Park Service, Santa Fe, NM 87504, ☎ 505–988–6888

TRAIL OF TEARS HISTORIC TRAIL

Length: 2,200 miles ☛ After many years of pressure from white settlers, 16,000 Chero-kee from the southeastern states were moved by the U.S. Army in the late 1830s to lands west of the Mississippi River. Various detachments followed different routes west to the Oklahoma Territory. Thousands died along the way. Today the designated trail follows two of the principal routes: a water trail (1,226 miles) along the Tennessee, Ohio, Mississippi, and Arkansas rivers; and an overland route (826 miles) from Chattanooga, Tenn., to Tahlequah, Okla.

✐ National Park Service, Santa Fe, NM 87504, ☎ 505–988–6888

CALIFORNIA NATIONAL HISTORIC TRAIL

Length: 5,665 miles ☛ The California Trail is commonly thought of as a single and direct line across the western United States that was trampled by fortune seekers during the gold rush of 1849. In fact, it was a collection of routes developed in the decade prior to the gold rush by land-seeking immigrants. Officially opened in 1992, the system includes an estimated 320 historical sites and the natural landmarks that guided immigrants.

✐ Oregon-California Trails Association, Independence, MO 64050 ☎ 816–252–2276

THE PONY EXPRESS TRAIL

Length: 1,666 miles ☛ During its 18 months of operation, riders for the privately owned Pony Express carried mail between St. Joseph, Mo., and San Francisco in an unprecedented 10 days. The horse-and-rider relay system became the most direct and practical means of east-west communications before the invention of the telegraph. The trail proved the feasibility of a central overland transportation route that could be used year-round, paving the way for a cross-country railroad. About one-third of the 150 relay stations, where the riders were allowed exactly two minutes to exchange mail with the stationmaster, show identifiable remains and are historical sites along the trail.

✐ National Park Service, Salt Lake City, UT 84145, ☎ 801–539–4093

CHAPTER SEVEN

ENTERTAINMENT

EXPERT QUOTES

"If one opens one's heart and ears to the music [in Handel's *Rinaldo*], it can work like a tonic against the burdens of daily life."
—Cecilia Bartoli, opera singer
Page 477

"Drawing is a way of thinking and learning to see in a different way."
—Ed Emberley, award-winning children's book illustrator
Page 503

"The most important requirements for great home movies are a good idea and a little planning."
—Rebecca Cardoza, video production expert
Page 512

■ **WHAT'S AHEAD:** **CHOOSE** a prizewinning title for your neighborhood book club... **EVALUATE** the benefits of CD mail-order programs... **CHECK OUT** the World Wide Web for the latest in music news... **TEACH** your child the simple pleasure of drawing... **ENJOY** stories that give R. L. Stine the shivers... **RIDE** the new hair-raising roller coasters opening across America...

BOOKS & MUSIC

ONLINE BOOKS

A TREK TO AMAZON.COM

The huge online bookstore has zillions of titles to pick from

Fears that the popularity of the Internet signaled the demise of great literature have proved to be unfounded. In fact, the success of online bookstores, such as Amazon.com, shows that the printed word is still very much in vogue.

In its few short years on the World Wide Web, Amazon.com *(http://www.amazon.com)*, has become perhaps the world's biggest bookstore. The company claims to be more than fourteen times the size of the largest bricks and mortar super bookstore. The number of titles it offers is staggering: 2.5 million book titles on hand and access to another 1.5 million books in print. In addition, Amazon offers 1 million popular, but hard-to-find or out-of-print titles.

Bookworms are visiting online book sites in swarms: Of the total $10 billion worth of books sold in 1996, $38.3 million were bought online, up from $11.4 million in 1995. Research analysts expect the online market to reach $255 million by the year 2000.

Much of the allure of online book buying is its convenience. At Amazon.com, you can plug your name, e-mail address, and literary preferences into a number of services that apprise you of the latest titles. For example, give Amazon.com's Eyes and Editors service the names of your favorite authors and areas of interest, and you will find a steady stream of recommendations in your e-mail box, including the latest titles in your chosen subject, as well as names of authors whose style and expertise might tweak your curiosity. Another service called Matchmaker asks customers to rate a series of books on a five-point scale. Using collaborative filtering technology, the service then recommends books that are most likely to match your interests.

The site strives to be interactive, encouraging customers to weigh in regularly with book reviews and personal favorites. An ongoing site contest offers $100 in free books to the best book reviews. Authors and publishers often discuss their books on site, and, just as in any local bookshop, the Amazon staff flags its own recommendations.

Amazon sells most books at a discount, which varies from time to time. In spring 1997, Amazon was taking 40 percent off the retail prices of the top 50 sellers in categories, such as science fiction, mystery, lit-

CYBER SOURCES

BOOK SALONS THAT BECKON

Amazon.com's presence hasn't gone unnoticed. New online bookstores are popping up quickly. Here are some other worthwhile online book salons.

BARNES & NOBLE

http://www.barnesandnoble.com

■ The bookstore's site offers all hardbacks in stock at a 30 percent discount; paperbacks are discounted 20 percent. But the site is low on amenities like e-mail.

BOOKSMITH IN SAN FRANCISCO

http://www.sirius.com/books

■ The Web site of this top independent bookstore in Haight-Ashbury is impressive, containing vast amounts of literary information. Books signed by authors are often available at no extra charge. Gift-wrapping is free but shipping is steep: $4.50 for the first book, $1 for each additional one.

BOOKSITE

http://www.booksite.com

■ Meet a virtual personal librarian who encourages you to describe a book and then helps you conduct a search. Shipping fees are figured by the weight of your order: $3.50 for the first pound, 75¢ for each additional one.

BOOKSERVE INTERNATIONAL BOOKSELLERS

http://www.bookserve.com

■ Brothers David and Michael Mason started this operation out of a family garage in Tennessee. The site sells more than 1 million international titles a year.

BOOK STACKS UNLIMITED

http://www.books.com

■ Offers a 15 percent discount on 300,000 of its 425,000 available titles. It touts itself as the world's largest book club, featuring online discussions of novels.

BORDERS

http://www.borders.com

■ This well-known bookstore is still getting its feet wet in the realm of online ordering. For now, you can order only a handful of featured books, although the company is working to expand the site.

CBOOKS EXPRESS

http://www.cbooks.com/home.html

■ International customers account for 30 percent of the site's sales. Often they can pick up books more cheaply here than in their neighborhood stores in Poland or Chile, for example.

HUNGRY MIND REVIEW

http://www.bookwire.com/HMR

■ Buy books and read witty reviews from this independent shop based in St. Paul, Minn.

---

erature, and computers. The same discount was offered on the Amazon.com 500 titles, which include bestsellers and books that Amazon editors deemed likely to become bestsellers.

Generous as those discounts are, they can sometimes be offset by hefty shipping fees, which come to $3 per order and an additional 95¢ per book. Settling the account can also make some online shoppers uncomfortable. Many shoppers are leery of revealing credit card numbers on the Net. Amazon gets around that concern by giving customers the option of charging purchases by phone.

Amazon is one of the few online companies to capitalize on what's referred to as communities of interest. If you have created a Web site for marathoners, for example, you can link your site to Amazon and let fellow runners order books on the sport. Amazon will then reward you with a 3 to 8 percent commission on any resulting sales. Amazon aims to please. About the only thing missing is a cup of tea—and a cozy armchair for perusing a new tome.

PRIZEWINNERS THAT SPEAK VOLUMES

Legions of literary offerings vie for coveted book awards each year. The following titles distinguished themselves recently by winning a prestigious prize such as the National Book Awards, National Book Critics Circle, the PEN/Faulkner, and Pulitzer prizes. The titles run the gamut from fiction to poetry, biography, and history.

NATIONAL BOOK AWARDS

A $10,000 award goes to the best book in each of the following categories.

Fiction
SHIP FEVER AND OTHER STORIES
by Andrea Barrett (W.W.Norton, $21)
■ The title novella is the tale of refugees from the Irish potato famine quarantined on a Canadian island. The remaining seven stories weave in fictional and historical characters from the 19th century.

Nonfiction
AN AMERICAN REQUIEM: GOD, MY FATHER, AND THE WAR THAT CAME BETWEEN US
by James Carroll (Houghton Mifflin, $24)
■ A seminary student and former priest, Carroll discusses the civil rights and Vietnam war protests, his father's disillusionment, and how the family coped with the upheaval of a tumultuous era.

Poetry
SCRAMBLED EGGS AND WHISKEY: POEMS, 1991–1995
by Hayden Carruth (Copper Canyon Press, $25)
■ Carruth's simple lines of poetry tackle his daughter's struggle against cancer, his late-life romance, poverty, and racism.

Young People's Literature
PARROT IN THE OVEN: MI VIDA
by Victor Martinez (Harper-Collins, $15)
A Mexican American adolescent comes of age in this first novel full of evocative imagery about neighborhood feuds, gawky teen love, and gritty schools.

NATIONAL BOOK CRITICS CIRCLE

Professional book reviewers chose the following favorites in these categories.

General Nonfiction
BAD LAND: AN AMERICAN ROMANCE
by Jonathan Raban (Pantheon, $25)
■ In his first book as a United States resident, Raban, an English expatriate, combines history and travel in this memoir, in which he researches the struggles of an earlier wave of immigrants to the west while making a series of road trips to Montana.

Fiction
WOMEN IN THEIR BEDS
by Gina Berriault (Counterpoint, $25)
■ A collection of 35 short stories. Her rich prose and brilliant use of language inspired one critic to recommend this book to "every reading group and writing workshop in the country."

Poetry
SUN UNDER WOOD
by Robert Haas (Ecco Press, $22)
■ The poet explores family, life, nature, and literature in this collection of thoughtful poems about the limitations and deceptions of thought.

Criticism
FINDING A FORM: ESSAYS
by William Gass (Knopf, $26)
■ The author discusses everything from the life of Nietzsche and Ezra Pound to the difficulties of writing an autobiography to various dimensions of the avant-garde movement.

PEN/FAULKNER AWARD

This award honors the year's best work of fiction by

an American writer. The prize is $15,000 for the winner, and $5,000 to each of four other nominees.

Winner
WOMEN IN THEIR BEDS
by Gina Berriault (Counterpoint Press, $25)
■ Berriault's collection of short stories also won the National Book Critics Circle. "One struggles to find a sentence that is anything less than jewel-box perfect," wrote a *New York Times* critic.

Runners-up
ST. BURL'S OBITUARY
by Daniel Akst (Harvest Books, $12)
■ Burleigh Bennett's life of moral virtue and culinary vice is upset when he stumbles upon a gangland killing. The character conjures up images of Ignatius Reilly in *A Confederacy of Dunces.*

THE BOOK OF MERCY
by Kathleen Cambor (Farrar, Straus & Giroux, $22)
■ The narrator, Edmund Mueller, and his daughter, Anne, take turns telling stories of Edmund's fascination with alchemy, Anne's psychiatry stories, and her brother's adventures in the Third World.

ATTICUS
by Ron Hansen (HarperCollins, $12)
■ This murder mystery set on the Caribbean coast of

Mexico illustrates a father's love for his son.

THE AUTOBIOGRAPHY OF MY MOTHER
by Jamaica Kincaid (Plume, $11)
■ The story of Zuela, a 70-year-old West Indian woman reflecting on her life, from the moment her mother died. *The Washington Post Book World* said Kincaid's work is "most comparable, perhaps, to Camus's *The Stranger.*"

THE PULITZER PRIZE

Joseph Pulitzer, publisher of the New York World, *set up this award as a bequest to Columbia University. The $3,000 prize is awarded annually for achievements in disciplines from journalism to drama. Here are the literary winners:*

Fiction
MARTIN DRESSLER: THE TALE OF AN AMERICAN DREAMER
by Steven Millhauser (Vintage, $12)
■ A young man begins as a clerk in his dad's cigar store on Broadway and becomes a 19th-century New York City hotel entrepreneur.

General Nonfiction
ASHES TO ASHES: AMERICA'S HUNDRED-YEAR CIGARETTE WAR, THE PUBLIC HEALTH, AND THE UNABASHED TRIUMPH OF PHILIP MORRIS
by Richard Kluger (Random House, $35)

■ This former reporter for *The Wall Street Journal* includes 200 interviews with tobacco insiders in this 800-page chronicle of how industry officials were able to downplay the dangers of smoking.

Biography
ANGELA'S ASHES
by Frank McCourt (Scribners, $23)
■ This New York City public school teacher and master storyteller weighs in with his first book, a funny, heartbreaking tale of his childhood voyage from Brooklyn to the slums of Limerick during the Great Depression.

Poetry
ALIVE TOGETHER: NEW AND SELECTED POEMS
by Lisel Mueller (Louisiana State University Press, $17.95)
■ An emigrant from Nazi Germany, Mueller writes of family relations and the contradictory wonders of nature.

History
ORIGINAL MEANINGS: POLITICS AND IDEAS IN THE MAKING OF THE CONSTITUTION
by Jack N. Rakove (Knopf, $35)
■ A Stanford University American History professor traces the critical debates and the early Congresses to illustrate the clash of politics and ideas that shaped the document.

CYBER SOURCES

THE SOUND OF CYBER MUSIC

The Internet is jammed with sites that cater to music lovers. You can download samples of the hottest songs, order recordings and concert tickets, check out the musical musings of other fans, or find out your favorite artist's shoe size—you name it. Artists of all stripes, from Abba to Zappa, have sites or pages on the World Wide Web. To help you sort through the cacophony, here is a guide to music sites that are worth a visit:

ON THE CHARTS

HITSWORLD
http://www.hitsworld.com

■ Lists of nationwide and international music charts, and of music most frequently requested or played by radio stations. One feature lets you vote on your favorites.

BILLBOARD MAGAZINE ONLINE
http://www.billboard.com

■ Official site of the industry's most trusted charts, it also offers samples of musical selections from its lists. Other features include daily music news updates and a trivia quiz. Winners get free CDs.

WORLD MUSIC CHARTS
http://www.musicscene.com/new/index.cgi

■ Enter the name of a country on this site and it will produce a variety of local and national record charts.

SPECIAL GENRES

DIRTY LINEN MAGAZINE
http://www.dirtynelson.com:80//linen/

■ An electronic magazine for folk and traditional-music fans, offering album reviews, as well as revealing interviews with artists.

BLUE HIGHWAY
http://www.magicnet.net:80/~curtis/

■ *The* blues site, it features tributes to legendary blues artists, local radio listings for blues-oriented shows, and The Gutbucket, a feature displaying rare photos from blues history.

EARLY 80'S CHEESE
http://www.mit.edu:8001/people/tobye/cheezy80's.htm/

■ All the scoop on '80s rock music, lists of the decade's top songs, and links to the Web sites of artists like Cyndi Lauper, Duran Duran, and Tears for Fears.

HIP-HOP HITLIST
http://www.hitlist.com

■ This is the stop for hip-hop lovers, featuring a listening booth with current hits, as well as news and reviews on hip-hop music and urban culture.

THE JAZZ PHOTOGRAPHS OF RAY AVERY
http://www.book.vci.edu/jazz/jazz.html

■ Ray Avery's beautiful black-and-white photos from the '50s West Coast jazz scene are found here. The pictures were taken at gigs, recording sessions, TV shows, and in more candid moments. They document legends like Billie Holiday, Chet Baker, Miles, Dave Brubeck, and others.

CLASSICAL MUSIC
http://www.einet.net/galaxy/leisure-and-recreation/music/douglas-bell/composers.html

■ Your link to sites for classical composers from Bach to Wagner.

RECORDINGS AND COLLECTIBLES

MUSIC BLVD.
http://www.musicblvd.com/

■ This online record store boasts more than 150,000 titles on CD and cassette. You can order releases in advance, so that you'll get them the same day the records hit the stores.

BOOTHAVEN BOOTLEG TRADERS PAGE
http://home.earthlink.net/~rraczkowski/bootlegs/

■ Visitors can trade—not sell—live recordings and concert videotapes of their favorite bands. The page specializes in performances by Van Halen, the Beatles, the Doors, the Rolling Stones, and Ozzy Osbourne.

POSTERS AND ROCK MEMORABILIA
http://www.teleport.com/
~legends/

■ Posters, records, and rare collectors' items are posted here, including great pieces of memorabilia from the Bill Graham venues and the Family Dog promotions. Online visitors can also buy shirts, posters, and backstage passes from rock, jazz, and blues concerts.

RARE AND USED RECORDS
http://users.aol.com/lp45btr/pri-vate/rock-k-l.txt

■ Nearly 500,000 used records are available, generally at a 10 percent discount. A great place to find records that have eluded you.

ROCKAWAY RECORDS
http://www.rockaway.com:80/

■ This site for the nearly 20-year-old store with locations in Arizona, Los Angeles, and Australia, specializes in records by the Beatles and Beach Boys. A good selection of records and CDs by artists from Cannonball Adderly to Tori Amos.

DADDY'S JUNKY MUSIC
http://www.daddys.com/

■ This site for the huge used-equipment dealer includes a full catalog of their wares. A large selection makes it the perfect place to shop for instruments, for novices and collectors. Buy, sell, or trade.

MISCELLANEOUS

REAL AUDIO
http://www.real audio.com

■ Before you dish out top dollar for concert tickets, check this site to download free software that provides access to audio snippets of concerts, record previews, and radio simulcasts.

ROCK AND ROLL HALL OF FAME
http://www.rockhall.com

■ A fun and informative site, featuring a "today in rock" section with tidbits about rock history events and lists of rock stars celebrating birthdays. Other features include the complete list of the Hall of Fame's 500 most influential songs, and names of those being inducted.

WHATEVER HAPPENED TO...?
http://www.hype.com/nostalgia/onehit/nearone.html

■ One-hit wonders like Aha, Bonnie Tyler, and Devo, with space to submit your own additions. Where else can you learn that the Captain and Tenille are still married?

ROCK AROUND THE WORLD RADIO SHOW SITE
http://www.ratw.com

■ News, interviews, and bootleg recordings from this legendary '70s rock radio show, Rock Around the World. Great pictures, sound clips, and more.

AUDIONET
http://www.audionet.com

■ This site offers links to online radio stations across the country, as well as occasional connections to concert broadcasts.

POLLSTAR
http://www.pollstar.com

■ This self-described bible for touring acts, includes a search function that allows you to search for concerts by artist, venue, or location.

ULTIMATE BAND LIST
http://www.ubl.com

■ Enter your favorite artist's name and this site will provide links to the appropriate Web site, news group, radio press, fan club site, and more.

MUSIC NEWS

MUSIC NEWS OF THE WORLD
http://www.addict.com/html/hifi/MNOTW

■ An online magazine of alternative rock news, well-written and updated daily. It covers most groups heard on modern-rock radio.

ALL STAR MAGAZINE
http://www.allstarmag.com/news

■ The *People* magazine of music Web sites, with great gossip. It's updated daily and covers mostly alternative rock.

CD CLUBS

DO CD CLUBS MAKE SENSE?

For the very vigilant they do, but it can be a tricky business

I f the ubiquitous ads touting "10 CDs for one penny," sound too good to be true, well, they are—sort of. The thicket of catches and fine print make participating in CD music clubs a tricky business. But for those who tread carefully and make the best of the gimmicks, CD clubs can actually give you a good value for your music dollar. And they can be a highly convenient way to build your music library.

The most important decision is to pick the right club. The two major clubs, Columbia House and BMG Music Service, have some notable distinctions (see box, facing page below). Both sell recordings from a variety of musical genres, but Columbia House has a larger stable. It stocks artists in 15 categories; BMG offers 14. Not included in the BMG lineup are recordings of artists on the Sony music label, which rules out popular stars like Bruce Springsteen, Billy Joel, and Isaac Stern, to mention a few.

You really do get the 10 or so advertised recordings, but in exchange you must buy one selection within a specified time period at regular club prices. Not surprisingly, the prices—$12.98 to $16.98 for CDs and $7.98 to $10.98 for cassettes—are sometimes higher than those in local music stores. Furthermore, the term "free" is a bit misleading. Members pay shipping and handling costs of up to $4 on each recording ordered, which is no bargain when you have 10 CDs coming. Nor do you get all your picks right away. Columbia House holds back on two of the promised CDs until you fulfill your membership obligations; BMG witholds three.

CD clubs require some vigilance. Every month, members are offered a selection chosen by the club. You can refuse the selection, but unless you notify the club in advance that you are declining, you will automatically be charged for it. A better option is to ask for a so-called positive option membership, which means that the monthly selection will be sent to you only if you specifically request it. This option is a good way to avoid having to pay for recordings you don't want. The irksome side effect, however, is that if you don't order a selection for an extended period, you get frequent letters reminding you to place an order to keep your membership active.

Columbia House rarely runs sales on all its catalog selections. BMG does so monthly. Take advantage of the sales—they can save you up to 65 percent off regular prices and are by far the best way to get great deals from these clubs. There are a few catches, of course. The sales are often reserved only for club members who have already fulfilled their membership obligations. And while BMG offers straight discounts, Columbia House requires you to buy one selection in order to get another (or occasionally two additional selections) for free. You can get additional free selections by recruiting family and friends to join the clubs. But with Columbia House, the member you recruit could be excluded from getting in on the company's best sales.

While the variety of offerings is good at the clubs, it's not exhaustive. One reason the clubs can afford to sell some selections at rock-bottom sale prices is that they pay lower royalties to artists. As a result, many artists, including the Beatles, the Rolling Stones, and Hootie and the Blowfish, put a limit on which of their more popular selections, if any, can be sold through music clubs. Furthermore, the clubs can't satisfy every musical taste. If you are in the market for more obscure tunes, or eclectic artists and albums, music clubs are not the place to shop.

GENERATIONAL JUKEBOX

Even Baby Boomers are getting tired of Classic Rock radio stations that play the same 300 songs over and over again. Thankfully, those who had their sensibilities forged in the Sixties can find plenty to like in today's music. From Jewel to Pavement and D'Angelo, here's a musical travel guide for the '90s:

IF YOU LIKE:	THEN YOU OUGHT TO HEAR:
THE BAND, VAN MORRISON	Counting Crows, The Wallflowers
THE CARS, THE SPECIALS	No Doubt, Goldfinger, 311, Sublime
JONI MITCHELL	Jewel, Paula Cole
MARVIN GAYE, LUTHER VANDROSS	Keith Sweat, Brian McKnight
BLONDIE, ABBA	The Cardigans
CHAKA KHAN, DONNA SUMMER	Toni Braxton, Mary J. Blige
BOB DYLAN, WOODY GUTHRIE	Beck, Haden
BARRY WHITE, TEDDY PENDERGRASS	R. Kelly, Babyface, The Tony Rich Project; Tony! Toni! Toné!
VELVET UNDERGROUND	Pavement
STEVIE WONDER	Jamiroquai, Sweetback
ROLLING STONES	Black Crowes, Railroad Jerk
NEIL YOUNG, THE BYRDS	Wilco, Son Volt, Dinosaur Jr.
TOM PETTY	Pete Droge and the Sinners
PATSY CLINE, EMMY LOU HARRIS	LeAnn Rimes, Deana Carter
THE CLASH, THE RAMONES	The Offspring, Green Day
PRINCE	Maxwell, D'Angelo
BOB MARLEY	Ziggy Marley, Buju Banton, Shabba Ranks
BLACK SABBATH	Alice in Chains, Soundgarden
THE KINKS, DAVID BOWIE	Blur, Spacehog
BEACH BOYS, THE BEATLES	Oasis, Matthew Sweet

SOURCE: Jamie Krents.

■ SINGING A DIFFERENT TUNE

Columbia House has a bigger selection than BMG but requires a 3-year deal.

BMG		COLUMBIA HOUSE
317–692–9200	☎	800–457–0500
7007.1532@compuserve.com	Internet	www.columbiahouse.com
10 free selections (3 held back)	Introductory offer	13 free selections (2 held back)
Buy 1 selection within 12 months at regular club prices	Membership obligations	Buy 5 selections within 36 months at regular club prices
$14.98–$16.98 for CDs $9.98–$10.98 for cassettes	Club's regular prices	$12.98–$16.98 for CDs $7.98–$10.98 for cassettes
14 musical genres	Overall selection	15 musical genres
Must decline by mail	To decline monthly selection	Can decline by phone 24 hours a day
4 free selections	Referral bonuses	4 free selections
$58.98 over 12 months (includes $4 shipping and handling per selection)	Minimum cost to join and fulfill obligations	$136.90 over 36 months (includes $4 shipping and handling per selection)

SOURCES: BMG; Columbia House.

INDIE LABELS
▼

TO FIND THE NEXT PEARL JAM...

To catch the next wave, the place to look is the independent labels

Heard of the new Tortoise record, or the latest release by Palace Music? If these bands are wholly unfamiliar to you, don't condemn yourself to the category of completely unhip just yet! You might never have heard of these bands because they release their recordings on small, independently owned record labels.

Largely unknown to the average music consumer, independent record labels are privately owned and smaller than well-known major labels like Sony or Geffen Records. But "indie" labels are home to some of the most exciting and innovative music being created. If you're looking for tomorrow's great bands, there are thousands of indie labels releasing music of every genre. Groups as diverse as the Smashing Pumpkins, Otis Redding, and Nirvana got their start on indie labels.

For many of these labels, making money from the music is only a secondary consideration. Says Chris Taquino, the head of UP Records, a successful Seattle-based independent: "We just want to put out great music without paying too much attention to whether it's commercially viable." Indies almost always give their artists total creative control, so what you hear on an indie release may well be truer to its artist's vision. Major label releases are more likely to reflect not only a band's tastes, but that of record company executives as well.

Indie labels can be difficult to find in retail outlets, but their albums are usually available through mail-order catalogs at a discount. Here, indie executive Taquino and Drew Hauser, director of college radio promotions at Advanced Alternative Media, provide their takes on a few of their favorite labels:

SUB POP RECORDS

■ Perhaps the most prominent indie label today, Sub Pop has been home to bands like Nirvana and Soundgarden. Current Sub Pop bands include the aggressive pop group Six Finger Satellite and the L.A.-based dense, heavy rock trio, Plexi. Specializing in the most cutting-edge rock music being played today, the Seattle-based Sub Pop sold 49 percent of its shares to Time Warner, and the result has been a huge increase in the promotion and availability of Sub Pop releases. The Sub Pop catalog comes with a coupon worth $1.00 off your first order and can be obtained by sending $1.00 to:
✆ Sub Pop Catalog, 1932 First Ave., Suite 1103, Seattle, WA 98101

EPITAPH RECORDS

■ Owned and run by Brett Gurewitz of the rock group Bad Religion, Epitaph has had great success recently with its distinctive brand of punk-tinged rock. Fans of Epitaph's superstar rock bands, like L7, and Rancid, may want to check out its less well known groups like Pennywise, Wayne Kramer (of the 1960s rock legends the MC5), the Cramps, and the Red Aunts. Epitaph's free catalog, which includes the releases from 12 other indie labels, can be ordered by sending a request to:
✆ 2140 Hyperion Ave., Los Angeles, CA 90027, ☎ 213–413–7325

RYKODISK

■ This indie's motto, "Big enough to matter, small enough to care," is reflected in the quality and in the wide variety of records it releases. In addition to reissuing rock classics by artists like Jimi Hendrix, Frank Zappa, and David Bowie, Rykodisk is also home to some of today's most innovative new rock bands like Sugar and Morphine. Rykodisk is far more than merely a rock record label, however; it also releases funk, jazz, folk, reggae, blues, hip-hop, and world music albums by artists from all over the world. Rykodisk's free catalog can be obtained by writing:
✆ Rykodisk USA, Pickering Wharf, Bldg. C, Salem, MA 01970

FOR R&B AND JAZZ LOVERS

Been through everything in the racks at your local music retailer's?
Try these mail-order music gold mines.

CADENCE, THE REVIEW OF JAZZ & BLUES

Cadence Bldg.
Redwood, NY 13679
☎ 315-287-2852

■ *Cadence* is both a catalog and a magazine. Every month it dedicates about 100 pages to jazz. There are features, extensive artist interviews, and dozens of record reviews. But it's the 40 pages of rare albums for sale that really make *Cadence* special. Each title is listed in a no-nonsense, phonebook style; over 9,000 titles indexed and alphabetized by record label.

Write or call to order a monthly subscription ($3 per issue, $30 per year).

DOUBLE TIME JAZZ RECORDS

1211 Aebersold Dr.
New Albany, IN 47150

■ Another well-organized jazz outlet, it offers nearly 5,000 titles. All eras of jazz are represented, but Double Time is especially good at locating out-of-print items. Write to receive a catalog.

RHINO CATALOG

10635 Santa Monica Blvd.
Los Angeles, CA 90025
☎ 800-357-4466

■ The label bills itself as the top archival record label in the country—and the extensive catalog bears out that claim. It covers music from the '50s to the '90s, with a great selection of funk anthologies and rock compilation albums. Catalogs may feature thick sections devoted to Cajun music, zydeco, New Orleans r&b, folk, world music, country and western, blues, jazz, vocals, and a lot more. The catalog is free for the asking, and requests are handled at the 800 number.

Rykodisk also offers a CD-ROM featuring an interactive tour through the label's full catalog as well as samples of Rykodisk artists' recordings and videos. The CD-ROM also enables travelers of the information superhighway to order Rykodisk products directly from the company via the Internet. Consumers can receive the CD-ROM, Surf This Disc, by sending $3.00 to:
✆ Rykodisk, Dept. S1, 530 N. 3rd St.
Minneapolis, MN 55401
e-mail: info@rykodisc.com

ALLIGATOR RECORDS

■ *The New York Times* calls Alligator "the leading record label for blues," adding that Alligator has "succeeded where the giants have failed." Founded by Bruce Iglauer in Chicago in 1971, Alligator has released albums from blues legends like Buddy Guy and Johnny Winter and continues to put out some of the finest blues being recorded. The folks at Alligator recently released a special silver anniversary collection. Their free catalog can be obtained by writing:
✆ Alligator Records, P.O. Box 60234, Chicago, IL 60660
☎ 800-344-5609

DISCHORD RECORDS

■ The ultimate indie label, Dischord shuns all corporate trappings and sells its punk rock releases as cheaply as possible. Founded by Ian Mackaye, the label, based in the nation's capital, is home to some of the biggest and best punk and hard-core rock bands like Fugazi and Slant 6. You can get Dischord's free catalog by sending a self-addressed stamped envelope to:
✆ Dischord Records, Dept. S,
3819 Beecher Street, Washington, D.C. 20007-1802

CLASSICS
▼

LIVING WITH THE MUSIC MASTERS

Building blocks for a classical CD collection, from Bach to Gershwin

"Music is about emotions," says Ted Libbey, who appears in the weekly National Public Radio show *Performance Today*. "It helps us grow." And classical music "has a particular richness because it goes back centuries," says Libbey, who is author of *The NPR Guide to Building a Classical CD Collection* (Workman Publishing Co., 1994). Following are the composers who Libbey believes would form the building blocks of any classical music collection, and why he thinks so.

JOHANN SEBASTIAN BACH (1685–1750)

Bach has had a huge influence on music history, much greater than any of his contemporaries would have guessed. He was known mainly as an astounding keyboard virtuoso and a very prolific composer. What has emerged in the two-and-a-half centuries since his death, however, is the absolutely amazing spiritual power of his compositions. There is a beauty of construction and a kind of clarity of conception and detail that goes far beyond what any other composer of the Baroque period achieved.

WOLFGANG AMADEUS MOZART (1756–1791)

Mozart is his favorite, Libbey says, because of the sense of humanity that comes out in the music. People say he was a divine genius, and it's true. But he was also very human. With all the formality of the 18th century, he could evoke tragedy in music and make it burn with emotion. He was a virtuoso keyboardist, the greatest of his age. At the same time he played the violin well enough that he could have had a career as Europe's leading violinist. In his operas he conveys to the listener an understanding of an emotional or dramatic state probably more acutely than any other composer of all time.

FRANZ JOSEPH HAYDN (1732–1809)

Haydn was the most powerful innovator of the later 18th century. In the field of symphonies, he was the leader. He grew the form from a lightweight suite to a very thoroughly worked-out and highly contrasted musical expression for a large orchestra. For Haydn, music was something of a game, and so there are wonderful jokes in his music. He didn't probe the tragic dimension as much as Mozart did, but he was a pioneer in creating the classical style.

LUDWIG VAN BEETHOVEN (1770–1827)

Beethoven was a classical composer who can also be called the first Romantic. He made things more subjective. His music not only conveyed emotions or imagery, but very precise emotions from his own soul as well. Working on the basis of what Mozart and Haydn had done, Beethoven reinvented the string quartet and symphony and expanded their meaning dramatically. His instrumentals set the standards for the entire 19th and 20th centuries. Like an undertow in the ocean, they pull you in.

FRANZ SCHUBERT (1797–1828)

Schubert was the great songwriter in music history; his melodies pin down a state of emotion so effectively. His music is more concerned with contemplation than drama. It puts a very high value on the beauty of sound. Indeed, what you hear in Schubert's music is the beginning of a Romantic concept of sound as color. His music inhabits regions. It's not in a hurry to go from one place to another in a straight line. It's like seeing a strange landscape.

FREDERIC CHOPIN (1810–1849)

There has never been a closer connection between a composer and an instrument than with Chopin and the piano. There is an Italian quality to some of his works: he treated the piano as a human voice. There is an undertone of darkness in much of what he wrote, but also a surreal beauty and lightness to it all—an imaginative release from life.

PIOTR ILYICH TCHAIKOVSKY (1840–1893)

Tchaikovsky has been diminished by the musicologists as a little bit too hysterical and trite in his music. But when you listen to his music, you're not surprised that it's among the most popular. It is music of immediate emotional impact. His ballets—*Sleeping Beauty*, *Swan Lake*, *The Nutcracker* —are among the greatest ever written. His symphonic music has a richness and translucency to it. Many of his musical ideas are almost commonplace, like a simple scale, but he clothed them so gloriously that they come out as very powerful expressions.

CLAUDE DEBUSSY (1862–1918)

Debussy was one of the most profound thinkers in the history of music. He did so much to create modernity. He had an ear for sonority that was completely original. He was influenced by the orchestra of cymbals and gongs from Indonesia that he heard at the World's Fair in Paris. It revolutionized his thinking about sound and resulted in some of the most extraordinary writing for the piano ever. The essential Debussy is in the quiet floating pieces like "Prelude to the Afternoon of a Faun." People tend to compare Debussy to the impressionist painters, but it's more accurate to compare him to the symbolist poets. Most of his work takes a literary point of departure.

GEORGE GERSHWIN (1898–1937)

Gershwin was a lot like Schubert. He was a wonderful melodist. His tunes are all over our musical consciousness. He wrote "Rhapsody in Blue" when he was 25. As he got older, he got more of a sense of organization and structure without losing that freshness he always possessed. His opera, *Porgy and Bess*, is probably the great American opera. It's a tragedy his life ended so early. He still conveys something of the American spirit, especially of the roaring '20s, that no one else has captured in quite the same way.

CYBER SOURCE

Why do classical music buffs love the genre? Classical Is Cool, a music Web site, polled its audience to find out. Here are the site's favorite five reasons, confirming that not all Wagner aficionados are devoid of humor:

5. German is less obscure than rap music lyrics.

4. You can make up your own words to a Beethoven string quartet.

3. Listening to classical music is the most fun you'll have wearing a suit.

2. It costs less and works better than Prozac.

1. The macarena doesn't exist in classical music.

To find Classical is Cool, go to:

http://www.classicaliscool.com/ cCoolTalk.html

CECILIA BARTOLI'S GUIDE TO OPERA

The Italian diva wants to share her favorite operas with all of you

Cecilia Bartoli is one of the most celebrated classical singers performing today. Highly acclaimed for her concert, opera, and recital appearances, she is known to an even wider audience through her immensely popular recordings (see box, next page), which have won numerous awards around the world. Here, the Italian mezzo-soprano known for the warmth and expressiveness of her singing recommends a list of 10 operas for opera-novices and opera lovers alike. She explains:

In trying to compile a list of 10 operas which are my recommendations for seducing people to become opera lovers, I would like to choose only one opera from each of 10 different composers, although each of them has written many other wonderful stage works. They are mentioned here not necessarily in the recommended order for listening.

■ MOZART'S *Le Nozze di Figaro*

Le Nozze di Figaro is a wonderful marriage of perfect music and a perfect story. Some people will chide me for not choosing *Don Giovanni* or *The Magic Flute* as his most perfect opera. I say, start with *Nozze* and then listen to ALL of Mozart's operas.

■ ROSSINI'S *La Cenerentola*

La Cenerentola is Rossini's scintillating setting of the Cinderella fairy tale. It also happens to be one of my favorite roles. And if you like the sparkle of *La Cenerentola*, you will find champagne in such other works as his *Barbiere di Siviglia* or *L'Italiana in Algieri*. Eventually you will find your way also to his serious operas.

■ PUCCINI'S *La Bohème*

Puccini's *La Bohème* is probably the most directly appealing opera. It's about youth, love, and tragedy in the most realistic terms, set to glorious music. And from *La Bohème* one goes so easily to all the other works of this great composer.

■ BIZET'S *Carmen*

Many consider the adventures of the Spanish gypsy to be the perfect opera. This is a timeless story set to timeless music. One could say that it is the first really realistic opera— a path to what later became *verismo* in opera.

■ MASCAGNI'S *Cavalleria Rusticana*

This opera is considered the most important step into the *verismo* era in music. In *verismo*, best translated as "stark reality," there are no gods, no mythical beings, no royalty, no *deus ex machina*—just everyday people in some very realistic, and often violent, circumstances. If it were not for its emotionally charged music, it might be a play or a movie.

■ VERDI'S *Otello*

This is a perfect example of an opera being more powerful than its source. Shakespeare's play is weak in that the jealousy motive built on the missing handkerchief is rather unbelievable. Through Verdi's absolutely glorious music the story becomes not only completely believable but in the end truly heart-wrenching.

■ RICHARD STRAUSS'S *Elektra*

Elektra is probably the prime shocker in music and there will be raised eyebrows as to why I have included it in a 10-most-accessible-operas list. This searing score is built on the Sophocles tragedy and it is unsparing in its assault on our senses. But our senses have become accustomed to so much violence in entertainment that *Elektra* may be the very subject matter that has an immediate audience appeal.

I've purposely left three of the earliest operas for the end of my list. They are from the early Baroque era, the beginning of the 18th century. Strange as it may seem, to some listeners this early music is the most accessible of all, because of its "logic" in composition. To others it is an acquired taste. My advice is that every listener should do his own experimenting.

■ HANDEL'S *Rinaldo*

Written in 1711, *Rinaldo* is based on the text of Torquato Tasso's *Liberation of Jerusalem*. Although it demands female and male singers capable of extraordinary bravura singing, its music has an almost "healing" quality. If one opens one's heart and ears to this music, it can work like a tonic against the burdens of daily life. Let us not forget that because of "Messiah," Handel is no stranger to most of us.

■ PERGOLESI'S *La Serva Padrona*

La Serva Padrona was written in 1733 and its success, in so many countries in addition to its native Italy, established it as ground-breaking in the area of comic opera—or *opera buffa*. The music is inventive, charming, and often "witty." It is extremely easy on the ears, which is a quality to be cherished.

■ VIVALDI'S *Orlando Furioso*

Orlando Furioso, which premiered in 1727, is based on Ariosto's epic poem, which was also the inspiration for the three Handel operas: *Orlando*, *Ariodante*, and *Alcina*. Like Handel's *Rinaldo*, this is an *opera seria*—but listen to the differences in composing styles. To my ears, it takes more liberties within the musical boundaries of that era, just like Vivaldi's "The Four Seasons" is looser in concept than Handel's "Water Music" and "Fireworks Music."

I hope that we will have a real revival of Vivaldi in opera soon—and that I will be part of it.

THE ART AND SOUL OF A SONGBIRD

If you haven't enjoyed Cecilia Bartoli's singing on CDs, you're in for a treat. Here are some highlights and sources for those who can't get enough:

■ CDs	Cecilia Bartoli: A Portrait	London Records	1995
	Haydn: Orfeo ed Euridice	Oiseau Lyre London/Decca	1997
	If You Love Me	London Records	1993
	The Impatient Lover	London Records	1993
	Mozart Arias	London Records	1991
	Mozart: La Clemenza di Tito	London Records	1995
	Mozart: Le Nozze di Figaro	Deutsche Grammophon	1996
	Mozart Portraits	London Records	1994
	Pergolesi: Stabat Mater	London Records	1990
	Rossini Arias	London Records	1989
	Rossini Heroines	London Records	1992
	Rossini: Il Barbiere di Siviglia	London Records	1989
	Rossini: Il Barbiere di Siviglia (excerpt)	London Records	1993
	Rossini: La Cenerentola	London Records	1993
	Rossini Recital	London Records	1991
	Rossini: Stabat Mater	Philips	1990
■ VIDEOS	Cecilia Bartoli: A Portrait	London Records	1992
	Rossini: Il Barbiere di Siviglia	RCA	1993
	Rossini: La Cenerentola	London Records	1996
:// WWW	Cecilia Bartoli FanWeb	http://www.lochnet.com/client/gs/cb.html	

MOVIES

STUDIO TOURS
▼

BACKLOT THRILLS AND SPILLS

Here's a chance to schmooze with your favorite celluloid creatures

I f your kids have a say in the matter, your next vacation may find you face to knees with King Kong or zooming in a car heading Back to the Future. Each year 23 million people descend on the major movie-studio theme parks: Universal Studios in Universal City, Calif., and Orlando, Fla., and MGM Studios, also in Orlando. Elbowing visitors may not be everyone's idea of fun, but for movie buffs and seekers of amusement park thrills, movie-studio tours can be just the ticket.

Besides the usual rides, tours, and exhibits based on movie blockbusters and popular television shows, the parks also put on special concerts and holiday celebrations that often attract huge crowds. Find out about them in advance and schedule your visit accordingly.

A trip to these studios doesn't have to plunder you. The parks offer attractive package deals that include air fare, hotel accommodations, and park passes. The deals can be an economical way to visit—if you plan to stay for several days. Otherwise, you'll do better by buying a one-day pass and staying in a hotel a few miles away from the park. Here's how the studios compare:

UNIVERSAL STUDIOS

Universal City, Calif. ☛ *9 a.m. to 7 p.m.; summer: 7 a.m. to 11 p.m.; every day except Thanksgiving and Christmas.*

■ A fisherman's boat capsizes and you watch him disappear into the murky depths. Moments later you're heading toward a huge shark with jagged teeth. It veers away seconds before you approach. The Jaws ride, based on the old hit movie, is still one of the park's best offerings. Other popular rides include ET, in which the audience is lifted aboard starbound bicycles, and Back to the Future, a special effects ride in a flashy DeLorean sports car. A newly added attraction, based on the hit movie *Jurassic Park*, opened in the summer of 1997. Movie buffs will relish the 500 outdoor sets and facades depicting locations such as the Old West and Europe. Nestled between the Hollywood hills and the San Fernando Valley, this 420-acre studio lot may be the granddaddy of movie theme parks, but a recent face-lift has given it new vigor
■ **TICKETS:** $34 for 12 and over; $26 for 3–11; under 3 admitted free. Parking: $6
☎ 818–622–3801

UNIVERSAL STUDIOS

Orlando, Fla. ☛ *9 a.m. to 7 p.m.; 9 a.m. to 11 p.m. from June to September and during*

MOVIE BUFFS: TEST YOUR METTLE

Mired in a movie trivia contest? Brendan's Magnificent Movie Quote Trivia Page at http://www.mosquito.com/~uofmich/movies.html *can help. Try this quiz of famous quotes, gleaned from the site. Who said...*

1. *"Sweetheart, you can't buy the necessities of life with cookies."*

2. *"Oh, I forgot. You were sick the day they taught law at law school."*

3. *"The city that he builds shall bear my name, the woman that he loves shall bear my child. So let it be written, so let it be done."*

4. *"I'm only laughing on the outside. My smile is just skin deep. If you could see inside I'm really crying. You might join me for a weep."*

5. *"Your eyes are full of hate, forty-one. That's good. Hate keeps a man alive."*

6. *"It's the story of my life. I always get the fuzzy end of the lollipop."*

ANSWERS: 1. Alan Arkin, *Edward Scissorhands* **2.** Tom Cruise, *A Few Good Men* **3.** Yul Brynner, *The Ten Commandments* **4.** Jack Nicholson, *Batman* **5.** Jack Hawkins, *Ben Hur* **6.** Marilyn Monroe, *Some Like It Hot*

---

holidays. Open every day.

■ At this newer version of Universal Studios, you can confront the massive King Kong on the streets of a pseudo New York City. If your tastes run to newer action movies, you should check out the Terminator II video attraction in which Arnold Schwarzenegger, the Terminator himself, reveals how the movie's special effects were created. Younger visitors will relish the World of Hanna-Barbera, where they can cuddle with characters like Yogi Bear and the Jetsons. At Nickelodeon Studios you can watch tapings of shows like *All That* and *Global Guts,* or peek behind the scenes into editing and makeup rooms. The Animal Actors Stage features amazing performances by chimps and Mr. Ed the talking horse. Or, if cowboy movies are your thing, head for the Wild West Show and watch stunt people perform like celluloid bronco busters.

You can combine your visit with trips to nearby Sea World and Wet 'n Wild water park by buying a special combination ticket.

■ **TICKETS:** $39.75; $32 for ages 3–9; under three admitted free. Parking: $6
☎ 407–363–8000

MGM STUDIOS

Orlando, Fla. ☛ *9 a.m. to 7 p.m.; 9 a.m. to 9:30 p.m. June through August and during holidays. Open every day.*

■ A fully operational television, animation, and radio studio, this park was added to the huge Disney World complex in Orlando in 1986. Rides feature Indiana Jones' Epic Adventure in which stunt performers enact scenes from *Raiders of the Lost Ark*—often getting a little help from the audience—and Jim Henson's Muppet Vision 4-D, a combination puppet theater and 3-D movie. Characters from movies like *Toy Story* wander the park to meet, greet, and take photos with guests.

A popular spot is Superstar Television, in which you can act along with the cast of *Cheers* and *Home Improvement* and with legends like Lucille Ball—all made possible through high-tech video technology. If you're a *Star Wars* fan don't miss the chance to ride Star Tours, which includes a flight simulator for you to test.

■ **TICKETS:** $39.75; $32.00 for ages 3–9; under three are admitted free. Parking: $5
☎ 407–934–7639

WELCOME TO ONLINE HOLLYWOOD

Judging a movie by its blurbs is like taking the claims in "personal ads" at face value. Your salvation may lie in pulling a few quick movie reviews off the Internet. There's no shortage of opinions on the World Wide Web. The Yahoo index, one of a number of programs that catalog and steer Internet users to what they're looking for, recently showed more than 120 sources of movie reviews, with new sites constantly cropping up. Everything from two- to three-sentence reviews with letter grades for the latest releases to scholarly discourses are within a click of your mouse. Here are a few of your scouting options and what they serve up.

MOVIE REVIEWS

THE INTERNET MOVIE DATABASE
http://us.imdb.com

■ This sort of cinema bible is a vast compendium of movie-related information compiled by movie buffs' contributions and then repackaged for easy electronic retrieval by fellow enthusiasts. Users are invited to update the database and post their own reviews. You can engage in a kind of running plebiscite by having your ratings of any of the thousands of films on the site factored into the scores posted for each title. If you're trying to decide whether or not to see *Jerry Maguire*, for instance, you can check how database users rated it.

MR. SHOWBIZ
http://www.mrshowbiz.com

■ Mr. Showbiz is a spirited entertainment magazine in cyberspace. You'll find movie, television, and music reviews, and lots of celeb features, showbiz news, and dishy gossip. One nice feature of the movie reviews: If you're in a hurry to make the show, there's a quick one- or two-sentence assessment, followed by a numerical ranking for each film so you don't have to read the full review. Mr. S. is very clever. One recent entry in his Haiku page, for example: "Tom Cruise: pilot, spy/Vampire, lawyer, barkeep, star./All in a day's work."

PATHFINDER
http://www.pathfinder.com

■ All the movie reviews that appear in the Time Warner magazine family, including *Time, People,* and *Entertainment Weekly*. Need more be said?

HOLLYWOOD ONLINE
http://www.hollywood.com

■ A list of all the current movies links you to reviews and official film sites. A good base for launching off into everything Tinseltown has to offer: star news, movie-themed games, interviews with celebs, and more.

MOVIE LINK
http://www.777film.com

■ This useful, practical site tells you when the latest movies will show at your local theater and lets you order tickets (but expect to pay a premium). You get a movie rating guide, as well as synopses of plots.

CINEMANIA ONLINE
http://www.msn.com/cinemania

■ A wide-ranging site featuring current reviews by "two thumbs up" byline superstar Roger Ebert, as well as Leonard Maltin and Cinemania's own in-house reviewers. Film star biographies, highbrow essays, movie award-winners—it's all here.

MR. CRANKY
http://internet-plaza.net/zone/mrcranky

■ You might never go to the movies again if you listen to Mr. Cranky, but he's sure to put you in a better mood anyway. The ratings system he uses is unique: "Almost Tolerable" (1 cherry bomb); "Consistently Annoying" (2 cherry bombs); "Will Require Therapy After Viewing" (3 cherry bombs); "As Good As A Poke In The Eye With A Sharp Stick" (4 cherry bombs); "So Godawful That It Ruptured The

■ CYBER SOURCES

Very Fabric Of Space And Time With The Sheer Overpowering Force Of Its Mediocrity" (1 bundle of dynamite).

E! ONLINE
http://www.eonline.com

■ This site dishes out the latest Hollywood gossip about entertainment celebrities. Its saving grace is its sense of humor.

CELEBRITY SITES

The following were chosen by Yahoo! *magazine as the top movie star sites.*

ELVIS
sunsite.unc.edu/elvis/elvishom.html

■ Forget the visit to Graceland, you can get a virtual tour of the King's mansion at this site. Plus: a monthly calendar of Elvis-related happenings like TV shows and movies, links to other Elvis sites, and, last but not least, a copy of the King's last will and testament.

KEANU REEVES
http://www.empirenet.com/-rdaeley/skc/index.html

■ Another facet of actor Reeves's talents are on display here: his creed for raising consciousness through spiritual enlightenment. Says Yahoo!, with tongue firmly in cheek, "All Keanuisms are religiously probed for spiritual meaning."

THE SIMPSONS
http://www.eden.com/maverick/

MEET THE BLURB WRITERS

Trying to spend your movie-ticket dollar wisely? The blurbs in movie ads can be as deceptive as cineplex popcorn "butter." If the names attached to "Heartwarming," and "Best of the Year" mean nothing to you, here's the skinny on the critics who do the dissin'.

■ **MICHAEL MEDVED,** *New York Post:* Medved's tastes favor family-styled fare. Trust him when you're taking the kids.

■ **TERRENCE RAFFERTY,** *The New Yorker:* Rafferty has inherited the mantle of his predecessor, Pauline Kael, as Hollywood's most demanding critic. If he likes a major studio film, it's probably good. He's much less discriminating with art flicks.

■ **CARRIE RICKEY,** *Philadelphia Enquirer:* Tough to please. She gets more excited by risk-takers (good or bad) than recycled formulas.

■ **JOEL SIEGEL,** *Good Morning America:* Call him an optimist, but he loves almost everything. If you're going to the theater based only on his blurb, you're asking for it.

■ **GENE SHALIT,** *Today:* He's not "blurbed" as much as he used to be, which means he's become more critical of big films.

■ **KENNETH TURAN,** *Los Angeles Times:* Turan is pretty cynical, as befits a critic in Hollywood's backyard. But when he praises a movie, he means it.

simpsons.html

■ Among the zillions of online sites that pay tribute to the irreverent and zany TV cartoon family, this is the best. It has a well-organized page that features a great collection of Simpsons audio bites, including Bart's "I was myself with a rag on a stick."

XENA
http://www.xenafan.com

■ The sword-swinging Princess Xena, played by Lucy Lawless, is now queen of the Internet. Homage is paid at this site with Xena fan art, bloopers, and snippets from old TV shows revealing the raven-haired Lawless was once a blonde.

MOVIES THAT MADE IT TO THE HALL OF FAME

On your next trip to the video store, bring back something that's really worth watching. Listed below are feature films in the National Film Registry, including those inducted in 1996, marked by an asterisk. The films are organized by category, along with a brief description of the entries and any Oscars they may have won. Not included are films made before the 1927 inception of the Academy Awards. Only those films that are generally available on videocassette have been selected.

COMEDY

ANNIE HALL
Woody Allen, color, 1977, 94m

■ One of the best romantic comedies ever made. Woody Allen stars and directs himself, Diane Keaton, and Tony Roberts through the minefield of relationships in New York and Los Angeles.

■ **OSCARS:** Best Actress, Director, Screenplay, Picture.

THE APARTMENT
Billy Wilder, B&W, 1960, 125m

■ Jack Lemmon stars in this fantastic satire as an insurance clerk who lends his apartment to his superiors for their extra-marital affairs. All's well until he falls for one of the women. Shirley MacLaine and Fred MacMurray co-star.

■ **OSCARS:** Best Art Direction/Set Decoration, Director, Editing, Screenplay.

THE AWFUL TRUTH*
Leo McCarey, B&W, 1937, 90m

■ Cary Grant and Irene Dunne star in this classic 1930 screwball comedy about a series of marriage misadventures.

■ **OSCARS:** Best Director.

BRINGING UP BABY
Howard Hawks, B&W, 1938, 102m

■ Katharine Hepburn and Cary Grant star in the kind of great slapstick comedy that just doesn't get made anymore.

DAVID HOLZMAN'S DIARY
Jim McBride, B&W, 1967, 71m

■ Clever satire on the pretensions of cinema verité. A filmmaker explores the truth in his life by making a film about himself.

DR. STRANGELOVE (OR, HOW I LEARNED TO STOP WORRYING AND LOVE THE BOMB)
Stanley Kubrick, B&W, 1964, 93m

■ Peter Sellers plays three roles in this brilliant black comedy about nuclear bombs. George C. Scott, Slim Pickens, and James Earl Jones contribute great comic performances, too. Nominated for Best Picture.

DUCK SOUP
Leo McCarey, B&W, 1933, 70m

■ The best of the Marx Brothers films. Strangely, it was a box-office disaster when first released.

HIS GIRL FRIDAY
Howard Hawks, B&W, 1940, 92m

■ Based on the oft-filmed Ben Hecht and Charles MacArthur play, *The Front Page*. Cary Grant and Rosalind Russell have combustible chemistry as a battling reporter and her editor.

THE HOSPITAL
Arthur Hiller, color, 1971, 102m

■ Very black hit-and-miss comedy, scripted by Paddy Chayefsky, with a magisterial performance from George C. Scott as a depressed hospital boss faced with a raft of professional crises.

■ **OSCAR:** Best Screenplay.

IT HAPPENED ONE NIGHT
Frank Capra, B&W, 1934, 105m

■ Clark Gable and Claudette Colbert fall in love one night. Frank Capra directs in the patent "feel-good" style he invented.

■ **OSCARS:** Best Screenplay, Actor, Actress, Director, Picture.

MODERN TIMES
Charlie Chaplin, B&W, *1936, 87m*

■ Chaplin's classic industrial satire features the Little Tramp stuck in an automated nightmare. It probably means more to today's technology-flooded viewers than it did to the moviegoers of 1936.

A NIGHT AT THE OPERA
Sam Wood, B&W, *1935, 92m*

■ A Marx Brothers musical comedy with a love story tacked on for good measure. Fortunately, the romance doesn't spoil the Brothers' weird brand of antic fun.

NINOTCHKA
Ernst Lubitsch, B&W, *1939, 110m*

■ A comedy starring Greta Garbo? The lady with the scowl plays a Soviet commissar checking up on some comrades in Paris. It's still good lightweight entertainment.

THE PHILADELPHIA STORY
George Cukor, B&W, *1940, 112m*

■ Donald Ogden Stewart's adaptation of Philip Barry's hit Broadway comedy, about a socialite wedding threatened by scandal, fires on every cylinder. Katharine Hepburn, Cary Grant, and notably James Stewart are in peak, sophisticated form.
■ **OSCARS:** Best Screenplay, Actor.

THE PRODUCERS*
Mel Brooks, color, 1968, 88m

■ Zero Mostel stars as a louse who is amazed when his intentionally tasteless play, *Springtime for Hitler,* becomes a hit.
■ **OSCAR:** Mel Brooks, Best Screenplay.

ROAD TO MOROCCO*
David Butler, B&W *1942, 83m*

■ Bob Hope and Bing Crosby are the comedic duo hamming it up as lone survivors of a shipwreck trekking back to civilization.

SOME LIKE IT HOT
Billy Wilder, B&W, *1959, 120m*

■ A classic. Jack Lemmon and Tony Curtis witness a mob hit and flee to the safe haven of an all-girl band— as girls. Marilyn Monroe is the lead singer of the band in her best performance.
■ **OSCAR:** Best Costume Design.

SULLIVAN'S TRAVELS
Preston Sturges, B&W, *1941, 90m*

■ Sturges sends a jaded Hollywood director out into the real world with nothing but a dime in his pocket. Clever satire featuring Veronica Lake.

TO BE OR NOT TO BE*
Ernst Lubitsch, B&W *1942, 99m*

■ At the time of its release, some thought this searing satire of the Nazi regime was in bad taste. Today, it is seen as an insight-

---

FACT FILE:

OSCAR'S LATEST FAVORITES

■ *From* Gone With the Wind *to* The English Patient, *Hollywood has always loved epic romances in historical settings.*
In 1997, The English Patient, *a romance set in World War II, took home Best Picture, Best Directing, Best Supporting Actress, and eight additional Oscars. Big category winners for 1997 included:*

Geoffrey Rush, Best Actor, Shine
Frances McDormand, Best Actress, Fargo
Cuba Gooding, Jr., Best Supporting Actor, Jerry Maguire
Juliette Binoche, Best Supporting Actress, The English Patient

ful and hilarious political commentary.

TROUBLE IN PARADISE
Ernst Lubitsch, B&W, 1932, 83m

■ The story of two jewel thieves who fall in and out of love.

DRAMA
THE ADVENTURES OF ROBIN HOOD
Michael Curtiz and William Keighley, color, 1938, 105m

■ The old yarn is retold with flamboyant gusto on great sets. Errol Flynn and Basil Rathbone duel with unsurpassed panache.
■ **OSCARS:** Best Music, Art Direction, Editing.

THE AFRICAN QUEEN
John Huston, color, 1951, 105m

■ Bogart and Hepburn travel downriver through Africa. Scripted by James Agee. A near-perfect film.
■ **OSCAR:** Best Actor.

ALL ABOUT EVE
Joseph L. Mankiewicz, B&W, 1950, 138m

■ This look at the New York theater scene features a great leading performance from Bette Davis. Also stars Anne Baxter and George Sanders.
■ **OSCARS:** Best Director, Picture, Sound, Supporting Actor.

ALL THAT HEAVEN ALLOWS
Douglas Sirk, color 1955, 89m

■ Glossy weepie that runs a stiletto into the heart of the American Dream. Jane Wyman is the wealthy widow who has an ill-fated affair with young Rock Hudson, her bohemian gardener. Lurid and harrowing.

AMERICAN GRAFFITI
George Lucas, color, 1973, 110m

■ Breakthrough, and very taking, nostalgia picture about California teenage life on a small-town strip in 1962. With Ron Howard, Richard Dreyfuss, and Harrison Ford in top form at the start of their careers. You'll remember the songs.

THE BLOOD OF JESUS
Spencer Williams, Jr., color, 1941, 50m

■ Williams wrote, directed, and starred in this story of a husband who accidentally shoots his wife.

BONNIE AND CLYDE
Arthur Penn, color, 1967, 111m

■ Warren Beatty and Faye Dunaway reinvented the gangster picture as the infamous crime duo. The final shoot-out in slow motion is one of the most memorable scenes in American film. Also stars Gene Hackman and Estelle Parsons.
■ **OSCARS:** Best Cinematography, Supporting Actress.

CASABLANCA
Michael Curtiz, B&W, 1942, 102m

■ The standard by which every movie romance will forever be judged. Bogart and Bergman are magic at every turn.
■ **OSCARS:** Best Director, Picture, Screenplay.

CITIZEN KANE
Orson Welles, B&W, 1941, 119m

■ The single most influential American film. The story of newspaper tycoon Charles Foster Kane still tops many lists of the greatest films of all time, and it established Orson Welles as the premier talent of his generation.
■ **OSCAR:** Best Original Screenplay.

CITY LIGHTS
Charlie Chaplin, B&W, 1931, 81m

■ Considered Chaplin's masterpiece, the actor's little tramp befriends a blind woman and does all he can to help her. The finale will bring tears to your eyes.

THE CROWD
King Vidor, B&W, 1928, 90m
■ An examination of a working-class family in a wealthy world. Vidor's best work.

THE DEER HUNTER*
Michael Cimino, Technicolor 1978, 182m

■ This epic film examines the effect of the Vietnam war on a small Pennsylvania community, and its slow readjustment in the conflict's aftermath. Starring: Robert De Niro, Christopher Walken, and Meryl Streep.

■ **OSCARS:** Best Picture, Best Director, Best Supporting Actor.

DODSWORTH
William Wyler, B&W, 1936, 101m

■ From the Sinclair Lewis novel of the same name. The finely crafted story follows Walter Huston as Dodsworth, a self-made millionaire and automobile mogul.

■ **OSCAR:** Best Interior Decoration.

EL NORTE
Gregory Nava, color, 1983, 140m

■ A brother and sister flee political persecution in Guatemala for sweated labor in California. Obvious and on the long side, but not unaffecting.

FURY
Fritz Lang, B&W, 1936, 94m

■ Atmospheric thriller somewhat softened by MGM in which Spencer Tracy, wrongly accused of kidnapping, escapes a lynch mob and a burning jail, and turns the tables on his "killers." The first and most famous U.S. film by the German master of psychological suspense.

THE GODFATHER
Francis Ford Coppola,
color, 1972, 175m

■ The unforgettable first chapter in the Corleone family saga. Marlon Brando stars as the title character, with Al Pacino, James Caan, Talia Shire, Diane Keaton, and Robert Duvall. A great film.

■ **OSCARS:** Best Actor, Adapted Screenplay, Picture.

THE GODFATHER, PART II
Francis Ford Coppola, color, 1974, 200m

■ Robert De Niro joins the star-studded cast as the young Don Corleone, but it's Al Pacino as Michael who eclipses everyone with a skillful, complicated performance. The sequel is just as good as the original.

■ **OSCARS:** Best Adapted Screenplay, Art Direction/Set Decoration, Director, Picture, Supporting Actor, Screenplay.

GONE WITH THE WIND
Victor Fleming, color, 1939, 222m

■ Clark Gable and Vivien Leigh star in the epic telling of the last days of the Civil War. Politically incorrect? Sure. But it remains a beautiful, compelling, and thoroughly entertaining film.

■ **OSCARS:** Best Color Cinematography, Interior Deco-

FACT FILE:

WHO IS OSCAR, ANYWAY?

■ *We've all seen the ebullient Academy Award winners clutching their goldplated Oscars as they deliver breathless acceptance speeches. But who is Oscar? The stiff figure of a man holding a sword and standing atop a reel of film was designed by famed art director/production designer Cedric Gibbons (his credits include* **A Night at the Opera** *and* **An American in Paris**). *For many years after the 1927 inception of the awards ceremony, the statue was nameless.*

Then, as Hollywood legend goes, an Academy secretary noticed that the statue's face bore a resemblance to her uncle Oscar, and hence the figure was christened. To recipients, an Oscar is undoubtedly priceless. In fact, the 13 1/2-inch-tall statuette is worth about $300.

ration, Screenplay, Editing, Supporting Actress, Actress, Director, Picture.

THE GRADUATE*
Mike Nichols, Technicolor 1967, 105m

■ Dustin Hoffman has an affair with his father's friend (Anne Bancroft), then falls in love with her daughter in this '60s classic ■ **OSCAR:** Best Director.

THE GRAPES OF WRATH
John Ford, B&W, 1940, 129m

■ Henry Fonda is brilliant and Ford is at his best. Adapted from the Steinbeck classic about Okies fleeing the Dust Bowl.
■ **OSCARS:** Best Supporting Actress, Director.

THE HEIRESS*
William Wyler, B&W 1949, 115m

■ In this adaptation of a Henry James tale, a young, wealthy woman takes revenge on her gold-digging lover.

HOW GREEN WAS MY VALLEY
John Ford, color, 1941, 118m

■ The story of a Welsh mining family told by 13-year-old Roddy McDowall.
■ **OSCARS:** Best Interior Decoration, Black and White Cinematography, Supporting Actor, Director, Picture.

I AM A FUGITIVE FROM A CHAIN GANG
Mervyn Leroy, B&W, 1932, 90m

■ An honest man convicted of a crime he didn't commit. One of the first films to explore this subject, Paul Muni's performance pulls it all together.

IT'S A WONDERFUL LIFE
Frank Capra, B&W, 1946, 129m

■ Jimmy Stewart finds out what the world would be like if he had never been born. A Christmas classic with an ending as sweet as Santa himself.

THE LADY EVE
Preston Sturges, B&W, 1941, 94m

■ Barbara Stanwyck stars as a con making the moves on the wealthy but nerdy Henry Fonda. Subtle humor and first-rate lead performances.

LASSIE COME HOME
Fred Wilcox, color 1943, 90m

■ Elizabeth Taylor and Roddy McDowall star, but Lassie steals the show. Perfect family viewing, even 50 years later.

LAWRENCE OF ARABIA
David Lean, color, 1962, 221m

■ Peter O'Toole gives one of the greatest debut performances in film history as T. E. Lawrence, and David Lean tells the lengthy story with remarkable ease. See it on a large screen if possible.
■ **OSCARS:** Best Art Direction, Set Decoration, Color

Cinematography, Sound, Score, Editing, Director, Picture.

THE LEARNING TREE
Gordon Parks, color, 1969, 107m

■ Gordon Parks became the first black director of a major studio film with this autobiographical project. The former *Life* photographer directed, produced, wrote the script, and scored the film himself.

LETTER FROM AN UNKNOWN WOMAN
Max Ophüls, B&W, 1948, 90m

■ Romance starring Joan Fontaine and Louis Jourdan. Director Ophüls gives the film a European feel and stylized look.

THE MAGNIFICENT AMBERSONS
Orson Welles, B&W, 1942, 88m

■ Orson Welles's dark portrait of a midwestern family in decline, from the Booth Tarkington novel. Was nominated for Best Picture; don't miss it.

MARTY
Delbert Mann, B&W, 1955, 91m

■ The tiny but touching story of a Bronx butcher (Ernest Borgnine) who finds love unexpectedly. Borgnine gives (by far) his best performance.
■ **OSCARS:** Best Screenplay, Actor, Director, Picture.

■ **EXPERT LIST**

M*A*S*H*
Robert Altman, color
1970,116m

■ The film that launched the long-running television series about the comedic medics coping with the tragedies of the Korean war.
■ **OSCAR:** Best Screenplay.

MIDNIGHT COWBOY
John Schlesinger, color,
1969, 113m

■ The only X-rated film to win Best Picture, *Cowboy* is hardly as shocking today as it was then. Dustin Hoffman and Jon Voight star as small-time hustlers. New York never looked seamier than through director Schlesinger's lens.
■ **OSCARS:** Best Adapted Screenplay, Director, Picture.

MILDRED PIERCE*
Michael Curtiz, B&W, 1945,
113m

■ This soap-operatic drama follows housewife Joan Crawford as she breaks with her husband, becomes a restaurant owner, and endures her ingrate-of-a-daughter.
■ **OSCAR:** Best Actress.

MOROCCO
Josef von Sternberg, B&W,
1930, 92m

■ Marlene Dietrich's first Hollywood film casts her as a cabaret singer stuck in Morocco. Gary Cooper goes along for the ride.

MR. SMITH GOES TO WASHINGTON
Frank Capra, B&W, 1939,
129m

■ Capra and Jimmy Stewart (as Jefferson Smith) team up to tell the story of a scoutmaster turned senator who brings old-fashioned values back to Capitol Hill. It's every politician's dream role.
■ **OSCAR:** Best Screenplay.

NASHVILLE
Robert Altman, color, 1975,
159m

■ Altman at his best. With a large ensemble cast at his disposal, the director examines American life and the way it was lived in the '70s with acute wit and style.
■ **OSCAR:** Best Song.

NOTHING BUT A MAN
Michael Roemer, B&W, 1964,
95m

■ A quiet look at racial prejudice in the South. Melodrama is kept to a minimum, as director Roemer examines the complexities of black life.

ON THE WATERFRONT
Elia Kazan, B&W, 1954,
108m

■ Marlon Brando stars as Terry Malloy, a boxer-turned-longshoreman. Disgusted by the mob corruption that his older brother (Rod Steiger) has introduced him to, Brando sums himself up with one of the most desperate lines in the movies: "I coulda' been a contender."
■ **OSCARS:** Best Art Direction/Set Decoration, Black

FACT FILE:

THE FIRST TIME IS THE CHARM

■ *First-time nominees took home the Oscar in four top talent categories in 1997:*
Juliette Binoche, *Best Supporting Actress,* and Anthony Minghella, *director,* **The English Patient**
Geoffrey Rush, *Best Actor,* **Shine**
Billy Bob Thornton, *writing,* **Sling Blade**

■ *In 1955, all four acting winners were freshmen and all went on to have successful movie careers:*
Ernest Borgnine, **Marty;** Anna Magnani, **The Rose Tattoo;** Jack Lemmon, **Mister Roberts,** *and* Jo Van Fleet, **East of Eden**

and White Cinematography, Editing, Screenplay, Supporting Actress, Actor, Director, Picture.

ONE FLEW OVER THE CUCKOO'S NEST
Milos Forman, color, 1975, 129m

■ *Cuckoo's Nest* and *It Happened One Night* are the only two films to have swept the five major Oscar categories. Jack Nicholson is an inmate at a mental institution who brings the other patients back to life. Based on Ken Kesey's novel. Look for a great early-career performance from Danny DeVito.
■ **OSCARS:** Best Screenplay, Actor, Actress, Director, Picture.

PATHS OF GLORY
Stanley Kubrick, B&W, 1957, 86m

■ Kubrick's specialty, an antiwar movie. Kirk Douglas stars as a World War I sergeant forced to

defend three of his troops against charges of cowardice.

A PLACE IN THE SUN
George Stevens, B&W, 1951, 120m

■ Elizabeth Taylor, Montgomery Clift, and Shelley Winters star as the three points of a love triangle.
■ **OSCARS:** Best Black and White Cinematography, Costume Design, Score, Editing, Screenplay, Director.

THE PRISONER OF ZENDA
John Cromwell, B&W, 1937, 101m

■ From the Anthony Hope novel about a power struggle in a small European kingdom. Ronald Colman stars, and Mary Astor, Douglas Fairbanks, Jr., and David Niven also put in appearances.

RAGING BULL
Martin Scorsese, B&W, 1980, 128m

■ Many critics hailed this drama about boxer Jake LaMotta as the best film of the '80s. Robert De Niro gives a fantastic performance as LaMotta, portraying the character from his 20s as a fighting machine to his dissolute later years.
■ **OSCARS:** Best Editing, Actor.

REBEL WITHOUT A CAUSE
Nicholas Ray, color, 1955, 111m

■ The classic tale of teen angst and alienation. James Dean stars in the role that made him an American legend.

SALT OF THE EARTH
Herbert Biberman, B&W, 1954, 94m

■ Deals with a miners' strike in New Mexico from a staunchly pro-union perspective. During the McCarthy era it was attacked as Communist propaganda.

SCARFACE
Howard Hawks, B&W, 1932, 93m

■ Like the remake, it was censored at first because of its violent content. Hawks's film was the best gangster film until *The Godfather*. Paul Muni plays a Capone-like mob man with deep affection for his sister.

SHADOWS
John Cassavetes, B&W, 1959, 87m

FACT FILE:

IT HAPPENED THRICE

■ *Only three films have ever won Oscar's quintuple crown by being honored in all five top categories: Best Picture, Directing, Screenplay, Actor, and Actress. They were:*

It Happened One Night *(1934)*
One Flew Over the Cuckoo's Nest *(1975)*
Silence of the Lambs *(1991)*

■ Cassavetes's first directorial effort. The film follows a light-skinned black girl through life in New York City. Lelia Goldoni turns in a strong lead performance.

SHE DONE HIM WRONG*
Lowell Sherman, B&W, 1933, 68m

■ Mae West in her heyday as a barkeep who falls for an undercover cop.

SHOCK CORRIDOR*
Samuel Fuller, B&W, 1963, 101m

■ A reporter gets himself admitted to a mental institution to solve the case of a murdered inmate.

STAGECOACH
John Ford, B&W, 1939, 96m

■ A stagecoach of assorted characters jolts across Monument Valley under threat of Indian attack. John Wayne collaborated with John Ford for the first time in this classic and still matchless Western.
■ **OSCARS:** Best Music, Supporting Actor.

SUNSET BOULEVARD
Billy Wilder, B&W, 1950, 100m

■ A cavalcade of Hollywood's greats appear in this black comedy about Norma Desmond, played by Gloria Swanson in her defining role, a silent film star who's got nothing left. As a Broadway musical starring Glenn Close, it was a hit in 1994.

■ **OSCARS:** Best Art Direction/Set Decoration, Screenplay, Score.

SWEET SMELL OF SUCCESS
Alexander Mackendrick, B&W, 1957, 96m

■ Burt Lancaster and Tony Curtis star in a story about a newspaper gossip columnist (Lancaster) and the press agent who'll do anything for him (Curtis). An excellent musical score by Elmer Bernstein of *Magnificent Seven* fame.

TABU
F. W. Murnau and Robert Flaherty, B&W, 1931, 81m

■ The story follows a young diver and his unrequited love for a woman declared "taboo" by the gods.
■ **OSCAR:** Best Cinematography.

TAXI DRIVER
Martin Scorsese, color, 1976, 112m

■ Robert De Niro plays Travis Bickle, a disturbed taxi driver who can't stand New York and goes berserk. Scorsese's portrait of vigilantism was cited by John Hinckley as an influence for his assassination attempt on Ronald Reagan. Costars Jodie Foster, Cybill Shepherd, and Harvey Keitel.

TEVYE
Maurice Schwartz, B&W, 1939, 96m

■ Later known as *Fiddler on the Roof*, this is the story of a Jewish dairyman whose lifestyle is changed by his daughter's wishes to marry outside the faith. From the Sholom Aleichem story.

TO KILL A MOCKINGBIRD
Robert Mulligan, B&W, 1962, 129m

■ Horton Foote's righteous adaptation of Harper Lee's novel about a Southern lawyer, Gregory Peck, who defends a black man wrongly accused of rape.
■ **OSCARS:** Best Actor, Screenplay.

THE WIND
Victor Seastrom, B&W, 1928, 74m

■ Lillian Gish as a girl who marries a farmer to escape her family. One of the last great silent films.

A WOMAN UNDER THE INFLUENCE
John Cassavetes, color, 1974, 147m

■ Gena Rowlands and Peter Falk star in the story of a woman who is cracking up.

HORROR
CAT PEOPLE
Jacques Tourneur, B&W, 1942, 73m

■ Simone Simon is a dressmaker who believes she's infected with a panther curse in this creepy, well-directed thriller.

FRANKENSTEIN
James Whale, B&W, 1931, 71m

■ Boris Karloff's performance as Mary Shelley's monster is still the best, Robert De Niro's friendly monster in the Kenneth Branagh version included.

FREAKS
Tod Browning, B&W, 1932, 64m

■ Director Browning explores relationships between sideshow freaks in this strange horror film. The real story is the humanity of the freak characters, many of whom are real-life sideshow performers.

KING KONG
Merian Cooper and Ernest Shoedsack, B&W, 1933, 105m

■ Big ape rampages through New York until he reaches the Empire State Building. A camp classic.

PSYCHO
Alfred Hitchcock, B&W, 1960, 109m

■ Anthony Perkins stars as Norman Bates, motel proprietor and neighborhood psychotic. Thirty years and several hundred slasher imitators later, *Psycho* still provides some terrifyingly good screams.

MUSICALS
AN AMERICAN IN PARIS
Vincente Minnelli, color, 1951, 113m

■ Gene Kelly stars in this entertaining musical as a GI-turned-painter. Features a stunning, 17-minute ballet sequence with classic Kelly dancing.

■ **OSCARS:** Best Art Direction/Set Decoration, Color Cinematography, Score, Screenplay, Picture.

THE BAND WAGON
Vincente Minnelli, color, 1953, 112m

■ Witty backstage Broad-

way drama with Cyd Charisse and comeback star Fred Astaire dancing up a storm, and Jack Buchanan as their temperamental producer. "By Myself," "A Shine on Your Shoes," "Dancing in the Dark," and many more. A champagne pick-me-up.

CABARET
Bob Fosse, color, 1972, 128m

■ Glittering if sometimes crude adaptation of John Kander's musical of Christopher Isherwood's prewar Berlin stories, notable for Fosse's stylish choreography and Joel Grey's silky performance as the Kit Kat Klub's cynical MC.

■ **OSCARS:** Eight in all, including Best Director, Photography, Score Adaptation, and Actress.

CARMEN JONES
Otto Preminger, color, 1954, 105m

■ Oscar Hammerstein II adapted the film from Bizet's opera. Harry Belafonte and Dorothy Dandridge turn in good performances.

FOOTLIGHT PARADE
Lloyd Bacon, B&W, 1933, 100m

■ James Cagney plays a struggling stage director trying to outdo himself (and sound movies) with every musical number.

FACT FILE:

NIGHTS TO REMEMBER

■ The **English Patient**'s nine Oscars placed it in a tie with **Gigi** and **The Last Emperor** for third place on the all-time biggest Oscar winners. The distinction for collecting the most Oscars ever is shared by:

Ben Hur, 1959
West Side Story, 1961

Each was honored in 11 categories, including Best Picture and Directing. So striking was the dancing in West Side Story that a special Oscar was awarded for choreography.

■ **EXPERT LIST**

GIGI
Vincente Minnelli, color,
1958, 116m

■ Leslie Caron plays Gigi, a young harlot-in-training who has Louis Jourdan on her mind. One of the last great movie musicals.

■ **OSCARS:** Best Art Direction, Color Cinematography, Costume Design, Score, Song, Screenplay, Director, Picture.

LOVE ME TONIGHT
Rouben Mamoulian, B&W,
1932, 104m

■ The Rodgers & Hart musical that introduced "Isn't It Romantic" (sung by Maurice Chevalier) to the film world.

SHOW BOAT*
James Whale, B&W, 1936,
110m

■ An actress on the floating theater flees when she learns she is half-black. The captain's daughter and a gambler step in to fill the acting roles, and fall in love with each other.

SINGIN' IN THE RAIN
Gene Kelly and Stanley Donen, color, 1952, 103m

■ This is the greatest movie musical ever. Kelly's performance of the title song is deservedly one of the most famous scenes in film. Donald O'Connor, Debbie Reynolds, Cyd Charisse, and Jean Hagen also give great performances.

TOP HAT
Mark Sandrich, B&W, 1935,
97m

■ Ginger Rogers and Fred Astaire in their best form. "Cheek to Cheek" and "Top Hat, White Tie, and Tails" are just two of the great songs performed. Look for Lucille Ball in a small early role.

THE WIZARD OF OZ
Victor Fleming, color/ B&W,
1939, 101m

■ An American cinema classic based on L. Frank Baum's children's novel of the same name. Judy Garland stars as Dorothy in the role of a lifetime. The music is instantly hummable, the performances are unforgettable. A perfect film.

■ **OSCARS:** Best Song, Score.

YANKEE DOODLE DANDY
Michael Curtiz, B&W, 1942,
126m

■ James Cagney stars in the story of popular song composer George M. Cohan. Cagney proved that he could play something other than a gangster in this sweet musical.

■ **OSCARS:** Best Score, Sound, Actor.

MYSTERY & SUSPENSE
BADLANDS
Terrence Malick, color,
1974, 94m

■ Before there was Oliver Stone's *Natural Born Killers*, there was *Badlands*. Director

Malick's creepy thriller stars Martin Sheen and Sissy Spacek as a murderer and his companion. Loosely inspired by a Nebraska killing spree in 1958.

CHAN IS MISSING
Wayne Wang, B&W,
1981, 80m

■ Very off-the-wall Chinese-American San Francisco mystery, by turns funny, suspenseful, and melancholy. There's no payoff, but it's fresh and full of surprises.

CHINATOWN
Roman Polanski, color,
1974, 131m

■ Jack Nicholson and Faye Dunaway in one of Hollywood's greatest executions of film noir. John Huston, Diane Ladd, and Burt Young co-star.

■ **OSCAR:** Best Original Screenplay.

THE CONVERSATION
Francis Ford Coppola, color,
1974, 113m

■ A master surveillance man cannot find the bug planted on him. Gene Hackman is wholly compelling as the hero of this riveting psychological thriller.

DETOUR
Edgar Ulmer, B&W,
1946, 69m

■ Ulmer was one of the first low-budget, independent filmmakers. His craft is at its sharpest in this film noir about a drifter, played superbly by Tom Neal.

DOUBLE INDEMNITY
Billy Wilder, B&W, 1944, 106m

■ Fred MacMurray stars as an insurance salesman who joins Barbara Stanwyck in a plot to kill her husband for his insurance. Suspense films don't get any better than this.

FORCE OF EVIL
Abraham Polonsky, B&W, 1948, 100m

■ Noir classic starring John Garfield as a mob lawyer caught between crime and brotherly love. A tremendous performance by Garfield, a too-often underrated actor.

THE MALTESE FALCON
John Huston, B&W, 1941, 101m

■ Bogart is Sam Spade, a P.I. investigating the web of deceit and murder spun around a priceless statue. With a supporting cast featuring Peter Lorre, Mary Astor, and Sydney Greenstreet, this is the best of P.I. flicks.

THE MANCHURIAN CANDIDATE
John Frankenheimer, B&W, 1962, 126m

■ Frank Sinatra gives his best film performance as an Army man who knows more than he thinks he does in Frankenheimer's thrilling adaptation of the Richard Condon novel. The plot revolves around conspiracy and brainwashing at the highest levels of American government.

THE NIGHT OF THE HUNTER
Charles Laughton, B&W, 1955, 93m

■ Robert Mitchum plays a terrifying preacher trying to kill his step-kids. This is one scary flick, and Mitchum turns in a creepy, career-defining performance.

NORTH BY NORTHWEST
Alfred Hitchcock, color, 1959, 136m

■ Cary Grant is the nonchalant advertising executive who escapes abduction and goes on the run across America. An extraordinary mix of comedy and paranoia, and a faultless Hitchcock classic, climaxing on the slippery stone face of a U.S. president.

OUT OF THE PAST
Jacques Tourneur, B&W, 1947, 97m

■ A small film noir starring Robert Mitchum and Kirk Douglas. Mitchum plays a P.I. who gets involved with a gangster's girl. Douglas plays the formidable gangster.

SHADOW OF A DOUBT
Alfred Hitchcock, B&W, 1943, 108m

■ Joseph Cotten stars as Uncle Charlie, a loving relative who may have a murderous secret to hide. This is Hitchcock's personal favorite.

TOUCH OF EVIL
Orson Welles, B&W, 1958, 108m

■ In this film, director Welles also stars as the corrupt sheriff of a seedy Mexican border

FACT FILE:

NIGHTS TO FORGET

■ *Two pictures,* **The Turning Point** *and* **The Color Purple,** *were nominated for 11 Oscars and came up empty-handed.* **Judgment at Nuremberg** *did slightly better. It had 13 nominations but managed to win two, for Best Actor (Maximilian Schell) and Writing (based on material from another medium). It would have done better had it not been up against* **West Side Story,** *which virtually swept the field in 1961.*

town. Charlton Heston, Janet Leigh, and a host of other stars also appear.

THE TREASURE OF THE SIERRA MADRE
John Huston, B&W, 1948, 126m

■ Humphrey Bogart, Walter Huston, and Tim Holt go prospecting for gold and discover the worst in human nature.
■ **OSCARS:** Best Screenplay, Supporting Actor, Director.

VERTIGO
Alfred Hitchcock, color, 1958, 126m

■ Jimmy Stewart is an ex-cop hired to shadow Kim Novak. He has vertigo. To reveal anything more would be criminal.

WESTERNS
DESTRY RIDES AGAIN*
George Marshall, B&W 1939, 94m

■ In this western classic, James Stewart is a sheriff who refuses to wear a gun and drinks milk at the bar, which is frequented by Marlene Dietrich's character—until he gets fed up with local corruption.

HIGH NOON
Fred Zinneman, B&W, 1952, 85m

■ The clock ticks down on sheriff Gary Cooper as an old nemesis turns his wedding day into a nightmare. Great suspense and good acting; Cooper won his sec-

ond Oscar for the role.
■ **OSCARS:** Best Editing, Song, Score, Actor.

MY DARLING CLEMENTINE
John Ford, B&W, 1946, 97m

■ Henry Fonda plays Wyatt Earp in the best version of the oft-filmed shoot-out at the O.K. Corral.

THE OUTLAW JOSEY WALES*
Clint Eastwood, color 1976, 135 m

■ Eastwood stars as a new type of western hero in this film, a vulnerable guy who seeks healing, closure, and a little revenge after the murder of his wife.

RED RIVER
Howard Hawks, B&W, 1948, 133m

■ One of the most frequently underrated Westerns. John Wayne plays a leathery rancher with surprising skill. Montgomery Clift co-stars in his first film role.

RIDE THE HIGH COUNTRY
Sam Peckinpah, color, 1962, 93m

■ Two gunmen are hired to guard a stash of gold. One has honorable intentions, one doesn't. Starring Randolph Scott and Joel McCrea in their final screen roles.

THE SEARCHERS
John Ford, color, 1956, 119m

■ John Wayne plays a

racist old Confederate in search of his niece (Natalie Wood) who was abducted by Indians. Both Wayne and director Ford are in peak form.

SHANE
George Stevens, color, 1953, 117m

■ A great drama from the Jack Schaeffer novel of the same name. Alan Ladd as the lonely gunfighter is fantastic.
■ **OSCAR:** Best Color Cinematography.

SCIENCE FICTION
BLADE RUNNER
Ridley Scott, color, 1982, 122m

■ An art-house favorite starring Harrison Ford as an everyday cop in a nightmarish future that resembles L.A. Cast features Daryl Hannah, Sean Young, Edward James Olmos, and Rutger Hauer. The production design is superb.

THE DAY THE EARTH STOOD STILL
Robert Wise, B&W, 1951, 92m

■ The story: Alien robot lands in Washington, D.C., with a dire warning of what will happen if mankind fails to mend its warlike ways. A sci-fi classic, strange and menacing.

E.T. THE EXTRA TERRESTRIAL
Steven Spielberg, color, 1982, 115m

■ **EXPERT LIST**

■ This touching adventure of a boy and his alien friend could only come from the imagination of Steven Spielberg. Henry Thomas as Eliot gives one of the best performances by a child ever in a film, and the superior cast (including actress Debra Winger as the voice of E.T.) makes this the classic of '80s pop-cinema.
■ OSCARS: Best Sound, Visual Effects, Score.

FLASH GORDON*
Frederick Stephani, B&W, 1936, 97m
■ In this example of science-fiction triumph, Flash has his hands full struggling to save the earth from destruction at the hands of evil Ming the Merciless and his cadre of giant lobsters, shark men, and horned gorillas.

INVASION OF THE BODY SNATCHERS
Don Siegel, B&W, 1956, 80m
■ One of the most influential sci-fi horror movies. Aliens replace people with duplicates hatched from pods. Don't watch it alone.

STAR WARS
George Lucas, color, 1977, 121m
■ "A long time ago, in a galaxy far, far away," science-fiction fantasies were drive-in jokes. Then director George Lucas came along and made outer space into a world populated by heroes and monsters drawn from Greek mythology. The special effects set a new standard for film technology.
■ OSCARS: Best Art Direction, Set Decoration, Costume Design, Editing, Sound, Visual Effects, Score.

2001: A SPACE ODYSSEY
Stanley Kubrick, color, 1968, 139m
■ The groundbreaking film that took viewers into a future where machine and man are equals. Besides being a visual feast, the philosophical and theological issues raised within make it one of the touchstone films of a generation.
■ OSCAR: Best Visual Effects.

VIDEOS THAT ARE HARD TO FIND

The variety of unusual videos that can be ordered through the mail is staggering. While Blockbuster Video might have 140 copies of True Lies, *very often the major video rental chains don't carry a single copy of harder-to-find films. For those videophiles looking for the obscure, whether for rental or purchase, mail-order houses are often the best bet. Some outlets rent and sell only through membership deals, while others are happy to deal with onetime customers.*

ALTERNATIVE VIDEOS
P.O. Box 270797
Dallas, TX 75227
☎ 214–823–6030

■ Specializes in films for those who are interested in the African American experience. The catalog costs $2.

COLUMBIA HOUSE
1400 N. Fruitridge Avenue
Terre Haute, IN 47811
☎ 800–262–2001

■ Good deals at first, but read the agreement and respond to your mail—monthly selections are sent unless you say in advance that you don't want them. Free catalog.

CRITICS' CHOICE VIDEO
P.O. Box 749
Itasca, IL 60143
☎ 800–367–7765

■ The free quarterly catalog of 2,500 titles is the tip of the iceberg; some 55,000 unlisted titles are available via another special 900 number, including titles in areas of interest such as Japanimation, the bizarre, railroading, aviation, and Spanish movies. Searches for films can be done by title, individual stars, or subject matter (☎ 800–729–0833). You can request a search for a film even if you don't know the title.

DAVE'S VIDEO, THE LASER PLACE
12144 Ventura Blvd.
Studio City, CA 91604
☎ 800–736–1659

■ Ten percent discount on all discs. Dave's insists it can and will find any title currently available on the laser disc format. Catalog comes with purchase or is available for $4.95 and comes with coupon towards future purchase.

FACETS MULTIMEDIA
517 West Fullerton Ave.
Chicago, IL 60614
☎ 773–281–9075

■ The Whole Toon Catalog is sheer heaven for lovers of animated film. Catalog is free.

FESTIVAL FILMS
6115 Chestnut Terrace
Shorewood, MN 55331
☎ 612–470–2172

■ Specializes in foreign titles at lower-than-average prices. The price of the $2 catalog is applied to your first purchase.

FILMIC ARCHIVES
The Cinema Center
Botsford, CT 06404
☎ 800–366–1920

■ One of the few mail-order houses that only sells to teachers. Three free catalogs: one each for teachers of English, history, and kindergarten through 8th grade.

KEN CRANE'S LASER DISC SUPERSTORE
15251 Beach Blvd.
Westminster, CA 92683
☎ 800–624–3078

■ The superstore claims to have over 100,000 titles available—with an updated list every week. Every purchase is automatically discounted by 20 percent.

MONDO MOVIES
255 W. 26th St.
New York, NY 10001
☎ 212–929–2560

■ The avant-garde specialists, from raunchy B-movies to hard-to-find, experimental art-shorts. Free catalog.

SCIENCE FICTION CONTINUUM
P.O. Box 154
Colonia, NJ 07067
☎ 800–232–6002

■ The name says it all. The catalog costs $1.

JUST FOR KIDS

RATINGS
▼

KEEPING TABS ON KIDS' TV

TV ratings and V-chips give parents new screening tools

For parents upset with TV violence and sexual explicitness, the V-chip that will be built into all new TV sets beginning in 1998 is a kind of quick fix. The electronic device lets parents block programs they consider inappropriate. But the key to the V-chip is the TV rating system, which was introduced in early 1997 and is stirring controversy. The system, similar to that used by the motion picture business, rates shows by age appropriateness. For example, a rating of TV-PG indicates a show that may contain some violence, sexual material, or coarse language; parental guidance is therefore suggested. An "M" rating is assigned to a show for mature audiences and is not suitable for anyone under 17. A "G" rating is suitable for general audiences, and a "K-7" for children over 7. At the start of each TV program, a rating appears for 15 seconds on the upper left-hand corner of the TV screen.

But many parents, media watchdogs, and children's advocacy groups complain that these ratings don't provide enough information to be useful. For instance, they don't indicate why a show is given a TV-14, making it inappropriate for kids under 14. Does it contain nudity, profanity, violence? This ambiguity, they argue, results in inconsistently rated shows. Critics are pressing for a more detailed rating system that gives parents the basis for deciding on which grounds they want to limit their children's TV viewing. As this book went to press in mid-1997, the television industry and parent organizations were negotiating a deal to modify the ratings system by adding warnings for shows containing violence, sex, or strong language. Stay tuned for the next ratings episode, which may arrive just in time for the V-chip.

Here, David Kleeman, executive director of the American Center for Children's Television, and David Moulton, chief of staff for Congresssman Edward Markey, author of the V-chip legislation, answer questions on the TV-rating system and the upcoming V-chip.

■ **Why are programmers rating their own shows? Why isn't there an independent review board, similar to the one that rates movies, to rate TV shows?**

There are about 500 television programs aired every day. That's more than the total number of movies released in a year. It wouldn't be practical, or even feasible, to set up an outside review board to rate every episode of every program. The producers and programmers know their programs and are the most logical and appropriate source for the ratings. (DK)

Why are the ratings so inconsistent?

There *are* lots of inconsistencies—Jay Leno is rated TV-14, David Letterman is TV-PG, for example. But you have to remember that this is a new system and given more time, we'll see fewer inconsistencies. In many cases, though, it's also a judgment call. There may be a fine line between what programmers believe parents would consider appropriate for a 14-year-old but inappropriate for a 13-year-old. (DK)

Are there indications that parents are using these ratings to change their children's viewing choices?

Polls show that most parents are aware of the ratings system, but few have modified their kids' viewing habits because of it. The real results will show when the V-chip is released. If parents choose to block categories of shows with certain ratings, then you'll see the audience numbers change. (DK)

It's hard to know why some shows are rated as they are. Wouldn't a more specific system help answer those questions?

Definitely. A description of why the show is given a certain rating tells you more about its content. And that helps parents make choices. Some parents care more about their children being exposed to violence than to rough language, for example.

Another problem with age-based ratings is that they imply that the material is suitable for all children of a certain age, which is false. Some children at 10 are ready for material that may be too mature for some 18-year-olds. The rating levels should be a jumping-off point, not a black-and-white decision. (DK)

Will I need to buy a new television to get the V-chip?

No, all new TVs will come standardly equipped with the chip, but you will be able to modify an existing TV with an add-on

system that will cost about $40. (DM)

Will the V-chip make TV sets more expensive?

No. Manufacturers can build onto existing platforms already in place for closed-captioning for about $1 per set. (DM)

What if I want to watch a show after my children are asleep and the show is rated above the level I set for them to watch?

The V-chip will come equipped with a pin-number, or access code, which makes it easy to modify, override, or turn off the censoring device. (DM)

How can parents best use these ratings and the V-chip technology to make good choices about television viewing?

Even with the best technology, parents will have to play an active role in determining what and how much TV their children watch. Parents need to view the programs and discuss with their children which shows are appropriate or inappropriate for their age. What parents really need is not a way to block out what they don't want, but a way to find what they do want. (DK)

FACT FILE:

THE RATING GAME

How does your favorite show rate?

BAYWATCH	
SEINFELD	TV-PG
THE SIMPSONS	TV-PG
POWER RANGERS	TV-PG
NYPD BLUE	K-7
BEAVIS AND BUTTHEAD	TV-14
FRIENDS	TV-14
TOUCHED BY AN ANGEL	TV-PG
SPECIAL: WORLD'S MOST DANGEROUS ANIMALS III	TV-G
JAY LENO	TV-14
DAVID LETTERMAN	TV-14
SUPER BOWL	TV-PG
	UNRATED

A MOVIE MOM'S FAVORITE FLICKS

Whether your kids are tiny or teens, they'll love these

Watching a movie with your child is not just a way to spend time together, says children's film critic Nell Minow, it's also a way to teach children about the past, to expose them to ideas and points of view that will help them grow, and to share with them some of the stories, characters, and music that meant the most to you as a child. Author of *The Movie Mom's Guide to Family Movies* (Avon, 1997), Minow offers a movie and video review service on the World Wide Web (*http://pages.prodigy.com/VA/rcpj55a/moviemom.html*). Here the Movie Mom™ recommends some of her favorite children's movies in a variety of categories from animal movies to screwball comedies. All selections are generally available in video and are arranged by age appropriateness.

ANIMALS

THE ADVENTURES OF MILO AND OTIS (1989) *For 4 and up*

■ A charming film for the whole family, this is the story of Milo the cat and Otis the dog. The two best friends live on a farm until Milo is swept away down a stream and Otis tries to rescue him. The two have many adventures, funny and exciting, as they make their way home. Dudley Moore provides the witty narration. Themes for family discussion include cooperation, loyalty, and growing up.

BABE (1995) *For 4 and up*

■ A lovely story about a pig who lives his dream—and saves his life—by learning to herd sheep. Babe, the pig, treats all species of animals as friends, even though they are prejudiced against each other and him. The sheep accuse the dogs (whom they call wolves) of being ignorant; the dogs counter that the sheep are stupid. The movie does a good job of illustrating the importance of kindness and how it can transform both the giver and the recipient.

MISTY (1961) *For 4 and up*

■ This faithful adaptation of the classic children's book *Misty of Chincoteague*, by Marguerite Henry, is about two children who fall in love with a wild horse, a descendent of Spanish ponies that escaped from a sinking ship and swam to Asateague, an island off the coast of Virginia. Each year residents of nearby Chincoteague go to Asateague to capture ponies. The film depicts very nicely the challenge of teaching the foal independence and the love the process entails.

SO DEAR TO MY HEART (1948) *For 5 and up*

■ A gentle Disney musical set on a farm, this is the story of a boy who wants to enter his black sheep in the state fair. Along with nicely handled themes of the importance of persistence and believing in yourself and those you love, there are some classic musical numbers, including Burl Ives singing "Lavender Blue (Dilly Dilly)."

BORN FREE (1966) *For 6 and up*

■ This film is based on the true story of George and Joy Adamson, and Elsa, the lion they adopted and tamed when George was a game warden in Kenya. When Elsa accidentally causes an elephant stampede, they are ordered to send her to a zoo. Instead, Joy resolves to try to undo the effects of domestication and teach Elsa how to live in the wild. Kids may like to talk about methods parents use to prepare their children for life "in the wild," and how difficult that is, when their inclination is to protect them. (Warning: There is a subtle but benignly arrogant colonialism in the subtext of this movie.)

LASSIE COME HOME (1943)
For 6 and up

■ This is the classic boy-and-dog story, starring a young boy, played by Roddy McDowall, his friend (a young Elizabeth Taylor), and the dog, Lassie. The father of Lassie's young master loses his job and sells the dog. But Lassie escapes repeatedly, encountering many adventures on his way home. This is one of at least 10 films featuring Lassie, including *Son of Lassie*, in which he helps to win World War II, and *The Magic of Lassie*, co-starring Jimmy Stewart.

THE THREE LIVES OF THOMASINA (1964)
For 8 and up

■ This is a film about a little girl in Scotland whose father, a veterinarian, has little ability to communicate his feelings. When the girl's beloved cat, Thomasina, gets hurt, her father is unable to cure the cat and puts her to sleep. But Thomasina has used only one of her nine lives. After a trip to Cat Heaven she reunites with the little girl and her father, teaching them lessons about the importance of communicating one's feelings.

OLD YELLER (1957)
For 8 and up

■ One of the finest of the early Disney dramas, this movie is the story of a young boy who grows fond of a stray dog and adopts him from his real owner. Soon the pair is inseparable until the dog, Yeller, becomes sick. The dog is shot but the young boy takes comfort in Yeller's pup. The fighting scenes are exciting; the family scenes are sensitive and evocative. A talk between the boy and his father shows parental wisdom, understanding, and patience at its best.

THE BLACK STALLION (1979)
For 8 and up

■ This is one of the most beautiful and genuinely magical movies ever made. There are long stretches of film without a single word, just exquisite cinematography. The story is about a young boy who is shipwrecked with a wild and beautiful black horse. He tames the horse, which returns home with him when they are rescued. The boy meets a former trainer named Henry, played by Mickey Rooney, and they enter the horse in a race and triumph over two champions. (Warning: Although the movie is rated G, the shipwreck and loss of the little boy's father may be too frightening for younger children.)

REAL AMERICAN LIVES
THE JACKIE ROBINSON STORY (1950)
For 8 and up

■ The primary appeal of this movie is that Robinson plays himself. The film is forthright about the racial issues but inevitably appears somewhat naive by today's standards. Ruby Dee, who plays his wife, appears as Robinson's mother in a worthwhile made-for-TV movie called *The Court-Martial of Jackie Robinson,* based on Robinson's experiences with racism in the Army.

HOUDINI (1953)
For 10 and up

■ Tony Curtis plays the title role in this fictionalized account of the greatest of all magicians and escape artists. The stunts, including an attempt to escape from an "escape-proof" British prison, are great fun to watch. Very touching is Houdini's devotion to his mother and to his wife, played by Curtis's then-wife Janet Leigh.

SERGEANT YORK (1941)
For 10 and up

■ Gary Cooper won an Oscar for this performance as World War I hero, Alvin York, a pacifist from the Tennessee hills who carried out one of the most extraordinary missions in military history. York captured 132 men by himself, a figure that remains the record of the most men ever captured by a single soldier. In addition to the exciting story of his war record, this is also the thoughtful story of a man's spiritual journey. He opposed fighting but believed that what he was doing was ultimately saving lives, thereby making his extraordinary achievements even more meaningful.

SUNRISE AT CAMPOBELLO (1960)
For 10 and up

■ Ralph Bellamy plays the role of President

Franklin Delano Roosevelt. When Franklin, a vigorous man, was disabled by polio and forced to reconsider his future, his close friend and political adviser Louis Howe (played by Hume Cronyn) told him he had two choices: become a country squire and write books, or get back into politics. Roosevelt's compassion for others is deepened by the experience, and his wife Eleanor learns to overcome her shyness and becomes his eyes and ears by giving speeches and meeting people. This inspiring story raises important questions about public service, what it means, and ways in which the public interest is best determined and served.

YOUNG MR. LINCOLN (1939) and ABE LINCOLN IN ILLINOIS (1940)
For 10 and up

■ Henry Fonda in the first and Raymond Massey in the second both portray beautifully this icon of American history. The first movie shows his early law practice and his tragic romance with Ann Rutledge. The second covers 30 years of his career, from shopkeeper to lawyer, through the debates with Stephen Douglas, and ending with his election to the presidency.

THE RIGHT STUFF (1983)
For 12 and up

■ This brilliant movie about astronaut John Glenn and the early days of the space program is outstanding in every detail, from the script to performances by a number of future stars, including Dennis Quaid, Ed Harris, Scott Glenn, and Fred Ward. Not just a thrilling story about an exciting and successful American adventure, the film is also a thoughtful commentary on the American spirit. Topics for discussion include loyalty, maintaining integrity under commercial and political pressure, problem solving, and what "the right stuff" really is. (Warning: This film contains references to infidelity and some locker-room humor.)

THE TEEN YEARS
BYE BYE BIRDIE (1961)
For 8 and up

■ In this musical satire of 1950s popular culture and suburban life, America's most popular rock singer, Conrad Birdie, has been drafted, just as Elvis had in real life. A fan, played by Ann-Margret, is picked at random to kiss him good-bye on the *Ed Sullivan Show*. The ensuing chaos involves her parents, her boyfriend, and a songwriter-biochemist, played by Dick Van Dyke. The film gives kids a glimpse, albeit idealized and amplified, of how teenagers once behaved and how they felt about things like rock stars, going steady, and growing up. Kids and parents can draw parallels to the way parents think about kids in the 1990s, and speculate about the conflicts today's kids may have with their future children.

REBEL WITHOUT A CAUSE (1955)
For 11 and up

■ This ultimate classic of teenage angst is an excellent movie for families to watch together. James Dean plays Jim, a new kid in town who must find a place for himself. By reaching out to another lost teen, played by Sal Mineo, Jim tries to become everything he wishes his own ineffectual father could be for him. He stands up for his friend with the police and promises to take care of everything. But when his friend is killed, Jim tragically learns a little about what it's like to be a parent. A generation later, James Dean's performance in this film still has resonance for teenagers and others who feel insecure, frustrated, lonely, and angry. They can identify with Jim's feelings as they begin to establish their own identities and take responsibility for their own choices.

BREAKING AWAY (1979)
For 12 and up

■ This movie is about four friends, recent high school graduates in the college town of Bloomington, Ind., and how they stick together as they struggle with adulthood. The film focuses on Dave, played by Dennis Christopher, who has tested well enough to go to college, but spends his time racing his bicycle and trying to emulate his heroes, the Italian bicycle racing team. When the university for the first time invites local teams to participate in their annual "Little 500" bicycle race, Dave and his friends enter to show the college that the locals can compete with the college kids. When Dave is injured, the others prove their friendship in different ways.

THE FLAMINGO KID (1984)
For 14 and up
■ Matt Dillon stars in the role of a young man from grimy Brooklyn who gets a job at the fancy El Flamingo Club on Long Island, where everything is sleek and spotless. At the club he meets a car dealer and card player and is awed by the man's wealth and charm. But the boy later discovers that the man is dishonest to his friends and to himself. (Warning: There is some rough language and brief nudity in this film.)

GREGORY'S GIRL (1981)
For 12 and up
■ Gregory is a gangling but amiable Scottish teenager who is mildly befuddled by just about everything, especially a young girl named Dorothy, who takes his place on the soccer team. By contrast, most of the girls he knows, including his 10-year-old sister, seem to understand everything. This is a sweet, endearing comedy with a great deal of insight and affection for its characters.

LUCAS (1986)
For 14 and up
■ This exceptionally intelligent and sensitive movie about an intelligent and sensitive kid evokes the range of emotions of the high school years: terror, exhilaration, swings from confidence to self-doubt. Lucas is a very bright 14-year-old, academically accelerated so that he is in high school with older kids. He befriends Maggie, a pretty girl who is new in town and vulnerable because of her parents' recent divorce. But Lucas is heartbroken when Maggie is attracted to his friend Cappie, the captain of the school football team. He then takes desperate action to assuage his feelings of frustration and jealousy. (Warning: There is some strong language and an occasional mild sexual reference.)

JUST PLAIN FUN
IT'S A MAD, MAD, MAD, MAD WORLD (1963)
For all ages
■ Every comedian in Hollywood—plus Spencer Tracy—appears in this story of a mad dash to buried treasure by an assortment of people becoming increasingly insane with greed. Deliriously chaotic and wildly funny.

THE COURT JESTER (1956)
For 5 and up
■ This is Danny Kaye's best movie, and also one of the funniest comedies ever made, with a plot that is both exciting and hilarious. The "vessel with the pestle" scene is a classic, but just as good are the scenes in which a snap of the fingers puts Kaye in and out of his hypnotic state and the ones in which he must qualify as a knight to be eligible to enter a jousting match. This is terrific family fun, with an exceptionally active and competent heroine.

HELP (1965)
For 6 and up
■ The Beatles' second film is a wild chase over a ruby ring worn by sacrificial victims of an obscure Eastern religion and sent to Ringo by an adoring fan. That is just the excuse for sublime silliness. (If they hadn't been able to sing, the Beatles could have been the modern-day Marx brothers.) A sensational musical score features "Ticket to Ride," "Another Girl," "You've Got to Hide Your Love Away," and the title tune, plus Beethoven's 9th.

THE GENERAL (1927)
For 8 and up
■ In this silent classic, based on a real incident during the Civil War, Confederate engineer Buster Keaton must rescue both his train and his girlfriend when they are captured by Union soldiers. Breathtaking split-second timing of the gags and the action leave you concluding that sound in movies may be superfluous.

BOOKS THAT GIVE R. L. STINE GOOSEBUMPS

"I'm basically a 10-year-old," says writer R. L. Stine, which would put the author of the Goosebumps *series and America's most popular children's author squarely in the middle of his intended audience of children 8 to 12 years old. For readers 10 to 13, Stine has the* Fear Street *series. Between the two series, Stine has written some 100 scary books for children at last count. Quite a phenomenon for someone whose first writing job was for a soft-drink industry magazine and who sells about a million books a month. Here, Stine tells which children's books he loves most, and why:*

PINOCCHIO
by Carlo Collodi

■ My first book. Pinocchio smashes the advice-giving cricket with a mallet, then falls asleep near the stove and burns his feet off! Obviously, a big influence on me.

WHERE THE WILD THINGS ARE
by Maurice Sendak

■ Very wild—and very dangerous. That's why it's so wonderful.

HUCKLEBERRY FINN
by Mark Twain

■ I loved it as a kid; even

more as an adult. Not really a children's book, but it has to go on any list because it's the best American novel.

SOMETHING WICKED THIS WAY COMES
by Ray Bradbury

■ About a midwestern boy who sneaks off to a weird, menacing circus. Scariest book I ever read.

TREASURE ISLAND
by Robert Louis Stevenson

■ A great, gripping adventure written from a boy's point of view. As a kid, I

found it absolutely thrilling.

INTERSTELLAR PIG
by William Sleator

■ Inventive, chilling sci-fi thriller by one of my favorite young-adult writers.

WHERE THE SIDEWALK ENDS
by Shel Silverstein

■ Uncle Shelby is hilarious for all ages.

SKINNYBONES
by Barbara Park

■ Wise and very funny. The only author my son ever wrote a fan letter to!

MINE'S THE BEST
by Crosby Bonsall

■ Hilarious picture book that captures the way kids argue better than any book I ever read.

TIGER EYES
by Judy Blume

■ A book that's really about something. Simply the best young-adult novel ever.

EXPERT QUOTE

"I always loved stories in which a ventriloquist dummy comes to life. So in *Night of the Living Dummy* (*Goosebumps* #7) I tried to double the suspense in this book by having TWO dummies come to life and battle it out.

I was pleased with this book because it has the mix of fear and humor I try for, along with a lot of big surprises."

A BOOST FOR A BUDDING PICASSO

*Unleashing the artist in your child
is easier than you might think*

Adults who feel artistically challenged can still teach their children to draw, pick up a few pointers along the way, and enjoy the process to boot. The key is to approach drawing from another perspective—that is, to realize that drawing isn't merely an ability to make realistic depictions. "Drawing is a way of thinking and learning to see in a different way," says Ed Emberley, author and illustrator of 60 picture books and 15 drawing books. A winner of the prized Caldecott book award, Emberley says there isn't just one method of drawing. On the contrary, "I draw about 10 or 15 different ways myself. Look at Picasso's art and the many ways he drew," he says.

Emberley's method uses a small alphabet of shapes, letters, and numbers to create basic images that you can build upon. When finished, you will recognize a smiling fish or a baby bat, for example. Explains Emberley: "My drawings come from looking at the way children draw naturally. You never actually see all four legs of an animal at the same time, but that's what children draw." Most important, says Emberley, is for adults to create what he calls "a habit of success," by encouraging a child's interest in putting images down on paper. Here, Emberley offers more advice on ways to unleash the artist in your child:

■ **DON'T FORCE A CHILD TO DRAW.** Adults should not be drill sergeants. Children only draw if they want to and if they truly enjoy it. Your

job is to keep the atmosphere unthreatening and encourage the child to continue drawing because it is an enjoyable activity. For some children the only encouragement needed is a pleasant room, music, or a snack. Stress the fun of drawing, and if children are enjoying what they're doing, you won't need to push them. If you take pleasure in drawing, teach the pleasure of drawing by your example.

■ **DON'T CRITICIZE.** Most children draw when they are very young, through about the third or fourth grade. The problem isn't that you have to teach them to draw, the question is why do they stop? Usually it's because someone compared them to someone else and they developed a fear of art. Maybe they were pushed toward an adult standard too soon. The key is to recognize interest at any age and encourage it, not push it.

Art for children should not be a contest. There are no winners, no losers. Parents should avoid making it into a competition between themselves and the child. Yet many parents unintentionally do just that.

Avoid being critical, even in the smallest or well-meaning way. Praise the picture. Good hard criticism may be appropriate for someone studying to become a professional artist, but there's no place for that from an adult working with a child.

■ **COPY TO LEARN.** Does copying destroy creativity? Michelangelo didn't think so. He spent many afternoons copying the work of Giotto. And Van Gogh didn't think so either. He writes in one of his letters, "Lots of people copy, lots of people don't copy. I copy. I find it teaches me things and above all it gives me consolation." Were these artists creative? Of course. Copying didn't hinder their creativity.

Teaching a child to draw doesn't mean you will produce a Michelangelo. Drawing relates to creativity as typing does to writing. It's just one skill to master in order to become an artist. Practically anyone can be taught

PUT YOUR TALENTS TO THE TEST

Nearly everyone would like to be able to draw a wise owl, a mischievous frog, or a smiling lion. To draw the lion, for example, artist Ed Emberley starts with a rectangle and builds onto it by adding other shapes, including a triangle, a letter "V," and circles. Then, voila!, a happy lion. Here, the artist provides a sampler of other characters that children and adults can create. They are derived from a variety of his drawing books, including Ed Emberley's Drawing Book of Animals *(Little, Brown, 1970, $5.95).*

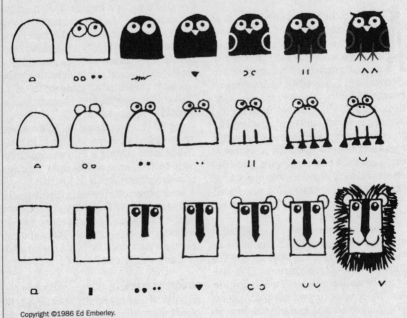

how to draw but to become an artist is something different. It's probably the one thing that can't be taught.

■ **CHOOSE MATERIALS CAREFULLY.** There are many kinds of art materials available, but the hands-down favorites are the kind of markers you can find at any big drug store. They are relatively cheap, easy to use, and portable. All my drawing books have been created using markers.

Avoid crayons. There is nothing more miserable than trying to draw with them. You can't put one color on top of another.

Graphite pencils and white paper may be close at hand, but they're limiting, because you end up drawing outlines, and that's not how we see things. Most things don't actually have a visible outline. Colored pencils are good if they are of superior quality, such as Prismacolor. Tiny, hard, thin, and cheap lead pencils are frustrating to use.

Computers are convenient because you never run out of paper. And, if you have a color monitor, you never run out of color. Unfortunately, unless you have a printer, you don't have anything tangible in your hand when you're done.

EXPERT LIST

HAIR-RAISING RIDES OF A LIFETIME

Roller coasters, cotton candy, Ferris wheels, and bumper cars. Parks these days are a mix of trendy themes and old-fashioned rides, appealing to both the coaster thrill-seeker and the carousel fan. For the past 10 years, Mark Wyatt has made a full-time job of checking out amusement parks. "I've loved this since I was a little kid," Wyatt says. He is the author of White Knuckle Ride *(Random House, 1996) and editor of* Inside Track *(☎ 302–737–3667), a publication that rates amusement parks and their attractions.*

AMUSEMENT PARKS

Following are the results of Inside Track's 10th annual readers' poll of the best traditional amusement parks in America—in order of preference—and Wyatt's commentary on the winners:

1. CEDAR POINT
Sandusky, OH
Season: May 10 to Labor Day. Admission: $25–$30

■ This 364-acre park on Lake Erie has the most rides of any amusement park in the world. There are over 50 rides, including 12 roller coasters. One of the hottest rides is the Mantis, the second tallest standing roller coaster in the world. The Magnum XL-200, which is over 200 feet high, was ranked the ninth-best roller coaster in America by *Inside Track* readers in 1996. "It's everything you'd ever want in a park," says Wyatt.

2. KNOEBELS AMUSEMENT RESORT
Elysburg, PA
Season: Late April to third week in September. Admission: Free for the park; individual rides are extra.

■ One of the very few free-admission parks left in the world. Knoebels charges by the ride, so park visitors can also picnic or walk around for free. Old-fashioned rides, such as bumper cars, are mixed with attractions such as a haunted house. There's a huge swimming pool and campground, and the whole park is shaded by large trees.

3. KENNYWOOD
West Mifflin, PA

Season: Mid-April to Labor Day. Admission: $14–$16

■ Although Dollywood, the Tennessee theme park, is actually named after country star Dolly Parton, Kennywood has no affiliation with her sometimes singing partner Kenny Rogers. At over age 100, Kennywood is one of the oldest amusement parks in the United States. It has four excellent roller coasters, and Wyatt notes that it is the best park for french fries.

EXPERT PICKS

In 1996, *Inside Track* readers rated these waterparks the best to get a soak:

1. Blizzard Beach, Lake Buena Vista, FL
2. Schlitterbahn, New Braunfels, TX
3. Wildwater Kingdom, Allentown, PA
4. Typhoon Lagoon, Lake Buena Vista, FL
5. The Beach, Mason, OH
6. Six Flags Wet 'n Wild, Arlington, TX
7. Wet 'n Wild, Orlando, FL
8. Soak City, Sandusky, OH
9. Splashin' Safari, Santa Claus, IN
10. Hyland Hills Water World, Denver, CO

Source: Inside Track *(January 1997).*

4. HOLIDAY WORLD
Santa Claus, IN
Season: May 4 to the second week in September
Admission: $16–$18

■ Holiday World opened in 1946 as a park with a Santa Claus theme, which the town's name suggests. Now the park has three sections: permanent versions of Christmas, Fourth of July, and Halloween. Among the park's draws are its number-three-ranked roller coaster, the Raven, and its waterpark, Splashin' Safari.

5. CANOBIE LAKE PARK
Salem, NH
Season: May to September.
Admission: $15–$20

■ One of the most beautiful traditional amusement parks in New England, with lush landscaping and a family atmosphere throughout.

The park offers games, food, and a variety of rides, including a vintage wooden roller coaster called the Yankee Cannonball.

THEME PARKS

Here are Inside Track *readers' choices for the top five theme parks in America:*

1. BUSCH GARDENS
Williamsburg, VA
Season: Late March to October. Admission: $25–$30

■ One of the most beautifully landscaped parks in the world, Busch Gardens has a European theme, which means that you can explore the food and culture of Germany, France, England, and Italy. Beer fans can take a tour of the Anheuser-Busch brewery, complete with tastings. The Busch Clydesdale

horses are mascots of the park. It also boasts five world-class roller coasters.

2. PARAMOUNT'S KINGS ISLAND
King's Island, OH
Season: April 19 to October 26. Admission: $30–$35

■ This 25-year-old park features more than 350 acres of rides, shows, and a newly expanded WaterWorks waterpark. Among the thrilling rides: the Beast, the longest wooden-track roller coaster in the world at 7,400 feet long.

3. WALT DISNEY WORLD
Lake Buena Vista, FL
Season: Every day. Admission: $40–$45

■ The biggest theme park in the world. The sprawling complex actually features three world-class theme parks (another one, Disney's Animal Kingdom, is set to open in 1998), three themed waterparks, restaurants, hotels, shopping facilities, an island of nightclubs, and much more. Fireworks every night.

4. SIX FLAGS MAGIC MOUNTAIN
Valencia, CA
Season: Year round. Admission: $25–$30

■ Six Flags is best known for its thrill rides, including 10 roller coasters. Its latest is a 415-foot-high ride called Superman: The Escape. Like all the Six Flags

EXPERT PICKS

The baddest roller coasters in the entire nation, according to *Inside Track*'s coaster riders:

1. Comet, The Great Escape, Lake George, NY
2. Raptor, Cedar Point, Sandusky, OH
3. Raven, Holiday World, Santa Claus, IN
4. Wildcat, Hersheypark, Hershey, PA
5. Steel Phantom, Kennywood, West Mifflin, PA
6. Phoenix, Knoebels Resort, Elysburg, PA
7. Texas Giant, Six Flags Over Texas, Arlington, TX
8. Timber Wolf, Worlds of Fun, Kansas City, MO
9. Magnum XL-200, Cedar Point, Sandusky, OH
10. Montu, Busch Gardens, Tampa, FL

Source: Inside Track *(January 1997).*

parks, this one is owned by Time Warner—hence the many Warner Bros. characters ambling around the park.

5. UNIVERSAL STUDIOS FLORIDA
Orlando, FL
Season: Every day. Admission: $30–$35

■ Here you can "ride the movies" in attractions like Jaws, Earthquake, and Back to the Future. The $60 million Terminator 2 3-D show combines live actors with a multi-sensory 3-D movie. This park is a must-see if you're visiting central Florida; it's the largest active movie studio outside California and is also home to TV's *Nickelodeon*.

RIDES
From the man who makes a living visiting amusement parks, here are Mark Wyatt's personal favorites when it comes to rides:

1. THE BIG SHOT
Stratosphere Tower
Las Vegas, NV

■ This ride starts you off at 930 feet above the ground, then propels you straight up another 200 feet.

2. MONTU
Busch Gardens, Williamsburg, VA

■ A 150-foot-tall inverted coaster where riders hang from overhead tracks in ski-lift style chairs and negotiate a series of loops,

rollovers, twists, and turns at high speeds. Totally disorienting and thrilling from beginning to end.

3. ALPENGEIST
Busch Gardens, Williamsburg, VA

■ Similar to Montu but taller and faster, with an alpine skiing theme and different course.

4. THE GREAT WHITE
Wild Wheels Pier, Wildwood, NJ

■ Classic-style wooden

roller coaster located on a boardwalk amusement pier. Starts off with a very fast tunnel and continues with great drops and turns throughout. Also provides a scenic view of the Atlantic Ocean at no extra charge.

5. TIDAL WAVE
Hersheypark, Hershey, PA

■ A 20-passenger boat is pulled up a 100-foot-tall hill and then hurdles down a chute into the water. It's like jumping into the ocean with your clothes on.

EXPERT PICKS
The top amusement park attractions in America, according to *Inside Track* readers:

1. Twilight Zone Tower of Terror, Disney–MGM Studios, Lake Buena Vista, FL
2. Big Shot, Stratosphere Tower, Las Vegas, NV
3. Escape From Pompeii, Busch Gardens, Williamsburg, VA
4. Haunted House, Knoebels Amusement Resort, Elysburg, PA
5. Back to the Future—The Ride, Universal Studios, Orlando, FL, and Hollywood, CA
6. Indiana Jones Adventure, Disneyland, Anaheim, CA
7. Terminator 2 3-D, Universal Studios, Orlando, FL
8. Drop Zone Stunt Tower, Paramount's Carowinds, Charlotte, NC
9. Jurassic Park—The Ride, Universal Studios, Hollywood, CA
10. Bumper cars, Knoebel's Amusement Resort, Elysburg, PA

Source: Inside Track *(January 1997).*

GEAR & GADGETS

TVS: Picture and sound are still major considerations, but bigger isn't always better, PAGE 509   **HOME VIDEOS:** An expert's tips on producing great home movies, PAGE 512   **SOUND SYSTEMS:** The latest equipment, PAGE 514   **SPEAKERS:** How to set up a concert hall at home, PAGE 515   **CAMERAS:** What's new in the compact camera market, PAGE 516   **TECHNOLOGY:** Cameras that use computers and don't need film, PAGE 516

VIDEO
▼

NOW WATCH THIS, TV SHOPPERS

Tiny satellite dishes and huge TV sets serve up everything but dinner

For most people, buying home entertainment equipment is a nerve-racking ordeal. "Will I end up with an obsolete system?" "Am I being taken for a ride?" What looks good and sounds great in the showroom can turn out to be disappointing when you get it home.

The key to avoiding disillusionment is to be prepared. Magazines like *Videomaker, Video Magazine, Stereo Review,* and, of course, *Consumer Reports* are great sources. The following guide should also help get you started.

SATELLITE TV

Those unsightly backyard satellite dishes are about to become dinosaur carcasses, as digital satellite systems (DSS) take off. In the four years since small satellite dishes were introduced, sales have soared, making them one of the most successful new electronic products

of all time. The dishes are surprisingly tiny, about 18 inches in diameter, but the result is picture and sound that are superior to cable-TV, and immune to static, noise, and interference. Digital satellite services, meanwhile, serve up a smorgasbord of programs.

Despite the many advantages, there are some downsides, including still-stiff prices. But if you'd like to roam the programming firmament freely, then satellite TV is for you. Here are some factors to consider before making the investment:

■ **INSTALLATION.** To install a digital satellite disk requires a professional, who will charge about $200, depending on the difficulty of the job. Kits are available for do-it-yourselfers at a cost of about $100. You'll spare yourself some cash, but be forewarned: the task can be daunting.

■ **PROGRAMMING PACKAGES.** DSS subscribers purchase monthly packages of programs, in addition to the more than 150 standard channels. Package options are numerous, including hundreds of sports programs, extensive pay-per-view choices, and a slew of movie channels. One provider, DirecTV (☎800–347–3288), offers basic cable channels and pay-per-view sports packages and audio channels. USSB (☎800–238–8378) delivers movie channels, as well as additional pay-per-view stations. Subscribers can also get 30 commercial-free, audio-only channels that offer a variety of musical genres. This service also lets parents install restricted viewing mechanisms to prevent children from tuning in to objectionable films. Packages can be expensive—up to $100 or more per month.

■ **MULTIPLE TVS.** The basic satellite dish will not allow viewers of more than one TV under one roof to watch different programs simultaneously. Multiple TV viewing requires a more costly dish called a dual-LNB, and a separate receiver. Expect to shell out another $500 or so for these elements.

■ **LOCAL CHANNELS AND INDEPENDENT CHANNELS.** DSS does not generally deliver local network and cable channels. In most cases an additional antenna is required. Or you can subscribe to a local cable TV service. Local cable providers generally extend a discounted cable subscription for the service, which comes to about $8.00 per month for channels 2 to 13. A onetime service charge applies as well.

SOME BRANDS WORTH CONSIDERING:

$250–$350	Toshiba, Sony
$350–$500	Toshiba, Sony
$500 and up	Sony, RCA, Magnavox

TELEVISION

The past decade has seen an incredible reduction in the cost of wide screen televisions and the near elimination of black-and-white models. Today, one of the most important considerations when you are choosing a new TV is its compatibility with the rest of your entertainment system. Will your TV remote work with cable stations? Will you be able to input speakers and a receiver for "surround sound"?

Picture and sound quality are still major considerations, but the next trend is to merge audio and video into one large home theater. You'll want to make sure the investment you make in equipment now will position you for the future.

Most people decide what size TV to buy by how much money they have to spend. But

Don't be coerced by smooth-talking salespeople into purchasing extended warranties for audio and video equipment. Says Dan Kumin, a contributor to *Stereo Review* and *Audio Magazine*, "Chances are if components will need repair, they will break down during the first 10 to 20 hours of operation. At that stage, they will still be fully covered by the manufacturer's warranty."

too often, people discover that bigger is not always better. Within a few inches, screen size is not going to vastly improve the viewing experience, and you could end up just paying for special features that you may not want.

Regardless of what size TV you plan to buy, there are several features every set should have, and some you can do without. Here's a rundown:

■ **INTERNAL SPEAKERS.** Built-in stereo loudspeakers provide a higher quality sound than traditional mono, but external speakers do the best job. Most high-end sets are going to come with built-in stereo sound, but if you're planning on speakers anyway, don't worry about them.

■ **SLEEP-TIMER.** A built-in timer that turns TV off after a preset amount of time. Good for people who like to fall asleep in front of the TV.

■ **CLOSE-CAPTIONING.** This feature is required by law on all sets 13 inches or larger. The subtitles are a plus for the hearing-impaired, or people just learning English.

■ **PREVIOUS CHANNEL.** Just press this button,

and the TV automatically returns to the last channel viewed. Great for people who like to flip from channel to channel during commercials.

■ **PRESET AUDIO/VISUAL.** You'll be glad you have this feature after you've mucked around with the treble or brightness. It automatically returns the color and sound to their original settings.

■ **CABLE READY.** Common in better sets, this option allows your TV to accept cable TV directly, without the need for a costly cable converter box. There are certain premium services, however, like Pay-Per-View, that cannot be ordered without the box.

■ **PICTURE-IN-PICTURE.** Allows your TV to display two images simultaneously from different feeds (e.g., TV and VCR). A nice feature, but a baseball game in the corner of a movie love scene can be distracting. Two-tuner sets are also available and can display two broadcast channels at a time—a boon for news junkies.

■ **REMOTE CONTROL LOCATOR.** Remote emits sound when TV set is turned on. Perfect for people who are always misplacing the clicker.

■ **VOLUME ADAPTER.** Automatically adjusts the sound to a reasonable level, even when the broadcast suddenly changes volume. A good feature for people who are irritated by loud commercials.

■ **CHANNEL BLOCK-OUT.** Allows you to skip over certain channels while channel-surfing. A good option for parents with young children, or people who hate CNN.

SOME BRANDS WORTH CONSIDERING:

20-INCH COLOR TV (with stereo sound):
$200–$250 ....Sharp, Goldstar
$250–$300 ....RCA, Toshiba, Zenith
$300–$350 ....Hitachi, JVC, Sony
REAR PROJECTION TV (with stereo sound):
$2,000–$2,500 ....Pioneer
$3,000–$3,200 ....Sony, Hitachi
$3,200–$3,500 ....Toshiba

VIDEOCASSETTE RECORDERS

 With digital video players now on the market, you might be reluctant to buy a traditional VCR. But just as the advent of the compact disc didn't mean the end of audiocassettes, videotapes will be around long enough for you to get your money's worth from any VCR you buy in the next few years. Nor are VCR manufacturers sitting on their laurels waiting to become obsolete. Video technology is constantly being improved and options are being added to recorders to meet consumer demand.

Already available are machines with automatic clocks that keep time even if the power is shut off (no more blinking 12:00!) and others that can tape and replay images from digital satellite sources. One word of warning: If you are interested in stereo sound, be sure to get a stereo VCR. Even if your TV has speakers, anything recorded on a mono VCR will sound muffled.

Any decent VCR should come equipped with a range of features to make recording and viewing easier, including preset recording options, remote control, and fast forward at double speed. There are also a number of optional features that true video aficionados might be interested in. They include:

■ **AUTO-TRACKING:** Automatically adjusts tracking to provide optimal image. Perfect for people who hate having to jump up every few minutes to fix the picture.

■ **AUTOMATIC TURN-ON:** Instantly turns on VCR and begins playing when a tape is inserted. A nice, but nonessential labor-saving option.

■ **GO-TO:** Allows you to go to a predetermined point on the tape. Cuts down on time wasted checking fast-forward.

■ **POWER-BACKUP:** Preserves preset records and VCR clock in case of power outage.

SOME BRANDS WORTH CONSIDERING:

$300–$350 ....Sony, Panasonic, GE
$350–$400 ....Panasonic, Quasar, RCA
$400–$450 ....Mitsubishi, Toshiba

HELP FOR THE VCR-IMPAIRED

With VCR PLUS+, even neophytes should be able to record TV shows

If you are among the legions of Americans who still find setting a VCR's clock daunting, programming the machine to tape a show while you're away may seem truly impossible. But don't give up hope just yet: manufacturers have begun to attack the VCR conundrum with simple, on-screen programming and easy-to-follow manuals.

One of the best weapons in the war against VCR illiteracy is a system called VCR PLUS+, offered as a built-in feature on the better VCRs of better brands and now in selected television sets.

Here's how VCR PLUS+ works: Start by looking at the daily listings in *TV Guide* or other participating publications. You will notice there a long series of numbers following each individual show. These are the PlusCode numbers that must be entered with a special remote to let VCR PLUS+ know what you want to tape. Your machine will ask if you wish to record your program once, daily, or weekly. If any problems arise, you can call 800–432–1VCR or 900–454–PLUS for the PlusCode number to any show (95¢ a minute). A word of warning, though: Although VCR PLUS+ makes taping easier in the long run, there is a monotonous, onetime process of calibrating the system to your local listings. In addition, some machines with VCR PLUS+ cannot adapt to cable boxes, making recording a nuisance for some cable subscribers.

A number of other, similar services to VCR PLUS+ are now on the market. One of the most user-friendly is VideoGuide. A remote control tuned in to the VideoGuide box allows you to record programming with a touch of a button. VideoGuide also allows you to scan TV listings up to a week in advance, as well as get up-to-the-minute sports and news information. Its cost: under $100.

VIDEO CAMERAS

With camcorders there are two basic choices for the typical amateur: 8mm and VHS-C video cameras. While 8mm film allows for more filming time (about two hours, compared to 30 minutes at regular speed for VHS-C), VHS-C is easier to play back. Both formats weigh around two pounds and cost about the same ($650–$1,000).

More demanding consumers with fatter wallets may prefer higher-end versions of both models, HI8 and Super-VHS-C, which offer better picture quality. A more recent entry is the digital video cassette (DVC) format. It can capture images at 500 lines of resolution, by far the highest quality available for consumers. All higher-end camcorders should come with standard features, such as auto-focus, built-in microphone, and self-timer. A color monitor, rather than a black-and-white one, is a nice feature: It gives the cameraperson a more realistic idea of what the finished product will look like. Some other useful options available:

■ **TITLES:** Allows you to spruce up footage with a pregenerated title sequence.

■ **DIGITAL ZOOM:** Allows you to zoom up to 100X as opposed to the standard zoom's 10X.

■ **IMAGE STABILIZATION:** Takes some of the jerkiness out of handheld shots. Useful, but a tripod is a good alternative.

■ **FADE:** Lets you stop a sequence without a quick cutoff.

■ **FLYING ERASE HEAD:** Allows you to edit or record over previous film without creating unsightly glitches on the videotape.

■ **SPECIAL EFFECTS:** Luxury features that add

a professional quality to home movies. Among the things you can do is tint images in sepia tones or create an effect that gives your movies the look of old black-and-white films. A wipes feature provides ways to segue from one shot to another, giving you more film editing options than just cutting or fading.

SOME BRANDS WORTH CONSIDERING:

$300–$350 ....Magnavox, GE, Samsung
$600–$800 ....RCA, Sony (8mm and VHS-C)
$800–$1,000 ..Magnav.(VHS-C), Hitachi (8mm)
$1,000–$1,50........Canon (HI8), JVC (S-VHS-C)

DIGITAL CAMCORDERS

Sony, Panasonic, JVC, Sharp, and Canon have all released digital mini-camcorders. Their popularity is due to their convenient size and higher resolution than analog cameras. Consumers can now produce good quality videos with a camera that is no bigger than a box of crayons. Models run from $700 to $1,500 for a fully loaded version. Two useful features to look for are image stabilization, which improves picture clarity, and a color view-finder, which allows you to see while filming the picture as it will look on a playback.

PRODUCING YAWN-FREE HOME VIDEOS

Make movies that won't clear out the house

Home movies generally share some common problems: poor camerawork, little if any editing, and an unparalleled ability to bore viewers. It doesn't have to be that way, says Rebecca Cardozo, head of Cardozo Productions, a video production company, and producer of the videotape *Home Video Hits: Great Ideas for Creating Better Home Videos* (☎888–625–2448; $25). Cardozo has taken up the crusade of teaching amateurs how to make professional home movies that are actually fun to watch. Here Cardozo shares some of her home-video expertise.

■ The most important requirements for great home movies are a good idea and a little planning. To get a more professional look, use the zoom sparingly and with a purpose. Often people zoom in and out too much, which is distracting. There is also a tendency to move the camera from side-to-side too fast. The remedy is to pan slowly. Another common mistake is to let the camera run too long. Keep your shots short—about 5 to 10 seconds each.

■ Vary your angles. Instead of filming the dog while you're standing up, get down to the dog's eye level. Get up on a chair and film as someone opens presents, for example, or shoot up in a column to make a dramatic shot. When documenting a vacation, record the packing, show the car filling up rapidly, and then during the drive show scenery, as well as shots of the kids and the dog sleeping.

■ You don't need sophisticated equipment—only a camcorder. Nor do you need external lighting. The best light the room has to offer will do. External microphones are great and not very expensive, but not absolutely necessary. Just be aware that the microphone on the camera is picking up all noises.

A tripod isn't always vital either; many cameras today have built-in stabilizers. But if you're filming wildlife, a tripod might be necessary.

■ f you plan ahead, you won't need to edit. Most people don't want to spare the time and expense of editing after they've finished filming anyway. The best editing comes in the planning stage.

■ When you're ready to film, be sure the batteries are charged and the owner's manual is handy, in case you need to consult it.

BUILDING YOURSELF A HOME THEATER

For true audio/video connoisseurs, the home theater is even better than a trip to the multiplex.

The combination TV/VCR/Stereo comes close to approximating the feel of a movie theater without the expensive candy and sticky floors. The only limit is your imagination…and your pocketbook.

■ For a simple and inexpensive home theater, all you need is a VCR, a stereo TV with audio inputs, and maybe a pair of external speakers.

■ For something more advanced, consider investing in a special A/V receiver with more power and speaker outlets than your basic television. These receivers start as cheaply as $300–$400, and are a good choice if you plan to upgrade your home theater in the future. The Dolby sound of most movie sound tracks and television shows is wasted on many basic stereo receivers.

Receivers with Pro Logic circuitry, available on most receivers over $350, can create acoustics once found only in movie theaters and Pavarotti's shower.

■ If the very best is what you want, get a system with THX sound. Developed by Lucasfilm, THX is replacing Dolby sound in movie theaters. THX is not a piece of machinery, but rather a set of criteria for realistically reproducing film sound tracks. Originally begun as a certification program for theaters, THX broke into the personal stereo market when manufacturers of high-end audio equipment began sending components to LucasArts for certification. Among other things, true THX sound diffuses the output of surround sound, so that the source cannot be located by ear.

■ **JUST LIKE BEING THERE**

Here's the basic setup for turning your entertainment room into a home theater.

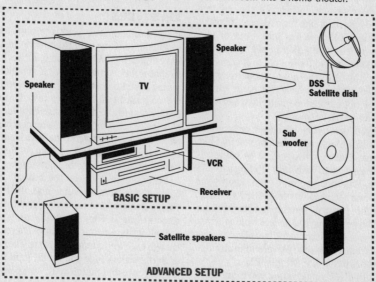

SOUND TIPS ON SOUND SYSTEMS

Speakers matter, but so do the other components of a music center

Boom boxes and rack stereos have their time and place in every music lover's life, but when you get serious about sound quality, you'll want to consider a stereo system with separate components. Consider these tips when shopping for great sound:

CD PLAYERS

Some CD players are better at reducing background noise; others can locate and play a track quickly. Those killer speakers won't do you any good if all they amplify is some hissing and skipping. When you visit a store, try listening to a high-end CD player through a top-of-the-line receiver and speakers. Then test CD players in your price range through the same system, looking for the one that sounds the most like the expensive player.

You should also test how a player performs when playing a scratched or damaged disc. Does it skip like an old hi-fi stereo, or jump ahead to the next readable space? Higher-end models have disc error correction, which can deduce material when faced with a scratch or smudge.

If you have a portable player, or your system's in a high-traffic area, or you just like to have dance parties—you'd be better off getting a system with antiskipping capabilitites. Whether you do or not, keep your player on a flat, stable surface OFF the floor.

Before you can even think about buying a CD player, you have to decide which format suits you. In just a short time, players have gone from single-disc players to multi-disc changers to 100-disc CD jukeboxes.

Multi-disc changers allow you to queue up several (usually five or six) CDs at once and choose among them, without having to reload the machine. The two basic formats are carousel changers—with a lazy Susan–style drawer that slides halfway out for loading, and magazine changers—with a loadable cartridge that actually pops out of the machine. Which is better for you is a matter of personal preference, although carousel changers tend to jam less and give you the luxury of listening to one CD while changing others.

CD jukeboxes are only practical if you have a gargantuan CD collection or are a professional party-thrower. Other features worth considering in a CD player are:

■ **FADE OUT/FADE IN:** Adjusts pauses between tracks, making them less noticeable.

■ **SAMPLING:** Lets you listen to a few seconds of each track on a disc.

■ **FAVORITE TRACKS:** Remembers selected tracks on a disc.

SOME BRANDS WORTH CONSIDERING:

CAROUSEL-CHANGERS:

$150–$200	JVC, Sony
$200–$300	Sony, Onkyo, Denon
$300–$400	Denon, Onkyo, Kenwood

MAGAZINE LOADING:

$180–$230	Sony, Technics
$240–$300	Technics, Pioneer

RECEIVERS

If you only plan to use your receiver to listen to music, most any on the market should have digital FM and AM tuning, with at least 20 spaces for channel presets. If you like listening to audiocassettes, consider a receiver with a built-in tape deck (or two). Graphic equalizers are nice, but the basic bass and treble buttons are usually enough for most beginners. Also, some receivers come with loudness compensation, meaning you can get the full bass without cranking the volume up.

Unfortunately, unless you buy all your components from the same manufacturer, you're liable to end up with a grab bag of remote controls. For most people this is only a small irritation, but for others it's reason enough to go with compatible parts. The price or performance edge you might gain from playing mix-and-match with components won't do you any good if you're driven to dis-

■ **THAT CARNEGIE HALL SOUND IN YOUR OWN HOME**
The ins and outs of arranging speakers for perfect performances

■ Always try to form a triangle with your sound sources if you want great sound.

■ Speaker placements depend on how many speakers you have, their size, and the kind of sound you like.

■ To get the most out of smaller speakers, try putting them on speaker stands. It will diminish the bass slightly, but provide a more uniform sound.

■ Keep speakers clear of walls and corners, and try to maintain a uniform distance from the stereo unit itself.

■ If you like to lie in bed while listening to music, position the speakers about 10 feet away from the bed and separated from each other as well. Additional speakers should line the perpendicular walls, not the opposite wall.

■ Do what works best for you. Every space has unique acoustics, so play around with speaker placement to find the best sound for your room.

---

traction over remote control incompatibility

SOME BRANDS WORTH CONSIDERING:

$150–$200	Sony, Sherwood
$200–$300	Technics, JVC
$300–$400	Yamaha, Onkyo

SPEAKERS

Important features to examine when comparing speakers include clarity, bass, bandwidth, and distortion. Bring a favorite CD to the store showroom, preferably something with a variety of styles, and a heavy bass. Classical music and acid jazz are good possibilities. Any reputable dealer will allow you to gauge the speakers' performance before making a decision. But make sure the speakers are connected to a stereo comparable to your own. There's no point in buying speakers that sound great with a $1,000 system, when all you have at home is a Sony Discman.

Another important speaker feature is size. Most other stereo components are more or less the same size, but speakers can vary from ones that fit on your desk to ones as big as filing cabinets. For music lovers working

with a budget and size constraints, there are two basic categories. Bookshelf speakers (surprise!) are small enough to fit on a shelf—under 3 feet tall—and run under $100. But you do sacrifice bass quality and general sound richness with smaller speakers. At around 3 to 4 feet in height, mini-tower speakers are more expensive (from $100 to $1,000) and generally occupy a square foot of floor space. The sound quality is better, but any imperfections in the music will be amplified.

There are also speakers that specialize in producing exceptional bass, speakers for outside listening, even wireless speakers for that uncluttered look. But you're likely to pay upwards of $300 for some of these options. Don't be afraid to do a lot of research before buying—this is a big investment. And keep in mind how much available space you have—or you could end up sleeping on a subwoofer.

SOME BRANDS WORTH CONSIDERING:

$200–$250	Bose, Sony
$300–$400	Boston Acoustics, Jensen
$400–$600	Bose, Infinity, Koss

HERE COME THE HOT SHOTS

*Picture this: Easy-to-use cameras
that perform well*

Photos of red-eyed relatives and fuzzy friends are mainly a thing of the past. Most cameras are powered by microchips these days, making it easy to take a good shot. The other good news: you won't need to spend a fortune for a good point-and-shoot camera. The question now becomes, which is right for you? Here are your options:

35MM COMPACTS

Compacts are generally available in the following types:

■ **Single-Use Disposable.** These handy cameras use ISO 400-speed film and can take surprisingly good photos. To develop the film, turn in the entire camera. Disposable panoramic versions take extra-wide shots. **Price:** $5–$13.

■ **Fixed-Focus.** These compacts shoot through a very small lens opening and work best when taking pictures in daylight. **Price:** $50–$400.

■ **Auto-Focus.** The most popular type of compact camera, these use an infrared beam to determine the distance between the camera and its subject, then adjust the lens accordingly for the best picture. **Price:** $80–$600.

35MM SINGLE-LENS REFLEX

These versatile cameras are equipped with a variety of lenses—telephoto, zoom, super wide-angle, etc. Long the standard for professional photographers, these cameras allow you to tackle any lighting conditions. **Price:** $300–$2,000.

ADVANCED PHOTO SYSTEM

Introduced in 1996, advanced photo system cameras are generally smaller than their 35 mm counterparts and have an easy and exposure-proof loading system that labels and protects negatives. They also offer three print sizes. The cameras produce pretty good photos, but there is a drawback: they take only APS film, which is neither as common nor as widely processed as 35mm film. **Price:** $190–$300.

NO FILM? NO PROBLEM

With the help of your computer you can turn out fine photos

Want photos that look good, can be computer-altered, and are ready in less than a half-hour? It's all possible with a digital camera, a new gadget that looks much like its traditional 35mm counterpart but works through your computer. Fast becoming popular, these cameras go for $250 to $1,000.

Here's how digital cameras work: When a photo is taken, the light patterns are recorded on the camera's charge-coupled devices, which are used instead of film. The readings are compressed into a group of pixel values at a predetermined resolution. When the camera is full, it needs to be emptied before more pictures can be taken. The images are transferred to a computer by using software that comes with the camera. Once on the computer, the images can be tinkered with before you print them out.

There are some downsides to this new technology. The resolution on large images isn't ideal, and colors and tones aren't as crisp as with traditional slide and print film. But for aspiring photographers who have a computer but no darkroom, or for photographers who want fast photos, these cameras are great tools.

CHAPTER EIGHT

COMPUTERS

"When something bad happens to your computer, the best thing to do is leave the power on and walk away for a few minutes."
—Alfred Poor, author of *The Underground Guide to Troubleshooting PC Hardware,*
Page 529

"Most kids' software is better played with a friend, sibling, or parent."
—Cathy Miranker and Alison Elliott, authors of *The Computer Museum Guide to the Best Software for Kids,*
Page 538

"The most common misconception is that it's all about sex."
—Alfred and Emily Glossbrenner, authors of *The Little Web Book,*
Page 550

■ **WHAT'S AHEAD: BUY** a computer in January, when the prices drop after the holidays... **BROWSE** the newstand for a computer magazine that fits the bill... **DECIDE** whether you really want a Macintosh... **CONSIDER** buying a recycled, less expensive PC... **LEARN** how to troubleshoot common computer glitches... **JUMPSTART** your kids' education with fun and informative software... **INVESTIGATE** the wealth of resources on the Internet...

HARDWARE

STRATEGIES
▼

THE SMART WAY TO BUY A PC

Buy the latest model, a name brand, and remember prices dip in January

Personal computers don't last forever. It's not that computers die—though some parts will fail eventually—but they become long in the tooth. The technology changes so rapidly that after a few years, a PC can't run the new crop of software. Three to five years is about how long you can expect to be satisfied with your PC. Mary Kathleen Flynn, cyberspace correspondent for MSNBC, a new cable channel, offers some buying tips:

■ **STRETCH YOUR BUDGET.** It may sound extravagant, but in fact the most prudent approach to buying a new PC is to spend as much as you possibly can to get the most leading-edge machine you can afford. Prices are dropping all the time, but generally that's to make way for the next set of PCs with new features. The planned obsolescence cycle in the computer industry is about every six months. Be wary of last year's, or last season's models.

PCs aren't like televisions or other appliances, where the new features are often just bells and whistles (though there's some of that as you'll see below). The brain and guts of PCs are improving all the time, with new product lines introduced each spring and fall. To get a modern complete system (PC, monitor, and printer), you'll have to pay about $3,000.

It's tempting to keep delaying purchasing a PC. After all, the longer you wait, the more power your $3,000 will buy. But don't make the mistake some people have made with camcorders; they waited so long to buy one that they miss documenting their kids' toddler years. Post-holiday price drops make January an especially good time to buy.

■ **WHAT TO LOOK FOR.** Pass up the bargain-priced entry-level models and move right on to the middle of the product line. Currently, the configuration you should choose is a 200 megahertz Pentium processor with MMX multimedia extensions, 32 megabytes of memory, a 2.5-gigabyte hard disk, a 12-speed CD-ROM drive and a 33.6 Kilobits-per-second modem.

PC makers are adding more and more fancy features to their machines. Some may be very useful—such as a built-in scanner for photos or documents—while others may seem redundant for home users, like an answering machine. Don't cut corners on the key components listed above to buy an extra frill unless you've really got your heart set on it.

■ SPECS TO INSIST ON

Basic computing requires no more than a keyboard, a mouse, a monitor, and a central processing unit (CPU). To make sure a potential purchase has the right features in the right amounts and speeds, keep this in mind when you shop for a new system.

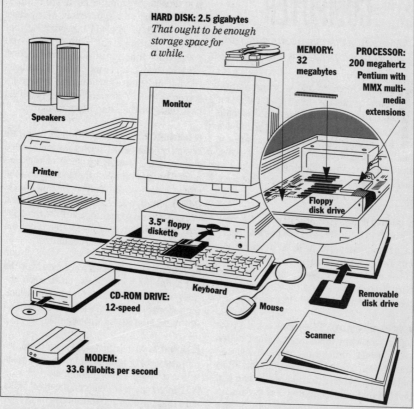

HARD DISK: 2.5 gigabytes
That ought to be enough storage space for a while.

MEMORY: 32 megabytes

PROCESSOR: 200 megahertz Pentium with MMX multi-media extensions

Speakers

Monitor

Printer

Floppy disk drive

3.5" floppy diskette

Keyboard

CD-ROM DRIVE: 12-speed

Mouse

Removable disk drive

Scanner

MODEM: 33.6 Kilobits per second

■ **CHOOSE A NAME BRAND.** Although sophisticated computer owners may ask a favorite local company to build them a PC—or they may even "grow their own"—less technically savvy buyers should always choose a name brand. You don't need to stick with the top 10, but make sure the manufacturer you're considering is distributed nationally. Check the reviews in *PC Magazine* and other computer publications to find reputable companies.

Even with a big name there's no guarantee of smooth sailing. PCs are complicated, and things do go wrong from time to time. But at least with a bigger company, chances are better that it will still be in business a few years later and that it will have a technical staff to help you solve problems.

■ **CONSIDER MAIL ORDER.** Many PC buyers may find the idea of walking into a store more comfortable than buying over the phone. And today, computer warehouses, such as CompUSA, offer deals comparable to mail-order houses. But the big advantage to working with a company like Gateway 2000, which doesn't sell through stores, is that you can pick and choose exactly the features you want.

THE ANATOMY OF A COMPUTER

Master a few basic terms and you sound like a nerd, not a neophyte

You don't have to take a programming course or lock yourself up for days on end attempting to decode technical manuals to understand the basic principles that make computers run. There are virtually no moving parts inside a computer, just electronic messages zipping from place to place. Here's a quick course on basic computer components.

■ **CD-ROM DRIVE:** Virtually all new PCs come with CD-ROM drives, and most new software programs come on CD-ROM disks. When buying a new drive, insist on at least an 8X speed drive, which makes for smoother video clips. Drives of up to 16X are available but their performance is no better than the 8X.

■ **EXPANSION SLOTS:** There may come a time when you want to add extra stuff, called peripherals, onto your computer—stereo sound, a CD-ROM drive, a scanner, an internal modem. When this time comes, you will be glad that your computer has expansion slots, which are simply empty slots that are usually located at the back of your computer. The slots are designed to accommodate special expansion cards that either add functionality to your computer by themselves or allow peripherals like modems and CD-ROMs to "talk" to your computer.

■ **HARD DISK:** You'll probably never see your hard disk—it's nestled inside your computer—but you'll use it all the time. The hard disk is your computer's electronic filing cabinet; it stores all the documents that you work on, as well as all the software that makes it possible for you to create those documents.

The amount of storage space a hard disk has is measured in megabytes (MB); 1,000 megabytes is a gigabyte. Hard-disk size should be as great as you can afford but at least 2.5 gigabytes for today's PCs.

■ **KEYBOARD:** A computer keyboard is different from that of a typewriter. Many have "function" keys labeled F1 through F12 that you can program to carry out various—you guessed it—functions. Most have "arrow" keys that let you move the cursor (that blinking bar or square) around the monitor's screen, a "delete" key, and other specialized keys that give the computer information.

■ **MEGAHERTZ:** Near the CPU there is a little crystal called a clock—it whirs around, which speeds up the processing power of the computer. The speed at which the clock whirs—the clock speed—is measured in megahertz (MHz). When you see an advertisement for a PC, and it reads something like P133, the "133" part refers to the clock speed—the faster the clock speed, the faster the computer.

■ **MODEM:** It lets you exchange data over the telephone lines and allows you access to the Internet. When shopping for a new one, look for a speed of at least 33.6 kilobits per second (for more buying tips, see page 525).

■ **MONITOR:** Also called screens or displays, monitors come in different sizes and resolutions (for more information, see page 523). A 17-inch screen is easier on the eyes. Make sure that the monitor you choose has a "dot pitch" rating of .28 mm or less, which provides greater clarity.

■ **MOTHERBOARD:** This circuit board is where the CPU, RAM, and the other "brains" of the computer live. It's called the motherboard because it has to do the most work.

■ **PROCESSOR:** This chip is the brain of the computer. It comes in different speeds. For a Windows PC, you should go for a Pentium processor, running at 166 MHz or 200 MHz, which is fast enough for running most computer tasks, playing games, and using the

RIFLING THROUGH THE RACKS

Computer magazines have overrun the bookstores. Which do you choose?

Few industries generate as much old-fashioned paper and ink as the computer business. Dozens of magazines report on the computer industry, ranging from mega-titles like *PC Magazine* to ultra-specialized publications like the *Journal of Object-Oriented Programming,* and even *Laser Focus World.*

Which to read? That depends on what you need, of course. When it comes to IBM-compatible computers and peripherals, such as printers and modems, *PC Magazine* is the undisputed king. You'll find hundreds of pages of reviews of hardware, software, and Internet tools. *PC World,* another big name, tends to specialize by selecting a single product family to examine in detail each month. For an office computer user's perspective, try *PC Computing,* which covers the latest hardware, software, and Internet developments for professionals.

A slew of publications, including *FamilyPC, Home PC,* or *Computer Life* offer a lighter, less technical resource. Their target is the home-computing audience and within that niche, *FamilyPC* and *Home PC* are geared to parents trying to manage the family computer. A recent issue of *Home PC,* for example, featured articles on online investment clubs, computer repair, and ways to construct a family Web site. *Computer Life* is aimed at PC "enthusi-asts," such as computer game lovers.

If you're in the market for a particular product, say, a laptop computer, or tax software, the best strategy is to visit the computer section at your bookstore and scan the covers. Very often one of the dozens of magazines devoted to computer paraphernalia will feature a shopper's comparison guide to the product you're after. Two magazines, *Windows Sources* and *Windows Magazine,* for example, focus exclusively on software for IBM-compatible machines running the Windows operating system.

The most thorough source for keeping track of what's going on in the world of computers that use the Macintosh format is *MacWeek.* Two others, *MacUser* and *MacWorld,* feature a wealth of product reviews for both hardware and software—in particular for graphics "power users." A fairly recent addition, *MacAddict,* takes a more aggressive and lively approach to promoting the Macintosh platform.

In recent years, however, coverage of the computer world has moved beyond specialized publications and into mainstream newspapers and business magazines. Three of the best emerging sources of news and reviews about computing are also mainstays of business news: *The Wall Street Journal, The New York Times,* and *Business Week.*

Internet. Also, be sure the chip is an MMX model, which can support some of the newer multimedia software.

■ **RANDOM ACCESS MEMORY (RAM):** This serves as the computer's memory, or the capacity to hold material it is working on. RAM is measured in megabytes (MB) and the more memory, the more programs you can use more quickly and simultaneously. Memory capacity is critical. Your PC should have at least 16 megabytes of memory, but 32 megabytes is better.

■ **SPEAKERS:** Today's multimedia PCs come with a sound card and a pair of speakers. (If you've got an old computer and are shopping for new speakers, make sure that they are "self-powered.") Typically, speakers are separate units that sit on your desk, but in some new PCs, the speakers are attached to the monitor.

DO YOU REALLY WANT A MAC?

PC or Mac? A tough decision that gets easier as Apple's woes worsen

Even if you don't own a computer, chances are you've heard about the troubles facing Apple Computer, maker of Macintosh computers. The company has reported huge losses, as rivals selling computers based on the Windows operating system have grabbed nearly 95 percent of the market. For many experts, the question is not whether Apple will fold, but when.

Loyal fans of the Mac stand by their Apples, which they say are high-quality and easy to use. But while software stores are clogged with scores of computer programs, usually no more than a few dozen titles are for the Mac. That's because software publishers are reluctant to produce programs for the small Mac market, when there are so many more potential buyers in the Windows world.

The Mac's biggest threat is the popularity of the Windows operating system from Microsoft. Though debate still rages about which operating system is easier to use, even Apple loyalists concede that Windows erases many of Mac's traditional advantages. Furthermore, Microsoft has introduced new features and capabilities to its interface, such as integrating access to the Internet into the user's basic environment. As of mid-1997, other advanced features were being developed for the next generation of Windows.

If you buy a Mac, don't expect any major updating of the operating system. Apple has not produced an overhaul for years, and it's doubtful that recently announced ambitious upgrade plans will materialize. But all the news isn't grim. While Windows-based systems have been catching up in ease of use, the Mac has taken the lead in the speed and power of its machines. Further, with all the competition, high-end Macs have become much more affordable. Besides, Apple maintains a fanatically devoted user population in certain key markets, such as education and publishing.

What's the lesson for computer shoppers? Buying a Mac is a risky move. Apple's poor financial health makes it ripe for a takeover by another company, which could end the Macintosh platform. On the other hand, no matter what happens, the 6 million Mac users worldwide represent a major market that won't disappear overnight. And whether you buy a Mac or a Windows computer, chances are that, in any case, it will be outdated in six months and obsolete in two to three years.

PICKING UP A PC AT CUT-RATE PRICES

Sky-high prices for a well-equipped new computer are a big deterrent for many potential PC owners. And buying one of the bottom-of-line, $1,000 or so, computers may be unappealing to many. One solution might be to buy a recycled machine. Re-Compute (☎ 800–510–8414), an Austin, Texas–based mail order house, takes PCs with 486 or Pentium processors and refurbishes and sells them for $600 to $1,000.

The company gets its computers from businesses that upgrade continually and then installs parts as needed, such as memory, hard drives, and modems. Then it adds its own interface. With the computer you get a versatile bundle of software, including Microsoft Works and Money, Eudora for e-mail, and some games and utilities. Though the recycled PCs may fall short of the souped-up, high-end models, reviewers say they are fine for day-to-day business—and are likely to appeal to the same buyers who prefer a second-hand Jaguar to a new Yugo.

WHAT YOU'LL ALSO NEED

A computer isn't complete without a monitor, printer, and modem

Buying a home computing system often doesn't end with the purchase of a spanking new PC. There are some extras you may desire—especially if you bought the machine a few years ago. A faster modem and a bigger monitor are common reasons to return to the computer store. Many families find that a color printer, which sometimes comes bundled with a new PC for a low price, is a must. Here are the buying strategies from well-known experts on how to pick the three devices.

MONITORING MONITORS

Multimedia maven John R. Quain has been staring at monitors for over 12 years in the course of testing and evaluating all kinds of computer products for a variety of magazines, including Entertainment Weekly, Fast Company, *and* PC Magazine. *Here are his views on monitors.*

■ **What's the most important thing to look for?**

The best monitor is the one that looks good to you. Carefully examine a potential purchase in the store. Make sure the onscreen image is not bowed or blurry.

■ **What are the key specs?**

For sharp, detailed images, get a resolution of at least 800 by 600 pixels and a dot pitch (the distance between pixels of the same color) of .28 or smaller. Also look for a "refresh rate"—how often the monitor can redraw the screen—of 72 Hertz or higher, which causes less eyestrain than lower ones. These days most monitors are "noninterlaced," which is what you want.

■ **What size monitor should you buy?**

The biggest one you can afford. A 15-inch unit (around $300) is adequate for most people but not for those who want to view several open windows onscreen at the same time. A better choice, budget permitting, is 17 inches (between $600 and $700).

■ **Should you be concerned about radiation?**

The type of radiation in question is called extremely low frequency (ELF), which is emitted in low doses from computer monitors. No studies have proven that health problems arise directly from using monitors frequently, but ELF from other sources (such as electrical transmission and distribution lines) has been linked with increased incidence of cancer. Current monitors emit low radiation and are considered reasonably safe.

■ **Do you recommend antiglare filters?**

No. Most monitors have some form of antiglare treatment, so extra filters, which cost $50 to $150, are not necessary—unless you work in an especially bright room.

CYBER SOURCE

Can't understand why your modem isn't working up to speed, or just want to learn more about the world of modems? Check out Curt's High-Speed Modem Page online at *http://elaine.teleport. com/~curt/modems.htm.*

Detailed information at this site includes: how to set up a modem under Windows, buying tips, links to modem manufacturers, and much more.

■ **Do you need to know anything special to hook up a laptop to a monitor?**

Make sure the laptop can accept an external monitor and that it is able to display the image on both screens at the same time.

■ **What's the state of the art?**

Professional artists and serious game players will appreciate a 21-inch monitor with 1600 by 1200 resolution and a refresh rate of 85 Hz. Two popular brands are Nanao and Nokia for the high end. These monitors start at $2,000.

PICKING A PRINTER

As the director and principal analyst of electronic printer services at Dataquest, a market research firm in San Jose, Calif., Bob Fennell's middle name is hard copy. This is how he shops for the perfect printer.

■ **How do you choose between a laser printer and an inkjet?**

If you're only interested in printing text, then a laser printer is the best option. But for those planning to print color and graphics, you're better off with an inkjet. Try to get a salesperson to print out a test document you designed yourself. A family newsletter or greeting card will do nicely.

■ **How much will you have to spend?**

A good laser printer will cost around $300 and up for faster machines. For a decent color inkjet, expect to spend between $200 and $450.

■ **What's the best speed?**

A decent laser printer should print between 6 and 8 pages per minute. A color inkjet printer prints between 4 and 8 pages per minute in monochrome. You should get the fastest printer you can afford. To test color printing speed, print out one color page. Bear in mind that it takes longer to print a document that has highly detailed graphics. Color printouts can take less than one minute; some printers can print color up to 7 pages per minute.

■ **What about the resolution?**

Resolution in printers is measured in dots per inch (dpi). Resolutions start at 300 dpi, but for crisp, professional-looking output, look for 600 or 720 dpi. Advanced inkjets can print up to 1440 dpi.

■ **Do you recommend multipurpose devices that combine printer, copier, and fax machine?**

Make sure that you're not buying anything you don't need; your PC may already have fax capability, for example. One advantage of a multipurpose machine is that it is less expensive than buying all the features separately, and it requires less space. A disadvantage is that when one feature malfunctions, the others may also fail.

■ **What are the best brands?**

For laser: Apple, Brother, Hewlett-Packard, Lexmark, NEC, Okidata, Panasonic, Texas Instruments, and Xerox. For inkjets: Hewlett-Packard, Canon, Apple, Epson, and Lexmark.

EXPERT TIP

According to the Sierra Club, a PC that is consuming electricity but ignored for three hours a day is responsible for some 200 pounds of carbon dioxide pollution every year. That's about 2 percent of the annual carbon dioxide that is emitted by a car that is idling or being driven. To help reduce the CO_2 emissions from your computer, be sure to turn it off if it is sitting idle for long stretches.

■ Should anyone even consider a dot matrix printer these days?

The cost of paper and ink or toner is lower for a dot matrix than for inkjet and laser printers, but the print quality is also lower. Dot matrix printers are most appropriate for those who need to print continuous-form paper and multiple-part forms.

LINKING UP WITH A MODEM

As the technical editor at Communications Week, *Oliver Rist knows modems inside and out. Here's his communications strategy for the rest of us.*

■ Why buy a modem?

With all the new online services popping up, a modem has become as necessary a device as the telephone. A modem allows you to exchange electronic mail with friends and relatives, surf the Internet, receive updated software, and shop without leaving the comfort of home.

■ What should you look for in a modem?

Get the fastest standard modem available. It transfers data at 33.6 Kilobits per second.

■ Should you replace a slow modem?

Yes, if you think it's likely you'll spend much time on the Internet. Viewing sites on the Web is painfully slow at speeds lower than 28.8 Kbps.

■ How easy is it to hook up a modem to a PC?

To install an internal modem ($100 and up), you need to open up the computer and replace the old one with it, which could be a hassle. An external modem ($150 and up) would be a better choice for beginners. Windows 95, which comes installed on most systems sold since the fall of 1995, makes adding an external modem especially simple: just plug the device into the back of the PC and reboot.

■ What are the most popular brands?

Hayes and U.S. Robotics.

■ What are cable modems and when will they be available?

Instead of the phone lines, cable modems use cable TV wires, which at 128 Kbps are much faster than regular modems. Manufacturers are still test-marketing cable modems. Trial runs involve buying the device for about $200 and paying a monthly rental fee of $40. Don't expect to see cable modems widely available before mid-1998.

■ What about Integrated Services Digital Network (ISDN) lines?

ISDN lines also transmit data at 128 Kbps and can carry voice and data simultaneously. For instance, you can talk on the phone and receive a fax at the same time. To get this service, however, the phone company has to install special lines (for a fee of $100 to $250), and the monthly fees ($30 to $85, plus additional per-minute fees) are too costly for casual users.

■ WHAT YOUR MODEM IS TELLING YOU

A guide to those blinking lights, be they vertical or horizontal.

✳ **HS** HIGH SPEED—Your modem is set to communicate at its highest speed.

✳ **AA** AUTO ANSWER—Your modem is set to answer incoming calls.

✳ **CD** CARRIER DETECT—Your modem is connected to another modem.

✳ **OH** OFF HOOK—Your modem is in use, either answering an incoming call or placing an outgoing one.

✳ **RT** or **RX** RECEIVE DATA—Your modem is receiving data from another modem.

✳ **ST** or **SX** SEND DATA—Your modem is sending data to another modem.

✳ **MR** MODEM READY—Your modem is on.

✳ **TR** TERMINAL READY— A hardware connection exists between your computer and your modem.

PUMPING UP YOUR PC

You don't necessarily need to buy a new computer to be up to speed

If your computer is out-of-date, you can't run the newest software programs. For people who only use the computer to balance their budgets or to write letters, that's fine. But if you're frustrated because you don't have access to the nifty programs your friends are talking about, or you aren't able to log onto the Internet or send electronic mail, it's time to upgrade your PC. You may even need to replace it altogether.

■ **MULTIMEDIA.** Today, all new PCs have built-in multimedia—a sound card and speakers and a CD-ROM drive. Get at least a 12X or 16X CD-ROM drive and a 16-bit Sound Blaster compatible sound card; for even better sound quality, you can get a card with wavetable synthesis. Installing the upgrades is not easy and best done by your dealer. Note that not all your current software may be compatible with the new products you are installing.

To take advantage of the latest products and services, you need multimedia. If you have an older PC that lacks sound and a CD-ROM drive, you can buy a multimedia upgrade kit for a few hundred dollars. Today, 16X speed drives are standard, although high-end drives have surpassed the 20X speed mark. Unlike earlier models of CD-ROM drives, the new drives are usually variable speed drives; the speed quoted, i.e., 16X, is the maximum speed the drive can achieve. Although Digital Video Disc software for the PC—or DVD-ROM software—is not plentiful, you can get a head start by buying a DVD-ROM upgrade kit for about $500 to $600.

People who bought early multimedia systems may want to update the components. If you've got an 8-bit sound card, consider swapping it out for a 16-bit one. If the CD-ROM drive is "double-speed," you may want a faster one—though many of the current programs work adequately on a double-speed drive. The norm for upgrade kits is an 8X speed drive.

■ **PROCESSOR.** Those buying a new system shouldn't look at anything slower than a Pentium with MMX technology or PowerPC chip on the Mac side, but if you've got a PC or Mac that you purchased three to four years ago, you can still run some software just fine. If you do need to upgrade, consider getting a new machine. Although it's often possible to upgrade a processor, it's not easy to do, and the old components may slow the new processor down, canceling out the reason you upgraded in the first place.

■ **OPERATING SYSTEM.** To be sure you can run the latest software programs, you need the latest operating systems. For IBM-type PC owners, that means Windows 95 (about $100) and for Macintosh owners, System 7.5 (also around $100). Be forewarned: Upgrading an operating system can take several hours and a fair amount of tinkering to get everything up and running again.

■ **MEMORY.** To upgrade to a modern operating system like Windows 95 or Macintosh System 7.5—and the programs that require them—you'll need at least 16 MB of memory (32 MB is even better). Check with your PC manufacturer, or a tech-savvy friend, to see if your computer's memory can be expanded and to see what kind of memory it takes (SIMMs are standard, but some machines require proprietary memory made by the system manufacturer). You can buy memory from a computer store; a megabyte will probably cost less than $40.

■ **MODEM SPEED.** If you want to surf the Web, you'll need to upgrade your 9,600 Kilobits-per-second or 14.4 Kilobits-per-second modem to at least a 33.6 Kilobits-per-second unit. The 56.6 Kilobits-per-second modems offer even greater speeds; however, not all Internet service providers can support them yet.

EXPERT Q & A

SIZING UP THE SMALL COMPUTERS

Portable computers are hot. Here's what you need to know

Seems like everybody's going mobile. With more and more people working away from the office—at home, on the road, in planes and trains, and other far-flung locations—portable computers are compact, convenient, and are getting so powerful that many people are using them as their primary computers. But other than the size difference, what's to know about portable computers? Here's the lowdown on sized-down machines from some of the editors of *PC Magazine*.

■ What's the difference between portable and desktop computers?

Portables are smaller. It sounds like a ridiculously obvious point, but if you're talking components, that's about the only real difference between desktops and portables. You will, however, have to pay more for those components in miniature. While prices of portables are falling steadily, you'll still pay about a third more for a portable (specifically, a notebook) than you would for a desktop. Why? It's the price of design ingenuity; it takes some pretty fancy engineering to cram all those goodies into a compact package. The other difference is power. By and large, turbo-powered computing always hits the desktop market before it shrinks to portable sizes. In other words, don't expect the same kinds of bells and whistles that you see on desktops now to be standard fare on a portable at least until 1998.

Tempted to buy a notebook instead of a desktop—even though you don't plan to take it on the road much? Reconsider. The undersize keyboard and display will cause you discomfort if a notebook is your only home PC.

■ What's the difference between a PowerBook, laptop, notebook, and sub-notebook?

Portable computers come in varying sizes and weights. The terms "laptop" and "notebook" tend to be used interchangeably. Notebooks are the most popular, practical kind of portable. They're relatively slim, and weigh between five and nine pounds; heavier models generally come with larger screens and many multimedia features, putting them on par with powerful desktop PCs. Subnotebooks are smaller, more compact, and weigh about four pounds. These systems are great for road warriors, assiduous notetakers, and e-mail users, but because of their cramped keyboards and smaller screens, subnotebooks are not appropriate for people who write all the time. And subs are definitely not right for budget buyers, who find better bargains in notebook computers.

PowerBooks are Apple's Macintosh notebooks. The latest and most powerful powerbooks use the PowerPC chip, roughly comparable to the Pentium chip used in PCs.

■ What should you look for in a notebook?

The typical configuration in an average notebook now includes the fol-

---

FACT FILE:

TOP FIVE PORTABLES

■ *The leading brands in the United States by percentage of market:*

1. TOSHIBA	18.9
2. IBM	11.0
3. COMPAQ	10.7
4. NEC CORP.	9.2
5. DELL COMPUTER	6.4

SOURCE: Computer Intelligence.

BATTERIES THAT KEEP ON GOING...AND GOING

Learning about how batteries work can save you trouble on the road, or wherever you're tethered to your computer. Here's what the experts advise:

■ **PUT IT TO SLEEP.** If you're not going to be working on a file for several minutes, don't turn off the laptop (the energy required to boot it up again drains battery juice). Most portable computers have energy-saving utilities that will lull the machine into "sleep mode" after several minutes of non-use, but if you don't have this feature, simply close the cover or use the Suspend/Resume switch.

■ **KEEP THE LIGHT LOW.** A bright monitor setting drains 20 to 65 percent of your computer's energy; keep your screen as dim as is comfortable.

■ **AVOID USING PERIPHERALS.** Switching among your CD-ROM drive, modem— even floppy drive—wastes energy. Try to work only from your hard disk, and save files as infrequently as possible; constant saving can eat up to 80 percent of a battery's power.

■ **TREAD LIGHTLY ON YOUR HARD DRIVE.** The type of software you use and the amount of RAM in your computer affect how often the disk drive is used and therefore the running time of the battery. If you increase the amount of RAM on your computer, say, from 4 MB to 8 MB, the battery will last longer. Also, some programs rely more heavily on the hard drive than others.

■ **PREVENTIVE CARE.** When you buy a new, uncharged battery, charge and discharge it two to four times before taking it on a trip. To discharge a battery, unplug your AC-adapter and leave your laptop on (idle) for a few hours. Discharge it fully before recharging. Also, don't let batteries go dormant too long; unplug your AC-adapter every so often while you're working on your laptop at home, and always disconnect it when you're not using the machine. Discharging and recharging your battery periodically will lengthen its life.

■ **WATCH FOR NEW DEVELOPMENTS.** New technologies are producing lighter batteries that run longer on a single charge. Lithium ion batteries, which last longer, can be recharged more often, and retain more of their charge during storage than nickel-metal hydride batteries. They are, however, more expensive and are usually found in mid- and high-end laptops.

lowing: 16MB RAM, 1 gigabyte hard disk, 133 MHz Pentium processor, 10X CD-ROM, 11.3-inch or 12-inch active matrix monitor, a PC slot (credit card–sized drives for modems), a 3$^1/_2$-inch floppy drive, and a "pointing stick." The average time for battery life on notebooks and PowerBooks is about three hours. Remember, though, that heavy-duty batteries can saddle you down—they weigh up to half a pound. Make sure that the weight you're quoted for the portable machine includes the weight of the battery and its adapter.

■ **What if I wait until next year to get a notebook?**

Waiting will get you more computing power for less money. A typical notebook configuration will probably include: a 200-MHz Pentium, a 2.5- or 3.0-gigabyte hard disk, and a 14-inch active-matrix color screen. But if you know what you want and have the cash, why wait?

WHEN YOUR PC WON'T PURR

Troubleshooting tips for when bad things happen to your computer

When a computer works the way it should, life is good. But when your mouse pointer freezes on the screen, or when the dreaded "Fatal error..." message appears in a window, it can make you long for the days of the abacus and slide rule.

In some cases, the best solution is to pack up the system and get professional help. Most of the time, however, you may be able to solve the problem yourself. Alfred Poor, *PC Magazine* contributing editor and author of *The Underground Guide to Troubleshooting PC Hardware* (Addison Wesley, 1996), has made a career of helping people with computer problems. Here are some tips from Poor:

■ **APPROACH THE PROBLEM SLOWLY.** Avoid jumping to conclusions and trying a fix that may turn out to make matters much worse. When something bad happens to your computer, the best thing to do is to leave the power on and walk away for a few minutes. Think about your alternatives before you start, and when in doubt, do nothing. Wait until you're certain of the next step to take.

■ **DON'T RISK MORE THAN YOU HAVE TO.** If you don't have a current backup when something goes wrong, don't do anything that will jeopardize that data. If you can't afford to lose the information, then make a backup immediately if you can still access it. If your problem is with the hard disk, consider removing the drive right away and sending it to a professional data recovery service; if you try to recover the data on your own, you may make it impossible to retrieve the information.

■ **FIRST, CHECK THE OBVIOUS.** If the problem occurs when you first turn on the computer, check that all cables and expansion cards are firmly seated in their connectors, and press firmly on all socketed chips to make sure they are in place. If the failures occur after the computer has been running for a while, the problem could be a failing chip, or the computer may just be too hot. Make sure the computer's ventilation fans are working properly and that there is no dust accumulation inside.

■ **PUT THE COMPONENTS TO THE TEST.** If you have a component that you think might be faulty, try a different unit, which you know works on another computer, in its place. Or try the suspect component in another computer that is known to work reliably. This test isn't conclusive, but can provide a strong indication of whether or not a component is working correctly or not. If this approach doesn't find the problem, take out all the components except the floppy disk and graphics adapter, disconnect all peripherals, and see if the system will boot. If it will, then add back one piece at a time and check to see if the machine will boot. When the system fails to boot, you know that the last part added at the least plays a part in the problem.

■ **SOFTWARE PROBLEMS CAN BE CAUSED BY HARDWARE.** You can run into error messages that may appear to be caused by software conflicts, but they may be caused by hardware problems. Try removing part of your system's memory (if possible); bad memory chips can cause problems that look like software problems. Another step to try is to disable or remove the system cache (L2 cache) on your computer's circuitboard, if it has one. An "overclocked" processor—one that is configured to run faster than its specifications—can also cause intermittent problems that would appear to be software problems.

■ **FIND HELP ONLINE.** There are dozens of excellent sites on the Web where you can get detailed computer troubleshooting information. Among the best are Microsoft's site *(http://www.microsoft.com/kb/)* and the ZDNet site *(http://www.zd.com/)*.

WARNING: COMPUTING CAN BE HAZARDOUS TO YOUR HEALTH

If you type 50 words a minute for an hour, you'll have pecked out some 18,000 keystrokes. Keep that up all day, five days a week, and you're giving your digits and wrists a hard-core workout. Typing's repetitive movements can lead to muscle strain, pain, and weakness in the hands, arms, and wrists—all of which are signs of carpal tunnel syndrome and other repetitive stress injuries (RSI). And that's not all. A bad chair or posture can cause back and neck strain, and staring at your monitor (especially if it's a flickery one) is a great way to give yourself a pounding headache, not to mention ruin your eyes.

PREVENTING REPETITIVE STRESS INJURIES

Behavior modification:

■ Make sure that your keyboard is lower than your elbows; your wrists should be slightly higher than your fingers.

■ Don't over-curl your fingers, drop, or twist your wrists—you'll put too much stress on your hands' muscles and tendons. When you're at the keyboard, keep your fingers just slightly curled and sit up straight.

■ Avoid tendonitis in the elbow (a condition also known as tennis elbow) by making sure that your arms rest comfortably on the armrests of your chair and that your elbows do not jut out at an awkward angle. Ideally, your elbows should bend at 90 degrees. The best chairs let you adjust the armrests to fit your body size.

■ Do you peck at the keyboard, using only a few fingers to do all the work? This can cause muscle strain. If you learn to touch-type, you'll reduce the pain—and double your typing speed at the same time.

■ Take plenty of breaks (five minutes every hour if possible).

Products to try:

■ Investing in a wrist-rest—a device that elevates your hands so that your wrists remain straight while typing—is a great way to help prevent repetitive stress injuries in your hands and wrists. They range from the simple (a foam pad, which costs about $10) to the sophisticated (plastic supports, going for $25 and above). You can find wrist-rests at many computer stores. Don't want to spend the dough? Try a rolled up towel instead.

■ Dozens of keyboards claim to be ergonomic, and some of them actually deliver on that promise. The most comfortable keyboards are Kinesis Ergonomic Keyboard (☎ 206–402–8100) and Microsoft's keyboard.

■ KEYBOARDING

Three common incorrect practices and their symptoms:

TWISTING: Long muscles forced to stretch around elbow, stressing muscles in hands and arms.
SYMPTOMS: Elbow inflammation, throbbing forearm, loss of dexterity in ring and little fingers.

OVER-CURLED FINGERS: Continuously flexed muscles that contract cause nerve compression in the wrist.
SYMPTOMS: Pain in the wrist and forearm, tingling or numbness in the fingers.

DROPPED WRISTS: Tendons press against the nerves in the wrist, weakening the thumb, index, and ring fingers.
SYMPTOMS: Numbness, tingling in the fingers at night, swelling of wrist and/or thumb.

PREVENTING EYESTRAIN

Behavior modification:

■ Keep at least 20 inches between your eyes and monitor, and adjust the monitor's angle so that you don't have to crane your neck to look at the screen. If you wear bifocals, adjust your monitor so that you're looking down.

■ The light that you work by should be diffuse and come from overhead. A light source that comes from the side, or worse, from behind, will make you squint; over time, you'll develop headaches from eyestrain.

■ It sounds kind of obvious, but have you adjusted the brightness and contrast on your screen? This often overlooked solution can save you from squinting at a screen that is either too dim or too bright.

■ Contact lenses may cause eyestrain in people who stare at a computer screen for hours on end. Try using your glasses instead. Photo-sensitive lenses soften the glare from the screen.

Products to try:

■ Nothing is harder to look at than a bright monitor; it can cause headaches as well as eyestrain. Look for add-on screen filters to correct that problem, such as the ones that are available from

Kensington (☎ 800–535–4242).

■ Is your monitor's screen flickering? If it is, it's causing strain on your eyes. A monitor that flickers usually has a low vertical refresh rate or a high dot pitch (see page 523); in either case, it's probably time to get a new monitor.

PREVENTING BACK AND NECK STRAIN

Behavior modification:

■ Bad posture is the most common reason for neck and upper back pain. So learn to sit straight, don't slouch, and keep your shoulders relaxed (but not dropped forward).

Products to try:

■ If you're looking for a computer desk (anything that costs more than $100 is probably called a worksta-

tion), keep a few important points in mind: Get one that you can raise and lower from 27 to 29 inches. Make sure it has an adjustable and sliding keyboard holder—one that is a couple of inches below the table level. Finally, spend the extra bucks and get something solid—there's nothing more likely to give you a headache than a wobbly PC.

■ If you tend to slouch in the chair at your desk, try the $49.95 Nada Chair, a contraption that forces you to sit straight. Call ☎ 800–722–2587 for more information.

■ Looking for a new chair? Make sure the backrest is adjustable and tilts backward. Also look for lumbar support, armrests, adjustable height, and easy-rolling wheels.

■ POSTURE

Computer workstations can be equipped to ensure good posture and proper alignment.

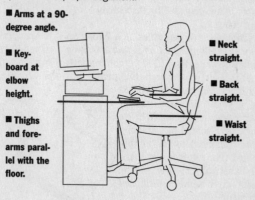

■ Arms at a 90-degree angle.

■ Keyboard at elbow height.

■ Thighs and forearms parallel with the floor.

■ Neck straight.

■ Back straight.

■ Waist straight.

SOFTWARE

EXPERT PICKS

THE 50 GREATEST CD-ROMS

With zillions to choose from, here are the best of the bunch in 11 areas

Book publishers, game developers, Hollywood types, even staid business applications programmers are packing their wares into multimedia CDs. Some 6,000 CD-ROMs were produced in 1996 alone. But just because the box says it's multimedia doesn't mean it's good. The bottom line: For every 100 multimedia CDs, there might be one worth buying.

To find the 50 best titles, Ron White, an executive editor at *PC Computing* magazine where he writes the "CD-RON" column each month, sorted through the proverbial haystack. You can find updated reviews at his Web site at *http://www.cdron.com*. White's picks are sorted by category, from business to the simply weird. The choices are listed alphabetically by title. All the prices given below are estimated street prices.

BUSINESS

ALLEGRO REFERENCE SERIES BUSINESS LIBRARY
Allegro New Media, $40

■ Includes 12 superb books on marketing, finance, real estate, international business, selling, and careers. Lacks multimedia niceties, but the material is easy to search and integrate into your own documents.

QUICKBOOKS PRO
Intuit, $200

■ The best solutions to most money problems, done with great simplicity. Every tool the entrepreneur will need: invoicing, bill paying, contact management, check tracking, online banking, payroll inventory, W-2s, job costing, bidding, and time tracking. Plus: worksheets, and legal and business advice.

QUICKEN TURBOTAX DELUXE EDITION
Intuit, $50

■ A tax program with great features and ease of use. EasyStep walks you through the information-gathering needed to produce completed tax returns. Tax Advisor gives money-saving advice, and Final Review checks for accuracy.

QUICKEN FINANCIAL SUITE
Intuit, $90

■ A wealth of functions include Internet links, expanded investment tracking, and online banking. The suite also features

Quicken's Financial Planner, RetireReady Deluxe, and an expanded version of Family Lawyer, an inexpensive way to take care of lots of life's little contracts.

CHILDREN
ARTHUR'S TEACHER TROUBLE
Living Books, $40

■ Great animation and clickables that are fresh and avoid the obvious. Click on a cuckoo clock, and the bird doesn't just come out and chirp the time—it announces a prizefight. Many of the titles in the Living Books series are based on top children's tales, including: *Harry and the Haunted House, Ruff's Bone, Stellaluna,* and *Dr. Seuss's ABCs.*

BIG JOB
Discovery Channel Multimedia, $40

■ A chance to play with trucks, construction machines, and big-job tools. Build your own town by clipping-and-dragging roads, houses, and factories. When you're through, you can blow it up.

GEORGE SHRINKS
HarperCollins Interactive, $40

■ When George wakes up in this instant classic by William Joyce, he is the size of a mouse. The story follows the clever ways in which he carries out the chores his mother has asked him to do. Great songs and clickables, and beautiful illustrations and animation.

THE LOGICAL JOURNEY OF THE ZOOMBINIS
Broderbund, $40

■ The coolest educational game around. Your goal is to help the Zoombinis escape Bloat's Island prison, by guiding them past blockades and obstacles. Kids learn math skills such as set theory, graphing, data analysis, and logic. Great fun for adults, too.

THE MAGIC SCHOOL BUS EXPLORES THE HUMAN BODY
Microsoft Home, $45

■ This full-screen, full-action animation features endless "hot" objects that do surprising things when you click on them. Click on some

odd morsel in the stomach and it turns into its preingestion state—a hamburger or a cheese puff, for example. A fun approach to learning.

MIXED-UP MOTHER GOOSE DELUXE
Sierra, $40

■ Mother Goose needs your help in finding objects that 18 characters have lost from their rhyme. Peter lost his wife, the old woman in the shoe can't find the broth, and Miss Muffett lost her tuffet. Excellent songs and graphics. Easy enough for even toddlers to enjoy.

STEPHEN BIESTY'S INCREDIBLE CROSS-SECTIONS STOWAWAY!
DK Multimedia, $30

■ Take a section of a sailing ship of yore and explore it in detail. Not just for budding engineers: Explorations include the roles of crew members and how they advanced as seamen, for example. Excellent illustrations and sound effects that seem to put the deck under your feet. The game of trying to find a young stowaway is a footnote.

WHERE IN THE WORLD IS CARMEN SANDIEGO?
Broderbund, $50

■ This game sneaks in geography lessons. You travel to exotic locations in a quest to track down Carmen's henchmen, who've swiped some of the world's treasures. Filled with photographs, animated characters, and folk music from around the world.

ENTERTAINMENT
A PASSION FOR ART
Corbis, $45

■ Corbis offers a guided tour of the Albert Barnes collection, a private cache of Impressionist, post-Impressionist, and early modern paintings. Zoom in on a masterpiece for a closer look, as text and audio explain each work.

MICROSOFT CINEMANIA
Microsoft Home, $35

■ Neither the most film listings nor the most

film clips, but its great design and well-chosen contents make it the only movie guide often more entertaining than watching a movie. You can connect to The Microsoft Network and download monthly updates with the latest movie reviews.

STAR TREK OMNIPEDIA
Simon & Schuster Interactive, $60

■ The ultimate Star Trek know-it-all, spanning the four TV series and all the films. Links to a generous collection of videos, minidocumentaries, and a diagram of the Enterprise. It's all put together with the look and voice of the Enterprise's computer. And you can control it with voice commands.

GAMES
DUKE NUKEM 3D
3D Realms Entertainment, $40

■ It's not wildly popular Doom, but urban-based Duke Nukem has served as the fix for the Doom-starved, at least until Quake came out. Most are still hooked.

ICEBREAKER
20th Century Fox and Magnet Enteractive, $40

■ The idea is to guide a little pyramid around the screen, shooting and smashing into other pyramids before the hunter pyramids catch up to you. Sometimes you fight. Sometimes you lead pursuers to their demises by tricking them into bottomless pits. An original and fascinating game.

MECHWARRIOR 2: MERCENARIES
Activision, $45

■ Afficionados will drool over the new mechanics, weapons, battle scenarios, and 30 new mechanical warriors. Novices will appreciate the improved multimedia training sessions. There are separate installations for DOS, Windows 3.x, and Windows 95; and there's even multiplayer gaming over the Internet when using the DOS version.

MICROSOFT FLIGHT SIMULATOR FOR WINDOWS 95
Microsoft, $60

■ This grandaddy is finally available for Windows 95. This version brings to the screen

the color and detail we imagined we saw with the original game. Some of the landscapes are still a little clunky, but that's offset by the range of locations. Now you can crash into the Golden Gate Bridge, the Empire State Building, and a host of other tall structures.

MICROSOFT FURY
Microsoft Home, $45

■ In this highly addictive game, you are in a flying vehicle, plowing through tunnels from one spot on a planet to another. Beneath you are 3-D textured landscapes of mountains, valleys, plains and seas, studded with cities and war machines marching to destroy civilization. The action is constant, the details amazingly realistic.

POD
UbiSoft Entertainment, Inc., $50

■ POD is a real-time, 3D racing simulation on a futuristic planet, where a deadly virus is rapidly destroying life. Players race customized superpower cars for the last seat on the last shuttle to safety. Up to eight players can race simultaneously by using a local area network, modem, direct connection or service provider to link to the Internet.

QUAKE
id Software, $45

■ Quake is rendered in true 3D. You can move anywhere within worlds so complex that you can go in circles and not realize it. Add to this state of bewilderment some of the scariest creatures and new ways to die, including my favorite—an exploding grenade.

HISTORY AND CURRENT EVENTS
THE COMPLETE MAUS
Voyager, $50

■ Art Spiegelman's memoir of his father's experiences during the Holocaust, a powerful work of history, first appeared in 1986. This version takes you through the historical and structural details behind the book. The pages of Maus are linked to sketches, archival photographs, and drawings made by Holocaust victims. Audio includes Spiegelman's commentary on the making of Maus, as well as the ideas, and history behind this work.

OUR TIMES MULTIMEDIA ENCYCLOPEDIA OF THE 20TH CENTURY
Vicarious, $70

■ All the events that shaped this century. A photo-studded timeline highlights the social, scientific, artistic, cultural, political, and international events that had the most impact each year starting from 1900. A video for each decade brings the highlights to life. (There's a hardcover book, too.) Thoughtfully chosen photos are matched by intelligently written text.

VIETNAM
Medio Multimedia, $35

■ No sound track can be more effective than stark silence as the video takes you to the Vietnam War Memorial, showing the names of men and women who died in that war. An excellent selection of videos, photos, narration, text, and interviews with people on both sides of the war.

HEALTH
ANNE HOOPER'S ULTIMATE SEX GUIDE
DK Multimedia, $40

■ Filled with tastefully presented information, this guide starts by asking you questions designed to search out your areas of sexual ignorance. It devotes a lot of time to the emotional side of sex, hygiene, sexual diseases, and sex techniques. Personal passwords prevent your kids from using the disk, although it is a good way to teach older children about sex.

DR. SCHUELER'S HOME MEDICAL ADVISOR PRO
Pixel Perfect, $60

■ The next best thing to a house call, this three-disc, Web-linked set packs information on thousands of diseases, injuries, and drugs. Give it your symptoms, and it tells you what's wrong—or asks you some more questions to narrow down your ailment. Like any home doctoring, the CD should be used with

some common sense. If you sense anything serious, see a real doctor.

THE ULTIMATE HUMAN BODY
DK Multimedia, $40

■ Of the many CDs that take you inside the human body, this is a standout. It explores the functions of individual organs, as well as the nervous system, skeletal systems, and six others. There are more than 1,000 illustrations and 90 animations that are not only effective teaching tools but also stunning works of art.

YOUR PREGNANCY, YOUR NEWBORN
Parenting Magazine, $32

■ Follow a couple from conception to the dirty diapers stage, while learning about all aspects of pregnancy—physical and mental health, lifestyle changes, even legal and workplace changes. Video demonstrations cover ultrasounds, vaginal and C-section births, and nursing and bathing the newborn.

ON THE HOME FRONT
3D LANDSCAPE
Books That Work, $50

■ Populate a yard using trees, shrubs, flowers, even ponds, boulders, and lawn chairs. See how shadows would be cast at different times of the day or year, and how plants will look after years of growth. There are tips on growing the plants—and you can even find out how much your sylvan fantasy will cost.

HOME IMPROVEMENT ENCYCLOPEDIA
Books That Work, $13

■ The answer to a do-it-yourself homeowner's prayers. An authoritative and comprehensive collection of videos, animations, and text that teaches you how to be handy around the house.

MICROSOFT PICTURE-IT
Microsoft Home, $80

■ Here's a complete factory for retouching, cropping, matting, framing, labeling, and printing photos. Scan directly or use a digital camera. Do some cropping, add a textured background, put in some cute captions and you've got a fancy photo. If you don't have a color printer, upload your pictures to Kodak and you'll get prints in the mail.

VISUAL HOME
Books That Work, $60

■ No other architectural CD matches Visual Home's ease of use and spectacular results. Create a 3D model you can walk though. An Internet link lets you download professional house plans you can modify. Or experiment with over 2 million combinations of fabrics, colors, and styles in appliances, furniture, carpeting, and other personal touches.

REFERENCE
MICROSOFT BOOKSHELF FOR WINDOWS
Microsoft Home, $70

■ The best way to dig up facts or spice up a dry report. It's all inclusive: the *American Heritage Dictionary*, with more than 350,000 entries and sound bites of 80,000 words, the *Columbia Dictionary of Quotations, Roget's Thesaurus, People's Chronology, Concise Columbia Encyclopedia, Hammond World Atlas, World Almanac, Book of Facts,* a zip code finder, and the year in review.

MICROSOFT ENCARTA ENCYCLOPEDIA DELUXE EDITION
Microsoft Home, $80

■ The ultimate in multimedia encyclopedias. By adding a second CD and Internet links, Microsoft has expanded its reach. There are: 14,000 photos, 68 videos, 978 maps, 800 charts, 2,300 clips, as well as some nifty multimedia shows. You also get 30,000 articles, monthly updates, and access to a news and periodical database, Encarta Online, worth the $7 a month.

THE MULTIMEDIA ENCYCLOPEDIA OF SCIENCE FICTION
Grolier Interactive, $40

■ One of the best combinations of content and presentation around. It lets you explore sci-fi by concept, for example, time travel, life forms, technology, as well as by author and title. Based

on an award-winning book, the text explores some of the genre's best-known writers.

RANDOM HOUSE UNABRIDGED ELECTRONIC DICTIONARY
Random House Reference and Electronic, $40

■ The best, most extensive dictionary you can get for your money. This enhanced version has a search engine that lets you get at the dictionary's 315,000 entries so many ways that you can misspell a word and still find it. Maps, illustrations, and an audio collection of 120,000 pronunciations are included.

SCIENCE AND TECHNOLOGY
A BRIEF HISTORY OF TIME
Creative Labs, $35

■ Take a quantum leap toward understanding how the universe began with this CD containing the entire text of Stephen Hawking's best-selling book. Explore the universe through the CD's animations and graphics narrated by physicists, including Hawking, who suffers from motor neuron disease and uses a computerized voice.

DISTANT SUNS FIRST LIGHT
Virtual Reality Laboratories, $60

■ Observe the stars, planets, comets, asteroids, and spacecraft, from any angle and at any time in the past or future. It lets you control the amount of detail you want to include. The program takes some getting used to, but it's worth it when you make that fly-by past Saturn.

EYEWITNESS ENCYCLOPEDIA OF NATURE
DK Multimedia, $40

■ Captures the wonder of nature, taking you back to when you were a child and were curious about the world. Explanations of everything from how viruses reproduce to how whales feed, all presented with a clarity that kids will understand and adults won't find patronizing. A must for all nature-lovers.

MICROSOFT DANGEROUS CREATURES
Microsoft Home, $35

■ Take guided tours to the Amazon, Africa, coral reefs, and other parts of the animal kingdom. It's hard to stay on a tour for long because there are so many distractions. Start out learning about male and female roles among animals and wind up learning how an octopus poisons its prey. Along the way, sample photographs, videos, and the sounds the creatures make.

MICROSOFT OCEANS
Microsoft Home, $35

■ You could drown in all the information here. There are guided tours, but the real joy comes from clicking away on the abundant links that take you from the depths of the oceans to the pirates who sailed the seas. A rich collection assembled with style and wit.

ORIGINS OF MANKIND
Maxis, $40

■ A CD of rare depth pulling all the multimedia stops to explore human evolution. It's packed with videos, maps, a tour of an actual dig, 3-D artwork, and even morphs that let you pick which cousins on the evolutionary train get transformed from one to the other. Just the right mix of learning tools and fun.

RED SHIFT
Maxis, $49

■ A great astronomy/planetarium Windows program. View the stars and planets any way you like—from vast panoramas to low, sweeping flybys over alien terrain. The color photography is beautiful, and the way you can play with the universe is totally absorbing.

THE WAY THINGS WORK
DK Multimedia,$40

■ An adaptation of David Macaulay's 1988 bestseller, explaining everything from simple levers to microprocessors. The CD adds a new section on inventors, a machine history timeline, and a Web site for the Young Inventors club. Explanations are lucid and fun.

SPORTS
FLY FISHING: GREAT RIVERS OF THE WEST
IVI Publishing, $35

Beautiful art, photos, and maps. Some of the multimedia gets a bit silly, such as the sounds

gallery, which treats you to noises like rowing and babbling water. But to the enthusiast, it's all part of the oneness of fly-fishing.

TRAVEL
BERLITZ, LIVE! JAPANESE
Sierra, $80

Just as helpful for those doing business in Japan as it is for tourists. The language instructor emphasizes business phrases you're most likely to use. You learn about body language, too, such as Japan's all-important bowing ritual during the exchange of meishi, or business cards.

RAND MCNALLY TRIPMAKER
Rand McNally, $40

■ A great map-making program. Enter a couple of locations and get a series of scaled maps, and then, with the help of StreetFinder, a separate CD, zero in on the neighborhood you want. Check out video clips, distance calculation, and alternate side trips. Plus, get the lowdown on restaurants, accommodations, and attractions along your route.

UTILITIES
SMARTSOUND FOR MULTIMEDIA
Sonic Desktop Software, $129

■ Need background music for a killer multimedia presentation? No problem. Tell the program how long the music should be, what emotional effect it should have, and whether you need an opener, segue, background, or finale. The software does the rest, creating an original musical score.

WEIRD
MONTY PYTHON & THE QUEST FOR THE HOLY GRAIL
7th Level, $50

■ More nutty antics from the BBC favorites. Try to register the CD, and you will be asked your name, address, and more than 100 other questions, including your favorite color and the capital of Assyria. The disc covers some familiar territory from the movie, but there are lots of surprise clickables, and several rousing games.

AN ELECTRONIC BABY-SITTER?

Don't just plop the kids in front of the computer. Lend a helping hand

The odds are better than even that your kids are more at home with a computer than you are. But in case they're not, Cathy Miranker and Alison Elliott, authors of *The Computer Museum Guide to the Best Software for Kids* (HarperCollins, 1995), offer some advice about how to make your home computer as comfy as a teddy bear.

■ How involved should parents be when kids play on the computer?

Very. If you want your kids to get the most from your home computer, don't limit your involvement to simply choosing software. Hold toddlers on your lap and be the audience for older kids' artwork and stories. Explore a topic of interest together. Challenge them to a game. Because in the end, the computer is not their teacher. You are.

■ What are some good ways to extend the longevity of a computer game?

Put the game away after two months or so. When you reintroduce it, your kids will be slightly different people. Chances are, they'll use the same software in a new and different way. Check the Web sites of your favorite children's software publishers, too. Their free online activities often let kids get more mileage out of a software title.

■ What kinds of programs are good for sharing?

Most kids' software is even better when played with a friend, sibling, or parent. For older kids, brainteasers, math challenges, thinking games, history simulations, and geography quests make great "together" activities. Children who are too young to play love watching siblings at the keyboard and helping them decide what to do next.

■ How can software reinforce classroom work?

Talk to your child's teacher to learn what the students are doing with computers in school. They may also recommend homework helpers like a writing program, spelling software, or electronic encyclopedia. Also consider programs that complement the subjects your child is studying. Software that presents classroom topics in unclassroom-like ways often sparks the most enthusiasm and discovery.

■ How should parents go about buying software?

Beware of programs that simply repackage movies, TV shows, and books. Too often, they ask kids to do little more than click and watch. Instead, look for software that encourages kids to create, experiment, make decisions, and solve problems. Beyond that, it helps to read reviews, talk to teachers and friends, and surf the Web. If possible, try before you buy—at a store, a children's museum, or an after-school computer center. Then buy from a source that will let you return the software

---

■ BEYOND THE COOL AND WHIZZY

These packages don't teach programming per se, but include intriguing activities that let kids master challenges that are central to programming. Here are some picks from Cathy Miranker and Alison Elliott:

MY MAKE BELIEVE CASTLE	Ages 4–7
Logo Computer Syst.	☎800–321–5646
ZURK'S ALASKAN TREK	Ages 6–10
Soleil	☎415–494–0114
THINKIN' THINGS COLLECTION	Ages 7–13
Edmark	☎800–691–2985
LOST MIND OF DR. BRAIN	Ages 9+
Sierra On-Line	☎800–757–7707
KLIK & PLAY	Ages 10 and up
Maxis	☎800–526–2947

HOW TO CHILDPROOF YOUR COMPUTER

It's easier than you think to keep kids away from things they shouldn't see

Sharing the home computer with your brood seems like a good idea, both financially and familially—until your seven-year-old deletes an important business report from your hard disk. And you probably don't want the kids wandering around the Internet's red-light district. Here are some inexpensive solutions.

■ **HARDWARE SOLUTIONS:** A solid hardware solution to kid intervention is hard disk partitioning. If you're a computer whiz, you've probably done this already; otherwise, take your computer to a good service store. Disk partitioning allows you to divide a single hard disk into separate drives, assigning one to kids, the other to adults. When kids turn the computer on, they're automatically routed into the drive assigned to them; password protection prevents them from accessing the adults' space.

If you decide on this option, just make sure that you have a hard drive that is large enough to divide so adults have enough hard disk space to run their applications and the kids have enough space to run their games. For true division, you can buy two external hard drives; one for parents and one for kids.

■ **SOFTWARE SOLUTIONS:** Give your kids their own desktop software. Kid Desk, from Edmark, ☎ 800–320–8378, makes the computer screen look like a child's desk. Like the Microsoft Windows or Macintosh desktop, Kid Desk displays icons for applications that your kids use, and identifies parents' territory with a single icon, which is password protected. The family edition lets kids leave messages and voice mail on the desktop for other family members.

Launch Pad, from Berkeley Systems, ☎ 510–540–5535, works in the same way, but kids are given the option of selecting one of several desktop wallpaper designs: dinosaurs, a spaceship, a castle, a unicorn, or a creepy old haunted house.

■ **INTERNET SOLUTIONS:** Several software programs are designed specifically to prevent kids from viewing adult material on the Internet. One of the best is SurfWatch, ☎ 800–458–6600, which blocks out thousands of Web sites that contain sexually explicit material and stuff you probably don't want your kids to see. With an annual subscription, you'll get monthly updates. Other Internet filtering utilities include Cyber Patrol, ☎ 800–828–2608, and Net-Nanny, ☎ 800–340–7177. (See also page 556.)

---

if it doesn't meet your expectations.

■ **What's the best way to avoid incompatibility surprises?**

Keep the vital statistics about your system on hand when you shop: type of processor, amount of RAM, CD-ROM drive speed, type of monitor, operating system version number, and types of sound card and speakers.

■ **Do most packages have enough facets to keep kids busy?**

Great kids' software has a long life span because smart publishers update successful titles to take advantage of new technology. So start with the software classics; they have a solid track record for keeping kids involved.

■ **What rules should parents enforce?**

Guide your child in striking a balance among homework, sports, after-school lessons, free play, chores, computer use, and TV watching. When you first introduce the Internet, you should always supervise children's online activities. Later, require older children to check with you before using the Internet and be specific about what they're planning to do and how long they'll be online.

BEST EDUCATIONAL SOFTWARE FOR THE UNDER-12 SET

Buying good software for your kids is a little like finding suitable television shows for them: You've got to weed out the junk, then make a parent-child compromise. To help you choose the best family-tested educational software in math, reading, social studies, and science, here are some of the best, chosen by the editors of FamilyPC *magazine—along with scores of teachers, parents, and kids.*

MATH

MIGHTY MATH CALCULATING CREW
Edmark, $39.99, ages 8–12

■ Using cartoon-style activities, this program uses thousands of problems to teach essential math concepts, including reasoning, money transactions, estimation and rounding, one- to four-digit addition and subtraction, one- to three-digit multiplication and division, and 3-D geometry. The teachers, parents, and kids who reviewed this program agreed its techniques were fun and successful.

SIERRA'S SCHOOL HOUSE: MATH
Sierra On-Line, $34.95, ages 6–12

■ Adi is an extraterrestrial tutor from the planet Zitron, situated 3 trillion light-years from Earth. The bald-headed, big-eared alien provides verbal encouragement as kids learn about numbers, calculation, measurement, patterns, and geometry. The two-disc set contains 4,000 questions and exercises, 100 videos, eight interactive games, and draw, paint, and print functions.

STICKYBEAR'S MATH SPLASH
Optimum Resource, $59.95, ages 5–10

■ Mixes together one large, friendly brown bear, 60 math skills, and lots of water scenes. The fun is built upon four activities designed to drill kids on math fundamentals. In one of these activities, for example, your child must click on correct answers attached to passing marine life. What makes Math Splash so useful are its multiple levels, which automatically serve up more challenging problems.

READING

JUMPSTART KINDERGARTEN READING
Knowledge Adventure. $39.95, ages 4–6

■ Alive with colorful characters such as Flash the surfin' dude and Count

Romulus, who lives on a ranch with dancing cows. Through interactive word games with these cartoons, kids are taught 10 concepts that help them learn to read, including learning letters, matching sounds with letters, and sorting sounds into vowels and consonants. The final step: reading.

SOCIAL STUDIES

WHERE IN THE USA IS CARMEN SANDIEGO?
Broderbund, $39.95, ages 9 and up

■ This third version in the series features eight levels and 40 cases to solve. Kids learn about cities, states, and regions, while hunting for clues to nab the crooks before the battery meter runs out. Along the way, they can search a database containing videos, maps, flags, and essays that highlight state geography, economy, historic events, landmarks, and famous citizens.

SCIENCE

THE UNIVERSE ACCORDING TO VIRGIL REALITY
7th Level, $39.99. ages 8 and up

■ In this smorgasbord of science studies, Professor

Virgil Reality pulls out all the stops to encourage your child to examine the inner workings of the world. For example, click on the frog in the Lab, and the prof provides a brief introduction to the natural history of the amphibian through text, graphics, and narration. Other features include hands-on activities such as how to make invisible ink.

A.D.A.M. THE INSIDE STORY 1997 EDITION
A.D.A.M. Software, $39.95, ages 8 and up

■ This edition contains an even more remarkable body of anatomical information than the previous edition. The program is renowned for its innovative use of multimedia, such as a fully rotatable 3-D graphics based on a real human cadaver. Other features: a pronunciation guide for 1,200 anatomical names, links to top medical Internet sites, and interactive quizzes to test your knowledge.

ENCYCLOPEDIA OF SPACE AND THE UNIVERSE
DK Multimedia, $39.95, ages 8 and up

■ This comprehensive multimedia encyclopedia contains 80,000 words, 400 full-color photographs and illustrations, 200 animations, 30 videos, and 2 hours of audios. Explore the night sky from 3,000 years ago to 7,000 years into the future,

and rotate the moon to observe its hidden far side. Or: listen to Sputnik's transmission signals, discover the effects of gravity on the universe, watch a space shuttle take off, and even learn about futuristic space colonies.

MULTIPLE SUBJECTS
JUMPSTART ADVENTURES 3RD GRADE
Knowledge Adventure, $39.95, ages 7–9

■ Bratty little Polly Spark has programmed 25 robots to alter history, and only your third-grader can stop the world from getting really weird. With Android XLT as an advisor and companion, your child must retrieve the robots by solving Polly's pop quizzes based on a comprehensive, interdisciplinary third-grade curriculum that includes language arts, math, science, music, history, and art.

JUMPSTART PRE-K
Knowledge Adventure, $34.95, ages 3–5

■ Help preschoolers gain confidence in language, math, and other skills. Set in colorful Our Town, it teaches letters, numbers, shapes, and colors, as well as advancing problem-solving and decision-making skills by playing timed activities with multiple choices in places such as the bakery, barber shop, and fire station. Also

teaches social concepts such as sharing, healthy eating, and good manners.

MADELINE: EUROPEAN ADVENTURES
Creative Wonders, $34.95, ages 5 and up

■ Spunky Madeline of storybook fame and her dog Genevieve take your child along on the trail of a thief who has stolen a magic lamp. The journey begins in France and winds through Switzerland, Italy, and Turkey. Along the way, your child can learn 100 French and Spanish words, write, decorate, and paint postcards, and the names, capitals, and flags of 19 European countries.

REFERENCE
RANDOM HOUSE KID'S ENCYCLOPEDIA
Random House Children's Media/Knowledge Adventure, $29.95, ages 7–12

■ The latest version of this encyclopedia has 4,000 articles and includes 60 days free access to the Electric Library, an online reference source. About 1,000 entries are narrated; a bibliography accompanies every entry. Nonreaders will enjoy the 250 movies and animations. Kids can locate facts five different ways: by geography, timeline, category, and key word, or alphabetically.

SOURCE: Reprinted from *FamilyPC* March 1997. Copyright ©1997 *FamilyPC*.

TAKING THE TEDIUM OUT OF LANGUAGE LEARNING

Gaining proficiency in a language may be handy when you're touring foreign lands, but when it comes to doing business abroad, talking like a native is a huge advantage. These software programs can help you master a foreign tongue.

POWER SERIES
Transparent Language, $99 each

■ Power Japanese and Power Spanish are among the most popular language tutors. The teaching philosophy deemphasizes rote memorization and helps you formulate your own sentences quickly. The courses are the equivalent of an entry, college-level course.

LANGUAGE! NOW SERIES
Transparent Language, $29.95 each

■ Less rigorous is the Language! Now series, available in Spanish, French, German, Italian, Latin, Russian, Portuguese, and English for Spanish speakers. Provides multimedia instruction and the fundamentals needed for basic conversational and reading skills, including the ability to record and compare your pronunciation with that of native speakers.

EASY LANGUAGE
IMSI, $29.95

■ This 17-language edition, double CD-ROM set includes vocabulary and pronunciation lessons for everyday words and phrases in Spanish, French, German, and English. Plus, there are 1,000 key words in Arabic, Chinese, Danish, Dutch, Greek, Hebrew, Indonesian, Italian, Japanese, Korean, Portuguese, and Russian.

LET'S TALK
Syracuse Language Systems, $44.95

■ Available languages include French, German, Italian, Spanish, and English (for students of English as a second language). Helps forge vocabulary and conversational skills for beginners and intermediate students. Syracuse also offers a 12-lesson interactive online Spanish I course through its Language Connect University. The cost of the course, including all materials and a CD-ROM, starts at $475.

THE ROSETTA STONE POWERPAC
Fairfield Language Technologies, $99

■ For those who want to sample a smattering of languages. You'll get an introduction to Dutch, English, French, German, Russian, and Spanish.

THE KEYS TO THE KINGDOM

Getting the most out of your computer means you'll need to have pretty good typing skills. Are they a bit rusty? Try these programs:

MAVIS BEACON TEACHES TYPING
Mindscape, about $39.99.

■ Have fun while hitting the keyboard. This package provides arcade-style games that teach 10-key typing skills and help improve your typing rhythm and accuracy. And to start them out young, there's Mavis Beacon Teaches Typing for Kids. The software comes with a 30-day money-back guarantee if you don't see results.   ☎ 800–234–3088

TYPING INSTRUCTOR DELUXE
Individual Software, about $29.95

■ Provides well-organized typing lessons jazzed up with lively graphics. This is about as exciting as typing gets.   ☎ 800–331–3313

SOFTWARE FOR LIST LOVERS

*Chances are the database program
you need already exists*

Many people need to keep lists, but they don't need a typical database program. While these programs can make short work of tasks that would take hours by hand, it's important to make sure that you're using the right tool for the job. Here are some tips for choosing the database you really need.

■ **YOU PROBABLY HAVE A DATABASE ALREADY:** If you have Microsoft Windows 3.1, you already have a simple "flat file" database program. Cardfile is like a set of 3x5 cards that you can use to keep simple lists of information. This program can't create complex reports, but it's a good place to start and to find out whether you need a more powerful program. (Cardfile is not included in Windows 95, but you can have a copy installed on your system if you upgraded from Windows 3.1.) Another easy way to create a quick and dirty list is to use a spreadsheet program such as Microsoft Excel or Lotus 1-2-3. Also, built-in programs, like Microsoft Works, and application suites, such as Microsoft Office Professional 97, Corel Office Professional 7, or Lotus Smart-Suite 97, typically include database features.

■ **LET SOMEONE ELSE DO THE WORK:** Chances are that someone else has already created a program to handle the specific task you have in mind. Rather than reinvent the wheel, consider taking advantage of their efforts. Want to track contacts and addresses? Try a sales management program such as Act! or Gold-Mine, or a personal information manager like Day-Timer Organizer. Need to handle your finances? Quicken, QuickBooks, and Managing Your Money are specialized database programs that can do the job with ease. Want to bring order to your hobbies? Whether it's antiques or genealogy, recipes or baseball-card collections, there are programs for dozens of different activities. Many are shareware programs that you can download for free from the Web; start your search at ZDNet Software Library at *http://www.hotfiles.com.*

■ **FLAT FILE VS. RELATIONAL:** Simple "flat file" programs can keep track of information that you might keep on 3x5 cards, one card for each piece of information, such as a name and address for one person. But this is not sufficient when the information is more complex. For example, consider a list of family addresses and birthdays. With a file card system, you'd have to make a separate card for every person, even if they live at the same address as someone else. A relational database such as Lotus Approach can handle more complicated data structures, by letting you link information from different files.

■ **LEADING PERSONAL
INFORMATION MANAGERS**
These programs can help you organize your contacts and schedules.

	☎
Act!	
Symantec Corp.	800–441–7234
AnyTime 3.0 for Windows	
Individual Software	800–822–3522
Ascend 5.0	
Franklin Quest Co.	800–360–5328
Day Runner Planner for Windows	
Day Runner	800–635–5544
Day–Timer Organizer 2.1	
Day–Timer Technologies	800–225–5005
Ecco 3.0	
NetManage	206–885–4272
GoldMine 3.2	
GoldMine Software Corp.	800–654–3526
Janna Contact Personal	
Janna Systems	800–268–6107
Lotus Organizer 2.1	
Lotus Development Corp.	800–343–5414
Sidekick Deluxe	
Starfish Software	800–765–7839

THE BOTTOM LINE ON SPREADSHEETS

It's hard to find a bad spreadsheet program, says PC Magazine *contributing editor Craig Stinson. All three of the major players—Corel Quattro Pro, Lotus 1-2-3, and Microsoft Excel—are powerful and versatile tools that can help you do anything from minute calculations to complex charts and data modeling. Here's Stinson's list of things to check before you buy.*

■ **ANALYSIS AND MODEL BUILDING:** A good spreadsheet application can analyze numbers and interpret them in a way that allows you to build models based on the data. Clues that tell you whether or not a spreadsheet can do this are number of data entry tools, function library, ability to annotate, special features that organize and consolidate data, and the degree to which you can access databases.

■ **CHARTING:** This feature transforms your data into different types of charts for presentation purposes. Look at the number and quality of chart formats that the spreadsheet offers, its ability to automate simple charting tasks, and options such as customizable titles, notes, multiple typefaces, objects, colors, shading.

■ **WORKSHEET PRESENTATION:** Make sure the application produces boardroom quality documents, on screen and on paper. Generally, if the program offers a print previewer, a number of pre-configured document styles, as well as a broad range of fonts, shading, ruling, and color options, it's up to snuff.

■ **WORKGROUP COMPUTING:** A good spreadsheet program should support e-mail so you can quickly route files to others, multiple versions, and conversion of tables to HTML format so you can post those materials on the Web. The ability for multiple users to work on the same file simultaneously is also a plus.

■ **CUSTOM DESIGN:** Once you become a spreadsheet whiz, you might want to have the option of making macros, or programming keys, on your keyboard to carry out certain functions automatically. Each spreadsheet application has its own "macro language" that allows you to do this. Before you buy the software, examine the macro language to ascertain how it can be implemented.

■ **APPLICATION DEVELOPMENT:** Ideally, a program's development language should work across other applications, thus allowing the spreadsheet to work with database programs, word processors, and presentation programs.

■ **YOU DON'T NEED A PROGRAMMING DEGREE:** If you can't find a program that does what you need, then it's time to consider creating your own with a database program. There are a number of programs that make it relatively easy to create, use, and maintain a database of information. Among the easiest, yet powerful, relational programs are Approach from Lotus, Alpha Five from Alpha Software, FileMaker Pro from Claris, and Access from Microsoft. Plan your database on paper carefully before you start to work on the computer. And before you enter all your data, test your files to be sure they do exactly what you want. Good programs will let you make changes to the database structure after you've entered the data, but it's always better to get it right from the start rather than have to fix it later.

MONEY MANAGING PROGRAMS YOU CAN BANK ON

Personal computers are great for helping with repetitive tasks and for keeping track of small bits of information. They can be especially valuable tools when it comes to keeping tabs on your finances. Good personal financial software can help you set up a budget, track expenses, balance your checkbook, plan for large expenditures and retirement, follow your investments, and, of course, help you prepare your tax returns. With so many financial programs available, it's easy to get confused. PC Magazine *contributing editor, Bruce Brown, picks the following programs as the best personal financial packages out there. (Prices indicated are suggested retail, except where otherwise indicated.)*

RECORD KEEPING AND BANKING

For day-to-day financial chores like recording expenses and tracking your budget, these general purpose programs fit the bill. But they also come with extra features such as tips on basic investment management and an ability to earmark tax-deductible expenses.

QUICKEN FOR WINDOWS
Intuit, $34.95

■ The top-selling personal finance software. Friendly to use, making it easy to pay bills, track expenses, graph the results, budget your income, and get current balances. Excels at budgeting and graphing what happens to your money. The latest edition makes online banking even easier. It gets current account balances, transfers funds between accounts, and pays bills online.
☎ 800–446–8848

MICROSOFT MONEY FOR WINDOWS 95
Microsoft Corp., $34.95 (street price)

■ Good for beginners who want to create a budget by using their spending patterns as a guide. Its online banking ability also makes it appealing to more sophisticated investors. Money provides checking account management, budgeting, and bill tracking, all within the framework of a highly graphical interface that makes it easy to follow the program's organization.
☎ 800–426–9400

FINANCIAL PLANNING

To plan for the future you need more than a budget assistant and check recorder. Good financial planning software helps you set goals, choose investments, and track your money's growth. Extra features like

insurance analysis add even more value.

QUICKEN FINANCIAL PLANNER
Intuit, $39.95

■ Complete with goal setting, mutual fund assessment and tracking, and the ability to do "what-if" analysis of various investment plans, Quicken Financial Planner may be all you need to prepare for a secure financial future.
☎ 800–446–8848

KIPLINGER'S SIMPLY MONEY 2.0
4Home Productions, $69.95

■ Simply Money 2.0 continues to build upon the good graphics and clear interface of earlier versions. The package includes Financial Advisor, Financial Scheduler, and automatic budgeting components. You can export data to major tax programs.
☎ 800–773–5445

MANAGING YOUR MONEY PLUS 2.0
MECA Software, $79.99 on

floppy disks; $99.99 on CD-ROM

■ You can set up home or business accounts, or both, with Managing Your Money Plus and work with them through graphics that resemble an office, by using a quick access toolbar, or with menus.

☎ 800–288–6322

TAX PREPARATION

Good tax software saves you time and helps you work through often complicated tax forms with integrated error checking and valuable tax planning features. Return consumer information cards to manufacturers, so that they can send you information about new editions on subsequent years' versions of the soft-

ware. And, don't forget, the price of tax software is tax deductible.

TURBOTAX DELUXE

Intuit, $49.95 federal; $24.95 each for 45 states

■ A perennial winner in tax preparation software. You can get right to the forms or use a thorough interview process that walks you through every line on every form. Built in self-auditing and forms checking help catch errors. In addition to getting videos of tax experts, you can also refer to an extensive reference library that includes many IRS publications and *Money Magazine's Income Tax Handbook.*

☎ 800–446–8848

KIPLINGER TAXCUT DELUXE MULTIMEDIA

Block Financial, $35 federal; $24.95 each for 23 states

■ TaxCut splits the screen to show you the current form while you answer questions in the other part of the screen. Packed with tips on tax planning and preparing your taxes.

☎ 800–235–4060

PERSONAL TAX EDGE

Parsons Technology, $19 federal; $19 each for 45 states

■ Because it lacks depth of reference information, Tax Edge is best for simpler returns. However, it does flag suspected errors and questionable entries as it walks you through the tax interview process.

☎ 888–883–0791

PORTFOLIO MANAGERS WORTH THE INVESTMENT

These programs for experienced investors let you screen stocks, bonds, or mutual funds, as well trade securities by modem.

CAPTOOLS CO.

Captool Individual Investor, $149

■ Performs sophisticated calculations, such as your stock, bond, or mutual fund portfolio's internal rate of return.

☎ 800–826–8082

REUTERS MONEY NETWORK

WealthBuilder's Reality

Online, $49.95 (plus $6 to $30 a month for additional information)

■ This software and online service package lets you screen a database of stocks, bonds, and CDs and suggests those that fit your investment goals. It also updates and analyzes Quicken and Microsoft Money portfolios.

☎ 800–346–2024

WINDOWS ON WALL STREET

Personal Investor, $49.95

■ For technically minded investors who need to chart and analyze portfolio performance. Updates of seven years of historical data are available for $59.95 per year. A deluxe version of the program goes for $128.

☎ 800–998–8439

FOR BUDDING PUBLISHERS

This software lets you design pages—from book to Web

Desktop publishing (DTP) software allows you to arrange words and pictures on a page in complex layouts. You can format text, resize and crop pictures, and move elements freely around a page. Luisa Simone, contributing editor of *PC Magazine* and author of *Microsoft Publisher by Design* (Microsoft Press, 1997) and *The Windows 95 Scanning Book* (John Wiley, 1996), helps beginning desktop publishers make some important decisions.

■ WORD PROCESSING VS. DESKTOP PUBLISHING
Word processing programs are geared toward a linear flow of text, while DTP programs allow for much more flexible placement of text and pictures. If you are producing a document where stories flow in sequence from page to page, a word processor is sufficient. If you want to produce a highly formatted document that includes three or more columns, lots of pictures, or stories that jump to noncontiguous pages, you should consider a DTP program so you can control typographic elements like interword and intercharacter spacing, align text across columns, control the way text wraps around pictures, and prepare files for high-resolution output at a service bureau or for commercial printing.

■ MAC OR PC? The Mac has long been the preferred platform for DTP, but Windows users no longer have to feel like second-class citizens. In fact, three of the top four desktop publishing programs—QuarkXpress, Adobe PageMaker, and Adobe Framemaker—are available for both the Mac and PC. And PC-based Corel Ventura should be shipping a Mac version by early 1998. If you are a PC user and are planning to send your projects to a service bureau or commercial printer, look for a program that has a Mac counterpart and produces what's called binary-compatible files. This means that the files you create on your PC can be opened directly on the Mac—without any special conversion routines.

■ COMPARISON SHOPPING: If you want to produce standard business publications for a small business, turn to products that offer both ease of use and low cost, like Microsoft Publisher, Serif PagePlus, or I Publish from Design Intelligence. To produce design-intensive documents that require a high degree of typographic control, full-color separations, and robust prepress functions, Adobe PageMaker and QuarkXpress are the programs of choice. For generating long documents like reference books or technical manuals, Adobe FrameMaker and Corel Ventura let you create and maintain complex cross-references, contents lists, and indexes.

■ PRICING: Prices will vary depending upon where you buy your software. In general, you can buy Microsoft Publisher, Serif PagePlus, and I Publish for well under $100. High-end programs, like Adobe PageMaker, QuarkXpress, Ventura, and FrameMaker hover between $600 and $700.

■ LEADING DESKTOP PUBLISHING PACKAGES

COREL VENTURA
Corel Corp.   ☎ 800–772–6735

FRAMEMAKER
Adobe Systems   ☎ 800–833–6687

I PUBLISH
Design Intelligence   ☎ 888–278–2547

MICROSOFT PUBLISHER
Microsoft Corp.   ☎ 800–426–9400

PAGEMAKER
Adobe Systems   ☎ 800–833–6687

SERIF PAGEPLUS PUBLISHING SUITE
Serif   ☎ 800–489–6719

QUARKXPRESS
Quark Inc.   ☎ 800–676–4575

SUITE DEALS ON SOFTWARE THAT DOES IT ALL

Why buy separate packages of word processing or spreadsheet software, for example, when you can buy them bundled, get other programs too, and save a bundle to boot? There are loads of good home office suites to pick from. The packages aren't cheap—expect to pay between $300 and $600. Then again, buying the separate pieces would run a whole lot more. Here are some of the more popular packages that suit a typical home user's needs. The features referred to were available as this book went to press in mid-1997.

FOR PCS
COREL WORDPERFECT SUITE 8
Corel Corp., $300 street price

■ This suite has it all: the ever-better WordPerfect word processor, the flexible Quattro Pro spreadsheet, and Corel graphics programs. Includes software for photo editing, viewing files, a personal planner, clip-art, fonts, and photos.
☎ 800–772–6735

LOTUS SMARTSUITE
Lotus Development Corp., $399

■ Combines six of the company's most popular programs, including 1-2-3 spreadsheet, word processor, database, presentation graphics, personal information manager, even software for creating screen movies.
☎ 800–782–7876

MICROSOFT OFFICE 97
Microsoft Corp., $500 street price

■ A potent combination of Word, Excel spreadsheet, PowerPoint graphics, an information manager, a computer camcorder and photo editor, and Internet links.
☎ 800–426–9400

MICROSOFT HOME ESSENTIALS
Microsoft Corp., $109

■ A handy set for family use. Includes everything you need to research and write reports, create greeting cards, and keep track of expenses. Also thrown in are five arcade games and Internet links.
☎ 800–426–9400

FOR MACS
CLARISWORKS 4.0
Claris Corp., $99

■ Package features a word processor, spreadsheet, and components for drawing and painting.
☎ 800–325–2747

MICROSOFT OFFICE (MAC)
Microsoft Corp., $499

■ The best suite for the Mac. Includes Word, Excel, Power Point, and Microsoft Mail.
☎ 800–426–9400

■ **HARDWARE:** Most DTP software runs fine on a 486 processor. However, if you are using a DTP program for business, you'll probably have to upgrade your hard disk (think in gigabytes, not megabytes), and you should also consider buying a high-capacity removable storage device, such as a Syquest drive or an Iomega Zip drive, in order to transport files to a service bureau.

■ **WEB PUBLISHING:** To publish documents on the Web, you must produce a standard format called HTML (HyperText Markup Language). While there are a number of dedicated HTML authoring programs (see page 562), you'll find that nearly all desktop publishing programs mentioned here, with the exception of QuarkXpress, can convert traditional paper-based designs to electronic documents in either HTML or the Adobe Portable Document formats. The latter format is gaining popularity on the Web because it maintains the organization of a page-based document and reproduces graphically rich designs well.

ONLINE

ONLINE SERVICES: A guide to your choices, PAGE 552 **TECH TALK:** The lingo of cyber-communication, PAGE 553 **E-MAIL:** Keeping your correspondence private, PAGE 554 **TOOLS:** Software and search engines to help you navigate online, PAGE 556 **WEB SITES:** The top places for a plethora of interests, PAGE 557 **HOME PAGES:** How to create your own, PAGE 563 **ESOTERICA:** Six Web sites for those who enjoy the strange, PAGE 564

CYBERSPACE
▼

YOUR GUIDE TO GETTING WIRED

Things you need to know about the online world

These days, you can't escape from symbols of the Internet: World Wide Web addresses are plastered on the sides of buses, displayed on television, and printed throughout books like this one. Only dyed-in-the-wool skeptics doubt that the Internet is the communications medium of the future and that the future is now.

But what exactly is the Internet? More to the point: how can you sign up, set up, and find out for yourself what all the hoopla is about? For the ABCs of the Internet, we talked with Alfred and Emily Glossbrenner, authors of more than 40 books about computers, software, and online communications. Their most recent titles include *The Little Web Book* (Peachpit Press, 1996), a comprehensive guide to getting connected and getting the most from the Internet, and *Search Engines for the World Wide Web: Visual QuickStart Guide,* (Peachpit Press, 1997). (For questions or comments, they can be reached via e-mail at gloss@gloss.com.) Here are their comments:

■ **What is the Internet?**
The Internet is really nothing more than the collection of wires, switches, and software that makes it possible for computers all over the world to "talk" to each other. The Internet was born nearly three decades ago when the military realized it needed a more decentralized communications system than the "hub and spoke" model, where communications had to pass through one central routing location to get from one point to another. The Internet concept connected all points to each other, offering a nearly limitless number of alternative paths for a message to travel from point to point.

Although the Internet has been around for nearly 30 years, it didn't really catch on in the public sector until the Cold War ended in the early 1990s. When the military safeguards became obsolete, the Internet went commercial, opening its doors to schools, homes, organizations, and businesses.

Even if the Internet had been available to the public 20 years ago, it wouldn't have had the incredible run that it's having now. Access came at just the right time—the hardware was available, computer literacy in the population was high, the desire was there, and when the door opened, the Internet took off like wildfire.

■ Of what benefit is the Internet to individuals?

There are lots of ways it can help you both professionally and personally—from sending letters to your child at college, to managing your investment portfolio, to discussing classical literature with readers and scholars all over the world. It comes in handy during tax time, too. A friend recently needed some out-of-state tax forms. Rather than calling the IRS, I went online and within 5 minutes had picture-perfect copies of both the federal and state forms she needed.

We use it for recreational purposes, too, to get movie reviews, home improvement tips, and even advice on how to get rid of annoying house-pecking woodpeckers. (The answer: Check for termites and hang up a plastic owl.)

■ What are the components of the Internet?

A lot of people confuse the World Wide Web, or the "Web," with the Internet, but they're not the same. The Web is a part of the Internet—the newest part in fact—but

is extremely popular because of its ability to display video, graphics, and sound data. And a truly salutary feature of the Web is the ability to click from one location to another via "hot links," with everything looking like a page from a slick magazine, complete with different type styles, color illustrations, and links to still other pages. These pages are called Web sites and allow surfers to view everything from great works of art *(http://sgwww.epfl.ch/BERGER/index.html)* to a complete rundown of the night's TV picks *(http://www.ultimatetv.com)*.

■ What are newsgroups?

I think newsgroups are one of the most important components of the Internet. These discussion groups are divided into more than 60,000 topics spanning the range from Beavis and Butt-Head to Jane Austen or tips on brewing your own beer. Virtually anybody can read a newsgroup's postings made by other readers on a particular subject—or contribute their own thoughts and ideas. And if you know what you're looking for, but aren't sure where to find it, you can go to a newsgroup research service *(http://www. dejanews.com/)*, which will search nearly all the existing newsgroups for any postings on a given topic—going back years and years.

■ What is the Internet's most popular feature?

Electronic mail, or e-mail, is without a doubt the most popular—and with good reason. First, you can contact virtually anyone who owns a personal computer and has an online account anywhere in the world. Second, you can do that for pennies. Say, for instance, you need to get a 30-page report to your boss across the country as soon as possible. You can send it by overnight mail for about $13, or you can pay about $2 in first-class mail, which hopefully will arrive in 3 to 5 days. But if you e-mail it, not only does it arrive seconds later, but it will cost less than a nickel.

■ What are the most common misconceptions about the Internet?

The most common misconception is that

FACT FILE:

CLOGGING THE E-WAVES

■ *There are an estimated 90 million e-mail addresses worldwide.*

■ *Nearly 80 percent of organizations use e-mail to communicate. Forty percent of the entire American workforce uses e-mail.*

■ *Personal e-mail messages will jump from 100 million a day in 1996 to 500 million in 2001. By 2005, 5 billion daily messages are projected.*

■ *Some 70 percent of Americans don't mind getting unsolicited e-mail, as long as it's tailored to their interests.*

it's all about sex. In reality, less than 1 percent of the material online is sex-related. People fear that they might be on the Internet checking stock quotes, and suddenly a sex page will pop up. That is patently untrue.

Another misconception is that if you're not online, you're a nobody. Something like 33 percent of American households have computers and only about half of those households are connected online. It's a much smaller number—though the number is growing—than most people generally assume. Lots of people don't have any compelling need to be on the Internet and if you're one of them, you probably have far better things to do with your life than spend it in front of a computer screen.

■ What is the difference betwen a commercial online service and an Internet service provider?

Commercial online services like America Online or CompuServe provide options beyond Internet access, such as chat rooms, Web-page design help, technical support, and other features that are proprietary to subscribers of that particular service. Internet Service Providers (ISPs), on the other hand, generally just offer no-frills direct Internet access. Think about the difference between the two like a shopping mall and a single retail outlet. The online service is like a mall—you may go there to buy a pair of jeans, see a movie, eat lunch, get a haircut, and hang out with your friends. An ISP is more like The Gap—where you go just to buy the pair of jeans.

Both commercial online services and ISPs cost about the same (generally about $20 a month) but provide different benefits. (See page 552 for a comparison of the top providers.) ISPs usually have fewer subscribers than online services, so you're less likely to get a busy signal when you try to log on. And customer service may be more personalized and helpful than the automated help lines that most commercial services offer. But the commercial services tend to provide more extras and are more user friendly, especially for kids or people who are new to the Internet.

■ What sort of equipment is needed to access the Internet?

Pretty much any garden variety of computer will do these days. The most recent high-powered computers will improve your navigation and speed, but basically any system can get you some kind of access. Most new computers come with a modem for connecting via a telephone line—but if you have an older model, buy an external modem at the highest speed available. (They are available for about $150 from a computer mail order catalog or electronics store.) You'll also need an account with either a commercial service or an ISP, and then software to connect to the service. Software is often supplied free by your provider.

■ How would someone get started?

Pick a service provider, hook up the modem, and check it out. Most online services have some sort of free-trial period to test out its features. To pick a provider, ask around for recommendations from friends or colleagues who are already online, or if you have a new computer, it may come already loaded with online software. Play around with the options—visit Web sites, read newsgroups— if you think you want to continue, you might want to invest in a user-friendly Internet beginners guidebook to help you learn how to make the most of your online experience.

■ What is a search engine and how is it used?

Since the invention of the Internet, search engines have turned out to be the most important tool. Basically, a search engine is an Internet directory that helps you find the information you need online. Among the more familiar names are Netscape, Alta Vista, Excite, Infoseek, Lycos, and Yahoo! (see also page 556). Each service has different ways of searching out information, but as a rule of thumb, try to think of the most unique word, phrase, or name that you would logically expect to find in any discussion of your target topic. Then use that as your search term. That's the best way to filter out the stuff you don't need and get the information you're looking for.

HOW THE TOP TEN ONLINE PROVIDERS STACK UP

Ready to go online? Use this comparison chart to help you decide which online service or Internet service provider is right for you. Most services offer a one-month free trial. Microsoft Network is only for Windows 95.

SERVICE	PROS	CONS
AMERICA ONLINE ☎ 800–827–6364 $ $19.95 for unlimited hours	Nontechnical, easy to use and install. Great features like chat rooms and instant messaging. Excellent content including *The New York Times* online; good parental control features.	Dismal call success rates. Slow on Web-browsing and file downloading. Technical support varies; getting live help can frustrate even the most determined seeker.
AT&T WORLDNET ☎ 800–967–5363 $ $19.95 for unlimited hours	Highest marks for network reliability and technical support. Call completion near 90%. Moderately fast downloads. Convenient billing for AT&T customers.	No support for ISDN (high-speed access) connections.
COMPUSERVE ☎ 800–848–8199 $ $24.95 for 20 hours; $1.95 each additional hour	Reliable access, fast e-mail, free utility files, the best technical support forums. Provides help with Web page design and offers 5 megabytes for Web page.	Comparatively expensive. Slow navigation, occasional lengthy download times.
CONCENTRIC NETWORK ☎ 800–939–4262 $ $19.95 for unlimited hours	User-friendly window menu; 5 megabytes to build your home page. Technical reps knowledgeable. Attracts users who enjoy playing online games.	Mediocre performance, speed and reliability. Requires steering a maze of automated options to reach a service person on the phone.
EARTHLINK ☎ 800–395–8425 $ $25 startup fee; $19.95 for unlimited hours	Call success rate of 90%. Easy to install. 600 high-speed ISDN local access numbers, 2 free megabytes for a Web page. Customize your startup page with links to your favorite Web sites. Lots of resources for rookies, access to tons of newsgroups.	Long waits for technical help (up to an hour in some cases).
MCI INTERNET ☎ 800–550–0927 $ $19.95 for unlimited hours	Easy installation; comes equipped with PointCast Network, an application that downloads the latest headlines from various Web sites.	Poor e-mail delivery, erratic tech support, and no space for Web pages. A long wait for installation software of up to a month, according to customer service reps.
MICROSOFT NETWORK ☎ 800–373–3676 $ $19.95 for unlimited hours	Conveniently preinstalled in Windows 95. Has a jazzy, graphics-intensive look and comes with strong content such as the *Encarta Encyclopedia*.	Erratic connection times, no Web page space. Installation and log-on are unwieldly, time-consuming. Toll-free help can take hours, even days, to reach. After you get through, it's not particularly helpful.
MINDSPRING ☎ 888–677–7464 $ $35 startup fee; $19.95 for unlimited hours	Loads of good software, good performance, high-speed ISDN access. For a slightly higher fee you get 10 megabytes for Web pages. Good tech support.	Average reliability and speed; 11 disks to install.
NETCOM ☎ 800–638–2661 $ $19.95 for unlimited hours	Reliable and prompt e-mail. Service is friendly and accurate, both live and online. ISDN access and good software. Gears itself toward more experienced users.	No toll-free help line, waiting for and getting help can run up your phone bill. Only 1 megabyte for a Web page.
PRODIGY INTERNET ☎ 800–776–3449 $ $19.95 for unlimited hours	Quick Web downloads. Changed recently from an online service to an ISP.	Low call success rate; installation not user-friendly. Poor technical support.

LEARNING THE ONLINE LINGO

A handy glossary of terms that will get you fluent online

You don't have to be a nerd to break the code of cyberspeak. In fact, the online world has become a low-tech mecca, attracting millions of nongeek men, women, and children. The first step toward learning the language is a mastery of basic technical vocabulary and some quirky terms that have cropped up in the online environment. Here are some of the most essential.

Browser—Software, such as Internet Explorer or Netscape Navigator, for PC Windows– or Mac-users that allows one to point and click one's way around the World Wide Web.

BBS—Bulletin board service. Cheaper than major online services, BBSes are generally run by a small number of people as a hobby bringing together people who share a common interest. Generally, you join a BBS by paying an annual fee (between $30 and $50 a year) as well as an hourly online fee (35¢ to $2.50 an hour). To find lists of BBSes (there are thousands of them), consult magazines such as *Boardwatch Magazine* (☎ 303–973–6038) or *Computer Shopper* (☎ 212–503–3800).

FAQ (Frequently Asked Questions)—Electronic handbooks filed at most Usenet newsgroups that answer most questions you'll have about that site; read them before you participate to avoid getting flamed (see below).

Flame—An inflammatory statement that is often rude, and occasionally crude. Newcomers sometimes are flamed for ignoring "netiquette."

Gopher—A search tool that helps you find files, services, and sites on the Internet by listing them in menu form. People at the University of Minnesota developed the software, so they got to name it (after their mascot).

Home page—The reception area for World Wide Web sites (see below). A home page welcomes you, lists the site's features and areas, and gives you a menu of choices about which to access.

Hypertext—Highlighted text in a file (a hyperlink) that is linked electronically to another file. Point and click on a word, and a new file pops up. Hypertext is the primary means of navigating the World Wide Web (see below).

Internet Relay Chat (IRC)—Instead of exchanging messages via e-mail, this tool lets you talk in "real time" with people: It's a typed, instead of spoken, conversation.

HTML (HyperText Markup Language)—The traditional computer programming language for developing documents on the World Wide Web, HTML identifies (or marks up) the various components, such as the title, and allows for hyperlinks to other pages.

Java—A newer computer programming language for embedding a mini program (or "applet"), such as an animation, into a document on the World Wide Web.

URL (Uniform Resource Locater)—A World Wide Web site's address, the URL typically looks something like this: http://www.somethingorother.

Usenet newsgroups—The group of over 7,000 Internet discussion groups, whose diverse topics range from Elvis to toxic waste to computer programming.

VRML (Virtual Reality Modeling Language)—A programming language for making 3-D images on the World Wide Web.

World Wide Web—The "cool" multimedia portion of the Internet, the Web is where all the action is these days.

KEEPING YOUR MAILBOX PRIVATE

How to keep spam and other junk messages out of your box

Instant electronic contact with friends, family, and co-workers may be a modern miracle, but it can also expose you and your messages to privacy invaders of all stripes. Some of the hype about the dangers of computer hackers and cyber-stalkers is doubtlessly overblown, but some privacy concerns are warranted. After all, personal information you provide online may get into the hands of undesirables and be used against you. At very least, once your e-mail address is in the public domain, you are likely to get a barrage of junk e-mail. Fortunately, there are steps you can take to ensure some degree of e-mail privacy.

Here are some, gleaned with the help of the Privacy Rights Clearinghouse, a Washington, D.C. group:

■ **TURN OFF YOUR COMPUTER WHEN NOT IN USE.** A basic safety measure may seem obvious: Turn off your home or office computer when you're not using it. A disconnected machine is a safe machine because no matter how clever Internet interlopers may be, they cannot find a way into your system if the power is down.

■ **CREATE UNUSUAL PASSWORDS.** Professional organizations that hack into corporate networks for a living claim that breaking into someone's computer or e-mail box is often

---

AN ONLINE RAMP FOR COUCH POTATOES

Surf the Web, or communicate by e-mail with this computer-free gizmo

All the buzz about the online world has piqued the curiosity of many folks who can't afford a computer—or don't want the hassle of learning to use one. Needless to say, inventive marketers have a solution: WebTV, offered by Sony, Philips, and others, a new category of devices that give any old television the power to browse the Web and use electronic mail.

The devices are technically called set-top boxes because they sit on your TV top, just like a cable converter. They work by taking the digital information describing a Web page on the Internet and translating it into an analog format that a TV can understand. WebTV dials up over your phone line into the company's own customized service to access the Internet. The rate is a standard $19.95 per month for unlimited hours of usage. And best of all, WebTV units sell for less than $350, a fraction of the cost of a full-fledged computer.

But before rushing out to invest in one of the gadgets, be warned that there are limitations. One problem is that even though the text-heavy Web pages are enlarged on the TV screen, some of them are hard to decipher. Another factor is that without a computer, you can't download software or play interactive games. The biggest problem may lie not in WebTV, but in the Web itself. Many observers say the Web just isn't as alluring as, say, the 50-plus cable channels.

Still, for immediate access to the Web at a minimal cost, WebTV is a logical answer. The device has become especially popular with people not familiar with the computer culture, such as retirees, for example. So far, WebTV has lured some 70,000 users, but by the year 2002, predicts research firm Jupiter Communications, 15.3 million households will be using some sort of Internet appliance.

simple because many people use their first names as a password. Even worse, many don't set up a password at all. You can easily avoid such pitfalls with a little diligence and creativity. Concoct passwords with unusual combinations of letters, numbers, and symbols. Change your e-mail password often and never give it out. Do not divulge phone numbers, credit card numbers, or other personal information in chat forums, postings or e-mail.

■ **BE CAREFUL OF PUBLIC POSTINGS.** Messages that you post on the Internet are often archived and can be retrieved by using search tools. Be wary of what you post so that it doesn't come back to haunt you. To safeguard your identity, ask your online provider to remove your personal data from the member directory. Better yet, don't list it in the first place.

■ **BE SURE YOUR MAIL IS ENCRYPTED.** Those concerned that e-mail messages are decipherable as they travel across the Internet should put their fears aside. Most of the popular e-mail packages, particularly those in well-known World Wide Web browsers, such as Netscape Navigator and Microsoft Internet Explorer, have foiled that possibility. The packages use so-called data encryption technology, which works to scramble the innards of your message, making it unreadable until it reaches its final destination. If you're feeling technically curious, you can check the kind of encryption your package uses by referring to the settings portion of your e-mail program.

■ **FILTER YOUR MESSAGES.** There are tools to help stop the avalanche of junk mail, or what's referred to as spam in cyberspeak. Web sites such as *http://www.getlost.com* and *http://www.junkbusters.com* will remove your name from spam lists. In addition, you can get a free version of Qualcomm's Eudora (download at *http://www.eudora.com*), which offers powerful filtering and is available for Mac, Windows 3.1, and Windows 95. At the very least, you can have all mail from specific addresses or domains routed directly

CYBER SOURCES

Concerned about what kind of personal information can be gleaned electronically? Here are some sites to help you maintain online privacy:

■ **CENTER FOR DEMOCRACY AND TECHNOLOGY.**
Informs consumers about the power and failings of technology.
http://www.cdt.org

■ **DISCREET DATA.**
Reveals how much personal data is available to online snoopers.
http://www.discreetdata.com

■ **ELECTRONIC PRIVACY INFORMATION CENTER.**
Keeps abreast of legislative, judicial, and other happenings regarding privacy issues.
http://www.epic.org

■ **THE STALKER'S HOME PAGE.**
Provides databases on Internet privacy. Lots of other resources.
http://pages.ripco.com8080/ glr/stalk.html

to the trash. Built-in filter systems are on the way; Netscape Communications Corp. and Microsoft Corp. are working on placing an e-mail filtering capability in upcoming releases of their browser software.

■ **BLOCK OBJECTIONABLE MAIL.** How do you keep objectionable mail out of your mailbox—and the minds of your children? And how do you ban access to unsavory newsgroups altogether? Fortunately, this is easier than it used to be. The major online services and Internet service providers offer software, which you can download for free that blocks access to objectionable newsgroup Web sites. (For other software solutions, see page 539.)

CYBER SOURCES

ONLINE TOOLS YOU CAN USE

NAVIGATION SOFTWARE

To surf the World Wide Web, you'll need a Web browser; if one of these is not included with your online access software, download a copy from the addresses listed below.

NETSCAPE COMMUNICATOR

Netscape Communications Corp., free

■ A software suite that includes Netscape Navigator, arguably the browser of choice.
http://www.netscape.com.

MICROSOFT INTERNET EXPLORER

Microsoft Corp., free

■ The next best thing to Netscape.
http://www.microsoft.com.

INTERNET UTILITIES

These tools help you perform many functions, including downloads.

REALAUDIO REALPLAYER

Progressive Networks, free

■ Plugs you into sites that offer sound and video (concerts, movie clips, etc.) without downloading huge audio and video files.
http://www.real.com

WEBWHACKER

The Forefront Group, $49.95

■ Lets you download single Web pages, groups of pages, or entire sites, retaining the pages' original format.
http://www.ffg.com.

SMART BOOKMARKS

First Floor Software, $24.95

■ Helps organize your browser's bookmarks. Can also monitor your favorite Web pages for changes, and download them.

CUTEFTP 1.5

GlobalSCAPE, $29.95

■ Handy for transferring files to and from the Net.

mIRC

Shareware, $15

■ The most flexible and user-friendly utility for chatting on the Internet.

PEGASUS MAIL

Shareware, free

■ Allows you to filter junk mail out of your mailbox.
http://www.pegasus.usa.com

FREE AGENT

Forte, free

■ A great package that lets you follow the latest Usenet newsgroup threads both online and offline.

WEBSEEKER

ForeFront Group, $49.95

■ Offers a single interface for searching up to 23 Web search engines.

VIRUSAFE WEB

EliaShim, free

■ Once integrated into your browser, ViruSafe scans all file downloads and rids them of viruses.

CYBER PATROL

Microsystems Software, $29.95

■ Helps control kids' online usage, blocking access to unwanted sites. Annual subscription for weekly updates: $29.95.

ONLINE DIRECTORIES

Search engines help locate what you want. Because each works differently, you may get varying results. To use any of the ones listed here, enter the Web address when you are online and follow the instructions.

■ **ALTA VISTA**
http://www.altavista.digital.com

■ **EXCITE**
http://www.excite.com.

■ **HOTBOT**
http://www.hotbot.com

■ **INFOSEEK GUIDE**
http://www.infoseek.com

■ **LYCOS**
http://www.lycos.com.

■ **YAHOO!**
http://www.yahoo.com

HOTTEST SITES IN THE WHOLE WIDE WEB

Finding the information you want on the World Wide Web is often like being on a scavenger hunt: You know you're looking for something, but you're not quite sure where to find it—or what you'll find when you get there. The editors of CMP Media's NetGuide Live site (http://www.netguide.com) comb through the ever-growing number of Web sites daily to ferret out the crème de la crème, and to help point you in the right direction. Here are NetGuide's favorites in 10 areas.

ARTS & ENTERTAINMENT

■ **BEST Music Community:** What's your favorite musical genre? Firefly wants to know so that you can be connected with those who share your musical tastes. Complete a user profile and Firefly's intelligent software agent will link you to musical soulmates, as well as other information you can use, such as artist bios, CD reviews, and sound samples.
http://www.ffly.com

■ **BEST Showbiz News & Gossip:** Catch the latest news, gossip, and trivia about movie stars, musicians, and other celebrities at E! Online, a spin-off of the popular cable channel. While you're getting the scoop, you can browse or submit your own reviews of CD-ROMs, CDs, and movies.
http://www.eonline.com

■ **BEST Couch Potato Companion:** Web surfing meets channel surfing at the Gist. Here, couch potatoes can search for their favorite TV events or create customized TV schedules and updates so they don't forget to tune in. Previews of miniseries and specials, actor interviews, and discussion forums.
http://www.gist.com

■ **BEST Place for Art Appreciation:** Splashed with memorable images, criticism, reports on the international art scene, and regular columns, ArtNet Worldwide paints a vivid picture of the contemporary art world. Visit hundreds of galleries worldwide, or list your own for a fee. Mingle at ArtNet's bulletin boards on Firefly *(www.ffly.com)* to discuss artists, exhibitions, and trends.
http://www.artnet.com

■ **BEST Zine:** The daily online magazine, Salon, neatly bundles substance, intelligence, grace, and wit into one provocative package. Salon's writers have an intriguing, West Coast take on books, TV, music, movies, and modern life, examining everything from online communities to foreign travel. Among Salon regulars are cartoonists, a word player and a mating etiquette maven. You can become a habitue by having your say in the Table Talk forums.
http://www.salon1999.com

■ **BEST Place for Jazz Fans:** Colorful and comprehensive, Jazz Central Station is replete with news and CD reviews. Board the listening car to sample tracks from new artists and recommended albums, or sit a while at the Jazz Cafe and enjoy RealAudio interviews with noted musicians. You'll even find artist profiles of jazz giants such as Ella Fitzgerald and Herbie Hancock, replete with photos and sound clips.
http://www.jazzcentralstation.com

■ **BEST Place to Find a Good Meal:** At CuisineNet, an online guide to food and restaurants, you can peruse a menu of reviews for eateries in New York, Boston, San Francisco, Seattle, and Chicago. Restaurants are graded on location, cuisine, and price. Visit Diner's Digest for fun food facts, articles on cooking, chef profiles, and more.
http://www.cuisinet.com

COMPUTING

■ **BEST All-around Technology Resource:** CMP Media's Tech-Web—NetGuide Live's sis-

ter site—is a one-stop source for computer and Internet-related news, product reviews, downloads, and tech support. It offers content from all of CMP's publications, including *Windows Magazine*, and *Home PC*. A handy search engine keeps information overload at bay.
http://www.techweb.com

■ BEST Place to Learn What Not to do on your Home Page: Sometimes the best way to learn how to do something is by looking at graphic examples of how not to do it. Web Pages That Suck is Web designer Vincent Flanders' vivid lesson in what's cliched, pretentious, or amateurish on the Web.
http://www.webpagesthat suck.com

■ BEST Place to Find a File: When you have to find a file fast, fire up this smart search engine and locate everything from software to multimedia files—even when you don't know the exact file name.
http://www.files.com

■ BEST Macintosh Resource: What snazzy new software is out there for the Mac? How do you get your "soft-power" Mac to restart after a power failure? What do system upgrades have in store for you? Adam and Tonya Engst, who started TidBITS, a free, weekly electronic newsletter in

1990, help answer your questions. You'll also find news and views about Apple and the Internet, along with helpful how-to's and reviews.
http://www.tidbits.com

■ BEST Collection of Winsock Software: The Ultimate Collection of Winsock Software site is an amazing place to download Winsock-compliant shareware and freeware for Windows 3.1, Windows 95, and Macintosh. Search for precisely what you need, or just graze. Browsable software categories include ActiveX plug-ins, antivirus scanners, compression utilities, diagnostic tools, and HTML accessories, along with games, MUDs, and, of course, MOOs. TUCOWS pulls up a list of relevant software, accompanied by descriptions and ratings.
http://www.tucows.com

HEALTH

■ BEST Place to Find Answers to your Health Questions: Check into Healthwise, Columbia University's terrific online health and wellness resource, for things you need to know about fitness and nutrition and anything else concerning the well-being of mind and body. Healthwise's wonderful "Go Ask Alice" archive of questions and answers covers all the bases.
http://www.columbia.edu/cu/healthwise/

■ BEST Heart-Friendly Site: Your heart beats about 100,000 times each day. Now's your chance to thank it for all its hard work. The official Web site of the American Heart Association can help you identify and reduce the risks of heart disease and stroke. Check out basic nutrition and exercise tips, downloadable brochures and a handy A-to-Z guide to medical terms and conditions.
http://www.amhrt.org

■ BEST Place to Find a Support Group: What did you promise to do for yourself this year—kick a habit, face a fear? Of the many excellent self-help resources online, the best is Mental Health Net, which offers the Self-Help Sourcebook Online and other pointers to information and support—both online and in the "real world."
http://www.cmhc.com/

■ BEST Nutritional Advice: How much food does the average American eat a day? What should shoppers look for on food labels? Registered dietitian and nutrition counselor Joanne Larsen dishes out advice on just about every aspect of healthy eating, from cooking to diet tips.
http://www.dietitian.com

■ BEST Runner's Resource: Runner's World Online is the Webzine for people on

the run. It offers guides for buying the right shoe, and sections on training and nutrition for all athletic levels. You'll also find tips on running in hot weather, information about mental fatigue, plus a home-remedy guide to injury prevention and treatment.
http://runnersworld.com

LIFE

■ **BEST Chat:** Whoever said online chat is a waste of time has never visited Talk City, a dynamic community made up of support groups, writers' workshops, legal advice forums, role-players, and even expeditions to ancient Mayan ruins.
http://www.talkcity.com

■ **BEST Place to Become a Volunteer:** Have you resolved to do more to help others? Well, becoming a volunteer is the perfect way to start. Impact Online is a great place to locate nonprofit organizations on the Web and in your neighborhood that could use your help.
http://www.impactonline.org

■ **BEST Family Site:** Famous for providing family-oriented entertainment, it's not surprising that Disney Online's Family.com is a great place to turn for help in raising children. A database of enlightening articles covers subjects such as food and home computing. Parents can share ideas on everything from home-

schooling to single parenting in chat session and message boards.
http://www.family.com

■ **BEST Relationship Advice:** Swoon embraces dating, mating, and relating. Articles and advice columns (some of which are culled from Conde Nast's *Details*, *Glamour*, *GQ*, and *Mademoiselle* magazines) address subjects like sibling rivalry, platonic friendships, and passionate relationships. Consult the Astrology section to see if you and your partner are a good match, or make a love connection at Interactive Personals. Some of the subjects may make you blush.
http://www.swoon.com

MONEY

■ **BEST Place to Grow Your Small Business:** What does it take to build a business? Confidence, canny market appraisal, cash, and all the help you can get. Inc. Online hands you many of the keys, including advice from Inc. magazine, marketing tips, software tools, and interactive worksheets. Make business contacts, and even do some self-promoting with a free home page for your business.
http://www.inc.com

■ **BEST Investment Advice:** America Online's classic, hip investment advisers the Motley Fool, are now on the Web. The site is a must-stop

for anyone thinking about investing some of their hard-earned cash.
http://www.fool.com/
America Online: Keyword fool

■ **BEST Business News:** A subscription to *The Wall Street Journal* Interactive edition will cost you $49 a year, or $29 for the paper's print subscribers, but it's well worth it. You'll get news, market data, and company briefing books, plus access to articles from the Dow Jones Publications Library, and more than 3,600 trade and business newswires, magazines, transcripts and newsletters.
http://www.wsj.com

NEWS

■ **BEST Place for News, Now:** CNN Interactive is not only an impressive complement to the cable news networks, it's also one of the Net's best sources for breaking news and analysis.
http://www.cnn.com

■ **BEST Place for the Times:** Whether you head straight for the auto section, scan the front page headlines or grab a pencil and puzzle over the crossword before you do anything else, *The New York Times* on the Web has all the daily content you could want, plus reader forums and special features.
http://www.nytimes.com

■ **BEST Alternative News:** What's going on in the

world? Check into OneWorld, originally created as a place where groups promoting human rights and sustainable development can share ideas and information. The site now brings you news reports that the mainstream media often miss, from 126 countries. Plus, you'll find issue guides, a multimedia gallery, discussion forums, and other resources.
http://www.oneworld.org

■ BEST Weather Resource: Whether you're traveling cross-country or planning a picnic, the Weather Channel is the place to get up-to-the-minute climate conditions. Pull-down menus help visitors quickly locate national and international forecasts and maps. Personalized home pages, weather safety tips, plus allergy and gardening maps are bonuses.
http://www.weather.com

REFERENCE

■ BEST Place to Look Up a Person: Trying to locate someone? Chances are you'll find them in Four11, a comprehensive e-mail, telephone, and Net phone directory with more than 10 million listings. Build your own online address book to keep up with your contacts or customize your own listing. Four11 also ties into the directory's free e-mail service.
http://www.four11.com

■ BEST Place to Look Up a Business: It's as easy as dialing 411. BigBook lets you search listings by name, business category, and location—right down to your very block. You might also find information such as a business's hours and prices, customer comments, or perhaps a review. There's even a personal address book for listings that you use often.
http://www.bigbook.com

■ BEST Place to Look Up a Word: Let OneLook Dictionaries sift through more than 250,000 words from 60 online dictionaries. Not sure of the spelling? Fire up the search engine and give it your best guess. If your word isn't in one of the "general dictionaries," OneLook will expand the search to include specialized resources—from the Online Dictionary of Computing to the Glossary of Pigeon Genetics.
http://www.onelook.com

■ BEST Place to Brush Up on Your Grammar: At the On-Line English Grammar site, you can take a hypertext course or an English as a second language test, get help with rules of usage, have your questions answered by teachers, and join in some friendly chat at the Grammar Cafe. At last, you'll get a grip on those gerunds and dangling participles.
http://www.edunet.com/english/grammar

■ BEST Place to Map a Course: Got your convertible and change for the tolls? MapQuest takes you anywhere in the continental U.S. with an Interactive Atlas that pinpoints any business or street address you type in. Zoom in and out, pan in any direction, and locate cash machines, gas stations, lodging, and all kinds of attractions. You also can personalize and file your maps, and get door-to-door driving directions between North American cities.
http://www.mapquest.com

■ BEST Place to Ask an Expert: Want to know why the Amish don't use electricity? Need some Web tips from a Java pro? Then, go straight to Ask an Expert. This directory of links will lead you to experts from all walks of life, whether high-tech or unplugged.
http://www.askanexpert.com

■ BEST Place to Learn How to Do Practically Anything: Often the most ordinary tasks are the most daunting. Find out how to tie a necktie properly, fix a leaky faucet, carve a turkey, and other life lessons at Learn2.com. What a brilliant idea for a Web site!
http://www.learn2.com

SHOPPING

■ BEST place to be a mall rat: The Internet Mall is home to more than 19,500 stores that offer a wide range of goods and services, from

flowers to greeting cards to political bumper stickers. Don't be intimidated by the enormous size of this virtual shopper's paradise; its search engine will help you locate just what you want.
http://www.internet-mall.com

■ **BEST place to Buy Vino:** Virtual Vineyards will help you relive the memory of that lovely California chardonnay your local liquor store doesn't stock. Thoughtful customer service, excellent wines from smaller vineyards, and tips from your host, "cork dork" Peter Granoff, might just make you a wine connoisseur.
http://www.virtualvin.com

■ **BEST place to Snag a CD:** If your CD collection is in need of new sounds, fast forward your browser to CDnow. This online store boasts more than 165,000 titles on CD and cassette and 8,500 music videos. Includes The All-Music Guide, a database of artist biographies and reviews.
http://www.cdnow.com

■ **BEST Automotive Consumer Guide:** For tips and advice on every aspect of buying a car online, try AutoWeb. Download information on particular makes and models, obtain customized price quotes, calculate financing options, and finalize a purchase—without putting a foot in a dealer's showroom.
http://www.autoweb.com

SPORTS

■ **BEST Place for Everything Sports:** By delivering knockout coverage of every major, and often minor, sport, CBS SportsLine is challenging ESPN SportsZone *(http://espnet.sportszone.com)* for the crown of heavyweight sports champion on the Web. In addition to hard-hitting news and feature stories, SportsLine delivers fan-friendly features, such as Internet-only radio and a Java-enhanced baseball scoreboard.
http://cbs.sportsline.com

■ **BEST Coverage of College Sports:** At FANSOnly's Total College Sports Network, you can meet tomorrow's professional all-stars and follow your personal favorites. In addition, TCS hosts official pages for athletic powerhouses such as Arizona, Kentucky, Notre Dame, and USC.
http://fansonly.com

■ **BEST Place for Outdoor Adventure:** Like its parent magazine, Outside Online offers articles and information about the great outdoors for the thrill-seeker in all of us. You'll find stories on everything from Mt. Kilimanjaro to the X games.
http://outside.starwave.com

■ **BEST Professional Wrestling Tribute:** The Professional Wrestling Online Museum holds the answers to any and all wrestling-related

questions. Includes interviews and a photo gallery of wrestling's most offbeat and memorable characters.
http://Adscape.com/wrestling

TRAVEL

■ **BEST Place to Make Travel Reservations:** Need a vacation? At Travelocity, you can book flights and hotels, tour cities around the world, and make an itinerary. Pick a location from the directory of cities and countries, and stop by the Registration Desk for airfares and flight schedules.
http://www.travelocity.com

■ **BEST Place to Start your Vacation:** Never mind the pointers to the Net's airfare bargains, the trip planner database, or the restaurant reviews—Condé Nast's Epicurious is in itself a wonderful destination for the virtual traveler.
http://www.epicurious.com

■ **BEST Place to Learn a New Language:** Select the language you speak and the one you want to learn from numerous options, including Bengali, French, Russian, Spanish and Swahili. You'll find basic vocabulary terms, pronunciation guides, translation dictionaries, slang guides, and other essentials that will help you get through your trip.
http://www.travlang.com

THE WEB
▼

SPINNING YOUR OWN WEB PAGE

Creating a Web page is easier than you might imagine

Thinking about staking a claim in the wild frontier of the World Wide Web? Why not? After all, the Web is populated by millions of people—men, women and children—who can't all be computer nerds. In fact, despite what many online novices may think, designing and publishing a Web page of your own is surprisingly simple.

Before you start constructing, you should first decide what you'd like your page to say and how you want it to look. Do you want to

CYBER SOURCES

Time to learn HTML? Check out these sites for HTML reference guides and Web design resources:

DESIGN CONSULTING. A complete HTML tutor, along with a gallery of images for Web use.
http://webcom.net~gmc/html/css.html

MICROSOFT'S WEB GALLERY. A wide range of multimedia goodies you can download for free.
http://www.microsoft.com

NETSCAPE'S CREATING NET SITES. The Page Wizard has templates, graphics to get your page started and links to other resources.
http://home.netscape.com

post news about a hobby? Promote a small business? Or do you just want to have fun and maybe show your prescience by predicting the winner of the Preakness? Once you've decided, you have several options for designing your home page. Choose the path that suits your level of expertise.

■ **THE GENERIC ROUTE.** Creating a Web page can be as easy as filling in the blanks. Some Internet providers and online services, such as America Online, CompuServe, and Prodigy, will design a page for you or give you the tools to do it easily yourself. Generally, the step-by-step process takes about 20 minutes and can be done at no extra charge beyond the monthly fee. By going through one of these services, you'll be given a reasonable amount of storage space on the service's computers, which will host your pages on a World Wide Web server. Going this route gets your page up and running quickly and easily.

■ **SOFTWARE THAT CUSTOMIZES.** If you find the online service route limited and uncreative, you may prefer one of the dozen or so software kits that allow you to create a more customized Web page. You can get professional-looking pages from packages such as Microsoft Front Page, Claris Home Page, Netscape Composer, and CorelWEB.Designer. All the packages start with a standard template, which you can then customize by clicking on menu choices. The programs let you create and edit text, import graphics, and add links to other sites on the Web. They convert your page into HTML, the standard language of the Internet, so that you never even need to know that HTML stands for Hypertext Markup Language. Also, keep in mind that many software programs, including desktop publishing packages, can generate HTML documents; word processors such as Corel WordPerfect 8 and Microsoft Word 97 even have integrated, graphical HTML editors.

■ **BUILDING FROM SCRATCH.** If you're determined to build your Web page from scratch, you'll need to learn the basics of HTML,

A WEB DESIGNER'S DECORATING MAXIMS

Ready to create your own page? Here are five design tips from Web page wizard Darrell Sano, a user-interface designer at Netscape Communications Corp. and author of Designing Large-Scale Web Sites: A Visual Design Methodology *(John Wiley & Sons, 1996).*

■ Plan your message and objective.

Focus your message toward your users. Building a Web site requires planning and forethought. Ask yourself, "Why am I creating this page? What would my readers find useful?" Remember, your home page is a direct reflection of you.

■ Start rough and slowly refine.

You don't have to be an artist to make rough sketches of your page. Sketching out Web pages is a quick, easy way to visualize alternative site layouts.

■ Don't let your users get lost.

Your visitors should always know where they are in your Web site, where they can go, and where they came from. Identify your pages and display a consistent manner so users won't have to scan the page looking for clues as to where they are.

■ Use images wisely.

Graphics should add value to the user's experience. It's a good practice to provide a text equivalent for any graphic link, especially large image maps, because many users temporarily defer image loading in exchange for greater speed when loading a Web page. Also, make sure backgrounds do not interfere with your text's legibility.

■ Keep it simple.

Simple designs are easier to understand than complex ones—a Web page packed with text and meaningless graphics can repel users. Because reading on a computer screen is more difficult than on paper, brevity is important. A simple Web page stands out from all the visual "noise" currently found on many Web sites.

---

which is not very difficult. HTML lets your Web browser graphically interpret a Web page and display it on your screen. The codes that make up HTML are used to apply different styles and attributes to a Web page, which in turn tell your Web browser how to display the page.

If you're a more advanced computer type, you can create your Web pages using a specialized word processor called an HTML editor. Some good bets are: Sausage Software's Hot Dog Standard Web Editor and SoftQuad's HotMetal Pro.

■ **GETTING PUBLISHED.** Once you've designed your page, you can have it posted online through any of the Internet service provid-

ers. But you might be able to get a free spot if you belong to an organization or association that makes space available to its members for personal Web sites. Check with groups you belong to and with your employer to see if you can get free space.

Another option is to join the ranks of rapidly growing Web communities at Geocities *(http://www.geocities.com)*, a company providing free home page space and e-mail to anyone who uses the Web. Geocities' homesteading program is supported by advertising and by fees for its commercial Web sites. With 34 themed neighborhoods to pick from, well over half a million online users have already staked their claim on the Web using Geocities.

CYBER SOURCES

WWW. WEIRD AND WACKY

Surfing the World Wide Web aimlessly doesn't always automatically turn up some of cyberspace's quirkiest inhabitants. If pretty strange sightings are what you're after, check out the sites below—six of the weirdest around. You can find lots more wacky sites listed in magazines like Yahoo!, The Net, *and* Wired. *Or, try* The World's Weirdest Web Pages and the People Who Create Them *(No Starch Press, 1996) by Hank Duderstadt.*

ASK MR. BAD ADVICE

http://www.echonyc.com/
~spingo/Mr.BA/

■ Mr. B.A. will entertain any and all manner of questions. But don't expect a logical response. He's bizarre, evasive, and sometimes funny. A recent question and answer:
"Dear Mr. B.A., During yesterday's jujitsu class, I hurt the little toe on my right foot in a bad landing breakfall. It didn't seem too bad at the time, but this morning, when I tried to walk, it hurt a lot. Should I go see a doctor? Regards, John"
"Dear John, That's kind of a boring name, isn't it? Mr. B.A."

DIRT MUSEUM

http://www.planet.com/dirtweb/
dirt.html

■ This award-winning site shovels up all the dirt there is to collect. Want to see a vial of dirt from the banks of the Chappaquiddick? Or, from Calvin Klein's beach house? It's all here in little jars lined up like a spice collection. You'll see tons of specimens—from Kenya, to Edith Piaf's grave site, to the Ed Sullivan Theater in New York.

Click on the vials for larger images and info on the sample.

THE NAKED DANCING LLAMA

http://www.frolic.org

■ NDL is a frolicking, tangoing, peanut-spitting llama who spews out advice on all sorts of problems, in the hopes that llama wisdom may bring you peace. A recent exchange:
"Dear NDL, How do you feel about the exploitation of llamas as pack animals? Sincerely, Llama Lover"
"Dear Llama Lover:
It is true that many llamas do like the Green Bay Packers, but I am pretty sure it is because their colors are yellow and an interesting shade of green. NDL."

OVI'S WORLD OF THE BIZARRE

http://www.ovis.com

■ A chronicle of the world's weirdest crimes and dumbest criminals, such as the three men who robbed a Liverpool post office armed with a gun and a tombstone. Also includes legends like the toilet clog that turned out to be a boa constrictor.

TALK LIKE A NATIVE

http://www.fas.harvard.edu/
~emolick/glass.html

■ Want to trick someone into believing that you're a native the next time you travel to a foreign country? Author Ethan Mollick says asking "Where is the bathroom?" is a dead give-away that you're not a local. So why not rattle off the phrase "I can eat glass, it doesn't hurt me." People will think you're insane and will treat you with respect. Learn how to say the phrase in 70 languages.

THE ULTIMATE LIGHT BULB JOKES

http://world.std.com/~olerin/
peter.html

■ Four parodies of Star Trek episodes pit the fearless crew against the perils of a dead 75-watt bulb. This could be the longest lightbulb joke ever.

CHAPTER NINE

AUTOS

■ **WHAT'S AHEAD: TAKE ADVANTAGE** of the revolution in used car selling... **READ** what experts are saying about the year's top new car models... **TRY** a professional auto-buying service for the best deal on your next car... **MAKE SURE** the motorcycle you buy is big enough... **CHECK** the credentials of a driving school before enrolling your teenager... **CRUISE** the Internet for driving and other car-related resources...

BUYING & LEASING

USED CARS
▼

NOT YOUR FATHER'S DEALER

Shopping at car superstores may be painless, but do you get a good deal?

Drive into one of the new auto super-stores and you're likely to feel as if you've reached a used-car nirvana. You drop off the kids at the store's daycare facility and browse the dealer's stock via a computer kiosk. You compile a list of suitable cars, and then move to the coffee bar to ponder your selections. Nary a plaid-suited salesman is visible. No one asks "What will it take to get you into a car today?" After you narrow down your choices to a few cars, you look for an "associate" for more information. You find that all the prices are set and non-negotiable. You make your selection, go directly to the dealer's financing department to work out the details, pick up the kids, and drive away in your new auto.

A consumer rebellion against high-pressure sales tactics and haggling over prices is responsible for this rev-olution in automobile retailing. Giant national chains, like CarMax (owned by Circuit City) and AutoNation USA (chaired by Blockbuster Video's founder, H. Wayne Huizenga), have created these auto havens, turning the used car market upside down. Traditional dealers, meanwhile, are scrambling to save their share of the trillion dollar market by banding together to form their own superstores or, at very least, by reassessing their high-pressure tactics. What does it mean for the consumer? Mostly good news. Here's a look at how superstores are changing the face of car buying:

■ **SELECTION:** One of the best features of buying at a superstore is the selection. While traditional dealers stock fewer than 100 cars, superstores offer as many as 700 automobiles of nearly every make and model. Most cars are relatively new, two- to five-year-old vehicles, which are the autos most used-car buyers crave. Cars five years or older are less reliable and more difficult to recondition. To maintain their inventories of the most desirable cars, supermarkets are striking alliances with car manufacturers and gaining access to the companies' closed auctions. Chrysler has transferred a dealership to CarMax. And AutoNation has hooked up with one of the largest Chevrolet dealerships.

■ **SERVICE:** A low-stress, customer-friendly shop-

■ WHAT WILL YOUR CAR BE WORTH DOWN THE ROAD?

The percentage to the right of each vehicle represents how much of its original value the vehicle will retain at the end of five years. Resale value is based on the car's rate of depreciation. Vehicles with better resale values have slower rates of depreciation.

HIGHEST RESALE VALUE

■ SUBCOMPACT

Honda Civic DX Coupe	66%
Honda Prelude	65
Acura Integra RS Coupe	64

■ COMPACT

Honda Accord DX	66
Saturn SL2	63
Toyota Corolla DX	59

■ MIDSIZE

Toyota Camry CE	60
Nissan Maxima GXE	58
Chevrolet Lumina	57

■ LARGE

Toyota Avalon XL	59
Buick LeSabre Custom	53
Pontiac Bonneville SE	53

■ NEAR LUXURY

Lexus ES 300	63
BMW 328 iS Coupe	61
Mercedes-Benz C220	60

■ LUXURY

Lexus SC 300	62
Lexus SC 400	61
Lexus GS 300	60

Mercedes-Benz SL320	60

■ BASE SPORT

Honda Civic del Sol S	59
Ford Mustang Cobra Coupe	59

■ SPORT

Mitsubishi 3000GT	59
BMW M3	58

■ SMALL WAGON

Saturn SW2	63
Honda Accord LX	61

■ MIDSIZE WAGON

Subaru Legacy L AWD	56
Volkswagen Passat GLX	52

LOWEST RESALE VALUES

■ SUBCOMPACT

Ford Probe GT	50
Subaru Impreza Brighton AWD Coupe	51

■ COMPACT

Buick Skylark Gran Sport Coupe	45
Oldsmobile Achieva SL Series II	46

■ MIDSIZE

Mercury Sable LS	46
Ford Taurus SHO	47

■ LARGE

Eagle Vision TSi	46
Dodge Intrepid ES	48

■ NEAR LUXURY

Chrysler LHS	44
Audi A6	47

■ LUXURY

Jaguar XJR	43
BMW 750iL	43

■ BASE SPORT

Pontiac Firebird Formula Convertible	53
Eagle Talon TSi Turbo AWD	54

■ SPORT

Subaru SVX L AWD	49
Toyota Supra Turbo	51

■ SMALL WAGON

Hyundai Elantra	49
Subaru Impreza Outback AWD	52

■ MIDSIZE WAGON

Ford Taurus LX	49
Mercury Sable LS	49

SOURCE: The Complete Car Cost Guide (Intellichoice, 1997).

ping environment is the superstores' key to winning customers. Salespeople work on salary, not on commission, and are generally polite and attentive. The stores stress cleanliness, efficiency, and convenience. Computer print-outs of autos include pictures of the cars, a list of equipment, fixed prices, and a map indicating where they can be found on the lot. You can browse the entire inventory on computer without having to walk the enormous lot. When you're ready to check out the car of your choice, you hop aboard a shuttle bus to the car's location.

■ REPAIRS AND WARRANTIES: Most of the extended services available from new car dealerships are also provided through the superstores, including warranties ranging from the existing manufacturer's warranty to options on extended warranties. Also available are fully equipped service centers and roadside assistance.

Superstores say that every car on their lot has been inspected and all necessary repairs have been made. Atlanta's CarMax gives a 30-day, 1,000-mile warranty on repairs, which is about what you would get with a traditional dealer. Another superstore, Car Choice, guarantees all repairs for one year or 12,000 miles, whichever comes first. Most superstores have a policy of taking back any car, no questions asked, within five days or 250 miles. It's hard to find a traditional dealer who rivals that policy; most never permit returns.

■ THE QUALITY LEADERS

The research firm J.D. Power and Associates in 1997 asked more than 43,000 owners of new cars, light trucks, and sports-utility vehicles to evaluate their autos 90 days after they had purchased them. The average number of new-car problems per 100 vehicles was 86 in 1997, an improvement of 22 percent from the previous year. Traditionally, outstanding quality scores have been awarded to low-volume, higher-priced vehicles, but J.D. Power found that the quality of high-volume vehicles increased dramatically in 1997. Here are the top three least problematic autos in each car category:

■ COMPACT CAR

Saturn SL	65
Toyota Tercel	65
Honda Civic	69

■ ENTRY MIDSIZE CAR

Nissan Altima	77
Buick Skylark	80
Chrysler Cirrus	80

■ PREMIUM MIDSIZE CAR

Honda Accord	51
Toyota Camry	53
Chevrolet Lumina	55

■ SPORTY CAR

Acura Integra	60
Honda Prelude	71
Nissan 200SX	87

■ ENTRY LUXURY CAR

Infiniti I30	46
Acura TL	52
Lexus ES300	61

■ PREMIUM LUXURY CAR

Lexus LS400	36
Lexus SC300/400	50
Acura RL	55

■ COMPACT PICKUP TRUCK

Toyota Tacoma	63
Ford Ranger	76
Nissan pickup	79

■ FULL-SIZE PICKUP

Ford F-Series	64
Chevrolet C/K	88
Toyota T100	90

■ COMPACT VAN

Honda Odyssey	52
Ford Windstar	68
Toyota Previa	72

■ COMPACT SPORTS UTILITY VEHICLE

Infiniti QX4	48
Toyota 4 Runner	64
Chevrolet Blazer	74

■ FULL-SIZE SPORTS UTILITY VEHICLE

Lexus LX450	75
Toyota Landcruiser	78
Chevrolet Suburban	97

SOURCE: J.D. Power and Associates, 1997.

Buyers of used cars generally like to know about a car's mechanical history. But a 1996 *Money* magazine survey showed that none of the superstores they contacted could supply them with data regarding a car's repairs. On the other hand, many of the traditional dealers *Money* contacted had such information on hand or on a computer database.

■ **COST:** While traditional dealers love to deal, chopping off a hundred dollars here and there, superstores stick to their policy of no-haggling on prices. Attempts to cut the fixed sticker prices will always be met with polite yet firm refusals.

Are superstore prices a better deal than traditional dealers' prices? Not always. Many superstores say they price their cars about $1,000 below the suggested manufacturer's retail price. But the *Money* magazine study found that that's not always the case. Five reporters were sent to CarMax and Car Choice superstores in Georgia, Michigan, North Carolina, Texas, and Virginia. The reporters then found similar cars at traditional dealers located within a few miles of the superstores. The upshot: although shopping at superstores was far more pleasant, dickering with a dealer always resulted in a better price, typically $100 to $300 below the superstores' price for a similar car.

The moral is: If you're not turned off by high-pressure tactics and you enjoy haggling with the best of them, then you're likely to nab the better bargain with a traditional dealer. In fact, a survey by the Dohring Co., a research firm, showed that consumer preferences for one-price selling fell from 39 percent in 1995 to 33 percent in 1996. "The only way consumers feel they can get a good deal is through negotiation," reported the survey. But when it comes to selection, service, and a money-back guarantee, most car buyers would agree that the unprecedented buying options available at superstores are finally putting the consumer in the driver's seat.

EXPERT PICKS

THE BEST CARS OF 1997

Everyone wants a car that starts when it's supposed to and gets you where you need to go. But many drivers expect an automobile to be more than just a reliable appliance. For drivers who love the road, the magazines Car and Driver *and* Automobile Magazine *are among the first places they turn for car evaluations. Here are the cars their editors picked as the very best of model year 1997.*

$13,000–$18,000
ACURA INTEGRA
Front-wheel drive, 3-door coupe or 4-door sedan; 24–25 mpg
Base: $16,520

■ The Integra is an outstanding example of the quality-over-quantity philosophy of car building. It's quick and its design is useful. The four-door sedans offer surprising room for four with decent luggage space. This performance and utility come in a compact package gifted with nimble handling, excellent fuel economy, and an attractive, ergonomically satisfying interior.

CAR AND DRIVER

CHRYSLER CIRRUS/ DODGE STRATUS/ PLYMOUTH BREEZE
Front-wheel drive, 4-door sedan, 19–25 mpg. Base: $15,330

■ Beauty is more than skin deep in these sedans, which represent the most advanced use of Chrysler's cab-forward design ethic. The transverse engine is pushed so far forward in the interest of maximizing passenger space that the battery is relegated to the left-front wheel well. As a result, these sedans offer the largest interior volume in their class, and a combination of features hard to beat at their mainstream prices.

CAR AND DRIVER

FORD CONTOUR MERCURY MYSTIQUE
Front-wheel drive, 4-door sedan, 21–24 mpg. Base: $14,405

■ These are among the most satisfying sedans in the United States, offering technical nuggets such as a range of double-overhead-camshaft, four-valves-per-cylinder, four- and six-cylinder engines, and optional four-wheel disc brakes and antilock control, at a price well below $20,000. Even when equipped with the standard four-cylinder engine, the drivelines are refined and responsive.

CAR AND DRIVER

HONDA CIVIC
Front-wheel drive coupe, 5-passenger, 2-door, 35 mpg. Base: $13,400

■ The Civic gives you a big small car with safety, performance, and environmental capabilities undreamed of more than two decades ago when the Civic was launched. Our favorite model is the HX coupe with Honda's own continuously

variable transmission, which is unobtrusive and totally transparent.

AUTOMOBILE MAGAZINE

$19,000–$25,000
AUDI A4
Front or 4-wheel drive, 4-door sedan. 19–21 mpg.
Base: $23,490

■ For a reasonable sum you gain entry into a line of exquisitely detailed sedans. The A4 is one of the sleekest four-doors on the road, graced with an interior in which every element is executed with style and taste. Although we wish the A4 offered a bit more rear-seat room, few sedans at any price provide more pure driving satisfaction.

CAR AND DRIVER

MAZDA MX-5 MIATA
Rear-wheel drive convertible, 2-passenger, 2-door, 23 mpg. Base: $19,125

■ The most successful sports car in history, the Miata is also the most automotive fun available for the price. Everything works. Flip the convertible top with one hand in seconds, and the car is quiet and dry. The Miata has grown a bit heavier with civility and safety features, but the engine has kept pace so that overall performance remains virtually unchanged.

AUTOMOBILE MAGAZINE

TOYOTA CAMRY V-6

Front-wheel drive, 4-door sedan, 19–20 mpg. Base: $19,668

■ The Camry offers a combination of a cushy ride and precise handling. Toyota has reduced the number of components in the front bumper and placed a cheaper surface finish on the underside of the gas tank, but these changes do not compromise the Camry's overall appeal. They do help to lower the price, however, by more than $1,000 on every model.

CAR AND DRIVER

$25,000–$35,000
BMW 328IM3

Rear-wheel drive, 2- or 4-door sedan, 19–20 mpg.
Base: $33,470

■ Better fuel economy and quicker acceleration enhance these definitive sports sedans. All the 3-series accommodate four adults, provide plenty of comfort, and deliver fuel economy commensurate with their light weight and efficient engines. An ideal all-around vehicle for discerning drivers who want more than two seats.

CAR AND DRIVER

CADILLAC CATERA

Rear-wheel drive, 4-door sedan, 5-passenger, 18 mpg.
Base: $29,995

■ The Catera feels European, thanks to its firm suspension, quick and accurate steering, nimble handling, and zippy acceleration. But it's been Cadillac-ized with optional leather seating, wood trim, polished wheels, and Caddy styling including full-width taillights and egg-crate grill. Aimed at baby boomers, the Catera is a kick to drive.

AUTOMOBILE MAGAZINE

HONDA PRELUDE SH

Front-wheel drive, 2-door coupe, 22 mpg. Base: $25,500

■ This is the sixth year that Preludes have made our list. This new model packs more horsepower than its predecessors, and its control-arm front and multilink rear suspensions deliver the best imitation of a Formula Ford that you can get in a street car with four seats. The bodywork is perhaps less exciting than in the past but it offers more interior space and a cleaner dashboard design.

CAR AND DRIVER

$35,000 AND ABOVE
BMW 5-series

Rear-wheel drive, 4-door sedan 15–19 mpg. Base: $38,828

■ It's rare to find a luxury sedan that provides full comfort and driver satisfaction. The BMW 5-series is an exception. It is the only sedan in its class that offers a manual transmission with six- and eight-cylinder engine options. Despite its

taut ride, the car's suspension soaks up everything from potholes to expansion joints. Leather upholstery is soft and door panels cosset your elbows. It's our luxury sedan of choice.

CAR AND DRIVER

JAGUAR XK8

Rear-wheel drive coupe, 2-door, 17 mpg. Base: $64,900

■ A car that takes your breath away whether it's streaking across the countryside or sitting in the garage. Its aluminum AJ-V8 engine is all new, and world-class, leading the field of 4.0-liter V-8s in specific output and compactness. The XK8 drives with silky deliberation, untroubled by any turmoil at the pavement level.

AUTOMOBILE MAGAZINE

LEXUS SC300

Rear-wheel drive coupe, 4-passenger, 2-door, 19 mpg.
Base: $39,000

■ The combination of the SC300's six-cylinder engine and five-speed manual gearbox is wonderful, placing it on our list for five years running. The SC300 transcends the sports car moniker; it approaches a luxury car because of its sumptuous interior appointments, comfortable seating for four, and plenty of quality leather.

AUTOMOBILE MAGAZINE

MERCEDES SLK

Rear-wheel drive, 2-door roadster, 22 mpg. Base: $41,123

■ The SLK has the responsive performance, sharp handling, and cozy interior we would expect from a tiny two-seater. Best of all, its convertible top shakes and rattles less than others, and there's even a decent trunk. One disappointment: Mercedes does not offer a manual gearbox. Despite that, the SLK defines a new paradigm for sports cars.

CAR AND DRIVER

PORSCHE 911 CARRERA

Rear-wheel drive coupe, 2-door, 17 mpg. Base: $63,750

■ Few cars are more satisfying to drive along twisting blacktop. The rear-engine location gives it supreme traction. The brake pedal is so perfectly weighted that you can feel exactly what the front tires are doing. No other sports cars this fast have as much luggage room or such good outward visibility. This is about as practical as a sports car gets, and it's so solidly built that it feels like it will last forever.

AUTOMOBILE MAGAZINE

SPORTS UTILITY
FORD EXPEDITION

Rear- and 4-wheel drive, 8-passenger, 4-door, 13 mpg.
Base: $38,875

■ The Expedition has finally arrived to challenge the already-excellent Chevrolet/GMC Suburbans, Tahoes, and Yukons. And what a challenger it is. It is an excellent long-distance cruiser, with quiet aerodynamics, good handling, and easy drivability. Inside are abundant luxuries, comforts, and conveniences.

AUTOMOBILE MAGAZINE

TOYOTA RAV 4

Four-wheel drive, 5-passenger, 4-door, 22 mpg. Base: $17,218

■ In the tradition of sports-utility vehicles, the RAV 4 carries the rakish aura of being able to tackle anything— trails over the Rockies, the drovers' roads in Wales. Toyota describes the vehicle as the first, and only, mass-produced sports utility vehicle with four-wheel independent suspension. Its

blend of the conventional sedan components and sport-utility looks make it capable of performing everything but the most arduous tasks.

AUTOMOBILE MAGAZINE

MINIVAN
CHRYSLER TOWN & COUNTRY/ DODGE CARAVAN/ PLYMOUTH VOYAGER

Front- or 4-wheel drive, 4- or 5-door sedan; 16–20 mpg.
Base: $17,815

■ Chrysler designers have transformed the minivan from a steamer trunk into a piece of Vuitton luggage. They have developed the suspension to soak up bumps and curves with aplomb and honed its steering to be more responsive and linear than most cars'. Add the industry's first left-side door, rolling seats, and outstanding space efficiency, and it's no wonder Chrysler's minivan has been selected to our list for the second year.

CAR AND DRIVER

■ CRUISIN' GETS COSTLIER

How much does it cost to own and operate a 1997 car? Here's the cost-per-mile picture by vehicle type based on driving 10,000 miles a year:

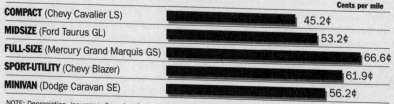

Cents per mile

COMPACT (Chevy Cavalier LS) 45.2¢
MIDSIZE (Ford Taurus GL) 53.2¢
FULL-SIZE (Mercury Grand Marquis GS) 66.6¢
SPORT-UTILITY (Chevy Blazer) 61.9¢
MINIVAN (Dodge Caravan SE) 56.2¢

NOTE: Depreciation, insurance, financing, fuel, oil, repairs, licenses, and taxes for 4-year, 60,000-mile ownership period.
SOURCE: Runzhaimer for the American Automobile Association.

WHAT DEALERS WON'T TELL YOU

With the right data, the salesman will be at your mercy

Most people approach buying a new car with the same apprehension as sitting in rush hour traffic with a car full of quarreling children. But there's no need to feel at the mercy of a car salesman, says Mark Eskeldson, author of *What Car Dealers Don't Want You to Know* (Technews, 1995) and *Leasing Lessons for Smart Shoppers* (Technews, 1997). Here, Eskeldson offers these tips on how to gain control of your car buying experience and save a great deal of money in the process:

■ **Knock 10 percent off the sticker price automatically.**

First and foremost, determine how much you can afford to spend. For a rough estimation, take a vehicle's sticker price and deduct 10 percent. For example, if you're interested in purchasing a vehicle listed at $20,000, estimate the monthly payments based on a purchase price of $18,000. After you've settled on an affordable price range, start shopping. Make a list of the cars that fit your style and budget. You don't necessarily need to visit dealerships to do this, you can make your list from television commercials or magazines. If you do visit a dealership, stay away from salesmen. If one approaches you, tell him or her, "I'm just looking and I am not buying a car."

To research the cars on your list, use consumer guides, reviewing cars for reliability, safety, performance, and the like. This is the area where people typically make their biggest mistakes. People who fail to research a car's reliability can lose a great deal of money to depreciation and the repair shop. If the car you like isn't among the top-rated,

try compromising style for reliability. Choose a car you find attractive, but that rates well in the car assessments.

■ **Don't begrudge a dealer a modest profit.**

Books and magazines provide very, very basic car cost numbers. For a number of reasons, the actual amount that a dealer pays for a vehicle can change from day to day. For accurate and daily up-to-date information on true dealer cost, you should consider phoning a service called Fighting Chance (☎ 800–288–1134). For a fee of $24.95, it will provide a complete package of buying and/or leasing information on one vehicle, including secret factory incentives and other market shifts that will affect the automobile's true price.

Once you have figured out a car's true cost, add in a reasonable amount for dealer profit. For cars costing $10,000–$15,000, allow $400–$500 for the dealer's profit. For cars in the $20,000 range, add on $600–$700. For luxury cars, a dealer typically won't accept an offer for less than $1,000 profit.

■ **Solicit bids by fax if possible.**

Before you tangle directly with the dealers, I encourage customers to first try the "fax strategy." Fax a form letter to a number of dealerships. Inform the dealer you've already done your research and you are shopping for the best offer. Describe in detail the automobile you intend to purchase and the names of the dealer's competitors. For example, "I'm looking for a blue '97 Taurus four-door sedan, with option package X, Y, Z. I am soliciting offers from Bob's Cars and Joe's Autos and will accept the lowest offer." Don't mention an amount, but let the dealer know you've done your homework. In closing, notify the dealer that if it is interested in selling a car, it should fax or call you with a price. In about three days you should hear from all interested parties.

Choose the offer you are most comfortable with and visit the dealer. You may only have to visit one dealer before closing a deal. I recently had great success using this method to purchase my own car. I sent out seven faxes, received three responses, and closed the deal without ever leaving my home. If this method fails, resort to plan B—visiting the dealer.

■ Be wary of "deals" at the end of the model year.

Most salespersons have quotas to meet at the end of each month. Whether he needs one more sale to keep his job or win a trip to Hawaii, the dealer may be willing to sell the car at little or no profit simply for the sale.

Beware of model year-end sales, however. Buying a model before the new versions arrive may appear to offer great savings, but it rarely makes up for the depreciation difference. Because the greatest depreciation occurs in an automobile's first two years, a year-end model has already lost 20 to 25 percent of its value.

■ Use walking out as a negotiating strategy.

You're never going to get the best price unless you're willing and ready to walk out. Don't waste your time fighting with dealers—you will always lose. Once you begin haggling, the dealer has gained the advantage. This is his specialty. The dealer makes his living haggling a deal; he does so nearly every single day.

When you visit the dealer, keep the process very impersonal. Submit an offer, and make it clear that if they turn you down, you are willing to offer their competitors the same deal. Usually the dealer will call your bluff and let you walk out. I'd be shocked if they didn't run out to catch you in the parking lot. At this point you have gained the advantage. Tell the salesman you will not go back inside unless they accept your price. The key ingredient to the strategy is competition. Most dealers accept the fact that a low-profit sale is better than no sale. Remember, it is a buyer's market. Use this to your advantage.

■ Keep the financing period as short as possible.

Never walk in and ask the salesperson for financial advice. A car dealer will always steer you toward the most expensive car and long-term financing. Don't be fooled by the low monthly payments. Financing a car is a "no pain, no gain" proposition—if it doesn't hurt, you haven't done it correctly. The intelligent way to finance a car is with a large

EXPERT SOURCES
WHERE TO GET A FIX ON PRICES

Invoice prices can be found in two annuals, The Complete Car Cost Guide *(IntelliChoice, Inc.) or* Edmund's New Car Price Guide *(Edmund Publications). The services below will mail or fax you that and more for $11 to $23.*

CAR PRICE NETWORK
■ Everything from dealer invoices and factory rebates to market overviews and negotiating tips.
☎ 800–227–3295

CENTER FOR THE STUDY OF SERVICES
■ A nonprofit organization. According to Mark Eskeldson, probably the

best service for getting a handle on car prices. Its biweekly newsletter, *Car Deals,* provides info on factory incentives for $7 a copy.
☎ 202–347–7283

CONSUMER REPORTS NEW CAR PRICING
■ Dealer invoice, factory rebates, negotiating tips.
☎ 800–933–5555

FIGHTING CHANCE
■ Like Car Price Network, it offers dealer invoices, factory rebates, market overviews, and negotiating tips.
☎ 800–288–1134

INTELLICHOICE
■ Dealer invoice, factory rebates, resale values, and ownership costs.
☎ 800–227–2665

WHEN DICKERING IS BEST LEFT TO THE PROS

The easiest way to spare yourself showroom face-offs with car salespersons you don't trust is to engage an auto-buying service that will do the negotiating for you. The best services are ones whose fees are paid by customers, not car dealers rewarding buying services for sending clients their way. Among the best-known national services are:

AUTO ADVISOR

■ This Seattle-based company's basic service costs $359, and the sales price it negotiates for a car is guaranteed. Its enhanced service ranges from $419 for four- to eight-week delivery to $679 for one-week delivery. The service permits customers to price more than one car at a time and includes an hour of consultation in the base fee. Extra advice costs $120 an hour.
☎ 800–326–1976

AUTOMOBILE CONSUMER SERVICES

■ Work begins with a $75-per-vehicle service fee. The final bill is based on a percentage of the savings between the sticker price and purchase price. Total costs average about $295.
☎ 800–223–4882

CAR BARGAINS

■ Operated by the Center for the Study of Services in Washington, D.C., on a nonprofit basis. For a fee of only $165, Car Bargains solicits bids from five dealers in your area. You get the actual dealer quote sheets as well as information on financing, service contracts, and the value of your used car.
☎ 800–475–7283

CONSUMERS AUTOMOTIVE

■ Fees are $195 for a car with a sticker price up to $15,000, $295 for a car between $15,000 and $30,000, and $395 for more expensive cars. Prices are guaranteed.
☎ 703–631–5161

down payment and as high monthly payments as possible.

Under no circumstance should you agree to a six-year car loan. A six-year loan is financial suicide. The interest will kill you. For example, if you purchased a $20,000 car, financed at 9 percent over three years, your total payment in interest will be $2,896. Paying the same price and rate, but agreeing to a six-year loan, your interest payment is now $5,963. If you can't afford at least a five-year loan, you are better off buying your car used or settling for a lower-priced model. A five-year loan is your compromise. Even there you'll save $1,000 in interest, while paying only $54 more a month than for a four-year loan.

■ Extended warranties are not always needed.

Extended warranties are where people make the biggest financial mistakes. If people do their homework and find a reliable car in the first place, an extended warranty becomes unnecessary. Statistically, you're better off banking or investing your money than purchasing a three-year warranty. But if you did buy a poorly rated car, then you should purchase an extended warranty for a reasonable price—$2,000 is not a reasonable price.

Most major insurance companies will sell you an extended warranty for well under $1,000. You can typically purchase an extended warranty for around $400. A credit union is your best bet. Of course these rates are contingent upon the reliability of your car. If your vehicle rates poorly, you will pay more. If you pay $1,800 at a credit union for your warranty, there is a very good chance your car is going to wind up in the repair shop.

NEGOTIATING A GREAT LEASE

Auto leasing is a cheap way to drive an expensive vehicle

Leasing a car can be a smooth ride if you map out your route in advance. But it can be one of the great auto scams of the 1990s if you don't understand how the lease you agree to really works. Here, Randall McCathren, executive vice president of Bank Lease Consultants, Inc., a consulting company that deals with auto lease financing, and the author of *Automobile Lending and Leasing Manual* (Warren, Gorham & Lamont, 1989), steers you toward your destination.

■ What is the difference between buying and leasing a car?

When you lease a car, you have no obligation for the car when you reach the end of the lease term on the closed-end lease (if you have observed the mileage and wear-and-tear restrictions). You have a guaranteed trade-in value equal to the end-of-term lease balance, and if you want to keep the car, you exercise your purchase option. When you buy a car, there is no guaranteed trade-in value any time you want to terminate the loan and trade in the car.

■ What are the advantages to leasing?

Leasing has become attractive to people who understand the benefits of cash conservation and guaranteed trade-in value. Leasing traditionally requires no down payment, though some special manufacturer lease programs require 5 to 10 percent down to get the financial terms being offered. Leasing has much lower payments than financing because the consumer only pays for depreciation, or the portion of the vehicle expected to be used up,

rather than for the total price of the vehicle. The higher the down payment on the lease, the lower the monthly payment. The guaranteed value means the customer can walk away from the vehicle when the lease is up without obligation even if the vehicle is worth less than projected.

Another benefit of leasing is deferring the purchase decision until after you've driven the vehicle for a while. Even consumers who think they want to keep the vehicle for 10 years are better off leasing it for 3 to 5 years first, then deciding whether or not they want to keep it for the full 10 years.

■ Why are people hesitant to lease a car?

Leasing can be very confusing. Unfamiliar words, lengthy contracts, and hard sales techniques can make it tough to shop for a lease. With no capitalized cost disclosure (which is analogous to the selling price in a purchase) and no annual percentage rate (APR) disclosure, it's difficult to be sure that you've gotten a good deal. Now, however, most of the largest lessors, such as Ford Credit, GMAC, Toyota Motor Credit, and General Electric Credit, require dealers to disclose the capitalized cost. Eleven states have also mandated capitalized cost disclosure. On October 1, 1997, a federal mandate for capitalized cost and other new disclosures will go into effect for all consumer leases. The disclosures will make it easier to shop for and understand leases.

■ What pitfalls should consumers avoid when leasing?

If consumers put down $1,000 less and pay $50 to $75 a month less on a five-year lease than a five-year loan, they can't expect to have the same lease balance after three years as they would have had on the loan.

Some lessees plan to terminate early when the structure of the lease is intended to avoid building equity. If lessees pay for 15,000 miles per year and drive 25,000, they can't expect to drop the car off with no obligation; if they had purchased the car, its trade-in value would be lower because of the extra mileage. The same is true in cases of excess wear and tear.

Finally, as in any business there are some unscrupulous lessors who try to take advan-

LEARNING THE LEASING LINGO

Monthly payments are just the beginning. Randall McCathren, executive vice president of Bank Lease Consultants Inc. (☎615–383–1930), a consulting firm that tracks trends in auto lease financing, advises that, in addition to monthly payment, which is the main shopping comparison consumers use, potential lessees shoud consider these variables:

■ **CAPITALIZED COST:** Don't lease a car without getting it in writing. Leasing has $300 to $500 of costs not found in loans (such as contingent liability insurance and credit insurance), so expect to pay at least that much more than for a purchase. The other benefits of leasing may also be worth a higher purchase price, particularly a highly subsidized rate, but the capitalized cost can be negotiated.

■ **RESIDUAL VALUE:** This is the predicted value of the car at the end of the lease term, and it's guaranteed. The higher it is, the more likely it is that the lessor will lose money at the end.

■ **PERMITTED MILEAGE:** Most deals are now only 10,000 or 12,000 miles a year, but don't choose the lower mileage if you're likely to end up paying excess mileage charges at lease end. You can select 15,000 or even 20,000 miles a year.

■ **EARLY TERMINATION RIGHT AND CHARGE:** Look for a lease that permits early termination and uses a constant yield or actuarial method (where interest is earned at the same rate every month and is precalculated), at least after the first 12 months.

■ **PURCHASE OPTION:** Look for a residual value fixed-price purchase option or, if you can find it, the lesser of the published wholesale value and the residual value.

■ **EXCESS MILEAGE CHARGE:** Make sure it is reasonable if you drive extra miles. For a car worth up to $15,000, you shouldn't pay more than 10¢ per extra mile. For a car worth $15,000 to $30,000, excess mileage shouldn't cost more than 15¢ a mile, and for cars above $30,000, no more than 18¢ a mile.

■ **TERM:** Don't sign a lease for longer than you plan to drive the car. The guaranteed value only benefits you at the end of the term. Never plan to terminate early. If you can't afford the payments on the shorter term, choose a less expensive car.

■ **LIABILITY AFTER CASUALTY LOSS:** If the lease doesn't include "gap insurance," don't pay more than $200 for coverage and consider self-insuring the risk.

tage of customers. Excessive charges for early termination and wear and tear are the two biggest areas of abuse. One or two bad apples can create a lot of negative publicity.

■ **How can I make sure I'm getting a good lease price?**
Negotiate the purchase price first. Get it in writing. Then negotiate the lease and get a statement of the capitalized cost in writing. If the dealer or independent leasing company says they don't know what the capitalized cost is or that there isn't one, take your business elsewhere. Shop around and talk to a number of lessors. Compare rates and terms before making a decision. When you're ready to lease, don't agree to a longer term than you expect to keep the vehicle. Don't choose a car so expensive that you won't be able to pay for early termination if you need to.

And make sure you're comfortable with the vehicle. A great lease on a car you don't really want is not a good deal.

CRASH TEST DUMMY'S GUIDE

HOW YOUR CAR DOES IN A CRUNCH

Each year the National Highway Traffic Safety Administration conducts crash tests of new cars under conditions that are the equivalent of having a head-on collision with an identical vehicle at 35 mph. The tables below include results for cars tested for the first time in 1997 as well as results for previously tested vehicles that were essentially the same cars being sold in model year 1997. Vehicles should be compared only to other vehicles in the same weight class—if a light vehicle collides head-on with a heavier vehicle at 35 mph, for example, the occupants in the lighter vehicle would experience a greater chance of injury than indicated. Vehicles are classified by the estimated chance of injury for the driver or passenger, and receive a one- to five-star rating, with five stars indicating the best protection.

VEHICLE	Driver / Passenger:	AIRBAG	CRASH RATING
■ MINI PASSENGER CARS			
GEO METRO		§	★★★★
4-dr. sedan, 1,986 lbs.		§	★★★★
■ LIGHT PASSENGER CARS			
FORD ASPIRE		§	★★★★
4-dr. HB, 2,086 lbs.		§	★★★★
HONDA CIVIC		§	★★★★
4-dr. sedan, 2,337 lbs.		§	★★★★★
HYUNDAI ACCENT		§	★★★
4-dr. sedan, 2,261 lbs.		§	★★★★
MAZDA MX-5		§	★★★★
2-dr. convertible, 2,312 lbs.		§	★★★
MAZDA PROTEGE		§	★★★★
4-dr. sedan, 2,429 lbs.		§	★★★
NISSAN SENTRA		§	★★★★
4-dr. sedan, 2,454 lbs.		§	★★★★
SATURN SL2		§	★★★★
4-dr. sedan, 2,332 lbs.		§	★★★★
TOYOTA PASEO		§	★★★★
2-dr., 2,050 lbs.		§	★★★★
TOYOTA TERCEL		§	★★★
4-dr. sedan, 2,176 lbs.		§	★★★★
■ COMPACT PASSENGER CARS			
BUICK SKYLARK		§	★★★★★
2-dr., 4-dr., 3,000 lbs.		§	★★★★
CHEVROLET CAVALIER		§	★★★★
4-dr. sedan, 2,731 lbs.		§	★★★
CHRYSLER SEBRING		§	★★★★★
2-dr., 3,400 lbs.		§	★★★★★
DODGE AVENGER		§	★★★★★
2-dr., 2,952 lbs.		§	★★★★★
DODGE NEON		§	★★★★
4-dr. sedan, 2,547 lbs.		§	★★★★
EAGLE TALON		§	★★★★
2-dr., 2,729 lbs.		§	★★★★

VEHICLE	Driver / Passenger:	AIRBAG	CRASH RATING
FORD ESCORT		§	★★★
4-dr. sedan, 2,509 lbs.		§	★★★★
FORD PROBE		§	★★★★★
2-dr., 2,773 lbs.		§	★★★★
HONDA ACCORD		§	★★★★
4-dr. sedan, 2,901 lbs.		§	★★★
HYUNDAI ELANTRA		§	★★★
4-dr., 2,500 lbs.		§	★★★
HYUNDAI SONATA		§	★★★
4-dr. sedan, 2,761 lbs.		§	★★★★
INFINITI I30		§	★★★★
4-dr., 3,150 lbs.		§	★★★
MAZDA MX-6		§	★★★★★
2-dr., 2,800 lbs.		§	★★★★
MITSUBISHI ECLIPSE		§	★★★★
2-dr., 2,853 lbs.		§	★★★★
MITSUBISHI GALANT		§	★★★★
4-dr. sedan, 2,832 lbs.		§	★★★★
NISSAN 240 SX		§	★★★
2-dr., 2,795 lbs.		§	★★★★
NISSAN ALTIMA		§	★★★★
4-dr. sedan, 2,941 lbs.		§	★★★★
NISSAN MAXIMA		§	★★★★
4-dr. sedan, 2,970 lbs.		§	★★★
OLDSMOBILE ACHIEVA		§	★★★★
2-dr., 4-dr., 2,900 lbs.		§	★★★★★
OLDSMOBILE CUTLASS		§	★★★★
4-dr., sedan, 3,000 lbs.		§	★★★★
PLYMOUTH NEON		§	★★★★
2-dr., 4-dr., 2,400 lbs.		§	★★★★
PONTIAC GRAND AM		§	★★★★★
4-dr. sedan, 2,987 lbs.		§	★★★★
PONTIAC GRAND AM		§	★★★★
2-dr. sedan, 2,987 lbs.		§	★★★★★
PONTIAC SUNFIRE		§	★★★★
2-dr., 4-dr., 2,650 lbs.		§	★★★★

■ CRASH TEST DUMMY'S GUIDE

VEHICLE	Driver / Passenger:	AIRBAG	CRASH RATING
SUBARU IMPREZA		§	★★★★
2-dr., 4-dr., 2,900 lbs.		§	★★★★
SUBARU LEGACY		§	★★★★
4-dr. sedan, 2,654 lbs.		§	★★★★
TOYOTA COROLLA		§	★★★★
4-dr. sedan, 2,553 lbs.		§	★★★★
VOLKSWAGEN GOLF		§	★★★
4-dr., 2,800 lbs.		§	★★★
VOLKSWAGEN JETTA III		§	★★★
4-dr. sedan, 2,950 lbs.		§	★★★

■ MEDIUM PASSENGER CARS

VEHICLE	Driver / Passenger:	AIRBAG	CRASH RATING
ACURA TL		§	★★★★
4-dr. sedan, 3,300 lbs.		§	★★★★
AUDI A4		§	★★★★
4-dr. sedan, 3,096 lbs.		§	★★★★★
AUDI A6		§	★★★★★
4-dr. sedan, 3,373 lbs.		§	★★★★★
BMW 328i		§	★★★★
4-dr. sedan, 3,234 lbs.		§	★★★★
CHEVROLET CAMARO		§	★★★★★
2-dr. HB, 3,408 lbs.		§	★★★★★
CHEVROLET LUMINA		§	★★★★★
4-dr. sedan, 3,344 lbs.		§	★★★★
CHEVROLET MALIBU		§	★★★★
4-dr., 3,100 lbs.		§	★★★★
CHEVROLET MONTE CARLO		§	★★★★
2-dr., 3,284 lbs.		§	★★★★
CHRYSLER CIRRUS		§	★★★
4-dr., 3,100 lbs.		§	NO DATA
CHRYSLER CONCORDE		§	★★★★
4-dr. sedan, 3,550 lbs.		§	★★★★
CHRYSLER SEBRING CONVERT.		§	★★★★
2-dr., 3,400 lbs.		§	★★★★
DODGE INTREPID		§	★★★★
4-dr. sedan, 3,254 lbs.		§	★★★★
DODGE STRATUS		§	★★★
4-dr. sedan, 3,144 lbs.		§	NO DATA
EAGLE VISION		§	★★★★
4-dr. sedan, 3,550 lbs.		§	★★★★
FORD CONTOUR		§	★★★★★
4-dr. sedan, 3,020 lbs.		§	★★★★★
FORD MUSTANG		§	★★★★
2-dr., 3,119 lbs.		§	★★★★
FORD MUSTANG		§	★★★★★
2-dr. convertible, 3,317 lbs.		§	★★★★★
FORD TAURUS		§	★★★★
4-dr. sedan, 3,368 lbs.		§	★★★★
FORD THUNDERBIRD		§	★★★★★
2-dr., 3,460 lbs.		§	★★★★★

VEHICLE	Driver / Passenger:	AIRBAG	CRASH RATING
HONDA ODYSSEY		§	★★★★
4-dr. wagon, 3,459 lbs.		§	★★★★
ISUZU OASIS		§	★★★★
4-dr., 3,450 lbs.		§	★★★★
MAZDA MILLENIA		§	★★★★
4-dr. sedan, 3,150 lbs.		§	★★★★★
MERCEDES-BENZ C220		§	★★★★
4-dr. sedan, 3,190 lbs.		§	★★★★
MERCURY COUGAR		§	★★★★
2-dr., 3,550 lbs.		§	★★★★
MERCURY MYSTIQUE		§	★★★★★
4-dr. sedan, 2,850 lbs.		§	★★★★
MERCURY SABLE		§	★★★★
4-dr., 3,388 lbs.		§	★★★★
PLYMOUTH BREEZE		§	★★★
4-dr. sedan, 2,900 lbs.		§	NO DATA
PONTIAC FIREBIRD		§	★★★★★
2-dr., 3,450 lbs.		§	★★★★★
PONTIAC GRAND PRIX		§	★★★★
2-dr., 3,210 lbs.		§	★★★★
SAAB 900		§	★★★★
4-dr. HB, 3,064 lbs.		§	★★★★
TOYOTA AVALON		§	★★★★
4-dr. sedan, 3,290 lbs.		§	★★★★★
TOYOTA CAMRY		§	★★★★
4-dr. sedan, 3,128 lbs.		§	★★★★
VOLKSWAGEN PASSAT		§	★★★★
4-dr. sedan, 3,124 lbs.		§	★★★★
VOLVO 850		§	★★★★★
4-dr. sedan, 3,241 lbs.		§	★★★★

■ HEAVY PASSENGER CARS

VEHICLE	Driver / Passenger:	AIRBAG	CRASH RATING
CADILLAC DEVILLE		§	★★★★
4-dr. sedan, 4,050 lbs.		§	★★★★
CHRYSLER LHS		§	★★★★
4-dr. sedan, 3,600 lbs.		§	★★★★
FORD CROWN VICTORIA		§	★★★★★
4-dr. sedan, 3,849 lbs.		§	★★★★★
LEXUS GS300		§	★★★
4-dr. sedan, 3,765 lbs.		§	★★★
LINCOLN CONTINENTAL		§	★★★★
4-dr. sedan, 3,900 lbs.		§	★★★★★
MERCURY GRAND MARQUIS		§	★★★★★
4-dr. sedan, 3,800 lbs.		§	★★★★★
OLDSMOBILE AURORA		§	★★★
4-dr. sedan, 3,883 lbs.		§	★★★
PONTIAC BONNEVILLE		§	★★★★★
4-dr. sedan, 3,558 lbs.		§	★★★
VOLVO 960		§	★★★★
4-dr., 3,500 lbs.		§	★★★★

■ CRASH TEST DUMMY'S GUIDE

VEHICLE	Driver / Passenger:	AIRBAG	CRASH RATING
■ SPORTS UTILITY VEHICLES			
ACURA SLX		§	★★★
4-dr., 4,200 lbs.		§	★★★
CHEVROLET BLAZER		§	★★★
4-dr. 4X4, 4,156 lbs.			★
CHEVROLET TAHOE		§	★★★★
4-dr. 4X4, 5,276 lbs.		§	★★★★
FORD EXPEDITION		§	★★★★
2-dr. 4X4, 4,763 lbs.		§	★★★★
FORD EXPLORER		§	★★★★
4-dr. 4X4, 4,242 lbs.		§	★★★★
GEO TRACKER		§	★★
2-dr., 4-dr., 2,600 lbs.		§	★★★
GMC JIMMY		§	★★★
4-dr. 4X4, 3,900 lbs.			★
HONDA PASSPORT		§	★★★★
4-dr., 4x4, 4,150 lbs.		§	★★★
INFINITI QX4		§	★★★
4-dr., 4,150 lbs.		§	★★★
ISUZU RODEO		§	★★★★
4-dr., 4x4, 4,105 lbs.		§	★★★
ISUZU TROOPER		§	★★★
4-dr., 4,200 lbs.		§	★★★
JEEP GRAND CHEROKEE		§	★★★
4-dr., 3,950 lbs.		§	★★★★
JEEP WRANGLER 4x4		§	★★★★
2-dr., 3,100 lbs.		§	★★★★★
MERCURY MOUNTAINEER		§	★★★★
4-dr., 4,200 lbs.		§	★★★★
NISSAN PATHFINDER 4x4		§	★★★
4-dr., 4,000 lbs.		§	★★★
OLDSMOBILE BRAVADA 4x4		§	★★★
4-dr., 4,000 lbs.			★
SUZUKI SIDEKICK 4x4		§	★★
4-dr., 2,950 lbs.		§	★★★
TOYOTA 4-RUNNER 4x4		§	★★★
4-dr., 3,850 lbs.		§	★★★
TOYOTA RAV4		§	★★★
2-dr., 4-dr., 2,850 lbs.		§	★★★
■ LIGHT TRUCKS			
CHEVROLET C/K		§	★★★★★
2-dr., 4,200 lbs.		§	★★★★
CHEVROLET C/K EXTEND. CAB		§	★★★★★
2-dr., 4,200 lbs.		§	★★★★
CHEVROLET S-10		§	★★★★★
2-dr., 3,091 lbs.		§	★★★★★
DODGE DAKOTA EXTEND. CAB		§	★★★★
2-dr., 3,500 lbs.		§	★★★★
DODGE RAM 1500		§	★★★★★
2-dr., 4,550 lbs.			NO DATA
DODGE RAM EXTEND. CAB		§	★★★★
2-dr., 4,550 lbs.			★★★
FORD F-150		§	★★★★
2-dr., 4,444 lbs.		§	★★★★★
FORD RANGER		§	★★★★
2-dr., 3,245 lbs.		§	★★★★
GMC SIERRA		§	★★★★★
2-dr., 4,200 lbs.		§	★★★★
GMC SIERRA EXTEND. CAB		§	★★★★★
2-dr., 4,200 lbs.		§	★★★★
GMC SONOMA PICKUP		§	★★★
2-dr., 3,350 lbs.			★★
MAZDA B-SERIES		§	★★★★
2-dr., 3,550 lbs.		§	★★★★
NISSAN 4x2 PICKUP		§	★★
2-dr., 2,950 lbs.			★★★★
TOYOTA TACOMA		§	★★
2-dr., 2,560 lbs.			★★★
■ VANS			
CHEVROLET ASTRO		§	★★★
4,200 lbs.		§	★★★
CHEVROLET VENTURE		§	★★★★
3,650 lbs.		§	★★★★
CHRYSLER TOWN & COUNTRY LX		§	★★★
3,900 lbs.		§	★★★★
DODGE CARAVAN		§	★★★★
3,800 lbs.		§	★★★★★
DODGE GRAND CARAVAN		§	★★★
4,000 lbs.		§	★★★★
DODGE RAM VAN/WAGON		§	★★★
4,100 lbs.			★★★★
FORD AEROSTAR VAN		§	★★★★
3,670 lbs.			★★★
FORD CLUB WAGON/ ECONOLINE		§	★★★
5,166 lbs.		§	★★★★
FORD WINDSTAR		§	★★★★★
3,801 lbs.		§	★★★★★
GMC SAFARI		§	★★★
4,500 lbs.		§	★★★
MAZDA MPV		§	★★★★
3,800 lbs.		§	★★★★
MERCURY VILLAGER		§	★★★★
3,862 lbs.		§	★★★
NISSAN QUEST		§	★★★★
3,850 lbs.		§	★★★
PLYMOUTH GRAND VOYAGER		§	★★★
3,700 lbs.		§	★★★★
PLYMOUTH VOYAGER		§	★★★★
3,700 lbs.		§	★★★★★
TOYOTA PREVIA		§	★★★★
3,644 lbs.		§	★★★

SOURCE: National Highway Traffic Safety Administration.

THE OTHER CAR PAYMENT TO REMEMBER

When you shop for a new car, considering the insurance cost of the make and model you select can give you a substantial savings over time

The ratings here show which cars are relative insurance bargains and which are not. Next to each model is State Farm Insurance Company's rating of that car's insurance cost when compared with other models in the same price range. If your make or model is not listed here, you should assume that it ranks as "average," and that you will be charged standard collision and comprehensive premiums. State Farm uses its actual claims payments to determine how likely a vehicle is to be stolen, or if it is damaged, how expensive it is to repair. Even if your car isn't insured by State Farm, the lists give an indication of how your own insurance company will evaluate your car.

Insurance rates for models that qualify for lower-than-average rates can range from 10 to 45 percent less than the standard collision and comprehensive premiums for cars in a comparable price range. Owners of models ranked higher than average can expect to pay between 10 and 45 percent more than the standard. However, these are "relative" insurance costs. Generally, the more expensive a car is, the more it costs to insure.

The examples below illustrate this relationship in three price ranges. For the sake of comparison, insurance costs were calculated using identical rating factors.

STICKER PRICE: $12,501–$15,000

LOWER THAN STANDARD	Chev. Cavalier 2 dr.	$845/yr.
STANDARD	Saturn SCl	$883
HIGHER THAN STANDARD	Honda Civic 2 dr.	$1,011

STICKER PRICE: $15,001–$20,000

LOWER THAN STANDARD	Buick Century	$883
STANDARD	Chrysler Cirrus	$1,011
HIGHER THAN STANDARD	Acura Integra 2 dr.	$1,118

STICKER PRICE: $20,001–$30,000

LOWER THAN STANDARD	Buick Park Avenue	$1,011
STANDARD	Infiniti I30	$1,186
HIGHER THAN STANDARD	Honda Prelude	$1,236

■ **1997 MAKE**

Model:	LOWER INSURANCE VALUE / HIGHER INSURANCE VALUE	STICKER PRICE
■ **ACURA**		
	Integra 2dr & 4dr	$16,100–$19,650
■ **AUDI**		
Audi A4 4dr		$22,990
Audi A6 4dr and sw		$32,600–$34,400
Audi A6 Quattro 4dr and sw		$32,000–$44,000
	Cabriolet cv	$35,000
■ **BMW**		
740i, 750i 4dr		$61,000–$94,000
	318i, 328i 2dr, 4dr, cv	$25,950–$41,390
	M3 2dr	$42,000
	840Ci, 850Ci 2dr	$76,000–$95,000
■ **BUICK**		
Century 4 dr		$17,845
LeSabre 4 dr		$22,000–$29,000
Park Avenue 4 dr		$30,000–$37,000
Regal 2 dr & 4 dr		$21,000–$30,000
Riviera 2 dr		$30,110
■ **CADILLAC**		
DeVille 4 dr		$37,000–$45,000
Eldorado 2 dr		$38,000–$49,000
Seville 4 dr		$40,000–$51,000
■ **CHEVROLET**		
Corvette 2dr		$37,495
Lumina 4 dr		$17,000–$22,000
Astro 2wd and 4wd van		$20,000–$29,000
Suburban K2500 spw		$25,000–$38,000
Tahoe 2wd and 4wd spw		$24,000–$35,000
	Camaro 2 dr and cv	$16,000–$29,000
	Cavalier 2 dr and 4 dr	$10,980–$11,180
	Blazer S10 2 and 4wd spw	$11,553–$14,353
	Blazer 2 and 4wd spw	$20,000–$24,116

■ **AUTO SHOPPER'S GUIDE**

■ 1997 MAKE

Model:	LOWER INSURANCE VALUE / HIGHER INSURANCE VALUE	STICKER PRICE

■ **CHRYSLER**

Concorde 4 dr	$20,435–$24,665
LHS 4dr	$30,255
Sebring cv	$20,150–$24,660
Town & Country 2 and 4wd van	$28,000–$35,000

■ **DODGE**

B1500, B2500, B3500 van	$18,000–$22,000
Caravan 2wd; 4wd van	$18,000–$32,000
Ram 3500 4 wd; pk	$19,740
Avenger 2 dr	$14,620–$17,490
Neon 2dr; 4 dr	$10,395–$10,595
Ram 1500 2wd; pk	$16,000

■ **FORD**

Crown Victoria 4dr	$21,475–$23,195
Taurus 2dr and sw	$18,000–$31,000
Aerostar 2wd and 4wd spw	$17,000–$28,000
Club Wagon van	$21,000–$28,000
Explorer 2wd and 4wd spw	$20,000–$38,000
F150, F250, F350 2 and 4wd pk	$14,000–$35,000
Windstar van	$21,000–$30,000
Aspire 2 dr and 4 dr	$9,915–$9,825
Escort 4 dr	$11,795
Mustang 2 dr cv	$16,000–$24,000
Probe 2dr	$15,000–$23,000
Ranger 2wd pk	$11,000–$25,000

■ **GEO**

Metro 2dr and 4dr	$8,580–$9,850
Prism 4dr	$12,840
Tracker 2wd and 4wd spw	$13,000–$20,000

■ **GMC**

G1500, G2500, G3500 van	$23,500–$27,000
Safari 2wd and 4wd van	$20,000–$29,000
Suburban C1500 spw	$25,000–$41,000
Suburban C2500 spw	$25,000–$41,000
Suburban K1500 spw	$25,000–$41,000
Suburban K2500 spw	$25,000–$41,000
Yukon 2wd and 4wd spw	$30,000–$31,000
S15 Jimmy 4wd spw	$21,000–$31,000
S15 Sonoma 2wd pk	$15,000–$24,000

■ 1997 MAKE

■ **HONDA**

Accord sw	$19,090
Civic 2dr and 4dr	$12,280–$12,635
del Sol 2dr	$15,000–$20,000
Prelude 2dr	$23,200

■ **HYUNDAI**

Elantra sw	$11,999
Elantra 4dr	$11,099
Sonata 4dr	$14,199

■ **INFINITY**

| Q45 4dr | $47,900–$49,400 |

■ **IZUSU**

| Hombre 2wd pk | $11,000–$16,000 |
| Trooper spw | $25,000–$39,000 |

■ **JAGUAR**

| Jaguar XJ6, XJR 4dr | $55,000–$71,000 |
| Jaguar XK8 2dr | $65,000–$76,000 |

■ **JEEP/EAGLE**

Vision 4dr	$20,305–$24,485
Grand Cherokee 4wd spw	$15,000–$28,000
Talon 2dr	$14,059
Talon 4wd 2dr	$18,015
Wrangler 4wd spw	$13,470

■ **LEXUS**

ES 300 4dr	$29,900
GS 300 4dr	$45,700
LS 400 4dr	$52,900
SC300 2dr	$40,000–$90,000

■ **LINCOLN**

Continental 4 dr	$37,280
Mark VIII 4dr	$38,000–$45,000
Town Car	$38,000–$48,000

■ **KEY TO ABBREVIATIONS:**

cv	convertible
dr	door
pk	pickup
spw	sports wagon
sw	station wagon
wd	wheel drive

■ AUTO SHOPPER'S GUIDE

■ 1997 MAKE

Model:	LOWER INSURANCE VALUE HIGHER INSURANCE VALUE	STICKER PRICE
■ MAZDA		
	626 4dr	$15,695
	MX6 2dr	$19,000–$27,000
	Protege 4dr	$12,145
	B2300, B4000 2wd pk	$10,000–$15,000
■ MERCEDES		
	C220, C280, C36 AMG 4dr	$30,450–$51,925
	E320 4dr and sw	$40,000–$57,000
	E300, E420 4dr	$40,000–$57,000
	S320, S320W, S420 4dr	$64,000–$137,000
	S500, S600 2dr and 4dr	$64,000–$137,000
■ MERCURY		
	Grand Marquis 4dr	$22,495–$24,000
	Mystique 4dr	$14,775
	Sable 4dr and sw	$19,000–$28,000
	Villager van	$21,000–$25,000
	Tracer 4dr	$11,145
■ MITSUBISHI		
	3000GT 2dr	$27,050
	3000GT 4wd 2dr	$44,590
	Eclipse 2dr	$15,140
	Eclipse 4wd and 2dr	$23,220
	Galant 4dr	$15,420
	Mirage 4dr	$12,090
	Montero spw	$30,000–$36,000
■ NISSAN		
	Quest van	$21,000–$29,000
	200 SX 2dr	$12,999
	240 SX 2dr	$18,359
	Altima 4dr	$15,649
	Sentra 4dr	$11,499
	Nissan 2wd and 4wd pk	$11,000–$18,00
	Pathfinder 4wd spw	$23,000–$36,000
■ OLDSMOBILE		
	Aurora 4dr	$35,735
	Cutlass 4dr	$17,325–$19,225
	Cutlass Supreme 2dr and 4dr	$19,000–$24,000
	Eighty-eight 4dr LSS 4dr	$23,000–$30,000

■ 1997 MAKE

Model:	LOWER INSURANCE VALUE HIGHER INSURANCE VALUE	STICKER PRICE
■ PLYMOUTH		
	Breeze 4 dr	$14,795
	Voyager 2wd van	$18,000–$21,000
	Neon 2dr and 4dr	$10,395–$10,595
■ PONTIAC		
	Bonneville 4dr	$22,119–$27,164
	Grand Prix 4dr	$18,029–$19,809
	Sunfire cv	$18,899
	Firebird 2dr and cv	$17,000–$23,000
	Sunfire 2dr and 4dr	$12,059–$12,199
■ PORSCHE		
	Porsche 911 2dr and cv	$64,000
■ SAAB		
	Saab 900 4dr and cv	$25,995–$40,995
■ SATURN		
	SW1, SW2 sw	$12,195–$13,095
	SC1, SC2 2dr	$12,495–$13,695
■ SUBARU		
	Impreza 2dr	$13,744
■ SUZUKI		
	Suzuki X90 2ws spw	$13,499
	Suzuki Swift 2 dr	$9,000–$10,000
	Suzuki Sidekick 2wd, 4wd spw	$15,000–$16,000
	Suzuki X90 4wd spw	$14,999–$16,000
■ TOYOTA		
	Avalon 4dr	$23,538–$27,048
	Landcruiser spw	$41,000–$49,000
	Previa 2wd and 4wd van	$25,000–$40,000
	Celica 2dr	$17,000–$34,000
	Corolla 4dr	$12,998
	Paseo 2dr	$13,208
	Supra 2dr	$39,000–$54,000
	Tercel 2dr and 4dr	$10,648–$12,108
	4 Runner 4wd spw	$20,000–$36,000
	Tacoma 2wd and 4wd pk	$12,000–$23,000
■ VOLKSWAGEN		
	Passat sw	$22,320
	Volkswagen Golf 4dr	$13,470
	Volkswagen GTI 2dr	$16,320
■ VOLVO		
	Volvo 960 4dr and sw	$35,000–$38,000

SOURCE: State Farm Insurance Companies, 1997.

TAKING A CYCLE FOR A SPIN

Learn to ride before you buy; you may spare yourself a big mistake

When Ed Youngblood describes motorcycling as "a spiritual activity, essential for maintaining a healthy mental perspective," he reflects a viewpoint shared by many motorcycle lovers. Youngblood's romance with the motorcycle began nearly 40 years ago, when he was just 14 and took the $60 he saved from doing odd jobs to purchase his first bike, a 1953 Harley-Davidson 165F. Youngblood has since gone on to become one of the great ambassadors of cycling. The president of the American Motorcyclist Association (AMA, ☎ 800–262–2643), Youngblood is a regular contributor to *American Motorcyclist*. For anyone interested in joining America's 6 million motorcycle enthusiasts, Youngblood has this advice:

■ How do you know if a motorcycle is right for you?

I don't believe motorcycles are right for everyone. So before you go out and buy yourself a $10,000 motorcycle, register in a motorcycle training course—preferably the Motorcycle Safety Foundation's (MSF). The course will take you through all aspects of motorcycle operation and maintenance. You'll also receive an excellent introduction to motorcycle makes and sizes, so if you do decide to buy a bike, you'll have an idea of the type of bike that fits your personality and needs.

■ What kinds of bikes are there for the motorcycle buyer to choose from?

First, you must decide whether you prefer an on-road or off-road motorcycle. In other words do you plan on riding over dirt trails or on the open highway? If you're in the market for an off-road, you can choose between a total dirt bike and a trail bike made street-legal. The latter comes with turning signals and other requirements of a highway vehicle. If you favor the highway, there are essentially three bike types. The sport bike is styled like a high-performance machine; it is light and quick, best suited for short rides. Cruisers are designed for comfort and local riding. These bikes provide an ideal fit for a commuter or the "weekend" rider. Touring bikes are made for the long-distance traveler. They're larger and often have built-in saddlebags for luggage.

Size is also important. Typically, trail bikes have much smaller engines than road bikes. Trail bike sizes usually top out at 600cc (cubic centimeters), while a touring bike can have an engine as large as 1500cc—comparable to a small automobile engine.

■ Which motorcycle best fits the first-time buyer?

Unlike automobiles, which are typically purchased with practicality in mind, motorcycle selection is determined by personal taste and style. You must remember: The motorcycle is a recre-

FACT FILE:

REBELS NO MORE

■ *Think of bikers and images of modern-day desperadoes come to mind. In reality, members of the American Motorcyclist Association (North America's largest motorcycle organization) are established, well educated, and financially successful:*

■ **Average household income: $57,300**

■ **Post-high school educational experience: 79 percent**

■ **Unemployed: 3 percent**

ational vehicle. Most AMA members own more than two cycles, and many own more than four.

As far as the leading brands or makes available in the U.S., you have Harley-Davidson, Honda, Kawasaki, Suzuki, Yamaha, Triumph, Ducati, BMW, and a variety of smaller manufacturers. Typically, all these manufacturers put out high-quality products. The choice among them usually comes down to brand loyalty. I know people who have driven Harleys for over 20 years and would never try anything else. The same is true for BMWs and most other brands. You can't explain a person's personal taste for motorcycles any more than you can explain a person's clothing selection. It's all up to the individual.

■ What is your favorite bike?

Hard to say. There aren't many I don't like. I guess it would depend upon the type of riding I'm doing. At this moment I own a Harley-Davidson FLHF touring bike and a Kawasaki 1500cc Vulcan Classic cruiser.

EXPERT PICKS

Every year for more than two decades, the editors of *Cycle World* magazine, the premier motorcycle publication, select their favorite new bike models. Here's the cream of the crop for 1997:

1. SUZUKI TL 1000S
2. HONDA VTR 1000 SUPER HAWK
3. HONDA VFR 750 F
4. HONDA CBR 600F
5. HONDA VALKYRIE TOURER
6. BMW R1100RT
7. SUZUKI BANDIT 1200S
8. KTM 620 R/XC
9. KTM 250 E/XC
10. YAMAHA YZ125

■ What should you ask the dealer when shopping for a bike?

As I said earlier, motorcycle selection is very personal, and today's selection is enormous. That's why it's so important to have an informative motorcycle introduction, such as the MSF's safety course, before you begin shopping for a bike. The dealer will actually depend upon you for information. In my early days, the choices were much simpler. The $60 I bought a Harley-Davidson 165 with when I was 14 would not buy me anything today, but at least I'd have more to look at.

■ What is the first-time buyer's most common mistake?

First-time buyers often purchase bikes that are too small. Going into the showroom, most first-timers lack confidence, so they choose the smaller bikes, which are easier to handle. After their first month, they're ready for a larger model. I'm not suggesting every first-time buyer needs a larger bike, but I would recommend some riding experience before going to the dealer.

■ Which, if any, accessories really matter?

This depends upon your cycling plans. If you intend on having a passenger, install a backrest for his or her comfort. A rider taking long trips should consider installing saddlebags. Personally, I prefer a windscreen, simply for the comfort. If you like camping, there are specially made motorcycle trailers, which many people use to haul their outdoor gear.

■ Any other critical advice for first-time cyclists?

A good source for information is a group called Discover Today's Motorcycling (☎ 800–833–3995). Again, I can't stress how important it is to enlist in motorcycle driving courses *before* you take to the road. For my first 20 years of riding, no instruction was available and I believed I didn't need any. After participating in my first course, I was horrified to learn of my poor technique and riding habits. I was so taken by the course, I became an instructor and lifelong advocate. If you don't intend to go through a training course, don't ride.

DRIVING & MAINTENANCE

EXPERT Q & A

JOHN ANDRETTI TAKES THE WHEEL

One of the world's great drivers shares his tips on the curves ahead

If avoiding the pesky pothole on your street corner is your biggest daily challenge, try stopping on a dime at over 200 mph or taking razor sharp curves at speeds that would make your hair stand on end. For premier race car driver, John Andretti, those feats are all in a day's work. The nephew of racing legend Mario Andretti (John's father, Aldo, is Mario's twin), Andretti says he's raced cars "practically since birth." Along the way, he's driven dragsters, midgets, dirt cars, sprint cars, you name it, winning such prestigious races as the 24 Hours of Daytona. Andretti is now a top driver on NASCAR's elite Winston Cup circuit. We asked Andretti for advice on becoming a safer driver.

■ **How did you first learn to drive and how did those formative years affect your driving on and off the track?**

I think I first learned to drive in my crib with my toy steering wheel. I've been racing competitively since I was nine years old. Before that I used to sit on my dad's lap and drive that way. I've had a steering wheel in front of me basically my whole life.

When you start driving at a young age, the mind logs in those early experiences, and you develop instincts. In driving, you have to take in things through your eyes and react instantaneously to what you've seen visually. What you see has to trigger a reaction in your mind. You learn to slow things down with your eyes and yet react to situations immediately.

■ **Is there anything a driver should do even before turning on the ignition?**

Make sure you and all your passengers are buckled in and that your mind is focused on the road. This holds true on and off the track. When I get in my race car, even before I put on my helmet, the first thing I do is make sure I'm buckled in.

■ **What is the best way to handle turns and curves?**

Always at a safe speed. When the road is dry and it's clear out, if the speed limit says 35 mph, a corner should be quite easily taken at 35. At the same time, you have to be aware that if there's a car coming from the other direction, that car may not be totally under control—it may be coming toward you at a high speed and maybe the driver has lost control of the vehicle. If you're not prepared and don't pull off to the side of the road, for example, it could be a deadly situation for all.

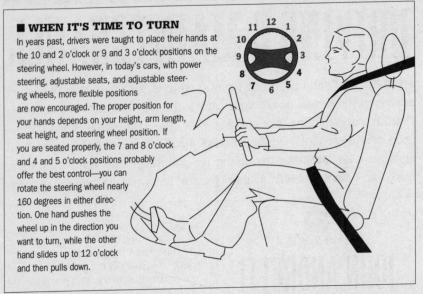

■ WHEN IT'S TIME TO TURN

In years past, drivers were taught to place their hands at the 10 and 2 o'clock or 9 and 3 o'clock positions on the steering wheel. However, in today's cars, with power steering, adjustable seats, and adjustable steering wheels, more flexible positions are now encouraged. The proper position for your hands depends on your height, arm length, seat height, and steering wheel position. If you are seated properly, the 7 and 8 o'clock and 4 and 5 o'clock positions probably offer the best control—you can rotate the steering wheel nearly 160 degrees in either direction. One hand pushes the wheel up in the direction you want to turn, while the other hand slides up to 12 o'clock and then pulls down.

■ What has racing taught you about tailgating and trailing other vehicles?

Appropriate distances between cars vary with the situation. With today's traffic, there are few opportunities to maintain large gaps between cars, therefore drivers really must pay attention.

My rule is: No matter how fast I'm driving, if someone wants to go faster, they're welcome to pass me. In fact, I try to make it easy for them to get by, which is the opposite of what 90 percent of drivers might do. Most would speed up, or become angry and tailgate. That makes no sense to me. When I'm not on the track, I'm not in a race.

■ What's the best way to change lanes or pass other vehicles?

Many drivers have trouble changing lanes safely. On the highway, for example, you often find the "left-lane hanger," who rides in the left lane no matter what. They make others pass them in the right lane, creating a difficult situation. Often, they speed up as people try to pass, making it worse. There are plenty of open spots in the slow lane. Let them pass you and then get behind them. Most of the time, you don't even have to slow down to allow them to pass.

■ Is a stick shift superior to an automatic transmission?

Both are equally safe in dry and sunny conditions. I find that in very snowy and icy conditions, a stick shift provides more control. Often in an automatic, when you approach a stop sign and the road is icy, if you don't put the car in neutral, you're really fighting the vehicle, because it wants to go forward. In a car with a stick-shift transmission, not only can you switch to a higher gear to get going and avoid wheel-spin, but you can also use the neutral position and the rear tire to slow you down a bit, giving you more control.

■ How do you alter your driving for various conditions such as poor visibility, bad weather, etc.?

You should drive within your control. Obviously that means different things for different people. The conditions I race in are not always ideal. Often I can hardly see ahead of me and I have to adapt to very difficult situations. On the road, you should drive at whatever speed is necessary for safety. However, if you feel you must drive at a very slow speed, it's important to put on your hazard lights so you won't get hit in the back because drivers can't see you. Extreme conditions require the smart driver

■ WHAT IT TAKES TO STOP IN TIME

Tailgaters beware: The stopping distance required for a car going 35 mph is just over half a football field, even when the road is dry. At 65 mph the distance required is equal to the length of one and a third football fields.

Stopping distances at selected speeds

WET
DRY

MOTORCYCLE
- 35 MPH: 225 ft. / 260 ft.
- 45 MPH: 315 ft. / 385 ft.
- 55 MPH: 435 ft. / 530 ft.
- 65 MPH: 575 ft. / 705 ft.

PASSENGER CAR
- 35 MPH: 160 ft. / 185 ft.
- 45 MPH: 225 ft. / 275 ft.
- 55 MPH: 310 ft. / 380 ft.
- 65 MPH: 410 ft. / 505 ft.

TRUCK
- 35 MPH: 190 ft. / 230 ft.
- 45 MPH: 280 ft. / 350 ft.
- 55 MPH: 490 ft. / 390 ft.
- 65 MPH: 525 ft. / 665ft.

SOURCE: National Highway Traffic Safety Administration.

to drive within his own means. Again, remember that even though you may be in control of your car, that doesn't mean everyone is, so be constantly aware of other drivers.

■ If you are approaching an accident or dangerous situation, what is the best way to proceed?

The whole time I drive, I'm always looking for escape routes from potential problems. That's become natural to me. As you go down the road, always be prepared for anything that might confront you. Be aware of the limitations of your car. Understand your

car and how it will respond to situations in order to avoid accidents. You could save a life or serious damage to the car by driving defensively.

■ What's your best advice for drivers?

Pay attention. I get more frustrated with drivers who aren't courteous and don't pay attention than with those who drive too fast. I just let the fast drivers pass so that I can see them. Don't get angry at situations that are beyond your control. A car takes more lives every year than guns. It can be a very deadly weapon and should be treated with respect.

SAFE AT ALL SPEEDS?

There's a right way to operate antilock brake systems and air bags

A mericans are driving more and dying less often. In 1950, an average of 7.6 Americans died behind the wheel for every 100 million miles driven. Today, the fatality rate has dropped to only 1.7 over the same distance. Much of the credit goes to motorists who demanded safer cars. But confusion about the proper use of air bags, antilock brakes, and other safety innovations still leads to unnecessary accidents. Here, safety specialist Norman Grimm of the American Automobile Association discusses how to make today's safety features work for you.

■ **Antilock brakes work, but only if they are held down, not pumped.**

It is true that in the short time we have had ABS there has not been any noticeable difference in the number of accidents. But the problem is not the system—it's the way it is used. There is a prevailing myth that in an emergency you should pump your brakes, but for antilock brakes to work effectively, the driver must press down hard and hold down. The grinding noise and pulsations indicate that ABS is functioning correctly.

■ **Air bags need to be used in tandem with seat belts to be effective.**

There have been times when air bags have deployed unnecessarily, and other instances when the bag is deployed with such force that it causes injury. Technology is now being developed that will correct these problems, but improvements will only help if the system is used properly. Without the assistance of seat belts, air bags lose their effectiveness.

When buckling your seat belt, use the lap

and shoulder harness simultaneously. The lap belt should be worn as low on the abdomen as possible. The shoulder harness should come across the chest and not up by the neck.

■ **The safest place to position a child is in the car's middle rear.**

Deployed passenger-side air bags have been implicated in some children's injuries and even fatalities. Children under 13 should always ride in the back seat, whether or not the car is equipped with air bags. Keep older children in seat belts and toddlers and infants in child seats, and always read a child seat's manufacturer instructions.

■ **Head restraints are a safety device, not a head rest.**

Most Americans drive cars with an adjustable head restraint. If used properly it can help prevent neck injuries such as whiplash: the head restraint should support the back of the head, not the neck or shoulders.

■ **If you suddenly lose your power steering, don't panic.**

You still have steering capabilities, only now you'll have to use more muscle. Any play in your power steering wheel when the car is off indicates a problem that should be checked.

■ **HELPING AIR BAGS DO THEIR JOB**

Despite all the controversy over air-bag safety, statistics show that the devices saved about 2,000 lives as of mid-1997. Nevertheless, some air-bag injuries can be serious, especially when someone gets in the path of an air bag early in its inflation. Here are some air-bag safety tips for the driver:

■ Sit at least 10 to 12 inches away from the steering wheel.

■ Hold the steering wheel from the sides so your arms aren't between your chest and the air bag cover.

■ If needed, use a booster cushion to help you see over the steering wheel.

■ HOLDING YOUR LIQUOR

Percentage of alcohol in the blood one hour after drinking

Examples of alcoholic drinks	Amount of alcohol (oz.)	Body weight (lbs.)					
		100	120	140	160	180	200
Three Dubonnet cocktails	3.0	.252	.208	.176	.152	.134	.119
Four Bloody Marys, Daiquiris, or Whiskey Sours	2.8	.234	.193	.163	.141	.124	.110
Two glasses Fish House Punch	2.6	.217	.178	.151	.130	.114	.101
Three Martinis or Manhattans or glasses malt liquor	2.4	.199	.163	.138	.119	.104	.092
Two Mai Tais or Mint Juleps	2.2	.181	.149	.125	.108	.094	.083
Four Champagne Cocktails	2.0	.163	.134	.113	.097	.084	.075
Two Margaritas	1.8	.146	.119	.100	.086	.057	.066
Two Martinis or Manhattans	1.6	.128	.104	.087	.075	.065	.057
Two highballs, Bloody Marys	1.4	.110	.089	.075	.063	.055	.048
Two 3 oz. glasses fortified wine (port, vermouth, etc.)	1.2	.092	.075	.062	.052	.045	.039
Two glasses beer	1.0	.075	.060	.049	.041	.035	.030
One Black Russian	0.8	.057	.045	.037	.030	.025	.021
One Sloe Gin Fizz	0.6	.039	.030	.024	.019	.015	.012
One 1 oz. cordial or liqueur	0.4	.021	.015	.011	.008	.006	.004

■ THE MEANING OF TIPSY

The bold figures represent the blood alcohol content past which you shouldn't drive:

BLOOD ALCOHOL CONTENT	EFFECTS ON FEELING AND BEHAVIOR	EFFECTS ON DRIVING ABILITY
.40 .20 .19 .18	At this point, most people have passed out.	Hopefully, driver passed out before trying to get into vehicle.
.17 .16 .15 .14 .13	Major impairment of all physical and mental functions. Irresponsible behavior. Euphoria. Some difficulty standing, walking, and talking.	Distortion of all perception and judgment. Driving erratic. Driver in a daze.
.12 .11 .10	Difficulty performing gross motor skills. Uncoordinated behavior. Definite impairment of mental abilities, judgment, and memory.	Judgment seriously affected. Physical difficulty in driving a vehicle.
.09 .08 .07	Feeling of relaxation. Mild sedation. Exaggeration of emotions and behavior. Slight impairment of motor skills. Increase in reaction time.	Drivers take too long to decide and act. Motor skills (such as braking) are impaired. Reaction time is increased.
.06 .05 .02	Absence of observable effects. Mild alteration of feelings, slight intensification of existing moods.	Mild changes. Most drivers seem a bit moody. Bad driving habits slightly pronounced.

SOURCES: National Clearinghouse for Alcohol and Drug Information; National Safety Council.

DRIVING SCHOOLS
▼

TRAINING TEENS FOR THE ROAD

Driver's ed has hit the skids. Here's how to find a good driving school

For teenagers, getting a driver's license is as much a rite of passage as learning to cavort with the opposite sex. For parents of new teen drivers, seeing their offspring slide behind the steering wheel can be a source of high anxiety. In fact, teenagers are seven times more likely to be involved in a fatal crash than adult drivers and 44 percent of teen drivers are involved in a collision before their 17th

birthday. Most disturbing, car crashes have become the number-one killer of teenagers between the ages of 16 and 19, and for the first time in years, teen fatalities and accidents are on the upswing.

Experts believe it's inexperience that is largely responsible for teen accidents. For many years, parents have relied on driver's education courses at public schools to teach their teens basic driving skills. But now, mainly because of school budget cuts and automobile liability costs, only about half of all high schools, or 8,200, offer driver's ed. The solution for many parents is to turn to professional driving schools.

Locating a driving school is the easy part. There are hundreds of them, ranging from one-man shops to nationwide operations. Besides checking the phone book for local driving schools, you can also get listings from the area chapter of the American Automobile Association (some AAAs operate their own driving schools) and from the Internet, where hundreds of regional driving schools have pages describing their programs. The more difficult part comes once you've zeroed in on a few candidates. How do you pick a reputable one? Here are some guidelines.

■ **FIND OUT IF THE SCHOOL IS ACCREDITED.** Call the schools that interest you and ask whether the school is affiliated with a state or national accrediting group. The most prominent seal of approval comes from the Driving School Association of the Americas (DSAA), with over 500 members nationwide. Robert Maxino, a past president of the DSAA and vice president of the Easy Method Driving School in Maryland, says that members of an association like the DSAA are guaranteed to be full-time driving schools, rather than part-time and possibly fly-by-night operations. Maxino adds that association members are provided with up-to-date technology and teaching methods.

■ **VISIT THE FACILITIES.** Once you've pared your list down to a few candidates, visit the driving schools. Check to see if the classroom is equipped with adequate

---

FACT FILE:

HANDING OVER THE KEYS

■ *In all 50 states, anyone applying for a first driver's license must take tests for vision, knowledge of state driving laws, and driving skills.*

■ *Only 31 states and the District of Columbia require learner's permits before getting a license. In Alaska, Arkansas, Michigan, Montana, Iowa, Kansas, and North and South Dakota, the minimum age for getting a permit is 14. In most other states the age is 15. In a few states, such as Delaware, Kentucky, Ohio, and New Jersey, new drivers must wait until 16.*

■ *In most states, the minimum age for getting a driver's license is 16. A few exceptions include: South Dakota, with the lowest minimum age of 14, and New Jersey, with the highest age of 17.*

CRUISE BEFORE YOU DRIVE

Most parents rely on two old standbys to pick a driving school—word of mouth or the yellow pages. But, a third option—surfing the Internet—is likely to turn up more information than you might expect. You can track down a local driving school, find out about state driving requirements, even get up-to-the minute traffic information in your hometown. Here are some Web sites worth the detour.

AAA ONLINE
http://www.aaa.com

■ This site of the American Automobile Association lists numerous free guides, such as *Choosing a Driving School*. Type in your zip code and you will be whisked directly to valuable driver information in your area.

TRAFFIC SAFETY INFORMATION VILLAGE
http://www.drivers.com

■ One of the Web's most comprehensive driving-related sites. Its page for new drivers is exhaustive, including driving laws, facts, and figures, as well as an extensive archive of articles on driving from various sources.

MR. TRAFFIC
http://www. mrtraffic.com

■ California driving authority Kenny Morse, also known as Mr. Traffic, dishes out all manner of driving advice for novices and more experienced drivers. Flashier than the Village but just as useful, it includes articles from choosing a good commercial school to the most stolen cars in America. The site has links to a teenage driving safety program and to state departments of motor vehicles.

NATIONAL HIGHWAY TRAFFIC SAFETY ADMINISTRATION
http://www.nhtsa.dot.gov

■ Find out about car safety, crash-test results, and vehicle recalls. Links to other safety and auto-related sites.

---

desks and audio and visual equipment. Make sure the textbooks are current.

■ **CHECK OUT THE CARS.** Driving courses include six to eight hours of on-the-road instruction, so be sure to look at the cars used. They should be no more than a few years old, and should include safety features such as a dual-control brake for the instructor, power steering and power brakes, and head restraints, in addition to safety belts and air bags, of course.

■ **TALK TO THE STAFF.** All instructors should have successfully completed driving courses from an association such as the DSAA, the American Driver and Traffic Safety Education Association, or the Association of Driver Educators for the Disabled. On top of that, says Maxino, choose an instructor who has completed at least two college-level courses in driver education.

■ **ASK ABOUT THE CURRICULUM.** Courses should last at least four to six weeks and include two to three hours of classroom instruction and two behind-the-wheel sessions of one-hour or more per week. Class size should be limited to 30 students. On-the-road instruction should include a variety of driving situations from city traffic to highways to rural roads.

■ **PROGRAMS TO AVOID.** Stay away from condensed or "intensive" courses, which do not provide enough time for students to learn the principles of controlling a car. Also be wary of cut-rate prices. A quality course costs $200 and up. Anyone charging less may be giving inadequate instructions, says Maxino.

EASY-AS-PIE CAR REPAIRS

Spare yourself grief; listen to "The Auto Repair Grandmother"

"Grandma" probably isn't the name that comes to mind when you need automotive repair advice, but then your grandmother isn't Lucille Treganowan. The 66-year-old auto-repair grandmother owns two Transmission by Lucille shops in Pittsburgh, hosts a weekly television show that can be seen throughout the country on HGTV, and writes an online auto column for *Microsoft Magazine*. Lucille first learned about fixing automobiles back in the '60s, while working as a bookkeeper for a local Pittsburgh garage. She began reading repair manuals and soon after began directing the shops' most difficult repairs. Now she's a legend in the automotive repair industry and also author of *Lucille's Car Care* (Hyperion, 1996). Here, the "grandmother of auto repair" sets you straight on the essentials of car maintenance:

■ **Whatever you do, change your oil.**

Today, with convenient and inexpensive drive-in oil-change outlets, you don't even need to bother with this procedure yourself. But don't rely completely on your 60-day visit for oil maintenance. Regularly check oil level yourself. It is one of the simplest things to do yet is often overlooked. Just remember, for an accurate reading you need to turn the car off and park it on level ground before checking the dipstick.

The frequency of your oil change depends upon the type of driving you do. If you're driving a family vehicle, where the majority of driving time is spent on short trips, then you should change the oil about every 60 days. People who spend more time driving highways and interstates, like salesmen, can go longer between changes.

■ **Check coolant colors as well as levels: They should be clear or green.**

The National Car Care Council reports over-heating as the number-one motorist complaint. This usually occurs due to low coolant level. Always make certain you allow the engine to cool for at least 20 minutes before removing the radiator cap. If the fluid level checks, the problem may be a faulty thermostat or even a bad radiator cap.

I like to change my radiator fluid every two years. But depending upon your driving habits, you can go much longer between changes. Get in the habit of checking all your fluids. If the coolant still looks clear and green, you can keep it.

■ **When you change one hose, change them all.**

With hoses you need to look at the condition of the rubber. Usually, when one goes, others will follow. If you find the hoses have lost their flexibility and feel brittle or stiff, there's the possibility they may split or crack in the near future. Residue around the clamps, caused by leaking, is also a sign a hose may need to be changed.

Unlike hoses, belt wear is much more difficult to see. To play it safe, change your belts every four years.

■ **Don't sacrifice quality for price when buying a battery.**

Batteries are like shoes—you can buy good ones or bad ones. The length of time they're good for varies, although typically they'll last three to four years. The complex electrical systems have made batteries much more important than simply a device to start the engine. In some newer cars, a bad battery can send your car into the limp mode—meaning it will limp and sputter its way into the repair shop. Even transmissions and steering have become dependent on the battery.

■ **Use your ears when it comes to brakes.**

To check your brakes you need to pull the wheels off. Most people aren't going to go

ALTERNATIVES TO KICKING THE TIRES

You don't have to get yourself covered with grease to tell quickly whether a car has been well maintained. The following tips for reading a car's history will save you lots of headaches later:

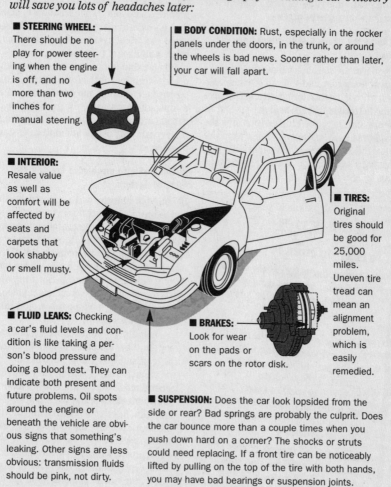

■ **STEERING WHEEL:** There should be no play for power steering when the engine is off, and no more than two inches for manual steering.

■ **BODY CONDITION:** Rust, especially in the rocker panels under the doors, in the trunk, or around the wheels is bad news. Sooner rather than later, your car will fall apart.

■ **INTERIOR:** Resale value as well as comfort will be affected by seats and carpets that look shabby or smell musty.

■ **TIRES:** Original tires should be good for 25,000 miles. Uneven tire tread can mean an alignment problem, which is easily remedied.

■ **FLUID LEAKS:** Checking a car's fluid levels and condition is like taking a person's blood pressure and doing a blood test. They can indicate both present and future problems. Oil spots around the engine or beneath the vehicle are obvious signs that something's leaking. Other signs are less obvious: transmission fluids should be pink, not dirty.

■ **BRAKES:** Look for wear on the pads or scars on the rotor disk.

■ **SUSPENSION:** Does the car look lopsided from the side or rear? Bad springs are probably the culprit. Does the car bounce more than a couple times when you push down hard on a corner? The shocks or struts could need replacing. If a front tire can be noticeably lifted by pulling on the top of the tire with both hands, you may have bad bearings or suspension joints.

through that. Luckily, your ears can pick out most brake problems. When brake pads need to be replaced, listen for a singing/whistling noise. A scratching/metal grinding noise indicates your pads or footings have worn away to the point where metal is rubbing against metal. In such cases, bring your car into a garage immediately. The time it takes for this to occur will depend upon your personal driving habits. I have a tendency to use my brakes a bit much, so I need to change my brake pads about once a year.

■ **Ignore smells at your own peril.**

A smoky smell is a good indication of oil leaking onto something hot. A nasty acid odor, like the smell of something caught in your vacuum cleaner, points to wires burning. In the case of the burning wires, you should first pull over, turn the car off, and if the smell persists, disconnect the battery, which will interrupt the flow of electrical currents through the battery.

■ Apply the penny test to check your tire tread.

If you place a Lincoln-head penny in a tire's lowest tread spot, and you can see the president's head, it's time for new tires. The variation in tread height is usually due to a tire's air pressure. If you overinflate your tires, the inside tread will tend to wear first. If your tire is low, the outside tread will wear first. By purchasing a $4 air gauge, you can check your tires for correct inflation.

FACT FILE:

FIX IT OR JUNK IT?

■ **ENGINE OVERHAUL:** *If the engine is worn out, making a lot of noise, blowing smoke, or has no power, it might need an overhaul. That's when an engine gets rebuilt to the manufacturer's specification. For a 4-cylinder engine, it might cost $2,000 to $3,000. For an 8-cylinder it can get up to $4,000. That's when you have to evaluate if it's worth putting that much money into the vehicle.*

■ **AUTOMATIC TRANSMISSION:** *The automatic transmission should be serviced every 25,000 miles. Symptoms of automatic transmission failure are that the vehicle feels as if it lacks power, is going nowhere, or is making grinding noises. The majority just won't drive. If you have a transmission failure, it could cost $1,200 to $3,000 to fix.*

■ Don't jump to jump-start a car that won't start.

If you turn the key, and the car slowly turns, or you hear only a series of clicks, you probably have a low battery. In this case, a jump start can remedy the situation, but before you try one, check your owner's manual to make sure it's safe. In many newer cars' sophisticated electrical systems jump starts can cause a number of problems.

When using jumper cables, connect the positive terminal of the fresh battery to the positive terminal of the dead battery, and the negative terminal of the fresh battery to a metal ground. Have the car with the fresh battery running before attempting to start the second.

■ Think of auto mechanics the way you think of doctors.

If you visit a doctor with a stomachache, and before any tests are taken, the doctor recommends immediate removal of your appendix, most people would think the doctor a quack and seek a second opinion. But, if the same person sees a mechanic with a battery problem, and before performing any tests the mechanic recommends replacing your alternator, most people would take the mechanic's advice.

Just like the stomachache, a low battery may have a number of causes. Something as simple as a loose fan belt could be the culprit. Simply taking your car to a second mechanic could end up saving you hundreds of dollars in repair bills—and the hassle of returning to the mechanic because the real problem was never fixed.

Approach with caution any mechanic who won't discuss price. After looking over your car, a competent and honest mechanic should have little problem offering a rough estimate on the cost of parts and labor. Repair scams occur when you allow the mechanic to begin work before discussing price; once they have your car torn apart, they'll tell you you already owe so much in labor that you might as well go ahead with the rest of the repairs.

CHAPTER TEN

SPORTS & GAMES

■ **WHAT'S AHEAD: SEND** for tickets today to see Tiger Woods at the next Masters... **IMPROVE** your odds of winning the next office pool... **CATCH** a preseason baseball game in Florida or Arizona... **TAKE A SWING** at one of America's 10 best public golf courses... **CLIMB** Astroman in Yosemite if you're up for a challenge... **HEAD OUT** to Looe Key to snorkel among sunken ships... **SKI** top-rated Whistler/Blackcomb, in British Columbia... **TRY** snowboarding, which is no longer just for the grunge set... **STRAP ON** snowshoes for a winter workout...

A FAN'S GUIDE

BEING THERE
▼

A TICKET FOR ALL SEASONS

Watch the game, not the box. Here's how to get a seat for big events

Most couch potatoes' idea of a good seat for the Super Bowl is in front of a wide-screen television. But for real sports fans, nothing beats being there—whether it's the Super Bowl, the World Series, the Masters, or whatever. Getting tickets to some of the nation's sporting events—like the Masters, for example—is next to impossible. But you can get in the door to some of the others if you do some advance planning and are prepared for a little hustle. Here's the lowdown on how and where to get tickets to some of the hottest sporting events.

THE SUPER BOWL
January 25, 1998
Jack Murphy Stadium, San Diego, Calif.

 Football's biggest game is the world's most-watched television event each year, but the Super Bowl itself is not all that hard to see in person, if you're willing to pay the hefty ticket price ($275 on average last year). Season-ticket holders of the participating teams have the best shot; the AFC and NFC champs split 35 percent of the Super Bowl ducats, most of which are made available to their faithful fans. The host team gets another 10 percent of the tickets, and every other NFL team gets hundreds of tickets, which they generally sell to their own ticket holders. The league also distributes several thousand tickets each year through a lottery it conducts. You can enter by sending a self-addressed stamped envelope to the league's office between February and June. The NFL's address is 410 Park Ave., New York, NY 10022.

WORLD SERIES
October 1998; Place to be determined

 The participating teams control virtually all the tickets to baseball's Fall Classic, so your best bet is to hold season tickets for your favorite team—and hope they make it all the way.

NCAA FINAL FOUR
March 28 and 30, 1998
Alamo Dome, San Antonio, Texas

 You practically have to jump through hoops to watch the best college-basketball teams fight for the national championship each year. Your chances of getting a Final Four ticket have improved since 1997 when the NCAA began holding championship games in aren-

SNAGGING A SEAT, WHEN THERE AREN'T ANY

Just because the game is sold out doesn't mean that you can't get a ticket. Here's a scalper's guide

Selling tickets at more than face value is illegal in many places. But it is the scalpers who face arrest, not the ticket buyers. And if a game is completely sold out—or so the newspaper says—buying a scalped tickets can be your best and only way to see the game in person.

Scalping, of course, is somewhat of a covert activity. Reselling tickets at any price on stadium grounds is illegal in some places, so much of the commerce takes place in surrounding areas. You may get a good deal here, but you're probably better off waiting.

The more scalpers you see, the more patient you should be; as game time approaches, the prices will drop. If the game is not sold out, or if demand is not high, try to wait until right before the game starts, and you'll discover a buyer's market. Desperate to unload tickets, scalpers will sell them for as little as a third of the price they paid.

If it's a very big game, the seekers will far outnumber the sellers, and prices may be steep. Scalped tickets at events like the Super Bowl and Final Four can run as high as $1,000. Try to bargain for the best price you can get. Most scalpers are trying to do brisk business, so they may take your reasonable offer.

Before you decide to buy, make sure to get a good look at the tickets; fake ones are often sold, and while you may not be able to recognize them, it's worth a try. Whatever you do, don't buy a press pass; it's probably fake, and even if it's not, you're almost sure to get discovered and thrown out.

---

as that seat over 30,000, but it's still going to be tough. In 1996, over 91,000 applicants vied for 1,000 available tickets in the Meadowlands Arena with 18,500 seats. While the 1997 games were held in the Hoosier Dome, which seats 47,000—more than twice the number of seats in the '96 games—just 16,000 went to the general public; the others went to the competing colleges and the host, coaches, corporate sponsors, and college sports officials. The NCAA received 167,900 applications for those 16,000 tickets—the second highest number of applicants in NCAA history. The NCAA begins taking applications just after the previous year's tournament. Write to NCAA, 6201 College Blvd., Overland Park, KS 66211.

THE MASTERS

April 9–12, 1998; Augusta, Ga.

 It's almost as hard to watch golf's big event in person as it is to play a round at Augusta National, the famous Georgia course on which it is played each year. Only the lucky few on Augusta National's "patron's list" are allowed to buy tickets each year. The list is made up primarily of people who had been attending the tournament before 1968, and those people who've been added to it off the very long waiting list—which itself was closed to new members in 1978. Your best chance of seeing top golfers play at Augusta National is to go a few days early for the practice rounds. Fans interested in those tickets should write the club just after the end of the previous year's tournament: Augusta National, P.O. Box 2086, Augusta, GA 30903.

If you care more about great golf than the majesty of the Masters, you might want to check out the U.S. Open. The 1998 Open, which will be held June 18–24 at the Olympic Club in San Francisco, sells tickets to the general public on a first-come, first-served basis. Tickets go on sale, by mail or fax, the day after the 1997 Open ends. For more information, contact the U.S. Golf Association's sales office at ☎ 800–336–4446, or write P.O. Box 1500, Far Hills, NJ 07931.

EXPERT TIPS

YOUR ODDS OF WINNING THE OFFICE POOL

Sports gambling is a losing proposition for all but the savviest—and luckiest—bettors. We asked Russ Culver, who runs the sports book at Palace Station Casino in Las Vegas, and helps set the Associated Press odds that appear in hundreds of newspapers, for tips on winning the office pool:

■ **Look for trends.** Statistics aren't as telling as shifts in a team's fortunes and ability. "Knowing that a team goes 8-1 on Thursdays probably isn't important, but knowing that the Bears haven't won a road game since 1987 may well be," says Culver.

■ **Ignore the polls.** Associated Press polls of the nation's best college basketball and football teams are "nothing more than beauty contest," Culver says. When you look at the NCAA tournament bracket in the office pool, bet against the glamour teams when they are playing a strong team that's not as popular.

■ **Momentum matters.** In baseball, focus on a pitcher's last five starts. In college hoops, look at how a team played down the stretch period just before the NCAA tournament. A team that finished third in its league in the regular season, but came on strong to win the conference, deserves a good look.

■ **Seedings mean little in the NCAA tournament.** "The NCAA will never admit it," says Culver, "but those seedings are gerrymandered to give them the best matchups for television. The No.1 and No.2 ranked teams are accurate, but from No.4 to about 12, they screw around with those for TV."

INDIANAPOLIS 500

May 24, 1998; Indianapolis Motor Speedway

Hundreds of thousands of people turn out every year for auto racing's big day, which is also one of the world's biggest parties. But despite the huge number of seats, it's still a tough ticket. About 95 percent of the 300,000 seats are filled through renewals—people who attend the race one year and, within a week, request renewals or upgrades for the next year's 500.

To request tickets for the first time, you must send a check or money order (no credit cards) to the Indianapolis Motor Speedway, 4790 W. 16th St., Indianapolis, IN 46222, immediately after the end of the prior year's race. Timing is crucial: Requests received before the race will be returned. New requests are considered in the order of the date received. The only seats that are ever available to new requesters are the least-expensive seats ($30 in 1998); all other seats are filled by repeaters. While many new requests get turned down, there is hope: If you're turned away one year, your request will get considered before other new requesters if you apply for tickets again the following year. And if you really want to see the race, the speedway sells general-admission, standing-room-only tickets the day of the race. But these are a last resort: Peggy Swalls, director of ticket operations, describes them as "partial view."

KENTUCKY DERBY

May 2, 1998; Churchilll Downs, Ky.

The infield is the place to be for the Run for the Roses; more than 80,000 people mill around inside the track oval drinking juleps each year, while about 48,000 sit in the cushier boxes.

The box seats (sold in sets of six) and the infield tickets are available by writing to the Kentucky Derby ticket office at 700 Central Ave., Louisville, KY 40208, at the conclusion of the previous year's race.

BASEBALL FAN'S GUIDE

TAKE ME OUT TO THE BALL GAME

You can still get peanuts and Cracker Jacks, of course. But the fare is getting fancier at a lot of America's ballparks. In Baltimore, you might try the crab cakes; in L.A., the sushi; in Miami, the empanadas and Cuban sandwiches. But the game is the same. Here's the batting order for the 1998 season. As always, the World Series is scheduled for October.

Team	LAST TITLE		Stadium	Capacity	Ticket information
	World Series	League			
AMERICAN LEAGUE EAST					
BALTIMORE ORIOLES	1983	1983	Oriole Park at Camden Yards	48,079	410–685–9500
BOSTON RED SOX	1918	1986	Fenway Park	33,871	617–267–8661
DETROIT TIGERS	1984	1984	Tiger Stadium	52,416	313–962–4000
NEW YORK YANKEES	1996	1996	Yankee Stadium	57,545	718–293–6000
TORONTO BLUE JAYS	1993	1993	Skydome	50,516	416–341–1111
AMERICAN LEAGUE CENTRAL					
CHICAGO WHITE SOX	1917	1959	Comiskey Park	44,321	312–924–1000
CLEVELAND INDIANS	1948	1995	Jacobs Field	42,400	216–241–5555
KANSAS CITY ROYALS	1985	1985	Kauffman Stadium	40,625	816–921–8000
MILWAUKEE BREWERS	—	1982	County Stadium	53,192	414–933–1818
MINNESOTA TWINS	1991	1991	Hubert H. Humphrey Metrodome	56,783	612–375–7444
AMERICAN LEAGUE WEST					
ANAHEIM ANGELS	—	—	Anaheim Stadium	64,593	714–940–2000
OAKLAND ATHLETICS	1989	1990	Oakland–Alameda County Stadium	47,313	510–638–0500
SEATTLE MARINERS	—	—	Kingdome	59,702	206–628–3555
TEXAS RANGERS	—	—	The Ballpark in Arlington	48,100	817–273–5222
NATIONAL LEAGUE EAST					
ATLANTA BRAVES	1995	1996	Turner Field	49,831	404–522–7630
FLORIDA MARLINS	—	—	Joe Robbie Stadium	46,238	305–626–7400
MONTREAL EXPOS	—	—	Olympic Stadium	46,500	800–463–9767
NEW YORK METS	1986	1986	Shea Stadium	55,601	718–507–8499
PHILADELPHIA PHILLIES	1980	1993	Veterans Stadium	62,238	215–463–1000
NATIONAL LEAGUE CENTRAL					
CHICAGO CUBS	1908	1945	Wrigley Field	38,765	312–404–2827
CINCINNATI REDS	1990	1990	Riverfront Stadium	52,952	513–421–7337
HOUSTON ASTROS	—	—	Astrodome	53,821	713–799–9555
PITTSBURGH PIRATES	1979	1979	Three Rivers Stadium	47,972	412–321–2827
ST. LOUIS CARDINALS	1982	1987	Busch Stadium	57,078	314–421–4060
NATIONAL LEAGUE WEST					
COLORADO ROCKIES	—	—	Coors Field	50,400	303–762–5437
LOS ANGELES DODGERS	1988	1988	Dodger Stadium	56,000	213–224–1400
SAN DIEGO PADRES	—	1984	San Diego Jack Murphy Stadium	46,510	619–881–6500
SAN FRANCISCO GIANTS	1954	1989	Candlestick Park	63,000	415–467–8000

CAL RIPKEN GETS UP TO BAT

*Advice from a legend on turning a
Little Leaguer into an All-Star*

With major-league baseball stars signing multimillion-dollar contracts and basking in the spotlight, it's tempting for parents to look at their little athletes and say: "Hmmm. If I just push him a little harder..."

Don't do it, says Cal Ripken, Jr. The Baltimore Orioles baseball star and author of the bestselling book *The Only Way I Know* (Viking, 1997) wowed the world with his gritty, gracious pursuit of Lou Gehrig's consecutive-game streak and understands the temptation that parents feel (he's got two kids of his own, after all). But he counsels parents to let kids develop an appreciation for baseball and other sports at their own pace. Pushing them won't help, he says. "In order to instill passion for the game, it has to be inside of you. And it's only going to develop if a kid comes to it on his or her own, and if it's fun."

Although Ripken grew up in a baseball family (his dad, Cal Sr., was a long-time coach for the Orioles), he was not pushed into playing the game. Still, his

desire to play in the big leagues burned inside him, and from an early age: The night before his first Little League game, he surreptitiously slept in his uniform, his glove by his side. He just wanted to be ready, he said.

Here are Ripken's tips for the nearly 3 million kids who play on Little League teams, and for their parents:

■ **What's the best way to get kids interested in baseball?**

Gear it to whatever makes kids enjoy playing. The worst thing you can see is to go to a Little League game and have parents yelling at the kids. Too much emphasis on winning saps a lot of the fun out of it. Kids should be encouraged to play any position they want, and to experiment.

■ **How do you make it fun?**

Just let them see how much you enjoy it. I take my young son to the batting cage, and he watches me having a good time. Be a good teacher to your kids, and they'll learn to love the game from you.

■ **What's the right age to start?**

My first competition was as an 8-year-old, which was the age when kids could really play the whole game—hitting, throwing, and running. I think it's great you're now shown parts of the game through T-ball and other games like that. Kids can learn how to slide and run a lot earlier than I did.

■ **A lot of kids love to play but hate to practice. How do you make practice fun?**

To learn baseball, like other things, you have to teach fundamentals, and then give kids time to practice them. Repetition is key, but it's boring. The answer is to figure out creative ways to make it fun—to find games within the games. Take a game like pepper, and come up with a system where you get points for catches and good throws and make it a competition. The kids won't even realize they've fielded 100 ground balls.

■ **How should young pitchers train?**

In order to develop your arm you need to develop arm strength, and the way you do

FACT FILE:

A GOLD MEDAL EVENT

■ *Although baseball is the American pastime, it wasn't an official Olympic sport until the 1992 Summer Games in Barcelona. A big difference: in Olympic baseball, you can use aluminum bats.*

FOLLOWING THE BOYS OF SUMMER

For spring training, fans have two choices: the Grapefruit League in Florida or the Cactus League in Arizona. Here are some places to catch a game before the regular season starts.

TEAM		STADIUM	CAPACITY	TICKET INFO
AMERICAN LEAGUE				
EAST	Baltimore Orioles	Fort Lauderdale Stadium, Fort Lauderdale, Fla.	8,340	954–776–1921
	Boston Red Sox	City of Palms Park, Fort Myers, Fla.	6,850	941–334–4700
	Detroit Tigers	Merchant Stadium, Lakeland, Fla.	7,027	941–499–8229
	New York Yankees	Legends Field, Tampa, Fla.	10,000	813–879–2244
	Toronto Blue Jays	Grant Field, Dunedin, Fla.	6,218	813–733–9302
CENTRAL	Chicago White Sox	Ed Smith Stadium, Sarasota, Fla.	7,500	813–287–8844
	Cleveland Indians	Chain O'Lakes Stadium, Winter Haven, Fla.	7,042	813–291–5803
	Kansas City Royals	Baseball City Stadium, Davenport, Fla.	7,000	407–839–3900
	Milwaukee Brewers	Compadre Stadium, Chandler, Ariz.	10,000	602–895–1200
	Minnesota Twins	Lee County Stadium, Fort Myers, Fla.	7,500	800–338–9467
WEST	Anaheim Angels	Diablo Stadium, Tempe, Ariz.	9,785	602–438–4300
	Oakland Athletics	Municipal Stadium, Phoenix, Ariz.	8,500	602–225–9400
	Seattle Mariners	Peoria Stadium, Peoria, Ariz.	10,000	602–784–4444
	Texas Rangers	Charlotte Co. Stadium, Port Charlotte, Fla.	6,026	813–625–9500
NATIONAL LEAGUE				
EAST	Atlanta Braves	Municipal Stadium, West Palm Beach, Fla.	7,200	561–683–6100
	Florida Marlins	Space Coast Stadium, Melbourne, Fla.	7,200	407–633–9200
	Montreal Expos	Municipal Stadium, West Palm Beach, Fla.	7,200	561–966–3309
	New York Mets	St. Lucie Co. Stadium, Port St. Lucie, Fla.	7,400	561–871–2115
	Philadelphia Phillies	Jack Russell Stadium, Clearwater, Fla.	7,195	813–442–8496
CENTRAL	Chicago Cubs	HoHoKam Park, Mesa, Ariz.	8,963	602–964–4467
	Cincinnati Reds	Reds Spring Training Complex, Plant City, Fla.	6,700	813–752–7337
	Houston Astros	Osceola Co. Stadium, Kissimmee, Fla.	5,100	407–839–3900
	Pittsburgh Pirates	McKechnie Field, Bradenton, Fla.	6,562	941–748–4610
	St. Louis Cardinals	Roger Dean Stadium, Jupiter, Fla.	6,950	561–775–1818
WEST	Colorado Rockies	Hi Corbett Field, Tucson, Ariz.	7,726	602–327–9467
	Los Angeles Dodgers	Holman Stadium, Vero Beach, Fla.	6,500	561–569–6858
	San Diego Padres	Peoria Stadium, Peoria, Ariz.	10,000	602–878–4337
	San Francisco Giants	Scottsdale Stadium, Scottsdale, Ariz.	10,000	602–784–4444

that is by throwing straight. Throwing curves doesn't help build up kids' arms. I don't think you want to not allow them to throw curve balls, but you should make sure that they throw 70 to 80 percent fastballs. You can always teach a kid who has a good arm to throw breaking balls, but if you don't have arm strength, you can't learn to throw a fastball.

■ **Major leaguers sometimes violate the fundamentals. What do you tell a kid?**

I'll be at a clinic telling kids how important it is to throw overhand, and a kid'll say, "On TV you threw the ball sidearm on a double play." I'll say, "When you get older, you can do these things to speed up your throws. When I was your age, I threw overhand." That's the truth, and it's all you can say.

FOOTBALL FAN'S GUIDE

GET READY FOR THE KICK-OFF

Not since the Romans put a gladiator in a ring with a lion has a sport been so brutal and so popular. Men and boys—and increasingly women and girls—huddle in front of the TV set to watch hulking grown men throw themselves at each other. But that experience doesn't compare to being at the stadium in person.

Team	LAST TITLE		Stadium	Capacity	Ticket information
	Super Bowl	Conference			
AMERICAN FOOTBALL CONFERENCE EAST					
BUFFALO BILLS	—	1994	Rich Stadium	80,091	716–649–0015
INDIANAPOLIS COLTS	1971	1971	RCA Dome	60,272	317–297–7000
MIAMI DOLPHINS	1974	1985	Pro Player Stadium	73,000	305–620–5000
NEW ENGLAND PATRIOTS	—	1997	Foxboro Stadium	60,794	508–543–1776
NEW YORK JETS	1969	1969	Giants Stadium	76,891	516–538–7200
AMERICAN FOOTBALL CONFERENCE CENTRAL					
BALTIMORE RAVENS	—	—	Memorial Stadium	60,020	410–547–5696
CINCINNATI BENGALS	—	1989	Cinergy Field	60,389	513–621–3550
HOUSTON OILERS	—	—	Astrodome	62,439	713–797–1000
JACKSONVILLE JAGUARS	—	—	Jacksonville Stadium	73,000	904–633–6000
PITTSBURGH STEELERS	1980	1996	Three Rivers Stadium	59,600	412–323–1200
AMERICAN FOOTBALL CONFERENCE WEST					
DENVER BRONCOS	—	1990	Mile High Stadium	76,273	303–433–7466
KANSAS CITY CHIEFS	1970	1970	Alltell Chiefs Stadium	77,872	816–924–9400
OAKLAND RAIDERS	1984	1984	Quallecomm Stadium, Jack Murphy Field	65,000	310–322–5901
SAN DIEGO CHARGERS	—	1995	San Diego Jack Murphy Stadium	60,836	619–280–2121
SEATTLE SEAHAWKS	—	—	Kingdome	66,400	206–827–9766
NATIONAL FOOTBALL CONFERENCE EAST					
ARIZONA CARDINALS	—	—	Sun Devil Stadium	73,521	602–379–0102
DALLAS COWBOYS	1996	1996	Texas Stadium	65,024	214–579–5000
NEW YORK GIANTS	1991	1991	Giants Stadium	77,311	201–935–8222
PHILADELPHIA EAGLES	—	1981	Veterans Stadium	65,187	215–463–5500
WASHINGTON REDSKINS	1992	1992	Jack Kent Cooke Stadium	78,000	202–546–2222
NATIONAL FOOTBALL CONFERENCE CENTRAL					
CHICAGO BEARS	1986	1986	Soldier Field	66,950	312–663–5100
DETROIT LIONS	—	—	Pontiac Silverdome	80,500	313–335–4151
GREEN BAY PACKERS	1997	1997	Lambeau Field	59,543	414–496–5719
MINNESOTA VIKINGS	—	1977	Metrodome	63,000	612–333–8828
TAMPA BAY BUCCANEERS	—	—	Houlihan Stadium	74,296	813–870–2700
NATIONAL FOOTBALL CONFERENCE WEST					
ATLANTA FALCONS	—	—	Georgia Dome	70,500	404–223–8000
CAROLINA PANTHERS	—	—	Ericcson Stadium	72,300	704–358–7000
NEW ORLEANS SAINTS	—	—	Louisiana Superdome	69,065	504–522–2600
SAN FRANCISCO 49ERS	1995	1995	Candlestick Park	66,513	415–468–2249
ST. LOUIS RAMS	—	1980	Trans World Dome	67,000	314–982–4267

PEEWEE FOOTBALL
▼

SHOULD KIDS PLAY FOOTBALL?

Is soccer a safer alternative? Our experts tackle the questions

Your eight-year-old comes home one day and proudly announces his intention to try out for the local peewee football team. You've just finished watching another NFL quarterback get carried off the field on a stretcher. It's hard not to picture your son in the same position some day. Do you let him play?

Dr. Jeffrey L. Brown, a clinical associate professor in pediatrics and psychiatry at New York Hospital–Cornell Medical Center, compares such a decision to the many other major choices parents must make each day about their children, from what kind of school they should attend to whether and when they should drive a car. "You take into account the child's wishes, and the risk or benefit for them. But ultimately, the decision should always be the parents'," says Brown.

Okay, so you know your child's wishes: He wants to play. What are the risks and benefits of letting him participate?

How you weigh the two varies to some extent from child to child, especially as they grow older. Participating in a sport like football may be more important for children who "need it for self-esteem," Brown says, because it makes them "stand out" in high school or is their "ticket to college." Those factors must be considered against the chances of "putting the body at risk."

How great is that risk? That, too, varies depending on the level of play. In general, football has become much safer in the last 25 years as equipment has improved and rules have been tightened to prevent certain kinds of hitting, says Frederick O. Mueller, who heads the National Center for Catastrophic Sports Injury Research at the University of North Carolina at Chapel Hill. The number of deaths and paralyzing injuries caused by football has dropped dramatically since the late 1960s. In 1968, 36 people died from football-related injuries; in 1994, the latest year for which statistics are available, just one person died. Similar declines in the number of permanently disabling head and neck injuries have brought the annual number down to fewer than 10 a year, says Mueller. "Those numbers are low," he says, though that won't be any consolation "if it's your son or daughter."

While catastrophic injuries are relatively rare these days, knee injuries and concussions appear to be on the rise. Knee injuries especially trouble doctors. "If you screw up your knees playing football," says Brown, "they're hurt for the rest of your life." Brown and Mueller both warn parents to be cautious, but neither aggressively discourages kids from playing football, especially at younger ages, when the level of play is less intense and knee injuries are generally less severe. Mueller advises parents to look carefully at the coach and the kind of program he runs— finding out what kind of emergency equipment is on the sidelines at games, for instance, and what kind of preparation is taken to prevent players from getting heat stroke, which has killed several football players in recent years.

Many other sports are just as dangerous as football, if not more so. Per capita, the rates of serious injury are higher in ice hockey, gymnastics, and pole vaulting. Indeed, soccer, often the alternative of choice for those who eschew football, has some drawbacks of its own. Recent studies suggest that soccer players may have abnormal brain-wave readings and lower IQs than other people, probably attributable to hitting the ball repeatedly with their heads. Repeated heading puts soccer players at the same kind of risk as boxers, the studies suggest. "I've been sending kids off to play soccer," Brown admits, "but the better choice may be lacrosse."

A WHO'S WHO OF HOOPSTERS

When the Basketball Association of America and National Basketball League merged just after the 1948–49 season, the National Basketball Association was born. But it wasn't until the early '80s that the NBA exploded in popularity. In 1995, the NBA added expansion teams in Vancouver and Toronto. As of the 1997 season, the Washington Bullets are known as the Wizards. Here's the line-up for the 1997–98 season.

Team	LAST TITLE League	Conference	Stadium	Capacity	Ticket information
EASTERN CONFERENCE ATLANTIC DIVISION					
BOSTON CELTICS	1986	1987	FleetCenter	18,400	617–523–3030
MIAMI HEAT	—	—	Miami Arena	15,200	305–577–4328
NEW JERSEY NETS	—	—	Byrne Meadowlands Arena	20,029	201–935–8888
NEW YORK KNICKERBOCKERS	1973	1994	Madison Square Garden	19,763	212–465–6000
ORLANDO MAGIC	—	1995	Orlando Arena	16,010	407–649–2255
PHILADELPHIA 76ERS	1983	1983	CoreStates Center	21,000	215–339–7676
WASHINGTON WIZARDS	1978	1978	MCI Center	20,000	301–622–3865
EASTERN CONFERENCE CENTRAL DIVISION					
ATLANTA HAWKS	1958	1961	The Omni	16,368	404–827–3865
CHARLOTTE HORNETS	—	—	Charlotte Coliseum	23,698	704–357–0489
CHICAGO BULLS	1997	1997	United Center	21,500	312–455–4000
CLEVELAND CAVALIERS	—	—	Gund Arena	21,500	216–420–2000
DETROIT PISTONS	1990	1990	The Palace of Auburn Hills	21,454	313–337–0100
INDIANA PACERS	—	—	Market Square Arena	16,530	317–263–2100
MILWAUKEE BUCKS	1971	1974	Bradley Center	18,633	414–227–0500
TORONTO RAPTORS	—	—	SkyDome	22,500	416–366–3865
WESTERN CONFERENCE MIDWEST DIVISION					
DALLAS MAVERICKS	—	—	Reunion Arena	17,502	214–939–2800
DENVER NUGGETS	—	—	McNichols Sports Arena	17,171	303–893–3865
HOUSTON ROCKETS	1995	1995	The Summit	16,611	713–627–0600
MINNESOTA TIMBERWOLVES	—	—	Target Center	19,006	612–673–1313
SAN ANTONIO SPURS	—	—	Alamodome	20,640	210–554–7787
UTAH JAZZ	—	1997	Delta Center	19,911	801–355–3865
WESTERN CONFERENCE PACIFIC DIVISION					
GOLDEN STATE WARRIORS	1975	1975	Oakland Coliseum Arena	15,025	510–638–6300
LOS ANGELES CLIPPERS	—	—	Los Angeles Memorial Sports Arena	16,005	213–748–0500
LOS ANGELES LAKERS	1988	1991	The Great Western Forum	17,505	213–480–3232
PHOENIX SUNS	—	1993	America West Arena	19,023	602–379–7867
PORTLAND TRAIL BLAZERS	1977	1992	Rose Garden	21,401	503–231–8000
SACRAMENTO KINGS	1951	1996	Arco Arena	17,317	916–928–6900
SEATTLE SUPERSONICS	1979	1979	Key Arena	17,102	206–283–3865
VANCOUVER GRIZZLIES	—	—	GM Place	20,004	604–688–5867

THE HOME COURT ADVANTAGE

What you need to know to build the hoop of your dreams

D r. James Naismith created the first home basketball hoop by nailing a peach basket to a pole more than a century ago. Designing your home court today is not so easy or inexpensive. But your options are many, ranging widely in quality, durability, and price.

Mobility is crucial to playing basketball. The traditional 10-foot mounted backboards and pole-secured backboards are still available for those who want to practice on a regulation hoop. But players trying to dunk like Michael Jordan or shoot three-pointers can get awfully frustrated if Dad pulls the car into the driveway under the hoop.

Portable baskets and baskets with adjustable heights are sturdier than they once were. Players who compete in leagues or gyms should be especially careful in selecting a rim. A springed rim (which gives a little when the ball hits it) will give the shooter a better bounce, but it can cause frustration when the player returns to a real court where tighter steel rims are the rule. To get the ultimate home-court advantage, here are the options:

MOUNTED BACKBOARD
Price: around $80

■ The most common of home-court hoops can be attached to the wall of a house or garage with a few nuts and bolts.
■ **PROS:** Very sturdy.
■ **CONS:** The backboard cannot be moved. The height can't be adjusted either.

PORTABLE BACKBOARD
Price: $200–$300

■ Wheels on the base of the basket allow you to move it easily by simply tilting the basket forward. The base should be filled with sand or a combination of water and antifreeze to keep the basket from moving. The height can be adjusted from 7 to the regulation 10 feet. Less expensive portable backboards are made of graphite. The more expensive ones have acrylic backboards that shake less and hold up better in inclement weather.
■ **PROS:** The basket can be easily moved to other locations, and the height can be easily adjusted for players of all ages.
■ **CONS:** The basket will still shake on hard shots. The base can at times be wobbly.

IN-GROUND HOOP
Price: around $300

■ The acrylic backboard is attached to a steel pole and inserted in the ground. The height can be adjusted from 7 to 10 feet.
■ **PROS:** With an acrylic backboard and base in the ground, this is the sturdiest option.
■ **CONS:** It's the most expensive option, and the game cannot be moved.

FACT FILE:

HERE COME THE HOOPSTER-ETTES

■ *The number of women playing basketball has risen 24 percent since 1990, thanks partly to the Gold Medal performance of the U.S. women's team in the '96 Summer Olympics.*

■ *The launching of two pro women's leagues, the American Basketball League and the Women's National Basketball Association, is likely to further increase women's participation in the game. Attendance at the '96–'97 ABL games averaged 3,500 fans per game, exceeding expectations by 20 percent.*

THE FASTEST GAME ON ICE

The top eight teams in each conference qualify for the Stanley Cup playoffs, the outcome of which determines the League's champion. At least one team from each division makes the playoffs. These division leaders are seeded first and second. One plays eight, two plays seven, and so on. The divisions:

TEAM	First season in NHL	Stanley Cups* (most recent win)	Stadium	Capacity	Ticket information
EASTERN CONFERENCE ATLANTIC DIVISION					
FLORIDA PANTHERS	1993–94	0	Miami Arena	14,500	305–358–5885
NEW JERSEY DEVILS	1974–75	1 (1995)	Meadowlands Arena	19,040	201–935–3900
NEW YORK ISLANDERS	1972–73	4 (1983)	Nassau Coliseum	16,927	516–888–9000
NEW YORK RANGERS	1926–27	4 (1994)	Madison Square Garden	18,200	212–465–6741
PHILADELPHIA FLYERS	1967–68	2 (1975)	The CoreStates Center	17,380	215–336–2000
TAMPA BAY LIGHTNING	1992–93	0	ThunderDome	26,000	813–229–8800
WASHINGTON CAPITALS	1974–75	0	MCI Center	20,000	301–386–7000
EASTERN CONFERENCE NORTHEAST DIVISION					
BOSTON BRUINS	1924–25	5 (1990)	The FleetCenter	17,200	617–227–3200
BUFFALO SABRES	1970–71	0	Crossroads Arena	19,500	716–856–8100
COLORADO AVALANCHE	1979–80	1 (1996)	McNichols Arena	16,058	303–893–6700
RALEIGH HURRICANES	1978–79	0	Greensboro Coliseum	23,500	910–218–5300
MONTREAL CANADIENS	1917–18	23 (1993)	Montreal Forum	21,400	514–932–2582
OTTAWA SENATORS	1993–94	0	Ottawa Paladium	18,500	613–721–4300
PITTSBURGH PENGUINS	1967–68	2 (1992)	Civic Arena	17,537	412–323–1919
WESTERN CONFERENCE CENTRAL DIVISION					
CHICAGO BLACKHAWKS	1926–27	3 (1961)	United Center	17,742	312–559–1212
DALLAS STARS	1967–68	0	Reunion Arena	16,914	214–467–8277
DETROIT RED WINGS	1926–27	8 (1997)	Joe Louis Arena	19,275	313–396–7544
ST. LOUIS BLUES	1967–68	0	Kiel Center	18,500	314–291–7600
TORONTO MAPLE LEAFS	1917–18	13 (1967)	Maple Leaf Gardens	15,642	416–977–1641
WINNIPEG JETS	1979–80	0	Winnipeg Arena	15,405	204–982–5304
WESTERN CONFERENCE PACIFIC DIVISION					
MIGHTY DUCKS OF ANAHEIM	1993–94	0	Arrowhead Pond of Anaheim	17,250	714–704–2500
CALGARY FLAMES	1972–73	1 (1989)	Olympic Saddledome	20,230	403–777–4646
EDMONTON OILERS	1979–80	5 (1988)	Northlands Coliseum	17,503	403–471–2191
LOS ANGELES KINGS	1967–68	0	Great Western Forum	16,005	310–419–3870
SAN JOSE SHARKS	1991–92	0	San Jose Arena	17,190	408–287–9200
VANCOUVER CANUCKS	1970–71	0	GM Place	19,056	604–280–4400

*As of the end of the 1996–97 season.

EXPERT Q & A

WHO MADE THE HALL OF FAME?

Over 1,000 shrines honor the great and—well—not-so-great

Pick a sport or pastime and, chances are, there's a hall of fame that honors its legends. Baseball, football, and basketball have their well-known and popular halls, of course, but so do bodybuilding, show jumping, and drag racing. Heck, there's even a dog musher's hall of fame in Knik, Alaska, and a jousting hall in Virginia.

Halls of fame are rare elsewhere in the world, but over 1,000 are spread across America. The vast majority are sports-themed, but scores of others feature leading lights in other fields. There's a Barbie Doll Hall of Fame in Palo Alto, Calif., for instance, and an Aviation Hall of Fame in New Jersey. The National Fresh Water Fishing Hall of Fame is housed in a five-story building shaped like a muskie.

Choosing which halls of fame to visit and which to skip can be a daunting task. We asked Paul Dickson, a co-author of the *Volvo Guide to Halls of Fame* (Living Planet Press, 1995), for some recommendations.

■ **Of the four major sports—baseball, basketball, football, and hockey—which has the best hall of fame?**

It's really hard to beat the baseball hall in Cooperstown, N.Y. It's got everything, and it keeps reinventing itself to stay vital. But all four of them are good, because they realize they're in show business. The day when a hall of fame was a room full of dusty trophies and exhibits is long gone.

■ **What are some of your favorites?**

The bowling hall is a real sleeper. I'm biased because I discovered a picture of my great-grandfather there. It's a great place to bowl and have some laughs, and there's a wonderful collection of bowling ceramics, and a collection of 60 antique beer steins all depicting bowling. The Indiana Basketball Hall of Fame and Museum gives you a chance to replicate the buzzer-beater from the movie *Hoosiers*.

■ **If you were planning a trip to see halls of fame, where would you go?**

Oklahoma City has three diverse ones: the National Cowboy Hall of Fame, which is spectacular and one of the biggest; the American Softball Association Hall of Fame, which is a real treat; and the International Photography Hall of Fame. Another prime spot is upstate New York, which has the baseball hall and the Corvette Americana museum in Cooperstown, boxing in Canastota, and soccer in Oneonta. And one of the great hall-of-fame trifectas is the Canton-Akron-Cleveland area: Canton has the football hall, Cleveland has the rock and roll hall, and Akron has Inventure Place, which honors great inventors, like the guy who invented MRI and the inventor of the Kevlar vest, which has saved about 1,100 cops.

■ **HOW DO YOU GET TO THE HALLS OF FAME?**

Practice, practice, practice. But if you need directions, call first.

International Photography Hall of Fame and Museum, Oklahoma City, OK ☎800–532–7652

Inventure Place—Home of the National Inventors Hall of Fame, Akron, OH ☎216–768–4463

Naismith Memorial Basketball Hall of Fame, Springfield, MA ☎413–781–6500

National Baseball Hall of Fame and Museum, Cooperstown, NY ☎607–547–7200

National Bowling Hall of Fame and Museum, St. Louis, MO ☎314–231–6340

National Cowboy Hall of Fame, Oklahoma City, OK ☎405–478–2250

National Fresh Water Fishing Hall of Fame, Hayward, WI ☎800–826–3474

National Jousting Hall of Fame, Mount Solon, VA ☎703–350–2510

National Soccer Hall of Fame, Oneonta, NY ☎607–432–3351

National Softball Hall of Fame, Oklahoma City, OK ☎405–424–5266

THE GREAT OUTDOORS

GOLF

GETTING A GRIP ON YOUR GAME

It's a new game, with lots more players and better equipment

Golf tournaments haven't quite attained Super Bowl status, but golf wunderkind Tiger Woods is helping to turn a ho-hum sport into one of the coolest games around. Estimates are that 500,000 to one million new golfers will be taking up the game during the next decade. Many of them are expected to be not rich suburbanites and retirees, but women and younger kids. "Golf is not just for fat cats," says Jim Frank, editor of *Golf* magazine. "Tiger Woods and others are helping bring in younger players, changing the dynamics of the game." We asked Frank for advice on buying equipment and ways to improve your swing.

■ Do you need to join a golf club to play?

No. There are lots of public, daily-fee courses, where you pay per round or for the day. There are about 14,000 golf courses in the country: about 7,000 are daily-fee courses and 2,000 are owned by localities. Private courses account for only about one-third of the total.

■ How expensive is it to play?

Fees at private clubs vary widely but are generally very expensive. At a daily-fee course, the fees are not insignificant. You can find some good ones in the $25 to $30 range and a lot of good ones in the $60 range.

■ What is the best way to learn the game?

Every newcomer should take some lessons very early on. After you've played a round or two of golf, you pretty much have your swing tendencies intact. Once you get into a bad habit, it's difficult to break.

■ How can you locate golf instructors?

Find a teacher at a course, a driving range, or an adult education program, or go to a golf school—there are thousands around the country, including ones for kids. The costs range from a few hundred dollars for a weekend to a few thousand dollars for all-inclusive golf vacations at fancy resorts. A good place to start is a book called *Golf Schools: The Complete Guide* (First Person Press, 1994). Many schools also advertise in golf magazines.

■ When should you invest in your own set of clubs?

You don't want to buy them right away for a couple of reasons. First, you have to figure out your swing, which you can only do after you've played a few times. Your shape, size, and attitude can pretty much tell you what your swing will look like. But all clubs are not the same. If you are short and round, you will need

GOLF COURSES FROM HADES

Here, according to Men's Health *magazine, are the world's 10 most dangerous golf courses:*

BEACHWOOD
Natal, South Africa
■ A few years back, a golfer was attacked by a monkey who tried to strangle her. She was rescued by an alert caddie.

COMPTON PAR-3
Compton, California
■ High-caliber excitement. Home to Crips versus Bloods gang competition.

ELEPHANT HILLS
Victoria Falls, Zimbabwe
■ The fairways are sometimes marked by craters caused by mortar shells fired across the Zambezi River.

LOST CITY
Sun City, South Africa
■ The 13th green is fronted by a stone pit filled with crocodiles.

LUNDIN LINKS
Fife, Scotland
■ A player in the 1950s was hit by a train while crossing the tracks beyond the fifth green.

MACHRIE HOTEL
Islay, Scotland
■ Nearly every drive and approach is blind, played over huge sand dunes.

PELHAM BAY
Bronx, N.Y.
■ Reportedly, 13 bodies were found in the environs in a recent 10-year period.

PLANTATION
Gretna, Louisiana
■ With 18 holes shoved into 61 acres (less than half the norm), players await their turn huddled against protective fencing.

SCHOOL CANYON
Glendale, California
■ Built on a landfill, golfers have snagged clubs on buried tires and methane gas has risen up from the divots.

SINGAPORE ISLAND
Singapore
■ Pro Jim Stewart encountered a 10-foot cobra here in 1982. He killed it—only to watch in horror as another emerged from its mouth.

SOURCE: *Men's Health*, April, 1997.

clubs that are constructed differently from those that suit a tall, thin person.

Once you've decided to play seriously and invest in clubs, you should have your clubs fitted. Most pros at clubs and driving ranges can lead you to someone who will watch the way you swing, take measurements, and determine what size clubs you need.

If you don't want to buy new equipment, you can buy used clubs at a lot of stores; pros and driving ranges often sell used sets too. My advice is: Don't buy any equipment until you've tried it out. At the very least try hitting with the clubs at a driving range.

■ How do you pick golf clubs?

First, it's important that you like the way the clubs look and that you feel comfortable with the size of the heads.

Anyone new to the game, and almost all players who aren't very advanced, should buy game-improvement clubs, or "perimeter-weighted" clubs. The weight of the head is placed around the club head so that even if you don't hit the ball at its "sweet" spot, the clubs will be as forgiving as possible.

■ How much can you expect to spend on golf clubs?

Very expensive clubs can cost $3,000 for a full set. But you can get good sets for under $200. You can only carry 14 or fewer clubs on the course: 3 woods, a putter, and 10 irons (a 3-iron, a 9-iron, and a few wedges). There's no reason why someone just starting out shouldn't go to a Kmart or Wal-Mart, or a local sporting goods chain like Sports Authority, and buy a good, adequate set of golf clubs for $150 to $250.

Some good brands in that price range are Wilson, MacGregor, and Dunlop. They are not state-of-the-art clubs, but they are perfectly good. And they are of game-improvement design. At the high-end, the good brands are Callaway, Taylor-Made, and Cobra. Callaway is the largest company on the high-end; it makes the famous Big Bertha driver.

■ Are there any brands to stay away from?

There really aren't a lot of bad clubs out there. One thing to watch out for is shafts made of cheap graphite. Graphite has become a popular replacement for steel because it's lighter than steel, making the head swing faster—and it absorbs the impact of hitting the ball. But graphite can and does break, and cheap graphite breaks easily. Quality graphite clubs should cost more than steel clubs.

EXPERT TIPS

For 31 years, Angelo Provenzano, owner of Angelo's Golf Shop (☎202-244-5105) in Washington, D.C., repaired broken shafts and otherwise gave old clubs new life. Here he offers tips:

■ **Scrape scum off the face after each round and rub it clean with water and the tip of a towel or a specially designed brush with two types of bristles—one for woods and one for irons.**

■ **At the first sign of fraying, replace the whipping around the hosel connecting the head and shaft, which protects the joint.**

■ **Varnish—don't shellac—the heads every year. Varnish is glossier and makes it easier to keep the heads clean.**

■ How often should a golfer play to see significant improvement?

You cannot improve if you only play once a week, which is what most golfers do. People who are serious practice every day. You should go to a driving range and work on something every few days. It's easier to have something ingrained in a series of shorter, regular periods than in longer, less frequent periods. A lot of the game is simply learning and mastering the swing.

■ What can a golfer do to improve his swing?

For 95 percent of golfers the solution is: swing slower and don't squeeze the grip so hard. You should hold the club just tight enough so that it doesn't fly out of your hands when you swing. When your grip is too tight, your arms and shoulders become tense, making it impossible to swing well. Slow your swing down. And then slow it down more.

At some point you will have to see a pro, who can tell you where you need help, teach you some drills, and put your swing on videotape so that you can analyze it.

■ What are some of the frustrations of the game?

Golf is a game of compensation. You have to play your errors. When you mess up, you have to play from where you messed up. You can be out there for six hours, slashing away, and you can hit 140 shots and out of those only one will be a good one. But that's the one that says, "I'll be back next week."

■ Where's the challenge after you've mastered your swing?

After a while you learn to play the course. That's when it gets to be more fun. One of the clichés is that you aren't playing anyone but yourself and the course. The course is your opponent and playing it intelligently becomes the challenge. You begin to make choices: Should I try to fly it over the stream or lay up short so I have a safer and easier shot? What kind of trouble is over the green? Is there water? Sand? Most novices won't have those experiences for a while, but it all adds to the enjoyment and complexity of the game.

GOLFER'S GUIDE

THE TEN BEST PUBLIC COURSES

Many of the best American golf courses are available to you for the price of a greens fee. Golf *magazine recently published a list of the "Top 100 You Can Play." The complete survey, based on the views of about 200 golf fanatics from around the country, is available from* Golf *(☎ 212-779-5000). Here are the top 10:*

1. PEBBLE BEACH
Pebble Beach, Calif.

■ *Golf*'s survey picked Pebble Beach as the most scenic public course as well as tops over all. But you pay for what you get at this stunning resort course overlooking Carmel Bay: It's the most expensive course in the survey.
■ $225 to $275
☎ 408-624-3811

2. PINEHURST (No. 2)
Pinehurst, N.C.

■ One of many multicourse facilities that placed more than one course on *Golf*'s list. *Golf* cites Pinehurst's clubhouse as the nicest in the survey, and its practice area, Maniac Hill, as one of the best.
■ $140 to $200
☎ 910-295-8141

3. BLACKWOLF RUN
(River Course)
Kohler, Wisc.

■ This resort course was designed by Pete Dye, an architect known for driving golfers mad with his challenging layouts. Its sister course, Meadow Valleys, which is part of the same facility, placed No. 46 on *Golf*'s list.
■ $140
☎ 414-457-4448

4. SPYGLASS HILL
Pebble Beach, Calif.

■ Pebble Beach's neighbor on California's Monterey coastline, this resort course was rated one of the best-groomed and toughest courses in the country. It's also one of the prettiest.
■ $175 to $225
☎ 408-624-3811

5. PUMPKIN RIDGE
(Ghost Creek)
Cornelius, Ore.

■ *Golf* singled out this daily-fee course, built on rolling farmland 20 miles outside Portland, as among the best-groomed in the country.
■ $75 to $90
☎ 503-647-4747

6. BETHPAGE
Farmingdale, N.Y.
■ *Golf*'s choice as the best value in the survey, this daily-fee course is part of a state park on Long Island, an hour's drive from Manhattan.
■ $20
☎ 516-249-0700

7. COG HILL (No. 4)
Lemont, Ill.

■ In its list of brutal courses, *Golf* describes this daily-fee course outside Chicago as one of a handful of "classic round-wreckers,

time-honored toughies."
■ $95
☎ 630-257-5872

8. TROON NORTH
(Monument)
Scottsdale, Ariz.

■ Voters picked this daily-fee course as perhaps the best-kept course in the survey, with impeccably groomed fairways and velvety smooth greens.
■ $75 and up (seasonal)
☎ 602-585-5300

9. TPC AT SAWGRASS
(Stadium)
Ponte Vedra Beach, Fla.

■ *Golf* picked this resort course, not far from Jacksonville, as one of the most challenging courses, but this Pete Dye course actually has been softened over the years.
■ $90
☎ 904-285-7888

10. WORLD WOODS
(Pine Barrens)
Brooksville, Fla.

■ This course, about 90 minutes from Tampa, features an unmatched practice facility that includes a four-sided, 700-yard driving range and several stunning practice holes.
■ $21 to $85
☎ 352-796-5500

IN-LINE SKATING

WHEN YOU'RE REALLY ON A ROLL

A glider's guide to the fastest-growing outdoor sport in America

A decade ago, in-line skating was a specialized training device for hockey players during the off-season. These days, in-line skating—also known as "rollerblading," after the popular skate manufacturer—is the fastest-growing outdoor sport in the country, with over 20 million participants. Kids ages 6 through 11 account for almost half of all skaters. But the sport is catching on among adults, too—people over 35 now account for about 20 percent of skaters.

There are four varieties of in-line skating. Most skaters simply do it for recreation.

Aggressive skating involves leaping, twisting moves on ramps and stairways. Roller speed skating is similar to the same event on ice. The fastest growing in-line activity is roller hockey, which is similar to the game played on ice. In fact, it is now more popular than baseball among California youths.

In-line skating is good exercise. A study published in the American College of Sports Medicine's journal found that in-line skating is as good as running for burning calories and aerobic conditioning.

Here are some pointers before you hit the pavement.

■ **SAFETY AND GEAR.** There's a reason in-line skaters should suit up with helmets, and pads for knees, elbows, and wrists. According to the International In-Line Skating Association, 103,000 trips to the emergency room in 1996 were caused by in-line injuries. The helmet and wrist guards are the most important gear. Head injuries are the most serious; wrist injuries, the most common.

Learning how to skate properly also increases safety. The International In-Line Skating Association (☎ 301–942–9770) and most YMCA chapters provide lessons for modest fees.

■ **THE SKATES.** Expect to spend at least $150 to ensure quality wheels, ball bearings, and frames. A decent pair of children's skates costs $50 to $90. Buying used skates is a money-saving option. Paula Caballero, a former editor of *In-Line Skater* magazine, recommends aluminum-framed skates for heavier skaters, because they will support weight better.

The more expensive skates may be too fast for inexperienced recreational skaters. Hockey players should stick with brands they know, such as Bauer and CCM. Aggressive skaters should buy cheaper skates, because the sport's wear and tear will break skate frames no matter how well they are made. Novice speed skaters should look into brands that can be converted from four wheels to five. With any skates, the wheels should be rotated to avoid wearing down the edges, and bearings should always be cleaned, particularly after skating in wet areas.

■ **THE DEVIL IS IN THE DETAILS**

There are hundreds of in-line skates available. Here are some things to look for when you pick yours:

■ **PLASTIC BOOT.** Supportive, durable, and designed to flex.

■ **RATCHET BUCKLES.** Faster to put on and off, and they tighten better.

■ **NYLON FRAME.** The material of choice—rigid and responsive, yet it absorbs shock.

■ **WHEELS.** Bigger isn't always better. Big wheels are faster, but less stable.

■ **HEEL BRAKE.** Works like a charm.

ROCK CLIMBING
▼

SCALING NEW HEIGHTS

For some, it's a sheer delight, for others sheer madness

Some hope to savor what the poet Alfred, Lord Tennyson called the "joy in steepness overcome ... [the] joy in breathing nearer heaven." For others, it is a way to overcome faint-heartedness. Rather than being daredevils, most climbers, in fact, work to reduce the dangers. "Climbers like to have control over their risks," explains George Bracksieck, editor of *Rock and Ice* (☎ 303–499–8410), a climbing magazine.

High-tech innovations developed during the past 30 years, like spring-loaded gadgets that lock into cracks and stop falls, help minimize the inherent risks of the sport. Besides, climbers can limit their risk according to what style of climbing they take on. Using "top roping," which employs a block and tackle system, a climber can only slip a few inches before the rope stops the fall. Mountaineering, which combines traditional climbing—in which each climber sets his or her own anchors—and ice climbing on high peaks, can be much more dangerous, mainly because of uncontrollable risks, such as avalanches and blizzards.

Climbers must always work in pairs, with one "belaying," protecting the other by controlling the rope. And because the belayer literally holds the climber's life in just one hand, it's crucial that climbers have proper training. Rock gyms and many college outdoor clubs offer instruction. The American Mountain Guides Association (☎ 303–271–0984) and the American Alpine Club (☎ 303–384–0110), willingly give out advice and guidance.

Across the country, there are plenty of cliffs to climb. Brent Bishop has climbed all over the United States and the world, including an ascent of Mt. Everest, which his late father also conquered. Currently, Bishop is the director of the Sagarmatha Environmental Foundation, which is dedicated to cleaning tons of expedition gear off Everest. Here are his favorite climbing spots in the U.S.

YOSEMITE NATIONAL PARK, *California*

■ A spectacular area with no rival in the U.S. Many climbs demand not only expertise, but also spending nights hanging in a bivouac sack, tied to the rock.
■ **CLASSIC ROUTE:** Astroman, possibly the best vertical crack climb in the world for its high degree of difficulty. It's well over 1,500 feet long.

OTHER DEATH-DEFYING DIVERSIONS

If rock climbing is no longer challenging, try one of these activities

BALLOONING
$100 to $175 per person
■ An hour flour, depending on the wind, can take you under a mile to over 10, reaching an average height of 500 feet.

SKYDIVING
$150 to $300 per person
■ Tandem ride: jumper is attached to instructor's harness—requires minimal ground training. Static line chute is deployed automatically. Accelerated free fall; instructors hold you until chute opens.

HANG GLIDING
$50 to $100 per person
■ Students can take one-day classes from flight instructors and take a number of glides off gently sloped terrain.

BUNGEE JUMPING
$10 to $25 per person
■ Jumper usually must weigh at least 80 pounds. Age restrictions may vary by state.

■ **OUTFITTER:** Yosemite Mountaineering School
☎ 209–372–1244

CITY OF ROCKS, *Idaho*

■ Scores of granite blocks, many 100 to 120 feet high, cater to every ability level and offer both awesome traditional crack climbs and hard-core sport routes, most of them safe and user-friendly.
■ **CLASSIC ROUTE:** Bloody Fingers, a 115-foot-long crack that just fits your fingers.
■ **OUTFITTER:** Exum Mountain Guides
☎ 307–733–2297

DEVIL'S TOWER, *Wyoming*

■ Every route up this 365-foot-high core of an ancient volcano requires a sustained crack climb. There's a voluntary hiatus on climbing in June, out of respect for Native Americans who consider this a sacred site.
■ **CLASSIC ROUTE:** Durrance. Though the climb is rated as moderate in difficulty, it's still an amazing route every foot of the way up.
■ **OUTFITTER:** Jackson Hole Mountain Guides
☎ 307–733–4979

SENECA ROCKS, *West Virginia*

■ There are more than 200 routes here, most of them challenging, up this bizarre slab of quartzite, which looks like two huge fins cutting through the forest. The summit is only 12 feet wide. The cliffs have some good sport climbs and also easy routes for beginners.
■ **CLASSIC ROUTE:** Castor and Pollux, two side-by-side cracks, which are steep and scary.
■ **OUTFITTER:** Seneca Rocks Climbing School
☎ 304–567–2600

SHAWANGUNK MOUNTAINS, *New York*

■ "The Gunks," as they are better known, are four major cliff areas spread over seven miles and offering more than 1,300 different ways up, each topping out anywhere between 30 and 200 feet high. A unique feature here is that beginners' routes are often right next to ones that can defy the proficient, giving everyone a great chance to mingle.
■ **CLASSIC ROUTE:** Foops, one of the best climbs in the country. It's a tough roof problem—you climb as if you're hanging on a ceiling.
■ **OUTFITTER:** High Angle Adventures.
☎ 800–777–2546

EXPERT SOURCES

READINGS ON THE ROCKS

Duane Raleigh, equipment editor for Climbing Magazine, *co-authored with Michael Benge* Rock, Tools, and Technique *(Climbing Magazine, 1995), a comprehensive, up-to-date climbing manual. He recommends the following how-to guides for safety-conscious climbers.*

KNOTS FOR CLIMBERS
Craig Luebben, Chockstone Press, 1993, $5.95.
■ Numerous, well-done illustrations and descriptions clarify how to tie the knots used in rock climbing and mountaineering.

SPORT AND FACE CLIMBING
John Long, Chockstone Press, 1994, $11.95.
■ Covers the nuances of face climbing and strategies for sport and indoor competition climbing.

MOUNTAINEERING, FREEDOM OF THE HILLS
Don Graydon, ed., Mountaineers, 1992, $22.95.
■ Textbook format covers everything you need to know for mountaineering, as well as for rock and snow climbing.

ROCK 'N ROAD: Rock Climbing Areas of North America
Tim Toula, Chockstone Press, 1995.
■ A comprehensive guide describing more than 2,000 places to climb.

■ For a listing of other books and guides, contact:
The Adventurous Traveler Bookstore
☎ 800–282–3963.

RADICAL RACES FOR THE HELL BENT

O.K, tough guy. Let's see how tough you really are. Sure, lots of Americans have run a marathon, a 26-mile race. But that's a cakewalk compared to the really tough endurance races out there. Outside magazine compiled a listing a few years ago of the toughest endurance races — rating the seven events on such factors as the toughness of the course, the rigor of the action, and the percentage of competitors who reach the finish line (it's often small). The events are presented here from easiest (relatively, of course) to most hell bent.

IRONMAN WORLD TRIATHLON COMPETITION

A 2.4-mile ocean swim, followed by 112 miles of cycling and a 26.2-mile marathon.

■ **WHERE:** Kailua-Kona, Hawaii
■ **WHEN:** October 1998
■ **HOW TOUGH:** The oldest and probably best-known of the endurance events. Eight to nine hours of grueling competition for some of the world's fittest men—and women.

BADWATER

A 139-mile run and walk from Badwater, Calif., the lowest point in the contiguous U.S., to near the top of Mount Whitney, the highest.

■ **WHERE:** Death Valley, Calif.
■ **WHEN:** July 1998
■ **HOW TOUGH:** Temperatures range from 130 degrees in the desert to 30 on the mountaintop. Runners can face everything from sandstorms to ice storms and take anywhere from 26 to 60 hours to finish the course.

LA TRAVERSEE INTERNATIONALE DU LAC SAINT-JEAN

A 25-mile swim across a lake in Northern Quebec

■ **WHERE:** About 500 miles north of Montreal
■ **WHEN:** July 1998
■ **HOW TOUGH:** Three-to-four-foot swells make for a rough ride, and no wetsuits are permitted during the nine-plus-hour swim, even though the water temperatures often fall to the low 60s.

RAID GAULOISE

A "wilderness endurance competition" in which five-person teams must navigate a 300-mile course and finish together.

■ **WHERE:** The site varies from year to year, and is kept secret until hours before the race.
■ **WHEN:** December 1998
■ **HOW TOUGH:** Recent races have been held over brutal terrain in Patagonia, Argentina, Costa Rica, Oman, and Madagascar. In this week-long event participants may engage in mountain climbing, kayaking, white-water canoeing, horseback riding, and skiing—among other things.

IDITAROD SLED DOG RACE

A 1,100-mile race through Alaskan wilderness that takes the mushers and their dogs 10 to 20 days to finish.

■ **WHERE:** Anchorage to Nome, Alaska.
■ **WHEN:** March 1998
■ **HOW TOUGH:** Like the Ironman, this race has become an icon. The wintry conditions can be brutal, but the race is even tougher on the dogs when it's overly warm.

VENDEE GLOBE

A four-month solo sailing race around the world.

■ **WHERE:** From France's Bay of Biscay, past Western Africa, Antarctica, and Cape Horn.
■ **WHEN:** Every four years; last in November 1996.
■ **HOW TOUGH:** Participants can't go ashore or get assistance, so they're totally on their own for four months.

RACE ACROSS AMERICA

A 2,900-mile bicycle race in 8 to 10 days.

■ **WHERE:** California to Savannah, Georgia.
■ **WHEN:** July 1998
■ **HOW TOUGH:** The winners cycle 350 miles in a day and sleep little more than an hour. About a third of the entrants finish.

BLAZING YOUR OWN TRAIL

A cycling pro's advice on the best deals on wheels

A stroll into today's bike shop is not for the faint of heart. The days of banana seats and coaster brakes are long gone, replaced by the likes of titanium steel frames and shock-absorbing suspension forks. But don't be intimidated—or fooled. Inside that shop, there is a bike that is exactly what you need—and lots more that you don't need. Here to guide you through the maze of bike styles and sizes and help you pick one that best suits your needs (and pocketbook) is the editor of *Bicycling* magazine, Geoff Drake.

■ How do I know what type of bike I need?

There are three types of bikes: road, mountain, and hybrid. Each is built for a certain type of riding. A breakdown:

ROAD BIKES: The lightest and fastest of the three bicycle types, these bikes are primarily for people who will be doing distance riding on smooth pavement. The skinny, smooth tires and low handlebars give riders speed and low wind resistance but also make some cyclists feel vulnerable in traffic. Most road bikes weigh between 20 and 30 pounds, but new high-end models can weigh as little as 18 pounds. The majority of people riding road bikes today are athletes who use them for training purposes.

MOUNTAIN BIKES: Mountain bikes, created by outdoors enthusiasts in Northern California, are now the most popular bike in the United States. The upright seating, fat, knobby tires, and easy gearing make these bikes ideal for off-road riding. But even if you

live in the heart of the city and only occasionally hit a trail, mountain bikes offer comfort and stability. If you use your bike only for riding with the kids or short trips around town, a mountain bike is probably better suited to your needs than a road bike.

HYBRID BIKES: Hybrids, relative newcomers to the bike market, are rapidly gaining in popularity. Hybrids combine the upright seating and shifting of mountain bikes, but offer the thin, smooth tires of road bikes for speed. Many people like the versatility a hybrid offers; you can ride on some less-challenging trails, and also make better time than you would on a mountain bike. But don't buy a hybrid if you are a serious cyclist: the limitations on both roads and trails will frustrate you. If you want to ride on tough trails, the hybrid's frame and thin tires can't handle the challenge. And if you want to take it on the open road, you'll be battling wind resistance the whole ride.

■ How much should I spend on a bike?

Bikes aren't cheap. You can spend anywhere from several hundred to several thousand dollars for a high-end model. It's hard to purchase a bad bike today, though—you can find a decent bike for $300 to $400. So don't worry if your budget is tight, but remember you get what you pay for. Don't expect a less-expensive bike to perform as well or last as long as a high-end model. Your extra money is buying lighter, sturdier frames, and components (like gears and brakes) that can take a beating and last a long time.

■ How do I know if my bike fits me?

One of the most common errors is buying a bike that is too large. The best advice is buy the smallest bike that you can comfortably ride. Tests to determine if the size is right for you include: straddling the bike frame and lifting the front tire up by the handlebars. There should be several inches of clearance between your crotch and the bike frame, 1 to 2 inches for a road bike, and at least 3 to 4 inches for a mountain bike.

When riding, you should be able to straighten—but not strain—your leg. Adjust-

■ THE NUTS AND BOLTS OF MOUNTAIN BIKES

Bike shops are dangerous places for those with an itchy wallet finger. There are hundreds of bike accessories you could purchase, but a much smaller number that you actually need. Here are a few of the basics, and some exotic innovations:

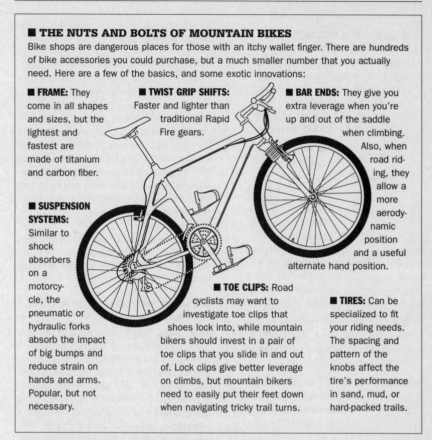

■ **FRAME:** They come in all shapes and sizes, but the lightest and fastest are made of titanium and carbon fiber.

■ **TWIST GRIP SHIFTS:** Faster and lighter than traditional Rapid Fire gears.

■ **BAR ENDS:** They give you extra leverage when you're up and out of the saddle when climbing. Also, when road riding, they allow you a more aerodynamic position and a useful alternate hand position.

■ **SUSPENSION SYSTEMS:** Similar to shock absorbers on a motorcycle, the pneumatic or hydraulic forks absorb the impact of big bumps and reduce strain on hands and arms. Popular, but not necessary.

■ **TOE CLIPS:** Road cyclists may want to investigate toe clips that shoes lock into, while mountain bikers should invest in a pair of toe clips that you slide in and out of. Lock clips give better leverage on climbs, but mountain bikers need to easily put their feet down when navigating tricky trail turns.

■ **TIRES:** Can be specialized to fit your riding needs. The spacing and pattern of the knobs affect the tire's performance in sand, mud, or hard-packed trails.

---

ing the seat height can help this. Also, especially on road bikes, be sure that you can comfortably reach the handlebars and that your knees are just barely brushing your elbows as you pedal.

■ There are so many frames to choose from. What's best for me?

Frames vary in price and expense, with the heaviest and least expensive being a steel frame. More expensive and lighter are aluminum, carbon fiber, and titanium steel frames, in that order. One-piece, molded composite frames are the lightest of all and are a hot new item, but they also carry a hefty price tag. Some composite-frame bikes cost as much as $3,250.

If you are planning on racing with your bike, a light frame is a necessity. But for weekend riders, it is merely a luxury that will make your ride somewhat more enjoyable.

■ Which bikes do you recommend?

Bike models come and go, and what's hot this year may be outdated by next year. The surest way to purchase a quality bike is to avoid the hot gimmicks and new names, and stick with companies that produce high-quality bikes year-in and year-out.

For mountain and hybrid bikes, try Trek and Cannondale, two of the biggest American companies. Bikes made by GT, Specialized, and Schwinn are also good.

For road bikes: Specialized and Trek are always reliable. For sure-fire winners , look to the Italian-made bikes. Some bike shops carry Pinarello and De Rosa, which are top of the line. They often cost as much as $5,000.

■ BUYING A HELMET

Wearing a bike helmet is no longer nerdy. In fact, in many cities it's the law. The majority of bike-related deaths are caused by head injuries—injuries that could easily be avoided if cyclists wore helmets. But a helmet won't do you any good if it doesn't fit properly.

■ The experts suggest buying a helmet that feels snug, but not uncomfortable.

■ The strap under your chin should feel snug, but loose enough to open your mouth wide enough to take a drink of water.

■ The helmet should touch the head at the crown, sides, front, and back and should not roll backward or forward on the head when you push up.

■ Remember that you can make a tight helmet looser by inserting smaller sizing pads or sanding down existing pads.

■ I'd like a better bike, but don't have the money for a new one. Can I upgrade my bike?

Absolutely. If you have a mountain bike, the first thing to add would be a suspension fork if you don't already have one—it absorbs the impact of big bumps and gives you a smoother ride. Also, clipless pedals make riding a lot nicer. If you're looking at replacing an entire component group (gears, brakes, etc.), you may want to look into a new bike. There are significant cost savings on individual components when you buy them as part of a bike, as opposed to individually.

If you have a road bike, look into clipless pedals. Also, a cycle computer that goes on your handlebars can tell you your speed, distance, time, and sometimes your heart rate. Computers run $20 to $100. For greater speed on your road bike, you could also buy new, lighter wheels.

■ How do all those gears work?

Just as a car has an ideal rpm range, you have an ideal rpm range for your legs, which is about 80 to 100 rpms. The idea is to spin at a high cadence with light pressure, rather than pedaling slowly. Just as you shift your car to maintain that rpm, you should be constantly shifting on your bike to keep within the ideal rpm range. New advances in shifting technology (like Rapid Fire gears and twist grip shifters on your handlebars) are great because they make it easier to stay within that ideal range.

Remember, a higher gear is a harder gear, and if you're in a high gear, you're in a smaller sprocket in the back or a bigger sprocket in the front.

■ What are some easy bike repairs I can do myself?

Everyone should be able to fix a flat tire. Always carry a pump, a patch kit, and a spare tire tube. If you get a flat on the road or trail, put on a new tube. If you get a second flat, you can find the hole and patch it. Patching takes practice and you should try it at home a few times before you go on a trail—you don't want to be stuck out in the woods with a flat and no way to fix it. You should always carry what is called a mini tool—the Swiss Army knife of the bike world. It's an all-in-one tool, including an Allen wrench and spoke wrench, and it can be bought at any bike shop.

People often forget to keep their bike chains clean and lubricated. If you have a really grimy chain, first spray the chain and derailleurs with degreaser, then wet an old sponge with warm, soapy water and hold it around the chain as you spin the wheels. Continue this until the chain is clean, then dry with rags. Instead of using a sponge, you could buy a chain cleaning kit that snaps around your chain and then cleans and degreases it. Remember to regularly lubricate your chain—lubricants made specifically for bike chains are available at all bike shops. If you ride in the rain, be sure to lubricate your chain every time.

TENNIS
▼

A PRO'S PRIMER ON TENNIS

Getting kids on the court, whether they're tots or teens

Tennis pro Todd Martin knows a thing or two about tennis. He started playing competitively when he was nine and has become a top player on the ATP Tour. Martin reached the semifinals at Wimbledon and the finals at the Australian Open. Respected on and off the court, Martin has twice won the ATP tour sportsmanship award and is president of its player's council. He recently founded the Todd Martin Development Fund, dedicated to fostering an interest in tennis and academics in his hometown of Lansing, Michigan. We asked Martin for advice on when to get kids involved in tennis and ways to improve your game, whether you're a novice or an ace.

■ When should kids start playing tennis?

There is no appropriate age. If a child is interested in being a professional tennis player, then the earlier the better, as long as the parents don't overdo it. The earlier they start, the more likely the kids are to learn and understand the fundamentals. But one of the beauties of tennis is that it can be learned and played later in life. You can pick it up and still enjoy it as an adult.

■ Where should you look for a good tennis instructor?

Unless you get a referral, you pretty much have to take what you get at the local tennis center. There are certain criteria for good tennis teachers. The better a teacher plays, the more potential the teacher will have to teach. Obviously there are some exceptions to that but I think that if a teacher doesn't really play well, then it's going to be tough for him or her to really teach someone else.

Once you've found a good coach, then you will have to make some choices. You can do as I did and live a normal life at home, playing tennis when you can. Or you could go to a tennis academy where the idea is to get you on the court against great competitors every day for hours and hours. The decision depends on the level of intensity a player is comfortable with.

■ What's the best way to get children interested in playing tennis?

With kids the more you can incorporate games, the more they're going to pay attention. A businesslike structure at a young age is not always good. Once the kids are really interested in playing better tennis, then you can start using more structure.

■ When should a child start playing competitively?

I don't think it's essential to compete at an early age. It's much more essential to learn the fundamentals, enjoy the game and figure out if this is something you want to do. If the child wants to play tournaments just for the sake of competing, that's great. If the motivation is to get ranked and there's a concern with numbers, then it's a problem. You can't compete just to compare yourself to others. You have to play because you love the game.

■ How does a player improve his game?

It helps to play against other players who are better than you. The cliché is that you learn more from losing than you do from winning, which is often true. However, you still are capable of learning a great deal from winning and from being better. In order to win at any level, you need to know how to win and you need to have experienced winning before.

A guy like Pete Sampras probably never practices with anyone who's better than he is, but he continues to improve. If you're losing all the time, then you're forced to make things better. If you're always better than someone, you can continue to evolve and learn how to win in other ways. It's only within the last few years, for example, that Steffi Graf has learned to hit a top-spin backhand, even though she's been beating her competition 6–1, 6–0.

■ What can tennis players do to avoid injuries?

For kids, it's important to participate in other sports and to develop athletic ability. I played soccer and basketball growing up and both of those helped different aspects of my foot movement, which is a big part of tennis.

For adults, getting to the gym a few times a week and making sure that your muscles are balanced is crucial. If your elbow hurts, it's probably due to a lack of strength in your shoulder, If your wrist hurts, it's probably due to a lack of strength in the elbow. Obviously, players should stretch as well. Make sure you don't go out there physically unprepared for the wear and tear that the surface will put on your body.

■ What's the most important thing a player can do to improve his game?

I learned early that the Jimmy Connors mode of practicing is the most beneficial. Jimmy would practice for one hour and make more progress in that hour than 10 guys who were out there for three hours, because he would really focus and concentrate for the whole hour. That approach saves you time and mental capacity, and is beneficial for players of any level. Rather than being on the court for hours, hitting balls brainlessly, go out there, focus, and do the work in one hour.

Of course, for people to really enjoy sports, there has to be some competitiveness in their blood. The more that you can strike a chord with that competitiveness, the better.

EXPERT TIPS

PICKING A TENNIS RACQUET

You look for an exact fit in shoes and clothes. Do the same with racquets, which are individualized instruments that must be chosen carefully. Any racquet can be made more or less powerful by adjusting the three systems— handle size and shape, overall weight and balance, and string type and tension. Warren Bosworth is a racquet consultant to stars like Pete Sampras, Ivan Lendl, and Martina Navratilova, and chairman of Bosworth International, a racquet-testing company. His suggestions:

■ **BODY:** Today's wide-body racquets may provide power, but the more conventional racquets offer more control.

■ **WEIGHT:** Too heavy a racquet will strain your wrist, arm, elbow, or shoulder, but the new ultralights have also been a principal cause of injury because they are just too light to overcome the impact of the ball.

■ **STRING:** Strings are the most important part of the racquet in regard to storing energy and influencing the spin of the ball. Basically, you have two choices: gut and synthetics. Synthetics, which are cheaper, are thought to last longer, but you have to take into account climate and humidity (dry weather is better for strings), surface (clay is harder on strings), the type of racquet (some have grommets, or string-holds, that are harder on strings than others) and the type of player you are (spin players are harder on their strings).

Gauge, or string thickness, is as critical as string type. Thicker gauges last longer. Thinner ones provide more feel.

Tension is another factor. The looser the strings, the more power. Tighter strings may give you more spin control, but may also add shock.

■ **COST.** Expect to spend $150 to $250 for a standard retail purchase. Look for the previous year's model, which is often just as good as the new ones.

EXPERT TIPS

A PRIVATE LESSON WITH ZINA

A Wimbledon finalist's five-step program to playing a better game

Zina Garrison-Jackson has been one of the best and most-popular players on the women's tennis tour for more than a decade, winning more than a dozen tournaments and well over $4 million during that time, including a second-place finish to Martina Navratilova at Wimbledon in 1990. Here is her advice for preparing to play smart tennis, mentally and physically.

Step 1: ASSESS YOUR OPPONENT

If you get the chance, watch your opponent play or practice before your next match, Garrison-Jackson says. "Watch their movements and their strokes to figure out where their weaknesses are," she says. Once you've identified those failings, shape your game to determine "how you'll be able to maneuver him or her to take advantage of the weaknesses."

That advice is somewhat self-evident: If the player has a much weaker backhand than forehand, hit to the weaker side. But don't go too far, Garrison-Jackson says, that you change your own game. "If you're primarily a baseline player, and you're playing a hardcore baseliner, don't suddenly become a serve-and-volleyer that match. Instead, hit a lot of balls around the court, a lot in the corners and a lot of deep balls, so you'll force mistakes and be in a position to move in occasionally and attack."

Step 2: VISUALIZE

Yogi Berra once said that half of baseball is 90 percent mental. Well, you know what he meant, and tennis is, too. Like many top athletes, Garrison-Jackson is a strong believer in visualization, in which she prepares for a

match by playing it out, point by point, in her mind. She closes her eyes and pictures herself "hitting the strokes exactly the way I want to." She takes this process to its logical end, "to the point where I'm smiling after the match rather than frowning."

Step 3: HAVE A GAME PLAN

Say you've developed a good game plan based on your strengths and your opponent's failings. But once the match begins, you fall behind five games to one. Do you dump your plan and try something else? "You should believe enough in your game plan to stick with it win, lose, or draw," Garrison-Jackson says. That doesn't mean that you don't adapt if you find a bigger hole in your challenger's game than the ones you spotted in practice. But if you were thorough and thoughtful going in, you probably picked the right game plan for you, and dumping it probably won't produce a better one, says Garrison-Jackson.

Step 4: HIT WINNERS

A lot of tennis players actively try to hit winners: They rear back and try to rip a hole in the opponent's racquet, or try desperately to drop a ball daintily over the net. Bad idea, Garrison-Jackson says. "Your best bet is to learn the basics of tennis first, and concentrate on making your opponent miss. Do that until you get to the point where you place that ball so well that you get your opponent totally out of position. That's how you hit winners. You basically do it without trying to."

Step 5: ASSUME THE RIGHT ATTITUDE

Garrison-Jackson says she sees a lot of players who are either over- or underconfident. The overconfident types, she says, believe they're better than they really are and try shots they have no business trying, usually unsuccessfully. "The other type of player says, 'Oh, I'm a hacker,'" Garrison-Jackson says. The hacker assumes he'll lose, while the overconfident player assumes he'll win. Both mind-sets are equally damaging to good, smart tennis, Garrison-Jackson says. "The key is not to think about the level of the person you're playing, but just to go out and compete as hard as you can, one point at a time."

AN AVID ANGLER'S FAVORITE STREAMS

A talented author and illustrator picks his special trout spots

James Prosek makes you want to fly-fish, even if you've never had the slightest inclination to do so. He doesn't do it purposefully: He's not a salesman or a shill for the sport. But his appreciation for fly-fishing, and for everything that surrounds it, is infectious.

He lovingly describes the trout as "elegant, streamlined, and beautiful." He details the remarkable, brief life of the mayfly, which arises from the water as a nymph, hatches in the air, mates, and dies in the course of a single day. And he places himself as a fisherman in the context of the awesome natural cycle of the fishing stream. "It's a big immortal cycle, and you're the mortal angler," he says. "You step into that water and see your reflection, and you've become part of that cycle. It's powerful."

Prosek shares his love for fly-fishing in *Trout: An Illustrated History* (Alfred A. Knopf, 1996), a book of watercolor paintings and text describing about 70 types of trout. Here he volunteers some of his favorite fishing streams.

HOUSATONIC RIVER, *Cornwall Bridge, Conn.*

■ This is Prosek's "home" stream, located not far from where he lives. The trout season here is short because the water warms up by late June, making it inhospitable for trout. But from late April through June, the green rolling hills make it a perfect place to catch some big rainbows and brown trout, as well as take in some terrific scenery. Phil Demetri at the Housatonic Meadows Fly Shop (☎ 203–672–6064) will set you up with all you need.

CONNECTICUT RIVER, *Pittsburgh, N.H.*

■ This fishing hole near the river's headwaters in northern New Hampshire offers a delightful surprise. Wild rainbow and brown trout are the dominant catch, but the river also contains a nice population of landlocked salmon. When you catch one, they leap around wildly.

ANDROSCOGGIN RIVER, *Lewiston, Me.*

■ The alder fly hatches in early to mid-June, and trout just gobble up the fat fly with the zebra-colored wings.

LITTLE KENNEBAGO RIVER, *Rangeley, Me.*

■ Prosek's recommended spot is where the river flows into Mooselookmeguntic Lake, one of the Rangeley Lakes. Each September, landlocked salmon go there to spawn, though Prosek admits that he has never been present at quite the right moment himself.

FALLING SPRINGS CREEK, *Chambersburg, Pa.*

■ This is Prosek's favorite among the unusual spring-fed creeks in central Pennsylvania. The creeks are fed by cold, slightly chalky water that pours forth from limestone outcroppings. The limestone raises the pH of the streams, which increases plant life and, in turn, fattens up the trout. Don't fish these streams with traditional mayflies or other flies, Prosek warns; use imitations of insects such as ants, beetles, or cicadas.

MADISON RIVER, *Ennis, Mont.*

■ This very famous river lives up to its reputation. Prosek suggests taking a guided float trip the first time you fish it; after that you can pull off the road and fish your favorite spots yourself. There's a big hatch of stoneflies at the end of June; flies based on this huge two-inch-long insect attract large brown trout.

ROCK CREEK, *Missoula, Mont.*

■ Buffalo and elk frequently stroll along the banks of this stream in west central Montana. Look for the striking-looking West Slope cutthroat trout; cutthroats get their name from the two red slashes below their neck.

SEARCHING FOR BIGGER, MEANER FISH

Landing a tarpon or a bonefish with a fly rod poses quite a challenge

Fly-fishing has stood the test of time. It's always been popular with serious anglers and, of course, still is. But these days, stream fishing is having to share the limelight with its coastal cousin: saltwater fly-fishing. While fly-fishing on the high seas may lack the bucolic beauty and some of the fly-making artistry of fly-rodding in the streams of Montana, what it offers instead is simple: "Bigger, meaner fish," says Art Scheck, an editor of *Saltwater Fly-Fishing* magazine.

Tarpon, bonefish, striped bass, and sailfish are the hard-running—and often mammoth—quarry of saltwater fly-rodding. Big trout, a primary target of stream fishers, run to 20 pounds; tarpon and sailfish can easily tip the scales at 100 pounds or more. But saltwater fly-fishing isn't just about size; striped bass and bonefish can take your line and tear away from you at dazzling speeds, and the fight to reel them in can give you a workout that'll make a day in the gym look like a walk in the park.

Ocean fly-fishing isn't as accessible as stream fishing, which you can dabble in in most states in the country. And to do some of the best saltwater fly-rodding, you have to travel to exotic locales like the Florida Keys. But you can find good ocean fishing up and down the East Coast, and a few other places besides. (Unfortunately, if you live on the West Coast, most experts say the Pacific Ocean fly-fishing just doesn't measure up.)

It's nice to have an expensive boat that can take you to more far-flung, and less-fished, spots. But shallow water is in many ways the best place to fly-fish, and you can do so successfully off beaches and cliffs, and in and around estuaries. This is not a sport of kings.

Some of the equipment you'll need can cost a princely sum, though. The specialized gear is much heavier and stronger than for stream fishing, reflecting the bigness and meanness of your foe. The high-end equipment can be outrageously expensive, but you don't have to spend a fortune for quality gear.

For most of the fishing that you'll probably do, you'll need a saltwater-grade graphite rod in the 8/9 or 9/10 weight class, which typically runs anywhere from about $100 to $400. Big-game rods, for going after tarpon or sailfish, say, will run a little more. The rest of the equipment that you'll need—line, leader, flies, etc.—will probably run you at least a few hundred dollars more.

GREEN RIVER, *Pinedale, Wyo.*

■ Prosek raves about the fishing and hiking in the mountains of the Wind River Range in central Wyoming. The lakes that feed off the headwaters of the Green River get stocked regularly by airplane drops; the fish get deposited as fingerlings and are left to develop in the wild. Any tackle store in Pinedale will be able to outfit you for a several-day pack trip.

FRYING PAN RIVER, *Western Colo.*

■ Freshwater springs are so plentiful in the Colorado mountains that you can pull off Highway 70 and fish in ditches and do well. A better bet, however, is this beautiful river that runs through brick-red hills. It features some enormous brown and rainbow trout, but the native fish here is the Colorado River cutthroat.

PROVO RIVER, *Heber City, Utah*

■ Utah may be best known for its salt lakes, but this stream in the central part of the state, not far from Brigham Young University, has some of the prettiest wild trout ever seen.

SNORKELING
▼

A MASK, FINS, AND THE DEEP BLUE

Top spots where the underwater views are nothing if not spectacular

Jacques Cousteau was best known for his scuba diving adventures. The television films he produced made the ocean come alive, revealing the teeming life and incredible vibrancy of the world's waters. His own eyes, however, were opened not by scuba diving—which he invented—but by snorkeling. In 1936, he first donned a pair of goggles and floated on the surface of the sea. "Sometimes we are lucky enough to know that our lives have been changed, to discard the old, embrace the new and run headlong down an immutable course. It happened to me on that summer's day, when my eyes were opened to the sea," he later wrote.

Today, the sport of scuba diving has largely supplanted snorkeling in the public imagination. But snorkeling still has the power to captivate, and more people actually snorkel each year than scuba. Partisans say snorkeling offers more freedom than scuba diving, which requires clunky gear and sometimes keeps you tethered to a boat. For snorkeling, all you need are fins, a mask, and a snorkel. It's much cheaper, and you don't need the certification that scuba diving requires.

David Taylor, executive editor of *Scuba Diving* magazine (☎ 912-351-0855), has some tips for getting started with snorkeling. Take great care in picking a mouthpiece and mask that fit comfortably. To test whether a mask fits, hold it to your face, sniff slightly to hold it in place, and let go. If the mask stays on and there are no leaks, the fit is sufficient. Try on as many as five masks with different shapes to see which fits best. Buy fins that cover your entire feet, instead of the open-heeled fins. And buy your equipment in a dive store, not in some discount department store, Taylor

says: "You are buying serious sports equipment, not tennis shoes." Ready to plunge in? Taylor suggests these top destinations:

LOOE KEY, FLORIDA
Best time to go: Year-round, though winds can limit visibility during the winter.

■ There are dozens of incredible snorkeling spots in the Florida Keys, the most popular diving location in the world. Looe Key features a national marine sanctuary, and stands out for its remarkable fish life and the numerous sunken ships that the schoolmasters, snappers, and barracuda dart through.
■ **CONTACT:** Outcast Charters and Florida Keys House, ☎ 305-872-4680.

BAHAMAS, OUT ISLANDS
Best time to go: February–September.

■ More than 30 hotels on Abaco, Bimini, Eleuthera, and the other smaller islands in the Bahamas offer a snorkeling package that is top-notch. The Out Islands don't have the posh hotels and casinos of Freeport and the other main tourist islands, but the snorkeling sights are sure luxurious.
■ **CONTACT:** Out Island Tourism ☎ 305-359-8097.

BONAIRE MARINE PARK, NETHERLANDS ANTILLES
Best time to go: Year-round.

■ This island off Venezuela's coast is less famous than neighboring Aruba and Curaçao. But its snorkeling—from its coral gardens to its tube sponges, which are as long as a person—is unmatched. The island's license plate says it all: "Diver's Paradise."
■ **CONTACT:** Sand Dollar Dive and Photo ☎ 800-288-4773.

HERON ISLAND, AUSTRALIA
Best time to go: April–July.

■ One of about 900 islands that make up the 1,200-mile Great Barrier Reef, Heron sits amid a protected marine sanctuary, so the diversity of fish life is virtually unmatched in the world. Park rangers are accessible and knowledgeable, so you learn as you dive.
■ **CONTACT:** P & O Resorts, Ltd. ☎ 800-225-9849.

PROVIDENTIALES, TURKS AND CAICOS
Best time to go: June–August.

■ These eight British colonial islands offer terrific diving in an unspoiled setting. The reefs around Providentiales sit on a shallow shelf surrounded by deep water, so snorkelers can see sharks, turtles, and other marine life that usually swim in far deeper water.

■ **CONTACT:** Turks and Caicos Tourist Board ☎ 809–94–64970.

GULF OF AQABA, RED SEA
Best time to go: June–October.

■ Deep walls of coral reef begin in just 18 inches of water near the gulf's mouth, so snorkelers can glimpse up close sights typically seen only by scuba divers. Those who make the trip to what *Scuba Diving* magazine calls the "most-unexplored of the world's divable seas" can also see unusual regional fishlife, like the bump-head wrasse. Hard to get to, but worth it.

■ **CONTACT:** Sinai Divers, ☎ 011–2062–600158.

MADANG, PAPUA NEW GUINEA
Best time to go: Year-round, though monsoons can hit from November–April, and are worst in January.

■ Madang is bounded by a tropical rain forest and the Bismarck Sea. The turquoise waters here contain some of the world's last primitive reefs, largely untouched and unspoiled by human encroachment. The corals and sea life are astounding, matched by the remarkable ancient land creatures found in the rain forest.

■ **CONTACT:** Trans Nuigini Tours ☎ 800–521–7242.

DELOS, GREECE
Best time to go: April–September, except mid-August, when the the seas can be rough.

■ Scuba diving is now banned here, because scavengers have taken off with many of the cultural artifacts that lie just below the surface, remnants of Greece's Golden Age more than 2,000 years ago. Snorkelers, however, can view what remains, including pieces of mosaic and sunken temple columns.

■ **CONTACT:** Hard to get to, so see your local travel agent.

■ HOW TO SWIM LIKE A FISH

Terry Laughlin, a world-class swimming coach who runs a camp in Goshen, N.Y., (☎ 914–294–3510) offers this advice:

1. BALANCE YOUR BODY.
Many swimmers find that the lower half of their body lags beneath the surface when they swim, like excess baggage in a boat. They kick harder—but it won't help. The solution is pushing your chest down into the water as you swim, which lifts your hips and hence your legs. It takes some practice to master this, but it works.

2. SWIM TALL. This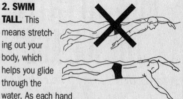
means stretching out your body, which helps you glide through the water. As each hand enters the water, reach forward—not down—before starting your pull. This will be difficult: Your inclination will be to automatically reach for the bottom as your hand hits the water. To fight that tendency, begin each stroke as if you're reaching for the wall at the end of a lap.

3. SWIM ON YOUR SIDE.
Yachts move more easily through the water than barges do. Yet most of us swim more like barges—which lie flat in the water—than like yachts, which are frequently leaning to the side, leaving only a narrow sliver in the water. So when you swim, roll from side to side as you stroke. It's not natural, and your body will fight it because you'll feel unbalanced. Master it and you'll swim more fluidly with less effort.

WINTER FUN

SNOWBOARDING: Essential gear to take some air, PAGE 628
SKIING: The top resorts for ski bums and ski bunnies, PAGE 630
EQUIPMENT: Hourglass skis are taking over the slopes, PAGE 633
ONLINE: Best ski sites on the Web, PAGE 633   **ESCAPADES:** From curling to ice climbing, other sports for cold weather, PAGE 635   **HUNTING:** A guide to bagging a duck and bringing home the venison, PAGE 638

PAGE 628, PAGE 630, PAGE 633, PAGE 633, PAGE 635, PAGE 638

FIGURE SKATING
▼

HOW TO ENTER THE ICE AGE

A top coach's tips on teaching kids to figure skate

Watching 14-year-old Tara Lipinski win the world figure skating title in 1997—the youngest "woman" ever to do so—no doubt raised the hopes of countless girls skating in circles in local arenas. But what are the odds that the hard work of any given child in America will pay off with incredible fame and riches? Not great, but also not impossible.

What does it take to make it in ice-skating? "Talent, motivation, and a serious interest in the sport," says Audrey Weisiger, an ice-skating coach, judge, and former competitor who has spent nearly her entire life in the rink, earning double gold medals in the United States Figure Skating Association in figures and freestyle. Weisinger currently coaches Michael Weiss, the country's number-two ranked skater in the senior men's division, and a strong contender for a 1998 Olympic team berth and the 1998 world team. We asked Weisinger her advice for budding ice-skaters.

■ **How old should a child be to start learning to figure skate?**

Anyone can learn to skate and enjoy it as a recreational sport at any age. If you're thinking of a competitive career, though, you have to start young enough to make it feasible — around 6 or 7 for girls, maybe 8 to 10 for boys. But starting young is no guarantee of success, of course.

■ **How do you get children interested in the sport?**

You can't. If they're not interested in skating on their own, you can't make them interested. You may not want to let your child quit after the first lesson, but be reasonable. If the child has a temper tantrum every day about practicing or going to lessons, it's time to reevaluate continuing.

A parent's role is to be supportive and encouraging—regardless of the skater's ability. Most skaters don't get to the Olympic or "elite" level of competition, but they can still enjoy the benefits of skating recreationally. Parents should facilitate improvement, but not manage it. And they should separate their own goals and desires from their child's. They should provide the opportunities for growth, but not demand it. If your child's not enjoying himself, back off.

■ **When should you invest in good skates?**

A basic pair of beginners skates is perfectly fine to start off with. When and if your child shows an interest in learning new skills,

ANATOMY OF AN ICE SKATE

Keys to putting your best foot forward

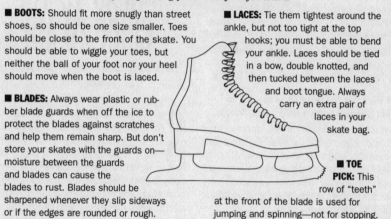

■ **BOOTS:** Should fit more snugly than street shoes, so should be one size smaller. Toes should be close to the front of the skate. You should be able to wiggle your toes, but neither the ball of your foot nor your heel should move when the boot is laced.

■ **BLADES:** Always wear plastic or rubber blade guards when off the ice to protect the blades against scratches and help them remain sharp. But don't store your skates with the guards on—moisture between the guards and blades can cause the blades to rust. Blades should be sharpened whenever they slip sideways or if the edges are rounded or rough.

■ **LACES:** Tie them tightest around the ankle, but not too tight at the top hooks; you must be able to bend your ankle. Laces should be tied in a bow, double knotted, and then tucked between the laces and boot tongue. Always carry an extra pair of laces in your skate bag.

■ **TOE PICK:** This row of "teeth" at the front of the blade is used for jumping and spinning—not for stopping.

begins skating more than once a week, and is motivated to practice to improve, then that's the time to invest in a moderately good pair of skates. Good skates have boots and blades that are mounted separately. They cost about $150 to $250.

■ How much time should children spend practicing?

That depends on the child's goals. To learn the basics for recreational skating requires

EXPERT SOURCES

To find out about ice-skating lessons and rinks in your area besides those offered by local skating rinks and the Department of Parks and Recreation, try:

Ice Skating Institute of America (ISIA) ☎ 708-808-7528

Professional Skaters Association ☎ 507-281-5122

United States Figure Skating Assn. (USFSA) ☎ 719-635-5200

about one hour of lessons per week with another two or three spent practicing. But a beginner who is 10, let's say, and has competitive goals in mind, should practice at least one hour a day with additional time spent on dance and endurance training. Skaters at the top competitive level devote the majority of their day to becoming a champion—two or three coaching sessions supplemented by hours of practice and one or two daily lessons in ballet or weight training. But no matter what level of competition they reach, children need to take some time off. I would suggest at least one day a week off to relax, pursue other interests, and to spend time with family and friends.

■ How do you find a good coach?

A good coach is one whose primary interest is in the well-being of the child, not winning medals. The coach should be properly trained as a skater—a future can be ruined by starting off with a poor foundation. And a good coach should teach the child according to the child's agenda, not his or her own.

■ What kind of expenses can a competitive skater expect?

Serious recreational skaters can expect to

pay about $60 for three lessons per week, and then another $7 a day for practice sessions. At the highest level of competition, though, expenses can reach $50,000 a year, including lessons, ice time, costumes, traveling to competitions, etc. The boots alone for custom-made skates can cost $500. For the "elite" class skaters, scholarships and fundraisers may offset some of the costs, but until a skater reaches that level, the family foots the bill.

■ What are the benefits of skating for kids who don't reach elite competition?

After every winter Olympics, we see a surge of kids sign up for lessons, and then quit when they realize how much work it takes. But kids who don't reach a high level still learn invaluable life skills. I've seen many skaters who persevered, despite not reaching the top, who then went on to become successful doctors, lawyers, and bankers, because they can apply the concentration and drive they learned from skating to other areas of life.

■ What are the downsides to a successful skating career?

When a skater reaches the elite level, especially at a very young age, the pressure and expectations can become overwhelming. He or she is trying to please the coach, or parents, or agent, or all of the above. But one of the biggest downsides for top figure skaters is the disruption of normal school and family life. With only a few top training facilities in the country, families often make great sacrifices, including uprooting or dividing the family to move closer to the coach.

■ What advice would you give parents about introducing their kids to the sport?

Go for it! Encourage them to always try to do something a little better, even if it's just for fun. And if your child does aspire to climb the competitive ladder, try to find adequate coaching in your own back yard. Keep your family intact and your child in school. If this isn't possible where you live, and if by 6th or 7th grade, your child has shown a lot of promise and determination, then maybe you owe your child the chance to pursue his or her dream.

SNOWBOARDING
▼

A HEAD-TO-TOE GUIDE TO AIR

Boarding is no longer just for the grunge set

Sixteen-year-old grunge boarders are still the norm, but now some of their parents are buying snowboards and joining them. Some skiers, attracted by the prospect of fewer knee blowouts and familiar with the slalom movements of snowboarding, are making the switch. Other adults, simply eager to spend time outdoors and get a good workout, are seeking advice from their teenagers.

Meet 40-something Paul Graves, who began snowboarding in 1964 on one huge wooden ski with a leather belt binding. Graves and partner Gordon Robbins run snowboard camps that cater mainly to middle-aged beginners. Here, Graves offers a guide to snowboard gear that will get you up and skying fat in no time!

■ **THE BOARD:** The first thing you'll need is, of course, a board. (A board with bindings costs about $500.) There are two styles of boards: freestyle and alpine. Freestyle is more common in the U.S. There is no true front or back of a freestyle board, as boarders can ride "fakie"—spin and reverse the direction of the board. Alpine, which is popular in Europe, is done on a thinner board designed to carve the snow and work the board's edges more.

■ **BINDINGS AND BOOTS:** Freestyle boards use boots that are similar to regular snow boots. Alpine boards use a rubber-soled hard boot that resembles a ski boot. The binding of the back foot is quickly released, as boarders must skate themselves through the lift line. Boarders either ride regular (left foot forward, right foot skates) or goofy (right foot forward, left foot skates).

■ BASIC MOVES

All you do is work just one edge at a time, heel or toe side. Traversing **1**, the board will hold a line like a ski when tilted on edge;

Release the edge **2**, and the board will sideslip down the fall line.

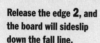

HEEL-SIDE TURN

TOE-SIDE TURN

To make the basic turn, from heel edge to toe edge, say, release the heel edge **3**,

pivot the back foot in the direction of the turn **4**,

engaging and weighting the toe edge **5**. The board's sidecut draws a curve in the snow.

SOURCE: *Men's Journal*, Dec. 1994/Jan. 1995.

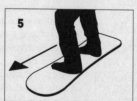

■ SNOWBOARD LINGO

■ **Bomb hole.** *If you land so hard after a jump that you leave a dent/hole in the snow.*

■ **Butt rocker.** *Being on your butt a lot.*

■ **Catching air.** *As in, "You caught some awesome air that time!" Catching air is the time spent in the air after a jump.*

■ **Doing hits.** *Any kind of move.*

■ **Fresh powder hits.** *A powder hit happens when you attack a jump that's all powder snow. When you hit, the jump "explodes" into a blur of white powder.*

■ **Headin' to the half-pipe?** *Many mountains have half-pipes built in where snowboarders can show off their moves.*

■ **Laying down an arc.** *Being so far over on your board's edges that you're almost lying flat on the snow and your body is almost parallel to the ground. Done at high speeds.*

■ **Poser.** *One who walks the walk and talks the talk, but can't catch air.*

■ **Sky fatter.** *If someone is sky-ing fatter than you, they are going higher and catching more air.*

■ **$%&#*!!!.** *Foul language is common and welcome in the snowboard world.*

■ **LEGS AND BUTT:** Loose-fitting clothing is a must. Snowboard pants come with reinforced knees because you'll spend a lot of time on your knees, either after a fall or resting. Some snowboard companies sell extra padding for your butt. But no matter how much you pad, beginners will spend a majority of time falling on their butt and knees and will feel it afterward. Also, your lead quad and upper thigh will begin to burn before too long.

■ **TORSO AND ARMS:** Most jackets come with a butt flap that makes sitting on a chilly chairlift more comfortable. Thick gloves with gaiters that come up to the elbows are important, as your hands will be on the snow a lot.

■ **HEAD:** Many snowboarders wear elaborate headgear. They wear sunglasses and goggles for the same reason that skiers do, but many opt for sunglasses all the time for the total look.

IT'S DOWNHILL FROM HERE

Our annual look at the best resorts for ski bums and ski bunnies

A ski resort's charms are often in the eye of the beholder. One skier's Heavenly is another's Purgatory. And so it goes for Sun Valley, Steamboat, Vail, and many other resorts. According to *Skiing* magazine, experts rank Whistler/Blackcomb, Vail, and Alta as their top choices, while *Ski* magazine gives Whistler/Blackcomb, Aspen,

---

■ HOW THEY RANKED

Each year, the editors of *Ski*, *Snow Country*, and *Skiing* magazines ask their readers to rank the nation's top resorts. Here are the '96–'97 results. We've included each magazine's top 10 and, if applicable, the corresponding rank on the other surveys.

AREA	SKI	SNOW COUNTRY	SKIING
Whistler/Blackcomb, B.C.	1	1	1
Aspen, Colo.	2	3	N/A
Vail, Colo.	3	2	2
Lake Louise, Alberta	4	24	N/A
Crested Butte, Colo.	5	13	N/A
Snowmass, Colo.	6	5	N/A
Squaw Valley, Calif.	7	12	N/A
Deer Valley, Utah	8	14	N/A
Jackson Hole, Wyo.	9	18	5
Park City, Utah	10	8	N/A
Sun Valley, Idaho	23	9	4
Steamboat, Colo.	19	6	7
Snowbird, Utah	14	26	8
Telluride, Colo.	17	20	6
Alta, Utah	15	29	3
Beaver Creek, Colo.	16	4	N/A
Taos, N.M.	22	25	10
Mammoth, Calif.	18	7	N/A

---

and Vail gold medals for terrain. *Snow Country* magazine ranked Beaver Creek and Mammoth among their top 10, which don't show up on the other two top 10 lists. The rankings in the box on this page show the top ten resorts for each of the three major ski magazines (and, where applicable, how those resorts ranked in the two other surveys.) Below are some of the pros and cons of the ski areas that made *Ski* magazine's top 10 list.

1. WHISTLER/BLACKCOMB, B.C.

TOP RANKINGS: Terrain, lifts and lines, value, challenge, food, lodging, après-ski

■ For the past few seasons, American ski resorts have been playing catch-up with this brash new player from the wilds of British Columbia. Number one for the second year in a row, the resort offers an awesome vertical drop, and some of the most breathtaking scenery around and a base village with a European feel. Its proximity to the Pacific, however, can lead to rain, fog, and wet snow. The sheer size—7,000 acres of accessible ski terrain and 30 lifts—however, more than compensates for a few days of bad weather.

2. ASPEN, COLO.

TOP RANKINGS: Snow conditions, terrain, challenge, fair weather, food, lodging, après-ski

■ Up from 10th place last year, Aspen is steep, compact, and covered with moguls. Skiers (no snowboarders allowed) can count on plenty of snow, 75 trails, and abundant sunshine. Beginners shouldn't even consider the mountain's challenging terrain. They might prefer nearby Buttermilk, or roaming around Aspen, replete with 300 stores, 30 art galleries, and plenty of nightclubs.

3. VAIL, COLO.

TOP RANKINGS: Snow conditions, terrain, challenge, fair weather, food, lodging, après-ski

■ It's no fluke that Vail is a consistent frontrunner on *Ski*'s lists. The mountain's front side offers run after run of groomed, forested trails, and the back side offers seven bowls to keep experts busy. A car-free alpine village is famous for shopping, food, and high prices.

■ SNOW STATS FOR SKIERS

Here are the key stats on some of the top-rated resorts by the three leading ski magazines. For lift ticket prices and travel and lodging information, call the individual resorts.

Resort		Vertical rise (ft.)	Skiable acres	% of runs that are...			Lifts/ gondolas	Snowfall (in./yr.)
				Exp.	Int.	Beg.		
WHISTLER/BLACKCOMB, B.C.	☎ 604–932–3141	5,280	3,340	30	55	15	13/1	400
ASPEN, Colo.	☎ 800–923–8920	3,267	6,310	65	35	0	7/1	300
VAIL, Colo.	☎ 800–525–8930	3,330	4,112	32	36	32	25/1	335
LAKE LOUISE, Alberta	☎ 800–661–1676	3,230	4,000	30	45	25	11/11	144
CRESTED BUTTE, Colo.	☎ 800–544–8448	2,775	1,162	58	29	13	13/0	270
SNOWMASS, Colo.	☎ 800–923–8920	4,087	2,560	38	52	10	18/0	300
SQUAW VALLEY, Calif.	☎ 800–545–4350	2,850	4,000	30	45	25	30/2	450
DEER VALLEY, Utah	☎ 800–424–DEER	2,200	1,100	35	50	15	14/0	300
JACKSON HOLE, Wyo.	☎ 800–443–6931	4,139	2,500	50	40	10	9/1	400
PARK CITY, Utah	☎ 800–545–7669	3,100	2,000	17	44	39	13/1	350
SUN VALLEY, Idaho	☎ 800–786–8259	3,400	2,067	17	45	38	17/0	220
STEAMBOAT, Colo.	☎ 800–879–6111	3,668	2,500	31	54	15	19/1	300
SNOWBIRD, Utah	☎ 800–453–3000	3,240	2,000	45	10	25	8/1	500
TELLURIDE, Colo.	☎ 800–525–2717	3,522	1,050	32	47	21	11/0	300
ALTA, Utah	☎ 801–942–0404	2,100	2,200	35	40	25	8/0	500
BEAVER CREEK, Colo.	☎ 800–525–8930	3,340	1,191	43	39	18	11/0	330
TAOS, N.M.	☎ 505–776–2291	2,612	1,094	51	25	24	11/0	312
MAMMOTH MOUNTAIN, Calif.	☎ 800–832–7320	3,100	3,500	30	40	30	27/2	335

The biggest downside is the crowds. Long lift lines are commonplace.

4. LAKE LOUISE, ALBERTA

TOP RANKINGS: Snow conditions, terrain, value, lifts and lines, challenge, lodging

■ This colossal playground north of the border makes its first appearance on *Ski*'s top 10 list. Thanks to its European-inspired terrain access policy, for about $30, you can ski 4,000 acres and take in Banff National Park's incredible scenery. About 35 miles away is Banff, a bustling Western-style resort town. Readers ranked Lake Louise low on accessiblity; count on long snowy drives, they reported.

5. CRESTED BUTTE, COLO.

TOP RANKINGS: Snow conditions, terrain, value, lifts and lines, challenge

■ There's something for all levels of skiers here. The Butte's terrain includes nearly 700 spacious beginner acres; an abundance of tree- and mogul-studded bowls for top skiers; and a network of intermediate and less expert runs. Overall, however, the skiing surface can't compare with some other Colorado resorts. A hippie-like atmosphere is evident in town—plenty of tie-dyed clothing and dreadlocks.

6. SNOWMASS, COLO.

TOP RANKINGS: Snow conditions, terrain, challenge, fair weather, food, lodging

■ While Snowmass is a great family resort with lots of beginner and intermediate runs, there are also plenty of bumps and extreme runs for the more advanced. Big Burn is a long, intermediate cruising run—one of the state's most famous. Located up the road from Aspen, Snowmass has more than its share of excellent dining and lodging, without the "Aspen scene."

7. SQUAW VALLEY, CALIF.

TOP RANKINGS: Snow conditions, terrain, challenge

■ Squaw's steeps are legendary but they are only part of the scene: 33 lifts cover 4,000 acres. In between are six peaks for the adven-

GREAT RUNS EAST OF THE ROCKIES

Eastern ski resorts may not be blessed with the West's waist-deep snowfall, but many skiers found lots to like east of the Rockies. A survey of readers by *Snow Country* magazine turned up a dozen of the most popular Eastern resorts, chosen primarily for the snow quality, terrain, scenery, and the resort's programs for children. Less enticing were the food, après-ski activities, and around-town transportation. Here are the favorites:

- **Sugarloaf,** *Me., 2,837-ft. vert. drop, 1,400 acres,* ☎ 207–237–2000
- **Killington,** *Vt., 3,150-ft. vert. drop, 918 acres,* ☎ 802–422–3333
- **Mont Tremblant,** *Quebec, 2,131-ft. vert. drop, 493 acres,* ☎ 800–461–8711
- **Sugarbush,** *Vt., 2,650-ft. vert. drop, 412 acres,* ☎ 802–583–2381
- **Sunday River,** *Me., 2,350-ft. vert. drop, 640 acres,* ☎ 207–824–3000
- **Stowe,** *Vt., 2,360-ft. vert. drop, 480 acres,* ☎ 802–253–3000
- **Mount Snow/Haystack,** *Vt., 1,700-ft. vert. drop, 750 acres,* ☎ 802–464–3333
- **Whiteface/Lake Placid,** *N.Y., 3,216-ft. vert. drop, 170 acres,* ☎ 518–523–1655
- **Okemo,** *Vt., 2,150-ft. vert. drop, 470 acres,* ☎ 802–228–4041
- **Smugglers' Notch,** *Vt., 2,610-ft. vert. drop, 246 acres,* ☎ 802–644–8851
- **Stratton,** *Vt., 2,003-ft. vert. drop, 478 acres,* ☎ 802–297–2200
- **Loon,** *N.H., 2,100-ft. vert. drop, 250 acres,* ☎ 603–745–8111

turous, cruising valleys for intermediates, and a sunny plateau for beginners. For night skiing, try the 3¹/₂-mile long, 2,000-ft. Mountain Run. Nightlife migrates to nearby Tahoe City, but it's hard to avoid the traffic and crowds.

8. DEER VALLEY, UTAH

TOP RANKINGS: Snow conditions, lifts and lines, fair weather, accessibility, food, lodging

■ Deer Valley consistently ranks number one in the food category. You can find homemade granola as easily as Chilean sea bass with fresh ginger sauce. Pampering is the name of the game all around, from the 1,100 well-groomed acres to luxury lodgings. Ski valets help you unload and load your car. But, it comes at a price, of course. Deer Valley ranked near the bottom when it comes to value.

9. JACKSON HOLE, WYO.

TOP RANKINGS: Snow conditions, terrain, challenge

■ For years, families and intermediate skiers have shied away from Jackson Hole, the single toughest ski mountain in the country. But a booming town, spectacular views of the Tetons, and half a mountain of beginner and intermediate runs are changing all that. If you still want to tackle the expert black diamonds, help yourself to 1,250 acres and 4,139 vertical feet of terrain. Jets are a common sight at Jackson's airport, but flights fill up fast and securing a seat can be difficult.

10. PARK CITY, UTAH

TOP RANKINGS: Terrain, challenge, accessibility

■ No matter what curves the weather throws, Park City lays down a world-class carpet of snow. This future site of the 2002 Olympic snowboarding events strives to maintain its family-friendly reputation. But that doesn't mean the slopes are boring. Steep chutes and powder-rich bowls off Jupiter Peak offer plenty of challenge. (History buffs can bring along a map and explore silver mining sites on the mountain.) Reader complaints included a lift system that warrants some improvement.

SUPER SKIS TO LIFT YOUR SKILLS

"Hourglass" skis can make an expert out of an intermediate

There's a revolution under way in the world of skiing. For years, ski manufacturers have fiddled with ski technology, producing faster, lighter, safer equipment, but the fundamental shape of the ski has remain unchanged. Now, parabolic or hourglass skis are challenging the traditional ski design. "Hourglass skis will do for skiing what the Prince oversized rackets did for tennis and the Big Bertha oversized driver did for golf," says Steve Still, director of the Vail Ski School. Still is such a proponent of hourglass skis that the Vail Ski School has converted to them. We asked Still about some of the whys and wherefores.

■ **What are hourglass skis?**

Hourglass skis are a new style of ski that is narrow in the middle and wider at the tip and tail. They're also sometimes called "super-sidecut" or "parabolic" skis.

■ **How do they work?**

All skis have sidecut (a tapering in the middle). When a ski is turned on edge, the sidecut helps to make the turn. Without sidecut, skis would not turn at all. On traditional skis, the sidecut is not extreme and skiers must shift their weight and lift their legs and feet in order to turn their skis. On hourglass skis, however, the sidecut is so extreme that skiers just shift their weight from ski to ski.

■ **What type of skiers would benefit most?**

All skiers. Because less energy is needed to turn hourglass skis, all skiers will feel less

---

CYBER SOURCES

SKIING IN CYBERSPACE

Snow reports, trail maps, and other skiing information is a computer keystroke away. Here are some of the better skiing Web sites:

SKICENTRAL
http://www.skicentral.com/ skimaps.html
■ Visit the Web sites of various ski resorts and locate trail maps.

SKI GATE
http://www.skigate.com/
■ Everything from equipment to ski products and resort information.

SKINET
http://www.skinet.com
■ This site of *Ski* and *Skiing* magazines offers vital

stats on resorts, equipment reviews, snow conditions, same-day race results, chat forums, travel information, links to other ski pages, and a resort finder, to help you choose the resort that suits your interests and ability.

SOUTHLAND SKI SERVER
http://www.cccd.edu/ski.html
■ Creator Mark Bixby has made it his own personal crusade to keep California skiers informed and

entertained. Bixby provides a wealth of information on most California resorts and offers links to nearly every ski resource. *Snow Country* magazine dubbed his page "the best ski link out there."

SKI WEB HOME PAGE
http://diamond.sierra.net:80/ skiweb/
■ Offers links to most major ski resorts and information on discount tickets.

fatigued and will be able to ski longer and safer. Beginners will see improvement almost immediately; intermediates will soon be skiing effortlessly; experts will be able to get more performance out of their skis while expending less energy; even pros can benefit— many of today's World Cup skiers have switched to hourglass skis.

■ Do they work better in some conditions?

Soft, cruising runs with room were made for hourglass skis. Some complain the sidecut on hourglass skis makes it tough to run them fast and straight on quick runs.

■ What are the disadvantages?

Hourglass skis are funny-looking. If you can handle the muffled giggles in the lift lines, you may have overcome the biggest challenge facing hourglass skis.

■ Are all hourglass skis the same?

The severity of the sidecut varies by ski. Many rental shops now carry hourglass skis, so you can comparison-shop before you buy. Elan and Head are two of the biggest producers of hourglass skis, but expect the hourglass market to expand rapidly.

■ Do they cost the same as regular skis?

Skis aren't cheap. If you're not used to dropping $500 on a pair of skis, you may be turned off by the cost of hourglass. Expect to spend between $450 and $550.

EXPERT TIPS

HOW LONG SHOULD YOUR SKIS BE?

Some skis are too big, some are too small, and some are just right. Greenwood's Ski Haus in Boise, Idaho—consistently rated one of the best ski shops in the country by Snow Country *magazine—offers these sizing tips*

■ The first question you need to ask yourself is: What type of skier are you?
• If you are a beginner to intermediate skier, you should probably buy skis about 4 inches taller than yourself
• If you are a more accomplished, aggressive skier, you could go 4 to 8 inches over your head.
• If you are very, very aggressive, you could venture up to 12 inches over your head.

■ If you are buying hourglass skis, they may be much shorter.

AT A GLANCE:

BEGINNER: 4" longer

EXPERIENCED: 4-8" longer

VERY AGGRESSIVE: 12" longer

■ In general, you should buy skis that are on the long side. In the old days, beginners and intermediates were steered toward very short skis. Not anymore.

■ The longer the ski, the faster the ride. Add 5 cm. for fast skiing on groomed slopes. Subtract 5 cm. for skiing mostly bumps, or if you are a slow, conservative skier.

■ Intermediate skiers looking for a basic, all-purpose ski should use the chart below as a general guide.

HEIGHT	SKI LENGTH (cm.)
5'0" – 5'1"	158
5'2" – 5'3"	168
5'4" – 5'5"	178
5'6" – 5'7"	183
5'8" – 5'9"	188
5'10" – 5'11"	193
6'0" – 6'1"	198
6'2" – 6'3"	201
6'3" +	201

POLAR CHILLS AND THRILLS

Who says you have to stay in and get fat? Try curling, for example

J ust because winter is here doesn't mean you should settle for riding a stationary bike or climbing a fake set of steps in a gym. But what if skiing isn't your thing? Here's a guide to other winter activities that team up well with ice, snow, and chilly weather.

CURLING

Curling is a team sport played on ice. Teams of four shove "rocks" down the ice toward a target. Team members slide along the ice with the rock, steering it by sweeping long-handled brooms in front of it. While curling is found mostly in the colder northern tier of the country, there are curling clubs as far west as San Francisco and as far south as Houston. More than 15,000 curling enthusiasts do their stuff all winter long, some of those with dreams of gold: Curling will debut as a full-medal sport in the 1998 Olympics.

■ **GEAR:** Clubs are also good places to start because many lend equipment to beginners. Once you're serious, you'll need your own Teflon slider (about $18); a broom (about $40); and curling shoes (about $80), but flat sneakers will also do.

■ **TRAINING TIP:** Sweeping (the rapid back and forth with the broom in front of the curling rock) is an exhaustive workout for the arms and shoulders. But don't forget about your quads: curling is done primarily in a squat.

■ **KEEP AN EYE ON:** The skip (the "captain" of the four-person team). The skip is the strategist and controls the flow of the shots and movement.

■ **WHO TO CALL:** U.S. Curling Association ☎ 715-344-1199. Curling is a club-oriented sport. Your first step is to get in touch with one of the 130 area clubs. Most clubs also offer instruction for beginners.

SNOWSHOEING

Snowshoes are no longer relics of the Nordic past. In fact, snowshoe sales have tripled of late and snowshoers are popping up at ski resorts the way snowboarders did in the '80s. New lightweight equipment is making snowshoeing easier and faster for experts and beginners alike. Many serious athletes now do their winter training on snowshoes and there is an annual snowshoe marathon, but you don't need to be an iron man to snowshoe. It is, perhaps, the world's simplest sport: If you can walk, you can snowshoe.

■ **GEAR:** One of snowshoeing's most appealing aspects is its lack of cumbersome gear. The old-fashioned wood and rawhide snowshoes have given way to lightweight aluminum shoes with crampons. But in deeper powder, you need more flotation and the new running snowshoes are not as effective. A set of Nordic ski poles will give you more balance and stability and also add an upper-body workout. Like cross-country skiers, snowshoers should dress in layers that will keep out the cold but allow you to strip down once you really start sweating— which you will. Top-of-the-line snowshoes can cost about $250, but many outdoors stores rent them.

■ **TRAINING TIP:** Snowshoeing is an excellent cardiovascular workout. In steep terrain, a 150-pound snowshoer can burn up to 500 calories per mile. A simple way to get in shape for snowshoeing is walking up and down hills. When you first start, you'll feel a burn in the tops of the legs at the hip and groin area from lifting a snow-filled shoe.

■ **KEEP AN EYE ON:** The scenery. Snowshoeing can take you places you couldn't get to on skis or in boots. But if you're in the mountains, be careful in the backcountry and keep an eye out for avalanches.

■ **WHO TO CALL:** There is no national snowshoe association, but check local newspapers and local outdoors stores for information on any clubs in your area. For further information, you could call self-appointed sport spokesman Dave Felkley ☎303–258–3157, a snowshoe guide in Boulder, Colorado.

HOCKEY

Want to be more than a hockey parent? Want to relive those glory days of Pee Wee hockey? Then strap on your skates and join an amateur hockey league. There are organized hockey leagues all over the country (no checking, or blocking an opponent, is allowed in older leagues) and the amateur popularity of the sport continues to rise.

■ **GEAR:** You'll need a lot. Hockey requires a fair amount of equipment. You can't play league hockey in your college sweatshirt and a pair of skates; you'll need all the proper body padding (including shoulder pads, shin pads and elbow pads), gloves, a stick, and a helmet. Plan on spending anywhere from $200 to $700. You might want to check with used sports stores for good prices on skates and equipment.

■ **TRAINING TIP:** Hockey is a grueling cardiovascular workout, so don't hit the ice without some preconditioning. Also, although most over-35 leagues outlaw checking, expect to take some knocks and spills—and not complain. Before you even think about joining a team, make sure you're confident on your skates—forward, backward, and stopping.

■ **KEEP AN EYE ON:** The obvious—the puck, your teammates, and the opposing team. If you're playing hockey to relieve a little stress and aggression, you may want to throw the occasional hip check. But if you're playing

for pure cardiovascular reasons, watch out so you don't end up with your face plastered against the Plexiglas.

■ **WHO TO CALL:** USA Hockey ☎719–599–5500 is the national governing body for hockey in the United States. USA Hockey can provide information on area leagues. For more information on old-timers' leagues in your areas, check the Yellow Pages for ice rinks.

SNOWMOBILING

A nice, noisy snowmobile can take you everywhere a wimpy pair of cross country skis can—and make a lot more noise doing it too. There are about 1.4 million registered snowmobiles in the U.S. Tour operators offer everything from half-day to three- to four-day trips. Women-only trips are a sign of the sports growing popularity.

■ **GEAR:** The average snowmobile costs between $5,000 and $6,000, but used ones can be found for about $2,000. Daily rentals can run from $50 to several hundred dollars, depending on the package. If you don't own them, you'll also need to rent a snowmobile suit, gloves, and a helmet.

■ **TRAINING TIP:** Always wear a helmet and follow general safety guidelines. There are a number of snowmobile deaths every year, caused mostly by drunk and reckless driving. Just like cars, snowmobiles must abide by a set of operating laws. Most operators offer a free lesson on mechanics, handling, and safety. Physically, riding a snowmobile may not seem taxing, but controlling a large machine for several hours at a time wears out anyone. Don't be too ambitious and be sure to head back before you're beat.

■ **KEEP AN EYE ON:** Where you are. Snowmobiling on private land without prior consent could land you in jail. There are over 100,000 miles of groomed, marked snowmobile trails in North America. Always be extra cautious about snowmobiling on frozen lakes. And if you're snowmobiling near a road, don't assume the traffic can see you.

■ **WHO TO CALL:** The American Council of Snowmobile Associations ☎517–351–4362 is the best place to start. The council can help you organize a trip or direct you to one of 27 state organizations for more region-specific information. The council also offers a variety of snowmobiling publications, including safety manuals and a complete North American snowmobile directory.

POLAR BEAR SWIMMING

Jump in a body of water in the middle of January and you're called a nut. Do it with a club and you're called a polar bear swimmer. Polar bears have been gathering on frozen U.S. shores for close to 100 years and today's polar bears claim that the therapeutic benefits of cold-water swimming keep them healthy and happy. It's one of winter's least complicated sports. All you need is a swimsuit, a brisk winter day, a body of water, and the determination to walk (or run) into icy cold waves.

■ **GEAR:** A swimsuit, goggles, water-proof booties optional, a big warm towel.

■ **TRAINING TIP:** Those with heart troubles should check with their physicians before jumping in icy water. The sudden drastic change in temperature could cause problems, but many polar bears are octogenarians who claim the cold water is precisely what keeps them going.

■ **KEEP AN EYE ON:** Frolickers. Polar bear swimming is as much about frolicking and splashing in the icy water as it is about exercise. Polar bears swim together because it's fun. If you want a serious, competitive workout, turn down the temperature in the pool and do some laps.

■ **WHO TO CALL:** Although you could jump in any old frozen water, it's more fun to do it with a club. The Coney Island Polar Bears (at 91 years old) is the nation's oldest club, ☎718–748–1674. If you're in or near Boston, there's the L Street Swimming Club and Brownies, ☎617–635–5106. On the West Coast,

jump in with San Francisco's Dolphin Swimming and Boating Club ☎415–441–9329.

ICE CLIMBING

Ice climbing was invented by restless rock climbers looking for a way to pass the winter months. It is similar to rock climbing, but climbers scale frozen waterfalls, instead of sheer cliffs. Climbers can be found anywhere the temperature drops. The mecca for ice climbers is the San Juan Range, near Telluride, Colorado, but East Coasters can find excellent ice climbing outside North Conway, N.H., and midwestern diehards have been known to ice silos for a good climb. The sport's popularity has soared in recent years, mostly due to rock climbing's popularity and advances in safety equipment.

■ **GEAR:** To be properly outfitted, you'll need: ice climbing boots, which are plastic versions of stiff hiking boots and run $200–$250; crampons, the stiff iron spikes you strap to your boots that cost $125–$150; two hand tools, basically handles with fancy picks on them that cost about $200; a helmet. Most climbers stick to low climbs, but anything higher requires ropes and harnesses.

■ **TRAINING TIP:** Climbing is done with all parts of your body, not just the arms, as many people assume. Women often make excellent climbers because they lack upper body strength, and are forced to use ingenuity instead of brawn.

■ **KEEP AN EYE ON:** Melting ice, so you can avoid it. A sunny, warm day may tempt you outside, but resign yourself to the fact that ice climbing is best—and safest—on chilly, cloudy days.

■ **WHO TO CALL:** There are no organized ice climbing organizations, but your local outdoors clubs and retail outlets are good sources. In the San Juans, call Ryder–Walker Alpine Adventures in Telluride, Colorado ☎970–728–6481. In New England call International Mountain Equipment in North Conway, New Hampshire ☎603–356–6316.

THE HUNTER AND HIS PREY

Choose your target, dress warmly, and head for the woods

Mention hunting and most people picture a middle-aged man in an orange vest wielding a rifle and, perhaps, a beer can. But the sport of hunting has become so popular that hunters—many of them women—are too diverse to be easily stereotyped. The United States Fish and Wildlife Service estimates that some 40 million Americans hunt or fish. The average hunter spends about $1,000 a year, making the sport a $40.9 billion annual industry. (For more information about fishing, see The Great Outdoors, page 622.)

Hunting is a sport of precision, skill, challenge, and being outdoors. You have four sports to choose from. You can hunt waterfowl (ducks and geese), upland birds (quail, dove, grouse, and pheasant), deer, or elk. Each sport has its own seasons, locations, and pros and cons. Dave Petzal, editor-in-chief of *Field and Stream,* has compiled a beginner's guide to the basics of hunting.

WATERFOWL

Waterfowl are, of course, found near water. Duck hunters spend their time crouched in fields and blinds (structures that hunters erect to conceal them from the ducks) alongside lakes, ponds, and marshes.

The North American geese population is larger than the duck population. One reason: Many geese have adapted to their surroundings and may stay in one spot all year long, rather than migrating. Hunting geese is similar to hunting ducks. The only differences are the seasons and limits. Check with your local fish and wildlife department or a good sporting goods store for local information.

■ **WHERE TO HUNT:** There are four principal North American migration routes. So no matter where you live, you're not more than a state or two away from a duck thoroughfare. Much of the best duck hunting land is private. You will need to stick to public land or pay a user's fee for the private land.

■ **WHEN TO HUNT:** Early in the morning. You can't shoot until the first daylight, but plan on starting your day about 3 a.m., so you can get set up and ready by sunrise. The best shooting is generally at sunrise and sunset.

Duck hunting seasons vary by region, but you can plan on hunting somewhere between November and January, depending on how far south you live. Seasons are set each August by the local fish and wildlife department.

■ **ESSENTIAL GEAR:** A license and (in many states) proof of a hunting safety course. The limits on ducks are generally very small and some species are limited or restricted. It's essential you have a license and are within local limits. For information on licenses, check with your local sporting goods store.
• **12-gauge shotgun**—the accepted gun of choice for all duck hunters. Shotguns actually fire hundreds of tiny pellets, which make them ideal for moving targets, but they don't shoot far, so don't fire at ducks beyond your 40-yard range.
• **Camouflage raingear and hip boots.** Plan on being cold and wet. The best duck hunting is always in the worst weather.
• **A duck call,** very important and worth any investment. A good one costs about $30.
• **Decoys** made of lightweight plastic help lure ducks within range.
• **A good retriever dog** is crucial. Labrador retrievers are best, followed by golden retrievers.

■ **HUNTING TIP:** Don't shoot at anything more than 40 yards away. Wait until the ducks are lured into your decoys, and then pull the trigger as they're descending. Also, the hunting is best on rainy, overcast days.

UPLAND BIRDS

Upland generally refers to the hunting of inland birds. The most popular targets are dove, followed by quail, grouse, and pheasant.

■ **WHERE TO HUNT:** Upland hunters generally stand around in fields and prairies, near where birds eat, and wait for the birds to descend and take off. Upland hunting is common in all parts of the country, but find out where the private and public lands are.

■ **WHEN TO HUNT:** Upland seasons are generally in the fall and early winter months. The bird populations are more dense than waterfowl populations, so seasons are longer and limits are larger. Inland birds feed at all times of day, so you don't necessarily need to be shooting at sunrise or sunset.

■ **ESSENTIAL GEAR:** Proper licenses and safety courses, of course. Unlike waterfowl, no calls or decoys are necessary.
• **Any type of shotgun,** from a 12-gauge to a .410-gauge shotgun, will do.
• **Brush pants** (heavy canvas pants faced with leather or nylon) for trudging through briers and thickets. A jacket of the same material is also essential.
• **A game vest with multiple pockets** provides a handy place to store shells and also a place to stuff the game you shoot.
• **A good dog,** either a pointer (to track down birds), a retriever (to bring back your kill), or a springer (to flush the birds up).

■ **HUNTING TIP:** Because you're using a shotgun, don't shoot at anything beyond 40 yards.

DEER

Two deer species are hunted: the white-tail (the most commonly hunted and found throughout the U.S.) and the mule (only found west of the Mississippi).

■ **WHERE TO HUNT:** You can hunt as far south as South Carolina and as far north as Canada. Access to hunting on private land can easily cost several hundred dollars. In some areas, membership in a hunting club grants you access to private areas.

■ **WHEN TO HUNT:** Deer hunting seasons tend to be short, simply because the deer can't handle constant hunting pressure.

Depending on your latitude, deer season is somewhere between August and January.

■ **ESSENTIAL GEAR:** License and proof of hunter-safety course. Safety courses are usually conducted by the local fish and game department at a shooting range.
• **Weapon of choice.** There are three types of weapons to hunt deer, each having its own season. Most common is the modern rifle. But more primitive weapons—bow and arrows and muzzle-loading rifles—are also used. The primitive weapons offer a greater challenge and demand a higher skill level—though animal rights activists argue that bow-hunting in particular can be more cruel to the animals. Proficiency in all three weapons prolongs your hunting season.
• **Camouflage gear** made of soft fabrics. Your clothes must not rustle when you move or bump into trees. The slightest noise can ruin a day of tracking.
• **A bright orange hunting vest** is required in most states.
• **A telescopic scope on your rifle** will help you track your target.
• **A good set of binoculars** is a must. Using your scope exclusively can lead to misfires.
• **Survival kit,** including equipment to start a fire. The woods can be cold, and you may end up spending a full day or night outdoors.
        • **Compass.** Don't assume

FACT FILE:

BRINGING HOME THE VENISON

■ *Expenses for a day of deer hunting:*   **$50** — *license*
                        $200 — *proper clothes*
                        $500 — *rifle*
                        $300 — *scope*
     $500–$1,000 — *Either a trespassing fee on private land, or lodging near public land*
                        $300 — *binoculars*
     $1,850–$2,350 — *total*

FALCONRY: A SPORT OF SULTANS

An ancient field sport favored by kings and sultans is making a modest modern-day comeback of sorts. There are 2,000 or so falconers in the U.S. currently, but their numbers are soaring. Falconers spend years training falcons and red-tailed hawks to respond to commands, hunt prey, and then return to their masters. They track down and kill everything from duck and pheasant to rabbits and squirrels. The thrill of the sport, falconers say, is spending time outside and the awesome sight of a falcon diving at 200 mph to attack its prey.

Wannabe falconers must spend several years in training—earning first the title of apprentice, then general, then master falconer. You can't just purchase a falcon, you must find a master who is willing to be your sponsor. There are strict state and federal regulations (designed to protect the birds) and multiple levels of examinations to pass. In response to the sport's growing popularity, several resort areas now offer day- or week-long falconry schools. The North American Falconers Association (125 S. Woodstock Drive, Cherry Hill, NJ 08034) can put you in touch with your local falconers club.

■ **WHERE TO HUNT:** Falconry is currently outlawed in Delaware, Hawaii, and Connecticut, but you can take your falcon pretty much anywhere else. (Falcons generally hunt game birds; red-tailed hawks generally hunt smaller land animals.)

■ **WHEN TO HUNT:** There is no set falconry season. Indeed, if you own a falcon, you must work with, train, and care for it every day. You also must first pass a written exam and housing inspection before you can begin training your own bird.

■ **ESSENTIAL GEAR:** A falcon or hawk. Apprentice falconers trap wild birds and spend two years training them. Once you are a master or general, you can buy a bred bird.

• **Appropriate housing** for your bird.
• **Classic falconers' bells** alert you to the whereabouts of your bird when it is off hunting.
• **Leather glove** allows the bird to rest on your arm.
• **Game bag** (sack) to bring home your catch.
• **Lure to bring your bird back.** If properly trained, your falcon will identify the lure with a food-reward and promptly return.

■ **HUNTING TIP:** These birds of prey are not pets. They are working animals and will only return to you because they want to.

you can find your way back to your car. Trees start to look alike after a while.

■ **HUNTING TIP:** Rifles are more precise than shotguns, but you only get one chance. Unlike shotguns, rifles shoot a single, conical-shaped bullet. A careless shot can ruin an entire day of tracking and scare off all deer within earshot, and deer have great ears.

ELK

Hunting elk is similar to hunting deer, but it's harder, you need to travel farther to do it, and you need more expensive stuff.

■ **ESSENTIAL GEAR:** Elk are found in the western and Alaskan mountains, so factor in a plane ride if you don't live in the Rocky Mountains or the 49th state.

• **A big-game rifle,** which can cost about $2,000, is essential.
• **A guide who knows the area.** It's not worth the money to fly out there and spend three days getting the lay of the land.
• **An out-of-state elk hunting license,** if you don't live in one of the Rocky Mountain states, which runs about $300–$500.
• **An access fee.** It's not uncommon to pay $5,000 for prime elk country.

PARLOR GAMES

MONOPOLY: The most landed-on sites, PAGE 642   **SCRABBLE:** Seven tips from a Scrabble master on winning the war of words, PAGE 643 **BOARD GAMES:** The rules for checkers, chess, and backgammon, PAGE 644   **CARD GAMES:** A primer on poker, gin rummy, spades, and solitaire, PAGE 647   **BLACKJACK:** When to stick and when to take a hit, PAGE 649   **BRIDGE:** Essential reading for the enthusiast, PAGE 651

STRATEGIES
▼

SECRETS OF A MONOPOLY CHAMP

Don't buy Boardwalk, skimp on hotels, and gobble up the orange

At the Monopoly Game Championship in New York City in the fall of 1995, Roger Craig astonished onlookers when, on his first pass around the board, he opted not to buy Boardwalk, the most expensive property in the game and one highly coveted by lesser players. But about 90 minutes later, Craig, a tire salesman from Harrisburg, Ill., emerged as the U.S. Monopoly champion for the next four years. We tracked Craig down and asked him to share some of his secrets of success. Craig's strategy is based on the "traditional" game, in which each player starts with $1,500 and gives all tax and fine money over to the bank. (Nontournament matches often include the "untraditional" $500 bonus pot into which all taxes and fines are placed—a bounty awarded to any player landing directly on Free Parking.)

■ **An important tactical question first. Do you prefer a particular token?**

I use the iron. It's the smallest piece on the board, and as you're moving it around you can hide it behind hotels and get away without paying rent. It's amazing how much money I've saved over the years using that piece. Once the dice are rolled by two people beyond yourself, you can't be caught for owing money on your last move. In the championship final they announced every move to the crowd, so I couldn't get away with it.

■ **What is your basic strategy in acquiring property?**

You buy everything you can, until you get around to the three most expensive sets of properties—the yellow ones (Atlantic, Ventnor, Marvin Gardens), green ones (Pacific, North Carolina, Pennsylvania) and blue ones (Park Place, Boardwalk). They cost too much to buy, get a monopoly on, then have to improve with houses and hotels. If I get one of the green ones or the yellow ones, that's all I'm interested in. It blocks the other monopolies, and it gives me something to trade later in the game.

■ **Which properties are the best to acquire?**

The orange ones—St. James, Tennessee and New York. The two most common numbers rolled on the dice are six and eight—and rolling them just pops you onto the orange ones. You get those three or the red ones—Kentucky, Indiana, and Illinois—and you're going to win 75 percent or more of the time unless you roll very poorly. They don't cost

■ THE MOST LANDED-ON MONOPOLIES

In the 1980s, Parker Brothers, Monopoly's manufacturer, made a list of the most frequently landed-upon monopolies. The list shows the odds a player is going to land on one property of a monopoly in one trip around the board.

■ GO DIRECTLY TO JAIL...

1	**RAILROADS** – B&O, Reading, Short Line, Penn	**64%**
2	**ORANGES** – N.Y., St. James, Tennessee	**50%**
3	**REDS** – Illinois, Indiana, Kentucky	**49%**
4	**YELLOWS** – Marvin Gardens, Atlantic, Ventnor	**45%**
5	**GREENS** – Pacific, Pennsylvania, N. Carolina	**44%**
6	**LIGHT PURPLES** – St. Charles, States, Virginia	**43%**
7	**LIGHT BLUES** – Oriental, Connecticut, Vermont	**39%**
8	**UTILITIES** – Water Works, Electric Co.	**32%**
9	**DARK BLUES** – Boardwalk, Park Place	**27%**
10	**DARK PURPLES** – Mediterranean, Baltic	**24%**

■ DO NOT PASS GO, DO NOT COLLECT $200...

Using a computer, Irvin Hentzel, a mathematics professor at Iowa State University and a frustrated Monopoly player, calculated the 10 spaces you can count on landing on more than others. (The most landed-upon space was Jail, but Hentzel deleted that from his list, since a player in Jail had to remain there for three turns or roll doubles to get out.) Upon making his findings in 1973, Hentzel promptly quit playing. "It was no fun anymore," he explained. "I had figured it out."

1. Illinois Avenue
2. Go
3. B&O Railroad
4. Free Parking
5. Tennessee Avenue
6. New York Avenue
7. Reading Railroad
8. St. James Place
9. Water Works
10. Pennsylvania Railroad

too much to build up, and they bring in the best return for what you spend.

Knowing that, if you have one of the yellows and two of the greens—or vice-versa—you can trade them for oranges or reds to people who don't know what it takes to win. They see the yellows and greens cost more, and they're only thinking about how much they'll get when someone lands there—not how much it will cost to build them up. I figure how much cash a player can generate. I would never make such a trade if a guy was sitting there with $1,000 in cash.

■ How does your strategy change once you have a monopoly?

If you can get a monopoly of your own without having to trade for it, you ought to have the game in hand. Then you can spend the rest of your time blocking everybody else—making a trade that doesn't help any opponent and gets you a piece of property that will block someone else. If you're holding all the single cards to a bunch of monopolies and you've got one monopoly yourself, they can't beat you. The only time I will make a trade that gives someone a monopoly is if I get an outright monopoly itself in exchange.

It usually takes eight or nine times around for everything to be bought up. When all the properties are sold, you start looking around at all the deals you can make. Hardly anybody ever tries to get Boardwalk or Park Place as part of a deal, because they cost so much to improve—and at that stage of the game you don't have any money.

■ How much should you build up your properties with houses and hotels?

Everybody wants to build up as many houses as they can—as fast as they can. A good rule is to only build up to the three-house level—as quickly as possible. Your return on your money from one house to two houses is

A-D-V-I-C-E FROM A SCRABBLE MASTER

Seven things you can do to score big

Joe Edley was already a self-admitted games guru when he began playing Scrabble. After two years of "fanatical study," he won the National Scrabble Championship in 1978. Since then, he has won another national title (1992) and consistently has been one of the 15 top-ranked players in the U.S. Edley is the co-author, with John Williams, of *Everything Scrabble* (Pocket Books, 1985). Both men are officials with the National Scrabble Organization (☎ 516-477-0033). The words Edley suggests mastering can all be found in the *Official Scrabble Players Dictionary* (Merriam-Webster, 1993). The third edition, published in 1996, contains approximately 1,200 more words than the 1991 second edition—but without some 100 "offensive" words that have been removed from the game.

■ Learn the 94 two-letter words.

■ Learn the 996 three-letter words.

■ Learn the 17 "Q without U" words. Seven of them (Faqir, Qintar, Qanat, Tranq, Qoph, Qaid, Qat) can also be made plural with the addition of an "S", and "Qindar" (an Albanian monetary unit) can become "Qindarka."

■ Learn the approximately 1,200 four- and five-letter words containing a J, Q, X, or Z.

■ Learn to use "vowel dumps"—words containing multiple vowels such as "ourie" (shivering with cold) and "warison" (a battle cry) that get four or more low-scoring vowels out of your rack in one move.

■ "S" and "A" are "hook letters" that can often be used to form two words off of one existing word (e.g., "board" can lead to "aboard" and "ape").

■ Learn "bingos"—words that by using all seven of your tiles earn a 50-point bonus. Included in the bingo list are about 200 "six to make seven" words that can all be built off just three six-letter words (saltine, satire, retain) and one blank tile.

almost nothing, but once you make the jump to the third house—that's where your real money is made. The jump from the third to the fourth house and the fourth house to a hotel isn't that big. So save your money for something else.

The biggest mistake I saw people make during the championships was that as soon as they got a monopoly, they would spend everything in front of them to build their land up—without regard to where they or the other players were on the board. You need to leave yourself enough money to cover yourself. If there are several monopolies out, I'll take whatever money I figure I can spend and put it aside, then see where everyone else is on the board. As soon as they get real

close to my property, then I'll build on the property and take a chance they'll land there. I also wait until I pass opposing monopolies before spending cash.

■ **What else should players keep in mind?**

Don't always go for cash. Say an opponent lands on your property, and they owe you $800. You can see by what they have in front of them that they can raise that much cash with what they have on hand and by mortgaging properties. It's not always smart to let them do that, because if you leave them with three or four mortgaged properties, the next person who lands there is going to be able to get those properties. So a lot of times, I'll take whatever property they have instead of cash.

WHERE KINGS AND QUEENS REIGN

The rules that rule the pieces in checkers, chess, and backgammon

The most exciting board games require a unique mix of brains and imaginative brawn. In the best of matches, the rules metamorphose from simple mathematical variations into the physics of a new world in which pawns become warriors and you are the mastermind behind a war in which everything good and decent is at stake. Here are the rules that govern the battlefield.

HOPSCOTCHING THE CHECKER BOARD

Learning to play checkers is child's play, but devising strategies to triumph over a good player takes skill and lots of practice. The winner, of course, is the first player to capture all of an opponent's men or to block them so that they can't move anywhere on the board. To test your mettle, follow these instructions:

RANK AND FILE: In both checkers and chess, the rows across are known as ranks; the columns as files. In checkers, only the dark squares are used.

■ Opponents face each other across the board, which has eight rows of eight squares each, alternately red and black. One player takes the red pieces, or men, and puts them on the black squares in the three horizontal rows nearest him. The opponent places the black checkers on the black squares in the three rows facing him.

■ The opponents take turns—black goes first, then red—moving a man forward diagonally toward the opponent's side. Only the black squares are used. With each turn, a player moves one man to an adjacent empty square. When one player's man comes up against an enemy checker and there is an empty space behind it, the player jumps over the enemy, landing on the unoccupied square. The captured checker is removed from the board.

■ One man can jump two or more enemy pieces consecutively, by moving diagonally left or right after the first jump, as long as there are empty spaces to land on between each jump. A checker that makes it to any square in the opponent's first row becomes a king—at which time it gets crowned by a man of the same color that is not in play. The king can now move, and jump, forward and backward.

THE MIND FIELDS OF CHESS

When it comes to drama, intrigue, and byzantine rules, few games can match chess, which is thought to date back to sixth-century India or China. Odds are you won't become the next Bobby Fischer, who at age 15 was the youngest international grandmaster in history, but here are the rules that will take you to the endgame: capturing the enemy's king.

■ Opponents face each other across the board, which has eight rows of eight squares each, alternately white and black. Each player gets 16 pieces of one color, black or white. From least to most important, the pieces are: 8 pawns, 2 knights, 2 bishops, 2 rooks (or castles), 1 queen, and 1 king.

■ Place the board so that each player has a light square at the nearest right-hand corner.

King moves   **Queen moves**   **Bishop moves**

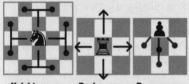

Knight moves   **Rook moves**   **Pawn moves**

MANEUVERS: As shown here, the six chess pieces can move in a variety of ways. The knight, however, is the only one that can actually move through, or jump over, other pieces. That ability, combined with its unusual L-shaped moving pattern, makes it an endgame linchpin.

In the row closest to you, place in order from left to right: rook, knight, bishop, queen, king, bishop, knight, and rook. Line up the pawns next to each other in the row directly in front these pieces.

■ A piece can move only into a square that's not occupied by another piece owned by the same player. If an enemy piece occupies the square, it is captured. You remove the captured piece from the board and put your piece in its place.

■ A pawn moves forward one square at a time, except for its first move when it can go one or two squares. A knight makes an L-shaped move, going two squares forward, backward, or sideways, then another square at a right angle. It's the only piece that can jump over another piece. A bishop goes diagonally forward or backward, but has to stay on the same color. A rook moves forward, backward, or sideways, for any distance. The queen is a potent force. She moves forward, backward, sideways, and diagonally for any number of squares in one direction. The king's moves are like the queen's except that he moves one square at a time, as long as it's unoccupied or not under attack by an enemy piece.

■ When a king is under attack by an enemy piece, the king is in check. The player whose king is in check has several options: to move the king to safety, to capture the attacker, or to move another piece to a square between the king and the attacker. If a player can't take any of these moves, the king is captured or "checkmated," and the game is over.

■ Pieces capture an opponent's man by moving as they normally do, except for the pawn. It can capture any of its opponent's pieces that are diagonally next to and ahead of it.

■ A pawn can also take an enemy pawn "en passant," or in passing. Say an opponent starts by moving his pawn two squares, instead of one, putting it next to one's pawn. You can take that piece by moving diagonally to the square directly behind it. But do it immediately: you can't wait for your next turn.

■ Once in each game, in a move called castling, a king gets to move two spaces. Castling is done only if the king is not in check, there are no pieces between the king and a rook, and neither piece has yet made a move. The two-part move is done by moving the king two squares toward the rook and then putting the rook on the square passed over by the king. Castling counts as one move.

THE FINER POINTS OF BACKGAMMON

Backgammon is a game played by two players, each with 15 markers or stones—but these days checkers can be used in a pinch. The object is to be the first player to move all one's markers around the board and then off it.

■ To set up, the markers are placed on the board as shown in the diagram below. The board is divided into four "tables" with numbered triangular spaces, or "points." The bar in the middle is also used in the game.

■ Each player rolls a die to determine who goes first. The higher one starts. Players then take turns rolling two dice to determine how many spaces to move the stones, with black moving around the board in one direction and white moving in the opposite direction. The numbers on each die can be combined so that one piece moves the total amount indicated. Alternatively, each die's value can be applied separately to a single marker.

■ Throwing "doubles" (for example, two 4s), allows a player to move twice as many points as shown on the dice—in this case, either four markers can be moved four spaces each, one can be moved four spaces and one 12 spaces, two can be moved 8 spaces each, or one marker can be moved 16 spaces.

■ There is no limit to the number of markers of the same color that may stay on one point, but markers of opposite colors may not occupy the same point. If two or more markers are on a point, the point is closed—a marker of the opposite color can't land there. However, a point that is occupied by only one marker is open and is called a "blot." If an opponent lands on a blot, the other player must move his or her man to the bar between the two halves of the board and can play no other man till the one on the bar re-enters. To do so, the player must make a roll of the dice that corresponds to a space on the other player's inner table that is open or blotted.

■ Once all of a player's 15 men have entered his or her "inner table" (the opposite side of the board from which the player began), the player may begin bearing them off the board by rolling the dice and removing any men that occupy spaces indicated by the roll. If a player rolls 5 and 4, for example, he or she may remove one of the men that occupies point 5 and one of the men that occupies point 4. If the number is higher than any of the occupied points, the player may remove a man from the next highest point. Double 6s are an especially good roll at this point. Play continues until one of the players has removed all of his or her men.

**BACKGAMMON:
Board is shown in the starting position. The goal is to move your men from your opponent's inner table to your own inner table on the opposite side of the board. White moves in the direction indicated by the arrows, black moves in the opposite direction. When all of your men reach your inner**

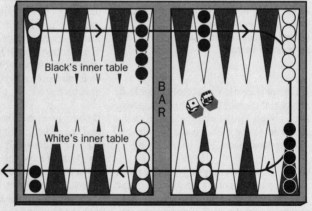

table, you may begin bearing them off by throwing dice that (hopefully) correspond to the number assigned each point.

CUT THE DECK, PLEASE

A quick review of how to play poker, gin rummy, spades, and solitaire

I f you want to learn how to play bridge, you need to either read a book or take lessons. But here are the rules—and some tricks of the trade—for popular card games that almost anyone can play. That's no guarantee, of course, that you'll draw good cards, but at least you'll be prepared to call the other guy's bet.

■ POKER (FIVE-CARD DRAW)

Poker pits one player against another. Casinos that provide poker tables make their money by taking a percentage of the winnings or charging by the hour for the use of their table and dealer. Unless you're an expert, you're better off wagering chips or change in the comfort of your own home.

There are hundreds of card games based on slight modifications of standard poker or "five-card draw." Variations include adding wild cards, changing the way players bet, and altering the size of each hand. The goal is always the same: to get a better hand (selection of cards) than the other players.

To play five-card draw, shuffle a regular 52-card deck and deal 5 cards to each of three to seven players. Typically each player pays a small sum, called an "ante," for the privilege of seeing his or her hand. All bets (and antes) are placed in the pot, a pile of money in the center of the table.

Players bet on their cards in a clockwise fashion, starting at the dealer's left. The first player has several betting options:

■ **FOLD:** Throwing in the cards and sitting out the rest of the hand. Any time a player folds at this stage, the ante remains in the pot and goes to winner.

■ **BET:** Placing a wager in the pot.
■ **PASS:** Choosing not to make a wager and allowing the next player to go.

If the first player doesn't make a bet, then the next player has the same options. Once a player has made a bet, however, other players may no longer pass, and are required to do one of the following:

■ **FOLD:** And lose one's bets and ante.
■ **CALL:** Match the other player's bets by placing an equal wager into the pot.
■ **RAISE:** Place a higher wager than others have bet into the pot. All other players will need to match this raised bet in order to stay in the game.

After a round of betting, all remaining players are then allowed to exchange up to three of their cards with those from the top of the remaining deck in the same order that the cards were dealt. At this time, the players have a second round of betting. After this round, all remaining players show their cards to each other. The player with the highest hand wins the entire pot.

Cards are ranked in the following order, from lowest to highest: 2, 3, 4, 5, 6, 7, 8, 9, 10, Jack, Queen, King, Ace. The box on the next page helps illustrate the ranking. Each level of the table beats ALL hands below it. For example, even the lowest straight (2, 3, 4, 5, 6) will beat the highest three of a kind (Ace, Ace, Ace, King, Queen). In many games, Aces can be both the highest and lowest card, at the player's discretion.

If two players have the same type of hand, the one who has the higher cards wins the hand. For example, a player with a 9, 9, 9, Jack, 2 (three 9s) would beat a player with a 6, 6, 6, Ace, Queen (three 6s). Extra cards, such as the Ace, Queen, Jack, and 2 in this example, only matter when two players have identical winning combinations. For example, a player with a 9, 9, 5, 5, King (two pair, with a King) would beat a player with a 9, 9, 5, 5, Queen (two pair, with a Queen).

■ LOW-HAND POKER

The rules for this game are identical to poker,

■ WHAT BEATS WHAT

Hand	Number possible	Odds of obtaining
ROYAL FLUSH The highest straight flush— 10, J, Q, K, A all of the same suit	4	1:649,739
STRAIGHT FLUSH A straight, and all five cards are of the same suit	40	1:64,973
FOUR OF A KIND Four cards of the same value with one extra	624	1:4,164
FULL HOUSE Three cards of one value and two of another	3,744	1:693
FLUSH Five cards of the same suit, such as five spades	5,108	1:508
STRAIGHT Five cards in a sequence of different suits, such as 5-6-7-8-9	10,200	1:254
THREE OF A KIND Three cards of the same value with two extra	54,912	1:46
TWO PAIR Two pairs of cards with one extra	123,552	1:20
ONE PAIR (Two of a kind) Two cards of the same value with three extra	1,098,240	1:1.37
HIGH CARD In a hand with no winning combination of cards, the highest card	1,302,540	1:1

except for an exciting 180-degree switch. In low-hand poker, it is the player with the lowest (and not the highest) hand who wins. The lowest hand possible is an Ace, 2, 3, 4, 6—known as a "perfect low." The next best low is Ace, 2, 3, 5, 6. In this game, it is common to see players discarding pairs of cards to rid themselves of their beastly hand.

■ HIGH-LOW POKER

Two players split the pot—the one with the highest hand and the one with the lowest hand. If all but one player folds, then the entire pot goes to the winner.

■ FIVE-CARD STUD

Unlike draw, five-card stud begins by dealing only two cards to each player. One of these cards is placed facedown and one is placed face up, in plain view of all players at the table. Each player is allowed to look at his or her facedown card, after which a round of betting ensues. Betting starts with the player showing the highest card. After this round, another card is placed faceup for each player (so that each player has two cards showing and one hidden card) and there is another round of betting. Again, betting starts with the player showing the highest cards. This pattern continues until each player has five cards. At any time during the game, a player can fold and the person with the highest hand at the end wins.

■ SEVEN-CARD STUD

This is an extremely lively and often high-stakes game. It is played in a similar fashion to five-card stud, except that the game begins by dealing three cards to each player—two are facedown and one is face up. Rounds of betting are then interspersed with receiving additional faceup cards until each player has two facedown cards and four faceup cards. At this time, a final card is dealt facedown and the final round of betting occurs.

Players can use any of their seven cards to make their best five-card hand. The catch to this game is that the odds are thrown haywire. Having seven cards makes it much easier to achieve good hands. It is common to see full houses, straights, and flushes.

■ BASEBALL

Baseball is a popular variation on seven-card stud, which makes the chances of achieving a high hand ridiculously easy. The game has wild cards, ones that can represent any other card in the deck at the player's discretion. In the game, all 3s and 9s (the number of strikes and innings in baseball) are wild. But they come with a price; players must either purchase 3s and 9s (at a predetermined price) if they are dealt these cards faceup or they must fold the hand. If a player is dealt a 4 faceup (the number of balls in baseball), the player is immediately dealt another card facedown.

Because of the wild cards in baseball, and the possibility of having more than seven cards (if a 4 is dealt), it is common for players to obtain the absurd "five of a kind." For example, a hand of 5, 5, 5, 3, 9 would be five 5s. Five of a kind is the highest hand possible, and beats a royal flush.

■ BLACKJACK

The object of blackjack is to have a hand with a point value that is higher than the dealer's. You must do this without going over 21 points, which is why the game is also known as Twenty-one. A player or dealer with 22 points or more has busted and automatically loses the hand. All numbered cards are worth their face value; picture cards (Jacks, Queens, and Kings) are worth 10 points each; and Aces are worth either 1 or 11—which the player gets to determine. Suits and colors are disregarded in the game.

Before each deal, all players make their bets, if you're playing at a casino. Two cards are then dealt to everybody including the dealer, who is dealt one card facedown. A player whose first two cards add up to 21 (e.g., an Ace and a Queen) has a Blackjack and is immediately paid 3–2, unless the dealer also has a Blackjack. Whenever a dealer and player tie, it is known as a push, and neither one wins the hand.

Once everyone has been dealt, players have several options to choose from. The best move depends both on what you have been dealt and on the one exposed card of the dealer's hand. A player can:

- **HIT:** Take an additional card.
- **STAND:** Take no additional cards.
- **DOUBLE DOWN:** Double the original bet and take only one additional card.
- **SPLIT:** When a player has been dealt two cards of identical value (e.g., two 9s), he can choose to double the original bet and play the two cards as separate hands.

HOW TO WIN AT BLACKJACK

You got to know when to hold 'em, and know when to fold 'em.

■ **Always hit when you have been dealt 8 or less.** You have no chance of busting, and you need to get closer to 21.

■ **Always stand on hard hands of 17 or more, regardless of what the dealer is showing.** A hard hand is a hand that either has no Aces or has an Ace or Aces that must be worth only one point because to be worth more would mean a bust (e.g., a 6, a Jack, and an Ace). If you hit, odds are you will bust.

■ **Always hit if you have 16 or less and the dealer's card is a 7, 8, 9, 10, or Ace.** These are the best cards and it is likely that the dealer will beat you. Although you have a good chance of busting, it is worth the risk of getting closer to 21.

■ **Always stand on hard hands of 12 or more if the dealer's first card is a 2, 3, 4, 5, or 6.** These are the worst cards and it is likely that the dealer will bust. But, you don't win if you bust first!

■ **Always stand on soft 19s and 20s.** A soft hand is one that has an Ace that can still be valued at either 1 or 11. Don't risk losing the good hand.

■ **CLAIM INSURANCE:** When a dealer is showing an Ace, players are invited to claim insurance that the next dealer's card will be worth 10 (and thus Blackjack). Insurance involves risking half the amount of the original bet and pays off at two to one, if the dealer has a Blackjack.

■ **SURRENDER:** Forfeit the hand and lose half of the original bet. (Not an option in many casinos.)

Once all the players are either satisfied with their hands or have busted, the dealer proceeds. Unlike the players, who get to make choices, the dealer must proceed according to set rules: drawing on any hand that is less than 17 and standing on anything 17 or higher.

■ GIN RUMMY

Gin Rummy (or simply "Gin") is one of the most popular two-handed card games. It can be played for fun or for money. All 52 cards are used. Suits, however, do not play a role in the game. Face cards are worth 10 points each; numbered cards are worth their face value; and Aces are worth one point each. One common variation, however, is to allow Aces to be either high or low. Usually when this is done, Aces are worth 15 points instead of one. The object is to get rid of the cards in your hand by creating sets of three or more cards that can be "melded." Timing is important, though—the sets are played differently depending on who melds his or her cards first. The sets can be formed in two ways:

■ **SERIES:** Three or more cards form a series in sequential order, such as a 4-5-6-7 or a 10-J-Q.

■ **MATCHING SETS:** This is when cards are put in groups of the same value, such as an 8-8-8 or an A-A-A-A.

To play, 10 cards are dealt to each of two players and the remainder of the deck is placed in a pile between them. The dealer turns over the top card from this pile and places it faceup to begin a discard pile. The second player then has the option of taking this card and switching it with one of the cards in his hand or passing and giving the dealer the same option. If the dealer also passes, the second player takes the card that is on the top of the pile—so that momentarily there are 11 cards in his hand. One of the 11 cards is then placed faceup on top of the discard pile.

The dealer must then either take the card that has been discarded or the next card from the deck. This continues until a player decides to end the round of play by melding his or her cards to reveal the hand.

Here's where it gets complicated. The first player to meld or "knock" must have fewer than 10 points in hand that are not part of sets. For example, after several rounds of drawing cards, a player might knock with the following hand: 5-5-5 (a set), 8-9-10-J (another set), and A, 2, 2, K (not a set). This player can discard the King and then meld with the set of 5s, the 8 through Jack sequence, and five points (A+2+2).

The second player then must meld his or her cards, too. In doing so, the second player has the added advantage of being able to play cards off the first player's hand.

For example, the second player might have the following hand: 2-3-4, 9-9-9, 4, 5, 8, Q. The 2 through 4 sequence and the 9s would be played in their own right. However, the Q could also be played off the 8 through Jack sequence of the first player, as would the 5 with the three 5s. This would leave the second player with only 12 unused points (4+8). The player who knocked would earn the difference between the two hands, or seven points (12–5).

If a player knocks and then is beat (or underscored), then the second player gets an additional 25 points for the feat. If a player melds an entire hand, with no extra cards, then he is entitled to say "gin" and obtains an extra 25 points. The winner of each round deals the next hand.

The game continues until one player reaches 100 points (or any score that the players have agreed to before the game). To play for money, players typically bet a certain sum per point. For example, a final score of 105 to 80 would result in 25 points to the winner.

■ SPADES

Spades can be played by three people, but four

EXPERT SOURCES

THE BOOKS ON BRIDGE

We asked Bob Hamman, a championship player who's won the Bermuda Bowl, the Olympiad, and World Open Pairs, to choose the volumes that best teach the game. He has played with and against many authors on this list.

WHY YOU LOSE AT BRIDGE
S. J. Simon (Devyn, reprinted 1997, $9.95)
■ A classic with great humor. Not really a book about bridge but about how to be a competitor.

KILLING DEFENSE AT BRIDGE
Hugh Kelsey (Houghton Mifflin, 1966, $9.95)
■ All Kelsey's books are good. He does an excellent job of laying out a problem and putting you in the position of the player, then allowing you to make the decision along with the player.

ADVENTURES IN CARD PLAY
Hugh Kelsey and Geza Ottlik (Trafalgar, 1983, $19.95)
■ The high end of books on card-playing. This is stuff that's tough for

everyone, including myself. Ottlik was a mediocre player at the table, but an excellent theorist.

MASTER PLAY IN CONTRACT BRIDGE
Terrence Reese (Dover 1974, $3.95)
■ Reese has worked on over 50 books as an author and collaborator, and this is the best (also published as *The Expert Game*). A classic for the high-level player.

RIGHT THROUGH THE PACK
Robert Darvas and Norman de V. Hart (Devyn, 1947, out of print)
■ Problems cast in a narrative form, with interesting hands that give you other things to think about. Very good for the moderate player.

HOW TO READ YOUR OPPONENTS' CARDS
Mike Lawrence (Devyn, 1991, $9.95)
and **COMPLETE DEFENSIVE BRIDGE PLAY**
Eddie Kantar (Wilshire, 1974, $20)
■ The best of the modern high-tech theorists who are still living and playing. Beginning players can't go wrong reading anything by Lawrence and Kantar, who have both won a couple of world championships.

THE LAWS OF TOTAL TRICKS
Larry Cohen (Cohen, 1992, $12.95)
■ Excellent for a basic understanding of the game. It's about bidding, not card play, and will really help someone who has played just a little bit.

is ideal. The goal is to score as many points as possible by collecting "tricks."

To begin, the entire 52-card deck is dealt evenly to each of the players. If there are four players, each will have 13 cards. The first round is begun by whoever has the 2 of clubs, which is laid in the center of the table. The player to his or her left then must lay down any card of the same suit. The next player does likewise, and the next, till each has laid a card. The highest card wins the trick. (Aces are played high in spades; 2 is the lowest.)

If a player doesn't have a card in the suit

that is being played, he or she may trump the trick by playing a spade. However, if any of the following players in that round also has no cards in the original suit, he or she may "trump the trump" with a higher spade. (No one may open with a spade until spades have been "broken"—that is, played as a trump.) The winner of the book plays the next card, and the round continues till all 13 books have been played.

Scoring is what makes spades challenging. Each trick is worth 10 points. After a hand is dealt, players must make a bid on how many tricks they expect to get based on the strength of the cards they were dealt. Because each player in a four-person game has 13 cards, there are 13 possible tricks (130 points). A player who found among his or her 13 cards a couple of Kings, some Queens, and several spades of any value would rightly feel justified in making a high bid because those cards are all likely to make a trick. The catch: If a player has a strong hand and so bids, say, 6 tricks, that player must make at least those 6. If not, he or she will instead lose 60 points (–10 points for each trick bid).

On the other hand, if the player makes over the amount bid, say 7 tricks instead of the 6 bid, he or she receives only a single point for each extra trick—in this case 61 points. Another catch: if a player receives more than 10 of those extra single points, he or she loses 100 points. This is called "sandbagging."

A player who is behind by more than 100 points may bid "blind six," a bid of six made before the cards are even dealt. If the six are made, the player receives 100 points; if not, the player loses 100 points.

Players can play as many hands as they like to a preset score. About 500 points is a good goal for a satisfying evening.

■ SOLITAIRE

Klondike is the most common form of solitaire in the United States—so common, in fact, that it is often known simply as "solitaire." In reality, there are many varieties of solitaire which, as the name implies, refers to any card game played by one person.

To play Klondike, deal one card faceup from a standard deck. Then deal six additional cards facedown, to form a row to the right of the first card. Next a card is dealt faceup on top of the second card in the row, and five more cards are dealt facedown on top of the remaining piles to the right. This pattern continues until 28 cards have been used and there are seven piles or columns of cards, ranging from one card (in the left column) to seven cards (in

the right column). The remainder of the deck is placed facedown on the table.

Cards can be moved onto the next higher card of a different color to form descending sets that alternate by color. In the example below, the red 8 can be placed on top of a black 9, allowing the card beneath the 8 to be flipped over and brought into play. If a red 10 were to appear, then the 9 and 8 could be moved together on top of the 10, allowing the player to flip over more cards.

Aces are removed from the layout when they appear, and are used as starting points to build ascending sets. These sets follow suit, rather than the black-red pattern already described. In this example, the Ace of diamonds has been set aside. If the two of diamonds appears, it will be placed on top of the Ace, and then the 3 of diamonds, and so on. The game is won if all four of these Ace piles are built into Ace-through-King sequences.

If one of the seven columns becomes empty because all of its cards have been shifted, any King (and anything stacked on it) can be moved into the empty column, allowing any card under the King to be flipped. After making every possible move on the board, the first card from the remainder of the deck is turned over and played off on any of the columns, if possible. When the entire deck has been played through, the game is over.

A variation on the game involves flipping the remainder three cards at a time. If you can play the top card, you can play the next one as well. When the pile has been gone through, the discard pile can be turned over and gone through a second time, or even a third time before calling it a loss.

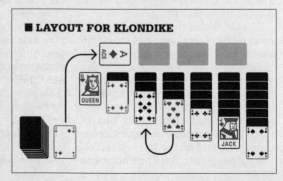

■ LAYOUT FOR KLONDIKE

CHAPTER ELEVEN

FACTS FOR LIFE

EXPERT QUOTES

"The beauty of the night sky can only be appreciated by the naked eye."
—Geoff Chester, astronomer, U.S. Naval Observatory
Page 662

"When you remove your shoes in a Japanese house, place them so the toes face the door."
—Norine Dresser, author of *Multicultural Manners*
Page 705

"People with unlisted numbers have definite opinions about some issues."
—Peter Hart, pollster
Page 758

■ **WHAT'S AHEAD: LOOK FOR** new technology to improve the accuracy of weather forecasting... **GET READY** for the Chinese Year of the Tiger... **ANTICIPATE** a total eclipse to occur in Siberia... **IMPROVE** your relationships with neighbors from other cultures... **LEARN** how to be prepared in the face of natural disasters... **START** tracing your family tree...

WEATHER

PREDICTIONS

THE FINE ART OF FORECASTING

How meteorologists are improving short-range and seasonal forecasts

Remember the winter of 1996–97, when the Northwest was punished by severe flooding that caused over $1 billion in damages? Forecasters were unable to predict the floods until about a week before they occurred. On the other hand, during the 1996 Summer Olympics in Atlanta, athletes and fans from around the world sweltered during the two-week event. And guess what? Long-range weather forecasters had predicted a year in advance that it was going to be hotter than usual for the Games.

Why are some long-range forecasts right on while others miss by a mile? Forecasters who make seasonal predictions have a daunting task. Imagine a person going outside and waving his hands in the air. According to Kerry Emanuel, a meteorologist at the Massachusetts Institute of Technology, the weather that results, at least in the northern hemisphere, will be different two or three weeks hence. "People think that scenario is metaphoric," he says, "but it's probably literal

that small perturbations eventually grow."

That means that from a scientific perspective the atmosphere is unpredictable beyond a certain time frame. For the one- to five-day predictions you hear on the nightly news, scientists believe the best they can ever deliver is two weeks. For long-range forecasts of precipitation and temperature trends, the limit on their prognostications is thought to be two years.

Forecasters who make long-range seasonal forecasts have two types of weather modeling systems running on their supercomputers. One type, the statistical model, tries to correlate present conditions in the atmosphere and in the ocean with past weather data and with the climatic trends that followed. Newer models actually simulate the physical interaction between atmosphere and ocean. These dynamic models employ the principles of physics such as Newton's laws and the laws of thermodynamics, says meteorologist Huug Vandendool at the Climate Predictions Center in Camp Springs, Md.

Sea surface temperatures drive the planet's weather. Most weather watchers have heard of El Niño and know that it can cause areas of the globe to experience severe droughts while others suffer extreme flooding. It takes from three to seven years to cycle through an El Niño and its cool counterpart, La Niña.

Being able to predict these warming and cooling trends in the ocean is a crucial part of making accurate seasonal predictions. And forecasters are just now discovering

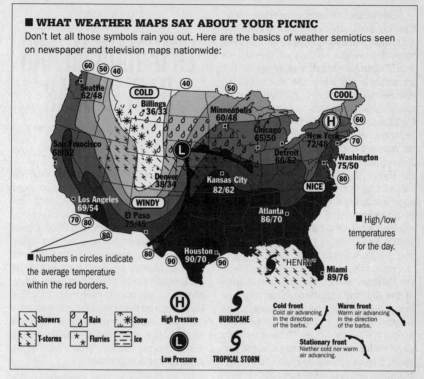

■ WHAT WEATHER MAPS SAY ABOUT YOUR PICNIC

Don't let all those symbols rain you out. Here are the basics of weather semiotics seen on newspaper and television maps nationwide:

■ Numbers in circles indicate the average temperature within the red borders.

■ High/low temperatures for the day.

| Showers | Rain | Snow | High Pressure | HURRICANE |
| T-storms | Flurries | Ice | Low Pressure | TROPICAL STORM |

Cold front Cold air advancing in the direction of the barbs.

Warm front Warm air advancing in the direction of the barbs.

Stationary front Niether cold nor warm air advancing.

new temperature cycles in the world's oceans. Columbia University meteorologist Yves M. Tourre's research led scientists recently to discover that El Niño is not confined solely to the tropical Pacific. It is a worldwide cycle termed El Niño Southern Oscillation, or ENSO. "We find the ENSO in the Indian as well as the Pacific oceans, and then 12 to 18 months later in the equatorial Atlantic," says Tourre. A very warm tropical Atlantic led scientists to make their accurate forecast of 1995's hurricane season, he explains.

Researchers recently have also discovered new temperature oscillations in northern sections of the Atlantic and Pacific. Tourre calls this phenomenon interdecadal variability for it takes about 20 years to complete a cycle. Scientists are in the process of figuring out how this cycle affects world weather.

While some meteorologists are trying to simulate these ocean oscillations on supercomputers, still others are exploring how the land itself influences the weather and climate. Many satellite missions that NASA proposes focus on trying to measure soil moisture, says Vandendool. Wet soil tends to have a cooling effect as a result of evaporation. With dry soil, there is a lot less water vapor available to the atmosphere, which can create warmer and drier conditions. Says Vandendool: "Some people have speculated for 50 years that continental droughts may actually be reacting to feedback from the soil."

The implication is that dry soil conditions are self-perpetuating on the local level, and that this may lead to larger regional or even continental effects. This is difficult to establish, however, since meteorologists do not routinely measure soil moisture as they do ocean temperatures. Says MIT's Emanuel: "There's some hope that if we understand land/atmosphere interactions better and perfect techniques to measure soil properties, that might give us a leg up on seasonal weather forecasting."

Short-range forecasters who make one- to five-day predictions are also starting to assimilate more land property data in their computer models. In the past, forecasters would note how much water was on the ground or how much of the land was snow-covered. If a blast of Arctic air was coming out of Canada to a snow-covered region of New England, they knew to extend low temperature forecasts, because the cold is better retained than if the ground were bare. According to Dave Olson, chief forecaster at the Hydrometeorological Prediction Center in Camp Springs, Md., short-term modeling is starting to include this information in its guidance. "Whether it does it adequately or not, we'll have to see. We haven't seen a lot of output from [these models] yet," cautions Olson.

Forecasters also have more data due to the National Weather Services' installation of the Automated Surface Observing System (ASOS), which provides computerized weather beacons in many new locations across the United States. This equipment supplies information on pressure, temperature, moisture, cloud height and coverage, visibility, and rain- and snowfall.

One of the newest innovations to help forecasters analyze conditions and predict changes is the Advanced Weather Interactive Process System (AWIPS), which the weather service began installing in 1997. Twenty-one computer terminals will link at a single workstation data received from new Doppler radars, automated ground observing systems, and satellites. The system, says former Weather Service director Elbert W. Friday, will enable forecasters "to rapidly gather and assess the most meaningful information needed to issue critical forecasts and warnings."

But don't expect miracles. "I don't see real breakthroughs," says Vandendool of the Climate Predictions Center. "When we got satellites in the 1960s, that was seen as very exciting—and that development in itself has only contributed incrementally to the improvement of forecasts. On the other hand," he adds, "37 years of incremental advances add up to significant overall improvement."

FOLKLORE

LIMP HAIR MEANS RAIN IS NEAR

The science behind the farmers' and sailors' maxims

Weather folklore has been passed down through the ages by mariners and farmers who relied on their own observations of astronomical events, animal behaviors, and atmospheric changes to predict upcoming weather. Today, while the average person's ability to observe the natural world has declined, much of the folklore still exists, partly because of a psychological yearning to keep in touch with a time when humans seemed more in tune with their environment. Here, meteorology lecturer Mark Wysocki of Cornell University helps discern what of today's remaining weather lore is still viable.

■ **Red sky at night, sailors delight. Red sky in the morning, sailor take warning.**

Much of the weather folklore based on observations of atmospheric phenomena is a fairly good predictor of short-range weather changes, Wysocki says. In the mid-latitude regions, the general flow of storm systems follows the jet stream from west to east. The red color at night is due to the reflection of the red colors from the sun as it lowers in the western sky. This signals that the jet stream has pushed the storm systems out of your area. If clouds appear red in the morning, this means that the sun is rising in clear skies to the east with clouds approaching from the west, indicating the storm system is to your west and moving your way.

■ **Mackerel clouds in the sky, expect more wet than dry.**

Wysocki cites this as another good example of accurate weather folklore based on atmospheric observations. Mackerel clouds refer to cirrocumulus clouds that appear pearly white with scaly formations akin to the scales on a fish. Ancient mariners knew that these clouds presaged the approach of a warm front that would produce rain or snow within the next 12 to 18 hours, Wysocki says.

■ When round the moon there is a halo, the weather will be cold and rough.

The halo, according to Wysocki, is generated by cirrostratus clouds 15,000 to 20,000 feet up in the atmosphere. These clouds cover large areas with a uniform thickness of ice crystals, which are responsible for many optical wonders. A halo around the moon generally means stormy weather within the next 24 hours.

■ If bees stay at home, rain will soon come.

Wysocki likens this folklore to stories that associate approaching storms with ants lining up to go back to their nest, cows lying down in a field, and frogs singing more than usual. He admits that these examples are difficult to prove or disprove, because scientists can't isolate what in the environment would be causing these behaviors. However, he says he would have to err on the side of beekeepers who swear by the ability of their bees to predict rain. With cows, though, he jokingly asks, "If 25 cows are lying down in a field, and 25 are standing up, does this mean there's a 50 percent chance of rain?"

■ Crickets are a poor man's thermometer.

Counting the chirps of a cricket, Wysocki asserts, is an accurate way of determining temperatures above 40 degrees Fahrenheit. Below 40 degrees, a cricket's metabolism is too slow. To get the current air temperature within one degree Fahrenheit, count the number of chirps in a 14-second period and then add 40 to this number.

■ When hornets build their nest close to the ground, expect a hard winter.

Folklore that deals with animals and long-term weather forecasts generally is false, says Wysocki. He believes that if people observed the hornet's activities over a long period of time, they would find no correlation between the hornet's behavior and seasonal forecasts. The same is true for folklore that links a squirrel's very bushy tail or a large black band on a woolly-bear caterpillar with an upcoming severe winter.

■ When smoke hangs low, a storm is approaching.

Wysocki attributes the phenomenon of smoke hanging low to low-pressure systems that cause the atmosphere to be unstable and can signal the approach of stormy weather. However, sometimes near lakes and in valleys, local air circulation can dominate the larger-scale circulation that can give a false reading, he warns.

■ The air smells sweet before a storm.

Science definitely has an explanation for this folklore, Wysocki says. Before a storm, lower pressure predominates, which causes plants' stomatic openings to enlarge and emit more gases, including ones that are aromatic.

■ When human hair becomes limp, rain is near.

Human hair—especially blond hair—becomes thicker and longer when exposed to increases in humidity, which sometimes mean rain is near. In fact, says Wysocki, early hygrometers designed to determine the moisture content of the air relied on measuring the changes in the length of a human hair.

■ Sinus and joint pain signals stormy weather.

This folklore, at least for arthritis sufferers, has been proved to signal rapid changes in the weather, says Wysocki. Pressure changes, the cause of the pain, signal the unstable atmospheric conditions that typically precede a storm.

SUNNY OR COLD, WINDY OR WET

W. C. Fields may have made jokes about Philadelphia, but there are a lot worse places in the United States when it comes to weather. For a coast-to-coast tour of the weather horizon, see the following breakdown of recent weather patterns in selected major American cities.

City	Average annual sunshine (%)	Mean days below freezing	AVERAGE ANNUAL TEMPERATURE (F) High	Low	Average annual rain (in.)	AVERAGE RELATIVE HUMIDITY (%) Annual a.m.	p.m.	January a.m.	p.m.	July a.m.	p.m.
Albany, N.Y.	52	14.9	58.1	36.6	36.17	79	57	76	63	84	55
Albuquerque, N.M.	76	11.9	70.1	42.2	8.88	60	29	70	40	60	27
Atlanta, Ga.	61	5.3	71.2	51.3	50.77	77	56	74	59	85	60
Atlantic City, N.J.	56	11.0	63.2	42.8	40.29	82	56	76	58	87	57
Baltimore, Md.	57	9.7	65.0	45.2	40.70	75	54	69	57	81	53
Bismarck, N.D.	59	18.6	53.8	29.4	15.47	74	56	75	66	74	46
Boise, Idaho	64	12.4	62.8	39.1	12.11	69	43	81	70	54	21
Boston, Mass.	58	9.8	59.0	43.6	41.51	72	58	65	57	77	56
Buffalo, N.Y.	49	13.2	55.8	39.5	38.58	79	63	77	72	79	55
Burlington, Vt.	49	15.5	54.0	35.2	34.47	77	59	70	63	82	53
Charleston, W.V.	40	10.0	65.8	44.2	42.53	79	56	74	63	90	60
Charlotte, N.C.	63	6.6	70.4	49.7	43.09	76	54	72	56	83	57
Cheyenne, Wyo.	65	17.2	58.0	33.2	14.40	65	44	57	50	70	35
Chicago, Ill.	54	13.3	58.6	39.5	35.82	77	60	75	67	79	56
Cincinnati, Ohio	52	10.8	63.2	43.2	41.33	77	59	75	67	83	57
Cleveland, Ohio	49	12.3	58.7	40.5	36.63	77	62	75	69	81	57
Columbia, S.C.	64	6.0	75.1	50.9	49.91	83	51	78	54	87	54
Columbus, Ohio	49	11.9	61.2	41.6	38.09	77	59	74	67	82	56
Concord, N.H.	54	17.3	57.0	33.1	36.37	82	54	74	58	90	51
Dallas-Fort Worth, Texas	63	4.0	76.3	54.6	33.70	72	56	73	60	67	49
Denver, Colo.	70	15.7	64.2	36.2	15.40	67	40	63	49	68	34
Des Moines, Iowa	59	13.5	59.8	40.0	33.12	75	60	74	67	76	57
Detroit, Mich.	53	13.6	58.1	39.0	32.62	79	60	78	69	81	53
Duluth, Minn.	52	18.5	47.9	29.0	30.0	77	63	74	70	82	59
El Paso, Texas	84	6.5	77.5	49.0	8.81	57	28	66	35	63	30
Great Falls, Mont.	61	15.7	56.4	33.1	15.21	67	45	66	60	66	29
Hartford, Conn.	56	13.5	60.2	39.5	44.14	76	52	69	56	82	51
Honolulu, Hawaii	69	0	84.4	70.0	22.02	76	56	81	61	73	51
Houston, Texas	56	2.1	78.6	57.3	46.07	86	60	82	64	86	58
Indianapolis, Ind.	55	11.8	62.1	42.4	39.94	80	62	78	70	84	59
Jackson, Miss.	60	5.0	76.4	52.0	55.37	87	58	84	65	90	59
Jacksonville, Fla.	63	1.5	78.9	57.1	51.32	86	56	85	57	88	58
Juneau, Alaska	30	14.1	46.9	34.1	54.31	86	73	81	77	87	70

■ WEATHER WATCHER'S GUIDE

City	Average annual sunshine (%)	Mean days below freezing	AVERAGE ANNUAL TEMPERATURE (F)		Average annual rain (in.)	AVERAGE RELATIVE HUMIDITY (%)					
			High	Low		Annual a.m.	p.m.	January a.m.	p.m.	July a.m.	p.m.
Kansas City, Mo.	62	11.0	63.6	43.7	37.62	74	59	72	63	75	56
Little Rock, Ark.	62	6.0	72.5	51.0	50.86	79	57	76	61	83	56
Los Angeles, Calif.	73	0	70.4	55.5	12.01	79	64	70	59	86	68
Louisville, Ky.	56	8.9	66.0	46.0	44.39	76	58	72	64	81	58
Memphis, Tenn.	64	5.7	72.1	52.4	52.10	76	57	75	63	79	57
Miami, Fla.	72	0	82.8	69.0	55.91	81	61	81	59	82	63
Milwaukee, Wis.	54	14.1	54.3	37.9	32.93	78	64	75	68	80	61
Minn.-St. Paul, Minn.	58	15.6	54.3	35.3	28.32	73	60	72	67	74	54
Mobile, Ala.	59	2.2	77.4	57.4	63.96	83	57	79	61	87	60
Nashville, Tenn.	56	7.6	69.8	48.4	47.30	79	57	75	63	85	57
New Orleans, La.	59	1.3	77.6	58.5	61.88	85	63	82	66	89	66
New York, N.Y.	58	7.9	62.3	47.4	47.25	70	56	65	60	74	55
Norfolk, Va.	61	5.4	67.8	50.6	44.64	78	57	72	59	84	59
Oklahoma City, Okla.	NA	7.7	71.1	48.8	33.36	72	54	72	59	70	49
Omaha, Neb.	60	14.1	61.5	39.5	29.86	76	59	75	65	78	57
Peoria, Ill.	57	12.9	60.4	41.0	36.25	79	62	78	68	82	59
Philadelphia, Pa.	56	9.7	63.4	45.1	41.41	76	55	71	59	81	54
Phoenix, Ariz.	86	0.8	85.9	59.3	7.66	51	23	66	32	45	20
Pittsburgh, Pa.	46	12.3	59.9	40.7	36.85	75	57	73	65	80	54
Portland, Maine	57	15.7	54.9	35.8	44.34	82	59	74	60	89	59
Portland, Ore.	48	4.3	62.6	44.5	36.30	86	60	86	75	82	45
Providence, R.I.	58	11.8	59.8	41.0	45.53	76	55	69	56	83	56
Raleigh, N.C.	59	7.8	70.1	48.4	41.43	80	54	73	55	88	58
Reno, Nev.	79	17.4	66.8	34.7	7.53	70	31	79	50	63	18
Richmond, Va.	62	8.5	68.8	46.6	43.16	82	53	77	57	88	56
Sacramento, Calif.	78	1.7	73.5	48.1	17.52	82	45	90	70	76	28
Salt Lake City, Utah	66	12.5	63.6	40.3	16.18	67	43	79	69	52	22
San Diego, Calif.	68	0	70.8	57.6	9.90	76	62	70	56	82	66
San Francisco, Calif.	NA	0.2	65.2	49.0	19.70	84	62	86	66	86	59
San Juan, P.R.	66	0	86.4	74.0	52.34	83	65	82	64	84	67
Sault Ste. Marie, Mich.	47	18.1	49.6	29.8	34.23	85	67	81	75	90	61
Seattle-Tacoma, Wash.	46	3.1	59.4	44.6	37.19	83	62	81	74	82	49
Sioux Falls, S.D.	63	16.8	56.8	34.2	23.86	76	60	75	68	75	53
Spokane, Wash.	54	13.9	57.5	36.9	16.49	78	52	85	78	64	27
St. Louis, Mo.	57	10.0	65.4	46.7	37.51	76	59	77	66	77	56
Washington, D.C.	56	7.0	66.9	49.2	38.63	72	53	67	55	77	53
Wichita, Kan.	65	11.1	67.4	45.0	29.33	73	55	76	63	67	48
Wilmington, Del.	NA	10.0	63.6	44.8	40.84	78	55	73	60	83	54

THE BAROMETER

KNOW WHICH WAY THE WIND BLOWS

Forecast the weather by gauging changes in atmospheric pressure

With a simple aneroid barometer, available at a local hardware store or marine supply center, you can make fairly accurate short-range weather predictions for $20 to $50. Generally, when the barometer is high and rising, it means high pressure is approaching. High pressure systems typically are associated with fair weather—light and variable winds, dry air, and temperatures below seasonal averages. When the barometer is low and falling, it typically means low pressure is on the way. Low pressure systems tend to bring inclement weather—strong winds, high humidity, clouds, and storm fronts.

An aneroid barometer has one pointer, similar to the hand on a clock, which measures atmospheric pressure in inches of mercury and another pointer which is used to reference pressure changes. Rising pressure causes the reading pointer to move clockwise, while falling pressure causes it to move counterclockwise.

Once or twice a day, the reference pointer should be placed to correspond with the reading pointer. Over the course of the day, you can track pressure changes by noting how the reading pointer moves in relation to the reference hand.

To ensure accurate readings, aneroid barometers, and even some electronic ones, occasionally need to be calibrated. A call to the local branch of the Weather Service or listening to the weather report on TV provides the current pressure adjusted to what it would read at sea level. Adjustments should be made on days with settled winds, which usually indicate the pressure is changing slowly.

Many amateur forecasters find useful the chart on the facing page, which bases its weather predictions on barometric changes and wind direction. However, meteorologists caution these are general rules that don't hold true for all locations and situations. For example, west winds off the Great Lakes can bring terrible lake-effect snows even when the barometer is high. Similarly, in the Northeast near the Atlantic Ocean, a sea breeze can bring cooler air, clouds, drizzle, and fog when the pressure is high.

CYBER SOURCE
EL NIÑO, COMING TO A COMPUTER NEAR YOU

Twenty years ago, forecasters thought that the weather was driven by something in the atmosphere. Now, most people understand the importance of ocean and atmospheric interactions. Forecasters assimilate ocean data on their supercomputers, while amateur weather enthusiasts have to wait for them to churn out predictions.

These days, however, weather watchers can have instant access to ocean data via the the World Wide Web. Meteorologist Yves M. Tourre and his colleagues at Columbia University's Lamont-Doherty Earth Observatory have established a web page for viewing ocean temperatures collected from satellites and ocean buoys. The page provides color maps and monthly analyses of the earth's waters. According to Tourre, "It's the most advanced prototype of its kind." The site is 100 percent interactive and people can even download the data. Check out the site at:

http://rainbow.ldeo.columbia.edu/igoss/ productsbulletin.

■ BE YOUR OWN FORECASTER

Basic barometer reading for amateur meteorologists

Barometer reduced to sea level	Wind direction	Character of weather indicated
30.10 to 30.20 and steady	SW → NW	Fair, slight temperature changes for one to two days.
30.10 to 30.20 and rising rapidly	SW → NW	Fair followed within two days by warmer air and rain.
30.10 to 30.20 and falling slowly	SW → NW	Warmer with rain in 24 to 36 hours.
30.10 to 30.20 and falling rapidly	SW → NW	Warmer with rain in 18 to 24 hours.
30.20 and above and stationary	SW → NW	Continued fair with no decided temperature change.
30.20 and above and falling slowly	SW → NW	Slowly rising temperature and fair for two days.
30.10 to 30.20 and falling slowly	S → SE	Rain within 24 hours.
30.10 to 30.20 and falling rapidly	S → SE	Wind increasing in force with rain within 12 to 24 hrs.
30.10 to 30.20 and falling slowly	SE → NE	Increasing wind with rain within 12 hours.
30.10 and above and falling slowly	E → NE	In summer with light winds, rain may not fall for several days. In winter rain within 24 hours.
30.10 and above and falling rapidly	E → NE	In summer rain probable within 12 to 24 hours. In winter rain or snow, increasing winds will often set in.
30 or below and falling slowly	SE → NE	Rain will continue one to two days.
30 or below and falling rapidly	SE → NE	Rain with high wind, followed within 24 hours by clearing and cooler.
30 or below and rising slowly	S → SW	Clearing in a few hours, continued fair for some days.
29.80 or below and falling rapidly	S → E	Severe storm of wind and rain or snow imminent, followed within 24 hours by clearing and colder.
29.80 or below and falling rapidly	E → N	Severe northeast gales and heavy rain or snow, followed in winter by a cold wave.
29.80 or below and rising rapidly	Going → W	Clearing and colder.

■ WHEN PUTTING A FINGER TO THE WIND WON'T DO

The Beaufort Scale of Wind Effects can help you estimate wind speed from simple observations. It also gives the basis for converting the wind descriptions used in weather reports to wind speed equivalents, and vice versa.

Wind speed (mph)	Beaufort number	Wind effect on land	Official description
Less than 1	0	Calm; smoke rises vertically.	LIGHT
1 to 3	1	Wind direction is seen in direction of smoke but is not revealed by weather vane.	LIGHT
4 to 7	2	Wind can be felt on face; leaves rustle; wind vane moves.	LIGHT
8 to 12	3	Leaves, small twigs in motion; wind extends light flag.	GENTLE
13 to 18	4	Wind raises dust, loose papers. Small branches move.	MODERATE
19 to 24	5	Small trees with leaves begin to sway; crested wavelets appear on inland waters.	FRESH
25 to 31	6	Large branches move; telegraph wires whistle; umbrellas become difficult to control.	STRONG
32 to 38	7	Whole trees sway, walking into the wind becomes difficult.	STRONG
39 to 46	8	Twigs break off trees; cars veer in roads.	STRONG
47 to 54	9	Slight structural damage occurs; roof slates may blow away.	STRONG
55 to 63	10	Trees uprooted; considerable structural damage caused.	WHOLE GALE
64 to 72	11	Widespread damage is caused.	WHOLE GALE
73 or more	12	Widespread damage is caused.	HURRICANE

STARS & TIDES

THE NIGHT SKY
▼

STARGAZING WITH THE NAKED EYE

You don't need a telescope to roam the heavens on a starry evening

In a world of space stations and orbiting telescopes, stargazing with the naked eye may seem a quaint notion. Not so, insists astronomer Geoff Chester of the U.S. Naval Observatory in Washington, D.C. "The beauty and majesty of the night sky can only be appreciated by the naked eye." Even without binoculars and telescopes, it can be quite easy to enjoy some of nature's most extraordinary spectacles—if you know what to look for, as Chester explains here.

To familiarize yourself with the stars, constellations, and other astronomical phenomena, you'll need a celestial map and a red-filtered flashlight to help you read. You can find such maps at planetariums and astronomy clubs, in specialty publications such as *Astronomy Magazine*, and in this book on pages 665 to 670. The red filter helps your night vision. Make a filter by covering your flashlight lens with any porous red paper, or buy a red LED bulb at Radio Shack.

The best locations for viewing the night sky are usually in rural areas, where there is little gazing interference from artificial light and pollution. Begin your celestial search by seeking out the brightest stars. Use the sky's brightest patterns, such as the Summer Triangle, for reference points to the constellations and other celestial

---

■ **TEST PATTERNS IN THE SKY**
The Summer Triangle and the Winter Circle will help you find your way in the firmament.

■ **THE SUMMER TRIANGLE.**
Consists of the stars Vega, Deneb, and Altair (left).

■ **THE GREAT WINTER CIRCLE.**
Use Orion's belt to point to Sirius. Then, clockwise, go to Procyon, Pollux, Castor, Capella, Aldebaran, and Rigel (right).

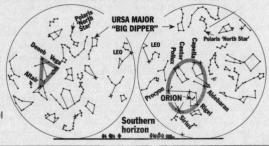

objects. The Summer Triangle, found directly overhead in the summer months, is formed by stars in the Vega, Deneb, and Altair constellations.

In winter, use the Great Winter Circle, which boasts 9 of the 21 brightest stars in the winter sky. To find it, start with Orion's belt, which lies in the middle of the Circle and points to Sirius. Move clockwise from there to Procyon, Pollux, Castor, Capella, Aldebaran, and Rigel. To bring the night sky even more alive, check out George Lovi's and Wil Tirion's book, *Men, Monsters and the Modern Universe* (Willmann–Bell, 1989), an excellent guide to the mythological universe.

■ THE PLANETS

Stars twinkle and planets don't, yet planets, not stars, are generally the brightest objects in the sky. Four planets—Venus, Jupiter, Mars, and Saturn—can be seen easily with the naked eye. Venus is the third-brightest object in the sky after the sun and moon and displays a milky white glow. Jupiter, usually the fourth-brightest object, appears creamy or yellow. Mars follows Jupiter in visibility and is the only planet whose color, a pinkish hue, represents its surface color and not its atmosphere. Saturn is the faintest of the naked-eye planets and is yellowish.

Mercury can also be seen if you're skilled, but it's very difficult because of its close proximity to the sun. Most astronomers believe Copernicus, the grandfather of modern astronomy, never spotted Mercury.

■ SHOOTING STARS AND COMETS

Ever seen a shooting star? Think of what you viewed as a grain of sand hitting the earth's atmosphere at tremendous speed and bursting into flames. A meteor shower occurs when such debris, usually from a comet, enters the earth's atmosphere.

A really bright shooting star is called a fireball. It's not uncommon for such a phenomenon to illuminate an entire state. In the last major fireball sighting in the United States several years ago, thousands of high school football fans in North Carolina were treated to a highly unexpected and spectacular show on a fall Friday night. The

celestial headliner came to a 20-pound thud on top of a car in Peekskill, New York.

Comets, like meteors, are random visitors to our world. But comets can remain in view from a few days to several months. The brightest comet in decades, the recently discovered Hale–Bopp comet, was visible from February through April in 1997.

■ ECLIPSES

"A total solar eclipse is the single most spectacular sight in the natural world," says Chester, and the next total eclipse will occur on February 26, 1998, in Siberia. (For other celestial highlights in 1998, see page 664.) Such extravaganzas owe their occurrence to the fact that the moon is 400 times smaller than the sun, but 400 times closer to earth—hence the moon and sun appear to have equal diameters. So when the moon comes between the sun and earth, we are left with an awe-inspiring sight of a pearly halo around a black disc.

Total lunar eclipses may not be as impressive, but they more than reward the small effort required to see one. At least once a year the moon passes into the the earth's shadow and completely disappears from the night sky. Unlike a solar eclipse, a lunar eclipse can be enjoyed across an entire hemisphere.

STARGAZER'S GUIDE

CELESTIAL HIGHLIGHTS FOR 1998

The single best highlight of 1998, according to Geoff Chester of the U.S. Naval Observatory, is the total solar eclipse on February 26. The path of totality stretches from the Pacific Ocean near the Galapagos Islands to the northern edge of South America and across the Caribbean Sea. This will be the last total solar eclipse visible in the Americas until 2017. Other astronomical events in 1998 are listed below. Times are expressed in Universal Time (UT), which is five hours ahead of Eastern Standard Time.

■ JANUARY
1. Moon near Jupiter. Venus low on the horizon; much fainter Mars between the two bright planets.
3. Quadrantid meteor shower peaks in predawn hours.
4. Earth is at perihelion, (closest point to the sun) at 21:00 UT, 147,099,400 km (91,407,600 mi.).

■ FEBRUARY
23. Venus highest and brightest in predawn.
26. Total solar eclipse, visible in Caribbean Sea.

■ MARCH
1. Moon near Saturn in evening sky.
20. Vernal equinox, 19:56 UT. Mercury at its best in evening twilight sky.
24. Moon near Venus in morning sky.

■ APRIL
23. Venus and Jupiter very close in predawn.

■ MAY
5. Eta Aquarid meteor shower peaks in morning sky.
22. Moon near Venus in morning sky.

29. Venus and Saturn very close together in predawn.

■ JUNE
17. Moon near Jupiter in morning sky.
19. Moon near Saturn in morning sky.
21. Summer solstice, 14:03 UT. Moon near Venus in morning sky.

■ JULY
4. Earth at aphelion (farthest point from the sun), 00:00 UT, 152,096,700 km (94,512,300 mi).
14. Moon near Jupiter in morning sky.
17. Moon near Saturn in morning sky.
21. Mercury near Venus in morning sky.

■ AUGUST
11. Moon near Jupiter in morning sky.
12. Perseid meteor shower peaks in morning sky.
19. Moon near Mars in morning sky.
22. Annular solar eclipse in Malaysia and Indonesia.

■ SEPTEMBER
1. Mercury at its best in predawn. Mars and Venus also bright.
6. Moon near Jupiter all night.
9. Moon near Saturn in morning sky.

16. Jupiter at opposition, visible from sunset to sunrise.
22. Autumnal equinox, 5:39 UT.

■ OCTOBER
3. Moon near Jupiter all night.
22. Orionid meteor shower peaks in morning sky.
23. Saturn at opposition, visible in sky all night.
26. Venus near Mars in late evening twilight.
31. Moon near Jupiter all night.

■ NOVEMBER
3. Moon near Saturn all night.
13. Moon near Mars in morning sky.
27. Moon near Jupiter in evening sky.
30. Moon near Saturn in evening sky.

■ DECEMBER
3. Moon near Venus in evening sky.
4. Moon near Jupiter in evening sky.
12. Moon near Mars in morning sky.
14. Geminid meteor shower peaks.
22. Winter solstice, 1:58 UT.
27. Moon near Saturn in evening sky.

■ **STARGAZER'S GUIDE**

■ STARS AND CONSTELLATIONS

The explosion that created the Universe gave birth to trillions of stars, but only 5,000 are visible to the naked eye. Since only half the sky can be seen at any one time, that means only 2,500 stars will be in your field of vision on the next clear night. Constellations are groups of stars whose patterns remind stargazers of familiar shapes. Today, astronomers recognize 88 such patterns. Their names and meanings:

Andromeda	Chained Maiden
Antila	Air Pump
Apus	Bird of Paradise
Aquarius	Water Bearer
Aquila	Eagle
Ara	Altar
Aries	Ram
Auriga	Charioteer
Bootes	Herdsman
Caelum	Chisel
Camelopardalis	Giraffe
Cancer	Crab
Canes Venatici	Hunting Dogs
Canis Major	Great Dog
Canis Minor	Little Dog
Capricornus	Sea-goat
Carina	Keel
Cassiopeia	Queen
Centaurus	Centaur
Cepheus	King
Cetus	Whale
Chamaeleon	Chameleon
Circinus	Compasses (art)
Columba	Dove
Coma Berenices	Bernice's Hair
Corona Australis	Southern Crown
Corona Borealis	Northern Crown
Corvus	Crow
Crater	Cup
Crux	Cross (southern)
Cygnus	Swan
Delphinus	Dolphin
Dorado	Goldfish
Draco	Dragon

■ THE NIGHT SKY IN JANUARY

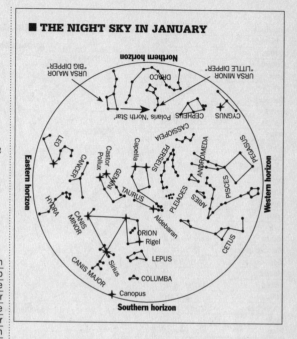

■ THE NIGHT SKY IN FEBRUARY

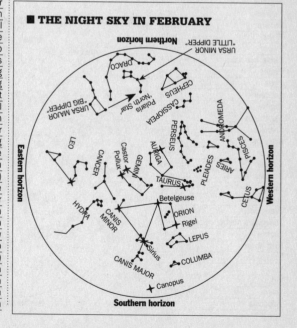

■ **STARGAZER'S GUIDE**

Equuieus	Little Horse
Eridanus	River
Fomax	Furnace
Gemini	Twins
Grus	Crane (bird)
Hercules	Hercules
Horologium	Clock
Hydra	Water Snake (female)
Hydrus	Water Snake (male)
Indus	Indian
Lacerta	Lizard
Leo	Lion
Leo Minor	Little Lion
Lepus	Hare
Libra	Balance
Lupus	Wolf
Lynx	Lynx
Lyra	Lyre
Mensa	Table Mountain
Microscopium	Microscope
Monoceros	Unicorn
Musca	Fly
Norma	Square (rule)
Octans	Octant
Ophiuchus	Serpent Bearer
Orion	Hunter
Pavo	Peacock
Pegasus	Flying Horse
Perseus	Hero
Phoenix	Phoenix
Pictor	Painter
Pisces	Fishes
Piscis Austrinius	Southern Fish
Puppis	Stern (deck)
Pyxis	Compass (sea)
Reticulum	Reticle
Sagitta	Arrow
Sagittarius	Archer
Scorpius	Scorpion
Sculptor	Sculptor
Scutum	Shield
Serpens	Serpent
Sextans	Sextant
Taurus	Bull
Telescopium	Telescope
Triangulum	Triangle
Triangulum Australe	South. Triangle
Tucana	Toucan
Ursa Major	Great Bear
Ursa Minor	Little Bear
Vela	Sail
Virgo	Maiden
Volans	Flying Fish
Vulpecula	Fox

■ **THE NIGHT SKY IN MARCH**

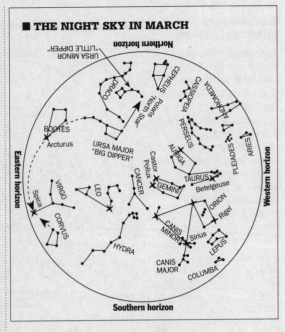

■ **THE NIGHT SKY IN APRIL**

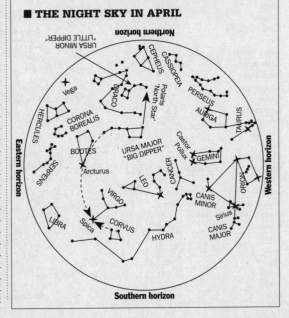

■ THE NIGHT SKY IN MAY

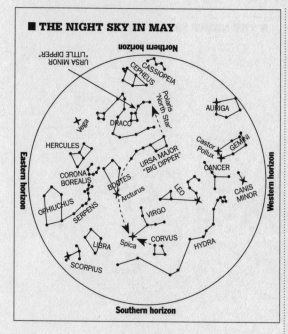

Northern horizon

Eastern horizon

Western horizon

Southern horizon

■ THE NIGHT SKY IN JUNE

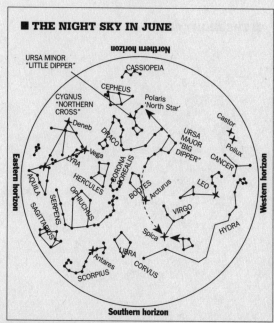

Northern horizon

Eastern horizon

Western horizon

Southern horizon

■ PLANETS

There are nine planets in the solar system, including Earth, but only four besides our own are visible to the naked eye: Venus, Mars, Jupiter, and Saturn.

■ **MERCURY:** The smallest of the planets is Mercury. Its diameter is less than half the earth's. Named for the winged messenger of the gods, it is the planet closest to the sun and has no satellites. It is believed that Mercury always turns the same side toward the sun and that the sunlit part of Mercury has a temperature hotter than 600 degrees Fahrenheit. By contrast, the temperature on the side away from the sun is thought to be –460 degrees Fahrenheit.

■ **VENUS:** Named for the goddess of love and beauty, Venus is almost the same size as Earth and is often called Earth's "sister planet." The brightest of all planets, Venus is shadowed only by the sun and the moon. It is the first "star" to appear in the evening sky and the last to disappear in the morning. At its brightest, Venus may even be visible during the day. Many astronomers believe that the core of Venus is largely metallic, mostly iron and nickel. Because of the dense carbon dioxide clouds enveloping the planet, the surface of Venus can't be seen.

■ **STARGAZER'S GUIDE**

■ **EARTH:** This is the third-closest planet to the sun—they are only 93 million miles apart. Seen from space, the planet appears as a blue ocean sphere with brown and green areas marking the location of its continents. Its diameter at the equator is 7,900 miles, and its atmosphere contains 78 percent nitrogen and 21 percent oxygen, in addition to traces of water in gaseous form, carbon dioxide, and other gases. By measuring the radioactive decay of elements in the earth's crust, scientists estimate that the planet is about 4.5 billion years old.

■ **MARS:** Like Earth, Mars has four seasons, but its diameter is just about half that of Earth's, and its mass is only about a tenth of ours. Named for the god of war, Mars takes 687 days to complete one revolution of the sun. About 80 percent of the planet's atmosphere is carbon dioxide. The white caps that cover its poles increase in size during the Martian winter and shrink during the summer. Martian seasons are about twice as long as Earth's.

■ **JUPITER:** Next to the sun, Jupiter is the largest and most massive object in the solar system. Named for the leader of the gods, Jupiter has a mass more than twice that of all other planets

■ **THE NIGHT SKY IN JULY**

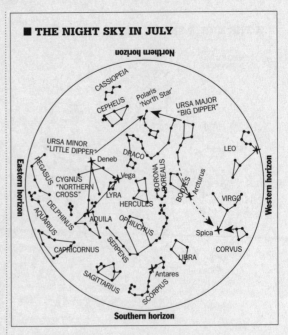

■ **THE NIGHT SKY IN AUGUST**

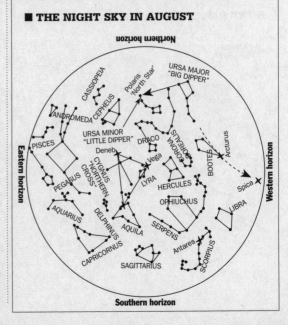

■ **STARGAZER'S GUIDE**

■ THE NIGHT SKY IN SEPTEMBER

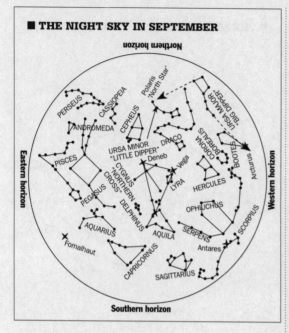

■ THE NIGHT SKY IN OCTOBER

combined. A body on the surface of Jupiter would weigh 2.64 times what it would weigh on Earth. Jupiter completes a revolution every 10 hours, giving it the shortest day in the solar system. It also has 12 satellites, the largest number of any planet in the solar system. It is perhaps most famous for its Great Red Spot, which scientists believe is a storm that has been going on for 300 years.

■ **SATURN:** The second-largest planet in the solar system, Saturn is named for Titan, the father of Jupiter and the god of sowing. It is best known for its system of concentric rings, which are not visible to the naked eye. The rings are probably composed of debris from a shattered satellite. Saturn is the least dense of all the planets but one of the brightest.

■ **URANUS:** Visible by the naked eye on a dark, clear night, Uranus is unique because its axis of rotation lies almost in the plane of its orbit. The planet was discovered by the German-English astronomer William Herschel in 1781. Herschel proposed to name the planet Georgium Sidu, in honor of England's King George III. But in keeping with the tradition of naming planets after Greek gods, it was eventually named after the father of

Titan and the grandfather of Jupiter. Uranus has five known satellites and a mass over 14 times that of Earth. Its temperature is thought to be below –300 degrees Fahrenheit.

■ **NEPTUNE:** Named for the god of the sea, Neptune requires 165 years to complete one revolution of the sun. Its atmosphere is made of methane, hydrogen, ammonia, and helium, and its mass is about 17 times that of Earth. The planet was discovered as a result of a mathematical prediction. Two mathematicians, John Couch Adams and Urbain Leverrier, calculated that there must be an unknown planet more distant from the sun than Uranus because they could detect the gravitational pull on Uranus.

■ **PLUTO:** There is probably little or no atmosphere on Pluto because of its extreme temperature, which is nearly –400 degrees Fahrenheit. From Pluto the sun would only appear as a bright star. Named for the god of the underworld, the planet's first two letters are also the initials of Percival Lowell, whose research on gravitational forces led him to predict the planet's existence around the beginning of this century. However, the planet wasn't discovered until after Lowell's death.

■ **THE NIGHT SKY IN NOVEMBER**

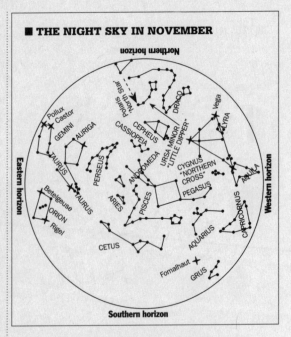

■ **THE NIGHT SKY IN DECEMBER**

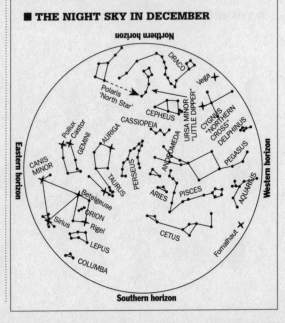

MOONLIGHT BECOMES YOU

The moon has no light of its own; it merely reflects the light of the sun. If the moon did not rotate as it revolves around the earth, we would see all its sides; as it is, we always see the same side. Here's a calendar for the moon's phases in 1998 in Universal Time (EST plus five hours):

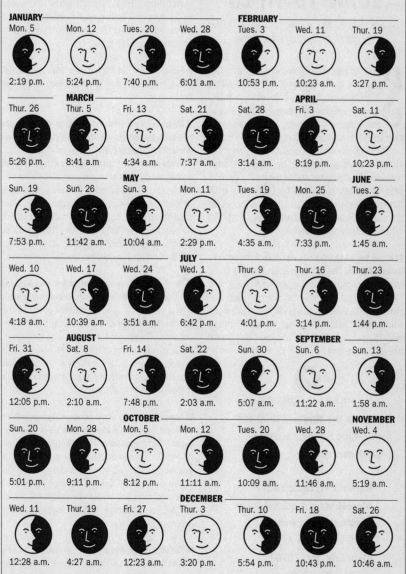

JANUARY

Mon. 5	Mon. 12	Tues. 20	Wed. 28
2:19 p.m.	5:24 p.m.	7:40 p.m.	6:01 a.m.

FEBRUARY

Tues. 3	Wed. 11	Thur. 19
10:53 p.m.	10:23 a.m.	3:27 p.m.

MARCH

Thur. 26	Thur. 5	Fri. 13	Sat. 21
5:26 p.m.	8:41 a.m	4:34 a.m.	7:37 a.m.

APRIL

Sat. 28	Fri. 3	Sat. 11
3:14 a.m.	8:19 p.m.	10:23 p.m.

MAY

Sun. 19	Sun. 26	Sun. 3	Mon. 11
7:53 p.m.	11:42 a.m.	10:04 a.m.	2:29 p.m.

JUNE

Tues. 19	Mon. 25	Tues. 2
4:35 a.m.	7:33 p.m.	1:45 a.m.

JULY

Wed. 10	Wed. 17	Wed. 24	Wed. 1
4:18 a.m.	10:39 a.m.	3:51 a.m.	6:42 p.m.

Thur. 9	Thur. 16	Thur. 23
4:01 p.m.	3:14 p.m.	1:44 p.m.

AUGUST

Fri. 31	Sat. 8	Fri. 14	Sat. 22
12:05 p.m.	2:10 a.m.	7:48 p.m.	2:03 a.m.

SEPTEMBER

Sun. 30	Sun. 6	Sun. 13
5:07 a.m.	11:22 a.m.	1:58 a.m.

OCTOBER

Sun. 20	Mon. 28	Mon. 5	Mon. 12
5:01 p.m.	9:11 p.m.	8:12 p.m.	11:11 a.m.

NOVEMBER

Tues. 20	Wed. 28	Wed. 4
10:09 a.m.	11:46 a.m.	5:19 a.m.

DECEMBER

Wed. 11	Thur. 19	Fri. 27	Thur. 3
12:28 a.m.	4:27 a.m.	12:23 a.m.	3:20 p.m.

Thur. 10	Fri. 18	Sat. 26
5:54 p.m.	10:43 p.m.	10:46 a.m.

A BEACHGOER'S GUIDE TO TIDES

Skim this to know more about tidal effects than most fishermen

Some ancient myth-makers held that the earth's pulse caused the tides. The Greeks began to notice the moon's influence when they began venturing out of the relatively tideless Mediterranean. Our modern understanding of tides is based on Sir Isaac Newton's equilibrium theory of tides, which described the gravitational attractions of the sun and moon on the earth's waters. Today, tides can be predicted with astronomical precision and need no longer be a mystery. Here's what landlubbers will find when they are at the beach:

■ **If you live on the East Coast, expect the tides to be semidiurnal.** That's when high and low tides occur twice per lunar day, and the heights of both the first and second set of tides are roughly the same. A lunar day is 50 minutes longer than a day on planet Earth, which is why in many places high and low tides occur about 50 minutes later than the corre-

EXPERT SOURCE

To obtain the tide and tidal current tables for your coastal region, contact:

National Oceanic and Atmospheric Administration Distribution Branch 6501 Lafayette Ave. Riverdale, MD 20737 ☎ 301–436–6990

sponding tides of the previous day.

■ **If you live on the West Coast, expect mixed tides.** The tides on America's left coast rise and fall twice per lunar day, but the heights of the second set of tides differ from the first. The different tides each day are termed higher high water, lower high water, higher low water, and lower low water. Their order of occurrence varies over the course of the month and from place to place.

■ **Along the Gulf of Mexico, the tides are diurnal.** Here, high and low tides appear only once every day.

■ **About twice a month, near the time of the new and full moon, the tidal range between high and low tides is usually 20 percent above average.** These tides, known as spring tides, occur when the sun and moon are in a straight line with the earth. When the sun and moon are at right angles to each other with respect to the earth, tidal ranges between high and low tides are about 20 percent less than average. These tides, known as neap tides, occur around the time of the first and third quarters of the moon.

■ **For another big swing in height between high and low tide, wait until the moon is at perigee.** That's when the moon is at its closest point to the earth each month and is when the tidal range between high and low tide is greatest. Roughly two weeks later the moon is at apogee, which is its farthest point from the earth for the month. That's when the moon's influence is at a minimum.

■ **During the course of the month, daily inequalities between successive high or low tides also can occur.** This happens as the moon moves from about 28 degrees north of the equator to 28 degrees south. When the moon is at one of these extremes, the difference in height between morning and evening tides is greatest. When the moon is at the equator, tides are roughly equal.

■ **The tidal range also increases in January.** That's when the earth's elliptical orbit around the sun brings the planet closest to the sun, in

■ THE MOON AND TIDES

The tide is the rise and fall of water throughout the earth's oceans. Occurring every 12 hours and 26 minutes, tides are created primarily by the moon's pull of gravity on the water.

High tides are produced when the earth is nearer the moon and water is pulled toward the moon. This happens on the opposite side of the earth at the same time.

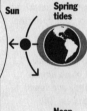

Spring tides occur when the sun and the moon are directly in line. The moon is either in front of or behind the earth. This produces a very high tide twice a month.

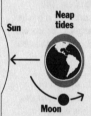

Neap tides do not rise as high as normal because the moon is at right angles to the sun. A neap tide occurs twice a month.

high and low tide. There, the funnel-like opening of the bay concentrates the energy and increases the height of the incoming tide, resulting in average tidal ranges of about 45 feet.

■ Meteorological conditions can also disrupt normal tide patterns. While tide tables provide accurate times and heights of high and low tide, strong and persistent winds and the low atmospheric pressure associated with storm systems can alter the time and height of high or low tide. If you are planning to go clamming or to collect seashells at low tide and there is a strong onshore breeze, you may want to play it safe and delay for as long as an hour after the predicted time of low tide.

■ Horizontal water movements, known as tidal currents, are generally strongest midway between high and low tide. When the tide rises and water flows in to fill estuaries and inlets, the water is called a flood current. When the tide goes out and water drains from these coastal areas, the flow is called an ebb current. Slack currents are found around the time of both high and low tide.

■ Surf fishing is best done when tidal currents are strongest. Strong flood currents force bait fish up closer to the beach and cause them to school up tighter and hide behind features such as rocks or jetties. Game fish such as bluefish or striped bass take advantage of these conditions, and so should knowledgeable surf fishermen, advises marine fisheries biologist Gregg Skomal. Game fish lie in wait for the bait fish to be swept in and out of inlets, estuaries, and bays by flood and ebb currents. Slack water is usually the worst time to fish.

■ Boaters shouldn't rely on the tidal charts in coastal newspapers. While most coastal newspapers list the times and heights of high and low tide, boaters need more tidal information than the newspapers provide in order to ensure safe passage over the ocean floor and to know where to anchor. They should consult the tide and tidal current tables that are published each year by the government.

what astronomers call the state of perihelion. In July, when the earth is farthest away from the sun in what astronomers refer to as the state of aphelion, the tidal range decreases.

■ The shape and depth of ocean basins change tidal ranges, too. The smallest differences in the heights between high and low tides occur along open coasts. For example, spring tidal ranges (near the time of the new and full moon) vary from about 2 feet on the Gulf Coast to as much as 8 or 9 feet on the California coast. The largest tidal ranges are found in tidal inlets, estuaries, and salt marshes. The Bay of Fundy in Canada has the greatest difference in the world between

SAFETY FOR SWIMMERS AND SURFERS

Lifeguards recommend swimming off sheltered beaches such as those found in coves or behind a point or peninsula. Swimming is easiest out beyond the breakwaters and away from where the biggest sets of waves are breaking. Eyeball how longshore currents are flowing by watching floating debris or swimmers, and swim with the current to limit fatigue and frustration. We asked Karl Tallman, a lifeguard for the California Department of Parks and Recreation, for some additional tips:

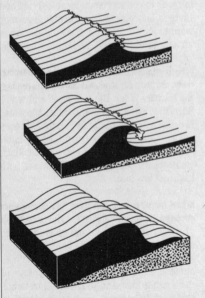

■ **Spilling breakers** provide body or board surfers with the longest ride. Such waves commonly occur on relatively flat beaches and are characterized by foam and bubbles that spill down the front of the wave.

■ **Plunging breakers** can break with great force right on top of an unsuspecting surf swimmer. They are found on moderately steep beaches. The crests of these waves curl over a pocket of air and result in splash-up. As waves, they are short-lived and are not the best for surfing.

■ **Surging breakers** slide up and down the beach creating very few challenges for the surf swimmer. They occur on steep beaches and produce little or no bubbles.

■ **Rip currents** can endanger even the most experienced swimmer. Remember to swim parallel to the shore to escape the current or allow it to carry you out to where its strength diminishes.

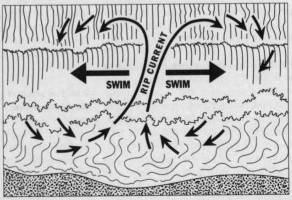

TIMES & DATES

TIME ZONES: Telling time across America, PAGE 677   **INTERNATIONAL DAYS:** Some festive observances from around the world, PAGE 678   **RELIGIOUS DAYS:** Selected sacred celebrations, PAGE 680   **SHOPPING:** A guide to what's on sale throughout the year, PAGE 681   **CALENDAR:** Keeping time through the ages, PAGE 682   **HOROSCOPE:** An astrologer's look at 1998, PAGE 690   **CHINESE ZODIAC:** The animal signs that affect your personality, PAGE 692

HOLIDAYS

HOLY DAYS AND OTHER DAYS '98

Stories behind the days that come but once a year

Merchants like holidays because they provide a good shopping opportunity. Greeting-card makers want to invent special occasions when they don't exist. The religious faithful take their Holy Days seriously. And those who need a break cheer at the prospect of a day free of the normal routines. Here is the holiday calendar for 1998:

MAJOR AMERICAN HOLIDAYS

* NEW YEAR'S DAY, Jan. 1

Roman mythology says two-faced Janus, the god of beginnings for whom our first month is named, looked back on the old year and

---

* = FEDERAL HOLIDAYS
Holidays in which federal government offices nationwide, and schools, banks, and offices in Washington, D.C., are closed. In practice, most states also declare a legal holiday on these days.

---

ahead to the new. In the United States, we ring out the old year at midnight with champagne and a few bars of that cryptic Scottish melody, Auld Lang Syne ("The Good Old Days").

* DR. MARTIN LUTHER KING, JR., BIRTHDAY, Jan. 19
Third Monday in January

The civil rights activist, minister, and advocate of nonviolent protest was born on January 15, 1929. A bill to make his birthday a federal holiday was first introduced in 1968, the year King was assassinated. Some states added it to their calendar while waiting for Congress to approve it; Ronald Reagan signed the bill in 1983.

GROUNDHOG DAY, Feb. 2

Rumor has it that if a groundhog comes out of his hole on this day and sees his shadow, winter will last for six more weeks. But if the sky is overcast and the groundhog is shadowless, mild weather is on its way. Pennsylvania's Punxsutawney Phil is the country's most famous rodent meteorologist. Since 1887, the Punxsutawney Groundhog Club has gone to Gobbler's Knob to watch successive generations of Phils offer their predictions.

VALENTINE'S DAY, Feb. 14

The origin of this romantic holiday is uncertain, but it may have been inspired by the martyrdom of St. Valentine in A.D. 270. The first commercial Valentine's Day cards in the United States hit the shops in the 1840s; in the early 1900s, when risqué cards were "in," the Chicago postal service refused to deliver 25,000 valentines it deemed unfit to be mailed.

✳ PRESIDENTS' DAY, Feb. 16
Third Monday in February

Honors two of our most famous presidents, George Washington (born Feb. 22, 1732) and Abraham Lincoln (born Feb. 12, 1809), whose birthdays used to be celebrated separately. These larger-than-life figures stood out in the crowd even by today's standards: Washington was 6 feet tall, and lanky Lincoln was 6 feet 4 inches.

ST. PATRICK'S DAY, March 17

The patron saint of Ireland was born in England around A.D. 389, and immigrants who came to America from the Emerald Isle brought his holiday with them. So many of George Washington's troops were Irish that the secret password during one Revolutionary War battle was "Saint Patrick."

VERNAL EQUINOX, March 20

Day and night are equally long on this first day of spring.

APRIL FOOLS' DAY, April 1

No one is sure when or why the first of April turned into a day for making friends look like fools, but the tradition dates back at least to the early 18th century. April fools are labeled "gowks" (cuckoos) in Scotland, and "gobs" or "noddies" in England; the French call April 1 pranks "poisson d'avril," or April fish.

EARTH DAY, April 22

In 1970 the Environmental Protection Agency first asked us to "Give Earth a Chance." Congress has passed laws that protect our natural resources, and curbside recycling is now common. But the EPA reports that we still produce more solid waste per person every day than any other nation—4.4 pounds.

MOTHER'S DAY, May 10
Second Sunday in May

Julia Ward Howe, author of the Battle Hymn

of the Republic, first floated the idea of a national holiday to honor mothers in 1872. But Philadelphian Anna Jarvis, whose mother had wanted such a day to comfort families after the Civil War, launched the campaign that made it a reality. President Woodrow Wilson officially established the holiday in 1914.

✳ MEMORIAL DAY, May 25
Last Monday in May

The government bowed in 1868 to the campaign of a Union veterans group that wanted to honor soldiers who died in the Civil War. The holiday has now become a tribute to all fallen soldiers and deceased loved ones.

FLAG DAY, June 14

The Second Continental Congress adopted the official flag design on June 14, 1777. Protocol dictates that the American flag may not touch the ground, nor may it be dipped to anyone or anything while being carried in a parade. The star-spangled banner Francis Scott Key saw by the dawn's early light was hit by 11 bullets as it flew above Baltimore's Fort McHenry; it is preserved at the Smithsonian Institution.

FATHER'S DAY, June 21
Third Sunday in June

The daughter of a Civil War veteran whose wife died giving birth to their sixth child persuaded her church in Spokane, Wash., to conduct a special service in honor of fathers. That was in 1910, and though the idea soon became popular around the nation, it wasn't made an official holiday until 1966.

SUMMER SOLSTICE, June 21

The first day of summer; the year's longest.

✳ INDEPENDENCE DAY, July 4

With many fireworks and much fanfare, Fourth of July festivities commemorate the 1776 signing of the Declaration of Independence. Two of the signers were loyal to it even in death: On July 4, 1826, John Adams, the second president, died at age 90, and Thomas Jefferson, president number three, died at age 83.

■ U.S. TIME ZONES AND DAYLIGHT SAVINGS TIME

Daylight Savings Time begins the first Sunday in April: move your clock ahead one hour. On the last Sunday in October, Standard Time returns: move the clock back again.

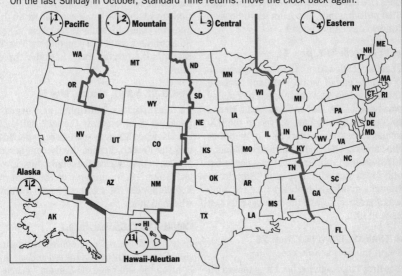

WOMEN'S EQUALITY DAY, Aug. 26

The 19th Amendment to the Constitution was passed on this day in 1920, giving women the right to vote. In Tennessee's House of Representatives, the last vote needed to ratify the amendment was cast by 24-year-old Harry Burns, who, though his district opposed the measure, promised his mother he would vote for it to break a tie.

✳ LABOR DAY, Sept. 7

First Monday in September

During the Industrial Revolution, a bad time for laborers, union leader Peter McGuire proposed a day that honored America's workers. He chose early September for its fine weather, and because no other legal holiday broke up the stretch between Independence Day and Thanksgiving. It's always been thought of as the end of summer vacation.

AUTUMNAL EQUINOX, Sept. 23

The first day of fall.

✳ COLUMBUS DAY, Oct. 12

Christopher Columbus and his entourage first touched American soil on October 12, 1492, probably on Samana Cay in the Bahamas. At sea, Columbus kept an accurate private log of the miles traveled each day, but subtracted miles for the ship's official log. He did so to avoid mutinies caused by sailors who didn't want to be so far from home, and to make sure his directions to Asia, which turned out to be wildly inaccurate, wouldn't fall into the wrong hands.

UNITED NATIONS DAY, Oct. 24

When the United Nations was founded in 1945, it had 51 member countries. Now it has more than 150. Its six official languages are Arabic, Chinese, English, French, Russian, and Spanish.

HALLOWEEN, Oct. 31

The attendant ghouls and goblins stem from the myths of the ancient Celts, who thought witches, ghosts, and the souls of the dead wandered about on the last night of their harvest season. The name comes from the Catholic Church, which in the ninth century declared the first of November All

Saints' Day and called the previous evening All Hallow Even. Candy-loving children benefit from the combination of influences, as does UNICEF, which has earned more than $100 million since 1950 from its Halloween fundraising campaign.

* VETERANS DAY, Nov. 11

Formerly called Armistice Day, it commemorated the end of World War I and honored those who had died fighting it. The holiday was renamed in 1954 and its scope widened to include all who have served in the U.S. armed forces. For a short time in the 1970s, the date was changed to the fourth Monday in November to add another three-day weekend to the calendar. But many Americans thought making the observance movable was disrespectful, and the date was changed back in 1978.

* THANKSGIVING DAY, Nov. 26

Fourth Thursday in November

The first Thanksgiving feast was cooked up around 1621 when pilgrims and Native Americans sat down together to enjoy the fruits of harvest. The day after Thanksgiving marks the start of the Christmas shopping season.

WINTER SOLSTICE, Dec. 22

First day of winter; shortest day of the year.

KWANZAA, Dec. 26 to Jan. 1

The name of this holiday means "first fruits" in Swahili, and the holiday is based on African harvest festivals. Brought to America in the mid-1960s by Maulana Karenga, a civil rights leader who wanted black Americans to learn about their ancestors' cultures, Kwanzaa celebrates the history and culture of African Americans.

SELECTED INTERNATIONAL HOLIDAYS

NEW YEAR, China, Jan. 29

Second new moon after winter solstice

In Chinese tradition, 1998 is the year of the tiger. Families gather on New Year's Eve for a sumptuous banquet (the fish dish served last is not eaten, symbolizing the hope that there will be food left at the end of the year) and children awaken the next morning to find red envelopes filled with money under their pillows. Chinese tradition says babies are one year old at birth, and everyone's birthday is New Year's Day. So a child born at 11:59 p.m. on New Year's Eve hits the terrible twos in under three minutes.

CINCO DE MAYO, Mexico, May 5

Parades, parties, bullfights, and beauty pageants commemorate the 1862 Battle of Puebla, when Mexican soldiers beat the odds and the French. France finally conquered Mexico in 1864, but lost the country just three years later. A monument in the town of Puebla honors the soldiers of both armies who died there.

CANADA DAY, Canada, July 1

In honor of the nation's confederation in 1867, fireworks (heavy on the red and white) light up the skies and "O Canada!" echoes through the capital city of Ottawa, which hosts an annual concert on Parliament Hill. Across the country, Canadians trot out their flags and firecrackers.

OBON FESTIVAL, Japan, July 13–15 or Aug. 13–15 (varies by region)

The souls of the dead are said to return for a visit during this festival, so the Japanese go to cemeteries and decorate their ancestors' graves in anticipation. Drummers and folk dancers perform, and lanterns and bonfires are lit to comfort the spiritual guests.

BASTILLE DAY, France, July 14

A Parisian mob stormed the famous fortress and prison in 1789, not satisfied to just eat cake and hell-bent on releasing the political prisoners they thought were held there. They freed seven inmates, none of whom was actually a political prisoner, but the action marked the lower classes' entry into the French Revolution. Today, the Bastille is gone and the Parisians are slightly tamer: they light firecrackers, decorate their neighborhoods with paper lanterns, and waltz in the streets to accordion music.

■ INTERNATIONAL TIME ZONES

The 24 time zones are figured in relation to their distance from the prime meridian, which is the longitudinal position of the Royal Observatory in Greenwich, England. Anyone crossing the International Date Line going west should move the calendar ahead one day; if the line is crossed going east, the date moves back one day.

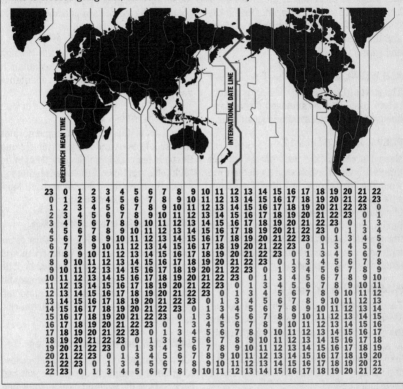

23	0	1	2	3	4	5	6	7	8	9	10	11	12	13	14	15	16	17	18	19	20	21	22
0	1	2	3	4	5	6	7	8	9	10	11	12	13	14	15	16	17	18	19	20	21	22	23
1	2	3	4	5	6	7	8	9	10	11	12	13	14	15	16	17	18	19	20	21	22	23	0
2	3	4	5	6	7	8	9	10	11	12	13	14	15	16	17	18	19	20	21	22	23	0	1
3	4	5	6	7	8	9	10	11	12	13	14	15	16	17	18	19	20	21	22	23	0	1	3
4	5	6	7	8	9	10	11	12	13	14	15	16	17	18	19	20	21	22	23	0	1	3	4
5	6	7	8	9	10	11	12	13	14	15	16	17	18	19	20	21	22	23	0	1	3	4	5
6	7	8	9	10	11	12	13	14	15	16	17	18	19	20	21	22	23	0	1	3	4	5	6
7	8	9	10	11	12	13	14	15	16	17	18	19	20	21	22	23	0	1	3	4	5	6	7
8	9	10	11	12	13	14	15	16	17	18	19	20	21	22	23	0	1	3	4	5	6	7	8
9	10	11	12	13	14	15	16	17	18	19	20	21	22	23	0	1	3	4	5	6	7	8	9
10	11	12	13	14	15	16	17	18	19	20	21	22	23	0	1	3	4	5	6	7	8	9	10
11	12	13	14	15	16	17	18	19	20	21	22	23	0	1	3	4	5	6	7	8	9	10	11
12	13	14	15	16	17	18	19	20	21	22	23	0	1	3	4	5	6	7	8	9	10	11	12
13	14	15	16	17	18	19	20	21	22	23	0	1	3	4	5	6	7	8	9	10	11	12	13
14	15	16	17	18	19	20	21	22	23	0	1	3	4	5	6	7	8	9	10	11	12	13	14
15	16	17	18	19	20	21	22	23	0	1	3	4	5	6	7	8	9	10	11	12	13	14	15
16	17	18	19	20	21	22	23	0	1	3	4	5	6	7	8	9	10	11	12	13	14	15	16
17	18	19	20	21	22	23	0	1	3	4	5	6	7	8	9	10	11	12	13	14	15	16	17
18	19	20	21	22	23	0	1	3	4	5	6	7	8	9	10	11	12	13	14	15	16	17	18
19	20	21	22	23	0	1	3	4	5	6	7	8	9	10	11	12	13	14	15	16	17	18	19
20	21	22	23	0	1	3	4	5	6	7	8	9	10	11	12	13	14	15	16	17	18	19	20
21	22	23	0	1	3	4	5	6	7	8	9	10	11	12	13	14	15	16	17	18	19	20	21
22	23	0	1	3	4	5	6	7	8	9	10	11	12	13	14	15	16	17	18	19	20	21	22

SINTER KLAAS, the Netherlands, Dec. 5

St. Nicholas is the patron saint of children, so the Dutch celebrate his birthday to please them. Legend has it that he wears a red cape, rides a white horse, and delivers presents via chimneys. Children leave their shoes out overnight (as well as carrots for the horse) and find them filled with trinkets in the morning.

SANTA LUCIA, Sweden, Dec. 13

St. Lucia wore a crown of candles to bring light during the darkest day of the bleak Swedish winter. At dawn in homes across the country, one girl dons a wreath topped with burning white candles (electric ones are available for wobbly Lucias) and a long white dress with a red sash. She and her white-clad siblings bring coffee and saffron bread to their parents, singing carols as they go. Students often organize "Lucia trains" and visit the homes of their teachers as well.

BOXING DAY, United Kingdom, Dec. 26

Churches used to open their collection boxes the day after Christmas and distribute the contents to the poor. Now Britons use the occasion to give gifts to the people who have helped them throughout the year—those who deliver mail, newspapers, and milk bottles are the big winners.

SELECTED RELIGIOUS HOLIDAYS

RAMADAN, Islamic, begins Dec. 30, 1997

The fourth of the five pillars of Islam is to keep the fast of Ramadan, which celebrates Muhammad's reception of the divine revelations recorded in the Koran. During the monthlong fast, Muslims (except soldiers and the sick) may not eat between sunrise and sunset.

ASH WEDNESDAY, Christian, Feb. 25

The start of Lent, a fast that begins 40 days before Easter. Ashes smudged on the foreheads of the faithful symbolize penitence.

PURIM, Jewish, March 12

Named for the lots, or "pur," that the Persian king's adviser Haman cast to determine when the Jews should be killed. The king's wife, Esther, who was Jewish, uncovered his plot and Haman was killed instead. During Purim, Jews dress in costumes and act out the story of Esther. In synagogue, children with noisemakers try to drown out Haman's name whenever it is read.

PASSOVER, Jewish, April 11

The eight-day holiday reminds Jews that Moses led the Israelites from Egypt, where they had been slaves under the Pharaoh. At special dinners called seders, everyone takes part in reading the Israelites' story and tasting foods that symbolize aspects of their journey.

EASTER, Christian, April 12

The Christian religion's most important holiday, Easter, celebrates the resurrection of Jesus Christ. It is the last day of Holy Week, which includes Palm Sunday, Maundy Thursday, and Good Friday, and it marks the end of Lent. The traditional Easter eggs are thought to represent new life and immortality.

BAISAKHI, Hindu, April 13

Hindus bathe in the Ganges or in other holy waters during the celebration of their new year. Charitable acts performed throughout the following month are deemed especially good, so people give generously to the poor.

ROSH HASHANAH, Jewish, Sept. 21

The start of the Jewish new year is the first of the 10 High Holy Days, during which Jews reflect on their sins of the past year and seek forgiveness. A hollowed-out ram's horn, called the shofar, is sounded in synagogue to remind people of the trumpets of Judgment Day.

YOM KIPPUR, Jewish, Sept. 30

The Day of Atonement ends the 10 High Holy Days that begin on Rosh Hashanah. It is a day of fasting and prayer, repentance and forgiveness.

SUKKOTH, Jewish, Oct. 5

The "feast of tabernacles" commemorates the Israelites' wanderings after fleeing Egypt. In homes and synagogues, Jews build "sukkahs," replicas of the small shelters in which the Israelites lived during their journey. Also a harvest celebration.

DEWALI, Hindu, late Oct./early Nov.

The five-day festival of lights celebrates the human desire to move toward truth and light from ignorance and darkness. The streets are strewn with festive lamps and homes are decorated with flowers and colored paper. Festivities include fireworks, parties, and gift giving.

HANUKKAH, Jewish, begins Dec. 14

After a group of Jews led by Judah Maccabee recaptured a temple in Jerusalem that had been seized by Syrian-Greeks, they had enough oil to light the temple's lamp for a day. But the lamp burned for eight days, and Jews celebrate this miracle and the Maccabees' victory by lighting candles in the menorah (a special candelabra), adding one each night until all eight candles are lit.

CHRISTMAS DAY, Christian, Dec. 25

Christians celebrate the birth of Jesus Christ on this day (though his birth date is much debated among theologians and historians), but many Christmas traditions actually have pagan origins. The ancient Druids, for example, worshiped holly and mistletoe, and Norsemen burned yule logs in the winter to scare off demons.

SHOP TILL YOU DROP

For every retail item, there's a season. White sales are big on Columbus Day and silverware sales flourish in the June wedding season. Here's when the following items are likely to go on sale across the United States.

JANUARY
- Holiday-related products, including wrapping paper, cards, lights, candles, holiday decorations
- Cookware
- Curtains
- Dishes
- Housewares, small appliances, including toaster ovens, blenders, food processors, coffee makers, etc.
- Rugs
- Silverware
- Toys
- White sales, including linens
- Winter apparel, including coats, furs, sweaters

FEBRUARY
- Presidents' Day sales, big for the electronics industry
- Candy
- Jewelry
- Lingerie
- Stereos
- Televisions
- VCRs
- Winter clothes

MARCH
- Best time to buy winter clothes as retailers make room for spring lines
- Camping gear
- Gardening
- Spring fashion promotions

APRIL
- Bicycles
- Jewelry
- Lingerie
- Personal care products

MAY
- Furniture (bedroom sets, sofas, dining room tables)
- Gardening supplies
- Home furnishings
- Luggage
- Mattresses
- Outdoor furniture
- Refrigerators
- Spring clothing
- Stereos
- Televisions
- Tires
- VCRs
- Washer/dryers

JUNE
- Father's Day promotions

- Electronics
- Silverware (for wedding season)
- Sporting goods
- Summer recreational gear

JULY
- Bathing suits
- Bicycles
- Furniture
- Mattresses
- Refrigerators
- Tires
- Washer/dryers

AUGUST
- Back-to-school promotions for children's and juniors' clothing
- Office supplies
- School supplies
- Undergarments
- Wardrobe basics

SEPTEMBER
- Labor Day "last chance" promotions on summer wear
- Air conditioners
- Cookware
- Dishes

- Lamps
- Musical instruments (pianos, guitars, flutes, etc.)
- Recreational gear
- Stereos
- Televisions
- Tires
- VCRs

OCTOBER
- Columbus Day white sales
- Fall apparel
- Home textiles

NOVEMBER
- Curtains
- Fall apparel
- Holiday promotions
- Lamps
- Rugs
- Winter recreational gear

DECEMBER
- Consumer electronics
- Cookware
- Cosmetics
- Furniture
- Home appliances
- Jewelry
- Luggage
- Perfume
- Toys
- Washer/dryers
- Winter apparel

SOURCE: National Retail Federation.

THE CALENDAR
▼

COUNTDOWN TO A NEW MILLENNIUM

Time won't stand still, and the datebooks must reflect that

By definition, New Year's Day has always marked the start of a new calendar year, but that calendar year hasn't always been in January. Until the 16th century in Western Europe, New Year's Day was rung in on the vernal equinox, the start of spring in the Northern hemisphere. But other, non-Christian cultures have always had festivals to celebrate the birth of the sun around the time of the winter solstice in the dead of December, and in 1582 Pope Gregory XIII rearranged the calendar that is now universally used and decreed that the Christian New Year should commence on January 1.

While today's calendar may divide history into the years B.C. ("Before Christ") and A.D. (Latin for "year of the Lord"), that doesn't mean that when New Year's 1998 rolls around, it will have been 1998 years since Christ was born. Biblical historians now believe that Jesus of Nazareth was born around 6 B.C. and most likely not on December 25th. A sixth-century monk named Dionysius Exiguus suggested that date to commemorate Jesus' birthday, and others went along, at least in part because it didn't interfere with Passover, which occurs around the time of the vernal equinox.

If you are planning a big millennial celebration for December 31, 1999, think again. Since there is no year zero, the new millennium doesn't actually begin until January 1, 2001.

■ THE PERPETUAL CALENDAR

The letter shown for each year indicates which calendar to use. For the years 1803 to 1820, use the letters for 1983 to 2000, respectively.

Year		Year		Year		Year		Year		Year		Year		Year	
1821	L	1850	M	1879	N	1908	G	1937	B	1973	L	2009	A	2045	K
1822	M	1851	N	1880	H	1909	B	1938	C	1974	M	2010	B	2046	L
1823	N	1852	H	1881	C	1910	C	1939	K	1975	N	2011	C	2047	M
1824	H	1853	C	1882	K	1911	K	1940	E	1976	H	2012	D	2048	G
1825	C	1854	K	1883	L	1912	E	1941	N	1977	C	2013	M	2049	B
1826	K	1855	L	1884	F	1913	N	1942	A	1978	K	2014	N	2050	C
1827	L	1856	F	1885	A	1914	A	1943	B	1979	L	2015	A	2051	K
1828	F	1857	A	1886	B	1915	B	1944	J	1980	F	2016	I	2052	E
1829	A	1858	B	1887	C	1916	J	1945	L	1981	A	2017	K	2053	N
1830	B	1859	C	1888	D	1917	L	1946	M	1982	B	2018	L	2054	A
1831	C	1860	D	1889	M	1918	M	1947	N	1983	C	2019	M	2055	B
1832	D	1861	M	1890	N	1919	N	1948	H	1984	D	2020	G	2056	J
1833	M	1862	N	1891	A	1920	H	1949	C	1985	M	2021	B	2057	C
1834	N	1863	A	1892	I	1921	C	1950	K	1986	N	2022	C	2058	M
1835	A	1864	I	1893	K	1922	K	1951	L	1987	A	2023	K	2059	N
1836	I	1865	K	1894	L	1923	L	1952	F	1988	I	2024	E	2060	H
1837	K	1866	L	1895	M	1924	F	1953	A	1989	K	2025	C	2061	C
1838	L	1867	M	1896	G	1925	A	1954	B	1990	L	2026	A	2062	K
1839	M	1868	G	1897	B	1926	B	1955	C	1991	M	2027	B	2063	L
1840	G	1869	B	1898	C	1927	C	1956	D	1992	G	2028	J	2064	F
1841	B	1870	C	1899	K	1928	D	1957	M	1993	B	2029	L	2065	A
1842	C	1871	K	1900	L	1929	M	1958	N	1994	C	2030	M	2066	B
1843	D	1872	E	1901	M	1930	N	1959	A	1995	K	2031	N	2067	C
1844	E	1873	N	1902	N	1931	A	1960	I	1996	E	2032	H	2068	D
1845	N	1874	A	1903	A	1932	I	1961	K	1997	N	2033	C	2069	M
1846	A	1875	B	1904	I	1933	K	1962	L	1998	A	2034	K	2070	N
1847	B	1876	J	1905	K	1934	L	1963	M	1999	B	2035	M	2071	A
1848	J	1877	L	1906	L	1935	M	1964	G	2000	J	2036	F	2072	I
1849	L	1878	M	1907	M	1936	G	1965	B	2001	L	2037	A	2073	K
								1966	C	2002	M	2038	B	2074	L
								1967	N	2003	N	2039	C	2075	M
								1968	E	2004	H	2040	D	2076	G
								1969	N	2005	C	2041	M	2077	B
								1970	A	2006	K	2042	N	2078	C
								1971	B	2007	L	2043	A	2079	K
								1972	J	2008	F	2044	I	2080	E

A — 1998 1987

JANUARY
S	M	T	W	T	F	S
				1	2	3
4	5	6	7	8	9	10
11	12	13	14	15	16	17
18	19	20	21	22	23	24
25	26	27	28	29	30	31

FEBRUARY
S	M	T	W	T	F	S
1	2	3	4	5	6	7
8	9	10	11	12	13	14
15	16	17	18	19	20	21
22	23	24	25	26	27	28

MARCH
S	M	T	W	T	F	S
1	2	3	4	5	6	7
8	9	10	11	12	13	14
15	16	17	18	19	20	21
22	23	24	25	26	27	28
29	30	31				

APRIL
S	M	T	W	T	F	S
			1	2	3	4
5	6	7	8	9	10	11
12	13	14	15	16	17	18
19	20	21	22	23	24	25
26	27	28	29	30		

MAY
S	M	T	W	T	F	S
					1	2
3	4	5	6	7	8	9
10	11	12	13	14	15	16
17	18	19	20	21	22	23
24	25	26	27	28	29	30
31						

JUNE
S	M	T	W	T	F	S
	1	2	3	4	5	6
7	8	9	10	11	12	13
14	15	16	17	18	19	20
21	22	23	24	25	26	27
28	29	30				

JULY
S	M	T	W	T	F	S
			1	2	3	4
5	6	7	8	9	10	11
12	13	14	15	16	17	18
19	20	21	22	23	24	25
26	27	28	29	30	31	

AUGUST
S	M	T	W	T	F	S
						1
2	3	4	5	6	7	8
9	10	11	12	13	14	15
16	17	18	19	20	21	22
23	24	25	26	27	28	29
30	31					

SEPTEMBER
S	M	T	W	T	F	S
		1	2	3	4	5
6	7	8	9	10	11	12
13	14	15	16	17	18	19
20	21	22	23	24	25	26
27	28	29	30			

OCTOBER
S	M	T	W	T	F	S
				1	2	3
4	5	6	7	8	9	10
11	12	13	14	15	16	17
18	19	20	21	22	23	24
25	26	27	28	29	30	31

NOVEMBER
S	M	T	W	T	F	S
1	2	3	4	5	6	7
8	9	10	11	12	13	14
15	16	17	18	19	20	21
22	23	24	25	26	27	28
29	30					

DECEMBER
S	M	T	W	T	F	S
		1	2	3	4	5
6	7	8	9	10	11	12
13	14	15	16	17	18	19
20	21	22	23	24	25	26
27	28	29	30	31		

B — 1999 1993

JANUARY
S	M	T	W	T	F	S
					1	2
3	4	5	6	7	8	9
10	11	12	13	14	15	16
17	18	19	20	21	22	23
24	25	26	27	28	29	30
31						

FEBRUARY
S	M	T	W	T	F	S
	1	2	3	4	5	6
7	8	9	10	11	12	13
14	15	16	17	18	19	20
21	22	23	24	25	26	27
28						

MARCH
S	M	T	W	T	F	S
	1	2	3	4	5	6
7	8	9	10	11	12	13
14	15	16	17	18	19	20
21	22	23	24	25	26	27
28	29	30	31			

APRIL
S	M	T	W	T	F	S
				1	2	3
4	5	6	7	8	9	10
11	12	13	14	15	16	17
18	19	20	21	22	23	24
25	26	27	28	29	30	

MAY
S	M	T	W	T	F	S
						1
2	3	4	5	6	7	8
9	10	11	12	13	14	15
16	17	18	19	20	21	22
23	24	25	26	27	28	29
30	31					

JUNE
S	M	T	W	T	F	S
		1	2	3	4	5
6	7	8	9	10	11	12
13	14	15	16	17	18	19
20	21	22	23	24	25	26
27	28	29	30			

JULY
S	M	T	W	T	F	S
				1	2	3
4	5	6	7	8	9	10
11	12	13	14	15	16	17
18	19	20	21	22	23	24
25	26	27	28	29	30	31

AUGUST
S	M	T	W	T	F	S
1	2	3	4	5	6	7
8	9	10	11	12	13	14
15	16	17	18	19	20	21
22	23	24	25	26	27	28
29	30	31				

SEPTEMBER
S	M	T	W	T	F	S
			1	2	3	4
5	6	7	8	9	10	11
12	13	14	15	16	17	18
19	20	21	22	23	24	25
26	27	28	29	30		

OCTOBER
S	M	T	W	T	F	S
					1	2
3	4	5	6	7	8	9
10	11	12	13	14	15	16
17	18	19	20	21	22	23
24	25	26	27	28	29	30
31						

NOVEMBER
S	M	T	W	T	F	S
	1	2	3	4	5	6
7	8	9	10	11	12	13
14	15	16	17	18	19	20
21	22	23	24	25	26	27
28	29	30				

DECEMBER
S	M	T	W	T	F	S
			1	2	3	4
5	6	7	8	9	10	11
12	13	14	15	16	17	18
19	20	21	22	23	24	25
26	27	28	29	30	31	

C · 2005 · 1994

JANUARY
S	M	T	W	T	F	S
						1
2	3	4	5	6	7	8
9	10	11	12	13	14	15
16	17	18	19	20	21	22
23	24	25	26	27	28	29
30	31					

MAY
S	M	T	W	T	F	S
1	2	3	4	5	6	7
8	9	10	11	12	13	14
15	16	17	18	19	20	21
22	23	24	25	26	27	28
29	30	31				

SEPTEMBER
S	M	T	W	T	F	S
				1	2	3
4	5	6	7	8	9	10
11	12	13	14	15	16	17
18	19	20	21	22	23	24
25	26	27	28	29	30	

FEBRUARY
S	M	T	W	T	F	S
		1	2	3	4	5
6	7	8	9	10	11	12
13	14	15	16	17	18	19
20	21	22	23	24	25	26
27	28					

JUNE
S	M	T	W	T	F	S
			1	2	3	4
5	6	7	8	9	10	11
12	13	14	15	16	17	18
19	20	21	22	23	24	25
26	27	28	29	30		

OCTOBER
S	M	T	W	T	F	S
						1
2	3	4	5	6	7	8
9	10	11	12	13	14	15
16	17	18	19	20	21	22
23	24	25	26	27	28	29
30	31					

MARCH
S	M	T	W	T	F	S
		1	2	3	4	5
6	7	8	9	10	11	12
13	14	15	16	17	18	19
20	21	22	23	24	25	26
27	28	29	30	31		

JULY
S	M	T	W	T	F	S
					1	2
3	4	5	6	7	8	9
10	11	12	13	14	15	16
17	18	19	20	21	22	23
24	25	26	27	28	29	30
31						

NOVEMBER
S	M	T	W	T	F	S
		1	2	3	4	5
6	7	8	9	10	11	12
13	14	15	16	17	18	19
20	21	22	23	24	25	26
27	28	29	30			

APRIL
S	M	T	W	T	F	S
					1	2
3	4	5	6	7	8	9
10	11	12	13	14	15	16
17	18	19	20	21	22	23
24	25	26	27	28	29	30

AUGUST
S	M	T	W	T	F	S
	1	2	3	4	5	6
7	8	9	10	11	12	13
14	15	16	17	18	19	20
21	22	23	24	25	26	27
28	29	30	31			

DECEMBER
S	M	T	W	T	F	S
				1	2	3
4	5	6	7	8	9	10
11	12	13	14	15	16	17
18	19	20	21	22	23	24
25	26	27	28	29	30	31

D · 2012 · 1984

JANUARY
S	M	T	W	T	F	S
1	2	3	4	5	6	7
8	9	10	11	12	13	14
15	16	17	18	19	20	21
22	23	24	25	26	27	28
29	30	31				

MAY
S	M	T	W	T	F	S
		1	2	3	4	5
6	7	8	9	10	11	12
13	14	15	16	17	18	19
20	21	22	23	24	25	26
27	28	29	30	31		

SEPTEMBER
S	M	T	W	T	F	S
						1
2	3	4	5	6	7	8
9	10	11	12	13	14	15
16	17	18	19	20	21	22
23	24	25	26	27	28	29
30						

FEBRUARY
S	M	T	W	T	F	S
			1	2	3	4
5	6	7	8	9	10	11
12	13	14	15	16	17	18
19	20	21	22	23	24	25
26	27	28	29			

JUNE
S	M	T	W	T	F	S
					1	2
3	4	5	6	7	8	9
10	11	12	13	14	15	16
17	18	19	20	21	22	23
24	25	26	27	28	29	30

OCTOBER
S	M	T	W	T	F	S
	1	2	3	4	5	6
7	8	9	10	11	12	13
14	15	16	17	18	19	20
21	22	23	24	25	26	27
28	29	30	31			

MARCH
S	M	T	W	T	F	S
				1	2	3
4	5	6	7	8	9	10
11	12	13	14	15	16	17
18	19	20	21	22	23	24
25	26	27	28	29	30	31

JULY
S	M	T	W	T	F	S
1	2	3	4	5	6	7
8	9	10	11	12	13	14
15	16	17	18	19	20	21
22	23	24	25	26	27	28
29	30	31				

NOVEMBER
S	M	T	W	T	F	S
				1	2	3
4	5	6	7	8	9	10
11	12	13	14	15	16	17
18	19	20	21	22	23	24
25	26	27	28	29	30	

APRIL
S	M	T	W	T	F	S
1	2	3	4	5	6	7
8	9	10	11	12	13	14
15	16	17	18	19	20	21
22	23	24	25	26	27	28
29	30					

AUGUST
S	M	T	W	T	F	S
			1	2	3	4
5	6	7	8	9	10	11
12	13	14	15	16	17	18
19	20	21	22	23	24	25
26	27	28	29	30	31	

DECEMBER
S	M	T	W	T	F	S
						1
2	3	4	5	6	7	8
9	10	11	12	13	14	15
16	17	18	19	20	21	22
23	24	25	26	27	28	29
30	31					

E · 2012 · 1996

JANUARY

S	M	T	W	T	F	S
	1	2	3	4	5	6
7	8	9	10	11	12	13
14	15	16	17	18	19	20
21	22	23	24	25	26	27
28	29	30	31			

FEBRUARY

S	M	T	W	T	F	S
				1	2	3
4	5	6	7	8	9	10
11	12	13	14	15	16	17
18	19	20	21	22	23	24
25	26	27	28	29		

MARCH

S	M	T	W	T	F	S
					1	2
3	4	5	6	7	8	9
10	11	12	13	14	15	16
17	18	19	20	21	22	23
24	25	26	27	28	29	30
31						

APRIL

S	M	T	W	T	F	S
	1	2	3	4	5	6
7	8	9	10	11	12	13
14	15	16	17	18	19	20
21	22	23	24	25	26	27
28	29	30				

MAY

S	M	T	W	T	F	S
		1	2	3	4	
5	6	7	8	9	10	11
12	13	14	15	16	17	18
19	20	21	22	23	24	25
26	27	28	29	30	31	

JUNE

S	M	T	W	T	F	S
						1
2	3	4	5	6	7	8
9	10	11	12	13	14	15
16	17	18	19	20	21	22
23	24	25	26	27	28	29
30						

JULY

S	M	T	W	T	F	S
	1	2	3	4	5	6
7	8	9	10	11	12	13
14	15	16	17	18	19	20
21	22	23	24	25	26	27
28	29	30	31			

AUGUST

S	M	T	W	T	F	S
			1	2	3	
4	5	6	7	8	9	10
11	12	13	14	15	16	17
18	19	20	21	22	23	24
25	26	27	28	29	30	31

SEPTEMBER

S	M	T	W	T	F	S
1	2	3	4	5	6	7
8	9	10	11	12	13	14
15	16	17	18	19	20	21
22	23	24	25	26	27	28
29	30					

OCTOBER

S	M	T	W	T	F	S
		1	2	3	4	5
6	7	8	9	10	11	12
13	14	15	16	17	18	19
20	21	22	23	24	25	26
27	28	29	30	31		

NOVEMBER

S	M	T	W	T	F	S
					1	2
3	4	5	6	7	8	9
10	11	12	13	14	15	16
17	18	19	20	21	22	23
24	25	26	27	28	29	30

DECEMBER

S	M	T	W	T	F	S
1	2	3	4	5	6	7
8	9	10	11	12	13	14
15	16	17	18	19	20	21
22	23	24	25	26	27	28
29	30	31				

F · 1980 · 2008

JANUARY

S	M	T	W	T	F	S
		1	2	3	4	5
6	7	8	9	10	11	12
13	14	15	16	17	18	19
20	21	22	23	24	25	26
27	28	29	30	31		

FEBRUARY

S	M	T	W	T	F	S
					1	2
3	4	5	6	7	8	9
10	11	12	13	14	15	16
17	18	19	20	21	22	23
24	25	26	27	28	29	

MARCH

S	M	T	W	T	F	S
						1
2	3	4	5	6	7	8
9	10	11	12	13	14	15
16	17	18	19	20	21	22
23	24	25	26	27	28	29
30	31					

APRIL

S	M	T	W	T	F	S
		1	2	3	4	5
6	7	8	9	10	11	12
13	14	15	16	17	18	19
20	21	22	23	24	25	26
27	28	29	30			

MAY

S	M	T	W	T	F	S
				1	2	3
4	5	6	7	8	9	10
11	12	13	14	15	16	17
18	19	20	21	22	23	24
25	26	27	28	29	30	31

JUNE

S	M	T	W	T	F	S
1	2	3	4	5	6	7
8	9	10	11	12	13	14
15	16	17	18	19	20	21
22	23	24	25	26	27	28
29	30					

JULY

S	M	T	W	T	F	S
		1	2	3	4	5
6	7	8	9	10	11	12
13	14	15	16	17	18	19
20	21	22	23	24	25	26
27	28	29	30	31		

AUGUST

S	M	T	W	T	F	S
					1	2
3	4	5	6	7	8	9
10	11	12	13	14	15	16
17	18	19	20	21	22	23
24	25	26	27	28	29	30
31						

SEPTEMBER

S	M	T	W	T	F	S
	1	2	3	4	5	6
7	8	9	10	11	12	13
14	15	16	17	18	19	20
21	22	23	24	25	26	27
28	29	30				

OCTOBER

S	M	T	W	T	F	S
			1	2	3	4
5	6	7	8	9	10	11
12	13	14	15	16	17	18
19	20	21	22	23	24	25
26	27	28	29	30	31	

NOVEMBER

S	M	T	W	T	F	S
						1
2	3	4	5	6	7	8
9	10	11	12	13	14	15
16	17	18	19	20	21	22
23	24	25	26	27	28	29
30						

DECEMBER

S	M	T	W	T	F	S
	1	2	3	4	5	6
7	8	9	10	11	12	13
14	15	16	17	18	19	20
21	22	23	24	25	26	27
28	29	30	31			

G   1992   2020

JANUARY
S	M	T	W	T	F	S
			1	2	3	4
5	6	7	8	9	10	11
12	13	14	15	16	17	18
19	20	21	22	23	24	25
26	27	28	29	30	31	

FEBRUARY
S	M	T	W	T	F	S
						1
2	3	4	5	6	7	8
9	10	11	12	13	14	15
16	17	18	19	20	21	22
23	24	25	26	27	28	29

MARCH
S	M	T	W	T	F	S
1	2	3	4	5	6	7
8	9	10	11	12	13	14
15	16	17	18	19	20	21
22	23	24	25	26	27	28
29	30	31				

APRIL
S	M	T	W	T	F	S
			1	2	3	4
5	6	7	8	9	10	11
12	13	14	15	16	17	18
19	20	21	22	23	24	25
26	27	28	29	30		

MAY
S	M	T	W	T	F	S
					1	2
3	4	5	6	7	8	9
10	11	12	13	14	15	16
17	18	19	20	21	22	23
24	25	26	27	28	29	30
31						

JUNE
S	M	T	W	T	F	S
	1	2	3	4	5	6
7	8	9	10	11	12	13
14	15	16	17	18	19	20
21	22	23	24	25	26	27
28	29	30				

JULY
S	M	T	W	T	F	S
			1	2	3	4
5	6	7	8	9	10	11
12	13	14	15	16	17	18
19	20	21	22	23	24	25
26	27	28	29	30	31	

AUGUST
S	M	T	W	T	F	S
						1
2	3	4	5	6	7	8
9	10	11	12	13	14	15
16	17	18	19	20	21	22
23	24	25	26	27	28	29
30	31					

SEPTEMBER
S	M	T	W	T	F	S
		1	2	3	4	5
6	7	8	9	10	11	12
13	14	15	16	17	18	19
20	21	22	23	24	25	26
27	28	29	30			

OCTOBER
S	M	T	W	T	F	S
				1	2	3
4	5	6	7	8	9	10
11	12	13	14	15	16	17
18	19	20	21	22	23	24
25	26	27	28	29	30	31

NOVEMBER
S	M	T	W	T	F	S
1	2	3	4	5	6	7
8	9	10	11	12	13	14
15	16	17	18	19	20	21
22	23	24	25	26	27	28
29	30					

DECEMBER
S	M	T	W	T	F	S
		1	2	3	4	5
6	7	8	9	10	11	12
13	14	15	16	17	18	19
20	21	22	23	24	25	26
27	28	29	30	31		

H   2004   1976

JANUARY
S	M	T	W	T	F	S
				1	2	3
4	5	6	7	8	9	10
11	12	13	14	15	16	17
18	19	20	21	22	23	24
25	26	27	28	29	30	31

FEBRUARY
S	M	T	W	T	F	S
1	2	3	4	5	6	7
8	9	10	11	12	13	14
15	16	17	18	19	20	21
22	23	24	25	26	27	28
29						

MARCH
S	M	T	W	T	F	S
	1	2	3	4	5	6
7	8	9	10	11	12	13
14	15	16	17	18	19	20
21	22	23	24	25	26	27
28	29	30	31			

APRIL
S	M	T	W	T	F	S
				1	2	3
4	5	6	7	8	9	10
11	12	13	14	15	16	17
18	19	20	21	22	23	24
25	26	27	28	29	30	

MAY
S	M	T	W	T	F	S
						1
2	3	4	5	6	7	8
9	10	11	12	13	14	15
16	17	18	19	20	21	22
23	24	25	26	27	28	29
30	31					

JUNE
S	M	T	W	T	F	S
		1	2	3	4	5
6	7	8	9	10	11	12
13	14	15	16	17	18	19
20	21	22	23	24	25	26
27	28	29	30			

JULY
S	M	T	W	T	F	S
				1	2	3
4	5	6	7	8	9	10
11	12	13	14	15	16	17
18	19	20	21	22	23	24
25	26	27	28	29	30	31

AUGUST
S	M	T	W	T	F	S
1	2	3	4	5	6	7
8	9	10	11	12	13	14
15	16	17	18	19	20	21
22	23	24	25	26	27	28
29	30	31				

SEPTEMBER
S	M	T	W	T	F	S
			1	2	3	4
5	6	7	8	9	10	11
12	13	14	15	16	17	18
19	20	21	22	23	24	25
26	27	28	29	30		

OCTOBER
S	M	T	W	T	F	S
					1	2
3	4	5	6	7	8	9
10	11	12	13	14	15	16
17	18	19	20	21	22	23
24	25	26	27	28	29	30
31						

NOVEMBER
S	M	T	W	T	F	S
	1	2	3	4	5	6
7	8	9	10	11	12	13
14	15	16	17	18	19	20
21	22	23	24	25	26	27
28	29	30				

DECEMBER
S	M	T	W	T	F	S
			1	2	3	4
5	6	7	8	9	10	11
12	13	14	15	16	17	18
19	20	21	22	23	24	25
26	27	28	29	30	31	

I — 2016   1988

JANUARY
S	M	T	W	T	F	S
					1	2
3	4	5	6	7	8	9
10	11	12	13	14	15	16
17	18	19	20	21	22	23
24	25	26	27	28	29	30
31						

FEBRUARY
S	M	T	W	T	F	S
	1	2	3	4	5	6
7	8	9	10	11	12	13
14	15	16	17	18	19	20
21	22	23	24	25	26	27
28	29					

MARCH
S	M	T	W	T	F	S
		1	2	3	4	5
6	7	8	9	10	11	12
13	14	15	16	17	18	19
20	21	22	23	24	25	26
27	28	29	30	31		

APRIL
S	M	T	W	T	F	S
					1	2
3	4	5	6	7	8	9
10	11	12	13	14	15	16
17	18	19	20	21	22	23
24	25	26	27	28	29	30

MAY
S	M	T	W	T	F	S
1	2	3	4	5	6	7
8	9	10	11	12	13	14
15	16	17	18	19	20	21
22	23	24	25	26	27	28
29	30	31				

JUNE
S	M	T	W	T	F	S
			1	2	3	4
5	66	7	8	9	10	11
12	13	14	15	16	17	18
19	20	21	22	23	24	25
26	27	28	29	30		

JULY
S	M	T	W	T	F	S
					1	2
3	4	5	6	7	8	9
10	11	12	13	14	15	16
17	18	19	20	21	22	23
24	25	26	27	28	29	30
31						

AUGUST
S	M	T	W	T	F	S
	1	2	3	4	5	6
7	8	9	10	11	12	13
14	15	16	17	18	19	20
21	22	23	24	25	26	27
28	29	30	31			

SEPTEMBER
S	M	T	W	T	F	S
				1	2	3
4	5	6	7	8	9	10
11	12	13	14	15	16	17
18	19	20	21	22	23	24
25	26	27	28	29	30	

OCTOBER
S	M	T	W	T	F	S
						1
2	3	4	5	6	7	8
9	10	11	12	13	14	15
16	17	18	19	20	21	22
23	24	25	26	27	28	29
30	31					

NOVEMBER
S	M	T	W	T	F	S
		1	2	3	4	5
6	7	8	9	10	11	12
13	14	15	16	17	18	19
20	21	22	23	24	25	26
27	28	29	30			

DECEMBER
S	M	T	W	T	F	S
				1	2	3
4	5	6	7	8	9	10
11	12	13	14	15	16	17
18	19	20	21	22	23	24
25	26	27	28	29	30	31

J — 2000   1972

JANUARY
S	M	T	W	T	F	S
						1
2	3	4	5	6	7	8
9	10	11	12	13	14	15
16	17	18	19	20	21	22
23	24	25	26	27	28	29
30	31					

FEBRUARY
S	M	T	W	T	F	S
		1	2	3	4	5
6	7	8	9	10	11	12
13	14	15	16	17	18	19
20	21	22	23	24	25	26
27	28	29				

MARCH
S	M	T	W	T	F	S
		1	2	3	4	
5	6	7	8	9	10	11
12	13	14	15	16	17	18
19	20	21	22	23	24	25
26	27	28	29	30	31	

APRIL
S	M	T	W	T	F	S
						1
2	3	4	5	6	7	8
9	10	11	12	13	14	15
16	17	18	19	20	21	22
23	24	25	26	27	28	29
30						

MAY
S	M	T	W	T	F	S
	1	2	3	4	5	6
7	8	9	10	11	12	13
14	15	16	17	18	19	20
21	22	23	24	25	26	27
28	29	30	31			

JUNE
S	M	T	W	T	F	S
				1	2	3
4	5	6	7	8	9	10
11	12	13	14	15	16	17
18	19	20	21	22	23	24
25	26	27	28	29	30	

JULY
S	M	T	W	T	F	S
						1
2	3	4	5	6	7	8
9	10	11	12	13	14	15
16	17	18	19	20	21	22
23	24	25	26	27	28	29
30	31					

AUGUST
S	M	T	W	T	F	S
		1	2	3	4	5
6	7	8	9	10	11	12
13	14	15	16	17	18	19
20	21	22	23	24	25	26
27	28	29	30	31		

SEPTEMBER
S	M	T	W	T	F	S
					1	2
3	4	5	6	7	8	9
10	11	12	13	14	15	16
17	18	19	20	21	22	23
24	25	26	27	28	29	30

OCTOBER
S	M	T	W	T	F	S
1	2	3	4	5	6	7
8	9	10	11	12	13	14
15	16	17	18	19	20	21
22	23	24	25	26	27	28
29	30	31				

NOVEMBER
S	M	T	W	T	F	S
			1	2	3	4
5	6	7	8	9	10	11
12	13	14	15	16	17	18
19	20	21	22	23	24	25
26	27	28	29	30		

DECEMBER
S	M	T	W	T	F	S
					1	2
3	4	5	6	7	8	9
10	11	12	13	14	15	16
17	18	19	20	21	22	23
24	25	26	27	28	29	30
31						

K — 2006 1995

JANUARY
S	M	T	W	T	F	S
1	2	3	4	5	6	7
8	9	10	11	12	13	14
15	16	17	18	19	20	21
22	23	24	25	26	27	28
29	30	31				

FEBRUARY
S	M	T	W	T	F	S
			1	2	3	4
5	6	7	8	9	10	11
12	13	14	15	16	17	18
19	20	21	22	23	24	25
26	27	28				

MARCH
S	M	T	W	T	F	S
			1	2	3	4
5	6	7	8	9	10	11
12	13	14	15	16	17	18
19	20	21	22	23	24	25
26	27	28	29	30	31	

APRIL
S	M	T	W	T	F	S
						1
2	3	4	5	6	7	8
9	10	11	12	13	14	15
16	17	18	19	20	21	22
23	24	25	26	27	28	29
30						

MAY
S	M	T	W	T	F	S
	1	2	3	4	5	6
7	8	9	10	11	12	13
14	15	16	17	18	19	20
21	22	23	24	25	26	27
28	29	30	31			

JUNE
S	M	T	W	T	F	S
				1	2	3
4	5	6	7	8	9	10
11	12	13	14	15	16	17
18	19	20	21	22	23	24
25	26	27	28	29	30	

JULY
S	M	T	W	T	F	S
						1
2	3	4	5	6	7	8
9	10	11	12	13	14	15
16	17	18	19	20	21	22
23	24	25	26	27	28	29
30	31					

AUGUST
S	M	T	W	T	F	S
		1	2	3	4	5
6	7	8	9	10	11	12
13	14	15	16	17	18	19
20	21	22	23	24	25	26
27	28	29	30	31		

SEPTEMBER
S	M	T	W	T	F	S
					1	2
3	4	5	6	7	8	9
10	11	12	13	14	15	16
17	18	19	20	21	22	23
24	25	26	27	28	29	30

OCTOBER
S	M	T	W	T	F	S
1	2	3	4	5	6	7
8	9	10	11	12	13	14
15	16	17	18	19	20	21
22	23	24	25	26	27	28
29	30	31				

NOVEMBER
S	M	T	W	T	F	S
			1	2	3	4
5	6	7	8	9	10	11
12	13	14	15	16	17	18
19	20	21	22	23	24	25
26	27	28	29	30		

DECEMBER
S	M	T	W	T	F	S
					1	2
3	4	5	6	7	8	9
10	11	12	13	14	15	16
17	18	19	20	21	22	23
24	25	26	27	28	29	30
31						

L — 2001 1990

JANUARY
S	M	T	W	T	F	S
	1	2	3	4	5	6
7	8	9	10	11	12	13
14	15	16	17	18	19	20
21	22	23	24	25	26	27
28	29	30	31			

FEBRUARY
S	M	T	W	T	F	S
				1	2	3
4	5	6	7	8	9	10
11	12	13	14	15	16	17
18	19	20	21	22	23	24
25	26	27	28			

MARCH
S	M	T	W	T	F	S
				1	2	3
4	5	6	7	8	9	10
11	12	13	14	15	16	17
18	19	20	21	22	23	24
25	26	27	28	29	30	31

APRIL
S	M	T	W	T	F	S
1	2	3	4	5	6	7
8	9	10	11	12	13	14
15	16	17	18	19	20	21
22	23	24	25	26	27	28
29	30					

MAY
S	M	T	W	T	F	S
		1	2	3	4	5
6	7	8	9	10	11	12
13	14	15	16	17	18	19
20	21	22	23	24	25	26
27	28	29	30	31		

JUNE
S	M	T	W	T	F	S
					1	2
3	4	5	6	7	8	9
10	11	12	13	14	15	16
17	18	19	20	21	22	23
24	25	26	27	28	29	30

JULY
S	M	T	W	T	F	S
1	2	3	4	5	6	7
8	9	10	11	12	13	14
15	16	17	18	19	20	21
22	23	24	25	26	27	28
29	30	31				

AUGUST
S	M	T	W	T	F	S
			1	2	3	4
5	6	7	8	9	10	11
12	13	14	15	16	17	18
19	20	21	22	23	24	25
26	27	28	20	30	31	

SEPTEMBER
S	M	T	W	T	F	S
						1
2	3	4	5	6	7	8
9	10	11	12	13	14	15
16	17	18	19	20	21	22
23	24	25	26	27	28	29
30						

OCTOBER
S	M	T	W	T	F	S
	1	2	3	4	5	6
7	8	9	10	11	12	13
14	15	16	17	18	19	20
21	22	23	24	25	26	27
28	29	30	31			

NOVEMBER
S	M	T	W	T	F	S
				1	2	3
4	5	6	7	8	9	10
11	12	13	14	15	16	17
18	19	20	21	22	23	24
25	26	27	28	29	30	

DECEMBER
S	M	T	W	T	F	S
						1
2	3	4	5	6	7	8
9	10	11	12	13	14	15
16	17	18	19	20	21	22
23	24	25	26	27	28	29
30	31					

M 2002 1991

JANUARY
S	M	T	W	T	F	S
		1	2	3	4	5
6	7	8	9	10	11	12
13	14	15	16	17	18	19
20	21	22	23	24	25	26
27	28	29	30	31		

FEBRUARY
S	M	T	W	T	F	S
					1	2
3	4	5	6	7	8	9
10	11	12	13	14	15	16
17	18	19	20	21	22	23
24	25	26	27	28		

MARCH
S	M	T	W	T	F	S
					1	2
3	4	5	6	7	8	9
10	11	12	13	14	15	16
17	18	19	20	21	22	23
24	25	26	27	28	29	30
31						

APRIL
S	M	T	W	T	F	S
	1	2	3	4	5	6
7	8	9	10	11	12	13
14	15	16	17	18	19	20
21	22	23	24	25	26	27
28	29	30				

MAY
S	M	T	W	T	F	S
			1	2	3	4
5	6	7	8	9	10	11
12	13	14	15	16	17	18
19	20	21	22	23	24	25
26	27	28	29	30	31	

JUNE
S	M	T	W	T	F	S
						1
2	3	4	5	6	7	8
9	10	11	12	13	14	15
16	17	18	19	20	21	22
23	24	26	27	27	28	29
30						

JULY
S	M	T	W	T	F	S
	1	2	3	4	5	6
7	8	9	10	11	12	13
14	15	16	17	18	19	20
21	22	23	24	25	26	27
28	29	30	31			

AUGUST
S	M	T	W	T	F	S
				1	2	3
4	5	6	7	8	9	10
11	12	13	14	15	16	17
18	19	20	21	22	23	24
25	26	27	28	29	30	31

SEPTEMBER
S	M	T	W	T	F	S
1	2	3	4	5	6	7
8	9	10	11	12	13	14
15	16	17	18	19	20	21
22	23	24	25	26	27	28
29	30					

OCTOBER
S	M	T	W	T	F	S
		1	2	3	4	5
6	7	8	9	10	11	12
13	14	15	16	17	18	19
20	21	22	23	24	25	26
27	28	29	30	31		

NOVEMBER
S	M	T	W	T	F	S
					1	2
3	4	5	6	7	8	9
10	11	12	13	14	15	16
17	18	19	20	21	22	23
24	25	26	27	28	29	30

DECEMBER
S	M	T	W	T	F	S
1	2	3	4	5	6	7
8	9	10	11	12	13	14
15	16	17	18	19	20	21
22	23	24	25	26	27	28
29	30	31				

N 1997 1986

JANUARY
S	M	T	W	T	F	S
			1	2	3	4
5	6	7	8	9	10	11
12	13	14	15	16	17	18
19	20	21	22	23	24	25
26	27	28	29	30	31	

FEBRUARY
S	M	T	W	T	F	S
						1
2	3	4	5	6	7	8
9	10	11	12	13	14	15
16	17	18	19	20	21	22
23	24	25	26	27	28	

MARCH
S	M	T	W	T	F	S
						1
2	3	4	5	6	7	8
9	10	11	12	13	14	15
16	17	18	19	20	21	22
23	24	25	26	27	28	29
30	31					

APRIL
S	M	T	W	T	F	S
		1	2	3	4	5
6	7	8	9	10	11	12
13	14	15	16	17	18	19
20	21	22	23	24	25	26
27	28	29	30			

MAY
S	M	T	W	T	F	S
				1	2	3
4	5	6	7	8	9	10
11	12	13	14	15	16	17
18	19	20	21	22	23	24
25	26	27	28	29	30	31

JUNE
S	M	T	W	T	F	S
1	2	3	4	5	6	7
8	9	10	11	12	13	14
15	16	17	18	19	20	21
22	23	24	25	26	27	28
29	30					

JULY
S	M	T	W	T	F	S
		1	2	3	4	5
6	7	8	9	10	11	12
13	14	15	16	17	18	19
20	21	22	23	24	25	26
27	28	29	30	31		

AUGUST
S	M	T	W	T	F	S
					1	2
3	4	5	6	7	8	9
10	11	12	13	14	15	16
17	18	19	20	21	22	23
24	25	26	27	28	29	30
31						

SEPTEMBER
S	M	T	W	T	F	S
	1	2	3	4	5	6
7	8	9	10	11	12	13
14	15	16	17	18	19	20
21	22	23	24	25	26	27
28	29	30				

OCTOBER
S	M	T	W	T	F	S
			1	2	3	4
5	6	7	8	9	10	11
12	13	14	15	16	17	18
19	20	21	22	23	24	25
26	27	28	29	30	31	

NOVEMBER
S	M	T	W	T	F	S
						1
2	3	4	5	6	7	8
9	10	11	12	13	14	15
16	17	18	19	20	21	22
23	24	25	26	27	28	29
30						

DECEMBER
S	M	T	W	T	F	S
	1	2	3	4	5	6
7	8	9	10	11	12	13
14	15	16	17	18	19	20
21	22	23	24	25	26	27
28	29	30	31			

HOROSCOPE
▼

WHAT'S IN THE STARS FOR 1998?

A revolution in the American image, predicts a British astrologer

Astrology is about cycles—the sun, moon, and eight planets moving at different speeds through the twelve signs in the heavens. The zodiac is effectively a map, a circle drawn in the heavens and divided with mathematical exactness, as British astrologer Marjorie Orr puts it. "The complexity and contradictory nature of human life is mirrored in the mix and muddle of the different astrological cycles," says Orr.

An astrologer for nearly 20 years, and a former journalist and award-winning documentary producer, Orr specializes in the astrological analysis of politicians, celebrities, and world events. She appears frequently on British radio and television to discuss her expertise. We asked Orr to devise a horoscope for the United States for 1998, from her perspective across the Atlantic. Here's her forecast for the former colonies.

■ The brave new world signaled in 1996 by Uranus's entry into Aquarius is alive, challenging, and vibrating to a higher pitch in

EXPERT QUOTE

Grounding is the key to success in 1998. Too much high voltage mental energy, electrical input, and computer speed thinking could lead to burnout. Worry levels could be higher than in 1997, so a strict schedule of wind-down and relaxation breaks are needed.

1998. Aquarius is associated in the astrological trade with new information, computers, astrology, new humanitarian movements, and a tolerance for racial differences.

■ Neptune joining Uranus in Aquarius from the end of January for several years to come will herald new spiritual growth, perhaps the birth of new religious movements. Neptune is mystical and creates direct experience but is prone to self-deception and delusion. Fundamentalist religious conflicts will continue to create anxiety in the United States, with Pluto still in Sagittarius for a few years to come.

Pluto deepens and transforms thinking about morality governing social behavior, tears down old structures to clear space for new ones. This is a time of immense intellectual challenge and excitement. But tolerance is not a strong point for Pluto. It is controlling and fanatical. Power struggles are inevitable as people battle over whose beliefs take precedence in fields such as law, science, psychology, and religion.

■ The major planetary influence in 1998 on the U.S. chart is Pluto and Sagittarius opposing Uranus in Gemini, which occurs in the spring and again in December. This brings about drastic changes, causing social and political upheaval. There could be outbursts of violence, some economic instability, temporary dislocation of working situations. It could also affect the American image and sense of identity, as well as the country's relations with other nations. The United States will be examining its values as a nation: How well has it kept its commitment to freedom, fairness, and family values? Some answers may be uncomfortable but the result will be a thorough reworking of the basic agreements within American society.

■ Russia is a continuing point of stress throughout the year, with moments of sinking panic, some harsh words being exchanged, and a general jostling for the upper hand. There are also tensions with China. Uranus squares Pluto in the Sino-U.S. relationship chart, indicating that old agreements will not hold and that new ones will have to be negotiated through a time of upheaval. Even relations with the United Kingdom are irritable with concealed resentments emerging. The long-term result will be to clear the air but that end may not be in sight until 1999. The United Nations, which has been a source of gloom as far as U.S. policy is concerned, is proving a stickier problem to solve than had been expected.

■ Bill Clinton is also facing a year of sweeping changes in his circumstances. If he can be flexible, then he will begin a whole new phase of life with new awareness. If he cannot adapt, this could be a time of great turmoil and stress as he tries to hold on to possessions, relationships, and situations that really belong to the past. As the national figurehead, he will, to some extent, live out a process that is also affecting mainstream American society.

■ Children born in 1998 will have the potential to be scientific pioneers, reformers, and explorers in the intellectual realms. With scientific, computer-obsessed Uranus next to mystical Neptune, and both far from deep-thinking Pluto in Sagittarius, these children will find rational evidence for what their parents consider supernatural or mere hocus-pocus. Alternative medicine will be mainstream for them. They will be an interesting mix of sentimentality, kindness, and thriftiness—and highly conscious of personal security.

■ The fixed sign children—Taurus, Leo, Scorpio, and Aquarius—will be zany, stimulating,

■ CHECK OUT YOUR SIGN

Twelve astrological signs that shape what happens in a year. They are:

 ARIES
The Ram
March 21–April 19

 TAURUS
The Bull
April 20–May 20

 GEMINI
The Twins
May 21–June 20

 CANCER
The Crab
June 21–July 22

 LEO
The Lion
July 23–Aug 22

 VIRGO
The Virgin
Aug 23–Sept 22

 LIBRA
The Scales
Sept 23–Oct 22

 SCORPIO
The Scorpion
Oct 23–Nov 21

 SAGITTARIUS
The Archer
Nov 22–Dec 21

 CAPRICORN
The Goat
Dec 22–Jan 19

 AQUARIUS
The Water Bearer
Jan 20–Feb 18

PISCES
The Fish
Feb 19–March 20

restless, high-strung, and rebellious. Mutable children—Gemini, Virgo, Sagittarius, and Pisces—will be more controlled, keen on power, and secretive. Cardinal signs—Aries, Cancer, Libra, and Capricorn—will be the go-betweens, the fixers. The Fire signs—Aries, Leo, Sagittarius—will thrive. The most favorable sign to be born under in 1998 is Pisces. Those children will be lucky, confident, and blessed with a guardian angel throughout their lives.

■ For the United States, 1998 is a year for courage, creativity, and a wholehearted approach to the unknown. "May you live in interesting times" was the old Chinese curse. Never was it more appropriate as the Uranus-Neptune conjunction heads for the millennium with the epochal 2000 year Age of Aquarius unfolding. Whatever roller-coaster rides or anxieties in the financial sphere that Uranus-Neptune bring to American life, it will provide an equal amount of spiritual healing. New forms of intimate relationships will develop and be fostered. Aquarius is tolerant of all facets of humanity.

■ Enlightenment is possible with moments of great compassion. But chaos lurks not far away. There is a fine line between the inspirational genius of Uranus-Neptune and complete self-deception. That is why stolid Saturn in earthy Taurus will be so useful—to provide ballast. Jupiter adds tenderness. The astrological mix for 1998 is somewhat disjointed but not unappealing for the adventuruous in spirit.

CHINESE ZODIAC

IN THE YEAR OF THE TIGER

Are you faithful as a Dog, witty as a Monkey, or wise as a Snake?

The Chinese zodiac is based on a 12-year cycle, with each year of the cycle represented by a different animal. Are you a rat, monkey, or tiger? Your sign depends on the year you were born, and if the ancient Chinese were right about the personality traits they ascribed to their calendrical animals, then Leonardo da Vinci was charismatic and witty because he was born in the Year of the Monkey. Confucius, on the other hand, would have been a pleasing fellow, though perhaps a trifle too sentimental since his birthdate in 551 B.C. would have made him a rabbit. For the key to understanding Benjamin Franklin, Joan of Arc, and Richard Nixon, read on.

TIGER
1926, 1938, 1950, 1962, 1974, 1986, 1998

You are sensitive, emotional, and capable of great love. However, you have a tendency to get carried away and be stubborn about what you think is right. Others often see you as a "hothead" or rebel. You would be excellent as a boss, explorer, race car driver, or matador. Some Tigers: Marco Polo, Mary Queen of Scots, Dwight D. Eisenhower, Marilyn Monroe.

BUFFALO
1925, 1937, 1949, 1961, 1973, 1985, 1997

A Buffalo is a born leader. You inspire confidence in everyone around you. You are conservative, methodical, and good with your hands.

Guard against being chauvinistic and always demanding your own way. The Buffalo would be successful as a skilled surgeon, general, or hairdresser. Some Buffalos: Napoleon, Van Gogh, Walt Disney, Clark Gable, Richard Nixon.

RAT
1936, 1948, 1960, 1972, 1984, 1996

You are imaginative, charming, and truly generous to the person you love. However, you have a tendency to be quick-tempered and overly critical. You are also inclined to be somewhat of an opportunist. Born under this sign, you should be happy in sales or as a writer, critic, or publicist. Some Rats: Shakespeare, Mozart, Winston Churchill, George Washington, Truman Capote.

PIG
1935, 1947, 1959, 1971, 1983, 1995

You are a splendid companion, an intellectual with a very strong need to set difficult goals and carry them out. You are sincere, tolerant, and honest but by expecting the same from others, you are incredibly naive. Your quest for material goods could be your downfall. A Pig would be best in the arts as an entertainer, or possibly a lawyer. Some Pigs: Albert Schweitzer, Ernest Hemingway.

DOG
1934, 1946, 1958, 1970, 1982, 1994

The Dog will never let you down. Born under this sign, you are honest and faithful to those you love. However, you are plagued by constant worry, a sharp tongue, and a tendency to be a fault finder. You would make an excellent businessperson, activist, teacher, or secret agent. Some Dogs: Socrates, George Gershwin, Benjamin Franklin, Herbert Hoover, David Niven.

ROOSTER
1933, 1945, 1957, 1969, 1981, 1993

The Rooster is a hard worker; shrewd and definite in decision making, often speaking his mind. Because of this, you tend to seem boastful to others. You are a dreamer, flashy dresser, and extravagant to an extreme. Born under this sign, you should be happy as a restaurant owner, publicist, soldier, or world traveler. Some Roosters: Rudyard Kipling, Caruso, Groucho Marx, Peter Ustinov.

MONKEY
1932, 1944, 1956, 1968, 1980, 1992

You are very intelligent and a have a clever wit. Because of your magnetic personality, you are always well-liked. The Monkey, however, must guard against being an opportunist and distrustful of other people. Your sign promises success in any field you try. Some Monkeys: Julius Caesar, Leonardo da Vinci, Harry S Truman, and Elizabeth Taylor.

GOAT
1931, 1943, 1955, 1967, 1979, 1991

Except for the knack of always getting off on the wrong foot with people, the Goat can be charming company. You are elegant and artistic—but the first to complain about things. Put aside your pessimism and worry, and try to be less dependent on material comforts. You would be best as an actor, gardener, or beachcomber. Some Goats: Michelangelo, Rudolph Valentino, Mark Twain, Orville Wright.

HORSE
1930, 1942, 1954, 1966, 1978, 1990

Your capacity for hard work is amazing. You are your own person—very independent. While intelligent and friendly, you have a strong streak of selfishness and sharp cunning and should guard against being egotistical. Your sign suggests that you would be successful as an adventurer, scientist, poet, or politician. Some Horses: Rembrandt, Chopin, Davy Crockett, Teddy Roosevelt.

SNAKE
1929, 1941, 1953, 1965, 1977, 1989

Rich in wisdom and charm, you are romantic and deep-thinking and your intuition guides you strongly. Avoid procrastination and your stingy attitude toward money. Maintain your sense of humor about life. The Snake would be most content as a teacher, philosopher, writer, psychiatrist, or fortune teller. Some Snakes: Charles Darwin, Edgar Allan Poe, Abraham Lincoln.

DRAGON
1928, 1940, 1952, 1964, 1976, 1988

Full of vitality and enthusiasm, the Dragon is a popular individual even with the reputation of being foolhardy and a "big mouth" at times. You are intelligent, gifted, and a perfectionist but these qualities make you unduly demanding on others. You would be well-suited to be an artist, priest, or politician. Some Dragons: Joan of Arc, Pearl Buck, Sigmund Freud.

RABBIT
1927, 1939, 1951, 1963, 1975, 1987

The Rabbit is the kind of person that people like to be around: affectionate, obliging, always pleasant. You have a tendency, though, to get too sentimental and seem superficial. Being cautious and conservative, you would be successful in business but would also make a good lawyer, diplomat, or actor. Some Rabbits: Rudolph Nureyev, Confucius, Orson Welles, Albert Einstein.

TRADITIONS

BELIEVER'S GUIDE
▼

FAITHS LIVED ROUND THE WORLD

The text and tenets that guide many of the best-known religions

More often than not these days, media coverage of religion beyond the shores of the United States is quick to demonize many faiths for having political agendas that threaten American interests. But for the billions of religiously devout around the world, the daily sustenance that comes from the practice of their faith is what makes life worth living. Here is a guide to the religious doctrines that inform some of the most common world religions:

BUDDHISM

 Its roughly 300 million adherents live mainly in India and eastern Asia. In recent times, Buddhism has gained a growing following in the West.

■ **HISTORY:** Now one of the world's major religions, Buddhism began as an outgrowth of Hinduism. It was founded by Siddhartha Gautama, the Buddha, who lived in northern India from about 560 to about 480 B.C. Today it is generally divided into two branches: the more conservative Theravada or "Way of the Elders," and the Mahayana or "Great Vehicle," a more liberal and diverse tradition.

■ **TENETS:** Basic Buddhist belief centers on four main doctrines or "Noble Truths" taught by the Buddha: first, that all beings are caught in a cycle of rebirth and suffering, or samsara, in which their actions, or karma, keep them wandering; second, that all suffering has a specific cause; third, that samsara can be escaped in what is called nirvana; and fourth, the way to nirvana is through practice of the "Eightfold Path," which combines ethical and disciplinary practices with meditation and faith and which leads to enlightened wisdom.

CHRISTIANITY

The world's largest religion with about 1 billion adherents. A strongly proselytizing religion, Christianity exists in all parts of the world.

■ **HISTORY:** Arising out of 1st-century Judaism in Palestine, Christianity quickly spread through the Mediterranean world and in the 4th century became the official religion of the Roman Empire. Christians have tended to separate into rival groups, but the main body of the Christian church was united under the Roman emperors. During the Middle Ages, this main church was divided into a Latin, or Western European, and a Byzantine, or

■ HOW THE WORLD WORSHIPS
Geographic distribution of the principal religions of the world

⊞ Roman Catholic ▨ Protestant ◺ Eastern Orthodox ▢ Islam ⋯ Buddhism ◼ Hindu

◼ Chinese (Taoism, Buddhism, Confucianism superimposed) ▮ Japanese (Shinto and Buddhism superimposed) ✡ Judaism Ⓣ Tribal religion ▢ Undifferentiated

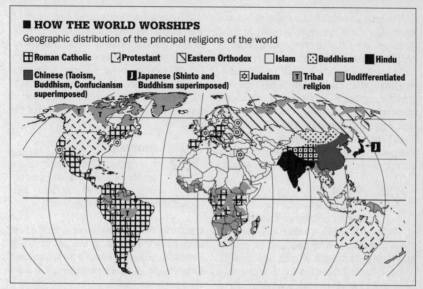

Orthodox, branch. The Western church was in turn divided by the Reformation of the 16th century into the Roman Catholic church and a large number of smaller Protestant churches (see pages 697–700).

■ **TENETS:** Christianity is based on the teachings of Jesus of Nazareth, whom Christians believe to be the Messiah or Christ whose coming was foretold in the Hebrew Bible.

Christians generally believe that Jesus was divine and that his death and resurrection in about A.D. 33 provided forgiveness from sin and eternal salvation for those who believe in him. Many look for his second coming and, with it, the inauguration of God's divine rule on earth. Christian beliefs are derived mainly from the New Testament, which contains the teachings of Jesus and some of his apostles. Those teachings include instructions for ethical behavior, devotion to God, and selfless love for all humanity. Most Christians also believe in a final judgment and in eternal reward and punishment.

HINDUISM
One of the great religions of the world. The bulk of its approximately 650 million followers are in India and south Asia.

■ **HISTORY:** Developed over about 4,000 years, Hinduism consists of a vast variety of beliefs and practices, has no single founder or creed, no hierarchy, and minimal organization. While two large movements are devoted to worship of the gods Vishnu and Siva, Hindu belief holds that there are many gods. Hindu "scriptures" also are diverse, beginning with the ancient Vedas, dating to about 800 B.C., and continuing with the Upanishads, written between 600 and 200 B.C.

■ **TENETS:** Common in classical Hinduism is the belief in the transmigration of souls, or samsara, from body to body in a cycle of birth, death, and reincarnation. The nature of one's birth and life is determined by one's karma, or actions, in a previous life. Liberation from this cycle is achieved through the practice of yoga and by seeking dharma, the ideal way of life, which is defined by the "duties of one's class and station." Ancient texts suggest four great classes, or castes: the Brahmins, or priests; the Ksatriyas, or warriors and rulers; the Vaisyas, or merchants and farmers; and the Sudras, or peasants and laborers. A fifth class, Panchamas, or "untouchables," includes those whose occupations require them to handle unclean objects. Each caste has its own distinct duties.

The texts also outline four stages of life: studentship, or brahmacarya, from five to eight years of age until marriage; householdership, or grihasthya, when one marries and raises a family; forest dwelling, or vanaprasthya, after one's children have grown; and renunciation, or samnyasa, when one gives up attachment to all worldly things and seeks spiritual liberation. Hinduism entails both house worship and temple worship and the performance of rituals associated with births, deaths, marriages, and other events.

ISLAM

Islam is the second largest of the world's religions with more than 950 million adherents, most of them in the eastern hemisphere, especially the Middle East, Asia, Africa, and parts of Europe. In the United States, their number is estimated at about 6 million. Many are of Middle Eastern or Asian origin or ancestry, but in recent decades, the religion has found growing numbers of converts among African Americans and others.

■ **HISTORY:** The Arabic word *al-islam* means to submit oneself to the one and only God, Allah. Those who do so, and who accept the 7th-century prophet Muhammad as God's final messenger, are known as Muslims. The two main branches of Islam are the Sunnites and the Shiites. The two branches arose shortly after the death of the prophet Muhammad in a dispute over succession to Muslim leadership.

■ **TENETS:** Muslims draw their doctrines from the Koran, a book that Muslims believe was dictated to Muhammad by the angel Gabriel. Mainstream Islamic doctrines include belief in heaven, hell, and a final judgment, and the necessity of combining faith and good works. It is the duty of all Muslims to observe the "five pillars" of Islam: shahada, the profession of faith in God and allegiance to his prophet; salat, the ritual prayer performed five times daily; zakat, almsgiving; sawm, abstaining from food and drink during daylight hours of the month of Ramadan; and hajj, the pilgrimage to Mecca, a holy site in

Saudi Arabia, which is incumbent upon all who are physically and financially able. Besides the salat, Muslim worship and devotion are expressed in personal prayers, in collective worship in the mosque on Fridays, and in the celebration of Id al-Fitr, the festival of the breaking of the fast at the end of Ramadan, and Id al-Adha, the festival of the sacrifice.

JUDAISM

The oldest living religion in the western world, Judaism, the religion of the Jews, claims 17 million adherents throughout the world.

■ **HISTORY:** Widely considered to be the first monotheistic religion, it teaches that God entered a special covenant with the ancient Israelites to be God's messengers and an example to the world.

■ **TENETS:** While belief in a coming messiah is central to most Jews, Judaism generally emphasizes conduct rather than creed or doctrine. Differences of opinion are found on such matters as immortality and the messianic hope. Most Jewish belief is drawn from the Hebrew Bible, especially the first five books, called the Torah, or Pentateuch, which Jews believe to be the law of God. The laws were clarified and elaborated upon in the Mishnah and the Talmud, written and compiled over many years.

The Jewish system of laws, called halachah, regulates civil and criminal justice, family relationships, personal ethics and manners, social responsibilities, and religious observances. Individual practices regulated include dietary laws, marriage, daily prayer and study, and the recital of blessings. The sabbath and festivals are observed both in the home and in the synagogue.

In the United States, Judaism is generally divided into three movements: orthodox, which teaches strict adherence to the ancient Jewish laws and traditions; conservative, which upholds ritual observance but seeks to adapt it to modern life; and reform, which goes even further by excluding many traditional beliefs and observances.

THE FAITHS OF A NATION

In a state based on religious freedom, Americans enjoy its fruits

A culture that once inspired a newsmagazine to ask, "Is God Dead?" on its cover, recently saw all three major newsweeklies, *Time*, *Newsweek*, and *U.S. News & World Report*, devote their cover stories during Easter week to the search for the historical Jesus. And no wonder. Churches and pollsters bear witness to the fact that the 1990s are shaping up as The Great Awakening when it comes to public interest in religion. Below is a guide to some of the most popular Christian denominations in the United States today. Many other religions, of course, have their followings nationwide.

ASSEMBLIES OF GOD

With a worldwide membership of more than 25 million, the Assemblies of God fellowship is the largest denomination in the Pentecostal movement, a Christian revival that spread through the United States early in the 20th century. Founded in 1914, the Assemblies of God have more than 11,000 churches in the U.S. with a membership of 2.3 million.

■ **TENETS AND WORSHIP:** Like other Pentecostal groups, the Assemblies of God emphasize the baptism in the Holy Spirit, an experience in which Christians are filled with the Spirit in a manner described in Acts 2:4 as having occurred to the disciples of Jesus. One of the signs of this Spirit baptism is glossolalia, or the "speaking in an unknown language." The Assemblies of God affirm belief in the Trinity and in the need for personal salvation through the life, death, and resurrection of Jesus Christ. They believe the Bible to be the infallible Word of God and observe two ordinances: adult baptism by immersion and the Lord's Supper.

Worship is generally informal, with the singing of hymns and lively "praise songs," scripture-reading, a sermon, and opportunities for worshipers to participate in vocal prayer, glossolalia, and other spiritual gifts.

BAPTIST

Baptists, with more than 38 million members worldwide, outnumber any other single Protestant denomination. Independent and distrustful of ecclesiastical authority, they are divided among a variety of loosely knit organizations with little power over the affairs of local congregations. The largest U.S. Baptist body is the Southern Baptist Convention with some 15.6 million members, followed by the National Baptist Convention USA with 8.2 million members, and the National Baptist Convention of America with 3.5 million members, both historically black churches.

■ **TENETS AND WORSHIP:** Baptists trace their ancestry to the Anabaptists of the Reformation period in Europe and to the Rhode Island colonist Roger Williams, who started the first Baptist congregation in America. They are distinguished from other Protestant churches by their insistence on baptism by immersion of adult believers only, their concern for freedom of speech and individual conscience, the primacy they give to scrip-

---

■ **WHO BELIEVES IN WHAT**

In 1967, two thirds of Americans were Protestants. In 1993, only 56 percent are. Slightly over a quarter of Americans are Catholics, about the same as 25 years ago. There are 4 to 6 million Muslims in the U.S. today, greater than the number of Episcopalians.

Protestant	56%
Catholic	26%
Jewish	2%
Other	7%
None	9%

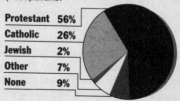

ture on matters of faith, doctrine, and morals and the authority they vest in local congregations in church affairs. Baptist worship is generally informal and scripture-centered with the sermon as the focal point.

ROMAN CATHOLIC

The Roman Catholic Church is the largest of the Christian denominations, with more than 900 million members worldwide and 60.2 million in the United States.

■ **TENETS AND WORSHIP:** Catholicism is identified as Roman because of its historical roots in Rome and the primacy it places upon the ministry of the bishop of Rome, the pope, who is considered to be the representative of Christ. Roman Catholics attach special significance to the rites of baptism, a sacramental entry into Christian life, and the Eucharist, a memorial of Christ's death and resurrection in which he is believed to be sacramentally present.

Also regarded as sacraments by Catholics are confession, ordination to ministry, marriage, confirmation, and the anointing of the sick. Public worship consists of the liturgy, principally the Eucharist, which is also called the mass, and includes the recitation of prayers, readings from the Bible, and a sermon or homily. The church observes a liturgical calendar similar to that of other Christians, following a cycle of Advent, Christmas, Epiphany, Lent, Easter, and Pentecost. It also follows a cycle of commemoration of the saints.

CHURCHES OF CHRIST

Churches of Christ are independent and autonomous congregations with no interlinking organization or headquarters. There are about 13,400 Church of Christ congregations in the U.S. with about 1.6 million members. The Churches of Christ are not to be confused with the United Church of Christ, a slightly smaller mainline denomination.

■ **TENETS AND WORSHIP:** Churches of Christ share a common belief that the Bible alone is the sufficient rule of faith and practice. Its members believe in the verbal inspiration

and inerrancy of the Bible, the divinity of Jesus and a firm hope of everlasting life for those who accept Jesus as personal Savior.

Worship is Bible-centered with preaching and a cappella singing. No musical instruments are used in worship. The Lord's Supper is observed each Sunday.

EPISCOPAL

The Episcopal Church in the United States is a part of the worldwide Anglican communion. It has about 2.5 million members in some 7,000 parishes and missions and about 14,000 clergy. It entered the colonies with the earliest settlers at Jamestown, Va., in 1607, as the Church of England. After the American Revolution, it became autonomous as the Protestant Episcopal Church in the United States and changed its name to the Episcopal Church in 1967.

■ **TENETS AND WORSHIP:** Its beliefs and practices are both Catholic and Reformed. Its clergy is composed of priests, bishops, and deacons, both male and female, and celibacy is not required. The church considers the Bible the primary authority, though it is further governed by a constitution, canon law, and the Book of Common Prayer. It recognizes two sacraments: baptism and the Eucharist. Episcopal worship generally is liturgical with the Eucharist as its centerpiece.

LUTHERAN

From its origins in Germany, Lutheranism spread to Scandinavia and, in the 18th century, to America and elsewhere. Its worldwide membership stands at more than 70 million. Its 7.8 million U.S. members are divided between the Evangelical Lutheran Church in America, 5.2 million, and the more conservative Lutheran Church–Missouri Synod, 2.6 million.

■ **TENETS AND WORSHIP:** Lutheranism is a branch of Protestantism that generally follows the teachings of the 16th-century reformer Martin Luther. An Augustinian monk, Luther was troubled by corruption and immorality in the Roman Catholic Church. His theological studies led him to

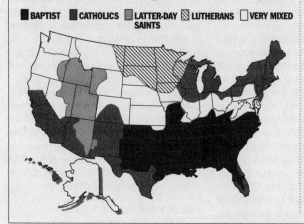

■ **HOW CHURCH AND STATE MIX**
Utah is the most religiously homogeneous state; 70 percent of its population is Mormon. Rhode Island is 61 percent Catholic. Mississippi, Alabama, and Georgia are more than half Baptist.

■ BAPTIST ■ CATHOLICS ■ LATTER-DAY ▨ LUTHERANS ☐ VERY MIXED
SAINTS

■ **WHERE CHURCHES ARE EMPTY**
In 1967, only 2 percent of Americans said they had no religion. That number was 11 percent in 1991. States with the largest percent of population with no religious identification:

OREGON	17.2%
WASHINGTON	14.0%
WYOMING	13.5%
NEVADA	13.2%
CALIFORNIA	13.0%
ARIZONA	12.2%
IDAHO	11.9%
COLORADO	11.4%
VERMONT	11.4%
MONTANA	10.2%

challenge much in the medieval tradition regarding the nature of faith and the Bible.

Luther's teachings centered on his belief in justification by grace through faith alone, in contrast to Catholic teachings that based favor with God partly on good deeds. He also taught that the Bible alone, not church tradition or papal pronouncements, is the sole authority for doctrine and practice. Lutherans recognize just two sacraments: baptism and the Eucharist. Lutheran worship generally follows a modified version of the Catholic liturgy.

METHODIST

Although centered in the British Isles and North America, Methodism has spread worldwide with total membership of about 26 million. Methodists are the second-largest Protestant group in the United States with some 8.5 million members in the United Methodist Church, the largest Methodist body. Besides the United Methodists, denominations in the U.S. include the African Methodist Episcopal Church, with some 3.5 million members, the African Methodist Episcopal Zion Church with 1.2 million members, and the Free Methodist Church with 60,000 members.

■ **TENETS AND WORSHIP:** Methodism arose from the 18th-century Wesleyan movement in England, led by John and Charles Wesley and George Whitefield. They organized small "societies" within the Church of England for religious sharing, Bible study, prayer, and preaching. Doctrine emphasized the personal experience of conversion, assurance, and sanctification. Eventually, the societies joined together and split from the Church of England. Methodist missionaries established the church in colonial America.

Methodist worship generally follows a traditional Protestant format with prayers, hymns and anthems, scripture readings, and a sermon, along with periodic baptisms and celebration of communion.

MORMON

The Church of Jesus Christ of Latter-day Saints, also known as the Mormon Church, is American in origin but global in its constituency. It has 9.4 million members worldwide, slightly less than half of them in the United States.

■ **TENETS AND WORSHIP:** The church teaches that the Christian church lost its authority from the second century until the 1820s when

Joseph Smith received a divine "latter day" revelation aimed at restoring the church. The revelation was translated into the Book of Mormon. The Mormon Church began in New York and eventually migrated to Utah, where it established its base for what would become a worldwide missionary endeavor.

Mormons use the Bible, the Book of Mormon, and two other books of revelations to Smith—Doctrine and Covenants and the Pearl of Great Price—as scriptures. They share many traditional Christian beliefs, but with some key modifications. Mormons believe, for example, that God was once human, has a wife, and that Jesus was their offspring. They believe humans can progress to divinity. The church baptizes by immersion. Vicarious baptism for those who have died and marriage for eternity are two distinctive practices. The church lays great emphasis on genealogical research so that members may undergo baptismal rites on behalf of their ancestors.

Congregations have separate weekly meetings for men, women, children and young people, and two meetings, Sunday School and Sacrament, for the entire church body. Each year, over 37,000 young people devote two years of their lives as missionaries.

ORTHODOX

Orthodox Christianity, sometimes referred to as "Eastern Orthodox" Christianity, is the third major division of the Christian church. It is composed of 15 independent churches united in faith, sacraments, and canonical discipline but each enjoying the right to elect its own head and its bishops. Worldwide membership is 100 to 200 million, with about 4 million in the United States. The largest fellowships are the Orthodox Church in America (Russian) with 2 million members and the Greek Orthodox Church with 1.9 million members.

■ **TENETS AND WORSHIP:** Orthodox Christianity developed historically from the church of the Byzantine Empire. It claims to have preserved the original and apostolic faith after the Great Schism of 1054, precipitated by disputes over the papacy and wording of the Nicene creed, which divided Christianity into an Eastern and a Western church.

The Patriarch of Constantinople, also known as the Ecumenical Patriarch, is given primacy over other Orthodox patriarchs but has no authority comparable to that of the pope. The Orthodox church accepts the early traditions of Christianity, including the same sacraments as the Roman Catholic Church, the episcopate, and the priesthood. Married men may become priests, but bishops and monks may not marry.

The veneration of Mary as Mother of God is central to Orthodox worship, and the intercession of saints is emphasized in liturgy. The liturgy used most often in the Orthodox church is the Divine Liturgy of John Chrysostom, and is always sung. The Eucharist is distributed to the congregation in both kinds, bread and wine.

PRESBYTERIAN

Presbyterianism emerged in the 16th-century Reformation as an effort to recapture the form as well as the message of the New Testament church. There are several Presbyterian denominations in the United States. The largest is the Presbyterian Church (USA), with about 2.7 million members.

■ **TENETS AND WORSHIP:** The church's name is derived from the Greek word *presbyteros*, or elder. Presbyterian churches are governed by elders elected by the congregation. They, in turn, elect regional governing bodies called presbyteries, which elect delegates to a national General Assembly. The representative structure grew out of the teachings of John Calvin, the Reformed leader in Geneva, who concluded after studying the Bible that Jesus Christ himself is the sole ruler of the church and that he exercises that rule through elected officers.

Presbyterian theology also is heavily influenced by Calvin, along with Luther and other reformers. It affirms the sovereignty of God, the Lordship of Jesus Christ, the authority of the scriptures, justification by grace through faith, the priesthood of all believers, and the efficacy of only two sacraments: baptism and the Lord's Supper. Presbyterian worship is structured and modestly liturgical.

GENEALOGY

▼

TRACING YOUR FAMILY TREE

It's amazing how much you can learn about ancestors if you look

Descended from the Highlands? Ascended from the Lowlands? Are there drops of blood from Genghis Khan, Dr. Livingston, or Sor Juana de la Cruz coursing through your veins? Does that racy family secret really have any truth to it?

Whatever your reason for peering into your family's past, you need not be alone in your quest. Thanks to the growing popularity of genealogical research, there is a wealth of resources for tracing family origins, as Erma Angevine, director of the National Genealogical Society's Home Study Program, points out below. For information on how to find professional research assistance, see the Expert Source on page 703.

■ FAMILY RECORDS

Gather all the information you can from relatives and family memorabilia before delving into published sources. The more clues you have to begin with, the better. One of the first pitfalls for a genealogist can be overeagerness. Learn early in the process to write down—in as much detail as possible—where, when, and why a search was made and the results of that search.

Remember that much of what you discover will be clues, not facts. Experienced researchers caution that word-of-mouth lore should be verified by consulting official records. Valuable family items include: birth, death, and marriage certificates; baptism and christening records; family

bibles, diaries, and letters, as well as newspaper clippings, photographs, school records, scrapbooks, military discharge papers, naturalization records, and passports. Pay attention to names of places, as they will be especially useful to you.

■ GENEALOGICAL SOCIETIES AND LIBRARIES

Check the local archives to see what they might have before hitting the road in search of important documents. Certain genealogical societies and libraries have copies of records that are normally available only through government sources.

The Church of Jesus Christ of Latter-day Saints has the largest genealogical collection in the country. Besides maintaining a library open to the public in Salt Lake City, Utah, the church runs local family centers throughout the country where you can order microfilm and copies of many types of records. These centers are open to all interested parties, regardless of religious affiliation. They can be located by calling a local Mormon organization.

The Church of the Latter-day Saints also has a Family Search CD-ROM program available through the LDS Family Centers, the Library of Congress, and other genealogical societies and libraries. Consult a local society or library to find out how you can access this program and what others might be available and helpful to you.

The next two largest collections are maintained by the New York Public Library Research Libraries and the Library of Congress. Other noteworthy collections are kept by the Daughters of the American Revolution and the National Genealogical Society in Washington, D.C., the Newberry Library in Chicago, the New England Historic Genealogical Society in Boston, the Bancroft Library at the University of California's Berkeley campus, the Western Reserve Historical

Society in Cleveland, and the Fort Wayne Public Library in Indiana.

To find out whether there is a genealogical society with a good library in your vicinity, consult the Directory of Historical Societies and Agencies in the United States and Canada, published by the American Association for State and Local History.

■ LOCAL AND FAMILY HISTORIES

Tap into local references early in your research. You may discover that another member of your family has investigated and documented the lineage of a certain branch of your family, thus saving you much time. Many local histories were commissioned by local leaders or written with the purpose of being sold in the community; they are full of "good upstanding Americans," "hardworking farmers," and "devout Christian mothers." If you're lucky enough to run across unusual details of your family, keep in mind that the information may not be accurate and should be verified through other sources.

To see if a history has been published of the county or locality in which your ancestors lived, consult Marion J. Kaminkow's *United States Local Histories in the Library of Congress* and P. William Filby's *A Bibliography of American County Histories*. To find out if a genealogy has been published on your family, also look in Kaminkow's *Genealogies in the Library of Congress* or in Netti Schreiner-Yantis's *Genealogical and Local History Books in Print*. (For publication information on all book titles, see page 704.)

■ U.S. CENSUS

Use census records not only to pinpoint an ancestor's location in a given year, but also to glean detailed information about a person's life. Depending on the year of the census, records might include data such as birthdates for each individual in the family, number of years married for each couple, number of children, whether a residence was rented or owned, whether the residence was a home or farm, and whether it was mortgaged. For foreign-born individuals, a census may have included the year of immigration and whether the person was natu-

ralized or not. The National Archives has microfilmed all existing census records for the period from 1790 to 1920 (conducted every 10 years). Begin in 1920 and work backwards.

To find your relatives' records, consult a census index if there is one. Look up your ancestor's name within the state and county in which he or she lived. If the name is not indexed, you may have to search all the names in a county. Published indexes are now available for all states for censuses from 1790 to 1830 and can be found in many libraries. The 1880, 1900, 1920, and 1940 censuses are coded in a different way from earlier ones; for a full explanation of this system, you will need the National Archives' free booklet "Getting Started: Beginning Your Genealogical Research in the National Archives."

Once you have figured out which census records are the most likely to bear fruit, you can obtain and use census microfilm in the following ways:

■ Visit the National Archives in Washington, D.C., or one of the 12 regional archives. The Microfilm Reading Rooms are open to all researchers, Monday and Wednesday, 8:45 a.m. to 5:00 p.m.; Tuesday, Thursday, and Friday, 8:45 a.m. to 9:00 p.m.; and Saturday, 8:45 a.m. to 4:45 p.m.

■ Rent census microfilm through your local library from the Census Microfilm Rental Program.

■ Purchase microfilm from the National Archives.

■ Use census microfilm at the LDS Family History Library in Salt Lake City and at its family history centers throughout the country. You do not need to belong to the Church of the Latter-day Saints to use the LDS Family History Library or its family centers.

■ Census microfilm can also be found at many state libraries, state archives, and historical and genealogical society libraries.

■ VITAL RECORDS

Write to state agencies or county and town offices for copies of their vital records once you have learned approximate dates and places for the births, marriages, and deaths of your ancestors.

Records of births, deaths, and marriages, wills, estate settlements, and deeds are among the most useful sources for genealogical information. These documents may be housed in different government agencies. Records created by the state or kept at the state level may be found in the state archives, the state vital records office, the state land office, or the state adjutant general's office. The state archives may also keep older county records. County records not transferred to the state archives are usually found in county courthouses. In some parts of the country, vital records are kept in town halls.

For help on the types of records kept and where to find them, you should consult a published guide. The National Genealogical Society suggests the following books: *Ancestry's Red Book; American State, County & Town Sources*, which contains an overview of the records in each state and the year of the earliest birth, marriage, death, land, probate, and court records in each county; *Bentley's County Courthouse Book*, which gives the address of each county courthouse in the United States; and *Kemp's International Vital Records Handbook*, which includes vital records order forms used in each state that can be photocopied.

■ MILITARY RECORDS

Don't overlook compiled military service records and pension application files. Compiled Military Service Records consist of rank, military unit, dates of service, presence on payrolls, and dates of discharge, desertion, or death. Pension application files are likely to include much more information, such as spouse's name, maiden name, certified vital records, birthplace, place of residence, and names and ages of children.

Indexes to these records can be viewed at the National Archives in Washington, D.C., as well as at certain genealogical libraries. While the federal government stores the most military records, certain state archives and libraries hold additional records and thus should also be consulted.

■ PASSENGER ARRIVAL RECORDS

Search passenger arrival records to find your immigrant ancestor. Between 1607 and 1920, over 30 million immigrants came to the shores of America, but Congress did not enact a law requiring ships' masters to file passenger lists until 1817.

The National Archives and its regional archives have some helpful records, including passenger and arrival records from the early 19th century through the 1950s. There are very few lists prior to 1820. All passenger arrival records and indexes have been microfilmed and are available in the Microfilm Reading Room. Depending on the year and circumstance of immigration, records may or may not exist.

The easiest way to access these records is to have key information such as the year your ancestor arrived, the port through which he or she entered this country, and the name of the ship. If you don't know this information, try consulting P. William Filby and Mary K. Meyer's three-volume work, *Passenger and Immigration Lists Index*. While the list is not complete, their index is the largest of its kind, currently including over one million names consolidated from nearly 1,000 sources.

EXPERT SOURCE

If you don't want to do it yourself, you can hire a genealogical sleuth. There are professional genealogists with a vast array of specialties, from those who work in untranslated Spanish archives to experts in tracking indentured servants. For a list of certified genealogists in your area, write:

**Board for Certification
of Genealogists
P.O. Box 14291
Washington, DC 20044**

WHERE TO FIND FAMILY GHOSTS

If you're ready to track down the family history, the following publications and archives are valuable sources to help you identify and locate all kinds of genealogical information

PUBLICATIONS

ANCESTRY'S RED BOOK: AMERICAN STATE, COUNTY & TOWN SOURCES
Alice Eichholz, ed., Ancestry Publications, 1992, $49.95

THE ARCHIVES: A GUIDE TO THE NATIONAL ARCHIVES FIELD BRANCHES
Loretto Dennis Szucs and Sandra Hargreaves Luebking, Ancestry Publications, 1988, $39.95

A BIBLIOGRAPHY OF AMERICAN COUNTY HISTORIES
P. William Filby, Genealogical Publishing Co., 1985, $24.95

COMPUTER GENEALOGY: A GUIDE TO RESEARCH THROUGH HIGH TECHNOLOGY
Richard A. Pence, ed., Ancestry, 1991, $12.95

COUNTY COURTHOUSE BOOK
Elizabeth Petty Bentley, Genealogical Publishing Co., 1990, $34.95

DIRECTORY OF GENEALOGICAL AND HISTORICAL SOCIETY PUBLICATIONS IN THE UNITED STATES AND CANADA
Dina C. Carson, Iron Gate Pub., 1994, $85

DIRECTORY OF HISTORICAL ORGANIZATIONS AND AGENCIES IN THE UNITED STATES AND CANADA
Mary K. Meyer, AASLH, 1990, $79.95

GENEALOGICAL AND LOCAL HISTORY BOOKS IN PRINT
Netti Schreiner-Yantis, GBIP, 1981, $15

GENEALOGIES IN THE LIBRARY OF CONGRESS
Marion J. Kaminkow, Magna Carta Book Co., 1981, $95

PASSENGER AND IMMIGRATION LISTS INDEX
P. William Filby and Mary K. Meyer, Gale Research Co., 1980, 3 vols., $440

WHERE TO WRITE FOR VITAL RECORDS: BIRTHS, DEATHS, MARRIAGES, AND DIVORCES
U.S. Department of Health and Human Services, Publication PHS-93-1142, 1993, $1.75

LIBRARIES

ALLEN COUNTY LIBRARY
Fred J. Reynolds Historical Genealogical Department
900 Webster St.
Fort Wayne, IN 46802
☎ 219-424-7241

BANCROFT LIBRARY
University of California
Berkeley, CA 94720
☎ 415-642-3773

FAMILY HISTORY LIBRARY
The Church of Jesus Christ of Latter-day Saints
35 N. Temple
Salt Lake City, UT 84150
☎ 801-240-2584

LIBRARY OF CONGRESS
Local History and Genealogy
Washington, D.C. 20540
☎ 202-707-5537

NATIONAL ARCHIVES
Genealogy Division
Washington, D.C. 20408
☎ 202-501-5410

SOCIETIES

AFRICAN AMERICAN FAMILY HISTORY ASSOCIATION
P.O. Box 115268
Atlanta, GA 30310
☎ 404-730-4001

NATIONAL SOCIETY OF THE DAUGHTERS OF THE AMERICAN REVOLUTION
1776 D St. NW
Washington, D.C. 20006
☎ 202-628-1776

NATIONAL GENEALOGICAL SOCIETY
4527 17th St. North
Arlington, VA 22207
☎ 703-525-0050

ETIQUETTE

MINDING CULTURAL MANNERS

Never give yellow flowers to a friend from Iran, and other gaffes to avoid

More than ever before, a new neighbor, classmate, or business associate is apt to be a recent immigrant whose social traditions are unfamiliar to most Americans. The latest census taken in 1990 showed that more than 19 million people in the United States were foreign-born, the highest number in a decade. Today's changing demographics call for new rules that will preclude cross-cultural misunderstandings.

As a folklorist, Norine Dresser studies customs, rituals, and beliefs of different cultures. The author of *Multicultural Manners* (John Wiley & Sons, Inc. 1996), Dresser dispenses etiquette advice in a column on cultural manners for the *Los Angeles Times*. Here are Dresser's do's and don'ts for avoiding cultural faux pas.

■ **What are some of the biggest multicultural gaffes Americans make?**

Our major problems are that we get too friendly and too informal, too fast. Our use of first names when we first meet someone, for example, is very offensive to most people in other parts of the world. It is interpreted as disrespectful. Americans also have a habit of getting right down to business. If you're dealing with Asian and Latin American cultures, you don't march in with your product and expect an order after a sales spiel. First, you establish rapport by introducing yourself and your company, then you leave a token, such as a company pen or calendar. Finally, you follow up with a phone call later in the week.

■ **Can you give us some examples of communications blunders?**

Americans should avoid asking questions that require direct "yes" or "no" responses. For example, we often say when asking for something, "Please feel free to say no, but would you..." In many cultures, responding no directly to a request is unheard of, so the newcomer becomes confused. Another point is that newcomers might be too embarrassed to say they don't understand because of language differences. Rather than ask, "Do you understand what I mean?" Say, "Please tell me what you don't understand."

■ **Would a recent immigrant really be offended by American blunders, knowing that customs are different here?**

Sure, the newcomers are being acculturated, but your efforts to pay attention to what's important to them show that you respect them. For example, you should never send yellow flowers to an Iranian. In that culture yellow flowers mean "I hate you and wish you were dead." One Iranian woman I know was given yellow flowers by a guest. She politely excused herself, threw the flowers on the floor, and cried.

Yellow also has bad connotations for many Peruvians and Mexicans. On the other hand, yellow flowers say "I miss you" in the Armenian culture.

■ **Are there other colors to avoid?**

Most Asian cultures respond negatively to white, which has death connotations. It would be safer not to give white flowers as a gift to an Asian friend.

Guests to an Indian wedding should avoid wearing white. It is thought to bring bad luck, even death, to the bride and groom. Many Chinese people believe wedding guests shouldn't wear black or white, which both represent death in their culture.

■ **What are some other customs that Americans should be aware of?**

Removing shoes before you enter the home of a Japanese person is fairly well known. Less known is the fact that when you remove your shoes in a Japanese house, you should place the shoes so that the toes face the door. Removing shoes is also a tradition among some Filipinos, Thais, Iranians, and Indian Buddhists.

Sometimes what you wear can be misunderstood. For example, jewelry made of bright cobalt blue ceramic beads from the Middle East were fashionable at one time in the United States. But an Iranian would laugh at the thought of women wearing such jewelry—in Iran, peddlers decorate their donkeys with the necklaces, known as donkey beads.

■ Are there foods that should not be served to guests from certain cultures?

Most people know that eating pork is taboo for religious Jews and Muslims, but fewer people are aware that orthodox Jews and Muslims also don't eat shellfish, or any fish without fins. Hindus don't eat beef and Seventh Day Adventists don't eat meat. Muslims, Hindus, and Mormons, of course, do not drink alcoholic beverages.

■ What should you do if you think you've offended someone?

If you make a mistake, do your best to rectify it. Here's an example: A Mexican student in my class befriended a Chinese girl, who invited her to a special birthday dinner. As a gift, the Mexican girl brought a black and white clock. When they opened the gifts, the Chinese family was horrified. Giving someone a clock in China means that you wish they were dead—that every moment brings them closer to death. And the black and white funeral colors exacerbated the problem. The Mexican girl was humiliated over her blunder. She later purchased another gift—a red blouse. Red is a more favorable color for the Chinese. With this gesture she was able to cement a friendship.

■ What's the best way to approach an unfamiliar multicultural situation?

It helps to be very observant. When in doubt, ask. It's best to ask someone of your own sex, so that it's less awkward for both of you in situations where there are significant male-female differences. Age matters too; young people may feel reluctant to tell older people what to do.

It all gets back to the main point: making an effort to understand, and showing others that you're trying to learn from them.

NEW RULES FOR NEW TOOLS

Savoir-faire today means faring with newfangled devices

New techology and the inevitable passing of time have revamped our lifestyles, creating an age of etiquette confusion. What's the protocol for call-waiting? What do you do when your beeper goes off during a meeting? Image consultants and manners experts are bustling to finesse the particulars of high-tech etiquette. Some old-fashioned rules never go out of date, however. Judith Martin, author of *Miss Manners' Basic Training: Communication* (Crown, 1997), advises that handwritten thank-you notes are almost always a must. For those who want to maintain their polish in the face of new devices that test our good manners almost daily, here's our own primer.

■ **ANSWERING MACHINE:** Keep outgoing messages clear and brief. When leaving a message on an answering machine, follow the same rules: be brief and clear, and leave all the information requested in the outgoing message. Try not to hold an extended one-way conversation unless you really don't want to talk to the person you're calling.

■ **CALL WAITING:** The best advice is not to succumb to the rudeness of this service at all. But if you must and your conversation is interrupted by another call on your line, apologize to the person with whom you are talking. Switch to the other caller and tell him or her that you'll call back. Then return to the original conversation and apologize again.

■ ***69:** When you press *69 on the telephone keypad, a recording gives you the phone number of your last caller, in case you didn't get to the ringing phone in time and the caller left

■ NETIQUETTE

Online etiquette requires knowing the language spoken on the Internet. Many emotions are expressed online with "emoticons," symbols that denote happiness, sadness, anger, etc. Here are some of the commonly used emoticons.

:-) Smile; happy; "I'm joking."

:-(Frown; sadness; "Bummer."

:-| Can't decide how to feel; no feelings either way.

:-O Yelling, or completely shocked.

:-() Can't (or won't) stop talking.

:-& Tongue-tied.

:-X Lips are sealed.

|-O Yawning or snoring.

%-(Confused, unhappy.

:'-(Crying.

:'-) Crying happy tears.

:-} or :-] Sarcastic smile.

:-D Big, delighted grin.

{} or [] Hug.

* Kiss.

FREQUENTLY USED ABBREVIATIONS

\<g> or \<G>	Grin.
AFKB	Away from keyboard.
BTW	By the way.
f2f	Face to face, used when you're referring to meeting an online friend in person, or when you'd like to.
FAQ	Frequently Asked Questions
IMHO	In my humble opinion.
IMNSHO	In my not so humble opinion.
IRL	In real life.
ITRW	In the real world.
LOL	Laughing out loud.
MorF?	Male or female? Used when your online name is gender-neutral.
OTF	On the floor (laughing).

no message. However, a sticky situation arises when you are given a number that you don't recognize. Say you dial the number and get a strange voice. What do you say without revealing your identity? The proper protocol, according to Susan Bixler, president of Professional Image Inc. of Atlanta, Ga., is to say: "Hello, this is (your phone number). I noticed you called and wondered if there is anything I can help you with?" It may well have been a wrong number, but, says Bixler, you don't want to miss out on opportunities either.

■ **BEEPERS:** If you are paged, turn off your beeper immediately and then politely excuse yourself to make the necessary phone calls. You do not need to reveal the nature of the call unless you must leave the meeting, dinner party, show, or other event immediately.

■ **FAX MACHINES:** Use the fax only for communicating business or nonconfidential information quickly. Never use the fax to send a thank-you note after a job interview.

■ **CELLULAR PHONES:** When calling a car phone or another cellular phone, remember that the person receiving the call is paying dearly for it, so keep the conversation brief. Remember, no cell phone conversation is completely private—your voice may be picked up on another cell phone. And most important—stay focused on your driving while using a car phone.

■ **SPEAKER PHONES:** These devices allow a group of people in a room to hear someone on the other end of the phone. Use speaker phones as infrequently as possible, because they tend to make the person who is not in the room feel uncomfortable. Always apologize for having to use the speaker phone and be sure to end the call with your handset.

■ **E-MAIL:** When sending electronic messages, make the header specific so recipients know immediately whether the message is important. It is acceptable to acknowledge an impromptu missive, such as "Congratulations on your new job," with an e-mail note of thanks, according to Judith Martin. E-mail is not confidential, however, so personal or controversial messages have no place in office e-mail.

FIGURES & FORMULAS

WEIGHTS & MEASURES: Measurements to live by, PAGE 708   **RULERS:** How some everyday objects measure up, PAGE 709   **TEMPERATURE:** From Fahrenheit to Celsius, PAGE 711   **CLOTHING CONVERSION:** How big is your head when you go to Paris? PAGE 713   **MATHEMATICS:** Placing math on a timeline, PAGE 714   **SYMBOLS:** The elegant language of mathematics, PAGE 716   **CHEMISTRY:** The building blocks of life, PAGE 718

WEIGHTS & MEASURES
▼

MEASUREMENTS THAT FIT A KING

Sizing up the world around you, from round holes to square pegs

Weights and measures have been a matter for pharaohs, emperors, and kings to establish and for practical men and women to follow for thousands of years. The Egyptians based their system of measurement on the human body: the little finger to the thumb tip was considered a span, and two spans were the equivalent of one cubit, which was the distance from a person's fingertips to the elbow. The mile was a Roman unit of measure: it came from the word "mille," which stood for "1,000 paces."

There are several legends to explain where the English unit of measure, the yard, came from. One is that it was the same length as King Henry I's arm. Another is that it represented the distance from the tip of Henry's nose to the end of his thumb. Yet another version suggests that it was inspired by the length of the arrows used by the King's archers. In any case, the state's role in setting standards has never been in doubt. For many centuries the weights and measures that Americans inherited from Britain were referred to as "the king's standard."

Americans have moved a fair way, however, from the Queen's English and what has come to be known as the British Imperial System of weights and measures, and in the United States today, weights and measures are usually referred to by the name "U.S. Customary System."

Most of the rest of the world, of course, follows the International (or Metric) System, which is a decimal system in which units of measurement increase by multiples of 10. First developed by ancient Hindu mathematicians and then embraced by the Arabs in the 10th century, the Metric System came into gradual use in Europe after 1100, and was officially adopted by the French in the late 1700s, about the time Louis XVI and Marie Antoinette faced the guillotine.

Led by the scientific and engineering communities, metrics are gradually winning wider acceptance in U.S. industry. But the day when the rulebook states that the proper height of a basketball hoop is 3.048 meters is still many years away.

■ LINEAR MEASURE
Use to measure lines and distances.
CUSTOMARY U.S. UNITS:

12 inches = 1 foot
3 feet = 1 yard
1,760 yards = 1 statute mile

5½ yards = 1 rod
40 rods = 1 furlong = 220 yards
8 furlongs = 5,280 feet = 1 statute mile

METRIC UNITS:
10 millimeters = 1 centimeter
10 centimeters = 1 decimeter
10 decimeters = 1 meter
10 meters = 1 decameter
10 decameters = 1 hectometer
10 hectometers = 1 kilometer

CUSTOMARY U.S. UNITS TO METRIC UNITS:
1 inch = 2.54 centimeters = 0.0254 meter
1 foot = 30.48 centimeters = 0.3048 meter
1 yard = 91.44 centimeters = 0.9144 meter
1 statute mile = 1,609.344 meters=
= 1.609344 kilometers

METRIC UNITS TO CUSTOMARY U.S. UNITS:
1 centimeter = 0.3937 inch
1 meter = 3.28084 feet
= 1.093613 yards
1 kilometer = 0.62137 mile

■ **MARINERS' MEASURE**
To measure distance, depth, or speed at sea.
CUSTOMARY U.S. UNITS:
6 feet = 1 fathom
1,000 fathoms (approx.) = 1 nautical mile
1 nautical mile = 1.151 statute miles
3 nautical miles = 1 league
60 nautical miles = 1 degree
1 knot = 1 nautical mile
per hour

■ **SQUARE MEASURE**
Multiply length by width in units of the same denomination to find surface area.
CUSTOMARY U.S. UNITS:
144 square inches = 1 square foot
9 square feet = 1 square yard
30 ¼ square yards = 2 square rods
160 square rods = 1 acre
640 acres = 1 square mile

METRIC UNITS:
100 square millimeters = 1 square
centimeter
100 square centimeters = 1 square
decimeter

■ **ROUGH YARDSTICKS WHEN YOU'RE IN A PINCH**
A little ingenuity can go a long way when you need a measurement, albeit an approximate one, in a hurry. For example, if you need to know the dimensions of a room it might help to know that most floor tile is 9 x 9 or 12 x 12 inches. If you know the length of your tie, belt, or shoelace, you can multiply that by the number of times it covers the area to be measured.

QUARTER
approximately
1 inch diameter

PENNY
approximately
¾ inch diameter

DOLLAR BILL
6⅛ x 2⅝ inches

BUSINESS CARD
generally 3⅝ x 2 inches

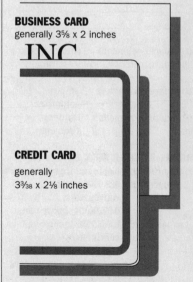

CREDIT CARD
generally
3³⁄₃₈ x 2⅛ inches

■ FRACTIONS AND THEIR DECIMAL EQUIVALENTS

Rounded to the nearest four decimals

½	.5	4/7	.5714
⅓	.3333	4/9	.4444
¼	.25	4/11	.3636
⅕	.2	5/6	.8333
⅙	.1667	5/7	.7143
1/7	.1429	5/8	.625
⅛	.125	5/9	.5556
1/9	.1111	5/11	.4545
1/10	.1	5/12	.4167
1/11	.0909	5/16	.3125
1/12	.0833	6/7	.8571
1/16	.0625	7/8	.875
1/32	.0313	7/9	.7778
1/64	.0156	7/10	.7
⅔	.6667	7/11	.6364
⅖	.4	7/12	.5833
2/7	.2857	7/16	.4375
2/9	.2222	8/9	.8889
2/11	.1818	8/11	.7273
¾	.75	9/10	.9
⅗	.6	9/11	.8182
3/7	.4286	9/16	.5625
⅜	.375	10/11	.9091
3/10	.3	11/12	.9167
3/11	.2727	11/16	.6875
3/16	.1875	13/16	.8125
⅘	.8	15/16	.9375

100 square decimeters = 1 square meter
100 square meters = 1 square decameter
= 1 acre
100 square decameters = 1 square hectometer
100 square hectometers = 1 square kilometer

CUSTOMARY U.S. UNITS TO METRIC UNITS:

1 square inch = 6.4516 square centimeters
1 square foot = 929.0304 square centimeters
= 0.09290304 square meter
1 square yard = 8,361.2736 square centimeters
= 0.83612736 square meter
1 acre = 4,046.8564 square meters
= 0.40468564 square hectometer
1 square mile = 2,589,988.11 square meters
= 258.998811 square hectometer
= 2.58998811 square kilometers

METRIC UNITS TO CUSTOMARY U.S. UNITS:

1 square centimeter = 0.1550003 square inch
1 square meter = 1,550.003 square inches
= 10.76391 square feet
= 1.195990 square yards
1 hectare = 107,639.1 square feet
= 11,959.90 square yards
= 2.4710538 acres
= 0.003861006 square mile
1 square kilometer = 247.10538 acres
= 0.3861006 square mile

■ CUBIC MEASURE

Multiply length by breadth by thickness to find cubic content or volume.

CUSTOMARY U.S. UNITS:

1,728 cubic inches = 1 cubic foot
27 cubic feet = 1 cubic yard

METRIC UNITS:

1,000 cubic millimeters = 1 cubic centimeter
1,000 cubic centimeters = 1 cubic decimeter
1,000 cubic decimeters = 1 cubic meter

■ SURVEYORS' MEASURE

Use to measure the borders and dimensions of a tract of land.

CUSTOMARY U.S. UNITS:

7.92 inches = 1 link
100 links = 1 chain
1 chain = 4 rods = 66 feet
80 chains = 1 survey mile = 5,280 feet

■ SURVEYORS' SQUARE MEASURE

Multiply length by breadth to find surface area of land.

CUSTOMARY U.S. UNITS:

272¼ square feet = 1 square rod
16 square rods = 1 square chain

160 square rods = 10 square chains
= 1 acre
640 acres = 1 square mile = 1 section
36 square miles = 36 sections
= 1 township

■ LIQUID MEASURE
Use to measure a vessel's capacity to hold liquids.

CUSTOMARY U.S. UNITS:
4 gills = 2 cups = 1 pint
2 pints = 1 quart
4 quarts = 1 gallon
31½ gallons = 1 barrel
2 barrels = 1 hogshead

METRIC UNITS:
10 milliliters = 1 centiliter
10 centiliters = 1 deciliter
10 deciliters = 1 liter
10 liters = 1 decaliter
10 decaliters = 1 hectoliter
10 hectoliters = 1 kiloliter

■ APOTHECARIES' FLUID MEASURE
Use in mixing medicines.

CUSTOMARY U.S. UNITS:
60 minims = 1 fluid dram
8 fluid drams = 1 fluid ounce
16 fluid ounces = 1 pint
2 pints = 1 quart
4 quarts = 1 gallon

CUSTOMARY U.S. UNITS TO METRIC UNITS:
1 fluid ounce = 29.573528 milliliters
= 0.02957 liter
1 cup = 236.588 milliliters
= 0.236588 liter
1 pint = 473.176 milliliters
= 0.473176 liter
1 quart = 946.3529 milliliters
= 0.9463529 liter
1 gallon = 3,785.41 milliliters
= 3.78541 liters

METRIC UNITS TO CUSTOMARY U.S. UNITS:
1 milliliter = 0.0338 fluid ounce
1 liter = 33.814 fluid ounces
= 4.2268 cups = 2.113 pints
= 1.0567 quarts = 0.264 gallons

■ TEMPERATURE CONVERSIONS

To convert temperatures from Fahrenheit to Celsius, subtract 32 degrees and multiply by 5, then divide by 9. To go from Celsius to Fahrenheit, multiply by 9, divide by 5, then add 32 degrees.

Celsius = Fahrenheit	Fahrenheit = Celsius
−45 = −49	−45 = −42.8
−40 = −40	−40 = −40.0
−35 = −31	−35 = −37.2
−25 = −13	−30 = −34.4
−30 = −8.5	−25 = −31.7
−20 = −4	−20 = −28.9
−15 = 5	−15 = −26.1
−10 = 14	−10 = −23.3
−5 = 23	−5 = −20.6
0 = 32	0 = −17.8
5 = 41	5 = −15.0
10 = 50	10 = −12.2
15 = 59	15 = −9.4
20 = 68	20 = −6.7
25 = 77	25 = −3.9
30 = 86	30 = −1.1
35 = 95	32 = 0.0
40 = 104	35 = 1.7
45 = 113	40 = 4.4
50 = 122	45 = 7.2
55 = 131	50 = 10.0
60 = 140	55 = 12.8
65 = 149	60 = 15.6
70 = 158	65 = 18.3
75 = 167	70 = 21.1
80 = 176	75 = 23.9
85 = 185	80 = 26.7
90 = 194	85 = 29.4
95 = 203	90 = 32.2
100 = 212	95 = 35.0
125 = 257	100 = 37.8
150 = 302	105 = 40.6
175 = 347	110 = 43.3
200 = 392	212 = 100.0
225 = 437	225 = 107.2
250 = 482	250 = 121.1
275 = 527	275 = 135.0
300 = 572	300 = 148.9
325 = 617	325 = 162.8
350 = 662	350 = 176.7
375 = 707	375 = 190.6
400 = 752	400 = 204.4
425 = 797	425 = 218.3
450 = 842	450 = 232.2
475 = 887	475 = 246.1

■ DRY MEASURE

Use to measure a vessel's capacity to hold solids such as grain.

CUSTOMARY U.S. UNITS:

2 pints = 1 quart
8 quarts = 1 peck
4 pecks = 1 bushel

CUSTOMARY U.S. UNITS TO METRIC UNITS:

1 pint = 33,600 cubic inches = 0.551 liter
1 quart = 67.201 cubic inches = 1.101 liters

■ COOKING MEASUREMENT EQUIVALENTS

3 teaspoons = 1 tablespoon
1 tablespoon = $\frac{1}{16}$ cup
4 tablespoons = $\frac{1}{4}$ cup
5 tablespoons = $\frac{1}{3}$ cup + 1 teaspoon
6 tablespoons = $\frac{3}{8}$ cup
8 tablespoons = $\frac{1}{2}$ cup
10 tablespoons = $\frac{2}{3}$ cup + 2 teaspoons
12 tablespoons = $\frac{3}{4}$ cup
16 tablespoons = 1 cup
32 tablespoons = 2 cups
48 teaspoons = 1 cup
2 cups = 1 pint
4 cups = 1 quart
2 pints = 1 quart
4 quarts = 1 gallon

■ WOOD MEASURE

To measure the volume of a pile of wood.

CUSTOMARY U.S. UNITS:

16 cubic feet = 1 cord foot = a wood pile
4 feet high by 4 feet wide by 1 foot long
8 cord feet = 1 cord = a wood pile 8 feet
long by 4 feet wide by 4 feet high

■ TIME MEASURE

Use to measure the passage of time.

CUSTOMARY U.S. UNITS:

60 seconds = 1 minute
60 minutes = 1 hour
24 hours = 1 day
7 days = 1 week
4 weeks (28 to 31 days) = 1 month
12 months (365 or 366 days) = 1 year
100 years = 1 century

■ ANGULAR AND CIRCULAR MEASURE

Use in surveying, navigating, astronomy, geography, reckoning latitude and longitude, and computing differences in time.

CUSTOMARY U.S. UNITS:

60 seconds = 1 minute
60 minutes = 1 degree
90 degrees = 1 right angle
180 degrees = 1 straight angle
360 degrees = 1 circle

The length of a degree of longitude on the earth's surface at the Equator is 69.16 miles.

■ TROY WEIGHT

Use in weighing gold, silver, and jewels.

CUSTOMARY U.S. UNITS:

24 grains = 1 pennyweight
20 pennyweights = 1 ounce
12 ounces = 1 pound

■ AVOIRDUPOIS WEIGHT

Use for weighing heavy articles such as grain and groceries.

CUSTOMARY U.S. UNITS:

$27\frac{11}{32}$ grains = 1 dram
16 drams = 1 ounce
16 ounces = 1 pound
100 pounds = 1 short hundredweight
20 short hundredweight = 1 short ton

■ APOTHECARIES' WEIGHT

For weighing medicines for prescriptions.

CUSTOMARY U.S. UNITS:

20 grains = 1 scruple
3 scruples = 1 dram
8 drams = 1 ounce
12 ounces = 1 pound

■ METRIC WEIGHT

Use for measuring weights, distances, areas, and both dry and liquid capacities.

METRIC UNITS:

10 milligrams = 1 centigram
10 centigrams = 1 decigram
10 decigrams = 1 gram
10 grams = 1 decagram
10 decagrams = 1 hectogram
10 hectograms = 1 kilogram

■ THE LONG AND THE SHORT OF CLOTHING SIZES

Men in Europe don't have huge heads and exceptionally large feet—they just have a different system for sizing hats and shoes. A look at how clothing sizes compare:

WOMEN

BLOUSES AND SWEATERS

	U.S.	32	34	36	38	40	42	44
	British	34	36	38	40	42	44	46
	Continental	40	42	44	46	48	50	52

COATS AND DRESSES

	U.S.	8	10	12	14	16	18	20
	British	30	32	34	36	38	40	42
	Continental	36	38	40	42	44	46	48

SHOES

		U.S.	5–5½	6–6½	7–7½	8–8½	9
		British	3½–4	4½–5	5½–6	6½–7	7½
		Continental	36	37	38	39	40

STOCKINGS

	U.S. and British	8	8½	9	9½	10	10½
	Continental	0	1	2	3	4	5

MEN

HATS

	U.S.	6⅝	6¾	6⅞	7	7⅛	7¼	7⅜	7½
	British	6½	6⅝	6¾	6⅞	7	7⅛	7¼	7⅜
	Continental	53	54	55	56	57	58	59	60

SHIRTS

	U.S. and British	14	14½	15	15½	16	16½	17
	Continental	36	37	38	39	41	42	43

SHOES

	U.S.	7	7½	8	8½	9	9½	10	10½	11
	British	6½	7	7½	8	8½	9	9½	10	10½
	Continental	39	40	41	42	43	43	44	44	45

SOCKS

	U.S. and British	9½	10	10½	11	11½	12	12½
	Continental	39	40	41	42	43	44	45

SUITS AND COATS

	U.S. and British	34	36	38	40	42	44	46
	Continental	44	46	48	50	52	54	56

100 kilograms = 1 quintal
10 quintals = 1 ton

■ MASS AND WEIGHT

Though they are not the same thing, mass and weight are identical in standard conditions (sea level on Earth), meaning that grams and other metric units of mass can be used as measures of weight or converted into customary units of weight.

CUSTOMARY U.S. UNITS TO METRIC UNITS:

1 ounce = 28.3495 grams
1 pound = 453.59 grams
= 0.453569 kilogram
1 short ton = 907.18 kilograms
= 0.907 metric ton

METRIC UNITS TO CUSTOMARY U.S. UNITS:

1 milligram = 0.000035 ounce
1 gram = 0.03527 ounce
1 kilogram = 35.27 ounces
= 2.2046 pounds
1 metric ton = 2,204.6 pounds
= 1.1023 short tons

MATHEMATICS
▼

THE NUMERICAL MARCH OF TIME

The study of math has been both practical and sublime for millennia

Without numbers it would be impossible to set a clock, keep score, or create a symphony. If numbers had not been needed, the civilizations of ancient Mesopotamia, Egypt, and China would not have felt it necessary to invent counting systems, which they then applied to their commerce and government. An early appreciation for the principles of geometry helped the Egyptians construct the pyramids and accurately record their boundaries.

By the sixth century B.C., the Greeks took the practical math that they had learned from the Babylonians and Egyptians and ventured into more abstract investigations. The Greek philosopher Pythagoras and his disciples proposed a theorem, for instance, that showed the mathematical relationship among the three sides of a right triangle (see page 717). Another Greek, Euclid, was the first to suggest that geometry possessed a single set of logical rules. Archimedes laid the conceptual groundwork for integral calculus in the third century B.C., and the celebrated astronomer Ptolemy played a leading role in developing trigonometry.

The Romans largely contented themselves with the use of math to solve practical problems, but the more ethereal inquiries into the nature of numbers by the Greeks were taken up by Islamic thinkers in the 9th and 10th centuries. One of them, an astronomer named Muhammad ibn M-us-a al-Khw-arizmi, laid many of the foundations for algebra.

Beginning in the 11th century, Islamic advances in mathematics gradually made their way to Europe. But it was not until the Renaissance in the 15th century that Europeans contributed to the breakthroughs, with astronomers such as Nicolaus Copernicus, Galileo Galilei, and Johannes Kepler making major contributions. Working independently, Sir Isaac Newton, an Englishman, and Baron Gottfried Wilhelm Leibniz invented calculus in the 1680s, which effectively ushered in the modern age of mathematics.

Following is a ready reference to many of the most commonly used mathematical concepts and operations.

ALGEBRA

Algebra is based on five fundamental laws, which govern the operations of addition, subtraction, multiplication, and division. Each of the laws is expressed in letter variables. Where variables a, b, and c are all real numbers, any number can be substituted for a variable without conflicting with the way the rule works.

■ THE COMMUTATIVE LAW OF ADDITION

$$a + b = b + a$$

Under this law, the order in which two numbers are added has no bearing on the sum derived. Thus,
$6+7 = 7+6$, or $(-10)+(-2) = (-2)+(-10)$

■ THE ASSOCIATIVE LAW OF ADDITION

$$a + (b + c) = (a + b) + c$$

Under this law, it does not matter which combination of numbers are added first, the sum remains the same. Thus,
$1+(8+2) = (1+8)+2$

■ THE COMMUTATIVE LAW OF MULTIPLICATION

$$ab = ba$$

Under this law, it does not matter which order numbers are multiplied in, the product is the same. Thus, $6.7 = 7.6$

■ THE ASSOCIATIVE LAW OF MULTIPLICATION:

$$a \cdot (bc) = (ab) \cdot c$$

Under this law, numbers can be multiplied in any sequence without affecting the final product. Thus, $5.(4.3)=(5.4).3$

■ THE DISTRIBUTIVE LAW OF MULTIPLICATION OVER ADDITION:

$$a(b+c) = ab + ac$$

Under this law, if a number multiplies a sum, the total is the same as the sum of the separate products of the multiplier and each of the addends represented by b and c. Thus, $3.(2+9) = 3.2 + 3.9$

■ THE QUADRATIC EQUATION

Another key algebraic equation is the quadratic equation, in which the highest power to which the unknown quantity is raised is the second. Assuming a, b, and c are real numbers, and a does not equal zero, the formula is as follows:

$$If: ax^2 + bx + c = 0$$

$$Then: x = \frac{-b \pm \sqrt{b^2 - 4ac}}{2a}$$

Thus, if a=1, b=4, and c=3, and we know that $1x^2 + 4x + 3 = 0$, then we can find the value of x as follows:

$$x = \frac{-4 \pm \sqrt{4^2 - (4 \cdot 1 \cdot 3)}}{2 \cdot 1} = (-1, -3)$$

GEOMETRY

This branch of mathematics deals with points, lines, planes, and figures and their properties, measurement, and spatial relationships.

■ ANGLES

Angles are expressed in degrees, which are fractions of a circle. A circle has 360 degrees.

 An **acute angle** is greater than zero degrees and less than 90.

 A **right angle** has 90 degrees. The lines forming the angle run perpendicular to each other.

 An **obtuse angle** has more than 90 degrees but less than 180 degrees.

 A **straight angle** has 180 degrees and forms a straight line.

WHEN IN ROME...

The Roman system of recording numbers lasted considerably longer than the Roman Empire. As recently as 500 years ago, Roman numerals were still being used for addition and subtraction throughout Europe. But the Roman approach to numbers didn't translate well to higher math, and by the late 1500s Arabic numerals were being adopted in the West.

The Roman system uses only seven symbols, individually or in combination. When more than one symbol is used to form a number, the value of each symbol generally is added together, reading from left to right.

To multiply a numeral by 1,000, place a bar over the symbol like a long vowel sound. For instance, X with a bar across its top would stand for 10,000.

ROMAN NUMERALS

1	**I**	300	CCC
2	II	400	CD
3	III	**500**	**D**
4	IV	600	DC
5	**V**	700	DCC
6	VI	800	DCCC
7	VII	900	CM
8	VIII	**1000**	**M**
9	IX	1500	MD
10	**X**	1900	MCM or
15	XV		MDCCCC
20	XX	1910	MCMX
25	XXV	1940	MCMXL
30	XXX	1950	MCML
40	XL	1960	MCMLX
50	**L**	1990	MCMXC
60	LX	1996	MCMXCVI
70	LXX	2000	MM
80	LXXX	3000	MMM
90	XC	5000	$\overline{\text{V}}$
100	**C**	10,000	$\overline{\text{X}}$
150	CL	100,000	$\overline{\text{C}}$
200	CC	1,000,000	$\overline{\text{M}}$

■ READING THE SIGNS

No science is more elegant when it comes to explaining the world around us than mathematics. To assist its examination of the properties, relations, and measurement of quantities, it relies on a system of mathematical signs, or directions. The most commonly used ones appear below:

+	plus or positive	≤	less than or equal to
−	minus or negative	≫	much greater than
±	plus or minus, positive or negative	≪	much less than
·	multiplied by	√	square root
÷ or /	divided by	∞	infinity
=	equal to	∝	proportional to
≠	not equal to	Σ	sum of
≈	approximately equal to	∏	product of
		Δ	difference
∼	of the order of or similar to	∴	therefore
>	greater than	∠	angle
<	less than	‖	parallel to
≥	greater than or equal to	:	is to (ratio)

 Complementary angles exist when two angles total 90 degrees.

 Supplementary angles occur when two angles add up to 180 degrees.

 Conjugate angles add up to 360 degrees when combined.

■ TRIANGLES

The sum of the internal angles of a triangle is always 180 degrees.

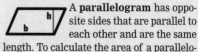 An **equilateral triangle** has sides that are of equal length and internal angles that are all 60 degrees.

 An **isosceles triangle** has two sides that are of equal length and two equal angles.

 A **scalene triangle** has no sides and no angles of equal size.

 A **right triangle** has one internal angle of 90 degrees.

 An **obtuse triangle** has one obtuse angle, which is an angle greater than 90 degrees but less than 180 degrees.

 An **acute-angle** triangle has three acute angles, meaning that all are under 90 degrees.

 To calculate the area of a triangle, multiply the base by the height by one-half:

$$A = (\tfrac{1}{2})bh$$

■ QUADRILATERALS

A quadrilateral is a four-sided polygon.

 A **square** has four equal sides and four right angles. To calculate the area of a square, square the length of one side:

$$A = a^2$$

 A **rectangle** has equal opposite sides and all right angles. To calculate a rectangle's area, multiply base by height:

$$A = bh$$

 A **rhombus** has equal sides and no right angles. To calculate its area, multiply base by height:

$$A = bh$$

 A **parallelogram** has opposite sides that are parallel to each other and are the same length. To calculate the area of a parallelogram, multiply the base by the height:

$$A = bh$$

■ OTHER POLYGONS

A **pentagon** is a five-sided polygon. To calculate the approximate area of a pentagon, multiply the square of the length of one side by 1.721:

$$A = 1.721\,a^2$$

A **hexagon** is a six-sided polygon. To calculate the approximate area of a hexagon, multiply the square of the length of one side by 2.598:

$$A = 2.598\,a^2$$

An **octagon** is an eight-sided polygon. To calculate the approximate area of an octagon: multiply the square of the length of one side by 4.828:

$$A = 4.828\,a^2$$

A **circle** is a figure in which every point on its boundary is equidistant from the center. The radius is that distance to the center. The diameter is twice the radius, or the longest distance across the circle. The circumference is the total distance around the boundary of the circle. To calculate the area, multiply the square of the radius by pi (3.1416…):

$$A = \pi r^2$$

To calculate the circumference of a circle, multiply radius of the circle by 2 and by pi (3.1416…):

$$C = 2\pi r$$

■ SOLIDS

Solids are three-dimensional geometric objects that exist in space.

A **cube** is a solid with six equal, square sides. To calculate a cube's surface area, multiply the square of the length of a side by 6:

$$S = 6a^2$$

■ THE RIGHT WAY TO VIEW RIGHT TRIANGLES

The relationships between the angles of a right triangle and its sides have been studied by mathematicians for millennia. Among the important trigonometric concepts are:

■ **SINE:** In a right triangle, the ratio of the opposite side of a given acute angle to the hypotenuse is known as the sine of that angle.

SINE OF ANGLE $A = a \div c$

■ **COSINE:** In a right triangle, the ratio of the adjacent side of an acute angle to the hypotenuse is known as the cosine of that angle.

COSINE OF ANGLE $A = b \div c$

■ **TANGENT:** In a right triangle, the ratio of the opposite to the adjacent side of an acute angle is known as the angle's tangent.

TANGENT OF $A = a \div b$

■ **COTANGENT:** In a right triangle, the ratio of the adjacent side of an acute angle to the opposite side is known as the angle's cotangent.

COTANGENT OF ANGLE $A = b \div a$

■ THE PYTHAGOREAN THEOREM:

In a right triangle the square of the hypotenuse is equal to the sum of the square of the other two sides.

$$c^2 = a^2 + b^2$$

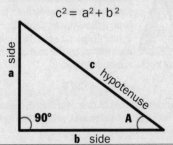

To calculate the volume of a cube, cube the length of one side:

$$V = a^3$$

A **sphere** is a body whose surface is equally distant from the center at all points. To calculate the surface area, multiply 4 by pi by the square of the radius:

$$S = 4\pi r^2$$

To calculate the volume of a sphere, multiply the cube of the radius by pi by 4/3:

$$V = (4/3)\pi r^3$$

A **pyramid** has a square base and four sloping triangular sides meeting at the top. To calculate the surface area, multiply base by length, and multiply 2 by the base and the height. Add the results:

$$S = bl + 2bh$$

To calculate a pyramid's volume, multiply the base's area by height and by $1/3$:

$$V = (1/3)bh$$

A **cylinder** is a solid described by a line that always has a point in common with a given closed curve. The surface area of a right, circular cylinder: multiply 2 by pi by radius by height:

$$S = 2\pi rh$$

To calculate the volume, multiply the square of the radius of the base by pi by height:

$$V = \pi r^2 h$$

A **cone** is a flat-based, single-pointed solid formed by a rotating straight line that traces out a base from a fixed vertex point. To calculate the surface area of a cone, multiply pi by the radius of the base by the slant height (s):

$$S = \pi rs$$

To calculate the volume, multiply the square of the radius of the base by pi by height by $1/3$.

$$V = (1/3)\pi r^2 h$$

WHAT MATTERS IN THE WORLD

The periodic table of elements tells what we're made of

The periodic table of the elements was first devised in the 19th century to show the atomic weights of the elements and to group them by similar properties. The discovery of protons and electrons in atoms in the early 20th century gave rise to a new and more accurate arrangement of the elements in a periodic table. This new arrangement is based on the atomic number, which is the number of protons (positively charged particles) present in the atomic nucleus of an element.

The table lists the elements in horizontal rows (or periods), according to their atomic numbers. Each vertical column (except hydrogen in the first column) groups elements that have related properties and are likely to behave similarly in chemical reactions. Except for hydrogen, the elements on the left side of the table are metals while those in the last six columns are predominantly nonmetals. In those columns, a heavier, stepped boundary line separates the metals from the nonmetals.

Hydrogen is the lightest and simplest element in the table. It has many properties that are different from all other elements. For example, in chemical reactions, it can give up or acquire an electron from other elements, which are incapable of transferring electrons both ways.

Besides the atomic number, the periodic table also lists each element's name, chemical symbol, and atomic weight (or atomic mass). Atomic weight is the mass of an atom relative to the mass of an atom of carbon-12, which is arbitrarily assigned an atomic weight of 12 by an international convention.

THE PERIODIC TABLE OF ELEMENTS

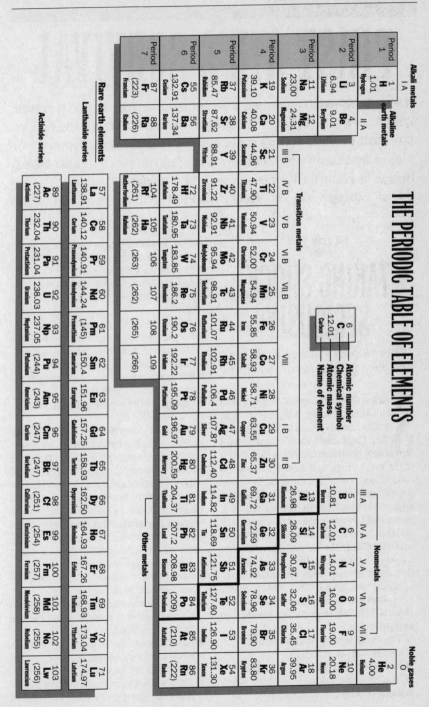

FIRST AID & SURVIVAL

RESCUE BREATHING: Timing and procedures for all ages, PAGE 724 **POISON:** What to do in a crisis, PAGE 730 **BURNS:** Treating skin that's singed, PAGE 731 **HOME SECURITY:** A cop's guide, PAGE 732 **SELF-DEFENSE:** Improve your odds of fending off an attacker by having a plan, PAGE 734 **EARTHQUAKE:** How to be ready for the big one, PAGE 736 **TORNADO:** Getting out of the way of a twister, PAGE 738 **FLOOD:** What to do if the river rises, PAGE 740

INJURIES
▼

TAKING SHOCK SERIOUSLY

When the body shuts down because of injury, immediate care is critical

Shock is the body's way of trying to deal with a bad situation. When a body experiences trauma from a serious injury, it often finds itself unable to maintain proper blood flow to all its organs. Shock is the mechanism that allows the body to ration blood flow so that the most important organs such as the brain, heart, lungs, and kidneys get the blood they need, even when that means that less vital parts, such as arms, legs, and skin have to make do with less. This natural triage cannot be sustained for very long, however, without causing potentially life-threatening damage to the brain and heart.

Shock, says the Red Cross, "can't be managed effectively by first aid alone. A victim of shock requires advanced medical care as soon as possible."

The early signs of shock include:
■ Restlessness or irritability.
■ Altered or confused consciousness.
■ Pale, cool, moist skin.
■ Rapid breathing and rapid pulse.

The proper response to shock is to:
■ Stretch the victim out on his or her back.
■ Treat any open bleeding.
■ Help the injured restore normal body temperature, covering him or her if there is chilling.
■ Talk to the victim reassuringly.
■ Prop the legs up about a foot unless there are possible head, neck, or back injuries, or broken bones in the hips or legs.
■ Withhold food or drink, even though the victim probably feels thirsty.
■ Call the rescue service immediately.

When the emergency that requires your assistance involves heavy bleeding, it's important to protect yourself against the risk of infection—especially if you have a cut, scrape, or sore that could allow the victim's blood to mix with yours. One of the easiest ways for an infectious disease such as the AIDS virus or hepatitis B to be transmitted is through direct blood-to-blood exchange. To reduce risk, the American Red Cross advises the following:
■ Avoid blood splashes.
■ Keep and use disposable latex gloves in emergencies involving bleeding.
■ If gloves are unavailable, cover the wound with a dressing or other available barrier such as plastic wrap.
■ Avoid any contact in which the victim's blood touches any cuts, scrapes, or skin irritations you may have.
■ Always wash your hands as soon as possible, whether or not you wore gloves.

CONTROL BLEEDING FROM A MAJOR OPEN WOUND

Pressure is the key to stopping blood loss from a serious injury. Bearing down on arterial pressure points may be necessary.

IF A PERSON IS BLEEDING...

STEP 1. Do not waste time washing wound. Cover it with sterile dressing or clean cloth and press firmly against the wound with hand.

STEP 2. Elevate the wound, if possible, above the level of the heart.

STEP 3. Apply a roller bandage snugly over the dressing to keep pressure on the wound. If bleeding doesn't stop...

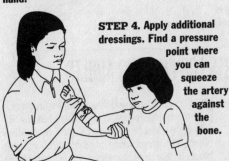

STEP 4. Apply additional dressings. Find a pressure point where you can squeeze the artery against the bone.

If bleeding is from the leg, press with the heel of your hand where the leg bends at the hip.

■ A ROLLER BANDAGE USED TO CONTROL BLEEDING

To apply a pressure bandage, start by securing the bandage over the dressing. Use overlapping turns to cover the dressing completely.

Tie or tape the bandage in place. If blood soaks through, put on more dressings and bandages. Do not remove bloodsoaked ones.

Check fingers or toes for warmth, color, and feeling. If they are pale and cold, bandage is too tight. Loosen it.

CHECKING AN UNCONSCIOUS VICTIM

When a victim does not respond to you, assume he or she is unconscious. Call for an ambulance at once, if possible. Then check to see if the victim is breathing, has a pulse, or is bleeding severely.

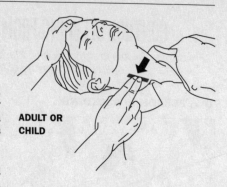

ADULT OR CHILD

■ **To check for breathing,** look, listen, and feel for breathing for about five seconds. Watch the chest to see if it rises.

■ **To find out if the heart is beating,** check the victim's pulse. Check the pulse of an adult or a child at the side of the neck. Check the pulse of an infant at the inside of the arm between the shoulder and the elbow.

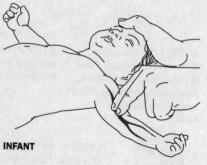

■ **Check for bleeding** by looking over the victim's body from head to foot. Bleeding is severe when blood spurts out of a wound. Often the situation may look worse than it is.

INFANT

ABDOMINAL THRUSTS FOR CHOKING ADULTS

Choking is a common breathing emergency. A conscious person who is choking has the airway blocked by a piece of food or another object. The airway may be partly or completely blocked. If a choking person is coughing forcefully, encourage him or her to cough up the object.

IF THE PERSON IS UNABLE TO COUGH, SPEAK, OR BREATHE...

STEP 1. Place thumb side of fist against middle of abdomen just above the navel. Grasp fist with other hand.

STEP 2. Give quick upward thrusts.

REPEAT until object is coughed up or person becomes unconscious.

Give chest thrusts when the choking victim is too large for you to reach around or is noticeably pregnant.

GIVE BACK BLOWS AND CHEST THRUSTS TO BABIES WHO ARE CHOKING

Choking is a leading cause of death and injury in infants, who love to put small objects such as pebbles, coins, beads, and parts of toys, in their mouth.

Babies also choke often while eating because they have not yet fully mastered chewing and swallowing. Foods like grapes and nuts are particularly risky. Never let an infant eat or drink alone, the American Red Cross advises.

IF AN INFANT IS UNABLE TO CRY, COUGH, OR BREATHE...

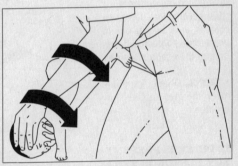

STEP 1. With infant facedown on forearm so that the head is lower than the chest, give five back blows with heel of hand between the infant's shoulder blades.

STEP 2. Holding the infant firmly between both forearms, turn the infant to a faceup position on forearm.

STEP 3. Using two fingers, give five chest thrusts on about the center of the breastbone.

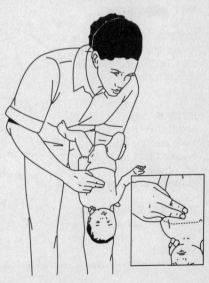

REPEAT the sequence of five back blows and five chest thrusts alternately until the object is coughed up, the infant begins to breathe on his own, or the infant becomes unconscious.

Stop as soon as the object is coughed up or the infant starts to breathe or cough. Watch the infant and make sure that he or she is breathing freely again.

Call the local emergency number if you haven't already done so. The infant should be taken to the local emergency department to be checked, even if the infant seems to be breathing well.

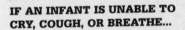

RESCUE BREATHING FOR ADULTS AND CHILDREN

The timing intervals for administering artificial respiration to adults and children are somewhat different, but the mechanics are the same

IF AN ADULT IS UNABLE TO BREATHE...

STEP 1. Begin by tilting the head back and lifting the chin to move the tongue away from the back of the throat. Pinch the nose shut.

STEP 2. Make a tight seal around the victim's mouth with your mouth. Breathe slowly into the victim until chest gently rises. Give two breaths, each lasting one to two seconds. Pause between breaths to let the air flow out.

STEP 3. Check for pulse after the two initial slow breaths.

IF PULSE IS PRESENT BUT PERSON IS STILL NOT BREATHING...

STEP 4. Give one slow breath about every five seconds. Do this for about one minute (12 breaths).

STEP 5. After 10 or 12 breaths, recheck pulse to make sure the heart is still beating. Check the pulse and breathing about every minute or 10 to 12 breaths.

CONTINUE rescue breathing as long as a pulse is present but the person is not breathing.

IF A CHILD IS UNABLE TO BREATHE...

STEP 1. Begin by tilting the head back and lifting the chin to move the tongue away from the back of the throat. Pinch the nose shut.

STEP 2. Make a tight seal around the victim's mouth with your mouth. Breathe slowly into the victim until chest gently rises. Give two breaths, each lasting one to two seconds. Pause between breaths to let the air flow out.

STEP 3. Check for pulse after the two initial slow breaths.

IF PULSE IS PRESENT BUT PERSON IS STILL NOT BREATHING...

STEP 4. Give one slow breath about every three seconds. Do this for about one minute (20 breaths).

STEP 5. Recheck pulse and breathing about every minute, or 20 breaths.

CALL the local emergency number if you have not already done so. Then, continue rescue breathing as long as a pulse is present but the child is not breathing.

RESCUE BREATHING FOR INFANTS

Because a baby's mouth is very small, you need to seal your mouth over both the infant's mouth and nose

IF AN INFANT IS NOT BREATHING...

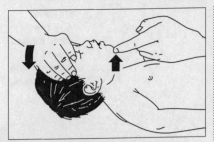

STEP 1. Begin by tilting the head back and lifting the chin to move the tongue away from the back of the throat.

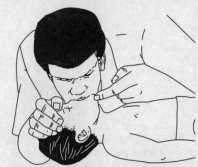

STEP 2. Make a tight seal around the infant's nose and mouth with your mouth.

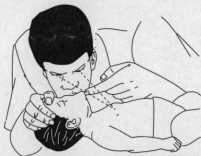

STEP 3. Breathe slowly into the victim until chest gently rises. Give two breaths, each lasting one to two seconds. Pause between breaths to let the air flow out.

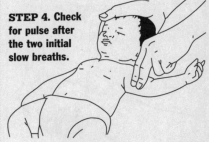

STEP 4. Check for pulse after the two initial slow breaths.

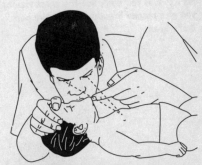

STEP 5. Give one slow breath about every three seconds. Do this for about one minute (20 breaths).

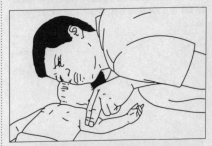

STEP 6. Recheck pulse and breathing about every minute. Call the local emergency number if you haven't already done so. Continue rescue breathing as long as a pulse is present but the child is not breathing.

CLEARING AN OBSTRUCTION WITH ABDOMINAL THRUSTS

When an unconscious person's airway is obstructed, getting air in is more important than removing the object

IF AIR DOES NOT GO IN...

STEP 1. If you don't see the chest rise as you give rescue breathing, retilt the person's head.

STEP 2. Give two breaths, each lasting one to two seconds. Pause between breaths to let the air flow out. If air still won't go in...

STEP 3. Straddling the victim's legs, place the heel of one hand just above the navel. Place your other hand on top of the first. Point the fingers of both hands toward the victim's head.

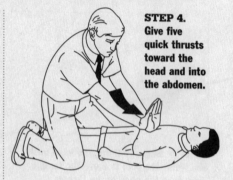

STEP 4. Give five quick thrusts toward the head and into the abdomen.

STEP 5. After giving five thrusts, lift the victim's lower jaw and tongue with your fingers and thumb. Slide one finger down the inside of the cheek and try to hook the object out.

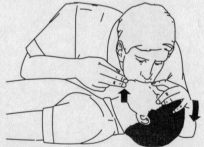

STEP 6. Tilt head back, lift chin, and give two slow breaths again. Repeat breaths, thrusts, and sweeps until breaths go in.

WHEN IT'S AN INFANT WITH THE BLOCKAGE

The technique for clearing an unconscious baby's airway is the same as for one who is choking

IF YOU ARE UNABLE TO BREATHE INTO AN INFANT...

STEP 1. Retilt the infant's head, lifting the chin.

STEP 2. Give two breaths again. If air still won't go in...

STEP 3. Position infant on forearm, then turn him facedown.

STEP 4. While holding infant facedown on forearm so that the head is lower than the chest, give five back blows with heel of hand between the infant's shoulder blades.

STEP 5. Holding the infant firmly between both forearms, turn the infant to a faceup position on forearm.

STEP 6. Give five chest thrusts on about the center of the breastbone.

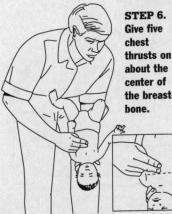

STEP 7. Lift the infant's lower jaw and tongue and check for object. Sweep one finger inside the mouth to hook the object out.

STEP 8. Tilt head back and give two breaths again. Repeat back blows, chest thrusts, sweeps, and breaths until breaths go in.

BASIC CPR FOR ADULTS AND CHILDREN

Give CPR when there is no breathing and no pulse. Without CPR, brain damage can set in within four minutes.

IF A PERSON IS NOT BREATHING AND HAS NO PULSE...

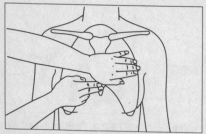

STEP 1. Find hand position–the notch where the ribs meet the lower breastbone. Place the heel of your hand on the breastbone just above your index finger.

STEP 2. Place your other hand on top of the first. Use the heel of your bottom hand to apply pressure on the breastbone. Position your shoulders directly over your hands with elbows locked. Press the chest down about two inches, and then release. Repeat 15 times keeping a smooth even rhythm.

STEP 3. Retilt the head, lift the chin and give two slow breaths.

STEP 4. Do three more sets of 15 compressions and 2 breaths. Each cycle takes about 15 seconds.

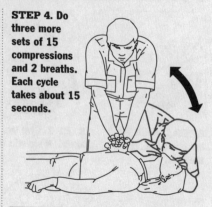

STEP 5. Recheck pulse and breathing for about five seconds. If there is no pulse...

STEP 6. Continue sets of 15 compressions and two breaths, pausing to check for pulse every few minutes. If you find a pulse, check breathing and give rescue breathing if necessary.

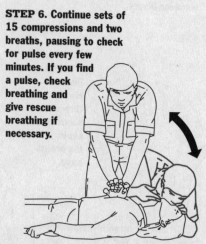

CPR FOR INFANTS HAS IMPORTANT DIFFERENCES

Babies require lighter chest pressure delivered in shorter, more frequent cycles than do older children and adults.

IF AN INFANT IS NOT BREATHING AND HAS NO PULSE...

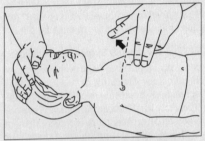

STEP 1. Place the infant on his or her back on a hard surface such as the floor or table. Place two fingers on the breastbone just below an imaginary line between the nipples.

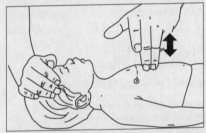

STEP 2. Give five compressions, about 3 seconds each. Count to help keep a regular, even rhythm.

STEP 3. Placing your mouth over the infant's mouth and nose, give one slow breath, about 1.5 seconds.

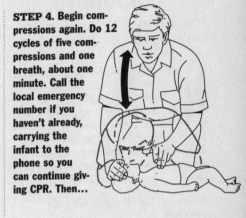

STEP 4. Begin compressions again. Do 12 cycles of five compressions and one breath, about one minute. Call the local emergency number if you haven't already, carrying the infant to the phone so you can continue giving CPR. Then...

STEP 5. Recheck pulse and breathing for about five seconds. If there is still no pulse...

STEP 6. Continue sets of five compressions and one breath. Recheck pulse and breathing every few minutes. Continue CPR until help arrives.

COPING WITH POISONING

Most cases involve children, but most deaths occur among adults

Ninety percent of all poisonings happen in the home. Most cases involve young children swallowing household or garden products or inappropriate medications. But the greatest number of fatalities involve adults and are frequently drug-related suicides. Here are the American Red Cross's suggestions on what to do in most cases of suspected poisoning.

■ **How can I tell if someone's been poisoned?**

The physical clues to poisoning include nausea, vomiting, diarrhea, pain in the chest or abdomen, difficulty breathing, sweating, seizures, and shifts in consciousness. When the victim is conscious and old enough to communicate, ask him or her what happened. When this is not possible, inspect the scene for clues. Do you see any open or overturned containers, any plants that don't look right, or any medicine cabinet that is opened? Are there any flames, smoke, or unusual smells?

■ **What if I strongly suspect a poisoning?**

Move the victim away from the poison source if necessary. Check his or her level of consciousness, breathing condition, and pulse. Treat any life-threatening factors. Then call a poison control center or emergency rescue with any information on what the victim may have been exposed to or swallowed.

■ **What if the poison has been swallowed?**

Never have a victim eat or drink unless medical professionals advise it. If you can't locate the poison source and the victim vomits, save some of the vomit for the hospital to test.

THE TRUTH ABOUT INSECT STINGS

A wasp or yellow jacket at a picnic could send you to the hospital

Insect stings are responsible for inducing severe allergic reactions in one to two million people in the United States every year. An estimated 3 percent of the population is susceptible to such a reaction, and about 50 deaths occur each year.

The usual reaction to an insect sting is mild redness and pain, which normally disappears within one to two hours without treatment. But people with immune systems that are sensitive to insect venom can have allergic reactions lasting as long as a full week.

A severe allergic reaction can produce symptoms that include dizziness, weakness, and nausea. Stomach cramps and diarrhea may occur, as well as generalized hives, itching, wheezing, mental confusion, shock, and, finally, unconsciousness—and death, if medical treatment is not obtained immediately.

In the past, the only products available for treatment were processed from the whole body of an insect. It was found, however, that these extracts did not contain enough pure venom for reliable diagnosis and treatment. Highly potent pure venoms are now available for most stinging insects. They are given in gradually stronger doses to stimulate the patient's immune system until it is able to become more resistant to the insect sting.

For those subject to severe reactions, a physician may recommend a self-treatment kit, containing a syringe with epinephrine (adrenaline), which works within minutes to tighten the blood vessels and keep the airways open.

If you know the poison, contact a poison control center for precise instructions on administering an antidote. If vomiting must be induced, syrup of ipecac is generally recommended. For someone over 12 years of age, the normal dosage is two tablespoons of syrup, followed by two glasses of water. For children under 12, the dosage normally is one tablespoon followed by two glasses of water. The intended result should come within 20 minutes.

■ When is inducing vomiting a bad idea?

Never induce vomiting when the victim has taken an acid or alkali, which can burn the esophagus, throat, and mouth tissues. The same is true for petroleum products such as gasoline or kerosene.

■ What is the role of activated charcoal in treating poisoning?

A solution made from activated charcoal is often used to help neutralize poison that remains in the stomach even after vomiting. The charcoal comes in both liquid and powder forms and is sold in pharmacies over the counter. The powder form needs mixing with water so that it becomes milk shake–like in its consistency. Young children have a hard time swallowing the mixture and often need it dispensed to them at a hospital.

■ How should toxic fumes be handled?

When the victim's skin is pale or bluish, it's a tip-off that toxic fumes may have been inhaled. The most common toxic fumes are carbon monoxide from car exhaust, carbon dioxide from wells or sewers, and chlorine from swimming pools. Glues, cleaning solvents, and paints also give off fumes, as do drugs such as crack cocaine. The most important thing you can do for a toxic-fume victim is to get the person to breathe fresh air as soon as possible. If the victim has lost consciousness, start rescue breathing.

■ How should chemicals on skin be handled?

Flush the area with running water and call the rescue service. If the chemical is dry and there's no water available, brush it off and see a doctor as soon as possible.

TREATING BURNS
Don't use ice unless it's slight

Burns are classified as first, second, or third degree by how deeply the skin is damaged. It's not always easy to tell how serious a burn is at first inspection. Electrical burns frequently look small, for instance, but they may be much deeper than suspected. You can't always tell how bad a burn is from pain, either, because really serious burns may destroy tissue nerve endings, leaving a victim with no feeling in the burned area. And burns whose severity is underestimated may end up needlessly infected. Here are the rules of the road when it comes to burns, courtesy of the American Red Cross.

■ **FIRST-DEGREE BURN.** A first-degree burn is on the skin's surface. It turns the skin red and dry, may cause swelling, and can be quite painful. The damage should heal within a week without leaving permanent scars.

■ **SECOND-DEGREE BURN.** A second-degree burn affects several top layers of skin, and not only reddens the skin but leaves blisters that may pop and leak clear fluid. Pain and swelling are common, and the burned skin sometimes appears blotchy. Healing usually takes three to four weeks.

■ **THIRD-DEGREE BURN.** A third-degree burn not only destroys every skin layer but goes deep enough to destroy other underlying tissue such as fat, muscles, nerves, and even bones sometimes. The pain can be intense to relatively minor if nerve endings are destroyed. Unless quickly treated, the risk of infection soars, and fluid loss can destroy the body's thermostat and impair breathing, making the situation potentially life-threatening.

CRIME FOILS

▼

A COP'S GUIDE TO HOME SECURITY

Know what crooks look for so you don't become a crime statistic

Washington, D.C., has the dubious distinction of being known as not only the nation's capital, but the country's crime capital as well. Not that the federal city has any monopoly on crime, of course; there is a burglary every 10 seconds in the United States. With the right knowledge, however, you can make your house far more crime-proof.

D.C. police officer Steven Jackson is the ultimate insider: His job is to teach ordinary citizens in Washington how to stay safe. He's analyzed the burglar's mind and warns, "The thief is riding around looking for people who are careless." Jackson's do's and don'ts of crime-fighting may seem simple, but they are often disregarded with disastrous consequences.

DO'S:

■ **Do** keep doors and windows locked, even when you're at home. Most burglars enter a home through the front door, either by breaking a lock or opening an unlocked door.

■ **Do** identify visitors through a peephole or window before letting someone in. Never allow a stranger in to use your phone. Instead, offer to call the police or tow truck.

Women who live alone should only list their last names and first initials on mailboxes, telephone directories, and doors.

■ **Do** make your house look occupied when you are away. Timed lights that go on before it gets dark are a good idea. Place a timer in the living room, kitchen, and main bedroom. When you go on vacation, have someone pick up your mail and newspapers. Parking a car in the driveway may suggest you are home, but it also leaves the car vulnerable. Put your car in the garage, if you have one.

■ **Do** vary your schedule. Don't jog, open the

LEAVING A CHILD HOME ALONE

Teaching kids how to deal with an emergency is the best way to avoid one

■ **To decide if a child is ready to be left home alone, ask yourself, can the child:**

- Be trusted to go straight home after school.
- Easily use the telephone, locks, and kitchen appliances.
- Stay alone without being afraid or lonely.

■ **Before leaving a child home alone, make sure he or she knows:**

- How to call your area's

emergency number.
- How to give directions to your home.
- How to use the door, window locks and alarm system if you have one.
- How to escape in case of fire.
- To check in with you or a neighbor after arriving home.
- To never accept gifts or rides from strangers.
- To never let anyone into the home without your permission.

- To never let a caller at the door or on the phone know they are alone (say, "Mom can't come to the phone now.").
- To not go into an empty house if things don't look right, such as a broken window, ripped screen, or open door.
- To let you know about anything that frightens them or makes them feel uncomfortable.

SOURCE: The National Crime Prevention Council, Washington, D.C.

door to pick up the paper, or do yard work every day at the same time. Criminals like to prey on victims who are easy to predict.

■ **Do** participate in a neighborhood watch program. Programs in which neighbors keep an eye on each other's houses can be very effective in deterring crime. Call your local police department for more information.

DON'TS:

■ **Don't** plant bushes around your front door. A criminal can hide in the bushes until someone comes home. Don't put a house key under an outside doormat, either. Instead, give a copy of your keys to a trusted neighbor.

■ **Don't** confuse your address when calling 911. The biggest problem with the emergency number is that people often don't know where they are when they call or don't give directions.

■ **Don't** forget your lines—or your exit strategy—if you are at home when a person with a weapon breaks in. If you feel the person is going to harm you, pretending to comply will give you some time to gain control and plot your escape route or determine what you can grab as a weapon.

A HOME IS WHERE YOU FEEL SAFE

Here are some simple steps you can take to make your home a castle:

1. Don't leave ladders or other tools outside where they can be used by an intruder to reach or pry open windows.

2. Outdoor lighting can be an effective deterrent. Install economical, high-pressure sodium lights. Motion detector spotlights also are good.

3. Keep your garage door locked at all times. If you have a door that opens mechanically, remove the disconnect rope from the bar when you're on vacation. If you have an electric door opener, turn the system off and put a padlock on the inside.

4. Put large, reflective numbers on your home or mailbox so police and other emergency vehicles can locate your home.

5. The weakest part of a door is where the locks are installed. Don't depend on door chains to keep out intruders. Invest in a door reinforcer such as the MAG Install-A-Lock. Install an anti-pry plate on the outside of the door. If there is glass within 40 inches of the lock, replace it with unbreakable glazing. Also install a wide-angle door viewer so you can see who is on the other side.

6. Prepare your master bedroom for use as an emergency refuge in the event that an intruder comes into your home while you are there. Install a solid wood door with a good lock. Equip the room with a phone, a fire extinguisher, first aid kit, and noisemaker.

7. Windows should be kept closed and locked. To make a lock for a double-sashed window, drill a hole at a slight downward angle where the sashes overlap and insert a sturdy eyebolt. To secure a single-sashed window, install a lock similar to a Blasi lock, two per window.

8. Sliding glass doors should be secured by a special steel or wood bar that you can buy at the hardware store to prevent jimmying or prying. Install a series of roundhead screws and angle irons to secure the stationary panel.

SOURCE: Adapted from "The 10-Minute Crime Safety Audit," Aetna Insurance Company and the National Crime Prevention Institute.

WHEN A WOLF IS AT YOUR THROAT

You up the odds of fending off an attacker when you have a plan

Remember the movie *Paper Chase*, in which the haughty Harvard law professor played by John Houseman told his first-year students on the first day of class to look to their left and then to their right because one or the other of their neighbors would not be graduating? Well, Houseman's character might better have told his class to consider that one out of three women in America will be attacked in her lifetime, according to the Justice Department.

It's no wonder that women—and men, too—are anxious about walking to their cars in parking lots, going somewhere by themselves at night, or even opening their front door at the end of the day. But no one wants to go through life being paranoid, and learning self-defense is a viable way to reach a balanced awareness.

The first step in self-defense, says Rosalind Wiseman, author of *Defending Ourselves* (Noonday Press, 1995), is to figure out a plan, whether it is running to safety or delivering a crippling blow. "Just as you have a fire escape plan in your house, you should have a plan for physical safety," she advises. Wiseman, who has a second-degree black belt in karate, is the founder of a self-defense school in Washington, D.C., called Woman's Way, where she trains everyone from Girl Scout troops to civil servants. "The techniques are easy—teaching your brain that you can do them is the hard part," says Wiseman. Her tips:

■ Women should be conscious of their body language when they are walking in public places. A confident stride, with eyes up and shoulders down, is preferable. Avoid carrying numerous bags or otherwise showing that you could not immediately fight back.

■ If a person stops you to ask for directions while you are walking, make sure you can see his feet in your peripheral vision. That means he's a safe distance away. If he asks you for help, volunteer to call the police rather than going anywhere with him.

■ Carrying Mace or pepper spray can be an effective defense tool, but only if you are both prepared to use it and have practiced. A can of Mace in your purse with a safety latch you've never tried isn't going to do you much good in an emergency.

■ If someone with a weapon demands your wallet, you should comply—whatever you have in there is not worth your life. Wiseman suggests throwing the wallet away from you at a 45-degree angle. When the attacker goes after it, run to safety. Go where other people are—to a neighbor, a store, a gas station, but be sure to think about your destination instead of running blindly. Without a plan, a woman robbed in a parking garage, for example, might run into a stairwell, setting herself up for a second attack.

■ If you are being followed, use verbal self-defense. State loudly and clearly what you want the person to do, such as: "Go away! Leave me alone!" Fighting back should only be used as a last resort, but it can be a very powerful tool because it greatly reduces your chances of being raped or otherwise harmed. Says Wiseman: "Most assailants aren't looking for someone who will be a tough fight."

■ If you are a woman fighting back, remember that your lower body is five times stronger than your upper body. When using self-defense techniques, aim for the attacker's eyes, nose, throat, groin, knees, or feet. If it seems you can't defend yourself— if the attacker has a knife to your throat, for example—try to lull the assailant into thinking he has control. Convince him he's got you but needs to put down the knife. When he does, strike.

SOME BASIC MOVES IN YOUR OWN DEFENSE

There are two times when experts say you should fight back physically right away. One is if the attacker has rope or duct tape or another means of tying your hands and feet, which will probably make it impossible for you to escape. The other is if someone wants to take you somewhere else; chances of surviving are lower if you are moved to a second location.

■ **A FRONTAL ATTACK.** The palm strike has the power of a punch but reduces injury to your hand and fingers. The primary target is the nose, but you can hit the mouth, chin, throat, ear, or Adam's apple.

■ The proper hand position is shown at far left.
■ Strike quickly and return quickly to prevent the attacker from swatting or grabbing your hand. Don't telegraph your intentions (i.e., don't let him see you *preparing* to strike). The element of surprise is critically important in self-defense.

■ **CLOSE QUARTERS.** You can use your knee if you are at a close distance to the attacker. The two main targets with the knee are the attacker's groin and his head.

■ As you knee the groin, pull the attacker toward you. At the same time, pull your body to his side to minimize his ability to strike you.
■ A knee to the head is for when his body is partially bent—for example, after he's been kneed in the groin. To do this, hold the attacker's head with both hands as you would a basketball.

■ **ATTACKS FROM BEHIND.** If you are attacked from behind or the side, you need to break the attacker's hold and create space between you. When you are touched, immediately yell and round your shoulders to protect your lungs and sternum.

■ Crossing your wrists in front of you will help you round your shoulders, minimizing injury to your upper body from the force of someone grabbing you from behind.
■ Then look for his closest foot and stomp on it. For best results, stomp across (not parallel to) his foot. If you stomp hard enough, you might break a bone, making it difficult for him to chase you.

SOURCE: *Defending Ourselves*, Rosalind Wiseman (Noonday Press, 1995), reprinted by permission.

EXPERT Q & A

GETTING READY FOR THE BIG ONE

Not a Californian? The biggest U.S. quake ever was in Missouri

The sheer force of the earth's shifting tectonic plates is tough to imagine. Most people don't realize that 39 states are at risk from earthquakes, and the threat isn't confined to towns on fault lines. Carl Mortensen, a geophysicist with the U.S. Geological Survey in California, fields questions for an earthquake hotline in Menlo Park, California. Here are some of the most important answers he has provided:

■ **Where are earthquakes most likely to hit?**

California, of course, is the most at risk—the San Francisco Bay area and Los Angeles represent the greatest urban earthquake threats. Seattle could also be at risk for a sizable earthquake in the next 30 years, and Alaska has had its share of earthquakes in Fairbanks, Anchorage, and the Aleutian Islands. But most people don't realize that the biggest earthquake in the United States was in New Madrid, Missouri, in 1811. It caused so much disturbance that the Mississippi River's current ran in another direction. In the early 19th century, Charleston, South Carolina, also got hit hard. There have also been some small earthquakes in upstate New York, but they're more of a curiosity.

■ **How does the system for measuring earthquake strength work?**

The Richter scale is actually a pretty arbitrary, old-fashioned scale. We now use a new magnitude rating system that ranges roughly from zero to 10. There's such a huge range of amplitudes for earthquakes that we use logarithms—that is, a one is ten times more powerful than a zero on the scale, while a two is 100 times more powerful than zero. So when you get into the sevens, those are powerful earthquakes. Anything above an eight is considered a "great" earthquake. The earthquake in Kobe, Japan, in 1995 was a 6.9. The San Francisco earthquake of 1906 was a 7.8. The last great earthquake in the U.S. was in Alaska in 1964. The largest recorded reading was in Chile in 1960—it reached over 9 in magnitude.

■ **How long do aftershocks last?**

We know that there's only so much energy that an earthquake can expend, through the size of the fault and the strength of the rock. Depending on how big the quake is, aftershocks can last 9 or 10 years. Typically, in California for example, a magnitude seven earthquake, like San Francisco in 1989, can have aftershocks for 7 or 8 years. Most people might feel one but not associate it with an earthquake that happened a few years ago and think of it as a minor quake, and not what it is—an aftershock.

■ **Who needs to worry about tsunamis?**

Anyone along the coast, particularly in Hawaii and Northern California. Tsunamis, giant sea waves caused by earthquakes, can travel through the ocean at a speed of 600 mph and they travel far. Earthquakes in Alaska have caused tsunamis in Crescent City, California.

■ **What should be done to prepare for an earthquake?**

The collapse of a house isn't very likely, unless the house is located near a ledge where a landslide is possible. Fire as a result of ripping a gas line or shaking water heaters is much more likely. So the first step you should take if you live in an earthquake-prone area is to find and repair faulty electrical wiring, leaky gas, and inflexible utility connections. Bolt down water heaters and gas appliances, and put heavy objects on lower shelves, then fasten the shelves to the walls. Store bottled foods, glass, and china on low shelves that can be fastened shut. If you live in apartments built before the 1980s,

EARLY WARNINGS PREVENT FIRE TRAGEDIES

Each year, fires kill 5,500 Americans and injure 30,000. The flames are less dangerous than the super-hot air that can sear your lungs, or the poisonous smoke and gases that make you drowsy and disoriented. Here are some tips from the U.S. Fire Administration to make sure you're never trapped in a burning house:

■ **Put smoke detectors on every floor of your house.** Smoke detectors double your chances of living through a fire. They should be near bedrooms and away from air vents. To ensure that they're not shielded from smoke, keep them at least four to six inches away from walls and corners. Replace batteries at least once a year, at the same time perhaps as you're changing clocks for daylight savings.

■ **Ask your local fire department to inspect your house for fire safety.** Often, local fire houses provide the service. They could help you identify faulty furnaces or stoves, chimneys with buildup, and places where home insulation is touch-ing electrical wiring—all potential fire-starters. They can also give you advice on choosing and using fire extinguishers.

■ **Don't overlook basic fire hazards.** Be wary of frayed or cracked wiring, and don't put wiring under rugs, over nails, or in high traffic areas. Avoid overloading outlets—if you're not sure, check to make sure they're staying cool to the touch. Never fill kerosene heaters with gasoline or camp stove fuel. Plug electric space heaters directly into the wall socket, not into extension cords. For woodstoves and fireplaces, use only seasoned wood, and always use a protective screen. Don't let old newspapers and maga-zines accumulate in storage areas. In the kitchen, keep appliances free of crumbs and grease.

■ **Plan your escape before the emergency.** If you have children, teach them two escape routes from every room. Keep emergency numbers, a whistle, and a flashlight near the phone. Sleeping with doors closed helps delay the spread of fire. If you hear the alarm, feel your door. If it's cool, open it to exit, but crawl to avoid the smoke that rises. Stop, drop, and roll if your clothes are on fire—teach it to your kids. If you're trapped in a room, hang a white sheet or light-colored material outside the window so firefighters can locate you.

there are engineering retrofits that can fix "soft" first floors — buildings with garages on the first floor, where the foundation would be most likely to collapse. You may want to check to see if your building has had that done. If you live in a house, make sure you have it anchored to your foundation.

■ **Where are the most dangerous places to be in a quake?**

In your home, it's a bad idea to be near anything that can topple over, like tall bookcases, and light fixtures that can fall. You should also stay away from windows where the glass can shatter, and from fireplaces—the brick or stone could crumble. If you're inside, get under a sturdy desk, table, or bench, or hold on to an inside wall. In crowded public places, don't rush for a doorway, since other people will be doing the same thing. Take cover and move away from display shelves and anything else that could fall on you. Stay on the same floor, and don't use elevators. If you're outside, stay there. Move away from buildings, street lights, and utility poles and wires.

WHEN A TWISTER ISN'T ON FILM

Get to the lowest floor, crawl under a table away from windows

Tornadoes are nature's most violent and erratic storms, as the movie *Twister* dramatized. In an average year, 800 tornadoes are reported nationwide, according to the Federal Emergency Management Agency, and 80 people die and 1,500 are injured as a result of twisters. The most violent of these storms are capable of reaching wind speeds of 250 mph or more, creating damage paths that can be over one mile wide and 50 miles long.

Mike Aculow is the Warning Coordination Meteorologist for the National Weather Service in Topeka, Kansas, in charge of severe weather programs. A seasoned tornado veteran, Aculow has, in his 25 years with the National Weather Service, trained tornado spotters, inspected damage sites, and experienced the storm's forces firsthand. In 1983, his house was destroyed by a tornado—Aculow wasn't home. His tornado tips:

■ **Plan ahead no matter where you live.** You are at greatest risk for tornadoes if you live in the Midwest, particularly in the plains and the Mississippi Valley, but during the spring and summer, tornadoes have been spotted across the United States. The Northeast is least likely to be hit by tornadoes—Maine had 82 between 1950 and 1995, compared to Texas's 5,490. Alaska, with one recorded tornado in 45 years, and the District of Columbia, with zero, have the best tornado track records. But tornadoes do hit cities, the worst-hit ever being Topeka, Kansas, in 1966.

■ **Know the warning signs.** Regardless of where you are, tornadoes rarely arrive unannounced. There's usually thunder, light-ning and dark skies. Figure out ahead of time where you would seek shelter if a tornado occurs, and practice this emergency maneuver with your family on a sunny day. Be sure to keep on hand the call numbers for your severe weather station. If you have a special weather radio, you'll find warnings between 162.400 and 162.55 on the dial. Since this band isn't available on most radios, know where the closest local station is, and tune in—this is particularly helpful if you are in a car, or have already sought shelter in a room where television is unavailable and you need a tornado update.

■ **Understand the difference between tornado watches and tornado warnings.** Communities issue tornado watches when the weather is favorable for the formation of tornadoes, particularly during severe thunderstorms. Tornado warnings are released after a funnel cloud has been sighted, or after a radar has picked it up.

■ **Don't open your windows to equalize pressure in the house.** This is one of the biggest myths of tornado preparation. Houses cannot explode from pressure, and letting in strong winds can cause additional damage.

■ **Get to the lowest floor of the building you're in.** But don't get caught in an elevator trying to do it. If the building has no basement, find the bathroom. The pipes in the walls usually reinforce the building structure. Be sure to avoid windows—flying glass is a major cause of tornado injury.

■ **Find a heavy table or workbench to get under.** If you have no basement, go to an inside room on the lowest floor, like a closet, hallway, or bathroom with no windows. If possible, cover your body with a blanket, sleeping bag, or pillows to protect yourself from fallling debris. Again, stay away from windows.

■ **Escape to the east if you're in a car and have time.** Tornadoes generally run from west to east. If the storm is over a mile away, drive away from it, heading east or south. As it nears, however, do not stay in your car, and do not seek shelter under any car, bus, or truck.

EXPERT TIPS

PREPARING FOR A HURRICANE

As hurricanes approach the coast, a huge dome of water called a storm surge crashes into the coastline—9 out of 10 people killed in hurricanes are victims of these storm surges. Jerry Jarrell, the Deputy Director of the National Hurricane Center in Miami, has the following tips for minimizing your risks of injury:

To be considered a hurricane, a tropical storm must make winds that reach speeds of at least 74 mph and blow counterclockwise around a center eye. Hurricane winds have been clocked at 155 mph, and the combination of the winds and torrential rains can spawn tornadoes and cause severe flooding, affecting areas hundreds of miles inland. Know what the evacuation plan is for your family, and include one for the family pet.

■ **Know how little time a hurricance watch or warning gives you.** If a hurricane watch is issued, you have 24 to 36 hours before the hurricane hits land. A hurricane warning means that hurricane winds and storm tides are expected in a specific coastal area within 24 hours. A NOAA Weather Radio with a warning alarm and battery back-up is useful in case the power goes out.

■ **Ask your local emergency management office about community evacuation plans.** Learn your evacuation routes, and plan a place for your family to meet in case you are separated. As part of this plan, choose an out-of-state contact for everyone to call and say they're okay.

■ **Cover your windows.** People who live in Florida, Texas, and along the Gulf Coast should have shutters in their homes. If you don't have them, you should cover your windows with 5/8-inch marine plywood, cut to fit and ready to install. Put some sort of slugs in the wall, or lagbolts, to secure the wood.

■ **If you live right on the ocean, go inland.** Fill up your car's gas tank ahead of time if there's a chance you might need to evacuate. Once the storm has arrived, service stations may be closed.

■ **Know how to shut off your utilities.** It's important that you know where the shut-off devices are for the gas, plumbing, and electrical lines in the house. Before leaving your home, turn these systems off.

■ **Make arrangements for housing your pets.** Many emergency shelters don't allow pets. Call your local humane society for more information.

High-force winds can easily lift cars—even 18-wheelers. The most dangerous place to be during a tornado is in a car or under one.

■ **Find a gully, ditch, or low spot on the ground if you are caught outside.** Lie flat and put your arms over your head. If possible, cover yourself with a blanket or sweater. Culverts, the drainage pipes that run under roads, are good places to be if you're caught outside. Boards and stones whipped around at high speeds become quite dangerous. Flying pieces of glass and metal are like razors when they're caught by tornado winds. The winds are just unimaginably strong, and I've heard stories of people who were picked up by tornadoes and carried several miles from where they were.

SURVIVING A DELUGE

Floods cause more damage nationwide than any other natural disaster. Often the result of hurricanes, floods occur most frequently during the hurricane season, which runs roughly from July through November. Here are some tips from the Federal Emergency Management Agency (FEMA) to help you survive the rising waters and minimize flood damage to your home.

BEFORE THE FLOOD

■ Make an itemized list of your furnishings, clothing, and valuables. Photos can help insurance adjusters settle your claims, as well as help you verify uninsured losses, which are tax deductible.

■ Keep your insurance policies and the inventory of your personal property in a secure place, such as a safety-deposit box.

DURING THE FLOOD

■ Have a battery-operated radio on hand and keep it tuned to a local station for announcements regarding evacuation plans.

■ Turn off all utilities at the main switch. Do not touch electrical equipment unless it is dry or you are standing on a piece of dry wood and are wearing rubber gloves and rubber footwear.

■ Open basement windows to equalize the water pressure on the foundation and walls.

■ If you are caught in the house and flood waters are suddenly rising around your house, move to the second floor and, if necessary, to the roof. Take warm clothing, a flashlight, and the radio with you. Do not try to swim to safety.

■ If you evacuate your home, avoid areas that are already flooded. Do not attempt to cross any stretch of flood waters on foot if the water is above your knees.

■ Do not drive through flooded roads. Rapidly rising water could carry your car away, possibly trapping you inside.

■ Be careful if you must evacuate at night, when flooded areas are harder to see. If your car stalls, get out and climb to higher ground.

AFTER THE FLOOD

■ Call your insurance broker, and have your policy and list of posessions handy. Take pictures of the damage to your house and its contents.

■ Before you enter your house, get an expert's opinion to be sure that there is no structural damage that may cause it to collapse.

■ Once inside, open windows and doors to let air circulate and protect you from escaping gas. During this time, do not strike any matches or use open flames.

■ Make sure the electrical current is turned off. Do not turn on any electrical appliances until an electrician has inspected your system.

■ Throw out perishable foods; they may be contaminated. Hose down major appliances and furniture; keep everything until the adjuster has completed an inspection.

■ Pump out the basement if there is standing water. To minimize structural damage, drain only one third of the water each day.

■ Shovel out mud while it is still moist; dry rugs and carpets thoroughly.

WALKING AWAY FROM A CRASH

An airplane crash survivor shares lessons she learned

Robin Fech was the only flight attendant aboard a 30-seat twin-engine Atlantic Southeast Airlines turboprop on August 21, 1995. That was the day it careened to the ground, crashed, and burst into flames on a Georgia hayfield, killing 8 of the 27 people on board. The surviving passengers praised Fech's remarkable composure, crediting her ability to maintain calm and order as the reason they came out of the crash alive. Fech has thought a lot about her ordeal, and here she offers advice on safety measures to take before flying, during a troubled flight, and in the aftermath of a crash.

■ **WEAR LOOSE-FITTING COTTON CLOTHING.** Jogging pants may not be fashionable, Fech notes, but they allow you ease of movement and removal. And opt for natural fibers. "Synthetic materials are often highly flammable. People who are really concerned about crashing don't wear nail polish, hair spray, or perfume, which are also flammable," she explains. Fech would add tennis shoes to that list. In the crash, she spotted a man whose jeans were on fire, but she couldn't remove them because the soles of his shoes had melted and stuck to his feet. She herself was wearing panty hose, which melted on her legs.

Fech recommends comfortable, flat shoes that are easy to slip off, yet offer support to your feet if you need to climb, for example.

■ **AS YOU BOARD A PLANE, LOOK AROUND.** Touch the seats and count them until you reach yours. This helps you to feel your way out in case of darkness or smoke. Locate not only the exit nearest you, but alternates as well. "Our passenger door wouldn't open," Fech recalls,

"but in our case, we didn't really need the exit, because the plane had split in half."

■ **PAY CLOSE ATTENTION DURING THE SAFETY DEMONSTRATION.** "Frequent-flyers are the worst offenders," says Fech. "Some of the survivors on our flight later remembered that they were reading their books instead of paying attention to the safety demonstration." Fortunately, Fech had time to demonstrate the crash position before the plane hit the ground: lean forward, cross your arms on the seat in front of you, and place your hands on your arms. If there's room in front of you, grab your ankles, put your chest on your thigh and your head between your knees. The intent is to lean forward as much as possible. Seat belts should be low and tight. Legs should be uncrossed and both feet should be flat on the floor.

Fech also asked passengers to empty their pockets; items there could cause injury upon impact. "Anything in your lap, like a computer, becomes a flying javelin," says Fech. Things like eyeglasses, pens, and pencils, should be removed and put in the seat pocket.

■ **USE COMMON SENSE AND TRY TO STAY CALM.** The same rules of escaping a house fire or some other emergency also apply to plane crashes. Most likely, the plane will be very smoky upon impact, and fires are common. "The emergency lighting system is a godsend, but it could still be pitch-black," says Fech. "Follow the lights, stay low, and crawl out on your hands and knees. Get out calmly and quickly."

■ **PREPARE TO BE DISORIENTED.** "It's probably the last thing you can prepare for," says Fech, "but you're going to be disoriented. I was unconscious for several minutes. Also, in our case, the back half of the plane rolled on its side, so there were people hanging from their seatbelts sideways, looking at other people down below them."

■ **MAINTAIN CONTACT WITH OTHER SURVIVORS.** Finally, says Fech, "I highly suggest getting together with others who shared your experience in the aftermath. It's helped me. It helps put all the pieces together and to deal with the disbelief and the grief."

CITIZEN'S GUIDE

CITIZENSHIP
▼

PROUD TO BE AN AMERICAN

How to become a citizen, get a passport, register to vote or for the draft

Who is an American? Certainly not everyone who lives in the United States. The population of the U.S. is now 261 million. But only about 241 million are citizens. If one of your parents is an American citizen, no matter where you're born, you're entitled to claim American citizenship. Even if your parents are not Americans but you were lucky enough to be born on American soil, you can claim citizenship. Otherwise, the process of applying for citizenship can be a lot more complex and rigorous. (See how to become a U.S. citizen, below.) But it's not impossible. The melting pot is still simmering. In 1996 alone, more than 1 million immigrants became U.S. citizens. Today, almost 20 million American residents, 8 percent of the population, were born outside of the U.S., up from 14 million in 1980.

Being an American—especially if you take the obligations of citizenship seriously—can be a time-consuming endeavor. Most important, you get to vote—in federal, state, and local elections. You're eligible for Social Security. All citizens and non-citizens who are residents of the U.S. are required, of course, to pay taxes. You can, if you so choose, volunteer to serve in the U.S. armed forces. Whether or not you intend to volunteer, all males at 18 years old have to register for the military. American citizens also have the right and privilege of serving on jury duty (see page 745). Here's a citizen's guide to being a citizen.

HOW TO BECOME A U.S. CITIZEN

An immigrant must meet several criteria in order to become a citizen: live in the U.S. for five years (three years for spouses of U.S. citizens), be conversant in English, and have a general knowledge of the principles of American government. Applications are available at the local office of the Immigration and Naturalization Service (INS).

People who are over 50 and have been permanent residents of the U.S. for 20 years, or who are over 55 and have been permanent residents for 20 years, are exempt from being tested on their English skills. However, everyone must pass the citizenship exam. You can take the test as many times as you need to. The test includes questions on the three branches of government and voting requirements.

There are prep courses for the test through public schools, community and private groups, as well as by mail. The federal goverment also publishes citizenship study guides containing all of the information that appears on the citizenship test. They are

THE STATUE OF LIBERTY

This monument, designed by Frédéric-Auguste Bartholdi, was a gift from France in 1886. On its base is engraved a sonnet by Emma Lazarus entitled "The New Colossus." For years it greeted immigrants passing through the New York City harbor to Ellis Island.

NOT LIKE THE BRAZEN GIANT OF GREEK FAME,
WITH CONQUERING LIMBS ASTRIDE FROM LAND TO LAND,
HERE AT OUR SEA-WASHED, SUNSET GATES SHALL STAND
A MIGHTY WOMAN WITH A TORCH, WHOSE FLAME
IS THE IMPRISONED LIGHTNING, AND HER NAME
MOTHER OF EXILES. FROM HER BEACON-HAND
GLOWS WORLD-WIDE WELCOME; HER MILD EYES COMMAND
THE AIR-BRIDGED HARBOR THAT TWIN CITIES FRAME.
"KEEP ANCIENT LANDS, YOUR STORIED POMP!" CRIES SHE
WITH SILENT LIPS. "GIVE ME YOUR TIRED, YOUR POOR,
YOUR HUDDLED MASSES YEARNING TO BREATHE FREE,
THE WRETCHED REFUSE OF YOUR TEEMING SHORE.
SEND THESE, THE HOMELESS, TEMPEST-TOST TO ME,
I LIFT MY LAMP BESIDE THE GOLDEN DOOR!"

available from the Superintendent of Documents, Government Printing Office, Washington, DC 20402.

■ **GREEN CARDS.** Officially known as the Alien Registration Receipt Card (Form I-551), green cards are issued to anyone who has become a permanent resident. They are valid for 10 years. Legal immigrants must present them when applying for jobs, and for state and federal entitlements, and when they reenter the United States. Curiously, green cards are no longer green. In 1996, the color was changed to pink. All green cards and alien registration cards issued before 1979 are no longer valid.

■ **FINAL STEPS TO CITIZENSHIP.** After legal immigrants have lived in the U.S. for a minimum of five years without being jailed for over 180 days, or convicted of an aggravated felony or murder, and have passed the citizenship tests and interviews with an INS officer, there is a further 30-day wait before you can become a citizen. If your application is approved, you take the Oath of Allegiance, agreeing to defend the Constitution and fight in wars.

SOCIAL SECURITY CARDS

Social Security cards are a relatively recent invention. The Social Security Administration came into existence in 1935, in the midst of the Great Depression. You need a Social Security number to open a bank account, buy savings bonds, or apply for some kinds of government services for your child. Legal immigrants are also entitled to Social Security, and need a number to receive benefits.

Since 1985, any child you claim as a dependent on your income tax return must have a Social Security number. The easiest way for a child to get a number is at birth. When your hospital asks for the information needed to complete your newborn's birth certificate, ask to have your state's vital statistics office share that information with the Social Security Administration. A Social Security card will be mailed to you directly.

If you decide to wait or your child does not yet have a number, you can get one by contacting the nearest Social Security office. You will then be asked to provide evidence that you are the child's parent or legal custodian, and furnish a birth certificate with proof of your child's age, identity, and citizenship.

To replace a lost Social Security card, change the name on your card, or request a new card, call Social Security (☎800–772–1213) for an appointment with your local office.

REGISTERING TO VOTE

Registering to vote recently became easier for residents of 46 states to whom the 1995 Motor Voter bill applies. The law mandates states to allow eligible voters to register by mail, at motor vehicle registries (hence the name), and at certain other state agencies including bureaus of public assistance. Minnesota, Wisconsin, and Wyoming were exempt from the law because they already offer same-day registration on Election Day. North Dakota, which does not register its small voting population, also was exempt.

Eligible voters should contact their State Secretary's office, town hall or county election office, or local League of Women Voters branch for more information. For those who are housebound or will be out of their district on voting day, absentee ballots usually are available from the same sources.

MAKING A CAMPAIGN CONTRIBUTION

Money seems to amplify the voice of the electorate substantially, so you may want to consider supporting the candidate that supports your views. But before you write a check to your favorite candidate or political party, be aware of federal election laws. Individuals may give no more than as follows: $1,000 to each candidate or candidate committee in an election (primaries and general elections count separately); $20,000 to a national party committee per calendar year, and $5,000 to any other political committee per calendar year. Foreign nationals are prohibited from donating to campaigns in the United States. For more information, contact the Federal Election Commission, ☎ 800–424–9530.

REGISTERING FOR THE DRAFT

By their 18th birthday, all young men must register for selective service. In the event of a national draft, names from the Selective Service System are drawn to provide additional soldiers needed to fight wars. Men remain on the list until they turn 26.

Registration forms are available at local post offices and high schools. You must sign the form in the presence of a postal clerk, show identification, and have the post office stamp the form. A postal clerk can mail it for you, or you can drop the form into any mail box without an envelope or stamp.

You should receive a registration acknowledgment in 90 days, and if you don't, it is your responsibility to contact the Selective Service System (☎ 847–688–6888).

GETTING A PASSPORT

It is illegal to leave or enter the country without a valid passport, and getting a passport is so time-consuming that it's best to apply several months before your departure. If you need visas from foreign embassies, you should allow even more time. Also, some countries require that your passport be valid at least 6 months beyond the date of your stay. Check with the country's nearest embassy or consulate before you plan your trip.

If you have never had a passport, apply in person at a post office or in one of the 13 passport agencies across the country. Complete the DSP-11 application form and bring proof of U.S. citizenship, such as a certified copy of your birth certificate or a Certificate of Naturalization.

You must also bring two 2x2-inch photographs, taken within the past 6 months. They may be color or black and white but must have a plain light background and show a frontal view of your face. Also, bring a picture ID, including a valid driver's license, government or military ID, or previous passport. The fee is $65 for a 10-year passport, or $40 for a 5-year passport. Make your check or money order payable to Passport Services.

If you are renewing an expired passport, the process is easier. You may apply by mail if your passport was issued within the past 12 years and you were over 18 when you received it. You can get an application form from your post office or travel agent. Attach your most recent passport, two identical passport photos, and a $55 check or money order, and mail to: National Passport Center, P.O. Box 371971, Pittsburgh, PA 15250–7971. Your old passport will be returned with your new one.

EXPERT Q & A

JURY DUTY: THE WHOLE TRUTH

O.J.'s consultant reveals the ins and outs of serving on a jury

To meet your civic responsibility when you get a summons for jury duty, work and family schedules often need to be revised. As O.J. Simpson's jury consultant in the criminal trial, Jo-Ellan Dimitrius of Forensic Technologies, Inc., advised Simpson's lawyers on which potential jury members were most likely to give their client a fair hearing. Here, she sheds some light on what to expect when you receive a summons.

■ **What should people know when they show up for jury duty?**

Jurors have the right to ask questions: what days will we have off, will I be sequestered, will I remain anonymous? Also, if you anticipate legitimate conflicts, like a long-planned family vacation, the court may be able to work around them.

■ **Who makes the best jurors for criminal and civil cases?**

For a defendant in a criminal trial, or a plaintiff in a civil trial, you look for jurors who are liberal. Someone who is a member of the Sierra Club or of PETA (People for the Ethical Treatment of Animals), for example, or church members and minorities. For defendants in civil cases, or prosecutors in criminal cases, you look for the more conservative, older jurors, perhaps someone who had been the victim of a crime.

In all cases, you want to have one or two firm, authoritarian types who will lead in your direction during the deliberation process. And for the rest you want followers who will listen.

■ **What is the surest way to get excused from jury duty?**

It raises red flags anytime a juror walks in with sunglasses on, anytime anyone's hiding their eyes. I avoid jurors who give very brief answers on the questionnaire and during oral questioning. It makes me wonder what they are trying to hide. I look at body language—there have been times when jurors are giving me a positive response, but shaking their heads no. Also, the way they talk about the defendant. During the O.J. trial, for example, a juror was referring to Simpson as "the incarcerated"—not a good sign.

Finally, I'll avoid a person who clearly doesn't want to be there. We've had people make up weak excuses, like their dog is sick, and when it's clear they don't want to be there, the last thing I want to do is to put that person in the jury box.

FACT FILE:

WE, THE JURY

■ *An estimated 150,000 civil and criminal jury trials go on each year in state and federal courts.*

■ *Some 12 million people are notified to serve on jury duty each year. Of those, some 4.5 million report to courthouses. The rest cannot be located or are excused.*

■ *Roughly 1.5 million are actually sworn in as jurors.*

■ *Jury trials last an average 4 to 5 days nationwide, except in California, where they are slightly longer.*

■ *Juries prefer not to give out death penalties. Support for the death penalty drops from 77 percent to 41 percent if the alternative is a life sentence without parole.*

SOURCE: National Center for State Courts; Death Penalty Information Center.

A PARADE OF PRESIDENTS

So far, seventeen of the presidents served more than one term.

PRESIDENT	VICE PRESIDENT	TERM OF OFFICE		PARTY	AGE AT INAUG.
1. George Washington	John Adams	April 30, 1789	March 3, 1797	Federalist	57
2. John Adams	Thomas Jefferson	March 4, 1797	March 3, 1801	Federalist	61
3. Thomas Jefferson	Aaron Burr George Clinton	March 4, 1801	March 3, 1809	Dem.-Rep.	57
4. James Madison	Elbridge Gerry	March 4, 1809	March 3, 1817	Dem.-Rep.	57
5. James Monroe	Daniel D. Tompkins	March 4, 1817	March 3, 1825	Dem.-Rep.	58
6. John Quincy Adams	John C. Calhoun	March 4, 1825	March 3, 1829	Dem.-Rep.	57
7. Andrew Jackson	Martin Van Buren	March 4, 1829	March 3, 1837	Democrat	61
8. Martin Van Buren	Richard M. Johnson	March 4, 1837	March 3, 1841	Democrat	54
9. William Henry Harrison	John Tyler	March 4, 1841	April 4, 1841	Whig	68
10. John Tyler [1]		April 6, 1841	March 3, 1845	Whig	51
11. James K. Polk	George M. Dallas	March 4, 1845	March 3, 1849	Democrat	49
12. Zachary Taylor	Millard Fillmore	March 5, 1849	July 9, 1850	Whig	64
13. Millard Fillmore [1]		July 10, 1850	March 3, 1853	Whig	50
14. Franklin Pierce	William R. King	March 4, 1853	March 3, 1857	Democrat	48
15. James Buchanan	John C. Breckinridge	March 4, 1857	March 3, 1861	Democrat	65
16. Abraham Lincoln	Hannibal Hamlin Andrew Johnson [2]	March 4, 1861	April 15, 1865	Republican	52
17. Andrew Johnson [1]		April 15, 1865	March 3, 1869	Democrat	56
18. Ulysses S. Grant	Schuyler Colfax Henry Wilson	March 4, 1869	Nov. 22, 1875	Republican	46
19. Rutherford B. Hayes	William A. Wheeler	March 4, 1877	March 3, 1881	Republican	54
20. James A. Garfield	Chester A. Arthur	March 4, 1881	Sept. 19, 1881	Republican	49
21. Chester A. Arthur [1]		Sept. 20, 1881	March 3, 1885	Republican	50
22. Grover Cleveland	Thomas A. Hendricks	March 4, 1885	March 3, 1889	Democratic	47
23. Benjamin Harrison	Levi P. Morton	March 4, 1889	March 3, 1893	Republican	55
24. Grover Cleveland	Adlai E. Stevenson	March 4, 1893	March 3, 1897	Democrat	55
25. William McKinley	Garret A. Hobart Theodore Roosevelt	March 4, 1897	March 3, 1901	Republican	54
26. Theodore Roosevelt [1]	Charles W. Fairbanks	March 4, 1901	March 3, 1909	Republican	42
27. William Howard Taft	James S. Sherman	March 4, 1909	March 3, 1913	Republican	51
28. Woodrow Wilson	Thomas R. Marshall	March 4, 1913	March 3, 1921	Democrat	56
29. Warren G. Harding	Calvin Coolidge	March 4, 1921	Aug. 2, 1923	Republican	55
30. Calvin Cooolidge [1]	Charles G. Dawes	Aug. 3, 1923	March 3, 1929	Republican	51
31. Herbert Hoover	Charles Curtis	March 4, 1929	March 3, 1933	Republican	54
32. Franklin D. Roosevelt	John N. Garner Henry A. Wallace Harry S Truman	March 4, 1933	April 12, 1945	Democrat	51
33. Harry S Truman	Alben W. Barkley	April 12, 1945	Jan. 20, 1953	Democrat	60
34. Dwight D. Eisenhower	Richard M. Nixon	Jan. 20, 1953	Jan. 20, 1961	Republican	62
35. John F. Kennedy	Lyndon B. Johnson	Jan. 20, 1961	Nov. 22, 1963	Democrat	43
36. Lyndon B. Johnson [1]	Hubert H. Humphrey	Nov. 22, 1963	Jan. 20, 1969	Democrat	55
37. Richard M. Nixon	Spiro T. Agnew Gerald Ford	Jan. 20, 1969	Aug. 9, 1974	Republican	56
38. Gerald Ford [1]	Nelson Rockefeller	Aug. 9, 1974	Jan. 20, 1977	Republican	61
39. James Earl Carter	Walter F. Mondale	Jan. 20, 1977	Jan. 20, 1981	Democrat	52
40. Ronald Reagan	George Bush	Jan. 20, 1981	Jan. 20, 1989	Republican	69
41. George Bush	Dan Quayle	Jan. 20, 1989	Jan. 20, 1993	Republican	64
42. William J. Clinton	Al Gore	Jan. 20, 1993		Democrat	46

1. Term includes part of predecessor's term. 2. A Democrat elected as vice-president with the Republican Lincoln on the National Union ticket.

BEST PRESIDENTIAL BIOGRAPHIES

Historian and biographer Arthur J. Schlesinger, Jr., picks his favorites

Our greatest presidents served their citizens well and have been well served by scholars. Distinguished historian Arthur J. Schlesinger, Jr., has penned books about Andrew Jackson, Franklin Delano Roosevelt, and John F. Kennedy. Schlesinger's *The Imperial Presidency* (Houghton Mifflin, 1973) is among the most important books published on the American presidency. Here are his choices for the best single-volume biographies of some of the men who have occupied the White House.

■ **GEORGE WASHINGTON (1732–1799).** James T. Flexner's volumes, published from 1965 to 1972, is now available in a one-volume condensation, *Washington: The Indispensable Man* (Little, Brown, 1984). Flexner brings Washington to vigorous life and sets him solidly against the perils and hopes of the years that established the United States as an independent republic.

■ **THOMAS JEFFERSON (1743–1826).** The most complete one-volume biography is Merrill D. Peterson's *Thomas Jefferson and the New Nation* (Oxford University Press, 1970). A new biography, *American Sphinx: The Character of Thomas Jefferson* (Alfred A. Knopf, 1996) by Joseph J. Ellis skillfully illuminates Jefferson's qualities and contradictions.

■ **ANDREW JACKSON (1767–1845).** Biographies of Andrew Jackson illustrate the swings in opinions from one generation to the next: After James Parton's affectionate but skeptical

work, *Life of Andrew Jackson* (three volumes, 1860) came William Graham Sumner's able but hostile *Andrew Jackson as a Public Man* (1882), then J. S. Bassett's more favorable two-volume *The Life of Andrew Jackson* (1911), then the even more favorable account in two volumes by Marquis James (1933–37), and now three masterful and sympathetic volumes by Robert V. Remini (1977–84), available in a one-volume condensation, *The Life of Andrew Jackson* (Viking Penguin, 1988).

■ **ABRAHAM LINCOLN (1809–1865).** Even Abraham Lincoln, regarded by most historians as our greatest president, has had his ride on the reputation roller coaster. Long praised as the Great Emancipator, Lincoln was denounced as a racist in the excitable 1960s. Defenders soon restored his reputation as a leader ahead of his time in advocating the cause of emancipation. David Herbert Donald, in his new, shrewd, and capacious *Lincoln* (Simon & Schuster, 1995), has written the biography "for this generation."

■ **THEODORE ROOSEVELT (1858–1919) and WOODROW WILSON (1856–1924).** When I went to college in the 1930s, we were taught that Theodore Roosevelt was an adolescent braggart and Woodrow Wilson a Presbyterian zealot. Years later, fine presidential biographies ably vindicated their qualities as men and their influence as national leaders: W. H. Harbaugh's on *TR, Power and Responsibility* (1961) and August Heckscher's more recent single-volume *Woodrow Wilson* (Scribner, 1991), as well as John Milton Cooper's *The Warrior and the Priest* (Belknap, 1983), on the rivalry between the two.

■ **FRANKLIN D. ROOSEVELT (1882–1945).** A deeply controversial figure when he was in the White House, FDR has now survived partisan recriminations. Even Newt Gingrich, while tearing down FDR's New Deal, has pronounced FDR the greatest president of the century. Biographers can't make out FDR: he has been portrayed as a closet socialist and the savior of capitalism, as an

IN CASE YOU FORGOT HOW THE ELECTORAL COLLEGE WORKS

It's a complex system to simplify the way we elect a president.

The authors of the Constitution devised the Electoral College to act as a kind of buffer between the masses and the ultimate process of selecting a president. The voters would choose electors for their state on a predetermined election day and then those individuals, along with electors from other states, would take it upon themselves to choose the president.

Today, the Electoral College is a body of 538 people. Each state receives a number of electoral votes equal to the number of senators and representatives in its congressional delegation, and Washington, D.C., which has no congressional representation, gets three votes. A candidate needs 270 electoral votes, slightly more than a majority, to be elected president. The candidate who wins a majority of a state's popular vote wins all of its electoral votes. As a result, the electoral vote tends to exaggerate the popular support of the winner.

If no candidate receives a majority of the votes of the Electoral College, the election will be decided by the House of Representatives. This has only happened once, so far, when in 1824 Andrew Jackson won the popular vote in a four-way race but John Quincy Adams was elected president by the House. In 1876, Rutherford B. Hayes lost the popular vote but won the presidency by a single electoral vote.

■ **ELECTORAL COLLEGE VOTES, BY STATE**

California has the largest number of electoral votes.

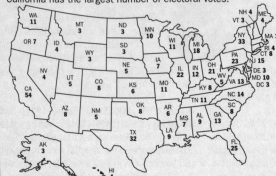

isolationist and an internationalist, as an appeaser and a warmonger, as an impetuous decision maker and as an incorrigible vacillator, and as a dreamer who thought he could charm Stalin and as a crafty imperialist serving the interests of American capitalism. The best one-volume life, favorable without being worshipful, is *Franklin D. Roosevelt: A Rendevous with Destiny* (Little, Brown), published in 1990 by the noted Roosevelt scholar Frank Freidel.

■ **HARRY TRUMAN (1884-1972).** Harry Truman has made an even more striking comeback. When he was president, his critics (and there were plenty) would say, "To err is Truman." Though he won a surprise reelection, not many stayed all that wild about Harry. At the end of his second term, his approval rating had sunk into the 20s. Yet no president is more popular in retrospect than the brave, candid, doughty, endearing man from Independence. Three recent biographies do justice to Harry Truman's improbable career. If you want the story and the portrait, read David McCullough's vivid and best-selling *Truman* (Simon & Schuster, 1992). If you want the presidency and the hard choices of the time, read Alonzo Hamby's analytical *Man of the People: The Life of Harry S. Truman* (Oxford University Press, 1995) or Robert H. Ferrell's cogent *Harry S. Truman: A Life* (University of Missouri Press, 1994).

THE LAW OF THE LAND

We all learned it in grade school, but for those of us who passed the civics test much too long ago, here's a refresher course on how laws are made. The Senate and the House of Representatives have equal voice in making laws, although revenue bills originate in the House. Differences in a piece of legislation between the two houses are reconciled by a joint committee that includes members of both chambers. A presidential veto of congressional legislation can be overrriden by a two-thirds vote in each chamber.

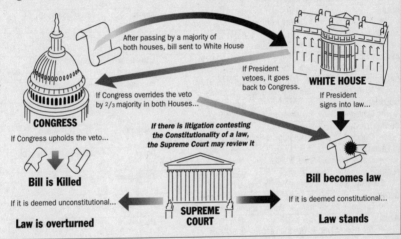

After passing by a majority of both houses, bill sent to White House

If President vetoes, it goes back to Congress.

WHITE HOUSE

If President signs into law...

If Congress overrides the veto by 2/3 majority in both Houses...

CONGRESS

If Congress upholds the veto...

If there is litigation contesting the Constitutionality of a law, the Supreme Court may review it

Bill is Killed

If it is deemed unconstitutional...

SUPREME COURT

If it is deemed constitutional...

Bill becomes law

Law is overturned

Law stands

HERE COME THE JUDGES

The nine justices who make up the U.S. Supreme Court are appointed by the president and serve lifetime tenures. Chief Justice, William H. Rehnquist, makes $171,500 a year; associate justices are paid $164,100. Decisions made by the court become law. As the following shows, the makeup of the Supreme Court reflects the legacy of several Republican administrations.

Justice	Born	Place of birth	Law school attended	Date appointed	Appointed by
William H. Rehnquist *Chief Justice*	Oct. 1, 1924	Milwaukee, Wis.	Stanford	1972 1986	Richard Nixon (R) Ronald Reagan (R)
John Paul Stevens	April 20, 1920	Chicago, Ill.	Northwestern	1975	Gerald Ford (R)
Sandra Day O'Connor	March 26, 1930	El Paso, Texas	Stanford	1981	Ronald Reagan (R)
Antonin Scalia	March 11, 1936	Trenton, N.J.	Harvard	1986	Ronald Reagan (R)
Anthony M. Kennedy	July 23, 1936	Sacramento, Calif.	Harvard	1987	Ronald Reagan (R)
David H. Souter	Sept. 17, 1939	Melrose, Mass.	Harvard	1990	George Bush (R)
Clarence Thomas	June 23, 1948	Savannah, Ga.	Yale	1991	George Bush (R)
Ruth Bader Ginsburg	March 15, 1933	Brooklyn, N.Y.	Columbia	1993	Bill Clinton (D)
Stephen Breyer	Aug. 15, 1945	San Francisco, Calif.	Yale	1994	Bill Clinton (D)

EXPERT LIST

THE PARADE OF STATES

From sea to shining sea, here are the 50 states at a glance.

State ☛ Nickname ❥ State bird ✿ State flower	Established	Rank (size in sq. miles)	Capital	Governor (party) * Term ends in 1998
ALABAMA ☛ The Heart of Dixie ❥ Yellowhammer ✿ Camellia	Dec. 4, 1819	28th (50,750)	Montgomery	Fob James, Jr. (R)*
ALASKA ☛ The Last Frontier ❥ Willow ptarmigan ✿ Forget-me-not	Jan. 3, 1959	1st (570,374)	Juneau	Tony Knowles (D)
ARIZONA ☛ Grand Canyon State ❥ Cactus wren ✿ Saguaro cactus flower	Feb. 14, 1912	6th (113,642)	Phoenix	Fife Symington (R)*
ARKANSAS ☛ Land of Opportunity ❥ Mockingbird ✿ Apple blossom	June 15, 1836	27th (52,075)	Little Rock	Mike Huckabee (R)
CALIFORNIA ☛ Golden State ❥ California valley quail ✿ Golden poppy	Sept. 9, 1850	3rd (155,973)	Sacramento	Pete Wilson (R)*
COLORADO ☛ Centennial State ❥ Lark bunting ✿ Columbine	Aug. 1, 1876	8th (103,729)	Denver	Roy Romer (D)*
CONNECTICUT ☛ Constitution or Nutmeg State ❥ American robin ✿ Mt. laurel	Jan. 9, 1788	48th (4,845)	Hartford	John G Rowland (R)*
DELAWARE ☛ First or Diamond State ❥ Blue hen chicken ✿ Peach blossom	Dec. 7, 1787	49th (1,955)	Dover	Thomas R. Carper (D)
FLORIDA ☛ Sunshine State ❥ Mockingbird ✿ Orange blossom	March 3, 1845	26th (53,997)	Tallahassee	Lawton Chiles (D)*
GEORGIA ☛ Empire or Peach State ❥ Brown thrasher ✿ Cherokee rose	Jan. 2, 1788	21st (57,919)	Atlanta	Zell Miller (D)*
HAWAII ☛ The Aloha State ❥ Hawaiian goose ✿ Hibiscus	Aug. 21, 1959	47th (16,423)	Honolulu	Benjamin J. Cayetano (D)
IDAHO ☛ Gem State ❥ Mountain bluebird ✿ Lilac	July 3, 1890	11th (82,751)	Boise	Philip E. Batt (R)*
ILLINOIS ☛ The Prairie State ❥ Cardinal ✿ Native violet	Dec. 3, 1818	24th (55,593)	Springfield	Jim Edgar (R)*
INDIANA ☛ Hoosier State ❥ Cardinal ✿ Peony	Dec. 11, 1816	38th (35,870)	Indianapolis	Frank O'Bannon (D)
IOWA ☛ Hawkeye State ❥ Eastern goldfinch ✿ Wild rose	Dec. 28, 1846	23rd (55,875)	Des Moines	Terry E. Branstad (R)*
KANSAS ☛ Sunflower or Free State ❥ Western meadowlark ✿ Native sunflower	Jan. 29, 1861	13th (81,823)	Topeka	Bill Graves (R)*
KENTUCKY ☛ Bluegrass State ❥ Cardinal ✿ Goldenrod	June 1, 1792	36th (39,732)	Frankfort	Paul E. Patton (D)
LOUISIANA ☛ Pelican State ❥ Eastern brown pelican ✿ Magnolia	April 30, 1812	33rd (43,566)	Baton Rouge	Mike Foster (R)
MAINE ☛ Pine Tree State ❥ Chickadee ✿ White pine cone and tassel	March 15, 1820	39th (30,865)	Augusta	Angus S. King, Jr. (I)*
MARYLAND ☛ Old Line or Free State ❥ Baltimore oriole ✿ Black-eyed Susan	April 28, 1788	42nd (9,775)	Annapolis	Parris N. Glendening (D)*
MASSACHUSETTS ☛ Bay State, Old Colony ❥ Chickadee ✿ Mayflower	Feb. 6, 1788	45th (7,838)	Boston	William F. Weld (R)*
MICHIGAN ☛ Great Lakes State, Wolverine State ❥ Robin ✿ Apple blossom	Jan. 26, 1837	22nd (56,809)	Lansing	John Engler (R)*
MINNESOTA ☛ North Star or Gopher State ❥ Common loon ✿ Lady-slipper	May 11, 1858	14th (79,617)	St. Paul	Arne H. Carlson (R)*
MISSISSIPPI ☛ Magnolia State ❥ Mockingbird ✿ Magnolia	Dec. 10, 1817	31st (46,914)	Jackson	Kirk Fordice (R)

■ EXPERT LIST

State ● Nickname ❥ State bird ✿ State flower	Established	Rank (size)	Capital	Governor (party) *Term ends in 1998
MISSOURI ● Show-Me State ❥ Bluebird ✿ White hawthorn	Aug. 10, 1821	18th (68,898)	Jefferson City	Mel Carnahan (D)
MONTANA ● Treasure State ❥ Western meadowlark ✿ Bitterroot	Nov. 8, 1889	4th (145,556)	Helena	Marc Racicot (R)
NEBRASKA ● Cornhusker State ❥ Western meadowlark ✿ Goldenrod	March 1, 1867	15th (76,878)	Lincoln	E. Benjamin Nelson (D)*
NEVADA ● Sagebrush, Battle or Silver State ✿ Mt. bluebird ✿ Sagebrush	Oct. 31, 1864	7th (109,806)	Carson City	Bob Miller (D)*
NEW HAMPSHIRE ● Granite State ❥ Purple finch ✿ Purple lilac	June 21, 1788	44th (8,969)	Concord	Jeanne Shaheen (D)*
NEW JERSEY ● Garden State ❥ Eastern goldfinch ✿ Violet	Dec. 8, 1787	46th (7,419)	Trenton	Christine Todd Whitman (R)
NEW MEXICO ● Land of Enchantment ❥ Piñon bird ✿ Yucca	Jan. 6, 1912	5th (121,365)	Sante Fe	Gary E. Johnson (R)*
NEW YORK ● Empire State ❥ Bluebird ✿ Rose	July 26, 1788	30th (47,224)	Albany	George E. Pataki (R)*
NORTH CAROLINA ● Tar Heel or Old North State ❥ Cardinal ✿ Dogwood	Nov. 21, 1789	29th (48,718)	Raleigh	James B. Hunt, Jr. (D)
NORTH DAKOTA ● Peace Garden State ❥ Western meadowlark ✿ Wild rose	Nov. 2, 1889	17th (68,994)	Bismarck	Edward T. Schafer (R)
OHIO ● Buckeye State ❥ Cardinal ✿ Scarlet carnation	March 1, 1803	35th (40,953)	Columbus	George V. Voinovich (R)*
OKLAHOMA ● Sooner State ❥ Scissor-tailed flycatcher ✿ Mistletoe	Nov. 16, 1907	19th (68,679)	Oklahoma City	Frank Keating (R)*
OREGON ● Beaver State ❥ Western meadowlark ✿ Oregon grape	Feb. 14, 1859	10th (96,003)	Salem	John A. Kitzhaber (D)*
PENNSYLVANIA ● Keystone State ❥ Ruffed grouse ✿ Mountain laurel	Dec. 12, 1787	32nd (44,820)	Harrisburg	Tom Ridge (R)*
RHODE ISLAND ● Little Rhody or Ocean State ❥ Rhode Island red ✿ Violet	May 29, 1790	50th (1,045)	Providence	Lincoln C. Almond (R)*
SOUTH CAROLINA ● Palmetto State ❥ Carolina wren ✿ Yellow jessamine	May 27, 1788	40th (30,111)	Columbia	David Beasley (R)*
SOUTH DAKOTA ● Coyote or Mt. Rushmore State ❥ Ring-neck pheasant ✿ Pasque	Nov. 2, 1889	16th (75,896)	Pierre	William J. Janklow (R)*
TENNESSEE ● Volunteer State ❥ Mockingbird ✿ Iris	June 1, 1796	34th (41,220)	Nashville	Don Sundquist (R)*
TEXAS ● Lone Star State ❥ Mockingbird ✿ Blue-bonnet	Dec. 28, 1845	2nd (261,914)	Austin	George W. Bush (R)*
UTAH ● Beehive State ❥ California seagull ✿ Sego lily	Jan. 4, 1896	12th (82,618)	Salt Lake City	Michael O. Leavitt (R)
VERMONT ● Green Mountain State ❥ Hermit thrush ✿ Red clover	March 4, 1791	43rd (9,249)	Montpelier	Howard Dean (D*)
VIRGINIA Old Dominion ❥ Cardinal ✿ Dogwood	June 25, 1788	37th (39,598)	Richmond	George F. Allen (R)
WASHINGTON ● Evergreen State ❥ Willow goldfinch ✿ Coast rhododendron	Nov. 11, 1889	20th (66,581)	Olympia	Gary Locke (D)
WEST VIRGINIA ● Mountain State ❥ Cardinal ✿ Big laurel	June 20, 1863	41st (24,087)	Charleston	Cecil Underwood (D)
WISCONSIN ● Badger State ❥ Robin ✿ Wood violet	May 29, 1848	25th (54,314)	Madison	Tommy G. Thompson (R)*
WYOMING ● Equality State ❥ Western meadowlark ✿ Indian paintbrush	July 10, 1890	9th (97,105)	Cheyenne	Jim Geringer (R)*
WASHINGTON, D.C. ● N/A ❥ Wood thrush ✿ American Beauty rose	Dec. 1, 1800	51st (61)	N/A	(Mayor) Marion Barry (D*)

THE GREAT MELTING POT

There are few countries more diverse than the United States. One study found that there is a 40 percent chance that two Americans picked at random are racially or ethnically different. The Southwest and West are the most diverse regions of the country, New England the least. New Hampshire, Vermont, and Maine are over 95 percent white. Native Americans compose 16 percent of Alaska's population, 9 percent of New Mexico's, and 8 percent of Oklahoma's.

	Population	Rank	White (%)	Black (%)	Hispanic (%)	Asian/ Pac. (%)	Males per 100 females (1992)	% 65 or older (1994)
			ETHNIC RATIO					
ALABAMA	4,218,792	22nd	73.6	25.3	0.6	0.5	92.19	13.1
ALASKA	606,276	49th	75.5	4.1	3.2	3.9	111.91	4.6
ARIZONA	4,075,052	24th	80.8	3.0	18.8	1.5	97.63	13.4
ARKANSAS	2,452,671	33rd	82.7	3.0	0.8	0.5	93.16	14.8
CALIFORNIA	31,430,697	1st	69.9	7.4	25.8	9.6	100.29	10.6
COLORADO	3,655,647	26th	88.2	4.0	12.9	1.8	98.34	10.1
CONNECTICUT	3,275,251	27th	87.0	8.3	6.5	1.5	94.03	14.2
DELAWARE	706,351	46th	80.3	16.9	2.4	1.4	94.63	12.7
D.C.	570,175	50th	30.0	65.8	5.4	1.8	87.86	13.5
FLORIDA	13,952,714	4th	83.1	13.6	12.2	1.2	93.96	18.4
GEORGIA	7,055,336	11th	71.0	27.0	1.7	1.2	94.50	10.1
HAWAII	1,178,564	41st	33.4	2.5	7.3	61.8	103.15	12.1
IDAHO	1,133,034	42nd	94.4	0.3	5.3	0.9	99.44	11.6
ILLINOIS	11,751,774	6th	78.3	14.8	7.9	2.5	94.69	12.6
INDIANA	5,752,073	14th	90.6	7.8	1.8	0.7	94.34	12.8
IOWA	2,829,252	30th	96.6	1.7	1.2	0.9	94.33	15.4
KANSAS	2,554,047	32nd	90.1	5.8	3.8	1.3	96.57	13.9
KENTUCKY	3,826,794	23rd	92.0	7.1	0.6	0.5	94.06	12.8
LOUISIANA	4,315,085	21st	67.3	30.8	2.2	1.0	92.93	11.4
MAINE	1,240,209	38th	98.4	0.4	0.6	0.5	95.10	13.9
MARYLAND	5,006,265	19th	71.0	24.9	2.6	2.9	94.45	11.2
MASSACHUSETTS	6,041,123	13th	89.8	5.0	4.8	2.4	92.65	14.1
MICHIGAN	9,496,147	8th	83.4	13.9	2.2	1.1	94.58	12.4
MINNESOTA	4,567,267	20th	94.4	2.2	1.2	1.8	96.54	12.5
MISSISSIPPI	2,669,111	31st	63.5	35.6	0.6	0.5	91.64	12.5
MISSOURI	5,227,640	15th	87.7	10.7	1.2	0.8	93.26	14.1
MONTANA	856,047	44th	92.7	0.3	1.5	0.5	98.55	13.3
NEBRASKA	1,622,858	36th	93.8	3.6	2.3	0.8	95.38	14.1
NEVADA	1,457,028	39th	84.3	6.6	10.4	3.2	103.84	11.3
NEW HAMPSHIRE	1,136,820	40th	98.0	0.6	1.0	0.8	95.94	11.9
NEW JERSEY	7,903,925	9th	79.3	13.4	9.6	3.5	93.61	13.6
NEW MEXICO	1,653,521	37th	75.6	2.0	38.2	0.9	97.13	11.0
NEW YORK	18,169,051	3rd	74.4	15.9	12.3	3.9	92.40	13.2
NORTH CAROLINA	7,069,836	10th	75.6	22.0	1.2	0.8	94.35	12.5
NORTH DAKOTA	637,988	47th	94.6	0.6	0.7	0.5	99.37	14.7
OHIO	11,102,198	7th	87.8	10.6	1.3	0.8	93.21	13.4

■ **EXPERT LIST**

	Population	Rank	ETHNIC RATIO				Males per 100 females (1992)	% 65 or older (1994)
			White (%)	Black (%)	Hispanic (%)	Asian/ Pac. (%)		
OKLAHOMA	3,258,069	28th	82.1	7.4	2.7	1.1	95.14	13.6
OREGON	3,086,188	29th	92.8	1.6	4.0	2.4	97.02	13.7
PENNSYLVANIA	12,052,367	5th	88.5	9.2	2.0	1.2	92.28	15.9
RHODE ISLAND	996,757	43rd	91.4	3.9	4.6	1.8	92.53	15.6
SOUTH CAROLINA	3,663,984	25th	69.0	29.8	0.9	0.6	94.02	11.9
SOUTH DAKOTA	721,164	45th	91.6	0.5	0.8	0.4	96.95	14.7
TENNESSEE	5,175,240	17th	83.0	16.0	0.7	0.7	93.01	12.7
TEXAS	18,378,185	2nd	75.2	11.9	25.5	1.9	97.15	10.2
UTAH	1,907,936	35th	93.8	0.7	4.9	1.9	98.90	8.8
VERMONT	580,209	48th	98.6	0.3	0.7	0.6	96.21	12.1
VIRGINIA	6,551,522	12th	77.4	18.8	2.6	2.6	96.25	11.1
WASHINGTON	5,343,090	18th	88.5	3.1	4.4	4.5	98.68	11.6
WEST VIRGINIA	1,822,021	34th	96.2	3.1	0.5	0.4	92.77	15.4
WISCONSIN	5,081,658	16th	92.2	5.0	1.9	1.1	96.12	13.4
WYOMING	475,981	51st	94.2	0.8	5.7	0.6	100.86	11.1

SOURCE: *Statistical Abstract of the United States*, 1996, U.S. Dept. of Commerce, Bureau of the Census.

FACT FILE

The highest ethnic populations in 1990

■ **AFRICAN AMERICANS**

1. Cook, IL	1,317,147
2. Los Angeles, CA	992,974
3. Brooklyn, NY	872,305
4. Wayne, MI	849,109
5. Philadelphia, PA	631,936

■ **NATIVE AMERICANS**
American Indian, Eskimo, or Aleut

1. Apache, AZ	47,803
2. Los Angeles, CA	45,508
3. McKinley, NM	43,570
4. Robeson, NC	40,511
5. Navajo, AZ	40,417

■ **HISPANICS**

1. Los Angeles	3,351,242
2. Dade, FL	953,407
3. Cook, IL	694,194
4. Harris, TX	644,935
5. Bexar, TX	589,180

SOURCE: *City and County Data Book*, U.S. Department of Commerce, 1994.

■ **THE CHANGING COLOR OF AMERICA**
Since 1980, the number of blacks, Asians, and Hispanics has risen steadily; this trend is expected to continue into the next century. The Asian population is expected to show the greatest increase by the middle of the next century.

Percentage American population increase by race

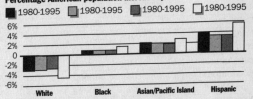

■ **THE GRAYING OF AMERICA**
The median age of the American population increased by about five years between 1970 and 1990. By 2050, the projected median age will have increased by 10 years compared to 1970.

Median age, fact and projection

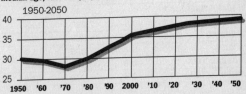

SOURCE: *Statistical Abstract of the U.S.*, Bureau of the Census, 1996.

FOR RICHER AND FOR POORER

Census bureau statisticians analyzed a two-year period (1990 to 1992), and determined that the incomes of most states remained constant. However, 12 states showed a significant decline in household income: Florida, Illinois, Kentucky, Maryland, Massachusetts, New Hampshire, New Jersey, New York, Rhode Island, South Carolina, Texas, and West Virginia.

	Percent of persons in poverty (1994)	Change in poverty rate (1992-1994)	Median Income (1994 $)	Unemploy- ment rate (1994)	SALES TAX (%)	GAS TAX (cents per gallon)	INCOME TAX (per $1,000)	Tax rank (based on tax per $1,000)
ALABAMA	16.4	−0.5	27,196	6.0	4	18	$64.05	35th
ALASKA	10.2	−	45,367	7.8	0	8	111.23	2nd
ARIZONA	15.9	−	31,293	6.4	5	18	78.46	13th
ARKANSAS	15.3	−1.1	25,565	5.3	4.5	18.5	74.93	19th
CALIFORNIA	17.9	0.8	35,331	8.6	6	18	73.81	23rd
COLORADO	9.0	−0.9	37,833	4.2	3	22	49.77	51st
CONNECTICUT	10.8	0.5	41,097	5.6	6	33	74.50	21st
DELAWARE	8.3	0.3	35,873	4.9	0	23	101.21	5th
D.C.	21.2	0.4	30,116	8.2	5.75	20	141.90	1st
FLORIDA	14.9	−0.3	29,294	6.6	6	4¹	58.95	42nd
GEORGIA	14.0	−1.9	31,467	5.2	4	7.5	61.38	39th
HAWAII	8.7	−1.3	42,255	6.1	4	16	102.46	4th
IDAHO	12.0	−1.6	31,536	5.6	5	22	83.72	6th
ILLINOIS	12.4	−1.6	35,081	5.7	6.25	19	56.51	43rd
INDIANA	13.7	0.9	27,858	4.9	5	15	67.51	30th
IOWA	10.7	−0.4	33,079	3.7	5	20	75.90	18th
KANSAS	14.9	1.9	28,322	5.3	4.9	18	66.76	32nd
KENTUCKY	18.5	−0.6	26,595	5.4	6	15	79.77	11th
LOUISIANA	25.7	0.6	25,676	8.0	4	20	54.97	48th
MAINE	9.4	−2.1	30,316	7.4	6	19	73.89	22nd
MARYLAND	10.7	−0.6	39,198	5.1	5	23.5	63.69	37th
MASSACHUSETTS	9.7	−0.3	40,500	6.0	5	21	71.62	26th
MICHIGAN	14.1	0.3	35,284	5.8	6	15	72.07	25th
MINNESOTA	11.7	−0.7	33,644	4.0	6	20	83.36	7th
MISSISSIPPI	19.9	−2.4	25,400	6.6	7	18	82.96	8th
MISSOURI	15.6	−	30,190	4.9	4.225	15	57.87	43rd
MONTANA	11.5	−1.2	27,631	5.1	0	27	75.91	17th
NEBRASKA	8.8	−0.9	31,794	2.9	5	24²	64.30	34th
NEVADA	11.1	−1.8	35,871	6.2	6.5	22.5	69.92	27th
NEW HAMPSHIRE	7.7	−0.5	35,245	4.6	0	18	52.29	50th
NEW JERSEY	9.2	−0.6	42,280	6.8	6	10.5	62.15	38th
NEW MEXICO	21.1	−0.3	26,905	6.3	5	17	108.10	3rd
NEW YORK	17.0	0.7	31,899	6.9	4	8	69.36	29th
NORTH CAROLINA	14.2	−0.8	30,114	4.4	4	22²	77.07	15th
NORTH DAKOTA	10.4	−0.8	28,278	3.9	5	18	77.82	14th
OHIO	14.1	0.8	31,855	5.5	5	22	61.00	40th
OKLAHOMA	16.7	−1.0	26,991	5.8	4.5	17	76.92	16th

■ **EXPERT LIST**

	Percent of persons in poverty (1994)	Change in poverty rate (1992-1994)	Median Income (1994 $)	Unemploy-ment rate (1994)	SALES TAX (%)	GAS TAX (cents per gallon)	INCOME TAX (per $1,000)	Tax rank (based on tax per $1,000)
OREGON	11.8	0.2	31,456	5.4	0	24	64.57	33rd
PENNSYLVANIA	12.5	0.3	32,066	6.2	6	22.35	64.00	36th
RHODE ISLAND	10.3	−1.1	31,928	7.1	7	28	55.54	46th
SOUTH CAROLINA	13.8	−2.6	29,846	6.3	5	16	69.73	28th
SOUTH DAKOTA	14.5	−0.3	29,733	3.3	4	18	59.37	41st
TENNESSEE	14.6	−1.2	28,639	4.8	6	22.4	56.74	44th
TEXAS	19.1	0.4	30,755	6.4	6.25	21	55.53	47th
UTAH	8.0	−0.7	35,716	3.7	4.875	19.5	82.49	10th
VERMONT	7.6	−1.5	35,802	4.7	4	16	67.30	31st
VIRGINIA	10.7	0.6	37,647	4.9	5.5	17.5	52.61	49th
WASHINGTON	11.7	0.3	33,533	6.4	6.5	23	74.91	20th
WEST VIRGINIA	18.6	−1.9	23,564	8.9	6	20.5	82.87	9th
WISCONSIN	9.0	−0.9	35,388	4.7	5	23.4[2]	78.88	12th
WYOMING	9.3	−0.5	33,140	5.3	4	9	73.15	24th

NOTES: **1.** Florida's gas tax rates vary by county. Counties may also add up to an additional 12%. **2.** Nebraska's gas tax rates are indexed and change quarterly. North Carolina's rate is indexed and changes every 6 months. Wisconsin's rate is indexed annually.
SOURCE: Tax Foundation, *Statistical Abstract of the United States.*

FACT FILE

There are wide discrepancies in the nation's towns and cities. Here are the five wealthiest and poorest areas:

■ **MONEY MAKERS**

City	Median Income (1990)
1. Washington, DC	$46,884
2. Anchorage, AK	$43,946
3. Poughkeepsie, NY	$42,250
4. San Francisco, CA	$41,459
5. Hartford, CT	$41,440

■ **CASH-STRAPPED**

City	Percent below poverty level (1990)
1. McAllen-Edinburg-Mission, TX	41.9%
2. Brownsville-Harlingen, TX	39.7%
3. Laredo, TX	38.2%
4. El Paso, TX	26.8%
5. Bryan-College Sta., TX	26.7%

SOURCE: *City and County Data Book,* U.S. Dept. of Census, 1994.

■ **THE WEALTH IS TRICKLING DOWN**

The rich-get-richer trend may be petering out. New data from the Federal Reserve Board show that in the first half of the 1990s, America's wealth was shared a bit more evenly. The Fed found that 14.4 percent of all families had a net worth—the value of assets minus debt—of more than $250,000 in 1995, down from 16.5 percent in 1989. By comparison, the share of families with net worth between $25,000 and $100,000 rose to 28.5 percent from 24.7 percent in 1989. Increased home ownership and retirement savings helped boost the wealth of the working class.

Family net worth by head of household, in thousands of 1995 dollars

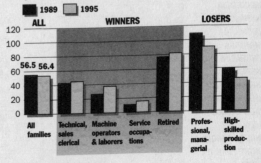

SOURCE: Federal Reserve Bulletin.

THE STATE OF EDUCATION, STATE-BY-STATE

A "boomlet" of high school graduates—children of baby boomers—is creating a surge in full-time school enrollment that is projected to reach almost 9 million students by 2004, up from 8.2 million in 1996. Over 43 percent of college students attend public two-year colleges and 38 percent are enrolled in public four-year colleges. Only 16 percent of college students attend private four-year schools.

	Average cost per pupil	HIGH SCHOOL graduates (%)	HIGH SCHOOL dropouts (%)	% Change in HS grads 1990-96	Some college or Assoc. degree (%)	Minority enrollment (%)	Bachelor's degree and above	Average in-state tuition 1995-96
U.S.	$5,767	75.2	14.4	3.1	45.2	24.6	20.3	$2,848
ALABAMA	$4,037	66.8	19.4	–6.9	37.4	25.5	15.6	$2,240
ALASKA	$8,882	86.5	8.2	14.8	57.8	18.7	23.0	$2,489
ARIZONA	$4,611	78.6	12.3	–2.8	52.5	24.0	20.3	$1,926
ARKANSAS	$4,280	66.4	18.4	3.0	33.7	17.1	13.4	$2,028
CALIFORNIA	$4,921	76.2	12.6	11.8	53.9	46.3	23.4	$2,666
COLORADO	$5,097	84.4	10.0	6.9	57.9	16.9	27.0	$2,473
CONNECTICUT	$8,473	79.2	12.4	–3.1	49.7	16.3	27.2	$3,845
DELAWARE	$6,621	77.5	15.3	6.1	44.8	18.0	21.4	$3,981
D.C.	$10,180	73.2	17.3	–20.6	52.0	45.2	33.3	$1,118
FLORIDA	$5,516	74.4	16.1	3.7	44.3	29.5	18.3	$1,767
GEORGIA	$4,915	70.9	17.1	–1.1	41.3	29.0	19.3	$2,103
HAWAII	$5,879	80.0	9.8	11.3	51.3	70.6	22.9	$1,576
IDAHO	$3,844	79.8	12.9	21.0	49.4	6.1	17.7	$1,682
ILLINOIS	$5,893	76.3	13.5	1.7	46.3	26.9	21.1	$3,352
INDIANA	$5,530	75.7	15.8	–0.4	37.5	10.5	15.6	$3,037
IOWA	$5,288	80.1	10.7	10.7	41.6	7.2	16.9	$2,565
KANSAS	$5,659	81.2	11.0	6.5	48.4	11.5	21.1	$2,120
KENTUCKY	$5,107	64.7	16.4	0.9	32.9	8.9	13.6	$2,161
LOUISIANA	$4,519	68.3	17.0	6.2	36.6	31.4	16.1	$2,221
MAINE	$6,069	78.9	12.4	–14.1	41.8	3.7	18.8	$3,474
MARYLAND	$6,958	79.4	13.7	6.6	50.3	30.0	26.5	$3,572
MASSACHUSETTS	$6,959	79.9	12.0	–1.1	50.2	16.5	27.2	$4,253
MICHIGAN	$6,658	76.7	15.5	–0.9	44.4	16.8	17.3	$3,895
MINNESOTA	$5,720	82.5	9.0	11.1	49.5	8.0	21.9	$3,216
MISSISSIPPI	$3,660	64.4	20.1	–2.3	36.9	31.2	14.8	$2,459
MISSOURI	$5,114	73.8	14.5	4.9	40.7	13.2	17.8	$3,015
MONTANA	$5,598	81.0	10.9	13.8	47.5	11.5	19.8	$2,367
NEBRASKA	$5,651	81.9	10.2	–1.6	47.2	7.4	19.0	$2,182
NEVADA	$5,049	78.8	15.2	13.4	47.3	19.5	15.3	$1,684
NEW HAMPSHIRE	$5,723	82.1	11.2	–12.1	50.4	4.6	24.3	$4,446
NEW JERSEY	$9,677	76.6	13.9	3.7	45.5	27.4	24.8	$3,972
NEW MEXICO	$4,261	75.0	13.5	–1.3	46.3	41.8	20.4	$1,940
NEW YORK	$9,175	74.8	15.0	2.7	45.3	29.8	23.1	$3,714
NORTH CAROLINA	$4,894	70.0	17.3	–10.1	41.0	24.1	17.4	$1,639
NORTH DAKOTA	$4,674	76.5	8.3	4.6	48.5	7.8	18.0	$2,248
OHIO	$5,971	75.6	16.4	2.5	39.3	13.2	17.0	$3,603

■ **EXPERT LIST**

	Average cost per pupil	HIGH SCHOOL		% Change in HS grads 1990-96	Some college or Assoc. degree (%)	Minority enrollment (%)	Bachelor's degree and above	Average in-state tuition 1995-96
		graduates (%)	dropouts (%)					
OKLAHOMA	$4,697	74.6	15.6	–0.4	44.1	19.9	17.8	$1,839
OREGON	$6,263	81.4	12.3	10.2	52.5	12.2	20.6	$3,233
PENNSYLVANIA	$6,983	74.6	15.9	3.6	36.0	13.2	17.9	$4,723
RHODE ISLAND	$7,333	72.1	16.9	–1.3	42.6	11.4	21.3	$3,856
SOUTH CAROLINA	$4,761	68.2	18.1	–1.5	38.7	24.7	16.6	$3,094
SOUTH DAKOTA	$4,586	77.1	9.5	22.7	43.4	8.6	17.2	$2,642
TENNESSEE	$4,149	67.0	17.0	–2.9	37.0	17.7	15.9	$1,990
TEXAS	$4,898	72.3	14.4	–3.4	46.7	35.1	20.4	$1,820
UTAH	$3,439	85.1	11.5	25.7	57.9	6.5	22.2	$2,011
VERMONT	$6,600	80.8	10.6	2.5	46.2	4.8	24.3	$5,898
VIRGINIA	$5,109	75.1	13.7	2.0	48.5	23.6	24.5	$3,907
WASHINGTON	$5,751	83.7	10.7	19.5	55.8	16.9	22.9	$2,791
WEST VIRGINIA	$5,713	65.9	17.3	–1.6	29.3	5.9	12.3	$2,024
WISCONSIN	$6,717	78.6	11.9	7.1	41.5	9.4	17.7	$2,614
WYOMING	$5,899	83.1	11.2	6.0	49.9	6.9	18.8	$2,005

SOURCE: *Digest of Education Statistics*, National Center for Education Statistics, U.S. Department of Education, 1996.

FACT FILE

Soon, parent-teacher e-mail could replace signed report cards.

■ **COMPUTER SURGE**

A decade ago there were 42 students per computer; in 1992 there were 14.

	1985	1989	1992
Average number of computers for instructional use in schools	10	26	37
Students per computer	42	20	14

■ **COMPUTER TUTORS**

The average number of instructional computers per school has almost quadrupled from 1985 to 1992.

	1992	1995
Schools w/ CD-ROMS	7%	37%
Schools with modems	16%	34%

■ **WHO HAS THE SHEEPSKINS**

Since 1960, the number of women who have completed high school has doubled, while the number of minority high school grads has increased from one fifth of those over 25 in 1960 to three quarters in 1995. The number of college grads over 25 has tripled to 23 percent.

High school completion or more for Americans 25 and over

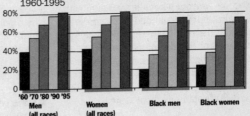

Completed 4 years of college or more for Americans 25 and over

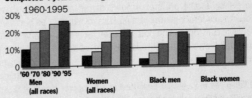

SOURCE: *Digest of Education Statistics*, National Center for Education Statistics, U.S. Department of Education, 1996.

HOW TO DECIPHER A POLL

Ah, the fickleness of the public's opinion. A pollster tells all

Polls putatively take the pulse of public opinion. But do they really tell us what we think? Well, yes and no. How reliable a gauge any poll is often depends on how large the sample size was, how the poll was taken, and, of course, precisely how the questions were posed.

Peter Hart has been taking polls for over 25 years. Currently, he samples public opinion for *NBC News* and *The Wall Street Journal*, among other organizations. He frequently appears on television and radio. Here are his tips for reading a poll.

■ **Take a look at how the poll was conducted.** One big problem in the polling business is that the word "survey" refers to anytime you talk to the American people. But questionnaires through the mail or phone-in surveys are self-selecting—anyone who calls a 900-number is a certain kind of person, and it won't make for an evenly distributed survey. Telephone surveys are probably the most accurate, and we do random-digit dialing to make sure we reach people with unlisted numbers, because they make up a segment of the population that has definite opinions about some issues.

■ **Find out the purpose of the poll, and who's doing the polling.** Is the pollster a news organization, an academic group, or a politician? And why are they doing the poll? Do they have an agenda? News organizations are one of the best sources for surveys.

■ **When you see a person described as a Democratic or Republican pollster, it means that they are specialists.** It doesn't mean their polls are going to be biased—because their client wants a very accurate picture of where they stand.

■ **Look for bias in the poll.** Look at the choice of answers that respondents were given. Are there four answers in one direction, and really only one choice for an answer if you feel differently? Also look at the order of questions. Questions should go from general to specific. If I say to you: give me your reaction to the fact that Bob Dole could be the oldest president ever elected—does that bother you a lot, a little, or not at all? You might answer "a little." Then I ask you who you would vote for if the election for president were tomorrow. The order changes how you think about the question. The previous question always influences the later question.

■ **Look at when the poll was done.** Maybe a candidate does a burst of media advertising, and I conduct a poll right after that blitz. The poll might show very favorable results that might be a temporary result of the media push. Also, sometimes polls are done before a major event, but not released until afterward. It's important to know when the poll was conducted, and to consider what has happened in the interim.

■ **The size of the sample, not the size of the universe, determines the accuracy of the poll.** If you poll 500 people in Nevada and 500 people in California, which poll is more accurate? They're both equally accurate. A good analogy is if you have a 300-pound linebacker and an 80-pound kid, and you need blood samples from both—there'll be no difference in the sampling.

■ **Polling price can determine a survey's accuracy.** A poll with an accuracy of plus or minus 3 percent means that if I tell you 50 percent of people favor welfare reform, that number could be between 53 and 47 percent. The more people you survey, the more accurate the poll. To get an accuracy of plus or minus 1 percent, you have to interview 9,000 people. I tell clients that each interview costs $30; they can save a lot of money by sticking with an accuracy range of plus or minus 4 percent. That's fine for most decisions you're going to make.

EXPERT SOURCES

MAKING YOUR VOICE HEARD IN POLITICS

How closely does that campaign rhetoric match the reality? You can't monitor every vote of your Representative personally, but there are organizations that do just that and more on a regular basis. We've listed some of the most influential interest groups in the country; whether you want to join their cause and lobby Congress or merely find out what your elected officials are up to, these organizations can help. An asterisk indicates groups that rate members of Congress.

BUSINESS AND LABOR

AFL-CIO COMMITTEE ON POLITICAL EDUCATION*
■ The nation's most powerful labor group. A federation of local, state, and national unions.
815 16th St., N.W.
Washington, D.C. 20006
☎ 202–637–5101

U.S. CHAMBER OF COMMERCE*
■ One of the big three pro-business lobbying groups.
1615 H St., N.W.
Washington, D.C. 20062
☎ 202–659–6000

NATIONAL ASSOCIATION OF MANUFACTURERS
■ The most politically middle-of-the-road of the big three. Members are large manufacturing firms.
1331 Pennsylvania Ave., N.W.
#1500 North Tower
Washington, D.C. 20004
☎ 202–637–3000

NATIONAL FEDERATION OF INDEPENDENT BUSINESS
■ Champions the interests of small, independent businesses. Closest to grass roots of the big three business groups.
600 Maryland Ave. S.W. #700
Washington, D.C. 20024
☎ 202–554–9000

CIVIL RIGHTS

NATIONAL RAINBOW COALITION
■ Founded by the Rev. Jesse Jackson, this group is best known for its advocacy of racial and ethnic tolerance.
1700 K St., N.W. #800
Washington, D.C. 20006
☎ 202–728–1180

CONSUMER GROUPS

COMMON CAUSE
■ Among other things, Common Cause advocates public financing of congressional campaigns and ethics in government. A player in the recent debate about campaign finance reform.
1250 Connecticut Ave., N.W.
Washington, D.C. 20036
☎ 202–833–1200

CONSUMER FEDERATION OF AMERICA*
■ This federation of 240 organizations claims to stand up for the rights of average consumers in Congress and before federal regulatory agencies.
1424 16th St., N.W. #604
Washington, D.C. 20036
☎ 202–387–6121

THE ENVIRONMENT

NATIONAL WILDLIFE FEDERATION
■ One of the most powerful public advocates for the environment and endangered species.
1400 16th St., N.W., #610
Washington, D.C. 20036
☎ 202–797–6800

FAMILY ISSUES

THE CHRISTIAN COALITION *
■ Supports a host of conservative issues. TV evangelist Pat Robertson is the power behind the scenes.
1801-L Sara Dr.
Chesapeake, VA 23320
☎ 757–424–2630

NATIONAL ABORTION REPRODUCTIVE RIGHTS ACTION LEAGUE*
■ Organization supports reproductive choice and safe, legal abortions.
1156 15th St., N.W., #700
Washington, D.C. 20005
☎ 202–973–3000

NATIONAL RIGHT TO LIFE COMMITTEE*
■ Opposes abortion, euthanasia, and infanticide; supports abortion alternative programs.
419 7th St., N.W. #500
Washington, D.C. 20004
☎ 202–626–8800

■ **EXPERT SOURCES**

GUNS

NATIONAL RIFLE ASSOCIATION*
■ The self-appointed defender of the Second Amendment. One of the most powerful political action groups in the country.
11250 Waples Mill Rd.
Fairfax, VA 22030
☎ 703-267-1000

JEWISH CAUSES

AMERICAN ISRAEL PUBLIC AFFAIRS COMMITTEE
■ A powerful voice in Congress on issues that affect the future of Israel
440 First St., N.W. #600
Washington, D.C. 20001
☎ 202-639-5200

AMERICAN JEWISH CONGRESS
■ Along with AIPAC, the most prominent lobbying force for Jewish affairs. Promotes civil rights and religious freedom.
2027 Massachusetts Ave., N.W.
Washington, D.C. 20036
☎ 202-332-4001

SENIOR CITIZENS

AMERICAN ASSOCIATION FOR RETIRED PERSONS
■ Arguably the most vocal public interest group of them all, and certainly one of the most powerful. Legendary for its legislative savvy. Its magazine, *Modern Maturity*, has the largest circulation of any in the country.
601 E St., N.W.
Washington, D.C. 20049
☎ 202-434-2277

CYBER SOURCES

WIRING INTO WASHINGTON

Your official representatives may be out of touch, but that doesn't mean they're out of reach. The Web sites listed here will help you find out who they are, what they're up to, and how to make your views known. After all, they work for you.

■ **U.S. HOUSE OF REPRESENTATIVES.** Provides access to your individual House members' home pages, as well as indexed Congressional Record updates.
http://www.house.gov

■ **U.S. SENATE.** A virtual tour of the Capitol, along with senators' bios and committee listings.
http://www.senate.gov

■ **WHITE HOUSE.** Features access to all of the Cabinet level sites and to an archive, updated daily, of more than 4,600 White House speeches, briefs, and reports. You can also get information on White House tours and other events at the mansion and send a message to the president.
http://www.whitehouse.gov

■ **COURTS.** The Federal Judicial Center offers general information about the court system.
http://www.uscourts.gov and *http://www.fjc.gov*

■ **MAJOR AGENCIES:**
Agriculture . . . . *http://www.usda.gov*
Commerce . . . . *http://www.doc.gov*
Defense . . . . *http://www.dtic.dla.mil/defenselink*
Education . . . . *http://www.ed.gov/index.html*
Environmental Protection Agency . . .*http://www.epa.gov*
Health and Human Services . . . .*http://www.os.dhhs.gov*
Housing and Urban Development . . . *http://www.hud.gov*
Justice . . . . *http://www.usdoj.gov*
Labor . *http://lcweb.loc.gov/global/executive/labor.html*
Library of Congress . . . . *http://www.loc.gov*
Postal Service . . . . *http://www.usps.gov*
State . . . .*http://dosfan.lib.uic.edu/dosfan.html*
Transportation . . . .*http://www.dot.gov*
Treasury . . . .*http://www.ustreas.gov*
Veterans Affairs . . . .*http://www.va.gov*

INDEX

Q

R

ACKNOWLEDGMENTS

The nourishment of a book as challenging to produce each year as *The Practical Guide to Practically Everything* requires many contributors, and we have benefited from a wealth of assistance in readying the third edition of this book for publication. Directing the editorial effort this year were our Managing Editor, Anna Isgro, our Senior Editor, Mary Yee, and our Editorial Design Director, Janice Olson. We cannot thank them enough for the dedication, skill, and initiative that they brought to the creation of this year's book.

Michele Turk added greatly to our efforts through her meticulous and exhaustive reporting on health matters. Writers Leila Kahn and Jamie Krents made a valuable contribution with their resourcefulness and skill in seeking out top experts. Our illustrator, Steve McCracken, our chart maker, David Merrill, our copy editors Eva Young and Evan Stone, and our indexer, Sydney Cohen and his associates, were again terrific. So, too, were our attorneys Robert Barnett and Jacqueline Davies, and our accountant, Richard Linden. Without all of their efforts, *The Practical Guide* would not continue to thrive.

Thanks as well to the hundreds of experts who made the time to share their expertise, including former First Lady Rosalynn Carter, Steve Thomas, host of the television series, *This Old House*, investment analyst Elaine Garzarelli and her colleague, Alida Melkonian, tennis pro Todd Martin, race car driver John Andretti, Dr. Susan Love, psychologist Barbara De Angelis, author Richard Bolles, and artist Ed Ember-ley, who generously offered his art work to illustrate the story on drawing. Among other experts who graciously shared their time and knowledge are John Marion, former chairman of Sotheby's; Mark Wyatt, editor of *Inside Track;* Huug Vandendool at the Climate Predictions Center; and Geoff Chester at the U.S. Naval Observatory.

Our gratitude also to historian Arthur Schlesinger, Jr., who contributed a special piece on presidential biographies, and to our friend Nell Minow, the Movie Mom. Our appreciation also to Morningstar Inc., the American Red Cross, the American Society of Plastic and Reconstructive Surgeons, Independent Sector, the New York Public Library, *U.S. News & World Report*, *PC Magazine*, *FamilyPC* magazine, and the scores of other institutions that so willingly provided us with valuable resources.

No author ever succeeds without the support and encouragement of a committed publisher and gifted editor, and we are fortunate to be published by the very best, Harry Evans and Jon Karp of Random House. Andy Carpenter, Liz Fogarty, and Sean Abbott also deserve a special thank you for their efforts on our behalf.

Most indispensable of all are our families. Thank you, Amy and Nathalie, Olivia, Rohan, Elisabeth, Alexander, Nicky, Bob, Helen, Sylvia, Jim, and Margaret, for practically everything.

Christopher Ma and Peter Bernstein